PRO FOOTBALL REGISTER

2004 EDITION

In association with

CONTENTS

EXPLANATION OF ABBREVIATIONS AND TERMS

LEAGUES: AFL: American Football League. **Ar.FL., Arena Football:** Arena Football League. **CFL:** Canadian Football League. **CoFL:** Continental Football League. **NFL:** National Football League. **NFLE:** NFL Europe League. **USFL:** United States Football League. **WFL:** World Football League. **W.L.:** World League. **WLAF:** World League of American Football.

TEAMS: Birm.: Birmingham. **Jack., Jax.:** Jacksonville. **L.A. Raiders:** Los Angeles Raiders. **L.A. Rams:** Los Angeles Rams. **New Eng.:** New England. **N.Y. Giants:** New York Giants. **N.Y. Jets:** New York Jets. **N.Y./N.J.:** New York/New Jersey. **San Ant.:** San Antonio. **San Fran.:** San Francisco. **Sask.:** Saskatchewan. **StL.:** St. Louis.

STATISTICS: Ast.: Assists. **Att.:** Attempts. **Avg.:** Average. **Blk.:** Blocked punts. **Cmp.:** Completions. **FGA**: Field goals attempted. **FGM:** Field goals made. **50+:** Field goals of 50 yards or longer. **F., Fum.:** Fumbles. **G:** Games. **In. 20:** Punts inside 20-yard line. **Int.:** Interceptions. **Lg.:** Longest made field goal. **L:** Lost. **Net avg.:** Net punting average. **No.:** Number. **Rat.:** Passer rating. **Pct.:** Percentage. **Pts.:** Points scored. **Skd.:** Times sacked. **Sks.:** Sacks. **T:** Tied. **TD:** Touchdowns. **Tk.:** Tackles. **2-pt.:** Two-point conversions. **W:** Won. **XPA:** Extra points attempted. **XPM:** Extra points made.**Yds.:** Yards.

POSITIONS: C: Center. **CB:** Cornerback. **DB:** Defensive back. **DE:** Defensive end. **DL:** Defensive lineman. **DT:** Defensive tackle. **FB:** Fullback. **G:** Guard. **K:** Kicker. **LB:** Linebacker. **OL:** Offensive lineman. **OT:** Offensive tackle. **P:** Punter. **QB:** Quarterback. **RB:** Running back. **S:** Safety. **TE:** Tight end. **WR:** Wide receiver.

SINGLE GAME HIGHS (regular season): If a player reached a single game high on numerous occasions—had one rushing touchdown in a game, for example—the most recent occurrence is listed.

EXPLANATION OF AWARDS

AWARDS: Butkus Award: Nation's top college linebacker. **Chuck Bednarik Award:** Nation's top college defensive player. **Davey O'Brien Award:** Nation's top college quarterback. **Doak Walker Award:** Nation's top college junior or senior running back. **Fred Biletnikoff Award:** Nation's top college wide receiver. **Harlon Hill Trophy:** Nation's top college Division II player. **Heisman Trophy:** Nation's top college player. **Jim Thorpe Award:** Nation's top college defensive back. **Lombardi Award:** Nation's top college lineman. **Lou Groza Award:** Nation's top college kicker. **Maxwell Award:** Nation's top college player. **Outland Trophy:** Nation's top college interior lineman. **Walter Payton Award:** Nation's top college Division I-AA player.

A Note on Tackles:

Nearly all of the numbers in the career section are official NFL statistics. However, tackle data is not official. For the sake of consistency, we use NFL game summaries to collect this information, assuming that the standards used in crediting tackles and assists are relatively uniform among the various stat crews at NFL game sites. However, for seasons before 1994 we list the team-supplied totals because no other data is available. For this reason, you may notice that many regular defenders' assist totals have dropped off substantially since 1994. One final note: a few teams never listed assists; instead, they threw them in with overall tackle numbers. This results in zeroes in the assists column for some players prior to 1995, which suggested that those players never assisted on tackles. In all likelihood they probably did pick up some assists, but it's impossible to find out how many.

Sporting News Contributors:
Editor: Dave Sloan; Programmers: Tim Chamberlain, Darin Kelkhoff; Designers: Michael Behrens, Chad Painter.
Stats Inc. Contributors:
Editor: Tony Nistler

ON THE COVER: Large photo of Peyton Manning by David Durochik for TSN; Ray Lewis by Bob Leverone/TSN; Torry Holt by TSN; Dante Hall by Albert Dickson/TSN. Spine photo of Brett Favre by TSN. Back cover photo of Tom Brady by Robert Seale/TSN.

NFL statistics compiled by STATS, Inc., a News Corporation company; 8130 Lehigh Avenue, Morton Grove, IL 60053. STATS is a trademark of Sports Team Analysis and Tracking Systems, Inc.

ISBN: 0-89204-737-2

10 9 8 7 6 5 4 3 2 1

VETERAN PLAYERS

Please note for statistical comparisons: In 1982, only nine of 16 games were played due to the cancellation of games because of a player's strike. In 1987, only 15 of 16 games were played due to the cancellation of games in the third week because of a player's strike. Most NFL players also missed games scheduled in the fourth, fifth and sixth weeks.

Sacks became an official NFL statistic in 1982.

Two-point conversions became an official NFL statistic in 1994.

* Indicates league leader.
† Indicates tied for league lead.
... Statistics unavailable, unofficial, or mathematically impossible to calculate.
‡ Indicates NFC leader.
§ Indicates AFC leader.
∞ Indicates tied for NFC lead.
▲ Indicates tied for AFC lead.

ABDULLAH, KHALID — LB — BENGALS

PERSONAL: Born March 6, 1979, in Jacksonville, Fla. ... 6-2/227. ... Brother of Rahim Abdullah, linebacker with Cleveland Browns (1999-2000).
HIGH SCHOOL: Fletcher (Jacksonville, Fla.).
COLLEGE: Mars Hill.
TRANSACTIONS/CAREER NOTES: Selected by Cincinnati Bengals in fifth round (136th pick overall) of 2003 NFL draft. ... Signed by Bengals (July 11, 2003).

			TOTALS			INTERCEPTIONS			
Year Team	**G**	**GS**	**Tk.**	**Ast.**	**Sks.**	**No.**	**Yds.**	**Avg.**	**TD**
2003—Cincinnati NFL	16	0	0	0	0.0	0	0	0.0	0

ABDULLAH, RABIH — RB — BEARS

PERSONAL: Born April 27, 1975, in Martinsville, Va. ... 6-0/220. ... Full name: Rabih Fard Abdullah. ... Name pronounced: RAH-bee ab-DUE-lah.
HIGH SCHOOL: Barham Clark (Roselle, N.J.).
COLLEGE: Lehigh.
TRANSACTIONS/CAREER NOTES: Signed as non-drafted free agent by Tampa Bay Buccaneers (April 20, 1998). ... Inactive for all 16 games (1998). ... On injured reserve with thumb injury (December 28, 1999-remainder of season). ... Granted free agency (March 2, 2001). ... Re-signed by Buccaneers (March 2, 2001). ... Granted unconditional free agency (March 1, 2002). ... Signed by Chicago Bears (March 6, 2002).
SINGLE GAME HIGHS (regular season): Attempts—10 (December 3, 2000, vs. Dallas); yards—38 (December 3, 2000, vs. Dallas); and rushing touchdowns—0.

			RUSHING				RECEIVING				KICKOFF RETURNS				TOTALS			
Year Team	**G**	**GS**	**Att.**	**Yds.**	**Avg.**	**TD**	**No.**	**Yds.**	**Avg.**	**TD**	**No.**	**Yds.**	**Avg.**	**TD**	**TD**	**2pt.**	**Pts.**	**Fum.**
1999—Tampa Bay NFL	15	1	5	12	2.4	0	2	11	5.5	0	0	0	0.0	0	0	0	0	0
2000—Tampa Bay NFL	12	0	16	70	4.4	0	2	14	7.0	0	1	16	16.0	0	0	0	0	0
2001—Tampa Bay NFL	16	0	11	40	3.6	0	2	26	13.0	0	5	92	18.4	0	0	0	0	0
2002—Chicago NFL	16	0	0	0	0.0	0	0	0	0.0	0	9	182	20.2	0	0	0	0	1
2003—Chicago NFL	15	0	18	37	2.1	0	8	55	6.9	0	5	62	12.4	0	0	0	0	0
Pro totals (5 years)	74	1	50	159	3.2	0	14	106	7.6	0	20	352	17.6	0	0	0	0	1

ABRAHAM, DONNIE — CB — JETS

PERSONAL: Born October 8, 1973, in Orangeburg, S.C. ... 5-10/192. ... Full name: Nathaniel Donnell Abraham.
HIGH SCHOOL: Orangeburg-Wilkinson (Orangeburg, S.C.).
COLLEGE: East Tennessee State.
TRANSACTIONS/CAREER NOTES: Selected by Tampa Bay Buccaneers in third round (71st pick overall) of 1996 NFL draft. ... Signed by Buccaneers (July 13, 1996). ... Released by Buccaneers (March 14, 2002). ... Signed by New York Jets (April 24, 2002).
CHAMPIONSHIP GAME EXPERIENCE: Played in NFC championship game (1999 season).
HONORS: Played in Pro Bowl (2000 season).
MISCELLANEOUS: Holds Tampa Bay Buccaneers all-time record for most interceptions (31).

			TOTALS			INTERCEPTIONS			
Year Team	**G**	**GS**	**Tk.**	**Ast.**	**Sks.**	**No.**	**Yds.**	**Avg.**	**TD**
1996—Tampa Bay NFL	16	12	50	8	0.0	5	27	5.4	0
1997—Tampa Bay NFL	16	16	44	10	0.0	5	16	3.2	0
1998—Tampa Bay NFL	13	13	32	6	0.0	1	3	3.0	0
1999—Tampa Bay NFL	16	16	65	14	2.0	†7	115	16.4	†2
2000—Tampa Bay NFL	16	16	46	11	0.0	7	82	11.7	0
2001—Tampa Bay NFL	15	5	29	10	0.0	6	98	16.3	0
2002—New York Jets NFL	16	16	47	6	0.0	4	49	12.3	0
2003—New York Jets NFL	8	2	11	0	0.0	1	12	12.0	0
Pro totals (8 years)	116	96	324	65	2.0	36	402	11.2	2

ABRAHAM, JOHN — DE — JETS

PERSONAL: Born May 6, 1978, in Timmonsville, S.C. ... 6-4/256.
HIGH SCHOOL: Lamar (Timmonsville, S.C.).
COLLEGE: South Carolina.
TRANSACTIONS/CAREER NOTES: Selected by New York Jets in first round (13th pick overall) of 2000 NFL draft. ... Signed by Jets (July 10, 2000). ... On injured reserve with hernia (November 17, 2000-remainder of season). ... On injured reserve with groin injury (December 15, 2003-remainder of season).

HONORS: Named defensive end on THE SPORTING NEWS NFL All-Pro team (2001). ... Played in Pro Bowl (2001 and 2002 seasons).

			TOTALS			INTERCEPTIONS			
Year Team	**G**	**GS**	**Tk.**	**Ast.**	**Sks.**	**No.**	**Yds.**	**Avg.**	**TD**
2000—New York Jets NFL	6	0	8	4	4.5	0	0	0.0	0
2001—New York Jets NFL	16	15	57	10	13.0	0	0	0.0	0
2002—New York Jets NFL	16	16	48	13	10.0	0	0	0.0	0
2003—New York Jets NFL	7	6	24	8	6.0	0	0	0.0	0
Pro totals (4 years)	45	37	137	35	33.5	0	0	0.0	0

ACKERMAN, TOM C/G

PERSONAL: Born September 6, 1972, in Bellingham, Wash. ... 6-4/295. ... Full name: Thomas Michael Ackerman.

HIGH SCHOOL: Nooksack (Wash.) Valley.

COLLEGE: Eastern Washington.

TRANSACTIONS/CAREER NOTES: Selected by New Orleans Saints in fifth round (145th pick overall) of 1996 NFL draft. ... Signed by Saints (July 14, 1996). ... Granted free agency (February 12, 1999). ... Re-signed by Saints (April 14, 1999). ... Granted unconditional free agency (February 11, 2000). ... Re-signed by Saints (February 15, 2000). ... Released by Saints (March 12, 2002). ... Signed by Oakland Raiders (May 22, 2002). ... Released by Raiders (September 1, 2002). ... Signed by Tennessee Titans (September 3, 2002). ... Granted unconditional free agency (February 28, 2003). ... Re-signed by Titans (April 2, 2003). ... Released by Titans (March 3, 2004).

PLAYING EXPERIENCE: New Orleans NFL, 1996-2001; Tennessee NFL, 2002-2003. ... Games/Games started: 1996 (2/0), 1997 (14/0), 1998 (15/10), 1999 (16/8), 2000 (15/0), 2001 (16/0), 2002 (11/3), 2003 (16/0). Total: 105/21.

CHAMPIONSHIP GAME EXPERIENCE: Played in AFC championship game (2002 season).

ADAMS, ANTHONY DT 49ERS

PERSONAL: Born August 18, 1980, in Detroit, Mich. ... 6-0/300. ... Full name: Anthony Adams Jr..

HIGH SCHOOL: Martin Luther King (Detroit).

COLLEGE: Penn State.

TRANSACTIONS/CAREER NOTES: Selected by San Francisco 49ers in second round (57th pick overall) of 2003 NFL draft. ... Signed by 49ers (July 25, 2003).

			TOTALS		
Year Team	**G**	**GS**	**Tk.**	**Ast.**	**Sks.**
2003—San Francisco NFL	14	1	20	6	1.5

ADAMS, BLUE CB JAGUARS

PERSONAL: Born October 15, 1979, in Miami, Fla. ... 5-9/182. ... Full name: Daniel L. Adams.

HIGH SCHOOL: Miami Senior (Fla.).

COLLEGE: Cincinnati.

TRANSACTIONS/CAREER NOTES: Selected by Detroit Lions in seventh round (220th pick overall) of 2003 NFL draft. ... Signed by Lions (July 22, 2003). ... Released by Lions (September 8, 2003). ... Signed by Tampa Bay Buccaneers to practice squad (September 10, 2003). ... Signed by Jacksonville Jaguars off Buccaneers practice squad (October 8, 2003).

			TOTALS			INTERCEPTIONS			
Year Team	**G**	**GS**	**Tk.**	**Ast.**	**Sks.**	**No.**	**Yds.**	**Avg.**	**TD**
2003—Jacksonville NFL	8	0	0	1	0.0	0	0	0.0	0

ADAMS, CHARLIE WR BRONCOS

PERSONAL: Born October 23, 1979, in Camp Hill, Pa. ... 6-2/190.

HIGH SCHOOL: Cumberland Valley (Mechanicsburg, Pa.).

COLLEGE: Hofstra.

TRANSACTIONS/CAREER NOTES: Signed as non-drafted free agent by Denver Broncos (April 29, 2002). ... Waived by Broncos (August 31, 2002). ... Re-signed by Broncos (December 31, 2002). ... Assigned by Broncos to Rhein Fire in 2003 NFL Europe enhancement allocation program (February 22, 2003). ... Released by Broncos (August 31, 2003). ... Re-signed by Broncos to practice squad (September 1, 2003). ... Signed by Broncos from practice squad (December 5, 2003). ... Re-signed by Broncos to practice squad (December 29, 2003).

			RECEIVING				TOTALS			
Year Team	**G**	**GS**	**No.**	**Yds.**	**Avg.**	**TD**	**TD**	**2pt.**	**Pts.**	**Fum.**
2003—Denver NFL	4	0	0	0	0.0	0	0	0	0	0

ADAMS, FLOZELL T COWBOYS

PERSONAL: Born May 18, 1975, in Chicago, Ill. ... 6-7/357. ... Full name: Flozell Jootin Adams.

HIGH SCHOOL: Proviso West (Hillside, Ill.).

COLLEGE: Michigan State.

TRANSACTIONS/CAREER NOTES: Selected by Dallas Cowboys in second round (38th pick overall) of 1998 NFL draft. ... Signed by Cowboys (July 17, 1998). ... Designated by Cowboys as franchise player (February 21, 2002). ... Granted unconditional free agency (February 28, 2003). ... Re-signed by Cowboys (February 28, 2003).

PLAYING EXPERIENCE: Dallas NFL, 1998-2003. ... Games/Games started: 1998 (16/12), 1999 (16/16), 2000 (16/16), 2001 (16/16), 2002 (16/16), 2003 (16/16). Total: 96/92.

HONORS: Played in Pro Bowl (2003 season). ... Named offensive tackle on THE SPORTING NEWS college All-America third team (1997).

ADAMS, KEITH — LB — EAGLES

PERSONAL: Born November 22, 1979, in Atlanta, Ga. ... 5-11/223.
HIGH SCHOOL: Westlake (Atlanta).
COLLEGE: Clemson.
TRANSACTIONS/CAREER NOTES: Selected after junior season by Tennessee Titans in seventh round (232nd pick overall) of 2001 NFL draft. ... Signed by Titans (July 13, 2001). ... Released by Titans (August 31, 2001). ... Signed by Dallas Cowboys to practice squad (November 8, 2001). ... Activated (November 21, 2001). ... Claimed on waivers by Philadelphia Eagles (October 21, 2002). ... Re-signed by Eagles (March 3, 2003). ... Granted free agency (March 3, 2004). ... Re-signed by Eagles (April 30, 2004).
CHAMPIONSHIP GAME EXPERIENCE: Played in NFC championship game (2002 and 2003 seasons).
HONORS: Named linebacker on THE SPORTING NEWS college All-America third team (1999). ... Named linebacker on THE SPORTING NEWS college All-America first team (2000).

			TOTALS			INTERCEPTIONS			
Year Team	**G**	**GS**	**Tk.**	**Ast.**	**Sks.**	**No.**	**Yds.**	**Avg.**	**TD**
2001—Dallas NFL	4	0	0	0	0.0	0	0	0.0	0
2002—Dallas NFL	6	5	15	3	0.0	0	0	0.0	0
—Philadelphia NFL	10	0	0	0	0.0	0	0	0.0	0
2003—Philadelphia NFL	15	0	3	1	0.0	0	0	0.0	0
Pro totals (3 years)	35	5	18	4	0.0	0	0	0.0	0

ADAMS, SAM — DT — BILLS

PERSONAL: Born June 13, 1973, in Houston, Texas. ... 6-4/335. ... Full name: Sam Aaron Adams. ... Son of Sam Adams Sr., guard with New England Patriots (1972-80) and New Orleans Saints (1981).
HIGH SCHOOL: Cypress Creek (Houston).
COLLEGE: Texas A&M.
TRANSACTIONS/CAREER NOTES: Selected after junior season by Seattle Seahawks in first round (eighth pick overall) of 1994 NFL draft. ... Signed by Seahawks (July 30, 1994). ... Granted unconditional free agency (February 11, 2000). ... Signed by Baltimore Ravens (April 17, 2000). ... Released by Ravens (March 1, 2002). ... Signed by Oakland Raiders (August 19, 2002). ... Released by Raiders (February 27, 2003). ... Signed by Buffalo Bills (March 23, 2003).
CHAMPIONSHIP GAME EXPERIENCE: Played in AFC championship game (2000 and 2002 seasons). ... Member of Super Bowl championship team (2000 season). ... Played in Super Bowl 37 (2002 season).
HONORS: Named defensive lineman on THE SPORTING NEWS college All-America first team (1993). ... Played in Pro Bowl (2000 and 2001 seasons).

			TOTALS			INTERCEPTIONS			
Year Team	**G**	**GS**	**Tk.**	**Ast.**	**Sks.**	**No.**	**Yds.**	**Avg.**	**TD**
1994—Seattle NFL	12	7	20	7	4.0	0	0	0.0	0
1995—Seattle NFL	16	5	16	10	3.5	0	0	0.0	0
1996—Seattle NFL	16	15	35	5	5.5	0	0	0.0	0
1997—Seattle NFL	16	15	37	15	7.0	0	0	0.0	0
1998—Seattle NFL	16	11	28	3	2.0	1	25	25.0	1
1999—Seattle NFL	13	13	31	7	1.0	0	0	0.0	0
2000—Baltimore NFL	16	16	23	4	2.0	0	0	0.0	0
2001—Baltimore NFL	14	14	18	5	2.0	0	0	0.0	0
2002—Oakland NFL	15	14	18	4	2.0	0	0	0.0	0
2003—Buffalo NFL	15	15	24	9	5.0	1	37	37.0	1
Pro totals (10 years)	149	125	250	69	34.0	2	62	31.0	2

AHANOTU, CHIDI — DE

PERSONAL: Born October 11, 1970, in Modesto, Calif. ... 6-2/285. ... Full name: Chidi Obioma Ahanotu. ... Name pronounced: CHEE-dee a-HA-noe-too.
HIGH SCHOOL: Berkeley (Calif.).
COLLEGE: California.
TRANSACTIONS/CAREER NOTES: Selected by Tampa Bay Buccaneers in sixth round (145th pick overall) of 1993 NFL draft. ... Signed by Buccaneers (July 9, 1993). ... Granted free agency (February 16, 1996). ... Re-signed by Buccaneers (February 20, 1996). ... On injured reserve with shoulder injury (October 27, 1998-remainder of season). ... Designated by Buccaneers as franchise player (February 12, 1999). ... Re-signed by Buccaneers (July 30, 1999). ... Released by Buccaneers (April 20, 2001). ... Signed by St. Louis Rams (August 20, 2001). ... Granted unconditional free agency (March 1, 2002). ... Signed by Buffalo Bills (August 19, 2002). ... Granted unconditional free agency (February 28, 2003). ... Signed by San Francisco 49ers (August 21, 2003). ... Granted unconditional free agency (March 3, 2004).
CHAMPIONSHIP GAME EXPERIENCE: Played in NFC championship game (1999 and 2001 seasons). ... Played in Super Bowl 36 (2001 season).

			TOTALS		
Year Team	**G**	**GS**	**Tk.**	**Ast.**	**Sks.**
1993—Tampa Bay NFL	16	10	15	16	1.5
1994—Tampa Bay NFL	16	16	31	15	1.0
1995—Tampa Bay NFL	16	15	36	12	3.0
1996—Tampa Bay NFL	13	13	37	10	5.5
1997—Tampa Bay NFL	16	15	38	10	10.0
1998—Tampa Bay NFL	4	4	9	8	0.0
1999—Tampa Bay NFL	16	15	24	9	6.5
2000—Tampa Bay NFL	16	16	28	19	3.5
2001—St. Louis NFL	16	16	21	8	2.0
2002—Buffalo NFL	16	14	30	14	5.0
2003—San Francisco NFL	16	1	21	6	4.0
Pro totals (11 years)	161	135	290	127	42.0

A

AIKEN, SAM — WR — BILLS

PERSONAL: Born December 14, 1980, in Clinton, N.C. ... 6-2/204. ... Full name: Samuel Aiken.
HIGH SCHOOL: James Kenan (Warsaw, N.C.).
COLLEGE: North Carolina.
TRANSACTIONS/CAREER NOTES: Selected by Buffalo Bills in fourth round (127th pick overall) of 2003 NFL draft. ... Signed by Bills (July 10, 2003). ... On injured reserve with knee injury (November 26, 2003-remainder of season).
SINGLE GAME HIGHS (regular season): Receptions—1 (November 16, 2003, vs. Houston); yards—19 (November 16, 2003, vs. Houston); and touchdown receptions—0.

			RECEIVING				TOTALS			
Year Team	G	GS	No.	Yds.	Avg.	TD	TD	2pt.	Pts.	Fum.
2003—Buffalo NFL	5	0	3	35	11.7	0	0	0	0	0

AKERS, DAVID — K — EAGLES

PERSONAL: Born December 9, 1974, in Lexington, Ky. ... 5-10/200. ... Full name: David Roy Akers. ... Name pronounced: A-kers.
HIGH SCHOOL: Tates Creek (Lexington, Ky.).
COLLEGE: Louisville.
TRANSACTIONS/CAREER NOTES: Signed as non-drafted free agent by Carolina Panthers (April 19, 1997). ... Released by Panthers (August 17, 1997). ... Signed by Atlanta Falcons (April 28, 1998). ... Released by Falcons (July 7, 1998). ... Re-signed by Falcons (July 21, 1998). ... Released by Falcons (August 24, 1998). ... Signed by Washington Redskins to practice squad (September 1, 1998). ... Activated (September 15, 1998). ... Released by Redskins (September 22, 1998). ... Signed by Philadelphia Eagles (January 11, 1999). ... Assigned by Eagles to Berlin Thunder in 1999 NFL Europe enhancement allocation program (February 22, 1999).
CHAMPIONSHIP GAME EXPERIENCE: Played in NFC championship game (2001-2003 seasons).
HONORS: Named kicker on THE SPORTING NEWS NFL All-Pro team (2001 and 2002). ... Played in Pro Bowl (2001 and 2002 seasons).

		FIELD GOALS							TOTALS		
Year Team	G	1-29	30-39	40-49	50+	Tot.	Pct.	Lg.	XPM	XPA	Pts.
1998—Washington NFL	1	0-0	0-0	0-2	0-0	0-2	0.0	0	2	2	2
1999—Philadelphia NFL	16	0-0	0-0	2-3	1-3	3-6	50.0	∞53	2	2	11
2000—Philadelphia NFL	16	7-7	14-15	7-10	1-1	29-33	87.9	51	34	36	121
2001—Philadelphia NFL	16	10-10	7-8	7-10	2-3	26-31	83.9	50	37	38	115
2002—Philadelphia NFL	16	9-9	14-16	6-7	1-2	30-34	88.2	51	43	43	133
2003—Philadelphia NFL	16	9-9	7-7	6-10	2-3	24-29	82.8	57	42	42	114
Pro totals (6 years)	81	35-35	42-46	28-42	7-12	112-135	83.0	57	160	163	496

AKINS, CHRIS — S — DOLPHINS

PERSONAL: Born November 29, 1976, in Little Rock, Ark. ... 5-11/200. ... Full name: Christopher Drew Akins. ... Name pronounced: A-kenz.
HIGH SCHOOL: Little Rock (Ark.) Hall.
COLLEGE: Arkansas-Pine Bluff.
TRANSACTIONS/CAREER NOTES: Selected by Green Bay Packers in seventh round (212th pick overall) of 1999 NFL draft. ... Signed by Packers (June 1, 1999). ... Released by Packers (September 5, 1999). ... Re-signed by Packers to practice squad (September 14, 1999). ... Signed by Dallas Cowboys off Packers practice squad (October 27, 1999). ... Assigned by Cowboys to Rhein Fire in 2000 NFL Europe enhancement allocation program (February 18, 2000). ... Claimed on waivers by Packers (November 2, 2000). ... Claimed on waivers by Cleveland Browns (December 11, 2001). ... Granted free agency (March 1, 2002). ... Re-signed by Browns (May 5, 2002). ... Granted unconditional free agency (February 28, 2003). ... Signed by New England Patriots (March 12, 2003). ... Granted unconditional free agency (March 3, 2004). ... Signed by Miami Dolphins (March 5, 2004).
CHAMPIONSHIP GAME EXPERIENCE: Member of Super Bowl championship team (2003 season). ... Played in AFC championship game (2003 season).

			TOTALS			INTERCEPTIONS			
Year Team	G	GS	Tk.	Ast.	Sks.	No.	Yds.	Avg.	TD
1999—Dallas NFL	9	0	0	0	0.0	0	0	0.0	0
2000—Dallas NFL	8	0	0	0	0.0	0	0	0.0	0
—Green Bay NFL	2	0	0	0	0.0	0	0	0.0	0
2001—Green Bay NFL	11	0	9	5	0.0	0	0	0.0	0
—Cleveland NFL	4	0	3	0	0.0	0	0	0.0	0
2002—Cleveland NFL	15	0	0	0	0.0	0	0	0.0	0
2003—New England NFL	12	0	4	4	0.0	0	0	0.0	0
Pro totals (5 years)	61	0	16	9	0.0	0	0	0.0	0

ALBRIGHT, ETHAN — C/LS — REDSKINS

PERSONAL: Born May 1, 1971, in Greensboro, N.C. ... 6-5/265. ... Full name: Lawrence Ethan Albright.
HIGH SCHOOL: Grimsley (Greensboro, N.C.).
COLLEGE: North Carolina.
TRANSACTIONS/CAREER NOTES: Signed as non-drafted free agent by Miami Dolphins (April 28, 1994). ... Released by Dolphins (August 22, 1994). ... Re-signed by Dolphins to practice squad (August 29, 1994). ... Released by Dolphins (September 14, 1994). ... Re-signed by Dolphins to practice squad (September 28, 1994). ... Released by Dolphins (November 2, 1994). ... Re-signed by Dolphins (February 16, 1995). ... On injured reserve with knee injury (November 15, 1995-remainder of season). ... Released by Dolphins (August 20, 1996). ... Signed by Buffalo Bills (August 26, 1996). ... Granted free agency (February 13, 1998). ... Re-signed by Bills (April 15, 1998). ... Granted unconditional free agency (February 12, 1999). ... Re-signed by Bills (April 1, 1999). ... Released by Bills (March 1, 2001). ... Signed by Washington Redskins (March 9, 2001). ... Released by Redskins (March 6, 2003). ... Re-signed by Redskins (March 7, 2003) ... Granted unconditional free agency (March 3, 2004). ... Re-signed by Redskins (March 4, 2004).
PLAYING EXPERIENCE: Miami NFL, 1995; Buffalo NFL, 1996-2000; Washington NFL, 2001-2003. ... Games/Games started: 1995 (10/0), 1996 (16/0), 1997 (16/0), 1998 (16/0), 1999 (16/0), 2000 (16/0), 2001 (16/0), 2002 (16/0), 2003 (16/0). Total: 138/0.

A

ALEXANDER, BRENT S

PERSONAL: Born July 10, 1971, in Gallatin, Tenn. ... 5-11/200. ... Full name: Ronald Brent Alexander.
HIGH SCHOOL: Gallatin (Tenn.).
COLLEGE: Tennessee State.
TRANSACTIONS/CAREER NOTES: Signed as non-drafted free agent by Arizona Cardinals (April 28, 1994). ... Granted unconditional free agency (February 13, 1998). ... Signed by Carolina Panthers (March 20, 1998). ... Released by Panthers (April 18, 2000). ... Signed by Pittsburgh Steelers (May 30, 2000). ... Released by Steelers (March 23, 2004).
CHAMPIONSHIP GAME EXPERIENCE: Played in AFC championship game (2001 season).

			TOTALS			INTERCEPTIONS			
Year Team	G	GS	Tk.	Ast.	Sks.	No.	Yds.	Avg.	TD
1994—Arizona NFL	16	7	26	10	0.0	0	0	0.0	0
1995—Arizona NFL	16	13	51	17	0.5	2	14	7.0	0
1996—Arizona NFL	16	15	52	29	0.0	2	3	1.5	0
1997—Arizona NFL	16	15	54	22	0.0	0	0	0.0	0
1998—Carolina NFL	16	16	68	29	0.0	0	0	0.0	0
1999—Carolina NFL	16	16	65	12	0.0	2	18	9.0	0
2000—Pittsburgh NFL	16	16	61	15	1.5	3	31	10.3	0
2001—Pittsburgh NFL	16	16	52	17	2.0	4	39	9.8	0
2002—Pittsburgh NFL	16	16	50	25	1.0	4	37	9.3	0
2003—Pittsburgh NFL	16	16	60	21	1.0	4	63	15.8	0
Pro totals (10 years)	160	146	539	197	6.0	21	205	9.8	0

ALEXANDER, DAN RB

PERSONAL: Born March 17, 1978, in Wentzville, Mo. ... 6-0/257.
HIGH SCHOOL: Wentzville (Mo.).
COLLEGE: Nebraska.
TRANSACTIONS/CAREER NOTES: Selected by Tennessee Titans in sixth round (192nd pick overall) of 2001 NFL draft. ... Signed by Titans (July 10, 2001). ... Released by Titans (September 6, 2001). ... Re-signed by Titans to practice squad (September 8, 2001). ... Activated (November 21, 2001). ... Claimed on waivers by Jacksonville Jaguars (August 29, 2002). ... Re-signed by Jaguars (March 15, 2003). ... Released by Jaguars (August 30, 2003). ... Signed by St. Louis Rams (November 5, 2003). ... Released by Rams (November 11, 2003).

			RUSHING				TOTALS			
Year Team	G	GS	Att.	Yds.	Avg.	TD	TD	2pt.	Pts.	Fum.
2001—Tennessee NFL	7	0	0	0	0.0	0	0	0	0	0
2002—Jacksonville NFL	3	0	0	0	0.0	0	0	0	0	0
2003—St. Louis NFL	1	0	0	0	0.0	0	0	0	0	0
Pro totals (3 years)	11	0	0	0	0.0	0	0	0	0	0

ALEXANDER, SHAUN RB SEAHAWKS

PERSONAL: Born August 30, 1977, in Florence, Ky. ... 5-11/225.
HIGH SCHOOL: Boone County (Ky.).
COLLEGE: Alabama.
TRANSACTIONS/CAREER NOTES: Selected by Seattle Seahawks in first round (19th pick overall) of 2000 NFL draft. ... Signed by Seahawks (July 20, 2000).
HONORS: Named running back on THE SPORTING NEWS college All-America second team (1999). ... Played in Pro Bowl (2003 season).
SINGLE GAME HIGHS (regular season): Attempts—35 (November 11, 2001, vs. Oakland); yards—266 (November 11, 2001, vs. Oakland); and rushing touchdowns—4 (September 29, 2002, vs. Minnesota).
STATISTICAL PLATEAUS: 100-yard rushing games: 2001 (4), 2002 (4), 2003 (7). Total: 15.

			RUSHING				RECEIVING				TOTALS			
Year Team	G	GS	Att.	Yds.	Avg.	TD	No.	Yds.	Avg.	TD	TD	2pt.	Pts.	Fum.
2000—Seattle NFL	16	1	64	313	4.9	2	5	41	8.2	0	2	0	12	2
2001—Seattle NFL	16	12	309	1318	4.3	*14	44	343	7.8	2	§16	0	96	4
2002—Seattle NFL	16	16	295	1175	4.0	‡16	59	460	7.8	2	‡18	0	108	3
2003—Seattle NFL	16	15	326	1435	4.4	14	42	295	7.0	2	16	0	96	4
Pro totals (4 years)	64	44	994	4241	4.3	46	150	1139	7.6	6	52	0	312	13

ALEXANDER, STEPHEN TE

PERSONAL: Born November 7, 1975, in Chickasha, Okla. ... 6-4/250.
HIGH SCHOOL: Chickasha (Okla.).
COLLEGE: Oklahoma.
TRANSACTIONS/CAREER NOTES: Selected by Washington Redskins in second round (48th pick overall) of 1998 NFL draft. ... Signed by Redskins (July 13, 1998). ... On injured reserve with ankle injury (December 26, 2001-remainder of season). ... Granted unconditional free agency (March 1, 2002). ... Signed by San Diego Chargers (March 21, 2002). ... On injured reserve with groin injury (December 20, 2003-remainder of season). ... Released by Chargers (March 2, 2004).
HONORS: Played in Pro Bowl (2000 season).
SINGLE GAME HIGHS (regular season): Receptions—8 (December 29, 2002, vs. Seattle); yards—129 (December 29, 2002, vs. Seattle); and touchdown receptions—2 (September 19, 1999, vs. New York Giants).
STATISTICAL PLATEAUS: 100-yard receiving games: 2002 (1). Total: 1.

			RECEIVING				TOTALS			
Year Team	G	GS	No.	Yds.	Avg.	TD	TD	2pt.	Pts.	Fum.
1998—Washington NFL	15	5	37	383	10.4	4	4	0	24	2

Year Team	G	GS	RECEIVING No.	Yds.	Avg.	TD	TOTALS TD	2pt.	Pts.	Fum.
1999—Washington NFL	15	15	29	324	11.2	3	3	0	18	0
2000—Washington NFL	16	16	47	510	10.9	2	2	0	12	2
2001—Washington NFL	7	5	9	85	9.4	0	0	0	0	0
2002—San Diego NFL	14	14	45	510	11.3	1	1	0	6	1
2003—San Diego NFL	3	0	0	0	0.0	0	0	1	2	0
Pro totals (6 years)	70	55	167	1812	10.9	10	10	1	62	5

ALLEN, BRIAN LB

PERSONAL: Born April 1, 1978, in Lake City, Fla. ... 6-0/232.
HIGH SCHOOL: Columbia (Lake City, Fla.).
COLLEGE: Florida State.
TRANSACTIONS/CAREER NOTES: Selected by St. Louis Rams in third round (83rd pick overall) of 2001 NFL draft. ... Signed by Rams (June 5, 2001). ... Selected by Houston Texans from Rams in NFL expansion draft (February 18, 2002). ... Claimed on waivers by Carolina Panthers (May 30, 2002). ... Granted free agency (March 3, 2004).
CHAMPIONSHIP GAME EXPERIENCE: Member of Rams for NFC championship game (2001 season); inactive. ... Member of Rams for Super Bowl 36 (2001 season); inactive. ... Played in NFC championship game (2003 season). ... Played in Super Bowl 38 (2003 season).

Year Team	G	GS	TOTALS Tk.	Ast.	Sks.	INTERCEPTIONS No.	Yds.	Avg.	TD
2001—St. Louis NFL	3	0	0	0	0.0	0	0	0.0	0
2002—Carolina NFL	16	5	27	6	0.0	0	0	0.0	0
2003—Carolina NFL	14	4	22	10	1.0	0	0	0.0	0
Pro totals (3 years)	33	9	49	16	1.0	0	0	0.0	0

ALLEN, BRIAN RB COLTS

PERSONAL: Born April 20, 1980, in Ontario, Calif. ... 5-9/205.
HIGH SCHOOL: Damien (Calif.).
COLLEGE: Stanford.
TRANSACTIONS/CAREER NOTES: Selected by Indianapolis Colts in sixth round (204th pick overall) of 2002 NFL draft. ... Signed by Colts (July 8, 2002). ... On injured reserve with knee injury (August 26, 2002-entire season). ... Released by Colts (September 9, 2003). ... Re-signed by Colts (October 14, 2003). ... Released by Colts (November 18, 2003). ... Re-signed by Colts (February 4, 2004).

Year Team	G	GS	RUSHING Att.	Yds.	Avg.	TD	RECEIVING No.	Yds.	Avg.	TD	KICKOFF RETURNS No.	Yds.	Avg.	TD	TOTALS TD	2pt.	Pts.	Fum.
2003—Indianapolis NFL	4	0	0	0	0.0	0	0	0	0.0	0	1	6	6.0	0	0	0	0	0

ALLEN, DAVID RB JAGUARS

PERSONAL: Born February 5, 1978, in Euless, Texas. ... 5-9/195.
HIGH SCHOOL: Liberty (Mo.).
COLLEGE: Kansas State.
TRANSACTIONS/CAREER NOTES: Signed as non-drafted free agent by San Francisco 49ers (April 27, 2001). ... Waived by 49ers (August 30, 2001). ... Signed by Minnesota Vikings (March 27, 2002). ... Waived by Vikings (September 1, 2002). ... Signed by Jacksonville Jaguars to practice squad (November 5, 2002). ... Released by Jaguars (November 12, 2002). ... Re-signed by Jaguars to practice squad (December 17, 2002). ... Activated (January 7, 2003). ... Assigned by Jaguars to Berlin Thunder in 2003 NFL Europe enhancement allocation program (February 22, 2003). ... Released by Jaguars (August 31, 2003). ... Re-signed by Jaguars to practice squad (September 1, 2003). ... Released by Jaguars (September 10, 2003). ... Re-signed by Jaguars (September 16, 2003).
SINGLE GAME HIGHS (regular season): Attempts—3 (December 7, 2003, vs. Houston); yards—5 (December 14, 2003, vs. New England); and rushing touchdowns—0.

Year Team	G	GS	RUSHING Att.	Yds.	Avg.	TD	RECEIVING No.	Yds.	Avg.	TD	PUNT RETURNS No.	Yds.	Avg.	TD	KICKOFF RETURNS No.	Yds.	Avg.	TD	TOTALS TD	2pt.	Pts.
2003—Jac. NFL	14	0	4	8	2.0	0	6	60	10.0	1	27	324	12.0	0	41	831	20.3	0	1	0	6

ALLEN, IAN T GIANTS

PERSONAL: Born July 22, 1978, in Newark, N.J. ... 6-4/310. ... Full name: Ian Ramon Allen.
HIGH SCHOOL: Westlake (Atlanta).
COLLEGE: Purdue.
TRANSACTIONS/CAREER NOTES: Signed as non-drafted free agent by Kansas City Chiefs (April 30, 2001). ... Released by Chiefs (August 28, 2001). ... Signed by Atlanta Falcons to practice squad (January 2, 2002). ... Signed by Chiefs from Falcons practice squad (January 8, 2002). ... Allocated by Chiefs to Scottish Claymores in 2002 NFL Europe enhancement allocation program (February 12, 2002). ... Released by Chiefs (September 1, 2002). ... Signed by New York Giants to practice squad (September 10, 2002). ... Activated (October 3, 2002).
PLAYING EXPERIENCE: New York Giants NFL, 2002-2003. ... Games/Games started: 2002 (3/0), 2003 (16/11). Total: 19/11.

ALLEN, JAMES LB SAINTS

PERSONAL: Born November 11, 1979, in Portland, Ore. ... 6-2/240.
HIGH SCHOOL: Thomas Jefferson (Portland, Ore.).
COLLEGE: Oregon State.
TRANSACTIONS/CAREER NOTES: Selected by New Orleans Saints in third round (82nd pick overall) of 2002 NFL draft. ... Signed by Saints (July 22, 2002).

Year	Team	G	GS	TOTALS Tk.	Ast.	Sks.	INTERCEPTIONS No.	Yds.	Avg.	TD
2002—New Orleans NFL		14	1	6	2	0.0	1	0	0.0	1
2003—New Orleans NFL		15	1	10	1	0.0	0	0	0.0	0
Pro totals (2 years)		29	2	16	3	0.0	1	0	0.0	1

A

ALLEN, KENDERICK DT SAINTS

PERSONAL: Born September 14, 1978, in Bogalusa, La. ... 6-6/318.
HIGH SCHOOL: Bogalusa (La.).
COLLEGE: Louisiana State.
TRANSACTIONS/CAREER NOTES: Signed as non-drafted free agent by New Orleans Saints (May 2, 2003).

Year	Team	G	GS	TOTALS Tk.	Ast.	Sks.
2003—New Orleans NFL		10	1	9	2	0.0

ALLEN, LARRY G COWBOYS

PERSONAL: Born November 27, 1971, in Los Angeles, Calif. ... 6-3/335. ... Full name: Larry Christopher Allen.
HIGH SCHOOL: Centennial (Compton, Calif.), then Vintage (Napa, Calif.).
JUNIOR COLLEGE: Butte (Calif.) C.c.
COLLEGE: Sonoma State (Calif.).
TRANSACTIONS/CAREER NOTES: Selected by Dallas Cowboys in second round (46th pick overall) of 1994 NFL draft. ... Signed by Cowboys (July 16, 1994). ... On injured reserve with ankle injury (November 21, 2002-remainder of season).
PLAYING EXPERIENCE: Dallas NFL, 1994-2003. ... Games/Games started: 1994 (16/10), 1995 (16/16), 1996 (16/16), 1997 (16/16), 1998 (16/16), 1999 (11/11), 2000 (16/16), 2001 (16/16), 2002 (5/5), 2003 (16/16). Total: 144/138.
CHAMPIONSHIP GAME EXPERIENCE: Played in NFC championship game (1994 and 1995 seasons). ... Member of Super Bowl championship team (1995 season).
HONORS: Named guard on THE SPORTING NEWS NFL All-Pro team (1995-97 and 1999). ... Played in Pro Bowl (1995-1998, 2000 and 2003 seasons). ... Named to play in Pro Bowl (1999 season); replaced by Adam Timmerman due to injury. ... Named offensive tackle on THE SPORTING NEWS NFL All-Pro team (1998). ... Named guard on THE SPORTING NEWS NFL All-Pro team (2000 and 2001). ... Named to play in Pro Bowl (2001 season); replaced by Adam Timmerman due to injury.

ALLEN, WILL CB GIANTS

PERSONAL: Born August 5, 1978, in Syracuse, N.Y. ... 5-10/196. ... Full name: Will D. Allen.
HIGH SCHOOL: Corcoran (Syracuse, N.Y.).
COLLEGE: Syracuse.
TRANSACTIONS/CAREER NOTES: Selected by New York Giants in first round (22nd pick overall) of 2001 NFL draft. ... Signed by Giants (July 26, 2001). ... On injured reserve with foot injury (December 2, 2003-remainder of season).
HONORS: Named cornerback to THE SPORTING NEWS college All-America third team (2000).

Year	Team	G	GS	TOTALS Tk.	Ast.	Sks.	INTERCEPTIONS No.	Yds.	Avg.	TD
2001—New York Giants NFL		13	12	38	4	0.0	4	27	6.8	0
2002—New York Giants NFL		15	15	50	5	0.0	1	0	0.0	0
2003—New York Giants NFL		12	12	33	7	0.0	2	23	11.5	0
Pro totals (3 years)		40	39	121	16	0.0	7	50	7.1	0

ALSTOTT, MIKE FB BUCCANEERS

PERSONAL: Born December 21, 1973, in Joliet, Ill. ... 6-1/248. ... Full name: Michael Joseph Alstott.
HIGH SCHOOL: Joliet (Ill.) Catholic.
COLLEGE: Purdue.
TRANSACTIONS/CAREER NOTES: Selected by Tampa Bay Buccaneers in second round (35th pick overall) of 1996 NFL draft. ... Signed by Buccaneers (July 21, 1996). ... On injured reserve with neck injury (October 7, 2003-remainder of season).
CHAMPIONSHIP GAME EXPERIENCE: Played in NFC championship game (1999 and 2002 seasons). ... Member of Super Bowl championship team (2002 season).
HONORS: Played in Pro Bowl (1997-2002 seasons).
SINGLE GAME HIGHS (regular season): Attempts—28 (October 28, 2001, vs. Minnesota); yards—131 (September 26, 1999, vs. Denver); and rushing touchdowns—3 (October 28, 2001, vs. Minnesota).
STATISTICAL PLATEAUS: 100-yard rushing games: 1998 (2), 1999 (2), 2001 (2), 2002 (1). Total: 7.
MISCELLANEOUS: Holds Tampa Bay Buccaneers all-time records for most rushing touchdowns (47) and most touchdowns (59).

Year	Team	G	GS	RUSHING Att.	Yds.	Avg.	TD	RECEIVING No.	Yds.	Avg.	TD	TOTALS TD	2pt.	Pts.	Fum.
1996—Tampa Bay NFL		16	16	96	377	3.9	3	65	557	8.6	3	6	0	36	4
1997—Tampa Bay NFL		15	15	176	665	3.8	7	23	178	7.7	3	10	0	60	5
1998—Tampa Bay NFL		16	16	215	846	3.9	8	22	152	6.9	1	9	0	54	5
1999—Tampa Bay NFL		16	16	242	949	3.9	7	27	239	8.9	2	9	0	54	6
2000—Tampa Bay NFL		13	13	131	465	3.5	5	13	93	7.2	0	5	0	30	3
2001—Tampa Bay NFL		16	16	165	680	4.1	10	35	231	6.6	1	11	2	70	2
2002—Tampa Bay NFL		16	9	146	548	3.8	5	35	242	6.9	2	7	0	42	4
2003—Tampa Bay NFL		4	3	27	77	2.9	2	10	83	8.3	0	2	0	12	0
Pro totals (8 years)		112	104	1198	4607	3.8	47	230	1775	7.7	12	59	2	358	29

AMATO, KEN — C/LS — TITANS

PERSONAL: Born May 18, 1977, in Puerto Rico. ... 6-2/245. ... Full name: Kenneth Carlos Amato.
HIGH SCHOOL: Braddock (Miami).
JUNIOR COLLEGE: Moorpark (Calif.).
COLLEGE: Montana State.
TRANSACTIONS/CAREER NOTES: Signed as non-drafted free agent by Carolina Panthers (February 11, 2003). ... Released by Panthers (June 11, 2003). ... Re-signed by Panthers (May 28, 2003). ... Released by Panthers (August 2, 2003). ... Signed by Tennessee Titans (August 12, 2003). ... Released by Titans (October 14, 2003). ... Re-signed by Titans (October 17, 2003).
PLAYING EXPERIENCE: Tennessee NFL, 2003. ... Games/Games started: 2003 (16/0). Total: 16/0.

AMBROSE, ASHLEY — CB — SAINTS

PERSONAL: Born September 17, 1970, in New Orleans, La. ... 5-11/190. ... Full name: Ashley Avery Ambrose.
HIGH SCHOOL: Alcee Fortier (New Orleans).
COLLEGE: Mississippi Valley State.
TRANSACTIONS/CAREER NOTES: Selected by Indianapolis Colts in second round (29th pick overall) of 1992 NFL draft. ... Signed by Colts (August 11, 1992). ... On injured reserve with leg injury (September 14-October 29, 1992); on practice squad (October 21-29, 1992). ... Granted free agency (February 17, 1995). ... Re-signed by Colts (April 29, 1995). ... Granted unconditional free agency (February 16, 1996). ... Signed by Cincinnati Bengals (February 25, 1996). ... Granted unconditional free agency (February 12, 1999). ... Signed by New Orleans Saints (July 13, 1999). ... Granted unconditional free agency (February 11, 2000). ... Signed by Atlanta Falcons (February 12, 2000). ... Released by Falcons (February 21, 2003). ... Signed by Saints (March 3, 2003).
CHAMPIONSHIP GAME EXPERIENCE: Played in AFC championship game (1995 season).
HONORS: Played in Pro Bowl (1996 season).

			TOTALS			INTERCEPTIONS			
Year Team	G	GS	Tk.	Ast.	Sks.	No.	Yds.	Avg.	TD
1992—Indianapolis NFL	10	2	6	2	0.0	0	0	0.0	0
1993—Indianapolis NFL	14	6	36	8	0.0	0	0	0.0	0
1994—Indianapolis NFL	16	4	31	4	0.0	2	50	25.0	0
1995—Indianapolis NFL	16	0	11	3	0.0	3	12	4.0	0
1996—Cincinnati NFL	16	16	44	6	0.0	8	63	7.9	1
1997—Cincinnati NFL	16	16	57	2	1.0	3	56	18.7	0
1998—Cincinnati NFL	15	15	36	4	0.0	2	0	0.0	0
1999—New Orleans NFL	16	16	51	6	0.0	6	27	4.5	0
2000—Atlanta NFL	16	16	37	1	0.0	4	‡139	34.7	1
2001—Atlanta NFL	16	16	49	3	0.0	5	43	8.6	0
2002—Atlanta NFL	16	16	42	2	0.0	3	25	8.3	0
2003—New Orleans NFL	16	12	41	6	0.0	3	78	26.0	1
Pro totals (12 years)	183	135	441	47	1.0	39	493	12.6	3

ANDERSEN, MORTEN — K — CHIEFS

PERSONAL: Born August 19, 1960, in Copenhagen, Denmark. ... 6-2/217.
HIGH SCHOOL: Ben Davis (Indianapolis).
COLLEGE: Michigan State.
TRANSACTIONS/CAREER NOTES: Selected by New Orleans Saints in fourth round (86th pick overall) of 1982 NFL draft. ... On injured reserve with sprained ankle (September 15-November 20, 1982). ... Designated by Saints as transition player (February 25, 1993). ... Released by Saints (July 19, 1995). ... Signed by Atlanta Falcons (July 21, 1995). ... Granted unconditional free agency (March 2, 2001). ... Signed by New York Giants (August 29, 2001). ... Granted unconditional free agency (March 1, 2002). ... Signed by Kansas City Chiefs (March 25, 2002). ... On injured reserve with knee injury (December 17, 2002-remainder of season). ... Granted unconditional free agency (February 28, 2003). ... Re-signed by Chiefs (March 18, 2003).
CHAMPIONSHIP GAME EXPERIENCE: Played in NFC championship game (1998 season). ... Played in Super Bowl 33 (1998 season).
HONORS: Named kicker on THE SPORTING NEWS college All-America first team (1981). ... Named kicker on THE SPORTING NEWS NFL All-Pro team (1985-1987 and 1995). ... Played in Pro Bowl (1985-1988, 1990, 1992 and 1995 seasons).
RECORDS: Holds NFL career records for most consecutive games scoring—316 (December 11, 1983-present); and for most made field goals of 50 or more yards—40. ... Holds NFL single-season record for most made field goals of 50 or more yards—8 (1995). ... Holds NFL single-game record for most made field goals of 50 or more yards—3 (December 10, 1995, vs. New Orleans). ... Shares NFL record for most seasons with 100 or more points—14 (1985-89, 1991-95, 1997-98 and 2002-03).

		FIELD GOALS							TOTALS		
Year Team	G	1-29	30-39	40-49	50+	Tot.	Pct.	Lg.	XPM	XPA	Pts.
1982—New Orleans NFL	8	0-0	1-1	1-3	0-1	2-5	40.0	45	6	6	12
1983—New Orleans NFL	16	10-10	3-4	2-6	3-4	18-24	75.0	52	37	38	91
1984—New Orleans NFL	16	9-9	4-5	5-10	2-3	20-27	74.1	53	34	34	94
1985—New Orleans NFL	16	4-5	13-14	11-12	3-4	31-35	‡88.6	§55	27	29	120
1986—New Orleans NFL	16	12-12	6-7	6-6	2-5	26-30	*86.7	53	30	30	108
1987—New Orleans NFL	12	9-9	9-9	8-12	2-6	*28-*36	77.8	52	37	37	121
1988—New Orleans NFL	16	12-13	8-11	5-8	1-4	26-36	72.2	51	32	33	110
1989—New Orleans NFL	16	7-8	10-11	3-6	0-4	20-29	69.0	49	44	45	104
1990—New Orleans NFL	16	5-5	5-6	8-12	3-4	21-27	77.8	52	29	29	92
1991—New Orleans NFL	16	6-6	11-13	6-9	2-4	25-32	78.1	*60	38	38	113
1992—New Orleans NFL	16	10-10	8-10	8-11	3-3	29-34	‡85.3	52	33	34	∞120
1993—New Orleans NFL	16	9-9	7-7	11-14	1-5	28-35	80.0	56	33	33	117
1994—New Orleans NFL	16	9-9	11-14	8-10	0-6	28-†39	71.8	48	32	32	116
1995—Atlanta NFL	16	9-9	11-11	3-8	8-9	‡31-37	83.8	*59	29	30	122
1996—Atlanta NFL	16	5-5	9-11	7-8	1-5	22-29	75.9	∞54	31	31	97
1997—Atlanta NFL	16	11-11	7-7	3-6	2-3	23-27	85.2	∞55	35	35	104
1998—Atlanta NFL	16	8-10	7-7	6-9	2-2	23-28	82.1	53	51	52	120

Year Team	G	FIELD GOALS 1-29	30-39	40-49	50+	Tot.	Pct.	Lg.	TOTALS XPM	XPA	Pts.
1999—Atlanta NFL	16	6-6	5-8	4-6	0-1	15-21	71.4	49	34	34	79
2000—Atlanta NFL	16	6-6	6-7	11-15	2-3	25-31	80.6	51	23	23	98
2001—New York Giants NFL	16	8-8	7-8	6-7	2-5	23-28	82.1	51	29	30	98
2002—Kansas City NFL	14	6-6	10-10	5-9	1-1	22-26	84.6	50	*51	*51	117
2003—Kansas City NFL	16	3-3	8-8	5-8	0-1	16-20	80.0	49	*58	*59	106
Pro totals (22 years)	338	164-169	166-189	132-195	40-83	502-636	78.9	60	753	763	2259

ANDERSON, BENNIE G RAVENS

PERSONAL: Born February 17, 1977, in St. Louis, Mo. ... 6-5/345. ... Full name: Tyrone Lamar Anderson.
HIGH SCHOOL: Cleveland Junior Naval Academy (St. Louis).
COLLEGE: Tennessee State.
TRANSACTIONS/CAREER NOTES: Signed as non-drafted free agent by St. Louis Rams (May 3, 2000). ... Released by Rams (July 19, 2000). ... Signed by Baltimore Ravens (June 14, 2001).
PLAYING EXPERIENCE: Baltimore NFL, 2001-2003. ... Games/Games started: 2001 (16/13), 2002 (16/16), 2003 (16/15). Total: 48/44.

ANDERSON, DAMIEN RB CARDINALS

PERSONAL: Born July 17, 1979, in Wilmington, Ill. ... 5-11/212. ... Full name: Damien Ramone Anderson.
HIGH SCHOOL: Wilmington (Ill.).
COLLEGE: Northwestern.
TRANSACTIONS/CAREER NOTES: Signed as non-drafted free agent by Arizona Cardinals (April 23, 2002). ... Released by Cardinals (September 1, 2002). ... Re-signed by Cardinals to practice squad (September 2, 2002). ... Activated (October 5, 2002).
SINGLE GAME HIGHS (regular season): Attempts—23 (October 6, 2002, vs. Carolina); yards—61 (October 6, 2002, vs. Carolina); and rushing touchdowns—0.

Year Team	G	GS	RUSHING Att.	Yds.	Avg.	TD	RECEIVING No.	Yds.	Avg.	TD	KICKOFF RETURNS No.	Yds.	Avg.	TD	TOTALS TD	2pt.	Pts.	Fum.
2002—Arizona NFL	10	1	24	65	2.7	0	3	36	12.0	0	12	227	18.9	0	0	0	0	0
2003—Arizona NFL	16	0	18	68	3.8	0	6	36	6.0	0	2	31	15.5	0	0	0	0	0
Pro totals (2 years)	26	1	42	133	3.2	0	9	72	8.0	0	14	258	18.4	0	0	0	0	0

ANDERSON, GARY K

PERSONAL: Born July 16, 1959, in Parys, South Africa. ... 5-11/193. ... Full name: Gary Allan Anderson.
HIGH SCHOOL: Brettonwood (Durban, South Africa).
COLLEGE: Syracuse.
TRANSACTIONS/CAREER NOTES: Selected by Buffalo Bills in seventh round (171st pick overall) of 1982 NFL draft. ... Signed by Bills for 1982 season. ... Claimed on waivers by Pittsburgh Steelers (September 7, 1982). ... Designated by Steelers as transition player (February 15, 1994). ... On reserve/did not report list (August 23-25, 1994). ... Free agency status changed by Steelers from transition to unconditional (February 17, 1995). ... Signed by Philadelphia Eagles (July 23, 1995). ... Released by Eagles (April 22, 1997). ... Signed by San Francisco 49ers (June 11, 1997). ... Granted unconditional free agency (February 13, 1998). ... Signed by Minnesota Vikings (February 20, 1998). ... Granted unconditional free agency (March 1, 2002). ... Re-signed by Vikings (September 17, 2002). ... Granted unconditional free agency (February 28, 2003). ... Signed by Tennessee Titans (September 11, 2003). ... Granted unconditional free agency (March 3, 2004).
CHAMPIONSHIP GAME EXPERIENCE: Played in AFC championship game (1984 and 1994 seasons). ... Played in NFC championship game (1997 and 1998 seasons). ... Member of Vikings for NFC Championship game (2000 season); did not play.
HONORS: Played in Pro Bowl (1983, 1985, 1993 and 1998 seasons). ... Named kicker on THE SPORTING NEWS NFL All-Pro team (1998).
RECORDS: Holds NFL career records for most points—2,346; most field goals attempted—650, and most field goals made—521. ... Holds NFL single-season record for most points scored without a touchdown—164 (1998). ... Shares NFL record for most seasons with 100 or more points—14 (1983-85, 1988, 1991-94, 1996-2000, 2003). ... Shares NFL single-season record for highest field-goal percentage—100.0 (1998).
POST SEASON RECORDS: Holds NFL postseason career record for most made field goals—32. ... Holds NFL postseason record for most consecutive made field goals—16 (1989-95).

Year Team	G	FIELD GOALS 1-29	30-39	40-49	50+	Tot.	Pct.	Lg.	TOTALS XPM	XPA	Pts.
1982—Pittsburgh NFL	9	4-4	1-2	5-5	0-1	10-12	83.3	48	22	22	52
1983—Pittsburgh NFL	16	10-11	9-10	8-10	0-0	27-31	87.1	49	38	39	§119
1984—Pittsburgh NFL	16	8-9	6-9	8-11	2-3	▲24-32	75.0	55	45	45	§117
1985—Pittsburgh NFL	16	13-14	14-15	5-9	1-4	*33-*42	78.6	52	40	40	§139
1986—Pittsburgh NFL	16	6-8	6-7	9-14	0-3	21-32	65.6	45	32	32	95
1987—Pittsburgh NFL	12	8-9	5-5	7-11	2-2	22-27	81.5	52	21	21	87
1988—Pittsburgh NFL	16	12-12	9-10	6-12	1-2	28-36	77.8	52	34	35	118
1989—Pittsburgh NFL	16	7-7	5-8	9-15	0-0	21-30	70.0	49	28	28	91
1990—Pittsburgh NFL	16	4-4	8-8	8-11	0-2	20-25	80.0	48	32	32	92
1991—Pittsburgh NFL	16	8-10	9-11	5-6	1-6	23-33	69.7	54	31	31	100
1992—Pittsburgh NFL	16	12-13	12-15	4-6	0-2	28-36	77.8	49	29	31	113
1993—Pittsburgh NFL	16	9-10	14-14	5-6	0-0	28-30	§93.3	46	32	32	*116
1994—Pittsburgh NFL	16	8-9	8-9	7-9	1-2	24-29	82.8	50	32	32	104
1995—Philadelphia NFL	16	5-5	9-10	8-12	0-3	22-30	73.3	43	32	33	98
1996—Philadelphia NFL	16	10-11	8-9	7-9	0-0	25-29	86.2	46	40	40	115
1997—San Francisco NFL	16	11-11	9-12	8-10	1-3	29-36	80.6	51	38	38	125
1998—Minnesota NFL	16	12-12	9-9	12-12	2-2	‡35-∞35	*100.0	53	*59	*59	*164
1999—Minnesota NFL	16	6-8	9-11	4-9	0-2	19-30	63.3	44	46	46	103
2000—Minnesota NFL	16	6-6	9-9	7-7	0-1	22-23	95.7	49	‡45	∞45	111
2001—Minnesota NFL	16	7-7	2-4	6-7	0-0	15-18	83.3	44	29	30	74
2002—Minnesota NFL	14	9-9	5-5	3-8	1-1	18-23	78.3	∞53	36	37	90
2003—Tennessee NFL	15	5-5	12-12	10-14	0-0	27-31	87.1	43	42	42	123
Pro totals (22 years)	338	180-194	178-204	151-213	12-39	521-650	80.2	55	783	790	2346

ANDERSON, MARQUES — S — PACKERS

PERSONAL: Born May 26, 1979, in Harbor City, Calif. ... 5-11/212. ... Full name: Marques Deon Anderson.
HIGH SCHOOL: Polytechnic (Pasadena, Calif.).
COLLEGE: UCLA.
TRANSACTIONS/CAREER NOTES: Selected by Green Bay Packers in third round (92nd pick overall) of 2002 NFL draft. ... Signed by Packers (July 9, 2002).

			TOTALS			INTERCEPTIONS			
Year Team	G	GS	Tk.	Ast.	Sks.	No.	Yds.	Avg.	TD
2002—Green Bay NFL	14	11	41	20	0.0	4	114	28.5	2
2003—Green Bay NFL	16	7	51	20	0.0	1	3	3.0	0
Pro totals (2 years)	30	18	92	40	0.0	5	117	23.4	2

ANDERSON, MIKE — RB — BRONCOS

PERSONAL: Born September 21, 1973, in Winnsboro, S.C. ... 6-0/230. ... Full name: Michael Moschello Anderson.
HIGH SCHOOL: Fairfield (S.C.).
JUNIOR COLLEGE: Mount San Jacinto Community College (Calif.).
COLLEGE: Utah.
TRANSACTIONS/CAREER NOTES: Selected by Denver Broncos in sixth round (189th pick overall) of 2000 NFL draft. ... Signed by Broncos (July 14, 2000). ... On suspended list for violating league substance abuse policy (November 11-December 14, 2003).
SINGLE GAME HIGHS (regular season): Attempts—37 (December 3, 2000, vs. New Orleans); yards—251 (December 3, 2000, vs. New Orleans); and rushing touchdowns—4 (December 3, 2000, vs. New Orleans).
STATISTICAL PLATEAUS: 100-yard rushing games: 2000 (6), 2001 (2). Total: 8.

			RUSHING				RECEIVING				TOTALS			
Year Team	G	GS	Att.	Yds.	Avg.	TD	No.	Yds.	Avg.	TD	TD	2pt.	Pts.	Fum.
2000—Denver NFL	16	12	297	1487	§5.0	§15	23	169	7.3	0	15	1	92	4
2001—Denver NFL	16	7	175	678	3.9	4	8	46	5.8	0	4	1	26	1
2002—Denver NFL	15	12	84	386	4.6	2	18	167	9.3	2	4	0	24	2
2003—Denver NFL	12	5	70	257	3.7	3	12	53	4.4	2	5	0	30	2
Pro totals (4 years)	59	36	626	2808	4.5	24	61	435	7.1	4	28	2	172	9

ANDERSON, RICHIE — FB — COWBOYS

PERSONAL: Born September 13, 1971, in Sandy Spring, Md. ... 6-2/230. ... Full name: Richard Darnoll Anderson II.
HIGH SCHOOL: Sherwood (Sandy Spring, Md.).
COLLEGE: Penn State.
TRANSACTIONS/CAREER NOTES: Selected after junior season by New York Jets in sixth round (144th pick overall) of 1993 NFL draft. ... Signed by Jets (June 10, 1993). ... On injured reserve with ankle injury (December 31, 1993-remainder of season). ... On injured reserve with ankle injury (November 30, 1995-remainder of season). ... Granted unconditional free agency (February 28, 2003). ... Signed by Dallas Cowboys (March 4, 2003).
CHAMPIONSHIP GAME EXPERIENCE: Member of Jets for AFC championship game (1998 season); did not play.
HONORS: Played in Pro Bowl (2000 season).
SINGLE GAME HIGHS (regular season): Attempts—9 (November 13, 1994, vs. Green Bay); yards—74 (November 13, 1994, vs. Green Bay); and rushing touchdowns—1 (November 27, 2003, vs. Miami).
STATISTICAL PLATEAUS: 100-yard receiving games: 2000 (3). Total: 3.

			RUSHING				RECEIVING				KICKOFF RETURNS				TOTALS			
Year Team	G	GS	Att.	Yds.	Avg.	TD	No.	Yds.	Avg.	TD	No.	Yds.	Avg.	TD	TD	2pt.	Pts.	Fum.
1993—New York Jets NFL	7	0	0	0	0.0	0	0	0	0.0	0	4	66	16.5	0	0	0	0	1
1994—New York Jets NFL	13	5	43	207	4.8	1	25	212	8.5	1	3	43	14.3	0	2	0	12	1
1995—New York Jets NFL	10	0	5	17	3.4	0	5	26	5.2	0	0	0	0.0	0	0	0	0	2
1996—New York Jets NFL	16	13	47	150	3.2	1	44	385	8.8	0	0	0	0.0	0	1	0	6	0
1997—New York Jets NFL	16	3	21	70	3.3	0	26	150	5.8	1	0	0	0.0	0	1	0	6	2
1998—New York Jets NFL	8	1	1	2	2.0	0	3	12	4.0	0	0	0	0.0	0	0	0	0	0
1999—New York Jets NFL	16	9	16	84	5.3	0	29	302	10.4	3	0	0	0.0	0	3	0	18	0
2000—New York Jets NFL	16	15	27	63	2.3	0	88	853	9.7	2	0	0	0.0	0	2	0	12	2
2001—New York Jets NFL	16	16	26	102	3.9	0	40	252	6.3	2	0	0	0.0	0	2	0	12	1
2002—New York Jets NFL	16	16	5	27	5.4	0	45	257	5.7	1	0	0	0.0	0	1	0	6	0
2003—Dallas NFL	15	8	70	306	4.4	1	69	493	7.1	4	0	0	0.0	0	5	0	30	1
Pro totals (11 years)	149	86	261	1028	3.9	3	374	2942	7.9	14	7	109	15.6	0	17	0	102	10

ANDERSON, SCOTTY — WR — LIONS

PERSONAL: Born November 24, 1979, in Jonesboro, La. ... 6-2/191. ... Brother of Stevie Anderson, wide receiver with New York Jets (1994) and Arizona Cardinals (1995 and 1996); and brother of Anthony Anderson, defensive back with San Diego Chargers (1987).
HIGH SCHOOL: Jonesboro-Hodge (Jonesboro, La.).
COLLEGE: Grambling.
TRANSACTIONS/CAREER NOTES: Selected by Detroit Lions in fifth round (148th pick overall) of 2001 NFL draft. ... Signed by Lions (July 16, 2001). ... On injured reserve with ankle injury (November 18, 2003-remainder of season). ... Granted free agency (March 3, 2004). ... Re-signed by Lions (April 19, 2004).
SINGLE GAME HIGHS (regular season): Receptions—5 (November 9, 2003, vs. Chicago); yards—87 (November 16, 2003, vs. Seattle); and touchdown receptions—1 (November 16, 2003, vs. Seattle).

Year Team	G	GS	RECEIVING No.	Yds.	Avg.	TD	TOTALS TD	2pt.	Pts.	Fum.
2001—Detroit NFL	9	4	12	211	17.6	1	1	0	6	0
2002—Detroit NFL	16	4	25	322	12.9	1	1	0	6	1
2003—Detroit NFL	9	0	17	325	19.1	2	2	1	14	0
Pro totals (3 years)	34	8	54	858	15.9	4	4	1	26	1

ANDERSON, WILLIE T BENGALS

PERSONAL: Born July 11, 1975, in Whistler, Ala. ... 6-5/340. ... Full name: Willie Aaron Anderson.
HIGH SCHOOL: Vigor (Prichard, Ala.).
COLLEGE: Auburn.
TRANSACTIONS/CAREER NOTES: Selected after junior season by Cincinnati Bengals in first round (10th pick overall) of 1996 NFL draft. ... Signed by Bengals (August 5, 1996).
PLAYING EXPERIENCE: Cincinnati NFL, 1996-2003. ... Games/Games started: 1996 (16/10), 1997 (16/16), 1998 (16/16), 1999 (14/14), 2000 (16/16), 2001 (16/16), 2002 (16/16), 2003 (16/16). Total: 126/120.
HONORS: Played in Pro Bowl (2003 season).

ANDRUZZI, JOE G PATRIOTS

PERSONAL: Born August 23, 1975, in Brooklyn, N.Y. ... 6-3/312. ... Full name: Joseph Dominick Andruzzi. ... Name pronounced: ann-DROOZ-ee.
HIGH SCHOOL: Tottenville (Staten Island, N.Y.).
COLLEGE: Southern Connecticut State.
TRANSACTIONS/CAREER NOTES: Signed as non-drafted free agent by Green Bay Packers (April 25, 1997). ... Inactive for all 16 games (1997). ... Assigned by Packers to Scottish Claymores in 1998 NFL Europe enhancement allocations program (February 18, 1998). ... On injured reserve with knee injury (November 23, 1999-remainder of season). ... Released by Packers (August 27, 2000). ... Signed by New England Patriots (September 9, 2000). ... On injured reserve with knee injury (December 7, 2000-remainder of season).
PLAYING EXPERIENCE: Green Bay NFL, 1998-1999; New England NFL, 2000-2003. ... Games/Games started: 1998 (15/1), 1999 (8/3), 2000 (11/11), 2001 (16/16), 2002 (13/13), 2003 (16/16). Total: 79/60.
CHAMPIONSHIP GAME EXPERIENCE: Member of Packers for NFC championship game (1997 season); inactive. ... Member of Packers for Super Bowl 32 (1997 season); inactive. ... Played in AFC championship game (2001 and 2003 seasons). ... Member of Super Bowl championship team (2001 and 2003 seasons).

ANGULO, RICHARD TE VIKINGS

PERSONAL: Born August 13, 1980, in Albuquerque, N.M. ... 6-7/260.
HIGH SCHOOL: Sandia (Albuquerque, N.M.).
COLLEGE: Western New Mexico.
TRANSACTIONS/CAREER NOTES: Selected by St. Louis Rams in seventh round (254th pick overall) of 2003 NFL draft. ... Signed by Rams (July 23, 2003). ... Claimed on waivers by Minnesota Vikings (November 25, 2003).

Year Team	G	GS	RECEIVING No.	Yds.	Avg.	TD	TOTALS TD	2pt.	Pts.	Fum.
2003—St. Louis NFL	5	0	0	0	0.0	0	0	0	0	0

ANTHONY, CORNELIUS LB 49ERS

PERSONAL: Born July 3, 1978, in Pinesville, La. ... 6-0/235. ... Full name: Cornelius Armand Anthony.
HIGH SCHOOL: Elkins (Missouri City, Texas).
COLLEGE: Texas A&M.
TRANSACTIONS/CAREER NOTES: Signed as non-drafted free agent by Washington Redskins (April 24, 2001). ... Released by Redskins (August 27, 2001). ... Signed by San Francisco 49ers (February 5, 2002). ... Assigned by 49ers to Frankfurt Galaxy in 2002 NFL Europe enhancement allocation program (February 12, 2002). ... Released by 49ers (August 31, 2002). ... Re-signed by 49ers (October 23, 2002). ... Given injury settlement by 49ers (September 2, 2003). ... Re-signed by 49ers (November 15, 2003).

Year Team	G	GS	TOTALS Tk.	Ast.	Sks.	INTERCEPTIONS No.	Yds.	Avg.	TD
2002—San Francisco NFL	10	0	0	0	0.0	0	0	0.0	0
2003—San Francisco NFL	7	0	0	0	0.0	0	0	0.0	0
Pro totals (2 years)	17	0	0	0	0.0	0	0	0.0	0

ARAGUZ, LEO P

PERSONAL: Born January 18, 1970, in Pharr, Texas. ... 5-11/190. ... Full name: Leobardo Jaime Araguz. ... Name pronounced: ara-GOOSE.
HIGH SCHOOL: Harlingen (Texas).
COLLEGE: Stephen F. Austin.
TRANSACTIONS/CAREER NOTES: Signed as non-drafted free agent by Miami Dolphins (March 28, 1994). ... Released by Dolphins prior to 1994 season. ... Signed by San Diego Chargers (1995). ... Released by Chargers prior to 1995 season. ... Signed by Rhein Fire of the World League for 1996 season. ... Signed by Oakland Raiders (December 4, 1996). ... Released by Raiders (August 27, 2000). ... Signed by St. Louis Rams (June 14, 2001). ... Released by Rams (August 27, 2001). ... Signed by Detroit Lions (November 27, 2001). ... Released by Lions (December 18, 2001). ... Signed by Kansas City Chiefs (May 12, 2003). ... Released by Chiefs (August 26, 2003). ... Signed by Minnesota Vikings (December 16, 2003). ... Granted free agency (March 3, 2004).
RECORDS: Holds NFL single-game record for most punts—16 (October 11, 1998, vs. San Diego).

Year Team	G	PUNTING No.	Yds.	Avg.	Net avg.	In. 20	Blk.
1996—Oakland NFL	3	13	534	41.1	34.5	4	0
1997—Oakland NFL	16	§93	§4189	‡45.0	*39.1	▲28	0
1998—Oakland NFL	16	§98	§4256	43.4	33.4	29	0
1999—Oakland NFL	16	76	3045	40.1	32.3	25	1
2000—		Did not play.					
2001—Detroit NFL	3	17	713	41.9	34.0	6	0
2003—Minnesota NFL	2	7	271	38.7	27.7	1	0
Pro totals (6 years)	56	304	13008	42.8	34.8	93	1

ARCHULETA, ADAM — S — RAMS

PERSONAL: Born November 27, 1977, in Chandler, Ariz. ... 6-0/223. ... Full name: Adam J. Archuleta.
HIGH SCHOOL: Chandler (Ariz.).
COLLEGE: Arizona State.
TRANSACTIONS/CAREER NOTES: Selected by St. Louis Rams in first round (20th pick overall) of 2001 NFL draft. ... Signed by Rams (July 29, 2001).
CHAMPIONSHIP GAME EXPERIENCE: Played in NFC championship game (2001 season). ... Played in Super Bowl 36 (2001 season).

			TOTALS			INTERCEPTIONS			
Year Team	G	GS	Tk.	Ast.	Sks.	No.	Yds.	Avg.	TD
2001—St. Louis NFL	13	12	47	9	2.0	0	0	0.0	0
2002—St. Louis NFL	16	16	94	14	2.5	1	2	2.0	0
2003—St. Louis NFL	13	13	71	7	5.0	1	22	22.0	0
Pro totals (3 years)	42	41	212	30	9.5	2	24	12.0	0

ARMSTEAD, JESSIE — LB — PANTHERS

PERSONAL: Born October 26, 1970, in Dallas, Texas. ... 6-1/237. ... Full name: Jessie W. Armstead.
HIGH SCHOOL: David W. Carter (Dallas).
COLLEGE: Miami (Fla.).
TRANSACTIONS/CAREER NOTES: Selected by New York Giants in eighth round (207th pick overall) of 1993 NFL draft. ... Signed by Giants (July 19, 1993). ... Released by Giants (February 28, 2002). ... Signed by Washington Redskins (March 1, 2002). ... Released by Redskins (February 24, 2004). ... Signed by Carolina Panthers (March 5, 2004).
CHAMPIONSHIP GAME EXPERIENCE: Played in NFC championship game (2000 season). ... Played in Super Bowl 35 (2000 season).
HONORS: Named outside linebacker on THE SPORTING NEWS NFL All-Pro team (1997). ... Played in Pro Bowl (1997-2001 seasons).

			TOTALS			INTERCEPTIONS			
Year Team	G	GS	Tk.	Ast.	Sks.	No.	Yds.	Avg.	TD
1993—New York Giants NFL	16	0	28	3	0.0	1	0	0.0	0
1994—New York Giants NFL	16	0	33	8	3.0	1	0	0.0	0
1995—New York Giants NFL	16	2	36	10	0.5	1	58	58.0	1
1996—New York Giants NFL	16	16	83	31	3.0	2	23	11.5	0
1997—New York Giants NFL	16	16	101	31	3.5	2	57	28.5	1
1998—New York Giants NFL	16	16	75	26	5.0	2	4	2.0	0
1999—New York Giants NFL	16	16	97	27	9.0	2	35	17.5	0
2000—New York Giants NFL	16	16	76	26	5.0	1	-2	-2.0	0
2001—New York Giants NFL	16	16	64	24	1.5	0	0	0.0	0
2002—Washington NFL	16	16	79	21	3.0	0	0	0.0	0
2003—Washington NFL	16	15	76	17	6.5	0	0	0.0	0
Pro totals (11 years)	176	129	748	224	40.0	12	175	14.6	2

ARMSTRONG, DERICK — WR — TEXANS

PERSONAL: Born April 2, 1979, in Jasper, Texas. ... 6-2/196.
JUNIOR COLLEGE: Tyler (Texas).
COLLEGE: Arkansas-Monticello.
TRANSACTIONS/CAREER NOTES: Signed by Saskatchewan Roughriders of CFL (2002). ... Signed by Houston Texans (January 7, 2003).
SINGLE GAME HIGHS (regular season): Receptions—2 (December 21, 2003, vs. Tennessee); yards—31 (December 21, 2003, vs. Tennessee); and touchdown receptions—1 (October 12, 2003, vs. Tennessee).

			RECEIVING				TOTALS			
Year Team	G	GS	No.	Yds.	Avg.	TD	TD	2pt.	Pts.	Fum.
2003—Houston NFL	8	1	7	75	10.7	1	1	0	6	0

ARMSTRONG, TRACE — DE

PERSONAL: Born October 5, 1965, in Bethesda, Md. ... 6-4/275. ... Full name: Raymond Lester Armstrong.
HIGH SCHOOL: John Carroll (Birmingham, Ala.).
COLLEGE: Florida.
TRANSACTIONS/CAREER NOTES: Selected by Chicago Bears in first round (12th pick overall) of 1989 NFL draft. ... Signed by Bears (August 18, 1989). ... On injured reserve with knee injury (September 24-November 3, 1991). ... Granted free agency (March 1, 1993). ... Re-signed by Bears (March 14, 1993). ... Traded by Bears to Miami Dolphins for second- (P Todd Sauerbrun) and third-round (G Evan Pilgrim) picks in 1995 draft (April 4, 1995). ... Granted unconditional free agency (March 2, 2001). ... Signed by Oakland Raiders (March 5, 2001). ... On injured reserve with Achilles' tendon injury (October 2, 2001-remainder of season). ... On injured reserve with groin injury (November 19, 2003-remainder of season). ... Released by Raiders (March 2, 2004).
HONORS: Named defensive lineman on THE SPORTING NEWS college All-America first team (1988). ... Played in Pro Bowl (2000 season).

Year Team	G	GS	TOTALS Tk.	Ast.	Sks.	INTERCEPTIONS No.	Yds.	Avg.	TD
1989—Chicago NFL	14	14	37	43	5.0	0	0	0.0	0
1990—Chicago NFL	16	16	33	49	10.0	0	0	0.0	0
1991—Chicago NFL	12	12	26	30	1.5	0	0	0.0	0
1992—Chicago NFL	14	14	40	35	6.5	0	0	0.0	0
1993—Chicago NFL	16	16	34	24	11.5	0	0	0.0	0
1994—Chicago NFL	15	15	31	10	7.5	0	0	0.0	0
1995—Miami NFL	15	0	21	5	4.5	0	0	0.0	0
1996—Miami NFL	16	9	22	11	12.0	0	0	0.0	0
1997—Miami NFL	16	16	25	22	5.5	0	0	0.0	0
1998—Miami NFL	16	0	20	2	10.5	0	0	0.0	0
1999—Miami NFL	16	2	16	9	7.5	0	0	0.0	0
2000—Miami NFL	16	0	24	10	§16.5	0	0	0.0	0
2001—Oakland NFL	3	0	1	3	0.5	0	0	0.0	0
2002—Oakland NFL	15	8	15	5	4.0	1	0	0.0	0
2003—Oakland NFL	10	7	15	1	3.0	0	0	0.0	0
Pro totals (15 years)	210	129	360	259	106.0	1	0	0.0	0

ARRINGTON, LAVAR — LB — REDSKINS

PERSONAL: Born June 20, 1978, in Pittsburgh, Pa. ... 6-3/253. ... Full name: LaVar RaShad Arrington.
HIGH SCHOOL: North Hills (Pittsburgh).
COLLEGE: Penn State.
TRANSACTIONS/CAREER NOTES: Selected after junior season by Washington Redskins in first round (second pick overall) of 2000 NFL draft. ... Signed by Redskins (July 22, 2000).
HONORS: Named linebacker on THE SPORTING NEWS college All-America first team (1998 and 1999). ... Butkus Award winner (1999). ... Played in Pro Bowl (2001-2003 seasons).

Year Team	G	GS	TOTALS Tk.	Ast.	Sks.	INTERCEPTIONS No.	Yds.	Avg.	TD
2000—Washington NFL	16	11	43	9	4.0	0	0	0.0	0
2001—Washington NFL	14	14	82	17	0.5	3	120	40.0	1
2002—Washington NFL	16	16	70	25	11.0	0	0	0.0	0
2003—Washington NFL	16	16	77	13	6.0	0	0	0.0	0
Pro totals (4 years)	62	57	272	64	21.5	3	120	40.0	1

ASHWORTH, TOM — T — PATRIOTS

PERSONAL: Born October 10, 1977, in Denver, Colo. ... 6-6/305. ... Full name: Thomas F. Ashworth.
HIGH SCHOOL: Cherry Creek (Englewood, Colo.).
COLLEGE: Colorado.
TRANSACTIONS/CAREER NOTES: Signed as non-drafted free agent by San Francisco 49ers (April 27, 2001). ... Released by 49ers (August 27, 2001). ... Signed by New England Patriots to practice squad (September 4, 2001). ... Released by Patriots (October 9, 2001). ... Re-signed by Patriots to practice squad (October 31, 2001). ... Re-signed by Patriots (April 8, 2003).
PLAYING EXPERIENCE: New England NFL, 2002-2003. ... Games/Games started: 2002 (1/0), 2003 (16/13). Total: 17/13.
CHAMPIONSHIP GAME EXPERIENCE: Played in AFC championship game (2003 season). ... Member of Super Bowl championship team (2003 season).

ASKEW, B.J. — FB — JETS

PERSONAL: Born August 19, 1980, in Cincinnati, Ohio. ... 6-3/233. ... Full name: Bobby DeAngelo Askew Jr..
HIGH SCHOOL: Colerain (Cincinnati).
COLLEGE: Michigan.
TRANSACTIONS/CAREER NOTES: Selected by New York Jets in third round (85th pick overall) of 2003 NFL draft. ... Signed by Jets (July 20, 2003).
SINGLE GAME HIGHS (regular season): Attempts—2 (October 12, 2003, vs. Buffalo); yards—9 (October 12, 2003, vs. Buffalo); rushing touchdowns—0.

Year Team	G	GS	RUSHING Att.	Yds.	Avg.	TD	TOTALS TD	2pt.	Pts.	Fum.
2003—New York Jets NFL	16	0	2	9	4.5	0	0	0	0	0

ASOMUGHA, NNAMDI — CB — RAIDERS

PERSONAL: Born July 6, 1981, in Lafayette, La. ... 6-3/215.
HIGH SCHOOL: Narbonne (Los Angeles).
COLLEGE: California.
TRANSACTIONS/CAREER NOTES: Selected by Oakland Raiders in first round (31st pick overall) of 2003 NFL draft. ... Signed by Raiders (July 24, 2003).

Year Team	G	GS	TOTALS Tk.	Ast.	Sks.	INTERCEPTIONS No.	Yds.	Avg.	TD
2003—Oakland NFL	15	1	17	8	0.0	0	0	0.0	0

A

ATKINS, JAMES — DT — TITANS

PERSONAL: Born June 23, 1978, in Brooklyn, N.Y. ... 6-5/325. ... Full name: James Hodges Atkins.
HIGH SCHOOL: Roosevelt (Yonkers, N.Y.).
JUNIOR COLLEGE: Holmes (Goodman, Miss.), then Nassau (N.Y.).
COLLEGE: Virginia Union.
TRANSACTIONS/CAREER NOTES: Signed as non-drafted free agent by Miami Dolphins (April 25, 2002). ... Claimed on waivers by Tennessee Titans (August 27, 2002). ... Released by Titans (September 10, 2002). ... Re-signed by Titans to practice squad (September 12, 2002). ... Activated (January 31, 2003).

			TOTALS		
Year Team	G	GS	Tk.	Ast.	Sks.
2003—Tennessee NFL	13	4	7	5	0.0

ATKINS, LARRY — LB

PERSONAL: Born July 21, 1975, in Santa Monica, Calif. ... 6-3/250. ... Full name: Larry Tabay Atkins III.
HIGH SCHOOL: Venice (Los Angeles).
COLLEGE: UCLA.
TRANSACTIONS/CAREER NOTES: Selected by Kansas City Chiefs in third round (84th pick overall) of 1999 NFL draft. ... Signed by Chiefs (July 15, 1999). ... Granted free agency (March 1, 2002). ... Re-signed by Chiefs (March 18, 2002). ... On injured reserve with knee injury (December 4, 2002-remainder of season). ... Granted unconditional free agency (February 28, 2003). ... Re-signed by Chiefs (April 17, 2003). ... Released by Chiefs (August 27, 2003). ... Signed by Oakland Raiders (November 19, 2003). ... Released by Raiders (December 24, 2003).
HONORS: Named free safety on THE SPORTING NEWS college All-America second team (1998).

			TOTALS			INTERCEPTIONS			
Year Team	G	GS	Tk.	Ast.	Sks.	No.	Yds.	Avg.	TD
1999—Kansas City NFL	9	0	0	0	0.0	0	0	0.0	0
2000—Kansas City NFL	15	0	0	0	0.0	0	0	0.0	0
2001—Kansas City NFL	12	0	1	0	0.0	0	0	0.0	0
2002—Kansas City NFL	10	0	7	0	0.0	0	0	0.0	0
2003—Oakland NFL	3	0	0	0	0.0	0	0	0.0	0
Pro totals (5 years)	49	0	8	0	0.0	0	0	0.0	0

AVERY, JOHN — RB — VIKINGS

PERSONAL: Born January 11, 1976, in Richmond, Va. ... 5-9/188. ... Full name: John Edward Avery III.
HIGH SCHOOL: Asheville (N.C.).
JUNIOR COLLEGE: Northwest Mississippi Community College.
COLLEGE: Mississippi.
TRANSACTIONS/CAREER NOTES: Selected by Miami Dolphins in first round (29th pick overall) of 1998 NFL draft. ... Signed by Dolphins (July 17, 1998). ... Traded by Dolphins to Denver Broncos for WR Marcus Nash (September 21, 1999). ... Released by Broncos (August 22, 2000). ... Signed by Dallas Cowboys (April 30, 2001). ... Released by Cowboys (September 2, 2001). ... Signed by Edmonton Eskimos of CFL (April 29, 2002). ... Signed by Minnesota Vikings (February 13, 2003). ... On injured reserve with knee injury (October 24, 2003-remainder of season).
SINGLE GAME HIGHS (regular season): Attempts—21 (November 8, 1998, vs. Indianapolis); yards—99 (November 8, 1998, vs. Seattle); and rushing touchdowns—1 (November 8, 1998, vs. Indianapolis).

			RUSHING				RECEIVING				KICKOFF RETURNS				TOTALS			
Year Team	G	GS	Att.	Yds.	Avg.	TD	No.	Yds.	Avg.	TD	No.	Yds.	Avg.	TD	TD	2pt.	Pts.	Fum.
1998—Miami NFL	16	0	143	503	3.5	2	10	67	6.7	1	43	1085	25.2	0	3	0	18	5
1999—Miami NFL	1	0	0	0	0.0	0	0	0	0.0	0	2	55	27.5	0	0	0	0	0
—Denver NFL	6	1	5	21	4.2	0	4	24	6.0	0	7	137	19.6	0	0	0	0	0
2003—Minnesota NFL	6	0	1	0	0.0	0	2	24	12.0	1	16	346	21.6	0	1	0	6	1
Pro totals (3 years)	29	1	149	524	3.5	2	16	115	7.2	2	68	1623	23.9	0	4	0	24	6

AYANBADEJO, BRENDON — LB — DOLPHINS

PERSONAL: Born September 6, 1976, in Chicago, Ill. ... 6-1/230. ... Full name: Oladele Brendon Ayanbadejo. ... Brother of Obafemi Ayanbadejo, running back, Arizona Cardinals.
HIGH SCHOOL: Santa Cruz (Calif.).
COLLEGE: UCLA.
TRANSACTIONS/CAREER NOTES: Signed as non-drafted free agent by Atlanta Falcons (April 19, 1999). ... Waived by Falcons (August 23, 1999). ... Signed by Winnipeg Blue Bombers of CFL (2000). ... Signed by British Columbia of CFL (2002). ... Signed by Miami Dolphins (February 4, 2003).

			RUSHING				TOTALS			
Year Team	G	GS	Att.	Yds.	Avg.	TD	TD	2pt.	Pts.	Fum.
2003—Miami NFL	16	0	0	0	0.0	0	0	0	0	0

AYANBADEJO, OBAFEMI — FB — CARDINALS

PERSONAL: Born March 5, 1975, in Chicago, Ill. ... 6-2/235. ... Name pronounced: oh-BUH-fem-me eye-an-buh-DAY-ho. ... Brother of Brendon Ayanbadejo, linebacker, Miami Dolphins.
HIGH SCHOOL: Santa Cruz (Calif.).
JUNIOR COLLEGE: Cabrillo College (Calif.).
COLLEGE: San Diego State.

TRANSACTIONS/CAREER NOTES: Signed as non-drafted free agent by Minnesota Vikings (April 25, 1997). ... Released by Vikings (August 18, 1997). ... Re-signed by Vikings (February 6, 1998). ... Assigned by Vikings to England Monarchs in 1998 NFL Europe enhancement allocation program (February 17, 1998). ... Released by Vikings (August 24, 1998). ... Re-signed by Vikings to practice squad (August 31, 1998). ... Activated (December 1, 1998). ... Released by Vikings (December 23, 1998). ... Re-signed by Vikings to practice squad (December 24, 1998). ... Released by Vikings (September 21, 1999). ... Signed by Baltimore Ravens (September 27, 1999). ... On injured reserve with toe injury (November 28, 2000-remainder of season). ... Granted free agency (March 1, 2002). ... Signed by Miami Dolphins (July 25, 2002). ... Released by Dolphins (September 1, 2002). ... Re-signed by Dolphins (January 15, 2003). ... Granted unconditional free agency (March 3, 2004). ... Signed by Arizona Cardinals (March 6, 2004).

SINGLE GAME HIGHS (regular season): Attempts—9 (October 21, 2001, vs. Cleveland); yards—48 (October 21, 2001, vs. Cleveland); and rushing touchdowns—1 (December 2, 2001, vs. Indianapolis).

			RUSHING				RECEIVING				TOTALS			
Year Team	G	GS	Att.	Yds.	Avg.	TD	No.	Yds.	Avg.	TD	TD	2pt.	Pts.	Fum.
1998—Minnesota NFL	1	0	0	0	0.0	0	0	0	0.0	0	0	0	0	0
1999—Minnesota NFL	2	0	0	0	0.0	0	0	0	0.0	0	0	0	0	0
—Baltimore NFL	12	0	0	0	0.0	0	1	2	2.0	0	0	0	0	0
2000—Baltimore NFL	8	4	15	37	2.5	1	23	168	7.3	1	2	0	12	0
2001—Baltimore NFL	16	5	46	173	3.8	1	24	121	5.0	1	2	0	12	1
2003—Miami NFL	16	2	1	-2	-2.0	0	12	53	4.4	0	0	0	0	1
Pro totals (5 years)	55	11	62	208	3.4	2	60	344	5.7	2	4	0	24	2

AYODELE, AKIN — LB — JAGUARS

PERSONAL: Born September 17, 1979, in Dallas, Texas. ... 6-2/251. ... Full name: Akinola James Ayodele.

HIGH SCHOOL: MacArthur (Irving, Texas).

COLLEGE: Purdue.

TRANSACTIONS/CAREER NOTES: Selected by Jacksonville Jaguars in third round (89th pick overall) of 2002 NFL draft. ... Signed by Jaguars (July 11, 2002).

			TOTALS			INTERCEPTIONS			
Year Team	G	GS	Tk.	Ast.	Sks.	No.	Yds.	Avg.	TD
2002—Jacksonville NFL	16	3	49	7	3.0	1	22	22.0	0
2003—Jacksonville NFL	16	16	85	28	1.0	2	15	7.5	0
Pro totals (2 years)	32	19	134	35	4.0	3	37	12.3	0

AZUMAH, JERRY — CB — BEARS

PERSONAL: Born September 1, 1977, in Oklahoma City, Okla. ... 5-10/195. ... Name pronounced: ah-ZOO-muh.

HIGH SCHOOL: St. Peter-Marian (Worcester, Mass.).

COLLEGE: New Hampshire.

TRANSACTIONS/CAREER NOTES: Selected by Chicago Bears in fifth round (147th pick overall) of 1999 NFL draft. ... Signed by Bears (June 8, 1999).

HONORS: Named kick returner on The Sporting News NFL All-Pro team (2003 season). ... Played in Pro Bowl (2003 season). ... Walter Payton Award winner (1998).

			TOTALS			INTERCEPTIONS				KICKOFF RETURNS				TOTALS			
Year Team	G	GS	Tk.	Ast.	Sks.	No.	Yds.	Avg.	TD	No.	Yds.	Avg.	TD	TD	2pt.	Pts.	Fum.
1999—Chicago NFL	16	2	17	2	0.0	0	0	0.0	0	0	0	0.0	0	0	0	0	0
2000—Chicago NFL	14	4	21	5	0.0	1	2	2.0	0	0	0	0.0	0	0	0	0	0
2001—Chicago NFL	16	5	42	7	2.0	1	14	14.0	0	4	65	16.3	0	0	0	0	0
2002—Chicago NFL	16	16	69	13	1.0	0	18	0.0	0	0	0	0.0	0	0	0	0	0
2003—Chicago NFL	16	13	68	11	1.0	4	44	11.0	0	41	1191	*29.0	†2	2	0	12	1
Pro totals (5 years)	78	40	217	38	4.0	6	78	13.0	0	45	1256	27.9	2	2	0	12	1

BABER, BILLY — TE — CHIEFS

PERSONAL: Born January 17, 1979, in Charlottesville, Va. ... 6-3/255. ... Full name: William Franklin Baber.

HIGH SCHOOL: Western Albermarle (Va.).

COLLEGE: Virginia.

TRANSACTIONS/CAREER NOTES: Selected by Kansas City Chiefs in fifth round (141st pick overall) of 2001 NFL draft. ... Signed by Chiefs (May 24, 2001). ... Released by Chiefs (September 2, 2001). ... Re-signed by Chiefs to practice squad (September 3, 2001). ... Activated (December 3, 2001).

SINGLE GAME HIGHS (regular season): Receptions—1 (December 28, 2003, vs. Chicago); yards—20 (December 28, 2003, vs. Chicago); and touchdown receptions—1 (September 29, 2002, vs. Miami).

			RECEIVING				TOTALS			
Year Team	G	GS	No.	Yds.	Avg.	TD	TD	2pt.	Pts.	Fum.
2001—Kansas City NFL	1	0	0	0	0.0	0	0	0	0	0
2002—Kansas City NFL	12	2	2	10	5.0	1	1	0	6	0
2003—Kansas City NFL	16	0	1	20	20.0	0	0	0	0	0
Pro totals (3 years)	29	2	3	30	10.0	1	1	0	6	0

BABERS, RODERICK — CB — LIONS

PERSONAL: Born October 6, 1980, in Houston, Texas. ... 5-9/190. ... Full name: Roderick Henri Babers.

HIGH SCHOOL: Lamar (Houston).

COLLEGE: Texas.

TRANSACTIONS/CAREER NOTES: Selected by New York Giants in fourth round (123rd pick overall) of 2003 NFL draft. ... Signed by Giants (July 24, 2003). ... Claimed on waivers by Detroit Lions (September 8, 2003). ... On injured reserve with shoulder injury (November 11, 2003-remainder of season).

			TOTALS			INTERCEPTIONS			
Year Team	G	GS	Tk.	Ast.	Sks.	No.	Yds.	Avg.	TD
2003—Detroit NFL	5	0	3	1	0.0	0	0	0.0	0

BACKUS, JEFF — T — LIONS

PERSONAL: Born September 21, 1977, in Midland, Mich. ... 6-5/305. ... Full name: Jeffrey Carl Backus.
HIGH SCHOOL: Norcross (Ga.).
COLLEGE: Michigan.
TRANSACTIONS/CAREER NOTES: Selected by Detriot Lions in first round (18th pick overall) of 2001 NFL draft. ... Signed by Lions (July 23, 2001).
PLAYING EXPERIENCE: Detroit NFL, 2001-2003. ... Games/Games started: 2001 (16/16), 2002 (16/16), 2003 (16/16). Total: 48/48.

B

BADGER, BRAD — T — RAIDERS

PERSONAL: Born January 11, 1975, in Corvallis, Ore. ... 6-4/320.
HIGH SCHOOL: Corvallis (Ore.).
COLLEGE: Stanford.
TRANSACTIONS/CAREER NOTES: Selected by Washington Redskins in fifth round (162nd pick overall) of 1997 NFL draft. ... Signed by Redskins (May 5, 1997). ... Granted free agency (February 11, 2000). ... Tendered offer sheet by Minnesota Vikings (April 10, 2000). ... Redskins declined to match offer (April 11, 2000). ... Released by Vikings (March 12, 2002). ... Signed by Oakland Raiders (April 12, 2002). ... Granted unconditional free agency (February 28, 2003). ... Re-signed by Raiders (March 4, 2003).
PLAYING EXPERIENCE: Washington NFL, 1997-1999; Minnesota NFL, 2000-2001; Oakland NFL, 2002-2003. ... Games/Games started: 1997 (12/1), 1998 (16/16), 1999 (14/4), 2000 (16/0), 2001 (13/12), 2002 (7/0), 2003 (16/11). Total: 94/44.
CHAMPIONSHIP GAME EXPERIENCE: Member of Vikings for NFC Championship game (2000 season); did not play. ... Member of Raiders for AFC championship game (2002 season); inactive. ... Played in Super Bowl 37 (2002 season).

BAILEY, BOSS — LB — LIONS

PERSONAL: Born October 14, 1979, in Folkston, Ga. ... 6-3/233. ... Brother of Champ Bailey, cornerback, Denver Broncos.
HIGH SCHOOL: Charlton County (Ga.).
COLLEGE: Georgia.
TRANSACTIONS/CAREER NOTES: Selected by Detroit Lions in second round (34th pick overall) of 2003 NFL draft. ... Signed by Lions (July 23, 2003).

			TOTALS			INTERCEPTIONS			
Year Team	G	GS	Tk.	Ast.	Sks.	No.	Yds.	Avg.	TD
2003—Detroit NFL	16	16	68	20	1.5	1	-2	-2.0	0

BAILEY, CHAMP — CB — BRONCOS

PERSONAL: Born June 22, 1978, in Folkston, Ga. ... 6-0/192. ... Full name: Roland Champ Bailey. ... Brother of Boss Bailey, linebacker, Detroit Lions.
HIGH SCHOOL: Charlton County (Folkson, Ga.).
COLLEGE: Georgia.
TRANSACTIONS/CAREER NOTES: Selected after junior season by Washington Redskins in first round (seventh pick overall) of 1999 NFL draft. ... Signed by Redskins (July 24, 1999). ... Designated by Redskins as franchise player (February 24, 2004). ... Traded by Redskins with a second-round pick (RB Tatum Bell) in 2004 draft to Denver for RB Clinton Portis (March 4, 2004).
HONORS: Named cornerback on THE SPORTING NEWS college All-America second team (1998). ... Named cornerback on THE SPORTING NEWS NFL All-Pro team (2003). ... Bronko Nagurski Award winner (1998). ... Played in Pro Bowl (2000-2003 seasons).

			TOTALS			INTERCEPTIONS				PUNT RETURNS				KICKOFF RETURNS				TOTALS			
Year Team	G	GS	Tk.	Ast.	Sks.	No.	Yds.	Avg.	TD	No.	Yds.	Avg.	TD	No.	Yds.	Avg.	TD	TD	2pt.	Pts.	Fum.
1999—Was. NFL	16	16	61	5	1.0	5	55	11.0	1	0	0	0.0	0	0	0	0.0	0	1	0	6	0
2000—Was. NFL	16	16	52	5	0.0	5	48	9.6	0	1	65	65.0	0	0	0	0.0	0	1	0	6	0
2001—Was. NFL	16	16	49	2	0.0	3	17	5.7	0	0	0	0.0	0	0	0	0.0	0	0	0	0	0
2002—Was. NFL	16	16	62	6	0.0	3	2	0.7	0	24	238	9.9	0	1	17	17.0	0	0	0	0	4
2003—Was. NFL	16	16	67	4	0.0	2	2	1.0	0	0	0	0.0	0	0	0	0.0	0	0	0	0	0
Pro totals (5 years)	80	80	291	22	1.0	18	124	6.9	1	25	303	12.1	0	1	17	17.0	0	2	0	12	4

BAILEY, KARSTEN — WR

PERSONAL: Born April 26, 1977, in Newman, Ga. ... 6-0/205. ... Full name: Karsten Mario Bailey.
HIGH SCHOOL: East Coweta (Sharpsburg, Ga.).
COLLEGE: Auburn.
TRANSACTIONS/CAREER NOTES: Selected by Seattle Seahawks in third round (82nd pick overall) of 1999 NFL draft. ... Signed by Seahawks (July 29, 1999). ... Released by Seahawks (September 2, 2001). ... Signed by Green Bay Packers (January 24, 2002). ... Granted free agency (February 28, 2003). ... Re-signed by Packers (March 3, 2003). ... Released by Packers (September 10, 2003).
SINGLE GAME HIGHS (regular season): Receptions—2 (September 29, 2002, vs. Carolina); yards—34 (December 23, 2000, vs. Buffalo); and touchdown receptions—1 (October 15, 2000, vs. Indianapolis).

Year Team	G	GS	RECEIVING No.	Yds.	Avg.	TD	TOTALS TD	2pt.	Pts.	Fum.
1999—Seattle NFL	2	0	0	0	0.0	0	0	0	0	0
2000—Seattle NFL	9	0	6	62	10.3	1	1	0	6	0
2002—Green Bay NFL	7	0	3	26	8.7	0	0	0	0	0
2003—Green Bay NFL	1	0	0	0	0.0	0	0	0	0	0
Pro totals (4 years)	19	0	9	88	9.8	1	1	0	6	0

BAILEY, RODNEY DE PATRIOTS

PERSONAL: Born October 7, 1979, in Cleveland, Ohio. ... 6-3/306. ... Full name: Rodney Dwayne Bailey.
HIGH SCHOOL: St. Edwards (Cleveland).
COLLEGE: Ohio State.
TRANSACTIONS/CAREER NOTES: Selected by Pittsburgh Steelers in sixth round (181st pick overall) of 2001 NFL draft. ... Signed by Steelers (June 6, 2001). ... Granted free agency (March 3, 2004). ... Tendered offer sheet by New England Patriots (March 4, 2004). ... Steelers declined to match offer (March 11, 2004).
CHAMPIONSHIP GAME EXPERIENCE: Played in AFC championship game (2001 season).

Year Team	G	GS	TOTALS Tk.	Ast.	Sks.
2001—Pittsburgh NFL	16	1	8	4	2.0
2002—Pittsburgh NFL	16	0	17	7	5.5
2003—Pittsburgh NFL	16	0	7	2	2.0
Pro totals (3 years)	48	1	32	13	9.5

BAKER, CHRIS TE JETS

PERSONAL: Born November 18, 1979, in Queens, N.Y. ... 6-3/258.
HIGH SCHOOL: Saline (Mich.).
COLLEGE: Michigan State.
TRANSACTIONS/CAREER NOTES: Selected by New York Jets in third round (88th pick overall) of 2002 NFL draft. ... Signed by Jets (July 16, 2002).
SINGLE GAME HIGHS (regular season): Receptions—3 (December 20, 2003, vs. New England); yards—31 (December 20, 2003, vs. New England); and touchdown receptions—0.

Year Team	G	GS	RECEIVING No.	Yds.	Avg.	TD	KICKOFF RETURNS No.	Yds.	Avg.	TD	TOTALS TD	2pt.	Pts.	Fum.
2002—New York Jets NFL	12	0	2	14	7.0	0	3	23	7.7	0	0	0	0	0
2003—New York Jets NFL	16	0	14	137	9.8	0	2	6	3.0	0	0	0	0	0
Pro totals (2 years)	28	0	16	151	9.4	0	5	29	5.8	0	0	0	0	0

BAKER, EUGENE WR PANTHERS

PERSONAL: Born March 18, 1976, in Monroeville, Pa. ... 6-2/183.
HIGH SCHOOL: Shady Side Academy (Monroeville, Pa.).
COLLEGE: Kent State.
TRANSACTIONS/CAREER NOTES: Selected by Atlanta Falcons in fifth round (164th pick overall) of 1999 NFL draft. ... Signed by Falcons (July 7, 1999). ... Released by Falcons (September 5, 1999). ... Re-signed by Falcons to practice squad (September 7, 1999). ... Activated (December 13, 1999). ... Released by Falcons (September 2, 2001). ... Re-signed by Falcons to practice squad (September 4, 2001). ... Released by Falcons (October 2, 2001). ... Signed by Buffalo Bills to practice squad (October 3, 2001). ... Granted free agency following 2001 season. ... Signed by St. Louis Rams (February 19, 2002). ... Released by Rams (August 23, 2002). ... Signed by Carolina Panthers (January 8, 2003).
CHAMPIONSHIP GAME EXPERIENCE: Member of Panthers for NFC championship game (2003 season); inactive. ... Member of Panthers for Super Bowl 38 (2003 season); inactive.
SINGLE GAME HIGHS (regular season): Receptions—5 (December 19, 1999, vs. Tennessee); yards—66 (December 19, 1999, vs. Tennessee); and touchdown receptions—0.

Year Team	G	GS	RECEIVING No.	Yds.	Avg.	TD	TOTALS TD	2pt.	Pts.	Fum.
1999—Atlanta NFL	3	1	7	118	16.9	0	0	0	0	0
2003—Carolina NFL	1	0	0	0	0.0	0	0	0	0	0
Pro totals (2 years)	4	1	7	118	16.9	0	0	0	0	0

BAKER, JASON P CHIEFS

PERSONAL: Born May 17, 1978, in Fort Wayne, Ind. ... 6-1/201.
HIGH SCHOOL: Wayne (Fort Wayne, Ind.).
COLLEGE: Iowa.
TRANSACTIONS/CAREER NOTES: Signed as non-drafted free agent by Philadelphia Eagles (April 23, 2001). ... Released by Eagles (August 28, 2001). ... Signed by San Francisco 49ers (August 29, 2001). ... Released by 49ers (November 26, 2002). ... Signed by Philadelphia Eagles (December 3, 2002). ... Released by Eagles (December 16, 2002). ... Signed by Kansas City Chiefs (May 14, 2003). ... Granted free agency (March 3, 2004). ... Re-signed by Chiefs (April 12, 2004).

Year Team	G	PUNTING No.	Yds.	Avg.	Net avg.	In. 20	Blk.
2001—San Francisco NFL	16	69	2813	40.8	35.4	21	0
2002—Philadelphia NFL	2	13	445	34.2	29.8	2	0
—San Francisco NFL	11	42	1688	40.2	32.0	12	0

Year Team	G	PUNTING No.	Yds.	Avg.	Net avg.	In. 20	Blk.
2003—Kansas City NFL	16	80	3156	39.5	33.2	21	1
Pro totals (3 years)	45	204	8102	39.7	33.5	56	1

BALL, JASON — C — CHARGERS

PERSONAL: Born March 21, 1979, in Fayetteville, N.C. ... 6-2/301.
HIGH SCHOOL: Londonderry (N.H.).
COLLEGE: New Hampshire.
TRANSACTIONS/CAREER NOTES: Signed as non-drafted free agent by San Diego Chargers (April 26, 2002).
PLAYING EXPERIENCE: San Diego NFL, 2002-2003. ... Games/Games started: 2002 (16/13), 2003 (8/8). Total: 24/21.

B

BANKS, MIKE — TE — CARDINALS

PERSONAL: Born November 5, 1979, in Mason City, Iowa. ... 6-4/262.
HIGH SCHOOL: Ogden (Iowa).
COLLEGE: Iowa State.
TRANSACTIONS/CAREER NOTES: Selected by Arizona Cardinals in seventh round (223rd pick overall) of 2002 NFL draft. ... Signed by Cardinals (May 28, 2002).

			RECEIVING				TOTALS			
Year Team	G	GS	No.	Yds.	Avg.	TD	TD	2pt.	Pts.	Fum.
2002—Arizona NFL	12	0	0	0	0.0	0	0	0	0	0
2003—Arizona NFL	6	0	0	0	0.0	0	0	0	0	0
Pro totals (2 years)	18	0	0	0	0.0	0	0	0	0	0

BANKS, TONY — QB — TEXANS

PERSONAL: Born April 5, 1973, in San Diego, Calif. ... 6-4/230. ... Full name: Anthony Lamar Banks.
HIGH SCHOOL: Herbert Hoover (San Diego).
JUNIOR COLLEGE: San Diego Mesa College.
COLLEGE: Michigan State.
TRANSACTIONS/CAREER NOTES: Selected by St. Louis Rams in second round (42nd pick overall) of 1996 NFL draft. ... Signed by Rams (July 15, 1996). ... On injured reserve list with knee injury (December 14, 1998-remainder of season). ... Granted free agency (February 12, 1999). ... Re-signed by Rams (April 17, 1999). ... Traded by Rams to Baltimore Ravens for fifth-round pick (G Cameron Spikes) in 1999 draft and seventh-round pick (traded to Chicago) in 2000 draft (April 17, 1999). ... Granted unconditional free agency (February 11, 2000). ... Re-signed by Ravens (February 17, 2000). ... Released by Ravens (March 1, 2001). ... Signed by Dallas Cowboys (March 28, 2001). ... Released by Cowboys (August 14, 2001). ... Signed by Washington Redskins (August 16, 2001). ... Granted unconditional free agency (March 1, 2002). ... Signed by Houston Texans (August 19, 2002). ... Granted unconditional free agency (February 28, 2003). ... Re-signed by Texans (April 3, 2003). ... On injured reserve with hand injury (December 1, 2003-remainder of season).
CHAMPIONSHIP GAME EXPERIENCE: Member of Ravens for AFC championship game (2000 season); did not play. ... Member of Super Bowl championship team (2000 season).
SINGLE GAME HIGHS (regular season): Attempts—49 (September 28, 1997, vs. Oakland); completions—29 (September 6, 1998, vs. New Orleans); yards—401 (November 2, 1997, vs. Atlanta); and touchdown passes—5 (September 10, 2000, vs. Jacksonville).
STATISTICAL PLATEAUS: 300-yard passing games: 1996 (2), 1997 (1), 1999 (1), 2001 (1). Total: 5.
MISCELLANEOUS: Regular-season record as starting NFL quarterback: 35-43 (.449).

			PASSING									RUSHING				TOTALS		
Year Team	G	GS	Att.	Cmp.	Pct.	Yds.	TD	Int.	Avg.	Skd.	Rat.	Att.	Yds.	Avg.	TD	TD	2pt.	Pts.
1996—St. Louis NFL	14	13	368	192	52.2	2544	15	15	6.91	48	71.0	61	212	3.5	0	0	1	2
1997—St. Louis NFL	16	16	487	252	51.7	3254	14	13	6.68	43	71.5	47	186	4.0	1	1	0	6
1998—St. Louis NFL	14	14	408	241	59.1	2535	7	14	6.21	41	68.6	40	156	3.9	3	3	1	20
1999—Baltimore NFL	12	10	320	169	52.8	2136	17	8	6.68	33	81.2	24	93	3.9	0	0	0	0
2000—Baltimore NFL	11	8	274	150	54.7	1578	8	8	5.76	20	69.3	19	57	3.0	0	0	0	0
2001—Washington NFL	15	14	370	198	53.5	2386	10	10	6.45	29	71.3	47	152	3.2	2	2	0	12
2002—Houston NFL	Did not play.																	
2003—Houston NFL	7	3	102	61	59.8	693	5	3	6.79	13	84.3	6	27	4.5	0	0	0	0
Pro totals (7 years)	89	78	2329	1263	54.2	15126	76	71	6.49	227	72.5	244	883	3.6	6	6	2	40

BANNAN, JUSTIN — DT — BILLS

PERSONAL: Born April 18, 1979, in Sacramento, Calif. ... 6-3/305.
HIGH SCHOOL: Bella Vista (Fair Oaks, Calif.).
COLLEGE: Colorado.
TRANSACTIONS/CAREER NOTES: Selected by Buffalo Bills in fifth round (139th pick overall) of 2002 NFL draft. ... Signed by Bills (June 21, 2002).

			TOTALS		
Year Team	G	GS	Tk.	Ast.	Sks.
2002—Buffalo NFL	15	0	15	6	1.0
2003—Buffalo NFL	14	1	9	6	0.0
Pro totals (2 years)	29	1	24	12	1.0

BANNISTER, ALEX — WR — SEAHAWKS

PERSONAL: Born April 23, 1979, in Cincinnati, Ohio. ... 6-5/207.
HIGH SCHOOL: Hughes Center (Cincinnati).
COLLEGE: Eastern Kentucky.
TRANSACTIONS/CAREER NOTES: Selected by Seattle Seahawks in fifth round (140th pick overall) of 2001 NFL draft. ... Signed by Seahawks (July 9, 2001). ... Granted free agency (March 3, 2004). ... Re-signed by Seahawks (May 3, 2004).
HONORS: Played in Pro Bowl (2003 season).
SINGLE GAME HIGHS (regular season): Receptions—2 (December 27, 2003, vs.San Francisco); yards—53 (December 27, 2003, vs. San Francisco); and touchdown receptions—1 (December 27, 2003, vs. San Francisco).

			RECEIVING				TOTALS			
Year Team	G	GS	No.	Yds.	Avg.	TD	TD	2pt.	Pts.	Fum.
2001—Seattle NFL	16	0	4	50	12.5	0	1	0	6	0
2002—Seattle NFL	16	1	0	0	0.0	0	0	0	0	0
2003—Seattle NFL	16	2	3	61	20.3	1	1	0	6	0
Pro totals (3 years)	48	3	7	111	15.9	1	2	0	12	0

B

BANTA, BRADFORD — TE/LS — LIONS

PERSONAL: Born December 14, 1970, in Baton Rouge, La. ... 6-6/253. ... Full name: Dennis Bradford Banta.
HIGH SCHOOL: University (Baton Rouge, La.).
COLLEGE: Southern California.
TRANSACTIONS/CAREER NOTES: Selected by Indianapolis Colts in fourth round (106th pick overall) of 1994 NFL draft. ... Signed by Colts (July 22, 1994). ... Granted free agency (February 14, 1997). ... Re-signed by Colts (May 14, 1997). ... Granted unconditional free agency (February 11, 2000). ... Re-signed by Colts (March 9, 2000). ... Released by Colts (August 27, 2000). ... Signed by New York Jets (August 29, 2000). ... Granted unconditional free agency (March 2, 2001). ... Signed by Detroit Lions (April 19, 2001). ... On injured reserve with broken clavicle (December 8, 2003-remainder of season).
PLAYING EXPERIENCE: Indianapolis NFL, 1994-1999; New York Jets NFL, 2000; Detroit NFL, 2001-2003. ... Games/Games started: 1994 (16/0), 1995 (16/2), 1996 (13/0), 1997 (15/0), 1998 (16/0), 1999 (16/0), 2000 (16/0), 2001 (16/0), 2002 (16/0), 2003 (13/0). Total: 153/2.
CHAMPIONSHIP GAME EXPERIENCE: Played in AFC championship game (1995 season).
SINGLE GAME HIGHS (regular season): Receptions—1 (November 1, 1998, vs. New England); yards—7 (November 1, 1998, vs. New England); and touchdown receptions—0.

BANTA-CAIN, TULLY — LB — PATRIOTS

PERSONAL: Born August 28, 1980, in Mountain View, Calif. ... 6-2/254.
HIGH SCHOOL: Fremont (Mountain View, Calif.).
COLLEGE: California.
TRANSACTIONS/CAREER NOTES: Selected by New England Patriots in seventh round (239th pick overall) of 2003 NFL draft. ... Signed by Patriots (July 21, 2003). ... On physically unable to perform list with groin injury (August 26-October 18, 2003).
CHAMPIONSHIP GAME EXPERIENCE: Played in AFC championship game (2003 season). ... Member of Super Bowl championship team (2003 season).

			TOTALS			INTERCEPTIONS			
Year Team	G	GS	Tk.	Ast.	Sks.	No.	Yds.	Avg.	TD
2003—New England NFL	9	0	1	1	1.0	0	0	0.0	0

BARBER, RONDE — CB — BUCCANEERS

PERSONAL: Born April 7, 1975, in Montgomery County, Va. ... 5-10/184. ... Full name: Jamael Oronde Barber. ... Name pronounced: RON-day. ... Twin brother of Tiki Barber, running back, New York Giants.
HIGH SCHOOL: Cave Spring (Roanoke, Va.).
COLLEGE: Virginia.
TRANSACTIONS/CAREER NOTES: Selected after junior season by Tampa Bay Buccaneers in third round (66th pick overall) of 1997 NFL draft. ... Signed by Buccaneers (July 18, 1997). ... Granted free agency (February 11, 2000). ... Re-signed by Buccaneers (June 13, 2000). ... Granted unconditional free agency (March 2, 2001). ... Re-signed by Buccaneers (April 10, 2001).
CHAMPIONSHIP GAME EXPERIENCE: Played in NFC championship game (1999 and 2002 seasons). ... Member of Super Bowl championship team (2002 season).
HONORS: Played in Pro Bowl (2001 season).

			TOTALS			INTERCEPTIONS			
Year Team	G	GS	Tk.	Ast.	Sks.	No.	Yds.	Avg.	TD
1997—Tampa Bay NFL	1	0	4	0	0.0	0	0	0.0	0
1998—Tampa Bay NFL	16	9	59	11	3.0	2	67	33.5	0
1999—Tampa Bay NFL	16	15	54	16	1.0	2	60	30.0	0
2000—Tampa Bay NFL	16	16	67	15	5.5	2	46	23.0	1
2001—Tampa Bay NFL	16	16	56	13	1.0	†10	86	8.6	1
2002—Tampa Bay NFL	16	16	63	12	3.0	2	9	4.5	0
2003—Tampa Bay NFL	16	16	80	19	1.5	2	53	26.5	1
Pro totals (7 years)	97	88	383	86	15.0	20	321	16.1	3

BARBER, SHAWN — LB — CHIEFS

PERSONAL: Born January 14, 1975, in Richmond, Va. ... 6-2/245.
HIGH SCHOOL: Hermitage (Richmond, Va.).
COLLEGE: Richmond.

TRANSACTIONS/CAREER NOTES: Selected by Washington Redskins in fourth round (113th pick overall) of 1998 NFL draft. ... Signed by Redskins (May 13, 1998). ... Granted free agency (March 2, 2001). ... Re-signed by Redskins (June 1, 2001). ... On injured reserve with knee injury (October 2, 2001-remainder of season). ... Granted unconditional free agency (March 1, 2002). ... Signed by Philadelphia Eagles (March 15, 2002). ... Granted unconditional free agency (February 28, 2003). ... Signed by Kansas City Chiefs (March 3, 2003).
CHAMPIONSHIP GAME EXPERIENCE: Played in NFC championship game (2002 season).

			TOTALS			INTERCEPTIONS			
Year Team	**G**	**GS**	**Tk.**	**Ast.**	**Sks.**	**No.**	**Yds.**	**Avg.**	**TD**
1998—Washington NFL	16	1	21	6	0.0	1	0	0.0	0
1999—Washington NFL	16	16	82	19	1.0	2	70	35.0	1
2000—Washington NFL	14	14	56	7	2.0	0	0	0.0	0
2001—Washington NFL	3	3	14	3	0.0	0	0	0.0	0
2002—Philadelphia NFL	16	16	69	22	1.0	2	81	40.5	1
2003—Kansas City NFL	16	16	93	20	5.0	1	28	28.0	0
Pro totals (6 years)	81	66	335	77	9.0	6	179	29.8	2

B

BARBER, TIKI — RB — GIANTS

PERSONAL: Born April 7, 1975, in Roanoke, Va. ... 5-10/200. ... Full name: Atiim Kiambu Barber. ... Name pronounced: TEE-kee. ... Twin brother of Ronde Barber, cornerback, Tampa Bay Buccaneers.
HIGH SCHOOL: Cave Spring (Roanake, Va.).
COLLEGE: Virginia.
TRANSACTIONS/CAREER NOTES: Selected by New York Giants in second round (36th pick overall) of 1997 NFL draft. ... Signed by Giants for 1997 season. ... Granted free agency (February 11, 2000). ... Re-signed by Giants (June 8, 2000). ... Granted unconditional free agency (March 2, 2001). ... Re-signed by Giants (March 8, 2001).
CHAMPIONSHIP GAME EXPERIENCE: Played in NFC championship game (2000 season). ... Played in Super Bowl 35 (2000 season).
SINGLE GAME HIGHS (regular season): Attempts—32 (December 28, 2002, vs. Philadelphia); yards—203 (December 28, 2002, vs. Philadelphia); and rushing touchdowns—2 (December 22, 2002, vs. Indianapolis).
STATISTICAL PLATEAUS: 100-yard rushing games: 1997 (1), 2000 (1), 2001 (3), 2002 (4), 2003 (4). Total: 13. 100-yard receiving games: 1999 (1). Total: 1.
MISCELLANEOUS: Holds New York Giants all-time record for most receptions (422).

			RUSHING				RECEIVING				PUNT RETURNS				KICKOFF RETURNS				TOTALS		
Year Team	**G**	**GS**	**Att.**	**Yds.**	**Avg.**	**TD**	**No.**	**Yds.**	**Avg.**	**TD**	**No.**	**Yds.**	**Avg.**	**TD**	**No.**	**Yds.**	**Avg.**	**TD**	**TD**	**2pt.**	**Pts.**
1997—NYG NFL	12	6	136	511	3.8	3	34	299	8.8	1	0	0	0.0	0	0	0	0.0	0	4	1	26
1998—NYG NFL	16	4	52	166	3.2	0	42	348	8.3	3	0	0	0.0	0	14	250	17.9	0	3	0	18
1999—NYG NFL	16	1	62	258	4.2	0	66	609	9.2	2	∞44	‡506	11.5	∞1	12	266	22.2	0	3	0	18
2000—NYG NFL	16	12	213	1006	4.7	8	70	719	10.3	1	‡39	332	8.5	0	1	28	28.0	0	9	0	54
2001—NYG NFL	14	9	166	865	5.2	4	72	577	8.0	0	38	338	8.9	0	0	0	0.0	0	4	1	26
2002—NYG NFL	16	15	304	1387	4.6	11	69	597	8.7	0	1	5	5.0	0	0	0	0.0	0	11	0	66
2003—NYG NFL	16	16	278	1216	4.4	2	69	461	6.7	1	0	0	0.0	0	0	0	0.0	0	3	1	20
Pro totals (7 years)	106	63	1211	5409	4.5	28	422	3610	8.6	8	122	1181	9.7	1	27	544	20.1	0	37	3	228

BARKER, BRYAN — P

PERSONAL: Born June 28, 1964, in Jacksonville Beach, Fla. ... 6-1/202. ... Full name: Bryan Christopher Barker.
HIGH SCHOOL: Miramonte (Orinda, Calif.).
COLLEGE: Santa Clara.
TRANSACTIONS/CAREER NOTES: Signed as non-drafted free agent by Denver Broncos (May 1988). ... Released by Broncos (July 19, 1988). ... Signed by Seattle Seahawks (1989). ... Released by Seahawks (August 30, 1989). ... Signed by Kansas City Chiefs (May 1, 1990). ... Released by Chiefs (August 28, 1990). ... Re-signed by Chiefs (September 26, 1990). ... Granted unconditional free agency (February 1-April 1, 1991). ... Re-signed by Chiefs for 1991 season. ... Granted unconditional free agency (February 1-April 1, 1992). ... Re-signed by Chiefs for 1992 season. ... Released by Chiefs (1994). ... Signed by Minnesota Vikings (May 18, 1994). ... Released by Vikings (August 30, 1994). ... Signed by Philadelphia Eagles (October 11, 1994). ... Granted unconditional free agency (February 17, 1995). ... Signed by Jacksonville Jaguars (March 7, 1995). ... Granted unconditional free agency (March 2, 2001). ... Signed by Washington Redskins (April 12, 2001). ... On injured reserve with head injury (December 4, 2002-remainder of season). ... Released by Redskins (February 24, 2004).
CHAMPIONSHIP GAME EXPERIENCE: Played in AFC championship game (1993, 1996 and 1999 seasons).
HONORS: Played in Pro Bowl (1997 season).

		PUNTING					
Year Team	**G**	**No.**	**Yds.**	**Avg.**	**Net avg.**	**In. 20**	**Blk.**
1990—Kansas City NFL	13	64	2479	38.7	33.3	16	0
1991—Kansas City NFL	16	57	2303	40.4	35.0	11	0
1992—Kansas City NFL	15	75	3245	43.3	35.2	16	1
1993—Kansas City NFL	16	76	3240	42.6	35.3	19	1
1994—Philadelphia NFL	11	66	2696	40.8	‡36.2	20	0
1995—Jacksonville NFL	16	82	3591	43.8	*38.6	19	0
1996—Jacksonville NFL	16	69	3016	43.7	35.6	16	0
1997—Jacksonville NFL	16	66	2964	44.9	38.8	27	0
1998—Jacksonville NFL	16	85	3824	45.0	38.5	28	0
1999—Jacksonville NFL	16	78	3260	41.8	36.9	32	0
2000—Jacksonville NFL	16	76	3194	42.0	34.4	29	0
2001—Washington NFL	16	90	3747	41.6	34.8	27	0
2002—Washington NFL	12	48	1924	40.1	30.0	13	0
2003—Washington NFL	16	84	3377	40.2	34.3	24	0
Pro totals (14 years)	211	1016	42860	42.2	35.7	297	2

BARLOW, KEVAN — RB — 49ERS

PERSONAL: Born January 7, 1979, in Pittsburgh, Pa. ... 6-1/238. ... Full name: Kevan C. Barlow.
HIGH SCHOOL: Peabody (Pittsburgh).
COLLEGE: Pittsburgh.

TRANSACTIONS/CAREER NOTES: Selected by San Francisco 49ers in third round (80th pick overall) of 2001 NFL draft. ... Signed by 49ers (July 25, 2001).

SINGLE GAME HIGHS (regular season): Attempts—30 (December 21, 2003, vs. Philadelphia); yards—154 (December 21, 2003, vs. Philadelphia); and rushing touchdowns—2 (December 14, 2003, vs. Cincinnati).

STATISTICAL PLATEAUS: 100-yard rushing games: 2003 (2). Total: 2.

			RUSHING				RECEIVING				TOTALS			
Year Team	**G**	**GS**	**Att.**	**Yds.**	**Avg.**	**TD**	**No.**	**Yds.**	**Avg.**	**TD**	**TD**	**2pt.**	**Pts.**	**Fum.**
2001—San Francisco NFL	15	0	125	512	4.1	4	22	247	11.2	1	5	0	30	1
2002—San Francisco NFL	14	0	145	675	4.7	4	14	136	9.7	1	5	0	30	2
2003—San Francisco NFL	16	4	201	1024	5.1	6	35	307	8.8	1	7	0	42	5
Pro totals (3 years)	45	4	471	2211	4.7	14	71	690	9.7	3	17	0	102	8

B

BARLOW, REGGIE WR/PR

PERSONAL: Born January 22, 1973, in Montgomery, Ala. ... 6-0/190. ... Full name: Reggie Devon Barlow.

HIGH SCHOOL: Lanier (Montgomery, Ala.).

COLLEGE: Alabama State.

TRANSACTIONS/CAREER NOTES: Selected by Jacksonville Jaguars in fourth round (110th pick overall) of 1996 NFL draft. ... Signed by Jaguars (May 28, 1996). ... Granted free agency (February 12, 1999). ... Re-signed by Jaguars (March 23, 1999). ... Released by Jaguars (February 27. 2001). ... Signed by Oakland Raiders (March 21, 2001). ... On injured reserve with foot injury (August 28, 2001-entire season). ... Released by Raiders (September 1, 2002). ... Signed by Tampa Bay Buccaneers (September 4, 2002). ... Granted unconditional free agency (February 28, 2003). ... Re-signed by Buccaneers (June 17, 2003). ... Granted unconditional free agency (March 3, 2004).

CHAMPIONSHIP GAME EXPERIENCE: Played in AFC championship game (1996 and 1999 seasons). ... Member of Buccaneers for NFC championship game (2002 season); inactive. ... Member of Super Bowl championship team (2002 season); inactive.

SINGLE GAME HIGHS (regular season): Receptions—4 (December 2, 1999, vs. Pittsburgh); yards—50 (October 12, 1998, vs. Miami); and touchdown receptions—1 (October 6, 2003, vs. Indianapolis).

			RECEIVING				PUNT RETURNS				KICKOFF RETURNS				TOTALS			
Year Team	**G**	**GS**	**No.**	**Yds.**	**Avg.**	**TD**	**No.**	**Yds.**	**Avg.**	**TD**	**No.**	**Yds.**	**Avg.**	**TD**	**TD**	**2pt.**	**Pts.**	**Fum.**
1996—Jacksonville NFL	7	0	0	0	0.0	0	0	0	0.0	0	0	0	0.0	0	0	0	0	0
1997—Jacksonville NFL	16	0	5	74	14.8	0	36	412	11.4	0	10	267	26.7	▲1	1	0	6	2
1998—Jacksonville NFL	16	2	11	168	15.3	0	43	*555	§12.9	1	30	747	24.9	0	1	0	6	1
1999—Jacksonville NFL	14	2	16	202	12.6	0	38	414	10.9	1	19	396	20.8	0	1	0	6	4
2000—Jacksonville NFL	15	0	1	28	28.0	0	29	200	6.9	0	11	224	20.4	0	0	0	0	0
2001—Oakland NFL	Did not play.																	
2002—Tampa Bay NFL	2	1	3	23	7.7	0	0	0	0.0	0	0	0	0.0	0	0	0	0	0
2003—Tampa Bay NFL	11	0	3	27	9.0	1	12	58	4.8	0	10	221	22.1	0	1	0	6	1
Pro totals (7 years)	81	5	39	522	13.4	1	158	1639	10.4	2	80	1855	23.2	1	4	0	24	8

BARNARD, BROOKS P BEARS

PERSONAL: Born November 4, 1979, in Arnold, Md. ... 6-2/188. ... Full name: Brooks Alexander Barnard.

HIGH SCHOOL: Broadneck (Arnold, Md.).

COLLEGE: Maryland.

TRANSACTIONS/CAREER NOTES: Signed as non-drafted free agent by Chicago Bears (April 29, 2003). ... Released by Bears (August 24, 2003). ... Signed by New England Patriots (December 3, 2003). ... Waived by Patriots (December 12, 2003). ... Signed by Bears (December 15, 2003).

		PUNTING					
Year Team	**G**	**No.**	**Yds.**	**Avg.**	**Net avg.**	**In. 20**	**Blk.**
2003—New England NFL	1	10	365	36.5	32.5	4	0

BARNES, DARIAN FB COWBOYS

PERSONAL: Born February 28, 1980, in Toms River, N.J. ... 6-2/250. ... Full name: Darian Durrell Barnes.

HIGH SCHOOL: North (Toms River, N.J.).

COLLEGE: Hampton.

TRANSACTIONS/CAREER NOTES: Signed as non-drafted free agent by New York Giants (July 24, 2002). ... Claimed on waivers by Tampa Bay Buccaneers (September 2, 2002). ... On injured reserve with shoulder injury (December 16, 2003-remainder of season). ... Traded by Buccaneers to Dallas Cowboys for future considerations (April 25, 2004).

CHAMPIONSHIP GAME EXPERIENCE: Played in NFC championship game (2002 season). ... Member of Super Bowl championship team (2002 season).

			RUSHING				RECEIVING				TOTALS			
Year Team	**G**	**GS**	**Att.**	**Yds.**	**Avg.**	**TD**	**No.**	**Yds.**	**Avg.**	**TD**	**TD**	**2pt.**	**Pts.**	**Fum.**
2002—Tampa Bay NFL	6	0	0	0	0.0	0	0	0	0.0	0	0	0	0	0
2003—Tampa Bay NFL	14	0	0	0	0.0	0	1	6	6.0	0	0	0	0	0
Pro totals (2 years)	20	0	0	0	0.0	0	1	6	6.0	0	0	0	0	0

BARNES, LIONEL DE JAGUARS

PERSONAL: Born April 19, 1976, in New Orleans, La. ... 6-5/260. ... Full name: Lionel Barnes Jr.

HIGH SCHOOL: Lakenheath American (Suffolk, England).

JUNIOR COLLEGE: Barton County Community College, Kan. (did not play football).

COLLEGE: Louisiana-Monroe.

TRANSACTIONS/CAREER NOTES: Selected by St. Louis Rams in sixth round (176th pick overall) of 1999 NFL draft. ... Signed by Rams (July 19, 1999). ... Claimed on waivers by Indianapolis Colts (October 12, 2000). ... Released by Colts (November 17, 2001). ... Re-signed by Colts (November 21, 2001). ... Granted free agency (March 1, 2002). ... Signed by Jacksonville Jaguars (January 9, 2003).
CHAMPIONSHIP GAME EXPERIENCE: Member of Rams for NFC championship game (1999 season); inactive. ... Member of Super Bowl championship team (1999 season); inactive.

			TOTALS		
Year Team	**G**	**GS**	**Tk.**	**Ast.**	**Sks.**
1999—St. Louis NFL	3	0	0	0	0.0
2000—St. Louis NFL	1	0	0	0	0.0
—Indianapolis NFL	1	0	0	0	0.0
2001—Indianapolis NFL	6	0	0	0	0.0
2002—			Did not play.		
2003—Jacksonville NFL	13	0	11	2	1.0
Pro totals (4 years)	24	0	11	2	1.0

B

BARNETT, NICK LB PACKERS

PERSONAL: Born May 27, 1981, in Fontana, Calif. ... 6-2/240. ... Full name: Nicholas Alexander Barnett.
HIGH SCHOOL: A.B. Miller (Fontana, Calif.).
COLLEGE: Oregon State.
TRANSACTIONS/CAREER NOTES: Selected by Green Bay Packers in first round (29th pick overall) of 2003 NFL draft. ... Signed by Packers (July 21, 2003).

			TOTALS			INTERCEPTIONS			
Year Team	**G**	**GS**	**Tk.**	**Ast.**	**Sks.**	**No.**	**Yds.**	**Avg.**	**TD**
2003—Green Bay NFL	15	15	84	25	2.0	3	21	7.0	0

BARRETT, DAVID CB JETS

PERSONAL: Born December 22, 1977, in Waterloo, Iowa. ... 5-10/208.
HIGH SCHOOL: Osceola (Ark.).
COLLEGE: Arkansas.
TRANSACTIONS/CAREER NOTES: Selected by Arizona Cardinals in fourth round (102nd pick overall) of 2000 NFL draft. ... Signed by Cardinals (June 15, 2000). ... Granted free agency (February 28, 2003). ... Re-signed by Cardinals (May 8, 2003). ... Granted unconditional free agency (March 3, 2004). ... Signed by New York Jets (March 6, 2004).

			TOTALS			INTERCEPTIONS			
Year Team	**G**	**GS**	**Tk.**	**Ast.**	**Sks.**	**No.**	**Yds.**	**Avg.**	**TD**
2000—Arizona NFL	16	0	6	2	0.0	0	0	0.0	0
2001—Arizona NFL	16	9	49	9	0.0	2	30	15.0	0
2002—Arizona NFL	14	14	57	17	0.0	3	40	13.3	0
2003—Arizona NFL	16	16	68	11	0.0	1	25	25.0	0
Pro totals (4 years)	62	39	180	39	0.0	6	95	15.8	0

BARROW, MIKE LB REDSKINS

PERSONAL: Born April 19, 1970, in Homestead, Fla. ... 6-2/245. ... Full name: Micheal Colvin Barrow.
HIGH SCHOOL: Homestead (Fla.) Senior.
COLLEGE: Miami (Fla.).
TRANSACTIONS/CAREER NOTES: Selected by Houston Oilers in second round (47th pick overall) of 1993 NFL draft. ... Signed by Oilers (July 30, 1993). ... Granted free agency (February 16, 1996). ... Re-signed by Oilers (August 9, 1996). ... Granted unconditional free agency (February 14, 1997). ... Signed by Carolina Panthers (February 20, 1997). ... Released by Panthers (February 22, 2000). ... Signed by New York Giants (March 2, 2000). ... Released by Giants (March 10, 2004). ... Signed by Washington Redskins (April 22, 2004).
CHAMPIONSHIP GAME EXPERIENCE: Played in NFC championship game (2000 season). ... Played in Super Bowl 35 (2000 season).
HONORS: Named linebacker on THE SPORTING NEWS college All-America first team (1992).

			TOTALS			INTERCEPTIONS			
Year Team	**G**	**GS**	**Tk.**	**Ast.**	**Sks.**	**No.**	**Yds.**	**Avg.**	**TD**
1993—Houston NFL	16	0	21	5	1.0	0	0	0.0	0
1994—Houston NFL	16	16	57	37	2.5	0	0	0.0	0
1995—Houston NFL	13	12	54	32	3.0	0	0	0.0	0
1996—Houston NFL	16	16	67	39	6.0	0	0	0.0	0
1997—Carolina NFL	16	16	68	21	8.5	0	0	0.0	0
1998—Carolina NFL	16	16	97	32	4.0	1	10	10.0	0
1999—Carolina NFL	16	16	81	25	4.0	0	0	0.0	0
2000—New York Giants NFL	15	15	72	22	3.5	1	7	7.0	0
2001—New York Giants NFL	16	16	91	44	6.0	0	0	0.0	0
2002—New York Giants NFL	15	14	73	37	2.5	0	0	0.0	0
2003—New York Giants NFL	16	16	111	39	2.0	0	0	0.0	0
Pro totals (11 years)	171	153	792	333	43.0	2	17	8.5	0

BARRY, KEVIN T PACKERS

PERSONAL: Born July 20, 1979, in Racine, Wis. ... 6-4/330.
HIGH SCHOOL: Washington Park (Racine, Wis.).
COLLEGE: Arizona.
TRANSACTIONS/CAREER NOTES: Signed as non-drafted free agent by Green Bay Packers (April 21, 2002).
PLAYING EXPERIENCE: Green Bay NFL, 2002-2003. ... Games/Games started: 2002 (14/3), 2003 (16/1). Total: 30/4.

BARTEE, WILLIAM — CB — CHIEFS

PERSONAL: Born June 25, 1977, in Daytona Beach, Fla. ... 6-1/200.
HIGH SCHOOL: Atlantic (Daytona Beach, Fla.).
JUNIOR COLLEGE: Butler County Community College (Kan.).
COLLEGE: Oklahoma.
TRANSACTIONS/CAREER NOTES: Selected by Kansas City Chiefs in second round (54th pick overall) of 2000 NFL draft. ... Signed by Chiefs (July 21, 2000). ... Granted unconditional free agency (March 3, 2004). ... Re-signed by Chiefs (March 19, 2004).

			TOTALS			INTERCEPTIONS			
Year Team	G	GS	Tk.	Ast.	Sks.	No.	Yds.	Avg.	TD
2000—Kansas City NFL	16	3	23	4	1.0	0	0	0.0	0
2001—Kansas City NFL	16	5	30	2	1.0	0	0	0.0	0
2002—Kansas City NFL	14	13	71	6	0.0	0	0	0.0	0
2003—Kansas City NFL	11	1	18	4	0.0	0	0	0.0	0
Pro totals (4 years)	57	22	142	16	2.0	0	0	0.0	0

B

BARTON, ERIC — LB — JETS

PERSONAL: Born September 29, 1977, in Alexandria, Va. ... 6-2/245.
HIGH SCHOOL: Thomas A. Edison (Alexandria, Va.).
COLLEGE: Maryland.
TRANSACTIONS/CAREER NOTES: Selected by Oakland Raiders in fifth round (146th pick overall) of 1999 NFL draft. ... Signed by Raiders for 1999 season. ... Granted unconditional free agency (March 3, 2004). ... Signed by New York Jets (March 6, 2004).
CHAMPIONSHIP GAME EXPERIENCE: Member of Raiders for AFC Championship game (2000 season); inactive. ... Played in AFC championship game (2002 season). ... Played in Super Bowl 37 (2002 season).

			TOTALS			INTERCEPTIONS			
Year Team	G	GS	Tk.	Ast.	Sks.	No.	Yds.	Avg.	TD
1999—Oakland NFL	16	3	20	2	3.0	0	0	0.0	0
2000—Oakland NFL	4	0	4	2	0.0	0	0	0.0	0
2001—Oakland NFL	16	1	19	5	0.0	0	0	0.0	0
2002—Oakland NFL	16	16	95	29	6.0	2	5	2.5	0
2003—Oakland NFL	16	16	99	34	0.5	0	0	0.0	0
Pro totals (5 years)	68	36	237	72	9.5	2	5	2.5	0

BARTRUM, MIKE — TE/LS — EAGLES

PERSONAL: Born June 23, 1970, in Gallipolis, Ohio. ... 6-4/245. ... Full name: Michael Weldon Bartrum.
HIGH SCHOOL: Meigs (Pomeroy, Ohio).
COLLEGE: Marshall.
TRANSACTIONS/CAREER NOTES: Signed as non-drafted free agent by Kansas City Chiefs (May 5, 1993). ... Released by Chiefs (August 30, 1993). ... Re-signed by Chiefs to practice squad (August 31, 1993). ... Activated (October 27, 1993). ... Released by Chiefs (August 23, 1994). ... Signed by Green Bay Packers (January 20, 1995). ... On injured reserve with broken arm (October 11, 1995-remainder of season). ... Traded by Packers with DE Walter Scott to New England Patriots for past considerations (August 25, 1996). ... On injured reserve with forearm injury (November 12, 1997-remainder of season). ... Granted unconditional free agency (February 13, 1998). ... Re-signed by Patriots (April 7, 1998). ... Released by Patriots (April 10, 2000). ... Signed by Philadelphia Eagles (April 17, 2000). ... Granted unconditional free agency (March 1, 2002). ... Re-signed by Eagles (March 6, 2002).
PLAYING EXPERIENCE: Kansas City NFL, 1993; Green Bay NFL, 1995; New England NFL, 1996-1999; Philadelphia NFL, 2000-2003. ... Games/Games started: 1993 (3/0), 1995 (4/0), 1996 (16/0), 1997 (9/0), 1998 (16/0), 1999 (16/0), 2000 (16/0), 2001 (16/0), 2002 (16/0), 2003 (16/0). Total: 128/0.
CHAMPIONSHIP GAME EXPERIENCE: Member of Chiefs for AFC championship game (1993 season); inactive. ... Played in AFC championship game (1996 season). ... Played in Super Bowl 31 (1996 season). ... Played in NFC championship game (2001-2003 seasons).
SINGLE GAME HIGHS (regular season): Receptions—1 (September 22, 2002, vs. Dallas); yards—8 (September 22, 2002, vs. Dallas); and touchdown receptions—1 (November 11, 2001, vs. Minnesota).

BASHIR, IDREES — S — COLTS

PERSONAL: Born December 7, 1978, in Decatur, Ga. ... 6-2/198.
HIGH SCHOOL: Dunwoody (Decatur, Ga.).
COLLEGE: Memphis.
TRANSACTIONS/CAREER NOTES: Selected by Indianapolis Colts in second round (37th pick overall) of 2001 NFL draft. ... Signed by Colts (July 25, 2001).
CHAMPIONSHIP GAME EXPERIENCE: Member of Colts for AFC championship game (2003 season); inactive.

			TOTALS			INTERCEPTIONS			
Year Team	G	GS	Tk.	Ast.	Sks.	No.	Yds.	Avg.	TD
2001—Indianapolis NFL	15	15	53	24	0.0	1	0	0.0	0
2002—Indianapolis NFL	14	14	36	14	0.0	2	4	2.0	0
2003—Indianapolis NFL	9	9	29	14	0.0	2	9	4.5	0
Pro totals (3 years)	38	38	118	52	0.0	5	13	2.6	0

BATCH, CHARLIE — QB — STEELERS

PERSONAL: Born December 5, 1974, in Pittsburgh, Pa. ... 6-2/220. ... Full name: Charles D'Donte Batch.
HIGH SCHOOL: Steel Valley (Munhall, Pa.).
COLLEGE: Eastern Michigan.

TRANSACTIONS/CAREER NOTES: Selected by Detroit Lions in second round (60th pick overall) of 1998 NFL draft. ... Signed by Lions (July 19, 1998). ... On injured reserve with back injury (December 24, 1998-remainder of season). ... On injured reserve with shoulder injury (December 5, 2001-remainder of season). ... Released by Lions (June 3, 2002). ... Signed by Pittsburgh Steelers (June 17, 2002). ... On physically unable to perform list with knee injury (July 25-26, 2002). ... Granted unconditional free agency (February 28, 2003). ... Re-signed by Steelers (March 19, 2003).

RECORDS: Holds NFL rookie-season record for lowest interception percentage—1.98.

SINGLE GAME HIGHS (regular season): Attempts—62 (November 18, 2001, vs. Arizona); completions—36 (November 18, 2001, vs. Arizona); yards—436 (November 18, 2001, vs. Arizona); and touchdown passes—3 (November 18, 2001, vs. Arizona).

STATISTICAL PLATEAUS: 300-yard passing games: 2001 (3). Total: 3.

MISCELLANEOUS: Regular-season record as starting NFL quarterback: 19-27 (.413).

			PASSING									RUSHING				TOTALS		
Year Team	G	GS	Att.	Cmp.	Pct.	Yds.	TD	Int.	Avg.	Skd.	Rat.	Att.	Yds.	Avg.	TD	TD	2pt.	Pts.
1998—Detroit NFL	12	12	303	173	57.1	2178	11	6	7.19	37	83.5	41	229	5.6	1	1	0	6
1999—Detroit NFL	11	10	270	151	55.9	1957	13	7	7.25	36	84.1	28	87	3.1	2	2	0	12
2000—Detroit NFL	15	15	412	221	53.6	2489	13	15	6.04	41	67.3	44	199	4.5	2	2	0	12
2001—Detroit NFL	10	9	341	198	58.1	2392	12	12	7.01	33	76.8	12	45	3.8	0	0	0	0
2002—Pittsburgh NFL						Did not play.												
2003—Pittsburgh NFL	4	0	8	4	50.0	47	0	0	5.88	1	68.2	1	11	11.0	0	0	0	0
Pro totals (5 years)	52	46	1334	747	56.0	9063	49	40	6.79	148	76.8	126	571	4.5	5	5	0	30

BATES, D'WAYNE — WR

PERSONAL: Born December 4, 1975, in Augusta, Ga. ... 6-2/212. ... Full name: D'Wayne Lavoris Bates.

HIGH SCHOOL: Silver Bluff (Aiken, S.C.).

COLLEGE: Northwestern.

TRANSACTIONS/CAREER NOTES: Selected by Chicago Bears in third round (71st pick overall) of 1999 NFL draft. ... Signed by Bears (July 22, 1999). ... Granted free agency (March 1, 2002). ... Tendered offer sheet by Minnesota Vikings (March 27, 2002). ... Offer matched by Bears (April 3, 2002). ... Claimed on waivers by Vikings (April 9, 2002). ... Released by Vikings (March 15, 2004).

SINGLE GAME HIGHS (regular season): Receptions—7 (December 21, 2002, vs. Miami); yards—107 (December 30, 2001, vs. Detroit); and touchdown receptions—1 (September 7, 2003, vs. Green Bay).

STATISTICAL PLATEAUS: 100-yard receiving games: 2001 (1). Total: 1.

MISCELLANEOUS: Selected by Toronto Blue Jays organization in 53rd round of free-agent draft (June 2, 1994); did not sign.

			RECEIVING				PUNT RETURNS				TOTALS			
Year Team	G	GS	No.	Yds.	Avg.	TD	No.	Yds.	Avg.	TD	TD	2pt.	Pts.	Fum.
1999—Chicago NFL	7	1	2	19	9.5	0	0	0	0.0	0	0	0	0	0
2000—Chicago NFL	5	0	4	42	10.5	0	0	0	0.0	0	0	0	0	0
2001—Chicago NFL	11	1	9	160	17.8	1	0	0	0.0	0	1	0	6	0
2002—Minnesota NFL	14	11	50	689	13.8	4	4	93	23.2	0	4	0	24	2
2003—Minnesota NFL	10	8	15	151	10.1	1	0	0	0.0	0	1	0	6	0
Pro totals (5 years)	47	21	80	1061	13.3	6	4	93	23.3	0	6	0	36	2

BATES, MICHAEL — RB

PERSONAL: Born December 19, 1969, in Tucson, Ariz. ... 5-10/189. ... Full name: Michael Dion Bates. ... Brother of Mario Bates, running back, with New Orleans Saints (1994-97), Arizona Cardinals (1998-99) and Detroit Lions (2000).

HIGH SCHOOL: Amphitheater (Tucson, Ariz.).

COLLEGE: Arizona.

TRANSACTIONS/CAREER NOTES: Selected after sophomore season by Seattle Seahawks in sixth round (151st pick overall) of 1992 NFL draft. ... Missed 1992 season due to contract dispute. ... Signed by Seahawks (March 7, 1993). ... Claimed on waivers by Carolina Panthers (August 28, 1995). ... Traded by Panthers to Cleveland Browns for LB Travis Hill (August 29, 1995). ... Granted unconditional free agency (February 16, 1996). ... Signed by Panthers (March 12, 1996). ... Granted unconditional free agency (February 13, 1998). ... Re-signed by Panthers (March 4, 1998). ... Granted unconditional free agency (March 2, 2001). ... Signed by Washington Redskins (July 10, 2001). ... Released by Redskins (March 12, 2002). ... Signed by Panthers (March 25, 2002). ... On injured reserve with ankle injury (August 26, 2002-entire season). ... Granted unconditional free agency (February 28, 2003). ... Signed by Panthers (March 27, 2003). ... Released by Panthers (August 31, 2003). ... Signed by New York Jets (September 10, 2003). ... On injured reserve with hand injury (November 11-December 22, 2003). ... Claimed on waivers by Dallas Cowboys (December 25, 2003). ... Granted unconditional free agency (March 3, 2004).

CHAMPIONSHIP GAME EXPERIENCE: Played in NFC championship game (1996 season).

HONORS: Named kick returner on THE SPORTING NEWS NFL All-Pro team (1996 and 1997). ... Played in Pro Bowl (1996-2000 seasons).

SINGLE GAME HIGHS (regular season): Attempts—2 (December 3, 2000, vs. St. Louis); yards—14 (November 7, 1999, vs. Philadelphia); and rushing touchdowns—0.

MISCELLANEOUS: Won bronze medal in 200-meter dash in 1992 Summer Olympics.

			RECEIVING				KICKOFF RETURNS				TOTALS			
Year Team	G	GS	No.	Yds.	Avg.	TD	No.	Yds.	Avg.	TD	TD	2pt.	Pts.	Fum.
1992—Seattle NFL						Did not play.								
1993—Seattle NFL	16	1	1	6	6.0	0	30	603	20.1	0	0	0	0	1
1994—Seattle NFL	15	0	5	112	22.4	1	26	508	19.5	0	1	0	6	3
1995—Cleveland NFL	13	0	0	0	0.0	0	9	176	19.6	0	0	0	0	0
1996—Carolina NFL	14	0	0	0	0.0	0	33	998	*30.2	1	1	0	6	2
1997—Carolina NFL	16	0	0	0	0.0	0	47	1281	*27.3	0	0	0	0	4
1998—Carolina NFL	14	0	0	0	0.0	0	59	1480	25.1	1	1	0	6	1
1999—Carolina NFL	16	0	1	2	2.0	0	52	1287	24.8	†2	2	0	12	1
2000—Carolina NFL	16	0	5	38	7.6	0	42	941	22.4	1	1	0	6	4
2001—Washington NFL	16	0	0	0	0.0	0	49	1150	23.5	0	0	0	0	4
2002—Carolina NFL						Did not play.								
2003—New York Jets NFL	8	0	0	0	0.0	0	22	596	27.1	0	0	0	0	0
—Dallas NFL	1	0	0	0	0.0	0	4	90	22.5	0	0	0	0	0
Pro totals (10 years)	145	1	12	158	13.2	1	373	9110	24.4	5	6	0	36	20

B

BATES, SOLOMON — LB — SEAHAWKS

PERSONAL: Born April 18, 1982, in Carver City, Calif. ... 6-1/243. ... Full name: Solomon Augustus Bates.
HIGH SCHOOL: Canyon Springs (Moreno Valley, Calif.).
COLLEGE: Arizona State.
TRANSACTIONS/CAREER NOTES: Selected by Seattle Seahawks in fourth round (135th pick overall) of 2003 NFL draft. ... Signed by Seahawks (July 24, 2003).

			TOTALS			INTERCEPTIONS			
Year Team	G	GS	Tk.	Ast.	Sks.	No.	Yds.	Avg.	TD
2003—Seattle NFL	7	0	0	0	0.0	0	0	0.0	0

BATTAGLIA, MARCO — TE

PERSONAL: Born January 25, 1973, in Queens, N.Y. ... 6-3/250. ... Name pronounced: buh-TAG-lee-uh.
HIGH SCHOOL: St. Francis (Fresh Meadows, N.Y.).
COLLEGE: Rutgers.
TRANSACTIONS/CAREER NOTES: Selected by Cincinnati Bengals in second round (39th pick overall) of 1996 NFL draft. ... Signed by Bengals (July 15, 1996). ... Granted free agency (February 12, 1999). ... Re-signed by Bengals (May 25, 1999). ... On non-football illness list with appendectomy (November 17-December 10, 2001). ... Claimed on waivers by Washington Redskins (December 11, 2001). ... Granted unconditional free agency (March 1, 2002). ... Signed by Tampa Bay Buccaneers (March 19, 2002). ... Released by Buccaneers (September 24, 2002). ... Signed by Pittsburgh Steelers (December 10, 2002). ... Granted unconditional free agency (February 28, 2003). ... Signed by Miami Dolphins (March 25, 2003). ... Released by Dolphins (September 6, 2003). ... Signed by Carolina Panthers (December 2, 2003). ... Granted unconditional free agency (March 3, 2004).
CHAMPIONSHIP GAME EXPERIENCE: Member of Panthers for NFC championship game (2003 season); inactive. ... Member of Panthers for Super Bowl 38 (2003 season); inactive.
HONORS: Named tight end on THE SPORTING NEWS college All-America first team (1995).
SINGLE GAME HIGHS (regular season): Receptions—4 (November 11, 2001, vs. Jacksonville); yards—57 (October 21, 2001, vs. Chicago); and touchdown receptions—1 (November 1, 1998, vs. Denver).

			RECEIVING				TOTALS			
Year Team	G	GS	No.	Yds.	Avg.	TD	TD	2pt.	Pts.	Fum.
1996—Cincinnati NFL	16	0	8	79	9.9	0	0	0	0	0
1997—Cincinnati NFL	16	0	12	149	12.4	1	1	0	6	2
1998—Cincinnati NFL	16	0	10	47	4.7	1	1	0	6	1
1999—Cincinnati NFL	16	0	14	153	10.9	0	0	0	0	0
2000—Cincinnati NFL	16	10	13	105	8.1	0	0	0	0	0
2001—Cincinnati NFL	8	1	13	118	9.1	0	0	0	0	1
—Washington NFL	3	0	1	9	9.0	0	0	0	0	0
2002—Pittsburgh NFL	1	0	0	0	0.0	0	0	0	0	0
—Tampa Bay NFL	2	0	0	0	0.0	0	0	0	0	0
2003—Carolina NFL	2	0	0	0	0.0	0	0	0	0	0
Pro totals (8 years)	96	11	71	660	9.3	2	2	0	12	4

BATTLE, ARNAZ — WR — 49ERS

PERSONAL: Born February 22, 1980, in Dallas, Texas. ... 6-1/217. ... Full name: Arnaz Jerome Battle.
HIGH SCHOOL: C.E. Byrd (Shreveport, La.).
COLLEGE: Notre Dame.
TRANSACTIONS/CAREER NOTES: Selected by San Francisco 49ers in sixth round (197th pick overall) of 2003 NFL draft. ... Signed by 49ers (July 24, 2003). ... On injured reserve with toe injury (December 10, 2003-remainder of season).

			RUSHING				RECEIVING				KICKOFF RETURNS				TOTALS			
Year Team	G	GS	Att.	Yds.	Avg.	TD	No.	Yds.	Avg.	TD	No.	Yds.	Avg.	TD	TD	2pt.	Pts.	Fum.
2003—San Francisco NFL	8	0	2	14	7.0	0	0	0	0.0	0	5	88	17.6	0	0	0	0	0

BATTLE, JULIAN — CB — CHIEFS

PERSONAL: Born July 11, 1981, in Royal Palm Beach, Fla. ... 6-2/205.
HIGH SCHOOL: Wellington (West Palm Beach, Fla.).
JUNIOR COLLEGE: Los Angeles Valley College.
COLLEGE: Tennessee.
TRANSACTIONS/CAREER NOTES: Selected by Kansas City Chiefs in third round (92nd pick overall) of 2003 NFL draft. ... Signed by Chiefs (May 12, 2003).

			TOTALS			INTERCEPTIONS			
Year Team	G	GS	Tk.	Ast.	Sks.	No.	Yds.	Avg.	TD
2003—Kansas City NFL	14	0	4	0	0.0	0	0	0.0	0

BAUMAN, RASHAD — CB — REDSKINS

PERSONAL: Born May 7, 1979, in Tempe, Ariz. ... 5-8/184. ... Full name: Leddure Rashad Bauman.
HIGH SCHOOL: South Mountain (Phoenix).
COLLEGE: Oregon.
TRANSACTIONS/CAREER NOTES: Selected by Washington Redskins in third round (79th pick overall) of 2002 NFL draft. ... Signed by Redskins (July 22, 2002).

Year	Team	G	GS	TOTALS Tk.	Ast.	Sks.	INTERCEPTIONS No.	Yds.	Avg.	TD
2002	Washington NFL	16	1	9	0	0.0	0	0	0.0	0
2003	Washington NFL	12	2	17	4	0.0	2	1	0.5	0
Pro totals (2 years)		28	3	26	4	0.0	2	1	0.5	0

BAXTER, FRED — TE

PERSONAL: Born June 14, 1971, in Brundidge, Ala. ... 6-3/268. ... Full name: Frederick Denard Baxter.

HIGH SCHOOL: Pike County (Brundidge, Ala.).

COLLEGE: Auburn.

TRANSACTIONS/CAREER NOTES: Selected by New York Jets in fifth round (115th pick overall) of 1993 NFL draft. ... Signed by Jets (July 13, 1993). ... On injured reserve with broken hand (November 21, 2000-remainder of season). ... Released by Jets (December 23, 2000). ... Signed by Chicago Bears (February 27, 2001). ... Released by Bears (November 12, 2002). ... Signed by New England Patriots (December 24, 2002). ... Granted unconditional free agency (February 28, 2003). ... Re-signed by Patriots (March 6, 2003). ... Granted unconditional free agency (March 3, 2004).

CHAMPIONSHIP GAME EXPERIENCE: Played in AFC championship game (1998 season). ... Member of Patriots for AFC championship game (2003 season); inactive. ... Member of Patriots for Super Bowl 38 (2003 season); inactive.

SINGLE GAME HIGHS (regular season): Receptions—6 (September 17, 1995, vs. Jacksonville); yards—99 (September 17, 1995, vs. Jacksonville); and touchdown receptions—1 (December 16, 2001, vs. Tampa Bay).

Year	Team	G	GS	RECEIVING No.	Yds.	Avg.	TD	TOTALS TD	2pt.	Pts.	Fum.
1993	New York Jets NFL	7	0	3	48	16.0	1	1	0	6	0
1994	New York Jets NFL	11	1	3	11	3.7	1	1	0	6	0
1995	New York Jets NFL	15	3	18	222	12.3	1	1	0	6	1
1996	New York Jets NFL	16	4	7	114	16.3	0	0	0	0	1
1997	New York Jets NFL	16	9	27	276	10.2	3	3	0	18	1
1998	New York Jets NFL	14	2	3	50	16.7	0	0	0	0	0
1999	New York Jets NFL	14	8	8	66	8.3	2	2	0	12	0
2000	New York Jets NFL	9	6	4	22	5.5	2	2	0	12	0
2001	Chicago NFL	14	14	22	148	6.7	2	2	0	12	0
2002	Chicago NFL	5	3	5	51	10.2	0	0	0	0	0
	—New England NFL	1	0	0	0	0.0	0	0	0	0	0
2003	New England NFL	12	0	0	0	0.0	0	0	0	0	0
Pro totals (11 years)		134	50	100	1008	10.1	12	12	0	72	3

BAXTER, GARY — CB — RAVENS

PERSONAL: Born November 24, 1978, in Tyler, Texas. ... 6-2/204. ... Full name: Gary Wayne Baxter.

HIGH SCHOOL: John Tyler (Tyler, Texas).

COLLEGE: Baylor.

TRANSACTIONS/CAREER NOTES: Selected by Baltimore Ravens in second round (62nd pick overall) of 2001 NFL draft. ... Signed by Ravens (July 20, 2001).

Year	Team	G	GS	TOTALS Tk.	Ast.	Sks.	INTERCEPTIONS No.	Yds.	Avg.	TD
2001	Baltimore NFL	6	0	0	0	0.0	0	0	0.0	0
2002	Baltimore NFL	16	14	69	9	0.0	1	0	0.0	0
2003	Baltimore NFL	16	16	71	12	1.0	3	41	13.7	0
Pro totals (3 years)		38	30	140	21	1.0	4	41	10.3	0

BEASLEY, AARON — CB — FALCONS

PERSONAL: Born July 7, 1973, in Pottstown, Pa. ... 6-0/205. ... Full name: Aaron Bruce Beasley.

HIGH SCHOOL: Pottstown (Pa.), then Valley Forge Military Academy (Wayne, Pa.).

COLLEGE: West Virginia.

TRANSACTIONS/CAREER NOTES: Selected by Jacksonville Jaguars in third round (63rd pick overall) of 1996 NFL draft. ... Signed by Jaguars (May 24, 1996). ... Granted free agency (February 12, 1999). ... Re-signed by Jaguars (March 3, 1999). ... Granted unconditional free agency (February 11, 2000). ... Re-signed by Jaguars (February 11, 2000). ... On injured reserve with shoulder injury (December 21, 2001-remainder of season). ... Released by Jaguars (February 28, 2002). ... Signed by New York Jets (March 8, 2002). ... Released by Jets (February 27, 2004). ... Signed by Atlanta Falcons (March 31, 2004).

CHAMPIONSHIP GAME EXPERIENCE: Played in AFC championship game (1996 and 1999 seasons).

MISCELLANEOUS: Holds Jacksonville Jaguars all-time record for most interceptions (15).

Year	Team	G	GS	TOTALS Tk.	Ast.	Sks.	INTERCEPTIONS No.	Yds.	Avg.	TD
1996	Jacksonville NFL	9	7	20	9	1.0	1	0	0.0	0
1997	Jacksonville NFL	9	7	25	0	0.0	1	5	5.0	0
1998	Jacksonville NFL	16	15	58	9	0.0	3	35	11.7	0
1999	Jacksonville NFL	16	16	57	9	1.5	6	*200	§33.3	†2
2000	Jacksonville NFL	14	14	45	7	5.0	1	39	39.0	0
2001	Jacksonville NFL	12	12	36	3	0.0	3	0	0.0	0
2002	New York Jets NFL	15	15	59	7	0.0	2	29	14.5	0
2003	New York Jets NFL	16	16	46	15	0.0	3	64	21.3	0
Pro totals (8 years)		107	102	346	59	7.5	20	372	18.6	2

BEASLEY, CHAD — T — BROWNS

PERSONAL: Born November 13, 1978, in Upper St. Clair, Pa. ... 6-5/300. ... Full name: Thomas Chad Beasley.
HIGH SCHOOL: Gate City (Va.).
COLLEGE: Virginia Tech.
TRANSACTIONS/CAREER NOTES: Selected by Minnesota Vikings in seventh round (218th pick overall) of 2002 NFL draft. ... Signed by Vikings (July 19, 2002). ... Released by Vikings (August 27, 2002). ... Re-signed by Vikings to practice squad (September 3, 2002). ... Signed by Cleveland Browns off Vikings practice squad (October 1, 2002). ... On injured reserve with ankle injury (December 9, 2003-remainder of season).
PLAYING EXPERIENCE: Cleveland NFL, 2003. ... Games/Games started: 2003 (8/3). Total: 8/3.

BEASLEY, FRED — FB — 49ERS

PERSONAL: Born September 18, 1974, in Montgomery, Ala. ... 6-0/246. ... Full name: Frederick Jerome Beasley.
HIGH SCHOOL: Robert E. Lee (Montgomery, Ala.).
COLLEGE: Auburn.
TRANSACTIONS/CAREER NOTES: Selected by San Francisco 49ers in sixth round (180th pick overall) of 1998 NFL draft. ... Signed by 49ers (July 18, 1998). ... Granted free agency (March 2, 2001). ... Re-signed by 49ers (March 2, 2001). ... Granted unconditional free agency (March 1, 2002). ... Re-signed by 49ers (March 12, 2002).
HONORS: Played in Pro Bowl (2003 season).
SINGLE GAME HIGHS (regular season): Attempts—12 (December 26, 1999, vs. Washington); yards—65 (December 26, 1999, vs. Washington); and rushing touchdowns—2 (December 12, 1999, vs. Atlanta).

			RUSHING				RECEIVING				TOTALS			
Year Team	G	GS	Att.	Yds.	Avg.	TD	No.	Yds.	Avg.	TD	TD	2pt.	Pts.	Fum.
1998—San Francisco NFL	16	0	0	0	0.0	0	1	11	11.0	0	0	0	0	0
1999—San Francisco NFL	13	11	58	276	4.8	4	32	282	8.8	0	4	0	24	2
2000—San Francisco NFL	15	15	50	147	2.9	3	31	233	7.5	3	6	0	36	0
2001—San Francisco NFL	15	12	23	73	3.2	1	16	99	6.2	0	1	0	6	1
2002—San Francisco NFL	16	14	26	75	2.9	0	22	152	6.9	1	1	0	6	0
2003—San Francisco NFL	16	11	17	24	1.4	0	19	184	9.7	1	1	0	6	0
Pro totals (6 years)	91	63	174	595	3.4	8	121	961	7.9	5	13	0	78	3

BECHT, ANTHONY — TE — JETS

PERSONAL: Born August 8, 1977, in Media, Pa. ... 6-5/272.
HIGH SCHOOL: Monsignor Bonner (Drexel Hill, Pa.).
COLLEGE: West Virginia.
TRANSACTIONS/CAREER NOTES: Selected by New York Jets in first round (27th pick overall) of 2000 NFL draft. ... Signed by Jets (May 26, 2000).
SINGLE GAME HIGHS (regular season): Receptions—6 (December 28, 2003, vs. Miami); yards—63 (November 23, 2003, vs. Jacksonville); and touchdown receptions—2 (October 12, 2003, vs. Buffalo).

			RECEIVING				TOTALS			
Year Team	G	GS	No.	Yds.	Avg.	TD	TD	2pt.	Pts.	Fum.
2000—New York Jets NFL	14	10	16	144	9.0	2	2	0	12	1
2001—New York Jets NFL	16	16	36	321	8.9	5	5	0	30	0
2002—New York Jets NFL	16	16	28	243	8.7	5	5	1	32	0
2003—New York Jets NFL	16	16	40	356	8.9	4	4	1	26	1
Pro totals (4 years)	62	58	120	1064	8.9	16	16	2	100	2

BECKETT, ROGERS — S — BENGALS

PERSONAL: Born January 31, 1977, in Apopka, Fla. ... 6-2/207.
HIGH SCHOOL: Apopka (Fla.).
COLLEGE: Marshall.
TRANSACTIONS/CAREER NOTES: Selected by San Diego Chargers in second round (43rd pick overall) of 2000 NFL draft. ... Signed by Chargers (July 24, 2000). ... Claimed on waivers by Cincinnati Bengals (June 10, 2003). ... Granted unconditional free agency (March 3, 2004). ... Re-signed by Bengals (March 25, 2004).
HONORS: Named free safety on THE SPORTING NEWS college All-America third team (1999).

			TOTALS			INTERCEPTIONS			
Year Team	G	GS	Tk.	Ast.	Sks.	No.	Yds.	Avg.	TD
2000—San Diego NFL	16	3	28	11	1.0	1	7	7.0	0
2001—San Diego NFL	16	16	73	21	0.0	1	8	8.0	0
2002—San Diego NFL	16	10	32	2	0.0	0	0	0.0	0
2003—Cincinnati NFL	16	9	51	16	3.0	2	11	5.5	0
Pro totals (4 years)	64	38	184	50	4.0	4	26	6.5	0

BECKHAM, TONY — CB — TITANS

PERSONAL: Born October 1, 1978, in Gainesville, Fla. ... 6-1/187.
HIGH SCHOOL: Forest (Ocala, Fla.).
COLLEGE: Wisconsin-Stout.
TRANSACTIONS/CAREER NOTES: Selected by Tennesse Titans in fourth round (115th pick overall) of 2002 NFL draft. ... Signed by Titans (July 18, 2002).

B

CHAMPIONSHIP GAME EXPERIENCE: Played in AFC championship game (2002 season).

Year Team	G	GS	TOTALS Tk.	Ast.	Sks.	INTERCEPTIONS No.	Yds.	Avg.	TD
2002—Tennessee NFL	14	0	1	1	0.0	0	0	0.0	0
2003—Tennessee NFL	16	3	14	2	0.0	1	0	0.0	0
Pro totals (2 years)	30	3	15	3	0.0	1	0	0.0	0

BEISEL, MONTY — LB — CHIEFS

PERSONAL: Born August 20, 1978, in Douglass, Kan. ... 6-3/254.
HIGH SCHOOL: Douglass (Kan.).
COLLEGE: Kansas State.
TRANSACTIONS/CAREER NOTES: Selected by Kansas City Chiefs in fourth round (107th pick overall) of 2001 NFL draft. ... Signed by Chiefs (July 23, 2001). ... Granted free agency (March 3, 2004). ... Re-signed by Chiefs (March 24, 2004).

Year Team	G	GS	TOTALS Tk.	Ast.	Sks.	INTERCEPTIONS No.	Yds.	Avg.	TD
2001—Kansas City NFL	16	0	3	3	0.0	0	0	0.0	0
2002—Kansas City NFL	16	0	0	0	0.0	0	0	0.0	0
2003—Kansas City NFL	12	0	8	0	1.0	0	0	0.0	0
Pro totals (3 years)	44	0	11	3	1.0	0	0	0.0	0

BELL, JASON — CB — TEXANS

PERSONAL: Born April 1, 1978, in Long Beach, Calif. ... 6-0/182. ... Full name: Jason Dewande Bell.
HIGH SCHOOL: Millikan (Long Beach, Calif.).
COLLEGE: UCLA.
TRANSACTIONS/CAREER NOTES: Signed as non-drafted free agent by Dallas Cowboys (April 27, 2001). ... Claimed on waivers by Houston Texans (September 2, 2002). ... Re-signed by Texans (March 18, 2003). ... Granted free agency (March 3, 2004). ... Re-signed by Texans (April 22, 2004).

Year Team	G	GS	TOTALS Tk.	Ast.	Sks.	INTERCEPTIONS No.	Yds.	Avg.	TD
2001—Dallas NFL	16	0	0	0	0.0	0	0	0.0	0
2002—Houston NFL	13	0	2	0	0.0	0	0	0.0	0
2003—Houston NFL	13	0	2	0	0.0	0	0	0.0	0
Pro totals (3 years)	42	0	4	0	0.0	0	0	0.0	0

BELL, KENDRELL — LB — STEELERS

PERSONAL: Born July 2, 1978, in Augusta, Ga. ... 6-1/254.
HIGH SCHOOL: Laney (August, Ga.).
JUNIOR COLLEGE: Middle Georgia College.
COLLEGE: Georgia.
TRANSACTIONS/CAREER NOTES: Selected by Pittsburgh Steelers in second round (39th pick overall) of 2001 NFL draft. ... Signed by Steelers (June 11, 2001).
CHAMPIONSHIP GAME EXPERIENCE: Played in AFC championship game (2001 season).
HONORS: Named NFL Rookie of the Year by THE SPORTING NEWS (2001). ... Played in Pro Bowl (2001 season). ... Named to play in Pro Bowl (2002 season); replaced by Donnie Edwards due to injury.

Year Team	G	GS	TOTALS Tk.	Ast.	Sks.	INTERCEPTIONS No.	Yds.	Avg.	TD
2001—Pittsburgh NFL	16	16	69	13	9.0	0	0	0.0	0
2002—Pittsburgh NFL	12	12	37	13	4.0	0	0	0.0	0
2003—Pittsburgh NFL	16	16	81	19	5.0	1	61	61.0	0
Pro totals (3 years)	44	44	187	45	18.0	1	61	61.0	0

BELL, MARCUS — DT — CARDINALS

PERSONAL: Born June 1, 1979, in Memphis, Tenn. ... 6-2/339.
HIGH SCHOOL: Kingsbury (Memphis, Tenn.).
COLLEGE: Memphis.
TRANSACTIONS/CAREER NOTES: Selected by Arizona Cardinals in fourth round (123rd pick overall) of 2001 NFL draft. ... Signed by Cardinals (June 4, 2001). ... Granted free agency (March 3, 2004). ... Re-signed by Cardinals (May 7, 2004).

Year Team	G	GS	TOTALS Tk.	Ast.	Sks.
2001—Arizona NFL	13	0	16	7	0.5
2002—Arizona NFL	16	4	25	9	2.0
2003—Arizona NFL	13	10	21	2	1.0
Pro totals (3 years)	42	14	62	18	3.5

BELLAMY, JAY — S — SAINTS

PERSONAL: Born July 8, 1972, in Perth Amboy, N.J. ... 5-11/200. ... Full name: John Jay Bellamy. ... Name pronounced: BELL-a-me.
HIGH SCHOOL: Matawan Regional (Aberdeen, N.J.).
COLLEGE: Rutgers.

TRANSACTIONS/CAREER NOTES: Signed as non-drafted free agent by Seattle Seahawks (April 27, 1994). ... On injured reserve with shoulder injury (November 11, 1994-remainder of season). ... Granted unconditional free agency (March 2, 2001). ... Signed by New Orleans Saints (April 4, 2001).

			TOTALS			INTERCEPTIONS			
Year Team	**G**	**GS**	**Tk.**	**Ast.**	**Sks.**	**No.**	**Yds.**	**Avg.**	**TD**
1994—Seattle NFL	3	0	0	0	0.0	0	0	0.0	0
1995—Seattle NFL	15	0	2	1	0.0	0	0	0.0	0
1996—Seattle NFL	16	0	16	2	0.0	3	18	6.0	0
1997—Seattle NFL	16	7	42	10	2.0	1	13	13.0	0
1998—Seattle NFL	16	16	80	18	1.0	3	40	13.3	0
1999—Seattle NFL	16	16	85	11	0.0	4	4	1.0	0
2000—Seattle NFL	16	16	69	18	2.0	4	132	33.0	1
2001—New Orleans NFL	16	16	69	22	2.0	3	21	7.0	0
2002—New Orleans NFL	16	16	67	19	1.5	3	39	13.0	0
2003—New Orleans NFL	16	16	77	17	1.0	3	19	6.3	0
Pro totals (10 years)	146	103	507	118	9.5	24	286	11.9	1

BENJAMIN, RYAN C/LS

PERSONAL: Born November 11, 1977, in New Port Richey, Fla. ... 6-1/242. ... Full name: Ryan Arthur Benjamin.

HIGH SCHOOL: River Ridge (New Port Richey, Fla.).

COLLEGE: South Florida.

TRANSACTIONS/CAREER NOTES: Signed as non-drafted free agent by Tampa Bay Buccaneers (April 23, 2001). ... Released by Buccaneers (June 7, 2001). ... Signed by New England Patriots (August 13, 2001). ... Released by Patriots (August 26, 2001). ... Signed by Chicago Bears (October 13, 2001). ... Released by Bears (October 16, 2001). ... Signed by Patriots (February 11, 2002). ... Released by Patriots (August 27, 2002). ... Signed by Buccaneers (October 14, 2002). ... Released by Buccaneers (May 20, 2004).

PLAYING EXPERIENCE: Chicago NFL, 2001; Tampa Bay NFL, 2002-2003. ... Games/Games started: 2001 (1/0), 2002 (10/0), 2003 (16/0). Total: 27/0.

CHAMPIONSHIP GAME EXPERIENCE: Played in NFC championship game (2002 season). ... Member of Super Bowl championship team (2002 season).

BENNETT, BRANDON RB/KR BUCCANEERS

PERSONAL: Born February 3, 1973, in Greenville, S.C. ... 5-11/220.

HIGH SCHOOL: Riverside (Greer, S.C.).

COLLEGE: South Carolina.

TRANSACTIONS/CAREER NOTES: Signed as non-drafted free agent by Cleveland Browns (July 25, 1995). ... Released by Browns (August 18, 1995). ... Signed by Chicago Bears to practice squad (December 6, 1995). ... Released by Bears (August 19, 1996). ... Re-signed by Bears to practice squad (September 24, 1996). ... Released by Bears (November 1, 1996). ... Signed by Miami Dolphins to practice squad (November 5, 1996). ... Activated (December 17, 1996); did not play. ... Released by Dolphins (August 12, 1997). ... Signed by Cincinnati Bengals (April 20, 1998). ... Released by Bengals (August 30, 1998). ... Re-signed by Bengals (September 7, 1998). ... Released by Bengals (June 3, 1999). ... Re-signed by Bengals (March 2, 2001). ... Granted unconditional free agency (March 3, 2004). ... Signed by Tampa Bay Buccaneers (March 18, 2004).

SINGLE GAME HIGHS (regular season): Attempts—25 (December 20, 1998, vs. Pittsburgh); yards—87 (December 13, 1998, vs. Indianapolis); and rushing touchdowns—1 (December 3, 2000, vs. Arizona).

STATISTICAL PLATEAUS: 100-yard receiving games: 1998 (1). Total: 1.

			RUSHING				RECEIVING				KICKOFF RETURNS				TOTALS			
Year Team	**G**	**GS**	**Att.**	**Yds.**	**Avg.**	**TD**	**No.**	**Yds.**	**Avg.**	**TD**	**No.**	**Yds.**	**Avg.**	**TD**	**TD**	**2pt.**	**Pts.**	**Fum.**
1995—Chicago NFL								Did not play.										
1996—Miami NFL								Did not play.										
1997—								Did not play.										
1998—Cincinnati NFL	14	1	77	243	3.2	2	8	153	19.1	0	3	61	20.3	0	2	0	12	1
1999—								Did not play.										
2000—Cincinnati NFL	16	0	90	324	3.6	3	19	168	8.8	0	0	0	0.0	0	3	0	18	2
2001—Cincinnati NFL	16	1	50	232	4.6	0	20	150	7.5	0	4	60	15.0	0	0	0	0	1
2002—Cincinnati NFL	12	0	33	155	4.7	0	18	109	6.1	0	49	1231	25.1	1	1	0	6	2
2003—Cincinnati NFL	16	0	56	173	3.1	0	25	176	7.0	1	53	1146	21.6	0	1	0	6	2
Pro totals (5 years)	74	2	306	1127	3.7	5	90	756	8.4	1	109	2498	22.9	1	7	0	42	8

BENNETT, DARREN P VIKINGS

PERSONAL: Born January 9, 1965, in Sydney, Australia. ... 6-5/235. ... Full name: Darren Leslie Bennett.

HIGH SCHOOL: Applecross (Perth, Western Australia).

COLLEGE: None.

TRANSACTIONS/CAREER NOTES: Played Australian Rules Football (1987-1993). ... Signed as non-drafted free agent by San Diego Chargers (April 14, 1994). ... Released by Chargers (August 28, 1994). ... Re-signed by Chargers to practice squad (August 29, 1994). ... Assigned by Chargers to Amsterdam Admirals in 1995 World League enhancement allocation program (February 20, 1995). ... Granted unconditional free agency (February 11, 2000). ... Re-signed by Chargers (March 7, 2000). ... Granted unconditional free agency (March 3, 2004). ... Signed by Minnesota Vikings (March 20, 2004).

HONORS: Named punter on THE SPORTING NEWS NFL All-Pro team (1995). ... Played in Pro Bowl (1995 and 2000 seasons).

		PUNTING					
Year Team	**G**	**No.**	**Yds.**	**Avg.**	**Net avg.**	**In. 20**	**Blk.**
1994—San Diego NFL			Did not play.				
1995—San Diego NFL	16	72	3221	44.7	36.6	28	0
1996—San Diego NFL	16	87	3967	45.6	37.2	23	0
1997—San Diego NFL	16	89	3972	44.6	37.7	26	1
1998—San Diego NFL	16	95	4174	43.9	36.8	27	0
1999—San Diego NFL	16	89	3910	43.9	*38.7	32	0

Year	Team	G	PUNTING No.	Yds.	Avg.	Net avg.	In. 20	Blk.
2000—San Diego NFL		16	92	4248	*46.2	36.2	23	0
2001—San Diego NFL		16	78	3308	42.4	36.9	25	0
2002—San Diego NFL		16	87	3540	40.7	34.3	31	2
2003—San Diego NFL		16	82	3436	41.9	36.2	28	0
Pro totals (9 years)		144	771	33776	43.8	36.7	243	3

BENNETT, DREW — WR — TITANS

PERSONAL: Born August 26, 1978, in Berkeley, Calif. ... 6-5/206. ... Full name: Andrew Russell Bennett.
HIGH SCHOOL: Miramonte (Calif.).
COLLEGE: UCLA.
TRANSACTIONS/CAREER NOTES: Singed as non-drafted free agent by Tennessee Titans (April 22, 2001). ... Granted free agency (March 3, 2004). ... Re-signed by Titans (March 3, 2004).
CHAMPIONSHIP GAME EXPERIENCE: Played in AFC championship game (2002 season).
SINGLE GAME HIGHS (regular season): Receptions—8 (September 21, 2003, vs. New Orleans); yards—105 (September 21, 2003, vs. New Orleans); and touchdown receptions—1 (December 21, 2003, vs. Houston).
STATISTICAL PLATEAUS: 100-yard receiving games: 2003 (1). Total: 1.

Year	Team	G	GS	RECEIVING No.	Yds.	Avg.	TD	TOTALS TD	2pt.	Pts.	Fum.
2001—Tennessee NFL		14	1	24	329	13.7	1	1	1	8	0
2002—Tennessee NFL		16	7	33	478	14.5	2	2	0	12	0
2003—Tennessee NFL		12	8	32	504	15.8	4	4	0	24	0
Pro totals (3 years)		42	16	89	1311	14.7	7	7	1	44	0

BENNETT, MICHAEL — RB — VIKINGS

PERSONAL: Born August 13, 1978, in Milwaukee, Wis. ... 5-9/211.
HIGH SCHOOL: Milwaukee Tech.
COLLEGE: Wisconsin.
TRANSACTIONS/CAREER NOTES: Selected after junior season by Minnesota Vikings in first round (27th pick overall) of 2001 NFL draft. ... Signed by Vikings (July 30, 2001). ... On physically unable to perform list with foot injury (August 25, 2003). ... Activated (October 31, 2003).
HONORS: Played in Pro Bowl (2002 season).
SINGLE GAME HIGHS (regular season): Attempts—29 (October 27, 2002, vs. Chicago); yards—167 (November 10, 2002, vs. New York Giants); and rushing touchdowns—2 (December 9, 2001, vs. Tennessee).
STATISTICAL PLATEAUS: 100-yard rushing games: 2001 (2), 2002 (5), 2003 (1). Total: 8.

Year	Team	G	GS	RUSHING Att.	Yds.	Avg.	TD	RECEIVING No.	Yds.	Avg.	TD	TOTALS TD	2pt.	Pts.	Fum.
2001—Minnesota NFL		13	13	172	682	4.0	2	29	226	7.8	1	3	0	18	0
2002—Minnesota NFL		16	16	255	1296	5.1	5	37	351	9.5	1	6	0	36	4
2003—Minnesota NFL		8	7	90	447	5.0	1	12	132	11.0	0	1	0	6	2
Pro totals (3 years)		37	36	517	2425	4.7	8	78	709	9.1	2	10	0	60	6

BENTLEY, KEVIN — LB — BROWNS

PERSONAL: Born December 29, 1979, in Northridge, Calif. ... 6-1/245. ... Full name: Kevin Kinte Bentley.
HIGH SCHOOL: Montclair (Calif.).
COLLEGE: Northwestern.
TRANSACTIONS/CAREER NOTES: Selected by Cleveland Browns in fourth round (101st pick overall) of 2002 NFL draft. ... Signed by Browns (July 16, 2002).

Year	Team	G	GS	TOTALS Tk.	Ast.	Sks.	INTERCEPTIONS No.	Yds.	Avg.	TD
2002—Cleveland NFL		12	0	20	14	0.0	0	0	0.0	0
2003—Cleveland NFL		16	14	55	36	0.0	1	25	25.0	0
Pro totals (2 years)		28	14	75	50	0.0	1	25	25.0	0

BENTLEY, LECHARLES — G/C — SAINTS

PERSONAL: Born November 7, 1979, in Cleveland, Ohio. ... 6-2/299.
HIGH SCHOOL: St. Ignatius (Cleveland).
COLLEGE: Ohio State.
TRANSACTIONS/CAREER NOTES: Selected by New Orleans Saints in second round (44th pick overall) of 2002 NFL draft. ... Signed by Saints (July 28, 2002). ... On injured reserve with knee injury (December 26, 2003-remainder of season).
PLAYING EXPERIENCE: New Orleans NFL, 2002-2003. ... Games/Games started: 2002 (14/14), 2003 (13/13). Total: 27/27.
HONORS: Named center on THE SPORTING NEWS college All-America first team (2001). ... Named to play in Pro Bowl (2003 season); replaced by Steve Hutchinson due to injury.

BERGER, MITCH — P — SAINTS

PERSONAL: Born June 24, 1972, in Kamloops, BC. ... 6-4/220.
HIGH SCHOOL: North Delta (Vancouver).
JUNIOR COLLEGE: Tyler (Texas) Junior College.

COLLEGE: Colorado.
TRANSACTIONS/CAREER NOTES: Selected by Philadelphia Eagles in sixth round (193rd pick overall) of 1994 NFL draft. ... Signed by Eagles (July 11, 1994). ... Released by Eagles (October 10, 1994). ... Signed by Cincinnati Bengals to practice squad (October 13, 1994). ... Released by Bengals (November 30, 1994). ... Signed by Chicago Bears (March 7, 1995). ... Released by Bears (May 4, 1995). ... Signed by Indianapolis Colts (May 16, 1995). ... Claimed on waivers by Green Bay Packers (August 24, 1995). ... Released by Packers (August 27, 1995). ... Signed by Bears (November 7, 1995). ... Released by Bears (November 13, 1995). ... Signed by Minnesota Vikings (April 19, 1996). ... Granted unconditional free agency (February 11, 2000). ... Re-signed by Vikings (February 21, 2000). ... On injured reserve with knee injury (December 18, 2001-remainder of season). ... Released by Vikings (February 22, 2002). ... Signed by St. Louis Rams (April 22, 2002). ... Granted unconditional free agency (February 28, 2003). ... Signed by New Orleans Saints (March 7, 2003).
CHAMPIONSHIP GAME EXPERIENCE: Played in NFC championship game (1998 and 2000 seasons).
HONORS: Named punter on THE SPORTING NEWS NFL All-Pro team (1999). ... Played in Pro Bowl (1999 season).

		PUNTING					
Year Team	**G**	**No.**	**Yds.**	**Avg.**	**Net avg.**	**In. 20**	**Blk.**
1994—Philadelphia NFL	5	25	951	38.0	31.3	8	0
1995—			Did not play.				
1996—Minnesota NFL	16	88	3616	41.1	32.3	26	2
1997—Minnesota NFL	14	73	3133	42.9	34.1	22	0
1998—Minnesota NFL	16	55	2458	44.7	37.0	17	0
1999—Minnesota NFL	16	61	2769	‡45.4	‡38.4	18	0
2000—Minnesota NFL	16	62	2773	‡44.7	36.2	16	0
2001—Minnesota NFL	12	47	2046	43.5	32.9	10	0
2002—St. Louis NFL	16	72	3020	41.9	32.7	26	0
2003—New Orleans NFL	16	71	3144	44.3	*38.2	28	1
Pro totals (9 years)	127	554	23910	43.2	34.9	171	3

BERLIN, EDDIE WR

PERSONAL: Born January 14, 1978, in Urbandale, Iowa. ... 5-11/195.
HIGH SCHOOL: Urbandale (Iowa).
COLLEGE: Northern Iowa.
TRANSACTIONS/CAREER NOTES: Selected by Tennessee Titans in fifth round (159th pick overall) of 2001 NFL draft. ... Signed by Titans (July 9, 2001). ... Granted free agency (March 3, 2004).
CHAMPIONSHIP GAME EXPERIENCE: Played in AFC championship game (2002 season).
SINGLE GAME HIGHS (regular season): Receptions—2 (September 23, 2001, vs. Jacksonville); yards—50 (October 19, 2003, vs. Carolina); and touchdown receptions—1 (October 19, 2003, vs. Carolina).

			RECEIVING				KICKOFF RETURNS				TOTALS			
Year Team	**G**	**GS**	**No.**	**Yds.**	**Avg.**	**TD**	**No.**	**Yds.**	**Avg.**	**TD**	**TD**	**2pt.**	**Pts.**	**Fum.**
2001—Tennessee NFL	11	0	2	28	14.0	0	13	253	19.5	0	0	0	0	0
2002—Tennessee NFL	16	0	1	14	14.0	0	13	260	20.0	0	0	0	0	0
2003—Tennessee NFL	14	0	1	50	50.0	1	4	73	18.3	0	1	0	6	2
Pro totals (3 years)	41	0	4	92	23.0	1	30	586	19.5	0	1	0	6	2

BERNARD, ROCKY DT SEAHAWKS

PERSONAL: Born April 19, 1979, in Baytown, Texas. ... 6-3/293. ... Full name: Robert Bernard.
HIGH SCHOOL: Sterling (Baytown, Texas).
COLLEGE: Texas A&M.
TRANSACTIONS/CAREER NOTES: Selected by Seattle Seahawks in fifth round (146th pick overall) of 2002 NFL draft. ... Signed by Seahawks (July 11, 2002).

			TOTALS		
Year Team	**G**	**GS**	**Tk.**	**Ast.**	**Sks.**
2002—Seattle NFL	16	2	34	15	4.0
2003—Seattle NFL	12	0	11	5	2.0
Pro totals (2 years)	28	2	45	20	6.0

BERRY, BERTRAND DE CARDINALS

PERSONAL: Born August 15, 1975, in Houston, Texas. ... 6-3/250. ... Full name: Bertrand Demond Berry.
HIGH SCHOOL: Humble (Texas).
COLLEGE: Notre Dame.
TRANSACTIONS/CAREER NOTES: Selected by Indianapolis Colts in third round (86th pick overall) of 1997 NFL draft. ... Signed by Colts (July 9, 1997). ... Granted free agency (February 11, 2000). ... Signed by St. Louis Rams (July 20, 2000). ... Released by Rams (August 20, 2000). ... Signed by Denver Broncos (January 3, 2001). ... Granted unconditional free agency (March 3, 2004). ... Signed by Arizona Cardinals (March 6, 2004).

			TOTALS		
Year Team	**G**	**GS**	**Tk.**	**Ast.**	**Sks.**
1997—Indianapolis NFL	10	1	4	7	0.0
1998—Indianapolis NFL	16	12	38	11	4.0
1999—Indianapolis NFL	16	0	5	2	1.0
2000—			Did not play.		
2001—Denver NFL	14	0	14	2	2.0
2002—Denver NFL	16	1	10	2	6.5
2003—Denver NFL	16	16	23	14	11.5
Pro totals (6 years)	88	30	94	38	25.0

BERTON, SEAN — TE — VIKINGS

PERSONAL: Born October 31, 1979, in Columbia, S.C. ... 6-4/272.
HIGH SCHOOL: Hempfield (Greensburg, Pa.).
COLLEGE: North Carolina State.
TRANSACTIONS/CAREER NOTES: Signed as non-drafted free agent by Minnesota Vikings (May 1, 2003).

			RECEIVING				TOTALS			
Year Team	G	GS	No.	Yds.	Avg.	TD	TD	2pt.	Pts.	Fum.
2003—Minnesota NFL	16	0	0	0	0.0	0	0	0	0	0

BETTIS, JEROME — RB — STEELERS

PERSONAL: Born February 16, 1972, in Detroit, Mich. ... 5-11/252. ... Full name: Jerome Abram Bettis.
HIGH SCHOOL: Mackenzie (Detroit).
COLLEGE: Notre Dame.
TRANSACTIONS/CAREER NOTES: Selected after junior season by Los Angeles Rams in first round (10th pick overall) of 1993 NFL draft. ... Signed by Rams (July 22, 1993). ... Rams franchise moved to St. Louis (April 12, 1995). ... Traded by Rams with third-round pick (LB Steven Conley) in 1996 draft to Pittsburgh Steelers for second-round pick (TE Ernie Conwell) in 1996 draft and fourth-round pick (traded to Miami) in 1997 draft (April 20, 1996). ... Granted unconditional free agency (February 14, 1997). ... Re-signed by Steelers (February 17, 1997). ... Granted unconditional free agency (March 2, 2001). ... Re-signed by Steelers (March 2, 2001).
CHAMPIONSHIP GAME EXPERIENCE: Played in AFC championship game (1997 and 2001 seasons).
HONORS: Named NFL Rookie of the Year by THE SPORTING NEWS (1993). ... Played in Pro Bowl (1993, 1994, 1996 and 1997 seasons). ... Named to play in Pro Bowl (2001 season); replaced by Corey Dillon due to injury.
SINGLE GAME HIGHS (regular season): Attempts—39 (January 2, 1994, vs. Chicago); yards—212 (December 12, 1993, vs. New Orleans); and rushing touchdowns—3 (November 30, 1997, vs. Arizona).
STATISTICAL PLATEAUS: 100-yard rushing games: 1993 (7), 1994 (4), 1996 (10), 1997 (10), 1998 (6), 1999 (2), 2000 (7), 2001 (5), 2002 (1), 2003 (2). Total: 54.

			RUSHING				RECEIVING				TOTALS			
Year Team	G	GS	Att.	Yds.	Avg.	TD	No.	Yds.	Avg.	TD	TD	2pt.	Pts.	Fum.
1993—Los Angeles Rams NFL	16	12	‡294	1429	4.9	7	26	244	9.4	0	7	0	42	4
1994—Los Angeles Rams NFL	16	16	319	1025	3.2	3	31	293	9.5	1	4	∞2	28	5
1995—St. Louis NFL	15	13	183	637	3.5	3	18	106	5.9	0	3	0	18	4
1996—Pittsburgh NFL	16	12	320	1431	4.5	11	22	122	5.5	0	11	0	66	7
1997—Pittsburgh NFL	15	15	*375	1665	4.4	7	15	110	7.3	2	9	0	54	6
1998—Pittsburgh NFL	15	15	316	1185	3.8	3	16	90	5.6	0	3	0	18	2
1999—Pittsburgh NFL	16	16	299	1091	3.6	7	21	110	5.2	0	7	0	42	2
2000—Pittsburgh NFL	16	16	355	1341	3.8	8	13	97	7.5	0	8	0	48	1
2001—Pittsburgh NFL	11	11	225	1072	§4.8	4	8	48	6.0	0	4	0	24	3
2002—Pittsburgh NFL	13	11	187	666	3.6	9	7	57	8.1	0	9	0	54	1
2003—Pittsburgh NFL	16	10	246	811	3.3	7	13	86	6.6	0	7	1	44	5
Pro totals (11 years)	165	147	3119	12353	4.0	69	190	1363	7.2	3	72	3	438	40

BETTS, LADELL — RB — REDSKINS

PERSONAL: Born August 27, 1979, in Blue Springs, Mo. ... 5-10/222. ... Full name: Matthew Betts.
HIGH SCHOOL: Blue Springs (Mo.).
COLLEGE: Iowa.
TRANSACTIONS/CAREER NOTES: Selected by Washington Redskins in second round (56th pick overall) of 2002 NFL draft. ... Signed by Redskins (July 23, 2002).
SINGLE GAME HIGHS (regular season): Attempts—20 (December 22, 2002, vs. Houston); yards—116 (December 22, 2002, vs. Houston); and rushing touchdowns—1 (September 28, 2003, vs. New England).
STATISTICAL PLATEAUS: 100-yard rushing games: 2002 (1). Total: 1.

			RUSHING				RECEIVING				KICKOFF RETURNS				TOTALS			
Year Team	G	GS	Att.	Yds.	Avg.	TD	No.	Yds.	Avg.	TD	No.	Yds.	Avg.	TD	TD	2pt.	Pts.	Fum.
2002—Washington NFL	11	0	65	307	4.7	1	12	154	12.8	0	28	690	24.6	0	1	0	6	2
2003—Washington NFL	9	1	77	255	3.3	2	15	167	11.1	0	3	59	19.7	0	2	0	12	0
Pro totals (2 years)	20	1	142	562	4.0	3	27	321	11.9	0	31	749	24.2	0	3	0	18	2

BEUERLEIN, STEVE — QB

PERSONAL: Born March 7, 1965, in Hollywood, Calif. ... 6-3/220. ... Full name: Stephen Taylor Beuerlein. ... Name pronounced: BURR-line.
HIGH SCHOOL: Servite (Anaheim, Calif.).
COLLEGE: Notre Dame.
TRANSACTIONS/CAREER NOTES: Selected by Los Angeles Raiders in fourth round (110th pick overall) of 1987 NFL draft. ... Signed by Raiders (July 24, 1987). ... On injured reserve with elbow and shoulder injuries (September 7, 1987-entire season). ... Granted free agency (February 1, 1990). ... Re-signed by Raiders (September 3, 1990). ... Granted roster exemption (September 3-16, 1990). ... Inactive for all 16 games (1990). ... Granted free agency (February 1, 1991). ... Re-signed by Raiders (July 8, 1991). ... Traded by Raiders to Dallas Cowboys for fourth-round pick (traded to Indianapolis) in 1992 draft (August 25, 1991). ... Granted unconditional free agency (March 1, 1993). ... Signed by Phoenix Cardinals (April 21, 1993). ... Cardinals franchise renamed Arizona Cardinals for 1994 season. ... Selected by Jacksonville Jaguars from Cardinals in NFL expansion draft (February 15, 1995). ... Granted free agency (February 16, 1996). ... Signed by Carolina Panthers (April 10, 1996). ... Released by Panthers (March 19, 2001). ... Signed by Denver Broncos (May 30, 2001). ... On injured reserve with elbow injury (October 5, 2001-remainder of season). ... On injured reserve with finger injury (October 21, 2003-remainder of season). ... Waived by Broncos (May 10, 2004).

CHAMPIONSHIP GAME EXPERIENCE: Member of Raiders for AFC championship game (1990 season); inactive. ... Played in NFC championship game (1992 season). ... Member of Super Bowl championship team (1992 season). ... Member of Panthers for NFC championship game (1996 season); did not play.

HONORS: Played in Pro Bowl (1999 season).

SINGLE GAME HIGHS (regular season): Attempts—53 (December 19, 1993, vs. Seattle); completions—34 (December 19, 1993, vs. Seattle); yards—431 (December 19, 1993, vs. Seattle); and touchdown passes—5 (January 2, 2000, vs. New Orleans).

STATISTICAL PLATEAUS: 300-yard passing games: 1988 (1), 1993 (2), 1999 (5), 2000 (3). Total: 11.

MISCELLANEOUS: Regular-season record as starting NFL quarterback: 47-55 (.461). ... Postseason record as starting NFL quarterback: 1-1 (.500). ... Holds Carolina Panthers all-time records for most passing yards (12,690) and touchdown passes (86).

			PASSING									RUSHING				TOTALS		
Year Team	**G**	**GS**	**Att.**	**Cmp.**	**Pct.**	**Yds.**	**TD**	**Int.**	**Avg.**	**Skd.**	**Rat.**	**Att.**	**Yds.**	**Avg.**	**TD**	**TD**	**2pt.**	**Pts.**
1987—L.A. Raiders NFL						Did not play.												
1988—L.A. Raiders NFL	10	8	238	105	44.1	1643	8	7	6.90	26	66.6	30	35	1.2	0	0	0	0
1989—L.A. Raiders NFL	10	7	217	108	49.8	1677	13	9	7.73	22	78.4	16	39	2.4	0	0	0	0
1990—L.A. Raiders NFL						Did not play.												
1991—Dallas NFL	8	4	137	68	49.6	909	5	2	6.64	6	77.2	7	-14	-2.0	0	0	0	0
1992—Dallas NFL	16	0	18	12	66.7	152	0	1	8.44	0	69.7	4	-7	-1.7	0	0	0	0
1993—Phoenix NFL	16	14	418	258	61.7	3164	18	17	7.57	29	82.5	22	45	2.0	0	0	0	0
1994—Arizona NFL	9	7	255	130	51.0	1545	5	9	6.06	20	61.6	22	39	1.8	1	1	0	6
1995—Jacksonville NFL	7	6	142	71	50.0	952	4	7	6.70	17	60.5	5	32	6.4	0	0	0	0
1996—Carolina NFL	8	4	123	69	56.1	879	8	2	7.15	18	93.5	12	17	1.4	0	0	0	0
1997—Carolina NFL	7	3	153	89	58.2	1032	6	3	6.75	17	83.6	4	32	8.0	0	0	0	0
1998—Carolina NFL	12	12	343	216	63.0	2613	17	12	7.62	44	88.2	22	26	1.2	0	0	0	0
1999—Carolina NFL	16	16	571	*343	60.1	*4436	36	15	7.77	‡50	94.6	27	124	4.6	2	2	0	12
2000—Carolina NFL	16	16	533	324	60.8	3730	19	18	7.00	*62	79.7	44	106	2.4	1	1	1	8
2001—Denver NFL						Did not play.												
2002—Denver NFL	8	3	117	68	58.1	925	6	5	7.91	12	82.7	5	9	1.8	1	1	0	6
2003—Denver NFL	4	2	63	33	52.4	389	2	5	6.17	9	49.0	5	13	2.6	0	0	0	0
Pro totals (14 years)	147	102	3328	1894	56.9	24046	147	112	7.23	332	80.3	225	496	2.2	5	5	1	32

BEVERLY, ERIC — G — FALCONS

PERSONAL: Born March 28, 1974, in Cleveland, Ohio. ... 6-3/300. ... Full name: Eric Raymonde Beverly.

HIGH SCHOOL: Bedford Heights (Ohio).

COLLEGE: Miami (Ohio).

TRANSACTIONS/CAREER NOTES: Signed as non-drafted free agent by Detroit Lions (April 24, 1997). ... Released by Lions (August 24, 1997). ... Re-signed by Lions to practice squad (August 26, 1997). ... Activated (December 20, 1997). ... Active for one game (1997); did not play. ... Granted free agency (March 2, 2001). ... Tendered offer sheet by Miami Dolphins (March 8, 2001). ... Offer matched by Lions (March 15, 2001). ... On injured reserve with ankle injury (December 13, 2003-remainder of season). ... Granted unconditional free agency (March 3, 2004). ... Signed by Atlanta Falcons (March 10, 2004).

PLAYING EXPERIENCE: Detroit NFL, 1998-2003. ... Games/Games started: 1998 (16/0), 1999 (16/2), 2000 (16/7), 2001 (16/16), 2002 (15/3), 2003 (13/13). Total: 92/41.

BIBLA, MARTIN — G — FALCONS

PERSONAL: Born October 4, 1979, in Mountaintop, Pa. ... 6-3/306. ... Full name: Martin John Bibla.

HIGH SCHOOL: Crestwood (Mountaintop, Pa.).

COLLEGE: Miami (Fla.).

TRANSACTIONS/CAREER NOTES: Selected by Atlanta Falcons in fourth round (116th pick overall) of 2002 NFL draft. ... Signed by Falcons (June 19, 2002).

PLAYING EXPERIENCE: Atlanta NFL, 2002-2003. ... Games/Games started: 2002 (10/0), 2003 (10/2). Total: 20/2.

BICKERSTAFF, ERIK — RB — COWBOYS

PERSONAL: Born July 25, 1980, in Birmingham, Ala. ... 6-0/230.

HIGH SCHOOL: Waukesha (Wis.).

COLLEGE: Wisconsin.

TRANSACTIONS/CAREER NOTES: Signed as non-drafted free agent by Dallas Cowboys (August 5, 2003). ... Released by Cowboys (November 3, 2003). ... Re-signed by Cowboys to practice squad (November 5, 2003). ... Activated (December 2, 2003).

			RUSHING				KICKOFF RETURNS				TOTALS			
Year Team	**G**	**GS**	**Att.**	**Yds.**	**Avg.**	**TD**	**No.**	**Yds.**	**Avg.**	**TD**	**TD**	**2pt.**	**Pts.**	**Fum.**
2003—Dallas NFL	4	0	19	56	2.9	1	2	24	12.0	0	1	0	6	0

BIDWELL, JOSH — P — BUCCANEERS

PERSONAL: Born March 13, 1976, in Roseburg, Ore. ... 6-3/220. ... Full name: Joshua John Bidwell.

HIGH SCHOOL: Douglas (Winston, Ore.).

COLLEGE: Oregon.

TRANSACTIONS/CAREER NOTES: Selected by Green Bay Packers in fourth round (133rd pick overall) of 1999 NFL draft. ... Signed by Packers (July 27, 1999). ... On non-football illness list with cancer (September 5, 1999-entire season). ... Granted free agency (February 28, 2003). ... Re-signed by Packers (April 30, 2003). ... Granted unconditional free agency (March 3, 2004). ... Signed by Tampa Bay Buccaneers (March 13, 2004).

HONORS: Named punter on THE SPORTING NEWS college All-America second team (1998).

Year Team	G	PUNTING No.	Yds.	Avg.	Net avg.	In. 20	Blk.
1999—Green Bay NFL		Did not play.					
2000—Green Bay NFL	16	78	3003	38.5	34.6	22	0
2001—Green Bay NFL	16	82	3485	42.5	36.5	21	0
2002—Green Bay NFL	16	79	3296	41.7	35.7	26	0
2003—Green Bay NFL	16	69	2875	41.7	35.1	16	0
Pro totals (4 years)	64	308	12659	41.1	35.5	85	0

BIEKERT, GREG LB

PERSONAL: Born March 14, 1969, in Iowa City, Iowa. ... 6-2/253. ... Name pronounced: BEEK-ert.
HIGH SCHOOL: Longmont (Colo.).
COLLEGE: Colorado.
TRANSACTIONS/CAREER NOTES: Selected by Los Angeles Raiders in seventh round (181st pick overall) of 1993 NFL draft. ... Signed by Raiders (July 13, 1993). ... Raiders franchise moved to Oakland (July 21, 1995). ... Released by Raiders (September 1, 2002). ... Signed by Minnesota Vikings (September 2, 2002). ... Announced retirement (May 5, 2004).
CHAMPIONSHIP GAME EXPERIENCE: Played in AFC championship game (2000 season).

Year Team	G	GS	TOTALS Tk.	Ast.	Sks.	INTERCEPTIONS No.	Yds.	Avg.	TD
1993—Los Angeles Raiders NFL	16	0	8	2	0.0	0	0	0.0	0
1994—Los Angeles Raiders NFL	16	14	75	25	1.5	1	11	11.0	0
1995—Oakland NFL	16	14	69	16	1.0	0	0	0.0	0
1996—Oakland NFL	16	15	75	23	0.0	0	0	0.0	0
1997—Oakland NFL	16	16	73	26	2.5	0	0	0.0	0
1998—Oakland NFL	16	16	115	31	3.0	0	0	0.0	0
1999—Oakland NFL	16	16	104	32	2.0	2	57	28.5	0
2000—Oakland NFL	16	16	100	34	2.0	0	0	0.0	0
2001—Oakland NFL	16	16	81	27	3.0	0	0	0.0	0
2002—Minnesota NFL	16	16	70	31	0.0	4	26	6.5	0
2003—Minnesota NFL	16	16	61	16	1.0	0	0	0.0	0
Pro totals (11 years)	176	155	831	263	16.0	7	94	13.4	0

BINN, DAVID C/LS CHARGERS

PERSONAL: Born February 6, 1972, in San Mateo, Calif. ... 6-3/245. ... Full name: David Aaron Binn.
HIGH SCHOOL: San Mateo (Calif.).
COLLEGE: California.
TRANSACTIONS/CAREER NOTES: Signed as non-drafted free agent by San Diego Chargers (April 28, 1994). ... Granted unconditional free agency (February 13, 1998). ... Re-signed by Chargers (February 25, 1998). ... Granted unconditional free agency (February 11, 2000). ... Re-signed by Chargers (February 11, 2000). ... Granted unconditional free agency (March 1, 2002). ... Re-signed by Chargers (March 5, 2002). ... Granted unconditional free agency (February 28, 2003). ... Re-signed by Chargers (March 3, 2003). ... Granted unconditional free agency (March 3, 2004). ... Re-signed by Chargers (March 4, 2004).
PLAYING EXPERIENCE: San Diego NFL, 1994-2003. ... Games/Games started: 1994 (16/0), 1995 (16/0), 1996 (16/0), 1997 (16/0), 1998 (15/0), 1999 (16/0), 2000 (16/0), 2001 (16/0), 2002 (16/0), 2003 (16/0). Total: 159/0.
CHAMPIONSHIP GAME EXPERIENCE: Played in AFC championship game (1994 season). ... Played in Super Bowl 29 (1994 season).

BIRD, CORY S COLTS

PERSONAL: Born August 10, 1978, in Atlantic City, N.J. ... 5-10/213. ... Full name: Cory James Bird.
HIGH SCHOOL: Oakcrest (Mays Landing, N.J.).
COLLEGE: Virginia Tech.
TRANSACTIONS/CAREER NOTES: Selected by Indianapolis Colts in third round (91st pick overall) of 2001 NFL draft. ... Signed by Colts (July 25, 2001). ... On injured reserve with hip injury (November 20, 2002-remainder of season). ... Granted free agency (March 3, 2004). ... Re-signed by Colts (March 26, 2004).
CHAMPIONSHIP GAME EXPERIENCE: Played in AFC championship game (2003 season).

Year Team	G	GS	TOTALS Tk.	Ast.	Sks.	INTERCEPTIONS No.	Yds.	Avg.	TD
2001—Indianapolis NFL	14	0	20	5	0.5	0	0	0.0	0
2002—Indianapolis NFL	6	4	10	5	0.0	0	0	0.0	0
2003—Indianapolis NFL	12	0	2	0	0.0	0	0	0.0	0
Pro totals (3 years)	32	4	32	10	0.5	0	0	0.0	0

BIRK, MATT C VIKINGS

PERSONAL: Born July 23, 1976, in St. Paul, Minn. ... 6-4/300. ... Full name: Matthew Robert Birk.
HIGH SCHOOL: Cretin-Derham Hall (St. Paul, Minn.).
COLLEGE: Harvard.
TRANSACTIONS/CAREER NOTES: Selected by Minnesota Vikings in sixth round (173rd pick overall) of 1998 NFL draft. ... Signed by Vikings (June 24, 1998). ... Granted free agency (March 2, 2001). ... Re-signed by Vikings (March 6, 2001).
PLAYING EXPERIENCE: Minnesota NFL, 1998-2003. ... Games/Games started: 1998 (7/0), 1999 (15/0), 2000 (16/16), 2001 (16/16), 2002 (16/16), 2003 (16/16). Total: 86/64.
CHAMPIONSHIP GAME EXPERIENCE: Member of Vikings for NFC championship game (1998 season); did not play. ... Played in NFC championship game (2000 season).
HONORS: Named center on THE SPORTING NEWS NFL All-Pro team (2003). ... Played in Pro Bowl (2000 and 2003 seasons). ... Named to play in Pro Bowl (2001 season); replaced by Jeremy Newberry due to injury.

BLADE, WILLIE DT COWBOYS

PERSONAL: Born February 7, 1979, in Warner Robins, Ga. ... 6-3/315.
HIGH SCHOOL: Warner Robins (Ga.).
JUNIOR COLLEGE: Butler County Community College (Kan.).
COLLEGE: Mississippi State.
TRANSACTIONS/CAREER NOTES: Selected by Dallas Cowboys in third round (93rd pick overall) of 2001 NFL draft. ... Signed by Cowboys (July 23, 2001). ... On injured reserve with wrist injury (August 28, 2001-entire season). ... Claimed on waivers by Houston Texans (September 2, 2002). ... Released by Texans (December 24, 2002). ... Re-signed by Cowboys (January 7, 2003). ... Granted free agency (March 3, 2004). ... Re-signed by Cowboys (April 13, 2004).

			TOTALS		
Year Team	G	GS	Tk.	Ast.	Sks.
2003—Dallas NFL	15	14	11	5	1.0

B

BLAISE, KERLIN G

PERSONAL: Born December 25, 1974, in Orlando, Fla. ... 6-5/315.
HIGH SCHOOL: Maynard Evans (Orlando, Fla.).
COLLEGE: Miami (Fla.).
TRANSACTIONS/CAREER NOTES: Signed as non-drafted free agent by Detroit Lions (April 24, 1998). ... Released by Lions (August 30, 1998). ... Re-signed by Lions to practice squad (September 1, 1998). ... Activated (October 27, 1998); did not play. ... On injured reserve with knee injury (December 1, 1998-remainder of season). ... Granted free agency (March 2, 2001). ... Re-signed by Lions (April 26, 2001). ... Granted unconditional free agency (March 1, 2002). ... Re-signed by Lions (April 2, 2002). ... On injured reserve with knee injury (September 17, 2002-remainder of season). ... Granted unconditional free agency (February 28, 2003). ... Re-signed by Lions (November 11, 2003). ... Granted unconditional free agency (March 3, 2004).
PLAYING EXPERIENCE: Detroit NFL, 1999-2003. ... Games/Games started: 1999 (16/4), 2000 (12/0), 2001 (6/0), 2002 (2/2), 2003 (2/0). Total: 38/6.

BLAKE, JEFF QB

PERSONAL: Born December 4, 1970, in Daytona Beach, Fla. ... 6-1/223. ... Son of Emory Blake, running back with Toronto Argonauts of CFL (1974).
HIGH SCHOOL: Seminole (Sanford, Fla.).
COLLEGE: East Carolina.
TRANSACTIONS/CAREER NOTES: Selected by New York Jets in sixth round (166th pick overall) of 1992 NFL draft. ... Signed by Jets (July 14, 1992). ... Inactive for all 16 games (1993). ... Claimed on waivers by Cincinnati Bengals (August 29, 1994). ... Granted free agency (February 17, 1995). ... Re-signed by Bengals (May 8, 1995). ... On injured reserve with wrist injury (December 24, 1998-remainder of season). ... Granted unconditional free agency (February 11, 2000). ... Signed by New Orleans Saints (February 11, 2000). ... On injured reserve with broken foot (November 20, 2000-remainder of season). ... Released by Saints (March 1, 2002). ... Signed by Baltimore Ravens (April 24, 2002). ... Granted unconditional free agency (February 28, 2003). ... Signed by Arizona Cardinals (March 12, 2003). ... Released by Cardinals (February 4, 2004).
HONORS: Played in Pro Bowl (1995 season).
SINGLE GAME HIGHS (regular season): Attempts—50 (October 27, 2002, vs. Pittsburgh); completions—33 (September 10, 2000, vs. San Diego); yards—387 (November 6, 1994, vs. Seattle); and touchdown passes—4 (December 5, 1999, vs. San Francisco).
STATISTICAL PLATEAUS: 300-yard passing games: 1994 (2), 1995 (1), 1996 (2), 1997 (1), 1998 (1), 1999 (1), 2002 (2), 2003 (2). Total: 12.
MISCELLANEOUS: Regular-season record as starting NFL quarterback: 39-61 (.390).

			PASSING									RUSHING				TOTALS		
Year Team	G	GS	Att.	Cmp.	Pct.	Yds.	TD	Int.	Avg.	Skd.	Rat.	Att.	Yds.	Avg.	TD	TD	2pt.	Pts.
1992—New York Jets NFL	3	0	9	4	44.4	40	0	1	4.44	2	18.1	2	-2	1.0	0	0	0	0
1993—New York Jets NFL	Did not play.																	
1994—Cincinnati NFL	10	9	306	156	51.0	2154	14	9	7.04	19	76.9	37	204	5.5	1	1	1	8
1995—Cincinnati NFL	16	16	567	§326	57.5	3822	§28	17	6.74	24	82.1	53	309	5.8	2	2	1	14
1996—Cincinnati NFL	16	16	549	308	56.1	3624	24	14	6.60	44	80.3	72	317	4.4	2	2	0	12
1997—Cincinnati NFL	11	11	317	184	58.0	2125	8	7	6.70	39	77.6	45	234	5.2	3	3	0	18
1998—Cincinnati NFL	8	2	93	51	54.8	739	3	3	7.95	15	78.2	15	103	6.9	0	0	0	0
1999—Cincinnati NFL	14	12	389	215	55.3	2670	16	12	6.86	30	77.6	63	332	5.3	2	2	0	12
2000—New Orleans NFL	11	11	302	184	60.9	2025	13	9	6.71	24	82.7	57	243	4.3	1	1	0	6
2001—New Orleans NFL	1	0	1	0	0.0	0	0	0	0.00	0	39.6	1	-1	1.0	0	0	0	0
2002—Baltimore NFL	11	10	295	165	55.9	2084	13	11	7.06	30	77.3	39	106	2.7	1	1	0	6
2003—Arizona NFL	13	13	367	208	56.7	2247	13	15	6.12	19	69.6	30	177	5.9	2	2	1	14
Pro totals (11 years)	114	100	3195	1801	56.4	21530	132	98	6.74	246	78.1	414	2022	4.9	14	14	3	90

BLAYLOCK, DERRICK RB CHIEFS

PERSONAL: Born August 23, 1979, in Atlanta, Texas. ... 5-9/205.
HIGH SCHOOL: Atlanta (Texas).
COLLEGE: Stephen F. Austin.
TRANSACTIONS/CAREER NOTES: Selected by Kansas City Chiefs in fifth round (150th pick overall) of 2001 NFL draft. ... Signed by Chiefs (June 8, 2001). ... Granted free agency (March 3, 2004). ... Re-signed by Chiefs (March 24, 2004).
SINGLE GAME HIGHS (regular season): Attempts—7 (December 1, 2002, vs. Arizona); yards—40 (November 23, 2003, vs. Oakland); and rushing touchdowns—1 (November 23, 2003, vs. Oakland).
STATISTICAL PLATEAUS: 100-yard receiving games: 2003 (1). Total: 1.

			RUSHING				RECEIVING				KICKOFF RETURNS				TOTALS			
Year Team	G	GS	Att.	Yds.	Avg.	TD	No.	Yds.	Avg.	TD	No.	Yds.	Avg.	TD	TD	2pt.	Pts.	Fum.
2002—Kansas City NFL	12	0	16	72	4.5	0	5	47	9.4	0	3	49	16.3	0	0	0	0	0

Year Team	G	GS	RUSHING Att.	Yds.	Avg.	TD	RECEIVING No.	Yds.	Avg.	TD	KICKOFF RETURNS No.	Yds.	Avg.	TD	TOTALS TD	2pt.	Pts.	Fum.
2003—Kansas City NFL..........	16	0	22	112	5.1	2	15	181	12.1	1	1	32	32.0	0	3	0	18	1
Pro totals (2 years)...............	28	0	38	184	4.8	2	20	228	11.4	1	4	81	20.3	0	3	0	18	1

BLEDSOE, DREW — QB — BILLS

PERSONAL: Born February 14, 1972, in Ellensburg, Wash. ... 6-5/238.
HIGH SCHOOL: Walla Walla (Wash.).
COLLEGE: Washington State.
TRANSACTIONS/CAREER NOTES: Selected after junior season by New England Patriots in first round (first pick overall) of 1993 NFL draft. ... Signed by Patriots (July 6, 1993). ... Traded by Patriots to Buffalo Bills for first-round pick (traded to Chicago) in 2003 draft (April 21, 2002).
CHAMPIONSHIP GAME EXPERIENCE: Played in AFC championship game (1996 and 2001 seasons). ... Played in Super Bowl 31 (1996 season). ... Member of Super Bowl championship team (2001 season); did not play.
HONORS: Played in Pro Bowl (1994, 1996, 1997 and 2002 seasons).
RECORDS: Holds NFL single-season record for most passes attempted—691 (1994). ... Holds NFL single-game records for most passes completed—45; most passes attempted—70; and most passes attempted without an interception—70 (November 13, 1994, vs. Minnesota). ... Tied for most consecutive years leading league in passing attempts—3 (1994-1996).
SINGLE GAME HIGHS (regular season): Attempts—70 (November 13, 1994, vs. Minnesota); completions—45 (November 13, 1994, vs. Minnesota); yards—463 (September 15, 2002, vs. Minnesota); and touchdown passes—4 (September 29, 2002, vs. Chicago).
STATISTICAL PLATEAUS: 300-yard passing games: 1993 (1), 1994 (6), 1995 (2), 1996 (4), 1997 (3), 1998 (4), 1999 (5), 2000 (1), 2002 (7), 2003 (1). Total: 34.
MISCELLANEOUS: Regular-season record as starting NFL quarterback: 77-78 (.497). ... Postseason record as starting NFL quarterback: 3-3 (.500). ... Holds New England Patriots all-time record for most yards passing (29,657).

Year Team	G	GS	PASSING Att.	Cmp.	Pct.	Yds.	TD	Int.	Avg.	Skd.	Rat.	RUSHING Att.	Yds.	Avg.	TD	TOTALS TD	2pt.	Pts.
1993—New England NFL........	13	12	429	214	49.9	2494	15	15	5.81	16	65.0	32	82	2.6	0	0	0	0
1994—New England NFL........	16	16	*691	*400	57.9	*4555	25	*27	6.59	22	73.6	44	40	0.9	0	0	0	0
1995—New England NFL........	15	15	*636	323	50.8	3507	13	16	5.51	23	63.7	20	28	1.4	0	0	0	0
1996—New England NFL........	16	16	*623	*373	59.9	4086	27	15	6.56	30	83.7	24	27	1.1	0	0	0	0
1997—New England NFL........	16	16	522	314	60.2	3706	28	15	7.10	30	87.7	28	55	2.0	0	0	0	0
1998—New England NFL........	14	14	481	263	54.7	3633	20	14	7.55	36	80.9	28	44	1.6	0	0	0	0
1999—New England NFL........	16	16	§539	305	56.6	3985	19	§21	7.39	55	75.6	42	101	2.4	0	0	0	0
2000—New England NFL........	16	16	531	312	58.8	3291	17	13	6.20	45	77.3	47	158	3.4	2	2	0	12
2001—New England NFL........	2	2	66	40	60.6	400	2	2	6.06	5	75.3	5	18	3.6	0	0	0	0
2002—Buffalo NFL................	16	16	610	375	61.5	4359	24	15	7.15	54	86.0	27	67	2.5	2	2	0	12
2003—Buffalo NFL................	16	16	471	274	58.2	2860	11	12	6.07	*49	73.0	24	29	1.2	2	2	0	12
Pro totals (11 years).............	156	155	5599	3193	57.0	36876	201	165	6.59	365	76.7	321	649	2.0	6	6	0	36

BLY, DRE' — CB — LIONS

PERSONAL: Born May 22, 1977, in Chesapeake, Va. ... 5-9/185. ... Full name: Donald Andre Bly.
HIGH SCHOOL: Western Branch (Chesapeake, Va.).
COLLEGE: North Carolina.
TRANSACTIONS/CAREER NOTES: Selected after junior season by St. Louis Rams in second round (41st pick overall) of 1999 NFL draft. ... Signed by Rams (July 16, 1999). ... Granted unconditional free agency (February 28, 2003). ... Signed by Detroit Lions (March 1, 2003).
CHAMPIONSHIP GAME EXPERIENCE: Played in NFC championship game (1999 and 2001 seasons). ... Member of Super Bowl championship team (1999 season). ... Played in Super Bowl 36 (2001 season).
HONORS: Named cornerback on THE SPORTING NEWS college All-America first team (1996). ... Named cornerback on THE SPORTING NEWS college All-America third team (1997). ... Played in Pro Bowl (2003 season).

Year Team	G	GS	TOTALS Tk.	Ast.	Sks.	INTERCEPTIONS No.	Yds.	Avg.	TD	PUNT RETURNS No.	Yds.	Avg.	TD	KICKOFF RETURNS No.	Yds.	Avg.	TD	TOTALS TD	2pt.	Pts.	Fum.
1999—StL. NFL......................	16	2	16	1	0.0	3	53	17.7	1	0	0	0.0	0	1	1	1.0	0	1	0	6	0
2000—StL. NFL......................	16	3	39	4	1.0	3	44	14.7	0	0	0	0.0	0	9	163	18.1	0	0	0	0	1
2001—StL. NFL......................	16	4	28	2	0.0	6	150	25.0	†2	7	71	10.1	0	6	128	21.3	0	2	0	12	1
2002—StL. NFL......................	16	16	58	6	1.0	2	0	0.0	0	8	138	17.3	1	1	5	5.0	0	2	0	12	0
2003—Det. NFL......................	14	14	52	8	1.0	6	89	14.8	1	3	22	7.3	0	0	0	0.0	0	2	0	12	0
Pro totals (5 years)...............	78	39	193	21	3.0	20	336	16.8	4	18	231	12.8	1	17	297	17.5	0	7	0	42	2

BOBER, CHRIS — C — CHIEFS

PERSONAL: Born December 24, 1976, in Omaha, Neb. ... 6-5/310.
HIGH SCHOOL: South (Omaha, Neb.).
COLLEGE: Nebraska-Omaha.
TRANSACTIONS/CAREER NOTES: Signed as non-drafted free agent by New York Giants (April 20, 2000). ... Released by Giants (August 27, 2000). ... Re-signed by Giants to practice squad (August 29, 2000). ... Activated (November 6, 2000); did not play. ... Granted free agency (February 28, 2003). ... Re-signed by Giants (April 21, 2003). ... Granted unconditional free agency (March 3, 2004). ... Signed by Kansas City Chiefs (March 12, 2004).
PLAYING EXPERIENCE: New York Giants NFL, 2001-2003. ... Games/Games started: 2001 (16/0), 2002 (15/15), 2003 (16/16). Total: 47/31.

BODDEN, LEIGH — CB — BROWNS

PERSONAL: Born September 24, 1981, in Hyattsville, Md. ... 6-1/195. ... Full name: Leigh Edmond Bodden.
COLLEGE: Duquesne.
TRANSACTIONS/CAREER NOTES: Signed as non-drafted free agent by Cleveland Browns (May 2, 2003).

Year Team	G	GS	TOTALS Tk.	Ast.	Sks.	INTERCEPTIONS No.	Yds.	Avg.	TD
2003—Cleveland NFL	13	1	9	0	0.0	1	1	1.0	0

BOERIGTER, MARC WR CHIEFS

PERSONAL: Born May 4, 1978, in Hastings, Neb. ... 6-3/220. ... Full name: Marc Robert Boerigter.
HIGH SCHOOL: Hastings (Neb.).
COLLEGE: Hastings (Neb.).
TRANSACTIONS/CAREER NOTES: Signed by Calgary Stampeders of CFL (May 12, 2000). ... Signed as non-drafted free agent by Kansas City Chiefs (February 7, 2002).
CHAMPIONSHIP GAME EXPERIENCE: Member of CFL championship team (2001).
RECORDS: Shares NFL record for longest pass reception (from Trent Green)—99 yards, touchdown (December 22, 2002, vs. San Diego).
SINGLE GAME HIGHS (regular season): Receptions—5 (December 22, 2002, vs. San Diego); yards—144 (December 22, 2002, vs. San Diego); and touchdown receptions—2 (December 22, 2002, vs. San Diego).
STATISTICAL PLATEAUS: 100-yard receiving games: 2002 (1). Total: 1.

Year Team	G	GS	RECEIVING No.	Yds.	Avg.	TD	TOTALS TD	2pt.	Pts.	Fum.
2000—Calgary CFL	18	...	63	1092	17.3	8	8	0	48	0
2001—Calgary CFL	18	...	48	931	19.4	11	11	0	66	0
2002—Kansas City NFL	16	2	20	420	21.0	8	8	0	48	0
2003—Kansas City NFL	15	0	11	158	14.4	0	0	0	0	0
CFL Totals (2 years)	36	...	111	2023	18.2	19	19	0	114	0
NFL totals (2 years)	31	2	31	578	18.6	8	8	0	48	0
Pro totals (4 years)	67	...	142	2601	18.3	27	27	0	162	0

BOGLE, PHIL T CHARGERS

PERSONAL: Born September 27, 1979, in Spring Valley, N.Y. ... 6-2/332.
HIGH SCHOOL: Spring Valley (N.Y.).
COLLEGE: New Haven.
TRANSACTIONS/CAREER NOTES: Signed as non-drafted free agent by San Diego Chargers (May 2, 2003).
PLAYING EXPERIENCE: San Diego NFL, 2003. ... Games/Games started: 2003 (15/13). Total: 15/13.

BOIMAN, ROCKY LB TITANS

PERSONAL: Born January 24, 1980, in Cincinnati, Ohio. ... 6-4/236. ... Full name: Rocky Michael Boiman.
HIGH SCHOOL: St. Xavier (Cincinnati).
COLLEGE: Notre Dame.
TRANSACTIONS/CAREER NOTES: Selected by Tennessee Titans in fourth round (133rd pick overall) of 2002 NFL draft. ... Signed by Titans (July 24, 2002).
CHAMPIONSHIP GAME EXPERIENCE: Played in AFC championship game (2002 season).

Year Team	G	GS	TOTALS Tk.	Ast.	Sks.	INTERCEPTIONS No.	Yds.	Avg.	TD
2002—Tennessee NFL	16	0	1	0	0.0	0	0	0.0	0
2003—Tennessee NFL	16	2	23	13	1.5	2	70	35.0	1
Pro totals (2 years)	32	2	24	13	1.5	2	70	35.0	1

BOLDEN, JURAN CB JAGUARS

PERSONAL: Born June 27, 1974, in Washington, DC. ... 6-2/207.
HIGH SCHOOL: Hillsborough (Tampa).
JUNIOR COLLEGE: Mississippi Delta C.C.
TRANSACTIONS/CAREER NOTES: Signed by Winnipeg Blue Bombers of CFL (April 1995). ... Selected by Atlanta Falcons in fourth round (127th pick overall) of 1996 NFL draft. ... Signed by Falcons (July 20, 1996). ... On injured reserve with knee injury (December 9, 1996-remainder of season). ... Claimed on waivers by Green Bay Packers (September 30, 1998). ... Claimed on waivers by Carolina Panthers (October 27, 1998). ... Released by Panthers (February 12, 1999). ... Signed by Kansas City Chiefs (April 19, 1999). ... Released by Chiefs (September 5, 1999). ... Re-signed by Chiefs (September 21, 1999). ... Released by Chiefs (December 21, 1999). ... Signed by Blue Bombers of CFL (June 8, 2000). ... Signed by Atlanta Falcons (January 10, 2002). ... Granted unconditional free agency (February 28, 2003). ... Re-signed by Falcons (April 28, 2003), ... On active/physically unable to perform list with knee injury (July 25, 2003). ... Activated (October 31, 2003). ... Granted unconditional free agency (March 3, 2004). ... Signed by Jacksonville Jaguars (March 23, 2004).

Year Team	G	GS	TOTALS Tk.	Ast.	Sks.	INTERCEPTIONS No.	Yds.	Avg.	TD
1995—Winnipeg CFL	9	9	17	...	0.0	6	28	4.7	0
1996—Atlanta NFL	9	0	0	0	0.0	0	0	0.0	0
1997—Atlanta NFL	14	1	7	0	0.0	0	0	0.0	0
1998—Atlanta NFL	3	0	3	0	0.0	0	0	0.0	0
—Green Bay NFL	3	0	0	0	0.0	0	0	0.0	0
—Carolina NFL	6	0	0	0	0.0	0	0	0.0	0
1999—Kansas City NFL	7	0	0	0	0.0	0	0	0.0	0
2002—Atlanta NFL	14	6	23	6	0.0	4	25	6.3	0
2003—Atlanta NFL	8	8	22	3	0.0	3	61	20.3	1
CFL Totals (1 years)	9	9	17	...	0.0	6	28	4.7	0
NFL totals (6 years)	64	15	55	9	0.0	7	86	12.3	1
Pro totals (7 years)	73	24	72	9	0.0	13	114	8.8	1

BOLDIN, ANQUAN — WR — CARDINALS

PERSONAL: Born October 3, 1980, in Pahokee, Fla. ... 6-1/218.
HIGH SCHOOL: Pahokee (Fla.).
COLLEGE: Florida State.
TRANSACTIONS/CAREER NOTES: Selected after junior season by Arizona Cardinals in second round (54th pick overall) of 2003 NFL draft. ... Signed by Cardinals (July 24, 2003).
HONORS: Played in Pro Bowl (2003 season). ... Named NFL Rookie of the Year by THE SPORTING NEWS (2003).
RECORDS: Holds NFL single-season record for most receptions by a rookie—101 (2003).
SINGLE GAME HIGHS (regular season): Receptions—10 (December 21, 2003, vs. Seattle); yards—217 (September 7, 2003, vs. Detroit); and touchdown receptions—2 (November 23, 2003, vs. St. Louis).
STATISTICAL PLATEAUS: 100-yard receiving games: 2003 (5). Total: 5.

			RUSHING				RECEIVING				PUNT RETURNS				TOTALS			
Year Team	G	GS	Att.	Yds.	Avg.	TD	No.	Yds.	Avg.	TD	No.	Yds.	Avg.	TD	TD	2pt.	Pts.	Fum.
2003—Arizona NFL	16	16	5	40	8.0	0	101	1377	13.6	8	20	130	6.5	0	8	0	48	3

BOLLER, KYLE — QB — RAVENS

PERSONAL: Born June 17, 1981, in Burbank, Calif. ... 6-3/220.
HIGH SCHOOL: Hart (Newhall, Calif.).
COLLEGE: California.
TRANSACTIONS/CAREER NOTES: Selected by Baltimore Ravens in first round (19th pick overall) of 2003 NFL draft.
SINGLE GAME HIGHS (regular season): Attempts—43 (September 7, 2003, vs. Pittsburgh); completions—22 (September 7, 2003, vs. Pittsburgh); yards—302 (October 19, 2003, vs. Cincinnati); and touchdown passes—2 (October 19, 2003, vs. Cincinnati).
STATISTICAL PLATEAUS: 300-yard passing games: 2003 (1). Total: 1.
MISCELLANEOUS: Regular-season record as starting NFL quarterback: 5-4 (.556).

			PASSING									RUSHING				TOTALS		
Year Team	G	GS	Att.	Cmp.	Pct.	Yds.	TD	Int.	Avg.	Skd.	Rat.	Att.	Yds.	Avg.	TD	TD	2pt.	Pts.
2003—Baltimore NFL	11	9	224	116	51.8	1260	7	9	5.63	17	62.4	30	62	2.1	0	0	0	0

BOOKER, MARTY — WR — BEARS

PERSONAL: Born July 31, 1976, in Marrero, La. ... 6-0/212. ... Full name: Marty Montez Booker.
HIGH SCHOOL: Jonesboro-Hodge (Jonesboro, La.).
COLLEGE: Louisiana-Monroe.
TRANSACTIONS/CAREER NOTES: Selected by Chicago Bears in third round (78th pick overall) of 1999 NFL draft. ... Signed by Bears (July 22, 1999). ... Granted free agency (March 1, 2002). ... Re-signed by Bears (June 21, 2002).
HONORS: Played in Pro Bowl (2002 season).
SINGLE GAME HIGHS (regular season): Receptions—12 (October 7, 2002, vs. Green Bay); yards—198 (September 8, 2002, vs. Minnesota); and touchdown receptions—3 (November 18, 2001, vs. Tampa Bay).
STATISTICAL PLATEAUS: 100-yard receiving games: 1999 (1), 2001 (2), 2002 (3), 2003 (1). Total: 7.

			RECEIVING				TOTALS			
Year Team	G	GS	No.	Yds.	Avg.	TD	TD	2pt.	Pts.	Fum.
1999—Chicago NFL	9	4	19	219	11.5	3	3	0	18	0
2000—Chicago NFL	15	7	47	490	10.4	2	2	0	12	2
2001—Chicago NFL	16	16	100	1071	10.7	8	8	0	48	2
2002—Chicago NFL	16	16	97	1189	12.3	6	6	0	36	0
2003—Chicago NFL	13	13	52	715	13.8	4	4	0	24	1
Pro totals (5 years)	69	56	315	3684	11.7	23	23	0	138	5

BOONE, ALFONSO — DT — BEARS

PERSONAL: Born January 11, 1976, in Saginaw, Mich. ... 6-4/328.
HIGH SCHOOL: Arthur Hill (Saginaw, Mich.).
JUNIOR COLLEGE: Mount San Antonio J.C.
COLLEGE: Central State (did not play football).
TRANSACTIONS/CAREER NOTES: Selected after sophomore season by Detroit Lions in seventh round (253rd pick overall) of 2000 NFL draft. ... Signed by Lions (July 16, 2000). ... Released by Lions (August 27, 2000). ... Re-signed by Lions to practice squad (August 29, 2000). ... Signed by Chicago Bears off Lions practice squad (November 21, 2000). ... Inactive for five games (2000).

			TOTALS		
Year Team	G	GS	Tk.	Ast.	Sks.
2001—Chicago NFL	11	0	7	2	2.0
2002—Chicago NFL	16	5	19	2	1.5
2003—Chicago NFL	16	6	24	4	1.0
Pro totals (3 years)	43	11	50	8	4.5

BOSTON, DAVID — WR — DOLPHINS

PERSONAL: Born August 19, 1978, in Houston, Texas. ... 6-2/240.
HIGH SCHOOL: Humble (Texas).
COLLEGE: Ohio State.

TRANSACTIONS/CAREER NOTES: Selected after junior season by Arizona Cardinals in first round (eighth pick overall) of 1999 NFL draft. ... Signed by Cardinals (August 2, 1999). ... Granted unconditional free agency (February 28, 2003). ... Signed by San Diego Chargers (March 5, 2003). ... Suspended by Chargers for conduct detrimental to team (September 25, 2003). ... Reinstated (September 29, 2003). ... Traded by Chargers to Miami Dolphins for a sixth-round pick in 2005 draft and a player to be named (March 15, 2004). San Diego acquired CB Jamar Fletcher (March 16, 2004).

HONORS: Named wide receiver on THE SPORTING NEWS college All-America second team (1998). ... Named wide receiver on THE SPORTING NEWS NFL All-Pro team (2001). ... Played in Pro Bowl (2001 season).

SINGLE GAME HIGHS (regular season): Receptions—14 (October 5, 2003, vs. Jacksonville); yards—184 (December 3, 2000, vs. Cincinnati); and touchdown receptions—2 (November 23, 2003, vs. Cincinnati).

STATISTICAL PLATEAUS: 100-yard receiving games: 1999 (1), 2000 (4), 2001 (9), 2002 (2), 2003 (2). Total: 18.

			RUSHING				RECEIVING				PUNT RETURNS				TOTALS			
Year Team	G	GS	Att.	Yds.	Avg.	TD	No.	Yds.	Avg.	TD	No.	Yds.	Avg.	TD	TD	2pt.	Pts.	Fum.
1999—Arizona NFL	16	8	5	0	0.0	0	40	473	11.8	2	7	62	8.9	0	2	0	12	2
2000—Arizona NFL	16	16	3	9	3.0	0	71	1156	16.3	7	0	0	0.0	0	7	0	42	2
2001—Arizona NFL	16	16	5	35	7.0	0	98	*1598	16.3	8	0	0	0.0	0	8	0	48	1
2002—Arizona NFL	8	8	2	29	14.5	0	32	512	16.0	1	0	0	0.0	0	1	0	6	0
2003—San Diego NFL	14	14	3	18	6.0	0	70	880	12.6	7	0	0	0.0	0	7	1	44	2
Pro totals (5 years)	70	62	18	91	5.1	0	311	4619	14.9	25	7	62	8.9	0	25	1	152	7

B

BOULWARE, PETER — LB — RAVENS

PERSONAL: Born December 18, 1974, in Columbia, S.C. ... 6-4/255. ... Full name: Peter Nicholas Boulware. ... Name pronounced: BOWL-ware. ... Brother of Michael Boulware, linebacker, Seattle Seahawks.

HIGH SCHOOL: Spring Valley (Columbia, S.C.).

COLLEGE: Florida State.

TRANSACTIONS/CAREER NOTES: Selected after junior season by Baltimore Ravens in first round (fourth pick overall) of 1997 NFL draft. ... Signed by Ravens (August 16, 1997). ... On physically unable to perform list with ankle injury (July 26-August 16, 2002).

CHAMPIONSHIP GAME EXPERIENCE: Played in AFC championship game (2000 season). ... Member of Super Bowl championship team (2000 season).

HONORS: Named defensive end on THE SPORTING NEWS college All-America first team (1996). ... Played in Pro Bowl (1998, 1999 and 2002 seasons). ... Named to play in Pro Bowl (2003 season); replaced by Willie McGinest due to injury.

MISCELLANEOUS: Holds Baltimore Ravens all-time record for most sacks (67.5).

			TOTALS			INTERCEPTIONS			
Year Team	G	GS	Tk.	Ast.	Sks.	No.	Yds.	Avg.	TD
1997—Baltimore NFL	16	16	43	15	11.5	0	0	0.0	0
1998—Baltimore NFL	16	16	38	23	8.5	0	0	0.0	0
1999—Baltimore NFL	16	11	31	8	10.0	0	0	0.0	0
2000—Baltimore NFL	16	15	33	6	7.0	0	0	0.0	0
2001—Baltimore NFL	16	14	45	22	§15.0	0	0	0.0	0
2002—Baltimore NFL	16	16	57	16	7.0	1	6	6.0	0
2003—Baltimore NFL	15	14	42	16	8.5	0	0	0.0	0
Pro totals (7 years)	111	102	289	106	67.5	1	6	6.0	0

BOUMAN, TODD — QB — SAINTS

PERSONAL: Born August 1, 1972, in Ruthton, Minn. ... 6-2/229. ... Name pronounced: Bow-man.

HIGH SCHOOL: Ruthton (Minn.).

COLLEGE: St. Cloud State.

TRANSACTIONS/CAREER NOTES: Signed as non-drafted free agent by Minnesota Vikings (April 25, 1997). ... Released by Vikings (August 23, 1997). ... Re-signed by Vikings to practice squad (August 25, 1997). ... Activated (December 5, 1997). ... Inactive for all 16 games (1999). ... Assigned by Vikings to Barcelona Dragons in 1999 NFL Europe enhancement allocation program (February 22, 1999). ... Inactive for all 16 games (2000). ... Traded by Vikings to New Orleans Saints for sixth-round pick (LB Mike Nattiel) in 2003 draft (March 13, 2003).

CHAMPIONSHIP GAME EXPERIENCE: Member of Vikings for NFC championship game (1998 and 2000 seasons); inactive.

SINGLE GAME HIGHS (regular season): Attempts—38 (December 16, 2001, vs. Detroit); completions—21 (December 9, 2001, vs. Tennessee); yards—348 (December 9, 2001, vs. Tennessee); and touchdown passes—4 (December 9, 2001, vs. Tennessee).

STATISTICAL PLATEAUS: 300-yard passing games: 2001 (1). Total: 1.

MISCELLANEOUS: Regular-season record as starting NFL quarterback: 1-2 (.333).

			PASSING									RUSHING				TOTALS		
Year Team	G	GS	Att.	Cmp.	Pct.	Yds.	TD	Int.	Avg.	Skd.	Rat.	Att.	Yds.	Avg.	TD	TD	2pt.	Pts.
2000—Minnesota NFL							Did not play.											
2001—Minnesota NFL	5	3	89	51	57.3	795	8	4	8.93	4	98.3	9	61	6.8	0	0	0	0
2002—Minnesota NFL	1	0	6	3	50.0	85	0	0	14.17	2	95.8	1	9	9.0	0	0	0	0
2003—New Orleans NFL	4	0	13	7	53.8	81	1	0	6.23	2	98.6	3	1	0.3	0	0	0	0
Pro totals (3 years)	10	3	108	61	56.5	961	9	4	8.90	8	98.6	13	71	5.5	0	0	0	0

BOWEN, MATT — S — REDSKINS

PERSONAL: Born November 12, 1976, in Glen Ellyn, Ill. ... 6-1/207.

HIGH SCHOOL: Glenbard West (Glen Ellyn, Ill.).

COLLEGE: Iowa.

TRANSACTIONS/CAREER NOTES: Selected by St. Louis Rams in sixth round (198th pick overall) of 2000 NFL draft. ... Signed by Rams (July 7, 2000). ... On injured reserve with broken foot (October 3-November 6, 2001). ... Released by Rams (November 6, 2001). ... Signed by Green Bay Packers (November 30, 2001). ... Granted free agency (February 28, 2003). ... Tendered offer sheet by Washington Redskins (March 8, 2003). ... Packers declined to match offer (March 11, 2003).

Year Team	G	GS	TOTALS Tk.	Ast.	Sks.	INTERCEPTIONS No.	Yds.	Avg.	TD
2000—St. Louis NFL	16	2	14	2	0.0	0	0	0.0	0
2001—St. Louis NFL	1	0	0	0	0.0	0	0	0.0	0
—Green Bay NFL	5	0	0	0	0.0	0	0	0.0	0
2002—Green Bay NFL	16	6	29	16	0.0	1	0	0.0	0
2003—Washington NFL	16	16	76	9	0.0	3	44	14.7	0
Pro totals (4 years)	54	24	119	27	0.0	4	44	11.0	0

BOWENS, DAVID DE DOLPHINS

PERSONAL: Born July 3, 1977, in Denver, Colo. ... 6-3/260. ... Full name: David Walter Bowens.

HIGH SCHOOL: St. Mary's (Orchard Lake, Mich.).

COLLEGE: Western Illinois.

TRANSACTIONS/CAREER NOTES: Selected after junior season by Denver Broncos in fifth round (158th pick overall) of 1999 NFL draft. ... Signed by Broncos (July 22, 1999). ... Traded by Broncos to Green Bay Packers for fourth-round pick (C Ben Hamilton) in 2001 draft (February 24, 2000). ... Traded by Packers to Buffalo Bills for TE Bobby Collins (August 7, 2001). ... Claimed on waivers by Washington Redskins (September 3, 2001). ... Released by Redskins (September 26, 2001). ... Signed by Miami Dolphins (October 22, 2001). ... Granted unconditional free agency (February 28, 2003). ... Re-signed by Dolphins (March 6, 2003). ... On active/non-football injury list with knee injury (July 24-November 25, 2003).

Year Team	G	GS	TOTALS Tk.	Ast.	Sks.
1999—Denver NFL	16	0	7	0	1.0
2000—Green Bay NFL	14	0	19	7	3.5
2001—Miami NFL	8	0	5	1	1.0
2002—Miami NFL	14	0	9	7	1.5
2003—Miami NFL	4	0	2	0	1.0
Pro totals (5 years)	56	0	42	15	8.0

BOWENS, TIM DT DOLPHINS

PERSONAL: Born February 7, 1973, in Okolona, Miss. ... 6-4/325. ... Full name: Timothy L. Bowens.

HIGH SCHOOL: Okolona (Miss.).

JUNIOR COLLEGE: Itawamba Community College (Miss.).

COLLEGE: Mississippi.

TRANSACTIONS/CAREER NOTES: Selected after junior season by Miami Dolphins in first round (20th pick overall) of 1994 NFL draft. ... Signed by Dolphins (June 2, 1994). ... Designated by Dolphins as franchise player (February 13, 1998). ... Re-signed by Dolphins (August 21, 1998). ... On injured reserve with torn biceps muscle (January 3, 1999-remainder of playoffs). ... Released by Dolphins (February 28, 2002). ... Re-signed by Dolphins (February 28, 2002).

HONORS: Named to play in Pro Bowl (1998 season); replaced by Cortez Kennedy due to injury. ... Played in Pro Bowl (2002 season).

Year Team	G	GS	TOTALS Tk.	Ast.	Sks.	INTERCEPTIONS No.	Yds.	Avg.	TD
1994—Miami NFL	16	15	44	8	3.0	0	0	0.0	0
1995—Miami NFL	16	16	34	7	2.0	0	0	0.0	0
1996—Miami NFL	16	16	41	7	3.0	0	0	0.0	0
1997—Miami NFL	16	16	34	14	5.0	0	0	0.0	0
1998—Miami NFL	16	16	21	9	0.0	0	0	0.0	0
1999—Miami NFL	16	15	18	16	1.5	0	0	0.0	0
2000—Miami NFL	15	15	29	11	2.5	1	0	0.0	0
2001—Miami NFL	15	15	30	18	3.0	0	0	0.0	0
2002—Miami NFL	16	16	24	12	0.0	0	0	0.0	0
2003—Miami NFL	13	13	20	7	2.0	0	0	0.0	0
Pro totals (10 years)	155	153	295	109	22.0	1	0	0.0	0

BOWERS, R.J. RB BROWNS

PERSONAL: Born February 10, 1974, in Honolulu, Hawaii. ... 6-0/250. ... Full name: Raymond Keith Bowers Jr.

HIGH SCHOOL: West Middlesex (Pa.).

COLLEGE: Grove City (Pa.).

TRANSACTIONS/CAREER NOTES: Signed as non-drafted free agent by Carolina Panthers (April 23, 2001). ... Released by Panthers (August 28, 2001). ... Signed by Pittsburgh Steelers to practice squad (September 3, 2001). ... Activated (December 21, 2001). ... Claimed on waivers by Cleveland Browns (August 28, 2002). ... Released by Browns (October 2, 2002). ... Re-signed by Browns to practice squad (October 2, 2002). ... Activated (November 19, 2002). ... Released by Browns (November 26, 2002). ... Re-signed by Browns (November 29, 2002). ... On non-football injury list with knee injury (July 25, 2003). ... Activated (November 4, 2003). ... On injured reserve with ankle injury (November 26, 2003-remainder of season).

CHAMPIONSHIP GAME EXPERIENCE: Member of Steelers for AFC championship game (2001 season); inactive.

SINGLE GAME HIGHS (regular season): Attempts—11 (January 6, 2002, vs. Cleveland); yards—67 (January 6, 2002, vs. Cleveland); and rushing touchdowns—1 (January 6, 2002, vs. Cleveland).

Year Team	G	GS	RUSHING Att.	Yds.	Avg.	TD	RECEIVING No.	Yds.	Avg.	TD	TOTALS TD	2pt.	Pts.	Fum.
2001—Pittsburgh NFL	3	0	18	84	4.7	1	1	0	0.0	0	1	0	6	0
2002—Cleveland NFL	4	0	0	0	0.0	0	0	0	0.0	0	0	0	0	0
2003—Cleveland NFL	1	0	0	0	0.0	0	1	2	2.0	1	1	0	6	0
Pro totals (3 years)	8	0	18	84	4.7	1	2	2	1.0	1	2	0	12	0

BOYER, BRANT — LB — BROWNS

PERSONAL: Born June 27, 1971, in Ogden, Utah. ... 6-1/240. ... Full name: Brant T. Boyer.
HIGH SCHOOL: North Summit (Coalville, Utah).
JUNIOR COLLEGE: Snow College (Utah).
COLLEGE: Arizona.
TRANSACTIONS/CAREER NOTES: Selected by Miami Dolphins in sixth round (177th pick overall) of 1994 NFL draft. ... Signed by Dolphins (July 11, 1994). ... Released by Dolphins (September 21, 1994). ... Re-signed by Dolphins to practice squad (September 22, 1994). ... Activated (October 5, 1994). ... Selected by Jacksonville Jaguars from Dolphins in NFL expansion draft (February 15, 1995). ... Released by Jaguars (August 27, 1995). ... Re-signed by Jaguars (December 13, 1995). ... Released by Jaguars (August 25, 1996). ... Re-signed by Jaguars (September 24, 1996). ... Released by Jaguars (September 25, 1996). ... Re-signed by Jaguars (September 27, 1996). ... Granted free agency (February 13, 1998). ... Re-signed by Jaguars (March 18, 1998). ... On injured reserve with neck injury (December 2, 1998-remainder of season). ... Granted unconditional free agency (February 12, 1999). ... Re-signed by Jaguars (March 15, 1999). ... Released by Jaguars (March 1, 2001). ... Signed by Cleveland Browns (March 12, 2001).
CHAMPIONSHIP GAME EXPERIENCE: Played in AFC championship game (1996 and 1999 seasons).

			TOTALS			INTERCEPTIONS			
Year Team	**G**	**GS**	**Tk.**	**Ast.**	**Sks.**	**No.**	**Yds.**	**Avg.**	**TD**
1994—Miami NFL	14	0	1	1	0.0	0	0	0.0	0
1995—Jacksonville NFL	2	0	0	0	0.0	0	0	0.0	0
1996—Jacksonville NFL	12	0	4	1	0.0	0	0	0.0	0
1997—Jacksonville NFL	16	2	18	6	1.5	0	0	0.0	0
1998—Jacksonville NFL	11	0	10	2	1.0	0	0	0.0	0
1999—Jacksonville NFL	15	0	18	5	4.0	1	5	5.0	0
2000—Jacksonville NFL	12	5	19	4	3.5	1	12	12.0	0
2001—Cleveland NFL	16	1	50	15	0.0	2	12	6.0	0
2002—Cleveland NFL	16	1	34	7	3.0	1	1	1.0	0
2003—Cleveland NFL	15	7	39	16	0.0	1	4	4.0	0
Pro totals (10 years)	129	16	193	57	13.0	6	34	5.7	0

BRACKENS, TONY — DE

PERSONAL: Born December 26, 1974, in Fairfield, Texas. ... 6-4/267. ... Full name: Tony Lynn Brackens Jr.
HIGH SCHOOL: Fairfield (Texas).
COLLEGE: Texas.
TRANSACTIONS/CAREER NOTES: Selected after junior season by Jacksonville Jaguars in second round (33rd pick overall) of 1996 NFL draft. ... Signed by Jaguars (May 28, 1996). ... Designated by Jaguars as franchise player (February 11, 2000). ... On injured reserve with knee injury (October 15, 2002-remainder of season). ... Released by Jaguars (March 3, 2004).
CHAMPIONSHIP GAME EXPERIENCE: Played in AFC championship game (1996 and 1999 seasons).
HONORS: Named defensive lineman on THE SPORTING NEWS college All-America first team (1995). ... Played in Pro Bowl (1999 season).
MISCELLANEOUS: Holds Jacksonville Jaguars all-time record for most sacks (55).

			TOTALS			INTERCEPTIONS			
Year Team	**G**	**GS**	**Tk.**	**Ast.**	**Sks.**	**No.**	**Yds.**	**Avg.**	**TD**
1996—Jacksonville NFL	16	1	45	10	7.0	1	27	27.0	0
1997—Jacksonville NFL	15	3	41	3	7.0	0	0	0.0	0
1998—Jacksonville NFL	12	8	27	12	3.5	0	0	0.0	0
1999—Jacksonville NFL	16	15	55	13	12.0	2	16	8.0	1
2000—Jacksonville NFL	16	16	54	9	7.5	1	7	7.0	0
2001—Jacksonville NFL	12	12	39	3	11.0	0	0	0.0	0
2002—Jacksonville NFL	5	5	9	2	1.0	0	0	0.0	0
2003—Jacksonville NFL	15	15	33	6	6.0	1	4	4.0	0
Pro totals (8 years)	107	75	303	58	55.0	5	54	10.8	1

BRACKETT, GARY — LB — COLTS

PERSONAL: Born May 23, 1980, in Glassboro, N.J. ... 5-11/235.
COLLEGE: Rutgers.
TRANSACTIONS/CAREER NOTES: Signed as non-drafted free agent by Indianapolis Colts (May 2, 2003).
CHAMPIONSHIP GAME EXPERIENCE: Played in AFC championship game (2003 season).

			TOTALS			INTERCEPTIONS			
Year Team	**G**	**GS**	**Tk.**	**Ast.**	**Sks.**	**No.**	**Yds.**	**Avg.**	**TD**
2003—Indianapolis NFL	16	0	12	2	1.0	1	31	31.0	1

BRADFORD, COREY — WR — TEXANS

PERSONAL: Born December 8, 1975, in Baton Rouge, La. ... 6-1/197. ... Full name: Corey Lamon Bradford.
HIGH SCHOOL: Clinton (La.).
JUNIOR COLLEGE: Hinds Community College (Miss.).
COLLEGE: Jackson State.
TRANSACTIONS/CAREER NOTES: Selected by Green Bay Packers in fifth round (150th pick overall) of 1998 NFL draft. ... Signed by Packers (July 17, 1998). ... Granted free agency (March 2, 2001). ... Re-signed by Packers (March 20, 2001). ... Granted unconditional free agency (March 1, 2002). ... Signed by Houston Texans (March 11, 2002).
SINGLE GAME HIGHS (regular season): Receptions—7 (September 29, 2002, vs. Philadelphia); yards—127 (October 12, 2003, vs. Tennessee); and touchdown receptions—2 (October 20, 2002, vs. Cleveland).
STATISTICAL PLATEAUS: 100-yard receiving games: 1999 (1), 2001 (2), 2002 (1), 2003 (1). Total: 5.

MISCELLANEOUS: Holds Houston Texans all-time records for most touchdown receptions (10) and receiving yards (1,157).

Year	Team	G	GS	RECEIVING No.	Yds.	Avg.	TD	TOTALS TD	2pt.	Pts.	Fum.
1998	—Green Bay NFL	8	0	3	27	9.0	0	0	0	0	1
1999	—Green Bay NFL	16	2	37	637	17.2	5	5	1	32	1
2000	—Green Bay NFL	2	2	0	0	0.0	0	0	0	0	0
2001	—Green Bay NFL	16	6	31	526	17.0	2	2	0	12	1
2002	—Houston NFL	16	16	45	697	15.5	6	6	0	36	0
2003	—Houston NFL	16	6	24	460	19.2	4	4	0	24	0
Pro totals (6 years)		74	32	140	2347	16.8	17	17	1	104	3

B

BRADY, KYLE — TE — JAGUARS

PERSONAL: Born January 14, 1972, in New Cumberland, Pa. ... 6-6/278. ... Full name: Kyle James Brady.
HIGH SCHOOL: Cedar Cliff (Camp Hill, Pa.).
COLLEGE: Penn State.
TRANSACTIONS/CAREER NOTES: Selected by New York Jets in first round (ninth pick overall) of 1995 NFL draft. ... Signed by Jets (July 17, 1995). ... Designated by Jets as transition player (February 12, 1999). ... Tendered offer sheet by Jacksonville Jaguars (February 16, 1999). ... Jets declined to match offer (February 18, 1999).
CHAMPIONSHIP GAME EXPERIENCE: Played in AFC championship game (1998 and 1999 seasons).
HONORS: Named tight end on THE SPORTING NEWS college All-America second team (1994).
SINGLE GAME HIGHS (regular season): Receptions—10 (October 29, 2000, vs. Dallas); yards—138 (October 29, 2000, vs. Dallas); and touchdown receptions—2 (October 19, 1998, vs. New England).
STATISTICAL PLATEAUS: 100-yard receiving games: 2000 (2). Total: 2.

Year	Team	G	GS	RECEIVING No.	Yds.	Avg.	TD	TOTALS TD	2pt.	Pts.	Fum.
1995	—New York Jets NFL	15	11	26	252	9.7	2	2	0	12	0
1996	—New York Jets NFL	16	16	15	144	9.6	1	1	1	8	1
1997	—New York Jets NFL	16	14	22	238	10.8	2	2	0	12	1
1998	—New York Jets NFL	16	16	30	315	10.5	5	5	0	30	1
1999	—Jacksonville NFL	13	12	32	346	10.8	1	1	1	8	0
2000	—Jacksonville NFL	16	15	64	729	11.4	3	3	1	20	0
2001	—Jacksonville NFL	16	16	36	386	10.7	2	2	0	12	0
2002	—Jacksonville NFL	16	16	43	461	10.7	4	4	0	24	0
2003	—Jacksonville NFL	16	14	29	281	9.7	1	1	0	6	3
Pro totals (9 years)		140	130	297	3152	10.6	21	21	3	132	6

BRADY, TOM — QB — PATRIOTS

PERSONAL: Born August 3, 1977, in San Mateo, Calif. ... 6-4/225. ... Full name: Thomas Brady.
HIGH SCHOOL: Serra (San Mateo, Calif.).
COLLEGE: Michigan.
TRANSACTIONS/CAREER NOTES: Selected by New England Patriots in sixth round (199th pick overall) of 2000 NFL draft. ... Signed by Patriots (July 14, 2000).
CHAMPIONSHIP GAME EXPERIENCE: Played in AFC championship game (2001 and 2003 seasons). ... Member of Super Bowl championship team (2001 and 2003 seasons).
HONORS: Named Most Valuable Player of Super Bowl 36 (2001 season) and Super Bowl 38 (2003 season). ... Played in Pro Bowl (2001 and 2003 seasons).
SINGLE GAME HIGHS (regular season): Attempts—55 (November 10, 2002, vs. Chicago); completions—39 (September 22, 2002, vs. Kansas City); yards—410 (September 22, 2002, vs. Kansas City); and touchdown passes—4 (December 27, 2003, vs. Buffalo).
STATISTICAL PLATEAUS: 300-yard passing games: 2001 (1), 2002 (3), 2003 (2). Total: 6.
MISCELLANEOUS: Selected by Montreal Expos organization in 18th round of free-agent draft (June 1, 1995); did not sign. ... Regular-season record as starting NFL quarterback: 34-12 (.739). ... Postseason record as starting NFL quarterback: 6-0 (1.000).

Year	Team	G	GS	PASSING Att.	Cmp.	Pct.	Yds.	TD	Int.	Avg.	Skd.	Rat.	RUSHING Att.	Yds.	Avg.	TD	TOTALS TD	2pt.	Pts.
2000	—New England NFL	1	0	3	1	33.3	6	0	0	2.00	0	42.4	0	0	0.0	0	0	0	0
2001	—New England NFL	15	14	413	264	63.9	2843	18	12	6.88	41	86.5	36	43	1.2	0	0	0	0
2002	—New England NFL	16	16	601	373	62.1	3764	*28	14	6.26	31	85.7	42	110	2.6	1	1	0	6
2003	—New England NFL	16	16	527	317	60.2	3620	23	12	6.87	32	85.9	42	63	1.5	1	1	0	6
Pro totals (4 years)		48	46	1544	955	61.9	10233	69	38	6.63	104	85.9	120	216	1.8	2	2	0	12

BRAHAM, RICH — C/G — BENGALS

PERSONAL: Born November 6, 1970, in Morgantown, W.Va. ... 6-4/305. ... Name pronounced: BRAY-um.
HIGH SCHOOL: University (Morgantown, W.Va.).
COLLEGE: West Virginia.
TRANSACTIONS/CAREER NOTES: Selected by Arizona Cardinals in third round (76th pick overall) of 1994 NFL draft. ... Signed by Cardinals (July 30, 1994). ... Claimed on waivers by Cincinnati Bengals (November 18, 1994). ... On injured reserve with ankle injury (August 29, 1995-entire season). ... Granted free agency (February 14, 1997). ... Tendered offer sheet by New England Patriots (April 8, 1997). ... Offer matched by Bengals (April 15, 1997). ... On injured reserve with knee injury (December 3, 1998-remainder of season). ... Granted unconditional free agency (March 2, 2001). ... Re-signed by Bengals (March 12, 2001). ... Granted free agency (February 28, 2003). ... Re-signed by Bengals (April 30, 2003). ... Granted unconditional free agency (March 3, 2004). ... Re-signed by Bengals (March 8, 2004).
PLAYING EXPERIENCE: Cincinnati NFL, 1994-2003. ... Games/Games started: 1994 (3/0), 1996 (16/16), 1997 (16/16), 1998 (12/12), 1999 (16/16), 2000 (9/9), 2001 (16/16), 2002 (15/15), 2003 (16/15). Total: 119/115.
HONORS: Named offensive lineman on THE SPORTING NEWS college All-America second team (1993).

BRANCH, COLIN — S — PANTHERS

PERSONAL: Born March 2, 1980, in Carlsbad, Calif. ... 6-0/203. ... Brother of Calvin Branch, safety with Oakland Raiders (1997-2000).
HIGH SCHOOL: Carlsbad (Calif.).
COLLEGE: Stanford.
TRANSACTIONS/CAREER NOTES: Selected by Carolina Panthers in fourth round (119th pick overall) of 2003 NFL draft. ... Signed by Panthers (July 26, 2003).
CHAMPIONSHIP GAME EXPERIENCE: Played in NFC championship game (2003 season). ... Played in Super Bowl 38 (2003 season).

			TOTALS			INTERCEPTIONS			
Year Team	G	GS	Tk.	Ast.	Sks.	No.	Yds.	Avg.	TD
2003—Carolina NFL	16	0	2	0	0.0	0	0	0.0	0

BRANCH, DEION — WR — PATRIOTS

PERSONAL: Born July 18, 1979, in Albany, Ga. ... 5-9/193. ... Full name: Anthony Branch.
HIGH SCHOOL: Monroe (Ga.).
JUNIOR COLLEGE: Jones County Junior College (Miss.).
COLLEGE: Louisville.
TRANSACTIONS/CAREER NOTES: Selected by New England Patrios in second round (65th pick overall) of 2002 NFL draft.
CHAMPIONSHIP GAME EXPERIENCE: Played in AFC championship game (2003 season). ... Member of Super Bowl championship team (2003 season).
HONORS: Named wide receiver on THE SPORTING NEWS college All-America third team (2001).
SINGLE GAME HIGHS (regular season): Receptions—13 (September 29, 2002, vs. San Diego); yards—128 (September 29, 2002, vs. San Diego); and touchdown receptions—1 (November 30, 2003, vs. Indianapolis).
STATISTICAL PLATEAUS: 100-yard receiving games: 2002 (1), 2003 (1). Total: 2.

			RECEIVING				PUNT RETURNS				KICKOFF RETURNS				TOTALS			
Year Team	G	GS	No.	Yds.	Avg.	TD	No.	Yds.	Avg.	TD	No.	Yds.	Avg.	TD	TD	2pt.	Pts.	Fum.
2002—New England NFL	13	7	43	489	11.4	2	2	58	29.0	0	36	863	24.0	0	2	0	12	1
2003—New England NFL	15	12	57	803	14.1	3	4	26	6.5	0	0	0	0.0	0	3	0	18	0
Pro totals (2 years)	28	19	100	1292	12.9	5	6	84	14.0	0	36	863	24.0	0	5	0	30	1

BRANDON, SAM — S — BRONCOS

PERSONAL: Born July 5, 1979, in Toledo, Ohio. ... 6-2/200.
HIGH SCHOOL: Riverside (Calif.).
COLLEGE: UNLV.
TRANSACTIONS/CAREER NOTES: Selected by Denver Broncos in fourth round (131st pick overall) of 2002 NFL draft. ... Signed by Broncos (July 19, 2002).

			TOTALS			INTERCEPTIONS			
Year Team	G	GS	Tk.	Ast.	Sks.	No.	Yds.	Avg.	TD
2002—Denver NFL	16	2	14	3	0.0	0	0	0.0	0
2003—Denver NFL	16	10	33	14	0.0	1	0	0.0	0
Pro totals (2 years)	32	12	47	17	0.0	1	0	0.0	0

BRATZKE, CHAD — DE

PERSONAL: Born September 15, 1971, in Waukegan, Ill. ... 6-5/270. ... Full name: Chad Allen Bratzke. ... Name pronounced: BRAT-ski.
HIGH SCHOOL: Bloomingdale (Valrico, Fla.).
COLLEGE: Eastern Kentucky.
TRANSACTIONS/CAREER NOTES: Selected by New York Giants in fifth round (155th pick overall) of 1994 NFL draft. ... Signed by Giants (July 17, 1994). ... On injured reserve with knee injury (November 12, 1997-remainder of season). ... Granted unconditional free agency (February 12, 1999). ... Signed by Indianapolis Colts (March 1, 1999). ... Released by Colts (February 27, 2004).
CHAMPIONSHIP GAME EXPERIENCE: Played in AFC championship game (2003 season).

			TOTALS		
Year Team	G	GS	Tk.	Ast.	Sks.
1994—New York Giants NFL	2	0	0	0	0.0
1995—New York Giants NFL	6	0	2	3	0.0
1996—New York Giants NFL	16	16	43	9	5.0
1997—New York Giants NFL	10	10	23	12	3.5
1998—New York Giants NFL	16	16	57	22	11.0
1999—Indianapolis NFL	16	16	34	14	12.0
2000—Indianapolis NFL	16	16	45	19	7.5
2001—Indianapolis NFL	15	15	45	15	8.5
2002—Indianapolis NFL	16	16	34	11	6.0
2003—Indianapolis NFL	16	3	14	8	3.0
Pro totals (10 years)	129	108	297	113	56.5

BRAYTON, TYLER — DE — RAIDERS

PERSONAL: Born November 20, 1979, in Richland, Wash. ... 6-6/280.
HIGH SCHOOL: Pasco (Wash.).
COLLEGE: Colorado.

TRANSACTIONS/CAREER NOTES: Selected by Oakland Raiders in first round (32nd pick overall) of 2003 NFL draft. ... Signed by Raiders (July 24, 2003).

			TOTALS		
Year Team	G	GS	Tk.	Ast.	Sks.
2003—Oakland NFL	16	16	48	13	2.5

BREEDLOVE, KEVIN G/T BUCCANEERS

PERSONAL: Born June 25, 1980, in Arlington, Texas. ... 6-3/315.
HIGH SCHOOL: Daniel (Clemson, S.C.).
COLLEGE: Georgia.
TRANSACTIONS/CAREER NOTES: Signed as non-drafted free agent by San Diego Chargers (May 2, 2003). ... Released by Chargers (August 31, 2003). ... Re-signed by Chargers (September 25, 2003). ... Waived by Chargers (September 29, 2003). ... Re-signed by Chargers to practice squad (October 1, 2003). ... Activated (October 4, 2003). ... Released by Chargers (October 14, 2003). ... Re-signed by Chargers to practice squad (October 16, 2003). ... Waived by Chargers (October 21, 2003). ... Signed by Tampa Bay Buccaneers to practice squad (December 22, 2003). ... Assigned by Buccaneers to Rhein Fire in 2004 NFL Europe enhancement allocation program (February 9, 2004).
PLAYING EXPERIENCE: San Diego NFL, 2003. ... Games/Games started: 2003 (1/0). Total: 1/0.

BREES, DREW QB CHARGERS

PERSONAL: Born January 15, 1979, in Austin, Texas. ... 6-0/221. ... Full name: Drew Christopher Brees.
HIGH SCHOOL: Westlake (Austin, Texas).
COLLEGE: Purdue.
TRANSACTIONS/CAREER NOTES: Selected by San Diego Chargers in second round (32nd pick overall) of 2001 NFL draft. ... Signed by Chargers (August 7, 2001).
HONORS: Named quarterback to THE SPORTING NEWS college All-America third team (2000). ... Maxwell Award winner (2000).
SINGLE GAME HIGHS (regular season): Attempts—50 (November 17, 2002, vs. San Francisco); completions—29 (November 17, 2002, vs. San Francisco); yards—363 (December 14, 2003, vs. Green Bay); and touchdown passes—3 (October 5, 2003, vs. Jacksonville).
STATISTICAL PLATEAUS: 300-yard passing games: 2002 (3), 2003 (1). Total: 4.
MISCELLANEOUS: Regular-season record as starting NFL quarterback: 10-17 (.370).

			PASSING									RUSHING				TOTALS		
Year Team	G	GS	Att.	Cmp.	Pct.	Yds.	TD	Int.	Avg.	Skd.	Rat.	Att.	Yds.	Avg.	TD	TD	2pt.	Pts.
2001—San Diego NFL	1	0	27	15	55.6	221	1	0	8.19	2	94.8	2	18	9.0	0	0	0	0
2002—San Diego NFL	16	16	526	320	60.8	3284	17	16	6.24	24	76.9	38	130	3.4	1	1	0	6
2003—San Diego NFL	11	11	356	205	57.6	2108	11	15	5.92	21	67.5	21	84	4.0	0	1	0	6
Pro totals (3 years)	28	27	909	540	59.4	5613	29	31	6.17	47	73.7	61	232	3.8	1	2	0	12

BREWER, JACK S GIANTS

PERSONAL: Born January 8, 1979, in Fort Worth, Texas. ... 6-0/190.
HIGH SCHOOL: Grapevine (Texas).
COLLEGE: Minnesota.
TRANSACTIONS/CAREER NOTES: Signed as non-drafted free agent by Minnesota Vikings (April 24, 2002). ... On injured reserve with pectoral injury (November 12, 2003-remainder of season). ... Claimed on waivers by New York Giants (March 18, 2004).

			TOTALS			INTERCEPTIONS			
Year Team	G	GS	Tk.	Ast.	Sks.	No.	Yds.	Avg.	TD
2002—Minnesota NFL	15	1	8	2	0.0	2	24	12.0	0
2003—Minnesota NFL	6	0	0	0	0.0	0	0	0.0	0
Pro totals (2 years)	21	1	8	2	0.0	2	24	12.0	0

BREWER, SEAN TE FALCONS

PERSONAL: Born October 5, 1977, in Riverside, Calif. ... 6-4/255.
HIGH SCHOOL: Polytechnic (Riverside, Calif.).
JUNIOR COLLEGE: Riverside.
COLLEGE: San Jose State.
TRANSACTIONS/CAREER NOTES: Selected by Cincinnati Bengals in third round (66th pick overall) of 2001 NFL draft. ... Signed by Bengals (July 18, 2001). ... On injured reserve with leg injury (September 1, 2001-entire season). ... On injured reserve with knee injury (November 5, 2002-remainder of season). ... Claimed on waivers by Atlanta Falcons (September 1, 2003).

			RECEIVING				TOTALS			
Year Team	G	GS	No.	Yds.	Avg.	TD	TD	2pt.	Pts.	Fum.
2001—Cincinnati NFL					Did not play.					
2002—Cincinnati NFL	3	2	0	0	0.0	0	0	0	0	0
2003—Atlanta NFL	9	0	0	0	0.0	0	0	0	0	0
Pro totals (2 years)	12	2	0	0	0.0	0	0	0	0	0

BRIEN, DOUG K JETS

PERSONAL: Born November 24, 1970, in Bloomfield, N.J. ... 6-0/180. ... Full name: Douglas Robert Zachariah Brien.
HIGH SCHOOL: De La Salle Catholic (Concord, Calif.).
COLLEGE: California.

TRANSACTIONS/CAREER NOTES: Selected by San Francisco 49ers in third round (85th pick overall) of 1994 NFL draft. ... Signed by 49ers (July 27, 1994). ... Released by 49ers (October 16, 1995). ... Signed by New Orleans Saints (October 31, 1995). ... Granted free agency (February 14, 1997). ... Re-signed by Saints (July 17, 1997). ... Released by Saints (March 1, 2001). ... Signed by Indianapolis Colts (December 5, 2001). ... Released by Colts (December 15, 2001). ... Signed by Tampa Bay Buccaneers (December 27, 2001). ... Granted unconditional free agency (March 1, 2002). ... Signed by Minnesota Vikings (April 29, 2002). ... On physically unable to perform list with knee injury (July 27-August 2, 2002). ... Released by Vikings (October 23, 2002). ... Signed by New York Jets (March 21, 2003). ... Granted unconditional free agency (March 3, 2004). ... Re-signed by Jets (March 6, 2004).
CHAMPIONSHIP GAME EXPERIENCE: Played in NFC championship game (1994 season). ... Member of Super Bowl championship team (1994 season).
POST SEASON RECORDS: Shares Super Bowl single-game record for most extra points—7 (January 29, 1995, vs. San Diego).

		FIELD GOALS							TOTALS		
Year Team	G	1-29	30-39	40-49	50+	Tot.	Pct.	Lg.	XPM	XPA	Pts.
1994—San Francisco NFL	16	5-5	5-6	5-8	0-1	15-20	75.0	48	*60	*62	105
1995—San Francisco NFL	6	4-4	0-1	2-6	1-1	7-12	58.3	51	19	19	40
—New Orleans NFL	8	4-4	4-6	4-6	0-1	12-17	70.6	47	16	16	52
1996—New Orleans NFL	16	4-4	9-10	5-7	3-4	21-25	84.0	‡54	18	18	81
1997—New Orleans NFL	16	3-3	10-10	6-9	4-5	23-27	85.2	53	22	22	91
1998—New Orleans NFL	16	7-7	3-3	6-6	4-6	20-22	90.9	56	31	31	91
1999—New Orleans NFL	16	9-11	6-7	7-9	2-2	24-29	82.8	52	20	21	92
2000—New Orleans NFL	16	7-7	4-5	12-15	0-2	23-29	79.3	48	37	37	106
2001—Indianapolis NFL	1	0-0	0-0	0-0	0-0	0-0	0.0	0	0	0	0
—Tampa Bay NFL	2	2-2	1-1	2-3	0-0	5-6	83.3	42	2	2	17
2002—Minnesota NFL	6	3-3	1-1	1-2	0-0	5-6	83.3	42	5	7	20
2003—New York Jets NFL	16	5-5	15-15	7-8	0-4	27-32	84.4	48	24	24	105
Pro totals (10 years)	135	53-55	58-65	57-79	14-26	182-225	80.9	56	254	259	800

B

BRIGGS, LANCE LB BEARS

PERSONAL: Born November 12, 1980, in Sacramento, Calif. ... 6-1/245. ... Full name: Lance Marell Briggs.
HIGH SCHOOL: Elk Grove (Sacramento).
COLLEGE: Arizona.
TRANSACTIONS/CAREER NOTES: Selected by Chicago Bears in third round (68th pick overall) of 2003 NFL draft. ... Signed by Bears (July 25, 2003).

			TOTALS			INTERCEPTIONS			
Year Team	G	GS	Tk.	Ast.	Sks.	No.	Yds.	Avg.	TD
2003—Chicago NFL	16	13	62	13	0.0	1	45	45.0	1

BRIGHTFUL, LAMONT CB/KR RAVENS

PERSONAL: Born January 29, 1979, in Oak Harbor, Wash. ... 5-10/160. ... Full name: Lamont Eugene Brightful.
HIGH SCHOOL: Mariner (Everett, Wash.).
COLLEGE: Eastern Washington.
TRANSACTIONS/CAREER NOTES: Selected by Baltimore Ravens in sixth round (195th pick overall) of 2002 NFL draft. ... Signed by Ravens (July 25, 2002).

			TOTALS			INTERCEPTIONS				PUNT RETURNS				KICKOFF RETURNS				TOTALS			
Year Team	G	GS	Tk.	Ast.	Sks.	No.	Yds.	Avg.	TD	No.	Yds.	Avg.	TD	No.	Yds.	Avg.	TD	TD	2pt.	Pts.	Fum.
2002—Bal. NFL	12	0	0	0	0.0	0	0	0.0	0	15	241	16.1	1	34	701	20.6	0	1	0	6	3
2003—Bal. NFL	16	0	2	0	0.0	0	0	0.0	0	†45	351	7.8	0	29	716	24.7	0	0	0	0	2
Pro totals (2 years)	28	0	2	0	0.0	0	0	0.0	0	60	592	9.9	1	63	1417	22.5	0	1	0	6	5

BROCK, RAHEEM DE COLTS

PERSONAL: Born June 10, 1978, in Newark, N.J. ... 6-4/274.
HIGH SCHOOL: Dobbins (Germantown, Md.).
COLLEGE: Temple.
TRANSACTIONS/CAREER NOTES: Selected by Philadelphia Eagles in seventh round (238th pick overall) of 2002 NFL draft. ... Signed by Eagles (July 25, 2002). ... Released by Eagles (July 25, 2002). ... Signed by Indianapolis Colts (July 28, 2002).
CHAMPIONSHIP GAME EXPERIENCE: Played in AFC championship game (2003 season).

			TOTALS			INTERCEPTIONS			
Year Team	G	GS	Tk.	Ast.	Sks.	No.	Yds.	Avg.	TD
2002—Indianapolis NFL	13	6	12	7	1.0	0	0	0.0	0
2003—Indianapolis NFL	16	16	23	14	2.0	0	0	0.0	0
Pro totals (2 years)	29	22	35	21	3.0	0	0	0.0	0

BROCKERMEYER, BLAKE T

PERSONAL: Born April 11, 1973, in Fort Worth, Texas. ... 6-4/295. ... Full name: Blake Weeks Brockermeyer.
HIGH SCHOOL: Arlington Heights (Texas).
COLLEGE: Texas.
TRANSACTIONS/CAREER NOTES: Selected after junior season by Carolina Panthers in first round (29th pick overall) of 1995 NFL draft. ... Signed by Panthers (July 14, 1995). ... Granted unconditional free agency (February 12, 1999). ... Signed by Chicago Bears (February 27,

1999). ... Released by Bears (April 5, 2002). ... Signed by Denver Broncos (June 24, 2002). ... Released by Broncos (February 25, 2003). ... Re-signed by Broncos (August 1, 2003). ... Granted unconditional free agency (March 3, 2004).

PLAYING EXPERIENCE: Carolina NFL, 1995-1998; Chicago NFL, 1999-2001; Denver NFL, 2002-2003. ... Games/Games started: 1995 (16/16), 1996 (12/12), 1997 (16/13), 1998 (14/14), 1999 (15/15), 2000 (15/14), 2001 (16/16), 2002 (16/1), 2003 (16/2). Total: 136/103.

CHAMPIONSHIP GAME EXPERIENCE: Played in NFC championship game (1996 season).

HONORS: Named offensive lineman on THE SPORTING NEWS college All-America first team (1994).

BROMELL, LORENZO — DE — GIANTS

B

PERSONAL: Born September 23, 1975, in Georgetown, S.C. ... 6-6/260. ... Full name: Lorenzo Alexis Bromell.

HIGH SCHOOL: Choppee (Georgetown, S.C.).

JUNIOR COLLEGE: Georgia Military College.

COLLEGE: Clemson.

TRANSACTIONS/CAREER NOTES: Selected by Miami Dolphins in fourth round (102nd pick overall) of 1998 draft. ... Signed by Dolphins (July 10, 1998). ... Granted free agency (March 2, 2001). ... Re-signed by Dolphins (April 19, 2001). ... Granted unconditional free agency (March 1, 2002). ... Signed by Minnesota Vikings (April 12, 2002). ... Released by Vikings (August 31, 2003). ... Signed by Oakland Raiders (November 19, 2003). ... Granted unconditional free agency (March 3, 2004). ... Signed by New York Giants (April 5, 2004).

			TOTALS		
Year Team	**G**	**GS**	**Tk.**	**Ast.**	**Sks.**
1998—Miami NFL	14	0	16	7	8.0
1999—Miami NFL	15	1	10	7	5.0
2000—Miami NFL	8	0	11	1	2.0
2001—Miami NFL	16	1	20	12	6.5
2002—Minnesota NFL	16	1	22	7	4.0
2003—Oakland NFL	6	4	8	6	2.0
Pro totals (6 years)	75	7	87	40	27.5

BRONSON, ZACK — S — 49ERS

PERSONAL: Born January 28, 1974, in Jasper, Texas. ... 6-1/204. ... Full name: Robert Zack Bronson.

HIGH SCHOOL: Jasper (Texas).

COLLEGE: McNeese State.

TRANSACTIONS/CAREER NOTES: Signed as non-drafted free agent by San Francisco 49ers (May 2, 1997). ... On injured reserve with foot injury (December 29, 1999-remainder of season). ... Granted free agency (February 11, 2000). ... Re-signed by 49ers (June 15, 2000). ... Granted unconditional free agency (March 2, 2001). ... Re-signed by 49ers (May 15, 2001).

CHAMPIONSHIP GAME EXPERIENCE: Played in NFC championship game (1997 season).

			TOTALS			INTERCEPTIONS			
Year Team	**G**	**GS**	**Tk.**	**Ast.**	**Sks.**	**No.**	**Yds.**	**Avg.**	**TD**
1997—San Francisco NFL	16	0	18	6	0.0	1	22	22.0	0
1998—San Francisco NFL	11	1	17	0	0.0	4	34	8.5	0
1999—San Francisco NFL	15	2	17	6	0.0	0	0	0.0	0
2000—San Francisco NFL	9	7	31	7	0.0	3	75	25.0	0
2001—San Francisco NFL	16	16	57	6	0.0	7	‡165	23.6	†2
2002—San Francisco NFL	5	5	16	5	0.0	3	28	9.3	0
2003—San Francisco NFL	12	12	37	5	0.0	1	22	22.0	0
Pro totals (7 years)	84	43	193	35	0.0	19	346	18.2	2

BROOKING, KEITH — LB — FALCONS

PERSONAL: Born October 30, 1975, in Senoia, Ga. ... 6-2/245. ... Full name: Keith Howard Brooking.

HIGH SCHOOL: East Coweta (Sharpsburg, Ga.).

COLLEGE: Georgia Tech.

TRANSACTIONS/CAREER NOTES: Selected by Atlanta Falcons in first round (12th pick overall) of 1998 NFL draft. ... Signed by Falcons (June 29, 1998). ... On injured reserve with foot injury (November 1, 2000-remainder of season).

CHAMPIONSHIP GAME EXPERIENCE: Played in NFC championship game (1998 season). ... Played in Super Bowl 33 (1998 season).

HONORS: Played in Pro Bowl (2001 and 2003 seasons). ... Named to play in Pro Bowl (2002 season); replaced by Shelton Quarles due to injury.

			TOTALS			INTERCEPTIONS			
Year Team	**G**	**GS**	**Tk.**	**Ast.**	**Sks.**	**No.**	**Yds.**	**Avg.**	**TD**
1998—Atlanta NFL	15	0	21	5	0.0	1	12	12.0	0
1999—Atlanta NFL	13	13	73	21	2.0	0	0	0.0	0
2000—Atlanta NFL	5	5	28	8	1.0	0	0	0.0	0
2001—Atlanta NFL	16	16	‡102	25	3.5	2	17	8.5	0
2002—Atlanta NFL	16	16	111	29	0.0	2	24	12.0	0
2003—Atlanta NFL	16	16	†126	18	0.0	0	0	0.0	0
Pro totals (6 years)	81	66	461	106	6.5	5	53	10.6	0

BROOKS, AARON — QB — SAINTS

PERSONAL: Born March 24, 1976, in Newport News, Va. ... 6-4/205. ... Full name: Aaron Lafette Brooks.

HIGH SCHOOL: Homer L. Ferguson (Newport News, Va.).

COLLEGE: Virginia.

TRANSACTIONS/CAREER NOTES: Selected by Green Bay Packers in fourth round (131st pick overall) of 1999 NFL draft. ... Signed by Packers (July 27, 1999). ... Traded by Packers with TE Lamont Hall to New Orleans Saints for LB K.D. Williams and third-round pick (traded to San Francisco) in 2001 draft (July 31, 2000).

SINGLE GAME HIGHS (regular season): Attempts—54 (September 30, 2001, vs. New York Giants); completions—30 (December 3, 2000, vs. Denver); yards—441 (December 3, 2000, vs. Denver); and touchdown passes—5 (December 14, 2003, vs. New York Giants).
STATISTICAL PLATEAUS: 100-yard rushing games: 2000 (1). Total: 1. 300-yard passing games: 2000 (1), 2001 (3), 2002 (1), 2003 (1). Total: 6.
MISCELLANEOUS: Regular-season record as starting NFL quarterback: 27-26 (.509). ... Postseason record as starting NFL quarterback: 1-1 (.500).

			PASSING									RUSHING				TOTALS		
Year Team	**G**	**GS**	**Att.**	**Cmp.**	**Pct.**	**Yds.**	**TD**	**Int.**	**Avg.**	**Skd.**	**Rat.**	**Att.**	**Yds.**	**Avg.**	**TD**	**TD**	**2pt.**	**Pts.**
1999—Green Bay NFL			Did not play.															
2000—New Orleans NFL	8	5	194	113	58.2	1514	9	6	7.80	15	85.7	41	170	4.1	2	2	0	12
2001—New Orleans NFL	16	16	558	312	55.9	3832	26	∞22	6.87	‡50	76.4	80	358	4.5	1	1	0	6
2002—New Orleans NFL	16	16	528	283	53.6	3572	∞27	15	6.77	36	80.1	62	253	4.1	2	2	∞2	16
2003—New Orleans NFL	16	16	518	306	59.1	3546	24	8	6.85	34	88.8	54	175	3.2	2	2	0	12
Pro totals (4 years)	56	53	1798	1014	56.4	12464	86	51	6.93	135	82.1	237	956	4.0	7	7	2	46

BROOKS, DERRICK — LB — BUCCANEERS

PERSONAL: Born April 18, 1973, in Pensacola, Fla. ... 6-0/235. ... Full name: Derrick Dewan Brooks.
HIGH SCHOOL: Booker T. Washington (Pensacola, Fla.).
COLLEGE: Florida State.
TRANSACTIONS/CAREER NOTES: Selected by Tampa Bay Buccaneers in first round (28th pick overall) of 1995 NFL draft. ... Signed by Buccaneers (May 3, 1995).
CHAMPIONSHIP GAME EXPERIENCE: Played in NFC championship game (1999 and 2002 seasons). ... Member of Super Bowl championship team (2002 season).
HONORS: Named linebacker on THE SPORTING NEWS college All-America first team (1993 and 1994). ... Played in Pro Bowl (1997-2000 and 2002 seasons). ... Named linebacker on THE SPORTING NEWS NFL All-Pro team (1999, 2000, 2002 and 2003). ... Named to play in Pro Bowl (2001 season); replaced by Dexter Coakley due to injury. ... Named to play in Pro Bowl (2003 season); replaced by Dexter Coakley due to injury.

			TOTALS			INTERCEPTIONS			
Year Team	**G**	**GS**	**Tk.**	**Ast.**	**Sks.**	**No.**	**Yds.**	**Avg.**	**TD**
1995—Tampa Bay NFL	16	13	60	19	1.0	0	0	0.0	0
1996—Tampa Bay NFL	16	16	92	41	0.0	1	6	6.0	0
1997—Tampa Bay NFL	16	16	102	43	1.5	2	13	6.5	0
1998—Tampa Bay NFL	16	16	*123	35	0.0	1	25	25.0	0
1999—Tampa Bay NFL	16	16	‡118	36	2.0	4	61	15.3	0
2000—Tampa Bay NFL	16	16	*123	23	1.0	1	34	34.0	1
2001—Tampa Bay NFL	16	16	80	33	0.0	3	65	21.7	0
2002—Tampa Bay NFL	16	16	88	30	1.0	5	218	43.6	*3
2003—Tampa Bay NFL	16	16	73	30	1.0	2	56	28.0	1
Pro totals (9 years)	144	141	859	290	7.5	19	478	25.2	5

BROOKS, ETHAN — T — RAVENS

PERSONAL: Born April 27, 1972, in Hartford, Conn. ... 6-6/310.
HIGH SCHOOL: Westminster (Simsbury, Conn.).
COLLEGE: Williams.
TRANSACTIONS/CAREER NOTES: Selected by Atlanta Falcons in seventh round (229th pick overall) of 1996 NFL draft. ... Signed by Falcons (June 7, 1996). ... Assigned by Falcons to Frankfurt Galaxy in 1997 World League enhancement allocation program (February 19, 1997). ... Released by Falcons (August 27, 1997). ... Signed by St. Louis Rams (November 20, 1997). ... Inactive for five games (1997). ... Released by Rams (July 19, 1999). ... Signed by Arizona Cardinals (February 3, 2000). ... Granted unconditional free agency (March 2, 2001). ... Signed by Denver Broncos (March 15, 2001). ... Released by Broncos (August 28, 2001). ... Signed by Baltimore Ravens (August 2, 2002). ... Granted unconditional free agency (February 28, 2003). ... Re-signed by Ravens (March 13, 2003).
PLAYING EXPERIENCE: Atlanta NFL, 1996; St. Louis NFL, 1998; Arizona NFL, 2000; Baltimore NFL, 2002-2003. ... Games/Games started: 1996 (2/0), 1998 (15/0), 2000 (14/3), 2002 (15/13), 2003 (15/3). Total: 61/19.

BROOKS, JERMAINE — DT — COWBOYS

PERSONAL: Born April 11, 1979, in Pasadena, Calif. ... 6-3/285.
HIGH SCHOOL: Rancho Cucamonga (Calif.).
COLLEGE: Arkansas.
TRANSACTIONS/CAREER NOTES: Signed as non-drafted free agent by Dallas Cowboys and assigned to practice squad (October 27, 2003). ... Activated (December 24, 2003).

			TOTALS		
Year Team	**G**	**GS**	**Tk.**	**Ast.**	**Sks.**
2003—Dallas NFL	1	0	2	3	0.0

BROWN, ALEX — DE — BEARS

PERSONAL: Born June 4, 1979, in Jasper, Fla. ... 6-3/272. ... Full name: Alex James Brown.
HIGH SCHOOL: Hamilton County (White Springs, Fla.).
COLLEGE: Florida.
TRANSACTIONS/CAREER NOTES: Selected by Chicago Bears in fourth round (104th pick overall) of 2002 NFL draft. ... Signed by Bears (July 24, 2002).
HONORS: Named defensive end on THE SPORTING NEWS college All-America first team (1999). ... Named defensive end on THE SPORTING NEWS college All-America second team (2001).

Year	Team	G	GS	TOTALS Tk.	Ast.	Sks.	INTERCEPTIONS No.	Yds.	Avg.	TD
2002—Chicago NFL		15	9	31	9	2.5	0	0	0.0	0
2003—Chicago NFL		16	16	48	10	5.5	1	0	0.0	0
Pro totals (2 years)		31	25	79	19	8.0	1	0	0.0	0

BROWN, ANTONIO — WR — BILLS

PERSONAL: Born March 3, 1978, in Miami, Fla. ... 5-10/175. ... Full name: Antonio Duval Brown.
HIGH SCHOOL: Central (Miami, Fla.).
COLLEGE: West Virginia.
TRANSACTIONS/CAREER NOTES: Signed as non-drafted free agent by Buffalo Bills (March 25, 2003).

Year	Team	G	GS	RECEIVING No.	Yds.	Avg.	TD	PUNT RETURNS No.	Yds.	Avg.	TD	KICKOFF RETURNS No.	Yds.	Avg.	TD	TOTALS TD	2pt.	Pts.	Fum.
2003—Buffalo NFL		16	0	0	0	0.0	0	25	111	4.4	0	48	1046	21.8	0	0	0	0	1

BROWN, CHAD — LB — SEAHAWKS

PERSONAL: Born July 12, 1970, in Altadena, Calif. ... 6-2/245. ... Full name: Chadwick Everett Brown.
HIGH SCHOOL: John Muir (Pasadena, Calif.).
COLLEGE: Colorado.
TRANSACTIONS/CAREER NOTES: Selected by Pittsburgh Steelers in second round (44th pick overall) of 1993 NFL draft. ... Signed by Steelers (July 26, 1993). ... Granted unconditional free agency (February 14, 1997). ... Signed by Seattle Seahawks (February 15, 1997). ... On injured reserve with broken foot (November 12, 2002-remainder of season).
CHAMPIONSHIP GAME EXPERIENCE: Played in AFC championship game (1994 and 1995 seasons). ... Played in Super Bowl 30 (1995 season).
HONORS: Named linebacker on THE SPORTING NEWS NFL All-Pro team (1996 and 1998). ... Played in Pro Bowl (1996, 1998 and 1999 seasons).

Year	Team	G	GS	TOTALS Tk.	Ast.	Sks.	INTERCEPTIONS No.	Yds.	Avg.	TD
1993—Pittsburgh NFL		16	9	43	26	3.0	0	0	0.0	0
1994—Pittsburgh NFL		16	16	90	29	8.5	1	9	9.0	0
1995—Pittsburgh NFL		10	10	20	10	5.5	0	0	0.0	0
1996—Pittsburgh NFL		14	14	50	31	13.0	2	20	10.0	0
1997—Seattle NFL		15	15	75	29	6.5	0	0	0.0	0
1998—Seattle NFL		16	16	§117	32	7.5	1	11	11.0	0
1999—Seattle NFL		15	15	87	30	5.5	0	0	0.0	0
2000—Seattle NFL		16	16	71	23	6.0	1	0	0.0	0
2001—Seattle NFL		16	16	80	26	8.5	0	0	0.0	0
2002—Seattle NFL		8	8	42	8	6.0	0	0	0.0	0
2003—Seattle NFL		14	13	74	12	7.0	1	-1	-1.0	0
Pro totals (11 years)		156	148	749	256	77.0	6	39	6.5	0

BROWN, CHRIS — RB — TITANS

PERSONAL: Born April 17, 1981, in Winfield, Ill. ... 6-3/219. ... Full name: Christopher Rajean Brown.
HIGH SCHOOL: Naperville North (Ill.).
COLLEGE: Colorado.
TRANSACTIONS/CAREER NOTES: Selected after junior season by Tennessee Titans in third round (93rd pick overall) of 2003 NFL draft. ... Signed by Titans (July 21, 2003).
SINGLE GAME HIGHS (regular season): Attempts—12 (November 9, 2003, vs. Miami); yards—69 (December 21, 2003, Houston); and rushing touchdowns—0.

Year	Team	G	GS	RUSHING Att.	Yds.	Avg.	TD	RECEIVING No.	Yds.	Avg.	TD	TOTALS TD	2pt.	Pts.	Fum.
2003—Tennessee NFL		11	0	56	221	3.9	0	8	61	7.6	0	0	0	0	1

BROWN, CHRIS — CB — JAGUARS

PERSONAL: Born May 9, 1978, in Atlanta, Ga. ... 6-1/195. ... Full name: Christopher Dannell Brown.
HIGH SCHOOL: Avondale (Atlanta, Ga.).
COLLEGE: Alabama-Birmingham.
TRANSACTIONS/CAREER NOTES: Signed as non-drafted free agent by Jacksonville Jaguars (April 28, 2003). ... Released by Jaguars (August 31, 2003). ... Re-signed by Jaguars (September 1, 2003). ... Released by Jaguars (November 11, 2003). ... Re-signed by Jaguars to practice squad (November 13, 2003). ... Assigned by Jaguars to Frankfurt Galaxy in 2004 NFL Europe enhancement allocation program (February 9, 2004).

Year	Team	G	GS	TOTALS Tk.	Ast.	Sks.	INTERCEPTIONS No.	Yds.	Avg.	TD
2003—Jacksonville NFL		4	0	0	0	0.0	0	0	0.0	0

BROWN, CORNELL — LB — RAVENS

PERSONAL: Born March 15, 1975, in Englewood, N.J. ... 6-0/240. ... Full name: Cornell Desmond Brown. ... Brother of Ruben Brown, guard, Chicago Bears.
HIGH SCHOOL: E.C. Glass (Lynchburg, Va.).
COLLEGE: Virginia Tech.

TRANSACTIONS/CAREER NOTES: Selected by Baltimore Ravens in sixth round (194th pick overall) of 1997 NFL draft. ... Signed by Ravens (July 10, 1997). ... Granted free agency (February 11, 2000). ... Re-signed by Ravens (April 25, 2000) ... Granted unconditional free agency (March 2, 2001). ... Re-signed by Ravens (May 23, 2001). ... Released by Ravens (September 5, 2001). ... Signed by Oakland Raiders (February 21, 2002). ... Released by Raiders (June 10, 2002). ... Signed by Ravens (August 20, 2002). ... Granted unconditional free agency (February 28, 2003). ... Re-signed by Ravens (March 18, 2003).

CHAMPIONSHIP GAME EXPERIENCE: Member of Ravens for AFC Championship game (2000 season); inactive. ... Member of Super Bowl championship team (2000 season).

HONORS: Named defensive lineman on THE SPORTING NEWS college All-America first team (1995).

			TOTALS			INTERCEPTIONS			
Year Team	**G**	**GS**	**Tk.**	**Ast.**	**Sks.**	**No.**	**Yds.**	**Avg.**	**TD**
1997—Baltimore NFL	16	1	11	0	0.5	1	21	21.0	0
1998—Baltimore NFL	16	1	3	2	0.0	0	0	0.0	0
1999—Baltimore NFL	16	5	21	7	1.0	0	0	0.0	0
2000—Baltimore NFL	16	1	13	6	3.0	0	0	0.0	0
2001—				Did not play.					
2002—Baltimore NFL	16	14	36	23	1.5	0	0	0.0	0
2003—Baltimore NFL	16	3	16	2	1.0	0	0	0.0	0
Pro totals (6 years)	96	25	100	40	7.0	1	21	21.0	0

B

BROWN, COURTNEY DE BROWNS

PERSONAL: Born February 14, 1978, in Charleston, S.C. ... 6-4/280. ... Full name: Courtney Lanair Brown.

HIGH SCHOOL: Macedonia (Alvin, S.C.).

COLLEGE: Penn State.

TRANSACTIONS/CAREER NOTES: Selected by Cleveland Browns in first round (first pick overall) of 2000 NFL draft. ... Signed by Browns (May 10, 2000). ... On injured reserve with ankle injury (January 2, 2002-remainder of season). ... On injured reserve with knee injury (December 18, 2002-remainder of season). ... On injured reserve with biceps injury (December 9, 2003-remainder of season).

HONORS: Named defensive end on THE SPORTING NEWS college All-America first team (1999).

			TOTALS		
Year Team	**G**	**GS**	**Tk.**	**Ast.**	**Sks.**
2000—Cleveland NFL	16	16	61	8	4.5
2001—Cleveland NFL	5	5	14	7	4.5
2002—Cleveland NFL	11	11	30	12	2.0
2003—Cleveland NFL	13	13	29	9	6.0
Pro totals (4 years)	45	45	134	36	17.0

BROWN, DEE RB

PERSONAL: Born May 12, 1978, in Clearwater, Fla. ... 5-10/209. ... Full name: Dadrian L. Brown.

HIGH SCHOOL: Lake Brantley (Fla.).

COLLEGE: Syracuse.

TRANSACTIONS/CAREER NOTES: Selected by Carolina Panthers in sixth round (175th pick overall) of 2001 NFL draft. ... Signed by Panthers (July 18, 2001). ... On injured reserve with ankle injury (September 1, 2001-entire season). ... Released by Panthers (August 31, 2003). ... Signed by Pittsburgh Steelers (December 10, 2003). ... Released by Steelers (March 11, 2004). ... Signed by Atlanta Falcons (April 30, 2004). ... Waived by Falcons (May 18, 2004).

SINGLE GAME HIGHS (regular season): Attempts—27 (December 1, 2002, vs. Cleveland); yards—122 (December 1, 2002, vs. Cleveland); and rushing touchdowns—2 (December 22, 2002, vs. Chicago).

STATISTICAL PLATEAUS: 100-yard rushing games: 2002 (1). Total: 1.

			RUSHING				TOTALS			
Year Team	**G**	**GS**	**Att.**	**Yds.**	**Avg.**	**TD**	**TD**	**2pt.**	**Pts.**	**Fum.**
2002—Carolina NFL	14	3	102	360	3.5	4	5	0	30	4
2003—Pittsburgh NFL	1	0	0	0	0.0	0	0	0	0	0
Pro totals (2 years)	15	3	102	360	3.5	4	5	0	30	4

BROWN, ERIC S TEXANS

PERSONAL: Born March 20, 1975, in San Antonio, Texas. ... 6-1/210. ... Full name: Eric Jon Brown.

HIGH SCHOOL: Judson (Converse, Texas).

JUNIOR COLLEGE: Blinn College (Texas).

COLLEGE: Mississippi State.

TRANSACTIONS/CAREER NOTES: Selected by Denver Broncos in second round (61st pick overall) of 1998 NFL draft. ... Signed by Broncos (July 16, 1998). ... On injured reserve with knee injury (November 18, 1999-remainder of season). ... Granted unconditional free agency (March 1, 2002). ... Signed by Houston Texans (August 5, 2002). ... Granted unconditional free agency (February 28, 2003). ... Re-signed by Texans (March 17, 2003).

CHAMPIONSHIP GAME EXPERIENCE: Member of Broncos for AFC championship game (1998 season); inactive. ... Member of Super Bowl championship team (1998 season); inactive.

			TOTALS			INTERCEPTIONS			
Year Team	**G**	**GS**	**Tk.**	**Ast.**	**Sks.**	**No.**	**Yds.**	**Avg.**	**TD**
1998—Denver NFL	11	10	24	7	0.0	0	0	0.0	0
1999—Denver NFL	10	10	59	15	1.5	1	13	13.0	0
2000—Denver NFL	16	16	77	14	1.0	3	9	3.0	0
2001—Denver NFL	16	16	64	13	3.0	2	0	0.0	0
2002—Houston NFL	15	15	58	9	0.5	2	7	3.5	0
2003—Houston NFL	16	16	69	23	0.5	1	5	5.0	0
Pro totals (6 years)	84	83	351	81	6.5	9	34	3.8	0

BROWN, FAKHIR CB SAINTS

PERSONAL: Born September 21, 1977, in Detroit, Mich. ... 5-11/192. ... Full name: Fakhir Hamin Brown. ... Name pronounced: fah-KEAR.
HIGH SCHOOL: Mansfield (La.).
COLLEGE: Grambling.
TRANSACTIONS/CAREER NOTES: Signed by Toronto Argonauts of CFL (April 6, 1998). ... Signed as non-drafted free agent by San Diego Chargers (April 20, 1999). ... Released by Chargers (September 4, 1999). ... Re-signed by Chargers to practice squad (September 7, 1999). ... Activated (October 9, 1999). ... Released by Chargers (October 15, 1999). ... Re-signed by Chargers to practice squad (October 16, 1999). ... Activated (October 22, 1999). ... Released by Chargers (September 3, 2001). ... Signed by Oakland Raiders (January 24, 2002). ... Released by Raiders (April 26, 2002). ... Signed by New Orleans Saints (July 17, 2002).

B

			TOTALS			INTERCEPTIONS			
Year Team	G	GS	Tk.	Ast.	Sks.	No.	Yds.	Avg.	TD
1998—Toronto CFL	6	...	...	...	0.0	1	0	0.0	0
1999—San Diego NFL	9	3	29	2	0.0	0	0	0.0	0
2000—San Diego NFL	9	8	28	7	0.0	1	0	0.0	0
2002—New Orleans NFL	12	0	15	0	0.0	0	0	0.0	0
2003—New Orleans NFL	16	0	18	4	0.0	0	0	0.0	0
CFL Totals (1 years)	6	...	...	...	0.0	1	0	0.0	0
NFL totals (4 years)	46	11	90	13	0.0	1	0	0.0	0
Pro totals (5 years)	52	...	...	...	0.0	2	0	0.0	0

BROWN, GILBERT DT

PERSONAL: Born February 22, 1971, in Detroit, Mich. ... 6-2/340. ... Full name: Gilbert Jesse Brown.
HIGH SCHOOL: Mackenzie (Detroit).
COLLEGE: Kansas.
TRANSACTIONS/CAREER NOTES: Selected by Minnesota Vikings in third round (79th pick overall) of 1993 NFL draft. ... Signed by Vikings (July 16, 1993). ... Claimed on waivers by Green Bay Packers (August 31, 1993). ... On injured reserve with knee injury (December 6, 1994-remainder of season). ... Granted unconditional free agency (February 14, 1997). ... Re-signed by Packers (February 18, 1997). ... Granted unconditional free agency (February 11, 2000). ... Re-signed by Packers (March 23, 2001). ... Granted unconditional free agency (March 1, 2002). ... Re-signed by Packers (April 23, 2002). ... Granted unconditional free agency (February 28, 2003). ... Re-signed by Packers (July 29, 2003). ... Released by Packers (March 2, 2004).
CHAMPIONSHIP GAME EXPERIENCE: Played in NFC championship game (1995-97 seasons). ... Member of Super Bowl championship team (1996 season). ... Played in Super Bowl 32 (1997 season).

			TOTALS		
Year Team	G	GS	Tk.	Ast.	Sks.
1993—Green Bay NFL	2	0	1	0	0.0
1994—Green Bay NFL	13	1	25	6	3.0
1995—Green Bay NFL	13	7	17	6	0.0
1996—Green Bay NFL	16	16	38	13	1.0
1997—Green Bay NFL	12	12	15	12	3.0
1998—Green Bay NFL	16	16	9	17	0.0
1999—Green Bay NFL	16	15	22	18	0.0
2000—Green Bay NFL	Did not play.				
2001—Green Bay NFL	11	11	15	8	0.0
2002—Green Bay NFL	12	11	17	10	0.0
2003—Green Bay NFL	14	14	7	2	0.0
Pro totals (10 years)	125	103	166	92	7.0

BROWN, JOSH K SEAHAWKS

PERSONAL: Born April 29, 1979, in Tulsa, Okla. ... 6-0/202. ... Full name: Joshua Brown.
HIGH SCHOOL: Foyil (Okla.).
COLLEGE: Nebraska.
TRANSACTIONS/CAREER NOTES: Selected by Seattle Seahawks in seventh round (222nd pick overall) of 2003 NFL draft. ... Signed by Seahawks (June 20, 2003).

		FIELD GOALS							TOTALS		
Year Team	G	1-29	30-39	40-49	50+	Tot.	Pct.	Lg.	XPM	XPA	Pts.
2003—Seattle NFL	16	5-5	10-11	6-11	1-3	22-30	73.3	*58	48	48	114

BROWN, KRIS K TEXANS

PERSONAL: Born December 23, 1976, in Southlake, Texas. ... 5-11/206.
HIGH SCHOOL: Carroll (Southlake, Texas).
COLLEGE: Nebraska.
TRANSACTIONS/CAREER NOTES: Selected by Pittsburgh Steelers in seventh round (228th pick overall) of 1999 NFL draft. ... Signed by Steelers (June 29, 1999). ... Granted free agency (March 1, 2002). ... Signed by Houston Texans (March 25, 2002).
CHAMPIONSHIP GAME EXPERIENCE: Played in AFC championship game (2001 season).

		FIELD GOALS							TOTALS		
Year Team	G	1-29	30-39	40-49	50+	Tot.	Pct.	Lg.	XPM	XPA	Pts.
1999—Pittsburgh NFL	16	7-7	9-10	8-11	1-1	25-29	86.2	51	30	31	105
2000—Pittsburgh NFL	16	9-9	9-10	6-9	1-2	25-30	83.3	52	32	33	107
2001—Pittsburgh NFL	16	7-7	15-20	6-15	2-2	30-*44	68.2	†55	34	37	124
2002—Houston NFL	16	3-4	1-1	11-14	2-5	17-24	70.8	51	20	20	71
2003—Houston NFL	16	4-4	8-8	5-6	1-4	18-22	81.8	50	27	27	81
Pro totals (5 years)	80	30-31	42-49	36-55	7-14	115-149	77.2	55	143	148	488

BROWN, MARK — LB — JETS

PERSONAL: Born May 19, 1980, in Patterson, N.J. ... 6-0/238.
HIGH SCHOOL: Germantown (Tenn.).
COLLEGE: Auburn.
TRANSACTIONS/CAREER NOTES: Signed as non-drafted free agent by New York Jets (May 2, 2003). ... Released by Jets (August 31, 2003). ... Re-signed by Jets to practice squad (September 1, 2003). ... Released by Jets (October 16, 2003). ... Re-signed by Jets (November 11, 2003).

			TOTALS			INTERCEPTIONS			
Year Team	G	GS	Tk.	Ast.	Sks.	No.	Yds.	Avg.	TD
2003—New York Jets NFL	1	0	0	0	0.0	0	0	0.0	0

BROWN, MIKE — S — BEARS

PERSONAL: Born February 13, 1978, in Scottsdale, Ariz. ... 5-10/212.
HIGH SCHOOL: Saguaro (Scottsdale, Ariz.).
COLLEGE: Nebraska.
TRANSACTIONS/CAREER NOTES: Selected by Chicago Bears in second round (39th pick overall) of 2000 NFL draft. ... Signed by Bears (July 23, 2000).

			TOTALS			INTERCEPTIONS			
Year Team	G	GS	Tk.	Ast.	Sks.	No.	Yds.	Avg.	TD
2000—Chicago NFL	16	16	79	17	0.0	1	35	35.0	1
2001—Chicago NFL	16	16	51	11	3.0	5	81	16.2	†2
2002—Chicago NFL	16	15	72	12	0.0	3	16	5.3	0
2003—Chicago NFL	16	16	61	14	0.0	2	0	0.0	0
Pro totals (4 years)	64	63	263	54	3.0	11	132	12.0	3

BROWN, MILFORD — G — TEXANS

PERSONAL: Born August 15, 1980, in Montgomery, Ala. ... 6-4/320.
HIGH SCHOOL: Carver (Montgomery, Ala.).
JUNIOR COLLEGE: East Mississippi (Scooba, Miss.).
COLLEGE: Florida State.
TRANSACTIONS/CAREER NOTES: Selected by Houston Texans in sixth round of NFL supplemental draft (September 27, 2002). ... On injured reserve with knee injury (December 26, 2003-remainder of season).
PLAYING EXPERIENCE: Houston NFL, 2003. ... Games/Games started: 2003 (3/2). Total: 3/2.

BROWN, ORLANDO — T — RAVENS

PERSONAL: Born December 12, 1970, in Washington, DC. ... 6-7/360. ... Full name: Orlando Claude Brown.
HIGH SCHOOL: Howard D. Woodson (Washington, D.C.).
COLLEGE: South Carolina State.
TRANSACTIONS/CAREER NOTES: Signed as non-drafted free agent by Cleveland Browns (May 13, 1993). ... On injured reserve with shoulder injury (August 30, 1993-entire season). ... Browns franchise moved to Baltimore and renamed Ravens for 1996 season (March 11, 1996). ... Granted unconditional free agency (February 12, 1999). ... Signed by Browns (February 17, 1999). ... On suspended list for abusing an official (December 22, 1999-remainder of season). ... On physically unable to perform list with eye injury (August 27-September 19, 2000). ... Released by Browns (September 19, 2000). ... Signed by Baltimore Ravens (March 18, 2003). ... Granted unconditional free agency (March 3, 2004). ... Re-signed by Ravens (March 12, 2004).
PLAYING EXPERIENCE: Cleveland NFL, 1993-1995; Baltimore NFL, 1996-1998; Cleveland NFL, 1999; Baltimore NFL, 2003. ... Games/Games started: 1994 (14/8), 1995 (16/16), 1996 (16/16), 1997 (16/16), 1998 (13/13), 1999 (15/15), 2003 (16/13), Total: 106/97.

BROWN, RALPH — CB — REDSKINS

PERSONAL: Born September 16, 1978, in Hacienda Heights, Calif. ... 5-10/185. ... Full name: Ralph Brown II.
HIGH SCHOOL: Bishop Amat (La Puente, Calif.).
COLLEGE: Nebraska.
TRANSACTIONS/CAREER NOTES: Selected by New York Giants in fifth round (140th pick overall) of 2000 NFL draft. ... Signed by Giants (July 18, 2000). ... On injured reserve with kidney injury (October 3, 2000-remainder of season). ... Granted free agency (February 28, 2003). ... Re-signed by Giants (April 19, 2003). ... On injured reserve with shoulder injury (December 16, 2003-remainder of season). ... Granted unconditional free agency (March 3, 2004). ... Signed by Washington Redskins (March 18, 2004).
HONORS: Named cornerback on THE SPORTING NEWS college All-America first team (1999).

			TOTALS			INTERCEPTIONS			
Year Team	G	GS	Tk.	Ast.	Sks.	No.	Yds.	Avg.	TD
2000—New York Giants NFL	2	0	0	0	0.0	0	0	0.0	0
2001—New York Giants NFL	8	0	0	2	0.0	0	0	0.0	0
2002—New York Giants NFL	16	2	18	4	0.0	1	19	19.0	0
2003—New York Giants NFL	11	7	29	5	1.0	2	51	25.5	1
Pro totals (4 years)	37	9	47	11	1.0	3	70	23.3	1

BROWN, RAY — G

PERSONAL: Born December 12, 1962, in Marion, Ark. ... 6-5/318. ... Full name: Leonard Ray Brown Jr.

HIGH SCHOOL: Marion (Ark.).

COLLEGE: Arkansas State.

TRANSACTIONS/CAREER NOTES: Selected by St. Louis Cardinals in eighth round (201st pick overall) of 1986 NFL draft. ... Signed by Cardinals (July 14, 1986). ... On injured reserve with knee injury (October 17-November 21, 1986). ... Released by Cardinals (September 7, 1987). ... Re-signed by Cardinals as replacement player (September 25, 1987). ... On injured reserve with finger injury (November 12-December 12, 1987). ... Cardinals franchise moved to Phoenix (March 15, 1988). ... Granted unconditional free agency (February 1, 1989). ... Signed by Washington Redskins (March 10, 1989). ... On injured reserve with knee injury (September 5-November 4, 1989). ... On injured reserve with knee injury (September 4, 1990-January 4, 1991). ... Granted unconditional free agency (February 1-April 1, 1991). ... Re-signed by Redskins for 1991 season. ... On injured reserve with elbow injury (August 27, 1991-entire season). ... Granted unconditional free agency (February 16, 1996). ... Signed by San Francisco 49ers (March 1, 1996). ... Released by 49ers (June 3, 2002). ... Signed by Detroit Lions (August 20, 2002). ... Granted unconditional free agency (February 28, 2003). ... Re-signed by Lions (March 13, 2003). ... Granted unconditional free agency (March 3, 2004).

PLAYING EXPERIENCE: St. Louis NFL, 1986-1987; Phoenix NFL, 1988; Washington NFL, 1989-1995; San Francisco NFL, 1996-2001; Detroit NFL, 2002-2003. ... Games/Games started: 1986 (11/4), 1987 (7/3), 1988 (15/1), 1989 (7/0), 1992 (16/8), 1993 (16/14), 1994 (16/16), 1995 (16/16), 1996 (16/16), 1997 (15/15), 1998 (16/16), 1999 (16/16), 2000 (16/16), 2001 (16/16), 2002 (16/16), 2003 (16/16). Total: 231/189.

CHAMPIONSHIP GAME EXPERIENCE: Played in NFC championship game (1997 season).

HONORS: Played in Pro Bowl (2001 season).

B

BROWN, RUBEN — G — BEARS

PERSONAL: Born February 13, 1972, in Englewood, N.J. ... 6-3/300. ... Full name: Ruben Pernell Brown. ... Brother of Cornell Brown, linebacker, Baltimore Ravens.

HIGH SCHOOL: E.C. Glass (Lynchburg, Va.).

COLLEGE: Pittsburgh.

TRANSACTIONS/CAREER NOTES: Selected by Buffalo Bills in first round (14th pick overall) of 1995 NFL draft. ... Signed by Bills (June 20, 1995). ... Granted unconditional free agency (February 11, 2000). ... Re-signed by Bills (March 31, 2000). ... Released by Bills (March 1, 2004). ... Signed by Chicago Bears (April 2, 2004).

PLAYING EXPERIENCE: Buffalo NFL, 1995-2003. ... Games/Games started: 1995 (16/16), 1996 (14/14), 1997 (16/16), 1998 (13/13), 1999 (14/14), 2000 (16/16), 2001 (16/16), 2002 (16/16), 2003 (15/15). Total: 136/136.

HONORS: Named offensive lineman on THE SPORTING NEWS college All-America second team (1994). ... Played in Pro Bowl (1996-2003 seasons).

BROWN, SHELDON — CB — EAGLES

PERSONAL: Born March 19, 1979, in Lancaster, S.C. ... 5-10/196.

HIGH SCHOOL: Lewisville (Richburg, S.C.).

COLLEGE: South Carolina.

TRANSACTIONS/CAREER NOTES: Selected by Philadelphia Eagles in second round (59th pick overall) of 2002 NFL draft. ... Signed by Eagles (July 25, 2002).

CHAMPIONSHIP GAME EXPERIENCE: Played in NFC championship game (2002-2003 seasons).

			TOTALS			INTERCEPTIONS			
Year Team	G	GS	Tk.	Ast.	Sks.	No.	Yds.	Avg.	TD
2002—Philadelphia NFL	16	0	8	4	1.0	2	41	20.5	0
2003—Philadelphia NFL	16	3	37	6	1.0	1	10	10.0	0
Pro totals (2 years)	32	3	45	10	2.0	3	51	17.0	0

BROWN, TIM — WR — RAIDERS

PERSONAL: Born July 22, 1966, in Dallas, Texas. ... 6-0/195. ... Full name: Timothy Donell Brown.

HIGH SCHOOL: Woodrow Wilson (Dallas).

COLLEGE: Notre Dame.

TRANSACTIONS/CAREER NOTES: Selected by Los Angeles Raiders in first round (sixth pick overall) of 1988 NFL draft. ... Signed by Raiders (July 14, 1988). ... On injured reserve with knee injury (September 12, 1989-remainder of season). ... Granted free agency (February 1, 1992). ... Re-signed by Raiders (August 13, 1992). ... Designated by Raiders as transition player (February 25, 1993). ... Tendered offer sheet by Denver Broncos (March 11, 1994). ... Offer matched by Raiders (March 16, 1994). ... Raiders franchise moved to Oakland (July 21, 1995).

CHAMPIONSHIP GAME EXPERIENCE: Played in AFC championship game (1990, 2000 and 2002 seasons). ... Played in Super Bowl 37 (2002 season).

HONORS: Named wide receiver on THE SPORTING NEWS college All-America first team (1986 and 1987). ... Heisman Trophy winner (1987). ... Named College Football Player of the Year by THE SPORTING NEWS (1987). ... Named kick returner on THE SPORTING NEWS NFL All-Pro team (1988). ... Played in Pro Bowl (1988, 1991, 1993-1997 and 2001 seasons). ... Named wide receiver on THE SPORTING NEWS NFL All-Pro team (1997). ... Named to play in Pro Bowl (1999 season); replaced by Terry Glenn due to injury.

RECORDS: Holds NFL rookie-season record for most combined yards gained—2,317 (1988).

SINGLE GAME HIGHS (regular season): Receptions—14 (December 21, 1997, vs. Jacksonville); yards—190 (October 24, 1999, vs. New York Jets); and touchdown receptions—3 (August 31, 1997, vs. Tennessee).

STATISTICAL PLATEAUS: 100-yard receiving games: 1988 (1), 1991 (1), 1992 (1), 1993 (4), 1994 (4), 1995 (6), 1996 (2), 1997 (7), 1998 (3), 1999 (6), 2000 (2), 2001 (4), 2002 (1), 2003 (1). Total: 43.

MISCELLANEOUS: Holds Raiders franchise all-time record for most receptions (1,070), most yards receiving (14,734), most touchdowns (104) and most receiving touchdowns (99).

			RUSHING				RECEIVING				PUNT RETURNS				KICKOFF RETURNS				TOTALS		
Year Team	G	GS	Att.	Yds.	Avg.	TD	No.	Yds.	Avg.	TD	No.	Yds.	Avg.	TD	No.	Yds.	Avg.	TD	TD	2pt.	Pts.
1988—L.A. Raiders	16	9	14	50	3.6	1	43	725	16.9	5	§49	§444	9.1	0	†41	*1098	*26.8	†1	7	0	42
1989—L.A. Raiders	1	1	0	0	0.0	0	1	8	8.0	0	4	43	10.8	0	3	63	21.0	0	0	0	0
1990—L.A. Raiders	16	0	0	0	0.0	0	18	265	14.7	3	34	295	8.7	0	0	0	0.0	0	3	0	18
1991—L.A. Raiders	16	1	5	16	3.2	0	36	554	15.4	5	29	§330	11.4	▲1	1	29	29.0	0	6	0	36

Year Team	G	GS	RUSHING Att.	Yds.	Avg.	TD	RECEIVING No.	Yds.	Avg.	TD	PUNT RETURNS No.	Yds.	Avg.	TD	KICKOFF RETURNS No.	Yds.	Avg.	TD	TOTALS TD	2pt.	Pts.
1992—L.A. Raiders	15	12	3	-4	-1.3	0	49	693	14.1	7	37	383	10.4	0	2	14	7.0	0	7	0	42
1993—L.A. Raiders	16	16	2	7	3.5	0	80	§1180	14.8	7	40	§465	11.6	1	0	0	0.0	0	8	0	48
1994—L.A. Raiders	16	16	0	0	0.0	0	89	§1309	14.7	9	40	*487	12.2	0	0	0	0.0	0	9	0	54
1995—Oak. NFL	16	16	0	0	0.0	0	89	§1342	15.1	10	36	364	10.1	0	0	0	0.0	0	10	0	60
1996—Oak. NFL	16	16	6	35	5.8	0	90	1104	12.3	9	32	272	8.5	0	1	24	24.0	0	9	0	54
1997—Oak. NFL	16	16	5	19	3.8	0	†104	§1408	13.5	5	0	0	0.0	0	1	7	7.0	0	5	1	32
1998—Oak. NFL	16	16	1	-7	-7.0	0	81	1012	12.5	9	3	23	7.7	0	0	0	0.0	0	9	0	54
1999—Oak. NFL	16	16	1	4	4.0	0	90	1344	14.9	6	0	0	0.0	0	0	0	0.0	0	6	0	36
2000—Oak. NFL	16	16	3	12	4.0	0	76	1128	14.8	11	0	0	0.0	0	0	0	0.0	0	11	0	66
2001—Oak. NFL	16	16	4	39	9.8	0	91	1165	12.8	9	6	111	18.5	1	0	0	0.0	0	10	0	60
2002—Oak. NFL	16	16	6	19	3.2	0	81	930	11.5	2	10	55	5.5	0	0	0	0.0	0	2	0	12
2003—Oak. NFL	16	15	0	0	0.0	0	52	567	10.9	2	0	0	0.0	0	0	0	0.0	0	2	0	12
Pro totals (16 years)	240	198	50	190	3.8	1	1070	14734	13.8	99	320	3272	10.2	3	49	1235	25.2	1	104	1	626

B

BROWN, TRAVIS QB BILLS

PERSONAL: Born July 17, 1977, in Phoenix, Ariz. ... 6-3/215.
HIGH SCHOOL: Moon Valley (Phoenix).
COLLEGE: Northern Arizona.
TRANSACTIONS/CAREER NOTES: Signed as non-drafted free agent by Philadelphia Eagles (April 19, 2000). ... Released by Eagles (August 27, 2000). ... Signed by Seattle Seahawks to practice squad (August 30, 2000). ... Activated (November 21, 2000). ... Released by Seahawks (August 21, 2001). ... Signed by Buffalo Bills (August 22, 2001). ... On injured reserve with finger injury (August 31-September 4, 2003). ... Released by Bills (September 4, 2003). ... Re-signed by Bills (December 3, 2003). ... Granted free agency (March 3, 2004). ... Re-signed by Bills (April 22, 2004).
SINGLE GAME HIGHS (regular season): Attempts—33 (January 6, 2002, vs. Miami); completions—15 (January 6, 2002, vs. Miami); yards—201 (January 6, 2002, vs. Miami); and touchdown passes—1 (January 6, 2002, vs. Miami).

Year Team	G	GS	PASSING Att.	Cmp.	Pct.	Yds.	TD	Int.	Avg.	Skd.	Rat.	RUSHING Att.	Yds.	Avg.	TD	TOTALS TD	2pt.	Pts.
2000—Seattle NFL	1	0	1	0	0.0	0	0	0	0.00	0	39.6	0	0	0.0	0	0	0	0
2001—Buffalo NFL	1	0	33	15	45.5	201	1	2	6.09	1	50.2	1	10	10.0	0	0	0	0
2002—									Did not play.									
2003—Buffalo NFL	2	0	18	14	77.8	160	0	1	8.89	1	80.6	1	5	5.0	0	0	0	0
Pro totals (3 years)	4	0	52	29	55.8	361	1	3	6.94	2	59.9	2	15	7.5	0	0	0	0

BROWN, TROY WR PATRIOTS

PERSONAL: Born July 2, 1971, in Barnwell, S.C. ... 5-10/196. ... Full name: Troy Fitzgerald Brown.
HIGH SCHOOL: Blackville (S.C.)-Hilda.
JUNIOR COLLEGE: Lees-McRae College (N.C.).
COLLEGE: Marshall.
TRANSACTIONS/CAREER NOTES: Selected by New England Patriots in eighth round (198th pick overall) of 1993 NFL draft. ... Signed by Patriots (July 16, 1993). ... On injured reserve with quadriceps injury (December 31, 1993-remainder of season). ... Released by Patriots (August 28, 1994). ... Re-signed by Patriots (October 19, 1994). ... Granted unconditional free agency (February 14, 1997). ... Re-signed by Patriots (March 10, 1997). ... Granted unconditional free agency (February 11, 2000). ... Re-signed by Patriots (February 26, 2000).
CHAMPIONSHIP GAME EXPERIENCE: Played in AFC championship game (1996, 2001 and 2003 seasons). ... Member of Patriots for Super Bowl 31 (1996 season); inactive. ... Member of Super Bowl championship team (2001 and 2003 seasons).
HONORS: Played in Pro Bowl (2001 season).
SINGLE GAME HIGHS (regular season): Receptions—16 (September 22, 2002, vs. Kansas City); yards—176 (September 22, 2002, vs. Kansas City); and touchdown receptions—2 (October 1, 2000, vs. Denver).
STATISTICAL PLATEAUS: 100-yard receiving games: 1997 (2), 1999 (1), 2000 (4), 2001 (3), 2002 (2), 2003 (1). Total: 13.

Year Team	G	GS	RUSHING Att.	Yds.	Avg.	TD	RECEIVING No.	Yds.	Avg.	TD	PUNT RETURNS No.	Yds.	Avg.	TD	KICKOFF RETURNS No.	Yds.	Avg.	TD	TOTALS TD	2pt.	Pts.
1993—N.E. NFL	12	0	0	0	0.0	0	2	22	11.0	0	25	224	9.0	0	15	243	16.2	0	0	0	0
1994—N.E. NFL	9	0	0	0	0.0	0	0	0	0.0	0	24	202	8.4	0	1	14	14.0	0	0	0	0
1995—N.E. NFL	16	0	0	0	0.0	0	14	159	11.4	0	0	0	0.0	0	31	672	21.7	0	1	0	6
1996—N.E. NFL	16	0	0	0	0.0	0	21	222	10.6	0	0	0	0.0	0	29	634	21.9	0	0	0	0
1997—N.E. NFL	16	6	1	-18	-18.0	0	41	607	14.8	6	0	0	0.0	0	0	0	0.0	0	6	0	36
1998—N.E. NFL	10	0	0	0	0.0	0	23	346	15.0	1	17	225	13.2	0	0	0	0.0	0	1	0	6
1999—N.E. NFL	13	1	0	0	0.0	0	36	471	13.1	1	38	405	10.7	0	8	271	33.9	0	1	0	6
2000—N.E. NFL	16	15	6	46	7.7	0	83	944	11.4	4	39	504	12.9	1	2	15	7.5	0	5	0	30
2001—N.E. NFL	16	13	11	91	8.3	0	101	1199	11.9	5	29	413	*14.2	*2	1	13	13.0	0	7	0	42
2002—N.E. NFL	14	13	3	14	4.7	0	97	890	9.2	3	24	175	7.3	0	0	0	0.0	0	3	1	20
2003—N.E. NFL	12	10	6	27	4.5	0	40	472	11.8	4	29	293	10.1	0	0	0	0.0	0	4	0	24
Pro totals (11 years)	150	58	27	160	5.9	0	458	5332	11.6	24	225	2441	10.8	3	87	1862	21.4	0	28	1	170

BROWN, WILBERT G PATRIOTS

PERSONAL: Born May 9, 1977, in Texarkana, Texas. ... 6-2/320. ... Full name: Wilbert Lemon Brown.
HIGH SCHOOL: Hooks (Texas).
COLLEGE: Houston.
TRANSACTIONS/CAREER NOTES: Signed as non-drafted free agent by San Diego Chargers (April 20, 1999). ... Released by Chargers (September 4, 1999). ... Re-signed by Chargers to practice squad (September 6, 1999). ... Released by Chargers (September 14, 1999). ... Re-signed by Chargers to practice squad (September 21, 1999). ... Activated (December 4, 1999). ... Released by Chargers (August 27, 2000). ... Re-signed by Chargers to practice squad (August 29, 2000). ... Released by Chargers (November 25, 2000). ... Re-signed by Chargers to practice squad (November 27, 2000). ... Granted free agency following 2000 season. ... Signed by Tampa Bay Buccaneers (January 5, 2001).

... Assigned by Buccaneers to Frankfurt Galaxy in 2001 NFL Europe enhancement allocation program (February 19, 2001). ... Released by Buccaneers (September 2, 2001). ... Signed by Washington Redskins (July 16, 2002). ... Waived by Redskins (September 12, 2003). ... Re-signed by Redskins (September 16, 2003). ... Released by Redskins (September 19, 2003). ... Claimed on waivers by New England Patriots (September 22, 2003).

PLAYING EXPERIENCE: San Diego NFL, 1999; Washington NFL, 2002; New England NFL, 2003. ... Games/Games started: 1999 (5/0), 2002 (14/9), 2003 (1/0). Total: 20/9.

CHAMPIONSHIP GAME EXPERIENCE: Played in AFC championship game (2003 season). ... Member of Super Bowl championship team (2003 season).

BROWNING, JOHN — DT — CHIEFS

PERSONAL: Born September 30, 1973, in Miami, Fla. ... 6-4/297.

HIGH SCHOOL: North Miami (Fla.).

COLLEGE: West Virginia.

TRANSACTIONS/CAREER NOTES: Selected by Kansas City Chiefs in third round (68th pick overall) of 1996 NFL draft. ... Signed by Chiefs (July 24, 1996). ... On injured reserve with Achilles' tendon injury (September 1, 1999-entire season). ... Granted unconditional free agency (February 11, 2000). ... Re-signed by Chiefs (February 11, 2000). ... On injured reserve with shoulder injury (October 25, 2001-remainder of season).

			TOTALS			INTERCEPTIONS			
Year Team	G	GS	Tk.	Ast.	Sks.	No.	Yds.	Avg.	TD
1996—Kansas City NFL	13	2	17	4	2.0	0	0	0.0	0
1997—Kansas City NFL	14	13	29	4	4.0	0	0	0.0	0
1998—Kansas City NFL	8	8	20	10	0.0	0	0	0.0	0
1999—Kansas City NFL			Did not play.						
2000—Kansas City NFL	16	16	38	10	6.0	1	0	0.0	0
2001—Kansas City NFL	6	6	15	5	1.5	0	0	0.0	0
2002—Kansas City NFL	16	16	33	6	7.0	0	0	0.0	0
2003—Kansas City NFL	16	16	37	5	0.5	0	0	0.0	0
Pro totals (7 years)	89	77	189	44	21.0	1	0	0.0	0

BRUCE, ARLAND — WR — 49ERS

PERSONAL: Born November 23, 1977, in Olathe, Kan. ... 5-10/193. ... Full name: Arland R. Bruce III.

HIGH SCHOOL: Olathe North (Kansas City, Kan.).

JUNIOR COLLEGE: Hutchinson (Kan.).

COLLEGE: Minnesota.

TRANSACTIONS/CAREER NOTES: Signed as non-drafted free agent by Kansas City Chiefs (April 19, 2000). ... Released by Chiefs (August 27, 2000). ... Re-signed by Chiefs to practice squad (September 19, 2000). ... Released by Chiefs (October 12, 2000) ... Signed by Winnipeg Blue Bombers of CFL (2001). ... Signed by San Francisco 49ers (February 27, 2003). ... Released by 49ers (September 16, 2003). ... Re-signed by 49ers to practice squad (September 18, 2003).

			RECEIVING				PUNT RETURNS				KICKOFF RETURNS				TOTALS			
Year Team	G	GS	No.	Yds.	Avg.	TD	No.	Yds.	Avg.	TD	No.	Yds.	Avg.	TD	TD	2pt.	Pts.	Fum.
2003—San Francisco NFL	2	0	0	0	0.0	0	4	24	6.0	0	6	125	20.8	0	0	0	0	1

BRUCE, ISAAC — WR — RAMS

PERSONAL: Born November 10, 1972, in Fort Lauderdale, Fla. ... 6-0/188. ... Full name: Isaac Isidore Bruce.

HIGH SCHOOL: Dillard (Fort Lauderdale, Fla.).

JUNIOR COLLEGE: West Los Angeles Junior College, then Santa Monica (Calif.) Junior College.

COLLEGE: Memphis.

TRANSACTIONS/CAREER NOTES: Selected by Los Angeles Rams in second round (33rd pick overall) of 1994 NFL draft. ... Signed by Rams (July 13, 1994). ... On injured reserve with sprained right knee (December 9, 1994-remainder of season). ... Rams franchise moved to St. Louis (April 12, 1995). ... On injured reserve with hamstring injury (December 9, 1998-remainder of season).

CHAMPIONSHIP GAME EXPERIENCE: Played in NFC championship game (1999 and 2001 seasons). ... Member of Super Bowl championship team (1999 season). ... Played in Super Bowl 36 (2001 season).

HONORS: Named wide receiver on THE SPORTING NEWS NFL All-Pro team (1999). ... Played in Pro Bowl (1996 and 1999 season). ... Named to play in Pro Bowl (2000 season); replaced by Torry Holt due to injury. ... Named to play in Pro Bowl (2001 season); replaced by Joe Horn due to injury.

SINGLE GAME HIGHS (regular season): Receptions—15 (December 24, 1995, vs. Miami); yards—233 (November 2, 1997, vs. Atlanta); and touchdown receptions—4 (October 10, 1999, vs. San Francisco).

STATISTICAL PLATEAUS: 100-yard receiving games: 1995 (9), 1996 (5), 1997 (2), 1998 (2), 1999 (4), 2000 (4), 2001 (3), 2002 (2), 2003 (2). Total: 33.

MISCELLANEOUS: Holds St. Louis Rams all-time records for most receptions (688), most yards receiving (10, 461) and most receiving touchdowns (68).

			RUSHING				RECEIVING				TOTALS			
Year Team	G	GS	Att.	Yds.	Avg.	TD	No.	Yds.	Avg.	TD	TD	2pt.	Pts.	Fum.
1994—Los Angeles Rams NFL	12	0	1	2	2.0	0	21	272	13.0	3	3	0	18	0
1995—St. Louis NFL	16	16	3	17	5.7	0	119	1781	15.0	13	13	1	80	2
1996—St. Louis NFL	16	16	1	4	4.0	0	84	*1338	15.9	7	7	0	42	1
1997—St. Louis NFL	12	12	0	0	0.0	0	56	815	14.6	5	5	0	30	1
1998—St. Louis NFL	5	5	1	30	30.0	0	32	457	14.3	1	1	0	6	0
1999—St. Louis NFL	16	16	5	32	6.4	0	77	1165	15.1	12	12	1	74	0
2000—St. Louis NFL	16	16	1	11	11.0	0	87	1471	16.9	9	9	0	54	1
2001—St. Louis NFL	16	16	4	23	5.8	0	64	1106	17.3	6	6	0	36	4
2002—St. Louis NFL	16	16	3	18	6.0	0	79	1075	13.6	7	7	0	42	2

Year Team	G	GS	Rushing Att.	Rushing Yds.	Rushing Avg.	Rushing TD	Receiving No.	Receiving Yds.	Receiving Avg.	Receiving TD	Totals TD	Totals 2pt.	Totals Pts.	Totals Fum.
2003—St. Louis NFL	15	15	2	17	8.5	0	69	981	14.2	5	5	0	30	0
Pro totals (10 years)	140	128	21	154	7.3	0	688	10461	15.2	68	68	2	412	11

BRUENER, MARK — TE — TEXANS

PERSONAL: Born September 16, 1972, in Olympia, Wash. ... 6-4/260. ... Full name: Mark Frederick Bruener. ... Name pronounced: BREW-ner.
HIGH SCHOOL: Aberdeen (Wash.).
COLLEGE: Washington.
TRANSACTIONS/CAREER NOTES: Selected by Pittsburgh Steelers in first round (27th pick overall) of 1995 NFL draft. ... Signed by Steelers (July 25, 1995). ... On injured reserve with knee injury (November 29, 1996-remainder of season). ... On injured reserve with shoulder injury (November 21, 2001-remainder of season). ... On physically unable to perform list with foot injury (July 25-30, 2002). ... On injured reserve with knee injury (December 3, 2002-remainder of season). ... Released by Steelers (February 27, 2004). ... Signed by Houston Texans (March 22, 2004).
CHAMPIONSHIP GAME EXPERIENCE: Played in AFC championship game (1995 and 1997 seasons). ... Played in Super Bowl 30 (1995 season).
SINGLE GAME HIGHS (regular season): Receptions—5 (December 13, 1997, vs. New England); yards—51 (November 28, 1999, vs. Cincinnati); and touchdown receptions—1 (November 23, 2003, vs. Cleveland).

Year Team	G	GS	Receiving No.	Receiving Yds.	Receiving Avg.	Receiving TD	Totals TD	Totals 2pt.	Totals Pts.	Totals Fum.
1995—Pittsburgh NFL	16	13	26	238	9.2	3	3	0	18	0
1996—Pittsburgh NFL	12	12	12	141	11.8	0	0	1	2	0
1997—Pittsburgh NFL	16	16	18	117	6.5	6	6	0	36	1
1998—Pittsburgh NFL	16	16	19	157	8.3	2	2	0	12	0
1999—Pittsburgh NFL	14	14	18	176	9.8	0	0	0	0	0
2000—Pittsburgh NFL	16	16	17	192	11.3	3	3	0	18	0
2001—Pittsburgh NFL	9	9	12	98	8.2	0	0	0	0	0
2002—Pittsburgh NFL	12	12	13	66	5.1	1	1	0	6	0
2003—Pittsburgh NFL	14	0	2	12	6.0	1	1	0	6	0
Pro totals (9 years)	125	108	137	1197	8.7	16	16	1	98	1

BRUNELL, MARK — QB — REDSKINS

PERSONAL: Born September 17, 1970, in Los Angeles, Calif. ... 6-1/217. ... Full name: Mark Allen Brunell.
HIGH SCHOOL: St. Joseph (Santa Maria, Calif.).
COLLEGE: Washington.
TRANSACTIONS/CAREER NOTES: Selected by Green Bay Packers in fifth round (118th pick overall) of 1993 NFL draft. ... Signed by Packers (July 1, 1993). ... Traded by Packers to Jacksonville Jaguars for third- (FB William Henderson) and fifth-round (RB Travis Jervey) picks in 1995 draft (April 21, 1995). ... Traded by Jaguars to Washington Redskins for third-round pick (traded to Green Bay) in 2004 draft (March 3, 2004).
CHAMPIONSHIP GAME EXPERIENCE: Played in AFC championship game (1996 and 1999 seasons).
HONORS: Played in Pro Bowl (1996, 1997 and 1999 seasons). ... Named Outstanding Player of Pro Bowl (1996 season).
SINGLE GAME HIGHS (regular season): Attempts—52 (October 20, 1996, vs. St. Louis); completions—37 (October 20, 1996, vs. St. Louis); yards—432 (September 22, 1996, vs. New England); and touchdown passes—4 (November 29, 1998, vs. Cincinnati).
STATISTICAL PLATEAUS: 300-yard passing games: 1995 (2), 1996 (6), 1997 (3), 1998 (2), 1999 (3), 2000 (3), 2001 (2), 2002 (1). Total: 22.
MISCELLANEOUS: Regular-season record as starting NFL quarterback: 63-54 (.538). ... Postseason record as starting NFL quarterback: 4-4 (.500). ... Holds Jacksonville Jaguars all-time record for most yards passing (25,698) and most touchdown passes (144).

Year Team	G	GS	Passing Att.	Passing Cmp.	Passing Pct.	Passing Yds.	Passing TD	Passing Int.	Passing Avg.	Passing Skd.	Passing Rat.	Rushing Att.	Rushing Yds.	Rushing Avg.	Rushing TD	Totals TD	Totals 2pt.	Totals Pts.
1993—Green Bay NFL						Did not play.												
1994—Green Bay NFL	2	0	27	12	44.4	95	0	0	3.52	2	53.8	6	7	1.2	1	1	0	6
1995—Jacksonville NFL	13	10	346	201	58.1	2168	15	7	6.27	39	82.6	67	480	7.2	4	4	0	24
1996—Jacksonville NFL	16	16	557	353	§63.4	*4367	19	§20	*7.84	*50	84.0	80	396	5.0	3	3	2	22
1997—Jacksonville NFL	14	14	435	264	60.7	3281	18	7	§7.54	33	§91.2	48	257	5.4	2	2	0	12
1998—Jacksonville NFL	13	13	354	208	58.8	2601	20	9	7.35	28	89.9	49	192	3.9	0	0	0	0
1999—Jacksonville NFL	15	15	441	259	58.7	3060	14	9	6.94	29	82.0	47	208	4.4	1	1	†1	8
2000—Jacksonville NFL	16	16	512	311	60.7	3640	20	14	7.11	§54	84.0	48	236	4.9	2	2	0	12
2001—Jacksonville NFL	15	15	473	289	61.1	3309	19	13	7.00	*57	84.1	39	224	5.7	1	1	0	6
2002—Jacksonville NFL	15	15	416	245	58.9	2788	17	7	6.70	34	85.7	43	207	4.8	0	0	0	0
2003—Jacksonville NFL	3	3	82	54	65.9	484	2	0	5.90	9	89.7	8	19	2.4	1	1	0	6
Pro totals (10 years)	122	117	3643	2196	60.3	25793	144	86	7.08	335	85.2	435	2226	5.1	15	15	3	96

BRUSCHI, TEDY — LB — PATRIOTS

PERSONAL: Born June 9, 1973, in San Francisco, Calif. ... 6-1/247. ... Full name: Tedy Lacap Bruschi. ... Name pronounced: BREW-ski.
HIGH SCHOOL: Roseville (Calif.).
COLLEGE: Arizona.
TRANSACTIONS/CAREER NOTES: Selected by New England Patriots in third round (86th pick overall) of 1996 NFL draft. ... Signed by Patriots (July 17, 1996). ... Granted free agency (February 12, 1999). ... Re-signed by Patriots (June 1, 1999). ... Granted unconditional free agency (February 11, 2000). ... Re-signed by Patriots (March 22, 2000).
CHAMPIONSHIP GAME EXPERIENCE: Played in AFC championship game (1996, 2001 and 2003 seasons). ... Played in Super Bowl 31 (1996 season). ... Member of Super Bowl championship team (2001 and 2003 seasons).
HONORS: Named defensive lineman on THE SPORTING NEWS college All-America first team (1994 and 1995).

Year Team	G	GS	TOTALS Tk.	Ast.	Sks.	INTERCEPTIONS No.	Yds.	Avg.	TD
1996—New England NFL	16	0	10	1	4.0	0	0	0.0	0
1997—New England NFL	16	1	25	5	4.0	0	0	0.0	0
1998—New England NFL	16	7	48	26	2.0	0	0	0.0	0
1999—New England NFL	14	14	71	36	2.0	1	1	1.0	0
2000—New England NFL	16	16	68	38	1.0	0	0	0.0	0
2001—New England NFL	15	9	54	19	2.0	2	7	3.5	0
2002—New England NFL	11	9	45	20	4.5	2	75	37.5	▲2
2003—New England NFL	16	16	79	49	2.0	3	26	8.7	†2
Pro totals (8 years)	120	72	400	194	21.5	8	109	13.6	4

B

BRUTLEY, DARYON — CB

PERSONAL: Born May 31, 1979, in Eufaula, Ala. ... 5-11/187.
COLLEGE: Northern Iowa.
TRANSACTIONS/CAREER NOTES: Signed as non-drafted free agent by Buffalo Bills (April 26, 2002). ... Released by Bills (August 20, 2002). ... Selected by Berlin Thunder in 2003 NFL Europe draft (February 5, 2003). ... Signed by Philadelphia Eagles (June 17, 2003). ... Released by Eagles (August 31, 2003). ... Re-signed by Eagles (September 30, 2003). ... Released by Eagles (October 8, 2003).

Year Team	G	GS	TOTALS Tk.	Ast.	Sks.	INTERCEPTIONS No.	Yds.	Avg.	TD
2003—Philadelphia NFL	1	0	0	0	0.0	0	0	0.0	0

BRYANT, ANTONIO — WR — COWBOYS

PERSONAL: Born March 9, 1981, in Miami, Fla. ... 6-1/192.
HIGH SCHOOL: Miami Northwestern.
COLLEGE: Pittsburgh.
TRANSACTIONS/CAREER NOTES: Selected after junior season by Dallas Cowboys in second round (63rd pick overall) of 2002 NFL draft. ... Signed by Cowboys (July 26, 2002).
HONORS: Named wide receiver on THE SPORTING NEWS college All-America second team (2000).
SINGLE GAME HIGHS (regular season): Receptions—7 (December 29, 2002, vs. Washington); yards—170 (December 29, 2002, vs. Washington); and touchdown receptions—1 (November 27, 2003, vs. Miami).
STATISTICAL PLATEAUS: 100-yard receiving games: 2002 (1). Total: 1.

Year Team	G	GS	RUSHING Att.	Yds.	Avg.	TD	RECEIVING No.	Yds.	Avg.	TD	TOTALS TD	2pt.	Pts.	Fum.
2002—Dallas NFL	16	15	6	40	6.7	0	44	733	‡16.7	6	6	0	36	3
2003—Dallas NFL	16	5	2	0	0.0	0	39	550	14.1	2	2	0	12	0
Pro totals (2 years)	32	20	8	40	5.0	0	83	1283	15.5	8	8	0	48	3

BRYANT, FERNANDO — CB — LIONS

PERSONAL: Born March 26, 1977, in Albany, Ga. ... 5-10/174. ... Full name: Fernando Antoneiyo Bryant.
HIGH SCHOOL: Riverdale (Murfreesboro, Tenn.).
COLLEGE: Alabama.
TRANSACTIONS/CAREER NOTES: Selected by Jacksonville Jaguars in first round (26th pick overall) of 1999 NFL draft. ... Signed by Jaguars (August 9, 1999). ... On injured reserve with foot injury (January 1, 2002-remainder of season). ... Granted unconditional free agency (March 3, 2004). ... Signed by Detroit Lions (March 5, 2004).
CHAMPIONSHIP GAME EXPERIENCE: Played in AFC championship game (1999 season).

Year Team	G	GS	TOTALS Tk.	Ast.	Sks.	INTERCEPTIONS No.	Yds.	Avg.	TD
1999—Jacksonville NFL	16	16	61	9	0.0	2	0	0.0	0
2000—Jacksonville NFL	14	14	37	6	0.0	1	0	0.0	0
2001—Jacksonville NFL	10	9	49	5	0.0	0	0	0.0	0
2002—Jacksonville NFL	16	16	57	2	0.0	1	26	26.0	0
2003—Jacksonville NFL	16	16	61	9	0.0	1	0	0.0	0
Pro totals (5 years)	72	71	265	31	0.0	5	26	5.2	0

BRYANT, MATT — K — GIANTS

PERSONAL: Born May 29, 1975, in Orange, Texas. ... 5-9/200.
HIGH SCHOOL: Bridge City (Orange, Texas).
JUNIOR COLLEGE: Panola Junior College, then Trinity Valley Community College (Texas).
COLLEGE: Baylor.
TRANSACTIONS/CAREER NOTES: Signed as non-drafted free agent by New York Giants (January 15, 2002). ... Assigned by Giants to Frankfurt Galaxy in 2002 NFL Europe enhancement allocation program (February 12, 2002). ... Released by Giants (August 30, 2002). ... Re-signed by Giants to practice squad (September 2, 2002). ... Activated (September 3, 2002).

Year Team	G	FIELD GOALS 1-29	30-39	40-49	50+	Tot.	Pct.	Lg.	TOTALS XPM	XPA	Pts.
2002—New York Giants NFL	16	9-9	14-19	3-4	0-0	26-32	81.3	47	30	32	108
2003—New York Giants NFL	11	3-4	4-5	4-5	0-0	11-14	78.6	47	17	17	50
Pro totals (2 years)	27	12-13	18-24	7-9	0-0	37-46	80.4	47	47	49	158

BRYANT, WENDELL DT CARDINALS

PERSONAL: Born September 12, 1980, in St. Louis. ... 6-5/303.
HIGH SCHOOL: Ritenour (St. Louis).
COLLEGE: Wisconsin.
TRANSACTIONS/CAREER NOTES: Selected by Arizona Cardinals in first round (12th pick overall) of 2002 NFL draft. ... Signed by Cardinals (September 12, 2002).
HONORS: Named defensive tackle on THE SPORTING NEWS college All-America second team (2001).

			TOTALS		
Year Team	G	GS	Tk.	Ast.	Sks.
2002—Arizona NFL	14	4	12	8	1.5
2003—Arizona NFL	12	5	16	3	0.0
Pro totals (2 years)	26	9	28	11	1.5

B

BRYSON, SHAWN RB LIONS

PERSONAL: Born November 20, 1976, in Franklin, N.C. ... 6-1/228. ... Full name: Adrian Shawn Bryson.
HIGH SCHOOL: Franklin (N.C.).
COLLEGE: Tennessee.
TRANSACTIONS/CAREER NOTES: Selected by Buffalo Bills in third round (86th pick overall) of 1999 NFL draft. ... Signed by Bills (July 27, 1999). ... On injured reserve with knee injury (August 30, 1999-entire season). ... Granted free agency (March 1, 2002). ... Re-signed by Bills (May 6, 2002). ... On injured reserve with knee injury (October 18, 2002-remainder of season). ... Granted unconditional free agency (February 28, 2003). ... Signed by Detroit Lions (March 24, 2003). ... Granted unconditional free agency (March 3, 2004). ... Re-signed by Lions (March 23, 2004).
SINGLE GAME HIGHS (regular season): Attempts—28 (December 30, 2001, vs. New York Jets); yards—130 (December 23, 2001, vs. Atlanta); and rushing touchdowns—2 (December 23, 2001, vs. Atlanta).
STATISTICAL PLATEAUS: 100-yard rushing games: 2001 (2), 2003 (1). Total: 3.

			RUSHING				RECEIVING				KICKOFF RETURNS				TOTALS			
Year Team	G	GS	Att.	Yds.	Avg.	TD	No.	Yds.	Avg.	TD	No.	Yds.	Avg.	TD	TD	2pt.	Pts.	Fum.
1999—Buffalo NFL							Did not play.											
2000—Buffalo NFL	16	7	161	591	3.7	0	32	271	8.5	2	8	122	15.3	0	2	1	14	1
2001—Buffalo NFL	15	3	80	341	4.3	2	9	59	6.6	0	16	299	18.7	0	2	0	12	0
2002—Buffalo NFL	6	0	13	35	2.7	0	1	9	9.0	0	1	18	18.0	0	0	0	0	1
2003—Detroit NFL	16	13	158	606	3.8	3	54	340	6.3	0	0	0	0.0	0	3	0	18	2
Pro totals (4 years)	53	23	412	1573	3.8	5	96	679	7.1	2	25	439	17.6	0	7	1	44	4

BRZEZINSKI, DOUG G PANTHERS

PERSONAL: Born March 11, 1976, in Livonia, Mich. ... 6-4/305. ... Full name: Douglas Gregory Brzezinski. ... Name pronounced: bruh-ZHIN-skee.
HIGH SCHOOL: Detroit Catholic Central.
COLLEGE: Boston College.
TRANSACTIONS/CAREER NOTES: Selected by Philadelphia Eagles in third round (64th pick overall) of 1999 NFL draft. ... Signed by Eagles (July 28, 1999). ... Granted free agency (March 1, 2002). ... Re-signed by Eagles (March 28, 2002). ... Granted unconditional free agency (February 28, 2003). ... Signed by Carolina Panthers (March 12, 2003).
PLAYING EXPERIENCE: Philadelphia NFL, 1999-2002; Carolina NFL, 2003. ... Games/Games started: 1999 (16/16), 2000 (16/0), 2001 (16/1), 2002 (16/5), 2003 (1/0). Total: 65/22.
CHAMPIONSHIP GAME EXPERIENCE: Played in NFC championship game (2001 and 2002 seasons). ... Member of Panthers for NFC championship game (2003 season); inactive. ... Member of Panthers for Super Bowl 38 (2003 season); inactive.
HONORS: Named offensive guard on THE SPORTING NEWS college All-America first team (1998).

BUCHANAN, RAY CB RAIDERS

PERSONAL: Born September 29, 1971, in Chicago, Ill. ... 5-9/186. ... Full name: Raymond Louis Buchanan.
HIGH SCHOOL: Proviso East (Maywood, Ill.).
COLLEGE: Louisville.
TRANSACTIONS/CAREER NOTES: Selected by Indianapolis Colts in third round (65th pick overall) of 1993 NFL draft. ... Signed by Colts (July 26, 1993). ... Designated by Colts as transition player (February 13, 1997). ... Tendered offer sheet by Atlanta Falcons (February 25, 1997). ... Colts declined to match offer (March 3, 1997). ... Granted unconditional free agency (February 21, 2001). ... Re-signed by Falcons (February 21, 2001). ... On suspended list for violating league substance abuse policy (September 11-October 14, 2002). ... Released by Falcons (March 1, 2004). ... Signed by Oakland Raiders (April 5, 2004).
CHAMPIONSHIP GAME EXPERIENCE: Played in AFC championship game (1995 season). ... Played in NFC championship game (1998 season). ... Played in Super Bowl 33 (1998 season).
HONORS: Played in Pro Bowl (1998 season).

			TOTALS			INTERCEPTIONS				PUNT RETURNS				TOTALS			
Year Team	G	GS	Tk.	Ast.	Sks.	No.	Yds.	Avg.	TD	No.	Yds.	Avg.	TD	TD	2pt.	Pts.	Fum.
1993—Indianapolis NFL	16	5	44	21	0.0	4	45	11.3	0	0	0	0.0	0	0	0	0	0
1994—Indianapolis NFL	16	16	76	24	1.0	8	221	27.6	†3	0	0	0.0	0	3	0	18	0
1995—Indianapolis NFL	16	16	68	15	1.0	2	60	30.0	0	16	113	7.1	0	0	0	0	1
1996—Indianapolis NFL	13	13	53	9	0.5	2	32	16.0	0	12	201	16.8	0	0	0	0	0
1997—Atlanta NFL	16	16	48	4	0.0	5	49	9.8	0	0	37	0.0	0	0	0	0	0
1998—Atlanta NFL	16	16	54	7	0.0	7	102	14.6	0	1	4	4.0	0	0	0	0	0
1999—Atlanta NFL	16	16	59	5	1.0	4	81	20.2	1	0	0	0.0	0	1	0	6	0
2000—Atlanta NFL	16	16	69	11	0.0	6	114	19.0	0	0	0	0.0	0	0	0	0	0

Year	Team	G	GS	TOTALS Tk.	Ast.	Sks.	INTERCEPTIONS No.	Yds.	Avg.	TD	PUNT RETURNS No.	Yds.	Avg.	TD	TOTALS TD	2pt.	Pts.	Fum.
2001—Atlanta NFL		16	16	63	8	0.0	5	85	17.0	0	0	0	0.0	0	0	0	0	0
2002—Atlanta NFL		12	11	42	5	0.0	2	9	4.5	0	0	0	0.0	0	0	0	0	0
2003—Atlanta NFL		15	8	37	1	0.0	1	2	2.0	0	0	0	0.0	0	0	0	0	0
Pro totals (11 years)		168	149	613	110	3.5	46	800	17.4	4	29	355	12.2	0	4	0	24	1

BUCHANON, PHILLIP CB RAIDERS

PERSONAL: Born September 19, 1980, in Fort Myers, Fla. ... 5-10/185. ... Full name: Phillip Darren Buchanon.
HIGH SCHOOL: Lehigh (Fla.).
COLLEGE: Miami (Fla.).
TRANSACTIONS/CAREER NOTES: Selected after junior season by Oakland Raiders in first round (17th pick overall) of 2002 NFL draft. ... Signed by Raiders (July 25, 2002). ... On injured reserve with wrist injury (October 25, 2002-remainder of season).

Year	Team	G	GS	TOTALS Tk.	Ast.	Sks.	INTERCEPTIONS No.	Yds.	Avg.	TD	PUNT RETURNS No.	Yds.	Avg.	TD	KICKOFF RETURNS No.	Yds.	Avg.	TD	TOTALS TD	2pt.	Pts.	Fum.
2002—Oak. NFL		6	2	21	0	0.0	2	81	40.5	1	15	178	11.9	1	0	0	0.0	0	2	0	12	2
2003—Oak. NFL		16	10	42	2	0.0	6	§176	29.3	†2	36	491	13.6	†2	2	25	12.5	0	4	0	24	3
Pro totals (2 years)		22	12	63	2	0.0	8	257	32.1	3	51	669	13.1	3	2	25	12.5	0	6	0	36	5

BUCKHALTER, CORRELL RB EAGLES

PERSONAL: Born October 6, 1978, in Collins, Miss. ... 6-0/222.
HIGH SCHOOL: Collins (Miss.).
COLLEGE: Nebraska.
TRANSACTIONS/CAREER NOTES: Selected by Philadelphia Eagles in fourth round (121st pick overall) of 2001 NFL draft. ... Signed by Eagles (May 24, 2001). ... On physically unable to perform list with knee injury (July 27, 2002-entire season). ... Granted free agency (March 3, 2004). ... Re-signed by Eagles (April 30, 2004).
CHAMPIONSHIP GAME EXPERIENCE: Played in NFC championship game (2001 and 2003 seasons).
SINGLE GAME HIGHS (regular season): Attempts—23 (November 2, 2003, vs. Atlanta); yards—134 (October 7, 2001, vs. Arizona); and rushing touchdowns—2 (October 26, 2003, vs. New York Jets).
STATISTICAL PLATEAUS: 100-yard rushing games: 2001 (1), 2003 (2). Total: 3.

Year	Team	G	GS	RUSHING Att.	Yds.	Avg.	TD	RECEIVING No.	Yds.	Avg.	TD	TOTALS TD	2pt.	Pts.	Fum.
2001—Philadelphia NFL		15	6	129	586	4.5	2	13	130	10.0	0	2	0	12	2
2002—Philadelphia NFL		Did not play.													
2003—Philadelphia NFL		15	5	126	542	4.3	8	10	133	13.3	1	9	0	54	3
Pro totals (2 years)		30	11	255	1128	4.4	10	23	263	11.4	1	11	0	66	5

BUCKLEY, TERRELL CB

PERSONAL: Born June 7, 1971, in Pascagoula, Miss. ... 5-10/180. ... Full name: Douglas Terrell Buckley.
HIGH SCHOOL: Pascagoula (Miss.).
COLLEGE: Florida State.
TRANSACTIONS/CAREER NOTES: Selected after junior season by Green Bay Packers in first round (fifth pick overall) of 1992 NFL draft. ... Signed by Packers (September 11, 1992). ... Granted roster exemption for one game (September 1992). ... Traded by Packers to Miami Dolphins for past considerations (April 3, 1995). ... Granted unconditional free agency (February 11, 2000). ... Signed by Denver Broncos (July 20, 2000). ... Granted unconditional free agency (March 2, 2001). ... Signed by New England Patriots (July 13, 2001). ... Granted unconditional free agency (March 1, 2002). ... Signed by Tampa Bay Buccaneers (July 8, 2002). ... Released by Buccaneers (September 1, 2002). ... Signed by New England Patriots (September 5, 2002). ... Granted unconditional free agency (February 28, 2003). ... Signed by Dolphins (March 13, 2003). ... Granted unconditional free agency (March 3, 2004).
CHAMPIONSHIP GAME EXPERIENCE: Played in AFC championship game (2001 season). ... Member of Super Bowl championship team (2001 season).
HONORS: Named defensive back on THE SPORTING NEWS college All-America second team (1990). ... Jim Thorpe Award winner (1991). ... Named defensive back on THE SPORTING NEWS college All-America first team (1991).

Year	Team	G	GS	TOTALS Tk.	Ast.	Sks.	INTERCEPTIONS No.	Yds.	Avg.	TD	PUNT RETURNS No.	Yds.	Avg.	TD	TOTALS TD	2pt.	Pts.	Fum.
1992—Green Bay NFL		14	12	30	2	0.0	3	33	11.0	1	21	211	10.0	1	2	0	12	7
1993—Green Bay NFL		16	16	47	1	0.0	2	31	15.5	0	11	76	6.9	0	0	0	0	1
1994—Green Bay NFL		16	16	48	11	0.0	5	38	7.6	0	0	0	0.0	0	0	0	0	0
1995—Miami NFL		16	4	23	3	0.0	1	0	0.0	0	0	0	0.0	0	0	0	0	0
1996—Miami NFL		16	16	46	7	0.0	6	*164	27.3	1	3	24	8.0	0	1	0	6	1
1997—Miami NFL		16	16	67	18	0.0	4	26	6.5	0	4	58	14.5	0	1	0	6	0
1998—Miami NFL		16	16	44	7	0.0	8	157	19.6	1	29	354	12.2	0	1	0	6	1
1999—Miami NFL		16	11	30	5	1.0	3	3	1.0	0	8	13	1.6	0	0	0	0	1
2000—Denver NFL		16	16	35	3	0.0	6	110	18.3	1	2	10	5.0	0	1	0	6	0
2001—New England NFL		15	1	24	2	1.0	3	76	25.3	1	0	0	0.0	0	1	0	6	0
2002—New England NFL		16	2	21	0	0.0	4	50	12.5	0	0	0	0.0	0	0	0	0	1
2003—Miami NFL		16	5	39	11	0.0	2	75	37.5	1	1	2	2.0	0	1	0	6	1
Pro totals (12 years)		189	131	454	70	2.0	47	763	16.2	6	79	748	9.5	1	8	0	48	13

BUCKNER, BRENTSON DT PANTHERS

PERSONAL: Born September 30, 1971, in Columbus, Ga. ... 6-2/305. ... Full name: Brentson Andre Buckner. ... Name pronounced: BRENT-son.
HIGH SCHOOL: Carver (Columbus, Ga.).
COLLEGE: Clemson.
TRANSACTIONS/CAREER NOTES: Selected by Pittsburgh Steelers in second round (50th pick overall) of 1994 NFL Draft. ... Signed by Steelers (July 23, 1994). ... Traded by Steelers to Kansas City Chiefs for seventh-round pick (traded to San Diego) in 1997 draft (April 4, 1997). ...

Claimed on waivers by Cincinnati Bengals (August 25, 1997). ... Granted unconditional free agency (February 13, 1998). ... Signed by San Francisco 49ers (May 26, 1998). ... On physically unable to perform list with pulled quadricep muscle (July 17-August 15, 1998). ... Granted unconditional free agency (February 12, 1999). ... Re-signed by 49ers (April 7, 1999). ... Granted unconditional free agency (February 11, 2000). ... Re-signed by 49ers (August 8, 2000). ... Granted unconditional free agency (March 2, 2001). ... Signed by Carolina Panthers (April 21, 2001). ... On suspended list for violating league substance abuse policy (November 4-December 2, 2002). ... Activated (December 2, 2002).

CHAMPIONSHIP GAME EXPERIENCE: Played in AFC championship game (1994 and 1995 seasons). ... Played in NFC championship game (2003 season). ... Played in Super Bowl 30 (1995 season) and Super Bowl 38 (2003 season).

			TOTALS			INTERCEPTIONS			
Year Team	**G**	**GS**	**Tk.**	**Ast.**	**Sks.**	**No.**	**Yds.**	**Avg.**	**TD**
1994—Pittsburgh NFL	13	5	13	5	2.0	0	0	0.0	0
1995—Pittsburgh NFL	16	16	29	19	3.0	0	0	0.0	0
1996—Pittsburgh NFL	15	14	24	12	3.0	0	0	0.0	0
1997—Cincinnati NFL	14	5	32	7	0.0	0	0	0.0	0
1998—San Francisco NFL	13	0	10	6	0.5	0	0	0.0	0
1999—San Francisco NFL	16	6	29	15	1.0	0	0	0.0	0
2000—San Francisco NFL	16	16	41	14	7.0	0	0	0.0	0
2001—Carolina NFL	16	10	28	10	4.5	1	29	29.0	0
2002—Carolina NFL	12	12	24	8	5.0	0	0	0.0	0
2003—Carolina NFL	12	12	20	3	0.5	0	0	0.0	0
Pro totals (10 years)	143	96	250	99	26.5	1	29	29.0	0

BULGER, MARC — QB — RAMS

PERSONAL: Born April 5, 1977, in Pittsburgh, Pa. ... 6-3/215. ... Full name: Marc Robert Bulger.

HIGH SCHOOL: Central Catholic (Pittsburgh).

COLLEGE: West Virginia.

TRANSACTIONS/CAREER NOTES: Selected by New Orleans Saints in sixth round (168th pick overall) of 2000 NFL draft. ... Signed by Saints (July 13, 2000). ... Released by Saints (August 22, 2000). ... Signed by St. Louis Rams to practice squad (October 24, 2000). ... Released by Rams (October 31, 2000). ... Signed by Atlanta Falcons to practice squad (December 1, 2000). ... Released by Falcons (December 13, 2000). ... Re-signed by Rams (January 12, 2001). ... Granted free agency (March 3, 2004). ... Re-signed by Rams (May 4, 2004).

CHAMPIONSHIP GAME EXPERIENCE: Member of Rams for NFC championship game (2001 season); inactive. ... Member of Rams for Super Bowl 36 (2001 season); inactive.

HONORS: Played in Pro Bowl (2003 season). ... Named Outstanding Player of Pro Bowl (2003 season).

SINGLE GAME HIGHS (regular season): Attempts—48 (November 10, 2002, vs. San Diego); completions—36 (November 10, 2002, vs. San Diego); yards—453 (November 10, 2002, vs. San Diego); and touchdown passes—4 (November 10, 2002, vs. San Diego).

STATISTICAL PLATEAUS: 300-yard passing games: 2002 (3), 2003 (4). Total: 7.

MISCELLANEOUS: Regular-season record as starting NFL quarterback: 18-4 (.818). ... Post-season record as starting NFL quarterback: 0-1 (.000).

			PASSING									RUSHING				TOTALS		
Year Team	**G**	**GS**	**Att.**	**Cmp.**	**Pct.**	**Yds.**	**TD**	**Int.**	**Avg.**	**Skd.**	**Rat.**	**Att.**	**Yds.**	**Avg.**	**TD**	**TD**	**2pt.**	**Pts.**
2002—St. Louis NFL	7	7	214	138	64.5	1826	14	6	8.53	12	101.5	12	-13	-1.1	1	1	0	6
2003—St. Louis NFL	15	15	532	336	63.2	‡3845	22	†22	7.23	37	81.4	29	75	2.6	4	4	0	24
Pro totals (2 years)	22	22	746	474	63.5	5671	36	28	7.60	49	87.2	41	62	1.5	5	5	0	30

BULLARD, COURTLAND — LB — JAGUARS

PERSONAL: Born September 2, 1978, in Miami, Fla. ... 6-3/240.

HIGH SCHOOL: Southridge (Miami).

COLLEGE: Ohio State.

TRANSACTIONS/CAREER NOTES: Selected by St. Louis Rams in fifth round (167th pick overall) of 2002 NFL draft. ... Signed by Rams (July 10, 2002). ... Claimed on waivers by Jacksonville Jaguars (December 10, 2003).

			TOTALS			INTERCEPTIONS			
Year Team	**G**	**GS**	**Tk.**	**Ast.**	**Sks.**	**No.**	**Yds.**	**Avg.**	**TD**
2002—St. Louis NFL	11	1	1	0	0.0	0	0	0.0	0
2003—St. Louis NFL	9	0	0	0	0.0	0	0	0.0	0
Pro totals (2 years)	20	1	1	0	0.0	0	0	0.0	0

BULLUCK, KEITH — LB — TITANS

PERSONAL: Born April 4, 1977, in Suffern, N.Y. ... 6-3/235. ... Full name: Keith J. Bulluck.

HIGH SCHOOL: Clarkstown (New City, N.Y.).

COLLEGE: Syracuse.

TRANSACTIONS/CAREER NOTES: Selected by Tennessee Titans in first round (30th pick overall) of 2000 NFL draft. ... Signed by Titans (July 19, 2000).

CHAMPIONSHIP GAME EXPERIENCE: Played in AFC championship game (2002 season).

HONORS: Played in Pro Bowl (2003 season).

			TOTALS			INTERCEPTIONS			
Year Team	**G**	**GS**	**Tk.**	**Ast.**	**Sks.**	**No.**	**Yds.**	**Avg.**	**TD**
2000—Tennessee NFL	16	1	10	7	0.0	1	8	8.0	1
2001—Tennessee NFL	15	3	26	19	1.0	2	21	10.5	0
2002—Tennessee NFL	16	16	101	26	1.0	1	5	5.0	0
2003—Tennessee NFL	16	16	106	31	3.0	2	9	4.5	0
Pro totals (4 years)	63	36	243	83	5.0	6	43	7.2	1

B

BURGESS, DERRICK — LB/DE — EAGLES

PERSONAL: Born August 12, 1978, in Riverdale, Md. ... 6-2/266.
HIGH SCHOOL: Eleanor Roosevelt (Greenbelt, Md.).
COLLEGE: Mississippi.
TRANSACTIONS/CAREER NOTES: Selected by Philadelphia Eagles in third round (63rd pick overall) of 2001 NFL draft. ... Signed by Eagles (July 26, 2001). ... On injured reserve with Achilles injury (September 6, 2003—entire season).
CHAMPIONSHIP GAME EXPERIENCE: Played in NFC championship game (2001 season). ... Member of Eagles for NFC championship game (2002 season); inactive.

			TOTALS			INTERCEPTIONS			
Year Team	**G**	**GS**	**Tk.**	**Ast.**	**Sks.**	**No.**	**Yds.**	**Avg.**	**TD**
2001—Philadelphia NFL	16	4	24	6	6.0	0	0	0.0	0
2002—Philadelphia NFL	1	0	1	0	0.0	0	0	0.0	0
2003—Philadelphia NFL	Did not play.								
Pro totals (2 years)	17	4	25	6	6.0	0	0	0.0	0

BURLESON, NATE — WR — VIKINGS

PERSONAL: Born August 19, 1981, in Seattle, Wash. ... 6-0/192.
HIGH SCHOOL: O'Dea (Seattle).
COLLEGE: Nevada.
TRANSACTIONS/CAREER NOTES: Selected by Minnesota Vikings in third round (71st pick overall) of 2003 NFL draft. ... Signed by Vikings (July 23, 2003).
SINGLE GAME HIGHS (regular season): Receptions—3 (December 20, 2003, vs. Kansas City); yards—71 (October 5, 2003, vs. Atlanta); and touchdown receptions—1 (November 9, 2003, vs. San Diego).

			RECEIVING				PUNT RETURNS				KICKOFF RETURNS				TOTALS			
Year Team	**G**	**GS**	**No.**	**Yds.**	**Avg.**	**TD**	**No.**	**Yds.**	**Avg.**	**TD**	**No.**	**Yds.**	**Avg.**	**TD**	**TD**	**2pt.**	**Pts.**	**Fum.**
2003—Minnesota NFL	16	9	29	455	15.7	2	1	0	0.0	0	0	0	0.0	0	2	0	12	1

BURNETT, ROB — DE

PERSONAL: Born August 27, 1967, in East Orange, N.J. ... 6-4/265. ... Full name: Robert Barry Burnett.
HIGH SCHOOL: Newfield (Selden, N.Y.).
COLLEGE: Syracuse.
TRANSACTIONS/CAREER NOTES: Selected by Cleveland Browns in fifth round (129th pick overall) of 1990 NFL draft. ... Signed by Browns (July 22, 1990). ... Granted free agency (March 1, 1993). ... Re-signed by Browns (June 11, 1993). ... Browns franchise moved to Baltimore and renamed Ravens for 1996 season (March 11, 1996). ... Granted unconditional free agency (February 11, 2000). ... Re-signed by Ravens (February 17, 2000). ... Released by Ravens (February 27, 2002). ... Signed by Miami Dolphins (June 12, 2002). ... On injured reserve with knee injury (December 12, 2003-remainder of season). ... Granted unconditional free agency (March 3, 2004).
CHAMPIONSHIP GAME EXPERIENCE: Played in AFC championship game (2000 season). ... Member of Super Bowl championship team (2000 season).
HONORS: Played in Pro Bowl (1994 season).

			TOTALS			INTERCEPTIONS			
Year Team	**G**	**GS**	**Tk.**	**Ast.**	**Sks.**	**No.**	**Yds.**	**Avg.**	**TD**
1990—Cleveland NFL	16	6	38	19	2.0	0	0	0.0	0
1991—Cleveland NFL	13	8	17	14	3.0	0	0	0.0	0
1992—Cleveland NFL	16	16	37	23	9.0	0	0	0.0	0
1993—Cleveland NFL	16	16	39	37	9.0	0	0	0.0	0
1994—Cleveland NFL	16	16	41	13	10.0	0	0	0.0	0
1995—Cleveland NFL	16	16	40	15	7.5	0	0	0.0	0
1996—Baltimore NFL	6	6	21	2	3.0	0	0	0.0	0
1997—Baltimore NFL	15	15	33	7	4.0	0	0	0.0	0
1998—Baltimore NFL	16	16	37	12	2.5	0	0	0.0	0
1999—Baltimore NFL	16	16	39	17	6.5	0	0	0.0	0
2000—Baltimore NFL	16	16	40	9	10.5	1	3	3.0	0
2001—Baltimore NFL	13	13	16	10	0.0	0	0	0.0	0
2002—Miami NFL	15	0	10	5	4.0	0	0	0.0	0
2003—Miami NFL	12	0	7	6	2.0	0	0	0.0	0
Pro totals (14 years)	202	160	415	189	73.0	1	3	3.0	0

BURNS, CURRY — S — TEXANS

PERSONAL: Born February 12, 1981, in Miami, Fla. ... 6-0/216.
HIGH SCHOOL: Jackson (Miami).
COLLEGE: Louisville.
TRANSACTIONS/CAREER NOTES: Selected by Houston Texans in seventh round (217th pick overall) of 2003 NFL draft. ... Signed by Texans (June 4, 2003). ... Waived by Texans (August 25, 2003). ... Re-signed by Texans (December 2, 2003).

			TOTALS			INTERCEPTIONS			
Year Team	**G**	**GS**	**Tk.**	**Ast.**	**Sks.**	**No.**	**Yds.**	**Avg.**	**TD**
2003—Houston NFL	1	0	0	0	0.0	0	0	0.0	0

BURNS, JOE — RB — BILLS

PERSONAL: Born September 15, 1979, in Thomasville, Ga. ... 5-9/215. ... Full name: Joe Frank Burns.
HIGH SCHOOL: Thomas County (Ga.).
COLLEGE: Georgia Tech.
TRANSACTIONS/CAREER NOTES: Signed as non-drafted free agent by Buffalo Bills (April 26, 2002).
SINGLE GAME HIGHS (regular season): Attempts—8 (September 28, 2003, vs. Philadelphia); yards—29 (December 7, 2003, vs. New York Jets); and rushing touchdowns—0.

			RUSHING				RECEIVING				KICKOFF RETURNS				TOTALS			
Year Team	G	GS	Att.	Yds.	Avg.	TD	No.	Yds.	Avg.	TD	No.	Yds.	Avg.	TD	TD	2pt.	Pts.	Fum.
2002—Buffalo NFL	10	0	5	7	1.4	0	0	0	0.0	0	1	35	35.0	0	0	0	0	0
2003—Buffalo NFL	16	1	39	113	2.9	0	7	62	8.9	0	1	17	17.0	0	0	0	0	1
Pro totals (2 years)	26	1	44	120	2.7	0	7	62	8.9	0	2	52	26.0	0	0	0	0	1

B

BURNS, KEITH — LB — BUCCANEERS

PERSONAL: Born May 16, 1972, in Greeleyville, S.C. ... 6-2/235. ... Full name: Keith Bernard Burns.
HIGH SCHOOL: T. C. Williams (Alexandria, Va.).
JUNIOR COLLEGE: Navarro College (Texas).
COLLEGE: Oklahoma State.
TRANSACTIONS/CAREER NOTES: Selected by Denver Broncos in seventh round (210th pick overall) of 1994 NFL draft. ... Signed by Broncos (July 12, 1994). ... Granted free agency (February 14, 1997). ... Re-signed by Broncos (June 30, 1997). ... Granted unconditional free agency (February 12, 1999). ... Signed by Chicago Bears (April 6, 1999). ... Released by Bears (August 27, 2000). ... Signed by Broncos (September 19, 2000). ... Granted unconditional free agency (March 2, 2001). ... Re-signed by Broncos (April 6, 2001). ... Released by Broncos (February 26, 2003). ... Re-signed by Broncos (February 27, 2003). ... Granted unconditional free agency (March 3, 2004). ... Signed by Tampa Bay Buccaneers (March 9, 2004).
CHAMPIONSHIP GAME EXPERIENCE: Played in AFC championship game (1997 and 1998 seasons). ... Member of Super Bowl championship team (1997 and 1998 seasons).

			TOTALS			INTERCEPTIONS			
Year Team	G	GS	Tk.	Ast.	Sks.	No.	Yds.	Avg.	TD
1994—Denver NFL	11	1	15	3	0.0	0	0	0.0	0
1995—Denver NFL	16	0	10	3	1.5	0	0	0.0	0
1996—Denver NFL	16	0	1	0	0.0	0	0	0.0	0
1997—Denver NFL	16	0	1	0	0.0	0	0	0.0	0
1998—Denver NFL	16	0	7	2	0.0	0	0	0.0	0
1999—Chicago NFL	15	0	5	0	0.0	1	15	15.0	0
2000—Denver NFL	13	0	0	0	0.0	0	0	0.0	0
2001—Denver NFL	16	0	0	0	0.0	0	0	0.0	0
2002—Denver NFL	16	1	0	0	0.0	0	0	0.0	0
2003—Denver NFL	16	0	2	1	0.0	0	0	0.0	0
Pro totals (10 years)	151	2	41	9	1.5	1	15	15.0	0

BURRESS, PLAXICO — WR — STEELERS

PERSONAL: Born August 12, 1977, in Norfolk, Va. ... 6-5/226.
HIGH SCHOOL: Green Run (Virginia Beach, Va.).
COLLEGE: Michigan State.
TRANSACTIONS/CAREER NOTES: Selected after junior season by Pittsburgh Steelers in first round (eighth pick overall) of 2000 NFL draft. ... Signed by Steelers (July 20, 2000). ... On injured reserve with wrist injury (December 1, 2000-remainder of season).
CHAMPIONSHIP GAME EXPERIENCE: Played in AFC championship game (2001 season).
SINGLE GAME HIGHS (regular season): Receptions—9 (November 10, 2002, vs. Atlanta); yards—253 (November 10, 2002, vs. Atlanta); and touchdown receptions—2 (December 21, 2003, vs. San Diego).
STATISTICAL PLATEAUS: 100-yard receiving games: 2001 (4), 2002 (4), 2003 (3). Total: 11.

			RECEIVING				TOTALS			
Year Team	G	GS	No.	Yds.	Avg.	TD	TD	2pt.	Pts.	Fum.
2000—Pittsburgh NFL	12	8	22	273	12.4	0	0	0	0	1
2001—Pittsburgh NFL	16	16	66	1008	15.3	6	6	0	36	1
2002—Pittsburgh NFL	16	15	78	1325	17.0	7	7	1	44	2
2003—Pittsburgh NFL	16	16	60	860	14.3	4	4	0	24	1
Pro totals (4 years)	60	55	226	3466	15.3	17	17	1	104	5

BURRIS, JEFF — CB — PATRIOTS

PERSONAL: Born June 7, 1972, in Rock Hill, S.C. ... 6-0/190. ... Full name: Jeffrey Lamar Burris.
HIGH SCHOOL: Northwestern (Rock Hill, S.C.).
COLLEGE: Notre Dame.
TRANSACTIONS/CAREER NOTES: Selected by Buffalo Bills in first round (27th pick overall) of 1994 NFL draft. ... Signed by Bills (July 18, 1994). ... On injured reserve with knee injury (November 20, 1995-remainder of season). ... Granted unconditional free agency (February 13, 1998). ... Signed by Indianapolis Colts (February 18, 1998). ... Released by Colts (February 21, 2002). ... Signed by Cincinnati Bengals (March 26, 2002). ... Released by Bengals (March 10, 2004). ... Signed by New England Patriots (April 21, 2004).
HONORS: Named defensive back on THE SPORTING NEWS college All-America second team (1993).

Year Team	G	GS	TOTALS Tk.	Ast.	Sks.	INTERCEPTIONS No.	Yds.	Avg.	TD	PUNT RETURNS No.	Yds.	Avg.	TD	TOTALS TD	2pt.	Pts.	Fum.
1994—Buffalo NFL	16	0	13	3	0.0	2	24	12.0	0	32	332	10.4	0	0	0	0	2
1995—Buffalo NFL	9	9	28	6	0.0	1	19	19.0	0	20	229	11.5	0	0	0	0	0
1996—Buffalo NFL	15	15	41	9	0.0	1	28	28.0	0	27	286	10.6	0	0	0	0	1
1997—Buffalo NFL	14	14	39	6	0.0	2	19	9.5	0	21	198	9.4	0	0	0	0	3
1998—Indianapolis NFL	14	14	57	11	0.0	1	0	0.0	0	0	0	0.0	0	0	0	0	0
1999—Indianapolis NFL	16	16	67	16	2.0	2	83	41.5	0	0	0	0.0	0	0	0	0	0
2000—Indianapolis NFL	16	16	69	8	3.0	4	38	9.5	1	0	0	0.0	0	1	0	6	0
2001—Indianapolis NFL	15	15	54	4	0.0	3	69	23.0	1	0	0	0.0	0	1	0	6	0
2002—Cincinnati NFL	16	12	50	12	0.0	1	5	5.0	0	0	0	0.0	0	0	0	0	0
2003—Cincinnati NFL	13	8	33	3	0.0	2	17	8.5	0	5	58	11.6	0	0	0	0	0
Pro totals (10 years)	144	119	451	78	5.0	19	302	15.9	2	105	1103	10.5	0	2	0	12	6

BURTON, SHANE DT PANTHERS

PERSONAL: Born January 18, 1974, in Logan, W.Va. ... 6-6/305. ... Full name: Franklin Shane Burton.

HIGH SCHOOL: Bandys (Catawba, N.C.).

COLLEGE: Tennessee.

TRANSACTIONS/CAREER NOTES: Selected by Miami Dolphins in fifth round (150th pick overall) of 1996 NFL draft. ... Signed by Dolphins (June 18, 1996). ... Granted free agency (February 12, 1999). ... Re-signed by Dolphins (April 13, 1999). ... Claimed on waivers by Chicago Bears (August 24, 1999). ... Granted unconditional free agency (February 11, 2000). ... Signed by New York Jets (March 20, 2000). ... Released by Jets (February 26, 2002). ... Signed by Carolina Panthers (March 27, 2002).

CHAMPIONSHIP GAME EXPERIENCE: Played in NFC championship game (2003 season). ... Played in Super Bowl 38 (2003 season).

Year Team	G	GS	TOTALS Tk.	Ast.	Sks.	INTERCEPTIONS No.	Yds.	Avg.	TD
1996—Miami NFL	16	8	26	3	3.0	0	0	0.0	0
1997—Miami NFL	16	4	18	9	4.0	0	0	0.0	0
1998—Miami NFL	15	0	12	5	2.0	0	0	0.0	0
1999—Chicago NFL	15	0	7	4	3.0	1	37	37.0	0
2000—New York Jets NFL	16	16	31	18	1.0	0	0	0.0	0
2001—New York Jets NFL	15	13	24	16	2.0	1	0	0.0	0
2002—Carolina NFL	16	4	16	6	1.0	0	0	0.0	0
2003—Carolina NFL	16	4	12	5	2.0	1	10	10.0	0
Pro totals (8 years)	125	49	146	66	18.0	3	47	15.7	0

BUSH, STEVE TE CARDINALS

PERSONAL: Born July 4, 1974, in Paradise Valley, Ariz. ... 6-3/280. ... Full name: Steven Jack Bush.

HIGH SCHOOL: Paradise Valley (Phoenix).

COLLEGE: Arizona State.

TRANSACTIONS/CAREER NOTES: Signed as non-drafted free agent by Cincinnati Bengals (April 25, 1997). ... Granted free agency (February 11, 2000). ... Re-signed by Bengals (April 25, 2000). ... Granted unconditional free agency (March 2, 2001). ... Signed by St. Louis Rams (July 20, 2001). ... Released by Rams (August 27, 2001). ... Signed by Arizona Cardinals (November 6, 2001).

SINGLE GAME HIGHS (regular season): Receptions—4 (December 21, 2002, vs. San Francisco); yards—31 (December 24, 2000, vs. Philadelphia); and touchdown receptions—1 (December 28, 2003, vs. Minnesota).

Year Team	G	GS	RECEIVING No.	Yds.	Avg.	TD	TOTALS TD	2pt.	Pts.	Fum.
1997—Cincinnati NFL	16	0	0	0	0.0	0	0	0	0	0
1998—Cincinnati NFL	12	2	4	39	9.8	0	0	0	0	0
1999—Cincinnati NFL	13	0	1	4	4.0	0	0	0	0	0
2000—Cincinnati NFL	16	0	3	39	13.0	0	0	0	0	0
2001—Arizona NFL	9	7	8	80	10.0	0	0	0	0	0
2002—Arizona NFL	16	12	19	121	6.4	1	1	0	6	0
2003—Arizona NFL	16	4	11	71	6.5	1	1	0	6	0
Pro totals (7 years)	98	25	46	354	7.7	2	2	0	12	0

BUTLER, JERAMETRIUS CB RAMS

PERSONAL: Born November 28, 1978, in Dallas, Texas. ... 5-10/181.

HIGH SCHOOL: Carter (Dallas).

COLLEGE: Kansas State.

TRANSACTIONS/CAREER NOTES: Selected after junior season by St. Louis Rams in fifth round (145th pick overall) of 2001 NFL draft. ... Signed by Rams (June 27, 2001). ... Granted free agency (March 3, 2004). ... Tendered offer sheet by Washington Redskins (March 5, 2004). ... Offer matched by Rams (March 11, 2004).

CHAMPIONSHIP GAME EXPERIENCE: Played in NFC championship game (2001 season). ... Played in Super Bowl 36 (2001 season).

Year Team	G	GS	TOTALS Tk.	Ast.	Sks.	INTERCEPTIONS No.	Yds.	Avg.	TD
2001—St. Louis NFL	16	0	8	2	0.0	0	0	0.0	0
2002—St. Louis NFL	9	0	2	0	0.0	0	0	0.0	0
2003—St. Louis NFL	16	15	64	7	0.0	4	72	18.0	0
Pro totals (3 years)	41	15	74	9	0.0	4	72	18.0	0

CALDWELL, MIKE LB

PERSONAL: Born August 31, 1971, in Oak Ridge, Tenn. ... 6-2/235. ... Full name: Mike Isiah Caldwell.
HIGH SCHOOL: Oak Ridge (Tenn.).
COLLEGE: Middle Tennessee State.
TRANSACTIONS/CAREER NOTES: Selected by Cleveland Browns in third round (83rd pick overall) of 1993 NFL draft. ... Signed by Browns (July 14, 1993). ... Granted free agency (February 16, 1996). ... Browns franchise moved to Baltimore and renamed Ravens for 1996 season (March 11, 1996). ... Re-signed by Ravens for 1996 season. ... Granted unconditional free agency (February 14, 1997). ... Signed by Arizona Cardinals (July 16, 1997). ... Granted unconditional free agency (February 13, 1998). ... Signed by Philadelphia Eagles (April 9, 1998). ... Granted unconditional free agency (March 1, 2002). ... Signed by Chicago Bears (March 15, 2002). ... Released by Bears (August 31, 2003). ... Signed by Carolina Panthers (September 2, 2003). ... On injured reserve with hamstring injury (December 20, 2003-remainder of season). ... Released by Panthers (March 21, 2004).
CHAMPIONSHIP GAME EXPERIENCE: Played in NFC championship game (2001 season).

			TOTALS			INTERCEPTIONS			
Year Team	G	GS	Tk.	Ast.	Sks.	No.	Yds.	Avg.	TD
1993—Cleveland NFL	15	1	13	29	0.0	0	0	0.0	0
1994—Cleveland NFL	16	1	30	10	0.0	1	0	0.0	0
1995—Cleveland NFL	16	6	58	12	0.0	2	24	12.0	▲1
1996—Baltimore NFL	9	9	43	11	4.5	1	45	45.0	1
1997—Arizona NFL	16	0	24	5	2.0	1	5	5.0	0
1998—Philadelphia NFL	16	8	33	14	1.0	1	33	33.0	0
1999—Philadelphia NFL	14	2	19	9	1.0	1	12	12.0	0
2000—Philadelphia NFL	16	3	42	5	0.0	1	26	26.0	1
2001—Philadelphia NFL	16	16	72	23	3.0	0	0	0.0	0
2002—Chicago NFL	16	3	43	15	3.0	0	0	0.0	0
2003—Carolina NFL	9	0	2	0	0.0	0	0	0.0	0
Pro totals (11 years)	159	49	379	133	14.5	8	145	18.1	3

CALDWELL, RECHE WR CHARGERS

PERSONAL: Born March 28, 1979, in Tampa, Fla. ... 5-11/194. ... Full name: Donald Reche Caldwell Jr..
HIGH SCHOOL: Jefferson (Tampa, Fla.).
COLLEGE: Florida.
TRANSACTIONS/CAREER NOTES: Selected after junior season by San Diego Chargers in second round (48th pick overall) of 2002 NFL draft. ... Signed by Chargers (July 22, 2002).
SINGLE GAME HIGHS (regular season): Receptions—4 (December 14, 2003, vs. Green Bay); yards—53 (December 22, 2002, vs. Kansas City); and touchdown receptions—1 (November 17, 2002, vs. San Francisco).

			RUSHING				RECEIVING				PUNT RETURNS				KICKOFF RETURNS				TOTALS		
Year Team	G	GS	Att.	Yds.	Avg.	TD	No.	Yds.	Avg.	TD	No.	Yds.	Avg.	TD	No.	Yds.	Avg.	TD	TD	2pt.	Pts.
2002—S.D. NFL	16	2	2	9	4.5	0	22	208	9.5	3	2	-2	-1.0	0	9	220	24.4	0	3	1	20
2003—S.D. NFL	9	4	5	39	7.8	0	8	80	10.0	0	0	0	0.0	0	0	0	0.0	0	0	0	0
Pro totals (2 years)	25	6	7	48	6.9	0	30	288	9.6	3	2	-2	-1.0	0	9	220	24.4	0	3	1	20

CALICO, TYRONE WR TITANS

PERSONAL: Born November 9, 1980, in Millington, Tenn. ... 6-4/223.
HIGH SCHOOL: Millington (Tenn.).
COLLEGE: Middle Tennessee State.
TRANSACTIONS/CAREER NOTES: Selected by Tennessee Titans in second round (60th pick overall) of 2003 NFL draft. ... Signed by Titans (July 21, 2003).
SINGLE GAME HIGHS (regular season): Receptions—4 (October 12, 2003, vs. Houston); yards—92 (October 12, 2003, vs. Houston); and touchdown receptions—1 (November 9, 2003, vs. Miami).

			RUSHING				RECEIVING				TOTALS			
Year Team	G	GS	Att.	Yds.	Avg.	TD	No.	Yds.	Avg.	TD	TD	2pt.	Pts.	Fum.
2003—Tennessee NFL	14	2	1	5	5.0	0	18	297	16.5	4	4	1	26	0

CALMUS, ROCKY LB TITANS

PERSONAL: Born August 1, 1979, in Tulsa, Okla. ... 6-3/238.
HIGH SCHOOL: Jenks (Okla.).
COLLEGE: Oklahoma.
TRANSACTIONS/CAREER NOTES: Selected by Tennessee Titans in third round (77th pick overall) of 2002 NFL draft. ... Signed by Titans (July 24, 2002).
CHAMPIONSHIP GAME EXPERIENCE: Member of Titans for AFC championship game (2002 season); inactive.
HONORS: Named linebacker on THE SPORTING NEWS college All-America first team (2001). ... Butkus Award winner (2001).

			TOTALS			INTERCEPTIONS			
Year Team	G	GS	Tk.	Ast.	Sks.	No.	Yds.	Avg.	TD
2002—Tennessee NFL	13	1	7	4	0.0	0	0	0.0	0
2003—Tennessee NFL	10	9	35	9	1.0	2	26	13.0	0
Pro totals (2 years)	23	10	42	13	1.0	2	26	13.0	0

CAMPBELL, DAN — TE — COWBOYS

PERSONAL: Born April 13, 1976, in Clifton, Texas. ... 6-5/263. ... Full name: Daniel Allen Campbell.
HIGH SCHOOL: Glen Rose (Texas).
COLLEGE: Texas A&M.
TRANSACTIONS/CAREER NOTES: Selected by New York Giants in third round (79th pick overall) of 1999 NFL draft. ... Signed by Giants (July 29, 1999). ... Granted free agency (March 1, 2002). ... Re-signed by Giants (March 27, 2002). ... Granted unconditional free agency (February 28, 2003). ... Signed by Dallas Cowboys (March 11, 2003).
CHAMPIONSHIP GAME EXPERIENCE: Played in NFC championship game (2000 season). ... Played in Super Bowl 35 (2000 season).
SINGLE GAME HIGHS (regular season): Receptions—4 (November 10, 2002, vs. Minnesota); yards—35 (November 10, 2002, vs. Minnesota); and touchdown receptions—1 (November 9, 2003, vs. Buffalo).

			RECEIVING				TOTALS			
Year Team	G	GS	No.	Yds.	Avg.	TD	TD	2pt.	Pts.	Fum.
1999—New York Giants NFL	12	1	0	0	0.0	0	0	0	0	0
2000—New York Giants NFL	16	5	8	46	5.8	3	3	0	18	1
2001—New York Giants NFL	16	13	13	148	11.4	1	1	0	6	0
2002—New York Giants NFL	16	16	22	175	8.0	1	1	0	6	0
2003—Dallas NFL	16	16	20	195	9.8	1	1	0	6	0
Pro totals (5 years)	76	51	63	564	9.0	6	6	0	36	1

CAMPBELL, KELLY — WR — VIKINGS

PERSONAL: Born July 23, 1980, in Atlanta, Ga. ... 5-10/173.
HIGH SCHOOL: Mays (Atlanta).
COLLEGE: Georgia Tech.
TRANSACTIONS/CAREER NOTES: Signed non-drafted free agent by Minnesota Vikings (April 26, 2002). ... Released by Vikings (September 24, 2002). ... Re-signed by Vikings to practice squad (September 26, 2002). ... Activated (November 6, 2002).
SINGLE GAME HIGHS (regular season): Receptions—6 (November 24, 2002, vs. New England); yards—115 (November 16, 2003, vs. Oakland); and touchdown receptions—2 (December 29, 2002, vs. Detroit).
STATISTICAL PLATEAUS: 100-yard receiving games: 2003 (1). Total: 1.

			RECEIVING				TOTALS			
Year Team	G	GS	No.	Yds.	Avg.	TD	TD	2pt.	Pts.	Fum.
2002—Minnesota NFL	6	2	13	176	13.5	3	3	0	18	1
2003—Minnesota NFL	15	6	25	522	20.9	4	4	0	24	2
Pro totals (2 years)	21	8	38	698	18.4	7	7	0	42	3

CAMPBELL, KHARY — LB — REDSKINS

PERSONAL: Born April 4, 1979, in Brooklyn, N.Y. ... 6-1/230.
HIGH SCHOOL: Sylvania Southview (Toledo, Ohio).
COLLEGE: Bowling Green.
TRANSACTIONS/CAREER NOTES: Signed as non-drafted free agent by Dallas Cowboys (April 26, 2002). ... Released by Cowboys (August 27, 2002). ... Re-signed by Cowboys to practice squad (September 3, 2002). ... Signed by New York Jets off Cowboys practice squad (September 25, 2002). ... Re-signed by Jets (April 2, 2003). ... Waived by Jets (September 30, 2003). ... Signed by Washington Redskins (April 5, 2004).

			TOTALS			INTERCEPTIONS			
Year Team	G	GS	Tk.	Ast.	Sks.	No.	Yds.	Avg.	TD
2002—New York Jets NFL	9	0	0	0	0.0	0	0	0.0	0
2003—New York Jets NFL	4	0	3	0	0.0	0	0	0.0	0
Pro totals (2 years)	13	0	3	0	0.0	0	0	0.0	0

CAMPBELL, MARK — TE — BILLS

PERSONAL: Born December 6, 1975, in Clawson, Mich. ... 6-6/255.
HIGH SCHOOL: Bishop Foley (Madison Heights, Mich.).
COLLEGE: Michigan.
TRANSACTIONS/CAREER NOTES: Signed as non-drafted free agent by Cleveland Browns (April 23, 1999). ... On injured reserve with ankle injury (December 14, 1999-remainder of season). ... On injured reserve with leg injury (September 1, 2001-entire season). ... Traded by Browns to Buffalo Bills for undisclosed pick in 2004 draft (February 28, 2003).
SINGLE GAME HIGHS (regular season): Receptions—7 (October 27, 2002, vs. New York Jets); yards—55 (December 21, 2003, vs. Miami); and touchdown receptions—1 (December 14, 2003, vs. Tennessee).

			RECEIVING				KICKOFF RETURNS				TOTALS			
Year Team	G	GS	No.	Yds.	Avg.	TD	No.	Yds.	Avg.	TD	TD	2pt.	Pts.	Fum.
1999—Cleveland NFL	14	4	9	131	14.6	0	3	28	9.3	0	0	0	0	0
2000—Cleveland NFL	16	10	12	80	6.7	1	3	30	10.0	0	1	0	6	0
2002—Cleveland NFL	16	16	25	179	7.2	3	2	21	10.5	0	3	0	18	0
2003—Buffalo NFL	16	11	34	339	10.0	1	0	0	0.0	0	1	0	6	0
Pro totals (4 years)	62	41	80	729	9.1	5	8	79	9.9	0	5	0	30	0

CANIDATE, TRUNG — RB — REDSKINS

PERSONAL: Born March 3, 1977, in Phoenix, Ariz. ... 5-11/205. ... Full name: Trung Jered Canidate.
HIGH SCHOOL: Central (Phoenix).
COLLEGE: Arizona.

TRANSACTIONS/CAREER NOTES: Selected by St. Louis Rams in first round (31st pick overall) of 2000 NFL draft. ... Signed by Rams (July 20, 2000). ... On injured reserve with wrist injury (November 13, 2000-remainder of season). ... Traded by Rams to Washington Redskins for G David Loverne and fourth-round pick (DB DeJuan Groce) in 2003 draft (February 28, 2003).
CHAMPIONSHIP GAME EXPERIENCE: Played in NFC championship game (2001 season). ... Played in Super Bowl 36 (2001 season).
SINGLE GAME HIGHS (regular season): Attempts—23 (October 21, 2001, vs. New York Jets); yards—195 (October 21, 2001, vs. New York Jets); and rushing touchdowns—2 (October 21, 2001, vs. New York Jets).
STATISTICAL PLATEAUS: 100-yard rushing games: 2001 (2), 2003 (1). Total: 3. 100-yard receiving games: 2001 (1). Total: 1.

			RUSHING				RECEIVING				KICKOFF RETURNS				TOTALS			
Year Team	G	GS	Att.	Yds.	Avg.	TD	No.	Yds.	Avg.	TD	No.	Yds.	Avg.	TD	TD	2pt.	Pts.	Fum.
2000—St. Louis NFL	3	0	3	6	2.0	0	1	4	4.0	0	0	0	0.0	0	0	0	0	0
2001—St. Louis NFL	16	2	78	441	5.7	6	17	154	9.1	0	36	748	20.8	0	6	0	36	3
2002—St. Louis NFL	16	1	17	48	2.8	0	4	31	7.8	0	7	197	28.1	0	0	0	0	1
2003—Washington NFL	11	10	142	600	4.2	1	10	71	7.1	1	0	0	0.0	0	2	0	12	1
Pro totals (4 years)	46	13	240	1095	4.6	7	32	260	8.1	1	43	945	22.0	0	8	0	48	5

CARLISLE, COOPER G/T BRONCOS

PERSONAL: Born August 11, 1977, in Greenville, Miss. ... 6-5/295. ... Full name: Cooper Morrison Carlisle.
HIGH SCHOOL: McComb (Miss.).
COLLEGE: Florida.
TRANSACTIONS/CAREER NOTES: Selected by Denver Broncos in fourth round (112th pick overall) of 2000 NFL draft. ... Signed by Broncos (July 19, 2000).
PLAYING EXPERIENCE: Denver NFL, 2000-2003. ... Games/Games started: 2000 (13/0), 2001 (16/0), 2002 (1/0), 2003 (16/2). Total: 46/2.

CARNEY, JOHN K SAINTS

PERSONAL: Born April 20, 1964, in Hartford, Conn. ... 5-11/180. ... Full name: John Michael Carney.
HIGH SCHOOL: Cardinal Newman (West Palm Beach, Fla.).
COLLEGE: Notre Dame.
TRANSACTIONS/CAREER NOTES: Signed as non-drafted free agent by Cincinnati Bengals (May 1, 1987). ... Released by Bengals (August 10, 1987). ... Signed as replacement player by Tampa Bay Buccaneers (September 24, 1987). ... Released by Buccaneers (October 14, 1987). ... Re-signed by Buccaneers (April 5, 1988). ... Released by Buccaneers (August 23, 1988). ... Re-signed by Buccaneers (November 22, 1988). ... Granted unconditional free agency (February 1-April 1, 1989). ... Re-signed by Buccaneers (April 13, 1989). ... Released by Buccaneers (September 5, 1989). ... Re-signed by Buccaneers (December 13, 1989). ... Granted unconditional free agency (February 1, 1990). ... Signed by San Diego Chargers (April 1, 1990). ... Released by Chargers (August 28, 1990). ... Signed by Los Angeles Rams (September 21, 1990). ... Released by Rams (September 26, 1990). ... Signed by Chargers (October 3, 1990). ... Granted free agency (February 1, 1992). ... Re-signed by Chargers (July 27, 1992). ... Granted free agency (March 1, 1993). ... Re-signed by Chargers (June 9, 1993). ... Granted unconditional free agency (February 17, 1994). ... Re-signed by Chargers (April 6, 1994). ... On injured reserve with knee injury (November 15, 1997-remainder of season). ... Granted unconditional free agency (March 2, 2001). ... Signed by New Orleans Saints (August 5, 2001). ... Granted unconditional free agency (March 1, 2002). ... Re-signed by Saints (March 12, 2002). ... Granted unconditional free agency (February 28, 2003). ... Re-signed by Saints (March 7, 2003).
CHAMPIONSHIP GAME EXPERIENCE: Played in AFC championship game (1994 season). ... Played in Super Bowl 29 (1994 season).
HONORS: Named kicker on THE SPORTING NEWS NFL All-Pro team (1994). ... Played in Pro Bowl (1994 season).

		FIELD GOALS							TOTALS		
Year Team	G	1-29	30-39	40-49	50+	Tot.	Pct.	Lg.	XPM	XPA	Pts.
1988—Tampa Bay NFL	4	2-3	0-1	0-1	0-0	2-5	40.0	29	6	6	12
1989—Tampa Bay NFL	1	0-0	0-0	0-0	0-0	0-0	0.0	0	0	0	0
1990—Los Angeles Rams NFL	1	0-0	0-0	0-0	0-0	0-0	0.0	0	0	0	0
—San Diego NFL	12	10-10	6-7	3-3	0-1	19-21	90.5	43	27	28	84
1991—San Diego NFL	16	7-7	6-8	4-10	2-4	19-29	65.5	54	31	31	88
1992—San Diego NFL	16	13-14	5-7	7-8	1-3	26-32	81.3	50	35	35	113
1993—San Diego NFL	16	8-8	14-17	7-12	2-3	31-40	77.5	51	31	33	124
1994—San Diego NFL	16	12-12	15-15	5-9	2-2	†34-§38	89.5	50	33	33	*135
1995—San Diego NFL	16	8-8	10-11	3-5	0-2	21-26	80.8	45	32	33	95
1996—San Diego NFL	16	11-13	8-8	7-12	3-3	29-36	80.6	53	31	31	118
1997—San Diego NFL	4	3-3	2-2	2-2	0-0	7-7	100.0	41	5	5	26
1998—San Diego NFL	16	11-12	5-5	8-10	2-3	26-30	86.7	54	19	19	97
1999—San Diego NFL	16	15-15	6-8	9-12	1-1	31-36	86.1	50	22	23	115
2000—San Diego NFL	16	4-4	5-7	7-10	2-4	18-25	72.0	▲54	27	27	81
2001—New Orleans NFL	15	7-7	11-11	8-12	1-1	27-31	87.1	50	32	32	113
2002—New Orleans NFL	16	9-9	11-13	11-12	0-1	31-35	‡88.6	48	37	37	130
2003—New Orleans NFL	16	6-6	10-12	5-9	1-3	22-30	73.3	50	36	37	102
Pro totals (16 years)	213	126-131	114-132	86-127	17-31	343-421	81.5	54	404	410	1433

CARPENTER, DWAINE S 49ERS

PERSONAL: Born November 4, 1976, in Pinehurst, N.C. ... 6-1/203. ... Full name: Dwaine L. Carpenter.
HIGH SCHOOL: West Montgomery (Wadeville, N.C.).
COLLEGE: North Carolina A&T.
TRANSACTIONS/CAREER NOTES: Signed as non-drafted free agent by San Francisco 49ers (May 27, 2003).

			TOTALS			INTERCEPTIONS			
Year Team	G	GS	Tk.	Ast.	Sks.	No.	Yds.	Avg.	TD
2003—San Francisco NFL	15	2	18	1	0.0	0	0	0.0	0

CARPENTER, KEION — S — FALCONS

PERSONAL: Born October 31, 1977, in Baltimore, Md. ... 5-11/205. ... Full name: Keion Eric Carpenter.
HIGH SCHOOL: Woodlawn (Baltimore).
COLLEGE: Virginia Tech.
TRANSACTIONS/CAREER NOTES: Signed as non-drafted free agent by Buffalo Bills (April 19, 1999). ... Granted free agency (March 1, 2002). ... Signed by Atlanta Falcons (March 6, 2002). ... Granted unconditional free agency (February 28, 2003). ... Re-signed by Falcons (April 10, 2003). ... Granted unconditional free agency (March 3, 2004). ... Re-signed by Falcons (March 30, 2004).

			TOTALS			INTERCEPTIONS			
Year Team	G	GS	Tk.	Ast.	Sks.	No.	Yds.	Avg.	TD
1999—Buffalo NFL	10	0	0	0	0.0	0	0	0.0	0
2000—Buffalo NFL	12	12	30	3	0.0	5	63	12.6	0
2001—Buffalo NFL	15	10	24	10	0.0	0	0	0.0	0
2002—Atlanta NFL	16	16	43	6	0.0	4	82	20.5	1
2003—Atlanta NFL	15	8	29	2	0.0	3	22	7.3	0
Pro totals (5 years)	68	46	126	21	0.0	12	167	13.9	1

CARR, DAVID — QB — TEXANS

PERSONAL: Born July 21, 1979, in Bakersfield, Calif. ... 6-3/223.
HIGH SCHOOL: Stockdale (Bakersfield, Calf.).
COLLEGE: Fresno State.
TRANSACTIONS/CAREER NOTES: Selected by Houston Texans in first round (first pick overall) of 2002 NFL draft. ... Signed by Texans (April 20, 2002).
RECORDS: Holds NFL single-season record for most times sacked—76 (2002).
SINGLE GAME HIGHS (regular season): Attempts—42 (October 12, 2003, vs. Tennessee); completions—25 (October 12, 2003, vs. Tennessee); yards—371 (October 3, 2003, vs. Tennessee) and touchdown passes—2 (November 9 2003, vs. Philadelphia).
STATISTICAL PLATEAUS: 300-yard passing games: 2003 (1). Total: 1.
MISCELLANEOUS: Regular-season record as starting NFL quarterback: 7-20 (.259). ... Holds Houston Texans all-time records for most yards passing (4,605) and passing touchdowns (18).

			PASSING									RUSHING				TOTALS		
Year Team	G	GS	Att.	Cmp.	Pct.	Yds.	TD	Int.	Avg.	Skd.	Rat.	Att.	Yds.	Avg.	TD	TD	2pt.	Pts.
2002—Houston NFL	16	16	444	233	52.5	2592	9	15	5.84	*76	62.8	59	282	4.8	3	3	0	18
2003—Houston NFL	12	11	295	167	56.6	2013	9	13	6.82	15	69.5	27	151	5.6	2	2	0	12
Pro totals (2 years)	28	27	739	400	54.1	4605	18	28	6.23	91	65.5	86	433	5.0	5	5	0	30

CARROLL, TRAVIS — LB — TEXANS

PERSONAL: Born October 26, 1978, in Jacksonville, Fla. ... 6-4/240. ... Full name: Travis C. Carroll.
HIGH SCHOOL: The Bolles School (Jacksonville, Fla.).
COLLEGE: Florida.
TRANSACTIONS/CAREER NOTES: Signed as non-drafted free agent by New Orleans Saints (April 23, 2002). ... Waived by Saints (September 8, 2003). ... Signed by Houston Texans (December 1, 2003).

			TOTALS			INTERCEPTIONS			
Year Team	G	GS	Tk.	Ast.	Sks.	No.	Yds.	Avg.	TD
2002—New Orleans NFL	6	0	0	0	0.0	0	0	0.0	0
2003—New Orleans NFL	1	0	0	0	0.0	0	0	0.0	0
—Houston NFL	4	0	0	0	0.0	0	0	0.0	0
Pro totals (2 years)	11	0	0	0	0.0	0	0	0.0	0

CARSON, LEONARDO — DT — COWBOYS

PERSONAL: Born February 11, 1977, in Mobile, Ala. ... 6-2/305. ... Full name: Leonardo Tremayne Carson.
HIGH SCHOOL: Shaw (Mobile, Ala.).
COLLEGE: Auburn.
TRANSACTIONS/CAREER NOTES: Selected by San Diego Chargers in fourth round (113th pick overall) of 2000 NFL draft. ... Signed by Chargers (July 20, 2000). ... On injured reserve with shoulder injury (November 17, 2000-remainder of season). ... Granted free agency (February 28, 2003). ... Re-signed by Chargers (April 15, 2003). ... Released by Chargers (October 14, 2003). ... Signed by Dallas Cowboys (October 18, 2003). ... On injured reserve with triceps injury (December 16, 2003-remainder of season).

			TOTALS		
Year Team	G	GS	Tk.	Ast.	Sks.
2000—San Diego NFL	4	0	2	0	0.0
2001—San Diego NFL	16	13	24	9	3.0
2002—San Diego NFL	16	6	22	9	3.5
2003—San Diego NFL	5	0	2	0	0.0
—Dallas NFL	8	0	13	5	1.5
Pro totals (4 years)	49	19	63	23	8.0

CARSWELL, DWAYNE — TE — BRONCOS

PERSONAL: Born January 18, 1972, in Jacksonville, Fla. ... 6-3/260.
HIGH SCHOOL: University Christian (Jacksonville).
COLLEGE: Liberty.

TRANSACTIONS/CAREER NOTES: Signed as non-drafted free agent by Denver Broncos (May 2, 1994). ... Released by Broncos (August 26, 1994). ... Re-signed by Broncos to practice squad (August 30, 1994). ... Activated (November 25, 1994).
CHAMPIONSHIP GAME EXPERIENCE: Played in AFC championship game (1997 and 1998 seasons). ... Member of Super Bowl championship team (1997 and 1998 seasons).
HONORS: Played in Pro Bowl (2001 season).
SINGLE GAME HIGHS (regular season): Receptions—6 (December 16, 2001, vs. Kansas City); yards—68 (October 22, 2000, vs. Cincinnati); and touchdown receptions—1 (October 5, 2003, vs. Kansas City).

			RECEIVING				TOTALS			
Year Team	**G**	**GS**	**No.**	**Yds.**	**Avg.**	**TD**	**TD**	**2pt.**	**Pts.**	**Fum.**
1994—Denver NFL	4	0	0	0	0.0	0	0	0	0	0
1995—Denver NFL	9	2	3	37	12.3	0	0	0	0	0
1996—Denver NFL	16	2	15	85	5.7	0	0	0	0	0
1997—Denver NFL	16	3	12	96	8.0	1	1	0	6	0
1998—Denver NFL	16	1	4	51	12.8	0	0	0	0	0
1999—Denver NFL	16	11	24	201	8.4	2	2	0	12	0
2000—Denver NFL	16	16	49	495	10.1	3	3	0	18	0
2001—Denver NFL	16	16	34	299	8.8	4	4	1	26	0
2002—Denver NFL	16	7	21	189	9.0	1	1	0	6	0
2003—Denver NFL	16	10	6	53	8.8	1	1	0	6	0
Pro totals (10 years)	141	68	168	1506	9.0	12	12	1	74	0

CARTER, ANDRE — DE — 49ERS

PERSONAL: Born May 12, 1979, in Denver, Colo. ... 6-4/265.
HIGH SCHOOL: Oak Grove (San Jose, Calif.).
COLLEGE: California.
TRANSACTIONS/CAREER NOTES: Selected by San Francisco 49ers in first round (seventh pick overall) of 2001 NFL draft. ... Signed by 49ers (July 26, 2001).
HONORS: Named defensive end on THE SPORTING NEWS college All-America first team (2000).

			TOTALS		
Year Team	**G**	**GS**	**Tk.**	**Ast.**	**Sks.**
2001—San Francisco NFL	15	15	40	7	6.5
2002—San Francisco NFL	16	16	44	10	12.5
2003—San Francisco NFL	15	15	27	7	6.5
Pro totals (3 years)	46	46	111	24	25.5

CARTER, DALE — CB — RAVENS

PERSONAL: Born November 28, 1969, in Covington, Ga. ... 6-1/194. ... Full name: Dale Lavelle Carter. ... Brother of Jake Reed, wide receiver with Minnesota Vikings and New Orleans Saints (1991-2002).
HIGH SCHOOL: Newton County (Covington, Ga.).
JUNIOR COLLEGE: Ellsworth (Iowa) Community College.
COLLEGE: Tennessee.
TRANSACTIONS/CAREER NOTES: Selected by Kansas City Chiefs in first round (20th pick overall) of 1992 NFL draft. ... Signed by Chiefs (June 2, 1992). ... Designated by Chiefs as transition player (February 25, 1993). ... On injured reserve with broken arm (January 7, 1994-remainder of 1993 playoffs). ... Tendered offer sheet by Minnesota Vikings (July 12, 1996). ... Offer matched by Chiefs (July 19, 1996). ... Granted unconditional free agency (February 12, 1999). ... Signed by Denver Broncos (February 19, 1999). ... Suspended by NFL for violating league substance abuse policy (April 25, 2000-November 6, 2001). ... Released by Broncos (November 6, 2001). ... Signed by Minnesota Vikings (November 8, 2001). ... Granted unconditional free agency (March 1, 2002). ... Signed by New Orleans Saints (March 12, 2002). ... On suspended list for violating league substance abuse policy (July 19-November 4, 2002). ... On injured reserve with quad injury (December 6, 2003-remainder of season). ... Released by Saints (March 16, 2004). ... Signed by Baltimore Ravens (May 20, 2004).
HONORS: Named kick returner on THE SPORTING NEWS college All-America first team (1990). ... Named defensive back on THE SPORTING NEWS college All-America first team (1991). ... Played in Pro Bowl (1994, 1995 and 1997 seasons). ... Named cornerback on THE SPORTING NEWS NFL All-Pro team (1996). ... Named to play in Pro Bowl (1996 season); replaced by Terry McDaniel due to injury.

			TOTALS			INTERCEPTIONS				PUNT RETURNS				KICKOFF RETURNS				TOTALS			
Year Team	**G**	**GS**	**Tk.**	**Ast.**	**Sks.**	**No.**	**Yds.**	**Avg.**	**TD**	**No.**	**Yds.**	**Avg.**	**TD**	**No.**	**Yds.**	**Avg.**	**TD**	**TD**	**2pt.**	**Pts.**	**Fum.**
1992—K.C. NFL	16	9	39	16	0.0	7	65	9.3	1	38	398	10.5	†2	11	190	17.3	0	3	0	18	7
1993—K.C. NFL	15	11	43	15	0.0	1	0	0.0	0	27	247	9.1	0	0	0	0.0	0	0	0	0	4
1994—K.C. NFL	16	16	78	3	0.0	2	24	12.0	0	16	124	7.8	0	0	0	0.0	0	0	0	0	1
1995—K.C. NFL	16	14	48	5	0.0	4	45	11.3	0	0	0	0.0	0	0	0	0.0	0	0	0	0	0
1996—K.C. NFL	14	14	41	10	0.0	3	17	5.7	0	2	18	9.0	0	0	0	0.0	0	1	0	6	1
1997—K.C. NFL	16	15	49	6	0.0	2	9	4.5	0	0	0	0.0	0	0	0	0.0	0	0	0	0	0
1998—K.C. NFL	11	9	31	8	0.0	2	23	11.5	0	0	0	0.0	0	0	0	0.0	0	0	0	0	0
1999—Den. NFL	14	14	54	18	0.0	2	48	24.0	0	0	0	0.0	0	0	0	0.0	0	0	0	0	0
2000—Den. NFL	Did not play.																				
2001—Min. NFL	8	8	24	9	0.0	0	0	0.0	0	0	0	0.0	0	0	0	0.0	0	0	0	0	0
2002—N.O. NFL	7	7	26	4	0.0	1	25	25.0	0	0	0	0.0	0	0	0	0.0	0	0	0	0	0
2003—N.O. NFL	8	8	22	2	1.0	0	0	0.0	0	0	0	0.0	0	0	0	0.0	0	0	0	0	0
Pro totals (11 years)	141	125	455	96	1.0	24	256	10.7	1	83	787	9.5	2	11	190	17.3	0	4	0	24	13

CARTER, JONATHAN — WR — JETS

PERSONAL: Born March 20, 1979, in Anniston, Ala. ... 6-0/180.
HIGH SCHOOL: Lineville (Ala.).
COLLEGE: Troy State.

TRANSACTIONS/CAREER NOTES: Selected by New York Giants in fifth round (162nd pick overall) of 2001 NFL draft. ... Signed by Giants (July 26, 2001). ... Released by Giants (September 2, 2001). ... Re-signed by Giants to practice squad (September 3, 2001). ... Activated (December 29, 2001). ... Claimed on waivers by New York Jets (October 8, 2002). ... Re-signed by Jets (April 2, 2003) ... On injured reserve with knee injury (December 9, 2003-remainder of season).
SINGLE GAME HIGHS (regular season): Receptions—2 (November 23, 2003, vs. Jacksonville); yards—62 (November 16, 2003, vs. Indianapolis); and touchdown receptions—1 (November 16, 2003, vs. Indianapolis).

			RECEIVING				KICKOFF RETURNS				TOTALS			
Year Team	**G**	**GS**	**No.**	**Yds.**	**Avg.**	**TD**	**No.**	**Yds.**	**Avg.**	**TD**	**TD**	**2pt.**	**Pts.**	**Fum.**
2001—New York Giants NFL	2	0	0	0	0.0	0	8	155	19.4	0	0	0	0	0
2002—New York Giants NFL	1	0	0	0	0.0	0	1	14	14.0	0	0	0	0	0
2003—New York Jets NFL	9	0	4	93	23.3	1	18	517	28.7	1	2	0	12	0
Pro totals (3 years)	12	0	4	93	23.3	1	27	686	25.4	1	2	0	12	0

CARTER, KERRY — RB — SEAHAWKS

PERSONAL: Born December 19, 1980, in Port of Spain, Trinidad. ... 6-1/238.
HIGH SCHOOL: Henry Car (Ontario).
COLLEGE: Stanford.
TRANSACTIONS/CAREER NOTES: Signed as non-drafted free agent by Seattle Seahawks (May 1, 2003).
SINGLE GAME HIGHS (regular season): Attempts—3 (November 16, 2003, vs. Detroit); yards—2 (November 16, 2003, vs. Detroit); and rushing touchdowns—0.

C

			RUSHING				KICKOFF RETURNS				TOTALS			
Year Team	**G**	**GS**	**Att.**	**Yds.**	**Avg.**	**TD**	**No.**	**Yds.**	**Avg.**	**TD**	**TD**	**2pt.**	**Pts.**	**Fum.**
2003—Seattle NFL	16	0	3	-2	-0.7	0	8	185	23.1	0	0	0	0	0

CARTER, KEVIN — DE — TITANS

PERSONAL: Born September 21, 1973, in Miami, Fla. ... 6-5/290. ... Full name: Kevin Louis Carter. ... Brother of Bernard Carter, linebacker with Jacksonville Jaguars (1995).
HIGH SCHOOL: Lincoln (Tallahassee, Fla.).
COLLEGE: Florida.
TRANSACTIONS/CAREER NOTES: Selected by St. Louis Rams in first round (sixth pick overall) of 1995 NFL draft. ... Signed by Rams (July 17, 1995). ... Designated by Rams as franchise player (February 22, 2001). ... Traded by Rams to Tennessee Titans for first-round pick (DT Ryan Pickett) in 2001 draft (March 28, 2001).
CHAMPIONSHIP GAME EXPERIENCE: Played in NFC championship game (1999 season). ... Member of Super Bowl championship team (1999 season). ... Played in AFC championship game (2002 season).
HONORS: Named defensive lineman on THE SPORTING NEWS college All-America first team (1994). ... Named defensive end on THE SPORTING NEWS NFL All-Pro team (1999). ... Played in Pro Bowl (1999 and 2002 seasons).

			TOTALS		
Year Team	**G**	**GS**	**Tk.**	**Ast.**	**Sks.**
1995—St. Louis NFL	16	16	33	4	6.0
1996—St. Louis NFL	16	16	39	16	9.5
1997—St. Louis NFL	16	16	32	10	7.5
1998—St. Louis NFL	16	16	49	11	12.0
1999—St. Louis NFL	16	16	30	4	*17.0
2000—St. Louis NFL	16	13	31	4	10.5
2001—Tennessee NFL	16	16	28	8	2.0
2002—Tennessee NFL	16	16	27	15	10.0
2003—Tennessee NFL	16	16	29	19	5.5
Pro totals (9 years)	144	141	298	91	80.0

CARTER, KI-JANA — RB — SAINTS

PERSONAL: Born September 12, 1973, in Westerville, Ohio. ... 5-10/222. ... Full name: Kenneth Leonard Carter. ... Name pronounced: KEE-john-uh.
HIGH SCHOOL: Westerville (Ohio) South.
COLLEGE: Penn State.
TRANSACTIONS/CAREER NOTES: Selected after junior season by Cincinnati Bengals in first round (first pick overall) of 1995 NFL draft. ... Signed by Bengals (July 19, 1995). ... On injured reserve with knee injury (August 22, 1995-entire season). ... On injured reserve with wrist injury (September 7, 1998-remainder of season). ... On injured reserve with knee injury (September 29, 1999-remainder of season). ... Released by Bengals (June 1, 2000). ... Signed by Washington Redskins (July 31, 2001). ... Granted unconditional free agency (March 1, 2002). ... Signed by Green Bay Packers (June 14, 2002). ... Released by Packers (August 27, 2002). ... Signed by New Orleans Saints (August 18, 2003). ... Released by Saints (August 31, 2003). ... Re-signed by Saints (September 23, 2003). ... On injured reserve with toe injury (November 26, 2003-remainder of season). ... Granted unconditional free agency (March 3, 2004). ... Re-signed by Saints (May 20, 2004).
HONORS: Named running back on THE SPORTING NEWS college All-America first team (1994).
SINGLE GAME HIGHS (regular season): Attempts—19 (August 31, 1997, vs. Arizona); yards—104 (September 21, 1997, vs. Denver); and rushing touchdowns—2 (December 30, 2001, vs. New Orleans).
STATISTICAL PLATEAUS: 100-yard rushing games: 1997 (1). Total: 1.

			RUSHING				RECEIVING				TOTALS			
Year Team	**G**	**GS**	**Att.**	**Yds.**	**Avg.**	**TD**	**No.**	**Yds.**	**Avg.**	**TD**	**TD**	**2pt.**	**Pts.**	**Fum.**
1995—Cincinnati NFL							Did not play.							
1996—Cincinnati NFL	16	4	91	264	2.9	8	22	169	7.7	1	9	0	54	2
1997—Cincinnati NFL	15	10	128	464	3.6	7	21	157	7.5	0	7	0	42	3
1998—Cincinnati NFL	1	0	2	4	2.0	0	6	25	4.2	0	0	0	0	0
1999—Cincinnati NFL	3	0	6	15	2.5	1	3	24	8.0	0	1	0	6	0

Year Team	G	GS	RUSHING Att.	Yds.	Avg.	TD	RECEIVING No.	Yds.	Avg.	TD	TOTALS TD	2pt.	Pts.	Fum.
2000—						Did not play.								
2001—Washington NFL	14	0	63	308	4.9	3	13	83	6.4	0	3	0	18	1
2003—New Orleans NFL	8	0	19	72	3.8	1	1	11	11.0	0	1	0	6	0
Pro totals (6 years)	57	14	309	1127	3.6	20	66	469	7.1	1	21	0	126	6

CARTER, QUINCY QB COWBOYS

PERSONAL: Born October 13, 1977, in Decatur, Ga. ... 6-2/213.
HIGH SCHOOL: Southwest DeKalb (Decatur, Ga.).
COLLEGE: Georgia.
TRANSACTIONS/CAREER NOTES: Selected after junior season by Dallas Cowboys in second round (53rd pick overall) of 2001 NFL draft. ... Signed by Cowboys (July 19, 2001).
HONORS: Named College Football Freshman of the Year by THE SPORTING NEWS (1998).
SINGLE GAME HIGHS (regular season): Attempts—47 (December 28, 2003, vs. New Orleans); completions—29 (November 23, 2003, vs. Carolina); yards—321 (September 15, 2003, vs. New York Giants); and touchdown passes—3 (October 3, 2003, vs. Detroit).
STATISTICAL PLATEAUS: 300-yard passing games: 2003 (1). Total: 1.
MISCELLANEOUS: Regular-season record as starting NFL quarterback: 16-15 (.516). ... Post-season record as NFL starting quarterback: 0-1 (.000).

Year Team	G	GS	PASSING Att.	Cmp.	Pct.	Yds.	TD	Int.	Avg.	Skd.	Rat.	RUSHING Att.	Yds.	Avg.	TD	TOTALS TD	2pt.	Pts.
2001—Dallas NFL	8	8	176	90	51.1	1072	5	7	6.09	12	63.0	45	150	3.3	1	1	0	6
2002—Dallas NFL	7	7	221	125	56.6	1465	7	8	6.63	19	72.3	27	91	3.4	0	0	0	0
2003—Dallas NFL	16	16	505	292	57.8	3302	17	21	6.54	37	71.4	68	257	3.8	2	2	0	12
Pro totals (3 years)	31	31	902	507	56.2	5839	29	36	6.47	68	70.0	140	498	3.6	3	3	0	18

C

CARTER, TIM WR GIANTS

PERSONAL: Born September 21, 1979, in Atlanta, Ga. ... 6-0/200. ... Full name: Timothy M. Carter.
HIGH SCHOOL: Lakewood (St. Petersburg, Fla.).
COLLEGE: Auburn.
TRANSACTIONS/CAREER NOTES: Selected by New York Giants in second round (46th pick overall) of 2002 NFL draft. ... Signed by Giants (July 25, 2002). ... On injured reserve with Achilles' tendon injury (November 12, 2002-remainder of season). ... On injured reserve with concussion (December 12, 2003-remainder of season).
SINGLE GAME HIGHS (regular season): Receptions—1 (November 3, 2002, vs. Jacksonville); yards—27 (November 3, 2002, vs. Jacksonville); and touchdown receptions—0.

Year Team	G	GS	RUSHING Att.	Yds.	Avg.	TD	RECEIVING No.	Yds.	Avg.	TD	PUNT RETURNS No.	Yds.	Avg.	TD	KICKOFF RETURNS No.	Yds.	Avg.	TD	TOTALS TD	2pt.	Pts.
2002—NYG NFL	5	0	3	28	9.3	0	2	37	18.5	0	0	0	0.0	0	5	78	15.6	0	0	0	0
2003—NYG NFL	12	2	0	0	0.0	0	26	309	11.9	0	0	0	0.0	0	1	9	9.0	0	0	0	0
Pro totals (2 years)	17	2	3	28	9.3	0	28	346	12.4	0	0	0	0.0	0	6	87	14.5	0	0	0	0

CARTER, TYRONE S VIKINGS

PERSONAL: Born March 31, 1976, in Fort Lauderdale, Fla. ... 5-8/190.
HIGH SCHOOL: Ely (Pompano Beach, Fla.).
COLLEGE: Minnesota.
TRANSACTIONS/CAREER NOTES: Selected by Minnesota Vikings in fourth round (118th pick overall) of 2000 NFL draft. ... Signed by Vikings (July 5, 2000). ... Granted free agency (February 28, 2003). ... Signed by New York Jets (April 14, 2003). ... Released by Jets (March 1, 2004). ... Signed by Minnesota Vikings (March 11, 2004).
CHAMPIONSHIP GAME EXPERIENCE: Played in NFC championship game (2000 season).
HONORS: Jim Thorpe Award winner (1999). ... Named strong safety on THE SPORTING NEWS college All-America first team (1999).

Year Team	G	GS	TOTALS Tk.	Ast.	Sks.	INTERCEPTIONS No.	Yds.	Avg.	TD	KICKOFF RETURNS No.	Yds.	Avg.	TD	TOTALS TD	2pt.	Pts.	Fum.
2000—Minnesota NFL	15	7	29	9	0.0	0	0	0.0	0	17	389	22.9	0	0	0	0	0
2001—Minnesota NFL	15	7	45	5	1.0	0	0	0.0	0	0	0	0.0	0	1	0	6	0
2002—Minnesota NFL	16	7	42	6	0.0	1	13	13.0	0	17	350	20.6	0	0	0	0	0
2003—New York Jets NFL	16	10	59	23	0.0	2	37	18.5	0	0	0	0.0	0	0	0	0	0
Pro totals (4 years)	62	31	175	43	1.0	3	50	16.7	0	34	739	21.7	0	1	0	6	0

CARTWRIGHT, ROCK FB REDSKINS

PERSONAL: Born December 3, 1979, in Conroe, Texas. ... 5-7/223.
HIGH SCHOOL: Conroe (Texas).
JUNIOR COLLEGE: Trinity Valley Community College (Texas).
COLLEGE: Kansas State.
TRANSACTIONS/CAREER NOTES: Selected by Washington Redskins in seventh round (257th pick overall) of 2002 NFL draft.. ... Signed by Redskins (July 19, 2002).
SINGLE GAME HIGHS (regular season): Attempts—21 (December 14, 2003, vs. Dallas); yards—94 (December 14, 2003, vs. Dallas); and rushing touchdowns—1 (December 27, 2003, vs. Philadelphia).

Year Team	G	GS	RUSHING Att.	Yds.	Avg.	TD	RECEIVING No.	Yds.	Avg.	TD	KICKOFF RETURNS No.	Yds.	Avg.	TD	TOTALS TD	2pt.	Pts.	Fum.
2002—Washington NFL	16	0	3	22	7.3	0	11	121	11.0	1	10	169	16.9	0	1	0	6	1
2003—Washington NFL	15	3	107	411	3.8	4	18	176	9.8	0	2	26	13.0	0	4	0	24	2
Pro totals (2 years)	31	3	110	433	3.9	4	29	297	10.2	1	12	195	16.3	0	5	0	30	3

CASH, CHRISTOPHER — CB — LIONS

PERSONAL: Born July 13, 1980, in Stockton, Calif. ... 5-11/170. ... Full name: Chris Cash.
HIGH SCHOOL: Franklin (Stockton, Calif.).
JUNIOR COLLEGE: Palomar College (Calif.).
COLLEGE: Southern California.
TRANSACTIONS/CAREER NOTES: Selected by Detroit Lions in sixth round (175th pick overall) of 2002 NFL draft. ... Signed by Lions (July 23, 2002). ... On injured reserve with knee injury (August 25, 2003-entire season).

			TOTALS			INTERCEPTIONS			
Year Team	**G**	**GS**	**Tk.**	**Ast.**	**Sks.**	**No.**	**Yds.**	**Avg.**	**TD**
2002—Detroit NFL	16	12	79	12	0.0	1	11	11.0	0
2003—Detroit NFL	Did not play.								
Pro totals (1 year)	16	12	79	12	0.0	1	11	11.0	0

CASON, AVEION — RB — COWBOYS

PERSONAL: Born July 12, 1979, in St. Petersburg, Fla. ... 5-10/204. ... Full name: Aveion Marquel Cason.
HIGH SCHOOL: Lakewood (St. Petersburg, Fla.).
COLLEGE: Illinois State.
TRANSACTIONS/CAREER NOTES: Signed as non-drafted free agent by St. Louis Rams (April 23, 2001). ... Released by Rams (September 25, 2001). ... Re-signed by Rams to practice squad (September 26, 2001). ... Released by Rams (September 28, 2001). ... Signed by Detroit Lions (November 19, 2001). ... Traded by Lions to Dallas Cowboys for seventh-round pick (RB Brandon Drumm) in 2003 draft (April 27, 2003). ... On injured reserve with knee injury (December 10, 2003-remainder of season). ... Granted free agency (March 3, 2004). ... Re-signed by Cowboys (April 14, 2004).
SINGLE GAME HIGHS (regular season): Attempts—10 (December 15, 2002, vs. Tampa Bay); yards—77 (September 7, 2003, vs. Atlanta); and rushing touchdowns—1 (November 23, 2003, vs. Carolina).

			RUSHING				RECEIVING				KICKOFF RETURNS				TOTALS			
Year Team	**G**	**GS**	**Att.**	**Yds.**	**Avg.**	**TD**	**No.**	**Yds.**	**Avg.**	**TD**	**No.**	**Yds.**	**Avg.**	**TD**	**TD**	**2pt.**	**Pts.**	**Fum.**
2001—St. Louis NFL	1	0	0	0	0.0	0	0	0	0.0	0	4	73	18.3	0	0	0	0	1
—Detroit NFL	5	0	11	31	2.8	0	4	32	8.0	0	0	0	0.0	0	0	0	0	1
2002—Detroit NFL	10	3	26	107	4.1	0	19	288	15.2	2	2	48	24.0	0	2	0	12	0
2003—Dallas NFL	10	0	40	220	5.5	2	17	142	8.4	0	5	81	16.2	0	2	0	12	2
Pro totals (3 years)	26	3	77	358	4.6	2	40	462	11.6	2	11	202	18.4	0	4	0	24	4

CAVER, QUINTON — LB — CHIEFS

PERSONAL: Born August 22, 1978, in Anniston, Ala. ... 6-4/241.
HIGH SCHOOL: Anniston (Ala.).
COLLEGE: Arkansas.
TRANSACTIONS/CAREER NOTES: Selected by Philadelphia Eagles in second round (55th pick overall) of 2001 NFL draft. ... Signed by Eagles (July 27, 2001). ... Released by Eagles (October 21, 2002). ... Signed by Kansas City Chiefs (October 28, 2002). ... On injured reserve with shoulder injury (December 14, 2002-remainder of season). ... Released by Chiefs (August 31, 2003). ... Re-signed by Chiefs (September 16, 2003). ... Granted free agency (March 3, 2004). ... Re-signed by Chiefs (March 3, 2004).
CHAMPIONSHIP GAME EXPERIENCE: Played in NFC championship game (2001 season).

			TOTALS			INTERCEPTIONS			
Year Team	**G**	**GS**	**Tk.**	**Ast.**	**Sks.**	**No.**	**Yds.**	**Avg.**	**TD**
2001—Philadelphia NFL	11	0	7	2	0.0	0	0	0.0	0
2002—Kansas City NFL	1	0	0	0	0.0	0	0	0.0	0
—Philadelphia NFL	5	0	0	0	0.0	0	0	0.0	0
2003—Kansas City NFL	12	0	1	0	0.0	0	0	0.0	0
Pro totals (3 years)	29	0	8	2	0.0	0	0	0.0	0

CENTERS, LARRY — FB

PERSONAL: Born June 1, 1968, in Tatum, Texas. ... 6-0/225. ... Full name: Larry E. Centers.
HIGH SCHOOL: Tatum (Texas).
COLLEGE: Stephen F. Austin.
TRANSACTIONS/CAREER NOTES: Selected by Phoenix Cardinals in fifth round (115th pick overall) of 1990 NFL draft. ... Signed by Cardinals (July 23, 1990). ... On injured reserve with broken foot (September 11-October 30, 1991). ... Granted free agency (February 1, 1992). ... Re-signed by Cardinals (July 23, 1992). ... Granted unconditional free agency (February 17, 1994). ... Re-signed by Cardinals (March 15, 1994). ... Cardinals franchise renamed Arizona Cardinals for 1994 season. ... Granted unconditional free agency (February 14, 1997). ... Re-signed by Cardinals (March 14, 1997). ... Released by Cardinals (June 18, 1999). ... Signed by Washington Redskins (July 6, 1999). ... Released by Redskins (April 20, 2001). ... Signed by Buffalo Bills (May 8, 2001). ... Released by Bills (March 20, 2003). ... Signed by New England Patriots (July 30, 2003). ... Released by Patriots (October 18, 2003). ... Re-signed by Patriots (December 9, 2003). ... Granted unconditional free agency (March 3, 2004).
CHAMPIONSHIP GAME EXPERIENCE: Played in AFC championship game (2003 season). ... Member of Super Bowl championship team (2003 season).
HONORS: Played in Pro Bowl (1995, 1996 and 2001 seasons).
SINGLE GAME HIGHS (regular season): Attempts—15 (September 4, 1994, vs. Los Angeles Rams); yards—62 (November 26, 1995, vs. Atlanta); and rushing touchdowns—2 (December 4, 1994, vs. Houston).
STATISTICAL PLATEAUS: 100-yard receiving games: 1995 (2), 1996 (1). Total: 3.
MISCELLANEOUS: Holds Cardinals franchise all-time record for most receptions (535).

Year	Team	G	GS	RUSHING Att.	Yds.	Avg.	TD	RECEIVING No.	Yds.	Avg.	TD	KICKOFF RETURNS No.	Yds.	Avg.	TD	TOTALS TD	2pt.	Pts.	Fum.
1990—Phoenix NFL		6	0	0	0	0.0	0	0	0	0.0	0	16	272	17.0	0	0	0	0	1
1991—Phoenix NFL		9	2	14	44	3.1	0	19	176	9.3	0	16	330	20.6	0	0	0	0	4
1992—Phoenix NFL		16	1	37	139	3.8	0	50	417	8.3	2	0	0	0.0	0	2	0	12	1
1993—Phoenix NFL		16	9	25	152	6.1	0	66	603	9.1	3	0	0	0.0	0	3	0	18	1
1994—Arizona NFL		16	5	115	336	2.9	5	77	647	8.4	2	0	0	0.0	0	7	0	42	2
1995—Arizona NFL		16	10	78	254	3.3	2	101	962	9.5	2	1	15	15.0	0	4	0	24	2
1996—Arizona NFL		16	14	116	425	3.7	2	99	766	7.7	7	0	0	0.0	0	9	0	54	1
1997—Arizona NFL		15	14	101	276	2.7	1	54	409	7.6	1	0	0	0.0	0	2	0	12	1
1998—Arizona NFL		16	12	31	110	3.5	0	69	559	8.1	2	0	0	0.0	0	2	0	12	1
1999—Washington NFL		16	12	13	51	3.9	0	69	544	7.9	3	0	0	0.0	0	3	0	18	2
2000—Washington NFL		15	5	19	103	5.4	0	81	600	7.4	3	0	0	0.0	0	3	0	18	1
2001—Buffalo NFL		16	13	34	160	4.7	2	80	620	7.8	2	0	0	0.0	0	4	0	24	2
2002—Buffalo NFL		16	7	11	56	5.1	2	43	388	9.0	0	0	0	0.0	0	2	0	12	0
2003—New England NFL		9	3	21	82	3.9	0	19	106	5.6	1	0	0	0.0	0	1	0	6	0
Pro totals (14 years)		198	107	615	2188	3.6	14	827	6797	8.2	28	33	617	18.7	0	42	0	252	19

CESAIRE, JACQUES DT CHARGERS

PERSONAL: Born August 30, 1980, in Worcester, Mass. ... 6-2/295.
HIGH SCHOOL: Gardner (Mass.).
COLLEGE: Southern Connecticut State.
TRANSACTIONS/CAREER NOTES: Signed as non-drafted free agent by San Diego Chargers (May 2, 2003).

Year	Team	G	GS	TOTALS Tk.	Ast.	Sks.
2003—San Diego NFL		4	0	1	2	0.0

C

CHAMBERLAIN, BYRON TE BRONCOS

PERSONAL: Born October 17, 1971, in Honolulu, Hawaii. ... 6-1/250.
HIGH SCHOOL: Eastern Hills (Fort Worth, Texas).
COLLEGE: Wayne State (Neb.).
TRANSACTIONS/CAREER NOTES: Selected by Denver Broncos in seventh round (222nd pick overall) of 1995 NFL draft. ... Signed by Broncos (August 27, 1995). ... Released by Broncos (August 27, 1995). ... Re-signed by Broncos to practice squad (August 28, 1995). ... Activated (November 24, 1995). ... Assigned by Broncos to Rhein Fire in 1996 World League enhancement allocation program (February 19, 1996). ... Granted unconditional free agency (March 2, 2001). ... Signed by Minnesota Vikings (March 16, 2001). ... Granted unconditional free agency (March 1, 2002). ... Re-signed by Vikings (March 27, 2002). ... Released by Vikings (September 29, 2003). ... Signed by Washington Redskins (October 6, 2003). ... Released by Redskins (April 13, 2004). ... Signed by Broncos (May 14, 2004).
CHAMPIONSHIP GAME EXPERIENCE: Played in AFC championship game (1997 and 1998 seasons). ... Member of Super Bowl championship team (1997 season); did not play. ... Member of Super Bowl championship team (1998 season).
HONORS: Played in Pro Bowl (2001 season).
SINGLE GAME HIGHS (regular season): Receptions—7 (December 23, 2001, vs. Jacksonville); yards—123 (October 17, 1999, vs. Green Bay); and touchdown receptions—1 (December 30, 2001, vs. Green Bay).
STATISTICAL PLATEAUS: 100-yard receiving games: 1999 (1). Total: 1.

Year	Team	G	GS	RECEIVING No.	Yds.	Avg.	TD	TOTALS TD	2pt.	Pts.	Fum.
1995—Denver NFL		5	0	1	11	11.0	0	0	0	0	0
1996—Denver NFL		11	0	12	129	10.8	0	0	0	0	1
1997—Denver NFL		10	0	2	18	9.0	0	0	0	0	1
1998—Denver NFL		16	0	3	35	11.7	0	0	0	0	0
1999—Denver NFL		16	0	32	488	15.3	2	2	0	12	0
2000—Denver NFL		15	0	22	283	12.9	1	1	0	6	0
2001—Minnesota NFL		16	15	57	666	11.7	3	3	0	18	1
2002—Minnesota NFL		13	9	34	389	11.4	0	0	0	0	0
2003—Washington NFL		4	1	4	29	7.3	0	0	0	0	0
Pro totals (9 years)		106	25	167	2048	12.3	6	6	0	36	3

CHAMBERLIN, FRANK LB BENGALS

PERSONAL: Born January 2, 1978, in Mahwah, N.J. ... 6-1/235. ... Full name: Frank Jacob Chamberlin.
HIGH SCHOOL: Mahwah (N.J.).
COLLEGE: Boston College.
TRANSACTIONS/CAREER NOTES: Selected by Tennessee Titans in fifth round (160th pick overall) of 2000 NFL draft. ... Signed by Titans (July 7, 2000). ... Granted free agency (February 28, 2003). ... Re-signed by Titans (March 9, 2003). ... Released by Titans (September 2, 2003). ... Signed by Cincinnati Bengals (November 25, 2003).
CHAMPIONSHIP GAME EXPERIENCE: Played in AFC championship game (2002 season).

Year	Team	G	GS	TOTALS Tk.	Ast.	Sks.	INTERCEPTIONS No.	Yds.	Avg.	TD
2000—Tennessee NFL		12	0	0	1	0.0	0	0	0.0	0
2001—Tennessee NFL		16	0	8	3	1.0	0	0	0.0	0
2002—Tennessee NFL		15	3	11	5	0.0	0	0	0.0	0
2003—Cincinnati NFL		5	0	0	0	0.0	0	0	0.0	0
Pro totals (4 years)		48	3	19	9	1.0	0	0	0.0	0

CHAMBERS, CHRIS — WR — DOLPHINS

PERSONAL: Born August 12, 1978, in Cleveland, Ohio. ... 5-11/210.
HIGH SCHOOL: Bedford (Ohio).
COLLEGE: Wisconsin.
TRANSACTIONS/CAREER NOTES: Selected by Miami Dolphins in second round (52nd pick overall) of 2001 NFL draft. ... Signed by Dolphins (July 23, 2001).
SINGLE GAME HIGHS (regular season): Receptions—9 (December 28, 2003, vs. New York Jets); yards—153 (December 28, 2003, vs. New York Jets); and touchdown receptions—3 (November 27, 2003, vs. Dallas).
STATISTICAL PLATEAUS: 100-yard receiving games: 2001 (3), 2002 (2), 2003 (2). Total: 7.

			RUSHING				RECEIVING				TOTALS			
Year Team	**G**	**GS**	**Att.**	**Yds.**	**Avg.**	**TD**	**No.**	**Yds.**	**Avg.**	**TD**	**TD**	**2pt.**	**Pts.**	**Fum.**
2001—Miami NFL	16	7	1	-11	-11.0	0	48	883	*18.4	7	7	0	42	2
2002—Miami NFL	15	15	6	78	13.0	0	52	734	14.1	3	3	0	18	1
2003—Miami NFL	16	16	4	30	7.5	0	64	963	15.0	§11	11	0	66	1
Pro totals (3 years)	47	38	11	97	8.8	0	164	2580	15.7	21	21	0	126	4

CHANDLER, CHRIS — QB — RAMS

PERSONAL: Born October 12, 1965, in Everett, Wash. ... 6-4/224. ... Full name: Christopher Mark Chandler. ... Brother of Greg Chandler, catcher with San Francisco Giants organization (1978); and son-in-law of John Brodie, quarterback with San Francisco 49ers (1957-73).
HIGH SCHOOL: Everett (Wash.).
COLLEGE: Washington.
TRANSACTIONS/CAREER NOTES: Selected by Indianapolis Colts in third round (76th pick overall) of 1988 NFL draft. ... Signed by Colts (July 23, 1988). ... On injured reserve with knee injury (October 3, 1989-remainder of season). ... Traded by Colts to Tampa Bay Buccaneers for first round pick (LB Quentin Coryatt) in 1992 draft (August 7, 1990). ... Claimed on waivers by Phoenix Cardinals (November 6, 1991). ... Granted unconditional free agency (February 17, 1994). ... Signed by Los Angeles Rams (May 6, 1994). ... Granted unconditional free agency (February 17, 1995). ... Signed by Houston Oilers (March 10, 1995). ... Traded by Oilers to Atlanta Falcons for fourth- (WR Derrick Mason) and sixth-round (traded to New Orleans) picks in 1997 draft (February 24, 1997). ... Released by Falcons (February 25, 2002). ... Signed by Chicago Bears (April 12, 2002). ... Released by Bears (March 19, 2004). ... Signed by St. Louis Rams (March 23, 2004).
CHAMPIONSHIP GAME EXPERIENCE: Played in NFC championship game (1998 season). ... Played in Super Bowl 33 (1998 season).
HONORS: Played in Pro Bowl (1997 and 1998 seasons).
SINGLE GAME HIGHS (regular season): Attempts—50 (November 18, 2001, vs. Green Bay); completions—29 (November 18, 2001, vs. Green Bay); yards—431 (December 23, 2001, vs. Buffalo); and touchdown passes—4 (November 28, 1999, vs. Carolina).
STATISTICAL PLATEAUS: 300-yard passing games: 1992 (1), 1995 (1), 1998 (1), 1999 (2), 2001 (2). Total: 7.
MISCELLANEOUS: Regular-season record as starting NFL quarterback: 67-83 (.447). ... Postseason record as starting NFL quarterback: 2-1 (.667).

			PASSING									RUSHING				TOTALS		
Year Team	**G**	**GS**	**Att.**	**Cmp.**	**Pct.**	**Yds.**	**TD**	**Int.**	**Avg.**	**Skd.**	**Rat.**	**Att.**	**Yds.**	**Avg.**	**TD**	**TD**	**2pt.**	**Pts.**
1988—Indianapolis NFL	15	13	233	129	55.4	1619	8	12	6.95	18	67.2	46	139	3.0	3	3	0	18
1989—Indianapolis NFL	3	3	80	39	48.8	537	2	3	6.71	3	63.4	7	57	8.1	1	1	0	6
1990—Tampa Bay NFL	7	3	83	42	50.6	464	1	6	5.59	15	41.4	13	71	5.5	1	1	0	6
1991—Tampa Bay NFL	6	3	104	53	51.0	557	4	8	5.36	10	47.6	18	79	4.4	0	0	0	0
—Phoenix NFL	3	2	50	25	50.0	289	1	2	5.78	7	57.8	8	32	4.0	0	0	0	0
1992—Phoenix NFL	15	13	413	245	59.3	2832	15	15	6.86	29	77.1	36	149	4.1	1	1	0	6
1993—Phoenix NFL	4	2	103	52	50.5	471	3	2	4.57	4	64.8	3	2	0.7	0	0	0	0
1994—L.A. Rams NFL	12	6	176	108	61.4	1352	7	2	7.68	7	93.8	18	61	3.4	1	1	0	6
1995—Houston NFL	13	13	356	225	63.2	2460	17	10	6.91	21	87.8	28	58	2.1	2	2	1	14
1996—Houston NFL	12	12	320	184	57.5	2099	16	11	6.56	25	79.7	28	113	4.0	0	0	0	0
1997—Atlanta NFL	14	14	342	202	59.1	2692	20	7	7.87	39	95.1	43	158	3.7	0	0	0	0
1998—Atlanta NFL	14	14	327	190	58.1	3154	25	12	*9.65	45	100.9	36	121	3.4	2	2	0	12
1999—Atlanta NFL	12	12	307	174	56.7	2339	16	11	7.62	32	83.5	16	57	3.6	1	1	0	6
2000—Atlanta NFL	14	13	331	192	58.0	2236	10	12	6.76	40	73.5	21	60	2.9	0	0	0	0
2001—Atlanta NFL	14	14	365	223	61.1	2847	16	14	7.80	41	84.1	25	84	3.4	0	0	0	0
2002—Chicago NFL	9	7	161	103	64.0	1023	4	4	6.35	23	79.8	10	32	3.2	0	0	0	0
2003—Chicago NFL	8	6	192	107	55.7	1050	3	7	5.47	14	61.3	14	35	2.5	0	0	1	2
Pro totals (16 years)	175	150	3943	2293	58.2	28021	168	138	7.11	373	79.8	370	1308	3.5	12	12	2	76

CHANDLER, JEFF — K — JAGUARS

PERSONAL: Born June 18, 1979, in Jacksonville, Fla. ... 6-2/218. ... Full name: Jeffrey Robin Chandler.
HIGH SCHOOL: Mandarin (Jacksonville, Fla.).
COLLEGE: Florida.
TRANSACTIONS/CAREER NOTES: Selected by San Francisco 49ers in fourth round (102nd pick overall) of 2002 NFL draft. ... Signed by 49ers (July 21, 2002). ... Waived by 49ers (September 16, 2003). ... Signed by Jacksonville Jaguars (March 16, 2004).

		FIELD GOALS							TOTALS		
Year Team	**G**	**1-29**	**30-39**	**40-49**	**50+**	**Tot.**	**Pct.**	**Lg.**	**XPM**	**XPA**	**Pts.**
2002—San Francisco NFL	6	3-3	1-1	4-7	0-1	8-12	66.7	47	14	14	38
2003—San Francisco NFL	2	5-5	1-1	0-1	0-0	6-7	85.7	35	7	8	25
Pro totals (2 years)	8	8-8	2-2	4-8	0-1	14-19	73.7	47	21	22	63

CHAPMAN, DOUG — RB — CHARGERS

PERSONAL: Born August 22, 1977, in Chesterfield, Va. ... 5-10/213.
HIGH SCHOOL: Lloyd C. Bird (Chesterfield, Va.).
COLLEGE: Marshall.

TRANSACTIONS/CAREER NOTES: Selected by Minnesota Vikings in third round (88th pick overall) of 2000 NFL draft. ... Signed by Vikings (July 23, 2000). ... Inactive for 16 games (2000). ... On injured reserve with internal injury (October 23, 2002-remainder of season). ... Granted free agency (February 28, 2003). ... Re-signed by Vikings (April 1, 2003). ... Released by Vikings (November 25, 2003). ... Signed by San Diego Chargers (January 7, 2004).

CHAMPIONSHIP GAME EXPERIENCE: Member of Vikings for NFC championship game (2000 season); inactive.

SINGLE GAME HIGHS (regular season): Attempts—22 (October 21, 2001, vs. Green Bay); yards—90 (October 21, 2001, vs. Green Bay); and rushing touchdowns—0.

			RUSHING				RECEIVING				KICKOFF RETURNS				TOTALS			
Year Team	G	GS	Att.	Yds.	Avg.	TD	No.	Yds.	Avg.	TD	No.	Yds.	Avg.	TD	TD	2pt.	Pts.	Fum.
2000—Minnesota NFL							Did not play.											
2001—Minnesota NFL	16	3	63	195	3.1	0	16	135	8.4	1	0	0	0.0	0	1	0	6	1
2002—Minnesota NFL	6	0	12	89	7.4	0	0	0	0.0	0	11	225	20.5	0	0	0	0	1
2003—Minnesota NFL	4	0	15	33	2.2	0	1	8	8.0	0	4	51	12.8	0	0	0	0	0
Pro totals (3 years)	26	3	90	317	3.5	0	17	143	8.4	1	15	276	18.4	0	1	0	6	2

CHARLTON, IKE — CB — RAIDERS

PERSONAL: Born October 6, 1977, in Orlando, Fla. ... 5-11/199. ... Full name: Isaac C. Charlton IV.

HIGH SCHOOL: Dr. Phillips (Orlando, Fla.).

COLLEGE: Virginia Tech.

TRANSACTIONS/CAREER NOTES: Selected after junior season by Seattle Seahawks in second round (52nd pick overall) of 2000 NFL draft. ... Signed by Seahawks (July 20, 2000). ... Traded by Seahawks to Jacksonville Jaguars for conditional seventh-round draft pick (K Josh Brown) in 2003 draft (June 21, 2002). ... Released by Jaguars (August 30, 2003). ... Signed by New York Giants (November 11, 2003). ... Granted unconditional free agency (March 3, 2004). ... Signed by Oakland Raiders (March 10, 2004).

			TOTALS			INTERCEPTIONS				KICKOFF RETURNS				TOTALS			
Year Team	G	GS	Tk.	Ast.	Sks.	No.	Yds.	Avg.	TD	No.	Yds.	Avg.	TD	TD	2pt.	Pts.	Fum.
2000—Seattle NFL	16	0	11	2	0.0	0	0	0.0	0	0	0	0.0	0	0	0	0	0
2001—Seattle NFL	15	1	25	2	1.0	2	43	21.5	1	0	0	0.0	0	1	0	6	0
2002—Jacksonville NFL	15	0	22	0	1.0	0	0	0.0	0	10	236	23.6	0	0	0	0	1
2003—New York Giants NFL	7	2	9	3	0.0	0	0	0.0	0	0	0	0.0	0	0	0	0	0
Pro totals (4 years)	53	3	67	7	2.0	2	43	21.5	1	10	236	23.6	0	1	0	6	1

CHASE, MARTIN — DT — GIANTS

PERSONAL: Born December 19, 1974, in Lawton, Okla. ... 6-2/310. ... Full name: Cecil Martin Chase.

HIGH SCHOOL: Eisenhower (Lawton, Okla.).

COLLEGE: Oklahoma.

TRANSACTIONS/CAREER NOTES: Selected by Baltimore Ravens in fifth round (124th pick overall) of 1998 NFL draft. ... Signed by Ravens (July 17, 1998). ... On injured reserve with ankle injury (August 25, 1998-entire season). ... Assigned by Ravens to Frankfurt Galaxy in 2000 NFL Europe enhancement allocation program (February 18, 2000). ... Claimed on waivers by New Orleans Saints (August 28, 2000). ... Granted free agency (March 2, 2001). ... Re-signed by Saints (April 16, 2001). ... Traded by Saints to Washington Redskins for seventh-round pick (traded to Tampa Bay) in 2004 draft (August 20, 2003). ... Granted unconditional free agency (March 3, 2004). ... Signed by New York Giants (March 17, 2004).

			TOTALS		
Year Team	G	GS	Tk.	Ast.	Sks.
1998—Baltimore NFL		Did not play.			
1999—Baltimore NFL	3	0	0	1	0.0
2000—New Orleans NFL	9	0	3	0	0.0
2001—New Orleans NFL	16	3	16	6	1.0
2002—New Orleans NFL	13	1	15	4	0.0
2003—Washington NFL	13	2	12	2	0.0
Pro totals (5 years)	54	6	46	13	1.0

CHATHAM, MATT — LB — PATRIOTS

PERSONAL: Born June 28, 1977, in Sioux City, Iowa. ... 6-4/250.

HIGH SCHOOL: Sioux City (Iowa).

COLLEGE: South Dakota.

TRANSACTIONS/CAREER NOTES: Signed as non-drafted free agent by St. Louis Rams (April 26, 1999). ... Released by Rams (June 26, 1999). ... Signed by Rams (February 11, 2000). ... Claimed on waivers by New England Patriots (August 28, 2000). ... Released by Patriots (September 2, 2001). ... Re-signed by Patriots to practice squad (September 4, 2001). ... Activated (September 22, 2001). ... Released by Patriots (September 25, 2001). ... Re-signed by Patriots to practice squad (September 26, 2001). ... Activated (October 3, 2001). ... On injured reserve with hand injury (December 11, 2002-remainder of season). ... Granted free agency (February 28, 2003). ... Re-signed by Patriots (April 11, 2003).

CHAMPIONSHIP GAME EXPERIENCE: Played in AFC championship game (2001 and 2003 seasons). ... Member of Super Bowl championship team (2001 and 2003 seasons).

			TOTALS			INTERCEPTIONS			
Year Team	G	GS	Tk.	Ast.	Sks.	No.	Yds.	Avg.	TD
2000—New England NFL	6	0	0	0	0.0	0	0	0.0	0
2001—New England NFL	11	0	2	0	0.0	0	0	0.0	0
2002—New England NFL	13	0	2	0	0.0	0	0	0.0	0
2003—New England NFL	16	4	14	7	1.5	0	0	0.0	0
Pro totals (4 years)	46	4	18	7	1.5	0	0	0.0	0

CHATMAN, ANTONIO WR/KR PACKERS

PERSONAL: Born February 12, 1979, in Jackson, Ala. ... 5-9/177. ... Full name: Antonio Tavaras Chatman.
HIGH SCHOOL: Dorsey (Los Angeles, Calif.).
JUNIOR COLLEGE: El Camino (Torrence, Calif.).
COLLEGE: Cincinnati.
TRANSACTIONS/CAREER NOTES: Signed as non-drafted free agent by San Francisco 49ers (April 26, 2001). ... Released by 49ers (August 24, 2001). ... Signed by Green Bay Packers (June 2, 2003).

			RECEIVING				PUNT RETURNS				KICKOFF RETURNS				TOTALS			
Year Team	G	GS	No.	Yds.	Avg.	TD	No.	Yds.	Avg.	TD	No.	Yds.	Avg.	TD	TD	2pt.	Pts.	Fum.
2003—Green Bay NFL	16	0	0	0	0.0	0	33	277	8.4	0	36	804	22.3	0	0	0	0	0

CHATMAN, JESSE RB CHARGERS

PERSONAL: Born September 22, 1979, in Houston, Texas. ... 5-8/215.
HIGH SCHOOL: Franklin (Seattle).
COLLEGE: Eastern Washington.
TRANSACTIONS/CAREER NOTES: Signed as non-drafted free agent by San Diego Chargers (April 26, 2002).
SINGLE GAME HIGHS (regular season): Attempts—4 (September 28, 2003, vs. Oakland); yards—18 (November 24, 2002, vs. Miami); and rushing touchdowns—0.

C

			RUSHING				RECEIVING				TOTALS			
Year Team	G	GS	Att.	Yds.	Avg.	TD	No.	Yds.	Avg.	TD	TD	2pt.	Pts.	Fum.
2002—San Diego NFL	10	0	6	19	3.2	0	3	44	14.7	0	0	0	0	0
2003—San Diego NFL	16	0	8	17	2.1	0	5	54	10.8	0	0	0	0	0
Pro totals (2 years)	26	0	14	36	2.6	0	8	98	12.3	0	0	0	0	0

CHAVOUS, COREY S VIKINGS

PERSONAL: Born January 15, 1976, in Aiken, S.C. ... 6-1/205. ... Name pronounced: CHAY-vus.
HIGH SCHOOL: Silver Bluff (Aiken, S.C.).
COLLEGE: Vanderbilt.
TRANSACTIONS/CAREER NOTES: Selected by Arizona Cardinals in second round (33rd pick overall) of 1998 NFL draft. ... Signed by Cardinals (July 23, 1998). ... Granted free agency (March 2, 2001). ... Re-signed by Cardinals (July 13, 2001). ... Granted unconditional free agency (March 1, 2002). ... Signed by Minnesota Vikings (March 25, 2002).
HONORS: Played in Pro Bowl (2003 season).

			TOTALS			INTERCEPTIONS			
Year Team	G	GS	Tk.	Ast.	Sks.	No.	Yds.	Avg.	TD
1998—Arizona NFL	16	5	20	5	0.0	2	0	0.0	0
1999—Arizona NFL	15	4	28	8	0.0	1	1	1.0	0
2000—Arizona NFL	16	1	39	3	0.0	1	0	0.0	0
2001—Arizona NFL	14	14	59	12	0.0	1	0	0.0	0
2002—Minnesota NFL	16	16	66	17	1.0	3	76	25.3	1
2003—Minnesota NFL	16	16	74	11	0.0	8	143	17.9	1
Pro totals (6 years)	93	56	286	56	1.0	16	220	13.8	2

CHERRY, JE'ROD S PATRIOTS

PERSONAL: Born May 30, 1973, in Charlotte, N.C. ... 6-1/210. ... Full name: Je'Rod L. Cherry. ... Name pronounced: juh-ROD.
HIGH SCHOOL: Berkeley (Calif.).
COLLEGE: California.
TRANSACTIONS/CAREER NOTES: Selected by New Orleans Saints in second round (40th pick overall) of 1996 NFL draft. ... Signed by Saints (July 3, 1996). ... Granted free agency (February 12, 1999). ... Re-signed by Saints (July 21, 1999). ... Granted unconditional free agency (February 11, 2000). ... Signed by Oakland Raiders (February 19, 2000). ... Released by Raiders (August 27, 2000). ... Signed by Philadelphia Eagles (September 20, 2000). ... Granted unconditional free agency (March 2, 2001). ... Signed by New England Patriots (July 25, 2001). ... Granted unconditional free agency (February 28, 2003). ... Re-signed by Patriots (March 5, 2003). ... Granted unconditional free agency (March 3, 2004). ... Re-signed by Patriots (March 16, 2004).
CHAMPIONSHIP GAME EXPERIENCE: Played in AFC championship game (2001 and 2003 seasons). ... Member of Super Bowl championship team (2001 and 2003 seasons).

			TOTALS			INTERCEPTIONS			
Year Team	G	GS	Tk.	Ast.	Sks.	No.	Yds.	Avg.	TD
1996—New Orleans NFL	13	0	6	2	0.0	0	0	0.0	0
1997—New Orleans NFL	16	0	6	0	0.0	0	0	0.0	0
1998—New Orleans NFL	14	0	23	4	2.0	0	0	0.0	0
1999—New Orleans NFL	16	0	13	1	0.0	0	0	0.0	0
2000—Philadelphia NFL	13	0	0	0	0.0	0	0	0.0	0
2001—New England NFL	16	0	2	1	0.0	0	0	0.0	0
2002—New England NFL	16	0	1	0	0.0	0	0	0.0	0
2003—New England NFL	11	0	4	0	1.0	0	0	0.0	0
Pro totals (8 years)	115	0	55	8	3.0	0	0	0.0	0

CHESTER, LARRY DT DOLPHINS

PERSONAL: Born October 17, 1975, in Hammond, La. ... 6-2/325.
HIGH SCHOOL: Hammond (La.).
JUNIOR COLLEGE: Southwest Mississippi Junior College.

COLLEGE: Temple.
TRANSACTIONS/CAREER NOTES: Signed as non-drafted free agent by Indianapolis Colts (April 24, 1998). ... Released by Colts (August 31, 1998). ... Re-signed by Colts to practice squad (September 2, 1998). ... Activated (September 11, 1998). ... Granted free agency (March 2, 2001). ... Signed by Carolina Panthers (May 15, 2001). ... Granted unconditional free agency (March 1, 2002). ... Signed by Miami Dolphins (March 5, 2002).

			TOTALS		
Year Team	**G**	**GS**	**Tk.**	**Ast.**	**Sks.**
1998—Indianapolis NFL	14	2	20	3	3.0
1999—Indianapolis NFL	16	8	31	10	1.0
2000—Indianapolis NFL	15	0	10	6	2.5
2001—Carolina NFL	11	5	26	10	0.5
2002—Miami NFL	16	16	26	11	1.5
2003—Miami NFL	15	15	20	18	0.0
Pro totals (6 years)	87	46	133	58	8.5

CHREBET, WAYNE WR JETS

PERSONAL: Born August 14, 1973, in Garfield, N.J. ... 5-10/188. ... Name pronounced: kra-BET.
HIGH SCHOOL: Garfield (N.J.).
COLLEGE: Hofstra.
TRANSACTIONS/CAREER NOTES: Signed as non-drafted free agent by New York Jets (April 25, 1995). ... On injured reserve with post-concussion syndrome (November 12, 2003-remainder of season).
CHAMPIONSHIP GAME EXPERIENCE: Played in AFC championship game (1998 season).
SINGLE GAME HIGHS (regular season): Receptions—12 (October 13, 1996, vs. Jacksonville); yards—162 (October 13, 1996, vs. Jacksonville); and touchdown receptions—2 (December 29, 2002, vs. Green Bay).
STATISTICAL PLATEAUS: 100-yard receiving games: 1996 (1), 1997 (1), 1998 (5), 1999 (1), 2000 (2), 2001 (1). Total: 11.

			RECEIVING				PUNT RETURNS				TOTALS			
Year Team	**G**	**GS**	**No.**	**Yds.**	**Avg.**	**TD**	**No.**	**Yds.**	**Avg.**	**TD**	**TD**	**2pt.**	**Pts.**	**Fum.**
1995—New York Jets NFL	16	16	66	726	11.0	4	0	0	0.0	0	4	0	24	1
1996—New York Jets NFL	16	9	84	909	10.8	3	28	139	5.0	0	3	0	18	5
1997—New York Jets NFL	16	1	58	799	13.8	3	0	0	0.0	0	3	0	18	0
1998—New York Jets NFL	16	15	75	1083	14.4	8	0	0	0.0	0	8	0	48	0
1999—New York Jets NFL	11	11	48	631	13.1	3	0	0	0.0	0	3	0	18	0
2000—New York Jets NFL	16	16	69	937	13.6	8	0	0	0.0	0	8	0	48	0
2001—New York Jets NFL	15	15	56	750	13.4	1	0	0	0.0	0	1	0	6	0
2002—New York Jets NFL	15	15	51	691	13.5	9	0	0	0.0	0	9	0	54	2
2003—New York Jets NFL	7	5	27	289	10.7	1	0	0	0.0	0	1	0	6	0
Pro totals (9 years)	128	103	534	6815	12.8	40	28	139	5.0	0	40	0	240	8

CHRISTIE, STEVE K

PERSONAL: Born November 13, 1967, in Hamilton, Ont. ... 6-0/195. ... Full name: Geoffrey Stephen Christie.
HIGH SCHOOL: Trafalgar (Oakville, Ont.).
COLLEGE: William & Mary.
TRANSACTIONS/CAREER NOTES: Signed as non-drafted free agent by Tampa Bay Buccaneers (May 8, 1990). ... Granted unconditional free agency (February 1, 1992). ... Signed by Buffalo Bills (February 5, 1992). ... Granted unconditional free agency (March 2, 2001). ... Re-signed by Bills (April 22, 2001). ... On injured reserve with groin injury (September 8-October 3, 2001). ... Released by Bills (October 3, 2001). ... Signed by San Diego Chargers (November 29, 2001). ... Granted unconditional free agency (March 1, 2002). ... Re-signed by Chargers (March 29, 2002). ... Granted unconditional free agency (February 28, 2003). ... Re-signed by Chargers (April 7, 2003). ... Granted unconditional free agency (March 3, 2004).
CHAMPIONSHIP GAME EXPERIENCE: Played in AFC championship game (1992 and 1993 seasons). ... Played in Super Bowl 27 (1992 season) and Super Bowl 28 (1993 season).
POST SEASON RECORDS: Holds Super Bowl single-game record for longest field goal—54 yards (January 30, 1994, vs. Dallas). ... Shares NFL postseason single-game record for most field goals made—5; and most field goals attempted—6 (January 17, 1993, at Miami).

		FIELD GOALS							TOTALS		
Year Team	**G**	**1-29**	**30-39**	**40-49**	**50+**	**Tot.**	**Pct.**	**Lg.**	**XPM**	**XPA**	**Pts.**
1990—Tampa Bay NFL	16	7-7	10-13	4-5	2-2	23-27	85.2	54	27	27	96
1991—Tampa Bay NFL	16	5-5	7-11	3-4	0-0	15-20	75.0	49	22	22	67
1992—Buffalo NFL	16	11-11	3-6	7-8	3-5	24-30	80.0	†54	§43	§44	115
1993—Buffalo NFL	16	4-5	12-12	6-9	1-6	23-32	71.9	*59	36	37	105
1994—Buffalo NFL	16	11-12	6-7	5-7	2-2	24-28	85.7	52	§38	§38	110
1995—Buffalo NFL	16	13-14	13-15	3-6	2-5	31-40	77.5	51	33	35	126
1996—Buffalo NFL	16	5-6	12-14	7-8	0-1	24-29	82.8	48	33	33	105
1997—Buffalo NFL	16	6-6	9-12	8-10	1-2	24-30	80.0	†55	21	21	93
1998—Buffalo NFL	16	11-13	12-14	9-11	1-3	33-*41	80.5	52	41	41	§140
1999—Buffalo NFL	16	12-12	7-10	3-9	3-3	25-34	73.5	52	33	33	108
2000—Buffalo NFL	16	13-15	4-6	9-13	0-1	26-35	74.3	48	31	31	109
2001—San Diego NFL	5	4-4	3-5	2-2	0-0	9-11	81.8	41	6	6	33
2002—San Diego NFL	16	8-8	5-6	4-9	1-3	18-26	69.2	53	35	36	89
2003—San Diego NFL	16	7-7	3-3	3-7	2-3	15-20	75.0	51	36	36	81
Pro totals (14 years)	213	117-125	106-134	73-108	18-36	314-403	77.9	59	435	440	1377

CIURCIU, VINNY LB PANTHERS

PERSONAL: Born May 2, 1980, in Hackensack, N.J. ... 5-11/235. ... Full name: Vincenzo Ciurciu.
HIGH SCHOOL: St. Joseph (Paramus, N.J.).
COLLEGE: Boston College.

TRANSACTIONS/CAREER NOTES: Signed as non-drafted free agent by Carolina Panthers (May 2, 2003). ... Released by Panthers (August 31, 2003). ... Signed by Tampa Bay Buccaneers (October 7, 2003). ... Released by Buccaneers (December 2, 2003). ... Signed by Carolina Panthers to practice squad (December 5, 2003). ... Activated (December 20, 2003).

			TOTALS			INTERCEPTIONS			
Year Team	G	GS	Tk.	Ast.	Sks.	No.	Yds.	Avg.	TD
2003—Tampa Bay NFL	8	0	0	0	0.0	0	0	0.0	0
—Carolina NFL	2	0	0	0	0.0	0	0	0.0	0
Pro totals (1 years)	10	0	0	0	0.0	0	0	0.0	0

CLAIBORNE, CHRIS LB VIKINGS

PERSONAL: Born July 26, 1978, in San Diego, Calif. ... 6-3/259.
HIGH SCHOOL: John W. North (Riverside, Calif.).
COLLEGE: Southern California.
TRANSACTIONS/CAREER NOTES: Selected after junior season by Detroit Lions in first round (ninth pick overall) of 1999 NFL draft. ... Signed by Lions (July 24, 1999). ... Granted unconditional free agency (February 28, 2003). ... Signed by Minnesota Vikings (March 24, 2003).
HONORS: Butkus Award winner (1998). ... Named inside linebacker on THE SPORTING NEWS college All-America first team (1998).

C

			TOTALS			INTERCEPTIONS			
Year Team	G	GS	Tk.	Ast.	Sks.	No.	Yds.	Avg.	TD
1999—Detroit NFL	15	13	50	16	1.5	0	0	0.0	0
2000—Detroit NFL	16	14	65	39	0.5	1	1	1.0	0
2001—Detroit NFL	16	16	77	43	4.0	2	11	5.5	0
2002—Detroit NFL	16	15	72	29	4.5	3	63	21.0	1
2003—Minnesota NFL	12	12	61	19	3.0	1	3	3.0	0
Pro totals (5 years)	75	70	325	146	13.5	7	78	11.1	1

CLANCY, KENDRICK DT STEELERS

PERSONAL: Born September 17, 1978, in Tuscaloosa, Ala. ... 6-1/292.
HIGH SCHOOL: Holt (Tuscaloosa, Ala.).
JUNIOR COLLEGE: East Central Community College (Miss.).
COLLEGE: Mississippi.
TRANSACTIONS/CAREER NOTES: Selected by Pittsburgh Steelers in third round (72nd pick overall) of 2000 NFL draft. ... Signed by Steelers (July 16, 2000). ... Granted free agency (February 28, 2003). ... Re-signed by Steelers (April 16, 2003). ... Granted unconditional free agency (March 3, 2004). ... Re-signed by Steelers (April 28, 2004).
CHAMPIONSHIP GAME EXPERIENCE: Played in AFC championship game (2001 season).
HONORS: Named defensive tackle on THE SPORTING NEWS college All-America third team (1999).

			TOTALS			INTERCEPTIONS			
Year Team	G	GS	Tk.	Ast.	Sks.	No.	Yds.	Avg.	TD
2000—Pittsburgh NFL	9	0	5	3	0.0	0	0	0.0	0
2001—Pittsburgh NFL	16	4	6	4	0.0	1	3	3.0	0
2002—Pittsburgh NFL	7	0	1	0	0.0	0	0	0.0	0
2003—Pittsburgh NFL	10	0	3	0	0.0	0	0	0.0	0
Pro totals (4 years)	42	4	15	7	0.0	1	3	3.0	0

CLARIDGE, TRAVIS G/T PANTHERS

PERSONAL: Born March 23, 1978, in Detroit, Mich. ... 6-5/300.
HIGH SCHOOL: Fort Vancouver (Vancouver, Wash.).
COLLEGE: Southern California.
TRANSACTIONS/CAREER NOTES: Selected by Atlanta Falcons in second round (37th pick overall) of 2000 NFL draft. ... Signed by Falcons (May 16, 2000). ... On injured reserve with knee injury (November 4, 2003-remainder of season). ... Granted unconditional free agency (March 3, 2004). ... Signed by Carolina Panthers (April 19, 2004).
PLAYING EXPERIENCE: Atlanta NFL, 2000-2003. ... Games/Games started: 2000 (16/16), 2001 (14/11), 2002 (16/16), 2003 (6/6). Total: 52/49.
HONORS: Named guard on THE SPORTING NEWS college All-America third team (1999).

CLARK, DALLAS TE COLTS

PERSONAL: Born June 12, 1979, in Livermore, Iowa. ... 6-3/257.
HIGH SCHOOL: Twin River Valley (Livermore, Iowa).
COLLEGE: Iowa.
TRANSACTIONS/CAREER NOTES: Selected after junior season by Indianapolis Colts in first round (24th pick overall) of 2003 NFL draft. ... Signed by Colts (August 9, 2003).
CHAMPIONSHIP GAME EXPERIENCE: Played in AFC championship game (2003 season).
SINGLE GAME HIGHS (regular season): Receptions—5 (November 16, 2003, vs. New York Jets); yards—100 (November 16, 2003, vs. New York Jets); and touchdown receptions—1 (September 28, 2003, vs. New Orleans).
STATISTICAL PLATEAUS: 100-yard receiving games: 2003 (1). Total: 1.

			RECEIVING				TOTALS			
Year Team	G	GS	No.	Yds.	Avg.	TD	TD	2pt.	Pts.	Fum.
2003—Indianapolis NFL	10	10	29	340	11.7	1	1	0	6	0

CLARK, DANNY — LB — RAIDERS

PERSONAL: Born May 9, 1977, in Blue Island, Ill. ... 6-2/248. ... Full name: Daniel Clark IV.
HIGH SCHOOL: Hillcrest (Ill.).
COLLEGE: Illinois.
TRANSACTIONS/CAREER NOTES: Selected by Jacksonville Jaguars in seventh round (245th pick overall) of 2000 NFL draft. ... Signed by Jaguars (June 6, 2000). ... Granted free agency (February 28, 2003). ... Re-signed by Jaguars (May 5, 2003). ... Granted unconditional free agency (March 3, 2004). ... Signed by Oakland Raiders (March 12, 2004).

			TOTALS			INTERCEPTIONS			
Year Team	G	GS	Tk.	Ast.	Sks.	No.	Yds.	Avg.	TD
2000—Jacksonville NFL	16	0	4	0	0.0	0	0	0.0	0
2001—Jacksonville NFL	13	3	18	3	0.0	0	0	0.0	0
2002—Jacksonville NFL	16	16	69	22	2.0	1	7	7.0	0
2003—Jacksonville NFL	16	9	26	11	0.0	0	0	0.0	0
Pro totals (4 years)	61	28	117	36	2.0	1	7	7.0	0

CLARK, DESMOND — TE — BEARS

PERSONAL: Born April 20, 1977, in Bartow, Fla. ... 6-3/255. ... Full name: Desmond Darice Clark.
HIGH SCHOOL: Kathleen (Lakeland, Fla.).
COLLEGE: Wake Forest.
TRANSACTIONS/CAREER NOTES: Selected by Denver Broncos in sixth round (179th pick overall) of 1999 NFL draft. ... Signed by Broncos (June 14, 1999). ... Granted free agency (March 1, 2002). ... Re-signed by Broncos (April 16, 2002). ... Claimed on waivers by Miami Dolphins (September 2, 2002). ... Granted unconditional free agency (February 28, 2003). ... Signed by Chicago Bears (March 1, 2003).
SINGLE GAME HIGHS (regular season): Receptions—7 (November 5, 2001, vs. Oakland); yards—94 (October 28, 2001, vs. New England); and touchdown receptions—1 (November 9, 2003, vs. Detroit).

			RECEIVING				TOTALS			
Year Team	G	GS	No.	Yds.	Avg.	TD	TD	2pt.	Pts.	Fum.
1999—Denver NFL	9	0	1	5	5.0	0	0	0	0	0
2000—Denver NFL	16	2	27	339	12.6	3	3	0	18	0
2001—Denver NFL	16	4	51	566	11.1	6	6	0	36	3
2002—Miami NFL	11	0	2	42	21.0	0	0	0	0	0
2003—Chicago NFL	15	15	44	433	9.8	2	2	0	12	2
Pro totals (5 years)	67	21	125	1385	11.1	11	11	0	66	5

CLARK, KENNY — WR — VIKINGS

PERSONAL: Born May 14, 1978, in Gainesville, Fla. ... 6-1/217.
HIGH SCHOOL: Ocala Vanguard (Fla.).
COLLEGE: Central Florida.
TRANSACTIONS/CAREER NOTES: Signed as non-drafted free agent by Minnesota Vikings (April 23, 2001). ... Released by Vikings (September 2, 2001). ... Re-signed by Vikings to practice squad (September 11, 2001). ... On injured reserve with back injury (August 27, 2002-remainder of season). ... Released by Vikings (October 17, 2003). ... Re-signed by Vikings to practice squad (October 21, 2003).

			RECEIVING				KICKOFF RETURNS				TOTALS			
Year Team	G	GS	No.	Yds.	Avg.	TD	No.	Yds.	Avg.	TD	TD	2pt.	Pts.	Fum.
2003—Minnesota NFL	1	0	0	0	0.0	0	2	33	16.5	0	0	0	0	0

CLARK, RYAN — S

PERSONAL: Born October 12, 1979, in Marrero, La. ... 5-11/200. ... Full name: Ryan Terry Clark.
HIGH SCHOOL: Shaw (New Orleans).
COLLEGE: Louisiana State.
TRANSACTIONS/CAREER NOTES: Signed as non-drafted free agent by New York Giants (April 26, 2002). ... Released by Giants (October 21, 2002). ... Re-signed by Giants to practice squad (October 23, 2002). ... Activated (January 8, 2003). ... Released by Giants (May 26, 2004).

			TOTALS			INTERCEPTIONS			
Year Team	G	GS	Tk.	Ast.	Sks.	No.	Yds.	Avg.	TD
2002—New York Giants NFL	6	0	0	1	0.0	0	0	0.0	0
2003—New York Giants NFL	16	4	17	0	1.0	0	0	0.0	0
Pro totals (2 years)	22	4	17	1	1.0	0	0	0.0	0

CLAYBROOKS, DEVONE — DT — BUCCANEERS

PERSONAL: Born September 15, 1977, in Martinsville, Va. ... 6-3/292. ... Full name: Natravis DeVone Claybrooks. ... Cousin of Shawn Moore, quarterback with Denver Broncos (1991-93).
HIGH SCHOOL: Bassett (Va.).
COLLEGE: East Carolina.
TRANSACTIONS/CAREER NOTES: Signed as non-drafted free agent by Green Bay Packers (May 18, 2001). ... Released by Packers (September 2, 2001). ... Signed by Tampa Bay Buccaneers to practice squad (September 4, 2001). ... Released by Buccaneers (October 16, 2001). ... Signed by Cleveland Browns to practice squad (October 30, 2001). ... Activated (November 7, 2001); did not play. ... Assigned by Browns to Rhein Fire in 2002 NFL Europe enhancement allocation program (February 12, 2002). ... Released by Browns (July 26, 2002). ... Signed by Buccaneers to practice squad (November 6, 2002). ... Activated (November 15, 2002). ... Released by Buccaneers (November 18, 2002). ... Re-signed by Buccaneers to practice squad (November 20, 2002). ... Activated (November 23, 2002). ... Released by Buccaneers (August 31,

C

2003). ... Signed by San Francisco 49ers (September 30, 2003). ... Waived by 49ers (December 23, 2003). ... Signed by Atlanta Falcons (December 29, 2003). ... Waived by Falcons (March 9, 2004). ... Signed by Buccaneers (May 5, 2004).
CHAMPIONSHIP GAME EXPERIENCE: Played in NFC championship game (2002 season). ... Member of Super Bowl championship team (2002 season).

			TOTALS			INTERCEPTIONS			
Year Team	**G**	**GS**	**Tk.**	**Ast.**	**Sks.**	**No.**	**Yds.**	**Avg.**	**TD**
2002—Tampa Bay NFL	2	0	2	3	0.0	0	0	0.0	0
2003—San Francisco NFL	3	0	0	1	0.0	0	0	0.0	0
Pro totals (2 years)	5	0	2	4	0.0	0	0	0.0	0

CLAYBROOKS, FELIPE DE BROWNS

PERSONAL: Born January 22, 1978, in Decatur, Ga. ... 6-5/275.
HIGH SCHOOL: Decatur (Ga.).
COLLEGE: Georgia Tech.
TRANSACTIONS/CAREER NOTES: Signed as non-drafted free agent by Arizona Cardinals (May 4, 2001). ... Waived by Cardinals (August 27, 2001). ... Signed by Cleveland Browns to practice squad (November 7, 2001). ... Activated (December 11, 2001). ... On injured reserve with knee injury (September 1, 2002-entire season). ... Released by Browns (November 26, 2003). ... Signed by Browns to practice squad (November 27, 2003). ... Activated (December 10, 2003). ... Assigned by Browns to Cologne Centurions in 2004 NFL Europe enhancement allocation program (February 9, 2004).

			TOTALS		
Year Team	**G**	**GS**	**Tk.**	**Ast.**	**Sks.**
2001—Cleveland NFL	4	0	1	1	0.0
2003—Cleveland NFL	7	0	0	0	0.0
Pro totals (2 years)	11	0	1	1	0.0

C

CLEELAND, CAM TE

PERSONAL: Born August 15, 1975, in Sedro-Woolley, Wash. ... 6-4/272. ... Full name: Cameron Ross Cleeland.
HIGH SCHOOL: Sedro Woolley (Wash.).
COLLEGE: Washington.
TRANSACTIONS/CAREER NOTES: Selected by New Orleans Saints in second round (40th pick overall) of 1998 NFL draft. ... Signed by Saints (June 9, 1998). ... On injured reserve with Achilles injury (August 22, 2000-entire season). ... Granted free agency (March 2, 2001). ... Re-signed by Saints (March 19, 2001). ... On injured reserve with Achilles injury (December 26, 2001-remainder of season). ... Granted unconditional free agency (March 1, 2002). ... Signed by New England Patriots (March 28, 2002). ... Granted unconditional free agency (February 28, 2003). ... Signed by St. Louis Rams (April 4, 2003). ... Granted unconditional free agency (March 3, 2004).
SINGLE GAME HIGHS (regular season): Receptions—10 (December 27, 1998, vs. Buffalo); yards—112 (December 27, 1998, vs. Buffalo); and touchdown receptions—2 (October 14, 2001, vs. Carolina).
STATISTICAL PLATEAUS: 100-yard receiving games: 1998 (1). Total: 1.

			RECEIVING				TOTALS			
Year Team	**G**	**GS**	**No.**	**Yds.**	**Avg.**	**TD**	**TD**	**2pt.**	**Pts.**	**Fum.**
1998—New Orleans NFL	16	16	54	684	12.7	6	6	0	36	1
1999—New Orleans NFL	11	8	26	325	12.5	1	1	1	8	1
2000—New Orleans NFL						Did not play.				
2001—New Orleans NFL	9	7	13	138	10.6	4	4	0	24	1
2002—New England NFL	12	1	16	112	7.0	1	1	0	6	0
2003—St. Louis NFL	16	10	10	145	14.5	0	0	0	0	1
Pro totals (5 years)	64	42	119	1404	11.8	12	12	1	74	4

CLEMENT, ANTHONY T CARDINALS

PERSONAL: Born April 10, 1976, in Lafayette, La. ... 6-8/333.
HIGH SCHOOL: Cecilia (La.).
COLLEGE: Louisiana-Lafayette.
TRANSACTIONS/CAREER NOTES: Selected by Arizona Cardinals in second round (36th pick overall) of 1998 NFL draft. ... Signed by Cardinals (June 16, 1998). ... On injured reserve with back injury (November 17, 1998-remainder of season). ... Granted free agency (March 2, 2001). ... Re-signed by Cardinals (May 7, 2001). ... Granted unconditional free agency (March 1, 2002). ... Re-signed by Cardinals (March 3, 2002). ... On injured reserve with triceps injury (November 23, 2002-remainder of season).
PLAYING EXPERIENCE: Arizona NFL, 1998-2003. ... Games/Games started: 1998 (1/0), 1999 (16/14), 2000 (16/16), 2001 (16/16), 2002 (1/0), 2003 (16/16). Total: 66/62.

CLEMENTS, NATE CB BILLS

PERSONAL: Born December 12, 1979, in Shaker Heights, Ohio. ... 6-0/209.
HIGH SCHOOL: Shaker Heights (Ohio).
COLLEGE: Ohio State.
TRANSACTIONS/CAREER NOTES: Selected after junior season by Buffalo Bills in first round (21st pick overall) of 2001 NFL draft. ... Signed by Bills (July 28, 2001).

			TOTALS			INTERCEPTIONS				PUNT RETURNS				KICKOFF RETURNS				TOTALS			
Year Team	**G**	**GS**	**Tk.**	**Ast.**	**Sks.**	**No.**	**Yds.**	**Avg.**	**TD**	**No.**	**Yds.**	**Avg.**	**TD**	**No.**	**Yds.**	**Avg.**	**TD**	**TD**	**2pt.**	**Pts.**	**Fum.**
2001—Buf. NFL	16	11	55	10	1.0	3	48	16.0	1	4	81	20.2	1	30	628	20.9	0	2	0	12	1
2002—Buf. NFL	16	16	51	13	0.0	6	82	13.7	1	4	20	5.0	0	0	0	0.0	0	1	0	6	1
2003—Buf. NFL	16	16	51	11	0.0	3	54	18.0	1	14	137	9.8	0	0	0	0.0	0	1	0	6	3
Pro totals (3 years)	48	43	157	34	1.0	12	184	15.3	3	22	238	10.8	1	30	628	20.9	0	4	0	24	5

CLEMONS, CHARLIE LB

PERSONAL: Born July 4, 1972, in Griffin, Ga. ... 6-2/250. ... Full name: Charlie Fitzgerald Clemons.
HIGH SCHOOL: Griffin (Ga.).
JUNIOR COLLEGE: Northeast Oklahoma Junior College.
COLLEGE: Georgia.
TRANSACTIONS/CAREER NOTES: Signed by Winnipeg Blue Bombers of CFL (May 1994). ... Transferred to Ottawa Rough Riders of CFL (August 1995). ... Transferred back to Blue Bombers (January 1996). ... Signed as non-drafted free agent by St. Louis Rams (February 19, 1997). ... On injured reserve with hamstring injury (November 24, 1997-remainder of season). ... Granted free agency (February 11, 2000). ... Tendered offer sheet by New Orleans Saints (February 16, 2000). ... Rams declined to match offer (February 22, 2000). ... On injured reserve with Achilles' tendon injury (October 2, 2000-remainder of season). ... Granted unconditional free agency (February 28, 2003). ... Signed by Houston Texans (April 2, 2003). ... On injured reserve with ankle injury (December 8, 2003-remainder of season). ... Released by Texans (May 18, 2004).
CHAMPIONSHIP GAME EXPERIENCE: Played in NFC championship game (1999 season). ... Member of Super Bowl championship team (1999 season).

			TOTALS			INTERCEPTIONS			
Year Team	G	GS	Tk.	Ast.	Sks.	No.	Yds.	Avg.	TD
1994—Winnipeg CFL	7	...	28	...	0.0	...	...	0.0	...
1995—Winnipeg CFL	6	...	16	...	3.0	...	...	0.0	...
—Ottawa CFL	7	...	26	...	3.0	...	...	0.0	...
1996—Winnipeg CFL	14	...	37	...	6.0	...	...	0.0	...
1997—St. Louis NFL	5	0	1	0	0.0	0	0	0.0	0
1998—St. Louis NFL	16	0	13	2	2.0	0	0	0.0	0
1999—St. Louis NFL	16	0	30	4	3.0	1	0	0.0	0
2000—New Orleans NFL				Did not play.					
2001—New Orleans NFL	16	15	75	18	13.5	1	3	3.0	0
2002—New Orleans NFL	16	14	60	24	0.5	0	0	0.0	0
2003—Houston NFL	9	8	17	8	1.0	0	0	0.0	0
CFL Totals (3 years)	34	...	107	...	12.0	0	0	0.0	0
NFL totals (6 years)	78	37	196	56	20.0	2	3	1.5	0
Pro totals (9 years)	112	...	303	...	32.0	...	...	1.5	...

C

CLEMONS, DUANE DE BENGALS

PERSONAL: Born May 23, 1974, in Riverside, Calif. ... 6-5/275.
HIGH SCHOOL: John W. North (Riverside, Calif.).
COLLEGE: California.
TRANSACTIONS/CAREER NOTES: Selected after junior season by Minnesota Vikings in first round (16th pick overall) of 1996 NFL draft. ... Signed by Vikings (July 25, 1996). ... Granted unconditional free agency (February 11, 2000). ... Signed by Kansas City Chiefs (March 24, 2000). ... Released by Chiefs (February 26, 2003). ... Signed by Cincinnati Bengals (May 13, 2003).
CHAMPIONSHIP GAME EXPERIENCE: Played in NFC championship game (1998 season).

			TOTALS		
Year Team	G	GS	Tk.	Ast.	Sks.
1996—Minnesota NFL	13	0	2	5	0.0
1997—Minnesota NFL	13	3	23	1	7.0
1998—Minnesota NFL	16	3	17	8	2.5
1999—Minnesota NFL	16	9	29	7	9.0
2000—Kansas City NFL	12	12	47	9	7.5
2001—Kansas City NFL	16	15	37	12	7.0
2002—Kansas City NFL	16	16	28	8	2.0
2003—Cincinnati NFL	16	13	35	7	6.0
Pro totals (8 years)	118	71	218	57	41.0

CLIFTON, CHAD T PACKERS

PERSONAL: Born June 26, 1976, in Martin, Tenn. ... 6-5/330. ... Full name: Jeffrey Chad Clifton.
HIGH SCHOOL: Westview (Martin, Tenn.).
COLLEGE: Tennessee.
TRANSACTIONS/CAREER NOTES: Selected by Green Bay Packers in second round (44th pick overall) of 2000 NFL draft. ... Signed by Packers (July 24, 2000). ... On injured reserve with hip injury (December 4, 2002-remainder of season). ... Designated by Packers as franchise player (February 24, 2004). ... Re-signed by Packers (March 3, 2004).
PLAYING EXPERIENCE: Green Bay NFL, 2000-2003. ... Games/Games started: 2000 (13/10), 2001 (14/13), 2002 (10/9), 2003 (16/16). Total: 53/48.
HONORS: Named offensive tackle on THE SPORTING NEWS college All-America second team (1999).

CLOUD, MIKE RB PATRIOTS

PERSONAL: Born July 1, 1975, in Charleston, S.C. ... 5-10/205. ... Full name: Michael Alexander Cloud.
HIGH SCHOOL: Portsmouth (R.I.).
COLLEGE: Boston College.
TRANSACTIONS/CAREER NOTES: Selected by Kansas City Chiefs in second round (54th pick overall) of 1999 NFL draft. ... Signed by Chiefs (July 30, 1999). ... Granted unconditional free agency (February 28, 2003). ... Signed by New England Patriots (June 23, 2003). ... On suspended list for violating league substance abuse policy (August 31-October 5, 2003).
CHAMPIONSHIP GAME EXPERIENCE: Member of Patriots for AFC championship game (2003 season); inactive. ... Member of Patriots for Super Bowl 38 (2003 season); inactive.

SINGLE GAME HIGHS (regular season): Attempts—16 (December 22, 2002, vs. San Diego); yards—73 (October 5, 2003, vs. Tennessee); and rushing touchdowns—2 (November 30, 2003, vs. Indianapolis).

			RUSHING				RECEIVING				KICKOFF RETURNS				TOTALS			
Year Team	**G**	**GS**	**Att.**	**Yds.**	**Avg.**	**TD**	**No.**	**Yds.**	**Avg.**	**TD**	**No.**	**Yds.**	**Avg.**	**TD**	**TD**	**2pt.**	**Pts.**	**Fum.**
1999—Kansas City NFL	11	0	35	128	3.7	0	3	25	8.3	0	2	28	14.0	0	0	0	0	0
2000—Kansas City NFL	16	4	30	84	2.8	1	2	16	8.0	0	36	779	21.6	0	2	0	12	0
2001—Kansas City NFL	15	0	7	54	7.7	1	0	0	0.0	0	8	174	21.8	0	1	0	6	0
2002—Kansas City NFL	14	2	49	115	2.3	2	6	48	8.0	0	0	0	0.0	0	2	0	12	0
2003—New England NFL	5	1	27	118	4.4	5	1	8	8.0	0	2	38	19.0	0	5	0	30	0
Pro totals (5 years)	61	7	148	499	3.4	9	12	97	8.1	0	48	1019	21.2	0	10	0	60	0

COADY, RICH — S — RAMS

PERSONAL: Born January 26, 1976, in Dallas, Texas. ... 6-1/210. ... Full name: Richard Joseph Coady IV. ... Son of Rich Coady, tight end/center with Chicago Bears (1970-74).

HIGH SCHOOL: J.J. Pearce (Richardson, Texas).

COLLEGE: Texas A&M.

TRANSACTIONS/CAREER NOTES: Selected by St. Louis Rams in third round (68th pick overall) of 1999 NFL draft. ... Signed by Rams (July 16, 1999). ... On injured reserve with neck injury (December 13, 2000-remainder of season). ... Claimed on waivers by Tennessee Titans (August 29, 2002). ... Granted unconditional free agency (February 28, 2003). ... Signed by Indianapolis Colts (March 6, 2003). ... Traded by Colts to St. Louis Rams for seventh-round pick (K David Kimball) in 2004 draft (August 31, 2003). ... Granted unconditional free agency (March 3, 2004). ... Re-signed by Rams (March 23, 2004).

CHAMPIONSHIP GAME EXPERIENCE: Played in NFC championship game (1999 season). ... Member of Super Bowl championship team (1999 season). ... Member of Rams for NFC championship game (2001 season); inactive. ... Member of Rams for Super Bowl 36 (2001 season); inactive. ... Played in AFC championship game (2002 season).

			TOTALS			INTERCEPTIONS			
Year Team	**G**	**GS**	**Tk.**	**Ast.**	**Sks.**	**No.**	**Yds.**	**Avg.**	**TD**
1999—St. Louis NFL	16	0	3	0	0.0	1	11	11.0	0
2000—St. Louis NFL	12	2	17	1	0.0	0	0	0.0	0
2001—St. Louis NFL	12	2	18	3	1.0	0	0	0.0	0
2002—Tennessee NFL	14	2	10	3	0.0	1	24	24.0	1
2003—St. Louis NFL	13	5	26	3	0.0	0	0	0.0	0
Pro totals (5 years)	67	11	74	10	1.0	2	35	17.5	1

COAKLEY, DEXTER — LB — COWBOYS

PERSONAL: Born October 20, 1972, in Charleston, S.C. ... 5-10/236. ... Full name: William Dexter Coakley.

HIGH SCHOOL: Wando (Mt. Pleasant, S.C.), then Fork Union (Va.) Military Academy.

COLLEGE: Appalachian State.

TRANSACTIONS/CAREER NOTES: Selected by Dallas Cowboys in third round (65th pick overall) of 1997 NFL draft. ... Signed by Cowboys (July 14, 1997). ... Granted free agency (February 11, 2000). ... Re-signed by Cowboys (April 28, 2000). ... Granted unconditional free agency (March 2, 2001). ... Re-signed by Cowboys (March 8, 2001).

HONORS: Played in Pro Bowl (1999, 2001 and 2003 seasons).

			TOTALS			INTERCEPTIONS			
Year Team	**G**	**GS**	**Tk.**	**Ast.**	**Sks.**	**No.**	**Yds.**	**Avg.**	**TD**
1997—Dallas NFL	16	16	69	20	2.5	1	6	6.0	0
1998—Dallas NFL	16	16	55	17	2.0	1	18	18.0	0
1999—Dallas NFL	16	16	62	14	1.0	4	119	29.7	1
2000—Dallas NFL	16	16	75	12	0.0	0	0	0.0	0
2001—Dallas NFL	15	15	72	23	0.0	2	39	19.5	†2
2002—Dallas NFL	16	16	81	23	1.0	1	52	52.0	1
2003—Dallas NFL	16	16	71	25	1.0	1	24	24.0	0
Pro totals (7 years)	111	111	485	134	7.5	10	258	25.8	4

COATES, SHERROD — LB — BROWNS

PERSONAL: Born December 22, 1978, in Boynton Beach, Fla. ... 6-2/225.

HIGH SCHOOL: Santa Luces County (Boynton Beach, Fla.).

COLLEGE: Western Kentucky.

TRANSACTIONS/CAREER NOTES: Signed as non-drafted free agent by Cleveland Browns (May 2, 2003).

			TOTALS			INTERCEPTIONS			
Year Team	**G**	**GS**	**Tk.**	**Ast.**	**Sks.**	**No.**	**Yds.**	**Avg.**	**TD**
2003—Cleveland NFL	16	0	0	0	0.0	0	0	0.0	0

COBOURNE, AVON — RB — LIONS

PERSONAL: Born March 6, 1979, in Camden, N.J. ... 5-8/205.

HIGH SCHOOL: Holy Cross (N.J.).

COLLEGE: West Virginia.

TRANSACTIONS/CAREER NOTES: Signed as non-drafted free agent by Detroit Lions (May 2, 2003). ... Assigned by Lions to Cologne Centurions in 2004 NFL Europe enhancement allocation program (February 9, 2004).

SINGLE GAME HIGHS (regular season): Attempts—6 (November 9, 2003, vs. Chicago); yards—19 (September 28, 2003, vs. Denver); and rushing touchdowns—0.

Year	Team	G	GS	RUSHING Att.	Yds.	Avg.	TD	RECEIVING No.	Yds.	Avg.	TD	KICKOFF RETURNS No.	Yds.	Avg.	TD	TOTALS TD	2pt.	Pts.	Fum.
2003	—Detroit NFL	7	0	10	27	2.7	0	4	30	7.5	0	7	123	17.6	0	0	0	0	0

COCHRAN, ANTONIO — DE — SEAHAWKS

PERSONAL: Born June 21, 1976, in Montezuma, Ga. ... 6-4/299. ... Full name: Antonio Desez Cochran.
HIGH SCHOOL: Macon County (Montezuma, Ga.).
JUNIOR COLLEGE: Middle Georgia College.
COLLEGE: Georgia.
TRANSACTIONS/CAREER NOTES: Selected by Seattle Seahawks in fourth round (115th pick overall) of 1999 NFL draft. ... Signed by Seahawks (July 27, 1999). ... Granted free agency (March 1, 2002). ... Re-signed by Seahawks (May 2, 2002). ... Granted unconditional free agency (February 28, 2003). ... Re-signed by Seahawks (March 4, 2003).

Year	Team	G	GS	TOTALS Tk.	Ast.	Sks.	INTERCEPTIONS No.	Yds.	Avg.	TD
1999	—Seattle NFL	4	0	2	0	0.0	0	0	0.0	0
2000	—Seattle NFL	15	0	19	3	0.5	0	0	0.0	0
2001	—Seattle NFL	16	2	26	5	4.5	0	0	0.0	0
2002	—Seattle NFL	16	16	37	15	3.0	1	9	9.0	0
2003	—Seattle NFL	15	7	23	6	1.0	0	0	0.0	0
Pro totals (5 years)		66	25	107	29	9.0	1	9	9.0	0

CODY, TAY — CB

PERSONAL: Born October 6, 1977, in Colquitt, Ga. ... 5-9/180.
HIGH SCHOOL: Earl County (Blakely, Ga.).
COLLEGE: Florida State.
TRANSACTIONS/CAREER NOTES: Selected by San Diego Chargers in third round (67th pick overall) of 2001 NFL draft. ... Signed by Chargers (July 24, 2001). ... On injured reserve with toe injury (October 3, 2002-remainder of season). ... Released by Chargers (September 17, 2003).
HONORS: Named cornerback on THE SPORTING NEWS college All-America first team (2000).

Year	Team	G	GS	TOTALS Tk.	Ast.	Sks.	INTERCEPTIONS No.	Yds.	Avg.	TD
2001	—San Diego NFL	14	11	53	6	0.0	2	3	1.5	0
2002	—San Diego NFL	4	0	3	1	0.0	0	0	0.0	0
2003	—San Diego NFL	1	0	2	1	0.0	0	0	0.0	0
Pro totals (3 years)		19	11	58	8	0.0	2	3	1.5	0

COLE, CHRIS — WR — RAIDERS

PERSONAL: Born November 12, 1977, in Orange, Texas. ... 6-0/195. ... Full name: Charles Christopher Cole.
HIGH SCHOOL: West Orange-Stark (Orange, Texas).
COLLEGE: Texas A&M.
TRANSACTIONS/CAREER NOTES: Selected by Denver Broncos in third round (70th pick overall) of 2000 NFL draft. ... Signed by Broncos (July 21, 2000). ... On injured reserve with wrist injury (August 20, 2002-entire season). ... Granted free agency (February 28, 2003). ... Signed by Broncos (April 21, 2003). ... On injured reserve with shoulder and rib injuries (December 5, 2003-remainder of season). ... Granted unconditional free agency (March 3, 2004). ... Signed by Oakland Raiders (April 7, 2004).
SINGLE GAME HIGHS (regular season): Receptions—4 (December 2, 2001, vs. Miami); yards—43 (December 2, 2001, vs. Miami); and touchdown receptions—0.

Year	Team	G	GS	RUSHING Att.	Yds.	Avg.	TD	RECEIVING No.	Yds.	Avg.	TD	KICKOFF RETURNS No.	Yds.	Avg.	TD	TOTALS TD	2pt.	Pts.	Fum.
2000	—Denver NFL	8	0	0	0	0.0	0	0	0	0.0	0	11	264	24.0	0	0	0	0	0
2001	—Denver NFL	16	1	0	0	0.0	0	9	128	14.2	0	48	1127	23.5	0	0	0	0	2
2003	—Denver NFL	11	0	2	8	4.0	0	3	36	12.0	0	30	714	23.8	0	0	0	0	1
Pro totals (3 years)		35	1	2	8	4.0	0	12	164	13.7	0	89	2105	23.7	0	0	0	0	3

COLEMAN, CLARENCE — WR — BILLS

PERSONAL: Born June 4, 1980, in Miami, Fla. ... 5-10/193. ... Full name: Clarence Coleman Jr.
HIGH SCHOOL: Miramar (Fla.).
COLLEGE: Ferris State.
TRANSACTIONS/CAREER NOTES: Signed as non-drafted free agent by Buffalo Bills (April 26, 2002). ... Released by Bills (July 25, 2002). ... Re-signed by Bills (November 20, 2002).
SINGLE GAME HIGHS (regular season): Receptions—3 (December 27, 2003 vs. New England); yards—27 (October 12, 2003, vs. New York Jets); and touchdown receptions—0.

Year	Team	G	GS	RECEIVING No.	Yds.	Avg.	TD	TOTALS TD	2pt.	Pts.	Fum.
2003	—Buffalo NFL	14	0	8	69	8.6	0	0	0	0	0

COLEMAN, COSEY — G — BUCCANEERS

PERSONAL: Born October 27, 1978, in Clarkston, Ga. ... 6-4/322. ... Full name: Cosey Clinton Coleman.
HIGH SCHOOL: DeKalb (Clarkston, Ga.).
COLLEGE: Tennessee.

C

TRANSACTIONS/CAREER NOTES: Selected after junior season by Tampa Bay Buccaneers in second round (51st pick overall) of 2000 NFL draft. ... Signed by Buccaneers (July 23, 2000). ... Granted unconditional free agency (March 3, 2004). ... Re-signed by Buccaneers (March 23, 2004).
PLAYING EXPERIENCE: Tampa Bay NFL, 2000-2003. ... Games/Games started: 2000 (8/0), 2001 (16/16), 2002 (15/15), 2003 (16/16). Total: 55/47.
CHAMPIONSHIP GAME EXPERIENCE: Played in NFC championship game (2002 season). ... Member of Super Bowl championship team (2002 season).

COLEMAN, KENYON DE COWBOYS

PERSONAL: Born April 10, 1979, in Fontana, Calif. ... 6-5/285. ... Full name: Kenyon Octavia Coleman.
HIGH SCHOOL: Alta Loma (Calif.).
COLLEGE: UCLA.
TRANSACTIONS/CAREER NOTES: Selected by Oakland Raiders in fifth round (147th pick overall) of 2002 NFL draft. ... Signed by Raiders (July 24, 2002). ... Traded by Raiders to Dallas Cowboys for a seventh-round pick (later returned to Dallas) in 2004 draft (August 31, 2003).
CHAMPIONSHIP GAME EXPERIENCE: Member of Raiders for AFC championship game (2002 season); inactive. ... Member of Raiders for Super Bowl 37 (2002 season); inactive.
HONORS: Named defensive end on THE SPORTING NEWS college All-America third team (2001).

			TOTALS		
Year Team	G	GS	Tk.	Ast.	Sks.
2002—Oakland NFL	1	0	1	0	0.0
2003—Dallas NFL	16	0	10	4	1.0
Pro totals (2 years)	17	0	11	4	1.0

COLEMAN, MARCO DE BRONCOS

PERSONAL: Born December 18, 1969, in Dayton, Ohio. ... 6-3/286. ... Full name: Marco Darnell Coleman.
HIGH SCHOOL: Patterson Co-op (Dayton, Ohio).
COLLEGE: Georgia Tech.
TRANSACTIONS/CAREER NOTES: Selected after junior season by Miami Dolphins in first round (12th pick overall) of 1992 NFL draft. ... Signed by Dolphins (August 1, 1992). ... Designated by Dolphins as transition player (February 25, 1993). ... Tendered offer sheet by San Diego Chargers (February 28, 1996). ... Dolphins declined to match offer (March 7, 1996). ... Granted unconditional free agency (February 12, 1999). ... Signed by Washington Redskins (June 3, 1999). ... Granted unconditional free agency (February 11, 2000). ... Re-signed by Redskins (February 29, 2000). ... Released by Redskins (June 3, 2002). ... Signed by Jacksonville Jaguars (June 20, 2002). ... Released by Jaguars (August 30, 2003). ... Signed by Philadelphia Eagles (September 5, 2003). ... Granted unconditional free agency (March 3, 2004). ... Signed by Denver Broncos (March 11, 2004).
CHAMPIONSHIP GAME EXPERIENCE: Played in AFC championship game (1992 season). ... Played in NFC championship game (2003 season).
HONORS: Named linebacker on THE SPORTING NEWS college All-America second team (1991). ... Played in Pro Bowl (2000 season).

			TOTALS			INTERCEPTIONS			
Year Team	G	GS	Tk.	Ast.	Sks.	No.	Yds.	Avg.	TD
1992—Miami NFL	16	15	61	23	6.0	0	0	0.0	0
1993—Miami NFL	15	15	35	19	5.5	0	0	0.0	0
1994—Miami NFL	16	16	34	9	6.0	0	0	0.0	0
1995—Miami NFL	16	16	33	12	6.5	0	0	0.0	0
1996—San Diego NFL	16	15	34	8	4.0	0	0	0.0	0
1997—San Diego NFL	16	16	39	9	2.0	1	2	2.0	0
1998—San Diego NFL	16	16	46	5	3.5	0	0	0.0	0
1999—Washington NFL	16	16	54	13	6.5	0	0	0.0	0
2000—Washington NFL	16	16	41	11	12.0	0	0	0.0	0
2001—Washington NFL	12	12	33	6	4.5	0	0	0.0	0
2002—Jacksonville NFL	16	16	29	7	5.0	0	0	0.0	0
2003—Philadelphia NFL	13	0	11	2	0.5	0	0	0.0	0
Pro totals (12 years)	184	169	450	124	62.0	1	2	2.0	0

COLEMAN, MARCUS CB TEXANS

PERSONAL: Born May 24, 1974, in Dallas, Texas. ... 6-2/210.
HIGH SCHOOL: Lake Highlands (Dallas).
COLLEGE: Texas Tech.
TRANSACTIONS/CAREER NOTES: Selected by New York Jets in fifth round (133rd pick overall) of 1996 NFL draft. ... Signed by Jets (July 11, 1996). ... Granted unconditional free agency (February 11, 2000). ... Re-signed by Jets (February 14, 2000). ... Selected by Houston Texans from Jets in NFL expansion draft (February 18, 2002).
CHAMPIONSHIP GAME EXPERIENCE: Played in AFC championship game (1998 season).
MISCELLANEOUS: Holds Houston Texans all-time record for most interceptions (8).

			TOTALS			INTERCEPTIONS			
Year Team	G	GS	Tk.	Ast.	Sks.	No.	Yds.	Avg.	TD
1996—New York Jets NFL	13	4	25	6	0.0	1	23	23.0	0
1997—New York Jets NFL	16	2	8	2	0.0	1	24	24.0	0
1998—New York Jets NFL	14	0	5	1	0.0	0	0	0.0	0
1999—New York Jets NFL	16	10	51	11	0.0	6	165	27.5	1
2000—New York Jets NFL	16	16	50	6	0.0	4	6	1.5	0
2001—New York Jets NFL	16	16	58	11	0.0	2	41	20.5	0
2002—Houston NFL	16	16	60	12	0.0	1	0	0.0	0
2003—Houston NFL	15	15	57	12	0.0	▲7	95	13.6	0
Pro totals (8 years)	122	79	314	61	0.0	22	354	16.1	1

COLEMAN, ROD DT FALCONS

PERSONAL: Born August 16, 1976, in Vicksburg, Miss. ... 6-2/285. ... Full name: Roderick Coleman.
HIGH SCHOOL: Simon Gratz (Philadelphia).
COLLEGE: East Carolina.
TRANSACTIONS/CAREER NOTES: Selected by Oakland Raiders in fifth round (153rd pick overall) of 1999 NFL draft. ... Signed by Raiders (July 24, 1999). ... Granted unconditional free agency (March 3, 2004). ... Signed by Atlanta Falcons (March 8, 2004).
CHAMPIONSHIP GAME EXPERIENCE: Played in AFC championship game (2000 and 2002 seasons). ... Played in Super Bowl 37 (2002 season).

			TOTALS		
Year Team	G	GS	Tk.	Ast.	Sks.
1999—Oakland NFL	3	0	1	0	0.0
2000—Oakland NFL	13	1	16	4	6.0
2001—Oakland NFL	14	6	35	11	6.0
2002—Oakland NFL	14	2	33	5	11.0
2003—Oakland NFL	16	12	44	8	5.5
Pro totals (5 years)	60	21	129	28	28.5

COLES, LAVERANUES WR REDSKINS

PERSONAL: Born December 29, 1977, in Jacksonville, Fla. ... 5-11/193.
HIGH SCHOOL: Jean Ribault (Jacksonville).
COLLEGE: Florida State.
TRANSACTIONS/CAREER NOTES: Selected by New York Jets in third round (78th pick overall) of 2000 NFL draft. ... Signed by Jets (May 1, 2000). ... Granted free agency (February 28, 2003). ... Tendered offer sheet by Washington Redskins (March 13, 2003). ... Jets declined to match offer (March 19, 2003).
HONORS: Played in Pro Bowl (2003 season).
SINGLE GAME HIGHS (regular season): Receptions—11 (September 14, 2003, vs. Atlanta); yards—180 (September 14, 2003, vs. Atlanta); and touchdown receptions—2 (December 21, 2003, vs. Chicago).
STATISTICAL PLATEAUS: 100-yard receiving games: 2000 (1), 2001 (1), 2002 (4), 2003 (4). Total: 10.

			RUSHING				RECEIVING				KICKOFF RETURNS				TOTALS			
Year Team	G	GS	Att.	Yds.	Avg.	TD	No.	Yds.	Avg.	TD	No.	Yds.	Avg.	TD	TD	2pt.	Pts.	Fum.
2000—New York Jets NFL	13	3	2	15	7.5	0	22	370	16.8	1	11	207	18.8	0	1	1	8	0
2001—New York Jets NFL	16	16	10	108	10.8	0	59	868	14.7	7	9	211	23.4	0	7	0	42	1
2002—New York Jets NFL	16	16	6	39	6.5	0	89	1264	14.2	5	0	0	0.0	0	5	1	32	1
2003—Washington NFL	16	16	10	39	3.9	0	82	1204	14.7	6	0	0	0.0	0	6	0	36	0
Pro totals (4 years)	61	51	28	201	7.2	0	252	3706	14.7	19	20	418	20.9	0	19	2	118	2

COLLINS, JAVIAR T COWBOYS

PERSONAL: Born April 13, 1978, in St. Paul, Minn. ... 6-6/322.
HIGH SCHOOL: St. Thomas Academy (St. Paul, Minn.).
COLLEGE: Northwestern.
TRANSACTIONS/CAREER NOTES: Signed as non-drafted free agent by Dallas Cowboys (April 26, 2001). ... Inactive for all 16 games (2001). ... Assigned by Cowboys to Frankfurt Galaxy in 2002 NFL Europe enhancement allocation program (February 12, 2002). ... Granted free agency (March 3, 2004). ... Re-signed by Cowboys (April 22, 2004).
PLAYING EXPERIENCE: Dallas NFL, 2002-2003. ... Games/Games started: 2002 (9/4), 2003 (1/0). Total: 10/4.

COLLINS, KERRY QB RAIDERS

PERSONAL: Born December 30, 1972, in Lebanon, Pa. ... 6-5/248. ... Full name: Kerry Michael Collins.
HIGH SCHOOL: Wilson (West Lawn, Pa.).
COLLEGE: Penn State.
TRANSACTIONS/CAREER NOTES: Selected by Carolina Panthers in first round (fifth pick overall) of 1995 NFL draft. ... Signed by Panthers (July 17, 1995). ... Granted free agency (February 13, 1998). ... Re-signed by Panthers (July 24, 1998). ... Claimed on waivers by New Orleans Saints (October 14, 1998). ... Granted unconditional free agency (February 12, 1999). ... Signed by New York Giants (February 19, 1999). ... Released by Giants (April 28, 2004). ... Signed by Oakland Raiders (May 24, 2004).
CHAMPIONSHIP GAME EXPERIENCE: Played in NFC championship game (1996 and 2000 season). ... Played in Super Bowl 35 (2000 season).
HONORS: Maxwell Award winner (1994). ... Davey O'Brien Award winner (1994). ... Named quarterback on THE SPORTING NEWS college All-America first team (1994). ... Played in Pro Bowl (1996 season).
RECORDS: Shares NFL single-season record for most fumbles—23 (2001).
SINGLE GAME HIGHS (regular season): Attempts—59 (October 12, 2003, vs. New England); completions—36 (January 6, 2002, vs. Green Bay); passing yards—386 (January 6, 2002, vs. Green Bay); and touchdown passes—4 (December 22, 2002, vs. Indianapolis).
STATISTICAL PLATEAUS: 300-yard passing games: 1995 (2), 1996 (1), 1997 (1), 1998 (2), 1999 (2), 2000 (3), 2001 (5), 2002 (4), 2003 (3). Total: 23.
MISCELLANEOUS: Selected by Detroit Tigers organization in 26th round of free-agent draft (June 4, 1990); did not sign. ... Selected by Toronto Blue Jays organization in 48th round of free-agent draft (June 4, 1994); did not sign. ... Regular-season record as starting NFL quarterback: 59-58 (.504). ... Postseason record as starting NFL quarterback: 3-3 (.500).

			PASSING									RUSHING				TOTALS		
Year Team	G	GS	Att.	Cmp.	Pct.	Yds.	TD	Int.	Avg.	Skd.	Rat.	Att.	Yds.	Avg.	TD	TD	2pt.	Pts.
1995—Carolina NFL	15	13	433	214	49.4	2717	14	19	6.27	24	61.9	42	74	1.8	3	3	0	18
1996—Carolina NFL	13	12	364	204	56.0	2454	14	9	6.74	18	79.4	32	38	1.2	0	0	1	2
1997—Carolina NFL	13	13	381	200	52.5	2124	11	*21	5.57	27	55.7	26	65	2.5	1	1	0	6

C

Year Team	G	GS	PASSING Att.	Cmp.	Pct.	Yds.	TD	Int.	Avg.	Skd.	Rat.	RUSHING Att.	Yds.	Avg.	TD	TOTALS TD	2pt.	Pts.
1998—Carolina NFL	4	4	162	76	46.9	1011	8	5	6.24	10	70.8	7	40	5.7	0	0	1	2
—New Orleans NFL	7	7	191	94	49.2	1202	4	10	6.29	21	54.5	23	113	4.9	1	1	0	6
1999—New York Giants NFL	10	7	331	190	57.4	2318	8	11	7.00	16	73.3	19	36	1.9	2	2	1	14
2000—New York Giants NFL	16	16	529	311	58.8	3610	22	13	6.82	28	83.1	41	65	1.6	1	1	0	6
2001—New York Giants NFL	16	16	‡568	327	57.6	3764	19	16	6.63	36	77.1	39	73	1.9	0	0	0	0
2002—New York Giants NFL	16	16	545	335	61.5	‡4073	19	14	‡7.47	24	85.4	44	-3	-0.1	0	0	0	0
2003—New York Giants NFL	13	13	500	284	56.8	3110	13	16	6.22	28	70.7	17	49	2.9	0	0	1	2
Pro totals (9 years)	123	117	4004	2235	55.8	26383	132	134	6.59	232	73.1	290	550	1.9	8	8	4	56

COLLINS, MO — G — RAIDERS

PERSONAL: Born September 22, 1976, in Charlotte, N.C. ... 6-4/325. ... Full name: Damon Jamal Collins.

HIGH SCHOOL: West Charlotte.

COLLEGE: Florida.

TRANSACTIONS/CAREER NOTES: Selected after junior season by Oakland Raiders in first round (23rd pick overall) of 1998 NFL draft. ... Signed by Raiders (July 15, 1998). ... Granted unconditional free agency (February 28, 2003). ... Re-signed by Raiders (May 8, 2003). ... On injured reserve with knee injury (December 16, 2003-remainder of season).

PLAYING EXPERIENCE: Oakland NFL, 1998-2003. ... Games/Games started: 1998 (16/11), 1999 (13/12), 2000 (16/16), 2001 (6/5), 2002 (10/10), 2003 (10/10). Total: 71/64.

CHAMPIONSHIP GAME EXPERIENCE: Played in AFC championship game (2000 and 2002 seasons). ... Played in Super Bowl 37 (2002 season).

COLLINS, TODD — QB — CHIEFS

PERSONAL: Born November 5, 1971, in Walpole, Mass. ... 6-4/225.

HIGH SCHOOL: Walpole (Mass.).

COLLEGE: Michigan.

TRANSACTIONS/CAREER NOTES: Selected by Buffalo Bills in second round (45th pick overall) of 1995 NFL draft. ... Signed by Bills (July 10, 1995). ... Claimed on waivers by Kansas City Chiefs (August 25, 1998). ... Active for three games (1998); did not play. ... Active for all 16 games (1999); did not play. ... Active for all 16 games (2000); did not play. ... Granted unconditional free agency (February 28, 2003). ... Re-signed by Chiefs (March 24, 2003).

SINGLE GAME HIGHS (regular season): Attempts—44 (October 6, 1996, vs. Indianapolis); completions—25 (November 23, 1997, vs. Tennessee); yards—309 (October 6, 1996, vs. Indianapolis); and touchdown passes—3 (September 7, 1997, vs. New York Jets).

STATISTICAL PLATEAUS: 300-yard passing games: 1996 (1). Total: 1.

MISCELLANEOUS: Regular-season record as starting NFL quarterback: 7-10 (.412).

Year Team	G	GS	PASSING Att.	Cmp.	Pct.	Yds.	TD	Int.	Avg.	Skd.	Rat.	RUSHING Att.	Yds.	Avg.	TD	TOTALS TD	2pt.	Pts.
1995—Buffalo NFL	7	1	29	14	48.3	112	0	1	3.86	6	44.0	9	23	2.6	0	0	0	0
1996—Buffalo NFL	7	3	99	55	55.6	739	4	5	7.46	11	71.9	21	43	2.0	0	0	0	0
1997—Buffalo NFL	14	13	391	215	55.0	2367	12	13	6.05	39	69.5	30	77	2.6	0	0	0	0
1998—Kansas City NFL	Did not play.																	
1999—Kansas City NFL	Did not play.																	
2000—Kansas City NFL	Did not play.																	
2001—Kansas City NFL	1	0	4	3	75.0	40	0	0	10.00	0	106.2	2	6	3.0	0	0	0	0
2002—Kansas City NFL	3	0	6	5	83.3	73	1	0	12.17	0	156.9	1	7	7.0	0	0	0	0
2003—Kansas City NFL	5	0	12	9	75.0	74	0	0	6.17	0	90.3	8	-7	-0.9	0	0	0	0
Pro totals (6 years)	37	17	541	301	55.6	3405	17	19	6.29	56	70.5	71	149	2.1	0	0	0	0

COLOMBO, MARC — T — BEARS

PERSONAL: Born October 8, 1978, in Bridgewater, Mass. ... 6-7/320. ... Full name: Marc Edward Colombo.

HIGH SCHOOL: Bridgewater-Raynham (Bridgewater, Mass.).

COLLEGE: Boston College.

TRANSACTIONS/CAREER NOTES: Selected by Chicago Bears in first round (29th pick overall) of 2002 NFL draft. ... Signed by Bears (July 25, 2002). ... On injured reserve with knee injury (November 26, 2002-remainder of season). ... On physically unable to perform list with knee injury (August 27-November 4, 2003). ... On injured reserve with knee injury (November 4, 2003-remainder of season).

PLAYING EXPERIENCE: Chicago NFL, 2002-2003. ... Games/Games started: 2002 (10/5), Total: 10/5.

COLVIN, ROSEVELT — LB — PATRIOTS

PERSONAL: Born September 5, 1977, in Indianapolis, Ind. ... 6-3/250.

HIGH SCHOOL: Broad Ripple (Indianapolis).

COLLEGE: Purdue.

TRANSACTIONS/CAREER NOTES: Selected by Chicago Bears in fourth round (111th pick overall) of 1999 NFL draft. ... Signed by Bears (July 21, 1999). ... Granted free agency (March 1, 2002). ... Re-signed by Bears (April 19, 2002). ... Granted unconditional free agency (February 28, 2003). ... Signed by New England Patriots (March 11, 2003). ... On injured reserve with hip injury (September 22, 2003-remainder of season).

Year Team	G	GS	TOTALS Tk.	Ast.	Sks.	INTERCEPTIONS No.	Yds.	Avg.	TD
1999—Chicago NFL	11	0	10	2	2.0	0	0	0.0	0
2000—Chicago NFL	13	8	25	9	3.0	0	0	0.0	0
2001—Chicago NFL	16	13	60	10	10.5	2	22	11.0	0
2002—Chicago NFL	16	15	55	9	10.5	0	0	0.0	0
2003—New England NFL	2	2	3	2	2.0	0	0	0.0	0
Pro totals (5 years)	58	38	153	32	28.0	2	22	11.0	0

COMBS, DEREK CB PACKERS

PERSONAL: Born February 28, 1979, in Columbus, Ohio. ... 6-0/185.
HIGH SCHOOL: Grove City (Urbancrest, Ohio).
COLLEGE: Ohio State.
TRANSACTIONS/CAREER NOTES: Selected by Oakland Raiders in seventh round (228th pick overall) of 2001 NFL draft. ... Signed by Raiders (July 21, 2001). ... Released by Raiders (September 2, 2001). ... Signed by Tennessee Titans to practice squad (September 4, 2001). ... Released by Titans (September 5, 2001). ... Signed by Miami Dolphins to practice squad (September 11, 2001). ... Released by Dolphins (September 18, 2001). ... Re-signed by Dolphins to practice squad (September 26, 2001). ... Released by Dolphins (October 2, 2001). ... Signed by Raiders to practice squad (October 18, 2001). ... Released by Raiders (November 1, 2001). ... Re-signed by Raiders to practice squad (November 7, 2001). ... Released by Raiders (October 9, 2002). ... Signed by Kansas City Chiefs (February 1, 2003). ... Traded by Chiefs to Green Bay Packers for conditional pick in 2005 draft (April 24, 2003). ... Assigned by Packers to Amsterdam Admirals in 2004 NFL Europe enhancement allocation program (February 9, 2004).

			TOTALS			INTERCEPTIONS				KICKOFF RETURNS				TOTALS			
Year Team	G	GS	Tk.	Ast.	Sks.	No.	Yds.	Avg.	TD	No.	Yds.	Avg.	TD	TD	2pt.	Pts.	Fum.
2002—Oakland NFL	4	0	0	0	0.0	0	0	0.0	0	5	71	14.2	0	0	0	0	0
2003—Green Bay NFL	8	0	2	0	0.0	0	0	0.0	0	0	0	0.0	0	0	0	0	0
Pro totals (2 years)	12	0	2	0	0.0	0	0	0.0	0	5	71	14.2	0	0	0	0	0

COMELLA, GREG FB BUCCANEERS

C

PERSONAL: Born July 29, 1975, in Wellesley, Mass. ... 6-1/248. ... Name pronounced: Ka-MELL-uh.
HIGH SCHOOL: Xaverian Brothers (Westwood, Mass.).
COLLEGE: Stanford.
TRANSACTIONS/CAREER NOTES: Signed as non-drafted free agent by New York Giants (April 24, 1998). ... Granted free agency (March 2, 2001). ... Re-signed by Giants (April 18, 2001). ... Granted unconditional free agency (March 1, 2002). ... Signed by Tennessee Titans (April 19, 2002). ... Released by Titans (August 31, 2003). ... Signed by Houston Texans (September 1, 2003). ... Granted unconditional free agency (March 3, 2004). ... Signed by Tampa Bay Buccaneers (March 3, 2004).
CHAMPIONSHIP GAME EXPERIENCE: Played in NFC championship game (2000 season). ... Played in Super Bowl 35 (2000 season). ... Member of Titans for AFC championship game (2002 season); inactive.
SINGLE GAME HIGHS (regular season): Attempts—3 (November 5, 2000, vs. Cleveland); yards—19 (September 10, 2000, vs. Philadelphia); and rushing touchdowns—0.

			RUSHING				RECEIVING				TOTALS			
Year Team	G	GS	Att.	Yds.	Avg.	TD	No.	Yds.	Avg.	TD	TD	2pt.	Pts.	Fum.
1998—New York Giants NFL	16	0	1	6	6.0	0	1	3	3.0	0	0	0	0	0
1999—New York Giants NFL	16	3	1	0	0.0	0	8	39	4.9	0	0	0	0	0
2000—New York Giants NFL	16	12	10	45	4.5	0	36	274	7.6	0	0	0	0	2
2001—New York Giants NFL	16	13	4	15	3.8	0	39	253	6.5	1	1	0	6	2
2002—Tennessee NFL	12	7	1	0	0.0	0	10	70	7.0	0	0	0	0	1
2003—Houston NFL	5	0	0	0	0.0	0	0	0	0.0	0	0	0	0	0
Pro totals (6 years)	81	35	17	66	3.9	0	94	639	6.8	1	1	0	6	5

COMPTON, MIKE G/C JAGUARS

PERSONAL: Born September 18, 1970, in Richlands, Va. ... 6-6/310. ... Full name: Michael Eugene Compton.
HIGH SCHOOL: Richlands (Va.).
COLLEGE: West Virginia.
TRANSACTIONS/CAREER NOTES: Selected by Detroit Lions in third round (68th pick overall) of 1993 NFL draft. ... Signed by Lions (June 4, 1993). ... Granted unconditional free agency (March 2, 2001). ... Signed by New England Patriots (April 2, 2001). ... On injured reserve with foot injury (September 22, 2003-remainder of season). ... Granted unconditional free agency (March 3, 2004). ... Signed by Jacksonville Jaguars (March 9, 2004).
PLAYING EXPERIENCE: Detroit NFL, 1993-2000; New England NFL, 2001-2003. ... Games/Games started: 1993 (8/0), 1994 (3/0), 1995 (16/7), 1996 (15/15), 1997 (16/16), 1998 (16/16), 1999 (15/15), 2000 (16/16), 2001 (16/16), 2002 (16/16), 2003 (2/2). Total: 139/119.
CHAMPIONSHIP GAME EXPERIENCE: Played in AFC championship game (2001 season). ... Member of Super Bowl championship team (2001 season).
HONORS: Named center on THE SPORTING NEWS college All-America first team (1992).

CONWAY, BRETT K

PERSONAL: Born March 8, 1975, in Atlanta, Ga. ... 6-2/208. ... Full name: Brett Alan Conway.
HIGH SCHOOL: Parkview (Lilburn, Ga.).
COLLEGE: Penn State.
TRANSACTIONS/CAREER NOTES: Selected by Green Bay Packers in third round (90th pick overall) of 1997 NFL draft. ... Signed by Packers (July 8, 1997). ... On injured reserve with thigh injury (September 3, 1997-entire season). ... Traded by Packers to New York Jets for an undisclosed draft pick (August 21, 1998). ... Released by Jets (August 30, 1998). ... Re-signed by Jets to practice squad (September 1, 1998). ... Released by Jets (September 23, 1998). ... Signed by Washington Redskins (November 12, 1998). ... Granted free agency (February 11, 2000). ... Re-signed by Redskins (May 31, 2000). ... Released by Redskins (September 20, 2000). ... Signed by Oakland Raiders (November 11, 2000). ... Released by Raiders (November 21, 2000). ... Signed by Jets (December 18, 2000). ... Granted unconditional free agency (March 2, 2001). ... Signed by Redskins (March 15, 2001). ... On injured reserve with leg injury (September 10-December 5, 2002). ... Released by Redskins (December 5, 2002). ... Signed by Indianapolis Colts (January 23, 2003). ... Waived by Colts (August 31, 2003). ... Signed by New York Giants (October 6, 2003). ... Released by Giants (November 15, 2003). ... Signed by Cleveland Browns (December 10, 2003). ... Granted unconditional free agency (March 3, 2004).

		FIELD GOALS							TOTALS		
Year Team	G	1-29	30-39	40-49	50+	Tot.	Pct.	Lg.	XPM	XPA	Pts.
1997—Green Bay NFL	Did not play.										

Year Team	G	FIELD GOALS 1-29	30-39	40-49	50+	Tot.	Pct.	Lg.	TOTALS XPM	XPA	Pts.
1998—Washington NFL	6	0-0	0-0	0-0	0-0	0-0	0.0	0	0	0	0
1999—Washington NFL	16	7-9	6-7	6-7	3-9	22-∞32	68.8	51	49	50	115
2000—Washington NFL	2	3-3	0-0	0-0	0-0	3-3	100.0	26	3	3	12
—Oakland NFL	1	1-1	0-0	0-0	0-0	1-1	100.0	19	3	3	6
—New York Jets NFL	1	1-1	0-0	1-1	0-0	2-2	100.0	40	2	2	8
2001—Washington NFL	16	8-8	8-11	8-12	2-2	26-33	78.8	†55	22	22	100
2002—Washington NFL	1	0-0	1-1	0-0	0-0	1-1	100.0	35	4	4	7
2003—New York Giants NFL	5	3-3	5-6	1-3	0-0	9-12	75.0	44	6	6	33
—Cleveland NFL	3	1-1	1-3	3-3	0-0	5-7	71.4	48	3	3	18
Pro totals (6 years)	51	24-26	21-28	19-26	5-11	69-91	75.8	55	92	93	299

CONWAY, CURTIS WR

PERSONAL: Born January 13, 1971, in Los Angeles, Calif. ... 6-1/196. ... Full name: Curtis LaMont Conway.
HIGH SCHOOL: Hawthorne (Calif.).
JUNIOR COLLEGE: El Camino College (Calif.).
COLLEGE: Southern California.
TRANSACTIONS/CAREER NOTES: Selected after junior season by Chicago Bears in first round (seventh pick overall) of 1993 NFL draft. ... Signed by Bears (May 24, 1993). ... Granted free agency (February 16, 1996). ... Re-signed by Bears (March 4, 1996). ... On injured reserve with (shoulder) injury (December 22, 1999-remainder of season). ... Granted unconditional free agency (February 11, 2000). ... Signed by San Diego Chargers (February 22, 2000). ... Released by Chargers (February 27, 2003). ... Signed by New York Jets (March 20, 2003). ... Released by Jets (March 8, 2004).
HONORS: Named kick returner on THE SPORTING NEWS college All-America second team (1992).
SINGLE GAME HIGHS (regular season): Receptions—11 (December 30, 2001, vs. Seattle); yards—156 (December 30, 2001, vs. Seattle); and touchdown receptions—3 (October 15, 1995, vs. Jacksonville).
STATISTICAL PLATEAUS: 100-yard receiving games: 1994 (1), 1995 (3), 1996 (4), 1997 (3), 1999 (1), 2000 (2), 2001 (4), 2002 (3). Total: 21.

Year Team	G	GS	RUSHING Att.	Yds.	Avg.	TD	RECEIVING No.	Yds.	Avg.	TD	KICKOFF RETURNS No.	Yds.	Avg.	TD	TOTALS TD	2pt.	Pts.	Fum.
1993—Chicago NFL	16	7	5	44	8.8	0	19	231	12.2	2	21	450	21.4	0	2	0	12	1
1994—Chicago NFL	13	12	6	31	5.2	0	39	546	14.0	2	10	228	22.8	0	2	1	14	2
1995—Chicago NFL	16	16	5	77	15.4	0	62	1037	16.7	12	0	0	0.0	0	12	0	72	0
1996—Chicago NFL	16	16	8	50	6.3	0	81	1049	13.0	7	0	0	0.0	0	7	0	42	1
1997—Chicago NFL	7	7	3	17	5.7	0	30	476	15.9	1	0	0	0.0	0	1	0	6	0
1998—Chicago NFL	15	15	5	48	9.6	0	54	733	13.6	3	0	0	0.0	0	3	0	18	1
1999—Chicago NFL	9	8	1	-2	-2.0	0	44	426	9.7	4	0	0	0.0	0	4	0	24	2
2000—San Diego NFL	14	14	3	31	10.3	0	53	712	13.4	5	0	0	0.0	0	5	0	30	0
2001—San Diego NFL	16	16	7	116	16.6	1	71	1125	15.8	6	0	0	0.0	0	7	0	42	1
2002—San Diego NFL	13	13	7	53	7.6	2	57	852	14.9	5	0	0	0.0	0	7	0	42	2
2003—New York Jets NFL	16	15	0	0	0.0	0	46	640	13.9	2	0	0	0.0	0	2	0	12	0
Pro totals (11 years)	151	139	50	465	9.3	3	556	7827	14.1	49	31	678	21.9	0	52	1	314	10

CONWELL, ERNIE TE SAINTS

PERSONAL: Born August 17, 1972, in Renton, Wash. ... 6-2/265. ... Full name: Ernest Harold Conwell.
HIGH SCHOOL: Kentwood (Kent, Wash.).
COLLEGE: Washington.
TRANSACTIONS/CAREER NOTES: Selected by St. Louis Rams in second round (59th pick overall) of 1996 NFL draft. ... Signed by Rams (June 25, 1996). ... On injured reserve with knee injury (October 28, 1998-remainder of season). ... On physically unable to perform list with knee injury (August 30-November 9, 1999). ... Granted unconditional free agency (February 11, 2000). ... Re-signed by Rams (February 11, 2000). ... Granted unconditional free agency (February 28, 2003). ... Signed by New Orleans Saints (April 14, 2003). ... On injured reserve with ankle injury (November 20, 2003-remainder of season).
CHAMPIONSHIP GAME EXPERIENCE: Played in NFC championship game (1999 and 2001 seasons). ... Member of Super Bowl championship team (1999 season). ... Played in Super Bowl 36 (2001 season).
SINGLE GAME HIGHS (regular season): Receptions—6 (September 28, 2003, vs. Indianapolis); yards—88 (September 28, 2003, vs. Indianapolis); and touchdown receptions—1 (October 12, 2003, vs. Chicago).

Year Team	G	GS	RUSHING Att.	Yds.	Avg.	TD	RECEIVING No.	Yds.	Avg.	TD	TOTALS TD	2pt.	Pts.	Fum.
1996—St. Louis NFL	10	8	0	0	0.0	0	15	164	10.9	0	0	0	0	0
1997—St. Louis NFL	16	16	0	0	0.0	0	38	404	10.6	4	4	0	24	0
1998—St. Louis NFL	7	7	0	0	0.0	0	15	105	7.0	0	0	0	0	0
1999—St. Louis NFL	3	0	0	0	0.0	0	1	11	11.0	0	0	0	0	0
2000—St. Louis NFL	16	1	2	23	11.5	0	5	40	8.0	0	0	0	0	0
2001—St. Louis NFL	16	13	7	28	4.0	1	38	431	11.3	4	5	0	30	2
2002—St. Louis NFL	16	10	6	30	5.0	1	34	419	12.3	2	3	0	18	0
2003—New Orleans NFL	10	10	0	0	0.0	0	26	290	11.2	2	2	0	12	1
Pro totals (8 years)	94	65	15	81	5.4	2	172	1864	10.8	12	14	0	84	3

COOK, DAMION T

PERSONAL: Born April 16, 1979, in Nashville, Tenn. ... 6-5/335. ... Full name: Damion Lamar Cook.
HIGH SCHOOL: American Heritage (Fort Lauderdale, Fla.).
COLLEGE: Bethune-Cookman.
TRANSACTIONS/CAREER NOTES: Signed as non-drafted free agent by Baltimore Ravens (April 27, 2001). ... Released by Ravens (September 1, 2001). ... Signed by Chicago Bears (September 28, 2001). ... Inactive for 15 games (2001). ... Assigned by Bears to Barcelona Dragons in

2002 NFL Europe enhancement allocation program (February 12, 2002). ... Released by Bears (September 1, 2002). ... Signed by Miami Dolphins to practice squad (September 10, 2002). ... Signed by Ravens off Dolphins practice squad (September 23, 2002). ... Granted free agency (March 3, 2004).
PLAYING EXPERIENCE: Baltimore NFL, 2002-2003. ... Games/Games started: 2002 (3/0), 2003 (1/0). Total: 4/0.

COOK, JAMEEL — FB — BUCCANEERS

PERSONAL: Born February 8, 1979, in Miami, Fla. ... 5-10/237. ... Full name: Jameel A. Cook.
HIGH SCHOOL: Southridge (Miami).
COLLEGE: Illinois.
TRANSACTIONS/CAREER NOTES: Selected after junior season by Tampa Bay Buccaneers in sixth round (174th pick overall) of 2001 NFL draft. ... Signed by Buccaneers (July 16, 2001). ... Granted free agency (March 3, 2004). ... Re-signed by Buccaneers (April 19, 2004).
CHAMPIONSHIP GAME EXPERIENCE: Played in NFC championship game (2002 season). ... Member of Super Bowl championship team (2002 season).
SINGLE GAME HIGHS (regular season): Attempts—2 (October 28, 2001, vs. Minnesota); yards—2 (October 28, 2001, vs. Minnesota); and rushing touchdowns—0.

			RUSHING				RECEIVING				TOTALS			
Year Team	G	GS	Att.	Yds.	Avg.	TD	No.	Yds.	Avg.	TD	TD	2pt.	Pts.	Fum.
2001—Tampa Bay NFL	16	3	2	2	1.0	0	17	89	5.2	0	0	0	0	0
2002—Tampa Bay NFL	14	1	0	0	0.0	0	4	43	10.8	0	0	0	0	0
2003—Tampa Bay NFL	14	8	1	-1	-1.0	0	20	120	6.0	1	1	0	6	0
Pro totals (3 years)	44	12	3	1	0.3	0	41	252	6.1	1	1	0	6	0

C

COOPER, CHRIS — DE — RAIDERS

PERSONAL: Born December 27, 1977, in Lincoln, Neb. ... 6-5/275.
HIGH SCHOOL: Lincoln Southeast (Neb.).
COLLEGE: Nebraska-Omaha.
TRANSACTIONS/CAREER NOTES: Selected by Oakland Raiders in sixth round (184th pick overall) of 2001 NFL draft. ... Signed by Raiders (July 21, 2001).
CHAMPIONSHIP GAME EXPERIENCE: Played in AFC championship game (2002 season). ... Played in Super Bowl 37 (2002 season).

			TOTALS			INTERCEPTIONS			
Year Team	G	GS	Tk.	Ast.	Sks.	No.	Yds.	Avg.	TD
2001—Oakland NFL	11	1	14	8	2.0	1	0	0.0	0
2002—Oakland NFL	16	1	14	5	1.0	0	0	0.0	0
2003—Oakland NFL	16	9	40	9	2.5	0	0	0.0	0
Pro totals (3 years)	43	11	68	22	5.5	1	0	0.0	0

COOPER, DEKE — S — JAGUARS

PERSONAL: Born October 18, 1977, in Swainsboro, Ga. ... 6-3/215.
HIGH SCHOOL: Evansville (Ind.).
COLLEGE: Notre Dame.
TRANSACTIONS/CAREER NOTES: Signed as non-drafted free agent by Arizona Cardinals (April 18, 2000). ... Released by Cardinals (August 22, 2000). ... Re-signed by Cardinals (February 15, 2001). ... Assigned by Cardinals to Rhein Fire in 2001 NFL Europe enhancement allocation program (February 18, 2001). ... Released by Cardinals (September 1, 2001). ... Signed by Cleveland Browns to practice squad (September 20, 2001). ... Released by Browns (October 9, 2001). ... Signed by Carolina Panthers (January 16, 2002). ... Assigned by Panthers to Rhein Fire in 2002 NFL Europe enhancement allocation program (February 12, 2002). ... Released by Panthers (September 1, 2002). ... Re-signed by Panthers to practice squad (September 3, 2002). ... Activated (October 10, 2002). ... Waived by Panthers (August 31, 2003). ... Re-signed by Panthers to practice squad (September 3, 2003). ... Signed by Jacksonville Jaguars off Panthers practice squad (September 17, 2003).

			TOTALS			INTERCEPTIONS			
Year Team	G	GS	Tk.	Ast.	Sks.	No.	Yds.	Avg.	TD
2002—Carolina NFL	10	0	0	0	0.0	0	0	0.0	0
2003—Jacksonville NFL	14	10	35	16	0.0	1	12	12.0	0
Pro totals (2 years)	24	10	35	16	0.0	1	12	12.0	0

COOPER, JARROD — S — PANTHERS

PERSONAL: Born March 31, 1978, in Akron, Ohio. ... 6-0/210.
HIGH SCHOOL: Pearland (Texas).
COLLEGE: Kansas State.
TRANSACTIONS/CAREER NOTES: Selected by Carolina Panthers in fifth round (143rd pick overall) of 2001 NFL draft. ... Signed by Panthers (July 19, 2001). ... On injured reserve with knee injury (October 16, 2002-remainder of season). ... On suspended list for violating league substance abuse policy (November 19-December 15, 2003). ... Granted free agency (March 3, 2004). ... Re-signed by Panthers (May 15, 2004).
CHAMPIONSHIP GAME EXPERIENCE: Played in NFC championship game (2003 season). ... Played in Super Bowl 38 (2003 season).

			TOTALS			INTERCEPTIONS			
Year Team	G	GS	Tk.	Ast.	Sks.	No.	Yds.	Avg.	TD
2001—Carolina NFL	16	0	9	1	0.0	0	0	0.0	0
2002—Carolina NFL	6	0	2	0	0.0	0	0	0.0	0
2003—Carolina NFL	12	0	1	0	0.0	0	0	0.0	0
Pro totals (3 years)	34	0	12	1	0.0	0	0	0.0	0

COOPER, STEPHEN LB CHARGERS

PERSONAL: Born June 19, 1979, in Wareham, Mass. ... 6-1/235.
HIGH SCHOOL: Wareham (Mass.).
COLLEGE: Maine.
TRANSACTIONS/CAREER NOTES: Signed as non-drafted free agent by San Diego Chargers (May 2, 2003).

			TOTALS			INTERCEPTIONS			
Year Team	G	GS	Tk.	Ast.	Sks.	No.	Yds.	Avg.	TD
2003—San Diego NFL	16	0	5	3	1.0	1	25	25.0	0

CORTEZ, JOSE K

PERSONAL: Born May 27, 1975, in San Vicente, El Salvador. ... 5-11/200. ... Full name: Jose Antonio Cortez.
HIGH SCHOOL: Van Nuys (Calif.).
JUNIOR COLLEGE: Los Angeles Valley College.
COLLEGE: Oregon State.
TRANSACTIONS/CAREER NOTES: Signed as non-drafted free agent by Cleveland Browns (April 23, 1999). ... Released by Browns (June 3, 1999). ... Signed by San Diego Chargers (June 14, 1999). ... Released by Chargers (August 30, 1999). ... Signed by New York Giants to practice squad (December 14, 1999). ... Activated (December 17, 1999). ... Released by Giants (December 21, 1999). ... Signed by San Diego Chargers (January 18, 2000). ... Released by Chargers (August 27, 2000). ... Signed by San Francisco 49ers (May 9, 2001). ... Released by 49ers (November 26, 2002). ... Signed by Washington Redskins (December 2, 2002). ... Claimed on waivers by Kansas City Chiefs (March 14, 2003). ... Released by Chiefs (August 25, 2003). ... Signed by Minnesota Vikings (October 17, 2003). ... Released by Vikings (October 28, 2003).

C

		FIELD GOALS							TOTALS		
Year Team	G	1-29	30-39	40-49	50+	Tot.	Pct.	Lg.	XPM	XPA	Pts.
1999—New York Giants NFL	1	0-0	0-0	0-0	0-0	0-0	0.0	0	0	0	0
2001—San Francisco NFL	16	7-9	6-7	4-8	1-1	18-25	72.0	52	47	47	101
2002—San Francisco NFL	10	8-10	7-8	3-6	0-0	18-24	75.0	45	25	25	79
—Washington NFL	4	3-3	1-1	1-4	0-0	5-8	62.5	44	9	9	24
2003—Minnesota NFL	2	0-0	0-0	0-0	0-0	0-0	0.0	0	0	0	0
Pro totals (4 years)	33	18-22	14-16	8-18	1-1	41-57	71.9	52	81	81	204

COUCH, TIM QB BROWNS

PERSONAL: Born July 31, 1977, in Hyden, Ky. ... 6-4/220. ... Full name: Timothy Scott Couch.
HIGH SCHOOL: Leslie County (Hyden, Ky.).
COLLEGE: Kentucky.
TRANSACTIONS/CAREER NOTES: Selected after junior season by Cleveland Browns in first round (first pick overall) of 1999 NFL draft. ... Signed by Browns (April 17, 1999). ... On injured reserve with broken thumb (October 20, 2000-remainder of season).
HONORS: Named quarterback on THE SPORTING NEWS college All-America third team (1998).
SINGLE GAME HIGHS (regular season): Attempts—50 (September 22, 2002, vs. Tennessee); completions—36 (September 22, 2002, vs. Tennessee); passing yards—336 (December 30, 2001, vs. Tennessee); and touchdown passes—3 (November 17, 2002, vs. Cincinnati).
STATISTICAL PLATEAUS: 300-yard passing games: 2000 (1), 2001 (1), 2002 (1). Total: 3.
MISCELLANEOUS: Regular-season record as starting NFL quarterback: 22-37 (.373).

			PASSING									RUSHING				TOTALS		
Year Team	G	GS	Att.	Cmp.	Pct.	Yds.	TD	Int.	Avg.	Skd.	Rat.	Att.	Yds.	Avg.	TD	TD	2pt.	Pts.
1999—Cleveland NFL	15	14	399	223	55.9	2447	15	13	6.13	*56	73.2	40	267	6.7	1	1	1	8
2000—Cleveland NFL	7	7	215	137	63.7	1483	7	9	6.90	10	77.3	12	45	3.8	0	0	0	0
2001—Cleveland NFL	16	16	454	272	59.9	3040	17	21	6.70	51	73.1	38	128	3.4	0	0	0	0
2002—Cleveland NFL	14	14	443	273	61.6	2842	18	18	6.42	30	76.8	23	77	3.3	0	0	0	0
2003—Cleveland NFL	10	8	203	120	59.1	1319	7	6	6.50	19	77.6	11	39	3.5	1	1	0	6
Pro totals (5 years)	62	59	1714	1025	59.8	11131	64	67	6.49	166	75.1	124	556	4.5	2	2	1	14

COUSIN, TERRY CB GIANTS

PERSONAL: Born March 11, 1975, in Miami, Fla. ... 5-9/181.
HIGH SCHOOL: Miami Beach Senior.
COLLEGE: South Carolina.
TRANSACTIONS/CAREER NOTES: Signed as non-drafted free agent by Chicago Bears (April 25, 1997). ... Released by Bears (August 24, 1997). ... Re-signed by Bears to practice squad (August 26, 1997). ... Activated (October 25, 1997). ... Released by Bears (October 28, 1997). ... Re-signed by Bears to practice squad (October 30, 1997). ... Activated (November 15, 1997). ... Granted free agency (February 11, 2000). ... Re-signed by Bears (April 18, 2000). ... Claimed on waivers by Atlanta Falcons (August 28, 2000). ... Granted unconditional free agency (March 2, 2001). ... Signed by Miami Dolphins (March 15, 2001). ... Granted unconditional free agency (March 1, 2002). ... Signed by Carolina Panthers (March 19, 2002). ... Released by Panthers (March 5, 2004). ... Signed by New York Giants (March 24, 2004).
CHAMPIONSHIP GAME EXPERIENCE: Played in NFC championship game (2003 season). ... Played in Super Bowl 38 (2003 season).

			TOTALS			INTERCEPTIONS			
Year Team	G	GS	Tk.	Ast.	Sks.	No.	Yds.	Avg.	TD
1997—Chicago NFL	6	0	2	2	0.0	0	0	0.0	0
1998—Chicago NFL	16	12	50	12	0.0	1	0	0.0	0
1999—Chicago NFL	16	9	43	12	0.0	2	1	0.5	0
2000—Atlanta NFL	15	0	4	0	0.0	0	0	0.0	0
2001—Miami NFL	16	3	37	13	2.0	0	0	0.0	0
2002—Carolina NFL	16	16	44	15	1.0	2	4	2.0	0
2003—Carolina NFL	13	13	45	4	2.0	0	0	0.0	0
Pro totals (7 years)	98	53	225	58	5.0	5	5	1.0	0

COWART, SAM — LB — JETS

PERSONAL: Born February 26, 1975, in Jacksonville, Fla. ... 6-2/245.
HIGH SCHOOL: Mandarin (Jacksonville).
COLLEGE: Florida State.
TRANSACTIONS/CAREER NOTES: Selected by Buffalo Bills in second round (39th pick overall) of 1998 NFL draft. ... Signed by Bills (July 20, 1998). ... On injured reserve with Achilles' tendon injury (September 26, 2001-remainder of season). ... Granted unconditional free agency (March 1, 2002). ... Signed by New York Jets (March 6, 2002).
HONORS: Named outside linebacker on THE SPORTING NEWS college All-America first team (1997). ... Played in Pro Bowl (2000 season).

			TOTALS			INTERCEPTIONS			
Year Team	**G**	**GS**	**Tk.**	**Ast.**	**Sks.**	**No.**	**Yds.**	**Avg.**	**TD**
1998—Buffalo NFL	16	11	54	18	0.0	2	23	11.5	0
1999—Buffalo NFL	16	16	79	46	1.0	0	0	0.0	0
2000—Buffalo NFL	12	12	88	41	5.5	2	4	2.0	0
2001—Buffalo NFL	1	1	0	2	0.0	0	0	0.0	0
2002—New York Jets NFL	16	16	91	36	2.0	0	0	0.0	0
2003—New York Jets NFL	15	15	96	44	2.0	0	0	0.0	0
Pro totals (6 years)	76	71	408	187	10.5	4	27	6.8	0

COX, TORRIE — CB — BUCCANEERS

PERSONAL: Born October 29, 1980, in Miami. ... 5-9/181. ... Full name: Torrie Tywan Cox.
HIGH SCHOOL: Northwestern (Miami).
COLLEGE: Pittsburgh.
TRANSACTIONS/CAREER NOTES: Selected by Tampa Bay Buccaneers in sixth round (205th pick overall) of 2003 NFL draft. ... On injured reserve with knee injury (August 22, 2003-entire season).

		INTERCEPTIONS				PUNT RETURNS				KICKOFF RETURNS				TOTALS			
Year Team	**G**	**No.**	**Yds.**	**Avg.**	**TD**	**No.**	**Yds.**	**Avg.**	**TD**	**No.**	**Yds.**	**Avg.**	**TD**	**TD**	**2pt.**	**Pts.**	**Fum.**
2003—Tampa Bay NFL	Did not play.																

CRAFT, JASON — CB — SAINTS

PERSONAL: Born February 13, 1976, in Denver, Colo. ... 5-10/176. ... Full name: Jason Donell Andre Craft.
HIGH SCHOOL: Denver East.
JUNIOR COLLEGE: Denver Community College.
COLLEGE: Colorado State.
TRANSACTIONS/CAREER NOTES: Selected by Jacksonville Jaguars in fifth round (160th pick overall) of 1999 NFL draft. ... Signed by Jaguars (May 18, 1999). ... Granted free agency (March 1, 2002). ... Tendered offer sheet by New Orleans Saints (March 5, 2002). ... Offer sheet matched by Jaguars (March 12, 2002). ... On injured reserve with knee injury (December 19, 2003-remainder of season). ... Traded by Jaguars to New Orleans Saints for fifth-round pick (CB Chris Thompson) in 2004 draft (April 8, 2004).
CHAMPIONSHIP GAME EXPERIENCE: Played in AFC championship game (1999 season).

			TOTALS			INTERCEPTIONS			
Year Team	**G**	**GS**	**Tk.**	**Ast.**	**Sks.**	**No.**	**Yds.**	**Avg.**	**TD**
1999—Jacksonville NFL	16	0	2	0	0.0	0	0	0.0	0
2000—Jacksonville NFL	16	3	22	5	0.0	0	0	0.0	0
2001—Jacksonville NFL	16	8	45	6	0.0	2	4	2.0	0
2002—Jacksonville NFL	16	16	49	9	0.0	3	0	0.0	0
2003—Jacksonville NFL	6	6	17	9	0.0	2	29	14.5	0
Pro totals (5 years)	70	33	135	29	0.0	7	33	4.7	0

CRAVER, KEYUO — CB — SAINTS

PERSONAL: Born August 22, 1980, in Dallas, Texas. ... 5-10/195.
HIGH SCHOOL: Harleton (Texas).
COLLEGE: Nebraska.
TRANSACTIONS/CAREER NOTES: Selected by New Orleans Saints in fourth round (125th pick overall) of 2002 NFL draft. ... Signed by Saints (July 24, 2002). ... On suspended list for violating league substance abuse policy (October 7-November 11, 2003).
HONORS: Named cornerback on THE SPORTING NEWS college All-America first team (2001).

			TOTALS			INTERCEPTIONS				PUNT RETURNS				TOTALS			
Year Team	**G**	**GS**	**Tk.**	**Ast.**	**Sks.**	**No.**	**Yds.**	**Avg.**	**TD**	**No.**	**Yds.**	**Avg.**	**TD**	**TD**	**2pt.**	**Pts.**	**Fum.**
2002—New Orleans NFL	10	1	9	3	0.0	0	0	0.0	0	1	0	0.0	0	1	0	6	1
2003—New Orleans NFL	12	0	2	0	0.0	0	0	0.0	0	2	22	11.0	0	0	0	0	0
Pro totals (2 years)	22	1	11	3	0.0	0	0	0.0	0	3	22	7.3	0	1	0	6	1

CROCKER, CHRIS — S — BROWNS

PERSONAL: Born March 9, 1980, in Chesapeake, Va. ... 5-11/194. ... Full name: Christopher Alan Crocker.
HIGH SCHOOL: Deep Creek (Chesapeake, Va.).
COLLEGE: Marshall.
TRANSACTIONS/CAREER NOTES: Selected by Cleveland Browns in third round (84th pick overall) of 2003 NFL draft. ... Signed by Browns (July 31, 2003).

Year	Team	G	GS	TOTALS Tk.	Ast.	Sks.	INTERCEPTIONS No.	Yds.	Avg.	TD
2003—Cleveland NFL		16	1	21	4	0.0	0	0	0.0	0

CROCKETT, HENRI LB

PERSONAL: Born October 28, 1974, in Pompano Beach, Fla. ... 6-2/240. ... Full name: Henri W. Crockett. ... Brother of Zack Crockett, fullback, Oakland Raiders.
HIGH SCHOOL: Ely (Pompano Beach, Fla.).
COLLEGE: Florida State.
TRANSACTIONS/CAREER NOTES: Selected by Atlanta Falcons in fourth round (100th pick overall) of 1997 NFL draft. ... Signed by Falcons (July 14, 1997). ... Granted free agency (February 11, 2000). ... Re-signed by Falcons (June 1, 2000). ... Granted unconditional free agency (March 2, 2001). ... Signed by Denver Broncos (May 4, 2001). ... Traded by Broncos to Falcons for conditional pick in 2002 draft (August 2, 2001). ... Granted unconditional free agency (March 1, 2002). ... Signed by Minnesota Vikings (March 19, 2002). ... Released by Vikings (May 10, 2004).
CHAMPIONSHIP GAME EXPERIENCE: Played in NFC championship game (1998 season). ... Played in Super Bowl 33 (1998 season).

Year	Team	G	GS	TOTALS Tk.	Ast.	Sks.	INTERCEPTIONS No.	Yds.	Avg.	TD
1997—Atlanta NFL		16	10	26	4	2.0	0	0	0.0	0
1998—Atlanta NFL		10	10	22	7	1.0	0	0	0.0	0
1999—Atlanta NFL		16	14	30	12	1.5	0	0	0.0	0
2000—Atlanta NFL		15	12	34	6	2.0	0	0	0.0	0
2001—Atlanta NFL		16	15	46	8	0.0	1	7	7.0	0
2002—Minnesota NFL		14	11	47	14	1.0	0	0	0.0	0
2003—Minnesota NFL		16	15	32	2	0.0	0	0	0.0	0
Pro totals (7 years)		103	87	237	53	7.5	1	7	7.0	0

C

CROCKETT, ZACK FB RAIDERS

PERSONAL: Born December 2, 1972, in Pompano Beach, Fla. ... 6-2/240. ... Brother of Henri Crockett, linebacker with Atlanta Falcons (1997-2001) and Minnesota Vikings (2002-03).
HIGH SCHOOL: Ely (Pompano Beach, Fla.).
JUNIOR COLLEGE: Hinds Community College (Miss.).
COLLEGE: Florida State.
TRANSACTIONS/CAREER NOTES: Selected by Indianapolis Colts in third round (79th pick overall) of 1995 NFL draft. ... Signed by Colts (July 21, 1995). ... On injured reserve with knee injury (October 22, 1996-remainder of season). ... Granted free agency (February 13, 1998). ... Re-signed by Colts (July 23, 1998). ... Claimed on waivers by Jacksonville Jaguars (October 21, 1998). ... Granted unconditional free agency (February 12, 1999). ... Signed by Oakland Raiders (March 16, 1999). ... Granted unconditional free agency (February 28, 2003). ... Re-signed by Raiders (March 4, 2003).
CHAMPIONSHIP GAME EXPERIENCE: Played in AFC championship game (1995, 2000 and 2002 seasons). ... Played in Super Bowl 37 (2002 season).
SINGLE GAME HIGHS (regular season): Attempts—17 (October 28, 2001, vs. Philadelphia); yards—81 (November 2, 1997, vs. Tampa Bay); and rushing touchdowns—2 (November 16, 2003, vs. Minnesota).

Year	Team	G	GS	RUSHING Att.	Yds.	Avg.	TD	RECEIVING No.	Yds.	Avg.	TD	TOTALS TD	2pt.	Pts.	Fum.
1995—Indianapolis NFL		16	0	1	0	0.0	0	2	35	17.5	0	0	0	0	0
1996—Indianapolis NFL		5	5	31	164	5.3	0	11	96	8.7	1	1	0	6	2
1997—Indianapolis NFL		16	11	95	300	3.2	1	15	112	7.5	0	1	0	6	3
1998—Indianapolis NFL		2	1	2	5	2.5	0	1	1	1.0	0	0	0	0	1
—Jacksonville NFL		10	1	0	0	0.0	0	1	4	4.0	0	0	0	0	0
1999—Oakland NFL		13	1	45	91	2.0	4	8	56	7.0	1	5	0	30	0
2000—Oakland NFL		16	3	43	130	3.0	7	10	62	6.2	0	7	0	42	0
2001—Oakland NFL		16	1	57	145	2.5	6	2	10	5.0	0	6	0	36	1
2002—Oakland NFL		16	0	40	118	3.0	8	0	0	0.0	0	8	0	48	0
2003—Oakland NFL		16	6	48	145	3.0	7	7	53	7.6	0	7	0	42	1
Pro totals (9 years)		126	29	362	1098	3.0	33	57	429	7.5	2	35	0	210	8

CROSBY, CLIFF CB/S

PERSONAL: Born September 17, 1974, in Erie, Pa. ... 5-10/179. ... Full name: Clifton Crosby.
HIGH SCHOOL: East (Erie, Pa.).
COLLEGE: Maryland.
TRANSACTIONS/CAREER NOTES: Signed as non-drafted free agent by St. Louis Rams (April 20, 1999). ... Released by Rams (September 5, 1999). ... Re-signed by Rams (September 6, 1999). ... Released by Rams (September 13, 1999). ... Re-signed by Rams to practice squad (September 30, 1999). ... Released by Rams (August 27, 2000). ... Re-signed by Rams to practice squad (August 29, 2000). ... Released by Rams (October 24, 2000). ... Signed by Indianapolis Colts (November 1, 2000). ... Granted free agency (February 28, 2003). ... Re-signed by Colts (April 22, 2003). ... Granted unconditional free agency (March 3, 2004).
CHAMPIONSHIP GAME EXPERIENCE: Played in AFC championship game (2003 season).

Year	Team	G	GS	TOTALS Tk.	Ast.	Sks.	INTERCEPTIONS No.	Yds.	Avg.	TD
1999—St. Louis NFL		1	0	0	0	0.0	0	0	0.0	0
2001—Indianapolis NFL		14	0	2	0	0.0	0	0	0.0	0
2002—Indianapolis NFL		16	0	15	3	0.0	0	0	0.0	0
2003—Indianapolis NFL		14	0	3	1	0.0	0	0	0.0	0
Pro totals (4 years)		45	0	20	4	0.0	0	0	0.0	0

CROSBY, PHILLIP — FB — PATRIOTS

PERSONAL: Born November 5, 1976, in Bessemer City, N.C. ... 6-0/242. ... Full name: Phillip Jermaine Crosby.
HIGH SCHOOL: Bessemer City (N.C.).
JUNIOR COLLEGE: Coffeyville Community College.
COLLEGE: Tennessee.
TRANSACTIONS/CAREER NOTES: Signed as non-drafted free agent by Buffalo Bills (April 22, 2000). ... Released by Bills (August 21, 2000). ... Re-signed by Bills (April 24, 2001). ... On injured reserve with leg injury (September 27-November 19, 2003). ... Released from injured reserve (November 19, 2003). ... Signed by New England Patriots (February 6, 2004).

			RUSHING				RECEIVING				KICKOFF RETURNS				TOTALS			
Year Team	G	GS	Att.	Yds.	Avg.	TD	No.	Yds.	Avg.	TD	No.	Yds.	Avg.	TD	TD	2pt.	Pts.	Fum.
2001—Buffalo NFL	16	2	0	0	0.0	0	2	16	8.0	0	0	0	0.0	0	0	0	0	0
2002—Buffalo NFL	16	4	0	0	0.0	0	4	33	8.3	0	3	45	15.0	0	0	0	0	0
2003—Buffalo NFL	3	0	0	0	0.0	0	0	0	0.0	0	0	0	0.0	0	0	0	0	0
Pro totals (3 years)	35	6	0	0	0.0	0	6	49	8.2	0	3	45	15.0	0	0	0	0	0

CROWELL, ANGELO — LB — BILLS

PERSONAL: Born August 16, 1981, in Forsyth County, N.C. ... 6-1/235. ... Full name: Angelo Delvonne Crowell. ... Brother of Germane Crowell, wide receiver with Detroit Lions (1998-2002).
HIGH SCHOOL: North Forsyth (N.C.).
COLLEGE: Virginia.
TRANSACTIONS/CAREER NOTES: Selected by Buffalo Bills in third round (94th pick overall) of 2003 NFL draft. ... Signed by Bills (July 23, 2003).

			TOTALS			INTERCEPTIONS			
Year Team	G	GS	Tk.	Ast.	Sks.	No.	Yds.	Avg.	TD
2003—Buffalo NFL	6	0	0	0	0.0	0	0	0.0	0

C

CRUMPLER, ALGE — TE — FALCONS

PERSONAL: Born December 23, 1977, in Greenville, N.C. ... 6-2/262. ... Full name: Algernon Darius Crumpler.
HIGH SCHOOL: New Hanover (Wilmington, N.C.).
COLLEGE: North Carolina.
TRANSACTIONS/CAREER NOTES: Selected by Atlanta Falcons in second round (35th pick overall) of 2001 NFL draft. ... Signed by Falcons (May 29, 2001).
HONORS: Played in Pro Bowl (2003 season).
SINGLE GAME HIGHS (regular season): Receptions—5 (December 7, 2003, vs. Carolina); yards—94 (September 7, 2003, vs. Dallas); and touchdown receptions—1 (December 20, 2003, vs. Tampa Bay).

			RECEIVING				TOTALS			
Year Team	G	GS	No.	Yds.	Avg.	TD	TD	2pt.	Pts.	Fum.
2001—Atlanta NFL	16	12	25	330	13.2	3	3	0	18	1
2002—Atlanta NFL	16	9	36	455	12.6	5	5	0	30	0
2003—Atlanta NFL	16	16	44	552	12.5	3	3	0	18	1
Pro totals (3 years)	48	37	105	1337	12.7	11	11	0	66	2

CULPEPPER, DAUNTE — QB — VIKINGS

PERSONAL: Born January 28, 1977, in Ocala, Fla. ... 6-4/264.
HIGH SCHOOL: Vanguard (Ocala, Fla.).
COLLEGE: Central Florida.
TRANSACTIONS/CAREER NOTES: Selected by Minnesota Vikings in first round (11th pick overall) of 1999 NFL draft. ... Signed by Vikings (July 30, 1999).
CHAMPIONSHIP GAME EXPERIENCE: Played in NFC championship game (2000 season).
HONORS: Played in Pro Bowl (2000 and 2003 seasons).
RECORDS: Shares NFL single-season record for most fumbles—23 (2002).
SINGLE GAME HIGHS (regular season): Attempts—53 (September 29, 2002, vs. Seattle); completions—33 (November 30, 2003, vs. St. Louis); yards—396 (November 16, 2003, vs. Oakland); and touchdown passes—4 (November 9, 2003, vs. San Diego).
STATISTICAL PLATEAUS: 300-yard passing games: 2000 (5), 2001 (2), 2002 (2), 2003 (3). Total: 12.
MISCELLANEOUS: Selected by New York Yankees organization in 26th round of free-agent baseball draft (June 1, 1995); did not sign. ... Regular-season record as starting NFL quarterback: 28-29 (.491). ... Postseason record as starting NFL quarterback: 1-1 (.500).

			PASSING									RUSHING				TOTALS		
Year Team	G	GS	Att.	Cmp.	Pct.	Yds.	TD	Int.	Avg.	Skd.	Rat.	Att.	Yds.	Avg.	TD	TD	2pt.	Pts.
1999—Minnesota NFL	1	0	0	0	0.0	0	0	0	0.00	0	.0	3	6	2.0	0	0	0	0
2000—Minnesota NFL	16	16	474	297	62.7	3937	†33	16	8.31	34	98.0	89	470	5.3	7	7	0	42
2001—Minnesota NFL	11	11	366	235	64.2	2612	14	13	7.14	33	83.3	71	416	5.9	5	5	2	34
2002—Minnesota NFL	16	16	549	333	60.7	3853	18	*23	7.02	‡47	75.3	106	609	5.7	10	10	1	62
2003—Minnesota NFL	14	14	454	295	65.0	3479	25	11	‡7.66	37	‡96.4	73	422	5.8	4	4	0	24
Pro totals (5 years)	58	57	1843	1160	62.9	13881	90	63	7.53	151	88.0	342	1923	5.6	26	26	3	162

CUNDIFF, BILLY — K — COWBOYS

PERSONAL: Born March 30, 1980, in Valley Center, Calif. ... 6-1/201. ... Full name: Bill Cundiff.
HIGH SCHOOL: Harlan (Iowa).
COLLEGE: Drake.

TRANSACTIONS/CAREER NOTES: Signed as non-drafted free agent by Dallas Cowboys (April 26, 2002).
RECORDS: Shares NFL single-game record for most field goals—7 (September 15, 2003, vs. New York Giants (OT)).

		FIELD GOALS							TOTALS		
Year Team	G	1-29	30-39	40-49	50+	Tot.	Pct.	Lg.	XPM	XPA	Pts.
2002—Dallas NFL	16	3-3	5-7	4-8	0-1	12-19	63.2	48	25	25	61
2003—Dallas NFL	15	11-11	5-6	4-7	3-5	23-29	79.3	52	30	31	99
Pro totals (2 years)	31	14-14	10-13	8-15	3-6	35-48	72.9	52	55	56	160

CURLEY, DAN FB SAINTS

PERSONAL: Born April 25, 1978, in Tacoma, Wash. ... 6-4/254.
HIGH SCHOOL: Anacortes (Wash.).
COLLEGE: Eastern Washington.
TRANSACTIONS/CAREER NOTES: Selected by St. Louis Rams in fifth round (148th pick overall) of 2003 NFL draft. ... Signed by Rams (July 22, 2003). ... Released by Rams (October 9, 2003). ... Signed by New Orleans Saints (January 27, 2004).

			RECEIVING				TOTALS			
Year Team	G	GS	No.	Yds.	Avg.	TD	TD	2pt.	Pts.	Fum.
2003—St. Louis NFL	1	0	0	0	0.0	0	0	0	0	0

C

CURRY, DONTE' LB LIONS

PERSONAL: Born July 22, 1978, in Savannah, Ga. ... 6-1/233. ... Full name: Donte Curry.
HIGH SCHOOL: Savannah (Ga.).
JUNIOR COLLEGE: Middle Georgia Junior College.
COLLEGE: Morris Brown.
TRANSACTIONS/CAREER NOTES: Signed as non-drafted free agent by Green Bay Packers (April 24, 2001). ... Released by Packers (September 1, 2001). ... Re-signed by Packers to practice squad (September 3, 2001). ... Signed by Washington Redskins off Packers practice squad (October 3, 2001). ... Claimed on waivers by Detroit Lions (August 28, 2002). ... Re-signed by Lions (March 25, 2003). ... Granted free agency (March 3, 2004). ... Re-signed by Lions (April 21, 2004).

			TOTALS			INTERCEPTIONS			
Year Team	G	GS	Tk.	Ast.	Sks.	No.	Yds.	Avg.	TD
2001—Washington NFL	8	0	0	0	0.0	0	0	0.0	0
2002—Detroit NFL	16	10	39	16	3.0	0	0	0.0	0
2003—Detroit NFL	11	0	1	0	0.0	0	0	0.0	0
Pro totals (3 years)	35	10	40	16	3.0	0	0	0.0	0

CURRY, JULIUS CB LIONS

PERSONAL: Born May 17, 1979, in Detroit, Mich. ... 6-0/195. ... Full name: Julius Justin Curry.
HIGH SCHOOL: Bishop Gallagher (Detroit, Mich.).
COLLEGE: Michigan.
TRANSACTIONS/CAREER NOTES: Signed as non-drafted free agent by Chicago Bears (April 28, 2003). ... Released by Bears (August 25, 2003). ... Signed by Detroit Lions to practice squad (September 16, 2003). ... Released by Lions (November 4, 2003). ... Re-signed by Lions to practice squad (November 18, 2003). ... Activated (December 9, 2003).

			TOTALS			INTERCEPTIONS			
Year Team	G	GS	Tk.	Ast.	Sks.	No.	Yds.	Avg.	TD
2003—Detroit NFL	3	0	1	0	0.0	0	0	0.0	0

CURRY, RONALD WR RAIDERS

PERSONAL: Born May 28, 1979, in Hampton, Va. ... 6-2/220. ... Full name: Ronald Antonio Curry.
HIGH SCHOOL: Hampton (Va.).
COLLEGE: North Carolina.
TRANSACTIONS/CAREER NOTES: Selected by Oakland Raiders in seventh round (235th pick overall) of 2002 NFL draft. ... Signed by Raiders (July 26, 2002). ... Released by Raiders (September 1, 2002). ... Re-signed by Raiders to practice squad (September 3, 2002). ... Released by Raiders (November 2, 2002). ... Re-signed by Raiders to practice squad (January 22, 2003).
CHAMPIONSHIP GAME EXPERIENCE: Member of Raiders for Super Bowl 37 (2002 season); inactive.
SINGLE GAME HIGHS (regular season): Receptions—2 (October 5, 2003, vs. Chicago); yards—20 (September 22, 2003, vs. Denver); and touchdown receptions—0.

			RUSHING				RECEIVING				KICKOFF RETURNS				TOTALS			
Year Team	G	GS	Att.	Yds.	Avg.	TD	No.	Yds.	Avg.	TD	No.	Yds.	Avg.	TD	TD	2pt.	Pts.	Fum.
2002—Oakland NFL	1	0	0	0	0.0	0	0	0	0.0	0	3	68	22.7	0	0	0	0	1
2003—Oakland NFL	16	2	1	0	0.0	0	5	31	6.2	0	0	0	0.0	0	0	0	0	1
Pro totals (2 years)	17	2	1	0	0.0	0	5	31	6.2	0	3	68	22.7	0	0	0	0	2

CURTIS, KEVIN WR RAMS

PERSONAL: Born July 17, 1978, in Murray, Utah. ... 5-11/186.
HIGH SCHOOL: Bingham (South Jordan, Utah).
JUNIOR COLLEGE: Snow College (Utah).
COLLEGE: Utah State.

TRANSACTIONS/CAREER NOTES: Selected by St. Louis Rams in third round (74th pick overall) of 2003 NFL draft. ... Signed by Rams (July 23, 2003).

			RUSHING				RECEIVING				PUNT RETURNS				TOTALS			
Year Team	G	GS	Att.	Yds.	Avg.	TD	No.	Yds.	Avg.	TD	No.	Yds.	Avg.	TD	TD	2pt.	Pts.	Fum.
2003—St. Louis NFL	4	1	0	0	0.0	0	4	13	3.3	0	0	0	0.0	0	0	0	0	0

CUSHING, MATT — TE — STEELERS

PERSONAL: Born July 2, 1975, in Chicago, Ill. ... 6-4/255. ... Full name: Matt Jay Cushing.
HIGH SCHOOL: Mount Carmel (Chicago).
COLLEGE: Illinois.
TRANSACTIONS/CAREER NOTES: Signed as non-drafted free agent by Pittsburgh Steelers (April 24, 1998). ... Released by Steelers (August 24, 1998). ... Re-signed by Steelers (February 22, 1999). ... Assigned by Steelers to Amsterdam Admirals in 1999 NFL Europe enhancement allocation program (February 22, 1999). ... Released by Steelers (September 5, 1999). ... Re-signed by Steelers (October 28, 1999). ... Released by Steelers (August 27, 2000). ... Re-signed by Steelers (November 7, 2000). ... Granted free agency (March 1, 2002). ... Re-signed by Steelers (April 12, 2002). ... Released by Steelers (September 24, 2002). ... Re-signed by Steelers (October 22, 2002). ... Released by Steelers (November 5, 2002). ... Re-signed by Steelers (December 3, 2002). ... Granted unconditional free agency (February 28, 2003). ... Re-signed by Steelers (March 17, 2003). ... Granted unconditional free agency (March 3, 2004). ... Re-signed by Steelers (March 4, 2004).
CHAMPIONSHIP GAME EXPERIENCE: Played in AFC championship game (2001 season).
SINGLE GAME HIGHS (regular season): Receptions—2 (December 23, 2001, vs. Detroit); yards—29 (January 2, 2000, vs. Tennessee); and touchdown receptions—1 (December 23, 2001, vs. Detroit).

			RECEIVING				TOTALS			
Year Team	G	GS	No.	Yds.	Avg.	TD	TD	2pt.	Pts.	Fum.
1999—Pittsburgh NFL	7	1	2	29	14.5	0	0	0	0	0
2000—Pittsburgh NFL	6	1	4	17	4.3	0	0	0	0	0
2001—Pittsburgh NFL	13	3	5	24	4.8	1	1	0	6	0
2002—Pittsburgh NFL	6	0	1	4	4.0	0	0	0	0	0
2003—Pittsburgh NFL	4	0	0	0	0.0	0	0	0	0	0
Pro totals (5 years)	36	5	12	74	6.2	1	1	0	6	0

D

DACH, CARSON — C/LS — GIANTS

PERSONAL: Born September 29, 1980, in Flint, Mich. ... 6-1/253. ... Full name: Carson Elliot Dach.
HIGH SCHOOL: Grand Blanc (Mich.).
COLLEGE: Eastern Michigan.
TRANSACTIONS/CAREER NOTES: Signed as non-drafted free agent by Chicago Bears (June 9, 2003). ... Released by Bears (June 18, 2003). ... Re-signed by Bears (August 13, 2003). ... Claimed on waivers by New York Giants (August 26, 2003).
PLAYING EXPERIENCE: New York Giants NFL, 2003. ... Games/Games started: 2003 (16/0). Total: 16/0.

DALTON, LIONAL — DT — CHIEFS

PERSONAL: Born February 21, 1975, in Detroit, Mich. ... 6-1/315.
HIGH SCHOOL: Cooley (Detroit).
COLLEGE: Eastern Michigan.
TRANSACTIONS/CAREER NOTES: Signed as non-drafted free agent by Baltimore Ravens (April 23, 1998). ... Granted free agency (March 2, 2001). ... Re-signed by Ravens (March 29, 2001). ... Granted unconditional free agency (March 1, 2002). ... Signed by Denver Broncos (March 20, 2002). ... Traded by Broncos to Washington Redskins for sixth-round pick (WR Triandos Luke) in 2004 draft (August 26, 2003). ... Released by Redskins (February 24, 2004). ... Signed by Kansas City Chiefs (March 30, 2004).
CHAMPIONSHIP GAME EXPERIENCE: Played in AFC championship game (2000 season). ... Member of Super Bowl championship team (2000 season).

			TOTALS		
Year Team	G	GS	Tk.	Ast.	Sks.
1998—Baltimore NFL	2	0	3	1	0.0
1999—Baltimore NFL	16	2	12	5	1.0
2000—Baltimore NFL	16	1	9	1	0.0
2001—Baltimore NFL	16	3	12	4	0.0
2002—Denver NFL	16	13	24	5	1.0
2003—Washington NFL	12	9	11	3	1.0
Pro totals (6 years)	78	28	71	19	3.0

DANIELS, PHILLIP — DE — REDSKINS

PERSONAL: Born March 4, 1973, in Donalsonville, Ga. ... 6-5/285. ... Full name: Phillip Bernard Daniels.
HIGH SCHOOL: Seminole County (Donaldsonville, Ga.).
COLLEGE: Georgia.
TRANSACTIONS/CAREER NOTES: Selected by Seattle Seahawks in fourth round (99th pick overall) of 1996 NFL draft. ... Signed by Seahawks (July 17, 1996). ... Granted free agency (February 12, 1999). ... Re-signed by Seahawks (April 6, 1999). ... Granted unconditional free agency (February 11, 2000). ... Signed by Chicago Bears (February 12, 2000). ... On injured reserve with ankle injury (December 13, 2000-remainder of season). ... Released by Bears (March 1, 2004). ... Signed by Washington Redskins (March 2, 2004).

			TOTALS		
Year Team	G	GS	Tk.	Ast.	Sks.
1996—Seattle NFL	15	0	9	2	2.0
1997—Seattle NFL	13	10	24	10	4.0
1998—Seattle NFL	16	15	34	14	6.5

Year Team	G	GS	TOTALS Tk.	Ast.	Sks.
1999—Seattle NFL	16	16	40	8	9.0
2000—Chicago NFL	14	14	37	5	6.0
2001—Chicago NFL	16	16	43	7	9.0
2002—Chicago NFL	13	13	34	9	5.5
2003—Chicago NFL	16	16	41	12	2.5
Pro totals (8 years)	119	100	262	67	44.5

DANTZLER, WOODROW RB FALCONS

PERSONAL: Born October 4, 1979, in Orangeburg, S.C. ... 5-10/209.
HIGH SCHOOL: Wilkinsburg (Orangeburg, S.C.).
COLLEGE: Clemson.
TRANSACTIONS/CAREER NOTES: Signed as non-drafted free agent by Dallas Cowboys (April 26, 2002). ... Released by Cowboys (September 1, 2002). ... Re-signed by Cowboys to practice squad (September 3, 2002). ... Activated (November 27, 2002). ... Claimed on waivers by Atlanta Falcons (September 2, 2003).
SINGLE GAME HIGHS (regular season): Attempts—3 (September 28, 2003, vs. Carolina); yards—12 (September 28, 2003, vs. Carolina); and rushing touchdowns—1 (September 21, 2003, vs. Tampa Bay).

			RUSHING				KICKOFF RETURNS				TOTALS			
Year Team	G	GS	Att.	Yds.	Avg.	TD	No.	Yds.	Avg.	TD	TD	2pt.	Pts.	Fum.
2002—Dallas NFL	5	0	0	0	0.0	0	27	602	22.3	1	1	0	6	2
2003—Atlanta NFL	9	0	8	21	2.6	1	7	136	19.4	0	1	0	6	0
Pro totals (2 years)	14	0	8	21	2.6	1	34	738	21.7	1	2	0	12	2

DARBY, CHARTRIC DT BUCCANEERS

PERSONAL: Born October 22, 1975, in North, S.C. ... 6-0/270. ... Full name: Chartric Terrell Darby.
HIGH SCHOOL: North (S.C.).
COLLEGE: South Carolina State.
TRANSACTIONS/CAREER NOTES: Signed as non-drafted free agent by Baltimore Ravens (April 23, 1998). ... Released by Ravens (August 30, 1998). ... Re-signed by Ravens to practice squad (September 1, 1998). ... Granted free agency after 1998 season. ... Signed by Indianapolis Colts (January 19, 1999). ... Claimed on waivers by Carolina Panthers (April 28, 1999). ... Released by Panthers (August 30, 1999). ... Selected by Rhein Fire in 2000 NFL Europe draft (February 22, 2000). ... Signed by Buccaneers (July 10, 2000). ... Released by Buccaneers (August 27, 2000). ... Re-signed by Buccaneers to practice squad (August 28, 2000). ... Granted free agency (March 3, 2004). ... Re-signed by Tampa Bay (April 19, 2004).
CHAMPIONSHIP GAME EXPERIENCE: Played in NFC championship game (2002 season). ... Member of Super Bowl championship team (2002 season).

Year Team	G	GS	TOTALS Tk.	Ast.	Sks.
2001—Tampa Bay NFL	13	0	6	0	2.0
2002—Tampa Bay NFL	16	6	22	6	1.5
2003—Tampa Bay NFL	16	1	8	5	2.0
Pro totals (3 years)	45	7	36	11	5.5

DARCHE, JEAN-PHILIPPE C/LS SEAHAWKS

PERSONAL: Born February 28, 1975, in Montreal, PQ. ... 6-0/246. ... Full name: Jean-Philipe Darche. ... Brother of Mathieu Darche, left winger, Nashville Predators.
HIGH SCHOOL: Andre Grassett Junior College (Montreal).
COLLEGE: McGill.
TRANSACTIONS/CAREER NOTES: Signed as non-drafted free agent by Seattle Seahawks (May 11, 2000). ... Granted free agency (February 28, 2003). ... Re-signed by Seahawks (March 26, 2003).
PLAYING EXPERIENCE: Seattle NFL, 2000-2003. ... Games/Games started: 2000 (16/0), 2001 (16/0), 2002 (16/0), 2003 (16/0). Total: 64/0.

DARIUS, DONOVIN S JAGUARS

PERSONAL: Born August 12, 1975, in Camden, N.J. ... 6-1/225. ... Full name: Donovin Lee Darius.
HIGH SCHOOL: Woodrow Wilson (Camden, N.J.).
COLLEGE: Syracuse.
TRANSACTIONS/CAREER NOTES: Selected by Jacksonville Jaguars in first round (25th pick overall) of 1998 NFL draft. ... Signed by Jaguars (July 23, 1998). ... Designated by Jaguars as franchise player (February 20, 2003). ... Re-signed by Jaguars (March 25, 2003). ... Designated by Jaguars as franchise player (February 24, 2004). ... Re-signed by Jaguars (March 11, 2004).
CHAMPIONSHIP GAME EXPERIENCE: Played in AFC championship game (1999 season).
HONORS: Named free safety on THE SPORTING NEWS college All-America first team (1997).

			TOTALS			INTERCEPTIONS			
Year Team	G	GS	Tk.	Ast.	Sks.	No.	Yds.	Avg.	TD
1998—Jacksonville NFL	14	14	58	16	0.0	0	0	0.0	0
1999—Jacksonville NFL	16	16	56	19	0.0	4	37	9.3	0
2000—Jacksonville NFL	16	16	65	20	1.0	2	26	13.0	0
2001—Jacksonville NFL	11	11	64	12	0.0	1	39	39.0	0
2002—Jacksonville NFL	14	14	70	8	1.0	1	3	3.0	0
2003—Jacksonville NFL	16	16	55	27	0.0	1	4	4.0	0
Pro totals (6 years)	87	87	368	102	2.0	9	109	12.1	0

DARLING, JAMES — LB — CARDINALS

PERSONAL: Born December 29, 1974, in Denver, Colo. ... 6-1/247. ... Full name: James Jackson Darling.
HIGH SCHOOL: Kettle Falls (Wash.).
COLLEGE: Washington State.
TRANSACTIONS/CAREER NOTES: Selected by Philadelphia Eagles in second round (57th pick overall) of 1997 NFL draft. ... Signed by Eagles (July 16, 1997). ... Granted free agency (February 11, 2000). ... Re-signed by Eagles (April 10, 2000). ... Granted unconditional free agency (March 2, 2001). ... Signed by New York Jets (March 21, 2001). ... Granted unconditional free agency (February 28, 2003). ... Signed by Arizona Cardinals (March 12, 2003).
HONORS: Named inside linebacker on THE SPORTING NEWS college All-America second team (1996).

			TOTALS			INTERCEPTIONS			
Year Team	G	GS	Tk.	Ast.	Sks.	No.	Yds.	Avg.	TD
1997—Philadelphia NFL	16	6	20	8	0.0	0	0	0.0	0
1998—Philadelphia NFL	12	8	20	6	2.0	0	0	0.0	0
1999—Philadelphia NFL	15	10	40	18	0.0	1	33	33.0	0
2000—Philadelphia NFL	16	0	1	3	0.5	0	0	0.0	0
2001—New York Jets NFL	16	0	7	4	0.0	0	0	0.0	0
2002—New York Jets NFL	16	0	28	9	1.0	2	38	19.0	0
2003—Arizona NFL	16	0	21	0	2.0	0	0	0.0	0
Pro totals (7 years)	107	24	137	48	5.5	3	71	23.7	0

DAVENPORT, JOE DEAN — TE — COLTS

PERSONAL: Born October 29, 1976, in Springdale, Ark. ... 6-6/268. ... Full name: Joe Dean Davenport.
HIGH SCHOOL: Springdale (Ark.).
COLLEGE: Arkansas.
TRANSACTIONS/CAREER NOTES: Signed as non-drafted free agent by Indianapolis Colts (May 9, 2001).
CHAMPIONSHIP GAME EXPERIENCE: Played in AFC championship game (2003 season).
SINGLE GAME HIGHS (regular season): Receptions—3 (November 24, 2002, vs. Denver); yards—22 (December 15, 2002, vs. Cleveland); and touchdown receptions—0.

			RECEIVING				TOTALS			
Year Team	G	GS	No.	Yds.	Avg.	TD	TD	2pt.	Pts.	Fum.
2001—Indianapolis NFL	3	0	0	0	0.0	0	0	0	0	0
2002—Indianapolis NFL	10	7	8	70	8.8	0	0	0	0	0
2003—Indianapolis NFL	16	2	3	23	7.7	0	0	0	0	0
Pro totals (3 years)	29	9	11	93	8.5	0	0	0	0	0

D

DAVENPORT, NAJEH — RB — PACKERS

PERSONAL: Born February 8, 1979, in Raleigh, N.C. ... 6-1/245. ... Full name: Najeh Trenadious Monte Davenport.
HIGH SCHOOL: Miami Central (Fla.).
COLLEGE: Miami (Fla.).
TRANSACTIONS/CAREER NOTES: Selected by Green Bay Packers in fourth round (135th pick overall) of 2002 NFL draft. ... Signed by Packers (July 26, 2002). ... On injured reserve with eye injury (November 20, 2002-remainder of season).
SINGLE GAME HIGHS (regular season): Attempts—22 (September 22, 2002, vs. Detroit); yards— 84 (September 22, 2002, vs. Detroit); and rushing touchdowns—1 (October 19, 2003, vs. St. Louis).

			RUSHING				RECEIVING				KICKOFF RETURNS				TOTALS			
Year Team	G	GS	Att.	Yds.	Avg.	TD	No.	Yds.	Avg.	TD	No.	Yds.	Avg.	TD	TD	2pt.	Pts.	Fum.
2002—Green Bay NFL	8	0	39	184	4.7	1	5	33	6.6	0	6	130	21.7	0	1	0	6	1
2003—Green Bay NFL	15	0	77	420	5.5	2	6	38	6.3	0	16	505	31.6	0	2	0	12	4
Pro totals (2 years)	23	0	116	604	5.2	3	11	71	6.5	0	22	635	28.9	0	3	0	18	5

DAVEY, ROHAN — QB — PATRIOTS

PERSONAL: Born April 14, 1978, in Clarendon, Jamaica. ... 6-2/245. ... Full name: Rohan St. Patrick Davey.
HIGH SCHOOL: Miami Lakes (Fla.).
COLLEGE: Louisiana State.
TRANSACTIONS/CAREER NOTES: Selected by New England Patriots in fourth round (117th pick overall) of 2002 NFL draft. ... Signed by Patriots (July 21, 2002). ... Assigned by Patriots to Berlin Thunder in 2004 NFL Europe enhancement allocation program (February 9, 2004).
CHAMPIONSHIP GAME EXPERIENCE: Member of Patriots for AFC championship game (2003 season); inactive. ... Member of Patriots for Super Bowl 38 (2003 season); inactive.
SINGLE GAME HIGHS (regular season): Attempts—7 (September 7, 2003, vs. Buffalo); completions—3 (September 7, 2003, vs. Buffalo); yards—31 (September 7, 2003, vs. Buffalo); and touchdown passes—0.

			PASSING									RUSHING				TOTALS		
Year Team	G	GS	Att.	Cmp.	Pct.	Yds.	TD	Int.	Avg.	Skd.	Rat.	Att.	Yds.	Avg.	TD	TD	2pt.	Pts.
2002—New England NFL	2	0	2	1	50.0	3	0	0	1.50	0	56.2	2	-4	-2.0	0	0	0	0
2003—New England NFL	1	0	7	3	42.9	31	0	0	4.43	0	56.3	0	0	0.0	0	0	0	0
Pro totals (2 years)	3	0	9	4	44.4	34	0	0	3.78	0	54.9	2	-4	-2.0	0	0	0	0

DAVIS, ANDRA — LB — BROWNS

PERSONAL: Born December 23, 1978, in Live Oak, Fla. ... 6-1/255. ... Full name: Andra Raynard Davis.
HIGH SCHOOL: Suwanee (Live Oak, Fla.).
COLLEGE: Florida.

TRANSACTIONS/CAREER NOTES: Selected by Cleveland Browns in fifth round (141st pick overall) of 2002 NFL draft. ... Signed by Browns (July 18, 2002).
HONORS: Named linebacker on THE SPORTING NEWS college All-America second team (2001).

			TOTALS			INTERCEPTIONS			
Year Team	G	GS	Tk.	Ast.	Sks.	No.	Yds.	Avg.	TD
2002—Cleveland NFL	16	0	1	4	0.0	1	0	0.0	0
2003—Cleveland NFL	16	16	96	40	5.0	0	0	0.0	0
Pro totals (2 years)	32	16	97	44	5.0	1	0	0.0	0

DAVIS, ANDRE' WR BROWNS

PERSONAL: Born June 12, 1979, in Niskayuna, N.Y. ... 6-1/195. ... Full name: Andre' N. Davis.
HIGH SCHOOL: Niskayuna (N.Y.).
COLLEGE: Virginia Tech.
TRANSACTIONS/CAREER NOTES: Selected by Cleveland Browns in second round (47th pick overall) of 2002 NFL draft. ... Signed by Browns (July 22, 2002).
SINGLE GAME HIGHS (regular season): Receptions—7 (November 16, 2003, vs. Arizona); yards—117 (November 16, 2003, vs. Arizona); and touchdown receptions—2 (September 21, 2003, vs. San Francisco).
STATISTICAL PLATEAUS: 100-yard receiving games: 2003 (1). Total: 1.

			RUSHING				RECEIVING				PUNT RETURNS				KICKOFF RETURNS				TOTALS		
Year Team	G	GS	Att.	Yds.	Avg.	TD	No.	Yds.	Avg.	TD	No.	Yds.	Avg.	TD	No.	Yds.	Avg.	TD	TD	2pt.	Pts.
2002—Cle. NFL	16	4	3	7	2.3	0	37	420	11.4	6	7	33	4.7	0	50	1068	21.4	1	7	0	42
2003—Cle. NFL	16	8	5	28	5.6	0	40	576	14.4	5	1	7	7.0	0	38	803	21.1	0	5	0	30
Pro totals (2 years)	32	12	8	35	4.4	0	77	996	12.9	11	8	40	5.0	0	88	1871	21.3	1	12	0	72

DAVIS, CHRIS FB SEAHAWKS

PERSONAL: Born November 8, 1979, in Tampa, Fla. ... 5-11/235. ... Full name: Christopher Michael Davis.
HIGH SCHOOL: Hillsborough (Tampa).
COLLEGE: Syracuse.
TRANSACTIONS/CAREER NOTES: Selected by Seattle Seahawks in fifth round (165th pick overall) of 2003 NFL draft. ... Signed by Seahawks (July 23, 2003). ... On injured reserve with knee injury (September 9, 2003-remainder of season).

D

			RUSHING				TOTALS			
Year Team	G	GS	Att.	Yds.	Avg.	TD	TD	2pt.	Pts.	Fum.
2003—Seattle NFL	1	0	0	0	0.0	0	0	0	0	0

DAVIS, DOMANICK RB TEXANS

PERSONAL: Born October 1, 1980, in Lafayette, La. ... 5-9/216.
HIGH SCHOOL: Breaux Bridge (La.).
COLLEGE: Louisiana State.
TRANSACTIONS/CAREER NOTES: Selected by Houston Texans in fourth round (101st pick overall) of 2003 NFL draft. ... Signed by Texans (July 17, 2003).
SINGLE GAME HIGHS (regular season): Attempts—27 (October 19, 2003, vs. New York Jets); yards—129 (October 19, 2003, vs. New York Jets); and rushing touchdowns—2 (December 28, 2003, vs. Indianapolis).
STATISTICAL PLATEAUS: 100-yard rushing games: 2003 (4). Total: 4.
MISCELLANEOUS: Holds Houston Texans all-time records for most yards rushing (1,031) and most rushing touchdowns (8).

			RUSHING				RECEIVING				KICKOFF RETURNS				TOTALS			
Year Team	G	GS	Att.	Yds.	Avg.	TD	No.	Yds.	Avg.	TD	No.	Yds.	Avg.	TD	TD	2pt.	Pts.	Fum.
2003—Houston NFL	14	10	238	1031	4.3	8	47	351	7.5	0	3	61	20.3	0	8	0	48	4

DAVIS, DON LB PATRIOTS

PERSONAL: Born December 17, 1972, in Olathe, Kan. ... 6-1/235.
HIGH SCHOOL: Olathe (Kan.) South.
COLLEGE: Kansas.
TRANSACTIONS/CAREER NOTES: Signed as non-drafted free agent by New York Jets (April 28, 1995). ... Released by Jets (August 27, 1995). ... Signed by Kansas City Chiefs (January 9, 1996). ... Released by Chiefs (August 20, 1996). ... Signed by New Orleans Saints to practice squad (August 27, 1996). ... Activated (October 4, 1996). ... On injured reserve with wrist injury (November 19, 1997-remainder of season). ... Claimed on waivers by Tampa Bay Buccaneers (November 25, 1998). ... Granted free agency (February 12, 1999). ... Re-signed by Buccaneers (May 21, 1999). ... Released by Buccaneers (October 9, 1999). ... Re-signed by Buccaneers (October 19, 1999). ... Granted unconditional free agency (February 11, 2000). ... Re-signed by Buccaneers (July 1, 2000). ... Granted unconditional free agency (March 2, 2001). ... Signed by St. Louis Rams (March 3, 2001). ... Granted unconditional free agency (February 28, 2003). ... Signed by New England Patriots (May 16, 2003). ... Granted unconditional free agency (March 3, 2004). ... Re-signed by Patriots (March 5, 2004),
CHAMPIONSHIP GAME EXPERIENCE: Played in NFC championship game (1999 and 2001 seasons). ... Played in AFC championship game (2003 season). ... Played in Super Bowl 36 (2001 season). ... Member of Super Bowl championship team (2003 season).

			TOTALS			INTERCEPTIONS			
Year Team	G	GS	Tk.	Ast.	Sks.	No.	Yds.	Avg.	TD
1996—New Orleans NFL	11	0	0	0	0.0	0	0	0.0	0
1997—New Orleans NFL	11	0	0	0	0.0	0	0	0.0	0
1998—New Orleans NFL	4	0	2	2	0.0	0	0	0.0	0
—Tampa Bay NFL	5	0	0	0	0.0	0	0	0.0	0
1999—Tampa Bay NFL	14	0	0	1	0.0	0	0	0.0	0
2000—Tampa Bay NFL	16	0	2	5	0.0	0	0	0.0	0

Year Team	G	GS	TOTALS Tk.	Ast.	Sks.	INTERCEPTIONS No.	Yds.	Avg.	TD
2001—St. Louis NFL	12	8	16	9	0.0	0	0	0.0	0
2002—St. Louis NFL	16	7	33	6	0.0	1	29	29.0	0
2003—New England NFL	15	0	1	0	0.0	0	0	0.0	0
Pro totals (8 years)	104	15	54	23	0.0	1	29	29.0	0

DAVIS, DORSETT — DE/DT — BRONCOS

PERSONAL: Born January 24, 1979, in Shelby, Miss. ... 6-5/305. ... Full name: Dorsett Terrell Davis.
HIGH SCHOOL: East Side (Cleveland, Miss.).
JUNIOR COLLEGE: Mississippi Delta Community College.
COLLEGE: Mississippi State.
TRANSACTIONS/CAREER NOTES: Selected by Denver Broncos in third round (96th pick overall) of 2002 NFL draft. ... Signed by Broncos (July 19, 2002).

Year Team	G	GS	TOTALS Tk.	Ast.	Sks.
2003—Denver NFL	14	0	8	3	0.0

DAVIS, JAMES — LB — LIONS

PERSONAL: Born April 26, 1979, in Stuart, Fla. ... 6-1/221.
HIGH SCHOOL: Martin County (Stuart, Fla.).
COLLEGE: West Virginia.
TRANSACTIONS/CAREER NOTES: Selected by Detroit Lions in fifth round (144th pick overall) of 2003 NFL draft. ... Signed by Lions (July 15, 2003).

Year Team	G	GS	TOTALS Tk.	Ast.	Sks.	INTERCEPTIONS No.	Yds.	Avg.	TD
2003—Detroit NFL	8	1	6	0	0.0	0	0	0.0	0

DAVIS, JEROME — T — 49ERS

PERSONAL: Born February 4, 1974, in Detroit, Mich. ... 6-5/290.
HIGH SCHOOL: Chadsey (Detroit).
COLLEGE: Minnesota.
TRANSACTIONS/CAREER NOTES: Signed as non-drafted free agent by Detroit Lions (April 24, 1997). ... Released by Lions (August 19, 1997). ... Re-signed by Lions to practice squad (December 23, 1997). ... Assigned by Lions to Frankfurt Galaxy in 1998 NFL Europe enhancement allocation program (February 18, 1998). ... On injured reserve list with leg injury (August 17, 1998-entire season). ... Released by Lions (February 12, 1999). ... Signed by Carolina Panthers (August 2, 1999). ... Released by Panthers (August 30, 1999). ... Signed by Denver Broncos (February 16, 2000). ... Released by Broncos (August 21, 2000). ... Signed by Calgary Stampeders of CFL (October 2000). ... Released by Stampeders (June 27, 2001). ... Signed by San Francisco 49ers (August 7, 2001). ... Released by 49ers (September 3, 2001). ... Re-signed by 49ers (January 23, 2002). ... Assigned by 49ers to Frankfurt Galaxy in 2002 NFL Europe enhancement allocation program (February 12, 2002). ... Released by 49ers (September 7, 2002). ... Re-signed by 49ers to practice squad (September 9, 2002). ... Activated (December 30, 2002). ... Waived by 49ers (August 31, 2003). ... Re-signed by 49ers to practice squad (September 1, 2003). ... Activated (September 17, 2003).
PLAYING EXPERIENCE: Detroit NFL, 1998; Calgary CFL, 2000; San Francisco NFL, 2002-2003. ... Games/Games started: 2000 (2/0), 2002 (2/0), 2003 (2/0), Total: 4/0.

DAVIS, LEONARD — G — CARDINALS

PERSONAL: Born September 5, 1978, in Wortham, Texas. ... 6-6/384. ... Full name: Leonard Barnett Davis.
HIGH SCHOOL: Wortham (Texas).
COLLEGE: Texas.
TRANSACTIONS/CAREER NOTES: Selected by Arizona Cardinals in first round (second pick overall) of 2001 NFL draft. ... Signed by Cardinals (August 8, 2001). ... On injured reserve with knee injury (December 24, 2002-remainder of season).
PLAYING EXPERIENCE: Arizona NFL, 2001-2003. ... Games/Games started: 2001 (16/16), 2002 (15/15), 2003 (14/14). Total: 45/45.
HONORS: Named offensive tackle on THE SPORTING NEWS college All-America first team (2000).

DAVIS, NICK — WR — DOLPHINS

PERSONAL: Born October 6, 1979, in Manchester, Mich. ... 6-0/180.
HIGH SCHOOL: Manchester (Mich.).
COLLEGE: Wisconsin.
TRANSACTIONS/CAREER NOTES: Signed as non-drafted free agent by Minnesota Vikings (April 25, 2002). ... On physically unable to perform list with shoulder injury (August 25, 2003). ... Activated (October 24, 2003). ... Released by Vikings (December 2, 2003). ... Signed by Miami Dolphins (January 16, 2004). ... Assigned by Dolphins to Scottish Claymores in 2004 NFL Europe enhancement allocation program (February 9, 2004).

Year Team	G	GS	PUNT RETURNS No.	Yds.	Avg.	TD	KICKOFF RETURNS No.	Yds.	Avg.	TD	TOTALS TD	2pt.	Pts.	Fum.
2002—Minnesota NFL	15	0	24	190	7.9	0	18	368	20.4	0	0	0	0	4
2003—Minnesota NFL	1	0	0	0	0.0	0	0	0	0.0	0	0	0	0	0
Pro totals (2 years)	16	0	24	190	7.9	0	18	368	20.4	0	0	0	0	4

DAVIS, ROB — C/LS — PACKERS

PERSONAL: Born December 10, 1968, in Washington, DC. ... 6-3/284. ... Full name: Robert Emmett Davis.
HIGH SCHOOL: Eleanor Roosevelt (Greenbelt, Md.).
COLLEGE: Shippensburg (Pa.).
TRANSACTIONS/CAREER NOTES: Signed as non-drafted free agent by New York Jets (April 27, 1993). ... Released by Jets (August 24, 1993). ... Re-signed by Jets (April 29, 1994). ... Released by Jets (August 22, 1994). ... Signed by Baltimore Stallions of CFL (April 1995). ... Signed by Kansas City Chiefs (April 22, 1996). ... Released by Chiefs (August 20, 1996). ... Signed by Chicago Bears (August 28, 1996). ... Released by Bears (August 27, 1997). ... Signed by Green Bay Packers (November 4, 1997). ... On physically unable to perform list with back injury (July 18-August 10, 1998). ... Granted unconditional free agency (March 2, 2001). ... Re-signed by Packers (March 20, 2001).
PLAYING EXPERIENCE: Chicago NFL, 1996; Green Bay NFL, 1997-2003. ... Games/Games started: 1996 (16/0), 1997 (7/0), 1998 (16/0), 1999 (16/0), 2000 (16/0), 2001 (16/0), 2002 (16/0), 2003 (16/0). Total: 119/0.
CHAMPIONSHIP GAME EXPERIENCE: Played in NFC championship game (1997 season). ... Played in Super Bowl 32 (1997 season).

DAVIS, RUSSELL — DT — CARDINALS

PERSONAL: Born March 28, 1975, in Hampton, Va. ... 6-4/314. ... Full name: Russell Morgan Davis.
HIGH SCHOOL: E.E. Smith (Fayetteville, N.C.).
COLLEGE: North Carolina.
TRANSACTIONS/CAREER NOTES: Selected by Chicago Bears in second round (48th pick overall) of 1999 NFL draft. ... Signed by Bears (July 22, 1999). ... Claimed on waivers by Arizona Cardinals (August 28, 2000). ... Granted unconditional free agency (February 28, 2003). ... Re-signed by Cardinals (March 16, 2003).

			TOTALS		
Year Team	**G**	**GS**	**Tk.**	**Ast.**	**Sks.**
1999—Chicago NFL	11	8	13	4	2.0
2000—Arizona NFL	13	9	29	9	0.5
2001—Arizona NFL	16	16	37	17	2.0
2002—Arizona NFL	16	16	35	9	2.0
2003—Arizona NFL	15	15	29	9	1.0
Pro totals (5 years)	71	64	143	48	7.5

D

DAVIS, SAMMY — CB — CHARGERS

PERSONAL: Born April 8, 1980, in Humble, Texas. ... 6-0/190. ... Full name: Samuel J. Davis Jr..
HIGH SCHOOL: Humble (Texas).
COLLEGE: Texas A&M.
TRANSACTIONS/CAREER NOTES: Selected by San Diego Chargers in first round (30th pick overall) of 2003 NFL draft. ... Signed by Chargers (July 23, 2003).

			TOTALS			INTERCEPTIONS			
Year Team	**G**	**GS**	**Tk.**	**Ast.**	**Sks.**	**No.**	**Yds.**	**Avg.**	**TD**
2003—San Diego NFL	16	16	45	13	0.0	2	48	24.0	0

DAVIS, STEPHEN — RB — PANTHERS

PERSONAL: Born March 1, 1974, in Spartanburg, S.C. ... 6-0/230.
HIGH SCHOOL: Spartanburg (S.C.).
COLLEGE: Auburn.
TRANSACTIONS/CAREER NOTES: Selected by Washington Redskins in fourth round (102nd pick overall) of 1996 NFL draft. ... Signed by Redskins (July 16, 1996). ... Granted free agency (February 12, 1999). ... Re-signed by Redskins (May 12, 1999). ... Designated by Redskins as franchise player (February 11, 2000). ... Released by Redskins (February 26, 2003). ... Signed by Carolina Panthers (March 14, 2003).
CHAMPIONSHIP GAME EXPERIENCE: Played in NFC championship game (2003 season). ... Played in Super Bowl 38 (2003 season).
HONORS: Played in Pro Bowl (1999, 2000 and 2003 seasons).
SINGLE GAME HIGHS (regular season): Attempts—38 (January 6, 2002, vs. Arizona); yards—189 (December 12, 1999, vs. Arizona); and rushing touchdowns—3 (November 24, 2002, vs. St. Louis).
STATISTICAL PLATEAUS: 100-yard rushing games: 1999 (6), 2000 (5), 2001 (6), 2002 (1), 2003 (7). Total: 25. 100-yard receiving games: 1998 (1). Total: 1.

			RUSHING				RECEIVING				TOTALS			
Year Team	**G**	**GS**	**Att.**	**Yds.**	**Avg.**	**TD**	**No.**	**Yds.**	**Avg.**	**TD**	**TD**	**2pt.**	**Pts.**	**Fum.**
1996—Washington NFL	12	0	23	139	6.0	2	0	0	0.0	0	2	0	12	0
1997—Washington NFL	14	6	141	567	4.0	3	18	134	7.4	0	3	0	18	1
1998—Washington NFL	16	12	34	109	3.2	0	21	263	12.5	2	2	0	12	0
1999—Washington NFL	14	14	290	‡1405	4.8	*17	23	111	4.8	0	†17	1	104	4
2000—Washington NFL	15	15	332	1318	4.0	11	33	313	9.5	0	11	0	66	4
2001—Washington NFL	16	16	*356	‡1432	4.0	5	28	205	7.3	0	5	1	32	6
2002—Washington NFL	12	12	207	820	4.0	7	23	142	6.2	1	8	0	48	4
2003—Carolina NFL	14	14	318	1444	4.5	8	14	159	11.4	0	8	0	48	3
Pro totals (8 years)	113	89	1701	7234	4.3	53	160	1327	8.3	3	56	2	340	22

DAVISON, ANDREW — CB — COWBOYS

PERSONAL: Born December 9, 1979, in Detroit, Mich. ... 5-11/185.
HIGH SCHOOL: Chadsey (Detroit).
COLLEGE: Kansas.

TRANSACTIONS/CAREER NOTES: Signed as non-drafted free agent by New York Jets (April 26, 2002). ... Released by Jets (August 30, 2003). ... Signed by Dallas Cowboys (September 17, 2003).

			TOTALS			INTERCEPTIONS			
Year Team	G	GS	Tk.	Ast.	Sks.	No.	Yds.	Avg.	TD
2002—New York Jets NFL	6	0	1	0	0.0	0	0	0.0	0
2003—Dallas NFL	4	0	0	0	0.0	0	0	0.0	0
Pro totals (2 years)	10	0	1	0	0.0	0	0	0.0	0

DAWKINS, BRIAN S EAGLES

PERSONAL: Born October 13, 1973, in Jacksonville, Fla. ... 5-11/205.

HIGH SCHOOL: Raines (Jacksonville).

COLLEGE: Clemson.

TRANSACTIONS/CAREER NOTES: Selected by Philadelphia Eagles in second round (61st pick overall) of 1996 NFL draft. ... Signed by Eagles (July 17, 1996).

CHAMPIONSHIP GAME EXPERIENCE: Played in NFC championship game (2001-2003 seasons).

HONORS: Named defensive back on THE SPORTING NEWS college All-America second team (1995). ... Played in Pro Bowl (1999, 2001 and 2002 seasons). ... Named safety on THE SPORTING NEWS NFL All-Pro team (2001 and 2002).

			TOTALS			INTERCEPTIONS			
Year Team	G	GS	Tk.	Ast.	Sks.	No.	Yds.	Avg.	TD
1996—Philadelphia NFL	14	13	53	21	1.0	3	41	13.7	0
1997—Philadelphia NFL	15	15	61	13	0.0	3	76	25.3	1
1998—Philadelphia NFL	14	14	45	11	1.0	2	39	19.5	0
1999—Philadelphia NFL	16	16	58	20	1.5	4	127	31.7	1
2000—Philadelphia NFL	13	13	54	17	2.0	4	62	15.5	0
2001—Philadelphia NFL	15	15	58	12	1.5	2	15	7.5	0
2002—Philadelphia NFL	16	16	66	29	3.0	2	27	13.5	0
2003—Philadelphia NFL	7	7	28	7	0.5	1	0	0.0	0
Pro totals (8 years)	110	109	423	130	10.5	21	387	18.4	2

D

DAWSON, PHIL K BROWNS

PERSONAL: Born January 23, 1975, in West Palm Beach, Fla. ... 5-11/195.

HIGH SCHOOL: Lake Highlands (Dallas).

COLLEGE: Texas.

TRANSACTIONS/CAREER NOTES: Signed as non-drafted free agent by Oakland Raiders (April 24, 1998). ... Claimed on waivers by New England Patriots (August 21, 1998). ... Released by Patriots (August 30, 1998). ... Re-signed by Patriots to practice squad (August 31, 1998). ... Granted free agency after 1998 season. ... Signed by Cleveland Browns (March 25, 1999). ... Granted free agency (March 1, 2002). ... Re-signed by Browns (April 26, 2002). ... On injured reserve with arm injury (December 9, 2003-remainder of season).

		FIELD GOALS							TOTALS		
Year Team	G	1-29	30-39	40-49	50+	Tot.	Pct.	Lg.	XPM	XPA	Pts.
1999—Cleveland NFL	15	2-2	3-5	3-5	0-0	8-12	66.7	49	23	24	53
2000—Cleveland NFL	16	7-7	5-5	2-5	0-0	14-17	82.4	45	17	17	59
2001—Cleveland NFL	16	10-10	8-9	4-6	0-0	22-25	88.0	48	29	30	95
2002—Cleveland NFL	16	9-10	6-8	5-7	2-3	22-28	78.6	52	34	35	100
2003—Cleveland NFL	13	9-9	4-5	3-5	2-2	18-21	85.7	52	20	21	74
Pro totals (5 years)	76	37-38	26-32	17-28	4-5	84-103	81.6	52	123	127	381

DAYNE, RON RB GIANTS

PERSONAL: Born March 14, 1978, in Berlin, N.J. ... 5-10/250.

HIGH SCHOOL: Overbrook (Berlin, N.J.).

COLLEGE: Wisconsin.

TRANSACTIONS/CAREER NOTES: Selected by New York Giants in first round (11th pick overall) of 2000 NFL draft. ... Signed by Giants (July 21, 2000). ... Inactive for 16 games (2003).

CHAMPIONSHIP GAME EXPERIENCE: Played in NFC championship game (2000 season). ... Played in Super Bowl 35 (2000 season).

HONORS: Heisman Trophy winner (1999). ... Doak Walker Award winner (1999). ... Maxwell Award winner (1999). ... Named running back on THE SPORTING NEWS college All-America first team (1999). ... Named College Football Player of the Year by THE SPORTING NEWS (1999).

SINGLE GAME HIGHS (regular season): Attempts—25 (October 29, 2000, vs. Philadelphia); yards—111 (September 30, 2001, vs. New Orleans); and rushing touchdowns—2 (December 15, 2002, vs. Dallas).

STATISTICAL PLATEAUS: 100-yard rushing games: 2000 (1), 2001 (1). Total: 2.

			RUSHING				RECEIVING				TOTALS			
Year Team	G	GS	Att.	Yds.	Avg.	TD	No.	Yds.	Avg.	TD	TD	2pt.	Pts.	Fum.
2000—New York Giants NFL	16	4	228	770	3.4	5	3	11	3.7	0	5	0	30	1
2001—New York Giants NFL	16	7	180	690	3.8	7	8	67	8.4	0	7	1	44	2
2002—New York Giants NFL	16	1	125	428	3.4	3	11	49	4.5	0	3	0	18	1
2003—New York Giants NFL	Did not play.													
Pro totals (3 years)	48	12	533	1888	3.5	15	22	127	5.8	0	15	1	92	4

DEARTH, JAMES — TE/LS — JETS

PERSONAL: Born January 22, 1976, in Fort Ord, Calif. ... 6-4/270.
HIGH SCHOOL: Scurry (Texas)-Rosser.
COLLEGE: Tarleton State (Texas).
TRANSACTIONS/CAREER NOTES: Selected by Cleveland Browns in sixth round (191st pick overall) of 1999 NFL draft. ... Signed by Browns (July 22, 1999). ... Released by Browns (September 3, 1999). ... Re-signed by Browns to practice squad (November 23, 1999). ... Activated (December 14, 1999). ... Assigned by Browns to Scottish Claymores in 2000 NFL Europe enhancement allocation program (February 11, 2000). ... Released by Browns (April 18, 2000). ... Signed by Titans (July 14, 2000). ... Released by Titans (August 22, 2000). ... Re-signed by Titans to practice squad (November 8, 2000). ... Granted free agency following 2000 season. ... Signed by New York Jets (January 24, 2001).
PLAYING EXPERIENCE: Cleveland NFL, 1999; New York Jets NFL, 2001-2003. ... Games/Games started: 1999 (2/0), 2001 (16/0), 2002 (16/0), 2003 (16/0). Total: 50/0.
SINGLE GAME HIGHS (regular season): Receptions—1 (December 16, 2001, vs. Cincinnati); yards—9 (November 11, 2001, vs. Kansas City); and touchdown receptions—1 (December 16, 2001, vs. Cincinnati).

DEESE, DERRICK — T — BUCCANEERS

PERSONAL: Born May 17, 1970, in Culver City, Calif. ... 6-3/289.
HIGH SCHOOL: Culver City (Calif.).
JUNIOR COLLEGE: El Camino Junior College (Calif.).
COLLEGE: Southern California.
TRANSACTIONS/CAREER NOTES: Signed as non-drafted free agent by San Francisco 49ers (May 8, 1992). ... On injured reserve with elbow injury (August 4, 1992-entire season). ... Inactive for six games (1993). ... On injured reserve with broken wrist (October 23, 1993-remainder of season). ... Granted free agency (February 17, 1995). ... Tendered offer sheet by St. Louis Rams (April 20, 1995). ... Offer matched by 49ers (April 21, 1995). ... Granted unconditional free agency (February 16, 1996). ... Re-signed by 49ers (June 4, 1996). ... Granted unconditional free agency (February 14, 1997). ... Re-signed by 49ers (April 22, 1997). ... Released by 49ers (February 26, 2004). ... Signed by Tampa Bay Buccaneers (March 4, 2004).
PLAYING EXPERIENCE: San Francisco NFL, 1994-2003. ... Games/Games started: 1994 (16/15), 1995 (2/2), 1996 (16/0), 1997 (16/13), 1998 (16/16), 1999 (16/16), 2000 (13/13), 2001 (16/16), 2002 (14/14), 2003 (11/11). Total: 136/116.
CHAMPIONSHIP GAME EXPERIENCE: Played in NFC championship game (1994 and 1997 seasons). ... Member of Super Bowl championship team (1994 season).

DELHOMME, JAKE — QB — PANTHERS

PERSONAL: Born January 10, 1975, in Breaux Bridge, La. ... 6-2/205.
HIGH SCHOOL: Teurlings (La.).
COLLEGE: Louisiana-Lafayette.
TRANSACTIONS/CAREER NOTES: Signed as non-drafted free agent by New Orleans Saints (June 10, 1997). ... Released by Saints (August 18, 1997). ... Re-signed by Saints to practice sqaud (November 19, 1997). ... Assigned by Saints to Amsterdam Admirals in 1998 NFL Europe enhancement allocation program (February 18, 1998). ... Inactive for five games (1998). ... Released by Saints (October 14, 1998). ... Re-signed by Saints to practice squad (October 15, 1998). ... Assigned by Saints to Frankfurt Galaxy in 1999 NFL Europe enhancement allocation program (February 22, 1999). ... Released by Saints (September 5, 1999). ... Re-signed by Saints (November 23, 1999). ... Granted free agency (March 1, 2002). ... Re-signed by Saints (April 19, 2002). ... Granted unconditional free agency (February 28, 2003). ... Signed by Carolina Panthers (March 5, 2003).
CHAMPIONSHIP GAME EXPERIENCE: Played in NFC championship game (2003 season). ... Played in Super Bowl 38 (2003 season).
POST SEASON RECORDS: Holds Super Bowl record for longest pass completion (to Muhsin Muhammad)—85 yards (February 1, 2004, vs. New England).
SINGLE GAME HIGHS (regular season): Attempts—49 (October 19, 2003, vs. Tennessee); completions—31 (October 19, 2003, vs. Tennessee); passing yards—362 (October 19, 2003, vs. Dallas); and touchdown passes—3 (September 7, 2003, vs. Dallas).
STATISTICAL PLATEAUS: 300-yard passing games: 2003 (2). Total: 2.
MISCELLANEOUS: Regular-season record as starting NFL quarterback: 11-6 (.647). ... Post-season record as NFL starting quarterback: 3-1 (.750).

			PASSING									RUSHING				TOTALS		
Year Team	**G**	**GS**	**Att.**	**Cmp.**	**Pct.**	**Yds.**	**TD**	**Int.**	**Avg.**	**Skd.**	**Rat.**	**Att.**	**Yds.**	**Avg.**	**TD**	**TD**	**2pt.**	**Pts.**
1999—New Orleans NFL	2	2	76	42	55.3	521	3	5	6.86	6	62.4	11	72	6.5	2	2	0	12
2000—New Orleans NFL							Did not play.											
2002—New Orleans NFL	4	0	10	8	80.0	113	0	0	11.30	0	113.8	4	-2	-0.5	0	0	0	0
2003—Carolina NFL	16	15	449	266	59.2	3219	19	16	7.17	23	80.6	42	39	0.9	1	1	0	6
Pro totals (3 years)	22	17	535	316	59.1	3853	22	21	7.20	29	78.7	57	109	1.9	3	3	0	18

DELOACH, JERRY — DE — TEXANS

PERSONAL: Born July 17, 1977, in Sacramento, Calif. ... 6-2/315.
HIGH SCHOOL: Valley (Calif.).
COLLEGE: California.
TRANSACTIONS/CAREER NOTES: Singed as non-drafted free agent by Washington Redskins (April 28, 2000). ... Traded by Redskins to Houston Texans for QB Danny Wuerffel (March 4, 2002). ... Re-signed by Texans (March 21, 2003). ... Granted free agency (March 3, 2004). ... Re-signed by Texans (April 28, 2004).

			TOTALS		
Year Team	**G**	**GS**	**Tk.**	**Ast.**	**Sks.**
2001—Washington NFL	15	4	9	2	1.0
2002—Houston NFL	16	16	24	8	1.0
2003—Houston NFL	16	16	37	14	0.0
Pro totals (3 years)	47	36	70	24	2.0

DEMAR, ENOCH — T — BROWNS

PERSONAL: Born September 7, 1980, in Indianapolis... 6-4/317.
HIGH SCHOOL: Arsenal Tech (Indianapolis, Ind.).
COLLEGE: Indiana.
TRANSACTIONS/CAREER NOTES: Signed as non-drafted free agent by Cleveland Browns (May 2, 2003).
PLAYING EXPERIENCE: Cleveland NFL, 2003. ... Games/Games started: 2003 (5/2). Total: 5/2.

DEMPS, WILL — S — RAVENS

PERSONAL: Born November 7, 1979, in Charelston, S.C. ... 6-0/205. ... Full name: Will Henry Demps.
HIGH SCHOOL: Highlands (Palmdale, Calif.).
COLLEGE: San Diego State.
TRANSACTIONS/CAREER NOTES: Signed as non-drafted free agent by Baltimore Ravens (April 26, 2002).

			TOTALS			INTERCEPTIONS			
Year Team	G	GS	Tk.	Ast.	Sks.	No.	Yds.	Avg.	TD
2002—Baltimore NFL	14	10	43	6	1.0	1	18	18.0	0
2003—Baltimore NFL	16	9	31	8	0.0	2	57	28.5	0
Pro totals (2 years)	30	19	74	14	1.0	3	75	25.0	0

DEMULLING, RICK — G — COLTS

PERSONAL: Born July 21, 1977, in Cheney, Wash. ... 6-4/304. ... Full name: Rick Elwood DeMulling.
HIGH SCHOOL: Cheney (Wash.).
COLLEGE: Idaho.
TRANSACTIONS/CAREER NOTES: Selected by Indianapolis Colts in seventh round (220th pick overall) of 2001 NFL draft. ... Signed by Colts (June 19, 2001). ... Granted free agency (March 3, 2004). ... Re-signed by Colts (April 16, 2004).
PLAYING EXPERIENCE: Indianapolis NFL, 2001-2003. ... Games/Games started: 2001 (7/0), 2002 (14/14), 2003 (16/16). Total: 37/30.
CHAMPIONSHIP GAME EXPERIENCE: Played in AFC championship game (2003 season).

D

DENNEY, RYAN — DE — BILLS

PERSONAL: Born June 15, 1977, in Denver, Colo. ... 6-7/275.
HIGH SCHOOL: Horizon (Thornton, Colo.).
COLLEGE: Brigham Young.
TRANSACTIONS/CAREER NOTES: Selected by Buffalo Bills in second round (61st pick overall) of 2002 NFL draft. ... Signed by Bills (July 26, 2002).

			TOTALS			INTERCEPTIONS			
Year Team	G	GS	Tk.	Ast.	Sks.	No.	Yds.	Avg.	TD
2002—Buffalo NFL	8	0	6	3	0.0	0	0	0.0	0
2003—Buffalo NFL	16	13	27	16	3.5	0	0	0.0	0
Pro totals (2 years)	24	13	33	19	3.5	0	0	0.0	0

DETMER, KOY — QB — EAGLES

PERSONAL: Born July 5, 1973, in San Antonio, Texas. ... 6-1/195. ... Full name: Koy Dennis Detmer. ... Brother of Ty Detmer, quarterback, Atlanta Falcons.
HIGH SCHOOL: Mission (Texas).
COLLEGE: Colorado.
TRANSACTIONS/CAREER NOTES: Selected by Philadelphia Eagles in seventh round (207th pick overall) of 1997 NFL draft. ... Signed by Eagles (June 4, 1997). ... On injured reserve with knee injury (August 22, 1997-entire season). ... Granted free agency (February 11, 2000). ... Re-signed by Eagles (April 17, 2000).
CHAMPIONSHIP GAME EXPERIENCE: Played in NFC championship game (2001-2003 seasons).
SINGLE GAME HIGHS (regular season): Attempts—43 (December 20, 1998, vs. Dallas); completions—24 (December 20, 1998, vs. Dallas); yards—231 (December 20, 1998, vs. Dallas); and touchdown passes—3 (December 19, 1999, vs. New England).
MISCELLANEOUS: Regular-season record as starting NFL quarterback: 3-4 (.429).

			PASSING									RUSHING				TOTALS		
Year Team	G	GS	Att.	Cmp.	Pct.	Yds.	TD	Int.	Avg.	Skd.	Rat.	Att.	Yds.	Avg.	TD	TD	2pt.	Pts.
1997—Philadelphia NFL	Did not play.																	
1998—Philadelphia NFL	8	5	181	97	53.6	1011	5	5	5.59	5	67.7	7	20	2.9	0	0	0	0
1999—Philadelphia NFL	1	1	29	10	34.5	181	3	2	6.24	0	62.6	2	-2	-1.0	0	0	0	0
2000—Philadelphia NFL	16	0	1	0	0.0	0	0	1	0.00	0	.0	1	8	8.0	0	0	0	0
2001—Philadelphia NFL	16	0	14	5	35.7	51	0	1	3.64	1	17.3	8	6	0.8	0	0	0	0
2002—Philadelphia NFL	14	1	28	19	67.9	224	2	0	8.00	1	115.8	2	4	2.0	1	1	0	6
2003—Philadelphia NFL	16	0	5	3	60.0	32	0	0	6.40	0	78.8	0	0	0.0	0	0	0	0
Pro totals (6 years)	71	7	258	134	51.9	1499	10	9	5.81	7	68.0	20	36	1.8	1	1	0	6

DETMER, TY — QB — FALCONS

PERSONAL: Born October 30, 1967, in San Marcos, Texas. ... 6-0/189. ... Full name: Ty Hubert Detmer. ... Brother of Koy Detmer, quarterback, Philadelphia Eagles.
HIGH SCHOOL: Southwest (San Antonio).

COLLEGE: Brigham Young.

TRANSACTIONS/CAREER NOTES: Selected by Green Bay Packers in ninth round (230th pick overall) of 1992 NFL draft. ... Signed by Packers (July 22, 1992). ... Active for two games (1992); did not play. ... Active for five games (1994); did not play. ... On injured reserve with thumb injury (November 8, 1995-remainder of season). ... Granted unconditional free agency (February 16, 1996). ... Signed by Philadelphia Eagles (March 1, 1996). ... Granted unconditional free agency (February 13, 1998). ... Signed by San Francisco 49ers (March 12, 1998). ... Traded by 49ers with fourth-round pick (LB Wali Rainer) in 1999 draft to Cleveland Browns for fourth- (traded to Indianapolis) and fifth-round (traded to Miami) picks in 1999 draft (February 23, 1999). ... On injured reserve with Achilles' tendon injury (August 16, 2000-entire season). ... Traded by Browns to Detroit Lions for undisclosed pick in 2002 draft (September 2, 2001). ... Granted unconditional free agency (March 3, 2004). ... Signed by Atlanta Falcons (March 30, 2004).

HONORS: Heisman Trophy winner (1990). ... Maxwell Award winner (1990). ... Davey O'Brien Award winner (1990 and 1991). ... Named quarterback on THE SPORTING NEWS college All-America first team (1990 and 1991).

SINGLE GAME HIGHS (regular season): Attempts—51 (December 30, 2001, vs. Chicago); completions—31 (Decmeber 30, 2001, vs. Chicago); yards—342 (October 27, 1996, vs. Carolina); and touchdown passes—4 (October 20, 1996, vs. Miami).

STATISTICAL PLATEAUS: 300-yard passing games: 1996 (3), 2001 (1). Total: 4.

MISCELLANEOUS: Regular-season record as starting NFL quarterback: 11-14 (.440). ... Postseason record as starting NFL quarterback: 0-1.

			PASSING									RUSHING				TOTALS		
Year Team	**G**	**GS**	**Att.**	**Cmp.**	**Pct.**	**Yds.**	**TD**	**Int.**	**Avg.**	**Skd.**	**Rat.**	**Att.**	**Yds.**	**Avg.**	**TD**	**TD**	**2pt.**	**Pts.**
1992—Green Bay NFL						Did not play.												
1993—Green Bay NFL	3	0	5	3	60.0	26	0	0	5.20	0	73.7	1	-2	-2.0	0	0	0	0
1994—Green Bay NFL						Did not play.												
1995—Green Bay NFL	4	0	16	8	50.0	81	1	1	5.06	0	59.6	3	3	1.0	0	0	0	0
1996—Philadelphia NFL	13	11	401	238	59.4	2911	15	13	7.26	27	80.8	31	59	1.9	1	1	0	6
1997—Philadelphia NFL	8	7	244	134	54.9	1567	7	6	6.42	19	73.9	14	46	3.3	1	1	0	6
1998—San Francisco NFL	16	1	38	24	63.2	312	4	3	8.21	5	91.1	8	7	0.9	0	0	0	0
1999—Cleveland NFL	5	2	91	47	51.6	548	4	2	6.02	4	75.7	6	38	6.3	1	1	0	6
2000—Cleveland NFL						Did not play.												
2001—Detroit NFL	4	4	151	92	60.9	906	3	10	6.00	12	56.9	9	26	2.9	0	0	0	0
2002—Detroit NFL						Did not play.												
2003—Detroit NFL	1	0	0	0	0.0	0	0	0	0.00	0	.0	0	0	0.0	0	0	0	0
Pro totals (8 years)	54	25	946	546	57.7	6351	34	35	6.71	67	74.7	72	177	2.5	3	3	0	18

D

DEVRIES, JARED DE LIONS

PERSONAL: Born June 11, 1976, in Aplington, Iowa. ... 6-4/272.

HIGH SCHOOL: Aplington-Parkersburg (Aplington, Iowa).

COLLEGE: Iowa.

TRANSACTIONS/CAREER NOTES: Selected by Detroit Lions in third round (70th pick overall) of 1999 NFL draft. ... Signed by Lions (July 28, 1999). ... On physically unable to perform list with blood clot (July 24-October 27, 2001). ... Granted free agency (March 1, 2002). ... Re-signed by Lions (April 16, 2002). ... On injured reserve with foot injury (December 11, 2002-remainder of season). ... Granted unconditional free agency (February 28, 2003). ... Re-signed by Lions (March 5, 2003).

HONORS: Named defensive tackle on THE SPORTING NEWS college All-America third team (1997). ... Named defensive tackle on THE SPORTING NEWS college All-America first team (1998).

			TOTALS		
Year Team	**G**	**GS**	**Tk.**	**Ast.**	**Sks.**
1999—Detroit NFL	2	0	0	0	0.0
2000—Detroit NFL	15	1	14	8	0.0
2001—Detroit NFL	11	0	9	4	0.0
2002—Detroit NFL	10	0	5	5	1.0
2003—Detroit NFL	13	2	8	6	1.0
Pro totals (5 years)	51	3	36	23	2.0

DICKERSON, KORI TE EAGLES

PERSONAL: Born December 6, 1978, in Los Angeles, Calif. ... 6-4/235.

HIGH SCHOOL: Washington (Los Angeles, Calif.).

COLLEGE: Southern California.

TRANSACTIONS/CAREER NOTES: Signed as non-drafted free agent by Philadelphia Eagles (April 23, 2002). ... Released by Eagles (August 24, 2002). ... Re-signed by Eagles to practice squad for 2002 postseason (December 12, 2002). ... Released by Eagles (August 31, 2003). ... Re-signed by Eagles to practice squad (September 1, 2003). ... Activated (December 20, 2003).

CHAMPIONSHIP GAME EXPERIENCE: Member of Eagles for NFC championship game (2003 season); inactive.

			RECEIVING				TOTALS			
Year Team	**G**	**GS**	**No.**	**Yds.**	**Avg.**	**TD**	**TD**	**2pt.**	**Pts.**	**Fum.**
2003—Philadelphia NFL	2	0	0	0	0.0	0	0	0	0	0

DIEHL, DAVID G GIANTS

PERSONAL: Born September 15, 1980, in Chicago, Ill. ... 6-5/315. ... Full name: David Michael Diehl.

HIGH SCHOOL: Brother Rice (Oak Lawn, Ill.).

COLLEGE: Illinois.

TRANSACTIONS/CAREER NOTES: Selected by New York Giants in fifth round (160th pick overall) of 2003 NFL draft. ... Signed by Giants (June 12, 2003).

PLAYING EXPERIENCE: New York Giants NFL, 2003. ... Games/Games started: 2003 (16/16). Total: 16/16.

DIELMAN, KRIS — G — CHARGERS

PERSONAL: Born February 3, 1981, in Goshen, Ind. ... 6-4/310.
HIGH SCHOOL: Troy (Ohio).
COLLEGE: Indiana.
TRANSACTIONS/CAREER NOTES: Signed as non-drafted free agent by San Diego Chargers (May 2, 2003). ... Waived by Chargers (August 26, 2003). ... Re-signed by Chargers to practice squad (September 2, 2003). ... Activated (October 16, 2003).
PLAYING EXPERIENCE: San Diego NFL, 2003. ... Games/Games started: 2003 (6/0). Total: 6/0.

DIEM, RYAN — G — COLTS

PERSONAL: Born July 1, 1979, in Carol Stream, Ill. ... 6-6/331.
HIGH SCHOOL: Glenbard North (Carol Stream, Ill.).
COLLEGE: Northern Illinois.
TRANSACTIONS/CAREER NOTES: Selected by Indianapolis Colts in fourth round (118th pick overall) of 2001 NFL draft. ... Signed by Colts (July 19, 2001). ... Granted free agency (March 3, 2004). ... Re-signed by Colts (April 20, 2004).
PLAYING EXPERIENCE: Indianapolis NFL, 2001-2003. ... Games/Games started: 2001 (15/8), 2002 (16/16), 2003 (13/13). Total: 44/37.
CHAMPIONSHIP GAME EXPERIENCE: Played in AFC championship game (2003 season).

DIGGS, NA'IL — LB — PACKERS

PERSONAL: Born July 8, 1978, in Phoenix, Ariz. ... 6-4/238. ... Full name: Na'il Ronald Diggs.
HIGH SCHOOL: Dorsey (Los Angeles).
COLLEGE: Ohio State.
TRANSACTIONS/CAREER NOTES: Selected after junior season by Green Bay Packers in fourth round (98th pick overall) of 2000 NFL draft. ... Signed by Packers (June 19, 2000). ... Granted free agency (February 28, 2003). ... Tendered offer sheet by Detroit Lions (March 21, 2003). ... Offer matched by Packers (March 28, 2003).

			TOTALS			INTERCEPTIONS			
Year Team	**G**	**GS**	**Tk.**	**Ast.**	**Sks.**	**No.**	**Yds.**	**Avg.**	**TD**
2000—Green Bay NFL	13	12	24	9	0.0	0	0	0.0	0
2001—Green Bay NFL	16	16	51	16	2.0	0	0	0.0	0
2002—Green Bay NFL	16	16	65	19	3.0	2	62	31.0	0
2003—Green Bay NFL	16	16	76	11	1.0	2	13	6.5	0
Pro totals (4 years)	61	60	216	55	6.0	4	75	18.8	0

DILFER, TRENT — QB — SEAHAWKS

PERSONAL: Born March 13, 1972, in Santa Cruz, Calif. ... 6-4/225. ... Full name: Trent Farris Dilfer.
HIGH SCHOOL: Aptos (Calif.).
COLLEGE: Fresno State.
TRANSACTIONS/CAREER NOTES: Selected after junior season by Tampa Bay Buccaneers in first round (sixth pick overall) of 1994 NFL draft. ... Signed by Buccaneers (August 3, 1994). ... Granted unconditional free agency (January 25, 2000). ... Signed by Baltimore Ravens (March 8, 2000). ... Granted unconditional free agency (March 2, 2001). ... Signed by Seattle Seahawks (August 3, 2001). ... Granted unconditional free agency (March 1, 2002). ... Re-signed by Seahawks (March 5, 2002). ... On injured reserve with knee and Achillies' injuries (October 29, 2002-remainder of season).
CHAMPIONSHIP GAME EXPERIENCE: Member of Buccaneers for NFC championship game (1999 season); inactive. ... Played in AFC championship game (2000 season). ... Member of Super Bowl championship team (2000 season).
HONORS: Played in Pro Bowl (1997 season).
SINGLE GAME HIGHS (regular season): Attempts—48 (November 26, 1995, vs. Green Bay); completions—30 (November 17, 1996, vs. San Diego); yards—352 (September 15, 2002, vs. Arizona); and touchdown passes—4 (September 21, 1997, vs. Miami).
STATISTICAL PLATEAUS: 300-yard passing games: 1995 (1), 1996 (1), 1999 (1), 2002 (1). Total: 4.
MISCELLANEOUS: Regular-season record as starting NFL quarterback: 51-43 (.543). ... Postseason record as starting NFL quarterback: 5-1 (.833).

			PASSING									RUSHING				TOTALS		
Year Team	**G**	**GS**	**Att.**	**Cmp.**	**Pct.**	**Yds.**	**TD**	**Int.**	**Avg.**	**Skd.**	**Rat.**	**Att.**	**Yds.**	**Avg.**	**TD**	**TD**	**2pt.**	**Pts.**
1994—Tampa Bay NFL	5	2	82	38	46.3	433	1	6	5.28	8	36.3	2	27	13.5	0	0	0	0
1995—Tampa Bay NFL	16	16	415	224	54.0	2774	4	18	6.68	‡47	60.1	23	115	5.0	2	2	0	12
1996—Tampa Bay NFL	16	16	482	267	55.4	2859	12	19	5.93	28	64.8	32	124	3.9	0	0	0	0
1997—Tampa Bay NFL	16	16	386	217	56.2	2555	21	11	6.62	32	82.8	33	99	3.0	1	1	0	6
1998—Tampa Bay NFL	16	16	429	225	52.4	2729	21	15	6.36	27	74.0	40	141	3.5	2	2	0	12
1999—Tampa Bay NFL	10	10	244	146	59.8	1619	11	11	6.64	26	75.8	35	144	4.1	0	0	0	0
2000—Baltimore NFL	11	8	226	134	59.3	1502	12	11	6.65	23	76.6	20	75	3.8	0	0	0	0
2001—Seattle NFL	7	4	122	73	59.8	1014	7	4	8.31	10	92.0	11	17	1.5	0	0	0	0
2002—Seattle NFL	6	6	168	94	56.0	1182	4	6	7.04	7	71.1	10	27	2.7	0	0	0	0
2003—Seattle NFL	5	0	8	4	50.0	31	1	1	3.88	1	59.9	2	-1	-0.5	0	0	0	0
Pro totals (10 years)	108	94	2562	1422	55.5	16698	94	102	6.52	209	71.1	208	768	3.7	5	5	0	30

DILGER, KEN — TE — BUCCANEERS

PERSONAL: Born February 2, 1971, in Mariah Hill, Ind. ... 6-5/250. ... Full name: Kenneth Ray Dilger. ... Name pronounced: DIL-gur.
HIGH SCHOOL: Heritage Hills (Lincoln City, Ind.).
COLLEGE: Illinois.
TRANSACTIONS/CAREER NOTES: Selected by Indianapolis Colts in second round (48th pick overall) of 1995 NFL draft. ... Signed by Colts (July 15, 1995). ... Released by Colts (February 21, 2002). ... Signed by Tampa Bay Buccaneers (April 17, 2002).

CHAMPIONSHIP GAME EXPERIENCE: Played in AFC championship game (1995 season). ... Played in NFC championship game (2002 season). ... Member of Super Bowl championship team (2002 season).
HONORS: Played in Pro Bowl (2001 season).
SINGLE GAME HIGHS (regular season): Receptions—8 (September 10, 2000, vs. Oakland); yards—156 (September 8, 1996, vs. New York Jets); and touchdown receptions—3 (December 14, 1997, vs. Miami).
STATISTICAL PLATEAUS: 100-yard receiving games: 1995 (1), 1996 (1), 1997 (1). Total: 3.

			RECEIVING				TOTALS			
Year Team	**G**	**GS**	**No.**	**Yds.**	**Avg.**	**TD**	**TD**	**2pt.**	**Pts.**	**Fum.**
1995—Indianapolis NFL	16	13	42	635	15.1	4	4	0	24	0
1996—Indianapolis NFL	16	16	42	503	12.0	4	4	0	24	1
1997—Indianapolis NFL	14	14	27	380	14.1	3	3	0	18	0
1998—Indianapolis NFL	16	16	31	303	9.8	1	1	1	8	0
1999—Indianapolis NFL	15	15	40	479	12.0	2	2	0	12	1
2000—Indianapolis NFL	16	16	47	538	11.4	3	3	0	18	1
2001—Indianapolis NFL	16	16	32	343	10.7	1	1	1	8	2
2002—Tampa Bay NFL	16	15	34	329	9.7	2	2	0	12	1
2003—Tampa Bay NFL	15	15	22	244	11.1	1	1	0	6	1
Pro totals (9 years)	140	136	317	3754	11.8	21	21	2	130	7

DILLON, COREY — RB — PATRIOTS

PERSONAL: Born October 24, 1974, in Seattle, Wash. ... 6-1/225.
HIGH SCHOOL: Franklin (Seattle).
JUNIOR COLLEGE: Garden City (Kan.) Community College, then Dixie College (Utah).
COLLEGE: Washington.
TRANSACTIONS/CAREER NOTES: Selected after junior season by Cincinnati Bengals in second round (43rd pick overall) of 1997 NFL draft. ... Signed by Bengals (July 21, 1997). ... Granted free agency (February 11, 2000). ... Re-signed by Bengals (August 9, 2000). ... Designated by Bengals as transition player (February 12, 2001). ... Re-signed by Bengals (May 11, 2001). ... Traded by Bengals to New England Patriots for second-round pick (S Madieu Williams) in 2004 draft (April 19, 2004).
HONORS: Named running back on THE SPORTING NEWS college All-America second team (1996). ... Played in Pro Bowl (1999-2001 seasons).
SINGLE GAME HIGHS (regular season): Attempts—39 (December 4, 1997, vs. Tennessee); yards—278 (October 22, 2000, vs. Denver); and rushing touchdowns—4 (December 4, 1997, vs. Tennessee).
STATISTICAL PLATEAUS: 100-yard rushing games: 1997 (4), 1998 (4), 1999 (5), 2000 (5), 2001 (4), 2002 (5), 2003 (1). Total: 28.
MISCELLANEOUS: Selected by San Diego Padres organization in 34th round of free agent draft (June 3, 1993); did not sign. ... Holds Cincinnati Bengals all-time record for most yards rushing (8,061).

			RUSHING				RECEIVING				KICKOFF RETURNS				TOTALS			
Year Team	**G**	**GS**	**Att.**	**Yds.**	**Avg.**	**TD**	**No.**	**Yds.**	**Avg.**	**TD**	**No.**	**Yds.**	**Avg.**	**TD**	**TD**	**2pt.**	**Pts.**	**Fum.**
1997—Cincinnati NFL	16	6	233	1129	4.8	10	27	259	9.6	0	6	182	30.3	0	10	0	60	1
1998—Cincinnati NFL	15	15	262	1130	4.3	4	28	178	6.4	1	0	0	0.0	0	5	0	30	2
1999—Cincinnati NFL	15	15	263	1200	4.6	5	31	290	9.4	1	1	4	4.0	0	6	0	36	3
2000—Cincinnati NFL	16	16	315	1435	4.6	7	18	158	8.8	0	0	0	0.0	0	7	0	42	4
2001—Cincinnati NFL	16	16	§340	1315	3.9	10	34	228	6.7	3	0	0	0.0	0	13	0	78	5
2002—Cincinnati NFL	16	16	314	1311	4.2	7	43	298	6.9	0	0	0	0.0	0	7	0	42	5
2003—Cincinnati NFL	13	11	138	541	3.9	2	11	71	6.5	0	0	0	0.0	0	2	0	12	0
Pro totals (7 years)	107	95	1865	8061	4.3	45	192	1482	7.7	5	7	186	26.6	0	50	0	300	20

DINAPOLI, GENNARO — C — COWBOYS

PERSONAL: Born May 25, 1975, in Manhasset, N.Y. ... 6-3/287. ... Full name: Gennaro L. DiNapoli. ... Name pronounced: den-ah-POLE-e.
HIGH SCHOOL: Cazenovia (N.Y.), then Milford (Conn.) Academy.
COLLEGE: Virginia Tech.
TRANSACTIONS/CAREER NOTES: Selected by Oakland Raiders in fourth round (109th pick overall) of 1998 NFL draft. ... Signed by Raiders (July 24, 1998). ... Active for four games (1998); did not play. ... Traded by Raiders to Tennessee Titans for undisclosed pick (August 27, 2000). ... Granted unconditional free agency (March 1, 2002). ... Re-signed by Titans (April 19, 2002). ... Released by Titans (February 27, 2003). ... Signed by Dallas Cowboys (August 7, 2003). ... On injured reserve with ankle injury (October 29, 2003-remainder of season). ... Granted unconditional free agency (March 3, 2004). ... Re-signed by Cowboys (March 8, 2004).
PLAYING EXPERIENCE: Oakland NFL, 1999; Tennessee NFL, 2001-2002; Dallas NFL, 2003. ... Games/Games started: 1999 (11/9), 2001 (5/2), 2002 (16/16), 2003 (7/0). Total: 39/27.
CHAMPIONSHIP GAME EXPERIENCE: Played in AFC championship game (2002 season).

DINGLE, ADRIAN — DE — CHARGERS

PERSONAL: Born June 25, 1977, in Holly Hill, S.C. ... 6-3/272. ... Full name: Adrian Kennell Dingle.
HIGH SCHOOL: Holly Hill (S.C.)-Roberts.
COLLEGE: Clemson.
TRANSACTIONS/CAREER NOTES: Selected by San Diego Chargers in fifth round (139th pick overall) of 1999 NFL draft. ... Signed by Chargers (July 23, 1999). ... On physically unable to perform list with knee injury (August 31-November 17, 1999). ... Active for two games (1999); did not play. ... Granted free agency (March 1, 2002). ... Re-signed by Chargers (March 29, 2002). ... Granted unconditional free agency (February 28, 2003). ... Re-signed by Chargers (March 11, 2003).

			TOTALS		
Year Team	**G**	**GS**	**Tk.**	**Ast.**	**Sks.**
1999—San Diego NFL		Did not play.			
2000—San Diego NFL	14	1	15	1	2.5
2001—San Diego NFL	14	0	10	1	1.0
2002—San Diego NFL	16	3	24	1	4.0
2003—San Diego NFL	16	15	31	6	6.0
Pro totals (4 years)	60	19	80	9	13.5

DINKINS, DARNELL — TE — GIANTS

PERSONAL: Born January 20, 1977, in Pittsburgh, Pa. ... 6-3/255. ... Full name: Darnell Joseph Dinkins.
HIGH SCHOOL: Schenley (Pittsburgh).
COLLEGE: Pittsburgh.
TRANSACTIONS/CAREER NOTES: Signed as non-drafted free agent by New York Giants (January 31, 2002). ... Assigned by Giants to Rhein Fire in 2002 NFL Europe enhancement allocation program (February 12, 2002). ... On injured reserve with foot injury (November 1, 2002-remainder of season). ... Waived by Giants (August 31, 2003). ... Re-signed by Giants to practice squad (September 1, 2003). ... Activated (November 15, 2003).
SINGLE GAME HIGHS (regular season): Receptions—2 (December 28, 2003, vs. Carolina); yards—16 (December 28, 2003, vs. Carolina); and touchdown receptions—0.

			RECEIVING				TOTALS			
Year Team	**G**	**GS**	**No.**	**Yds.**	**Avg.**	**TD**	**TD**	**2pt.**	**Pts.**	**Fum.**
2002—New York Giants NFL	2	0	0	0	0.0	0	0	0	0	0
2003—New York Giants NFL	7	0	2	16	8.0	0	0	0	0	0
Pro totals (2 years)	9	0	2	16	8.0	0	0	0	0	0

DISHMAN, CHRIS — G

PERSONAL: Born February 27, 1974, in Cozad, Neb. ... 6-3/339.
HIGH SCHOOL: Cozad (Neb.).
COLLEGE: Nebraska.
TRANSACTIONS/CAREER NOTES: Selected by Arizona Cardinals in fourth round (106th pick overall) of 1997 NFL draft. ... Signed by Cardinals (July 9, 1997). ... Granted free agency (February 11, 2000). ... Re-signed by Cardinals (April 28, 2000) ... Granted unconditional free agency (March 2, 2001). ... Re-signed by Cardinals (March 5, 2001). ... Granted unconditional free agency (March 3, 2004).
PLAYING EXPERIENCE: Arizona NFL, 1997-2003. ... Games/Games started: 1997 (8/0), 1998 (12/11), 1999 (13/10), 2000 (15/12), 2001 (16/5), 2002 (14/14), 2003 (14/2). Total: 92/54.

DIXON, DAVID — G — VIKINGS

PERSONAL: Born January 5, 1969, in Papakura, New Zealand. ... 6-5/343. ... Full name: David Tukatahi Dixon.
HIGH SCHOOL: Pukekohe (New Zealand).
JUNIOR COLLEGE: Ricks College (Idaho).
COLLEGE: Arizona State.
TRANSACTIONS/CAREER NOTES: Selected by New England Patriots in ninth-round (232nd pick overall) of 1992 draft. ... Signed by Patriots for 1992 season. ... Released by Patriots (August 1992). ... Signed by Minnesota Vikings to practice squad (October 20, 1992). ... Released by Vikings (August 23, 1993). ... Signed by Dallas Cowboys to practice squad (September 8, 1993). ... Granted free agency after 1993 season. ... Signed by Vikings (July 12, 1994). ... Granted free agency (February 14, 1997). ... Re-signed by Vikings (May 1, 1997). ... Granted unconditional free agency (February 13, 1998). ... Re-signed by Vikings (February 17, 1998). ... On physically unable to perform list with knee injury (August 1-10, 1999).
PLAYING EXPERIENCE: Minnesota NFL, 1994-2003. ... Games/Games started: 1994 (1/0), 1995 (15/6), 1996 (13/6), 1997 (13/13), 1998 (16/16), 1999 (16/16), 2000 (16/16), 2001 (15/14), 2002 (15/15), 2003 (16/16). Total: 136/118.
CHAMPIONSHIP GAME EXPERIENCE: Played in NFC championship game (1998 and 2000 seasons).

DIXON, MARK — T

PERSONAL: Born November 26, 1970, in Charlottesville, N.C. ... 6-4/295. ... Full name: Mark Keller Dixon.
HIGH SCHOOL: Ragsdale (Jamestown, N.C.).
COLLEGE: Virginia.
TRANSACTIONS/CAREER NOTES: Signed as non-drafted free agent by Philadelphia Eagles (April 1994). ... Released by Eagles (August 1994). ... Played with Frankfurt Galaxy of World League (1995). ... Signed by Atlanta Falcons (July 18, 1995). ... Released by Falcons (August 21, 1995). ... Signed by Baltimore Stallions of CFL (August 30, 1995). ... Signed by Miami Dolphins (January 22, 1998). ... On injured reserve with neck injury (November 24, 1998-remainder of season). ... On injured reserve with broken leg (December 4, 2001-remainder of season). ... On injured reserve with ankle injury (November 4, 2003-remainder of season). ... Released by Dolphins (March 2, 2004).
PLAYING EXPERIENCE: Baltimore CFL, 1995; Montreal CFL, 1996-1997; Miami NFL, 1998-2003. ... Games/Games started: 1995 (8/...), 1996 (18/...), 1997 (7/...), 1998 (11/10), 1999 (13/13), 2000 (15/15), 2001 (10/10), 2002 (13/12), Total: 62/60.
CHAMPIONSHIP GAME EXPERIENCE: Member of CFL championship team (1995).

DIXON, TONY — S — COWBOYS

PERSONAL: Born June 18, 1979, in Tuscaloosa, Ala. ... 6-1/213.
HIGH SCHOOL: Pickens County (Reform, Ala.).
COLLEGE: Alabama.
TRANSACTIONS/CAREER NOTES: Selected by Dallas Cowboys in second round (56th pick overall) of 2001 NFL draft. ... Signed by Cowboys (July 21, 2001).

			TOTALS			INTERCEPTIONS			
Year Team	**G**	**GS**	**Tk.**	**Ast.**	**Sks.**	**No.**	**Yds.**	**Avg.**	**TD**
2001—Dallas NFL	8	0	5	2	1.0	0	0	0.0	0
2002—Dallas NFL	16	7	31	9	2.0	1	0	0.0	0
2003—Dallas NFL	16	0	0	0	0.0	0	0	0.0	0
Pro totals (3 years)	40	7	36	11	3.0	1	0	0.0	0

DOCKERY, DERRICK — G — REDSKINS

PERSONAL: Born September 7, 1980, in Garland, Texas. ... 6-6/345.
HIGH SCHOOL: Lakeview Centennial (Lakeview, Texas).
COLLEGE: Texas.
TRANSACTIONS/CAREER NOTES: Selected by Washington Redskins in third round (81st pick overall) of 2003 NFL draft. ... Signed by Redskins (July 28, 2003).
PLAYING EXPERIENCE: Washington NFL, 2003. ... Games/Games started: 2003 (16/13). Total: 16/13.

DOERING, CHRIS — WR — STEELERS

PERSONAL: Born May 19, 1973, in Gainesville, Fla. ... 6-4/202. ... Full name: Christopher Paul Doering. ... Name pronounced: DOOR-ing.
HIGH SCHOOL: P.K. Yonge (Gainesville, Fla.).
COLLEGE: Florida.
TRANSACTIONS/CAREER NOTES: Selected by Jacksonville Jaguars in sixth round (185th pick overall) of 1996 NFL draft. ... Signed by Jaguars (June 5, 1996). ... Claimed on waivers by New York Jets (August 20, 1996). ... Released by Jets (August 25, 1996). ... Signed by Indianapolis Colts to practice squad (August 27, 1996). ... Activated (December 20, 1996). ... Released by Colts (August 24, 1997). ... Re-signed by Colts to practice squad (August 25, 1997). ... Activated (December 5, 1997). ... Claimed on waivers by Cincinnati Bengals (February 25, 1998). ... Released by Bengals (September 2, 1998). ... Signed by Denver Broncos (February 3, 1999). ... Released by Broncos (August 7, 2000). ... Re-signed by Broncos (August 6, 2001). ... Released by Broncos (August 28, 2001). ... Signed by Washington Redskins (February 21, 2002). ... Granted free agency (February 28, 2003). ... Signed by Pittsburgh Steelers (May 20, 2003). ... Granted unconditional free agency (March 3, 2004). ... Re-signed by Steelers (March 4, 2004).
SINGLE GAME HIGHS (regular season): Receptions—4 (November 17, 2003, vs. San Francisco); yards—62 (November 9, 2003, vs. Arizona); and touchdown receptions—1 (November 9, 2003, vs. Arizona).

			RECEIVING				TOTALS			
Year Team	**G**	**GS**	**No.**	**Yds.**	**Avg.**	**TD**	**TD**	**2pt.**	**Pts.**	**Fum.**
1996—Indianapolis NFL	1	0	1	10	10.0	0	0	0	0	0
1997—Indianapolis NFL	2	0	2	12	6.0	0	0	0	0	0
1999—Denver NFL	3	0	3	22	7.3	0	0	0	0	0
2002—Washington NFL	15	3	18	192	10.7	2	2	1	14	1
2003—Pittsburgh NFL	16	0	18	240	13.3	1	1	0	6	0
Pro totals (5 years)	37	3	42	476	11.3	3	3	1	20	1

D

DOERING, JASON — S — GIANTS

PERSONAL: Born April 22, 1978, in Rhinelander, Wis. ... 6-0/201. ... Full name: Jason James Doering.
HIGH SCHOOL: Rhinelander (Wis.).
COLLEGE: Wisconsin.
TRANSACTIONS/CAREER NOTES: Selected by Indianapolis Colts in sixth round (193rd pick overall) of 2001 NFL draft. ... Signed by Colts (June 7, 2001). ... Granted unrestricted free agency (March 3, 2004). ... Signed by New York Giants (May 20, 2004).
CHAMPIONSHIP GAME EXPERIENCE: Played in AFC championship game (2003 season).

			TOTALS			INTERCEPTIONS			
Year Team	**G**	**GS**	**Tk.**	**Ast.**	**Sks.**	**No.**	**Yds.**	**Avg.**	**TD**
2001—Indianapolis NFL	16	1	10	1	0.0	0	0	0.0	0
2002—Indianapolis NFL	15	6	24	12	0.0	0	0	0.0	0
2003—Indianapolis NFL	16	0	6	0	0.0	0	0	0.0	0
Pro totals (3 years)	47	7	40	13	0.0	0	0	0.0	0

DONNALLEY, KEVIN — G

PERSONAL: Born June 10, 1968, in St. Louis, Mo. ... 6-5/310. ... Full name: Kevin Thomas Donnalley. ... Brother of Rick Donnalley, center with Pittsburgh Steelers (1982 and 1983), Washington Redskins (1984 and 1985) and Kansas City Chiefs (1986 and 1987).
HIGH SCHOOL: Athens Drive Senior (Raleigh, N.C.).
COLLEGE: North Carolina.
TRANSACTIONS/CAREER NOTES: Selected by Houston Oilers in third round (79th pick overall) of 1991 NFL draft. ... Signed by Oilers (July 10, 1991). ... Granted free agency (February 17, 1994). ... Tendered offer sheet by Los Angeles Rams (March 17, 1994). ... Offer matched by Oilers (March 23, 1994). ... Oilers franchise moved to Tennessee for 1997 season. ... Granted unconditional free agency (February 13, 1998). ... Signed by Miami Dolphins (February 17, 1998). ... Released by Dolphins (June 2, 2000). ... Re-signed by Dolphins (June 13, 2000). ... Granted unconditional free agency (March 2, 2001). ... Signed by Carolina Panthers (March 16, 2001). ... On injured reserve with knee injury (October 23, 2001-remainder of season). ... Announced retirement (February 16, 2004).
PLAYING EXPERIENCE: Houston NFL, 1991-1996; Tennessee NFL, 1997; Miami NFL, 1998-2000; Carolina NFL, 2001-2003. ... Games/Games started: 1991 (16/0), 1992 (16/2), 1993 (16/6), 1994 (13/11), 1995 (16/16), 1996 (16/16), 1997 (16/16), 1998 (14/14), 1999 (16/9), 2000 (16/16), 2001 (6/6), 2002 (16/16), 2003 (16/16). Total: 193/144.
CHAMPIONSHIP GAME EXPERIENCE: Played in NFC championship game (2003 season). ... Played in Super Bowl 38 (2003 season).

DORENBOS, JON — C/LS — BILLS

PERSONAL: Born July 21, 1980, in Humble, Texas. ... 6-0/250. ... Name pronounced: DORN-bahs.
HIGH SCHOOL: Pacifica (Garden Grove, Calif.).
JUNIOR COLLEGE: Golden West (Huntington Beach, Calif.).
COLLEGE: Texas-El Paso.
TRANSACTIONS/CAREER NOTES: Signed as non-drafted free agent by Buffalo Bills (April 28, 2003).
PLAYING EXPERIENCE: Buffalo NFL, 2003. ... Games/Games started: 2003 (16/0). Total: 16/0.

DORSETT, ANTHONY — S

PERSONAL: Born September 14, 1973, in Aliquippa, Pa. ... 5-11/205. ... Full name: Anthony Drew Dorsett Jr. ... Son of Tony Dorsett, Hall of Fame running back with Dallas Cowboys (1977-87) and Denver Broncos (1988).
HIGH SCHOOL: Richland (Dallas), then J.J. Pearce (Dallas).
COLLEGE: Pittsburgh.
TRANSACTIONS/CAREER NOTES: Selected by Houston Oilers in sixth round (177th pick overall) of 1996 NFL draft. ... Signed by Oilers (June 21, 1996). ... Assigned by Oilers to Barcelona Dragons in 1997 World League enhancement allocation program (February 19, 1997). ... Oilers franchise moved to Tennessee for 1997 season. ... Oilers franchise renamed Tennessee Titans for 1999 season (December 26, 1998). ... Granted free agency (February 12, 1999). ... Re-signed by Titans (June 15, 1999). ... Granted unconditional free agency (February 11, 2000). ... Signed by Oakland Raiders (March 21, 2000). ... Released by Raiders (February 27, 2003). ... Re-signed by Raiders (July 16, 2003). ... Granted unconditional free agency (March 3, 2004).
CHAMPIONSHIP GAME EXPERIENCE: Played in AFC championship game (1999, 2000 and 2002 seasons). ... Played in Super Bowl 34 (1999 season). ... Played in Super Bowl 37 (2002 season).

			TOTALS			INTERCEPTIONS			
Year Team	G	GS	Tk.	Ast.	Sks.	No.	Yds.	Avg.	TD
1996—Houston NFL	8	0	0	0	0.0	0	0	0.0	0
1997—Tennessee NFL	16	0	5	3	0.0	0	0	0.0	0
1998—Tennessee NFL	16	0	3	1	0.0	0	0	0.0	0
1999—Tennessee NFL	16	1	8	2	0.0	1	43	43.0	0
2000—Oakland NFL	16	16	52	20	1.0	0	0	0.0	0
2001—Oakland NFL	16	16	62	9	1.0	2	65	32.5	†2
2002—Oakland NFL	16	7	26	10	0.0	0	0	0.0	0
2003—Oakland NFL	14	6	40	8	0.0	0	0	0.0	0
Pro totals (8 years)	118	46	196	53	2.0	3	108	36.0	2

DORSEY, KEN — QB — 49ERS

PERSONAL: Born April 22, 1981, in Orinda, Calif. ... 6-5/208. ... Full name: Kenneth Simon Dorsey.
HIGH SCHOOL: Miramonte (Orinda, Calif.).
COLLEGE: Miami (Fla.).
TRANSACTIONS/CAREER NOTES: Selected by San Francisco 49ers in seventh round (241st pick overall) of 2003 NFL draft. ... Signed by 49ers (July 23, 2003).

			PASSING									RUSHING				TOTALS		
Year Team	G	GS	Att.	Cmp.	Pct.	Yds.	TD	Int.	Avg.	Skd.	Rat.	Att.	Yds.	Avg.	TD	TD	2pt.	Pts.
2003—San Francisco NFL	Did not play.																	

DOSS, MIKE — S — COLTS

PERSONAL: Born March 24, 1981, in Canton, Ohio. ... 5-10/207.
HIGH SCHOOL: McKinley (Canton, Ohio).
COLLEGE: Ohio State.
TRANSACTIONS/CAREER NOTES: Selected by Indianapolis Colts in second round (58th pick overall) of 2003 NFL draft. ... Signed by Colts (July 31, 2003).
CHAMPIONSHIP GAME EXPERIENCE: Played in AFC championship game (2003 season).

			TOTALS			INTERCEPTIONS			
Year Team	G	GS	Tk.	Ast.	Sks.	No.	Yds.	Avg.	TD
2003—Indianapolis NFL	15	15	68	29	0.0	1	15	15.0	0

DOUGLAS, HUGH — DE — JAGUARS

PERSONAL: Born August 23, 1971, in Mansfield, Ohio. ... 6-2/281.
HIGH SCHOOL: Mansfield (Ohio).
COLLEGE: Central State.
TRANSACTIONS/CAREER NOTES: Selected after junior season by New York Jets in first round (16th pick overall) of 1995 NFL draft. ... Signed by Jets (June 8, 1995). ... Traded by Jets to Philadelphia Eagles for second- (traded to Pittsburgh) and fifth-round (LB Casey Dailey) picks in 1998 draft (March 13, 1998). ... On injured reserve with bicep injury (October 20, 1999-remainder of season). ... Granted unconditional free agency (February 28, 2003). ... Signed by Jacksonville Jaguars (March 16, 2003).
CHAMPIONSHIP GAME EXPERIENCE: Played in NFC championship game (2001 and 2002 seasons).
HONORS: Named defensive end on THE SPORTING NEWS NFL All-Pro team (2000). ... Played in Pro Bowl (2000-2002 seasons).

			TOTALS			INTERCEPTIONS			
Year Team	G	GS	Tk.	Ast.	Sks.	No.	Yds.	Avg.	TD
1995—New York Jets NFL	15	3	25	8	10.0	0	0	0.0	0
1996—New York Jets NFL	10	10	28	8	8.0	0	0	0.0	0
1997—New York Jets NFL	15	15	31	8	4.0	0	0	0.0	0
1998—Philadelphia NFL	15	13	37	9	12.5	0	0	0.0	0
1999—Philadelphia NFL	4	2	5	3	2.0	0	0	0.0	0
2000—Philadelphia NFL	16	15	44	12	15.0	1	9	9.0	0
2001—Philadelphia NFL	15	15	39	8	9.5	0	0	0.0	0
2002—Philadelphia NFL	16	16	45	8	12.5	0	0	0.0	0
2003—Jacksonville NFL	16	16	22	5	3.5	0	0	0.0	0
Pro totals (9 years)	122	105	276	69	77.0	1	9	9.0	0

DOUGLAS, MARQUES — DE — RAVENS

PERSONAL: Born March 5, 1977, in Greensboro, N.C. ... 6-2/280. ... Full name: Marques Lamont Douglas.
HIGH SCHOOL: Dudley (Greensboro, N.C.).
COLLEGE: Howard.
TRANSACTIONS/CAREER NOTES: Signed by Baltimore Ravens as non-drafted free agent (April 23, 1999). ... Released by Ravens (September 4, 1999). ... Re-signed by Ravens (December 22, 1999). ... Claimed on waivers by New Orleans Saints (August 28, 2000). ... Released by Saints (September 14, 2000). ... Re-signed by Saints (September 20, 2000). ... On injured reserve with knee injury (October 12, 2000-remainder of season). ... Released by Saints (September 2, 2001). ... Re-signed by Saints to practice squad (September 3, 2001). ... Signed by Baltimore Ravens off Saints practice squad (November 28, 2001). ... Re-signed by Ravens (March 23, 2003). ... Granted free agency (March 3, 2004). ... Re-signed by Ravens (April 16, 2004).

			TOTALS		
Year Team	G	GS	Tk.	Ast.	Sks.
2000—New Orleans NFL	1	0	1	0	0.0
2001—Baltimore NFL	2	0	1	1	1.0
2002—Baltimore NFL	5	1	6	4	1.0
2003—Baltimore NFL	16	16	52	11	4.5
Pro totals (4 years)	24	17	60	16	6.5

DOWNING, ERIC — DT — CHIEFS

PERSONAL: Born September 16, 1978, in Ahoskie, N.C. ... 6-3/315. ... Full name: Eric Lamont Downing.
HIGH SCHOOL: John F. Kennedy (Paterson, N.J.).
JUNIOR COLLEGE: Coffeyville (Kan.) Community College.
COLLEGE: Syracuse.
TRANSACTIONS/CAREER NOTES: Selected by Kansas City Chiefs in third round (75th pick overall) of 2001 NFL draft. ... Signed by Chiefs (May 23, 2001). ... Granted free agency (March 3, 2004). ... Re-signed by Chiefs (March 24, 2004).

			TOTALS		
Year Team	G	GS	Tk.	Ast.	Sks.
2001—Kansas City NFL	15	9	13	6	1.5
2002—Kansas City NFL	13	4	10	4	0.5
2003—Kansas City NFL	14	0	7	3	0.0
Pro totals (3 years)	42	13	30	13	2.0

D

DRAFT, CHRIS — LB — FALCONS

PERSONAL: Born February 26, 1976, in Anaheim, Calif. ... 5-11/232.
HIGH SCHOOL: Valencia (Placentia, Calif.).
COLLEGE: Stanford.
TRANSACTIONS/CAREER NOTES: Selected by Chicago Bears in sixth round (157th pick overall) of 1998 NFL draft. ... Signed by Bears (June 16, 1998). ... Released by Bears (August 30, 1998). ... Re-signed by Bears to practice squad (August 31, 1998). ... Activated (December 2, 1998). ... Released by Bears (August 30, 1999). ... Signed by San Francisco 49ers to practice squad (September 29, 1999). ... Activated (November 19, 1999). ... Released by 49ers (February 10, 2000). ... Signed by Atlanta Falcons (February 14, 2000).

			TOTALS			INTERCEPTIONS			
Year Team	G	GS	Tk.	Ast.	Sks.	No.	Yds.	Avg.	TD
1998—Chicago NFL	1	0	0	0	0.0	0	0	0.0	0
1999—San Francisco NFL	7	0	0	0	0.0	0	0	0.0	0
2000—Atlanta NFL	13	8	41	15	1.0	0	0	0.0	0
2001—Atlanta NFL	13	10	53	19	0.0	0	0	0.0	0
2002—Atlanta NFL	15	5	49	15	3.5	2	12	6.0	0
2003—Atlanta NFL	16	16	102	20	2.0	1	4	4.0	0
Pro totals (6 years)	65	39	245	69	6.5	3	16	5.3	0

DRIVER, DONALD — WR — PACKERS

PERSONAL: Born February 2, 1975, in Houston, Texas. ... 6-0/188. ... Full name: Donald Jerome Driver.
HIGH SCHOOL: Milby (Houston).
COLLEGE: Alcorn State.
TRANSACTIONS/CAREER NOTES: Selected by Green Bay Packers in seventh round (213th pick overall) of 1999 NFL draft. ... Signed by Packers (June 2, 1999). ... Granted free agency (March 1, 2002). ... Re-signed by Packers (April 16, 2002).
HONORS: Played in Pro Bowl (2002 season).
SINGLE GAME HIGHS (regular season): Receptions—11 (November 10, 2002, vs. Detroit); yards—130 (November 10, 2002, vs. Detroit); and touchdown receptions—2 (September 29, 2002, vs. Carolina).
STATISTICAL PLATEAUS: 100-yard receiving games: 2002 (3), 2003 (1). Total: 4.

			RUSHING				RECEIVING				TOTALS			
Year Team	G	GS	Att.	Yds.	Avg.	TD	No.	Yds.	Avg.	TD	TD	2pt.	Pts.	Fum.
1999—Green Bay NFL	6	0	0	0	0.0	0	3	31	10.3	1	1	0	6	0
2000—Green Bay NFL	16	2	1	4	4.0	0	21	322	15.3	1	1	1	8	0
2001—Green Bay NFL	13	2	3	38	12.7	1	13	167	12.8	1	2	0	12	0
2002—Green Bay NFL	16	16	8	70	8.8	0	70	1064	15.2	9	9	0	54	1
2003—Green Bay NFL	15	15	5	51	10.2	0	52	621	11.9	2	2	0	12	0
Pro totals (5 years)	66	35	17	163	9.6	1	159	2205	13.9	14	15	1	92	1

DROUGHNS, REUBEN RB BRONCOS

PERSONAL: Born August 21, 1978, in Chicago, Ill. ... 5-11/207.
HIGH SCHOOL: Anaheim (Calif.).
JUNIOR COLLEGE: Merced (Calif.) College.
COLLEGE: Oregon.
TRANSACTIONS/CAREER NOTES: Selected by Detroit Lions in third round (81st pick overall) of 2000 NFL draft. ... Signed by Lions (July 15, 2000). ... On injured reserve with shoulder injury (August 22, 2000-entire season). ... Released by Lions (September 12, 2001). ... Signed by Miami Dolphins to practice squad (September 18, 2001). ... Signed by Lions off Dolphins practice squad (October 9, 2001). ... Granted free agency (March 1, 2002). ... Signed by Denver Broncos (April 1, 2002). ... Granted free agency (February 28, 2003). ... Re-signed by Broncos (April 24, 2003). ... Granted unconditional free agency (March 3, 2004). ... Re-signed by Broncos (March 19, 2004).
SINGLE GAME HIGHS (regular season): Attempts—13 (November 11, 2001, vs. Tampa Bay); yards—36 (November 4, 2001, vs. San Francisco); and rushing touchdowns—1 (September 30, 2002, vs. Baltimore).

			RUSHING				RECEIVING				KICKOFF RETURNS				TOTALS			
Year Team	G	GS	Att.	Yds.	Avg.	TD	No.	Yds.	Avg.	TD	No.	Yds.	Avg.	TD	TD	2pt.	Pts.	Fum.
2000—Detroit NFL							Did not play.											
2001—Detroit NFL	9	3	30	72	2.4	0	4	21	5.3	1	0	0	0.0	0	1	0	6	0
2002—Denver NFL	16	0	4	11	2.8	1	5	53	10.6	1	20	516	25.8	0	2	0	12	0
2003—Denver NFL	15	4	6	14	2.3	0	9	87	9.7	2	12	293	24.4	0	2	0	12	0
Pro totals (3 years)	40	7	40	97	2.4	1	18	161	8.9	4	32	809	25.3	0	5	0	30	0

DRUMMOND, EDDIE WR LIONS

PERSONAL: Born April 12, 1980, in Pittsburgh, Pa. ... 5-9/185.
HIGH SCHOOL: Linsley (Pittsburgh).
COLLEGE: Penn State.
TRANSACTIONS/CAREER NOTES: Signed as non-drafted free agent by Detroit Lions (April 26, 2002).
SINGLE GAME HIGHS (regular season): Receptions—1 (December 8, 2002, vs. Arizona); yards—-1 (December 8, 2002, vs. Arizona); and touchdown receptions—0.

			RUSHING				RECEIVING				PUNT RETURNS				KICKOFF RETURNS				TOTALS		
Year Team	G	GS	Att.	Yds.	Avg.	TD	No.	Yds.	Avg.	TD	No.	Yds.	Avg.	TD	No.	Yds.	Avg.	TD	TD	2pt.	Pts.
2002—Det. NFL	9	0	4	38	9.5	0	2	-3	-1.5	0	18	138	7.7	1	40	1039	26.0	0	1	0	6
2003—Det. NFL	6	0	1	1	1.0	0	0	0	0.0	0	12	151	12.6	1	21	469	22.3	0	1	0	6
Pro totals (2 years)	15	0	5	39	7.8	0	2	-3	-1.5	0	30	289	9.6	2	61	1508	24.7	0	2	0	12

D

DUCKETT, T.J. RB FALCONS

PERSONAL: Born February 17, 1981, in Kalamazoo, Mich. ... 6-0/254.
HIGH SCHOOL: Loy Norrix (Kalamazoo, Mich.).
COLLEGE: Michigan State.
TRANSACTIONS/CAREER NOTES: Selected after junior season by Atlanta Falcons in first round (18th pick overall) of 2002 NFL draft. ... Signed by Falcons (August 3, 2002).
SINGLE GAME HIGHS (regular season): Attempts—27 (December 20, 2003, vs. Tampa Bay); yards—100 (September 28, 2003, vs. Carolina); and rushing touchdowns—2 (November 9, 2003, vs. New York Giants).
STATISTICAL PLATEAUS: 100-yard rushing games: 2003 (1). Total: 1.

			RUSHING				RECEIVING				TOTALS			
Year Team	G	GS	Att.	Yds.	Avg.	TD	No.	Yds.	Avg.	TD	TD	2pt.	Pts.	Fum.
2002—Atlanta NFL	11	4	130	507	3.9	4	9	61	6.8	0	4	0	24	0
2003—Atlanta NFL	16	10	197	779	4.0	11	11	94	8.5	0	11	0	66	3
Pro totals (2 years)	27	14	327	1286	3.9	15	20	155	7.8	0	15	0	90	3

DUDLEY, RICKEY TE BUCCANEERS

PERSONAL: Born July 15, 1972, in Henderson, Texas. ... 6-6/255.
HIGH SCHOOL: Henderson (Texas).
COLLEGE: Ohio State.
TRANSACTIONS/CAREER NOTES: Selected by Oakland Raiders in first round (ninth pick overall) of 1996 NFL draft. ... Signed by Raiders (July 12, 1996). ... Granted unconditional free agency (March 2, 2001). ... Signed by Cleveland Browns (March 30, 2001). ... On injured reserve with foot injury (October 9, 2001-remainder of season). ... Released by Browns (September 1, 2002). ... Signed by Tampa Bay Buccaneers (September 17, 2002). ... Granted unconditional free agency (February 28, 2003). ... Re-signed by Buccaneers (April 25, 2003). ... Received injury settlement and released by Buccaneers (August 31, 2003). ... Re-signed by Buccaneers (November 11, 2003). ... Granted unconditional free agency (March 3, 2004). ... Re-signed by Buccaneers (March 5, 2004).
CHAMPIONSHIP GAME EXPERIENCE: Played in AFC championship game (2000 season). ... Played in NFC championship game (2002 season). ... Member of Super Bowl championship team (2002 season).
SINGLE GAME HIGHS (regular season): Receptions—6 (November 8, 1998, vs. Baltimore); yards—116 (November 9, 1997, vs. New Orleans); and touchdown receptions—2 (December 24, 2000, vs. Carolina).
STATISTICAL PLATEAUS: 100-yard receiving games: 1997 (2), 1998 (1). Total: 3.
MISCELLANEOUS: Member of Ohio State basketball team (1991-92 through 1993-94).

			RECEIVING				TOTALS			
Year Team	G	GS	No.	Yds.	Avg.	TD	TD	2pt.	Pts.	Fum.
1996—Oakland NFL	16	15	34	386	11.4	4	4	0	24	1
1997—Oakland NFL	16	16	48	787	16.4	7	7	0	42	0
1998—Oakland NFL	16	15	36	549	15.3	5	5	1	32	1
1999—Oakland NFL	16	16	39	555	14.2	9	9	0	54	0

Year	Team	G	GS	RECEIVING No.	Yds.	Avg.	TD	TOTALS TD	2pt.	Pts.	Fum.
2000—Oakland NFL		16	16	29	350	12.1	4	4	0	24	1
2001—Cleveland NFL		4	4	9	115	12.8	0	0	0	0	0
2002—Tampa Bay NFL		14	3	16	192	12.0	3	3	0	18	0
2003—Tampa Bay NFL		7	2	7	42	6.0	1	1	0	6	0
Pro totals (8 years)		105	87	218	2976	13.7	33	33	1	200	3

DUNBAR, LATARENCE WR FALCONS

PERSONAL: Born August 15, 1980, in Dallas, Texas. ... 5-11/196. ... Full name: LaTarence Eugene Dunbar.
HIGH SCHOOL: South Oak Cliff (Dallas).
COLLEGE: Texas Christian.
TRANSACTIONS/CAREER NOTES: Selected by Atlanta Falcons in sixth round (196th pick overall) of 2003 NFL draft. ... Signed by Falcons (June 16, 2003). ... On injured reserve with hamstring injury (December 4, 2003-remainder of season).

Year	Team	G	GS	RECEIVING No.	Yds.	Avg.	TD	TOTALS TD	2pt.	Pts.	Fum.
2003—Atlanta NFL		5	0	0	0	0.0	0	0	0	0	0

DUNCAN, JAMIE LB FALCONS

PERSONAL: Born July 20, 1975, in Wilmington, Del. ... 6-1/238. ... Full name: Jamie Robert Duncan.
HIGH SCHOOL: Christiana (Newark, Del.).
COLLEGE: Vanderbilt.
TRANSACTIONS/CAREER NOTES: Selected by Tampa Bay Buccaneers in third round (84th pick overall) of 1998 NFL draft. ... Signed by Buccaneers (July 10, 1998). ... Granted unconditional free agency (March 1, 2002). ... Signed by St. Louis Rams (March 7, 2002). ... Released by Rams (April 26, 2004). ... Signed by Atlanta Falcons (April 30, 2004).
CHAMPIONSHIP GAME EXPERIENCE: Played in NFC championship game (1999 season).
HONORS: Named inside linebacker on THE SPORTING NEWS college All-America second team (1997).

Year	Team	G	GS	TOTALS Tk.	Ast.	Sks.	INTERCEPTIONS No.	Yds.	Avg.	TD
1998—Tampa Bay NFL		14	6	30	6	0.0	0	0	0.0	0
1999—Tampa Bay NFL		15	0	0	0	0.0	0	0	0.0	0
2000—Tampa Bay NFL		15	15	48	17	0.0	4	55	13.8	1
2001—Tampa Bay NFL		15	15	66	21	2.0	1	9	9.0	0
2002—St. Louis NFL		16	12	47	16	0.0	0	0	0.0	0
2003—St. Louis NFL		16	6	17	10	1.0	1	0	0.0	0
Pro totals (6 years)		91	54	208	70	3.0	6	64	10.7	1

D

DUNCAN, TIM K EAGLES

PERSONAL: Born June 12, 1979, in Tulsa, Okla. ... 6-2/210.
HIGH SCHOOL: Clinton (Okla.).
COLLEGE: Oklahoma.
TRANSACTIONS/CAREER NOTES: Signed as non-drafted free agent by Arizona Cardinals (April 22, 2002). ... Released by Cardinals (August 31, 2002). ... Re-signed by Cardinals to practice squad (November 26, 2002). ... Activated (December 26, 2002). ... Released by Cardinals (August 30, 2003). ... Re-signed by Cardinals (October 3, 2003). ... Released by Cardinals (November 10, 2003). ... Signed by Philadelphia Eagles (March 30, 2004).

Year	Team	G	FIELD GOALS 1-29	30-39	40-49	50+	Tot.	Pct.	Lg.	TOTALS XPM	XPA	Pts.
2003—Arizona NFL		5	2-2	2-4	1-2	1-2	6-10	60.0	53	5	6	23

DUNN, ANTHONY DE TEXANS

PERSONAL: Born July 1, 1980, in Denver, Colo. ... 6-2/255.
HIGH SCHOOL: Centauri (Manassa, Colo.).
COLLEGE: Northern Colorado.
TRANSACTIONS/CAREER NOTES: Signed as non-drafted free agent by Tennessee Titans (April 28, 2003). ... Waived by Titans (September 3, 2003). ... Re-signed by Titans to practice squad (September 5, 2003). ... Activated (November 21, 2003). ... Waived by Titans (November 25, 2003). ... Re-signed by Titans to practice squad (November 26, 2003). ... Activated (November 29, 2003). ... Released by Titans (December 2, 2003). ... Re-signed by Titans to practice squad (December 4, 2003). ... Signed by Houston Texans off Titans practice squad (February 13, 2004).

Year	Team	G	GS	TOTALS Tk.	Ast.	Sks.
2003—Tennessee NFL		2	0	1	0	0.0

DUNN, JASON TE CHIEFS

PERSONAL: Born November 15, 1973, in Harrodsburg, Ky. ... 6-6/276. ... Full name: Jason Adam Dunn.
HIGH SCHOOL: Harrodsburg (Ky.).
COLLEGE: Eastern Kentucky.
TRANSACTIONS/CAREER NOTES: Selected by Philadelphia Eagles in second round (54th pick overall) of 1996 NFL draft. ... Signed by Eagles (July 17, 1996). ... On injured reserve with knee injury (December 1, 1998-remainder of season). ... Granted free agency (February 12, 1999).

... Re-signed by Eagles for 1999 season. ... Released by Eagles (June 17, 1999). ... Signed by Kansas City Chiefs (July 11, 2000). ... Granted unconditional free agency (March 2, 2001). ... Re-signed by Chiefs (March 26, 2001). ... On injured reserve with elbow injury (January 4, 2001-remainder of season). ... Granted unconditional free agency (March 3, 2004). ... Re-signed by Chiefs (March 18, 2004).

SINGLE GAME HIGHS (regular season): Receptions—4 (November 15, 1998, vs. Washington); yards—58 (September 22, 1996, vs. Atlanta); and touchdown receptions—1 (November 23, 2003, vs. Oakland).

			RECEIVING				TOTALS			
Year Team	G	GS	No.	Yds.	Avg.	TD	TD	2pt.	Pts.	Fum.
1996—Philadelphia NFL	16	12	15	332	22.1	2	2	0	12	0
1997—Philadelphia NFL	15	4	7	93	13.3	2	2	0	12	0
1998—Philadelphia NFL	10	10	18	132	7.3	0	0	0	0	1
2000—Kansas City NFL	14	2	2	26	13.0	0	0	0	0	0
2001—Kansas City NFL	15	5	4	54	13.5	1	1	0	6	0
2002—Kansas City NFL	11	4	2	16	8.0	0	0	0	0	0
2003—Kansas City NFL	16	4	5	35	7.0	3	3	0	18	0
Pro totals (7 years)	97	41	53	688	13.0	8	8	0	48	1

DUNN, WARRICK RB FALCONS

PERSONAL: Born January 5, 1975, in Baton Rouge, La. ... 5-9/180. ... Full name: Warrick De'Mon Dunn.

HIGH SCHOOL: Catholic (Baton Rouge, La.).

COLLEGE: Florida State.

TRANSACTIONS/CAREER NOTES: Selected by Tampa Bay Buccaneers in first round (12th pick overall) of 1997 NFL draft. ... Signed by Buccaneers (July 24, 1997). ... Granted unconditional free agency (March 1, 2002). ... Signed by Atlanta Falcons (March 15, 2002). ... On injured reserve with foot injury (November 25, 2003-remainder of season).

CHAMPIONSHIP GAME EXPERIENCE: Played in NFC championship game (1999 season).

HONORS: Named NFL Rookie of the Year by The Sporting News (1997). ... Played in Pro Bowl (1997 and 2000 seasons).

SINGLE GAME HIGHS (regular season): Attempts—30 (December 22, 2002, vs. Detroit); yards—210 (December 3, 2000, vs. Dallas); and rushing touchdowns—3 (December 18, 2000, vs. St. Louis).

STATISTICAL PLATEAUS: 100-yard rushing games: 1997 (5), 1998 (2), 2000 (3), 2002 (4), 2003 (2). Total: 16. 100-yard receiving games: 1997 (1), 1999 (1), 2001 (1), 2003 (1). Total: 4.

			RUSHING				RECEIVING				KICKOFF RETURNS				TOTALS			
Year Team	G	GS	Att.	Yds.	Avg.	TD	No.	Yds.	Avg.	TD	No.	Yds.	Avg.	TD	TD	2pt.	Pts.	Fum.
1997—Tampa Bay NFL	16	10	224	978	4.4	4	39	462	11.8	3	6	129	21.5	0	7	0	42	4
1998—Tampa Bay NFL	16	14	245	1026	4.2	2	44	344	7.8	0	1	25	25.0	0	2	0	12	1
1999—Tampa Bay NFL	15	15	195	616	3.2	0	64	589	9.2	2	8	156	19.5	0	2	0	12	3
2000—Tampa Bay NFL	16	14	248	1133	4.6	8	44	422	9.6	1	0	0	0.0	0	9	0	54	1
2001—Tampa Bay NFL	13	12	158	447	2.8	3	68	557	8.2	3	0	0	0.0	0	6	0	36	2
2002—Atlanta NFL	15	14	230	927	4.0	7	50	377	7.5	2	0	0	0.0	0	9	0	54	4
2003—Atlanta NFL	11	6	125	672	5.4	3	37	336	9.1	2	0	0	0.0	0	5	0	30	2
Pro totals (7 years)	102	85	1425	5799	4.1	27	346	3087	8.9	13	15	310	20.7	0	40	0	240	17

D

DWIGHT, TIM WR CHARGERS

PERSONAL: Born July 13, 1975, in Iowa City, Iowa. ... 5-9/180. ... Full name: Timothy John Dwight Jr.

HIGH SCHOOL: Iowa City (Iowa) High.

COLLEGE: Iowa.

TRANSACTIONS/CAREER NOTES: Selected by Atlanta Falcons in fourth round (114th pick overall) of 1998 NFL draft. ... Signed by Falcons (June 25, 1998). ... Granted free agency (March 2, 2001). ... Re-signed by Falcons (April 21, 2001). ... Traded by Falcons with first-(RB LaDainian Tomlinson) and third-round (DB Tay Cody) picks in 2001 draft and second-round pick in 2002 draft to San Diego Chargers for first-round pick (QB Michael Vick) in 2001 draft (April 20, 2001). ... On injured reserve with collapsed lung (November 26, 2003-remainder of season).

CHAMPIONSHIP GAME EXPERIENCE: Played in NFC championship game (1998 season). ... Played in Super Bowl 33 (1998 season).

HONORS: Named kick returner on THE SPORTING NEWS college All-America second team (1996). ... Named kick returner on THE SPORTING NEWS college All-America first team (1997).

POST SEASON RECORDS: Holds Super Bowl career record for highest kickoff return average (minimum four returns)—42.0. ... Shares Super Bowl single-game record for most touchdowns by kickoff return—1 (January 31, 1999, vs. Denver).

SINGLE GAME HIGHS (regular season): Receptions—7 (January 3, 2000, vs. San Francisco); yards—162 (January 3, 2000, vs. San Francisco); and touchdown receptions—2 (January 3, 2000, vs. San Francisco).

STATISTICAL PLATEAUS: 100-yard receiving games: 1999 (2). Total: 2.

			RUSHING				RECEIVING				PUNT RETURNS				KICKOFF RETURNS				TOTALS		
Year Team	G	GS	Att.	Yds.	Avg.	TD	No.	Yds.	Avg.	TD	No.	Yds.	Avg.	TD	No.	Yds.	Avg.	TD	TD	2pt.	Pts.
1998—Atl. NFL	12	0	8	19	2.4	0	4	94	23.5	1	31	263	8.5	0	36	973	27.0	1	2	0	12
1999—Atl. NFL	12	8	5	28	5.6	1	32	669	*20.9	7	20	220	11.0	∞1	44	944	21.5	0	9	0	54
2000—Atl. NFL	14	1	5	8	1.6	0	26	406	15.6	3	33	309	9.4	1	32	680	21.3	0	4	0	24
2001—S.D. NFL	10	2	2	24	12.0	1	25	406	16.2	0	24	271	11.3	1	0	0	0.0	0	2	0	12
2002—S.D. NFL	16	14	12	108	9.0	1	50	623	12.5	2	19	231	12.2	0	8	166	20.8	0	3	0	18
2003—S.D. NFL	9	3	9	88	9.8	0	14	193	13.8	0	2	0	0.0	0	22	488	22.2	0	0	0	0
Pro totals (6 years)	73	28	41	275	6.7	3	151	2391	15.8	13	129	1294	10.0	3	142	3251	22.9	1	20	0	120

DYSON, ANDRE CB TITANS

PERSONAL: Born May 25, 1979, in Logan, Utah. ... 5-10/183. ... Brother of Kevin Dyson, wide receiver, San Diego Chargers.

HIGH SCHOOL: Clearfield (Utah).

COLLEGE: Utah.

TRANSACTIONS/CAREER NOTES: Selected by Tennessee Titans in second round (60th pick overall) of 2001 NFL draft. ... Signed by Titans (July 24, 2001).

CHAMPIONSHIP GAME EXPERIENCE: Played in AFC championship game (2002 season).

Year Team	G	GS	TOTALS Tk.	Ast.	Sks.	INTERCEPTIONS No.	Yds.	Avg.	TD
2001—Tennessee NFL	14	12	54	4	0.0	3	36	12.0	0
2002—Tennessee NFL	16	16	56	5	1.0	3	27	9.0	1
2003—Tennessee NFL	16	16	54	11	0.0	4	62	15.5	†2
Pro totals (3 years)	46	44	164	20	1.0	10	125	12.5	3

DYSON, KEVIN WR CHARGERS

PERSONAL: Born June 23, 1975, in Logan, Utah. ... 6-1/208. ... Full name: Kevin Tyree Dyson. ... Brother of Andre Dyson, cornerback, Tennessee Titans.

HIGH SCHOOL: Clearfield (Utah).

COLLEGE: Utah.

TRANSACTIONS/CAREER NOTES: Selected by Tennessee Oilers in first round (16th pick overall) of 1998 NFL draft. ... Signed by Oilers (July 24, 1998). ... Oilers franchise renamed Tennessee Titans for 1999 season (December 26, 1998). ... On injured reserve with knee injury (September 29, 2000-remainder of season). ... On injured reserve with hamstring injury (December 20, 2002-remainder of season). ... Granted unconditional free agency (February 28, 2003). ... Signed by Carolina Panthers (March 19, 2003). ... On physically unable to perform list with Achilles injury (August 25, 2003). ... Activated (November 22, 2003). ... Granted unconditional free agency (March 3, 2004). ... Signed by San Diego Chargers (March 19, 2004).

CHAMPIONSHIP GAME EXPERIENCE: Played in AFC championship game (1999 season). ... Played in Super Bowl 34 (1999 season) and Super Bowl 38 (2003 season). ... Played in NFC championship game (2003 season).

SINGLE GAME HIGHS (regular season): Receptions—9 (September 12, 1999, vs. Cincinnati); yards—162 (September 12, 1999, vs. Cincinnati); and touchdown receptions—2 (November 17, 2002, vs. Pittsburgh).

STATISTICAL PLATEAUS: 100-yard receiving games: 1999 (1), 2000 (1), 2001 (2). Total: 4.

Year Team	G	GS	RECEIVING No.	Yds.	Avg.	TD	TOTALS TD	2pt.	Pts.	Fum.
1998—Tennessee NFL	13	9	21	263	12.5	2	2	0	12	0
1999—Tennessee NFL	16	16	54	658	12.2	4	4	0	24	0
2000—Tennessee NFL	2	2	6	104	17.3	1	1	0	6	0
2001—Tennessee NFL	16	16	54	825	15.3	7	7	1	44	0
2002—Tennessee NFL	11	11	41	460	11.2	4	4	0	24	1
2003—Carolina NFL	1	0	2	15	7.5	0	0	0	0	0
Pro totals (6 years)	59	54	178	2325	13.1	18	18	1	110	1

EASY, OMAR FB CHIEFS

PERSONAL: Born October 29, 1977, in Spanish Town, Jamaica. ... 6-1/245. ... Full name: Omar Xavier Easy.

HIGH SCHOOL: Everett (Mass.).

COLLEGE: Penn State.

TRANSACTIONS/CAREER NOTES: Selected by Kansas City Chiefs in fourth round (107th pick overall) of 2002 NFL draft. ... Signed by Chiefs (June 11, 2002).

Year Team	G	GS	RUSHING Att.	Yds.	Avg.	TD	RECEIVING No.	Yds.	Avg.	TD	TOTALS TD	2pt.	Pts.	Fum.
2002—Kansas City NFL	7	0	0	0	0.0	0	3	23	7.7	1	1	0	6	0
2003—Kansas City NFL	15	0	0	0	0.0	0	3	19	6.3	0	0	0	0	0
Pro totals (2 years)	22	0	0	0	0.0	0	6	42	7.0	1	1	0	6	0

EATON, CHAD DT

PERSONAL: Born April 6, 1972, in Exeter, N.H. ... 6-5/303. ... Full name: Chad Everett Eaton.

HIGH SCHOOL: Rogers (Puyallup, Wash.).

COLLEGE: Washington State.

TRANSACTIONS/CAREER NOTES: Selected by Arizona Cardinals in seventh round (241st pick overall) of 1995 NFL draft. ... Signed by Cardinals (July 24, 1995). ... Released by Cardinals (August 14, 1995). ... Signed by New York Jets (August 15, 1995). ... Released by Jets (August 27, 1995). ... Signed by Cleveland Browns to practice squad (September 28, 1995). ... Activated (December 15, 1995); did not play. ... Browns franchise moved to Baltimore and renamed Ravens for 1996 season (March 11, 1996). ... Released by Ravens (August 19, 1996). ... Signed by New England Patriots to practice squad (August 27, 1996). ... Activated (November 28, 1996). ... Granted unconditional free agency (March 2, 2001). ... Signed by Seattle Seahawks (March 9, 2001). ... On injured reserve with knee injury (August 26, 2003-entire season). ... Released by Seahawks (February 27, 2004).

CHAMPIONSHIP GAME EXPERIENCE: Played in AFC championship game (1996 season). ... Played in Super Bowl 31 (1996 season).

HONORS: Named defensive lineman on THE SPORTING NEWS college All-America second team (1994).

Year Team	G	GS	TOTALS Tk.	Ast.	Sks.
1995—Cleveland NFL			Did not play.		
1996—New England NFL	4	0	3	1	1.0
1997—New England NFL	16	1	13	8	1.0
1998—New England NFL	15	14	49	31	6.0
1999—New England NFL	16	16	38	18	3.0
2000—New England NFL	14	13	59	19	2.5
2001—Seattle NFL	16	16	44	13	1.0
2002—Seattle NFL	16	16	48	25	1.0
2003—Seattle NFL			Did not play.		
Pro totals (7 years)	97	76	254	115	15.5

E

ECHOLS, MIKE — CB — TITANS

PERSONAL: Born October 13, 1978, in Youngstown, Ohio. ... 5-10/190.
HIGH SCHOOL: Ursuline (Youngstown, Ohio).
COLLEGE: Wisconsin.
TRANSACTIONS/CAREER NOTES: Selected by Tennessee Titans in fourth round (110th pick overall) of 2002 NFL draft. ... Signed by Titans (July 26, 2002). ... On injured reserve with leg injury (November 27, 2002-remainder of season).

			TOTALS			INTERCEPTIONS			
Year Team	G	GS	Tk.	Ast.	Sks.	No.	Yds.	Avg.	TD
2002—Tennessee NFL	4	0	13	7	0.0	0	0	0.0	0
2003—Tennessee NFL	5	0	5	1	0.0	0	0	0.0	0
Pro totals (2 years)	9	0	18	8	0.0	0	0	0.0	0

EDINGER, PAUL — K — BEARS

PERSONAL: Born January 17, 1978, in Frankfort, Mich. ... 5-8/175. ... Full name: Paul E. Edinger.
HIGH SCHOOL: Kathleen (Lakeland, Fla.).
COLLEGE: Michigan State.
TRANSACTIONS/CAREER NOTES: Selected by Chicago Bears in sixth round (174th pick overall) of 2000 NFL draft. ... Signed by Bears (June 8, 2000). ... Granted free agency (February 28, 2003). ... Tendered offer sheet by Minnesota Vikings (March 9, 2003). ... Offer matched by Bears (March 12, 2003).

		FIELD GOALS							TOTALS		
Year Team	G	1-29	30-39	40-49	50+	Tot.	Pct.	Lg.	XPM	XPA	Pts.
2000—Chicago NFL	16	6-6	7-9	6-10	2-2	21-27	77.8	54	21	21	84
2001—Chicago NFL	16	6-7	7-8	13-16	0-0	26-31	83.9	48	34	34	112
2002—Chicago NFL	16	4-4	5-6	8-10	5-8	22-28	78.6	∞53	29	29	95
2003—Chicago NFL	16	5-5	9-13	9-14	3-4	26-36	72.2	54	27	27	105
Pro totals (4 years)	64	21-22	28-36	36-50	10-14	95-122	77.9	54	111	111	396

EDMONDS, CHRIS — FB

PERSONAL: Born January 1, 1978, in Newark, N.J. ... 6-3/250.
HIGH SCHOOL: Woodland Hills (Pittsburgh).
COLLEGE: West Virginia.
TRANSACTIONS/CAREER NOTES: Signed as non-drafted free agent by Cincinnati Bengals (April 24, 2001). ... Released by Bengals (September 2, 2001). ... Re-signed by Bengals to practice squad (September 3, 2001). ... Activated (December 18, 2001); did not play. ... Released by Bengals (September 1, 2002). ... Re-signed by Bengals to practice squad (September 2, 2002). ... Activated (November 5, 2002). ... Waived by Bengals (September 30, 2003).

			RUSHING				TOTALS			
Year Team	G	GS	Att.	Yds.	Avg.	TD	TD	2pt.	Pts.	Fum.
2002—Cincinnati NFL	8	0	0	0	0.0	0	0	0	0	0
2003—Cincinnati NFL	4	0	0	0	0.0	0	0	0	0	0
Pro totals (2 years)	12	0	0	0	0.0	0	0	0	0	0

E

EDWARDS, ANTUAN — S — DOLPHINS

PERSONAL: Born May 26, 1977, in Starkville, Miss. ... 6-1/212. ... Full name: Antuan Minye' Edwards. ... Name pronounced: AN-twan.
HIGH SCHOOL: Starkville (Miss.).
COLLEGE: Clemson.
TRANSACTIONS/CAREER NOTES: Selected by Green Bay Packers in first round (25th pick overall) of 1999 NFL draft. ... Signed by Packers (June 7, 1999). ... On injured reserve with knee injury (October 3, 2001-remainder of season). ... On injured reserve with hamstring injury (December 6, 2003-remainder of season). ... Granted unconditional free agency (March 3, 2004). ... Signed by Miami Dolphins (April 12, 2004).

			TOTALS			INTERCEPTIONS				PUNT RETURNS				TOTALS			
Year Team	G	GS	Tk.	Ast.	Sks.	No.	Yds.	Avg.	TD	No.	Yds.	Avg.	TD	TD	2pt.	Pts.	Fum.
1999—Green Bay NFL	16	1	26	4	0.0	4	26	6.5	1	10	90	9.0	0	1	0	6	1
2000—Green Bay NFL	13	3	21	4	0.0	2	4	2.0	0	0	0	0.0	0	0	0	0	0
2001—Green Bay NFL	3	0	2	0	0.0	0	0	0.0	0	0	0	0.0	0	0	0	0	0
2002—Green Bay NFL	12	4	25	14	1.0	0	0	0.0	0	1	0	0.0	0	0	0	0	0
2003—Green Bay NFL	10	10	42	8	1.0	1	5	5.0	0	0	0	0.0	0	0	0	0	0
Pro totals (5 years)	54	18	116	30	2.0	7	35	5.0	1	11	90	8.2	0	1	0	6	1

EDWARDS, DONNIE — LB — CHARGERS

PERSONAL: Born April 6, 1973, in San Diego, Calif. ... 6-2/227. ... Full name: Donnie Lewis Edwards Jr.
HIGH SCHOOL: Chula Vista (San Diego).
COLLEGE: UCLA.
TRANSACTIONS/CAREER NOTES: Selected by Kansas City Chiefs in fourth round (98th pick overall) of 1996 NFL draft. ... Signed by Chiefs (July 24, 1996). ... Released by Chiefs (March 1, 2002). ... Signed by San Diego Chargers (April 25, 2002).
HONORS: Played in Pro Bowl (2002).

			TOTALS			INTERCEPTIONS			
Year Team	G	GS	Tk.	Ast.	Sks.	No.	Yds.	Avg.	TD
1996—Kansas City NFL	15	1	8	3	0.0	1	22	22.0	0

Year Team	G	GS	TOTALS Tk.	Ast.	Sks.	INTERCEPTIONS No.	Yds.	Avg.	TD
1997—Kansas City NFL	16	16	80	20	2.5	2	15	7.5	0
1998—Kansas City NFL	15	15	80	44	6.0	0	0	0.0	0
1999—Kansas City NFL	16	16	98	25	3.0	5	50	10.0	1
2000—Kansas City NFL	16	16	114	18	1.0	2	45	22.5	1
2001—Kansas City NFL	16	16	98	32	2.0	0	0	0.0	0
2002—San Diego NFL	16	16	100	29	0.0	5	95	19.0	1
2003—San Diego NFL	16	16	†124	38	0.5	2	27	13.5	0
Pro totals (8 years)	126	112	702	209	15.0	17	254	14.9	3

EDWARDS, KALIMBA DE LIONS

PERSONAL: Born December 26, 1979, in East Point, Ga. ... 6-5/264.
HIGH SCHOOL: Tri-Cities (Atlanta).
COLLEGE: South Carolina.
TRANSACTIONS/CAREER NOTES: Selected by Detroit Lions in second round (35th pick overall) of 2002 NFL draft. ... Signed by Lions (July 23, 2002). ... On injured reserve with groin injury (December 23, 2003-remainder of season.)
HONORS: Named linebacker on THE SPORTING NEWS college All-America first team (2001).

Year Team	G	GS	TOTALS Tk.	Ast.	Sks.	INTERCEPTIONS No.	Yds.	Avg.	TD
2002—Detroit NFL	16	4	23	8	6.5	0	0	0.0	0
2003—Detroit NFL	15	0	15	1	2.0	0	0	0.0	0
Pro totals (2 years)	31	4	38	9	8.5	0	0	0.0	0

EDWARDS, MARC FB JAGUARS

PERSONAL: Born November 17, 1974, in Cincinnati, Ohio. ... 6-0/249. ... Full name: Marc Alexander Edwards.
HIGH SCHOOL: Norwood (Cincinnati).
COLLEGE: Notre Dame.
TRANSACTIONS/CAREER NOTES: Selected by San Francisco 49ers in second round (55th pick overall) of 1997 NFL draft. ... Signed by 49ers (July 23, 1997). ... On physically unable to perform list with back injury (July 17-August 10, 1998). ... Traded by 49ers to Cleveland Browns for fourth-round pick (DB Pierson Prioleau) in 1999 draft (April 18, 1999). ... Granted unconditional free agency (March 2, 2001). ... Signed by New England Patriots (March 19, 2001). ... Granted unconditional free agency (February 28, 2003). ... Signed by Jacksonville Jaguars (March 16, 2003).
CHAMPIONSHIP GAME EXPERIENCE: Played in NFC championship game (1997 season). ... Played in AFC championship game (2001 season). ... Member of Super Bowl championship team (2001 season).
SINGLE GAME HIGHS (regular season): Attempts—7 (September 15, 2002, vs. New York Jets); yards—41 (September 27, 1998, vs. Atlanta); and rushing touchdowns—1 (December 2, 2001, vs. New York Jets).

Year Team	G	GS	RUSHING Att.	Yds.	Avg.	TD	RECEIVING No.	Yds.	Avg.	TD	KICKOFF RETURNS No.	Yds.	Avg.	TD	TOTALS TD	2pt.	Pts.	Fum.
1997—San Francisco NFL	15	1	5	17	3.4	0	6	48	8.0	0	1	30	30.0	0	0	0	0	0
1998—San Francisco NFL	16	10	22	94	4.3	1	22	218	9.9	2	0	0	0.0	0	3	0	18	0
1999—Cleveland NFL	16	14	6	35	5.8	0	27	212	7.9	2	0	0	0.0	0	2	0	12	1
2000—Cleveland NFL	16	8	2	9	4.5	0	16	128	8.0	2	1	24	24.0	0	2	0	12	2
2001—New England NFL	16	13	51	141	2.8	1	25	166	6.6	2	1	23	23.0	0	3	0	18	3
2002—New England NFL	16	10	31	96	3.1	0	23	196	8.5	0	3	27	9.0	0	0	0	0	1
2003—Jacksonville NFL	16	16	7	13	1.9	1	31	226	7.3	0	2	44	22.0	0	1	0	6	0
Pro totals (7 years)	111	72	124	405	3.3	3	150	1194	8.0	8	8	148	18.5	0	11	0	66	7

EDWARDS, MARIO CB BUCCANEERS

PERSONAL: Born December 1, 1975, in Gautier, Miss. ... 6-0/199. ... Full name: Mario L. Edwards.
HIGH SCHOOL: Pascagoula (Miss.).
COLLEGE: Florida State.
TRANSACTIONS/CAREER NOTES: Selected by Dallas Cowboys in sixth round (180th pick overall) of 2000 NFL draft. ... Signed by Cowboys (July 14, 2000). ... Granted free agency (February 28, 2003). ... Re-signed by Cowboys (April 15, 2003). ... Granted unconditional free agency (March 3, 2004). ... Signed by Tampa Bay Buccaneers (April 4, 2004).

Year Team	G	GS	TOTALS Tk.	Ast.	Sks.	INTERCEPTIONS No.	Yds.	Avg.	TD
2000—Dallas NFL	11	1	5	0	0.0	0	0	0.0	0
2001—Dallas NFL	16	15	42	7	0.0	1	71	71.0	1
2002—Dallas NFL	15	15	53	4	0.0	2	29	14.5	0
2003—Dallas NFL	16	16	37	5	0.0	1	27	27.0	1
Pro totals (4 years)	58	47	137	16	0.0	4	127	31.8	2

EDWARDS, RON DT BILLS

PERSONAL: Born July 12, 1979, in Columbus, Ohio. ... 6-3/320.
HIGH SCHOOL: Klein Forest (Houston).
COLLEGE: Texas A&M.
TRANSACTIONS/CAREER NOTES: Selected by Buffalo Bills in third round (76th pick overall) of 2001 NFL draft. ... Signed by Bills (June 1, 2001). ... On injured reserve with shoulder injury (November 12, 2003-remainder of season). ... Granted free agency (March 3, 2004). ... Re-signed by Bills (2004).

Year	Team	G	GS	TOTALS Tk.	Ast.	Sks.
2001	—Buffalo NFL	7	3	7	3	0.0
2002	—Buffalo NFL	16	16	25	15	2.5
2003	—Buffalo NFL	5	0	5	2	0.5
Pro totals (3 years)		28	19	37	20	3.0

EDWARDS, STEVE — T — BEARS

PERSONAL: Born February 20, 1979, in Chicago, Ill. ... 6-5/340.
HIGH SCHOOL: Mount Carmel (Chicago).
JUNIOR COLLEGE: West Hills Community College (Calif.).
COLLEGE: Central Florida.
TRANSACTIONS/CAREER NOTES: Signed as non-drafted free agent by Philadelphia Eagles (April 23, 2002). ... Released by Eagles (September 1, 2002). ... Re-signed by Eagles to practice squad (September 3, 2002). ... Signed by Chicago Bears off Eagles practice squad (October 9, 2002).
PLAYING EXPERIENCE: Chicago NFL, 2002-2003. ... Games/Games started: 2002 (1/0), 2003 (16/16). Total: 17/16.

EDWARDS, TERRENCE — WR — FALCONS

PERSONAL: Born April 29, 1979, in Tennille, Ga. ... 6-0/176. ... Brother of Robert Edwards, running back with New England Patriots (1998-2000) and Miami Dolphins (2002).
HIGH SCHOOL: Washington County (Tennille, Ga.).
COLLEGE: Georgia.
TRANSACTIONS/CAREER NOTES: Signed as non-drafted free agent by Atlanta Falcons (April 29, 2003).
SINGLE GAME HIGHS (regular season): Receptions—1 (November 30, 2003, vs. Houston); yards—10 (November 30, 2003, vs. Houston); and touchdown receptions—0.

Year	Team	G	GS	RECEIVING No.	Yds.	Avg.	TD	TOTALS TD	2pt.	Pts.	Fum.
2003	—Atlanta NFL	6	0	1	10	10.0	0	0	0	0	0

EDWARDS, TROY — WR — JAGUARS

PERSONAL: Born April 7, 1977, in Shreveport, La. ... 5-10/191.
HIGH SCHOOL: Huntington (Shreveport, La.).
COLLEGE: Louisiana Tech.
TRANSACTIONS/CAREER NOTES: Selected by Pittsburgh Steelers in first round (13th pick overall) of 1999 NFL draft. ... Signed by Steelers (July 28, 1999). ... Traded by Steelers to St. Louis Rams for sixth-round pick (TE Matt Kranchick) in 2004 draft (September 1, 2002). ... Released by Rams (August 31, 2003). ... Signed by Jacksonville Jaguars (September 23, 2003).
CHAMPIONSHIP GAME EXPERIENCE: Played in AFC championship game (2001 season).
HONORS: Fred Biletnikoff Award winner (1998). ... Named wide receiver on THE SPORTING NEWS college All-America second team (1998).
SINGLE GAME HIGHS (regular season): Receptions—7 (November 28, 1999, vs. Cincinnati); yards—111 (September 28, 2003, vs. Houston); and touchdown receptions—1 (December 28, 2003, vs. Atlanta).
STATISTICAL PLATEAUS: 100-yard receiving games: 2003 (1). Total: 1.

Year	Team	G	GS	RUSHING Att.	Yds.	Avg.	TD	RECEIVING No.	Yds.	Avg.	TD	PUNT RETURNS No.	Yds.	Avg.	TD	KICKOFF RETURNS No.	Yds.	Avg.	TD	TOTALS TD	2pt.	Pts.
1999	—Pit. NFL	16	6	0	0	0.0	0	61	714	11.7	5	25	234	9.4	0	13	234	18.0	0	5	0	30
2000	—Pit. NFL	14	1	3	4	1.3	0	18	215	11.9	0	0	0	0.0	0	15	298	19.9	0	0	0	0
2001	—Pit. NFL	16	0	5	28	5.6	1	19	283	14.9	0	10	83	8.3	0	20	462	23.1	0	2	0	12
2002	—StL. NFL	14	0	3	21	7.0	0	18	157	8.7	2	0	0	0.0	0	10	211	21.1	0	2	0	12
2003	—Jac. NFL	13	11	3	-9	-3.0	0	35	487	13.9	3	0	0	0.0	0	1	20	20.0	0	3	0	18
Pro totals (5 years)		73	18	14	44	3.1	1	151	1856	12.3	10	35	317	9.1	0	59	1225	20.8	0	12	0	72

EKUBAN, EBENEZER — DE — BROWNS

PERSONAL: Born May 29, 1976, in Ghana, Africa. ... 6-3/265. ... Full name: Ebenezer Ekuban Jr. ... Name pronounced: ECK-you-bon.
HIGH SCHOOL: Bladensburg (Md.).
COLLEGE: North Carolina.
TRANSACTIONS/CAREER NOTES: Selected by Dallas Cowboys in first round (20th pick overall) of 1999 NFL draft. ... Signed by Cowboys (July 27, 1999). ... On injured reserve with back injury (December 21, 2001-remainder of season). ... Granted unconditional free agency (March 3, 2004). ... Signed by Cleveland Browns (March 11, 2004).

Year	Team	G	GS	TOTALS Tk.	Ast.	Sks.
1999	—Dallas NFL	16	2	20	3	2.5
2000	—Dallas NFL	12	2	22	7	6.5
2001	—Dallas NFL	1	1	1	1	0.0
2002	—Dallas NFL	16	15	26	5	1.0
2003	—Dallas NFL	15	14	19	8	2.5
Pro totals (5 years)		60	34	88	24	12.5

ELAM, JASON — K — BRONCOS

PERSONAL: Born March 8, 1970, in Ft. Walton Beach, Fla. ... 5-11/200. ... Name pronounced: EE-lum.
HIGH SCHOOL: Brookwood (Snellville, Ga.).
COLLEGE: Hawaii.
TRANSACTIONS/CAREER NOTES: Selected by Denver Broncos in third round (70th pick overall) of 1993 NFL draft. ... Signed by Broncos (July 12, 1993). ... Designated by Broncos as franchise player (February 21, 2002). ... Granted free agency (March 1, 2002). ... Re-signed by Broncos (July 25, 2002).
CHAMPIONSHIP GAME EXPERIENCE: Played in AFC championship game (1997 and 1998 seasons). ... Member of Super Bowl championship team (1997 and 1998 seasons).
HONORS: Named kicker on THE SPORTING NEWS college All-America second team (1989 and 1991). ... Played in Pro Bowl (1995, 1998 and 2001 seasons).
RECORDS: Holds NFL career record for most consecutive PATs made—371 (1993-2002). ... Holds NFL career record for highest PAT percentage—99.56. ... Shares NFL career record for longest field goal—63 yards (October 25, 1998, vs. Jacksonville).

		FIELD GOALS							TOTALS		
Year Team	G	1-29	30-39	40-49	50+	Tot.	Pct.	Lg.	XPM	XPA	Pts.
1993—Denver NFL	16	11-12	7-7	4-10	4-6	26-35	74.3	54	§41	§42	119
1994—Denver NFL	16	11-11	11-11	7-12	1-3	30-37	81.1	†54	29	29	119
1995—Denver NFL	16	7-9	14-15	5-7	5-7	31-38	81.6	§56	39	39	132
1996—Denver NFL	16	10-10	4-5	6-10	1-3	21-28	75.0	51	§46	§46	109
1997—Denver NFL	15	10-11	10-12	3-8	3-5	26-36	72.2	53	§46	§46	124
1998—Denver NFL	16	3-3	13-14	4-6	3-4	23-27	85.2	*63	§58	§58	§127
1999—Denver NFL	16	9-9	7-8	8-11	5-8	29-36	80.6	*55	29	29	116
2000—Denver NFL	13	7-7	6-7	4-9	1-1	18-24	75.0	51	*49	*49	103
2001—Denver NFL	16	11-11	8-8	10-13	2-4	*31-36	86.1	50	31	31	124
2002—Denver NFL	16	10-10	7-9	5-11	4-6	26-§36	72.2	55	42	43	120
2003—Denver NFL	16	10-11	6-6	9-11	2-3	27-31	87.1	51	39	39	120
Pro totals (11 years)	172	99-104	93-102	65-108	31-50	288-364	79.1	63	449	451	1313

ELLING, AARON — K — VIKINGS

PERSONAL: Born May 31, 1978, in Waconia, Minn. ... 6-2/201.
HIGH SCHOOL: Lander Valley (Lander, Wy.).
COLLEGE: Wyoming.
TRANSACTIONS/CAREER NOTES: Signed as non-drafted free agent by Seattle Seahawks (May 7, 2002). ... Released by Seahawks (August 30, 2002). ... Signed by Minnesota Vikings (March 21, 2003).

		FIELD GOALS							TOTALS		
Year Team	G	1-29	30-39	40-49	50+	Tot.	Pct.	Lg.	XPM	XPA	Pts.
2003—Minnesota NFL	16	7-7	6-8	4-7	1-3	18-25	72.0	51	48	48	102

E

ELLIS, ED — T — GIANTS

PERSONAL: Born October 13, 1975, in New Haven, Conn. ... 6-5/325. ... Full name: Edward Key Ellis.
HIGH SCHOOL: Hamden (Conn.).
COLLEGE: Buffalo.
TRANSACTIONS/CAREER NOTES: Selected by New England Patriots in fourth round (125th pick overall) of 1997 NFL draft. ... Signed by Patriots (June 19, 1997). ... Granted free agency (February 11, 2000). ... Assigned by Patriots to Barcelona Dragons in 2000 NFL Europe enhancement allocation program (February 18, 2000). ... Re-signed by Patriots (March 13, 2000). ... Released by Patriots (July 17, 2000). ... Signed by Washington Redskins (July 20, 2000). ... Granted unconditional free agency (March 2, 2001). ... Signed by San Diego Chargers (April 2, 2001). ... Released by Chargers (February 27, 2003). ... Signed by Denver Broncos (April 24, 2003). ... Released by Broncos (August 31, 2003). ... Signed by San Diego Chargers (December 17, 2003). ... Granted unconditional free agency (March 3, 2004). ... Signed by New York Giants (April 6, 2004).
PLAYING EXPERIENCE: New England NFL, 1997-1999; Washington NFL, 2000; San Diego NFL, 2001-2003. ... Games/Games started: 1997 (1/0), 1998 (7/0), 1999 (2/1), 2000 (12/0), 2001 (16/2), 2002 (15/3), 2003 (2/1). Total: 55/7.

ELLIS, GREG — DE — COWBOYS

PERSONAL: Born August 14, 1975, in Wendell, N.C. ... 6-6/277. ... Full name: Gregory Lemont Ellis.
HIGH SCHOOL: East Wake (Wendell, N.C.).
COLLEGE: North Carolina.
TRANSACTIONS/CAREER NOTES: Selected by Dallas Cowboys in first round (eighth pick overall) of 1998 NFL draft. ... Signed by Cowboys (July 13, 1998). ... On injured reserve with leg injury (December 16, 1999-remainder of season).
HONORS: Named defensive end on THE SPORTING NEWS college All-America second team (1996 and 1997).

			TOTALS			INTERCEPTIONS			
Year Team	G	GS	Tk.	Ast.	Sks.	No.	Yds.	Avg.	TD
1998—Dallas NFL	16	16	27	12	3.0	0	0	0.0	0
1999—Dallas NFL	13	13	37	7	7.5	1	87	87.0	1
2000—Dallas NFL	16	16	39	13	3.0	0	0	0.0	0
2001—Dallas NFL	16	16	45	16	6.0	0	0	0.0	0
2002—Dallas NFL	15	15	50	17	7.5	1	0	0.0	0
2003—Dallas NFL	16	15	35	14	8.0	0	0	0.0	0
Pro totals (6 years)	92	91	233	79	35.0	2	87	43.5	1

ELLIS, SHAUN — DE — JETS

PERSONAL: Born June 24, 1977, in Anderson, S.C. ... 6-5/294. ... Full name: MeShaunda Pizarrur Ellis.
HIGH SCHOOL: Westside (Anderson, S.C.).
COLLEGE: Tennessee.
TRANSACTIONS/CAREER NOTES: Selected by New York Jets in first round (12th pick overall) of 2000 NFL draft. ... Signed by Jets (July 10, 2000).
HONORS: Played in Pro Bowl (2003 season).

			TOTALS			INTERCEPTIONS			
Year Team	G	GS	Tk.	Ast.	Sks.	No.	Yds.	Avg.	TD
2000—New York Jets NFL	16	3	38	15	8.5	1	1	1.0	0
2001—New York Jets NFL	16	16	28	12	5.0	0	0	0.0	0
2002—New York Jets NFL	16	16	31	10	4.0	0	0	0.0	0
2003—New York Jets NFL	16	16	48	21	12.5	0	0	0.0	0
Pro totals (4 years)	64	51	145	58	30.0	1	1	1.0	0

ELLISS, LUTHER — DT — BRONCOS

PERSONAL: Born March 22, 1973, in Mancos, Colo. ... 6-5/318.
HIGH SCHOOL: Mancos (Colo.).
COLLEGE: Utah.
TRANSACTIONS/CAREER NOTES: Selected by Detroit Lions in first round (20th pick overall) of 1995 NFL draft. ... Signed by Lions (July 19, 1995). ... On injured reserve with ankle injury (December 19, 2002-remainder of season). ... On active/non-football injury list (July 23-November 15, 2003). ... Released by Lions (March 2, 2004). ... Signed by Denver Broncos (March 22, 2004).
HONORS: Named defensive lineman on THE SPORTING NEWS college All-America first team (1994). ... Played in Pro Bowl (1999 and 2000 seasons).

			TOTALS		
Year Team	G	GS	Tk.	Ast.	Sks.
1995—Detroit NFL	16	16	9	10	0.0
1996—Detroit NFL	14	14	26	23	6.5
1997—Detroit NFL	16	16	35	28	8.5
1998—Detroit NFL	16	16	38	12	3.0
1999—Detroit NFL	15	14	31	16	3.5
2000—Detroit NFL	16	16	23	16	3.0
2001—Detroit NFL	14	13	26	5	0.0
2002—Detroit NFL	14	14	19	7	2.5
2003—Detroit NFL	5	0	0	0	0.0
Pro totals (9 years)	126	119	207	117	27.0

EMMONS, CARLOS — LB — GIANTS

PERSONAL: Born September 3, 1973, in Greenwood, Miss. ... 6-5/250. ... Name pronounced: EM-mins.
HIGH SCHOOL: Greenwood (Miss.).
COLLEGE: Arkansas State.
TRANSACTIONS/CAREER NOTES: Selected by Pittsburgh Steelers in seventh round (242nd pick overall) of 1996 NFL draft. ... Signed by Steelers (July 16, 1996). ... Granted free agency (February 12, 1999). ... Re-signed by Steelers (April 23, 1999). ... Granted unconditional free agency (February 11, 2000). ... Signed by Philadelphia Eagles (March 23, 2000). ... On injured reserve with fibula injury (December 23, 2003-remainder of season). ... Granted unconditional free agency (March 3, 2004). ... Signed by New York Giants (March 5, 2004).
CHAMPIONSHIP GAME EXPERIENCE: Played in AFC championship game (1997 season). ... Played in NFC championship game (2001 and 2002 seasons).

			TOTALS			INTERCEPTIONS			
Year Team	G	GS	Tk.	Ast.	Sks.	No.	Yds.	Avg.	TD
1996—Pittsburgh NFL	15	0	5	2	2.5	0	0	0.0	0
1997—Pittsburgh NFL	5	0	1	0	0.0	0	0	0.0	0
1998—Pittsburgh NFL	15	14	46	17	3.5	1	2	2.0	0
1999—Pittsburgh NFL	16	16	51	16	6.0	1	22	22.0	0
2000—Philadelphia NFL	16	13	55	23	0.5	2	8	4.0	0
2001—Philadelphia NFL	16	15	61	18	1.0	0	0	0.0	0
2002—Philadelphia NFL	13	13	51	9	3.5	0	0	0.0	0
2003—Philadelphia NFL	15	15	65	20	0.0	0	0	0.0	0
Pro totals (8 years)	111	86	335	105	17.0	4	32	8.0	0

ENA, JUSTIN — LB — EAGLES

PERSONAL: Born November 20, 1977, in Shelton, Wash. ... 6-3/247.
HIGH SCHOOL: Shelton (Calif.).
COLLEGE: Brigham Young.
TRANSACTIONS/CAREER NOTES: Signed as non-drafted free agent by Philadelphia Eagles (April 23, 2002).
CHAMPIONSHIP GAME EXPERIENCE: Played in NFC championship game (2002 and 2003 seasons).

			TOTALS			INTERCEPTIONS			
Year Team	G	GS	Tk.	Ast.	Sks.	No.	Yds.	Avg.	TD
2002—Philadelphia NFL	9	0	1	0	0.0	0	0	0.0	0
2003—Philadelphia NFL	16	0	0	0	0.0	0	0	0.0	0
Pro totals (2 years)	25	0	1	0	0.0	0	0	0.0	0

ENGELBERGER, JOHN — DE — 49ERS

PERSONAL: Born October 18, 1976, in Heidelberg, Germany. ... 6-4/268. ... Full name: John Albert Engelberger.
HIGH SCHOOL: Robert E. Lee (Springfield, Va.).
COLLEGE: Virginia Tech.
TRANSACTIONS/CAREER NOTES: Selected by San Francisco 49ers in second round (35th pick overall) of 2000 NFL draft. ... Signed by 49ers (July 18, 2000). ... Granted unconditional free agency (March 3, 2004). ... Re-signed by 49ers (March 4, 2004).

			TOTALS		
Year Team	**G**	**GS**	**Tk.**	**Ast.**	**Sks.**
2000—San Francisco NFL	16	13	21	9	3.0
2001—San Francisco NFL	15	14	30	1	4.0
2002—San Francisco NFL	15	0	9	1	0.0
2003—San Francisco NFL	16	16	26	3	4.5
Pro totals (4 years)	62	43	86	14	11.5

ENGRAM, BOBBY — WR — SEAHAWKS

PERSONAL: Born January 7, 1973, in Camden, S.C. ... 5-10/188. ... Full name: Simon Engram III.
HIGH SCHOOL: Camden (S.C.).
COLLEGE: Penn State.
TRANSACTIONS/CAREER NOTES: Selected by Chicago Bears in second round (52nd pick overall) of 1996 NFL draft. ... Signed by Bears (July 17, 1996). ... Granted free agency (February 12, 1999). ... Re-signed by Bears (April 16, 1999). ... Granted unconditional free agency (February 11, 2000). ... Re-signed by Bears (April 26, 2000). ... On injured reserve with knee injury (September 19, 2000-remainder of season). ... Released by Bears (August 28, 2001). ... Signed by Seattle Seahawks (August 30, 2001). ... Granted unconditional free agency (February 28, 2003). ... Re-signed by Seahawks (March 5, 2003).
HONORS: Named wide receiver on THE SPORTING NEWS college All-America second team (1994 and 1995).
SINGLE GAME HIGHS (regular season): Receptions—13 (December 26, 1999, vs. St. Louis); yards—143 (December 26, 1999, vs. St. Louis); and touchdown receptions—2 (November 23, 2003, vs. Baltimore).
STATISTICAL PLATEAUS: 100-yard receiving games: 1998 (3), 1999 (2). Total: 5.

			RECEIVING				PUNT RETURNS				KICKOFF RETURNS				TOTALS			
Year Team	**G**	**GS**	**No.**	**Yds.**	**Avg.**	**TD**	**No.**	**Yds.**	**Avg.**	**TD**	**No.**	**Yds.**	**Avg.**	**TD**	**TD**	**2pt.**	**Pts.**	**Fum.**
1996—Chicago NFL	16	2	33	389	11.8	6	31	282	9.1	0	25	580	23.2	0	6	0	36	2
1997—Chicago NFL	11	11	45	399	8.9	2	1	4	4.0	0	2	27	13.5	0	2	1	14	1
1998—Chicago NFL	16	16	64	987	15.4	5	0	0	0.0	0	0	0	0.0	0	5	0	30	1
1999—Chicago NFL	16	14	88	947	10.8	4	0	0	0.0	0	0	0	0.0	0	4	0	24	2
2000—Chicago NFL	3	3	16	109	6.8	0	0	0	0.0	0	0	0	0.0	0	0	0	0	1
2001—Seattle NFL	16	4	29	400	13.8	0	6	96	16.0	0	1	6	6.0	0	0	0	0	0
2002—Seattle NFL	15	6	50	619	12.4	0	21	224	10.7	1	0	0	0.0	0	1	0	6	2
2003—Seattle NFL	16	7	52	637	12.3	6	31	320	10.3	1	1	18	18.0	0	7	0	42	5
Pro totals (8 years)	109	63	377	4487	11.9	23	90	926	10.3	2	29	631	21.8	0	25	1	152	14

EPHRAIM, ALONZO — C — EAGLES

PERSONAL: Born November 9, 1981, in Birmingham, Ala. ... 6-4/312. ... Full name: Alonzo Brandon Ephraim.
HIGH SCHOOL: Wenonah (Ala.).
COLLEGE: Alabama.
TRANSACTIONS/CAREER NOTES: Signed as non-drafted free agent by Philadelphia Eagles (April 28, 2003).
PLAYING EXPERIENCE: Philadelphia NFL, 2003. ... Games/Games started: 2003 (16/0). Total: 16/0.
CHAMPIONSHIP GAME EXPERIENCE: Played in NFC championship game (2003 season).

EVANS, DOUG — CB

PERSONAL: Born May 13, 1970, in Shreveport, La. ... 6-1/188. ... Full name: Douglas Edwards Evans. ... Brother of Bobby Evans, safety with Winnipeg Blue Bombers of the CFL (1990-94).
HIGH SCHOOL: Haynesville (La.).
COLLEGE: Louisiana Tech.
TRANSACTIONS/CAREER NOTES: Selected by Green Bay Packers in sixth round (141st pick overall) of 1993 NFL draft. ... Signed by Packers (July 9, 1993). ... Granted unconditional free agency (February 13, 1998). ... Signed by Carolina Panthers (February 18, 1998). ... On injured reserve with broken collarbone (November 10, 1998-remainder of season). ... Released by Panthers (February 22, 2002). ... Signed by Seattle Seahawks (April 10, 2002). ... Released by Seahawks (August 31, 2003). ... Re-signed by Seahawks (September 9, 2003), ... Released by Seahawks (October 11, 2003). ... Signed by Detroit Lions (October 31, 2003). ... Granted unconditional free agency (March 3, 2004).
CHAMPIONSHIP GAME EXPERIENCE: Played in NFC championship game (1995-1997 seasons). ... Member of Super Bowl championship team (1996 season). ... Played in Super Bowl 32 (1997 season).

			TOTALS			INTERCEPTIONS			
Year Team	**G**	**GS**	**Tk.**	**Ast.**	**Sks.**	**No.**	**Yds.**	**Avg.**	**TD**
1993—Green Bay NFL	16	0	9	5	0.0	1	0	0.0	0
1994—Green Bay NFL	16	15	46	12	1.0	1	0	0.0	0
1995—Green Bay NFL	16	16	74	15	1.0	2	24	12.0	0
1996—Green Bay NFL	16	16	62	16	3.0	5	102	20.4	1
1997—Green Bay NFL	15	15	66	10	1.0	3	33	11.0	0
1998—Carolina NFL	9	7	32	5	0.0	2	18	9.0	0
1999—Carolina NFL	16	16	60	10	0.0	2	1	0.5	0
2000—Carolina NFL	16	16	66	13	0.0	2	17	8.5	0
2001—Carolina NFL	16	16	60	7	0.0	8	126	15.8	1
2002—Seattle NFL	15	0	26	3	0.0	1	0	0.0	0

Year Team	G	GS	TOTALS Tk.	Ast.	Sks.	INTERCEPTIONS No.	Yds.	Avg.	TD
2003—Seattle NFL	2	0	1	0	0.0	0	0	0.0	0
—Detroit NFL	9	3	20	3	0.0	1	2	2.0	0
Pro totals (11 years)	162	120	522	99	6.0	28	323	11.5	2

EVANS, HEATH FB SEAHAWKS

PERSONAL: Born December 30, 1978, in West Palm Beach, Fla. ... 6-0/245. ... Full name: Bryan Heath Evans.
HIGH SCHOOL: Kings Academy (Miami).
COLLEGE: Auburn.
TRANSACTIONS/CAREER NOTES: Selected by Seattle Seahawks in third round (82nd pick overall) of 2001 NFL draft. ... Signed by Seahawks (July 26, 2001). ... Granted free agency (March 3, 2004). ... Re-signed by Seahawks (April 4, 2004).
SINGLE GAME HIGHS (regular season): Attempts—5 (December 29, 2002, vs. San Diego); yards—22 (December 29, 2002, vs. San Diego); and rushing touchdowns—0.

Year Team	G	GS	RUSHING Att.	Yds.	Avg.	TD	RECEIVING No.	Yds.	Avg.	TD	KICKOFF RETURNS No.	Yds.	Avg.	TD	TOTALS TD	2pt.	Pts.	Fum.
2001—Seattle NFL	16	0	2	11	5.5	0	0	0	0.0	0	3	40	13.3	0	0	0	0	0
2002—Seattle NFL	16	1	17	53	3.1	0	8	41	5.1	0	6	84	14.0	0	0	0	0	1
2003—Seattle NFL	14	0	7	24	3.4	0	2	34	17.0	0	1	14	14.0	0	0	0	0	0
Pro totals (3 years)	46	1	26	88	3.4	0	10	75	7.5	0	10	138	13.8	0	0	0	0	1

EVANS, JOSH DT JETS

PERSONAL: Born September 6, 1972, in Langdale, Ala. ... 6-3/280. ... Full name: Mijoshki Antwon Evans.
HIGH SCHOOL: Lanett (Ala.).
COLLEGE: Alabama-Birmingham.
TRANSACTIONS/CAREER NOTES: Signed as non-drafted free agent by Dallas Cowboys (April 27, 1995). ... Released by Cowboys (August 22, 1995). ... Signed by Houston Oilers to practice squad (September 1, 1995). ... Activated (November 10, 1995). ... On injured reserve with knee injury (November 29, 1996-remainder of season). ... Oilers franchise moved to Tennessee for 1997 season. ... Granted free agency (February 13, 1998). ... Re-signed by Oilers (July 25, 1998). ... Oilers franchise renamed Tennessee Titans for 1999 season (December 26, 1998). ... On suspended list for violating league substance abuse policy (September 6-October 4, 1999). ... On suspended list for violating league substance abuse policy (March 1, 2000-April 13, 2001). ... Granted unconditional free agency (March 1, 2002). ... Signed by New York Jets (July 17, 2002). ... On suspended list for violating league substance abuse policy (June 27-November 17, 2003).
CHAMPIONSHIP GAME EXPERIENCE: Played in AFC championship game (1999 season). ... Played in Super Bowl 34 (1999 season).

Year Team	G	GS	TOTALS Tk.	Ast.	Sks.
1995—Houston NFL	7	0	2	1	0.0
1996—Houston NFL	8	0	4	7	0.0
1997—Tennessee NFL	15	0	23	3	2.0
1998—Tennessee NFL	14	11	30	13	3.5
1999—Tennessee NFL	11	10	21	5	3.5
2000—Tennessee NFL	Did not play.				
2001—Tennessee NFL	16	16	41	12	5.5
2002—New York Jets NFL	16	16	40	7	6.0
2003—New York Jets NFL	6	0	10	4	1.0
Pro totals (8 years)	93	53	171	52	21.5

EVANS, TROY LB TEXANS

PERSONAL: Born December 3, 1977, in Bay City, Mich. ... 6-3/243. ... Full name: Troy Lyn Evans.
HIGH SCHOOL: Lakota (Cincinnati).
COLLEGE: Cincinnati.
TRANSACTIONS/CAREER NOTES: Signed as non-drafted free agent by St. Louis Rams (April 25, 2001). ... Released by Rams (August 27, 2001). ... Re-signed by Rams to practice squad (November 21, 2001). ... Granted free agency following 2001 season. ... Signed by Houston Texans (February 12, 2002). ... Released by Texans (September 23, 2002). ... Re-signed by Texans (October 30, 2002). ... Re-signed by Texans (April 1, 2003).

Year Team	G	GS	TOTALS Tk.	Ast.	Sks.	INTERCEPTIONS No.	Yds.	Avg.	TD
2002—Houston NFL	12	0	0	0	0.0	0	0	0.0	0
2003—Houston NFL	15	0	2	0	0.0	0	0	0.0	0
Pro totals (2 years)	27	0	2	0	0.0	0	0	0.0	0

FABINI, JASON T JETS

PERSONAL: Born August 25, 1974, in Fort Wayne, Ind. ... 6-7/304.
HIGH SCHOOL: Bishop Dwenger (Fort Wayne, Ind.).
COLLEGE: Cincinnati.
TRANSACTIONS/CAREER NOTES: Selected by New York Jets in fourth round (111th pick overall) of 1998 NFL draft. ... Signed by Jets (July 13, 1998). ... On injured reserve with knee injury (November 16, 1999-remainder of season). ... Granted free agency (March 2, 2001). ... Re-signed by Jets (May 30, 2001).
PLAYING EXPERIENCE: New York Jets NFL, 1998-2003. ... Games/Games started: 1998 (16/16), 1999 (9/9), 2000 (16/16), 2001 (16/16), 2002 (16/16), 2003 (16/16). Total: 89/89.
CHAMPIONSHIP GAME EXPERIENCE: Played in AFC championship game (1998 season).

F

FAGGINS, DEMARCUS — CB — TEXANS

PERSONAL: Born June 13, 1979, in Irving, Texas. ... 5-10/178. ... Full name: Demarcus Faggins.
HIGH SCHOOL: Irving (Texas).
JUNIOR COLLEGE: Navarro College (Texas).
COLLEGE: Kansas State.
TRANSACTIONS/CAREER NOTES: Selected by Houston Texans in sixth round (173rd pick overall) of 2002 NFL draft. ... Signed by Texans (July 13, 2002). ... Waived by Texans (August 31, 2003). ... Re-signed by Texans to practice squad (September 1, 2003). ... Activated (November 9, 2003).

			TOTALS			INTERCEPTIONS			
Year Team	**G**	**GS**	**Tk.**	**Ast.**	**Sks.**	**No.**	**Yds.**	**Avg.**	**TD**
2002—Houston NFL	2	0	0	0	0.0	0	0	0.0	0
2003—Houston NFL	8	1	12	1	0.0	0	0	0.0	0
Pro totals (2 years)	10	1	12	1	0.0	0	0	0.0	0

FAINE, JEFF — C — BROWNS

PERSONAL: Born April 6, 1981, in Milwaukie, Ore. ... 6-3/303. ... Full name: Jeffrey Kalei Faine.
HIGH SCHOOL: Seminole (Sanford, Fla.).
COLLEGE: Notre Dame.
TRANSACTIONS/CAREER NOTES: Selected after junior season by Cleveland Browns in first round (21st pick overall) of 2003 NFL draft. ... Signed by Browns (July 28, 2003). ... On injured reserve with ankle injury (November 26, 2003-remainder of season).
PLAYING EXPERIENCE: Cleveland NFL, 2003. ... Games/Games started: 2003 (9/9). Total: 9/9.

FAIR, TERRY — CB — STEELERS

PERSONAL: Born July 20, 1976, in Phoenix. ... 5-9/184. ... Full name: Terrance Delon Fair.
HIGH SCHOOL: South Mountain (Phoenix).
COLLEGE: Tennessee.
TRANSACTIONS/CAREER NOTES: Selected by Detroit Lions in first round (20th pick overall) of 1998 NFL draft. ... Signed by Lions (July 20, 1998). ... On non-football injury list with hand injury (December 14, 1999-remainder of season). ... On physically unable to perform list with foot injury (July 23-August 19, 2002). ... Released by Lions (September 1, 2002). ... Signed by Carolina Panthers (September 5, 2002). ... On injured reserve with broken ankle (September 24, 2002-remainder of season). ... Granted unconditional free agency (February 28, 2003). ... Signed by Pittsburgh Steelers (January 22, 2004).
HONORS: Named kick returner on THE SPORTING NEWS NFL All-Pro team (1998).

			TOTALS			INTERCEPTIONS				PUNT RETURNS				KICKOFF RETURNS				TOTALS			
Year Team	**G**	**GS**	**Tk.**	**Ast.**	**Sks.**	**No.**	**Yds.**	**Avg.**	**TD**	**No.**	**Yds.**	**Avg.**	**TD**	**No.**	**Yds.**	**Avg.**	**TD**	**TD**	**2pt.**	**Pts.**	**Fum.**
1998—Det. NFL	14	10	39	18	1.0	0	0	0.0	0	30	189	6.3	0	51	1428	*28.0	†2	2	0	12	5
1999—Det. NFL	11	11	46	6	0.0	3	49	16.3	1	11	97	8.8	0	34	752	22.1	0	2	0	12	2
2000—Det. NFL	15	15	46	11	0.0	2	0	0.0	0	2	15	7.5	0	6	149	24.8	0	0	0	0	1
2001—Det. NFL	12	12	37	6	0.0	2	29	14.5	1	4	37	9.3	0	10	187	18.7	0	1	0	6	0
2002—Car. NFL	3	0	0	0	0.0	0	0	0.0	0	0	0	0.0	0	0	0	0.0	0	0	0	0	0
2003—	Did not play.																				
Pro totals (5 years)	55	48	168	41	1.0	7	78	11.1	2	47	338	7.2	0	101	2516	24.9	2	5	0	30	8

FANECA, ALAN — G — STEELERS

PERSONAL: Born December 7, 1976, in New Orleans, La. ... 6-5/312. ... Full name: Alan Joseph Faneca Jr.
HIGH SCHOOL: John Curtis Christian (New Orleans), then Lamar (Houston).
COLLEGE: Louisiana State.
TRANSACTIONS/CAREER NOTES: Selected after junior season by Pittsburgh Steelers in first round (26th pick overall) of 1998 NFL draft. ... Signed by Steelers (July 29, 1998).
PLAYING EXPERIENCE: Pittsburgh NFL, 1998-2003. ... Games/Games started: 1998 (16/12), 1999 (15/14), 2000 (16/16), 2001 (15/15), 2002 (16/16), 2003 (16/16). Total: 94/89.
CHAMPIONSHIP GAME EXPERIENCE: Played in AFC championship game (2001 season).
HONORS: Named guard on THE SPORTING NEWS college All-America first team (1997). ... Named guard on THE SPORTING NEWS NFL All-Pro team (2001 and 2002). ... Played in Pro Bowl (2001-2003 seasons).

FARGAS, JUSTIN — RB — RAIDERS

PERSONAL: Born January 25, 1980, in Encino, Calif. ... 6-1/220.
HIGH SCHOOL: Notre Dame (Sherman Oaks, Calif.).
COLLEGE: Southern California.
TRANSACTIONS/CAREER NOTES: Selected by Oakland Raiders in third round (96th pick overall) of 2003 NFL draft. ... Signed by Raiders (July 24, 2003). ... On injured reserve with knee injury (November 19, 2003-remainder of season).
SINGLE GAME HIGHS (regular season): Attempts—16 (November 9, 2003, vs. New York Jets); yards—62 (November 9, 2003, vs. New York Jets); and rushing touchdowns—0.

			RUSHING				RECEIVING				KICKOFF RETURNS				TOTALS			
Year Team	**G**	**GS**	**Att.**	**Yds.**	**Avg.**	**TD**	**No.**	**Yds.**	**Avg.**	**TD**	**No.**	**Yds.**	**Avg.**	**TD**	**TD**	**2pt.**	**Pts.**	**Fum.**
2003—Oakland NFL	10	1	40	203	5.1	0	2	2	1.0	0	16	315	19.7	0	0	0	0	1

FARRIOR, JAMES — LB — STEELERS

PERSONAL: Born January 6, 1975, in Richmond, Va. ... 6-2/242. ... Full name: James Alfred Farrior.
HIGH SCHOOL: Matoaca (Ettrick, Va.).
COLLEGE: Virginia.
TRANSACTIONS/CAREER NOTES: Selected by New York Jets in first round (eighth pick overall) of 1997 NFL draft. ... Signed by Jets (July 20, 1997). ... Granted unconditional free agency (March 1, 2002). ... Signed by Pittsburgh Steelers (April 12, 2002).
CHAMPIONSHIP GAME EXPERIENCE: Played in AFC championship game (1998 season).

			TOTALS			INTERCEPTIONS			
Year Team	**G**	**GS**	**Tk.**	**Ast.**	**Sks.**	**No.**	**Yds.**	**Avg.**	**TD**
1997—New York Jets NFL	16	15	53	18	1.5	0	0	0.0	0
1998—New York Jets NFL	12	2	17	10	0.0	0	0	0.0	0
1999—New York Jets NFL	16	4	30	8	2.0	0	0	0.0	0
2000—New York Jets NFL	16	6	46	10	1.0	1	0	0.0	0
2001—New York Jets NFL	16	16	107	36	1.0	2	84	42.0	0
2002—Pittsburgh NFL	14	14	55	22	0.0	0	0	0.0	0
2003—Pittsburgh NFL	16	16	94	43	0.0	1	9	9.0	0
Pro totals (7 years)	106	73	402	147	5.5	4	93	23.3	0

FARRIS, JIMMY — WR — FALCONS

PERSONAL: Born April 13, 1978, in Lewiston, Idaho. ... 6-0/200.
HIGH SCHOOL: Lewiston (Id.).
COLLEGE: Montana.
TRANSACTIONS/CAREER NOTES: Signed as non-drafted free agent by San Francisco 49ers (April 26, 2001). ... Released by 49ers (September 2, 2001). ... Re-signed by 49ers to practice squad (September 4, 2001). ... Signed by New England Patriots off 49ers practice squad (January 11, 2002). ... Released by Patriots (August 27, 2002). ... Signed by Atlanta Falcons to practice squad (November 27, 2002). ... Activated (January 7, 2003).
SINGLE GAME HIGHS (regular season): Receptions—2 (September 14, 2003, vs. Washington); yards—58 (September 14, 2003, vs. Washington); and touchdown receptions—1 (October 5, 2003, vs. Minnesota).

			RECEIVING				TOTALS			
Year Team	**G**	**GS**	**No.**	**Yds.**	**Avg.**	**TD**	**TD**	**2pt.**	**Pts.**	**Fum.**
2003—Atlanta NFL	16	0	6	100	16.7	2	2	0	12	0

FATAFEHI, MARIO — DT — BRONCOS

PERSONAL: Born January 27, 1979, in Chicago, Ill. ... 6-2/300.
HIGH SCHOOL: Ferrington (Honolulu, Hawaii).
JUNIOR COLLEGE: Snow College (Utah).
COLLEGE: Kansas State.
TRANSACTIONS/CAREER NOTES: Selected by Arizona Cardinals in fifth round (133rd pick overall) of 2001 NFL draft. ... Signed by Cardinals (June 5, 2001). ... On injured reserve with hand injury (November 30, 2001-remainder of season). ... Released by Cardinals (October 5, 2002). ... Signed by Carolina Panthers (November 1, 2002). ... Waived by Panthers (July 14, 2003). ... Signed by Denver Broncos (July 28, 2003).

			TOTALS		
Year Team	**G**	**GS**	**Tk.**	**Ast.**	**Sks.**
2001—Arizona NFL	7	1	4	4	0.0
2002—Carolina NFL	6	0	0	0	0.0
2003—Denver NFL	16	9	22	9	2.5
Pro totals (3 years)	29	10	26	13	2.5

F

FAULK, KEVIN — RB — PATRIOTS

PERSONAL: Born June 5, 1976, in Lafayette, La. ... 5-8/202. ... Full name: Kevin Tony Faulk.
HIGH SCHOOL: Carencro (Lafayette, La.).
COLLEGE: Louisiana State.
TRANSACTIONS/CAREER NOTES: Selected by New England Patriots in second round (46th pick overall) of 1999 NFL draft. ... Signed by Patriots (July 28, 1999). ... On injured reserve with broken ankle (December 15, 1999-remainder of season). ... Granted unconditional free agency (March 3, 2004). ... Re-signed by Patriots (March 10, 2004).
CHAMPIONSHIP GAME EXPERIENCE: Played in AFC championship game (2001 and 2003 seasons). ... Member of Super Bowl championship team (2001 and 2003 seasons).
HONORS: Named kick returner on THE SPORTING NEWS college All-America second team (1998).
SINGLE GAME HIGHS (regular season): Attempts—23 (November 23, 2003, vs. Houston); yards—96 (October 26, 2003, vs. Cleveland); and rushing touchdowns—1 (November 3, 2002, vs. Buffalo).
STATISTICAL PLATEAUS: 100-yard receiving games: 2002 (1), 2003 (1). Total: 2.

			RUSHING				RECEIVING				PUNT RETURNS				KICKOFF RETURNS				TOTALS		
Year Team	**G**	**GS**	**Att.**	**Yds.**	**Avg.**	**TD**	**No.**	**Yds.**	**Avg.**	**TD**	**No.**	**Yds.**	**Avg.**	**TD**	**No.**	**Yds.**	**Avg.**	**TD**	**TD**	**2pt.**	**Pts.**
1999—N.E. NFL	11	2	67	227	3.4	1	12	98	8.2	1	10	90	9.0	0	39	943	24.2	0	2	0	12
2000—N.E. NFL	16	9	164	570	3.5	4	51	465	9.1	1	6	58	9.7	0	38	816	21.5	0	5	1	32
2001—N.E. NFL	15	1	41	169	4.1	1	30	189	6.3	2	4	27	6.8	0	33	662	20.1	0	3	0	18
2002—N.E. NFL	15	0	52	271	5.2	2	37	379	10.2	3	8	65	8.1	0	26	725	§27.9	†2	7	0	42
2003—N.E. NFL	15	8	178	638	3.6	0	48	440	9.2	0	5	66	13.2	0	10	207	20.7	0	0	0	0
Pro totals (5 years)	72	20	502	1875	3.7	8	178	1571	8.8	7	33	306	9.3	0	146	3353	23.0	2	17	1	104

FAULK, MARSHALL — RB — RAMS

PERSONAL: Born February 26, 1973, in New Orleans, La. ... 5-10/211. ... Full name: Marshall William Faulk.

HIGH SCHOOL: G. W. Carver (New Orleans).

COLLEGE: San Diego State.

TRANSACTIONS/CAREER NOTES: Selected after junior season by Indianapolis Colts in first round (second pick overall) of 1994 NFL draft. ... Signed by Colts (July 24, 1994). ... Traded by Colts to St. Louis Rams for second- (LB Mike Peterson) and fifth-round (DE Brad Scioli) picks in 1999 draft (April 15, 1999).

CHAMPIONSHIP GAME EXPERIENCE: Member of Colts for AFC championship game (1995 season); inactive due to injury. ... Played in NFC championship game (1999 and 2001 seasons). ... Member of Super Bowl championship team (1999 season). ... Played in Super Bowl 36 (2001 season).

HONORS: Named running back on THE SPORTING NEWS college All-America first team (1991-1993). ... Named NFL Rookie of the Year by THE SPORTING NEWS (1994). ... Played in Pro Bowl (1994, 1995, 1998, 1999, 2001 and 2002 seasons). ... Named Outstanding Player of Pro Bowl (1994 season). ... Named running back on THE SPORTING NEWS NFL All-Pro team (1999-2001). ... Named NFL Player of the Year by THE SPORTING NEWS (2000 and 2001). ... Named to play in Pro Bowl (2000 season); replaced by Stephen Davis due to injury.

RECORDS: Shares NFL single-game record for most two-point conversions—2 (October 15, 2000, vs. Atlanta).

SINGLE GAME HIGHS (regular season): Attempts—32 (October 20, 2002, vs. Seattle); yards—220 (December 24, 2000, vs. New Orleans); and rushing touchdowns—4 (December 10, 2000, vs. Minnesota).

STATISTICAL PLATEAUS: 100-yard rushing games: 1994 (4), 1995 (1), 1996 (1), 1997 (4), 1998 (4), 1999 (7), 2000 (4), 2001 (5), 2002 (3), 2003 (5). Total: 38. 100-yard receiving games: 1994 (1), 1998 (3), 1999 (1), 2000 (2), 2001 (1). Total: 8.

MISCELLANEOUS: Holds St. Louis Rams all-time record for most touchdowns (80).

			RUSHING				RECEIVING				TOTALS			
Year Team	**G**	**GS**	**Att.**	**Yds.**	**Avg.**	**TD**	**No.**	**Yds.**	**Avg.**	**TD**	**TD**	**2pt.**	**Pts.**	**Fum.**
1994—Indianapolis NFL	16	16	314	1282	4.1	11	52	522	10.0	1	▲12	0	72	5
1995—Indianapolis NFL	16	16	289	1078	3.7	11	56	475	8.5	3	14	0	84	8
1996—Indianapolis NFL	13	13	198	587	3.0	7	56	428	7.6	0	7	0	42	2
1997—Indianapolis NFL	16	16	264	1054	4.0	7	47	471	10.0	1	8	0	48	5
1998—Indianapolis NFL	16	15	324	1319	4.1	6	86	908	10.6	4	10	0	60	3
1999—St. Louis NFL	16	16	253	1381	*5.5	7	87	1048	12.0	5	12	†1	74	2
2000—St. Louis NFL	14	14	253	1359	*5.4	*18	81	830	10.2	8	*26	2	*160	0
2001—St. Louis NFL	14	14	260	1382	*5.3	‡12	83	765	9.2	9	*21	1	*128	3
2002—St. Louis NFL	14	10	212	953	4.5	8	80	537	6.7	2	10	0	60	4
2003—St. Louis NFL	11	11	209	818	3.9	10	45	290	6.4	1	11	0	66	0
Pro totals (10 years)	146	141	2576	11213	4.4	97	673	6274	9.3	34	131	4	794	32

FAURIA, CHRISTIAN — TE — PATRIOTS

PERSONAL: Born September 22, 1971, in Northridge, Calif. ... 6-4/250. ... Name pronounced: FOUR-ee-ah.

HIGH SCHOOL: Crespi Carmelite (Encino, Calif.).

COLLEGE: Colorado.

TRANSACTIONS/CAREER NOTES: Selected by Seattle Seahawks in second round (39th pick overall) of 1995 NFL draft. ... Signed by Seahawks (July 17, 1995). ... Granted free agency (February 13, 1998). ... Re-signed by Seahawks (April 20, 1998). ... Granted unconditional free agency (February 12, 1999). ... Re-signed by Seahawks (March 5, 1999). ... Granted unconditional free agency (March 1, 2002). ... Signed by New England Patriots (March 22, 2002).

CHAMPIONSHIP GAME EXPERIENCE: Played in AFC championship game (2003 season). ... Member of Super Bowl championship team (2003 season).

SINGLE GAME HIGHS (regular season): Receptions—6 (December 26, 1999, vs. Kansas City); yards—84 (December 26, 1999, vs. Kansas City); and touchdown receptions—2 (September 14, 2003, vs. Philadelphia).

F

			RECEIVING				TOTALS			
Year Team	**G**	**GS**	**No.**	**Yds.**	**Avg.**	**TD**	**TD**	**2pt.**	**Pts.**	**Fum.**
1995—Seattle NFL	14	9	17	181	10.6	1	1	0	6	0
1996—Seattle NFL	10	9	18	214	11.9	1	1	0	6	0
1997—Seattle NFL	16	3	10	110	11.0	0	0	0	0	0
1998—Seattle NFL	16	15	37	377	10.2	2	2	0	12	1
1999—Seattle NFL	16	16	35	376	10.7	0	0	0	0	1
2000—Seattle NFL	15	10	28	237	8.5	2	2	0	12	1
2001—Seattle NFL	16	11	21	188	9.0	1	1	1	8	2
2002—New England NFL	16	13	27	253	9.4	7	7	1	44	0
2003—New England NFL	16	12	28	285	10.2	2	2	0	12	0
Pro totals (9 years)	135	98	221	2221	10.0	16	16	2	100	5

FAVORS, GREG — LB — JAGUARS

PERSONAL: Born September 30, 1974, in Atlanta, Ga. ... 6-1/242. ... Full name: Gregory Bernard Favors.

HIGH SCHOOL: Southside (Atlanta).

COLLEGE: Mississippi State.

TRANSACTIONS/CAREER NOTES: Selected by Kansas City Chiefs in fourth round (120th pick overall) of 1998 NFL draft. ... Signed by Chiefs (July 17, 1998). ... Claimed on waivers by Tennessee Titans (September 8, 1999). ... Granted free agency (March 2, 2001). ... Re-signed by Titans (May 9, 2001). ... Granted unconditional free agency (March 1, 2002). ... Signed by Indianapolis Colts (April 9, 2002). ... Released by Colts (November 4, 2002). ... Signed by Buffalo Bills (November 19, 2002). ... Granted unconditional free agency (February 28, 2003). ... Signed by Carolina Panthers (March 25, 2003). ... Granted unconditional free agency (March 3, 2004). ... Signed by Jacksonville Jaguars (March 23, 2004).

CHAMPIONSHIP GAME EXPERIENCE: Played in AFC championship game (1999 season). ... Played in Super Bowl 34 (1999 season) and Super Bowl 38 (2003 season).

Year Team	G	GS	TOTALS Tk.	Ast.	Sks.	INTERCEPTIONS No.	Yds.	Avg.	TD
1998—Kansas City NFL	16	4	17	2	2.0	0	0	0.0	0
1999—Tennessee NFL	15	0	0	0	0.0	0	0	0.0	0
2000—Tennessee NFL	16	16	28	9	5.5	0	0	0.0	0
2001—Tennessee NFL	16	12	30	17	1.5	1	0	0.0	0
2002—Buffalo NFL	6	0	0	0	0.0	0	0	0.0	0
2003—Carolina NFL	16	12	56	20	0.0	0	0	0.0	0
Pro totals (6 years)	85	44	131	48	9.0	1	0	0.0	0

FAVRE, BRETT — QB — PACKERS

PERSONAL: Born October 10, 1969, in Gulfport, Miss. ... 6-2/225. ... Full name: Brett Lorenzo Favre. ... Name pronounced: FARVE.

HIGH SCHOOL: Hancock North Central (Kiln, Miss.).

COLLEGE: Southern Mississippi.

TRANSACTIONS/CAREER NOTES: Selected by Atlanta Falcons in second round (33rd pick overall) of 1991 NFL draft. ... Signed by Falcons (July 18, 1991). ... Traded by Falcons to Green Bay Packers for first-round pick (OT Bob Whitfield) in 1992 draft (February 11, 1992). ... Granted free agency (February 17, 1994). ... Re-signed by Packers (July 14, 1994).

CHAMPIONSHIP GAME EXPERIENCE: Played in NFC championship game (1995-1997 seasons). ... Member of Super Bowl championship team (1996 season). ... Played in Super Bowl 32 (1997 season).

HONORS: Played in Pro Bowl (1992, 1993, 1995 and 1996 seasons). ... Named NFL Player of the Year by THE SPORTING NEWS (1995 and 1996). ... Named quarterback on THE SPORTING NEWS NFL All-Pro team (1995-97). ... Named to play in Pro Bowl (1997 season); replaced by Chris Chandler due to injury. ... Named to play in Pro Bowl (2001 season); replaced by Donovan McNabb due to injury. ... Named to play in Pro Bowl (2002 season); replaced by Donovan McNabb due to injury. ... Named to play in Pro Bowl (2003 season); replaced by Matt Hasselbeck due to injury.

RECORDS: Shares NFL record for longest pass completion (to Robert Brooks)—99 yards, touchdown (September 11, 1995, at Chicago). ... Shares NFL record for most seasons leading league in touchdown passes—4 (1995-97, 2003).

SINGLE GAME HIGHS (regular season): Attempts—61 (October 14, 1996, vs. San Francisco); completions—36 (December 5, 1993, vs. Chicago); yards—402 (December 5, 1993, vs. Chicago); and touchdown passes—5 (September 27, 1998, vs. Carolina).

STATISTICAL PLATEAUS: 300-yard passing games: 1993 (1), 1994 (4), 1995 (7), 1996 (2), 1997 (2), 1998 (4), 1999 (6), 2000 (2), 2001 (4), 2002 (3), 2003 (1). Total: 36.

MISCELLANEOUS: Regular-season record as starting NFL quarterback: 125-64 (.661). ... Postseason record as starting NFL quarterback: 11-8 (.579). ... Active NFL leader in touchdown passes (346). ... Holds Green Bay Packers all-time records for most yards passing (45,646) and most touchdown passes (346).

Year Team	G	GS	PASSING Att.	Cmp.	Pct.	Yds.	TD	Int.	Avg.	Skd.	Rat.	RUSHING Att.	Yds.	Avg.	TD	TOTALS TD	2pt.	Pts.
1991—Atlanta NFL	2	0	5	0	0.0	0	0	2	0.00	1	.0	0	0	0.0	0	0	0	0
1992—Green Bay NFL	15	13	471	∞302	64.1	3227	18	13	6.85	34	85.3	47	198	4.2	1	1	0	6
1993—Green Bay NFL	16	16	‡522	‡318	60.9	3303	19	*24	6.33	30	72.2	58	216	3.7	1	1	0	6
1994—Green Bay NFL	16	16	582	363	62.4	3882	33	14	6.67	31	90.7	42	202	4.8	2	2	0	12
1995—Green Bay NFL	16	16	570	359	63.0	*4413	*38	13	‡7.74	33	‡99.5	39	181	4.6	3	3	0	18
1996—Green Bay NFL	16	16	‡543	‡325	59.9	‡3899	*39	13	7.18	40	95.8	49	136	2.8	2	2	0	12
1997—Green Bay NFL	16	16	513	‡304	59.3	‡3867	*35	16	7.54	25	92.6	58	187	3.2	1	1	0	6
1998—Green Bay NFL	16	16	‡551	*347	*63.0	*4212	31	‡23	7.64	38	87.8	40	133	3.3	1	1	0	6
1999—Green Bay NFL	16	16	*595	341	57.3	4091	22	23	6.86	35	74.7	28	142	5.1	0	0	0	0
2000—Green Bay NFL	16	16	‡580	338	58.3	3812	20	16	6.57	33	78.0	27	108	4.0	0	0	0	0
2001—Green Bay NFL	16	16	510	314	61.6	3921	32	15	7.69	22	94.1	38	56	1.5	1	1	0	6
2002—Green Bay NFL	16	16	‡551	‡341	61.9	3658	∞27	16	6.64	26	85.6	25	73	2.9	0	0	0	0
2003—Green Bay NFL	16	16	471	308	‡65.4	3361	*32	21	7.14	19	90.4	18	15	0.8	0	0	0	0
Pro totals (13 years)	193	189	6464	3960	61.3	45646	346	209	7.06	367	86.9	469	1647	3.5	12	12	0	72

FEAGLES, JEFF — P — GIANTS

PERSONAL: Born March 7, 1966, in Anaheim, Calif. ... 6-1/215. ... Full name: Jeffrey Allan Feagles.

HIGH SCHOOL: Gerard Catholic (Phoenix).

JUNIOR COLLEGE: Scottsdale (Ariz.) Community College.

COLLEGE: Miami (Fla.).

TRANSACTIONS/CAREER NOTES: Signed as non-drafted free agent by New England Patriots (May 1, 1988). ... Claimed on waivers by Philadelphia Eagles (June 5, 1990). ... Granted unconditional free agency (February 1-April 1, 1992). ... Re-signed by Eagles for 1992 season. ... Granted unconditional free agency (February 17, 1994). ... Signed by Phoenix Cardinals (March 2, 1994). ... Cardinals franchise renamed Arizona Cardinals for 1994 season. ... Granted unconditional free agency (February 13, 1998). ... Signed by Seattle Seahawks (March 4, 1998). ... Granted unconditional free agency (February 28, 2003). ... Signed by New York Giants (March 7, 2003).

HONORS: Played in Pro Bowl (1995 season).

Year Team	G	PUNTING No.	Yds.	Avg.	Net avg.	In. 20	Blk.
1988—New England NFL	16	▲91	3482	38.3	34.1	24	0
1989—New England NFL	16	63	2392	38.0	31.3	13	1
1990—Philadelphia NFL	16	72	3026	42.0	35.5	20	2
1991—Philadelphia NFL	16	*87	3640	41.8	34.0	*29	1
1992—Philadelphia NFL	16	‡82	‡3459	42.2	36.9	‡26	0
1993—Philadelphia NFL	16	83	3323	40.0	35.3	*31	0
1994—Arizona NFL	16	*98	‡3997	40.8	36.0	‡33	0
1995—Arizona NFL	16	72	3150	43.8	‡38.2	20	0
1996—Arizona NFL	16	76	3328	43.8	36.4	23	1
1997—Arizona NFL	16	91	4028	44.3	36.8	24	1
1998—Seattle NFL	16	81	3568	44.0	36.5	27	0
1999—Seattle NFL	16	84	3425	40.8	35.2	34	0
2000—Seattle NFL	16	74	2960	40.0	36.9	24	▲1
2001—Seattle NFL	16	85	3730	43.9	36.4	26	1

Year Team	G	PUNTING No.	Yds.	Avg.	Net avg.	In. 20	Blk.
2002—Seattle NFL	16	61	2542	41.7	37.0	22	0
2003—New York Giants NFL	16	90	3641	40.5	33.9	‡31	1
Pro totals (16 years)	256	1290	53691	41.6	35.7	407	9

FEELEY, A.J. — QB — DOLPHINS

PERSONAL: Born May 16, 1977, in Caldwell, Idaho. ... 6-3/217. ... Full name: Adam Joshua Feeley.
HIGH SCHOOL: Ontario (Ore.).
COLLEGE: Oregon.
TRANSACTIONS/CAREER NOTES: Selected by Philadelphia Eagles in fifth round (155th pick overall) of 2001 NFL draft. ... Signed by Eagles (June 6, 2001). ... Released by Eagles (September 26, 2002). ... Re-signed by Eagles to practice squad (September 28, 2002). ... Activated (October 8, 2002). ... Inactive for all 16 games (2003). ... Traded by Eagles to Miami Dolphins for second-round pick in 2005 draft (March 3, 2004).
CHAMPIONSHIP GAME EXPERIENCE: Member of Eagles for NFC championship game (2001-2003 seasons); inactive.
SINGLE GAME HIGHS (regular season): Attempts—35 (December 8, 2002, vs. Seattle); completions—21 (December 8, 2002, vs. Seattle); passing yards—253 (December 21, 2002, vs. Dallas); and touchdown passes—2 (December 15, 2002, vs. Washington).
MISCELLANEOUS: Regular-season record as starting NFL quarterback: 4-1 (.800).

Year Team	G	GS	PASSING Att.	Cmp.	Pct.	Yds.	TD	Int.	Avg.	Skd.	Rat.	RUSHING Att.	Yds.	Avg.	TD	TOTALS TD	2pt.	Pts.
2001—Philadelphia NFL	1	0	14	10	71.4	143	2	1	10.21	0	114.0	0	0	0.0	0	0	0	0
2002—Philadelphia NFL	6	5	154	86	55.8	1011	6	5	6.56	7	75.4	12	6	0.5	0	0	0	0
2003—Philadelphia NFL	Did not play.																	
Pro totals (2 years)	7	5	168	96	57.1	1154	8	6	6.87	7	79.3	12	6	0.5	0	0	0	0

FEELY, JAY — K — FALCONS

PERSONAL: Born May 23, 1976, in Odessa, Fla. ... 5-10/206.
HIGH SCHOOL: Tampa Jesuit (Fla.).
COLLEGE: Michigan.
TRANSACTIONS/CAREER NOTES: Signed as non-drafted free agent by Atlanta Falcons (April 12, 2001). ... Granted free agency (March 3, 2004). ... Re-signed by Falcons (May 20, 2004).

Year Team	G	FIELD GOALS 1-29	30-39	40-49	50+	Tot.	Pct.	Lg.	TOTALS XPM	XPA	Pts.
2001—Atlanta NFL	16	9-9	14-15	4-9	2-4	‡29-∞37	78.4	†55	28	28	115
2002—Atlanta NFL	16	8-10	12-14	11-13	1-3	†32-*40	80.0	52	42	43	‡138
2003—Atlanta NFL	16	6-6	9-11	4-7	0-3	19-27	70.4	46	32	33	89
Pro totals (3 years)	48	23-25	35-40	19-29	3-10	80-104	76.9	55	102	104	342

FENDERSON, JAMES — RB — FALCONS

PERSONAL: Born October 24, 1976, in Mililani, Hawaii. ... 5-9/200. ... Full name: James E. Fenderson.
HIGH SCHOOL: Mililani (Oahu, Hawaii).
COLLEGE: Hawaii.
TRANSACTIONS/CAREER NOTES: Signed as non-drafted free agent by New Orleans Saints (April 26, 2001). ... Released by Saints (September 7, 2001). ... Re-signed by Saints (December 14, 2001). ... On injured reserve with foot injury (December 10, 2003-remainder of season). ... Granted unconditional free agency (March 2, 2004). ... Signed by Atlanta Falcons (March 23, 2004).
SINGLE GAME HIGHS (regular season): Attempts—7 (November 24, 2002, vs. Cleveland); yards—35 (November 24, 2002, vs. Cleveland); and rushing touchdowns—1 (November 24, 2002, vs. Cleveland).

Year Team	G	GS	RUSHING Att.	Yds.	Avg.	TD	RECEIVING No.	Yds.	Avg.	TD	KICKOFF RETURNS No.	Yds.	Avg.	TD	TOTALS TD	2pt.	Pts.	Fum.
2001—New Orleans NFL	4	0	0	0	0.0	0	0	0	0.0	0	0	0	0.0	0	0	0	0	0
2002—New Orleans NFL	16	1	13	65	5.0	1	6	38	6.3	0	2	43	21.5	0	1	0	6	1
2003—New Orleans NFL	9	0	4	14	3.5	0	1	5	5.0	0	0	0	0.0	0	0	1	2	0
Pro totals (3 years)	29	1	17	79	4.6	1	7	43	6.1	0	2	43	21.5	0	1	1	8	1

F

FERGUSON, JASON — DT — JETS

PERSONAL: Born November 28, 1974, in Nettleton, Miss. ... 6-3/305. ... Full name: Jason O. Ferguson.
HIGH SCHOOL: Nettleton (Miss.).
JUNIOR COLLEGE: Itawamba Community College (Miss.).
COLLEGE: Georgia.
TRANSACTIONS/CAREER NOTES: Selected by New York Jets in seventh round (229th pick overall) of 1997 NFL draft. ... Signed by Jets (April 30, 1997). ... On suspended list for violating league substance abuse policy (November 24-December 22, 1999). ... Granted free agency (February 11, 2000). ... Re-signed by Jets (May 24, 2000). ... Granted unconditional free agency (March 2, 2001). ... Re-signed by Jets (March 11, 2001). ... On injured reserve with shoulder injury (September 3, 2001-entire season).
CHAMPIONSHIP GAME EXPERIENCE: Played in AFC championship game (1998 season).

Year Team	G	GS	TOTALS Tk.	Ast.	Sks.
1997—New York Jets NFL	13	1	23	8	3.5
1998—New York Jets NFL	16	16	42	21	4.0
1999—New York Jets NFL	9	9	23	10	1.0
2000—New York Jets NFL	15	11	34	11	1.0

	G	GS	Tk.	Ast.	Sks.
2001—New York Jets NFL	Did not play.				
2002—New York Jets NFL	16	16	42	21	3.0
2003—New York Jets NFL	16	16	52	23	4.5
Pro totals (6 years)	85	69	216	94	17.0

FERGUSON, NICK — S — BRONCOS

PERSONAL: Born November 27, 1974, in Miami, Fla. ... 5-11/201.
HIGH SCHOOL: Jackson (Miami).
COLLEGE: Georgia Tech.
TRANSACTIONS/CAREER NOTES: Signed as non-drafted free agent by Cincinnati Bengals (April 23, 1996). ... Released by Bengals (August 5, 1996). ... Signed by Sasketchewan Roughriders of CFL (September 27, 1996). ... Traded by Roughriders to Winnipeg Blue Bombers (May 9, 1997). ... Signed by Chicago Bears (February 12, 1999). ... Assigned by Bears to Rhein Fire in 1999 NFL Europe enhancement allocation program (February 22, 1999). ... Released by Bears (August 30, 1999). ... Signed by Buffalo Bills (July 6, 2000). ... Released by Bills (August 27, 2000). ... Re-signed by Bills to practice squad (August 28, 2000). ... Signed by New York Jets off Bills practice squad (November 7, 2000). ... Granted free agency (February 28, 2003). ... Signed by Denver Broncos (April 2, 2003). ... On injured reserve with forearm injury (December 24, 2003-remainder of season).

			TOTALS			INTERCEPTIONS			
Year Team	**G**	**GS**	**Tk.**	**Ast.**	**Sks.**	**No.**	**Yds.**	**Avg.**	**TD**
1996—Saskatchewan CFL	5	...	...	...	0.0	0	0	0.0	0
1997—Winnipeg CFL	15	...	...	...	0.0	2	35	17.5	0
1998—Winnipeg CFL	16	...	...	...	0.0	1	0	0.0	0
1999—Winnipeg CFL	3	...	...	...	0.0	0	0	0.0	0
2000—New York Jets NFL	7	0	5	4	0.0	1	20	20.0	0
2001—New York Jets NFL	16	1	10	3	0.0	0	0	0.0	0
2002—New York Jets NFL	16	0	7	2	0.0	0	0	0.0	0
2003—Denver NFL	15	10	53	11	1.0	0	0	0.0	0
CFL Totals (4 years)	39	...	...	...	0.0	3	35	11.7	0
NFL totals (4 years)	54	11	75	20	1.0	1	20	20.0	0
Pro totals (8 years)	93	...	...	...	1.0	4	55	13.8	0

FERGUSON, ROBERT — WR — PACKERS

PERSONAL: Born December 17, 1979, in Houston, Texas. ... 6-1/209.
HIGH SCHOOL: Spring Woods (Houston).
JUNIOR COLLEGE: Tyler (Texas) Junor College.
COLLEGE: Texas A&M.
TRANSACTIONS/CAREER NOTES: Selected after junior season by Green Bay Packers in second round (41st pick overall) of 2001 NFL draft. ... Signed by Packers (July 23, 2001).
SINGLE GAME HIGHS (regular season): Receptions—7 (December 7, 2003, vs. Chicago); yards—105 (December 8, 2002, vs. Minnesota); and touchdown receptions—2 (December 14, 2003, vs. San Diego).
STATISTICAL PLATEAUS: 100-yard receiving games: 2002 (1). Total: 1.

			RECEIVING				KICKOFF RETURNS				TOTALS			
Year Team	**G**	**GS**	**No.**	**Yds.**	**Avg.**	**TD**	**No.**	**Yds.**	**Avg.**	**TD**	**TD**	**2pt.**	**Pts.**	**Fum.**
2001—Green Bay NFL	1	0	0	0	0.0	0	2	32	16.0	0	0	0	0	0
2002—Green Bay NFL	16	1	22	293	13.3	3	6	113	18.8	0	3	0	18	0
2003—Green Bay NFL	15	12	38	520	13.7	4	7	148	21.1	0	4	0	24	0
Pro totals (3 years)	32	13	60	813	13.6	7	15	293	19.5	0	7	0	42	0

FERRARA, FRANK — DE — GIANTS

PERSONAL: Born December 7, 1975, in Brooklyn, N.Y. ... 6-3/280.
HIGH SCHOOL: New Dorp (N.Y.).
COLLEGE: Rhode Island.
TRANSACTIONS/CAREER NOTES: Signed as non-drafted free agent by New York Giants (April 19, 2000). ... Released by Giants (August 27, 2000). ... Re-signed by Giants to practice squad (August 29, 2000). ... Released by Giants (November 20, 2000). ... Re-signed by Giants to practice squad (December 13, 2000). ... Assigned by Giants to Amsterdam Admirals in 2000 NFL Europe enhancement allocation program (February 17, 2000). ... Waived by Giants (August 31, 2003). ... Re-signed by Giants (September 16, 2003). ... Released by Giants (September 30, 2003). ... Re-signed by Giants (November 19, 2003).

			TOTALS		
Year Team	**G**	**GS**	**Tk.**	**Ast.**	**Sks.**
2001—New York Giants NFL	9	0	4	3	1.0
2002—New York Giants NFL	16	1	20	6	2.5
2003—New York Giants NFL	2	0	0	0	0.0
Pro totals (3 years)	27	1	24	9	3.5

FIEDLER, JAY — QB — DOLPHINS

PERSONAL: Born December 29, 1971, in Oceanside, N.Y. ... 6-2/225. ... Full name: Jay Brian Fiedler.
HIGH SCHOOL: Oceanside (N.Y.).
COLLEGE: Dartmouth.
TRANSACTIONS/CAREER NOTES: Signed as non-drafted free agent by Philadelphia Eagles (April 29, 1994). ... Inactive for all 16 games (1994). ... Claimed on waivers by Cincinnati Bengals (July 31, 1996). ... Released by Bengals (August 25, 1996). ... Played for Amsterdam Admirals of World League (1997). ... Signed by Minnesota Vikings (April 3, 1998). ... Released by Vikings (August 30, 1998). ... Re-signed by Vikings (September 15, 1998). ... Granted free agency (February 12, 1999). ... Signed by Jacksonville Jaguars (April 16, 1999). ... Granted

unconditional free agency (February 11, 2000). ... Signed by Miami Dolphins (February 17, 2000). ... On physically unable to perform list with hip injury (July 26-31, 2002).

CHAMPIONSHIP GAME EXPERIENCE: Member of Vikings for NFC championship game (1998 season); inactive. ... Member of Jaguars for AFC championship game (1999 season); did not play.

SINGLE GAME HIGHS (regular season): Attempts—45 (September 29, 2002, vs. Kansas City); completions—30 (December 24, 2000, vs.New England); yards—328 (December 28, 2003, vs. New York Jets); and touchdown passes—3 (November 27, 2003, vs. Dallas).

STATISTICAL PLATEAUS: 300-yard passing games: 1999 (1), 2001 (1), 2002 (1), 2003 (1). Total: 4.

MISCELLANEOUS: Regular-season record as starting NFL quarterback: 36-17 (.679). ... Postseason record as starting NFL quarterback: 1-2 (.333).

			PASSING										RUSHING				TOTALS		
Year Team	**G**	**GS**	**Att.**	**Cmp.**	**Pct.**	**Yds.**	**TD**	**Int.**	**Avg.**	**Skd.**	**Rat.**	**Att.**	**Yds.**	**Avg.**	**TD**	**TD**	**2pt.**	**Pts.**
1994—Philadelphia NFL								Did not play.										
1995—Philadelphia NFL								Did not play.										
1996—								Did not play.										
1998—Minnesota NFL	5	0	7	3	42.9	41	0	1	5.86	0	22.6	4	-6	-1.5	0	0	0	0
1999—Jacksonville NFL	8	1	94	61	64.9	656	2	2	6.98	7	83.5	13	26	2.0	0	0	0	0
2000—Miami NFL	15	15	357	204	57.1	2402	14	14	6.73	23	74.5	54	267	4.9	1	1	0	6
2001—Miami NFL	16	16	450	273	60.7	3290	20	19	7.31	27	80.3	73	321	4.4	4	4	0	24
2002—Miami NFL	11	10	292	179	61.3	2024	14	9	6.93	13	85.2	28	99	3.5	3	3	0	18
2003—Miami NFL	12	11	314	179	57.0	2138	11	13	6.81	19	72.4	34	88	2.6	3	3	0	18
Pro totals (6 years)	67	53	1514	899	59.4	10551	61	58	6.97	89	78.1	206	795	3.9	11	11	0	66

FIELDS, MARK — LB — PANTHERS

PERSONAL: Born November 9, 1972, in Los Angeles. ... 6-2/244. ... Full name: Mark Lee Fields.

HIGH SCHOOL: Washington (Cerritos, Calif.).

JUNIOR COLLEGE: Los Angeles Southwest Community College.

COLLEGE: Washington State.

TRANSACTIONS/CAREER NOTES: Selected by New Orleans Saints in first round (13th pick overall) of 1995 NFL draft. ... Signed by Saints (July 20, 1995). ... Released by Saints (March 30, 2001). ... Signed by St. Louis Rams (April 10, 2001). ... Released by Rams (March 7, 2002). ... Signed by Carolina Panthers (March 21, 2002). ... On reserve/non-football injury list (August 18, 2003-entire season).

CHAMPIONSHIP GAME EXPERIENCE: Played in NFC championship game (2001 season). ... Played in Super Bowl 36 (2001 season).

HONORS: Played in Pro Bowl (2000 season).

			TOTALS			INTERCEPTIONS			
Year Team	**G**	**GS**	**Tk.**	**Ast.**	**Sks.**	**No.**	**Yds.**	**Avg.**	**TD**
1995—New Orleans NFL	16	3	31	9	1.0	0	0	0.0	0
1996—New Orleans NFL	16	15	85	22	2.0	0	0	0.0	0
1997—New Orleans NFL	16	15	88	20	8.0	0	0	0.0	0
1998—New Orleans NFL	15	15	82	27	6.0	0	0	0.0	0
1999—New Orleans NFL	14	14	63	18	4.0	2	0	0.0	0
2000—New Orleans NFL	16	14	63	21	2.0	0	0	0.0	0
2001—St. Louis NFL	14	12	48	15	0.0	1	30	30.0	0
2002—Carolina NFL	15	15	76	27	7.5	1	37	37.0	0
2003—Carolina NFL					Did not play.				
Pro totals (8 years)	122	103	536	159	30.5	4	67	16.8	0

FINLEY, CLINT — S — CHIEFS

F

PERSONAL: Born March 27, 1977, in Andrews, Texas. ... 6-0/210. ... Full name: Clint Cade Finley.

HIGH SCHOOL: Cuero (Texas).

COLLEGE: Nebraska.

TRANSACTIONS/CAREER NOTES: Signed as non-drafted free agent by Kansas City Chiefs (February 20, 2002). ... Released by Chiefs (September 1, 2002). ... Re-signed by Chiefs to practice squad (September 3, 2002). ... Activated (December 26, 2002). ... Assigned by Chiefs to Berlin Thunder in 2003 NFL Europe enhancement allocation program (February 4, 2003). ... Released by Chiefs (August 31, 2003). ... Re-signed by Chiefs to practice squad (September 1, 2003). ... Released by Chiefs (September 10, 2003). ... Re-signed by Chiefs to practice squad (September 12, 2003).

			TOTALS			INTERCEPTIONS			
Year Team	**G**	**GS**	**Tk.**	**Ast.**	**Sks.**	**No.**	**Yds.**	**Avg.**	**TD**
2002—Kansas City NFL	1	0	0	1	0.0	0	0	0.0	0
2003—Kansas City NFL	3	0	0	0	0.0	0	0	0.0	0
Pro totals (2 years)	4	0	0	1	0.0	0	0	0.0	0

FINN, JIM — FB — GIANTS

PERSONAL: Born December 2, 1976, in Teaneck, N.J. ... 6-0/245.

HIGH SCHOOL: Bergen Catholic (Oradell, N.J.).

COLLEGE: Pennsylvania.

TRANSACTIONS/CAREER NOTES: Selected by Chicago Bears in seventh round (253rd pick overall) of 1999 NFL draft. ... Signed by Bears (June 3, 1999). ... Released by Bears (August 30, 1999). ... Re-signed by Bears to practice squad (September 21, 1999). ... Released by Bears (October 11, 1999). ... Signed by Indianapolis Colts (January 25, 2000). ... Granted free agency (February 28, 2003). ... Signed by New York Giants (March 11, 2003).

SINGLE GAME HIGHS (regular season): Attempts—3 (November 10, 2002, vs. Philadelphia); yards—8 (November 3, 2002, vs. Tennessee); and rushing touchdowns—0.

Year Team	G	GS	RUSHING Att.	Yds.	Avg.	TD	RECEIVING No.	Yds.	Avg.	TD	KICKOFF RETURNS No.	Yds.	Avg.	TD	TOTALS TD	2pt.	Pts.	Fum.
2000—Indianapolis NFL	16	1	1	1	1.0	0	4	13	3.3	1	0	0	0.0	0	1	0	6	1
2001—Indianapolis NFL	15	0	0	0	0.0	0	0	0	0.0	0	3	29	9.7	0	0	0	0	0
2002—Indianapolis NFL	12	2	5	8	1.6	0	6	31	5.2	0	0	0	0.0	0	0	0	0	2
2003—New York Giants NFL	15	9	0	0	0.0	0	14	115	8.2	0	1	19	19.0	0	0	0	0	0
Pro totals (4 years)	58	12	6	9	1.5	0	24	159	6.6	1	4	48	12.0	0	1	0	6	3

FINNERAN, BRIAN — WR — FALCONS

PERSONAL: Born January 31, 1976, in Mission Viejo, Calif. ... 6-5/210.
HIGH SCHOOL: Santa Margarita (Mission Viejo, Calif.).
COLLEGE: Villanova.
TRANSACTIONS/CAREER NOTES: Signed as non-drafted free agent by Seattle Seahawks (April 21, 1998). ... Released by Seahawks (August 24, 1998). ... Selected by Barcelona Dragons in 1999 NFL Europe draft (February 18, 1999). ... Signed by Philadelphia Eagles (July 6, 1999). ... Released by Eagles (October 12, 1999). ... Signed by Atlanta Falcons to practice squad (December 13, 1999). ... Granted free agency (February 28, 2003). ... Re-signed by Falcons (March 23, 2003).
HONORS: Won Walter Payton Award (1997).
SINGLE GAME HIGHS (regular season): Receptions—6 (November 10, 2002, vs. Pittsburgh); yards—114 (December 1, 2002, vs. Minnesota); and touchdown receptions—2 (September 22, 2002, vs. Cincinnati).
STATISTICAL PLATEAUS: 100-yard receiving games: 2002 (2). Total: 2.

Year Team	G	GS	RECEIVING No.	Yds.	Avg.	TD	TOTALS TD	2pt.	Pts.	Fum.
1999—Philadelphia NFL	3	0	2	21	10.5	0	0	0	0	0
2000—Atlanta NFL	11	0	7	60	8.6	0	0	0	0	0
2001—Atlanta NFL	16	1	23	491	21.3	3	3	0	18	0
2002—Atlanta NFL	16	16	56	838	15.0	6	6	0	36	2
2003—Atlanta NFL	12	10	26	368	14.2	2	2	0	12	0
Pro totals (5 years)	58	27	114	1778	15.6	11	11	0	66	2

FIORE, DAVE — G — REDSKINS

PERSONAL: Born August 10, 1974, in Hackensack, N.J. ... 6-4/293. ... Full name: David Allan Fiore. ... Name pronounced: fee-OR-ee.
HIGH SCHOOL: Waldwick (N.J.).
COLLEGE: Hofstra.
TRANSACTIONS/CAREER NOTES: Signed as non-drafted free agent by San Francisco 49ers (April 23, 1996). ... Claimed on waivers by New York Jets (October 14, 1996). ... Active for nine games (1996); did not play. ... Released by Jets (July 31, 1997). ... Signed by 49ers (August 1, 1997). ... On injured reserve with knee injury (August 19, 1997-entire season). ... On injured reserve with knee injury (September 25, 2002-remainder of season). ... Released by 49ers (February 26, 2003). ... Signed by Washington Redskins (March 1, 2003). ... On injured reserve with knee injury (November 4, 2003-remainder of season).
PLAYING EXPERIENCE: San Francisco NFL, 1998-2002; Washington NFL, 2003. ... Games/Games started: 1998 (9/3), 1999 (16/16), 2000 (15/15), 2001 (16/16), 2002 (3/3), 2003 (3/3). Total: 62/56.

FISHER, BRYCE — DE — RAMS

PERSONAL: Born May 12, 1977, in Renton, Wash. ... 6-3/272.
HIGH SCHOOL: Seattle Prep.
COLLEGE: Air Force.
TRANSACTIONS/CAREER NOTES: Selected by Buffalo Bills in seventh round (248th pick overall) of 1999 NFL draft. ... Signed by Bills (July 27, 1999). ... On military reserve list (August 30, 1999-entire season). ... On military reserve list (August 27, 2000-entire season). ... Claimed on waivers by St. Louis Rams (September 3, 2002). ... Granted free agency (March 3, 2004). ... Re-signed by Rams (April 22, 2004).

Year Team	G	GS	TOTALS Tk.	Ast.	Sks.
1999—Buffalo NFL	Did not play.				
2000—	Did not play.				
2001—Buffalo NFL	13	2	19	13	3.0
2002—St. Louis NFL	4	0	2	1	0.0
2003—St. Louis NFL	16	1	21	3	2.0
Pro totals (3 years)	33	3	42	17	5.0

FISHER, LEVAR — LB — CARDINALS

PERSONAL: Born July 2, 1979, in Beaufort, N.C. ... 6-1/239.
HIGH SCHOOL: East Carteret (Beaufort, N.C.).
COLLEGE: North Carolina State.
TRANSACTIONS/CAREER NOTES: Selected by Arizona Cardinals in second round (49th pick overall) of 2002 NFL draft. ... Signed by Cardinals (July 22, 2002). ... On injured reserve with knee injury (December 18, 2002-remainder of season).
HONORS: Named linebacker on THE SPORTING NEWS college All-America third team (2001). ... Named linebacker on THE SPORTING NEWS college All-America second team (2000).

Year Team	G	GS	TOTALS Tk.	Ast.	Sks.	INTERCEPTIONS No.	Yds.	Avg.	TD
2002—Arizona NFL	7	0	18	2	0.0	0	0	0.0	0
2003—Arizona NFL	16	15	50	8	1.0	0	0	0.0	0
Pro totals (2 years)	23	15	68	10	1.0	0	0	0.0	0

FISHER, TONY — RB — PACKERS

PERSONAL: Born October 12, 1979, in Euclid, Ohio. ... 6-1/222. ... Full name: Antoine Maurice Fisher.
HIGH SCHOOL: Euclid (Ohio).
COLLEGE: Notre Dame.
TRANSACTIONS/CAREER NOTES: Signed as non-drafted free agent by Green Bay Packers (April 25, 2002). ... Granted unconditional free agency by Packers (March 3, 2004). ... Re-signed by Packers (April 16, 2004).
SINGLE GAME HIGHS (regular season): Attempts—25 (December 8, 2002, vs. Minnesota); yards—96 (December 8, 2002, vs. Minnesota); and rushing touchdowns—1 (October 5, 2003, vs. Seattle).

			RUSHING				RECEIVING				KICKOFF RETURNS				TOTALS			
Year Team	G	GS	Att.	Yds.	Avg.	TD	No.	Yds.	Avg.	TD	No.	Yds.	Avg.	TD	TD	2pt.	Pts.	Fum.
2002—Green Bay NFL	15	1	70	283	4.0	2	18	70	3.9	0	2	42	21.0	0	2	0	12	2
2003—Green Bay NFL	15	0	40	200	5.0	1	21	206	9.8	2	0	0	0.0	0	3	0	18	0
Pro totals (2 years)	30	1	110	483	4.4	3	39	276	7.1	2	2	42	21.0	0	5	0	30	2

FISHER, TRAVIS — CB — RAMS

PERSONAL: Born September 12, 1979, in Tallahassee, Fla. ... 5-10/189.
HIGH SCHOOL: Godby (Tallahassee, Fla.).
JUNIOR COLLEGE: Coffeyville (Kan.) Community College.
COLLEGE: Central Florida.
TRANSACTIONS/CAREER NOTES: Selected by St. Louis Rams in second round (64th pick overall) of 2002 NFL draft. ... Signed by Rams (June 21, 2002).

			TOTALS			INTERCEPTIONS			
Year Team	G	GS	Tk.	Ast.	Sks.	No.	Yds.	Avg.	TD
2002—St. Louis NFL	14	11	54	7	0.0	2	0	0.0	0
2003—St. Louis NFL	15	15	51	5	0.0	4	†205	51.3	†2
Pro totals (2 years)	29	26	105	12	0.0	6	205	34.2	2

FISK, JASON — DT — CHARGERS

PERSONAL: Born September 4, 1972, in Davis, Calif. ... 6-3/295.
HIGH SCHOOL: Davis (Calif.).
COLLEGE: Stanford.
TRANSACTIONS/CAREER NOTES: Selected by Minnesota Vikings in seventh round (243rd pick overall) of 1995 NFL draft. ... Signed by Vikings (July 24, 1995). ... Granted unconditional free agency (February 12, 1999). ... Signed by Tennessee Titans (March 3, 1999). ... Granted unconditional free agency (March 1, 2002). ... Signed by San Diego Chargers (March 8, 2002).
CHAMPIONSHIP GAME EXPERIENCE: Played in NFC championship game (1998 season). ... Played in AFC championship game (1999 season). ... Played in Super Bowl 34 (1999 season).

			TOTALS			INTERCEPTIONS			
Year Team	G	GS	Tk.	Ast.	Sks.	No.	Yds.	Avg.	TD
1995—Minnesota NFL	8	0	0	0	0.0	0	0	0.0	0
1996—Minnesota NFL	16	6	22	9	1.0	1	0	0.0	0
1997—Minnesota NFL	16	10	20	8	3.0	1	1	1.0	0
1998—Minnesota NFL	16	0	12	5	1.5	0	0	0.0	0
1999—Tennessee NFL	16	16	35	13	4.0	1	17	17.0	0
2000—Tennessee NFL	15	15	30	10	2.0	0	0	0.0	0
2001—Tennessee NFL	16	16	26	16	2.5	0	0	0.0	0
2002—San Diego NFL	16	14	28	10	3.0	0	0	0.0	0
2003—San Diego NFL	16	16	41	10	1.0	0	0	0.0	0
Pro totals (9 years)	135	93	214	81	18.0	3	18	6.0	0

FITZSIMMONS, CASEY — TE — LIONS

PERSONAL: Born October 10, 1980, in Wolf Point, Mont. ... 6-3/250.
HIGH SCHOOL: Chester (Mont.).
COLLEGE: Carroll (Mont.).
TRANSACTIONS/CAREER NOTES: Signed as non-drafted free agent by Detroit Lions (May 2, 2003).
SINGLE GAME HIGHS (regular season): Receptions—5 (November 9, 2003, vs. Chicago); yards—36 (December 28, 2003, vs. St. Louis); and touchdown receptions—1 (December 28, 2003, vs. St. Louis).

			RECEIVING				TOTALS			
Year Team	G	GS	No.	Yds.	Avg.	TD	TD	2pt.	Pts.	Fum.
2003—Detroit NFL	16	11	23	160	7.0	2	2	0	12	0

FLANAGAN, MIKE — C — PACKERS

PERSONAL: Born November 10, 1973, in Washington, DC. ... 6-5/297. ... Full name: Michael Christopher Flanagan.
HIGH SCHOOL: Rio Americano (Sacramento).
COLLEGE: UCLA.

TRANSACTIONS/CAREER NOTES: Selected by Green Bay Packers in third round (90th pick overall) of 1996 NFL draft. ... Signed by Packers (July 17, 1996). ... On injured reserve with leg injury (August 19, 1996-entire season). ... On physically unable to perform list with ankle injury (August 19, 1997-entire season). ... Traded by Packers to Carolina Panthers for an undisclosed draft pick (August 31, 1998); trade later voided because Flanagan failed physical (September 1, 1998). ... Granted free agency (February 12, 1999). ... Re-signed by Packers (March 25, 1999).

PLAYING EXPERIENCE: Green Bay NFL, 1998-2003. ... Games/Games started: 1998 (2/0), 1999 (15/0), 2000 (16/2), 2001 (16/16), 2002 (16/13), 2003 (16/16). Total: 81/47.

HONORS: Played in Pro Bowl (2003 season).

FLANIGAN, JIM — DT

PERSONAL: Born August 27, 1971, in Green Bay, Wis. ... 6-2/290. ... Full name: James Michael Flanigan. ... Son of Jim Flanigan, linebacker with Green Bay Packers (1967-70) and New Orleans Saints (1971).

HIGH SCHOOL: Southern Door (Brussels, Wis.).

COLLEGE: Notre Dame.

TRANSACTIONS/CAREER NOTES: Selected by Chicago Bears in third round (74th pick overall) of 1994 NFL draft. ... Signed by Bears (July 14, 1994). ... Granted free agency (February 14, 1997). ... Re-signed by Bears (June 1, 1997). ... Granted unconditional free agency (February 13, 1998). ... Re-signed by Bears (February 13, 1998). ... Released by Bears (April 26, 2001). ... Signed by Green Bay Packers (May 29, 2001). ... Granted unconditional free agency (March 1, 2002). ... Signed by San Francisco 49ers (June 13, 2002). ... Released by 49ers (August 31, 2003). ... Signed by Philadelphia Eagles (October 28, 2003). ... Granted unconditional free agency (March 3, 2004).

CHAMPIONSHIP GAME EXPERIENCE: Member of Eagles for NFC championship game (2003 season); inactive.

			TOTALS			INTERCEPTIONS			
Year Team	**G**	**GS**	**Tk.**	**Ast.**	**Sks.**	**No.**	**Yds.**	**Avg.**	**TD**
1994—Chicago NFL	14	0	10	1	0.0	0	0	0.0	0
1995—Chicago NFL	16	12	39	10	11.0	0	0	0.0	0
1996—Chicago NFL	14	14	36	5	5.0	0	0	0.0	0
1997—Chicago NFL	16	16	38	12	6.0	0	0	0.0	0
1998—Chicago NFL	16	16	32	14	8.5	0	0	0.0	0
1999—Chicago NFL	16	16	35	8	6.0	1	6	6.0	0
2000—Chicago NFL	16	14	33	13	4.0	0	0	0.0	0
2001—Green Bay NFL	16	8	26	14	4.5	0	0	0.0	0
2002—San Francisco NFL	15	1	7	5	1.0	0	0	0.0	0
2003—Philadelphia NFL	6	0	4	0	0.0	0	0	0.0	0
Pro totals (10 years)	145	97	260	82	46.0	1	6	6.0	0

FLEMISTER, ZERON — TE

PERSONAL: Born September 8, 1976, in Chicago, Ill. ... 6-4/250.

HIGH SCHOOL: West (Iowa).

COLLEGE: Iowa.

TRANSACTIONS/CAREER NOTES: Signed as non-drafted free agent by Washington Redskins (April 18, 2000). ... Claimed on waivers by Cleveland Browns (October 7, 2003). ... Released by Browns (October 11, 2003). ... Signed by Washington Redskins (October 14, 2003). ... Granted unconditional free agency (March 3, 2004).

SINGLE GAME HIGHS (regular season): Receptions—3 (September 22, 2002, vs. San Francisco); yards—57 (September 22, 2002, vs. San Francisco); and touchdown receptions—1 (November 28, 2002, vs. Dallas).

			RECEIVING				TOTALS			
Year Team	**G**	**GS**	**No.**	**Yds.**	**Avg.**	**TD**	**TD**	**2pt.**	**Pts.**	**Fum.**
2000—Washington NFL	5	0	1	8	8.0	0	0	0	0	0
2001—Washington NFL	16	1	18	196	10.9	2	2	0	12	0
2002—Washington NFL	15	7	10	146	14.6	2	2	0	12	1
2003—Washington NFL	12	9	9	89	9.9	0	0	0	0	1
Pro totals (4 years)	48	17	38	439	11.6	4	4	0	24	2

FLETCHER, JAMAR — CB — CHARGERS

PERSONAL: Born August 28, 1979, in St. Louis, Mo. ... 5-9/186. ... Full name: Jamar Mondell Fletcher.

HIGH SCHOOL: Hazelwood East (St. Louis).

COLLEGE: Wisconsin.

TRANSACTIONS/CAREER NOTES: Selected after junior season by Miami Dolphins in first round (26th pick overall) of 2001 NFL draft. ... Signed by Dolphins (July 25, 2001). ... On injured reserve with forearm injury (December 1, 2003-remainder of season). ... Traded by Dolphins to San Diego Chargers to complete March 15 trade that sent WR David Boston from San Diego to Miami (March 16, 2004).

HONORS: Named cornerback on THE SPORTING NEWS college All-America first team (1999). ... Named cornerback on THE SPORTING NEWS college All-America second team (2000). ... Jim Thorpe Award winner (2000).

			TOTALS			INTERCEPTIONS			
Year Team	**G**	**GS**	**Tk.**	**Ast.**	**Sks.**	**No.**	**Yds.**	**Avg.**	**TD**
2001—Miami NFL	14	2	8	2	0.0	0	0	0.0	0
2002—Miami NFL	16	4	35	2	0.0	2	30	15.0	0
2003—Miami NFL	11	0	5	3	0.0	0	0	0.0	0
Pro totals (3 years)	41	6	48	7	0.0	2	30	15.0	0

FLETCHER, LONDON — LB — BILLS

PERSONAL: Born May 19, 1975, in Cleveland, Ohio. ... 5-10/245. ... Full name: London Levi Fletcher.

HIGH SCHOOL: Villa Angela-St. Joseph (Cleveland).

COLLEGE: John Carroll.

TRANSACTIONS/CAREER NOTES: Signed as non-drafted free agent by St. Louis Rams (April 28, 1998). ... Granted free agency (March 2, 2001). ... Re-signed by Rams (May 9, 2001). ... Granted unconditional free agency (March 1, 2002). ... Signed by Buffalo Bills (March 7, 2002).

CHAMPIONSHIP GAME EXPERIENCE: Played in NFC championship game (1999 and 2001 seasons). ... Member of Super Bowl championship team (1999 season). ... Played in Super Bowl 36 (2001 season).

Year Team	G	GS	TOTALS Tk.	Ast.	Sks.	INTERCEPTIONS No.	Yds.	Avg.	TD
1998—St. Louis NFL	16	1	11	1	0.0	0	0	0.0	0
1999—St. Louis NFL	16	16	66	24	3.0	0	0	0.0	0
2000—St. Louis NFL	16	15	106	27	5.5	4	33	8.3	0
2001—St. Louis NFL	16	16	90	29	4.5	2	18	9.0	0
2002—Buffalo NFL	16	16	98	51	3.0	0	0	0.0	0
2003—Buffalo NFL	16	16	98	35	2.0	0	0	0.0	0
Pro totals (6 years)	96	80	469	167	18.0	6	51	8.5	0

FLORENCE, DRAYTON — CB — CHARGERS

PERSONAL: Born December 19, 1980, in Waycross, Ga. ... 6-0/195. ... Full name: Drayton Florence Jr..
HIGH SCHOOL: Richland Northeast (Columbia, S.C.), then Vanguard (Ocala, Fla.).
COLLEGE: Tuskegee.
TRANSACTIONS/CAREER NOTES: Selected by San Diego Chargers in second round (46th pick overall) of 2003 NFL draft. ... Signed by Chargers (July 23, 2003).

Year Team	G	GS	TOTALS Tk.	Ast.	Sks.	INTERCEPTIONS No.	Yds.	Avg.	TD	KICKOFF RETURNS No.	Yds.	Avg.	TD	TOTALS TD	2pt.	Pts.	Fum.
2003—San Diego NFL	16	0	16	0	0.0	0	0	0.0	0	4	47	11.8	0	0	0	0	0

FLOWERS, ERIK — LB — RAMS

PERSONAL: Born March 1, 1978, in San Antonio, Texas. ... 6-4/273. ... Full name: Erik Mathews Flowers.
HIGH SCHOOL: Theodore Roosevelt (San Antonio, Texas).
JUNIOR COLLEGE: Trinity Valley Community College (Texas).
COLLEGE: Arizona State.
TRANSACTIONS/CAREER NOTES: Selected by Buffalo Bills in first round (26th pick overall) of 2000 NFL draft. ... Signed by Bills (July 23, 2000). ... Claimed on waivers by Houston Texans (August 21, 2002). ... Claimed on waivers by Pittsburgh Steelers (September 3, 2003). ... Released by Steelers (September 16, 2003). ... Signed by St. Louis Rams (December 3, 2003).

Year Team	G	GS	TOTALS Tk.	Ast.	Sks.	INTERCEPTIONS No.	Yds.	Avg.	TD
2000—Buffalo NFL	16	0	11	9	2.0	1	0	0.0	0
2001—Buffalo NFL	15	5	15	6	2.0	0	0	0.0	0
2002—Houston NFL	14	0	0	1	0.0	0	0	0.0	0
2003—St. Louis NFL	4	0	0	0	0.0	0	0	0.0	0
Pro totals (4 years)	49	5	26	16	4.0	1	0	0.0	0

FLOYD, ANTHONY — CB — COLTS

PERSONAL: Born February 1, 1981, in Youngstown, Ohio. ... 5-10/202.
COLLEGE: Louisville.
TRANSACTIONS/CAREER NOTES: Signed as non-drafted free agent by Indianapolis Colts (May 2, 2003). ... Waived by Colts (September 26, 2003). ... Re-signed by Colts (November 11, 2003).
CHAMPIONSHIP GAME EXPERIENCE: Played in AFC championship game (2003 season).

Year Team	G	GS	TOTALS Tk.	Ast.	Sks.	INTERCEPTIONS No.	Yds.	Avg.	TD
2003—Indianapolis NFL	6	0	10	3	0.0	0	0	0.0	0

F

FLUTIE, DOUG — QB — CHARGERS

PERSONAL: Born October 23, 1962, in Manchester, Md. ... 5-10/180. ... Full name: Douglas Richard Flutie. ... Brother of Darren Flutie, wide receiver with San Diego Chargers (1998), B.C. Lions of CFL (1991-95), Edmonton Eskimos of CFL (1996 and 1997) and Hamilton Tiger-Cats of CFL (1998).
HIGH SCHOOL: Natick (Mass.).
COLLEGE: Boston College.
TRANSACTIONS/CAREER NOTES: Selected by New Jersey Generals in 1985 USFL territorial draft. ... Signed by Generals (February 4, 1985). ... Granted roster exemption (February 4-14, 1985). ... Activated (February 15, 1985). ... On developmental squad for three games with Generals (1985). ... Selected by Los Angeles Rams in 11th round (285th pick overall) of 1985 NFL draft. ... On developmental squad (June 10, 1995-remainder of season). ... Rights traded by Rams with fourth-round pick in 1987 draft to Chicago Bears for third- and sixth-round picks in 1987 draft (October 14, 1986). ... Signed by Bears (October 21, 1986). ... Granted roster exemption (October 21-November 3, 1986). ... Activated (November 4, 1986). ... Crossed picket line during players strike (October 13, 1987). ... Traded by Bears to New England Patriots for eighth-round pick in 1988 draft (October 13, 1987). ... Released by Patriots after 1989 season. ... Signed by B.C. Lions of CFL (June 1990). ... Granted free agency (February 1992). ... Signed by Calgary Stampeders of CFL (March 1992). ... Rights assigned to Toronto Argonauts of CFL (March 15, 1996). ... Signed by Buffalo Bills (January 16, 1998). ... Released by Bills (March 1, 2001). ... Signed by San Diego Chargers (March 9, 2001).
CHAMPIONSHIP GAME EXPERIENCE: Member of CFL championship team (1992, 1996 and 1997). ... Named Most Valuable Player of Grey Cup, CFL championship game (1992, 1996 and 1997). ... Played in Grey Cup (1993 and 1995).
HONORS: Heisman Trophy winner (1984). ... Named College Football Player of the Year by THE SPORTING NEWS (1984). ... Named quarterback on THE SPORTING NEWS college All-America first team (1984). ... Most Outstanding Player of CFL (1991-1994, 1996 and 1997). ... Played in Pro Bowl (1998 season).

SINGLE GAME HIGHS (regular season): Attempts—53 (December 30, 2001, vs. Seattle); completions—34 (December 30, 2001, vs. Seattle); yards—377 (December 30, 2001, vs. Seattle); and touchdown passes—4 (October 30, 1988, vs. Chicago).

STATISTICAL PLATEAUS: 300-yard passing games: 1998 (2), 1999 (1), 2000 (1), 2001 (4). Total: 8.

MISCELLANEOUS: Regular-season record as starting NFL quarterback: 37-28 (.569). ... Postseason record as starting NFL quarterback: 0-2 (.000).

			PASSING									RUSHING				TOTALS		
Year Team	G	GS	Att.	Cmp.	Pct.	Yds.	TD	Int.	Avg.	Skd.	Rat.	Att.	Yds.	Avg.	TD	TD	2pt.	Pts.
1985—New Jersey USFL	15	...	281	134	47.7	2109	13	14	7.51	...	67.8	65	465	7.2	6	6	0	36
1986—Chicago NFL	4	1	46	23	50.0	361	3	2	7.85	6	80.1	9	36	4.0	1	1	0	6
1987—Chicago NFL	1	0	0	0	0.0	0	0	0	0.00	0	.0	0	0	0.0	0	0	0	0
—New England NFL	1	1	25	15	60.0	199	1	0	7.96	1	98.6	6	43	7.2	0	0	0	0
1988—New England NFL	11	9	179	92	51.4	1150	8	10	6.42	11	63.3	38	179	4.7	1	1	0	6
1989—New England NFL	5	3	91	36	39.6	493	2	4	5.42	6	46.6	16	87	5.4	0	0	0	0
1990—British Columbia CFL	16	...	392	207	52.8	2960	16	19	7.55	...	71.0	79	662	8.4	3	3	0	18
1991—British Columbia CFL	18	...	730	466	63.8	6619	38	24	9.07	...	96.7	120	610	5.1	14	14	1	86
1992—Calgary CFL	18	...	688	396	57.6	5945	32	30	8.64	...	83.4	96	669	7.0	11	11	0	66
1993—Calgary CFL	18	...	703	416	59.2	6092	44	17	8.67	...	98.3	74	373	5.0	11	11	0	66
1994—Calgary CFL	18	...	659	403	61.2	5726	48	19	8.69	...	101.5	96	760	7.9	8	8	0	48
1995—Calgary CFL	12	...	332	223	67.2	2788	16	5	8.40	...	102.8	46	288	6.3	5	5	0	30
1996—Toronto CFL	18	...	677	434	64.1	5720	29	17	8.45	...	94.5	101	756	7.5	9	9	0	54
1997—Toronto CFL	18	18	673	430	63.9	5505	47	24	8.18	...	97.8	92	542	5.9	9	9	0	54
1998—Buffalo NFL	13	10	354	202	57.1	2711	20	11	7.66	12	87.4	48	248	5.2	1	1	0	6
1999—Buffalo NFL	15	15	478	264	55.2	3171	19	16	6.63	26	75.1	88	476	5.4	1	1	0	6
2000—Buffalo NFL	11	5	231	132	57.1	1700	8	3	7.36	10	86.5	36	161	4.5	1	1	0	6
2001—San Diego NFL	16	16	521	294	56.4	3464	15	18	6.65	25	72.0	53	192	3.6	1	1	0	6
2002—San Diego NFL	1	0	11	3	27.3	64	0	0	5.82	0	51.3	1	6	6.0	0	0	0	0
2003—San Diego NFL	7	5	167	91	54.5	1097	9	4	6.57	8	82.8	33	168	5.1	2	2	0	12
USFL Totals (1 years)	15	...	281	134	47.7	2109	13	14	7.51	...	67.8	65	465	7.2	6	6	0	36
CFL Totals (8 years)	136	...	4854	2975	61.3	41355	270	155	8.52	...	93.9	704	4660	6.6	70	70	1	422
NFL totals (10 years)	85	65	2103	1152	54.8	14410	85	68	6.85	105	76.3	328	1596	4.9	8	8	0	48
Pro totals (19 years)	236	...	7238	4261	58.9	57874	368	237	8.00	...	87.8	1097	6721	6.1	84	84	1	506

FLYNN, MIKE — C — RAVENS

PERSONAL: Born June 15, 1974, in Doylestown, Pa. ... 6-3/305. ... Full name: Michael Patrick Flynn.

HIGH SCHOOL: Cathedral (Springfield, Mass.).

COLLEGE: Maine.

TRANSACTIONS/CAREER NOTES: Signed as non-drafted free agent by Baltimore Ravens (April 25, 1997). ... Released by Ravens (August 24, 1997). ... Signed by Tampa Bay Buccaneers to practice squad (August 27, 1997). ... Released by Buccaneers (September 2, 1997). ... Signed by Jacksonville Jaguars to practice squad (November 4, 1997). ... Signed by Ravens off Jaguars practice squad (December 3, 1997). ... Granted free agency (March 2, 2001). ... Re-signed by Ravens (March 13, 2001).

PLAYING EXPERIENCE: Baltimore NFL, 1998-2003. ... Games/Games started: 1998 (2/0), 1999 (12/0), 2000 (16/16), 2001 (16/16), 2002 (15/15), 2003 (16/16). Total: 77/63.

CHAMPIONSHIP GAME EXPERIENCE: Played in AFC championship game (2000 season). ... Member of Super Bowl championship team (2000 season).

FOLAU, SPENCER — T — SAINTS

PERSONAL: Born April 5, 1973, in Nuku'alofa, Tonga. ... 6-5/315. ... Full name: Spencer Sione Folau. ... Name pronounced: fah-LOWE.

HIGH SCHOOL: Sequoia (Redwood City, Calif.).

COLLEGE: Idaho.

TRANSACTIONS/CAREER NOTES: Signed as non-drafted free agent by Baltimore Ravens (April 26, 1996). ... Released by Ravens (August 25, 1996). ... Re-signed by Ravens to practice squad (October 29, 1996). ... Assigned by Ravens to Rhein Fire in 1997 World League enhancement allocation program (February 1997). ... Released by Ravens (October 28, 1998). ... Re-signed by Ravens (November 3, 1998). ... Granted free agency (February 11, 2000). ... Tendered offer sheet by New England Patriots (April 10, 2000). ... Offer matched by Ravens (April 12, 2000). ... Released by Ravens (March 1, 2001). ... Signed by Miami Dolphins (July 28, 2001). ... Granted unconditional free agency (March 1, 2002). ... Signed by New Orleans Saints (April 1, 2002). ... On injured reserve with knee injury (December 19, 2003-remainder of season). ... Granted unconditional free agency (March 3, 2004). ... Re-signed by Saints (March 17, 2004).

PLAYING EXPERIENCE: Baltimore NFL, 1997-2000; Miami NFL, 2001; New Orleans NFL, 2002-2003. ... Games/Games started: 1997 (10/0), 1998 (3/3), 1999 (7/1), 2000 (11/4), 2001 (16/15), 2002 (16/16), 2003 (14/1). Total: 77/40.

CHAMPIONSHIP GAME EXPERIENCE: Played in AFC championship game (2000 season). ... Member of Super Bowl championship team (2000 season).

FOLEY, STEVE — LB — CHARGERS

PERSONAL: Born September 11, 1975, in Little Rock, Ark. ... 6-3/260.

HIGH SCHOOL: Hall (Little Rock, Ark.).

COLLEGE: Louisiana-Monroe.

TRANSACTIONS/CAREER NOTES: Selected by Cincinnati Bengals in third round (75th pick overall) of 1998 NFL draft. ... Signed by Bengals (July 19, 1998). ... On injured reserve with shoulder injury (September 1, 2002-entire season). ... Released by Bengals (August 31, 2003). ... Signed by Houston Texans (September 2, 2003). ... Granted unconditional free agency (March 3, 2004). ... Signed by San Diego Chargers (March 4, 2004).

			TOTALS			INTERCEPTIONS			
Year Team	G	GS	Tk.	Ast.	Sks.	No.	Yds.	Avg.	TD
1998—Cincinnati NFL	10	1	11	1	2.0	0	0	0.0	0
1999—Cincinnati NFL	16	16	34	3	3.5	0	0	0.0	0

Year Team	G	GS	TOTALS Tk.	Ast.	Sks.	INTERCEPTIONS No.	Yds.	Avg.	TD
2000—Cincinnati NFL	16	16	34	9	4.0	1	1	1.0	0
2001—Cincinnati NFL	12	12	25	14	0.0	0	0	0.0	0
2002—Cincinnati NFL				Did not play.					
2003—Houston NFL	13	3	21	5	1.0	0	0	0.0	0
Pro totals (5 years)	67	48	125	32	10.5	1	1	1.0	0

FONOTI, TONIU G CHARGERS

PERSONAL: Born November 26, 1981, in American Samoa. ... 6-4/349. ... Full name: Toniuolevaiavea Satele Fonoti.

HIGH SCHOOL: Kahuku (Hauula, Hawaii).

COLLEGE: Nebraska.

TRANSACTIONS/CAREER NOTES: Selected after junior season by San Diego Chargers in second round (39th pick overall) of 2002 NFL draft. ... Signed by Chargers (July 30, 2002). ... On injured reserve with foot injury (August 31, 2003-entire season).

PLAYING EXPERIENCE: San Diego NFL, 2002-2003. ... Games/Games started: 2002 (15/14), Total: 15/14.

FONTENOT, JERRY C SAINTS

PERSONAL: Born November 21, 1966, in Lafayette, La. ... 6-3/300. ... Full name: Jerry Paul Fontenot.

HIGH SCHOOL: Lafayette (La.).

COLLEGE: Texas A&M.

TRANSACTIONS/CAREER NOTES: Selected by Chicago Bears in third round (65th pick overall) of 1989 NFL draft. ... Signed by Bears (July 27, 1989). ... Granted free agency (March 1, 1993). ... Re-signed by Bears (June 16, 1993). ... Granted free agency (February 16, 1996). ... Re-signed by Bears (July 10, 1996). ... Granted unconditional free agency (February 14, 1997). ... Signed by New Orleans Saints (May 28, 1997). ... On injured reserve with knee injury (October 14, 1998-remainder of season). ... Granted unconditional free agency (February 12, 1999). ... Re-signed by Saints (February 15, 1999). ... Granted unconditional free agency (February 28, 2003). ... Re-signed by Saints (June 18, 2003). ... Granted unconditional free agency (March 3, 2004). ... Re-signed by Saints (May 13, 2004).

PLAYING EXPERIENCE: Chicago NFL, 1989-1996; New Orleans NFL, 1997-2003. ... Games/Games started: 1989 (16/0), 1990 (16/2), 1991 (16/7), 1992 (16/16), 1993 (16/16), 1994 (16/16), 1995 (16/16), 1996 (16/16), 1997 (16/16), 1998 (4/4), 1999 (16/16), 2000 (16/16), 2001 (16/16), 2002 (16/16), 2003 (16/16). Total: 228/189.

FOOTE, LARRY LB STEELERS

PERSONAL: Born June 12, 1980, in Detroit, Mich. ... 6-0/234. ... Full name: Lawrence Edward Foote Jr..

HIGH SCHOOL: Pershing (Detroit).

COLLEGE: Michigan.

TRANSACTIONS/CAREER NOTES: Selected by Pittsburgh Steelers in fourth round (128th pick overall) of 2002 NFL draft. ... Signed by Steelers (July 18, 2002).

HONORS: Named linebacker on THE SPORTING NEWS college All-America second team (2001).

Year Team	G	GS	TOTALS Tk.	Ast.	Sks.	INTERCEPTIONS No.	Yds.	Avg.	TD
2002—Pittsburgh NFL	14	3	11	7	0.0	0	0	0.0	0
2003—Pittsburgh NFL	16	0	0	0	0.0	0	0	0.0	0
Pro totals (2 years)	30	3	11	7	0.0	0	0	0.0	0

F

FORD, HENRY DT

PERSONAL: Born October 30, 1971, in Fort Worth, Texas. ... 6-3/295.

HIGH SCHOOL: Trimble Technical (Fort Worth, Texas).

COLLEGE: Arkansas.

TRANSACTIONS/CAREER NOTES: Selected by Houston Oilers in first round (26th pick overall) of 1994 NFL draft. ... Signed by Oilers (June 16, 1994). ... Oilers franchise moved to Tennessee for 1997 season. ... Granted unconditional free agency (February 13, 1998). ... Re-signed by Oilers (March 2, 1998). ... Oilers franchise renamed Tennessee Titans for 1999 season (December 26, 1998). ... Released by Titans (February 27, 2003). ... Signed by New Orleans Saints (July 28, 2003). ... Released by Saints (October 4, 2003). ... Re-signed by Saints (October 7, 2003). ... Released by Saints (December 3, 2003).

CHAMPIONSHIP GAME EXPERIENCE: Played in AFC championship game (1999 and 2002 seasons). ... Played in Super Bowl XXXIV (1999 season).

Year Team	G	GS	TOTALS Tk.	Ast.	Sks.
1994—Houston NFL	11	0	10	1	0.0
1995—Houston NFL	16	16	27	16	4.5
1996—Houston NFL	15	14	24	15	1.0
1997—Tennessee NFL	16	16	38	12	5.0
1998—Tennessee NFL	13	5	14	8	1.5
1999—Tennessee NFL	12	9	14	13	5.5
2000—Tennessee NFL	14	3	20	12	2.0
2001—Tennessee NFL	16	0	16	11	1.0
2002—Tennessee NFL	16	13	15	7	3.5
2003—New Orleans NFL	4	0	2	0	0.0
Pro totals (10 years)	133	76	180	95	24.0

FORDHAM, TODD — T — STEELERS

PERSONAL: Born October 9, 1973, in Atlanta, Ga. ... 6-5/320. ... Full name: Lindsey Todd Fordham.
HIGH SCHOOL: Tift County (Tifton, Ga.).
COLLEGE: Florida State.
TRANSACTIONS/CAREER NOTES: Signed as non-drafted free agent by Jacksonville Jaguars (April 21, 1997). ... Released by Jaguars (August 24, 1997). ... Re-signed by Jaguars to practice squad (August 25, 1997). ... Activated (September 23, 1997). ... On injured reserve with knee injury (August 31, 1999-entire season). ... Granted free agency (February 11, 2000). ... Re-signed by Jaguars (February 24, 2000). ... Granted unconditional free agency (March 2, 2001). ... Signed by Denver Broncos (April 13, 2001). ... Released by Broncos (September 2, 2001). ... Signed by Jaguars (October 2, 2001). ... Granted unconditional free agency (March 1, 2002). ... Re-signed by Jaguars (April 16, 2002). ... Granted unconditional free agency (February 28, 2003). ... Signed by Pittsburgh Steelers (March 18, 2003).
PLAYING EXPERIENCE: Jacksonville NFL, 1997-2002; Pittsburgh NFL, 2003. ... Games/Games started: 1997 (1/0), 1998 (11/1), 2000 (16/8), 2001 (12/12), 2002 (16/9), 2003 (11/6), Total: 67/36.

FOREMAN, JAY — LB — TEXANS

PERSONAL: Born February 18, 1976, in Eden Prairie, Minn. ... 6-1/240. ... Full name: Jamal A. Foreman. ... Son of Chuck Foreman, running back with Minnesota Vikings (1973-79) and New England Patriots (1980).
HIGH SCHOOL: Eden Prairie (Minn.).
COLLEGE: Nebraska.
TRANSACTIONS/CAREER NOTES: Selected by Buffalo Bills in fifth round (156th pick overall) of 1999 NFL draft. ... Signed by Bills (July 27, 1999). ... Granted free agency (March 1, 2002). ... Re-signed by Bills (April 17, 2002). ... Traded by Bills to Houston Texans for KR/PR Charlie Rogers (April 17, 2002). ... Granted unconditional free agency (February 28, 2003). ... Re-signed by Texans (March 4, 2003).

			TOTALS			INTERCEPTIONS			
Year Team	**G**	**GS**	**Tk.**	**Ast.**	**Sks.**	**No.**	**Yds.**	**Avg.**	**TD**
1999—Buffalo NFL	7	0	0	0	0.0	0	0	0.0	0
2000—Buffalo NFL	15	3	32	18	0.0	0	0	0.0	0
2001—Buffalo NFL	16	16	69	28	2.5	0	0	0.0	0
2002—Houston NFL	16	16	101	36	0.0	0	0	0.0	0
2003—Houston NFL	16	16	101	35	2.0	0	0	0.0	0
Pro totals (5 years)	70	51	303	117	4.5	0	0	0.0	0

FORNEY, KYNAN — G — FALCONS

PERSONAL: Born September 8, 1978, in Nacogdoches, Texas. ... 6-3/307.
HIGH SCHOOL: Nacogdoches (Texas).
JUNIOR COLLEGE: Trinity Valley Community College (Texas).
COLLEGE: Hawaii.
TRANSACTIONS/CAREER NOTES: Selected by Atlanta Falcons in seventh round (219th pick overall) of 2001 NFL draft. ... Signed by Falcons (May 21, 2001). ... Granted free agency (March 3, 2004). ... Re-signed by Falcons (April 6, 2004).
PLAYING EXPERIENCE: Atlanta NFL, 2001-2003. ... Games/Games started: 2001 (12/8), 2002 (14/12), 2003 (16/16). Total: 42/36.

FORSEY, BROCK — RB — BEARS

PERSONAL: Born February 11, 1980, in Meridian, Idaho. ... 5-11/203.
HIGH SCHOOL: Centennial (Meridian, Idaho).
COLLEGE: Boise State.
TRANSACTIONS/CAREER NOTES: Selected by Chicago Bears in sixth round (206th pick overall) of 2003 NFL draft. ... Signed by Bears (June 19, 2003).
SINGLE GAME HIGHS (regular season): Attempts—27 (November 30, 2003, vs. Arizona); yards—134 (November 30, 2003, vs. Arizona); and rushing touchdowns—1 (November 30, 2003, vs. Arizona).
STATISTICAL PLATEAUS: 100-yard rushing games: 2003 (1). Total: 1.

			RUSHING				RECEIVING				KICKOFF RETURNS				TOTALS			
Year Team	**G**	**GS**	**Att.**	**Yds.**	**Avg.**	**TD**	**No.**	**Yds.**	**Avg.**	**TD**	**No.**	**Yds.**	**Avg.**	**TD**	**TD**	**2pt.**	**Pts.**	**Fum.**
2003—Chicago NFL	9	2	50	191	3.8	2	3	37	12.3	0	0	0	0.0	0	2	0	12	0

FOSTER, DESHAUN — RB — PANTHERS

PERSONAL: Born January 10, 1980, in Charlotte, N.C. ... 6-0/222. ... Full name: DeShaun Xavier Foster.
HIGH SCHOOL: Tustin (Calif.).
COLLEGE: UCLA.
TRANSACTIONS/CAREER NOTES: Selected by Carolina Panthers in second round (34th pick overall) of 2002 NFL draft. ... Signed by Panthers (July 30, 2002). ... On injured reserve with knee injury (October 25, 2002-remainder of season).
CHAMPIONSHIP GAME EXPERIENCE: Played in NFC championship game (2003 season). ... Played in Super Bowl 38 (2003 season).
HONORS: Named running back on THE SPORTING NEWS college All-America second team (2001).
SINGLE GAME HIGHS (regular season): Attempts—22 (November 9, 2003, vs. Tampa Bay); yards—85 (October 12, 2003, vs. Indianapolis); and rushing touchdowns—0.

			RUSHING				RECEIVING				KICKOFF RETURNS				TOTALS			
Year Team	**G**	**GS**	**Att.**	**Yds.**	**Avg.**	**TD**	**No.**	**Yds.**	**Avg.**	**TD**	**No.**	**Yds.**	**Avg.**	**TD**	**TD**	**2pt.**	**Pts.**	**Fum.**
2002—Carolina NFL								Did not play.										
2003—Carolina NFL	14	2	113	429	3.8	0	26	207	8.0	2	0	0	0.0	0	2	0	12	3
Pro totals (1 years)	14	2	113	429	3.8	0	26	207	8.0	2	0	0	0.0	0	2	0	12	3

F

FOSTER, GEORGE — T — BRONCOS

PERSONAL: Born June 9, 1980, in Macon, Ga. ... 6-5/338.
HIGH SCHOOL: Southeast (Macon, Ga.).
COLLEGE: Georgia.
TRANSACTIONS/CAREER NOTES: Selected by Denver Broncos in first round (20th pick overall) of 2003 NFL draft. ... Signed by Broncos (July 24, 2003).
PLAYING EXPERIENCE: Denver NFL, 2003. ... Games/Games started: 2003 (1/0). Total: 1/0.

FOSTER, LARRY — WR

PERSONAL: Born November 7, 1976, in Harvey, La. ... 5-10/195.
HIGH SCHOOL: West Jefferson (La.).
COLLEGE: Louisiana State.
TRANSACTIONS/CAREER NOTES: Signed as non-drafted free agent by Detroit Lions (April 28, 2000). ... Released by Lions (August 27, 2000). ... Re-signed by Lions to practice squad (August 29, 2000). ... Activated (October 16, 2000). ... Granted free agency (February 28, 2003). ... Re-signed by Lions (April 27, 2003). ... Traded by Lions to Arizona Cardinals for seventh-round pick (DB Blue Adams) in 2003 draft (April 27, 2003). ... Reached injury settlement and released by Cardinals (October 3, 2003). ... Signed by Carolina Panthers (January 13, 2004). ... Assigned by Panthers to WLD in 2004 NFL Europe enhancement allocation program (February 9, 2004). ... Released by Panthers (March 9, 2004).
SINGLE GAME HIGHS (regular season): Receptions—8 (November 30, 2000, vs. Minnesota); yards—106 (November 30, 2000, vs. Minnesota); and touchdown receptions—1 (November 30, 2000, vs. Minnesota).
STATISTICAL PLATEAUS: 100-yard receiving games: 2000 (1). Total: 1.

			RUSHING				RECEIVING				PUNT RETURNS				KICKOFF RETURNS				TOTALS		
Year Team	G	GS	Att.	Yds.	Avg.	TD	No.	Yds.	Avg.	TD	No.	Yds.	Avg.	TD	No.	Yds.	Avg.	TD	TD	2pt.	Pts.
2000—Det. NFL	10	0	2	31	15.5	0	17	175	10.3	1	0	0	0.0	0	0	0	0.0	0	1	0	6
2001—Det. NFL	13	5	2	6	3.0	0	22	283	12.9	0	3	17	5.7	0	9	182	20.2	0	0	0	0
2002—Det. NFL	13	0	0	0	0.0	0	14	152	10.9	0	4	29	7.3	0	12	286	23.8	0	0	0	0
2003—Ari. NFL	1	1	0	0	0.0	0	1	7	7.0	0	0	0	0.0	0	0	0	0.0	0	0	0	0
Pro totals (4 years)	37	6	4	37	9.3	0	54	617	11.4	1	7	46	6.6	0	21	468	22.3	0	1	0	6

FOWLER, MELVIN — G/C — BROWNS

PERSONAL: Born March 31, 1979, in Brooklyn, N.Y. ... 6-3/310. ... Full name: Melvin Thaddeus Fowler Jr..
HIGH SCHOOL: Half Hollow Hills (Long Island, N.Y.).
COLLEGE: Maryland.
TRANSACTIONS/CAREER NOTES: Selected by Cleveland Browns in third round (76th pick overall) of 2002 NFL draft. ... Signed by Browns (July 22, 2002).
PLAYING EXPERIENCE: Cleveland NFL, 2002-2003. ... Games/Games started: 2002 (1/1), 2003 (14/10). Total: 15/11.

FOX, VERNON — S — CHARGERS

PERSONAL: Born October 9, 1979, in Las Vegas, Nev. ... 5-9/200. ... Full name: Vernon Lee Fox III.
HIGH SCHOOL: Caimarron-Memorial (Las Vegas).
COLLEGE: Fresno State.
TRANSACTIONS/CAREER NOTES: Signed as non-drafted free agent by San Diego Chargers (April 26, 2002).

			TOTALS			INTERCEPTIONS			
Year Team	G	GS	Tk.	Ast.	Sks.	No.	Yds.	Avg.	TD
2002—San Diego NFL	16	3	17	6	0.0	1	25	25.0	0
2003—San Diego NFL	12	2	18	4	0.0	0	0	0.0	0
Pro totals (2 years)	28	5	35	10	0.0	1	25	25.0	0

FRALEY, HANK — C/G — EAGLES

PERSONAL: Born September 21, 1977, in Gaithersburg, Md. ... 6-2/300.
HIGH SCHOOL: Gaithersburg (Md.).
COLLEGE: Robert Morris.
TRANSACTIONS/CAREER NOTES: Signed as non-drafted free agent by Pittsburgh Steelers (April 21, 2000). ... Claimed on waivers by Philadelphia Eagles (August 28, 2000). ... Inactive for all 16 games (2000).
PLAYING EXPERIENCE: Philadelphia NFL, 2001-2003. ... Games/Games started: 2001 (16/15), 2002 (16/16), 2003 (16/16). Total: 48/47.
CHAMPIONSHIP GAME EXPERIENCE: Played in NFC championship game (2001-2003 seasons).

FRANKLIN, AUBRAYO — DT — RAVENS

PERSONAL: Born August 27, 1980, in Johnson City, Tenn. ... 6-1/320. ... Full name: Aubrayo Razyo Franklin.
HIGH SCHOOL: Science Hill (Johnson City, Tenn.).
JUNIOR COLLEGE: Itawamba Community College (Miss.).
COLLEGE: Tennessee.
TRANSACTIONS/CAREER NOTES: Selected by Baltimore Ravens in fifth round (146th pick overall) of 2003 NFL draft.

Year Team	G	GS	TOTALS Tk.	Ast.	Sks.
2003—Baltimore NFL	1	0	1	0	0.0

FRANKLIN, BRAD — CB — SEAHAWKS

PERSONAL: Born December 22, 1979, in Baton Rouge, La. ... 6-1/184.
HIGH SCHOOL: Broadmoor (La.).
COLLEGE: Louisiana-Lafayette.
TRANSACTIONS/CAREER NOTES: Selected by Carolina Panthers in seventh round (258th pick overall) of 2002 NFL draft.. ... Signed by Panthers (July 9, 2002). ... Released by Panthers (October 10, 2002). ... Re-signed by Panthers to practice squad (October 12, 2002). ... Activated (December 12, 2002). ... Claimed on waivers by Jacksonville Jaguars (August 26, 2003). ... Waived by Jaguars (October 7, 2003). ... Signed by Tennessee Titans to practice squad (November 5, 2003). ... Released by Titans (November 11, 2003). ... Signed by Seattle Seahawks (January 28, 2004). ... Assigned by Seahawks to Scottish Claymores in 2004 NFL Europe enhancement allocation program (February 9, 2004).

			TOTALS			INTERCEPTIONS			
Year Team	G	GS	Tk.	Ast.	Sks.	No.	Yds.	Avg.	TD
2003—Jacksonville NFL	4	0	2	0	0.0	0	0	0.0	0

FRANKS, BUBBA — TE — PACKERS

PERSONAL: Born January 6, 1978, in Riverside, Calif. ... 6-6/263. ... Full name: Daniel Lamont Franks.
HIGH SCHOOL: Big Springs (Texas).
COLLEGE: Miami (Fla.).
TRANSACTIONS/CAREER NOTES: Selected after junior season by Green Bay Packers in first round (14th pick overall) of 2000 NFL draft. ... Signed by Packers (July 19, 2000).
HONORS: Named tight end on THE SPORTING NEWS college All-America first team (1999). ... Played in Pro Bowl (2001-2003 seasons).
SINGLE GAME HIGHS (regular season): Receptions—9 (September 22, 2002, vs. Detroit); yards—62 (September 22, 2002, vs. Detroit); and touchdown receptions—2 (December 23, 2001, vs. Cleveland).

			RECEIVING				TOTALS			
Year Team	G	GS	No.	Yds.	Avg.	TD	TD	2pt.	Pts.	Fum.
2000—Green Bay NFL	16	13	34	363	10.7	1	1	0	6	1
2001—Green Bay NFL	16	14	36	322	8.9	9	9	0	54	0
2002—Green Bay NFL	16	15	54	442	8.2	7	7	0	42	0
2003—Green Bay NFL	16	15	30	241	8.0	4	4	∞2	28	0
Pro totals (4 years)	64	57	154	1368	8.9	21	21	2	130	1

FRANZ, TODD — S — REDSKINS

PERSONAL: Born April 12, 1976, in Enid, Okla. ... 6-0/202. ... Full name: Stephen Todd Franz.
HIGH SCHOOL: Weatherford (Okla.).
COLLEGE: Tulsa.
TRANSACTIONS/CAREER NOTES: Selected by Detroit Lions in fifth round (145th pick overall) of 2000 NFL draft. ... Signed by Lions (July 15, 2000). ... Claimed on waivers by New Orleans Saints (August 28, 2000). ... Released by Saints (October 10, 2000). ... Signed by Cleveland Browns (November 14, 2000). ... Released by Browns (August 4, 2001). ... Signed by New York Jets (January 15, 2002). ... Claimed on waivers by Green Bay Packers (July 22, 2002). ... Released by Packers (September 1, 2002). ... Re-signed by Packers to practice squad (September 4, 2002). ... Released by Packers (September 9, 2002). ... Re-signed by Packers to practice squad (October 9, 2002). ... Activated (October 12, 2002). ... Released by Packers (October 23, 2002). ... Re-signed by Packers to practice squad (October 24, 2002). ... Released by Packers (November 13, 2002). ... Signed by Washington Redskins to practice squad (November 19, 2002). ... Activated (December 17, 2002).

			TOTALS			INTERCEPTIONS			
Year Team	G	GS	Tk.	Ast.	Sks.	No.	Yds.	Avg.	TD
2000—New Orleans NFL	5	0	0	0	0.0	0	0	0.0	0
—Cleveland NFL	2	0	2	0	0.0	0	0	0.0	0
2002—Green Bay NFL	2	0	2	1	0.0	0	0	0.0	0
2003—Washington NFL	16	1	21	5	0.0	0	0	0.0	0
Pro totals (3 years)	25	1	25	6	0.0	0	0	0.0	0

F

FREEMAN, ANTONIO — WR

PERSONAL: Born May 27, 1972, in Baltimore, Md. ... 6-1/198. ... Full name: Antonio Michael Freeman.
HIGH SCHOOL: Polytechnic (Baltimore).
COLLEGE: Virginia Tech.
TRANSACTIONS/CAREER NOTES: Selected by Green Bay Packers in third round (90th pick overall) of 1995 NFL draft. ... Signed by Packers (June 22, 1995). ... Granted free agency (February 13, 1998). ... Re-signed by Packers (June 16, 1998). ... Designated by Packers as franchise player (February 12, 1999). ... Released by Packers (June 3, 2002). ... Signed by Philadelphia Eagles (August 24, 2002). ... Granted unconditional free agency (February 28, 2003). ... Signed by Green Bay Packers (September 10, 2003). ... Granted unconditional free agency (March 3, 2004).
CHAMPIONSHIP GAME EXPERIENCE: Played in NFC championship game (1995-1997 and 2002 seasons). ... Member of Super Bowl championship team (1996 season). ... Played in Super Bowl 32 (1997 season).
HONORS: Named wide receiver on THE SPORTING NEWS NFL All-Pro team (1998). ... Played in Pro Bowl (1998 season).
POST SEASON RECORDS: Shares NFL postseason record for most touchdowns by punt return—1(December 31, 1995, vs. Atlanta).
SINGLE GAME HIGHS (regular season): Receptions—10 (December 14, 1997, vs. Carolina); yards—193 (November 1, 1998, vs. San Francisco); and touchdown receptions—3 (December 20, 1998, vs. Tennessee).
STATISTICAL PLATEAUS: 100-yard receiving games: 1996 (4), 1997 (3), 1998 (6), 1999 (3), 2000 (2), 2001 (2), 2002 (1). Total: 21.

Year Team	G	GS	RECEIVING No.	Yds.	Avg.	TD	PUNT RETURNS No.	Yds.	Avg.	TD	KICKOFF RETURNS No.	Yds.	Avg.	TD	TOTALS TD	2pt.	Pts.	Fum.
1995—Green Bay NFL	11	0	8	106	13.3	1	37	292	7.9	0	24	556	23.2	0	1	0	6	7
1996—Green Bay NFL	12	12	56	933	16.7	9	0	0	0.0	0	1	16	16.0	0	9	0	54	3
1997—Green Bay NFL	16	16	81	1243	15.3	12	0	0	0.0	0	0	0	0.0	0	12	0	72	1
1998—Green Bay NFL	15	15	84	*1424	17.0	14	0	0	0.0	0	0	0	0.0	0	14	1	86	0
1999—Green Bay NFL	16	16	74	1074	14.5	6	0	0	0.0	0	0	0	0.0	0	6	0	36	1
2000—Green Bay NFL	15	15	62	912	14.7	9	0	0	0.0	0	0	0	0.0	0	9	0	54	1
2001—Green Bay NFL	16	16	52	818	15.7	6	17	114	6.7	0	2	28	14.0	0	6	1	38	1
2002—Philadelphia NFL	16	1	46	600	13.0	4	0	0	0.0	0	0	0	0.0	0	4	0	24	0
2003—Green Bay NFL	15	0	14	141	10.1	0	0	0	0.0	0	0	0	0.0	0	0	0	0	0
Pro totals (9 years)	132	91	477	7251	15.2	61	54	406	7.5	0	27	600	22.2	0	61	2	370	14

FREEMAN, ARTURO — S — DOLPHINS

PERSONAL: Born October 27, 1976, in Orangeburg, S.C. ... 6-0/198. ... Full name: Arturo C. Freeman.
HIGH SCHOOL: Orangeburg-Wilkinson (Orangeburg, S.C.).
COLLEGE: South Carolina.
TRANSACTIONS/CAREER NOTES: Selected by Miami Dolphins in fifth round (152nd pick overall) of 2000 NFL draft. ... Signed by Dolphins (July 11, 2000). ... Granted free agency (February 28, 2003). ... Re-signed by Dolphins (March 2, 2003).

Year Team	G	GS	TOTALS Tk.	Ast.	Sks.	INTERCEPTIONS No.	Yds.	Avg.	TD
2000—Miami NFL	8	0	0	0	0.0	0	0	0.0	0
2001—Miami NFL	16	4	25	7	1.0	1	0	0.0	0
2002—Miami NFL	16	16	56	16	1.5	0	0	0.0	0
2003—Miami NFL	16	0	17	5	1.0	0	0	0.0	0
Pro totals (4 years)	56	20	98	28	3.5	1	0	0.0	0

FREEMAN, EDDIE — DE — CHIEFS

PERSONAL: Born January 4, 1978, in Mobile, Ala. ... 6-5/307.
HIGH SCHOOL: B.C. Rain (Mobile, Ala.).
COLLEGE: Alabama-Birmingham.
TRANSACTIONS/CAREER NOTES: Selected by Kansas City Chiefs in second round (43rd pick overall) of 2002 NFL draft. ... Signed by Chiefs (June 4, 2002).

Year Team	G	GS	TOTALS Tk.	Ast.	Sks.
2002—Kansas City NFL	15	0	13	4	4.0
2003—Kansas City NFL	5	0	2	0	0.0
Pro totals (2 years)	20	0	15	4	4.0

FREENEY, DWIGHT — DE — COLTS

PERSONAL: Born January 4, 1978, in Hartford, Conn. ... 6-1/268. ... Full name: Dwight Jason Freeney.
HIGH SCHOOL: Bloomfield (Conn.).
COLLEGE: Syracuse.
TRANSACTIONS/CAREER NOTES: Selected by Indianapolis Colts in first round (11th pick overall) of 2002 NFL draft. ... Signed by Colts (July 28, 2002).
CHAMPIONSHIP GAME EXPERIENCE: Played in AFC championship game (2003) season.
HONORS: Named defensive end on THE SPORTING NEWS college All-America first team (2001). ... Played in Pro Bowl (2003 season).

Year Team	G	GS	TOTALS Tk.	Ast.	Sks.
2002—Indianapolis NFL	16	8	45	1	13.0
2003—Indianapolis NFL	15	13	28	4	11.0
Pro totals (2 years)	31	21	73	5	24.0

FREITAS, MAKOA — T/G — COLTS

PERSONAL: Born November 23, 1979, in Honolulu, Hawaii. ... 6-4/307. ... Full name: Rockne Makoa Freitas. ... Son of Rocky Freitas, offensive tackle with Detroit Lions (1968-77) and Tampa Bay Buccaneers (1978).
HIGH SCHOOL: Kamehameha (Honolulu, Hawaii).
COLLEGE: Arizona.
TRANSACTIONS/CAREER NOTES: Selected by Indianapolis Colts in sixth round (208th pick overall) of 2003 NFL draft. ... Signed by Colts (July 25, 2003). ... Released by Colts (August 31, 2003). ... Re-signed by Colts (September 26, 2003).
PLAYING EXPERIENCE: Indianapolis NFL, 2003. ... Games/Games started: 2003 (12/6). Total: 12/6.
CHAMPIONSHIP GAME EXPERIENCE: Member of Colts for AFC championship game (2003 season); did not play.

FREROTTE, GUS — QB — VIKINGS

PERSONAL: Born July 31, 1971, in Kittanning, Pa. ... 6-3/237. ... Full name: Gustave Joseph Frerotte.
HIGH SCHOOL: Ford City (Pa.) Junior-Senior.
COLLEGE: Tulsa.

TRANSACTIONS/CAREER NOTES: Selected by Washington Redskins in seventh round (197th pick overall) of 1994 NFL draft. ... Signed by Redskins (July 19, 1994). ... Granted free agency (February 14, 1997). ... Re-signed by Redskins (July 18, 1997). ... On injured reserve with hip injury (December 2, 1997-remainder of season). ... Released by Redskins (February 11, 1999). ... Signed by Detroit Lions (March 3, 1999). ... Granted unconditional free agency (February 11, 2000). ... Signed by Denver Broncos (March 7, 2000). ... Granted unconditional free agency (March 2, 2001). ... Re-signed by Broncos (March 13, 2001). ... On injured reserve with shoulder injury (December 19, 2001-remainder of season). ... Granted unconditional free agency (March 1, 2002). ... Signed by Cincinnati Bengals (May 1, 2002). ... Granted unconditional free agency (February 28, 2003). ... Signed by Minnesota Vikings (March 19, 2003).

HONORS: Played in Pro Bowl (1996 season).

SINGLE GAME HIGHS (regular season): Attempts—58 (November 19, 2000, vs. San Diego); completions—36 (November 19, 2000, vs. San Diego); yards—462 (November 19, 2000, vs. San Diego); and touchdown passes—5 (November 19, 2000, vs. San Diego).

STATISTICAL PLATEAUS: 300-yard passing games: 1995 (1), 1996 (1), 1999 (2), 2000 (1). Total: 5.

MISCELLANEOUS: Regular-season record as starting NFL quarterback: 27-36-1 (.430). ... Postseason record as starting NFL quarterback: 0-2 (.000).

			PASSING									RUSHING				TOTALS		
Year Team	**G**	**GS**	**Att.**	**Cmp.**	**Pct.**	**Yds.**	**TD**	**Int.**	**Avg.**	**Skd.**	**Rat.**	**Att.**	**Yds.**	**Avg.**	**TD**	**TD**	**2pt.**	**Pts.**
1994—Washington NFL	4	4	100	46	46.0	600	5	5	6.00	3	61.3	4	1	0.3	0	0	0	0
1995—Washington NFL	16	11	396	199	50.3	2751	13	13	6.95	23	70.2	22	16	0.7	1	1	0	6
1996—Washington NFL	16	16	470	270	57.4	3453	12	11	7.35	22	79.3	28	16	0.6	0	0	0	0
1997—Washington NFL	13	13	402	204	50.7	2682	17	12	6.67	23	73.8	24	65	2.7	2	2	0	12
1998—Washington NFL	3	2	54	25	46.3	283	1	3	5.24	12	45.5	3	20	6.7	0	0	0	0
1999—Detroit NFL	9	6	288	175	60.8	2117	9	7	7.35	28	83.6	15	33	2.2	0	0	0	0
2000—Denver NFL	10	6	232	138	59.5	1776	9	8	7.66	12	82.1	22	64	2.9	1	1	0	6
2001—Denver NFL	4	1	48	30	62.5	308	3	0	6.42	3	101.7	10	9	0.9	1	1	0	6
2002—Cincinnati NFL	4	3	85	44	51.8	437	1	5	5.14	10	46.1	4	22	5.5	0	0	0	0
2003—Minnesota NFL	16	2	65	38	58.5	690	7	2	10.62	5	118.1	12	-2	-0.2	0	0	0	0
Pro totals (10 years)	95	64	2140	1169	54.6	15097	77	66	7.05	141	76.1	144	244	1.7	5	5	0	30

FRIEDMAN, LENNIE — G — REDSKINS

PERSONAL: Born October 13, 1976, in Livingston, N.J. ... 6-3/283. ... Full name: Leonard Lebrecht Friedman.

HIGH SCHOOL: West Milford (N.J.).

COLLEGE: Duke.

TRANSACTIONS/CAREER NOTES: Selected by Denver Broncos in second round (61st pick overall) of 1999 NFL draft. ... Signed by Broncos (June 14, 1999). ... On injured reserve with knee injury (August 31, 1999-entire season). ... Assigned by Broncos to Barcelona Dragons in 2000 NFL Europe enhancement allocation program (February 18, 2000). ... Released by Broncos (February 25, 2003). ... Signed by Washington Redskins (March 3, 2003).

PLAYING EXPERIENCE: Denver NFL, 1999-2002; Washington NFL, 2003. ... Games/Games started: 2000 (15/8), 2001 (15/14), 2002 (2/0), 2003 (16/8), Total: 48/30.

FROST, SCOTT — S — BUCCANEERS

PERSONAL: Born January 4, 1975, in Wood River, Neb. ... 6-3/218.

HIGH SCHOOL: Wood River (Neb.).

COLLEGE: Nebraska.

TRANSACTIONS/CAREER NOTES: Selected by New York Jets in third round (67th pick overall) of 1998 NFL draft. ... Signed by Jets (July 21, 1998). ... Granted free agency (March 2, 2001). ... Re-signed by Jets (April 12, 2001). ... On non-football injury list with ankle injury (July 28-August 18, 2001). ... Claimed on waivers by Cleveland Browns (August 29, 2001). ... Released by Browns (December 11, 2001). ... Signed by Green Bay Packers (December 19, 2001). ... On injured reserve with shoulder injury (August 14, 2002-entire season). ... Waived by Packers (December 18, 2002). ... Signed by San Francisco 49ers (June 16, 2003). ... Waived by 49ers (August 26, 2003). ... Signed by Tampa Bay Buccaneers (December 2, 2003).

CHAMPIONSHIP GAME EXPERIENCE: Played in AFC championship game (1998 season).

			TOTALS			INTERCEPTIONS			
Year Team	**G**	**GS**	**Tk.**	**Ast.**	**Sks.**	**No.**	**Yds.**	**Avg.**	**TD**
1998—New York Jets NFL	13	0	2	4	0.0	0	0	0.0	0
1999—New York Jets NFL	14	0	0	0	0.0	0	0	0.0	0
2000—New York Jets NFL	16	1	19	10	1.0	1	1	1.0	0
2001—Cleveland NFL	12	0	1	0	0.0	0	0	0.0	0
2003—Tampa Bay NFL	4	0	0	0	0.0	0	0	0.0	0
Pro totals (5 years)	59	1	22	14	1.0	1	1	1.0	0

FUAMATU-MA'AFALA, CHRIS — RB — JAGUARS

PERSONAL: Born March 4, 1977, in Honolulu, Hawaii. ... 5-11/254. ... Name pronounced: fu-ah-MAH-tu ma-ah-FAH-la.

HIGH SCHOOL: St. Louis (Honolulu).

COLLEGE: Utah.

TRANSACTIONS/CAREER NOTES: Selected after junior season by Pittsburgh Steelers in sixth round (178th pick overall) of 1998 NFL draft. ... Signed by Steelers (July 10, 1998). ... On injured reserve with broken foot (Decemeber 20, 2000-remainder of season). ... Granted free agency (March 2, 2001). ... Tendered offer sheet by New England Patriots (April 14, 2001). ... Offer matched by Steelers (April 19, 2001). ... Released by Steelers (August 31, 2003). ... Signed by Jacksonville Jaguars (September 3, 2003).

CHAMPIONSHIP GAME EXPERIENCE: Played in AFC championship game (2001 season).

SINGLE GAME HIGHS (regular season): Attempts—26 (December 23, 2001, vs. Detroit); yards—126 (December 23, 2001, vs. Detroit); and rushing touchdowns—1 (November 23, 2003, vs. New York Jets).

STATISTICAL PLATEAUS: 100-yard rushing games: 2001 (1). Total: 1.

			RUSHING				RECEIVING				TOTALS			
Year Team	**G**	**GS**	**Att.**	**Yds.**	**Avg.**	**TD**	**No.**	**Yds.**	**Avg.**	**TD**	**TD**	**2pt.**	**Pts.**	**Fum.**
1998—Pittsburgh NFL	12	0	7	30	4.3	2	9	84	9.3	1	3	0	18	0

Year Team	G	GS	RUSHING Att.	Yds.	Avg.	TD	RECEIVING No.	Yds.	Avg.	TD	TOTALS TD	2pt.	Pts.	Fum.
1999—Pittsburgh NFL	9	0	1	4	4.0	0	0	0	0.0	0	0	0	0	0
2000—Pittsburgh NFL	7	1	21	149	7.1	1	11	107	9.7	0	1	0	6	0
2001—Pittsburgh NFL	16	5	120	453	3.8	3	16	127	7.9	1	4	0	24	0
2002—Pittsburgh NFL	8	0	23	115	5.0	0	2	12	6.0	0	0	0	0	0
2003—Jacksonville NFL	13	0	35	144	4.1	1	1	2	2.0	0	1	0	6	0
Pro totals (6 years)	65	6	207	895	4.3	7	39	332	8.5	2	9	0	54	0

FUJITA, SCOTT — LB — CHIEFS

PERSONAL: Born April 28, 1979, in Ventura, Calif. ... 6-5/247.
HIGH SCHOOL: Rio Mesa (Calif.).
COLLEGE: California.
TRANSACTIONS/CAREER NOTES: Selected by Kansas City Chiefs in fifth round (143rd pick overall) of 2002 NFL draft. ... Signed by Chiefs (June 21, 2002).

Year Team	G	GS	TOTALS Tk.	Ast.	Sks.	INTERCEPTIONS No.	Yds.	Avg.	TD
2002—Kansas City NFL	16	9	50	5	1.0	0	0	0.0	0
2003—Kansas City NFL	16	16	98	16	4.0	1	8	8.0	0
Pro totals (2 years)	32	25	148	21	5.0	1	8	8.0	0

FULLER, COREY — CB — RAVENS

PERSONAL: Born May 1, 1971, in Tallahassee, Fla. ... 5-10/220.
HIGH SCHOOL: James S. Rickards (Tallahassee, Fla.).
COLLEGE: Florida State.
TRANSACTIONS/CAREER NOTES: Selected by Minnesota Vikings in second round (55th pick overall) of 1995 NFL draft. ... Signed by Vikings (July 24, 1995). ... Granted unconditional free agency (February 12, 1999). ... Signed by Cleveland Browns (February 18, 1999). ... Released by Browns (February 26, 2003). ... Signed by Baltimore Ravens (March 4, 2003).
CHAMPIONSHIP GAME EXPERIENCE: Played in NFC championship game (1998 season).

Year Team	G	GS	TOTALS Tk.	Ast.	Sks.	INTERCEPTIONS No.	Yds.	Avg.	TD
1995—Minnesota NFL	16	10	57	9	0.5	1	0	0.0	0
1996—Minnesota NFL	16	14	53	11	0.0	3	3	1.0	0
1997—Minnesota NFL	16	16	82	9	0.0	2	24	12.0	0
1998—Minnesota NFL	16	16	70	9	1.0	4	36	9.0	0
1999—Cleveland NFL	16	16	64	13	0.0	0	0	0.0	0
2000—Cleveland NFL	15	15	37	5	0.0	3	0	0.0	0
2001—Cleveland NFL	16	16	72	15	0.0	3	82	27.3	1
2002—Cleveland NFL	13	12	27	5	0.0	1	0	0.0	0
2003—Baltimore NFL	14	10	30	4	0.0	0	0	0.0	0
Pro totals (9 years)	138	125	492	80	1.5	17	145	8.5	1

FULLER, CURTIS — S — PACKERS

PERSONAL: Born July 25, 1978, in Fort Worth, Texas. ... 5-11/191.
HIGH SCHOOL: Christian (Fort Worth, Texas).
JUNIOR COLLEGE: Trinity Valley Community College (Texas).
COLLEGE: Texas Christian.
TRANSACTIONS/CAREER NOTES: Selected by Seattle Seahawks in fourth round (127th pick overall) of 2001 NFL draft. ... Signed by Seahawks (June 8, 2001). ... Claimed on waivers by Green Bay Packers (September 1, 2003).

Year Team	G	GS	TOTALS Tk.	Ast.	Sks.	INTERCEPTIONS No.	Yds.	Avg.	TD
2001—Seattle NFL	10	1	12	2	0.0	0	0	0.0	0
2002—Seattle NFL	16	1	22	11	0.0	1	3	3.0	0
2003—Green Bay NFL	9	0	2	3	0.0	0	0	0.0	0
Pro totals (3 years)	35	2	36	16	0.0	1	3	3.0	0

FURREY, MIKE — WR — RAMS

PERSONAL: Born May 12, 1977, in Grove City, Ohio. ... 6-0/185. ... Full name: Michael Thomas Furrey.
HIGH SCHOOL: Hillard (Ohio).
COLLEGE: Northern Iowa.
TRANSACTIONS/CAREER NOTES: Signed as non-drafted free agent by Indianapolis Colts (April 20, 2000). ... Released by Colts (August 27, 2000). ... Signed by New York Jets (July 27, 2002). ... Waived by Jets (October 3, 2002). ... Signed by St. Louis Rams (April 29, 2003).
SINGLE GAME HIGHS (regular season): Receptions—4 (December 14, 2003, vs. Seattle); yards—45 (December 14, 2003, vs. Seattle); and touchdown receptions—0.

Year Team	G	GS	RUSHING Att.	Yds.	Avg.	TD	RECEIVING No.	Yds.	Avg.	TD	PUNT RETURNS No.	Yds.	Avg.	TD	KICKOFF RETURNS No.	Yds.	Avg.	TD	TOTALS TD	2pt.	Pts.
2003—StL. NFL	13	0	3	5	1.7	0	20	189	9.5	0	11	119	10.8	0	7	140	20.0	0	0	0	0

GABRIEL, DOUG — WR — RAIDERS

PERSONAL: Born August 27, 1980, in Miami, Fla. ... 6-2/215. ... Full name: Douglas Gabriel.
HIGH SCHOOL: Dr. Phillips (Orlando).
JUNIOR COLLEGE: Mississippi Gulf Coast Junior College.
COLLEGE: Central Florida.
TRANSACTIONS/CAREER NOTES: Selected by Oakland Raiders in fifth round (167th pick overall) of 2003 NFL draft. ... Signed by Raiders (July 24, 2003).
SINGLE GAME HIGHS (regular season): Receptions—1 (September 22, 2003, vs. Denver); yards—17 (September 22, 2003, vs. Denver); and touchdown receptions—0.

			RUSHING				RECEIVING				KICKOFF RETURNS				TOTALS			
Year Team	G	GS	Att.	Yds.	Avg.	TD	No.	Yds.	Avg.	TD	No.	Yds.	Avg.	TD	TD	2pt.	Pts.	Fum.
2003—Oakland NFL	12	0	0	0	0.0	0	1	17	17.0	0	29	646	22.3	1	1	0	6	0

GADSDEN, ORONDE — WR

PERSONAL: Born August 20, 1971, in Charleston, S.C. ... 6-2/215. ... Full name: Oronde Benjamin Gadsden. ... Name pronounced: o-RON-day.
HIGH SCHOOL: Burke (Charleston, S.C.).
COLLEGE: Winston-Salem.
TRANSACTIONS/CAREER NOTES: Signed as non-drafted free agent by Dallas Cowboys (August 1995). ... Released by Cowboys (August 22, 1995). ... Re-signed by Cowboys to practice squad (August 30, 1995). ... Activated (January 8, 1996). ... On injured reserve with left ankle sprain (January 11, 1996-remainder of playoffs). ... Released by Cowboys (August 27, 1996). ... Signed by Pittsburgh Steelers (February 4, 1997). ... Released by Steelers (August 19, 1997). ... Signed by Cowboys (August 21, 1997). ... Released by Cowboys (August 24, 1997). ... Played with Portland Forest Dragons of Arena League (1998). ... Signed by Miami Dolphins (August 3, 1998). ... On injured reserve with wrist injury (October 21, 2002-remainder of season). ... Granted unconditional free agency (February 28, 2003). ... Re-signed by Dolphins (June 20, 2003). ... On injured reserve with ankle injury (August 31, 2003). ... Received injury settlement and released by Dolphins (September 5, 2003). ... Re-signed by Dolphins (November 19, 2003). ... Granted unconditional free agency (March 3, 2004).
SINGLE GAME HIGHS (regular season): Receptions—9 (January 2, 2000, vs. Washington); yards—153 (December 27, 1998, vs. Atlanta); and touchdown receptions—2 (October 1, 2000, vs. Cincinnati).
STATISTICAL PLATEAUS: 100-yard receiving games: 1998 (1), 1999 (3), 2000 (1), 2001 (2). Total: 7.

			RECEIVING				TOTALS			
Year Team	G	GS	No.	Yds.	Avg.	TD	TD	2pt.	Pts.	Fum.
1995—Dallas NFL				Did not play.						
1996—				Did not play.						
1997—				Did not play.						
1998—Miami NFL	16	12	48	713	14.9	7	7	0	42	2
1999—Miami NFL	16	7	48	803	16.7	6	6	0	36	0
2000—Miami NFL	16	16	56	786	14.0	6	6	0	36	0
2001—Miami NFL	14	14	55	674	12.3	3	3	0	18	1
2002—Miami NFL	6	6	16	228	14.3	0	0	0	0	0
2003—Miami NFL	6	0	4	48	12.0	0	0	0	0	0
Pro totals (6 years)	74	55	227	3252	14.3	22	22	0	132	3

GAFFNEY, JABAR — WR — TEXANS

PERSONAL: Born December 1, 1980, in San Antonio, Texas. ... 6-1/193. ... Full name: Derrick Jabar Gaffney.
HIGH SCHOOL: Raines (Jacksonville, Fla.).
COLLEGE: Florida.
TRANSACTIONS/CAREER NOTES: Selected after sophomore season by Houston Texans in second round (33rd pick overall) of 2002 NFL draft. ... Signed by Texans (July 19, 2002).
HONORS: Named College Football Freshman of the Year by THE SPORTING NEWS (2000). ... Named wide receiver on THE SPORTING NEWS college All-America first team (2001).
SINGLE GAME HIGHS (regular season): Receptions—6 (December 29, 2002, vs. Tennessee); yards—73 (December 29, 2002, vs. Tennessee); and touchdown receptions—1 (November 9, 2003, vs. Cincinnati).

			RECEIVING				PUNT RETURNS				TOTALS			
Year Team	G	GS	No.	Yds.	Avg.	TD	No.	Yds.	Avg.	TD	TD	2pt.	Pts.	Fum.
2002—Houston NFL	16	14	41	483	11.8	1	3	-3	-1.0	0	1	1	8	1
2003—Houston NFL	16	11	34	402	11.8	2	4	22	5.5	0	2	0	12	0
Pro totals (2 years)	32	25	75	885	11.8	3	7	19	2.7	0	3	1	20	1

GAGE, JUSTIN — WR — BEARS

PERSONAL: Born January 25, 1981, in Jefferson City, Mo. ... 6-4/208.
HIGH SCHOOL: Jefferson City (Mo.).
COLLEGE: Missouri.
TRANSACTIONS/CAREER NOTES: Selected by Chicago Bears in fifth round (143rd pick overall) of 2003 NFL draft. ... Signed by Bears (July 18, 2003).
SINGLE GAME HIGHS (regular season): Receptions—4 (December 21, 2003, vs. Washington); yards—100 (November 30, 2003, vs. Arizona); and touchdown receptions—1 (December 21, 2003, vs. Washington).
STATISTICAL PLATEAUS: 100-yard receiving games: 2003 (1). Total: 1.

			RECEIVING				TOTALS			
Year Team	G	GS	No.	Yds.	Avg.	TD	TD	2pt.	Pts.	Fum.
2003—Chicago NFL	10	3	17	338	19.9	2	2	0	12	1

GALLOWAY, JOEY — WR — BUCCANEERS

PERSONAL: Born November 20, 1971, in Bellaire, Ohio. ... 5-11/197.
HIGH SCHOOL: Bellaire (Ohio).
COLLEGE: Ohio State.
TRANSACTIONS/CAREER NOTES: Selected by Seattle Seahawks in first round (eighth pick overall) of 1995 NFL draft. ... Signed by Seahawks (July 20, 1995). ... On did not report list (September 4-November 9, 1999). ... Designated by Seahawks as franchise player (February 11, 2000). ... Traded by Seahawks to Dallas Cowboys for first-round pick (RB Shaun Alexander) in 2000 draft and first round pick (traded to San Francisco) in 2001 draft (February 12, 2000). ... On injured reserve with knee injury (September 8, 2000-remainder of season). ... Traded by Cowboys to Tampa Bay Buccaneers for WR Keyshawn Johnson (March 19, 2004).
SINGLE GAME HIGHS (regular season): Receptions—8 (October 6, 2002, vs. New York Giants); yards—146 (December 30, 2001, vs. San Francisco); and touchdown receptions—3 (October 26, 1997, vs. Oakland).
STATISTICAL PLATEAUS: 100-yard receiving games: 1995 (3), 1996 (2), 1997 (3), 1998 (4), 2001 (1), 2002 (3), 2003 (2). Total: 18.

			RUSHING				RECEIVING				PUNT RETURNS				KICKOFF RETURNS				TOTALS		
Year Team	**G**	**GS**	**Att.**	**Yds.**	**Avg.**	**TD**	**No.**	**Yds.**	**Avg.**	**TD**	**No.**	**Yds.**	**Avg.**	**TD**	**No.**	**Yds.**	**Avg.**	**TD**	**TD**	**2pt.**	**Pts.**
1995—Sea. NFL	16	16	11	154	14.0	1	67	1039	15.5	7	36	360	10.0	†1	2	30	15.0	0	9	0	54
1996—Sea. NFL	16	16	15	127	8.5	0	57	987	17.3	7	15	158	10.5	▲1	0	0	0.0	0	8	0	48
1997—Sea. NFL	15	15	9	72	8.0	0	72	1049	14.6	▲12	0	0	0.0	0	0	0	0.0	0	12	0	72
1998—Sea. NFL	16	16	9	26	2.9	0	65	1047	16.1	▲10	25	251	10.0	†2	0	0	0.0	0	12	0	72
1999—Sea. NFL	8	4	1	-1	-1.0	0	22	335	15.2	1	3	54	18.0	0	0	0	0.0	0	1	0	6
2000—Dal. NFL	1	1	0	0	0.0	0	4	62	15.5	1	1	2	2.0	0	0	0	0.0	0	1	0	6
2001—Dal. NFL	16	16	3	32	10.7	0	52	699	13.4	3	1	6	6.0	0	0	0	0.0	0	3	0	18
2002—Dal. NFL	16	16	4	31	7.8	0	61	908	14.9	6	15	181	12.1	0	0	0	0.0	0	6	0	36
2003—Dal. NFL	15	13	4	22	5.5	0	34	672	*19.8	2	20	178	8.9	0	2	38	19.0	0	2	0	12
Pro totals (9 years)	119	113	56	463	8.3	1	434	6798	15.7	49	116	1190	10.3	4	4	68	17.0	0	54	0	324

GAMBLE, TRENT — S

PERSONAL: Born July 24, 1977, in Denver, Colo. ... 5-9/195. ... Full name: Trent Ashford Gamble.
HIGH SCHOOL: Ponderosa (Parker, Colo.).
COLLEGE: Wyoming.
TRANSACTIONS/CAREER NOTES: Signed as non-drafted free agent by Miami Dolphins (April 25, 2000). ... On injured reserve with knee injury (October 23, 2001-remainder of season). ... On injured reserve with knee injury (November 10, 2003-remainder of season). ... Released by Dolphins (March 2, 2004).

			TOTALS			INTERCEPTIONS			
Year Team	**G**	**GS**	**Tk.**	**Ast.**	**Sks.**	**No.**	**Yds.**	**Avg.**	**TD**
2000—Miami NFL	16	0	2	1	0.0	0	0	0.0	0
2001—Miami NFL	1	0	0	0	0.0	0	0	0.0	0
2002—Miami NFL	13	0	6	2	0.0	0	0	0.0	0
2003—Miami NFL	9	1	0	0	0.0	0	0	0.0	0
Pro totals (4 years)	39	1	8	3	0.0	0	0	0.0	0

GAMMON, KENDALL — TE — CHIEFS

PERSONAL: Born October 23, 1968, in Wichita, Kan. ... 6-4/255. ... Full name: Kendall Robert Gammon.
HIGH SCHOOL: Rose Hill (Kan.).
COLLEGE: Pittsburg State.
TRANSACTIONS/CAREER NOTES: Selected by Pittsburgh Steelers in 11th round (291st pick overall) of 1992 NFL draft. ... Signed by Steelers (July 14, 1992). ... Released by Steelers (August 30, 1993). ... Re-signed by Steelers (August 31, 1993). ... Granted unconditional free agency (February 17, 1995). ... Re-signed by Steelers (May 8, 1995). ... Released by Steelers (August 26, 1996). ... Signed by New Orleans Saints (August 28, 1996). ... Granted unconditional free agency (February 11, 2000). ... Signed by Kansas City Chiefs (February 23, 2000). ... Granted unconditional free agency (February 28, 2003). ... Re-signed by Chiefs (March 23, 2003). ... Granted unconditional free agency (March 3, 2004). ... Re-signed by Chiefs (March 3, 2004).
CHAMPIONSHIP GAME EXPERIENCE: Played in AFC championship game (1994 and 1995 seasons). ... Played in Super Bowl 30 (1995 season).

			RECEIVING				TOTALS			
Year Team	**G**	**GS**	**No.**	**Yds.**	**Avg.**	**TD**	**TD**	**2pt.**	**Pts.**	**Fum.**
1992—Pittsburgh NFL	16	0	0	0	0.0	0	0	0	0	0
1993—Pittsburgh NFL	16	0	0	0	0.0	0	0	0	0	0
1994—Pittsburgh NFL	16	0	0	0	0.0	0	0	0	0	0
1995—Pittsburgh NFL	16	0	0	0	0.0	0	0	0	0	0
1996—New Orleans NFL	16	0	0	0	0.0	0	0	0	0	0
1997—New Orleans NFL	16	0	0	0	0.0	0	0	0	0	0
1998—New Orleans NFL	16	0	0	0	0.0	0	0	0	0	0
1999—New Orleans NFL	16	0	0	0	0.0	0	0	0	0	0
2000—Kansas City NFL	16	0	0	0	0.0	0	0	0	0	0
2001—Kansas City NFL	16	0	0	0	0.0	0	0	0	0	0
2002—Kansas City NFL	16	0	0	0	0.0	0	0	0	0	0
2003—Kansas City NFL	16	0	0	0	0.0	0	0	0	0	0
Pro totals (12 years)	192	0	0	0	0.0	0	0	0	0	0

GANDY, MIKE — T/G — BEARS

PERSONAL: Born January 3, 1979, in Rockford, Ill. ... 6-4/325. ... Full name: Michael Joseph Gandy.
HIGH SCHOOL: Garland (Texas).
COLLEGE: Notre Dame.

TRANSACTIONS/CAREER NOTES: Selected by Chicago Bears in third round (68th pick overall) of 2001 NFL draft. ... Signed by Bears (July 20, 2001). ... Inactive for all 16 games (2001). ... Granted free agency (March 3, 2004). ... Re-signed by Bears (March 19, 2004).
PLAYING EXPERIENCE: Chicago NFL, 2002-2003. ... Games/Games started: 2002 (13/11), 2003 (14/14). Total: 27/25.
HONORS: Named guard on THE SPORTING NEWS college All-America first team (2000).

GANDY, WAYNE — T — SAINTS

PERSONAL: Born February 10, 1971, in Haines City, Fla. ... 6-4/308. ... Full name: Wayne Lamar Gandy.
HIGH SCHOOL: Haines City (Fla.).
COLLEGE: Auburn.
TRANSACTIONS/CAREER NOTES: Selected by Los Angeles Rams in first round (15th pick overall) of 1994 NFL draft. ... Signed by Rams (July 23, 1994). ... Rams franchise moved to St. Louis (April 12, 1995). ... Granted unconditional free agency (February 12, 1999). ... Signed by Pittsburgh Steelers (April 6, 1999). ... Granted unconditional free agency (February 28, 2003). ... Signed by New Orleans Saints (March 2, 2003).
PLAYING EXPERIENCE: Los Angeles Rams NFL, 1994; St. Louis NFL, 1995-1998; Pittsburgh NFL, 1999-2002; New Orleans NFL, 2003. ... Games/Games started: 1994 (16/9), 1995 (16/16), 1996 (16/16), 1997 (16/16), 1998 (16/16), 1999 (16/16), 2000 (16/16), 2001 (15/15), 2002 (16/16), 2003 (16/16). Total: 159/152.
CHAMPIONSHIP GAME EXPERIENCE: Played in AFC championship game (2001 season).
HONORS: Named offensive lineman on THE SPORTING NEWS college All-America first team (1993).

GANNON, RICH — QB — RAIDERS

PERSONAL: Born December 20, 1965, in Philadelphia, Pa. ... 6-3/210. ... Full name: Richard Joseph Gannon.
HIGH SCHOOL: St. Joseph's Prep (Philadelphia).
COLLEGE: Delaware.
TRANSACTIONS/CAREER NOTES: Selected by New England Patriots in fourth round (98th pick overall) of 1987 NFL draft. ... Rights traded by Patriots to Minnesota Vikings for fourth- (WR Sammy Martin) and 11th-round (traded) picks in 1988 draft (May 6, 1987). ... Signed by Vikings (July 30, 1987). ... Active for 13 games (1989); did not play. ... Granted free agency (February 1, 1990). ... Re-signed by Vikings (July 30, 1990). ... Granted free agency (February 1, 1991). ... Re-signed by Vikings (July 25, 1991). ... Granted free agency (February 1, 1992). ... Re-signed by Vikings (August 8, 1992). ... Traded by Vikings to Washington Redskins for conditional draft pick (August 20, 1993). ... Granted unconditional free agency (February 17, 1994). ... Signed by Kansas City Chiefs (March 29, 1995). ... Released by Chiefs (February 15, 1996). ... Re-signed by Chiefs (April 3, 1996). ... Granted unconditional free agency (February 12, 1999). ... Signed by Oakland Raiders (February 16, 1999). ... On injured reserve with shoulder injury (November 12, 2003-remainder of season).
CHAMPIONSHIP GAME EXPERIENCE: Member of Vikings for NFC championship game (1987 season); did not play. ... Played in AFC championship game (2000 and 2002 seasons). ... Played in Super Bowl 37 (2002 season).
HONORS: Played in Pro Bowl (1999-2002 seasons). ... Named quarterback on THE SPORTING NEWS NFL All-Pro team (2000 and 2002). ... Named Outstanding Player of Pro Bowl (2000 and 2001). ... Named NFL Player of the Year by THE SPORTING NEWS (2002).
RECORDS: Holds NFL single-season record for most completions—418 (2002); and most games with 300 or more yards passing—10 (2002). ... Shares NFL record for most consecutive games with 300 or more yards passing—6 (September 15-October 27, 2002). ... Holds NFL single-game record for most consecutive completions—21 (November 11, 2002, vs. Denver).
POST SEASON RECORDS: Holds Super Bowl single-game record for most passes intercepted—5 (January 26, 2003, vs. Tampa Bay).
SINGLE GAME HIGHS (regular season): Attempts—64 (September 15, 2002, vs. Pittsburgh); completions—43 (September 15, 2002, vs. Pittsburgh); yards—403 (September 15, 2002, vs. Pittsburgh); and touchdown passes—5 (December 24, 2000, vs. Carolina).
STATISTICAL PLATEAUS: 300-yard passing games: 1991 (1), 1992 (1), 1997 (1), 1998 (1), 1999 (2), 2000 (2), 2001 (4), 2002 (10), 2003 (1). Total: 23.
MISCELLANEOUS: Regular-season record as starting NFL quarterback: 74-55 (.574). ... Postseason record as starting NFL quarterback: 4-3 (.571).

			PASSING									RUSHING				TOTALS		
Year Team	G	GS	Att.	Cmp.	Pct.	Yds.	TD	Int.	Avg.	Skd.	Rat.	Att.	Yds.	Avg.	TD	TD	2pt.	Pts.
1987—Minnesota NFL	4	0	6	2	33.3	18	0	1	3.00	0	2.8	0	0	0.0	0	0	0	0
1988—Minnesota NFL	3	0	15	7	46.7	90	0	0	6.00	3	66.0	4	29	7.3	0	0	0	0
1989—Minnesota NFL									Did not play.									
1990—Minnesota NFL	14	12	349	182	52.1	2278	16	16	6.53	34	68.9	52	268	5.2	1	1	0	6
1991—Minnesota NFL	15	11	354	211	59.6	2166	12	6	6.12	19	81.5	43	236	5.5	2	2	0	12
1992—Minnesota NFL	12	12	279	159	57.0	1905	12	13	6.83	25	72.9	45	187	4.2	0	0	0	0
1993—Washington NFL	8	4	125	74	59.2	704	3	7	5.63	16	59.6	21	88	4.2	1	1	0	6
1994—									Did not play.									
1995—Kansas City NFL	2	0	11	7	63.6	57	0	0	5.18	0	76.7	8	25	3.1	1	1	0	6
1996—Kansas City NFL	4	3	90	54	60.0	491	6	1	5.46	5	92.4	12	81	6.8	0	0	0	0
1997—Kansas City NFL	9	6	175	98	56.0	1144	7	4	6.54	13	79.8	33	109	3.3	2	2	0	12
1998—Kansas City NFL	12	10	354	206	58.2	2305	10	6	6.51	25	80.1	44	168	3.8	3	3	0	18
1999—Oakland NFL	16	16	515	304	59.0	3840	24	14	7.46	49	86.5	46	298	6.5	2	2	0	12
2000—Oakland NFL	16	16	473	284	60.0	3430	28	11	7.25	28	92.4	89	529	5.9	4	4	1	26
2001—Oakland NFL	16	16	549	§361	§65.8	3828	§27	9	6.97	27	§95.5	63	231	3.7	2	2	1	14
2002—Oakland NFL	16	16	*618	*418	67.6	*4689	26	10	7.59	36	97.3	50	156	3.1	3	3	0	18
2003—Oakland NFL	7	7	225	125	55.6	1274	6	4	5.66	17	73.5	6	18	3.0	0	0	0	0
Pro totals (15 years)	154	129	4138	2492	60.2	28219	177	102	6.82	297	84.7	516	2423	4.7	21	21	2	130

GARAY, ANTONIO — DE — BROWNS

PERSONAL: Born November 30, 1979, in Rahway, N.J. ... 6-4/300.
HIGH SCHOOL: Rahway (N.J.).
COLLEGE: Boston College.
TRANSACTIONS/CAREER NOTES: Selected by Cleveland Browns in sixth round (195th pick overall) of 2003 NFL draft. ... Signed by Browns (August 1, 2003). ... On injured reserve with knee injury (December 22, 2003-remainder of season).

G

Year Team	G	GS	TOTALS Tk.	Ast.	Sks.	INTERCEPTIONS No.	Yds.	Avg.	TD
2003—Cleveland NFL	4	0	2	2	0.0	0	0	0.0	0

GARCIA, FRANK C/G CARDINALS

PERSONAL: Born January 28, 1972, in Phoenix, Ariz. ... 6-2/302. ... Full name: Frank Christopher Garcia.

HIGH SCHOOL: Maryvale (Phoenix).

COLLEGE: Washington.

TRANSACTIONS/CAREER NOTES: Selected by Carolina Panthers in fourth round (132nd pick overall) of 1995 NFL draft. ... Signed by Panthers (July 14, 1995). ... Granted free agency (February 13, 1998). ... Re-signed by Panthers (March 16, 1998). ... Granted unconditional free agency (March 2, 2001). ... Signed by St. Louis Rams (April 26, 2001). ... Granted unconditional free agency (February 28, 2003). ... Signed by Arizona Cardinals (March 14, 2003). ... On suspended list for violating league substance abuse policy (August 30-October 3, 2003).

PLAYING EXPERIENCE: Carolina NFL, 1995-2000; St. Louis NFL, 2001-2002; Arizona NFL, 2003. ... Games/Games started: 1995 (15/14), 1996 (14/8), 1997 (16/16), 1998 (14/14), 1999 (16/16), 2000 (16/16), 2001 (13/2), 2002 (14/3), 2003 (7/3). Total: 125/92.

CHAMPIONSHIP GAME EXPERIENCE: Played in NFC championship game (1996 and 2001 seasons). ... Played in Super Bowl 36 (2001 season).

GARCIA, JEFF QB BROWNS

PERSONAL: Born February 24, 1970, in Gilroy, Calif. ... 6-1/195.

HIGH SCHOOL: Gilroy (Calif.).

JUNIOR COLLEGE: Gavilan College (Calif.).

COLLEGE: San Jose State.

TRANSACTIONS/CAREER NOTES: Signed by Calgary Stampeders of CFL (1994). ... Granted free agency (February 16, 1997). ... Re-signed by Stampeders (April 30, 1997). ... Signed as non-drafted free agent by San Francisco 49ers (February 16, 1999). ... Released by 49ers (March 2, 2004). ... Signed by Cleveland Browns (March 9, 2004).

CHAMPIONSHIP GAME EXPERIENCE: Played in Grey Cup (1995). ... Member of CFL Championship team (1998). ... Named Most Valuable Player of Grey Cup, CFL championship game (1998).

HONORS: Played in Pro Bowl (2000-2002 seasons).

SINGLE GAME HIGHS (regular season): Attempts—55 (December 8, 2002, vs. Dallas); completions—36 (December 8, 2002, vs. Dallas); passing yards—437 (December 5, 1999, vs. Cincinnati); and touchdown passes—4 (December 7, 2003, vs. Arizona).

STATISTICAL PLATEAUS: 300-yard passing games: 1999 (3), 2000 (6), 2001 (3), 2002 (1), 2003 (1). Total: 14.

MISCELLANEOUS: Regular-season record as starting NFL quarterback: 35-36 (.493). ... Postseason record as starting NFL quarterback: 1-2 (.333).

Year Team	G	GS	PASSING Att.	Cmp.	Pct.	Yds.	TD	Int.	Avg.	Skd.	Rat.	RUSHING Att.	Yds.	Avg.	TD	TOTALS TD	2pt.	Pts.
1994—Calgary CFL	7	...	3	2	66.7	10	0	0	3.33	...	71.5	2	3	1.5	0	0	...	0
1995—Calgary CFL	18	...	364	230	63.2	3358	25	7	9.23	...	108.1	61	396	6.5	5	5	...	30
1996—Calgary CFL	18	...	537	315	58.7	4225	25	16	7.87	...	86.9	92	657	7.1	6	6	...	36
1997—Calgary CFL	17	...	566	354	62.5	4573	33	14	8.08	...	97.0	135	727	5.4	7	7	1	44
1998—Calgary CFL	18	...	554	348	62.8	4276	28	15	7.72	...	92.2	94	575	6.1	6	6	...	36
1999—San Francisco NFL	13	10	375	225	60.0	2544	11	11	6.78	15	77.9	45	231	5.1	2	2	0	12
2000—San Francisco NFL	16	16	561	‡355	63.3	‡4278	‡31	10	7.63	24	97.6	72	414	5.8	4	4	0	24
2001—San Francisco NFL	16	16	504	316	62.7	3538	32	12	7.02	26	94.8	72	254	3.5	5	5	0	30
2002—San Francisco NFL	16	16	528	328	62.1	3344	21	10	6.33	17	85.6	73	353	4.8	3	3	1	20
2003—San Francisco NFL	13	13	392	225	57.4	2704	18	13	6.90	21	80.1	56	319	5.7	7	7	0	42
CFL Totals (5 years)	78	...	2024	1249	61.7	16442	111	52	8.12	...	94.9	384	2358	6.1	24	24	...	146
NFL totals (5 years)	74	71	2360	1449	61.4	16408	113	56	6.95	103	88.3	318	1571	4.9	21	21	1	128
Pro totals (10 years)	152	...	4384	2698	61.5	32850	224	108	7.49	...	91.4	702	3929	5.6	45	45	...	274

GARDENER, DARYL DT BRONCOS

PERSONAL: Born February 25, 1973, in Baltimore, Md. ... 6-6/295. ... Full name: Daryl Ronald Gardener.

HIGH SCHOOL: Lawton (Okla.).

COLLEGE: Baylor.

TRANSACTIONS/CAREER NOTES: Selected by Miami Dolphins in first round (20th pick overall) of 1996 NFL draft. ... Signed by Dolphins (June 6, 1996). ... On injured reserve with back injury (December 4, 2001-remainder of season). ... Released by Dolphins (July 19, 2002). ... Signed by Washington Redskins (July 30, 2002). ... Granted unconditional free agency (February 28, 2003). ... Signed by Denver Broncos (March 7, 2003). ... Inactive for five games (2003). ... Suspended three games for conduct detrimental to team (2003). ... On reserve/non-football injury list (December 9, 2003-remainder of season).

Year Team	G	GS	TOTALS Tk.	Ast.	Sks.	INTERCEPTIONS No.	Yds.	Avg.	TD
1996—Miami NFL	16	12	24	9	1.0	0	0	0.0	0
1997—Miami NFL	16	16	32	20	1.5	0	0	0.0	0
1998—Miami NFL	16	16	27	12	1.0	1	-1	-1.0	0
1999—Miami NFL	16	15	28	24	5.0	0	0	0.0	0
2000—Miami NFL	10	10	35	14	2.5	0	0	0.0	0
2001—Miami NFL	8	8	17	11	4.0	0	0	0.0	0
2002—Washington NFL	15	15	45	7	4.0	0	0	0.0	0
2003—Denver NFL	5	2	5	3	0.0	0	0	0.0	0
Pro totals (8 years)	102	94	213	100	19.0	1	-1	-1.0	0

GARDNER, BARRY — LB — BROWNS

PERSONAL: Born December 13, 1976, in Harvey, Ill. ... 6-1/245. ... Full name: Barry Allan Gardner.
HIGH SCHOOL: Thornton (Harvey, Ill.).
COLLEGE: Northwestern.
TRANSACTIONS/CAREER NOTES: Selected by Philadelphia Eagles in second round (35th pick overall) of 1999 NFL draft. ... Signed by Eagles (July 25, 1999). ... Granted unconditional free agency (February 28, 2003). ... Signed by Cleveland Browns (March 14, 2003).
CHAMPIONSHIP GAME EXPERIENCE: Played in NFC championship game (2001 and 2002 seasons).

			TOTALS			INTERCEPTIONS			
Year Team	**G**	**GS**	**Tk.**	**Ast.**	**Sks.**	**No.**	**Yds.**	**Avg.**	**TD**
1999—Philadelphia NFL	16	5	27	10	0.0	0	0	0.0	0
2000—Philadelphia NFL	16	13	42	15	1.0	0	0	0.0	0
2001—Philadelphia NFL	16	0	10	5	0.0	0	0	0.0	0
2002—Philadelphia NFL	16	0	19	9	1.0	0	0	0.0	0
2003—Cleveland NFL	16	0	13	6	0.0	0	0	0.0	0
Pro totals (5 years)	80	18	111	45	2.0	0	0	0.0	0

GARDNER, ROD — WR — REDSKINS

PERSONAL: Born October 26, 1977, in Jacksonville, Fla. ... 6-2/213. ... Full name: Roderick F. Gardner.
HIGH SCHOOL: Raines (Jacksonville, Fla.).
COLLEGE: Clemson.
TRANSACTIONS/CAREER NOTES: Selected by Washington Redskins in first round (15th pick overall) of 2001 NFL draft. ... Signed by Redskins (August 2, 2001).
SINGLE GAME HIGHS (regular season): Receptions—9 (October 12, 2003, vs. Tampa Bay); yards—208 (October 21, 2001, vs. Carolina); and touchdown receptions—1 (December 7, 2003, vs. New York Giants).
STATISTICAL PLATEAUS: 100-yard receiving games: 2001 (1), 2002 (2), 2003 (1). Total: 4.

			RECEIVING				TOTALS			
Year Team	**G**	**GS**	**No.**	**Yds.**	**Avg.**	**TD**	**TD**	**2pt.**	**Pts.**	**Fum.**
2001—Washington NFL	16	16	46	741	16.1	4	4	0	24	1
2002—Washington NFL	16	15	71	1006	14.2	8	8	0	48	1
2003—Washington NFL	16	16	59	600	10.2	5	5	0	30	1
Pro totals (3 years)	48	47	176	2347	13.3	17	17	0	102	3

GARDNER, TALMAN — WR — SAINTS

PERSONAL: Born March 10, 1980, in New Orleans, La. ... 6-1/205.
HIGH SCHOOL: McDonough (New Orleans).
COLLEGE: Florida State.
TRANSACTIONS/CAREER NOTES: Selected by New Orleans Saints in seventh round (231st pick overall) of 2003 NFL draft. ... Signed by Saints (July 23, 2003). ... Released by Saints (August 31, 2003). ... Re-signed by Saints to practice squad (September 3, 2003). ... Activated (October 4, 2003).
SINGLE GAME HIGHS (regular season): Receptions—2 (November 23, 2003, vs. Philadelphia); yards—18 (November 23, 2003, vs. Philadelphia); and touchdown receptions—0.

			RUSHING				RECEIVING				KICKOFF RETURNS				TOTALS			
Year Team	**G**	**GS**	**Att.**	**Yds.**	**Avg.**	**TD**	**No.**	**Yds.**	**Avg.**	**TD**	**No.**	**Yds.**	**Avg.**	**TD**	**TD**	**2pt.**	**Pts.**	**Fum.**
2003—New Orleans NFL	10	1	0	0	0.0	0	3	29	9.7	0	0	0	0.0	0	0	0	0	0

GARDOCKI, CHRIS — P — STEELERS

PERSONAL: Born February 7, 1970, in Stone Mountain, Ga. ... 6-1/200. ... Full name: Christopher Allen Gardocki.
HIGH SCHOOL: Redan (Stone Mountain, Ga.).
COLLEGE: Clemson.
TRANSACTIONS/CAREER NOTES: Selected after junior season by Chicago Bears in third round (78th pick overall) of 1991 NFL draft. ... Signed by Bears (June 24, 1991). ... On injured reserve with groin injury (August 27-November 27, 1991). ... Granted unconditional free agency (February 17, 1995). ... Signed by Indianapolis Colts (February 24, 1995). ... Granted unconditional free agency (February 12, 1999). ... Signed by Cleveland Browns (February 16, 1999). ... Granted unconditional free agency (March 3, 2004). ... Signed by Pittsburgh Steelers (March 6, 2004).
CHAMPIONSHIP GAME EXPERIENCE: Played in AFC championship game (1995 season).
HONORS: Named kicker on THE SPORTING NEWS college All-America second team (1990). ... Named punter on THE SPORTING NEWS NFL All-Pro team (1996). ... Played in Pro Bowl (1996 season).
RECORDS: Holds NFL career record for most consecutive punts without a block—978.

		PUNTING					
Year Team	**G**	**No.**	**Yds.**	**Avg.**	**Net avg.**	**In. 20**	**Blk.**
1991—Chicago NFL	4	0	0	0.0	0.0	0	0
1992—Chicago NFL	16	79	3393	42.9	36.2	19	0
1993—Chicago NFL	16	80	3080	38.5	36.6	28	0
1994—Chicago NFL	16	76	2871	37.8	32.3	23	0
1995—Indianapolis NFL	16	63	2681	42.6	33.3	16	0
1996—Indianapolis NFL	16	68	3105	45.7	§39.0	23	0
1997—Indianapolis NFL	16	67	3034	45.3	36.2	18	0
1998—Indianapolis NFL	16	79	3583	45.4	37.1	23	0
1999—Cleveland NFL	16	§106	*4645	43.8	34.6	20	0
2000—Cleveland NFL	16	*108	*4919	45.5	37.3	25	0

G

Year Team	G	PUNTING No.	Yds.	Avg.	Net avg.	In. 20	Blk.
2001—Cleveland NFL	16	*99	§4249	42.9	34.6	25	0
2002—Cleveland NFL	16	81	3388	41.8	35.3	27	0
2003—Cleveland NFL	16	72	3019	41.9	34.8	18	0
Pro totals (13 years)	196	978	41967	42.9	35.6	265	0

GARMON, KELVIN G BROWNS

PERSONAL: Born October 26, 1976, in Fort Worth, Texas. ... 6-2/350.
HIGH SCHOOL: Haltom (Fort Worth, Texas).
COLLEGE: Baylor.
TRANSACTIONS/CAREER NOTES: Selected by Dallas Cowboys in seventh round (243rd pick overall) of 1999 NFL draft. ... Signed by Cowboys (August 8, 1999). ... On non-football injury list with leg injury (August 31, 1999-entire season). ... Active for one game (2000); did not play. ... Traded by Cowboys to San Diego Chargers for conditional seventh-round pick (traded to Detroit) in 2003 draft (October 13, 2002). ... Granted unconditional free agency (March 3, 2004). ... Signed by Cleveland Browns (March 23, 2004).
PLAYING EXPERIENCE: Dallas NFL, 1999-2002; San Diego NFL, 2002-2003. ... Games/Games started: 2001 (16/16), 2002 (12/10), 2003 (16/16). Total: 44/42.

GARNER, CHARLIE RB BUCCANEERS

PERSONAL: Born February 13, 1972, in Fairfax, Va. ... 5-10/190.
HIGH SCHOOL: Jeb Stuart (Falls Church, Va.).
JUNIOR COLLEGE: Scottsdale (Ariz.) Community College.
COLLEGE: Tennessee.
TRANSACTIONS/CAREER NOTES: Selected by Philadelphia Eagles in second round (42nd pick overall) of 1994 NFL draft. ... Signed by Eagles (July 18, 1994). ... Granted free agency (February 14, 1997). ... Re-signed by Eagles (June 16, 1997). ... Granted unconditional free agency (February 13, 1998). ... Re-signed by Eagles (February 23, 1998). ... On injured reserve with rib injury (December 10, 1998-remainder of season). ... Released by Eagles (April 20, 1999). ... Signed by San Francisco 49ers (July 19, 1999). ... Granted unconditional free agency (March 2, 2001). ... Signed by Oakland Raiders (April 13, 2001). ... Granted unconditional free agency (March 3, 2004). ... Signed by Tampa Bay Buccaneers (March 9, 2004).
CHAMPIONSHIP GAME EXPERIENCE: Played in AFC championship game (2002 season). ... Played in Super Bowl 36 (2002 season).
HONORS: Played in Pro Bowl (2000 season).
SINGLE GAME HIGHS (regular season): Attempts—36 (September 24, 2000, vs. Dallas); yards—201 (September 24, 2000, vs. Dallas); and rushing touchdowns—3 (October 8, 1995, vs. Washington).
STATISTICAL PLATEAUS: 100-yard rushing games: 1994 (2), 1995 (1), 1997 (1), 1998 (1), 1999 (3), 2000 (3), 2002 (3). Total: 14. 100-yard receiving games: 2000 (1), 2003 (1). Total: 2.

			RUSHING				RECEIVING				KICKOFF RETURNS				TOTALS			
Year Team	G	GS	Att.	Yds.	Avg.	TD	No.	Yds.	Avg.	TD	No.	Yds.	Avg.	TD	TD	2pt.	Pts.	Fum.
1994—Philadelphia NFL	10	8	109	399	3.7	3	8	74	9.3	0	0	0	0.0	0	3	0	18	3
1995—Philadelphia NFL	15	3	108	588	*5.4	6	10	61	6.1	0	29	590	20.3	0	6	0	36	2
1996—Philadelphia NFL	15	1	66	346	5.2	1	14	92	6.6	0	6	117	19.5	0	1	0	6	1
1997—Philadelphia NFL	16	2	116	547	4.7	3	24	225	9.4	0	0	0	0.0	0	3	0	18	1
1998—Philadelphia NFL	10	3	96	381	4.0	4	19	110	5.8	0	0	0	0.0	0	4	0	24	1
1999—San Francisco NFL	16	15	241	1229	5.1	4	56	535	9.6	2	0	0	0.0	0	6	0	36	4
2000—San Francisco NFL	16	15	258	1142	4.4	7	68	647	9.5	3	0	0	0.0	0	10	0	60	4
2001—Oakland NFL	16	16	211	839	4.0	1	72	578	8.0	2	0	0	0.0	0	3	0	18	2
2002—Oakland NFL	16	15	182	962	5.3	7	91	941	10.3	4	0	0	0.0	0	11	0	66	0
2003—Oakland NFL	14	9	120	553	4.6	3	48	386	8.0	1	0	0	0.0	0	4	0	24	1
Pro totals (10 years)	144	87	1507	6986	4.6	39	410	3649	8.9	12	35	707	20.2	0	51	0	306	19

GARNES, SAM S

PERSONAL: Born July 12, 1974, in Bronx, N.Y. ... 6-3/225. ... Full name: Sam Aaron Garnes.
HIGH SCHOOL: DeWitt Clinton (Bronx, N.Y.).
COLLEGE: Cincinnati.
TRANSACTIONS/CAREER NOTES: Selected by New York Giants in fifth round (136th pick overall) of 1997 NFL draft. ... Signed by Giants for 1997 season. ... Granted free agency (February 11, 2000). ... Re-signed by Giants (February 12, 2000). ... Released by Giants (February 28, 2002). ... Signed by New York Jets (March 5, 2002). ... Released by Jets (March 1, 2004).

G

			TOTALS			INTERCEPTIONS			
Year Team	G	GS	Tk.	Ast.	Sks.	No.	Yds.	Avg.	TD
1997—New York Giants NFL	16	15	40	19	0.0	1	95	95.0	1
1998—New York Giants NFL	11	11	37	12	0.0	1	13	13.0	0
1999—New York Giants NFL	16	16	73	18	1.0	2	7	3.5	0
2000—New York Giants NFL	15	15	51	12	1.0	1	4	4.0	0
2001—New York Giants NFL	16	16	58	15	0.0	1	5	5.0	0
2002—New York Jets NFL	16	16	55	12	0.5	2	65	32.5	0
2003—New York Jets NFL	16	16	66	32	0.5	2	0	0.0	0
Pro totals (7 years)	106	105	380	120	3.0	10	189	18.9	1

GARRARD, DAVID QB JAGUARS

PERSONAL: Born February 14, 1978, in East Orange, N.J. ... 6-1/244. ... Full name: David Douglas Garrard.
HIGH SCHOOL: Southern Durham (N.C.).
COLLEGE: East Carolina.

TRANSACTIONS/CAREER NOTES: Selected by Jacksonville Jaguars in fourth round (108th pick overall) of 2002 NFL draft. ... Signed by Jaguars (July 22, 2002).
SINGLE GAME HIGHS (regular season): Attempts—26 (December 29, 2002, vs. Indianapolis); completions—13 (December 29, 2002, vs. Indianapolis); yards—135 (December 29, 2002, vs. Indianapolis); and touchdown passes—1 (October 26, 2003, vs. Tennessee).
MISCELLANEOUS: Regular-season record as starting NFL quarterback: 0-1 (.000).

			PASSING									RUSHING				TOTALS		
Year Team	**G**	**GS**	**Att.**	**Cmp.**	**Pct.**	**Yds.**	**TD**	**Int.**	**Avg.**	**Skd.**	**Rat.**	**Att.**	**Yds.**	**Avg.**	**TD**	**TD**	**2pt.**	**Pts.**
2002—Jacksonville NFL	4	1	46	23	50.0	231	1	2	5.02	7	53.8	25	139	5.6	2	2	0	12
2003—Jacksonville NFL	2	0	12	9	75.0	86	1	0	7.17	0	122.2	0	0	0.0	0	0	0	0
Pro totals (2 years)	6	1	58	32	55.2	317	2	2	5.47	7	68.0	25	139	5.6	2	2	0	12

GARRETT, JASON — QB — BUCCANEERS

PERSONAL: Born March 28, 1966, in Abington, Pa. ... 6-2/200. ... Full name: Jason Calvin Garrett. ... Son of Jim Garrett, scout, Dallas Cowboys; brother of John Garrett, wide receiver with Cincinnati Bengals (1989) and San Antonio Riders of World League (1991); and brother of Judd Garrett, running back with London of World League (1991-92).
HIGH SCHOOL: University (Chargin Falls, Ohio).
COLLEGE: Princeton.
TRANSACTIONS/CAREER NOTES: Signed as non-drafted free agent by New Orleans Saints (1989). ... Released by Saints (August 30, 1989). ... Re-signed by Saints to developmental squad (September 6, 1989). ... Released by Saints (December 29, 1989). ... Re-signed by Saints for 1990 season. ... Released by Saints (September 3, 1990). ... Signed by WLAF (January 3, 1991). ... Selected by San Antonio Riders in first round (seventh quarterback) of 1991 WLAF positional draft. ... Signed by Ottawa Rough Riders of CFL (1991). ... Released by San Antonio Riders (March 3, 1992). ... Signed by Dallas Cowboys (March 23, 1992). ... Released by Cowboys (August 31, 1992). ... Re-signed by Cowboys to practice squad (September 1, 1992). ... Granted unconditional free agency (February 16, 1996). ... Re-signed by Cowboys (April 3, 1996). ... Granted unconditional free agency (February 14, 1997). ... Re-signed by Cowboys (April 8, 1997). ... Granted unconditional free agency (February 11, 2000). ... Signed by New York Giants (February 22, 2000). ... Released by Giants (February 28, 2002). ... Re-signed by Giants (July 24, 2002). ... Granted unconditional free agency (February 28, 2003). ... Re-signed by Giants (March 4, 2003). ... Active for three games (2003); did not play. ... Granted unrestricted free agency (March 3, 2004). ... Signed by Tampa Bay Buccaneers (March 15, 2004).
CHAMPIONSHIP GAME EXPERIENCE: Member of Cowboys for NFC championship game (1993-1995 seasons); inactive. ... Member of Super Bowl championship team (1993 and 1995 seasons). ... Played in NFC championship game (2000 season). ... Member of Giants for Super Bowl 35 (2000 season); did not play.
SINGLE GAME HIGHS (regular season): Attempts—33 (September 27, 1998, vs. Oakland); completions—18 (September 27, 1998, vs. Oakland); yards—311 (November 24, 1994, vs. Green Bay); and touchdown passes—2 (November 14, 1999, vs. Green Bay).
STATISTICAL PLATEAUS: 300-yard passing games: 1994 (1). Total: 1.
MISCELLANEOUS: Regular-season record as starting NFL quarterback: 6-3 (.667).

			PASSING									RUSHING				TOTALS		
Year Team	**G**	**GS**	**Att.**	**Cmp.**	**Pct.**	**Yds.**	**TD**	**Int.**	**Avg.**	**Skd.**	**Rat.**	**Att.**	**Yds.**	**Avg.**	**TD**	**TD**	**2pt.**	**Pts.**
1991—Ottawa CFL	13	...	3	2	66.7	28	0	0	9.33	...	96.5	0	0	0.0	0	0	...	0
1992—Dallas NFL									Did not play.									
1993—Dallas NFL	5	1	19	9	47.4	61	0	0	3.21	1	54.9	8	-8	-1.0	0	0	0	0
1994—Dallas NFL	2	1	31	16	51.6	315	2	1	10.16	2	95.5	3	-2	-0.7	0	0	0	0
1995—Dallas NFL	1	0	5	4	80.0	46	1	0	9.20	0	144.6	1	-1	-1.0	0	0	0	0
1996—Dallas NFL	1	0	3	3	100.0	44	0	0	14.67	0	118.8	0	0	0.0	0	0	0	0
1997—Dallas NFL	1	0	14	10	71.4	56	0	0	4.00	2	78.3	0	0	0.0	0	0	0	0
1998—Dallas NFL	8	5	158	91	57.6	1206	5	3	7.63	10	84.5	11	14	1.3	0	0	0	0
1999—Dallas NFL	6	2	64	32	50.0	314	3	1	4.91	5	73.3	6	12	2.0	0	0	0	0
2000—New York Giants NFL	2	0	0	0	0.0	0	0	0	0.00	0	.0	4	-4	-1.0	0	0	0	0
2001—New York Giants NFL									Did not play.									
2003—New York Giants NFL									Did not play.									
CFL Totals (1 years)	13	...	3	2	66.7	28	0	0	9.33	...	96.5	0	0	0.0	0	0	...	0
NFL totals (8 years)	26	9	294	165	56.1	2042	11	5	6.95	20	83.2	33	11	0.3	0	0	0	0
Pro totals (9 years)	39	...	297	167	56.2	2070	11	5	6.97	...	83.3	33	11	0.3	0	0	...	0

GARRETT, KEVIN — CB — RAMS

PERSONAL: Born July 29, 1980, in San Benito, Texas. ... 5-10/194.
HIGH SCHOOL: Sweeney (Brazoria, Texas).
COLLEGE: Southern Methodist.
TRANSACTIONS/CAREER NOTES: Selected by St. Louis Rams in fifth round (172nd pick overall) of 2003 NFL draft. ... Signed by Rams (July 22, 2003).

			TOTALS			INTERCEPTIONS			
Year Team	**G**	**GS**	**Tk.**	**Ast.**	**Sks.**	**No.**	**Yds.**	**Avg.**	**TD**
2003—St. Louis NFL	9	0	0	0	0.0	0	0	0.0	0

GARY, OLANDIS — RB — LIONS

PERSONAL: Born May 18, 1975, in Washington, DC. ... 5-11/218. ... Full name: Olandis C. Gary.
HIGH SCHOOL: Riverdale Baptist (Upper Marlboro, Md.).
COLLEGE: Georgia.
TRANSACTIONS/CAREER NOTES: Selected by Denver Broncos in fourth round (127th pick overall) of 1999 NFL draft. ... Signed by Broncos (July 20, 1999). ... On injured reserve with knee injury (September 8, 2000-remainder of season). ... On injured reserve with broken leg (November 26, 2001-remainder of season). ... Granted free agency (March 1, 2002). ... Re-signed by Broncos (April 19, 2002). ... Granted unconditional free agency (February 28, 2003). ... Signed by Buffalo Bills (April 21, 2003). ... Traded by Bills to Detroit Lions for an undisclosed draft pick (August 31, 2003).
SINGLE GAME HIGHS (regular season): Attempts—37 (October 17, 1999, vs. Green Bay); yards—185 (December 25, 1999, vs. Detroit); and rushing touchdowns—2 (November 7, 1999, vs. San Diego).

STATISTICAL PLATEAUS: 100-yard rushing games: 1999 (4). Total: 4.

Year Team	G	GS	RUSHING Att.	Yds.	Avg.	TD	RECEIVING No.	Yds.	Avg.	TD	TOTALS TD	2pt.	Pts.	Fum.
1999—Denver NFL	12	12	276	1159	4.2	7	21	159	7.6	0	7	1	44	2
2000—Denver NFL	1	0	13	80	6.2	0	3	10	3.3	0	0	0	0	0
2001—Denver NFL	9	1	57	228	4.0	1	4	29	7.3	0	1	0	6	0
2002—Denver NFL	13	2	37	147	4.0	1	18	148	8.2	0	1	0	6	0
2003—Detroit NFL	13	1	113	384	3.4	2	13	69	5.3	0	2	0	12	1
Pro totals (5 years)	48	16	496	1998	4.0	11	59	415	7.0	0	11	1	68	3

GARZA, ROBERTO G/C FALCONS

PERSONAL: Born March 26, 1979, in Rio Hondo, Texas. ... 6-2/296. ... Full name: Robert Garza.

HIGH SCHOOL: Rio Hondo (Texas).

COLLEGE: Texas A&M-Kingsville.

TRANSACTIONS/CAREER NOTES: Selected by Atlanta Falcons in fourth round (99th pick overall) of 2001 NFL draft. ... Signed by Falcons (May 21, 2001). ... On injured reserve with knee injury (December 16, 2003-remainder of season). ... Granted free agency (March 3, 2004). ... Re-signed by Falcons (March 25, 2004).

PLAYING EXPERIENCE: Atlanta NFL, 2001-2003. ... Games/Games started: 2001 (16/4), 2002 (6/4), 2003 (14/8). Total: 36/16.

GASH, SAM FB SAINTS

PERSONAL: Born March 7, 1969, in Hendersonville, N.C. ... 6-0/242. ... Full name: Samuel Lee Gash Jr.

HIGH SCHOOL: Hendersonville (N.C.).

COLLEGE: Penn State.

TRANSACTIONS/CAREER NOTES: Selected by New England Patriots in eighth round (205th pick overall) of 1992 NFL draft. ... Signed by Patriots (June 10, 1992). ... Granted free agency (February 17, 1995). ... Re-signed by Patriots (May 5, 1995). ... On injured reserve with knee injury (December 10, 1996-remainder of season). ... Granted unconditional free agency (February 13, 1998). ... Signed by Buffalo Bills (March 5, 1998). ... Released by Bills (April 14, 2000). ... Signed by Baltimore Ravens (August 7, 2000). ... Granted unconditional free agency (March 2, 2001). ... Re-signed by Ravens (June 11, 2001). ... Released by Ravens (February 27, 2002). ... Re-signed by Ravens (September 2, 2002). ... Granted unconditional free agency (February 28, 2003). ... Signed by Bills (March 31, 2003). ... Granted unconditional free agency (March 3, 2004). ... Signed by New Orleans Saints (March 16, 2004).

CHAMPIONSHIP GAME EXPERIENCE: Played in AFC championship game (2000 season). ... Member of Super Bowl championship team (2000 season).

HONORS: Played in Pro Bowl (1998 and 1999 seasons).

SINGLE GAME HIGHS (regular season): Attempts—15 (December 18, 1994, vs. Buffalo); yards—56 (December 18, 1994, vs. Buffalo); and rushing touchdowns—1 (September 19, 1993, vs. Seattle).

Year Team	G	GS	RUSHING Att.	Yds.	Avg.	TD	RECEIVING No.	Yds.	Avg.	TD	TOTALS TD	2pt.	Pts.	Fum.
1992—New England NFL	15	0	5	7	1.4	1	0	0	0.0	0	1	0	6	1
1993—New England NFL	15	4	48	149	3.1	1	14	93	6.6	0	1	0	6	1
1994—New England NFL	13	6	30	86	2.9	0	9	61	6.8	0	0	0	0	1
1995—New England NFL	15	12	8	24	3.0	0	26	242	9.3	1	1	0	6	0
1996—New England NFL	14	9	8	15	1.9	0	33	276	8.4	2	2	1	14	0
1997—New England NFL	16	5	6	10	1.7	0	22	154	7.0	3	3	0	18	0
1998—Buffalo NFL	16	12	11	32	2.9	0	19	165	8.7	3	3	0	18	0
1999—Buffalo NFL	15	12	0	0	0.0	0	20	163	8.2	2	2	0	12	0
2000—Baltimore NFL	15	4	2	2	1.0	0	6	30	5.0	1	1	0	6	0
2001—Baltimore NFL	16	4	2	-1	-0.5	0	9	80	8.9	1	1	0	6	0
2002—Baltimore NFL	11	0	0	0	0.0	0	0	0	0.0	0	0	0	0	0
2003—Buffalo NFL	16	10	1	3	3.0	0	11	83	7.5	0	0	0	0	1
Pro totals (12 years)	177	78	121	327	2.7	2	169	1347	8.0	13	15	1	92	4

GATES, ANTONIO TE CHARGERS

PERSONAL: Born June 18, 1980, in Detroit, Mich. ... 6-4/260.

HIGH SCHOOL: Detroit Central (Mich.).

COLLEGE: Kent State.

TRANSACTIONS/CAREER NOTES: Signed as non-drafted free agent by San Diego Chargers (May 2, 2003).

SINGLE GAME HIGHS (regular season): Receptions—5 (December 21, 2003, vs. Pittsburgh); yards—117 (December 14, 2003, vs. Green Bay); and touchdown receptions—1 (November 30, 2003, vs. Kansas City).

STATISTICAL PLATEAUS: 100-yard receiving games: 2003 (1). Total: 1.

Year Team	G	GS	RECEIVING No.	Yds.	Avg.	TD	TOTALS TD	2pt.	Pts.	Fum.
2003—San Diego NFL	15	11	24	389	16.2	2	2	0	12	1

GBAJA-BIAMILA, AKBAR DE RAIDERS

PERSONAL: Born May 6, 1979, in Los Angeles, Calif. ... 6-5/270. ... Brother of Kabeer Gbaja-Biamila, defensive end, Green Bay Packers.

HIGH SCHOOL: Crenshaw (Los Angeles, Calif.).

COLLEGE: San Diego State.

TRANSACTIONS/CAREER NOTES: Signed as non-drafted free agent by Oakland Raiders (April 29, 2003).

Year	Team	G	GS	TOTALS Tk.	Ast.	Sks.
2003—Oakland NFL		13	0	4	3	1.0

GBAJA-BIAMILA, KABEER DE PACKERS

PERSONAL: Born September 24, 1977, in Los Angeles, Calif. ... 6-4/255. ... Full name: Muhammed-Kabeer Olarewaja Gbaja-Biamila. ... Brother of Akbar Gbaja-Biamila, defensive end, Oakland Raiders.
HIGH SCHOOL: Crenshaw (Los Angeles).
COLLEGE: San Diego State.
TRANSACTIONS/CAREER NOTES: Selected by Green Bay Packers in fifth round (149th pick overall) of 2000 NFL draft. ... Signed by Packers (July 17, 2000). ... Released by Packers (August 27, 2000). ... Re-signed by Packers to practice squad (August 28, 2000). ... Activated (October 10, 2000). ... Granted free agency (February 28, 2003). ... Re-signed by Packers (April 2, 2003).
HONORS: Played in Pro Bowl (2003 season).

			TOTALS			INTERCEPTIONS			
Year Team	G	GS	Tk.	Ast.	Sks.	No.	Yds.	Avg.	TD
2000—Green Bay NFL	7	0	3	1	1.5	0	0	0.0	0
2001—Green Bay NFL	16	0	19	5	13.5	0	0	0.0	0
2002—Green Bay NFL	15	11	35	11	12.0	1	72	72.0	1
2003—Green Bay NFL	16	16	36	11	10.0	0	0	0.0	0
Pro totals (4 years)	54	27	93	28	37.0	1	72	72.0	1

GEORGE, EDDIE RB TITANS

PERSONAL: Born September 24, 1973, in Philadelphia, Pa. ... 6-3/235. ... Full name: Edward Nathan George.
HIGH SCHOOL: Abington (Philadelphia), then Fork Union (Va.) Military Academy.
COLLEGE: Ohio State.
TRANSACTIONS/CAREER NOTES: Selected by Houston Oilers in first round (14th pick overall) of 1996 NFL draft. ... Signed by Oilers (July 20, 1996). ... Oilers franchise moved to Tennessee for 1997 season. ... Oilers franchise renamed Tennessee Titans for 1999 season (December 26, 1998). ... On physically unable to perform list with toe injury (July 28-31, 2001).
CHAMPIONSHIP GAME EXPERIENCE: Played in AFC championship game (1999 and 2002 seasons). ... Played in Super Bowl 34 (1999 season).
HONORS: Heisman Trophy winner (1995). ... Maxwell Award winner (1995). ... Doak Walker Award winner (1995). ... Named running back on THE SPORTING NEWS college All-America first team (1995). ... Named NFL Rookie of the Year by THE SPORTING NEWS (1996). ... Played in Pro Bowl (1997-2000 seasons).
SINGLE GAME HIGHS (regular season): Attempts—36 (November 19, 2000, vs. Cleveland); yards—216 (August 31, 1997, vs. Oakland); and rushing touchdowns—3 (December 17, 2000, vs. Cleveland).
STATISTICAL PLATEAUS: 100-yard rushing games: 1996 (4), 1997 (8), 1998 (6), 1999 (5), 2000 (6), 2001 (1), 2002 (4), 2003 (2). Total: 36. 100-yard receiving games: 2000 (1). Total: 1.
MISCELLANEOUS: Holds Titans franchise all-time record for most yards rushing (10,009) and most touchdowns (74).

			RUSHING				RECEIVING				TOTALS			
Year Team	G	GS	Att.	Yds.	Avg.	TD	No.	Yds.	Avg.	TD	TD	2pt.	Pts.	Fum.
1996—Houston NFL	16	16	335	1368	4.1	8	23	182	7.9	0	8	0	48	3
1997—Tennessee NFL	16	16	357	1399	3.9	6	7	44	6.3	1	7	1	44	4
1998—Tennessee NFL	16	16	348	1294	3.7	5	37	310	8.4	1	6	1	38	7
1999—Tennessee NFL	16	16	320	1304	4.1	9	47	458	9.7	4	13	0	78	5
2000—Tennessee NFL	16	16	*403	1509	3.7	14	50	453	9.1	2	16	0	96	5
2001—Tennessee NFL	16	16	315	939	3.0	5	37	279	7.5	0	5	0	30	8
2002—Tennessee NFL	16	16	343	1165	3.4	12	36	255	7.1	2	14	1	86	1
2003—Tennessee NFL	16	16	312	1031	3.3	5	22	163	7.4	0	5	0	30	1
Pro totals (8 years)	128	128	2733	10009	3.7	64	259	2144	8.3	10	74	3	450	34

GIBSON, AARON G/T BEARS

PERSONAL: Born September 27, 1977, in Indianapolis, Ind. ... 6-6/375.
HIGH SCHOOL: Decatur Central (Indianapolis).
COLLEGE: Wisconsin.
TRANSACTIONS/CAREER NOTES: Selected by Detroit Lions in first round (27th pick overall) of 1999 NFL draft. ... Signed by Lions (July 24, 1999). ... On injured reserve with shoulder injury (August 31, 1999-entire season). ... On injured reserve with shoulder injury (December 4, 2000-remainder of season). ... Claimed on waivers by Dallas Cowboys (October 31, 2001). ... Released by Cowboys (September 18, 2002). ... Signed by Chicago Bears (November 26, 2002).
PLAYING EXPERIENCE: Detroit NFL, 1999-2001; Dallas NFL, 2001-2002; Chicago NFL, 2003. ... Games/Games started: 2000 (10/10), 2001 (1/0), 2002 (7/5), 2003 (16/16), Total: 34/31.
HONORS: Named offensive tackle on THE SPORTING NEWS college All-America second team (1998).

G

GIBSON, DAVID S

PERSONAL: Born November 5, 1977, in Santa Ana, Calif. ... 6-1/210.
HIGH SCHOOL: Mater Dei (Santa, Ana, Calif.).
COLLEGE: Southern California.
TRANSACTIONS/CAREER NOTES: Selected by Tampa Bay Buccaneers in sixth round (193rd pick overall) of 2000 NFL draft. ... Signed by Buccaneers (July 10, 2000). ... Traded by Buccaneers to Indianapolis Colts for undisclosed draft pick (September 24, 2002). ... Granted free agency (February 28, 2003). ... Re-signed by Colts (May 6, 2003). ... Waived by Colts (August 31, 2003). ... Signed by Tampa Bay Buccaneers (October 29, 2003). ... Granted unconditional free agency (March 3, 2004).

Year Team	G	GS	TOTALS Tk.	Ast.	Sks.	INTERCEPTIONS No.	Yds.	Avg.	TD
2000—Tampa Bay NFL	9	0	2	0	0.0	0	0	0.0	0
2001—Tampa Bay NFL	13	0	4	2	0.0	0	0	0.0	0
2002—Indianapolis NFL	13	9	43	18	1.0	1	0	0.0	0
—Tampa Bay NFL	3	0	0	0	0.0	0	0	0.0	0
2003—Tampa Bay NFL	9	0	7	6	0.0	0	0	0.0	0
Pro totals (4 years)	47	9	56	26	1.0	1	0	0.0	0

GIBSON, DERRICK S RAIDERS

PERSONAL: Born March 22, 1979, in Miami, Fla. ... 6-2/215.
HIGH SCHOOL: Killian (Miami).
COLLEGE: Florida State.
TRANSACTIONS/CAREER NOTES: Selected by Oakland Raiders in first round (28th pick overall) of 2001 NFL draft. ... Signed by Raiders (July 21, 2001).
CHAMPIONSHIP GAME EXPERIENCE: Played in AFC championship game (2002 season). ... Played in Super Bowl 37 (2002 season).

Year Team	G	GS	TOTALS Tk.	Ast.	Sks.	INTERCEPTIONS No.	Yds.	Avg.	TD
2001—Oakland NFL	16	0	10	0	0.0	1	9	9.0	0
2002—Oakland NFL	16	11	50	14	0.0	0	0	0.0	0
2003—Oakland NFL	15	14	54	11	1.0	2	16	8.0	0
Pro totals (3 years)	47	25	114	25	1.0	3	25	8.3	0

GIBSON, OLIVER DT BILLS

PERSONAL: Born March 15, 1972, in Chicago, Ill. ... 6-2/304. ... Full name: Oliver Donnovan Gibson.
HIGH SCHOOL: Romeoville (Ill.).
COLLEGE: Notre Dame.
TRANSACTIONS/CAREER NOTES: Selected by Pittsburgh Steelers in fourth round (120th pick overall) of 1995 NFL draft. ... Signed by Steelers (July 18, 1995). ... Granted free agency (February 13, 1998). ... Re-signed by Steelers (June 9, 1998). ... Granted unconditional free agency (February 12, 1999). ... Signed by Cincinnati Bengals (March 9, 1999). ... On injured reserve with Achilles' injury (November 11, 2002-remainder of season). ... Released by Bengals (March 1, 2004). ... Signed by Buffalo Bills (March 29, 2004).
CHAMPIONSHIP GAME EXPERIENCE: Member of Steelers for AFC championship game (1995 season); inactive. ... Played in AFC championship game (1997 season).
HONORS: Earned first-team All-Independent honors from THE SPORTING NEWS (1994).

Year Team	G	GS	TOTALS Tk.	Ast.	Sks.	INTERCEPTIONS No.	Yds.	Avg.	TD
1995—Pittsburgh NFL	12	0	1	1	0.0	0	0	0.0	0
1996—Pittsburgh NFL	16	0	7	8	2.5	0	0	0.0	0
1997—Pittsburgh NFL	16	0	9	1	1.0	0	0	0.0	0
1998—Pittsburgh NFL	16	0	10	5	2.0	0	0	0.0	0
1999—Cincinnati NFL	16	16	31	10	4.5	0	0	0.0	0
2000—Cincinnati NFL	16	16	43	9	4.0	0	0	0.0	0
2001—Cincinnati NFL	16	16	45	10	3.0	0	0	0.0	0
2002—Cincinnati NFL	9	9	19	10	0.0	1	6	6.0	0
2003—Cincinnati NFL	16	0	17	7	0.5	0	0	0.0	0
Pro totals (9 years)	133	57	182	61	17.5	1	6	6.0	0

GILBERT, SEAN DT

PERSONAL: Born April 10, 1970, in Aliquippa, Pa. ... 6-5/318.
HIGH SCHOOL: Aliquippa (Pa.).
COLLEGE: Pittsburgh.
TRANSACTIONS/CAREER NOTES: Selected after junior season by Los Angeles Rams in first round (third pick overall) of 1992 NFL draft. ... Signed by Rams (July 28, 1992). ... Designated by Rams as transition player (February 25, 1993). ... Rams franchise moved to St. Louis (April 12, 1995). ... Traded by Rams to Washington Redskins for first-round pick (RB Lawrence Phillips) in 1996 draft (April 8, 1996). ... Designated by Redskins as franchise player (February 12, 1997). ... Sat out 1997 season due to contract dispute. ... Designated by Redskins as franchise player (February 11, 1998). ... Tendered offer sheet by Carolina Panthers (March 24, 1998). ... Redskins declined to match offer (April 21, 1998). ... On injured reserve with hip injury (November 21, 2002-remainder of season). ... Released by Panthers (March 10, 2003). ... Signed by Oakland Raiders (October 28, 2003). ... Granted unconditional free agency (March 3, 2004).
HONORS: Played in Pro Bowl (1993 season).

G

Year Team	G	GS	TOTALS Tk.	Ast.	Sks.	INTERCEPTIONS No.	Yds.	Avg.	TD
1992—Los Angeles Rams NFL	16	16	46	8	5.0	0	0	0.0	0
1993—Los Angeles Rams NFL	16	16	54	27	10.5	0	0	0.0	0
1994—Los Angeles Rams NFL	14	14	36	11	3.0	0	0	0.0	0
1995—St. Louis NFL	14	14	24	9	5.5	0	0	0.0	0
1996—Washington NFL	16	16	55	13	3.0	0	0	0.0	0
1997—Washington NFL				Did not play.					
1998—Carolina NFL	16	16	39	14	6.0	0	0	0.0	0
1999—Carolina NFL	16	16	36	11	2.5	1	4	4.0	0
2000—Carolina NFL	15	15	38	15	4.0	1	0	0.0	0
2001—Carolina NFL	9	9	23	2	2.0	0	0	0.0	0
2002—Carolina NFL	8	0	5	0	1.0	0	0	0.0	0
2003—Oakland NFL	6	0	4	3	0.0	0	0	0.0	0
Pro totals (11 years)	146	132	360	113	42.5	2	4	2.0	0

GILBERT, TONY — LB — JAGUARS

PERSONAL: Born October 16, 1979, in Macon, Ga. ... 6-1/257. ... Full name: Antonio C. Gilbert.
HIGH SCHOOL: Central (Macon, Ga.).
COLLEGE: Georgia.
TRANSACTIONS/CAREER NOTES: Selected by Arizona Cardinals in sixth round (210th pick overall) of 2003 NFL draft. ... Signed by Cardinals (June 2, 2003). ... Released by Cardinals (August 31, 2003). ... Re-signed by Cardinals to practice squad (September 1, 2003). ... Signed by Jacksonville Jaguars off Cardinals practice squad (October 29, 2003).

			TOTALS			INTERCEPTIONS			
Year Team	G	GS	Tk.	Ast.	Sks.	No.	Yds.	Avg.	TD
2003—Jacksonville NFL	8	0	0	0	0.0	0	0	0.0	0

GILDON, JASON — LB — STEELERS

PERSONAL: Born July 31, 1972, in Altus, Okla. ... 6-4/255. ... Full name: Jason Larue Gildon.
HIGH SCHOOL: Altus (Okla.).
COLLEGE: Oklahoma State.
TRANSACTIONS/CAREER NOTES: Selected by Pittsburgh Steelers in third round (88th pick overall) of 1994 NFL draft. ... Signed by Steelers (July 15, 1994). ... Granted free agency (February 14, 1997). ... Re-signed by Steelers (July 21, 1997). ... Granted unconditional free agency (February 13, 1998). ... Re-signed by Steelers (April 7, 1998). ... Designated by Steelers as franchise player (February 21, 2002). ... Re-signed by Steelers (February 25, 2002).
CHAMPIONSHIP GAME EXPERIENCE: Played in AFC championship game (1994, 1995, 1997 and 2001 seasons). ... Played in Super Bowl 30 (1995 season).
HONORS: Played in Pro Bowl (2000-2002 seasons).
MISCELLANEOUS: Holds Pittsburgh Steelers all-time record for most sacks (77).

			TOTALS			INTERCEPTIONS			
Year Team	G	GS	Tk.	Ast.	Sks.	No.	Yds.	Avg.	TD
1994—Pittsburgh NFL	16	1	4	0	2.0	0	0	0.0	0
1995—Pittsburgh NFL	16	0	8	4	3.0	0	0	0.0	0
1996—Pittsburgh NFL	14	13	47	12	7.0	0	0	0.0	0
1997—Pittsburgh NFL	16	16	41	12	5.0	0	0	0.0	0
1998—Pittsburgh NFL	16	16	42	12	11.0	0	0	0.0	0
1999—Pittsburgh NFL	16	16	42	15	8.5	0	0	0.0	0
2000—Pittsburgh NFL	16	16	58	19	13.5	0	0	0.0	0
2001—Pittsburgh NFL	16	16	43	13	12.0	1	0	0.0	0
2002—Pittsburgh NFL	16	16	45	22	9.0	0	0	0.0	0
2003—Pittsburgh NFL	16	16	42	19	6.0	1	1	1.0	0
Pro totals (10 years)	158	126	372	128	77.0	2	1	0.5	0

GILLIAM, DONDRE — WR

PERSONAL: Born February 9, 1977, in Baltimore, Md. ... 6-0/185.
HIGH SCHOOL: Aberdeen (Md.).
COLLEGE: Millersville (Pa.).
TRANSACTIONS/CAREER NOTES: Signed as non-drafted free agent by San Diego Chargers (April 24, 2001). ... On injured reserve with hip injury (August 28-September 8, 2001). ... Assigned by Chargers to Scottish Claymores in 2002 NFL Europe enhancement allocation program (February 12, 2002). ... Released by Chargers (September 1, 2002). ... Re-signed by Chargers to practice squad (September 3, 2002). ... Activated (November 14, 2002). ... Released by Chargers (November 19, 2002). ... Re-signed by Chargers to practice squad (November 21, 2002). ... Activated (December 21, 2002). ... Re-signed by Chargers (April 4, 2003). ... Waived by Chargers (August 26, 2003). ... Re-signed by Chargers (September 24, 2003). ... Waived by Chargers (October 21, 2003). ... Re-signed by Chargers to practice squad (October 23, 2003). ... Waived by Chargers (November 11, 2003). ... Re-signed by Chargers to practice squad (November 26, 2003). ... Activated (December 20, 2003). ... Released by Chargers (March 2, 2004).
SINGLE GAME HIGHS (regular season): Receptions—4 (September 28, 2003, vs. Oakland); yards—67 (September 28, 2003, vs. Oakland); and touchdown receptions—0.

			RECEIVING				KICKOFF RETURNS				TOTALS			
Year Team	G	GS	No.	Yds.	Avg.	TD	No.	Yds.	Avg.	TD	TD	2pt.	Pts.	Fum.
2002—San Diego NFL	2	0	0	0	0.0	0	0	0	0.0	0	0	0	0	0
2003—San Diego NFL	5	1	6	95	15.8	0	0	0	0.0	0	0	0	0	0
Pro totals (2 years)	7	1	6	95	15.8	0	0	0	0.0	0	0	0	0	0

GILMORE, BRYAN — WR — CARDINALS

PERSONAL: Born July 21, 1978, in Lufkin, Texas. ... 6-0/200.
HIGH SCHOOL: Lufkin (Texas).
COLLEGE: Midwestern State.
TRANSACTIONS/CAREER NOTES: Signed as non-drafted free agent by Arizona Cardinals (April 17, 2000). ... Released by Cardinals (August 27, 2000). ... Re-signed by Cardinals to practice squad (August 28, 2000). ... Activated (December 15, 2000). ... Assigned by Cardinals to Barcelona Dragons in 2001 NFL Europe enhancement allocation program (February 19, 2001). ... Released by Cardinals (September 2, 2001). ... Re-signed by Cardinals to practice squad (September 3, 2001). ... Activated (November 29, 2001). ... On injured reserve with ankle injury (October 30, 2002-remainder of season).
SINGLE GAME HIGHS (regular season): Receptions—3 (November 23, 2003, vs. St. Louis); yards—50 (November 23, 2003, vs. St. Louis); and touchdown receptions—1 (October 12, 2003, vs. Baltimore).

			RECEIVING				TOTALS			
Year Team	G	GS	No.	Yds.	Avg.	TD	TD	2pt.	Pts.	Fum.
2000—Arizona NFL	1	0	0	0	0.0	0	0	0	0	0

G

Year	Team	G	GS	RECEIVING No.	Yds.	Avg.	TD	TOTALS TD	2pt.	Pts.	Fum.
2001—Arizona NFL		2	0	0	0	0.0	0	0	0	0	0
2002—Arizona NFL		7	0	1	14	14.0	0	0	0	0	0
2003—Arizona NFL		14	10	17	208	12.2	2	2	0	12	0
Pro totals (4 years)		24	10	18	222	12.3	2	2	0	12	0

GILMORE, JOHN — TE — BEARS

PERSONAL: Born September 21, 1979, in Marquette, Mich. ... 6-4/260. ... Full name: John Henry Gilmore.

HIGH SCHOOL: Wilson (West Lawn, Pa.).

COLLEGE: Penn State.

TRANSACTIONS/CAREER NOTES: Selected by New Orleans Saints in sixth round (196th pick overall) of 2002 NFL draft. ... Signed by Saints (July 22, 2002). ... Released by Saints (September 1, 2002). ... Signed by Chicago Bears to practice squad (September 3, 2002). ... Activated (October 25, 2002).

SINGLE GAME HIGHS (regular season): Receptions—3 (December 15, 2002, vs. New York Jets); yards—32 (December 22, 2002, vs. Carolina); and touchdown receptions—0.

Year Team	G	GS	RECEIVING No.	Yds.	Avg.	TD	KICKOFF RETURNS No.	Yds.	Avg.	TD	TOTALS TD	2pt.	Pts.	Fum.
2002—Chicago NFL	8	4	10	130	13.0	0	0	0	0.0	0	0	0	0	0
2003—Chicago NFL	15	1	0	0	0.0	0	3	25	8.3	0	0	0	0	0
Pro totals (2 years)	23	5	10	130	13.0	0	3	25	8.3	0	0	0	0	0

GIVENS, DAVID — WR — PATRIOTS

PERSONAL: Born August 16, 1980, in Youngstown, Ohio. ... 6-0/212. ... Full name: David Lamar Givens.

HIGH SCHOOL: Humble (Texas).

COLLEGE: Notre Dame.

TRANSACTIONS/CAREER NOTES: Selected by New England Patriots in seventh round (253rd pick overall) of 2002 NFL draft. ... Signed by Patriots (July 21, 2002).

CHAMPIONSHIP GAME EXPERIENCE: Played in AFC championship game (2003 season). ... Member of Super Bowl championship team (2003 season).

SINGLE GAME HIGHS (regular season): Receptions—7 (December 27, 2003, vs. Buffalo); yards—87 (November 3, 2003, vs. Denver); and touchdown receptions—2 (December 20, 2003, vs. New York Jets).

Year Team	G	GS	RUSHING Att.	Yds.	Avg.	TD	RECEIVING No.	Yds.	Avg.	TD	KICKOFF RETURNS No.	Yds.	Avg.	TD	TOTALS TD	2pt.	Pts.	Fum.
2002—New England NFL	12	0	0	0	0.0	0	9	92	10.2	1	0	0	0.0	0	1	0	6	1
2003—New England NFL	13	5	0	0	0.0	0	34	510	15.0	6	2	31	15.5	0	6	0	36	0
Pro totals (2 years)	25	5	0	0	0.0	0	43	602	14.0	7	2	31	15.5	0	7	0	42	1

GLEASON, STEVE — S — SAINTS

PERSONAL: Born March 19, 1977, in Spokane, Wash. ... 5-11/215. ... Full name: Stephen Gleason.

HIGH SCHOOL: Gonzaga (Wash.) Prep.

COLLEGE: Washington State.

TRANSACTIONS/CAREER NOTES: Signed as non-drafted free agent by Indianapolis Colts (April 16, 2000). ... Released by Colts (August 27, 2000). ... Signed by New Orleans Saints to practice squad (November 21, 2000). ... Activated (December 3, 2000). ... Released by Saints (September 2, 2001). ... Re-signed by Saints (November 23, 2001). ... Granted free agency (March 3, 2004). ... Re-signed by Saints (May 5, 2004).

Year Team	G	GS	TOTALS Tk.	Ast.	Sks.	INTERCEPTIONS No.	Yds.	Avg.	TD
2000—New Orleans NFL	3	0	0	0	0.0	0	0	0.0	0
2001—New Orleans NFL	7	0	0	0	0.0	0	0	0.0	0
2002—New Orleans NFL	14	0	1	1	0.0	0	0	0.0	0
2003—New Orleans NFL	16	0	0	0	0.0	0	0	0.0	0
Pro totals (4 years)	40	0	1	1	0.0	0	0	0.0	0

GLENN, AARON — CB — TEXANS

G

PERSONAL: Born July 16, 1972, in Humble, Texas. ... 5-9/185. ... Full name: Aaron DeVon Glenn.

HIGH SCHOOL: Nimitz (Irving, Texas).

JUNIOR COLLEGE: Navarro College (Texas).

COLLEGE: Texas A&M.

TRANSACTIONS/CAREER NOTES: Selected by New York Jets in first round (12th pick overall) of 1994 NFL draft. ... Signed by Jets (July 21, 1994). ... Selected by Houston Texans from Jets in NFL expansion draft (February 18, 2002). ... On injured reserve with groin injury (December 10, 2003-remainder of season).

CHAMPIONSHIP GAME EXPERIENCE: Played in AFC championship game (1998 season).

HONORS: Named defensive back on THE SPORTING NEWS college All-America first team (1993). ... Played in Pro Bowl (1997 and 2002 seasons). ... Named to play in Pro Bowl (1998 season); replaced by Charles Woodson due to injury. ... Named cornerback on the THE SPORTING NEWS NFL All-Pro team (2002).

Year Team	G	GS	TOTALS Tk.	Ast.	Sks.	INTERCEPTIONS No.	Yds.	Avg.	TD	KICKOFF RETURNS No.	Yds.	Avg.	TD	TOTALS TD	2pt.	Pts.	Fum.
1994—New York Jets NFL	15	15	58	9	0.0	0	0	0.0	0	27	582	21.6	0	0	0	0	2
1995—New York Jets NFL	16	16	42	10	0.0	1	17	17.0	0	1	12	12.0	0	0	0	0	0

Year Team	G	GS	TOTALS Tk.	Ast.	Sks.	INTERCEPTIONS No.	Yds.	Avg.	TD	KICKOFF RETURNS No.	Yds.	Avg.	TD	TOTALS TD	2pt.	Pts.	Fum.
1996—New York Jets NFL	16	16	38	6	0.0	4	113	28.2	†2	1	6	6.0	0	2	0	12	0
1997—New York Jets NFL	16	16	54	11	0.0	1	5	5.0	0	28	741	§26.5	▲1	1	0	6	1
1998—New York Jets NFL	13	13	47	1	0.0	6	23	3.8	0	24	585	24.4	0	1	0	6	1
1999—New York Jets NFL	16	16	46	5	0.0	3	20	6.7	0	27	601	22.3	0	0	0	0	0
2000—New York Jets NFL	16	16	28	9	0.0	4	34	8.5	0	3	51	17.0	0	0	0	0	0
2001—New York Jets NFL	13	12	28	5	0.0	5	82	16.4	1	0	0	0.0	0	1	0	6	1
2002—Houston NFL	16	16	56	11	1.0	5	181	36.2	▲2	0	0	0.0	0	2	0	12	0
2003—Houston NFL	11	11	29	6	0.0	1	0	0.0	0	0	0	0.0	0	0	0	0	0
Pro totals (10 years)	148	147	426	73	1.0	30	475	15.8	5	111	2578	23.2	1	7	0	42	5

GLENN, JASON — LB — JETS

PERSONAL: Born August 20, 1979, in Aldine, Texas. ... 6-0/231.
HIGH SCHOOL: Nimitz (Aldine, Texas).
COLLEGE: Texas A&M.
TRANSACTIONS/CAREER NOTES: Selected by Detroit Lions in sixth round (173rd pick overall) of 2001 NFL draft. ... Signed by Lions (July 20, 2001). ... Claimed on waivers by New York Jets (September 3, 2001). ... Granted free agency (March 3, 2004). ... Re-signed by Jets (May 5, 2004).

Year Team	G	GS	TOTALS Tk.	Ast.	Sks.	INTERCEPTIONS No.	Yds.	Avg.	TD
2001—New York Jets NFL	15	0	0	0	0.0	0	0	0.0	0
2002—New York Jets NFL	16	0	0	0	0.0	0	0	0.0	0
2003—New York Jets NFL	14	1	29	11	0.0	0	0	0.0	0
Pro totals (3 years)	45	1	29	11	0.0	0	0	0.0	0

GLENN, TARIK — T — COLTS

PERSONAL: Born May 25, 1976, in Cleveland, Ohio. ... 6-5/332.
HIGH SCHOOL: Bishop O'Dowd (Oakland).
COLLEGE: California.
TRANSACTIONS/CAREER NOTES: Selected by Indianapolis Colts in first round (19th pick overall) of 1997 NFL draft. ... Signed by Colts (August 11, 1997). ... Granted free agency (March 1, 2002). ... Re-signed by Colts (March 15, 2002).
PLAYING EXPERIENCE: Indianapolis NFL, 1997-2003. ... Games/Games started: 1997 (16/16), 1998 (16/16), 1999 (16/16), 2000 (16/16), 2001 (16/16), 2002 (16/16), 2003 (10/10). Total: 106/106.
CHAMPIONSHIP GAME EXPERIENCE: Played in AFC championship game (2003 season).
HONORS: Named offensive tackle on THE SPORTING NEWS college All-America second team (1996).

GLENN, TERRY — WR — COWBOYS

PERSONAL: Born July 23, 1974, in Columbus, Ohio. ... 5-11/195.
HIGH SCHOOL: Brookhaven (Columbus, Ohio).
COLLEGE: Ohio State.
TRANSACTIONS/CAREER NOTES: Selected after junior season by New England Patriots in first round (seventh pick overall) of 1996 NFL draft. ... Signed by Patriots (July 12, 1996). ... On injured reserve with fractured ankle (December 18, 1998-remainder of season). ... On suspended list for violating league substance abuse policy (Sepetmber 9-October 7, 2001). ... On reserve/left squad list (August 15-September 13, 2001). ... Traded by Patriots to Green Bay Packers for fourth-round pick (DE Jarvis Green) in 2002 draft and conditional pick in 2003 draft (March 8, 2002). ... Traded by Packers to Dallas Cowboys for undisclosed draft pick (February 28, 2003).
CHAMPIONSHIP GAME EXPERIENCE: Played in AFC championship game (1996 season). ... Played in Super Bowl 31 (1996 season).
HONORS: Fred Biletnikoff Award winner (1995). ... Named wide receiver on THE SPORTING NEWS college All-America first team (1995).
SINGLE GAME HIGHS (regular season): Receptions—13 (October 3, 1999, vs. Cleveland); yards—214 (October 3, 1999, vs. Cleveland); and touchdown receptions—3 (October 19, 2003, vs. Detroit).
STATISTICAL PLATEAUS: 100-yard receiving games: 1996 (2), 1997 (1), 1998 (4), 1999 (4), 2000 (1), 2001 (1), 2002 (1), 2003 (2). Total: 16.

Year Team	G	GS	RUSHING Att.	Yds.	Avg.	TD	RECEIVING No.	Yds.	Avg.	TD	TOTALS TD	2pt.	Pts.	Fum.
1996—New England NFL	15	15	5	42	8.4	0	90	1132	12.6	6	6	0	36	1
1997—New England NFL	9	9	0	0	0.0	0	27	431	16.0	2	2	0	12	1
1998—New England NFL	10	9	2	-1	-0.5	0	50	792	15.8	3	3	0	18	0
1999—New England NFL	14	13	0	0	0.0	0	69	1147	16.6	4	4	0	24	2
2000—New England NFL	16	15	4	39	9.8	0	79	963	12.2	6	6	0	36	0
2001—New England NFL	4	1	0	0	0.0	0	14	204	14.6	1	1	0	6	0
2002—Green Bay NFL	15	14	0	0	0.0	0	56	817	14.6	2	2	0	12	1
2003—Dallas NFL	16	14	3	55	18.3	0	52	754	14.5	5	5	0	30	2
Pro totals (8 years)	99	90	14	135	9.6	0	437	6240	14.3	29	29	0	174	7

G

GLOVER, LA'ROI — DT — COWBOYS

PERSONAL: Born July 4, 1974, in San Diego, Calif. ... 6-2/285. ... Full name: La'Roi Damon Glover. ... Name pronounced: la-ROY.
HIGH SCHOOL: Point Loma (San Diego).
COLLEGE: San Diego State.
TRANSACTIONS/CAREER NOTES: Selected by Oakland Raiders in fifth round (166th pick overall) of 1996 NFL draft. ... Signed by Raiders (July 12, 1996). ... Assigned by Raiders to Barcelona Dragons in 1997 World League enhancement allocation program (February 19, 1997). ... Claimed on waivers by New Orleans Saints (August 25, 1997). ... Granted unconditional free agency (March 1, 2002). ... Signed by Dallas Cowboys (March 12, 2002).

HONORS: Named defensive tackle on THE SPORTING NEWS NFL All-Pro team (2000 and 2002). ... Played in Pro Bowl (2000-2003 seasons).

			TOTALS			INTERCEPTIONS			
Year Team	G	GS	Tk.	Ast.	Sks.	No.	Yds.	Avg.	TD
1996—Oakland NFL	2	0	2	0	0.0	0	0	0.0	0
1997—New Orleans NFL	15	2	24	9	6.5	0	0	0.0	0
1998—New Orleans NFL	16	15	59	8	10.0	1	0	0.0	0
1999—New Orleans NFL	16	16	46	16	8.5	0	0	0.0	0
2000—New Orleans NFL	16	16	53	14	*17.0	0	0	0.0	0
2001—New Orleans NFL	16	16	36	11	8.0	0	0	0.0	0
2002—Dallas NFL	16	16	39	11	6.5	1	7	7.0	0
2003—Dallas NFL	16	16	33	16	5.0	0	0	0.0	0
Pro totals (8 years)	113	97	292	85	61.5	2	7	3.5	0

GODFREY, RANDALL — LB — CHARGERS

PERSONAL: Born April 6, 1973, in Valdosta, Ga. ... 6-2/245. ... Full name: Randall Euralentris Godfrey.
HIGH SCHOOL: Lowndes County (Valdosta, Ga.).
COLLEGE: Georgia.
TRANSACTIONS/CAREER NOTES: Selected by Dallas Cowboys in second round (49th pick overall) of 1996 NFL draft. ... Signed by Cowboys (July 17, 1996). ... Granted free agency (February 12, 1999). ... Re-signed by Cowboys (June 25, 1999). ... Granted unconditional free agency (February 11, 2000). ... Signed by Tennessee Titans (February 16, 2000). ... Released by Titans (June 18, 2003). ... Signed by Seattle Seahawks (June 23, 2003). ... Granted unconditional free agency (March 3, 2004). ... Signed by San Diego Chargers (March 9, 2004).
CHAMPIONSHIP GAME EXPERIENCE: Played in AFC championship game (2002 season).

			TOTALS			INTERCEPTIONS			
Year Team	G	GS	Tk.	Ast.	Sks.	No.	Yds.	Avg.	TD
1996—Dallas NFL	16	6	25	3	0.0	0	0	0.0	0
1997—Dallas NFL	16	16	66	31	1.0	0	0	0.0	0
1998—Dallas NFL	16	16	70	16	3.0	1	0	0.0	0
1999—Dallas NFL	16	16	81	15	1.0	1	10	10.0	0
2000—Tennessee NFL	16	16	98	23	3.0	2	25	12.5	1
2001—Tennessee NFL	14	14	62	16	1.0	1	5	5.0	0
2002—Tennessee NFL	8	5	25	7	1.0	0	0	0.0	0
2003—Seattle NFL	15	14	45	14	0.0	1	7	7.0	0
Pro totals (8 years)	117	103	472	125	10.0	6	47	7.8	1

GOFF, MIKE — G — CHARGERS

PERSONAL: Born January 6, 1976, in Spring Valley, Ill. ... 6-5/306. ... Full name: Michael J. Goff.
HIGH SCHOOL: Lasalle-Peru (Peru, Ill.).
COLLEGE: Iowa.
TRANSACTIONS/CAREER NOTES: Selected by Cincinnati Bengals in third round (78th pick overall) of 1998 NFL draft. ... Signed by Bengals (July 20, 1998). ... Granted unconditional free agency (March 3, 2004). ... Signed by San Diego Chargers (March 5, 2004).
PLAYING EXPERIENCE: Cincinnati NFL, 1998-2003. ... Games/Games started: 1998 (10/5), 1999 (14/1), 2000 (16/16), 2001 (16/16), 2002 (13/13), 2003 (16/16). Total: 85/67.

GOINGS, NICK — RB — PANTHERS

PERSONAL: Born January 26, 1978, in Columbus, Ohio. ... 6-0/225. ... Full name: Nick Aaron Goings.
HIGH SCHOOL: Dublin Scioto (Ohio).
COLLEGE: Pittsburgh.
TRANSACTIONS/CAREER NOTES: Signed as non-drafted free agent by Carolina Panthers (April 23, 2001). ... Granted free agency (March 3, 2004). ... Re-signed by Panthers (April 8, 2004).
CHAMPIONSHIP GAME EXPERIENCE: Played in NFC championship game (2003 season). ... Played in Super Bowl 38 (2003 season).
SINGLE GAME HIGHS (regular season): Attempts—25 (September 9, 2001, vs. Minnesota); yards—86 (September 9, 2001, vs. Minnesota); and rushing touchdowns—0.

G

			RUSHING				RECEIVING				TOTALS			
Year Team	G	GS	Att.	Yds.	Avg.	TD	No.	Yds.	Avg.	TD	TD	2pt.	Pts.	Fum.
2001—Carolina NFL	13	2	66	197	3.0	0	8	39	4.9	0	0	0	0	1
2002—Carolina NFL	14	2	50	188	3.8	0	18	91	5.1	0	0	1	2	2
2003—Carolina NFL	15	0	10	69	6.9	0	12	97	8.1	1	1	0	6	0
Pro totals (3 years)	42	4	126	454	3.6	0	38	227	6.0	1	1	1	8	3

GOLD, IAN — LB — BUCCANEERS

PERSONAL: Born August 23, 1978, in Ann Arbor, Mich. ... 6-0/223. ... Full name: Ian Maurice Gold.
HIGH SCHOOL: Belleville (Mich.).
COLLEGE: Michigan.
TRANSACTIONS/CAREER NOTES: Selected by Denver Broncos in second round (40th pick overall) of 2000 NFL draft. ... Signed by Broncos (July 23, 2000). ... On injured reserve with knee injury (October 14, 2003-remainder of season). ... Granted unconditional free agency (March 3, 2004). ... Signed by Tampa Bay Buccaneers (April 28, 2004).
HONORS: Played in Pro Bowl (2001 season).

Year Team	G	GS	TOTALS Tk.	Ast.	Sks.	INTERCEPTIONS No.	Yds.	Avg.	TD
2000—Denver NFL	16	0	16	3	2.0	0	0	0.0	0
2001—Denver NFL	16	0	21	3	3.0	0	0	0.0	0
2002—Denver NFL	16	16	85	14	6.5	0	0	0.0	0
2003—Denver NFL	6	6	26	1	0.0	2	14	7.0	1
Pro totals (4 years)	54	22	148	21	11.5	2	14	7.0	1

GOLDEN, JACK LB

PERSONAL: Born January 28, 1977, in Harvey, Ill. ... 6-1/240.
HIGH SCHOOL: Thornton (Harvey, Ill.).
COLLEGE: Oklahoma State.
TRANSACTIONS/CAREER NOTES: Signed as non-drafted free agent by New York Giants (April 20, 2000). ... Claimed on waivers by Tampa Bay Buccaneers (April 4, 2002). ... Released by Buccaneers (September 4, 2002). ... Re-signed by Buccaneers (September 25, 2002). ... Granted free agency (February 28, 2003). ... Re-signed by Buccaneers (May 12, 2003). ... Released by Buccaneers (October 7, 2003).
CHAMPIONSHIP GAME EXPERIENCE: Played in NFC championship game (2000 and 2002 seasons). ... Played in Super Bowl 35 (2000 season). ... Member of Super Bowl championship team (2002 season).

Year Team	G	GS	TOTALS Tk.	Ast.	Sks.	INTERCEPTIONS No.	Yds.	Avg.	TD
2000—New York Giants NFL	16	0	0	0	0.0	0	0	0.0	0
2001—New York Giants NFL	16	0	0	0	0.0	0	0	0.0	0
2002—Tampa Bay NFL	13	0	0	0	0.0	0	0	0.0	0
2003—Tampa Bay NFL	4	0	1	0	0.0	0	0	0.0	0
Pro totals (4 years)	49	0	1	0	0.0	0	0	0.0	0

GONZALEZ, JOAQUIN T BROWNS

PERSONAL: Born September 7, 1979, in Miami, Fla. ... 6-5/310. ... Full name: Joaquin Antonio Gonzalez.
HIGH SCHOOL: Columbus (Miami).
COLLEGE: Miami (Fla.).
TRANSACTIONS/CAREER NOTES: Selected by Cleveland Browns in seventh round (227th pick overall) of 2002 NFL draft. ... Signed by Browns (July 16, 2002).
PLAYING EXPERIENCE: Cleveland NFL, 2002-2003. ... Games/Games started: 2002 (9/0), 2003 (16/3). Total: 25/3.
HONORS: Named offensive tackle on THE SPORTING NEWS college All-America second team (2001).

GONZALEZ, TONY TE CHIEFS

PERSONAL: Born February 27, 1976, in Torrance, Calif. ... 6-4/248. ... Full name: Anthony Gonzalez.
HIGH SCHOOL: Huntington Beach (Calif.).
COLLEGE: California.
TRANSACTIONS/CAREER NOTES: Selected by Kansas City Chiefs in first round (13th pick overall) of 1997 NFL draft. ... Signed by Chiefs (July 29, 1997). ... Designated by Chiefs as franchise player (February 21, 2002). ... Re-signed by Chiefs (August 30, 2002).
HONORS: Named tight end on THE SPORTING NEWS college All-America first team (1996). ... Named tight end on THE SPORTING NEWS NFL All-Pro team (1999-2003). ... Played in Pro Bowl (1999-2000 and 2002-2003 seasons). ... Named to play in Pro Bowl (2001 season); replaced by Ken Dilger due to injury.
SINGLE GAME HIGHS (regular season): Receptions—11 (December 4, 2000, vs. New England); yards—147 (December 4, 2000, vs. New England); and touchdown receptions—3 (September 29, 2002, vs. Miami).
STATISTICAL PLATEAUS: 100-yard receiving games: 2000 (6), 2001 (1), 2002 (1), 2003 (1). Total: 9.

Year Team	G	GS	RECEIVING No.	Yds.	Avg.	TD	TOTALS TD	2pt.	Pts.	Fum.
1997—Kansas City NFL	16	0	33	368	11.2	2	2	1	14	0
1998—Kansas City NFL	16	16	59	621	10.5	2	2	0	12	3
1999—Kansas City NFL	15	15	76	849	11.2	11	11	0	66	2
2000—Kansas City NFL	16	16	93	1203	12.9	9	9	0	54	0
2001—Kansas City NFL	16	16	73	917	12.6	6	6	1	38	0
2002—Kansas City NFL	16	16	63	773	12.3	7	7	0	42	0
2003—Kansas City NFL	16	16	71	916	12.9	10	10	0	60	0
Pro totals (7 years)	111	95	468	5647	12.1	47	47	2	286	5

GOOCH, JEFF LB BUCCANEERS

G

PERSONAL: Born October 31, 1974, in Nashville, Tenn. ... 5-11/226. ... Full name: Jeffery Lance Gooch.
HIGH SCHOOL: Overton (Nashville).
COLLEGE: Austin Peay.
TRANSACTIONS/CAREER NOTES: Signed as non-drafted free agent by Tampa Bay Buccaneers (April 23, 1996). ... On injured reserve with knee injury (December 17, 1996-remainder of season). ... Granted free agency (February 12, 1999). ... Re-signed by Buccaneers (April 13, 1999). ... Traded by Buccaneers to St. Louis Rams for fifth-round pick in 2001 draft (March 19, 2001); traded voided because Gooch failed physical (March 23, 2001). ... Released by Buccaneers (February 26, 2002). ... Signed by Detroit Lions (April 16, 2002). ... Granted unconditional free agency (March 3, 2004). ... Signed by Tampa Bay Buccaneers (March 10, 2004).
CHAMPIONSHIP GAME EXPERIENCE: Played in NFC championship game (1999 season).

Year Team	G	GS	TOTALS Tk.	Ast.	Sks.	INTERCEPTIONS No.	Yds.	Avg.	TD
1996—Tampa Bay NFL	15	0	4	2	0.0	0	0	0.0	0
1997—Tampa Bay NFL	14	5	18	8	0.0	0	0	0.0	0

Year Team	G	GS	TOTALS Tk.	Ast.	Sks.	INTERCEPTIONS No.	Yds.	Avg.	TD
1998—Tampa Bay NFL	16	16	35	18	1.0	0	0	0.0	0
1999—Tampa Bay NFL	15	0	3	1	0.0	0	0	0.0	0
2000—Tampa Bay NFL	16	0	6	1	0.0	0	0	0.0	0
2001—Tampa Bay NFL	13	0	6	5	0.5	0	0	0.0	0
2002—Detroit NFL	16	2	24	9	0.0	1	3	3.0	0
2003—Detroit NFL	16	0	11	3	0.0	0	0	0.0	0
Pro totals (8 years)	121	23	107	47	1.5	1	3	3.0	0

GOODMAN, ANDRE' CB LIONS

PERSONAL: Born August 11, 1978, in Greenville, S.C. ... 5-10/185.
HIGH SCHOOL: Eastwood (Greenville, S.C.).
COLLEGE: South Carolina.
TRANSACTIONS/CAREER NOTES: Selected by Detroit Lions in third round (68th pick overall) of 2002 NFL draft. ... Signed by Lions (July 16, 2002). ... On injured reserve with shoulder injury (September 25, 2003-remainder of season).

Year Team	G	GS	TOTALS Tk.	Ast.	Sks.	INTERCEPTIONS No.	Yds.	Avg.	TD
2002—Detroit NFL	14	6	34	8	0.0	1	2	2.0	0
2003—Detroit NFL	3	3	11	0	0.0	0	0	0.0	0
Pro totals (2 years)	17	9	45	8	0.0	1	2	2.0	0

GOODSPEED, JOEY FB RAMS

PERSONAL: Born February 22, 1978, in Berwyn, Ill. ... 6-1/247. ... Full name: Joey Allen Goodspeed.
HIGH SCHOOL: Oswego (Ill.).
COLLEGE: Notre Dame.
TRANSACTIONS/CAREER NOTES: Signed as non-drafted free agent by Pittsburgh Steelers (April 18, 2000). ... Released by Steelers (August 21, 2000). ... Re-signed by Steelers to practice squad (October 18, 2000). ... Granted free agency following 2000 season. ... Signed by New Orleans Saints (February 10, 2001). ... Released by Saints (September 1, 2001). ... Signed by San Diego Chargers (February 14, 2002). ... Re-signed by Chargers (April 4, 2003). ... Waived by Chargers (August 31, 2003). ... Signed by St. Louis Rams (October 28, 2003). ... Released by Rams (November 7, 2003). ... Re-signed by Rams (November 11, 2003).

Year Team	G	GS	RUSHING Att.	Yds.	Avg.	TD	TOTALS TD	2pt.	Pts.	Fum.
2002—San Diego NFL	12	0	0	0	0.0	0	0	0	0	0
2003—St. Louis NFL	8	4	0	0	0.0	0	0	0	0	0
Pro totals (2 years)	20	4	0	0	0.0	0	0	0	0	0

GOODWIN, HUNTER TE FALCONS

PERSONAL: Born October 10, 1972, in Bellville, Texas. ... 6-5/268. ... Full name: Robert Hunter Goodwin.
HIGH SCHOOL: Bellville (Texas).
COLLEGE: Texas A&M.
TRANSACTIONS/CAREER NOTES: Selected by Minnesota Vikings in fourth round (97th pick overall) of 1996 NFL draft. ... Signed by Vikings (July 20, 1996). ... Granted free agency (February 12, 1999). ... Tendered offer sheet by Miami Dolphins (April 8, 1999). ... Vikings declined to match offer (April 9, 1999). ... Released by Dolphins (March 14, 2001). ... Re-signed by Dolphins (March 16, 2001). ... Released by Dolphins (February 21, 2002). ... Signed by Vikings (April 23, 2002). ... Granted unconditional free agency (February 28, 2003). ... Re-signed by Vikings (April 2, 2003). ... Released by Vikings (March 23, 2004). ... Signed by Atlanta Falcons (March 25, 2004).
CHAMPIONSHIP GAME EXPERIENCE: Played in NFC championship game (1998 season).
SINGLE GAME HIGHS (regular season): Receptions—3 (December 27, 1999, vs. New York Jets); yards—24 (December 1, 1996, vs. Arizona); and touchdown receptions—1 (December 1, 2002, vs. Atlanta).

Year Team	G	GS	RECEIVING No.	Yds.	Avg.	TD	TOTALS TD	2pt.	Pts.	Fum.
1996—Minnesota NFL	9	6	1	24	24.0	0	0	0	0	0
1997—Minnesota NFL	16	5	7	61	8.7	0	0	0	0	0
1998—Minnesota NFL	15	0	3	16	5.3	0	0	0	0	0
1999—Miami NFL	15	5	8	55	6.9	0	0	0	0	1
2000—Miami NFL	16	16	6	36	6.0	1	1	0	6	0
2001—Miami NFL	16	11	4	27	6.8	0	0	0	0	0
2002—Minnesota NFL	16	6	4	20	5.0	1	1	0	6	0
2003—Minnesota NFL	16	5	4	26	6.5	0	0	1	2	0
Pro totals (8 years)	119	54	37	265	7.2	2	2	1	14	1

G

GOODWIN, JONATHAN G JETS

PERSONAL: Born December 2, 1978, in Columbia, S.C. ... 6-3/318. ... Full name: Jonathan Scott Goodwin.
HIGH SCHOOL: Lower Richland (S.C.).
COLLEGE: Michigan.
TRANSACTIONS/CAREER NOTES: Selected by New York Jets in fifth round (154th pick overall) of 2002 NFL draft. ... Signed by Jets (July 24, 2002).
PLAYING EXPERIENCE: New York Jets NFL, 2002-2003. ... Games/Games started: 2002 (12/0), 2003 (15/0). Total: 27/0.
HONORS: Named guard on THE SPORTING NEWS college All-America third team (2001).

GORDON, LAMAR — RB — RAMS

PERSONAL: Born January 7, 1980, in Milwaukee, Wis. ... 6-1/228.

HIGH SCHOOL: Cudahy (Milwaukee).

COLLEGE: North Dakota State.

TRANSACTIONS/CAREER NOTES: Selected by St. Louis Rams in third round (84th pick overall) of 2002 NFL draft. ... Signed by Rams (July 2, 2002).

SINGLE GAME HIGHS (regular season): Attempts—21 (September 28, 2003, vs. Arizona); yards—92 (October 13, 2003, vs. Atlanta); and rushing touchdowns—1 (September 28, 2003, vs. Arizona).

			RUSHING				RECEIVING				KICKOFF RETURNS				TOTALS			
Year Team	**G**	**GS**	**Att.**	**Yds.**	**Avg.**	**TD**	**No.**	**Yds.**	**Avg.**	**TD**	**No.**	**Yds.**	**Avg.**	**TD**	**TD**	**2pt.**	**Pts.**	**Fum.**
2002—St. Louis NFL	13	5	65	228	3.5	1	30	278	9.3	2	6	104	17.3	0	3	0	18	4
2003—St. Louis NFL	10	4	71	298	4.2	1	8	59	7.4	0	0	0	0.0	0	1	0	6	1
Pro totals (2 years)	23	9	136	526	3.9	2	38	337	8.9	2	6	104	17.3	0	4	0	24	5

GORIN, BRANDON — T — PATRIOTS

PERSONAL: Born July 17, 1978, in Muncie, Ind. ... 6-6/308. ... Full name: Brandon Michael Gorin.

HIGH SCHOOL: Southside (Ind.).

COLLEGE: Purdue.

TRANSACTIONS/CAREER NOTES: Selected by San Diego Chargers in seventh round (201st pick overall) of 2001 NFL draft. ... Signed by Chargers (June 21, 2001). ... Released by Chargers (August 25, 2002). ... Signed by New England Patriots to practice squad (September 5, 2002).

PLAYING EXPERIENCE: New England NFL, 2003. ... Games/Games started: 2003 (6/0). Total: 6/0.

CHAMPIONSHIP GAME EXPERIENCE: Played in AFC championship game (2003 season). ... Member of Patriots for Super Bowl 38 (2003 season); did not play.

GOSS, JASON — CB — CARDINALS

PERSONAL: Born October 4, 1979, in Fort Worth, Texas. ... 5-10/185. ... Full name: Jason Tamon Goss.

HIGH SCHOOL: O.D. Wyatt (Fort Worth, Texas).

COLLEGE: Texas Christian.

TRANSACTIONS/CAREER NOTES: Signed as non-drafted free agent by Chicago Bears (April 28, 2003). ... Claimed on waivers by Arizona Cardinals (September 1, 2003). ... Released by Cardinals (September 16, 2003). ... Re-signed by Cardinals to practice squad (September 17, 2003). ... Activated (November 26, 2003).

			TOTALS			INTERCEPTIONS			
Year Team	**G**	**GS**	**Tk.**	**Ast.**	**Sks.**	**No.**	**Yds.**	**Avg.**	**TD**
2003—Arizona NFL	4	0	0	0	0.0	0	0	0.0	0

GOWIN, TOBY — P — JETS

PERSONAL: Born March 30, 1975, in Jacksonville, Texas. ... 5-10/167. ... Name pronounced: GO-in.

HIGH SCHOOL: Jacksonville (Texas).

COLLEGE: North Texas.

TRANSACTIONS/CAREER NOTES: Signed as non-drafted free agent by Dallas Cowboys (April 24, 1997). ... Granted free agency (February 11, 2000). ... Tendered offer sheet by New Orleans Saints (April 6, 2000). ... Cowboys declined to match offer (April 6, 2000). ... Granted unconditional free agency (February 28, 2003). ... Signed by Cowboys (March 3, 2003). ... Released by Cowboys (March 10, 2004). ... Signed by New York Jets (March 31, 2004).

		PUNTING						
Year Team	**G**	**No.**	**Yds.**	**Avg.**	**Net avg.**	**In. 20**	**Blk.**
1997—Dallas NFL	16	86	3592	41.8	35.4	26	0
1998—Dallas NFL	16	77	3342	43.4	36.6	31	∞1
1999—Dallas NFL	16	81	3500	43.2	35.1	24	0
2000—New Orleans NFL	16	74	3043	41.1	32.3	22	0
2001—New Orleans NFL	16	76	3180	41.8	35.8	24	0
2002—New Orleans NFL	15	61	2553	41.9	36.9	15	0
2003—Dallas NFL	16	‡94	‡3665	39.0	34.9	25	0
Pro totals (7 years)	111	549	22875	41.7	35.2	167	1

GRAGG, SCOTT — T — 49ERS

PERSONAL: Born February 28, 1972, in Silverton, Ore. ... 6-8/315.

HIGH SCHOOL: Silverton (Ore.) Union.

COLLEGE: Montana.

TRANSACTIONS/CAREER NOTES: Selected by New York Giants in second round (54th pick overall) of 1995 NFL draft. ... Signed by Giants (July 23, 1995). ... Granted free agency (February 13, 1998). ... Re-signed by Giants (September 4, 1998). ... Released by Giants (March 28, 2000). ... Signed by San Francisco 49ers (July 19, 2000). ... Granted unconditional free agency (March 2, 2001). ... Re-signed by 49ers (April 5, 2001).

PLAYING EXPERIENCE: New York Giants NFL, 1995-1999; San Francisco NFL, 2000-2003. ... Games/Games started: 1995 (13/0), 1996 (16/16), 1997 (16/16), 1998 (16/16), 1999 (16/16), 2000 (16/16), 2001 (16/16), 2002 (16/16), 2003 (15/14). Total: 140/126.

GRAHAM, DANIEL — TE — PATRIOTS

PERSONAL: Born November 16, 1978, in Torrance, Calif. ... 6-3/257.
HIGH SCHOOL: Thomas Jefferson (Denver).
COLLEGE: Colorado.
TRANSACTIONS/CAREER NOTES: Selected by New England Patriots in first round (21st pick overall) of 2002 NFL draft. ... Signed by Patriots (July 21, 2002). ... On injured reserve with rib injury (December 24, 2002-remainder of season).
CHAMPIONSHIP GAME EXPERIENCE: Played in AFC championship game (2003 season). ... Member of Super Bowl championship team (2003 season).
HONORS: Named tight end on THE SPORTING NEWS college All-America first team (2001).
SINGLE GAME HIGHS (regular season): Receptions—7 (October 26, 2003, vs. Cleveland); yards—110 (October 26, 2003, vs. Cleveland); and touchdown receptions—1 (December 27, 2003, vs. Buffalo).
STATISTICAL PLATEAUS: 100-yard receiving games: 2003 (1). Total: 1.

			RECEIVING				TOTALS			
Year Team	G	GS	No.	Yds.	Avg.	TD	TD	2pt.	Pts.	Fum.
2002—New England NFL	12	6	15	150	10.0	1	1	0	6	0
2003—New England NFL	14	9	38	409	10.8	4	4	0	24	0
Pro totals (2 years)	26	15	53	559	10.5	5	5	0	30	0

GRAHAM, SHAYNE — K — BENGALS

PERSONAL: Born December 9, 1977, in Radford, Va. ... 6-0/197. ... Full name: Michael Shayne Graham.
HIGH SCHOOL: Pulaski County (Va.).
COLLEGE: Virginia Tech.
TRANSACTIONS/CAREER NOTES: Signed as non-drafted free agent by New Orleans Saints (June 30, 2000). ... Released by Saints (August 22, 2000). ... Signed by Seattle Seahawks (April 27, 2001). ... Released by Seahawks (September 2, 2001). ... Signed by Buffalo Bills (November 27, 2001). ... Released by Bills (April 24, 2002). ... Signed by Seattle Seahawks (May 13, 2002). ... Released by Seahawks (August 13, 2002). ... Signed by Carolina Panthers (September 28, 2002). ... Claimed on waivers by Cincinnati Bengals (September 1, 2003). ... Granted free agency (March 3, 2004). ... Tendered offer sheet by Jacksonville Jaguars (March 5, 2004). ... Offer matched by Bengals (March 11, 2004).

				FIELD GOALS					TOTALS		
Year Team	G	1-29	30-39	40-49	50+	Tot.	Pct.	Lg.	XPM	XPA	Pts.
2001—Buffalo NFL	6	4-4	0-0	2-4	0-0	6-8	75.0	41	7	7	25
2002—Carolina NFL	11	3-5	2-3	6-8	2-2	13-18	72.2	50	21	21	60
2003—Cincinnati NFL	16	5-5	10-10	7-8	0-2	22-25	88.0	48	40	40	106
Pro totals (3 years)	33	12-14	12-13	15-20	2-4	41-51	80.4	50	68	68	191

GRAMATICA, BILL — K — GIANTS

PERSONAL: Born July 10, 1978, in Buenos Aires, Argentina. ... 5-10/189. ... Full name: Guillermo Gramatica. ... Brother of Martin Gramatica, kicker, Tampa Bay Buccaneers.
HIGH SCHOOL: LaBelle (Fla.).
COLLEGE: South Florida.
TRANSACTIONS/CAREER NOTES: Selected by Arizona Cardinals in fourth round (98th pick overall) of 2001 NFL draft. ... Signed by Cardinals (June 4, 2001). ... On injured reserve with knee injury (December 18, 2001-remainder of season). ... On injured reserve with back injury (November 18, 2003-remainder of season). ... Granted unconditional free agency (March 3, 2004). ... Signed by New York Giants (May 14, 2004).

				FIELD GOALS					TOTALS		
Year Team	G	1-29	30-39	40-49	50+	Tot.	Pct.	Lg.	XPM	XPA	Pts.
2001—Arizona NFL	13	8-8	3-4	4-7	1-1	16-20	80.0	50	25	25	73
2002—Arizona NFL	16	6-7	2-2	6-8	1-4	15-21	71.4	50	29	29	74
2003—Arizona NFL	4	1-1	2-2	0-0	0-1	3-4	75.0	38	6	6	15
Pro totals (3 years)	33	15-16	7-8	10-15	2-6	34-45	75.6	50	60	60	162

GRAMATICA, MARTIN — K — BUCCANEERS

G

PERSONAL: Born November 27, 1975, in Buenos Aires, Argentina. ... 5-8/170. ... Name pronounced: mar-TEEN gruh-MAT-ee-ka. ... Brother of Bill Gramatica, kicker, New York Giants.
HIGH SCHOOL: La Belle (Fla.).
COLLEGE: Kansas State.
TRANSACTIONS/CAREER NOTES: Selected by Tampa Bay Buccaneers in third round (80th pick overall) of 1999 NFL draft. ... Signed by Buccaneers (July 29, 1999).
CHAMPIONSHIP GAME EXPERIENCE: Played in NFC championship game (1999 and 2002 seasons). ... Member of Super Bowl championship team (2002 season).
HONORS: Named kicker on THE SPORTING NEWS college All-America first team (1997). ... Named kicker on THE SPORTING NEWS college All-America second team (1998). ... Won Lou Groza Award (1997). ... Played in Pro Bowl (2000 season).

				FIELD GOALS					TOTALS		
Year Team	G	1-29	30-39	40-49	50+	Tot.	Pct.	Lg.	XPM	XPA	Pts.
1999—Tampa Bay NFL	16	8-8	10-12	6-8	3-4	‡27-∞32	84.4	∞53	25	25	106
2000—Tampa Bay NFL	16	8-8	8-10	7-9	5-7	28-34	82.4	*55	42	42	126
2001—Tampa Bay NFL	14	9-10	9-9	5-7	0-3	23-29	79.3	49	28	28	97
2002—Tampa Bay NFL	16	7-8	14-15	6-10	5-6	†32-39	82.1	∞53	32	32	128
2003—Tampa Bay NFL	16	9-9	3-6	3-8	1-3	16-26	61.5	50	33	34	81
Pro totals (5 years)	78	41-43	44-52	27-42	14-23	126-160	78.8	55	160	161	538

GRANT, CHARLES — DE — SAINTS

PERSONAL: Born September 3, 1978, in Colquitt, Ga. ... 6-3/282.
HIGH SCHOOL: Miller County (Colquitt, Ga.).
COLLEGE: Georgia.
TRANSACTIONS/CAREER NOTES: Selected by New Orleans Saints in first round (25th pick overall) of 2002 NFL draft. ... Signed by Saints (July 27, 2002).

			TOTALS		
Year Team	G	GS	Tk.	Ast.	Sks.
2002—New Orleans NFL	16	6	30	7	7.0
2003—New Orleans NFL	16	16	48	13	10.0
Pro totals (2 years)	32	22	78	20	17.0

GRANT, CIE — LB — SAINTS

PERSONAL: Born November 27, 1979, in New Philadelphia, Ohio. ... 6-0/228. ... Full name: Willie Grant.
HIGH SCHOOL: New Philadelphia (Ohio).
COLLEGE: Ohio State.
TRANSACTIONS/CAREER NOTES: Selected by New Orleans Saints in third round (86th pick overall) of 2003 NFL draft. ... Signed by Saints (July 25, 2003).

			TOTALS			INTERCEPTIONS			
Year Team	G	GS	Tk.	Ast.	Sks.	No.	Yds.	Avg.	TD
2003—New Orleans NFL	7	0	1	0	0.0	0	0	0.0	0

GRANT, DELAWRENCE — DE — RAIDERS

PERSONAL: Born November 18, 1979, in Compton, Calif. ... 6-3/280. ... Full name: DeLawrence Grant Jr..
HIGH SCHOOL: Centennial (Compton, Calif.).
JUNIOR COLLEGE: El Camino College (Calif.).
COLLEGE: Oregon State.
TRANSACTIONS/CAREER NOTES: Selected by Oakland Raiders in third round (89th pick overall) of 2001 NFL draft. ... Signed by Raiders (July 22, 2001).
CHAMPIONSHIP GAME EXPERIENCE: Played in AFC championship game (2002 season). ... Played in Super Bowl 37 (2002 season).
HONORS: Named defensive end on THE SPORTING NEWS college All-America second team (2000).

			TOTALS		
Year Team	G	GS	Tk.	Ast.	Sks.
2001—Oakland NFL	2	0	0	0	0.0
2002—Oakland NFL	16	14	21	5	3.0
2003—Oakland NFL	13	4	8	10	1.0
Pro totals (3 years)	31	18	29	15	4.0

GRANT, DEON — S — JAGUARS

PERSONAL: Born March 14, 1979, in Augusta, Ga. ... 6-2/207.
HIGH SCHOOL: Josey (Augusta, Ga.).
COLLEGE: Tennessee.
TRANSACTIONS/CAREER NOTES: Selected after junior season by Carolina Panthers in second round (57th pick overall) of 2000 NFL draft. ... Signed by Panthers (July 13, 2000). ... On injured reserve with hip injury (August 20, 2000-entire season). ... Granted unconditional free agency (March 3, 2004). ... Signed by Jacksonville Jaguars (March 10, 2004).
CHAMPIONSHIP GAME EXPERIENCE: Played in NFC championship game (2003 season). ... Played in Super Bowl 38 (2003 season).
HONORS: Named free safety on THE SPORTING NEWS college All-America first team (1999).

			TOTALS			INTERCEPTIONS			
Year Team	G	GS	Tk.	Ast.	Sks.	No.	Yds.	Avg.	TD
2000—Carolina NFL			Did not play.						
2001—Carolina NFL	16	16	59	12	1.0	5	96	19.2	0
2002—Carolina NFL	16	16	54	14	0.0	3	16	5.3	0
2003—Carolina NFL	16	16	65	12	1.0	3	25	8.3	0
Pro totals (3 years)	48	48	178	38	2.0	11	137	12.5	0

G

GRANT, ORANTES — LB

PERSONAL: Born March 18, 1978, in Atlanta, Ga. ... 6-0/228. ... Full name: Orantes Laquay Grant.
HIGH SCHOOL: Dunwoody (Atlanta).
COLLEGE: Georgia.
TRANSACTIONS/CAREER NOTES: Selected by Dallas Cowboys in seventh round (219th pick overall) of 2000 NFL draft. ... Signed by Cowboys (July 17, 2000). ... Released by Cowboys (September 1, 2002). ... Signed by Washington Redskins (December 4, 2002). ... Waived by Redskins (October 28, 2003). ... Signed by Cleveland Browns (November 26, 2003). ... Released by Browns (December 3, 2003).

			TOTALS			INTERCEPTIONS			
Year Team	G	GS	Tk.	Ast.	Sks.	No.	Yds.	Avg.	TD
2000—Dallas NFL	13	0	3	0	0.0	0	0	0.0	0
2001—Dallas NFL	10	1	8	3	0.0	0	0	0.0	0
2002—Washington NFL	1	0	0	0	0.0	0	0	0.0	0

Year Team	G	GS	TOTALS Tk.	Ast.	Sks.	INTERCEPTIONS No.	Yds.	Avg.	TD
2003—Washington NFL	1	0	0	0	0.0	0	0	0.0	0
—Cleveland NFL	1	0	0	0	0.0	0	0	0.0	0
Pro totals (4 years)	26	1	11	3	0.0	0	0	0.0	0

GRASMANIS, PAUL DT EAGLES

PERSONAL: Born August 2, 1974, in Grand Rapids, Mich. ... 6-3/298. ... Full name: Paul Ryan Grasmanis.
HIGH SCHOOL: Jenison (Mich.).
COLLEGE: Notre Dame.
TRANSACTIONS/CAREER NOTES: Selected by Chicago Bears in fourth round (116th pick overall) of 1996 NFL draft. ... Signed by Bears (June 13, 1996). ... Granted free agency (February 12, 1999). ... Re-signed by Bears (April 13, 1999). ... Released by Bears (September 5, 1999). ... Signed by St. Louis Rams (September 7, 1999). ... Inactive for one game with Rams (1999). ... Released by Rams (September 13, 1999). ... Signed by Denver Broncos (November 1, 1999). ... Granted unconditional free agency (February 11, 2000). ... Signed by Philadelphia Eagles (March 3, 2000). ... Granted unconditional free agency (March 2, 2001). ... Re-signed by Eagles (April 24, 2001). ... On injured reserve with Achilles injury (September 16, 2003-remainder of season). ... Granted unconditional free agency (March 3, 2004). ... Re-signed by Eagles (March 11, 2004).
CHAMPIONSHIP GAME EXPERIENCE: Played in NFC championship game (2001 and 2002 seasons).

Year Team	G	GS	TOTALS Tk.	Ast.	Sks.
1996—Chicago NFL	14	3	8	3	0.0
1997—Chicago NFL	16	1	9	5	0.5
1998—Chicago NFL	15	0	15	2	1.0
1999—Denver NFL	5	0	5	2	0.0
2000—Philadelphia NFL	16	0	30	5	3.5
2001—Philadelphia NFL	14	2	14	5	2.0
2002—Philadelphia NFL	16	3	20	11	4.0
2003—Philadelphia NFL	2	0	4	2	1.0
Pro totals (8 years)	98	9	105	35	12.0

GRAU, JEFF C/LS

PERSONAL: Born December 16, 1979, in Inglewood, Calif. ... 6-3/257. ... Full name: Jeffrey Alan Grau.
HIGH SCHOOL: Loyola (Torrance, Calif.).
COLLEGE: UCLA.
TRANSACTIONS/CAREER NOTES: Selected by Washington Redskins in seventh round (230th pick overall) of 2002 NFL draft. ... Signed by Redskins (July 22, 2002). ... Claimed on waivers by Dallas Cowboys (August 28, 2002). ... Traded by Cowboys to Tampa Bay Buccaneers for conditional pick in 2005 draft (August 7, 2003). ... Released by Buccaneers (August 24, 2003). ... Signed by Miami Dolphins (October 14, 2003). ... Released by Dolphins (March 3, 2004).
PLAYING EXPERIENCE: Dallas NFL, 2002; Miami NFL, 2003. ... Games/Games started: 2002 (16/0), 2003 (11/0). Total: 27/0.

GRAY, BOBBY S BEARS

PERSONAL: Born April 30, 1978, in Houston, Texas. ... 6-0/212. ... Full name: Bobby Wayne Gray.
HIGH SCHOOL: Aldine (Texas).
COLLEGE: Louisiana Tech.
TRANSACTIONS/CAREER NOTES: Selected by Chicago Bears in fifth round (140th pick overall) of 2002 NFL draft. ... Signed by Bears (July 19, 2002). ... On injured reserve with wrist injury (September 23, 2002-remainder of season).

Year Team	G	GS	TOTALS Tk.	Ast.	Sks.	INTERCEPTIONS No.	Yds.	Avg.	TD
2002—Chicago NFL	3	0	4	1	0.0	0	0	0.0	0
2003—Chicago NFL	16	9	41	11	1.0	0	0	0.0	0
Pro totals (2 years)	19	9	45	12	1.0	0	0	0.0	0

GRAY, CHRIS G/C SEAHAWKS

G

PERSONAL: Born June 19, 1970, in Birmingham, Ala. ... 6-4/308. ... Full name: Christopher William Gray.
HIGH SCHOOL: Homewood (Ala.).
COLLEGE: Auburn.
TRANSACTIONS/CAREER NOTES: Selected by Miami Dolphins in fifth round (132nd pick overall) of 1993 NFL draft. ... Signed by Dolphins (July 12, 1993). ... On injured reserve with ankle injury (November 15, 1995-remainder of season). ... On injured reserve with broken leg (November 19, 1996-remainder of season). ... Released by Dolphins (August 12, 1997). ... Signed by Chicago Bears (September 9, 1997). ... Granted unconditional free agency (February 13, 1998). ... Signed by Seattle Seahawks (February 20, 1998).
PLAYING EXPERIENCE: Miami NFL, 1993-1996; Chicago NFL, 1997; Seattle NFL, 1998-2003. ... Games/Games started: 1993 (5/0), 1994 (16/2), 1995 (10/10), 1996 (11/11), 1997 (8/2), 1998 (15/8), 1999 (16/10), 2000 (16/16), 2001 (16/16), 2002 (16/16), 2003 (16/16). Total: 145/107.

GREEN, AHMAN RB PACKERS

PERSONAL: Born February 16, 1977, in Omaha, Neb. ... 6-0/217.
HIGH SCHOOL: North (Omaha, Neb.), then Central Christian (Omaha, Neb.).
COLLEGE: Nebraska.

TRANSACTIONS/CAREER NOTES: Selected after junior season by Seattle Seahawks in third round (76th pick overall) of 1998 NFL draft. ... Signed by Seahawks (July 18, 1998). ... Traded by Seahawks with fifth-round pick (WR/KR Joey Jamison) in 2000 draft to Green Bay Packers for CB Fred Vinson and sixth-round pick (DT Tim Watson) in 2000 draft (April 14, 2000). ... Granted free agency (March 2, 2001). ... Re-signed by Packers (July 24, 2001).

HONORS: Named running back on THE SPORTING NEWS college All-America second team (1997). ... Played in Pro Bowl (2001 and 2003 seasons). ... Named to play in Pro Bowl (2002 season); replaced by Michael Bennett due to injury.

SINGLE GAME HIGHS (regular season): Attempts—31 (October 13, 2002, vs. New England); yards—218 (December 3, 2003, vs. Denver); and rushing touchdowns—3 (October 20, 2002, vs. Washington).

STATISTICAL PLATEAUS: 100-yard rushing games: 1998 (1), 2000 (3), 2001 (7), 2002 (4), 2003 (10). Total: 25.

			RUSHING				RECEIVING				KICKOFF RETURNS				TOTALS			
Year Team	**G**	**GS**	**Att.**	**Yds.**	**Avg.**	**TD**	**No.**	**Yds.**	**Avg.**	**TD**	**No.**	**Yds.**	**Avg.**	**TD**	**TD**	**2pt.**	**Pts.**	**Fum.**
1998—Seattle NFL	16	0	35	209	6.0	1	3	2	0.7	0	27	620	23.0	0	1	0	6	1
1999—Seattle NFL	14	0	26	120	4.6	0	0	0	0.0	0	36	818	22.7	0	0	0	0	2
2000—Green Bay NFL	16	11	263	1175	4.5	10	73	559	7.7	3	0	0	0.0	0	13	0	78	6
2001—Green Bay NFL	16	16	304	1387	4.6	9	62	594	9.6	2	0	0	0.0	0	11	0	66	5
2002—Green Bay NFL	14	14	286	1240	4.3	7	57	393	6.9	2	0	0	0.0	0	9	0	54	4
2003—Green Bay NFL	16	16	‡355	‡1883	5.3	‡15	50	367	7.3	5	0	0	0.0	0	‡20	0	120	7
Pro totals (6 years)	92	57	1269	6014	4.7	42	245	1915	7.8	12	63	1438	22.8	0	54	0	324	25

GREEN, BARRETT LB GIANTS

PERSONAL: Born October 29, 1977, in West Palm Beach, Fla. ... 6-0/225. ... Son of Joe Green, defensive back with New York Giants (1970 and 1971).

HIGH SCHOOL: Suncoast (West Palm Beach, Fla.).

COLLEGE: West Virginia.

TRANSACTIONS/CAREER NOTES: Selected by Detroit Lions in second round (50th pick overall) of 2000 NFL draft. ... Signed by Lions (July 15, 2000). ... Granted unconditional free agency (March 3, 2004). ... Signed by New York Giants (March 8, 2004).

			TOTALS			INTERCEPTIONS			
Year Team	**G**	**GS**	**Tk.**	**Ast.**	**Sks.**	**No.**	**Yds.**	**Avg.**	**TD**
2000—Detroit NFL	9	0	0	0	0.0	0	0	0.0	0
2001—Detroit NFL	14	10	51	24	1.0	0	0	0.0	0
2002—Detroit NFL	15	14	50	23	1.0	0	0	0.0	0
2003—Detroit NFL	16	16	65	29	3.0	0	0	0.0	0
Pro totals (4 years)	54	40	166	76	5.0	0	0	0.0	0

GREEN, CORNELL G/T BRONCOS

PERSONAL: Born August 25, 1976, in St. Petersburg, Fla. ... 6-6/315.

HIGH SCHOOL: Lakewood (St. Petersburg, Fla.).

COLLEGE: Central Florida.

TRANSACTIONS/CAREER NOTES: Signed as non-drafted free agent by Atlanta Falcons (May 18, 1999). ... Released by Falcons (August 30, 1999). ... Signed by Washington Redskins (July 14, 2000). ... Claimed on waivers by New York Jets (August 29, 2000). ... Released by Jets (September 6, 2000). ... Re-signed by Jets to practice squad (September 7, 2000). ... Activated (November 17, 2000); did not play. ... Released by Jets (December 3, 2001). ... Signed by Miami Dolphins to practice squad (December 11, 2001). ... Traded by Dolphins to Tampa Bay Buccaneers for seventh-round pick (traded to Carolina) in 2003 draft (August 20, 2002). ... Granted unconditional free agency (March 3, 2004). ... Signed by Denver Broncos (March 26, 2004).

PLAYING EXPERIENCE: Tampa Bay NFL, 2002-2003. ... Games/Games started: 2002 (16/3), 2003 (7/5). Total: 23/8.

CHAMPIONSHIP GAME EXPERIENCE: Played in NFC championship game (2002 season). ... Member of Super Bowl championship team (2002 season).

GREEN, HOWARD DT SAINTS

PERSONAL: Born January 12, 1979, in Donaldsonville, La. ... 6-2/320. ... Full name: Howard Green Jr..

HIGH SCHOOL: Donaldsonville (La.).

JUNIOR COLLEGE: Southwest Mississippi College.

COLLEGE: Louisiana State.

TRANSACTIONS/CAREER NOTES: Selected by Houston Texans in sixth round (190th pick overall) of 2002 NFL draft. ... Signed by Texans (June 19, 2002). ... Claimed on waivers by Baltimore Ravens (September 3, 2002). ... Released by Ravens (October 29, 2002). ... Signed by Texans to practice squad (October 31, 2002). ... Activated (December 18, 2002). ... Re-signed by Texans (March 24, 2003). ... Released by Texans (August 25, 2003). ... Signed by New Orleans Saints to practice squad (October 3, 2003). ... Activated (December 6, 2003).

			TOTALS		
Year Team	**G**	**GS**	**Tk.**	**Ast.**	**Sks.**
2002—Baltimore NFL	1	0	0	0	0.0
2003—New Orleans NFL	4	0	0	0	0.0
Pro totals (2 years)	5	0	0	0	0.0

G

GREEN, JAMAAL DE EAGLES

PERSONAL: Born June 5, 1980, in Camden, N.J. ... 6-2/272. ... Full name: Jamaal Hakeem Green.

HIGH SCHOOL: Woodrow Wilson (Camden, N.J.).

COLLEGE: Miami (Fla.).

TRANSACTIONS/CAREER NOTES: Selected by Philadelphia Eagles in fourth round (131st pick overall) of 2003 NFL draft. ... Signed by Eagles (May 29, 2003). ... On injured reserve with ankle injury (August 24, 2003-entire season).

Year Team	G	GS	TOTALS Tk.	Ast.	Sks.
2003—Philadelphia NFL			Did not play.		

GREEN, JARVIS — DE — PATRIOTS

PERSONAL: Born January 12, 1979, in Thibodaux, La. ... 6-3/290. ... Full name: Jarvis Pernell Green.
HIGH SCHOOL: Donaldsville (La.).
COLLEGE: Louisiana State.
TRANSACTIONS/CAREER NOTES: Selected by New England Patriots in fourth round (126th pick overall) of 2002 NFL draft. ... Signed by Patriots (July 18, 2002).
CHAMPIONSHIP GAME EXPERIENCE: Played in AFC championship game (2003 season). ... Member of Super Bowl championship team (2003 season).

			TOTALS		
Year Team	**G**	**GS**	**Tk.**	**Ast.**	**Sks.**
2002—New England NFL	15	4	14	7	2.5
2003—New England NFL	16	7	9	8	2.0
Pro totals (2 years)	31	11	23	15	4.5

GREEN, MIKE — S — BEARS

PERSONAL: Born December 6, 1976, in Ruston, La. ... 6-0/195.
HIGH SCHOOL: Ruston (La.).
COLLEGE: Northwestern State.
TRANSACTIONS/CAREER NOTES: Selected by Chicago Bears in seventh round (254th pick overall) of 2000 NFL draft. ... Signed by Bears (May 30, 2000). ... On injured reserve with groin injury (December 23, 2003-remainder of season).

			TOTALS			INTERCEPTIONS			
Year Team	**G**	**GS**	**Tk.**	**Ast.**	**Sks.**	**No.**	**Yds.**	**Avg.**	**TD**
2000—Chicago NFL	7	0	0	0	0.0	0	0	0.0	0
2001—Chicago NFL	16	2	53	4	3.0	0	0	0.0	0
2002—Chicago NFL	16	16	91	27	1.0	0	0	0.0	0
2003—Chicago NFL	10	8	36	7	0.5	1	3	3.0	0
Pro totals (4 years)	49	26	180	38	4.5	1	3	3.0	0

GREEN, RAY — CB — GIANTS

PERSONAL: Born March 22, 1977, in Queens, N.Y. ... 6-3/195.
HIGH SCHOOL: Burke (Charleston, S.C.).
COLLEGE: South Carolina.
TRANSACTIONS/CAREER NOTES: Signed as non-drafted free agent by Carolina Panthers (April 17, 2000). ... Released by Panthers (September 1, 2001). ... Signed by Miami Dolphins (October 23, 2001). ... On injured reserve with elbow injury (November 5, 2002-remainder of season). ... Granted free agency (February 28, 2003). ... Signed by New York Giants (March 12, 2003). ... Released by Giants (October 6, 2003). ... Signed by New York Jets (October 15, 2003). ... Released by Jets (December 9, 2003). ... Signed by New York Giants (December 16, 2003). ... Granted unconditional free agency (March 3, 2004). ... Re-signed by Giants (March 4, 2004).

			TOTALS			INTERCEPTIONS			
Year Team	**G**	**GS**	**Tk.**	**Ast.**	**Sks.**	**No.**	**Yds.**	**Avg.**	**TD**
2000—Carolina NFL	16	0	0	0	0.0	0	0	0.0	0
2001—Miami NFL	4	0	0	0	0.0	0	0	0.0	0
2002—Miami NFL	8	0	3	0	0.0	0	0	0.0	0
2003—New York Jets NFL	8	0	5	0	0.0	0	0	0.0	0
—New York Giants NFL	2	0	5	1	0.0	0	0	0.0	0
Pro totals (4 years)	38	0	13	1	0.0	0	0	0.0	0

GREEN, TRENT — QB — CHIEFS

G

PERSONAL: Born July 9, 1970, in St. Louis, Mo. ... 6-3/217. ... Full name: Trent Jason Green.
HIGH SCHOOL: Vianney (St. Louis).
COLLEGE: Indiana.
TRANSACTIONS/CAREER NOTES: Selected by San Diego Chargers in eighth round (222nd pick overall) of 1993 NFL draft. ... Signed by Chargers (July 15, 1993). ... Inactive for all 16 games (1993). ... Released by Chargers (August 22, 1994). ... Signed by Washington Redskins (April 5, 1995). ... Inactive for all 16 games (1995). ... Inactive for all 16 games (1996). ... Granted free agency (February 14, 1997). ... Re-signed by Redskins (June 6, 1997). ... Granted unconditional free agency (February 12, 1999). ... Signed by St. Louis Rams (February 16, 1999). ... On injured reserve with knee injury (August 30, 1999-entire season). ... Traded by Rams with fifth-round pick (RB Derrick Blaylock) in 2001 draft to Kansas City Chiefs for first-round pick (DT Damione Lewis) in 2001 draft (April 20, 2001).
HONORS: Played in Pro Bowl (2003 season).
RECORDS: Shares NFL record for longest pass completion (to Marc Boerigter)—99 yards, touchdown (December 22, 2002, vs. San Diego).
SINGLE GAME HIGHS (regular season): Attempts—54 (September 20, 1998, vs. Seattle); completions—34 (December 7, 2003, vs. Denver); yards—431 (November 5, 2000, vs. Carolina); and touchdown passes—5 (September 29, 2002, vs. Miami).
STATISTICAL PLATEAUS: 300-yard passing games: 1998 (2), 2000 (3), 2001 (3), 2002 (4), 2003 (5). Total: 17.
MISCELLANEOUS: Regular-season record as starting NFL quarterback: 35-32 (.522). ... Post-season record as starting NFL quarterback: 0-1 (.000).

Year Team	G	GS	PASSING									RUSHING				TOTALS		
			Att.	Cmp.	Pct.	Yds.	TD	Int.	Avg.	Skd.	Rat.	Att.	Yds.	Avg.	TD	TD	2pt.	Pts.
1993—San Diego NFL										Did not play.								
1994—										Did not play.								
1995—Washington NFL										Did not play.								
1996—Washington NFL										Did not play.								
1997—Washington NFL	1	0	1	0	0.0	0	0	0	0.00	0	39.6	0	0	0.0	0	0	0	0
1998—Washington NFL	15	14	509	278	54.6	3441	23	11	6.76	†49	81.8	42	117	2.8	2	2	0	12
1999—St. Louis NFL										Did not play.								
2000—St. Louis NFL	8	5	240	145	60.4	2063	16	5	8.60	24	‡101.8	20	69	3.5	1	1	0	6
2001—Kansas City NFL	16	16	523	296	56.6	3783	17	*24	7.23	39	71.1	35	158	4.5	0	0	1	2
2002—Kansas City NFL	16	16	470	287	61.1	3690	26	13	*7.85	26	92.6	31	225	7.3	1	1	1	8
2003—Kansas City NFL	16	16	523	330	63.1	4039	24	12	7.72	20	92.6	26	83	3.2	2	2	0	12
Pro totals (6 years)	72	67	2266	1336	59.0	17016	106	65	7.51	158	86.1	154	652	4.2	6	6	2	40

GREEN, VICTOR — S

PERSONAL: Born December 8, 1969, in Americus, Ga. ... 5-11/210. ... Full name: Victor Bernard Green.
HIGH SCHOOL: Americus (Ga.).
JUNIOR COLLEGE: Copiah-Lincoln Junior College (Miss.).
COLLEGE: Akron.
TRANSACTIONS/CAREER NOTES: Signed as non-drafted free agent by New York Jets (April 29, 1993). ... Released by Jets (August 30, 1993). ... Re-signed by Jets to practice squad (September 1, 1993). ... Activated (September 28, 1993). ... Released by Jets (February 28, 2002). ... Signed by New England Patriots (July 16, 2002). ... Granted free agency (February 28, 2003). ... Signed by New Orleans Saints (September 16, 2003). ... Granted unconditional free agency (March 3, 2004).
CHAMPIONSHIP GAME EXPERIENCE: Played in AFC championship game (1998 season).

Year Team	G	GS	TOTALS			INTERCEPTIONS			
			Tk.	Ast.	Sks.	No.	Yds.	Avg.	TD
1993—New York Jets NFL	11	0	0	0	0.0	0	0	0.0	0
1994—New York Jets NFL	16	0	16	1	1.0	0	0	0.0	0
1995—New York Jets NFL	16	12	103	34	2.0	1	2	2.0	0
1996—New York Jets NFL	16	16	*123	42	2.0	2	27	13.5	0
1997—New York Jets NFL	16	16	89	34	1.0	3	89	29.7	0
1998—New York Jets NFL	16	16	69	24	1.0	4	99	24.7	0
1999—New York Jets NFL	16	16	90	32	0.0	5	92	18.4	0
2000—New York Jets NFL	16	16	64	41	0.0	6	144	24.0	1
2001—New York Jets NFL	16	16	55	29	0.0	3	76	25.3	1
2002—New England NFL	16	6	62	22	0.0	1	90	90.0	1
2003—New Orleans NFL	14	1	13	3	0.0	0	24	0.0	0
Pro totals (11 years)	169	115	684	262	7.0	25	643	25.7	3

GREEN, WILLIAM — RB — BROWNS

PERSONAL: Born December 17, 1979, in Atlantic City, N.J. ... 6-0/215.
HIGH SCHOOL: Holy Spirit (Atlantic City, N.J.).
COLLEGE: Boston College.
TRANSACTIONS/CAREER NOTES: Selected after junior season by Cleveland Browns in first round (16th pick overall) of 2002 NFL draft. ... Signed by Browns (July 27, 2002). ... Suspended one game for conduct detrimental to team (November 9, 2003). ... On suspended list for violating league substance abuse policy (November 13, 2003-remainder of season).
HONORS: Named running back on THE SPORTING NEWS college All-America first team (2001).
SINGLE GAME HIGHS (regular season): Attempts—33 (October 5, 2003, vs. Pittsburgh); yards—178 (December 29, 2002, vs. Atlanta); and rushing touchdowns—2 (December 29, 2002, vs. Atlanta).
STATISTICAL PLATEAUS: 100-yard rushing games: 2002 (3), 2003 (2). Total: 5.

Year Team	G	GS	RUSHING				RECEIVING				TOTALS			
			Att.	Yds.	Avg.	TD	No.	Yds.	Avg.	TD	TD	2pt.	Pts.	Fum.
2002—Cleveland NFL	16	10	243	887	3.7	6	16	113	7.1	0	6	0	36	4
2003—Cleveland NFL	7	7	142	559	3.9	1	10	50	5.0	0	1	0	6	5
Pro totals (2 years)	23	17	385	1446	3.8	7	26	163	6.3	0	7	0	42	9

GREENWOOD, MORLON — LB — DOLPHINS

PERSONAL: Born July 17, 1978, in Jamaica, West Indies. ... 6-0/238. ... Full name: Morlon O'Neil Greenwood.
HIGH SCHOOL: Freeport (N.Y.).
COLLEGE: Syracuse.
TRANSACTIONS/CAREER NOTES: Selected by Miami Dolphins in third round (88th pick overall) of 2001 NFL draft. ... Signed by Dolphins (July 23, 2001). ... Granted free agency (March 3, 2004). ... Re-signed by Dolphins (April 19, 2004).

Year Team	G	GS	TOTALS			INTERCEPTIONS			
			Tk.	Ast.	Sks.	No.	Yds.	Avg.	TD
2001—Miami NFL	14	12	30	28	1.5	0	0	0.0	0
2002—Miami NFL	16	13	33	18	1.0	0	0	0.0	0
2003—Miami NFL	16	11	43	23	0.5	0	0	0.0	0
Pro totals (3 years)	46	36	106	69	3.0	0	0	0.0	0

G

GREGG, KELLY — DT — RAVENS

PERSONAL: Born November 1, 1976, in Wichita, Kan. ... 6-0/310.
HIGH SCHOOL: Edmond (Okla.).
COLLEGE: Oklahoma.
TRANSACTIONS/CAREER NOTES: Selected by Cincinnati Bengals in sixth round (173rd pick overall) of 1999 NFL draft. ... Signed by Bengals (June 23, 1999). ... Released by Bengals (September 6, 1999). ... Re-signed by Bengals to practice squad (September 7, 1999). ... Signed by Philadelphia Eagles off Bengals practice squad (December 7, 1999). ... Released by Eagles (September 12, 2000). ... Signed by Baltimore Ravens to practice squad (September 13, 2000). ... Assigned by Ravens to Rhein Fire in 2001 NFL Europe enhancement allocation program (February 19, 2001).

			TOTALS		
Year Team	**G**	**GS**	**Tk.**	**Ast.**	**Sks.**
1999—Philadelphia NFL	3	0	2	0	0.0
2000—Baltimore NFL			Did not play.		
2001—Baltimore NFL	8	1	7	3	1.0
2002—Baltimore NFL	16	16	45	11	2.0
2003—Baltimore NFL	16	15	63	17	3.0
Pro totals (4 years)	43	32	117	31	6.0

GREISEN, NICK — LB — GIANTS

PERSONAL: Born August 10, 1979, in Sturgeon Bay, Wis. ... 6-1/245.
HIGH SCHOOL: Sturgeon Bay (Wis.).
COLLEGE: Wisconsin.
TRANSACTIONS/CAREER NOTES: Selected by New York Giants in fifth round (152nd pick overall) of 2002 NFL draft.

			TOTALS			INTERCEPTIONS			
Year Team	**G**	**GS**	**Tk.**	**Ast.**	**Sks.**	**No.**	**Yds.**	**Avg.**	**TD**
2002—New York Giants NFL	8	1	3	0	1.0	0	0	0.0	0
2003—New York Giants NFL	15	0	0	1	0.0	0	0	0.0	0
Pro totals (2 years)	23	1	3	1	1.0	0	0	0.0	0

GRIESE, BRIAN — QB — BUCCANEERS

PERSONAL: Born March 18, 1975, in Miami, Fla. ... 6-3/215. ... Full name: Brian David Griese. ... Name pronounced: GREE-see. ... Son of Bob Griese, Hall of Fame quarterback with Miami Dolphins (1967-80).
HIGH SCHOOL: Columbus (Miami).
COLLEGE: Michigan.
TRANSACTIONS/CAREER NOTES: Selected by Denver Broncos in third round (91st pick overall) of 1998 NFL draft. ... Signed by Broncos (July 22, 1998). ... Granted free agency (March 2, 2001). ... Re-signed by Broncos (April 11, 2001). ... Waived by Broncos (June 2, 2003). ... Signed by Miami Dolphins (June 9, 2003). ... Released by Dolphins (March 2, 2004). ... Signed by Tampa Bay Buccaneers (March 19, 2004).
CHAMPIONSHIP GAME EXPERIENCE: Member of Broncos for AFC championship game (1998 season); inactive. ... Member of Super Bowl championship team (1998 season); inactive.
HONORS: Played in Pro Bowl (2000 season).
SINGLE GAME HIGHS (regular season): Attempts—53 (September 30, 2002, vs. Baltimore); completions—35 (September 30, 2002, vs. Baltimore); yards—376 (October 20, 2002, vs. Kansas City); and touchdown passes—3 (October 27, 2003, vs. San Diego).
STATISTICAL PLATEAUS: 300-yard passing games: 1999 (2), 2000 (5), 2001 (1), 2002 (4). Total: 12.
MISCELLANEOUS: Regular-season record as starting NFL quarterback: 30-26 (.536).

			PASSING									RUSHING				TOTALS		
Year Team	**G**	**GS**	**Att.**	**Cmp.**	**Pct.**	**Yds.**	**TD**	**Int.**	**Avg.**	**Skd.**	**Rat.**	**Att.**	**Yds.**	**Avg.**	**TD**	**TD**	**2pt.**	**Pts.**
1998—Denver NFL	1	0	3	1	33.3	2	0	1	0.67	0	2.8	4	-4	-1.0	0	0	0	0
1999—Denver NFL	14	13	452	261	57.7	3032	14	14	6.71	27	75.6	46	138	3.0	2	2	0	12
2000—Denver NFL	10	10	336	216	§64.3	2688	19	4	§8.00	17	*102.9	29	102	3.5	1	1	0	6
2001—Denver NFL	15	15	451	275	61.0	2827	23	19	6.27	38	78.5	50	173	3.5	1	1	0	6
2002—Denver NFL	13	13	436	291	66.7	3214	15	15	7.37	34	85.6	37	107	2.9	1	1	0	6
2003—Miami NFL	5	5	130	74	56.9	813	5	6	6.25	12	69.2	5	15	3.0	0	0	0	0
Pro totals (6 years)	58	56	1808	1118	61.8	12576	76	59	6.96	128	83.0	171	531	3.1	5	5	0	30

GRIFFIN, CORNELIUS — DT — REDSKINS

PERSONAL: Born December 3, 1976, in Brundidge, Ala. ... 6-3/300.
HIGH SCHOOL: Pike County (Brundidge, Ala.).
JUNIOR COLLEGE: Pearl River Community College (Miss.).
COLLEGE: Alabama.
TRANSACTIONS/CAREER NOTES: Selected by New York Giants in second round (42nd pick overall) of 2000 NFL draft. ... Signed by Giants (July 25, 2000). ... Granted unconditional free agency (March 3, 2004). ... Signed by Washington Redskins (March 4, 2004).
CHAMPIONSHIP GAME EXPERIENCE: Played in NFC championship game (2000 season). ... Played in Super Bowl 35 (2000 season).

			TOTALS		
Year Team	**G**	**GS**	**Tk.**	**Ast.**	**Sks.**
2000—New York Giants NFL	15	0	20	4	5.0
2001—New York Giants NFL	16	16	47	16	2.5
2002—New York Giants NFL	14	14	32	17	4.0
2003—New York Giants NFL	15	15	39	16	1.0
Pro totals (4 years)	60	45	138	53	12.5

GRIFFIN, QUENTIN — RB — BRONCOS

PERSONAL: Born January 12, 1981, in Houston, Texas. ... 5-7/195.
HIGH SCHOOL: Aldine-Nimitz (Aldine, Texas).
COLLEGE: Oklahoma.
TRANSACTIONS/CAREER NOTES: Selected by Denver Broncos in fourth round (108th pick overall) of 2003 NFL draft. ... Signed by Broncos (July 24, 2003).
SINGLE GAME HIGHS (regular season): Attempts—28 (December 21, 2003, vs. Indianapolis); yards—136 (December 21, 2003, vs. Indianapolis); and rushing touchdowns—0.
STATISTICAL PLATEAUS: 100-yard rushing games: 2003 (1). Total: 1.

			RUSHING				RECEIVING				TOTALS			
Year Team	G	GS	Att.	Yds.	Avg.	TD	No.	Yds.	Avg.	TD	TD	2pt.	Pts.	Fum.
2003—Denver NFL	10	1	94	345	3.7	0	8	61	7.6	0	0	0	0	3

GRIFFITH, JUSTIN — FB — FALCONS

PERSONAL: Born April 13, 1981, in Magee, Miss. ... 5-11/232. ... Full name: Justin Montrel Griffith.
HIGH SCHOOL: Magee (Sanatorium, Miss.).
COLLEGE: Mississippi State.
TRANSACTIONS/CAREER NOTES: Selected by Atlanta Falcons in fourth round (121st pick overall) of 2003 NFL draft. ... Signed by Falcons (July 21, 2003).
SINGLE GAME HIGHS (regular season): Attempts—9 (December 28, 2003, vs. Jacksonville); yards—38 (December 28, 2003, vs. Jacksonville); and rushing touchdowns—0.

			RUSHING				RECEIVING				TOTALS			
Year Team	G	GS	Att.	Yds.	Avg.	TD	No.	Yds.	Avg.	TD	TD	2pt.	Pts.	Fum.
2003—Atlanta NFL	16	11	38	168	4.4	0	21	122	5.8	2	2	0	12	0

GRIFFITH, ROBERT — S — BROWNS

PERSONAL: Born November 30, 1970, in Lanham, Md. ... 5-11/197. ... Full name: Robert Otis Griffith.
HIGH SCHOOL: Mount Miguel (Spring Valley, Calif.).
COLLEGE: San Diego State.
TRANSACTIONS/CAREER NOTES: Signed by Sacramento Gold Miners of CFL to practice squad (August 8, 1993). ... Granted free agency after 1993 season. ... Signed as non-drafted free agent by Minnesota Vikings (April 21, 1994). ... Granted free agency (February 14, 1997). ... Re-signed by Vikings (May 7, 1997). ... Granted unconditional free agency (March 1, 2002). ... Signed by Cleveland Browns (March 6, 2002).
CHAMPIONSHIP GAME EXPERIENCE: Played in NFC championship game (1998 and 2000 seasons).
HONORS: Named safety on THE SPORTING NEWS NFL All-Pro team (1998). ... Played in Pro Bowl (2000 season).

			TOTALS			INTERCEPTIONS			
Year Team	G	GS	Tk.	Ast.	Sks.	No.	Yds.	Avg.	TD
1994—Minnesota NFL	15	0	8	3	0.0	0	0	0.0	0
1995—Minnesota NFL	16	1	30	8	0.5	0	0	0.0	0
1996—Minnesota NFL	14	14	78	17	2.0	4	67	16.8	0
1997—Minnesota NFL	16	16	90	25	0.0	2	26	13.0	0
1998—Minnesota NFL	16	16	74	15	0.0	5	25	5.0	0
1999—Minnesota NFL	16	16	94	26	4.0	3	0	0.0	0
2000—Minnesota NFL	16	16	75	29	1.0	1	25	25.0	0
2001—Minnesota NFL	10	9	47	16	0.0	2	25	12.5	0
2002—Cleveland NFL	12	12	62	11	0.0	3	0	0.0	0
2003—Cleveland NFL	16	16	74	19	0.0	2	3	1.5	0
Pro totals (10 years)	147	116	632	169	7.5	22	171	7.8	0

GROCE, DEJUAN — CB — RAMS

PERSONAL: Born February 17, 1980, in Garfield Heights, Ohio. ... 5-10/192.
HIGH SCHOOL: St. Edward (Garfield Heights, Ohio).
COLLEGE: Nebraska.
TRANSACTIONS/CAREER NOTES: Selected by St. Louis Rams in fourth round (107th pick overall) of 2003 NFL draft. ... Signed by Rams (July 22, 2003).

			TOTALS			INTERCEPTIONS				PUNT RETURNS				TOTALS			
Year Team	G	GS	Tk.	Ast.	Sks.	No.	Yds.	Avg.	TD	No.	Yds.	Avg.	TD	TD	2pt.	Pts.	Fum.
2003—St. Louis NFL	16	1	11	0	0.0	1	7	7.0	0	19	135	7.1	0	0	0	0	5

GROSS, JORDAN — T — PANTHERS

PERSONAL: Born July 20, 1980, in Fruitland, Idaho. ... 6-4/300.
HIGH SCHOOL: Fruitland (Idaho).
COLLEGE: Utah.
TRANSACTIONS/CAREER NOTES: Selected by Carolina Panthers in first round (eighth pick overall) of 2003 NFL draft. ... Signed by Panthers (July 26, 2003).
PLAYING EXPERIENCE: Carolina NFL, 2003. ... Games/Games started: 2003 (16/16). Total: 16/16.
CHAMPIONSHIP GAME EXPERIENCE: Played in NFC championship game (2003 season). ... Played in Super Bowl 38 (2003 season).

GROSSMAN, REX QB BEARS

PERSONAL: Born August 23, 1980, in Bloomington, Ind. ... 6-1/222.
HIGH SCHOOL: Bloomington South (Bloomington, Ind.).
COLLEGE: Florida.
TRANSACTIONS/CAREER NOTES: Selected after junior season by Chicago Bears in first round (22nd pick overall) of 2003 NFL draft. ... Signed by Bears (July 25, 2003).
SINGLE GAME HIGHS (regular season): Attempts—32 (December 21, 2003, vs. Washington); completions—19 (December 21, 2003, vs. Washington); yards—249 (December 21, 2003, vs. Washington); and touchdown passes—2 (December 21, 2003, vs. Washington).
MISCELLANEOUS: Reguar-season record as starting NFL quarterback: 2-1 (.667).

			PASSING									RUSHING				TOTALS		
Year Team	G	GS	Att.	Cmp.	Pct.	Yds.	TD	Int.	Avg.	Skd.	Rat.	Att.	Yds.	Avg.	TD	TD	2pt.	Pts.
2003—Chicago NFL	3	3	72	38	52.8	437	2	1	6.07	4	74.8	3	-1	-0.3	0	0	0	0

GURODE, ANDRE G COWBOYS

PERSONAL: Born March 6, 1978, in Houston, Texas. ... 6-4/326.
HIGH SCHOOL: North Shore (Houston).
COLLEGE: Colorado.
TRANSACTIONS/CAREER NOTES: Selected by Dallas Cowboys in second round (37th pick overall) of 2002 NFL draft. ... Signed by Cowboys (July 26, 2002).
PLAYING EXPERIENCE: Dallas NFL, 2002-2003. ... Games/Games started: 2002 (14/14), 2003 (16/15). Total: 30/29.
HONORS: Named guard on THE SPORTING NEWS college All-America first team (2001).

GUTIERREZ, BROCK C 49ERS

PERSONAL: Born September 25, 1973, in Charlotte, Mich. ... 6-3/304.
HIGH SCHOOL: Charlotte (Mich.).
COLLEGE: Central Michigan.
TRANSACTIONS/CAREER NOTES: Signed as non-drafted free agent by Cincinnati Bengals (April 23, 1996). ... Active for two games (1996). ... Released by Bengals (August 30, 1998). ... Re-signed by Bengals (November 4, 1998). ... Released by Bengals (November 17, 1998). ... Signed by Jacksonville Jaguars to practice squad (November 30, 1998). ... Signed by Bengals off Jaguars practice squad (December 15, 1998). ... Granted free agency (February 11, 2000). ... Re-signed by Bengals (March 17, 2000). ... Released by Bengals (May 27, 2003). ... Signed by San Francisco 49ers (August 16, 2003). ... Granted unconditional free agency (March 3, 2004). ... Re-signed by 49ers (March 31, 2004).
PLAYING EXPERIENCE: Cincinnati NFL, 1997-2002; San Francisco NFL, 2003. ... Games/Games started: 1997 (5/0), 1998 (1/0), 1999 (16/0), 2000 (16/7), 2001 (14/0), 2002 (16/1), 2003 (12/0). Total: 80/8.

HAGGAN, MARIO LB BILLS

PERSONAL: Born March 3, 1980, in Clarksdale, Miss. ... 6-3/248. ... Full name: Mario Marcell Haggan.
HIGH SCHOOL: Clarksdale (Miss.).
COLLEGE: Mississippi State.
TRANSACTIONS/CAREER NOTES: Selected by Buffalo Bills in seventh round (228th pick overall) of 2003 NFL draft. ... Signed by Bills (July 22, 2003). ... Released by Bills (September 4, 2003). ... Re-signed by Bills to practice squad (September 8, 2003). ... Activated (November 14, 2003).

			TOTALS			INTERCEPTIONS			
Year Team	G	GS	Tk.	Ast.	Sks.	No.	Yds.	Avg.	TD
2003—Buffalo NFL	1	0	0	0	0.0	0	0	0.0	0

HAGGANS, CLARK LB STEELERS

PERSONAL: Born January 10, 1977, in Torrance, Calif. ... 6-3/251. ... Full name: Clark Cromwell Haggans.
HIGH SCHOOL: Peninsula (Torrance, Calif.).
COLLEGE: Colorado State.
TRANSACTIONS/CAREER NOTES: Selected by Pittsburgh Steelers in fifth round (137th pick overall) of 2000 NFL draft. ... Signed by Steelers (July 7, 2000). ... Granted free agency (February 28, 2003). ... Re-signed by Steelers (April 21, 2003). ... Granted unconditional free agency (March 3, 2004). ... Re-signed by Steelers (March 6, 2004).
CHAMPIONSHIP GAME EXPERIENCE: Played in AFC championship game (2001 season).

			TOTALS			INTERCEPTIONS			
Year Team	G	GS	Tk.	Ast.	Sks.	No.	Yds.	Avg.	TD
2000—Pittsburgh NFL	2	0	0	0	0.0	0	0	0.0	0
2001—Pittsburgh NFL	16	1	3	2	0.0	0	0	0.0	0
2002—Pittsburgh NFL	16	1	17	9	6.5	0	0	0.0	0
2003—Pittsburgh NFL	16	2	11	5	1.0	0	0	0.0	0
Pro totals (4 years)	50	4	31	16	7.5	0	0	0.0	0

HAKIM, AZ-ZAHIR WR LIONS

PERSONAL: Born June 3, 1977, in Los Angeles, Calif. ... 5-10/189. ... Full name: Az-Zahir Ali Hakim. ... Name pronounced: oz-za-HERE ha-KEEM.
HIGH SCHOOL: Fairfax (Los Angeles).
COLLEGE: San Diego State.

TRANSACTIONS/CAREER NOTES: Selected by St. Louis Rams in fourth round (96th pick overall) of 1998 NFL draft. ... Signed by Rams (July 13, 1998). ... Granted free agency (March 2, 2001). ... Re-signed by Rams (May 23, 2001). ... Granted unconditional free agency (March 1, 2002). ... Signed by Detroit Lions (March 7, 2002). ... On injured reserve with hip injury (November 20, 2002-remainder of season).
CHAMPIONSHIP GAME EXPERIENCE: Played in NFC championship game (1999 and 2001 seasons). ... Member of Super Bowl championship team (1999 season). ... Played in Super Bowl 36 (2001 season).
HONORS: Named punt returner on THE SPORTING NEWS NFL All-Pro team (2000).
SINGLE GAME HIGHS (regular season): Receptions—9 (September 8, 2002, vs. Miami); yards—147 (November 5, 2000, vs. Carolina); and touchdown receptions—3 (October 3, 1999, vs. Cincinnati).
STATISTICAL PLATEAUS: 100-yard receiving games: 1999 (1), 2000 (3), 2002 (1). Total: 5.

			RUSHING				RECEIVING				PUNT RETURNS				KICKOFF RETURNS				TOTALS		
Year Team	G	GS	Att.	Yds.	Avg.	TD	No.	Yds.	Avg.	TD	No.	Yds.	Avg.	TD	No.	Yds.	Avg.	TD	TD	2pt.	Pts.
1998—StL. NFL	9	4	2	30	15.0	1	20	247	12.4	1	0	0	0.0	0	0	0	0.0	0	2	0	12
1999—StL. NFL	15	0	4	44	11.0	0	36	677	18.8	8	∞44	461	10.5	∞1	2	35	17.5	0	9	0	54
2000—StL. NFL	16	4	5	19	3.8	0	53	734	13.8	4	32	‡489	‡15.3	1	1	2	2.0	0	5	0	30
2001—StL. NFL	16	2	11	50	4.5	0	39	374	9.6	3	36	330	9.2	0	0	0	0.0	0	3	0	18
2002—Det. NFL	10	10	4	3	0.8	0	37	541	14.6	3	10	148	14.8	1	0	0	0.0	0	4	0	24
2003—Det. NFL	14	12	3	51	17.0	0	49	449	9.2	4	9	85	9.4	0	0	0	0.0	0	4	1	26
Pro totals (6 years)	80	32	29	197	6.8	1	234	3022	12.9	23	131	1513	11.5	3	3	37	12.3	0	27	1	164

HALEY, JERMAINE DT REDSKINS

PERSONAL: Born February 23, 1973, in Fresno, Calif. ... 6-4/325.
HIGH SCHOOL: Hanford (Calif.).
JUNIOR COLLEGE: Butte (Calif.) J.C.
TRANSACTIONS/CAREER NOTES: Signed by Toronto Argonauts of CFL (May 1998). ... Selected by Miami Dolphins in seventh round (232nd pick overall) of 1999 NFL draft. ... Signed by Dolphins (March 2, 2000). ... Granted free agency (February 28, 2003). ... Tendered offer sheet by Washington Redskins (April 18, 2003). ... Dolphins declined to match offer (April 25, 2003). ... On injured reserve with hand injury (November 24, 2003-remainder of season).

			TOTALS			INTERCEPTIONS			
Year Team	G	GS	Tk.	Ast.	Sks.	No.	Yds.	Avg.	TD
1998—Toronto CFL	16	...	...	...	7.0	0	0	0.0	0
1999—Toronto CFL	15	...	...	...	3.0	1	0	0.0	0
2000—Miami NFL	15	4	15	7	1.5	0	0	0.0	0
2001—Miami NFL	12	5	10	8	0.5	0	0	0.0	0
2002—Miami NFL	16	0	13	14	0.5	1	0	0.0	0
2003—Washington NFL	6	5	11	2	0.0	0	0	0.0	0
CFL totals (2 years)	31	...	...	...	10.0	1	0	0.0	0
NFL totals (4 years)	49	14	49	31	2.5	1	0	0.0	0
Pro totals (6 years)	80	...	...	...	12.5	2	0	0.0	0

HALL, CARLOS DE TITANS

PERSONAL: Born January 16, 1979, in Marianna, Ark. ... 6-4/261.
HIGH SCHOOL: Lee (Mariana, Ark.).
COLLEGE: Arkansas.
TRANSACTIONS/CAREER NOTES: Selected by Tennessee Titans in seventh round (240th pick overall) of 2002 NFL draft. ... Signed by Titans (July 9, 2002).
CHAMPIONSHIP GAME EXPERIENCE: Played in AFC championship game (2002 season).

			TOTALS		
Year Team	G	GS	Tk.	Ast.	Sks.
2002—Tennessee NFL	15	13	27	15	8.0
2003—Tennessee NFL	16	4	29	8	3.0
Pro totals (2 years)	31	17	56	23	11.0

HALL, CORY S FALCONS

PERSONAL: Born December 5, 1976, in Bakersfield, Calif. ... 6-0/213.
HIGH SCHOOL: South (Bakersfield, Calif.).
COLLEGE: Fresno State.
TRANSACTIONS/CAREER NOTES: Selected by Cincinnati Bengals in third round (65th pick overall) of 1999 NFL draft. ... Signed by Bengals (May 7, 1999). ... Granted free agency (March 1, 2002). ... Re-signed by Bengals (April 23, 2002). ... On injured reserve with shoulder injury (December 17, 2002-remainder of season). ... Granted unconditional free agency (February 28, 2003). ... Signed by Atlanta Falcons (March 3, 2003).

			TOTALS			INTERCEPTIONS			
Year Team	G	GS	Tk.	Ast.	Sks.	No.	Yds.	Avg.	TD
1999—Cincinnati NFL	16	12	36	13	0.0	1	0	0.0	0
2000—Cincinnati NFL	16	6	36	5	4.0	1	12	12.0	0
2001—Cincinnati NFL	16	15	31	16	0.0	0	0	0.0	0
2002—Cincinnati NFL	14	14	43	15	2.0	1	2	2.0	0
2003—Atlanta NFL	11	10	26	5	0.0	0	0	0.0	0
Pro totals (5 years)	73	57	172	54	6.0	3	14	4.7	0

HALL, DANTE WR CHIEFS

PERSONAL: Born September 1, 1978, in Lufkin, Texas. ... 5-8/187. ... Full name: Damieon Dante Hall.
HIGH SCHOOL: Nimitz (Irving, Texas).
COLLEGE: Texas A&M.

TRANSACTIONS/CAREER NOTES: Selected by Kansas City Chiefs in fifth round (153rd pick overall) of 2000 NFL draft. ... Signed by Chiefs (July 6, 2000). ... Assigned by Chiefs to Scottish Claymores in 2001 NFL Europe enhancement allocation program (February 19, 2001).
HONORS: Played in Pro Bowl (2002-2003 seasons). ... Named punt returner on THE SPORTING NEWS NFL All-Pro team (2003).
RECORDS: Shares NFL single-season record for most kick returns for a touchdown—4 (2003).
POST SEASON RECORDS: Shares NFL postseason single-game record for most touchdowns by kickoff return—1 (January 11, 2004, vs. Indianapolis).
SINGLE GAME HIGHS (regular season): Receptions—11 (December 7, 2003, vs. Denver); yards—143 (December 15, 2002, vs. Denver); and touchdown receptions—2 (December 15, 2002, vs. Denver).
STATISTICAL PLATEAUS: 100-yard receiving games: 2002 (1), 2003 (2). Total: 3.

			RUSHING				RECEIVING				PUNT RETURNS				KICKOFF RETURNS				TOTALS		
Year Team	**G**	**GS**	**Att.**	**Yds.**	**Avg.**	**TD**	**No.**	**Yds.**	**Avg.**	**TD**	**No.**	**Yds.**	**Avg.**	**TD**	**No.**	**Yds.**	**Avg.**	**TD**	**TD**	**2pt.**	**Pts.**
2000—K.C. NFL	5	0	0	0	0.0	0	0	0	0.0	0	6	37	6.2	0	17	358	21.1	0	0	0	0
2001—K.C. NFL	13	0	2	10	5.0	0	0	0	0.0	0	32	235	7.3	0	43	969	22.5	0	0	0	0
2002—K.C. NFL	16	0	11	54	4.9	0	20	322	16.1	3	29	390	13.4	†2	57	1354	23.8	1	6	0	3
2003—K.C. NFL	16	2	16	73	4.6	0	40	423	10.6	1	29	472	*16.3	†2	57	§1478	25.9	†2	5	0	30
Pro totals (4 years)	50	2	29	137	4.7	0	60	745	12.4	4	96	1134	11.8	4	174	4159	23.9	3	11	0	66

HALL, JAMES DE LIONS

PERSONAL: Born February 4, 1977, in New Orleans, La. ... 6-2/270.
HIGH SCHOOL: St. Augustine (La.).
COLLEGE: Michigan.
TRANSACTIONS/CAREER NOTES: Signed as non-drafted free agent by Detroit Lions (April 28, 2000). ... Granted free agency (February 28, 2003). ... Re-signed by Lions (May 28, 2003).
HONORS: Named linebacker on THE SPORTING NEWS college All-America third team (1999).

			TOTALS		
Year Team	**G**	**GS**	**Tk.**	**Ast.**	**Sks.**
2000—Detroit NFL	5	0	1	0	1.0
2001—Detroit NFL	15	0	25	8	4.0
2002—Detroit NFL	16	14	34	15	2.0
2003—Detroit NFL	16	16	48	14	4.5
Pro totals (4 years)	52	30	108	37	11.5

HALL, JOHN K REDSKINS

PERSONAL: Born March 17, 1974, in Port Charlotte, Fla. ... 6-3/240.
HIGH SCHOOL: Port Charlotte (Fla.).
COLLEGE: Wisconsin.
TRANSACTIONS/CAREER NOTES: Signed as non-drafted free agent by New York Jets (April 25, 1997). ... Granted free agency (February 11, 2000). ... Re-signed by Jets (April 13, 2000). ... Granted unconditional free agency (February 28, 2003). ... Signed by Washington Redskins (March 2, 2003).
CHAMPIONSHIP GAME EXPERIENCE: Played in AFC championship game (1998 season).

		FIELD GOALS							TOTALS		
Year Team	**G**	**1-29**	**30-39**	**40-49**	**50+**	**Tot.**	**Pct.**	**Lg.**	**XPM**	**XPA**	**Pts.**
1997—New York Jets NFL	16	11-12	11-17	2-6	4-6	28-†41	68.3	†55	36	36	120
1998—New York Jets NFL	16	9-9	9-13	6-10	1-3	25-35	71.4	54	45	46	120
1999—New York Jets NFL	16	3-4	17-17	7-12	0-0	27-33	81.8	48	27	29	108
2000—New York Jets NFL	15	8-9	6-8	6-12	1-3	21-32	65.6	51	30	30	93
2001—New York Jets NFL	16	9-9	5-7	7-9	3-6	24-31	77.4	53	32	32	104
2002—New York Jets NFL	16	9-9	9-11	6-10	0-1	24-31	77.4	46	35	37	107
2003—Washington NFL	16	8-8	7-9	6-9	4-7	25-33	75.8	54	26	27	101
Pro totals (7 years)	111	57-60	64-82	40-68	13-26	174-236	73.7	55	231	237	753

HALL, TRAVIS DE FALCONS

PERSONAL: Born August 3, 1972, in Kenai, Alaska. ... 6-5/295.
HIGH SCHOOL: West Jordan (Utah).
COLLEGE: Brigham Young.
TRANSACTIONS/CAREER NOTES: Selected by Atlanta Falcons in sixth round (181st pick overall) of 1995 NFL draft. ... Signed by Falcons (June 30, 1995).
CHAMPIONSHIP GAME EXPERIENCE: Played in NFC championship game (1998 season). ... Played in Super Bowl 33 (1998 season).

			TOTALS		
Year Team	**G**	**GS**	**Tk.**	**Ast.**	**Sks.**
1995—Atlanta NFL	1	0	0	0	0.0
1996—Atlanta NFL	14	13	44	7	6.0
1997—Atlanta NFL	16	16	61	17	10.5
1998—Atlanta NFL	14	13	39	10	4.5
1999—Atlanta NFL	16	15	36	9	4.5
2000—Atlanta NFL	16	16	45	18	4.5
2001—Atlanta NFL	16	16	39	12	2.5
2002—Atlanta NFL	11	1	14	11	1.0
2003—Atlanta NFL	15	2	32	7	5.0
Pro totals (9 years)	119	92	310	91	38.5

HALLEN, BOB — C/G — PATRIOTS

PERSONAL: Born March 9, 1975, in Mentor, Ohio. ... 6-3/295. ... Full name: Robert Joseph Hallen.
HIGH SCHOOL: Mentor (Ohio).
COLLEGE: Kent State.
TRANSACTIONS/CAREER NOTES: Selected by Atlanta Falcons in second round (53rd pick overall) of 1998 NFL draft. ... Signed by Falcons (June 3, 1998). ... Granted unconditional free agency (March 1, 2002). ... Signed by San Diego Chargers (May 2, 2002). ... On injured reserve with pectoral injury (October 8, 2003-remainder of season). ... Granted unconditional free agency (March 3, 2004). ... Signed by New England Patriots (May 11, 2004).
PLAYING EXPERIENCE: Atlanta NFL, 1998-2001; San Diego NFL, 2002-2003. ... Games/Games started: 1998 (12/0), 1999 (16/14), 2000 (16/5), 2001 (15/12), 2002 (13/11), 2003 (3/2). Total: 75/44.
CHAMPIONSHIP GAME EXPERIENCE: Played in NFC championship game (1998 season). ... Played in Super Bowl 33 (1998 season).

HAMBRICK, TROY — RB — RAIDERS

PERSONAL: Born November 6, 1976, in Lacoochee, Fla. ... 6-1/233.
HIGH SCHOOL: Pasco (Fla.).
COLLEGE: Savannah State.
TRANSACTIONS/CAREER NOTES: Signed as non-drafted free agent by Dallas Cowboys (June 1, 2000). ... Released by Cowboys (August 27, 2000). ... Re-signed by Cowboys to practice squad (August 29, 2000). ... Activated (December 8, 2000). ... Released by Cowboys (May 13, 2004). ... Signed by Oakland Raiders (May 17, 2004).
SINGLE GAME HIGHS (regular season): Attempts—33 December 14, 2003, vs. Washington); yards—189 (December 14, 2001, vs. Washington); and rushing touchdowns—2 (December 14, 2003, vs. Washington).
STATISTICAL PLATEAUS: 100-yard rushing games: 2001 (2), 2003 (3). Total: 5.

			RUSHING				RECEIVING				TOTALS			
Year Team	G	GS	Att.	Yds.	Avg.	TD	No.	Yds.	Avg.	TD	TD	2pt.	Pts.	Fum.
2000—Dallas NFL	3	0	6	28	4.7	0	0	0	0.0	0	0	0	0	0
2001—Dallas NFL	16	11	113	579	5.1	2	4	62	15.5	0	2	0	12	1
2002—Dallas NFL	16	0	79	317	4.0	1	21	99	4.7	0	1	0	6	2
2003—Dallas NFL	16	16	275	972	3.5	5	17	99	5.8	0	5	0	30	4
Pro totals (4 years)	51	27	473	1896	4.0	8	42	260	6.2	0	8	0	48	7

HAMDAN, GIBRAN — QB — REDSKINS

PERSONAL: Born February 8, 1981, in San Diego, Calif. ... 6-6/240.
HIGH SCHOOL: Bishop O'Connell (North Potomac, Md.).
COLLEGE: Indiana.
TRANSACTIONS/CAREER NOTES: Selected by Washington Redskins in seventh round (232nd pick overall) of 2003 NFL draft. ... Signed by Redskins (July 25, 2003). ... Waived by Redskins (August 31, 2003). ... Re-signed by Redskins to practice squad (September 2, 2003). ... Activated (November 28, 2003). ... Assigned by Redskins to Amsterdam Admirals in 2004 NFL Europe enhancement allocation program (February 9, 2004).
SINGLE GAME HIGHS (regular season): Attempts—2 (December 27, 2003, vs. Philadelphia); completions—1 (December 27, 2003, vs. Philadelphia); yards—7 (December 27, 2003, vs. Philadelphia); touchdown passes—0.

			PASSING									RUSHING				TOTALS		
Year Team	G	GS	Att.	Cmp.	Pct.	Yds.	TD	Int.	Avg.	Skd.	Rat.	Att.	Yds.	Avg.	TD	TD	2pt.	Pts.
2003—Washington NFL	1	0	2	1	50.0	7	0	0	3.50	1	58.3	0	0	0.0	0	0	0	0

HAMILTON, BEN — C/G — BRONCOS

PERSONAL: Born August 18, 1977, in Minneapolis, Minn. ... 6-4/283. ... Son of Wes Hamilton, guard with Minnesota Vikings (1976-84).
HIGH SCHOOL: Wayzata (Minn.).
COLLEGE: Minnesota.
TRANSACTIONS/CAREER NOTES: Selected by Denver Broncos in fourth round (113th pick overall) of 2001 NFL draft. ... Signed by Broncos (July 10, 2001). ... Granted free agency (March 3, 2004). ... Re-signed by Broncos (May 7, 2004).
PLAYING EXPERIENCE: Denver NFL, 2002-2003. ... Games/Games started: 2002 (16/16), 2003 (16/16). Total: 32/32.
HONORS: Named center on THE SPORTING NEWS college All-America first team (1999 and 2000).

HAMILTON, BOBBY — DE — RAIDERS

PERSONAL: Born July 1, 1971, in Denver, Colo. ... 6-5/280.
HIGH SCHOOL: East Marion (Columbia, Miss.).
COLLEGE: Southern Mississippi.
TRANSACTIONS/CAREER NOTES: Signed as non-drafted free agent by Seattle Seahawks (April 19, 1994). ... On injured reserve with knee injury (August 17, 1994-entire season). ... Assigned by Seahawks to Amsterdam Admirals in 1995 World League enhancement allocation draft. ... Released by Seahawks (August 15, 1995). ... Signed by New York Jets (June, 1996). ... Released by Jets (August 24, 1996). ... Re-signed by Jets to practice squad (August 26, 1996). ... Activated (September 4, 1996). ... Granted unconditional free agency (February 11, 2000). ... Signed by New England Patriots (July 16, 2000). ... Granted unconditional free agency (March 3, 2004). ... Signed by Oakland Raiders (May 19, 2004).
CHAMPIONSHIP GAME EXPERIENCE: Played in AFC championship game (1998, 2001 and 2003 seasons). ... Member of Super Bowl championship team (2001 and 2003 seasons).

			TOTALS			INTERCEPTIONS			
Year Team	G	GS	Tk.	Ast.	Sks.	No.	Yds.	Avg.	TD
1994—Seattle NFL	Did not play.								

H

Year Team	G	GS	Tk.	Ast.	Sks.	No.	Yds.	Avg.	TD
1996—New York Jets NFL	15	11	32	17	4.5	0	0	0.0	0
1997—New York Jets NFL	16	0	13	11	1.0	0	0	0.0	0
1998—New York Jets NFL	16	1	13	8	0.0	0	0	0.0	0
1999—New York Jets NFL	7	0	4	2	0.0	0	0	0.0	0
2000—New England NFL	16	16	41	38	1.5	0	0	0.0	0
2001—New England NFL	16	15	31	21	7.0	0	0	0.0	0
2002—New England NFL	16	15	34	21	2.0	1	0	0.0	0
2003—New England NFL	16	16	30	16	0.0	0	0	0.0	0
Pro totals (8 years)	118	74	198	134	16.0	1	0	0.0	0

HAMILTON, KEITH DT

PERSONAL: Born May 25, 1971, in Paterson, N.J. ... 6-6/295. ... Full name: Keith Lamarr Hamilton.
HIGH SCHOOL: Heritage (Lynchburg, Va.).
COLLEGE: Pittsburgh.
TRANSACTIONS/CAREER NOTES: Selected after junior season by New York Giants in fourth round (99th pick overall) of 1992 NFL draft. ... Signed by Giants (July 21, 1992). ... On injured reserve with Achilles' tendon injury (October 15, 2002-remainder of season). ... Announced retirement (February 6, 2004).
CHAMPIONSHIP GAME EXPERIENCE: Played in NFC championship game (2000 season). ... Played in Super Bowl 35 (2000 season).

			TOTALS		
Year Team	**G**	**GS**	**Tk.**	**Ast.**	**Sks.**
1992—New York Giants NFL	16	0	15	6	3.5
1993—New York Giants NFL	16	16	40	11	11.5
1994—New York Giants NFL	15	15	27	14	6.5
1995—New York Giants NFL	14	14	29	13	2.0
1996—New York Giants NFL	14	14	31	6	3.0
1997—New York Giants NFL	16	16	40	17	8.0
1998—New York Giants NFL	16	16	35	12	7.0
1999—New York Giants NFL	16	16	36	18	4.0
2000—New York Giants NFL	16	16	43	14	10.0
2001—New York Giants NFL	13	13	19	16	6.0
2002—New York Giants NFL	6	6	11	3	0.0
2003—New York Giants NFL	15	15	43	14	1.5
Pro totals (12 years)	173	157	369	144	63.0

HAMILTON, LAWRENCE WR JETS

PERSONAL: Born August 31, 1980, in Marshall, Texas. ... 6-3/204.
HIGH SCHOOL: Marshall (Texas).
COLLEGE: Stephen F. Austin.
TRANSACTIONS/CAREER NOTES: Signed as non-drafted free agent by Arizona Cardinals (April 28, 2003). ... Claimed on waivers by Cincinnati Bengals (August 6, 2003). ... Released by Bengals (October 16, 2003). ... Re-signed by Bengals to practice squad (October 17, 2003). ... Signed by New York Jets off Bengals practice squad (December 8, 2003).

			RECEIVING				TOTALS			
Year Team	**G**	**GS**	**No.**	**Yds.**	**Avg.**	**TD**	**TD**	**2pt.**	**Pts.**	**Fum.**
2003—Cincinnati NFL	5	1	0	0	0.0	0	0	0	0	0

HAMLIN, KEN S SEAHAWKS

PERSONAL: Born January 20, 1981, in Memphis, Tenn. ... 6-2/209.
HIGH SCHOOL: Fraysar (Memphis, Tenn.).
COLLEGE: Arkansas.
TRANSACTIONS/CAREER NOTES: Selected after junior season by Seattle Seahawks in second round (42nd pick overall) of 2003 NFL draft. ... Signed by Seahawks (July 24, 2003).

			TOTALS			INTERCEPTIONS			
Year Team	**G**	**GS**	**Tk.**	**Ast.**	**Sks.**	**No.**	**Yds.**	**Avg.**	**TD**
2003—Seattle NFL	16	14	76	20	0.0	1	2	2.0	0

HAMPTON, CASEY DT STEELERS

PERSONAL: Born September 3, 1977, in Galveston, Texas. ... 6-1/320.
HIGH SCHOOL: Ball (Galveston, Texas).
COLLEGE: Texas.
TRANSACTIONS/CAREER NOTES: Selected by Pittsburgh Steelers in first round (19th pick overall) of 2001 NFL draft. ... Signed by Steelers (July 21, 2001).
CHAMPIONSHIP GAME EXPERIENCE: Played in AFC championship game (2001 season).
HONORS: Named defensive tackle on THE SPORTING NEWS college All-America second team (1999). ... Named defensive tackle on THE SPORTING NEWS college All-America first team (2000). ... Played in Pro Bowl (2003 season).

			TOTALS		
Year Team	**G**	**GS**	**Tk.**	**Ast.**	**Sks.**
2001—Pittsburgh NFL	16	11	10	13	1.0
2002—Pittsburgh NFL	16	15	24	17	2.0
2003—Pittsburgh NFL	16	16	27	12	1.0
Pro totals (3 years)	48	42	61	42	4.0

HAMPTON, WILLIAM CB PANTHERS

PERSONAL: Born March 7, 1975, in Little Rock, Ark. ... 5-10/190.
HIGH SCHOOL: McClellan (Little Rock, Ark.).
COLLEGE: Murray State.
TRANSACTIONS/CAREER NOTES: Signed as non-drafted free agent by Denver Broncos (January 25, 2000). ... Released by Broncos (August 21, 2000). ... Signed by Philadelphia Eagles to practice squad (August 31, 2000). ... Released by Eagles (August 31, 2002). ... Signed by Carolina Panthers (January 13, 2003).
CHAMPIONSHIP GAME EXPERIENCE: Played in NFC championship game (2001 season). ... Member of Panthers for NFC championship game (2003 season); inactive. ... Member of Panthers for Super Bowl 38 (2003 season); inactive.

			TOTALS			INTERCEPTIONS			
Year Team	G	GS	Tk.	Ast.	Sks.	No.	Yds.	Avg.	TD
2000—Philadelphia NFL			Did not play.						
2001—Philadelphia NFL	13	0	6	0	0.0	1	33	33.0	1
2003—Carolina NFL	5	0	2	0	0.0	0	0	0.0	0
Pro totals (2 years)	18	0	8	0	0.0	1	33	33.0	1

HAND, NORMAN DT GIANTS

PERSONAL: Born September 4, 1972, in Queens, N.Y. ... 6-3/310. ... Full name: Norman L. Hand.
HIGH SCHOOL: Walterboro (S.C.).
JUNIOR COLLEGE: Itawamba Community College (Miss.).
COLLEGE: Mississippi.
TRANSACTIONS/CAREER NOTES: Selected by Miami Dolphins in fifth round (158th pick overall) of 1995 NFL draft. ... Signed by Dolphins (May 17, 1995). ... Inactive for all 16 games (1995). ... Claimed on waivers by San Diego Chargers (August 25, 1997). ... Granted free agency (February 13, 1998). ... Re-signed by Chargers (July 14, 1998). ... Designated by Chargers as franchise player (February 11, 2000). ... Free agency status changed from franchise to unconditional (February 16, 2000). ... Signed by New Orleans Saints (February 23, 2000). ... On injured reserve with foot injury (January 4, 2002-remainder of season). ... Traded by Saints to Seattle Seahawks for sixth-round pick (WR Kareem Kelly) in 2003 draft (April 27, 2003). ... On injured reserve with arm injury (November 14, 2003-remainder of season). ... Released by Seahawks (March 29, 2004). ... Signed by New York Giants (April 7, 2004).

			TOTALS			INTERCEPTIONS			
Year Team	G	GS	Tk.	Ast.	Sks.	No.	Yds.	Avg.	TD
1995—Miami NFL			Did not play.						
1996—Miami NFL	9	0	2	3	0.5	0	0	0.0	0
1997—San Diego NFL	15	1	16	3	1.0	0	0	0.0	0
1998—San Diego NFL	16	16	42	7	6.0	2	47	23.5	0
1999—San Diego NFL	14	14	41	14	4.0	0	0	0.0	0
2000—New Orleans NFL	15	15	44	10	3.0	0	0	0.0	0
2001—New Orleans NFL	13	13	25	11	3.5	0	0	0.0	0
2002—New Orleans NFL	16	13	30	9	2.5	0	0	0.0	0
2003—Seattle NFL	6	4	4	6	1.0	0	0	0.0	0
Pro totals (8 years)	104	76	204	63	21.5	2	47	23.5	0

HAND, OMARI DE CHARGERS

PERSONAL: Born July 3, 1980, in Philadelphia, Pa. ... 6-4/265. ... Full name: Omari Sean Hand.
HIGH SCHOOL: Lincoln (Tallahassee, Fla.).
COLLEGE: Tennessee.
TRANSACTIONS/CAREER NOTES: Signed as non-drafted free agent by San Diego Chargers (May 2, 2003). ... Waived by Chargers (August 31, 2003). ... Re-signed by Chargers to practice squad (September 2, 2003). ... Waived by Chargers (November 4, 2003). ... Re-signed by Chargers to practice squad (November 12, 2003). ... Activated (November 29, 2003).

			TOTALS		
Year Team	G	GS	Tk.	Ast.	Sks.
2003—San Diego NFL	1	0	2	0	0.0

HANKTON, CORTEZ WR JAGUARS

PERSONAL: Born January 20, 1981, in New Orleans, La. ... 6-0/200.
HIGH SCHOOL: St. Augustine (New Orleans, La.).
COLLEGE: Texas Southern.
TRANSACTIONS/CAREER NOTES: Signed as non-drafted free agent by Jacksonville Jaguars (April 28, 2003).
SINGLE GAME HIGHS (regular season): Receptions—4 (December 7, 2003, vs. Houston); yards—49 (December 7, 2003, vs. Houston); and touchdown receptions—0.

			RECEIVING				TOTALS			
Year Team	G	GS	No.	Yds.	Avg.	TD	TD	2pt.	Pts.	Fum.
2003—Jacksonville NFL	16	0	17	166	9.8	0	0	0	0	0

HANKTON, KARL WR PANTHERS

PERSONAL: Born July 24, 1970, in New Orleans, La. ... 6-2/202.
HIGH SCHOOL: De La Salle (New Orleans), then Valley Forge Military Academy (Wayne, Penn.).
COLLEGE: Trinity (Ill.).

TRANSACTIONS/CAREER NOTES: Signed as non-drafted free agent by Washington Redskins (April 1, 1997). ... Released by Redskins (February 25, 1998). ... Signed by Philadelphia Eagles (April 9, 1998). ... Released by Eagles (August 31, 1998). ... Re-signed by Eagles to practice squad (September 2, 1998). ... Released by Eagles (August 31, 1998). ... Re-signed by Eagles to practice squad (September 25, 1998). ... Activated (September 25, 1998). ... Released by Eagles (September 7, 1999). ... Signed by Carolina Panthers (February 29, 2000). ... Granted free agency (March 2, 2001).

CHAMPIONSHIP GAME EXPERIENCE: Played in NFC championship game (2003 season). ... Played in Super Bowl 38 (2003 season).

SINGLE GAME HIGHS (regular season): Receptions—2 (November 24, 2002, vs. Atlanta); yards—38 (October 13, 2002, vs. Dallas); and touchdown receptions—0.

			RECEIVING				TOTALS			
Year Team	**G**	**GS**	**No.**	**Yds.**	**Avg.**	**TD**	**TD**	**2pt.**	**Pts.**	**Fum.**
1998—Philadelphia NFL	10	0	0	0	0.0	0	0	0	0	0
2000—Carolina NFL	16	0	4	38	9.5	0	0	0	0	0
2001—Carolina NFL	11	0	0	0	0.0	0	0	0	0	0
2002—Carolina NFL	16	1	9	146	16.2	0	0	0	0	0
2003—Carolina NFL	14	0	2	27	13.5	0	0	0	0	0
Pro totals (5 years)	67	1	15	211	14.1	0	0	0	0	0

HANNAM, RYAN — TE — SEAHAWKS

PERSONAL: Born February 24, 1980, in St. Ansgar, Iowa. ... 6-2/248.

HIGH SCHOOL: St. Ansgar (Iowa).

COLLEGE: Northern Iowa.

TRANSACTIONS/CAREER NOTES: Selected by Seattle Seahawks in fifth round (169th pick overall) of 2002 NFL draft. ... Signed by Seahawks (July 25, 2002). ... On injured reserve with knee injury (October 31, 2003-remainder of season).

SINGLE GAME HIGHS (regular season): Receptions—1 (November 10, 2002, vs. Arizona); yards—16 (November 10, 2002, vs. Arizona); and touchdown receptions—1 (November 10, 2002, vs. Arizona).

			RECEIVING				KICKOFF RETURNS				TOTALS			
Year Team	**G**	**GS**	**No.**	**Yds.**	**Avg.**	**TD**	**No.**	**Yds.**	**Avg.**	**TD**	**TD**	**2pt.**	**Pts.**	**Fum.**
2002—Seattle NFL	14	0	1	16	16.0	1	0	0	0.0	0	1	0	6	0
2003—Seattle NFL	5	0	0	0	0.0	0	1	17	17.0	0	0	0	0	0
Pro totals (2 years)	19	0	1	16	16.0	1	1	17	17.0	0	1	0	6	0

HANSON, CHRIS — P — JAGUARS

PERSONAL: Born October 25, 1976, in Riverdale, Ga. ... 6-2/223.

HIGH SCHOOL: East Coweta (Ga.).

COLLEGE: Marshall.

TRANSACTIONS/CAREER NOTES: Signed as non-drafted free agent by Cleveland Browns (April 23, 1999). ... Claimed on waivers by Green Bay Packers (September 1, 1999). ... Released by Packers (September 14, 1999). ... Re-signed by Packers to practice squad (September 16, 1999). ... Released by Packers (October 12, 1999). ... Signed by Miami Dolphins (February 8, 2000). ... Assigned by Dolphins to Barcelona Dragons in 2000 NFL Europe enhancement allocation program (February 18, 2000). ... On injured reserve with knee injury (July 21, 2000-entire season). ... Released by Dolphins (August 15, 2001). ... Signed by Jacksonville Jaguars (August 18, 2001). ... On injured reserve with leg injury (October 10, 2003-remainder of season).

HONORS: Played in Pro Bowl (2002 season).

		PUNTING					
Year Team	**G**	**No.**	**Yds.**	**Avg.**	**Net avg.**	**In. 20**	**Blk.**
1999—Green Bay NFL	1	4	157	39.2	38.5	0	0
2000—Miami NFL				Did not play.			
2001—Jacksonville NFL	16	82	3577	43.6	37.1	24	0
2002—Jacksonville NFL	16	81	3583	§44.2	§37.6	27	0
2003—Jacksonville NFL	5	23	1001	43.5	31.1	4	1
Pro totals (4 years)	38	190	8318	43.8	36.6	55	1

HANSON, JASON — K — LIONS

PERSONAL: Born June 17, 1970, in Spokane, Wash. ... 5-11/182. ... Full name: Jason Douglas Hanson.

HIGH SCHOOL: Mead (Spokane, Wash.).

COLLEGE: Washington State.

TRANSACTIONS/CAREER NOTES: Selected by Detroit Lions in second round (56th pick overall) of 1992 NFL draft. ... Signed by Lions (July 23, 1992). ... Designated by Lions as transition player (February 15, 1994).

HONORS: Named kicker on THE SPORTING NEWS college All-America first team (1989). ... Named kicker on THE SPORTING NEWS NFL All-Pro team (1993). ... Played in Pro Bowl (1997 and 1999 season).

		FIELD GOALS							TOTALS		
Year Team	**G**	**1-29**	**30-39**	**40-49**	**50+**	**Tot.**	**Pct.**	**Lg.**	**XPM**	**XPA**	**Pts.**
1992—Detroit NFL	16	5-5	10-10	4-6	2-5	21-26	80.8	52	30	30	93
1993—Detroit NFL	16	9-9	15-15	7-12	3-7	‡34-‡43	79.1	53	28	28	‡130
1994—Detroit NFL	16	6-7	7-7	5-8	0-5	18-27	66.7	49	39	40	93
1995—Detroit NFL	16	6-6	16-17	5-10	1-1	28-34	82.4	56	*48	†48	132
1996—Detroit NFL	16	4-4	4-5	3-5	1-3	12-17	70.6	51	36	36	72
1997—Detroit NFL	16	10-10	8-9	5-5	3-5	26-29	89.7	†55	39	40	117
1998—Detroit NFL	16	8-8	7-7	13-15	1-3	29-33	87.9	51	27	29	114
1999—Detroit NFL	16	8-8	4-4	10-12	4-8	26-∞32	81.3	52	28	29	106
2000—Detroit NFL	16	8-9	10-12	4-7	2-2	24-30	80.0	54	29	29	101
2001—Detroit NFL	16	3-3	8-8	6-12	4-7	21-30	70.0	54	23	23	86
2002—Detroit NFL	16	8-8	8-9	7-8	0-3	23-28	82.1	49	31	31	100
2003—Detroit NFL	16	7-7	6-6	5-6	4-4	22-23	‡95.7	54	26	27	92
Pro totals (12 years)	192	82-84	103-109	74-106	25-53	284-352	80.7	56	384	390	1236

HAPE, PATRICK — TE — BRONCOS

PERSONAL: Born June 6, 1974, in Killen, Ala. ... 6-4/262. ... Full name: Patrick Stephen Hape.
HIGH SCHOOL: Brooks (Killen, Ala.).
COLLEGE: Alabama.
TRANSACTIONS/CAREER NOTES: Selected by Tampa Bay Buccaneers in fifth round (137th pick overall) of 1997 NFL draft. ... Signed by Buccaneers (July 20, 1997). ... Granted free agency (February 11, 2000). ... Re-signed by Buccaneers (July 23, 2000). ... Granted unconditional free agency (March 2, 2001). ... Signed by Denver Broncos (March 14, 2001). ... Granted unconditional free agency (March 3, 2004). ... Re-signed by Broncos (April 15, 2004).
CHAMPIONSHIP GAME EXPERIENCE: Played in NFC championship game (1999 season).
SINGLE GAME HIGHS (regular season): Receptions—2 (December 14, 2003, vs. Cleveland); yards—35 (December 16, 2001, vs. Kansas City); and touchdown receptions—1 (November 17, 2002, vs. Seattle). ... Attempts—2 (September 10, 2001, vs. New York Giants); yards—1 (August 31, 1997, vs. San Francisco); and rushing touchdowns—0.

			RECEIVING				TOTALS			
Year Team	**G**	**GS**	**No.**	**Yds.**	**Avg.**	**TD**	**TD**	**2pt.**	**Pts.**	**Fum.**
1997—Tampa Bay NFL	14	3	4	22	5.5	1	1	0	6	1
1998—Tampa Bay NFL	16	2	4	27	6.8	0	0	1	2	1
1999—Tampa Bay NFL	15	1	5	12	2.4	1	1	0	6	0
2000—Tampa Bay NFL	16	2	6	39	6.5	0	0	0	0	0
2001—Denver NFL	15	8	15	96	6.4	3	3	0	18	0
2002—Denver NFL	16	0	6	26	4.3	2	2	0	12	0
2003—Denver NFL	16	0	3	30	10.0	0	0	0	0	0
Pro totals (7 years)	108	16	43	252	5.9	7	7	1	44	2

HARDY, KEVIN — LB — BENGALS

PERSONAL: Born July 24, 1973, in Evansville, Ind. ... 6-4/259. ... Full name: Kevin Lamont Hardy.
HIGH SCHOOL: Harrison (Evansville, Ind.).
COLLEGE: Illinois.
TRANSACTIONS/CAREER NOTES: Selected by Jacksonville Jaguars in first round (second pick overall) of 1996 NFL draft. ... Signed by Jaguars (July 17, 1996). ... On injured reserve with knee injury (December 11, 2001-remainder of season). ... Granted unconditional free agency (March 1, 2002). ... Signed by Dallas Cowboys (April 14, 2002). ... Granted unconditional free agency (February 28, 2003). ... Signed by Cincinnati Bengals (March 7, 2003).
CHAMPIONSHIP GAME EXPERIENCE: Played in AFC championship game (1996 and 1999 seasons).
HONORS: Butkus Award winner (1995). ... Named linebacker on THE SPORTING NEWS college All-America first team (1995). ... Named linebacker on THE SPORTING NEWS NFL All-Pro team (1999). ... Played in Pro Bowl (1999 season).

			TOTALS			INTERCEPTIONS			
Year Team	**G**	**GS**	**Tk.**	**Ast.**	**Sks.**	**No.**	**Yds.**	**Avg.**	**TD**
1996—Jacksonville NFL	16	15	64	22	5.5	2	19	9.5	0
1997—Jacksonville NFL	13	11	48	7	2.5	0	0	0.0	0
1998—Jacksonville NFL	16	16	87	25	1.5	2	40	20.0	0
1999—Jacksonville NFL	16	16	74	24	10.5	0	0	0.0	0
2000—Jacksonville NFL	16	16	72	14	3.0	1	0	0.0	0
2001—Jacksonville NFL	9	9	57	12	5.5	0	0	0.0	0
2002—Dallas NFL	16	15	60	15	2.0	0	0	0.0	0
2003—Cincinnati NFL	16	16	59	33	1.5	0	0	0.0	0
Pro totals (8 years)	118	114	521	152	32.0	5	59	11.8	0

HARPER, DEVERON — CB — SAINTS

PERSONAL: Born November 15, 1977, in Orangeburg, S.C. ... 5-11/187. ... Full name: Deveron Alfredo Harper.
HIGH SCHOOL: Orangeburg-Wilkinson (Orangeburg, S.C.).
COLLEGE: Notre Dame.
TRANSACTIONS/CAREER NOTES: Signed as non-drafted free agent by Carolina Panthers (April 17, 2000). ... Released by Panthers (August 1, 2002). ... Selected by Scottish Claymores in 2003 NFL Europe draft (February 5, 2003). ... Signed by New Orleans Saints (July 14, 2003).

			TOTALS			INTERCEPTIONS			
Year Team	**G**	**GS**	**Tk.**	**Ast.**	**Sks.**	**No.**	**Yds.**	**Avg.**	**TD**
2000—Carolina NFL	16	0	0	0	0.0	0	0	0.0	0
2001—Carolina NFL	8	1	3	0	0.0	0	0	0.0	0
2003—New Orleans NFL	14	0	2	1	0.0	0	0	0.0	0
Pro totals (3 years)	38	1	5	1	0.0	0	0	0.0	0

HARPER, NICK — CB — COLTS

PERSONAL: Born September 10, 1974, in Baldwin, Ga. ... 5-10/182. ... Full name: Nicholas Necosi Harper.
HIGH SCHOOL: Baldwin (Milledgeville, Ga.).
COLLEGE: Fort Valley (Ga.) State.
TRANSACTIONS/CAREER NOTES: Signed as non-drafted free agent by Indianapolis Colts (January 16, 2001). ... Granted free agency (March 3, 2004). ... Re-signed by Colts (April 23, 2004).
CHAMPIONSHIP GAME EXPERIENCE: Played in AFC championship game (2003 season).

			TOTALS			INTERCEPTIONS			
Year Team	**G**	**GS**	**Tk.**	**Ast.**	**Sks.**	**No.**	**Yds.**	**Avg.**	**TD**
2001—Indianapolis NFL	13	2	19	4	0.0	2	17	8.5	0
2002—Indianapolis NFL	16	1	35	5	0.0	0	0	0.0	0
2003—Indianapolis NFL	16	13	82	13	0.0	4	121	30.3	1
Pro totals (3 years)	45	16	136	22	0.0	6	138	23.0	1

H

HARRINGTON, JOEY QB LIONS

PERSONAL: Born October 21, 1978, in Portland, Ore. ... 6-4/220. ... Full name: John Joseph Harrington.
HIGH SCHOOL: Central Catholic (Portland, Ore.).
COLLEGE: Oregon.
TRANSACTIONS/CAREER NOTES: Selected by Detroit Lions in first round (third pick overall) of 2002 NFL draft. ... Signed by Lions (July 23, 2002).
HONORS: Named quarterback on THE SPORTING NEWS college All-America second team (2001).
SINGLE GAME HIGHS (regular season): Attempts—55 (September 14, 2003, vs. Green Bay); completions—26 (December 28, 2003, vs. St. Louis); yards—309 (October 13, 2002, vs. Minnesota); and touchdown passes—4 (September 7, 2003, vs. Arizona).
STATISTICAL PLATEAUS: 300-yard passing games: 2002 (1). Total: 1.
MISCELLANEOUS: Regular-season record as starting NFL quarterback: 8-20 (.286).

			PASSING										RUSHING				TOTALS		
Year Team	G	GS	Att.	Cmp.	Pct.	Yds.	TD	Int.	Avg.	Skd.	Rat.		Att.	Yds.	Avg.	TD	TD	2pt.	Pts.
2002—Detroit NFL	14	12	429	215	50.1	2294	12	16	5.35	8	59.9		7	4	0.6	0	0	0	0
2003—Detroit NFL	16	16	554	309	55.8	2880	17	†22	5.20	9	63.9		30	86	2.9	0	0	0	0
Pro totals (2 years)	30	28	983	524	53.3	5174	29	38	5.26	17	62.2		37	90	2.4	0	0	0	0

HARRIS, AL CB PACKERS

PERSONAL: Born December 7, 1974, in Pompano Beach, Fla. ... 6-1/185. ... Full name: Alshinard Harris.
HIGH SCHOOL: Ely (Pompano Beach, Fla.).
JUNIOR COLLEGE: Trinity Valley Community College (Texas).
COLLEGE: Texas A&M-Kingsville.
TRANSACTIONS/CAREER NOTES: Selected by Tampa Bay Buccaneers in sixth round (169th pick overall) of 1997 NFL draft. ... Signed by Buccaneers (July 1, 1997). ... Released by Buccaneers (August 24, 1997). ... Re-signed by Buccaneers to practice squad (August 26, 1997). ... Claimed on waivers by Philadelphia Eagles (August 31, 1998). ... Traded by Eagles to Green Bay Packers for second-round pick (traded to San Diego) in 2003 draft (March 1, 2003).
CHAMPIONSHIP GAME EXPERIENCE: Played in NFC championship game (2001 and 2002 seasons).

			TOTALS			INTERCEPTIONS			
Year Team	G	GS	Tk.	Ast.	Sks.	No.	Yds.	Avg.	TD
1998—Philadelphia NFL	16	7	40	1	0.0	0	0	0.0	0
1999—Philadelphia NFL	16	6	32	6	0.0	4	‡151	37.7	1
2000—Philadelphia NFL	16	4	25	2	0.0	0	1	0.0	0
2001—Philadelphia NFL	16	2	20	2	0.0	2	22	11.0	0
2002—Philadelphia NFL	16	2	22	2	0.0	1	0	0.0	0
2003—Green Bay NFL	16	16	46	2	0.0	3	89	29.7	1
Pro totals (6 years)	96	37	185	15	0.0	10	263	26.3	2

HARRIS, ANTWAN S

PERSONAL: Born May 29, 1977, in Raleigh, N.C. ... 5-9/194. ... Full name: Melvin Antwan Harris.
HIGH SCHOOL: Ravenscroft (Raleigh, N.C.).
COLLEGE: Virginia.
TRANSACTIONS/CAREER NOTES: Selected by New England Patriots in sixth round (187th pick overall) of 2000 NFL draft. ... Signed by Patriots (July 14, 2000). ... Granted unconditional free agency (March 3, 2004).
CHAMPIONSHIP GAME EXPERIENCE: Member of Patriots for AFC championship game (2003 season); inactive. ... Member of Patriots for Super Bowl 38 (2003 season); inactive.

			TOTALS			INTERCEPTIONS			
Year Team	G	GS	Tk.	Ast.	Sks.	No.	Yds.	Avg.	TD
2000—New England NFL	14	0	6	1	1.0	1	11	11.0	0
2001—New England NFL	11	1	2	2	0.0	0	0	0.0	0
2002—New England NFL	14	0	9	1	0.0	0	0	0.0	0
2003—New England NFL	13	1	5	5	0.0	0	0	0.0	0
Pro totals (4 years)	52	2	22	9	1.0	1	11	11.0	0

HARRIS, ARLEN RB RAMS

PERSONAL: Born April 22, 1980, in Chester, Pa. ... 5-10/212. ... Full name: Arlen Quincy Harris.
HIGH SCHOOL: Downingtown (Pa.).
COLLEGE: Hofstra.
TRANSACTIONS/CAREER NOTES: Signed as non-drafted free agent by St. Louis Rams (April 27, 2003).
SINGLE GAME HIGHS (regular season): Attempts—34 (September 7, 2003, vs. Pittsburgh); yards—85 (October 19, 2003, vs. Green Bay); and rushing touchdowns—3 (October 26, 2003, vs. Pittsburgh).

			RUSHING				RECEIVING				PUNT RETURNS				KICKOFF RETURNS				TOTALS		
Year Team	G	GS	Att.	Yds.	Avg.	TD	No.	Yds.	Avg.	TD	No.	Yds.	Avg.	TD	No.	Yds.	Avg.	TD	TD	2pt.	Pts.
2003—StL. NFL	16	2	85	255	3.0	4	15	102	6.8	0	7	36	5.1	0	51	1175	23.0	0	4	0	24

H

HARRIS, COREY S

PERSONAL: Born October 25, 1969, in Indianapolis, Ind. ... 5-11/213. ... Full name: Corey Lamont Harris.
HIGH SCHOOL: Ben Davis (Indianapolis).
COLLEGE: Vanderbilt.

TRANSACTIONS/CAREER NOTES: Selected by Houston Oilers in third round (77th pick overall) of 1992 NFL draft. ... Signed by Oilers (August 5, 1992). ... Claimed on waivers by Green Bay Packers (October 14, 1992). ... Granted free agency (February 17, 1995). ... Tendered offer sheet by Seattle Seahawks (March 3, 1995). ... Packers declined to match offer (March 10, 1995). ... Granted unconditional free agency (February 14, 1997). ... Signed by Miami Dolphins (March 17, 1997). ... Released by Dolphins (August 3, 1998). ... Signed by Baltimore Ravens (August 17, 1998). ... Granted unconditional free agency (February 12, 1999). ... Re-signed by Ravens (May 17, 1999). ... Granted unconditional free agency (February 11, 2000). ... Re-signed by Ravens (March 21, 2000). ... Granted unconditional free agency (March 1, 2002). ... Signed by Detroit Lions (April 2, 2002). ... On injured reserve with hamstring injury (December 8, 2003-remainder of season). ... Released by Lions (March 3, 2004).
CHAMPIONSHIP GAME EXPERIENCE: Played in AFC championship game (2000 season). ... Member of Super Bowl championship team (2000 season).
MISCELLANEOUS: Played wide receiver (1992 and 1993).

			TOTALS			INTERCEPTIONS				KICKOFF RETURNS				TOTALS			
Year Team	**G**	**GS**	**Tk.**	**Ast.**	**Sks.**	**No.**	**Yds.**	**Avg.**	**TD**	**No.**	**Yds.**	**Avg.**	**TD**	**TD**	**2pt.**	**Pts.**	**Fum.**
1992—Houston NFL	5	0	0	0	0.0	0	0	0.0	0	0	0	0.0	0	0	0	0	0
—Green Bay NFL	10	0	0	0	0.0	0	0	0.0	0	33	691	20.9	0	0	0	0	0
1993—Green Bay NFL	11	0	4	0	0.0	0	0	0.0	0	16	482	30.1	0	0	0	0	0
1994—Green Bay NFL	16	2	32	6	0.0	0	0	0.0	0	29	618	21.3	0	0	0	0	1
1995—Seattle NFL	16	16	76	9	0.0	3	-5	-1.7	0	19	397	20.9	0	1	0	6	0
1996—Seattle NFL	16	16	69	6	1.0	1	25	25.0	0	7	166	23.7	0	0	0	0	0
1997—Miami NFL	16	7	29	14	0.0	0	0	0.0	0	11	224	20.4	0	0	0	0	0
1998—Baltimore NFL	16	6	45	12	1.0	0	0	0.0	0	35	965	§27.6	▲1	1	0	6	2
1999—Baltimore NFL	16	0	31	6	1.0	1	24	24.0	1	38	843	22.2	0	1	0	6	0
2000—Baltimore NFL	16	0	31	3	0.0	2	44	22.0	0	39	907	23.3	0	0	0	0	1
2001—Baltimore NFL	16	16	74	10	0.0	2	1	0.5	0	11	235	21.4	0	0	0	0	0
2002—Detroit NFL	16	16	58	21	2.5	1	49	49.0	0	0	0	0.0	0	0	0	0	0
2003—Detroit NFL	13	13	43	8	1.0	1	-1	-1.0	0	0	0	0.0	0	1	0	6	0
Pro totals (12 years)	183	92	492	95	6.5	11	137	12.5	1	238	5528	23.2	1	4	0	24	4

HARRIS, COREY CB

PERSONAL: Born November 28, 1976, in Jacksonville, Fla. ... 5-10/187.
HIGH SCHOOL: Northside (Warner Robins, Ga.).
COLLEGE: North Alabama.
TRANSACTIONS/CAREER NOTES: Signed as non-drafted free agent by New Orleans Saints (May 20, 1999). ... Released by Saints (September 5, 1999). ... Re-signed by Saints to practice squad (September 6, 1999). ... Released by Saints (September 28, 1999). ... Re-signed by Saints to practice squad (October 27, 1999). ... Activated (December 17, 1999). ... Released by Saints (September 20, 2000). ... Assigned by Saints to Rhein Fire in 2001 NFL Europe enhancement allocation program (February 19, 2001). ... Released by Saints (May 8, 2001). ... Signed by Kansas City Chiefs (September 18, 2001). ... Released by Chiefs (August 31, 2003). ... Re-signed by Chiefs (September 10, 2003). ... Released by Chiefs (October 1, 2003).

			TOTALS			INTERCEPTIONS			
Year Team	**G**	**GS**	**Tk.**	**Ast.**	**Sks.**	**No.**	**Yds.**	**Avg.**	**TD**
1999—New Orleans NFL	3	0	0	0	0.0	0	0	0.0	0
2000—New Orleans NFL	3	1	0	0	0.0	0	0	0.0	0
2001—Kansas City NFL	4	0	0	0	0.0	0	0	0.0	0
2002—Kansas City NFL	14	0	15	2	1.0	0	0	0.0	0
2003—Kansas City NFL	3	0	1	0	0.0	0	0	0.0	0
Pro totals (5 years)	27	1	16	2	1.0	0	0	0.0	0

HARRIS, JOHNNIE S

PERSONAL: Born August 21, 1972, in Chicago, Ill. ... 6-0/215.
HIGH SCHOOL: Martin Luther King (Chicago).
JUNIOR COLLEGE: San Bernardino (Calif.) Valley.
COLLEGE: Mississippi State.
TRANSACTIONS/CAREER NOTES: Signed by San Antonio Texans of CFL (October 17, 1995). ... Selected by Edmonton Eskimos in 1996 U.S. Team Dispersal draft. ... Released by Eskimos (June 5, 1996). ... Played with Tampa Bay Storm of Arena League (1996-98). ... Signed by Toronto Argonauts of CFL (October 12, 1996). ... Released by Argonauts (May 15, 1997). ... Re-signed by Argonauts (June 2, 1997). ... Signed as non-drafted free agent by Oakland Raiders (February 28, 1999). ... Released by Raiders (September 5, 1999). ... Re-signed by Raiders to practice squad (September 7, 1999). ... Activated (December 1999). ... Released by Raiders (September 1, 2002). ... Signed by New York Giants (October 21, 2002). ... Granted unconditional free agency (March 3, 2004).
CHAMPIONSHIP GAME EXPERIENCE: Member of CFL championship team (1996). ... Played in AFC championship game (2000 season).

			TOTALS			INTERCEPTIONS			
Year Team	**G**	**GS**	**Tk.**	**Ast.**	**Sks.**	**No.**	**Yds.**	**Avg.**	**TD**
1996—Toronto CFL	4	...	...	...	0.0	0	0	0.0	0
1997—Toronto CFL	18	...	...	...	0.0	5	72	14.4	0
1998—			Did not play.						
1999—Oakland NFL	4	0	0	0	0.0	0	0	0.0	0
2000—Oakland NFL	15	2	27	6	0.0	0	0	0.0	0
2001—Oakland NFL	16	5	31	7	0.5	0	0	0.0	0
2002—New York Giants NFL	9	0	9	0	0.0	1	11	11.0	0
2003—New York Giants NFL	14	5	35	7	0.0	2	3	1.5	0
CFL totals (2 years)	22	...	...	...	0.0	5	72	14.4	0
NFL totals (5 years)	58	12	102	20	0.5	3	14	4.7	0
Pro totals (7 years)	80	...	...	...	0.5	8	86	10.8	0

HARRIS, KWAME — T — 49ERS

PERSONAL: Born March 15, 1982, in Jamaica. ... 6-7/310.
HIGH SCHOOL: Newark (Del.).
COLLEGE: Stanford.
TRANSACTIONS/CAREER NOTES: Selected after junior season by San Francisco 49ers in first round (26th pick overall) of 2003 NFL draft. ... Signed by 49ers (July 25, 2003).
PLAYING EXPERIENCE: San Francisco NFL, 2003. ... Games/Games started: 2003 (14/5). Total: 14/5.

HARRIS, NAPOLEON — LB — RAIDERS

PERSONAL: Born February 25, 1979, in Dixmoor, Ill. ... 6-2/255. ... Full name: Napoleon Bill Harris.
HIGH SCHOOL: Thornton (Harvey, Ill.).
COLLEGE: Northwestern.
TRANSACTIONS/CAREER NOTES: Selected by Oakland Raiders in first round (23rd pick overall) of 2002 NFL draft. ... Signed by Raiders (July 19, 2002).
CHAMPIONSHIP GAME EXPERIENCE: Played in AFC championship game (2002 season). ... Played in Super Bowl 37 (2002 season).

			TOTALS			INTERCEPTIONS			
Year Team	G	GS	Tk.	Ast.	Sks.	No.	Yds.	Avg.	TD
2002—Oakland NFL	15	13	59	22	0.5	0	0	0.0	0
2003—Oakland NFL	16	16	75	34	2.0	0	0	0.0	0
Pro totals (2 years)	31	29	134	56	2.5	0	0	0.0	0

HARRIS, NICK — P

PERSONAL: Born July 23, 1978, in Phoenix, Ariz. ... 6-2/218.
HIGH SCHOOL: Westview (Phoenix).
COLLEGE: California.
TRANSACTIONS/CAREER NOTES: Selected by Denver Broncos in fourth round (120th pick overall) of 2001 NFL draft. ... Signed by Broncos (May 22, 2001). ... Claimed on waivers by Cincinnati Bengals (August 29, 2001). ... Waived by Bengals (October 7, 2003). ... Signed by Detroit Lions (October 15, 2003). ... Granted free agency (March 3, 2004).

		PUNTING					
Year Team	G	No.	Yds.	Avg.	Net avg.	In. 20	Blk.
2001—Cincinnati NFL	16	84	3372	40.1	33.9	21	1
2002—Cincinnati NFL	15	65	2608	40.1	31.4	11	1
2003—Cincinnati NFL	5	28	1084	38.7	30.0	5	0
—Detroit NFL	11	63	2531	40.2	33.1	11	1
Pro totals (3 years)	47	240	9595	40.0	32.5	48	3

HARRIS, QUENTIN — S — CARDINALS

PERSONAL: Born January 26, 1977, in Wilkes-Barre, Pa. ... 6-1/214. ... Full name: Quentin Hugh Harris.
HIGH SCHOOL: Wilkes-Barre (Pa.).
COLLEGE: Syracuse.
TRANSACTIONS/CAREER NOTES: Signed as non-drafted free agent by Arizona Cardinals (April 22, 2002). ... Released by Cardinals (September 1, 2002). ... Re-signed by Cardinals to practice squad (September 3, 2002). ... Activated (November 14, 2002).

			TOTALS			INTERCEPTIONS			
Year Team	G	GS	Tk.	Ast.	Sks.	No.	Yds.	Avg.	TD
2002—Arizona NFL	6	0	0	0	0.0	0	0	0.0	0
2003—Arizona NFL	16	1	5	0	0.0	0	0	0.0	0
Pro totals (2 years)	22	1	5	0	0.0	0	0	0.0	0

HARRIS, WALT — CB — REDSKINS

PERSONAL: Born August 10, 1974, in LaGrange, Ga. ... 5-11/192. ... Full name: Walter Lee Harris.
HIGH SCHOOL: La Grange (Ga.).
COLLEGE: Mississippi State.
TRANSACTIONS/CAREER NOTES: Selected by Chicago Bears in first round (13th pick overall) of 1996 NFL draft. ... Signed by Bears (July 11, 1996). ... On injured reserve with knee injury (December 22, 1998-remainder of season). ... On injured reserve with knee injury (December 22, 2000-remainder of season). ... Granted unconditional free agency (March 2, 2001). ... Re-signed by Bears (April 25, 2001). ... Granted unconditional free agency (March 1, 2002). ... Signed by Indianapolis Colts (March 15, 2002). ... Released by Colts (February 27, 2004). ... Signed by Washington Redskins (March 18, 2004).
CHAMPIONSHIP GAME EXPERIENCE: Played in AFC championship game (2003 season).

			TOTALS			INTERCEPTIONS			
Year Team	G	GS	Tk.	Ast.	Sks.	No.	Yds.	Avg.	TD
1996—Chicago NFL	15	13	84	14	0.0	2	0	0.0	0
1997—Chicago NFL	16	16	76	7	0.0	5	30	6.0	0
1998—Chicago NFL	14	14	64	5	0.0	4	41	10.3	1
1999—Chicago NFL	15	15	60	10	1.0	1	-1	-1.0	0
2000—Chicago NFL	12	12	33	9	0.0	2	35	17.5	1
2001—Chicago NFL	15	13	49	2	0.0	1	45	45.0	1
2002—Indianapolis NFL	15	15	35	9	0.0	2	0	0.0	0
2003—Indianapolis NFL	16	15	36	19	0.0	0	0	0.0	0
Pro totals (8 years)	118	113	437	75	1.0	17	150	8.8	3

HARRISON, MARVIN — WR — COLTS

PERSONAL: Born August 25, 1972, in Philadelphia, Pa. ... 6-0/175. ... Full name: Marvin Daniel Harrison.
HIGH SCHOOL: Roman Catholic (Philadelphia).
COLLEGE: Syracuse.
TRANSACTIONS/CAREER NOTES: Selected by Indianapolis Colts in first round (19th pick overall) of 1996 NFL draft. ... Signed by Colts (July 8, 1996). ... On injured reserve with shoulder injury (December 2, 1998-remainder of season).
CHAMPIONSHIP GAME EXPERIENCE: Played in AFC championship game (2003 season).
HONORS: Named kick returner on THE SPORTING NEWS All-America first team (1995). ... Named wide receiver on THE SPORTING NEWS NFL All-Pro team (1999 and 2000-2003). ... Played in Pro Bowl (1999-2003 seasons).
RECORDS: Holds NFL single-season record for most pass receptions—143 (2002).
SINGLE GAME HIGHS (regular season): Receptions—14 (November 17, 2002, vs. Dallas); yards—196 (September 26, 1999, vs. San Diego); and touchdown receptions—3 (September 28, 2003, vs. New Orleans).
STATISTICAL PLATEAUS: 100-yard receiving games: 1996 (2), 1998 (2), 1999 (9), 2000 (8), 2001 (6), 2002 (10), 2003 (6). Total: 43.
MISCELLANEOUS: Holds Indianapolis Colts all-time records for most receptions (759), most yards receiving (10,072) and most touchdown receptions (83).

			RECEIVING				PUNT RETURNS				TOTALS			
Year Team	G	GS	No.	Yds.	Avg.	TD	No.	Yds.	Avg.	TD	TD	2pt.	Pts.	Fum.
1996—Indianapolis NFL	16	15	64	836	13.1	8	18	177	9.8	0	8	0	48	1
1997—Indianapolis NFL	16	15	73	866	11.9	6	0	0	0.0	0	6	2	40	2
1998—Indianapolis NFL	12	12	59	776	13.2	7	0	0	0.0	0	7	1	44	0
1999—Indianapolis NFL	16	16	115	*1663	14.5	§12	0	0	0.0	0	12	1	74	2
2000—Indianapolis NFL	16	16	†102	1413	13.9	§14	0	0	0.0	0	14	0	84	2
2001—Indianapolis NFL	16	16	109	§1524	14.0	§15	0	0	0.0	0	15	0	90	0
2002—Indianapolis NFL	16	16	*143	*1722	12.0	11	0	0	0.0	0	11	1	68	0
2003—Indianapolis NFL	15	15	94	1272	13.5	10	0	0	0.0	0	10	0	60	2
Pro totals (8 years)	123	121	759	10072	13.3	83	18	177	9.8	0	83	5	508	9

HARRISON, RODNEY — S — PATRIOTS

PERSONAL: Born December 15, 1972, in Markham, Ill. ... 6-1/220. ... Full name: Rodney Scott Harrison.
HIGH SCHOOL: Marian Catholic (Chicago Heights, Ill.).
COLLEGE: Western Illinois.
TRANSACTIONS/CAREER NOTES: Selected after junior season by San Diego Chargers in fifth round (145th pick overall) of 1994 NFL draft. ... Signed by Chargers (June 29, 1994). ... Released by Chargers (February 27, 2003). ... Signed by New England Patriots (March 12, 2003).
CHAMPIONSHIP GAME EXPERIENCE: Played in AFC championship game (1994 and 2003 seasons). ... Played in Super Bowl 29 (1994 season). ... Member of Super Bowl championship team (2003 season).
HONORS: Named safety on THE SPORTING NEWS NFL All-Pro team (1998 and 2001). ... Played in Pro Bowl (1998 and 2001 seasons).

			TOTALS			INTERCEPTIONS			
Year Team	G	GS	Tk.	Ast.	Sks.	No.	Yds.	Avg.	TD
1994—San Diego NFL	15	0	0	0	0.0	0	0	0.0	0
1995—San Diego NFL	11	0	21	3	0.0	5	22	4.4	0
1996—San Diego NFL	16	16	105	20	1.0	5	56	11.2	0
1997—San Diego NFL	16	16	96	36	4.0	2	75	37.5	1
1998—San Diego NFL	16	16	89	25	4.0	3	42	14.0	0
1999—San Diego NFL	6	6	30	11	1.0	1	0	0.0	0
2000—San Diego NFL	16	16	101	26	6.0	6	97	16.2	1
2001—San Diego NFL	14	14	91	17	3.5	2	51	25.5	0
2002—San Diego NFL	13	13	69	19	2.0	2	2	1.0	0
2003—New England NFL	16	16	93	32	3.0	3	0	0.0	0
Pro totals (10 years)	139	113	695	189	24.5	29	345	11.9	2

HARRISON, TYREO — LB — EAGLES

PERSONAL: Born May 15, 1980, in Sulphur Springs, Texas. ... 6-2/238. ... Full name: Tyreo Tremayne Harrison.
HIGH SCHOOL: Sulphur Springs (Texas).
COLLEGE: Notre Dame.
TRANSACTIONS/CAREER NOTES: Selected by Philadelphia Eagles in sixth round (198th pick overall) of 2002 NFL draft. ... Signed by Eagles (May 13, 2002). ... Released by Eagles (September 26, 2002). ... Re-signed by Eagles to practice squad (September 28, 2002). ... Activated (October 22, 2002).
CHAMPIONSHIP GAME EXPERIENCE: Member of Eagles for NFC championship game (2002 and 2003 seasons); inactive.

			TOTALS			INTERCEPTIONS			
Year Team	G	GS	Tk.	Ast.	Sks.	No.	Yds.	Avg.	TD
2002—Philadelphia NFL	2	0	0	0	0.0	0	0	0.0	0
2003—Philadelphia NFL	12	0	0	0	0.0	0	0	0.0	0
Pro totals (2 years)	14	0	0	0	0.0	0	0	0.0	0

HART, CLINTON — S — EAGLES

PERSONAL: Born July 20, 1977, in Dade City, Fla. ... 6-0/205. ... Full name: Clinton Glenn Hart.
HIGH SCHOOL: South Sumter (Bushnell, Fla.).
JUNIOR COLLEGE: Central Florida C.C.
TRANSACTIONS/CAREER NOTES: Signed as non-drafted free agent by Philadelphia Eagles (January 29, 2002). ... Assigned by Eagles to 2002 NFL Europe enhancement allocation program (February 7, 2002). ... Re-signed by Eagles (January 30, 2003).

CHAMPIONSHIP GAME EXPERIENCE: Played in NFC championship game (2003 season).

Year Team	G	GS	TOTALS Tk.	Ast.	Sks.	INTERCEPTIONS No.	Yds.	Avg.	TD
2003—Philadelphia NFL	16	9	38	8	1.0	0	0	0.0	0

HARTINGS, JEFF — C — STEELERS

PERSONAL: Born September 7, 1972, in St. Henry, Ohio. ... 6-3/301. ... Full name: Jeffrey Allen Hartings.
HIGH SCHOOL: St. Henry (Ohio).
COLLEGE: Penn State.
TRANSACTIONS/CAREER NOTES: Selected by Detroit Lions in first round (23rd pick overall) of 1996 NFL draft. ... Signed by Lions (September 27, 1996). ... Granted unconditional free agency (March 2, 2001). ... Signed by Pittsburgh Steelers (March 8, 2001).
PLAYING EXPERIENCE: Detroit NFL, 1996-2000; Pittsburgh NFL, 2001-2003. ... Games/Games started: 1996 (11/10), 1997 (16/16), 1998 (13/13), 1999 (16/16), 2000 (16/16), 2001 (16/16), 2002 (13/11), 2003 (16/16). Total: 117/114.
CHAMPIONSHIP GAME EXPERIENCE: Played in AFC championship game (2001 season).
HONORS: Named offensive lineman on THE SPORTING NEWS college All-America second team (1994). ... Named offensive lineman on THE SPORTING NEWS college All-America first team (1995).

HARTS, SHAUNARD — S — CHIEFS

PERSONAL: Born August 4, 1978, in Pittsburg, Calif. ... 6-0/207.
HIGH SCHOOL: Pittsburgh (Calif.).
COLLEGE: Boise State.
TRANSACTIONS/CAREER NOTES: Selected by Kansas City Chiefs in seventh round (212th pick overall) of 2001 NFL draft. ... Signed by Chiefs (July 3, 2001). ... Released by Chiefs (September 2, 2001). ... Re-signed by Chiefs to practice squad (September 3, 2001). ... Activated (December 22, 2001).

Year Team	G	GS	TOTALS Tk.	Ast.	Sks.	INTERCEPTIONS No.	Yds.	Avg.	TD
2001—Kansas City NFL	3	0	0	0	0.0	0	0	0.0	0
2002—Kansas City NFL	16	11	71	9	2.0	0	0	0.0	0
2003—Kansas City NFL	16	0	11	5	0.0	2	39	19.5	1
Pro totals (3 years)	35	11	82	14	2.0	2	39	19.5	1

HARTWELL, EDGERTON — LB — RAVENS

PERSONAL: Born May 27, 1978, in Las Vegas, Nev. ... 6-1/250.
HIGH SCHOOL: Cheyenne (Las Vegas, Nev.).
COLLEGE: Western Illinois.
TRANSACTIONS/CAREER NOTES: Selected by Baltimore Ravens in fourth round (126th pick overall) of 2001 NFL draft. ... Signed by Ravens (June 8, 2001). ... Granted free agency (March 3, 2004). ... Re-signed by Ravens (May 24, 2004).

Year Team	G	GS	TOTALS Tk.	Ast.	Sks.	INTERCEPTIONS No.	Yds.	Avg.	TD
2001—Baltimore NFL	16	0	0	0	0.0	0	0	0.0	0
2002—Baltimore NFL	16	16	§105	39	3.0	0	0	0.0	0
2003—Baltimore NFL	16	15	68	26	3.0	1	26	26.0	0
Pro totals (3 years)	48	31	173	65	6.0	1	26	26.0	0

HARTWIG, JUSTIN — C/G — TITANS

PERSONAL: Born November 21, 1978, in Mankato, Minn. ... 6-4/305.
HIGH SCHOOL: Valley (West Des Moines, Iowa).
COLLEGE: Kansas.
TRANSACTIONS/CAREER NOTES: Selected by Tennessee Titans in sixth round (187th pick overall) of 2002 NFL draft. ... Signed by Titans (July 11, 2002).
PLAYING EXPERIENCE: Tennessee NFL, 2002-2003. ... Games/Games started: 2002 (3/0), 2003 (16/16). Total: 19/16.
CHAMPIONSHIP GAME EXPERIENCE: Member of Titans for AFC championship game (2002 season); inactive.

HASSELBECK, MATT — QB — SEAHAWKS

PERSONAL: Born September 25, 1975, in Westwood, Mass. ... 6-4/223. ... Full name: Matthew Michael Hasselbeck. ... Son of Don Hasselbeck, tight end with New England Patriots (1977-85); and brother of Tim Hasselbeck, quarterback, Washington Redskins.
HIGH SCHOOL: Xaverian Brothers (Westwood, Mass.).
COLLEGE: Boston College.
TRANSACTIONS/CAREER NOTES: Selected by Green Bay Packers in sixth round (187th pick overall) of 1998 NFL draft. ... Signed by Packers (July 17, 1998). ... Released by Packers (September 3, 1998). ... Re-signed by Packers to practice squad (September 5, 1998). ... Traded by Packers with first-round pick (G Steve Hutchinson) in 2001 draft to Seattle Seahawks for first-round pick (DE Jamal Reynolds) in 2001 draft (March 2, 2001).
HONORS: Played in Pro Bowl (2003 season).
SINGLE GAME HIGHS (regular season): Attempts—55 (December 1, 2002, vs. San Francisco); completions—36 (December 29, 2002, vs. San Diego); passing yards—449 (December 29, 2002, vs. San Diego); and touchdown passes—5 (November 23, 2003, vs. Baltimore).
STATISTICAL PLATEAUS: 300-yard passing games: 2002 (4), 2003 (4). Total: 8.

MISCELLANEOUS: Regular-season record as starting NFL quarterback: 20-18 (.526). ... Post-season record as starting NFL quarterback: 0-1 (.000).

			PASSING									RUSHING				TOTALS		
Year Team	G	GS	Att.	Cmp.	Pct.	Yds.	TD	Int.	Avg.	Skd.	Rat.	Att.	Yds.	Avg.	TD	TD	2pt.	Pts.
1999—Green Bay NFL	16	0	10	3	30.0	41	1	0	4.10	1	77.5	6	15	2.5	0	0	0	0
2000—Green Bay NFL	16	0	19	10	52.6	104	1	0	5.47	1	86.3	4	-5	-1.2	0	0	0	0
2001—Seattle NFL	13	12	321	176	54.8	2023	7	8	6.30	38	70.9	40	141	3.5	0	0	0	0
2002—Seattle NFL	16	10	419	267	‡63.7	3075	15	10	7.34	26	87.8	40	202	5.1	1	1	1	8
2003—Seattle NFL	16	16	513	313	61.0	3841	26	15	7.49	42	88.8	36	125	3.5	2	2	0	12
Pro totals (5 years)	77	38	1282	769	60.0	9084	50	33	7.09	108	83.9	126	478	3.8	3	3	1	20

HASSELBECK, TIM QB REDSKINS

PERSONAL: Born April 6, 1978, in Norfolk, Mass. ... 6-1/211. ... Son of Don Hasselbeck, tight end with New England Patriots (1977-85); and brother of Matt Hasselbeck, quarterback, Seattle Seahawks.

HIGH SCHOOL: Xaverian Brothers (Westwood, Mass.).

COLLEGE: Boston College.

TRANSACTIONS/CAREER NOTES: Signed as non-drafted free agent by Buffalo Bills (April 24, 2001). ... Released by Bills (July 23, 2001). ... Signed by Baltimore Ravens (August 1, 2001). ... Released by Ravens (August 24, 2001). ... Signed by Philadelphia Eagles (February 6, 2002). ... Assigned by Eagles to Berlin Thunder in 2002 NFL Europe enhancement allocation program (February 12, 2002). ... Released by Eagles (September 1, 2002). ... Signed by Carolina Panthers to practice squad (October 22, 2002). ... Activated (October 25, 2002). ... Released by Panthers (October 29, 2002). ... Re-signed by Eagles to practice squad (November 19, 2002). ... Activated (November 27, 2002). ... Released by Eagles (August 31, 2003). ... Signed by Washington Redskins (October 23, 2003).

CHAMPIONSHIP GAME EXPERIENCE: Member of Eagles for NFC championship game (2002 season); inactive.

SINGLE GAME HIGHS (regular season): Attempts—42 (November 30, 2003, vs. New Orleans); completions—22 (November 30, 2003, vs. New Orleans); yards—231 (November 30, 2003, vs. New Orleans); and touchdown passes—2 (December 21, 2003).

MISCELLANEOUS: Regular-season record as starting NFL quarterback: 1-4 (.200).

			PASSING									RUSHING				TOTALS		
Year Team	G	GS	Att.	Cmp.	Pct.	Yds.	TD	Int.	Avg.	Skd.	Rat.	Att.	Yds.	Avg.	TD	TD	2pt.	Pts.
2002—Philadelphia NFL	2	0	0	0	0.0	0	0	0	0.00	0	.0	0	0	0.0	0	0	0	0
2003—Washington NFL	7	5	177	95	53.7	1012	5	7	5.72	9	63.6	15	41	2.7	0	0	0	0
Pro totals (2 years)	9	5	177	95	53.7	1012	5	7	5.72	9	63.6	15	41	2.7	0	0	0	0

HATCH, JEFF T

PERSONAL: Born September 28, 1979, in Annapolis, Md. ... 6-6/305.

HIGH SCHOOL: Severn (Millersville, Md.).

COLLEGE: Pennsylvania.

TRANSACTIONS/CAREER NOTES: Selected by New York Giants in third round (78th pick overall) of 2002 NFL draft. ... Signed by Giants (July 14, 2002). ... On injured reserve with back injury (August 26, 2002-entire season). ... Released by Giants (March 17, 2004).

PLAYING EXPERIENCE: New York Giants NFL, 2003. ... Games/Games started: 2003 (4/4). Total: 4/4.

HATCHETTE, MATTHEW WR JAGUARS

PERSONAL: Born May 1, 1974, in Cleveland, Ohio. ... 6-3/200. ... Full name: Matthew Isaac Hatchette.

HIGH SCHOOL: Jefferson (Delphos, Ohio).

COLLEGE: Langston (Okla.).

TRANSACTIONS/CAREER NOTES: Selected by Minnesota Vikings in seventh round (235th pick overall) of 1997 NFL draft. ... Signed by Vikings (June 20, 1997). ... Granted free agency (February 11, 2000). ... Re-signed by Vikings (April 11, 2000). ... Granted unconditional free agency (March 2, 2001). ... Signed by New York Jets (March 20, 2001). ... Released by Jets (February 25, 2002). ... Signed by Oakland Raiders (May 22, 2002). ... Released by Raiders (August 27, 2002). ... Selected by Amsterdam Admirals in 2003 NFL Europe draft (February 5, 2003). ... Signed by Jacksonville Jaguars (June 18, 2003). ... Released by Jaguars (December 10, 2003). ... Re-signed by Jaguars (December 17, 2003).

CHAMPIONSHIP GAME EXPERIENCE: Played in NFC championship game (1998 and 2000 seasons).

SINGLE GAME HIGHS (regular season): Receptions—6 (December 13, 1998, vs. Baltimore); yards—95 (December 13, 1998, vs. Baltimore); and touchdown receptions—1 (September 21, 2003, vs. Indianapolis).

			RECEIVING				TOTALS			
Year Team	G	GS	No.	Yds.	Avg.	TD	TD	2pt.	Pts.	Fum.
1997—Minnesota NFL	16	0	3	54	18.0	0	0	0	0	0
1998—Minnesota NFL	5	0	15	216	14.4	0	0	0	0	0
1999—Minnesota NFL	13	0	9	180	20.0	2	2	0	12	0
2000—Minnesota NFL	14	4	16	190	11.9	2	2	0	12	0
2001—New York Jets NFL	11	0	2	44	22.0	0	0	0	0	0
2003—Jacksonville NFL	6	4	15	203	13.5	2	2	0	12	0
Pro totals (6 years)	65	8	60	887	14.8	6	6	0	36	0

HAWKINS, ARTRELL CB PANTHERS

PERSONAL: Born November 24, 1976, in Johnstown, Pa. ... 5-10/190.

HIGH SCHOOL: Bishop McCort (Johnstown, Pa.).

COLLEGE: Cincinnati.

TRANSACTIONS/CAREER NOTES: Selected by Cincinnati Bengals in second round (43rd pick overall) of 1998 NFL draft. ... Signed by Bengals (May 14, 1998). ... Granted free agency (March 2, 2001). ... Re-signed by Bengals (April 4, 2001). ... Granted unconditional free agency (March

H

1, 2002). ... Re-signed by Bengals (March 18, 2002). ... Released by Bengals (March 5, 2004). ... Signed by Carolina Panthers (March 10, 2004).

			TOTALS			INTERCEPTIONS			
Year Team	G	GS	Tk.	Ast.	Sks.	No.	Yds.	Avg.	TD
1998—Cincinnati NFL	16	16	65	5	1.0	3	21	7.0	0
1999—Cincinnati NFL	14	13	61	7	0.0	0	0	0.0	0
2000—Cincinnati NFL	16	6	43	4	0.0	0	0	0.0	0
2001—Cincinnati NFL	14	13	49	10	0.0	3	26	8.7	0
2002—Cincinnati NFL	15	15	69	7	2.0	2	102	51.0	1
2003—Cincinnati NFL	14	9	50	5	0.0	1	8	8.0	0
Pro totals (6 years)	89	72	337	38	3.0	9	157	17.4	1

HAWTHORNE, MICHAEL S PACKERS

PERSONAL: Born January 26, 1977, in Sarasota, Fla. ... 6-3/200. ... Full name: Michael Seneca Hawthorne.

HIGH SCHOOL: Booker (Sarasota, Fla.).

COLLEGE: Purdue.

TRANSACTIONS/CAREER NOTES: Selected by New Orleans Saints in sixth round (195th pick overall) of 2000 NFL draft. ... Signed by Saints (June 23, 2000). ... On injured reserve with knee injury (December 22, 2002-remainder of season). ... Granted free agency (February 28, 2003). ... Re-signed by Saints (May 7, 2003). ... Waived by Saints (September 10, 2003). ... Signed by Green Bay Packers (September 15, 2003). ... Granted unconditional free agency (March 3, 2004). ... Re-signed by Packers (March 26, 2004).

			TOTALS			INTERCEPTIONS			
Year Team	G	GS	Tk.	Ast.	Sks.	No.	Yds.	Avg.	TD
2000—New Orleans NFL	11	1	6	1	0.0	0	0	0.0	0
2001—New Orleans NFL	11	2	15	3	0.0	0	0	0.0	0
2002—New Orleans NFL	6	4	25	9	0.0	1	0	0.0	0
2003—Green Bay NFL	14	2	22	6	1.0	2	8	4.0	0
Pro totals (4 years)	42	9	68	19	1.0	3	8	2.7	0

HAYES, DONALD WR PANTHERS

PERSONAL: Born July 13, 1975, in Madison, Wis. ... 6-4/220. ... Full name: Donald Ross Hayes Jr.

HIGH SCHOOL: Madison East (Wis.).

COLLEGE: Wisconsin.

TRANSACTIONS/CAREER NOTES: Selected by Carolina Panthers in fourth round (106th pick overall) of 1998 NFL draft. ... Signed by Panthers (July 8, 1998). ... Granted free agency (March 2, 2001). ... Re-signed by Panthers (March 2, 2001). ... Granted unconditional free agency (March 1, 2002). ... Signed by New England Patriots (March 12, 2002). ... Released by Patriots (February 21, 2003). ... Signed by Jacksonville Jaguars (March 11, 2003). ... Released by Jaguars (August 30, 2003). ... Signed by Panthers (April 26, 2004).

SINGLE GAME HIGHS (regular season): Receptions—7 (October 14, 2001, vs. New Orleans); yards—133 (November 28, 1999, vs. Atlanta); and touchdown receptions—1 (December 8, 2002, vs. Buffalo).

STATISTICAL PLATEAUS: 100-yard receiving games: 1999 (1), 2000 (1). Total: 2.

			RECEIVING				TOTALS			
Year Team	G	GS	No.	Yds.	Avg.	TD	TD	2pt.	Pts.	Fum.
1998—Carolina NFL	7	0	3	62	20.7	0	0	0	0	0
1999—Carolina NFL	13	1	11	270	24.5	2	2	0	12	0
2000—Carolina NFL	15	15	66	926	14.0	3	3	0	18	1
2001—Carolina NFL	16	15	52	597	11.5	2	2	0	12	1
2002—New England NFL	12	1	12	133	11.1	2	2	0	12	0
2003—	Did not play.									
Pro totals (5 years)	63	32	144	1988	13.8	9	9	0	54	2

HAYES, GERALD LB CARDINALS

PERSONAL: Born October 10, 1980, in Paterson, N.J. ... 6-1/237.

HIGH SCHOOL: Passaic County Technical Institute (Passaic, N.J.).

COLLEGE: Pittsburgh.

TRANSACTIONS/CAREER NOTES: Selected by Arizona Cardinals in third round (70th pick overall) of 2003 NFL draft. ... Signed by Cardinals (June 24, 2003).

			TOTALS			INTERCEPTIONS			
Year Team	G	GS	Tk.	Ast.	Sks.	No.	Yds.	Avg.	TD
2003—Arizona NFL	12	2	19	2	0.0	0	0	0.0	0

HAYNES, MICHAEL DE BEARS

PERSONAL: Born September 13, 1980, in Brooklyn, N.Y. ... 6-3/281. ... Full name: Michael Washington Augustis Haynes Jr.

HIGH SCHOOL: Balboa (Panama City, Fla.).

COLLEGE: Penn State.

TRANSACTIONS/CAREER NOTES: Selected by Chicago Bears in first round (14th pick overall) of 2003 NFL draft. ... Signed by Bears (July 25, 2003).

			TOTALS		
Year Team	G	GS	Tk.	Ast.	Sks.
2003—Chicago NFL	16	0	18	4	2.0

HAYNES, VERRON — RB — STEELERS

PERSONAL: Born February 17, 1979, in Woodstock, Ga. ... 5-10/223.
HIGH SCHOOL: North Springs (Atlanta).
COLLEGE: Georgia.
TRANSACTIONS/CAREER NOTES: Selected by Pittsburgh Steelers in fifth round (166th pick overall) of 2002 NFL draft. ... Signed by Steelers (July 24, 2002). ... On injured reserve with broken leg (December 17, 2002-remainder of season). ... On injured reserve with knee injury (December 10, 2003-remainder of season).
SINGLE GAME HIGHS (regular season): Attempts—11 (September 7, 2003, vs. Baltimore); yards—23 (October 27, 2002, vs. Baltimore); and rushing touchdowns—0.

			RUSHING				RECEIVING				TOTALS			
Year Team	G	GS	Att.	Yds.	Avg.	TD	No.	Yds.	Avg.	TD	TD	2pt.	Pts.	Fum.
2002—Pittsburgh NFL	14	0	10	51	5.1	0	3	10	3.3	0	0	0	0	0
2003—Pittsburgh NFL	12	0	20	63	3.2	0	7	57	8.1	0	0	0	0	2
Pro totals (2 years)	26	0	30	114	3.8	0	10	67	6.7	0	0	0	0	2

HAYNESWORTH, ALBERT — DT — TITANS

PERSONAL: Born June 17, 1981, in Hartsville, S.C. ... 6-6/320. ... Full name: Albert Haynesworth III.
HIGH SCHOOL: Hartsville (S.C.).
COLLEGE: Tennessee.
TRANSACTIONS/CAREER NOTES: Selected after junior season by Tennessee Titans in first round (15th pick overall) of 2002 NFL draft. ... Signed by Titans (July 29, 2002).
CHAMPIONSHIP GAME EXPERIENCE: Played in AFC championship game (2002 season).

			TOTALS		
Year Team	G	GS	Tk.	Ast.	Sks.
2002—Tennessee NFL	16	3	21	9	1.0
2003—Tennessee NFL	12	11	21	11	2.5
Pro totals (2 years)	28	14	42	20	3.5

HAYWARD, REGGIE — DE — BRONCOS

PERSONAL: Born March 14, 1979, in Chicago, Ill. ... 6-5/270.
HIGH SCHOOL: Thornridge (Dolton, Ill.).
COLLEGE: Iowa State.
TRANSACTIONS/CAREER NOTES: Selected by Denver Broncos in third round (87th pick overall) of 2001 NFL draft. ... Signed by Broncos (July 26, 2001). ... On injured reserve with hand injury (December 4, 2002-remainder of season). ... Granted free agency (March 3, 2004). ... Re-signed by Broncos (April 9, 2004).

			TOTALS		
Year Team	G	GS	Tk.	Ast.	Sks.
2001—Denver NFL	6	2	15	3	3.0
2002—Denver NFL	9	0	6	3	0.0
2003—Denver NFL	16	2	24	4	8.5
Pro totals (3 years)	31	4	45	10	11.5

HEAP, TODD — TE — RAVENS

PERSONAL: Born March 16, 1980, in Mesa, Ariz. ... 6-5/252. ... Full name: Todd Benjamin Heap.
HIGH SCHOOL: Mountain View (Mesa, Ariz.).
COLLEGE: Arizona State.
TRANSACTIONS/CAREER NOTES: Selected after junior season by Baltimore Ravens in first round (31st pick overall) of 2001 NFL draft. ... Signed by Ravens (July 28, 2001).
HONORS: Named tight end on THE SPORTING NEWS college All-America first team (2000). ... Played in Pro Bowl (2002 and 2003 seasons).
RECORDS: Shares NFL single-game record for most two-point conversions—2 (October 19, 2003, vs. Cincinnati).
SINGLE GAME HIGHS (regular season): Receptions—8 (November 16, 2003, vs. Miami); yards—146 (December 29, 2002, vs. Pittsburgh); and touchdown receptions—2 (October 20, 2002, vs. Jacksonville).
STATISTICAL PLATEAUS: 100-yard receiving games: 2002 (1), 2003 (1). Total: 2.

			RECEIVING				TOTALS			
Year Team	G	GS	No.	Yds.	Avg.	TD	TD	2pt.	Pts.	Fum.
2001—Baltimore NFL	12	7	16	206	12.9	1	1	0	6	1
2002—Baltimore NFL	16	16	68	836	12.3	6	6	1	38	0
2003—Baltimore NFL	16	16	57	693	12.2	3	3	*4	26	1
Pro totals (3 years)	44	39	141	1735	12.3	10	10	5	70	2

HEARD, RONNIE — S — 49ERS

PERSONAL: Born October 5, 1976, in Bay City, Texas. ... 6-3/215.
HIGH SCHOOL: Brazoswood (Clute, Texas).
COLLEGE: Mississippi.
TRANSACTIONS/CAREER NOTES: Signed as non-drafted free agent by San Francisco 49ers (April 20, 2000). ... Released by 49ers (August 27, 2000). ... Re-signed by 49ers to practice squad (August 29, 2000). ... Activated (October 16, 2000). ... Granted free agency (February 28, 2003). ... Released by 49ers (March 23, 2003). ... Re-signed by 49ers (May 16, 2003). ... Granted unconditional free agency (March 3, 2004). ... Re-signed by 49ers (March 4, 2004).

Year	Team	G	GS	TOTALS Tk.	Ast.	Sks.	INTERCEPTIONS No.	Yds.	Avg.	TD
2000	San Francisco NFL	13	3	13	3	2.0	0	0	0.0	0
2001	San Francisco NFL	16	0	24	6	1.0	0	0	0.0	0
2002	San Francisco NFL	12	6	34	8	0.0	4	60	15.0	0
2003	San Francisco NFL	12	1	7	4	0.5	1	0	0.0	0
Pro totals (4 years)		53	10	78	21	3.5	5	60	12.0	0

HEARST, GARRISON — RB — BRONCOS

PERSONAL: Born January 4, 1971, in Lincolnton, Ga. ... 5-11/215. ... Full name: Gerald Garrison Hearst.

HIGH SCHOOL: Lincoln County (Lincolnton, Ga.).

COLLEGE: Georgia.

TRANSACTIONS/CAREER NOTES: Selected after junior season by Phoenix Cardinals in first round (third pick overall) of 1993 NFL draft. ... Signed by Cardinals (August 28, 1993). ... On injured reserve with knee injury (November 4, 1993-remainder of season). ... Cardinals franchise renamed Arizona Cardinals for 1994 season. ... On physically unable to perform list with knee injury (August 23-October 13, 1994). ... Granted free agency (February 16, 1996). ... Re-signed by Cardinals (May 23, 1996). ... Claimed on waivers by Cincinnati Bengals (August 21, 1996). ... Granted unconditional free agency (February 14, 1997). ... Signed by San Francisco 49ers (March 7, 1997). ... On physically unable to perform list with leg injury (July 30, 1999-entire season). ... On physically unable to perform list with leg injury (August 22-November 21, 2000). ... Granted unconditional free agency (March 1, 2002). ... Re-signed by 49ers (March 19, 2002). ... Released by 49ers (February 26, 2004). ... Signed by Denver Broncos (March 24, 2004).

CHAMPIONSHIP GAME EXPERIENCE: Played in NFC championship game (1997 season).

HONORS: Doak Walker Award winner (1992). ... Named running back on THE SPORTING NEWS college All-America first team (1992). ... Named to play in Pro Bowl (1998 season); replaced by Emmitt Smith due to injury. ... Played in Pro Bowl (2001 season).

SINGLE GAME HIGHS (regular season): Attempts—31 (December 1, 2002, vs. Seattle); yards—198 (December 14, 1998, vs. Detroit); and rushing touchdowns—3 (December 1, 2002, vs. Seattle).

STATISTICAL PLATEAUS: 100-yard rushing games: 1995 (3), 1997 (3), 1998 (6), 2001 (4), 2002 (2), 2003 (1). Total: 19. 100-yard receiving games: 1998 (2), 2001 (1). Total: 3.

Year	Team	G	GS	RUSHING Att.	Yds.	Avg.	TD	RECEIVING No.	Yds.	Avg.	TD	TOTALS TD	2pt.	Pts.	Fum.
1993	Phoenix NFL	6	5	76	264	3.5	1	6	18	3.0	0	1	0	6	2
1994	Arizona NFL	8	0	37	169	4.6	1	6	49	8.2	0	1	0	6	0
1995	Arizona NFL	16	15	284	1070	3.8	1	29	243	8.4	1	2	0	12	12
1996	Cincinnati NFL	16	12	225	847	3.8	0	12	131	10.9	1	1	1	8	1
1997	San Francisco NFL	13	13	234	1019	4.4	4	21	194	9.2	2	6	0	36	2
1998	San Francisco NFL	16	16	310	1570	‡5.1	7	39	535	13.7	2	9	1	56	4
1999	San Francisco NFL	Did not play.													
2000	San Francisco NFL	Did not play.													
2001	San Francisco NFL	16	16	252	1206	4.8	4	41	347	8.5	1	5	0	30	1
2002	San Francisco NFL	16	16	215	972	4.5	8	48	317	6.6	1	9	1	56	4
2003	San Francisco NFL	12	12	178	768	4.3	3	25	211	8.4	1	4	0	24	2
Pro totals (9 years)		119	105	1811	7885	4.4	29	227	2045	9.0	9	38	3	234	28

HEIDEN, STEVE — TE — BROWNS

PERSONAL: Born September 21, 1976, in Rushford, Minn. ... 6-5/265. ... Full name: Steve Allen Heiden. ... Name pronounced: HIGH-den.

HIGH SCHOOL: Rushford-Peterson (Rushford, Minn.).

COLLEGE: South Dakota State.

TRANSACTIONS/CAREER NOTES: Selected by San Diego Chargers in third round (69th pick overall) of 1999 NFL draft. ... Signed by Chargers (July 22, 1999). ... Granted free agency (March 1, 2002). ... Re-signed by Chargers (April 3, 2002). ... Traded by Chargers to Cleveland Browns for seventh-round pick (traded to Dallas) in 2003 draft (September 1, 2002). ... On injured reserve with ankle injury (November 12, 2003-remainder of season).

SINGLE GAME HIGHS (regular season): Receptions—6 (October 26, 2003, vs. New England); yards—34 (October 26, 2003, vs. New England); and touchdown receptions—1 (November 3, 2002, vs. Pittsburgh).

Year	Team	G	GS	RECEIVING No.	Yds.	Avg.	TD	TOTALS TD	2pt.	Pts.	Fum.
1999	San Diego NFL	11	0	0	0	0.0	0	0	0	0	0
2000	San Diego NFL	15	3	6	32	5.3	1	1	0	6	0
2001	San Diego NFL	16	10	8	55	6.9	1	1	0	6	0
2002	Cleveland NFL	16	6	17	105	6.2	1	1	0	6	0
2003	Cleveland NFL	9	9	18	134	7.4	0	0	0	0	0
Pro totals (5 years)		67	28	49	326	6.7	3	3	0	18	0

HEINRICH, KEITH — TE — BROWNS

PERSONAL: Born March 19, 1979, in Houston, Texas. ... 6-5/255.

HIGH SCHOOL: Tomball (Texas).

COLLEGE: Sam Houston State.

TRANSACTIONS/CAREER NOTES: Selected by Carolina Panthers in sixth round (174th pick overall) of 2002 NFL draft. ... Signed by Panthers (July 12, 2002). ... On injured reserve with knee injury (October 17, 2002-remainder of season). ... Claimed on waivers by Cleveland Browns (August 28, 2003). ... Waived by Browns (August 31, 2003). ... Re-signed by Browns to practice squad (September 1, 2003). ... Activated (November 13, 2003).

SINGLE GAME HIGHS (regular season): Receptions—5 (November 16, 2003, vs. Arizona); yards—45 (November 16, 2003, vs. Arizona); and touchdown receptions—1 (December 14, 2003, vs. Denver).

Year Team	G	GS	RECEIVING No.	Yds.	Avg.	TD	TOTALS TD	2pt.	Pts.	Fum.
2002—Carolina NFL	4	0	0	0	0.0	0	0	0	0	0
2003—Cleveland NFL	7	3	8	64	8.0	2	2	0	12	0
Pro totals (2 years)	11	3	8	64	8.0	2	2	0	12	0

HEITMANN, ERIC — G — 49ERS

PERSONAL: Born February 24, 1980, in Brookshire, Texas. ... 6-3/305.
HIGH SCHOOL: Katy (Texas).
COLLEGE: Stanford.
TRANSACTIONS/CAREER NOTES: Selected by San Francisco 49ers in seventh round (239th pick overall) of 2002 NFL draft. ... Signed by 49ers (July 21, 2002).
PLAYING EXPERIENCE: San Francisco NFL, 2002-2003. ... Games/Games started: 2002 (16/12), 2003 (9/8). Total: 25/20.
HONORS: Named guard on THE SPORTING NEWS college All-America second team (2001).

HELLER, WILL — TE — BUCCANEERS

PERSONAL: Born February 28, 1981, in Dunwoody, Ga. ... 6-6/250. ... Full name: Will Sanders Heller.
HIGH SCHOOL: Marist (Ga.).
COLLEGE: Georgia Tech.
TRANSACTIONS/CAREER NOTES: Signed as non-drafted free agent by Tampa Bay Buccaneers (April 28, 2003).
SINGLE GAME HIGHS (regular season): Receptions—1 (October 19, 2003, vs. San Francisco); yards—11 (October 19, 2003, vs. San Francisco); and touchdown receptions—1 (October 12, 2003, vs. Washington).

Year Team	G	GS	RECEIVING No.	Yds.	Avg.	TD	TOTALS TD	2pt.	Pts.	Fum.
2003—Tampa Bay NFL	9	1	2	15	7.5	1	1	0	6	0

HENDERSON, E.J. — LB — VIKINGS

PERSONAL: Born August 3, 1980, in Aberdeen, Md. ... 6-1/245. ... Full name: Eric N. Henderson.
HIGH SCHOOL: Aberdeen (Md.).
COLLEGE: Maryland.
TRANSACTIONS/CAREER NOTES: Selected by Minnesota Vikings in second round (40th pick overall) of 2003 NFL draft. ... Signed by Vikings (July 25, 2003).

Year Team	G	GS	TOTALS Tk.	Ast.	Sks.	INTERCEPTIONS No.	Yds.	Avg.	TD
2003—Minnesota NFL	16	0	15	2	0.0	0	0	0.0	0

HENDERSON, JAMIE — CB

PERSONAL: Born January 1, 1979, in Carrollton, Ga. ... 6-2/202. ... Full name: Jamie Concepcion Henderson.
HIGH SCHOOL: Carrolton (Ga.).
JUNIOR COLLEGE: Mississippi Gulf Coast Junior College.
COLLEGE: Georgia.
TRANSACTIONS/CAREER NOTES: Selected by New York Jets in fourth round (101st pick overall) of 2001 NFL draft. ... Signed by Jets (June 28, 2001). ... On injured reserve with shoulder injury (October 8, 2002-remainder of season). ... Granted free agency (March 3, 2004).

Year Team	G	GS	TOTALS Tk.	Ast.	Sks.	INTERCEPTIONS No.	Yds.	Avg.	TD
2001—New York Jets NFL	16	0	8	4	0.0	1	5	5.0	0
2002—New York Jets NFL	2	0	3	0	0.0	0	0	0.0	0
2003—New York Jets NFL	14	0	10	2	0.0	0	0	0.0	0
Pro totals (3 years)	32	0	21	6	0.0	1	5	5.0	0

HENDERSON, JOHN — DT — JAGUARS

PERSONAL: Born January 9, 1979, in Nashville, Tenn. ... 6-7/328. ... Full name: John Nathan Henderson.
HIGH SCHOOL: Pearl-Cohn (Nashville, Tenn.).
COLLEGE: Tennessee.
TRANSACTIONS/CAREER NOTES: Selected by Jacksonville Jaguars in first round (ninth pick overall) of 2002 NFL draft. ... Signed by Jaguars (July 25, 2002).
HONORS: Named defensive tackle on THE SPORTING NEWS college All-America first team (2000 and 2001). ... Outland Trophy winner (2000).

Year Team	G	GS	TOTALS Tk.	Ast.	Sks.
2002—Jacksonville NFL	16	13	45	9	6.5
2003—Jacksonville NFL	16	16	47	11	3.5
Pro totals (2 years)	32	29	92	20	10.0

HENDERSON, WILLIAM FB PACKERS

PERSONAL: Born February 19, 1971, in Richmond, Va. ... 6-1/249. ... Full name: William Terrelle Henderson.

HIGH SCHOOL: Thomas Dale (Chester, Va.).

COLLEGE: North Carolina.

TRANSACTIONS/CAREER NOTES: Selected by Green Bay Packers in third round (66th pick overall) of 1995 NFL draft. ... Signed by Packers (July 17, 1995). ... Granted free agency (February 13, 1998). ... Re-signed by Packers (June 15, 1998). ... Granted unconditional free agency (February 12, 1999). ... Re-signed by Packers (April 6, 1999). ... Granted unconditional free agency (March 1, 2002). ... Re-signed by Packers (March 1, 2002).

CHAMPIONSHIP GAME EXPERIENCE: Played in NFC championship game (1995-1997 seasons). ... Member of Super Bowl championship team (1996 season). ... Played in Super Bowl 32 (1997 season).

SINGLE GAME HIGHS (regular season): Attempts—6 (December 29, 2002, vs. New York Jets); yards—40 (September 9, 1996, vs. Philadelphia); and rushing touchdowns—1 (September 8, 2002, vs. Atlanta).

			RUSHING				RECEIVING				KICKOFF RETURNS				TOTALS			
Year Team	G	GS	Att.	Yds.	Avg.	TD	No.	Yds.	Avg.	TD	No.	Yds.	Avg.	TD	TD	2pt.	Pts.	Fum.
1995—Green Bay NFL	15	1	7	35	5.0	0	3	21	7.0	0	0	0	0.0	0	0	0	0	0
1996—Green Bay NFL	16	11	39	130	3.3	0	27	203	7.5	1	2	38	19.0	0	1	0	6	1
1997—Green Bay NFL	16	14	31	113	3.6	0	41	367	9.0	1	0	0	0.0	0	1	0	6	1
1998—Green Bay NFL	16	10	23	70	3.0	2	37	241	6.5	1	0	0	0.0	0	3	0	18	1
1999—Green Bay NFL	16	13	7	29	4.1	2	30	203	6.8	1	2	23	11.5	0	3	0	18	1
2000—Green Bay NFL	16	6	2	16	8.0	0	35	234	6.7	1	5	80	16.0	0	1	0	6	1
2001—Green Bay NFL	16	8	6	11	1.8	0	21	193	9.2	0	6	62	10.3	0	0	0	0	0
2002—Green Bay NFL	15	12	7	27	3.9	1	26	168	6.5	3	0	0	0.0	0	4	0	24	0
2003—Green Bay NFL	16	12	0	0	0.0	0	24	214	8.9	3	3	33	11.0	0	3	0	18	0
Pro totals (9 years)	142	87	122	431	3.5	5	244	1844	7.6	11	18	236	13.1	0	16	0	96	5

HENDRICKS, TOMMY LB JAGUARS

PERSONAL: Born October 23, 1978, in Houston, Texas. ... 6-2/235. ... Full name: Thomas Emmett Hendricks III.

HIGH SCHOOL: Scarborough (Texas), then Eiserhower (Houston).

COLLEGE: Michigan.

TRANSACTIONS/CAREER NOTES: Signed as non-drafted free agent by Miami Dolphins (April 25, 2000). ... Released by Dolphins (August 27, 2000). ... Re-signed by Dophins (September 26, 2000). ... Released by Dolphins (October 2, 2000). ... Re-signed by Dolphins to practice squad (October 4, 2000). ... Activated (November 10, 2000). ... Granted unconditional free agency (March 3, 2004). ... Signed by Jacksonville Jaguars (March 6, 2004).

			TOTALS			INTERCEPTIONS			
Year Team	G	GS	Tk.	Ast.	Sks.	No.	Yds.	Avg.	TD
2000—Miami NFL	8	0	0	1	0.0	0	0	0.0	0
2001—Miami NFL	16	1	2	2	0.0	0	0	0.0	0
2002—Miami NFL	16	0	2	0	0.0	0	0	0.0	0
2003—Miami NFL	16	2	17	6	0.0	0	0	0.0	0
Pro totals (4 years)	56	3	21	9	0.0	0	0	0.0	0

HENRY, ANTHONY CB BROWNS

PERSONAL: Born November 3, 1976, in Fort Myers, Fla. ... 6-1/205. ... Full name: Anthony Daniel Henry.

HIGH SCHOOL: Estero (Fla.).

COLLEGE: South Florida.

TRANSACTIONS/CAREER NOTES: Selected by Cleveland Browns in fourth round (97th pick overall) of 2001 NFL draft. ... Signed by Browns (June 15, 2001).

			TOTALS			INTERCEPTIONS			
Year Team	G	GS	Tk.	Ast.	Sks.	No.	Yds.	Avg.	TD
2001—Cleveland NFL	16	2	37	9	0.0	†10	177	17.7	1
2002—Cleveland NFL	16	10	57	5	0.0	2	4	2.0	0
2003—Cleveland NFL	14	13	39	15	0.0	1	19	19.0	0
Pro totals (3 years)	46	25	133	29	0.0	13	200	15.4	1

HENRY, TRAVIS RB BILLS

PERSONAL: Born October 29, 1978, in Frostproof, Fla. ... 5-9/215. ... Full name: Travis Deion Henry.

HIGH SCHOOL: Frostproof (Fla.).

COLLEGE: Tennessee.

TRANSACTIONS/CAREER NOTES: Selected by Buffalo Bills in second round (58th pick overall) of 2001 NFL draft. ... Signed by Bills (July 26, 2001).

HONORS: Played in Pro Bowl (2002 season).

SINGLE GAME HIGHS (regular season): Attempts—35 (December 1, 2002, vs. Miami); yards—169 (December 7, 2003, vs. New York Jets); and rushing touchdowns—3 (September 14, 2003, vs. Jacksonville).

STATISTICAL PLATEAUS: 100-yard rushing games: 2001 (2), 2002 (6), 2003 (5). Total: 13.

			RUSHING				RECEIVING				TOTALS			
Year Team	G	GS	Att.	Yds.	Avg.	TD	No.	Yds.	Avg.	TD	TD	2pt.	Pts.	Fum.
2001—Buffalo NFL	13	12	213	729	3.4	4	22	179	8.1	0	4	0	24	5
2002—Buffalo NFL	16	16	325	1438	4.4	13	43	309	7.2	1	14	0	84	11
2003—Buffalo NFL	15	15	331	1356	4.1	10	28	158	5.6	1	11	0	66	7
Pro totals (3 years)	44	43	869	3523	4.1	27	93	646	6.9	2	29	0	174	23

HENTRICH, CRAIG — P/K — TITANS

PERSONAL: Born May 18, 1971, in Alton, Ill. ... 6-3/213. ... Full name: Craig Anthony Hentrich. ... Name pronounced: HEN-trick.
HIGH SCHOOL: Alton-Marquette (Ill.).
COLLEGE: Notre Dame.
TRANSACTIONS/CAREER NOTES: Selected by New York Jets in eighth round (200th pick overall) of 1993 NFL draft. ... Signed by Jets (July 14, 1993). ... Released by Jets (August 24, 1993). ... Signed by Green Bay Packers to practice squad (September 7, 1993). ... Activated (January 14, 1994); did not play. ... Granted unconditional free agency (February 13, 1998). ... Signed by Tennessee Oilers (February 19, 1998). ... Oilers franchise renamed Tennessee Titans for 1999 season (December 26, 1998). ... Desiganted by Titans as transition player (February 20, 2003).
CHAMPIONSHIP GAME EXPERIENCE: Played in NFC championship game (1995-1997 seasons). ... Member of Super Bowl championship team (1996 season). ... Played in Super Bowl 32 (1997 season) and Super Bowl 34 (1999 season). ... Played in AFC championship game (1999 and 2002 seasons).
HONORS: Named punter on THE SPORTING NEWS NFL All-Pro team (1998). ... Played in Pro Bowl (1998 and 2003 seasons).

		PUNTING						KICKING						TOTALS	
Year Team	G	No.	Yds.	Avg.	Net avg.	In. 20	Blk.	50+	Tot.	Pct.	Lg.	XPM	XPA	Pts.
1993—Green Bay NFL						Did not play.								
1994—Green Bay NFL	16	81	3351	41.4	35.5	24	0	0-0	0-0	0.0	0	0	0	0
1995—Green Bay NFL	16	65	2740	42.2	34.6	26	2	0-0	3-5	60.0	49	5	5	14
1996—Green Bay NFL	16	68	2886	42.4	36.2	28	0	0-0	0-0	0.0	0	0	0	0
1997—Green Bay NFL	16	75	3378	45.0	36.0	26	0	0-0	0-0	0.0	0	0	0	0
1998—Tennessee NFL	16	69	3258	*47.2	*39.2	18	0	0-0	0-1	0.0	0	0	0	0
1999—Tennessee NFL	16	90	3824	42.5	38.1	35	0	0-0	0-0	0.0	0	0	0	0
2000—Tennessee NFL	16	76	3101	40.8	36.3	33	0	0-1	0-1	0.0	0	0	0	0
2001—Tennessee NFL	16	85	3567	42.0	37.0	28	0	0-0	0-0	0.0	0	0	0	0
2002—Tennessee NFL	16	65	2725	41.9	33.9	28	1	0-0	0-0	0.0	0	0	0	0
2003—Tennessee NFL	16	71	3117	43.9	§37.8	26	0	0-1	4-5	80.0	49	1	1	13
Pro totals (10 years)	160	745	31947	42.9	36.5	272	3	0-2	7-12	58.3	49	6	6	27

HERNDON, KELLY — CB — BRONCOS

PERSONAL: Born November 3, 1976, in Bedford, Ohio. ... 5-10/180.
HIGH SCHOOL: Chamberlain (Ohio).
COLLEGE: Toledo.
TRANSACTIONS/CAREER NOTES: Signed as non-drafted free agent by San Francisco 49ers (April 23, 1999). ... Released by 49ers (September 6, 1999). ... Re-signed by 49ers (July 7, 2000). ... Released by 49ers (August 28, 2000). ... Signed by New York Giants (May 15, 2001). ... Released by Giants (September 2, 2001). ... Re-signed by Giants to practice squad (September 4, 2001). ... Released by Giants (September 18, 2001). ... Signed by Denver Broncos (October 24, 2001).

			TOTALS			INTERCEPTIONS			
Year Team	G	GS	Tk.	Ast.	Sks.	No.	Yds.	Avg.	TD
2002—Denver NFL	14	0	0	0	0.0	1	0	0.0	0
2003—Denver NFL	15	11	56	5	0.0	3	19	6.3	0
Pro totals (2 years)	29	11	56	5	0.0	4	19	4.8	0

HERNDON, STEVE — G — FALCONS

PERSONAL: Born May 25, 1977, in LaGrange, Ga. ... 6-4/292. ... Full name: Steven Marshall Herndon.
HIGH SCHOOL: Troup County (LaGrange, Ga.).
COLLEGE: Georgia.
TRANSACTIONS/CAREER NOTES: Signed as non-drafted free agent by Miami Dolphins (April 25, 2000). ... Released by Dolphins (August 22, 2000). ... Signed by Denver Broncos to practice squad (August 29, 2000). ... Assigned by Broncos to Barcelona Dragons in 2001 NFL Europe enhancement allocation program (February 17, 2001). ... Received no tender from Broncos (2004). ... Signed by Atlanta Falcons (March 8, 2004).
PLAYING EXPERIENCE: Denver NFL, 2001-2003. ... Games/Games started: 2001 (5/3), 2002 (15/9), 2003 (2/0). Total: 22/12.

HERRING, KIM — SS — BENGALS

PERSONAL: Born September 10, 1975, in Detroit. ... 200. ... Full name: Kimani Masai Herring.
HIGH SCHOOL: Solon (Ohio).
COLLEGE: Penn State.
TRANSACTIONS/CAREER NOTES: Selected by Baltimore Ravens in second round (58th pick overall) of 1997 NFL draft. ... Signed by Ravens (July 18, 1997). ... On injured reserve with shoulder injury (December 2, 1998-remainder of season). ... Granted free agency (February 11, 2000). ... Re-signed by Ravens (April 18, 2000) ... Granted unconditional free agency (March 2, 2001). ... Signed by St. Louis Rams (March 22, 2001). ... On injured reserve with forearm injury (August 31, 2003-entire season). ... Released by Rams (March 1, 2004). ... Signed by Cincinnati Bengals (March 4, 2004).
CHAMPIONSHIP GAME EXPERIENCE: Member of Ravens for AFC Championship game (2000 season); inactive. ... Member of Super Bowl championship team (2000 season). ... Played in NFC championship game (2001 season). ... Played in Super Bowl 36 (2001 season).
HONORS: Named free safety on THE SPORTING NEWS college All-America first team (1996).

			TOTALS			INTERCEPTIONS			
Year Team	G	GS	Tk.	Ast.	Sks.	No.	Yds.	Avg.	TD
1997—Baltimore NFL	15	4	44	8	1.0	0	0	0.0	0
1998—Baltimore NFL	7	7	20	7	0.0	0	0	0.0	0
1999—Baltimore NFL	16	16	48	10	0.0	0	0	0.0	0
2000—Baltimore NFL	16	16	47	7	1.0	3	74	24.7	0
2001—St. Louis NFL	16	15	49	6	0.0	1	15	15.0	0
2002—St. Louis NFL	16	16	66	9	0.0	3	38	12.7	0
2003—St. Louis NFL				Did not play.					
Pro totals (6 years)	86	74	274	47	2.0	7	127	18.1	0

HETHERINGTON, CHRIS — FB — RAIDERS

PERSONAL: Born November 27, 1972, in North Branford, Conn. ... 6-3/245. ... Full name: Christopher Raymond Hetherington.
HIGH SCHOOL: Avon (Conn.) Old Farms.
COLLEGE: Yale.
TRANSACTIONS/CAREER NOTES: Signed as non-drafted free agent by Cincinnati Bengals (April 23, 1996). ... Released by Bengals (August 21, 1996). ... Re-signed by Bengals to practice squad (August 26, 1996). ... Signed by Indianapolis Colts off Bengals practice squad (October 22, 1996). ... Released by Colts (August 24, 1998). ... Re-signed by Colts (August 31, 1998). ... Released by Colts (February 12, 1999). ... Signed by Carolina Panthers (March 5, 1999). ... Granted unconditional free agency (February 11, 2000). ... Re-signed by Panthers (February 23, 2000). ... Granted unconditional free agency (March 1, 2002). ... Signed by St. Louis Rams (April 30, 2002). ... Granted unconditional free agency (February 28, 2003). ... Signed by Oakland Raiders (March 19, 2003). ... Granted unconditional free agency (March 3, 2004). ... Re-signed by Raiders (March 4, 2004).
SINGLE GAME HIGHS (regular season): Attempts—5 (December 10, 2000, vs. Kansas City); yards—29 (December 24, 2000, vs. Oakland); and rushing touchdowns—1 (December 10, 2000, vs. Kansas City).

			RUSHING				RECEIVING				KICKOFF RETURNS				TOTALS			
Year Team	G	GS	Att.	Yds.	Avg.	TD	No.	Yds.	Avg.	TD	No.	Yds.	Avg.	TD	TD	2pt.	Pts.	Fum.
1996—Indianapolis NFL	6	0	0	0	0.0	0	0	0	0.0	0	1	16	16.0	0	0	0	0	0
1997—Indianapolis NFL	16	0	0	0	0.0	0	0	0	0.0	0	2	23	11.5	0	0	0	0	0
1998—Indianapolis NFL	14	1	0	0	0.0	0	0	0	0.0	0	5	71	14.2	0	0	0	0	1
1999—Carolina NFL	14	0	2	7	3.5	0	0	0	0.0	0	1	16	16.0	0	0	0	0	0
2000—Carolina NFL	16	5	23	65	2.8	2	14	116	8.3	1	2	21	10.5	0	3	0	18	0
2001—Carolina NFL	16	1	5	12	2.4	0	23	124	5.4	0	4	31	7.8	0	0	0	0	0
2002—St. Louis NFL	6	4	1	0	0.0	0	1	2	2.0	0	0	0	0.0	0	0	0	0	0
2003—Oakland NFL	14	1	0	0	0.0	0	2	23	11.5	0	0	0	0.0	0	0	0	0	0
Pro totals (8 years)	102	12	31	84	2.7	2	40	265	6.6	1	15	178	11.9	0	3	0	18	1

HICKS, ARTIS — T — EAGLES

PERSONAL: Born November 28, 1978, in Jackson, Tenn. ... 6-4/303. ... Full name: Artis Hicks Jr.
HIGH SCHOOL: Central Merry (Jackson, Tenn.).
COLLEGE: Memphis.
TRANSACTIONS/CAREER NOTES: Signed as non-drafted free agent by Philadelphia Eagles (April 23, 2002). ... Inactive for 16 games (2002).
PLAYING EXPERIENCE: Philadelphia NFL, 2003. ... Games/Games started: 2003 (10/4). Total: 10/4.
CHAMPIONSHIP GAME EXPERIENCE: Played in NFC championship game (2003 season).

HICKS, BRANDON — DT

PERSONAL: Born November 17, 1977, in Shields, Ill. ... 6-0/282.
COLLEGE: Bowling Green.
TRANSACTIONS/CAREER NOTES: Signed as non-drafted free agent by Indianapolis Colts (April 26, 2002). ... Waived by Colts (September 1, 2002). ... Re-signed by Colts to practice squad (September 3, 2002). ... Activated (January 6, 2003). ... Waived by Colts (October 25, 2003). ... Re-signed by Colts (November 5, 2003). ... Released by Colts (November 18, 2003).

			TOTALS			INTERCEPTIONS			
Year Team	G	GS	Tk.	Ast.	Sks.	No.	Yds.	Avg.	TD
2003—Indianapolis NFL	4	0	1	1	0.0	0	0	0.0	0

HICKS, DWONE — RB — TITANS

PERSONAL: Born April 25, 1981, in Huntsville, Ala. ... 5-10/222. ... Full name: Kenneth Dwone Hicks.
HIGH SCHOOL: Lee (Huntsville, Ala.).
COLLEGE: Middle Tennessee State.
TRANSACTIONS/CAREER NOTES: Signed as non-drafted free agent by Tennessee Titans (April 28, 2003). ... Waived by Titans (November 11, 2003). ... Re-signed by Titans to practice squad (November 13, 2003). ... Activated (December 30, 2003).

			RUSHING				TOTALS			
Year Team	G	GS	Att.	Yds.	Avg.	TD	TD	2pt.	Pts.	Fum.
2003—Tennessee NFL	3	0	0	0	0.0	0	0	0	0	0

HICKS, ERIC — DE — CHIEFS

PERSONAL: Born June 17, 1976, in Erie, Pa. ... 6-6/280. ... Full name: Eric David Hicks.
HIGH SCHOOL: Mercyhurst (Erie, Pa.).
COLLEGE: Maryland.
TRANSACTIONS/CAREER NOTES: Signed as non-drafted free agent by Kansas City Chiefs (April 25, 1998). ... Granted unconditional free agency (March 3, 2004). ... Re-signed by Chiefs (March 5, 2004).

			TOTALS		
Year Team	G	GS	Tk.	Ast.	Sks.
1998—Kansas City NFL	3	0	0	0	0.0
1999—Kansas City NFL	16	16	28	9	4.0
2000—Kansas City NFL	13	11	37	9	14.0
2001—Kansas City NFL	16	16	44	9	3.5
2002—Kansas City NFL	16	15	40	14	9.0
2003—Kansas City NFL	16	16	37	12	5.0
Pro totals (6 years)	80	74	186	53	35.5

HILL, DARRELL — WR — TITANS

PERSONAL: Born June 19, 1979, in Chicago, Ill. ... 6-3/200.
HIGH SCHOOL: Mount Carmel (Chicago).
COLLEGE: Northern Illinois.
TRANSACTIONS/CAREER NOTES: Selected by Tennessee Titans in seventh round (225th pick overall) of 2002 NFL draft. ... Signed by Titans (July 22, 2002).
CHAMPIONSHIP GAME EXPERIENCE: Member of Titans for AFC championship game (2002 season); inactive.

			RECEIVING				TOTALS			
Year Team	G	GS	No.	Yds.	Avg.	TD	TD	2pt.	Pts.	Fum.
2002—Tennessee NFL	7	0	0	0	0.0	0	0	0	0	0
2003—Tennessee NFL	12	0	0	0	0.0	0	0	0	0	0
Pro totals (2 years)	19	0	0	0	0.0	0	0	0	0	0

HILL, MATT — T — SEAHAWKS

PERSONAL: Born November 10, 1978, in Grangeville, Idaho. ... 6-6/304.
HIGH SCHOOL: Grangeville (Idaho).
COLLEGE: Boise State.
TRANSACTIONS/CAREER NOTES: Selected by Seattle Seahawks in fifth round (171st pick overall) of 2002 NFL draft. ... Signed by Seahawks (July 25, 2002).
PLAYING EXPERIENCE: Seattle NFL, 2002-2003. ... Games/Games started: 2002 (13/0), 2003 (13/2). Total: 26/2.

HILL, RENALDO — CB — CARDINALS

PERSONAL: Born November 12, 1978, in Detroit, Mich. ... 5-11/194.
HIGH SCHOOL: Chadsey (Mich.).
COLLEGE: Michigan State.
TRANSACTIONS/CAREER NOTES: Selected by Arizona Cardinals in seventh round (202nd pick overall) of 2001 NFL draft. ... Signed by Cardinals (May 29, 2001). ... Granted free agency (March 3, 2004). ... Re-signed by Cardinals (May 7, 2004).

			TOTALS			INTERCEPTIONS			
Year Team	G	GS	Tk.	Ast.	Sks.	No.	Yds.	Avg.	TD
2001—Arizona NFL	14	1	16	6	0.5	0	0	0.0	0
2002—Arizona NFL	14	7	52	4	1.0	2	4	2.0	0
2003—Arizona NFL	14	14	47	11	2.0	5	119	23.8	1
Pro totals (3 years)	42	22	115	21	3.5	7	123	17.6	1

HILLENMEYER, HUNTER — LB — BEARS

PERSONAL: Born October 28, 1980, in Nashville, Tenn. ... 6-4/238.
HIGH SCHOOL: Montgomery Bell (Nashville).
COLLEGE: Vanderbilt.
TRANSACTIONS/CAREER NOTES: Selected by Green Bay Packers in fifth round (166th pick overall) of 2003 NFL draft. ... Signed by Packers (July 18, 2003). ... Waived by Packers (September 10, 2003). ... Signed by Chicago Bears to practice squad (September 13, 2003). ... Activated (October 1, 2003).

			TOTALS			INTERCEPTIONS			
Year Team	G	GS	Tk.	Ast.	Sks.	No.	Yds.	Avg.	TD
2003—Chicago NFL	13	0	0	0	0.0	0	0	0.0	0

HILLIARD, IKE — WR — GIANTS

PERSONAL: Born April 5, 1976, in Patterson, La. ... 5-11/210. ... Full name: Isaac Jason Hilliard.
HIGH SCHOOL: Patterson (La.).
COLLEGE: Florida.
TRANSACTIONS/CAREER NOTES: Selected by New York Giants in first round (seventh pick overall) of 1997 NFL draft. ... Signed by Giants (July 19, 1997). ... On injured reserve with neck injury (September 30, 1997-remainder of season). ... On injured reserve with shoulder injury (November 1, 2002-remainder of season). ... Granted unconditional free agency (February 28, 2003). ... Re-signed by Giants (March 6, 2003).
CHAMPIONSHIP GAME EXPERIENCE: Played in NFC championship game (2000 season).
SINGLE GAME HIGHS (regular season): Receptions—9 (October 26, 2003, vs. Minnesota); yards—141 (November 30, 1998, vs. San Francisco); and touchdown receptions—2 (October 26, 2003, vs. Minnesota).
STATISTICAL PLATEAUS: 100-yard receiving games: 1998 (1), 1999 (3), 2000 (1), 2001 (2), 2003 (1). Total: 8.

			RECEIVING				TOTALS			
Year Team	G	GS	No.	Yds.	Avg.	TD	TD	2pt.	Pts.	Fum.
1997—New York Giants NFL	2	2	2	42	21.0	0	0	0	0	0
1998—New York Giants NFL	16	16	51	715	14.0	2	2	0	12	2
1999—New York Giants NFL	16	16	72	996	13.8	3	3	0	18	0
2000—New York Giants NFL	14	14	55	787	14.3	8	8	0	48	0
2001—New York Giants NFL	14	9	52	659	12.7	6	6	0	36	0
2002—New York Giants NFL	7	7	27	386	14.3	2	2	0	12	0
2003—New York Giants NFL	13	12	60	608	10.1	6	6	0	36	2
Pro totals (7 years)	82	76	319	4193	13.1	27	27	0	162	4

HILTON, ZACHARY — TE — SAINTS

PERSONAL: Born July 2, 1980, in Washington, DC. ... 6-8/262.
HIGH SCHOOL: Good Counsel (Wheaton, Md.).
COLLEGE: North Carolina.
TRANSACTIONS/CAREER NOTES: Signed as non-drafted free agent by New Orleans Saints (May 2, 2003).

			RECEIVING				TOTALS			
Year Team	G	GS	No.	Yds.	Avg.	TD	TD	2pt.	Pts.	Fum.
2003—New Orleans NFL	3	0	0	0	0.0	0	0	0	0	0

HOBSON, VICTOR — LB — JETS

PERSONAL: Born February 3, 1980, in Mount Laurel, N.J. ... 6-0/252.
HIGH SCHOOL: St. Joseph's Prep (Philadelphia).
COLLEGE: Michigan.
TRANSACTIONS/CAREER NOTES: Selected by New York Jets in second round (53rd pick overall) of 2003 NFL draft. ... Signed by Jets (July 20, 2003).

			TOTALS			INTERCEPTIONS			
Year Team	G	GS	Tk.	Ast.	Sks.	No.	Yds.	Avg.	TD
2003—New York Jets NFL	16	1	32	16	2.0	1	26	26.0	0

HOCHSTEIN, RUSS — G — PATRIOTS

PERSONAL: Born October 7, 1977, in Hartington, Neb. ... 6-4/305.
HIGH SCHOOL: Cedar Catholic (Hartington, Neb.).
COLLEGE: Nebraska.
TRANSACTIONS/CAREER NOTES: Selected by Tampa Bay Buccaneers in fifth round (151st pick overall) of 2001 NFL draft. ... Signed by Buccaneers (July 16, 2001). ... Inactive for 16 games (2001). ... Released by Buccaneers (September 17, 2002). ... Re-signed by Buccaneers (September 24, 2002). ... Released by Buccaneers (October 1, 2002). ... Re-signed by Buccaneers to practice squad (October 1, 2002). ... Released by Buccaneers (October 16, 2002). ... Signed by New England Patriots to practice squad (October 21, 2002). ... Activated (November 17, 2002). ... Released by Patriots (August 31, 2003). ... Re-signed by Patriots to practice squad (September 1, 2003). ... Activated (September 14, 2003).
PLAYING EXPERIENCE: New England NFL, 2002; Tampa Bay NFL, 2002; New England NFL, 2003. ... Games/Games started: 2002 (1/0), 2003 (14/1). Total: 15/1.
CHAMPIONSHIP GAME EXPERIENCE: Played in AFC championship game (2003 season). ... Member of Super Bowl championship team (2003 season).
HONORS: Named guard on THE SPORTING NEWS college All-America first team (2000).

HODEL, NATHAN — TE/LS — CARDINALS

PERSONAL: Born November 12, 1977, in Maryville, Ill. ... 6-2/249.
HIGH SCHOOL: East (Belleville, Ill.).
COLLEGE: Illinois.
TRANSACTIONS/CAREER NOTES: Signed as non-drafted free agent by Carolina Panthers (April 23, 2001). ... Released by Panthers (September 1, 2001). ... Re-signed by Panthers to practice squad (September 4, 2001). ... Released by Panthers (October 24, 2001). ... Signed by Arizona Cardinals to practice squad (October 26, 2001). ... Activated (December 27, 2001); did not play. ... Re-signed by Cardinals (March 26, 2004).
PLAYING EXPERIENCE: Arizona NFL, 2002-2003. ... Games/Games started: 2002 (16/0), 2003 (16/0). Total: 32/0.

HODGE, SEDRICK — LB — SAINTS

PERSONAL: Born September 13, 1978, in Fayetteville, Ga. ... 6-4/244. ... Full name: Sedrick Jamaine Hodge.
HIGH SCHOOL: Westminster (Atlanta).
COLLEGE: North Carolina.
TRANSACTIONS/CAREER NOTES: Selected by New Orleans Saints in third round (70th pick overall) of 2001 NFL draft. ... Signed by Saints (June 6, 2001). ... Granted free agency (March 3, 2004). ... Re-signed by Saints (May 7, 2004).

			TOTALS			INTERCEPTIONS			
Year Team	G	GS	Tk.	Ast.	Sks.	No.	Yds.	Avg.	TD
2001—New Orleans NFL	16	0	6	2	0.0	0	0	0.0	0
2002—New Orleans NFL	16	16	58	17	0.0	0	0	0.0	0
2003—New Orleans NFL	9	9	29	5	1.0	0	0	0.0	0
Pro totals (3 years)	41	25	93	24	1.0	0	0	0.0	0

HODGINS, JAMES — FB — CARDINALS

PERSONAL: Born April 30, 1977, in San Jose, Calif. ... 6-1/274.
HIGH SCHOOL: Oak Grove (San Jose, Calif.).
COLLEGE: San Jose State.
TRANSACTIONS/CAREER NOTES: Signed as non-drafted free agent by St. Louis Rams (April 20, 1999). ... Granted free agency (March 1, 2002). ... Tendered offer sheet by Denver Broncos (April 13, 2002). ... Offer matched by Rams (April 19, 2002). ... Released by Rams (February 27, 2003). ... Signed by Arizona Cardinals (March 12, 2003).

CHAMPIONSHIP GAME EXPERIENCE: Played in NFC championship game (1999 and 2001 seasons). ... Member of Super Bowl championship team (1999 season). ... Played in Super Bowl 36 (2001 season).
SINGLE GAME HIGHS (regular season): Attempts—3 (November 28, 1999, vs. New Orleans); yards—5 (December 15, 2002, vs. Arizona); and rushing touchdowns—1 (November 28, 1999, vs. New Orleans).

			RUSHING				RECEIVING				TOTALS			
Year Team	G	GS	Att.	Yds.	Avg.	TD	No.	Yds.	Avg.	TD	TD	2pt.	Pts.	Fum.
1999—St. Louis NFL	15	0	7	10	1.4	1	6	35	5.8	0	1	0	6	0
2000—St. Louis NFL	15	2	1	3	3.0	0	2	5	2.5	0	0	0	0	0
2001—St. Louis NFL	16	10	2	5	2.5	0	4	24	6.0	1	1	0	6	0
2002—St. Louis NFL	9	8	3	7	2.3	0	9	47	5.2	0	0	0	0	0
2003—Arizona NFL	16	8	2	6	3.0	0	14	58	4.1	2	2	0	12	1
Pro totals (5 years)	71	28	15	31	2.1	1	35	169	4.8	3	4	0	24	1

HOLCOMB, KELLY — QB — BROWNS

PERSONAL: Born July 9, 1973, in Fayetteville, Tenn. ... 6-2/212. ... Full name: Bryan Kelly Holcomb.
HIGH SCHOOL: Lincoln County (Fayetteville, Tenn.).
COLLEGE: Middle Tennessee State.
TRANSACTIONS/CAREER NOTES: Signed as non-drafted free agent by Tampa Bay Buccaneers (May 1, 1995). ... Released by Buccaneers (August 22, 1995). ... Re-signed by Buccaneers to practice squad (August 29, 1995). ... Released by Buccaneers (September 19, 1995). ... Re-signed by Buccaneers to practice squad (October 4, 1995). ... Released by Buccaneers (October 17, 1995). ... Re-signed by Buccaneers to practice squad (December 19, 1995). ... Played for Barcelona Dragons of World League (1996). ... Released by Buccaneers (August 19, 1996). ... Signed by Indianapolis Colts to practice squad (November 27, 1996). ... Activated (December 12, 1996). ... Active for all 16 games (1998); did not play. ... Granted free agency (February 11, 2000). ... Re-signed by Colts (February 26, 2000). ... Released by Colts (February 28, 2001) ... Signed by Cleveland Browns (March 2, 2001).
SINGLE GAME HIGHS (regular season): Attempts—44 (November 23, 2003, vs. Pittsburgh); completions—29 (November 16, 2003, vs. Arizona); yards—392 (November 16, 2003, vs. Arizona); and touchdown passes—3 (November 16, 2003, vs. Arizona).
STATISTICAL PLATEAUS: 300-yard passing games: 2002 (1), 2003 (1). Total: 2.
MISCELLANEOUS: Regular-season record as starting NFL quarterback: 3-8 (.273). ... Postseason record as starting NFL quarterback: 0-1.

			PASSING									RUSHING				TOTALS		
Year Team	G	GS	Att.	Cmp.	Pct.	Yds.	TD	Int.	Avg.	Skd.	Rat.	Att.	Yds.	Avg.	TD	TD	2pt.	Pts.
1995—Tampa Bay NFL								Did not play.										
1996—Indianapolis NFL								Did not play.										
1997—Indianapolis NFL	5	1	73	45	61.6	454	1	8	6.22	11	44.3	5	5	1.0	0	0	0	0
1998—Indianapolis NFL								Did not play.										
1999—Indianapolis NFL								Did not play.										
2000—Indianapolis NFL								Did not play.										
2001—Cleveland NFL	4	0	12	7	58.3	114	1	0	9.50	0	118.1	1	0	0.0	0	0	0	0
2002—Cleveland NFL	5	2	106	64	60.4	790	8	4	7.45	5	92.9	8	9	1.1	0	0	0	0
2003—Cleveland NFL	10	8	302	193	63.9	1797	10	12	5.95	21	74.6	8	7	0.9	0	0	0	0
Pro totals (4 years)	24	11	493	309	62.7	3155	20	24	6.40	37	74.2	22	21	1.0	0	0	0	0

HOLCOMBE, ROBERT — RB — TITANS

PERSONAL: Born December 11, 1975, in Houston, Texas. ... 5-11/208. ... Full name: Robert Wayne Holcombe.
HIGH SCHOOL: Jeff Davis Senior (Houston), then Mesa (Ariz.).
COLLEGE: Illinois.
TRANSACTIONS/CAREER NOTES: Selected by St. Louis Rams in second round (37th pick overall) of 1998 NFL draft. ... Signed by Rams (July 2, 1998). ... Granted unconditional free agency (March 1, 2002). ... Signed by Tennessee Titans (May 28, 2002).
CHAMPIONSHIP GAME EXPERIENCE: Played in NFC championship game (1999 and 2001 seasons). ... Member of Super Bowl championship team (1999 season). ... Played in Super Bowl 36 (2001 season). ... Played in AFC championship game (2002 season).
SINGLE GAME HIGHS (regular season): Attempts—21 (September 27, 1998, vs. Arizona); yards—86 (January 2, 2000, vs. Philadelphia); and rushing touchdowns—2 (September 27, 1998, vs. Arizona).

			RUSHING				RECEIVING				KICKOFF RETURNS				TOTALS			
Year Team	G	GS	Att.	Yds.	Avg.	TD	No.	Yds.	Avg.	TD	No.	Yds.	Avg.	TD	TD	2pt.	Pts.	Fum.
1998—St. Louis NFL	13	6	98	230	2.3	2	6	34	5.7	0	0	0	0.0	0	2	0	12	0
1999—St. Louis NFL	15	7	78	294	3.8	4	14	163	11.6	1	0	0	0.0	0	5	0	30	4
2000—St. Louis NFL	14	9	21	70	3.3	3	8	90	11.3	1	0	0	0.0	0	4	0	24	0
2001—St. Louis NFL	16	0	13	42	3.2	1	1	14	14.0	0	0	0	0.0	0	1	0	6	1
2002—Tennessee NFL	8	0	47	242	5.1	0	10	91	9.1	0	0	0	0.0	0	0	0	0	1
2003—Tennessee NFL	15	0	63	201	3.2	1	19	121	6.4	1	4	38	9.5	0	2	1	14	2
Pro totals (6 years)	81	22	320	1079	3.4	11	58	513	8.8	3	4	38	9.5	0	14	1	86	8

HOLDMAN, WARRICK — LB — BROWNS

PERSONAL: Born November 22, 1975, in Alief, Texas. ... 6-1/234. ... Full name: Warrick Donte Holdman.
HIGH SCHOOL: Elsik (Alief, Texas).
COLLEGE: Texas A&M.
TRANSACTIONS/CAREER NOTES: Selected by Chicago Bears in fourth round (106th pick overall) of 1999 NFL draft. ... Signed by Bears (July 25, 1999). ... On injured reserve with knee injury (November 21, 2000-remainder of season). ... Granted free agency (March 1, 2002). ... Tendered offer sheet by Kansas City Chiefs (April 16, 2002). ... Offer matched by Bears (April 19, 2002). ... On injured reserve with knee injury (October 1, 2002-remainder of season). ... Released by Bears (March 3, 2004). ... Signed by Cleveland Browns (April 16, 2004).

			TOTALS			INTERCEPTIONS			
Year Team	G	GS	Tk.	Ast.	Sks.	No.	Yds.	Avg.	TD
1999—Chicago NFL	16	5	47	13	2.0	0	0	0.0	0
2000—Chicago NFL	10	10	57	16	0.0	0	0	0.0	0

H

Year Team	G	GS	TOTALS Tk.	Ast.	Sks.	INTERCEPTIONS No.	Yds.	Avg.	TD
2001—Chicago NFL	16	15	95	14	1.5	1	0	0.0	0
2002—Chicago NFL	4	4	16	4	0.0	0	0	0.0	0
2003—Chicago NFL	13	13	57	14	0.0	0	0	0.0	0
Pro totals (5 years)	59	47	272	61	3.5	1	0	0.0	0

HOLLAND, DARIUS DT BRONCOS

PERSONAL: Born November 10, 1973, in Petersburg, Va. ... 6-5/330. ... Full name: Darius Jerome Holland.

HIGH SCHOOL: Mayfield (Las Cruces, N.M.).

COLLEGE: Colorado.

TRANSACTIONS/CAREER NOTES: Selected by Green Bay Packers in third round (65th pick overall) of 1995 NFL draft. ... Signed by Packers (July 18, 1995). ... Granted free agency (February 13, 1998). ... Re-signed by Packers (April 10, 1998). ... Traded by Packers to Kansas City Chiefs for DE Vaughn Booker (May 13, 1998). ... Released by Chiefs (October 13, 1998). ... Signed by Detroit Lions (October 19, 1998). ... Granted unconditional free agency (February 12, 1999). ... Signed by Cleveland Browns (April 23, 1999). ... Granted unconditional free agency (February 11, 2000). ... Re-signed by Browns (February 15, 2000). ... Released by Browns (September 1, 2001). ... Signed by Minnesota Vikings (March 12, 2002). ... Granted unconditional free agency (February 28, 2003). ... Signed by Denver Broncos (July 28, 2003).

CHAMPIONSHIP GAME EXPERIENCE: Played in NFC championship game (1995-1997 seasons). ... Member of Super Bowl championship team (1996 season). ... Played in Super Bowl 32 (1997 season).

Year Team	G	GS	TOTALS Tk.	Ast.	Sks.	INTERCEPTIONS No.	Yds.	Avg.	TD
1995—Green Bay NFL	14	4	9	8	1.5	0	0	0.0	0
1996—Green Bay NFL	16	0	9	1	0.0	0	0	0.0	0
1997—Green Bay NFL	12	1	5	7	0.0	0	0	0.0	0
1998—Kansas City NFL	6	0	0	0	0.0	0	0	0.0	0
—Detroit NFL	10	4	11	0	0.0	0	0	0.0	0
1999—Cleveland NFL	15	11	30	6	2.0	0	0	0.0	0
2000—Cleveland NFL	16	1	28	4	1.0	1	0	0.0	0
2002—Minnesota NFL	4	0	0	2	0.0	0	0	0.0	0
2003—Denver NFL	16	14	15	9	0.0	0	0	0.0	0
Pro totals (8 years)	109	35	107	37	4.5	1	0	0.0	0

HOLLAND, MONTRAE G SAINTS

PERSONAL: Born May 21, 1980, in Jefferson, Texas. ... 6-2/333.

HIGH SCHOOL: Jefferson (Ore City, Texas).

COLLEGE: Florida State.

TRANSACTIONS/CAREER NOTES: Selected by New Orleans Saints in fourth round (102nd pick overall) of 2003 NFL draft. ... Signed by Saints (July 25, 2003).

PLAYING EXPERIENCE: New Orleans NFL, 2003. ... Games/Games started: 2003 (16/7). Total: 16/7.

HOLLIDAY, VONNIE DE CHIEFS

PERSONAL: Born December 11, 1975, in Camden, S.C. ... 6-5/290. ... Full name: Dimetry Giovonni Holliday.

HIGH SCHOOL: Camden (S.C.).

COLLEGE: North Carolina.

TRANSACTIONS/CAREER NOTES: Selected by Green Bay Packers in first round (19th pick overall) of 1998 NFL draft. ... Signed by Packers (June 15, 1998). ... Granted unconditional free agency (February 28, 2003). ... Signed by Kansas City Chiefs (April 7, 2003).

Year Team	G	GS	TOTALS Tk.	Ast.	Sks.	INTERCEPTIONS No.	Yds.	Avg.	TD
1998—Green Bay NFL	12	12	34	18	8.0	0	0	0.0	0
1999—Green Bay NFL	16	16	47	20	6.0	0	0	0.0	0
2000—Green Bay NFL	12	9	22	13	5.0	1	3	3.0	0
2001—Green Bay NFL	16	16	47	25	7.0	0	0	0.0	0
2002—Green Bay NFL	10	10	18	8	6.0	1	3	3.0	0
2003—Kansas City NFL	16	16	30	8	5.5	0	0	0.0	0
Pro totals (6 years)	82	79	198	92	37.5	2	6	3.0	0

HOLLINGS, TONY RB TEXANS

PERSONAL: Born December 1, 1981, in Macon, Ga. ... 5-10/216. ... Full name: Tony Terrell Hollings.

HIGH SCHOOL: Twigs County (Jeffersonville, Ga.).

COLLEGE: Georgia Tech.

TRANSACTIONS/CAREER NOTES: Selected after junior season by Houston Texans in 2003 NFL supplemental draft. Texans forfeited their second-round pick (33rd overall) in 2004 regular draft. ... Signed by Texans (July 24, 2003).

SINGLE GAME HIGHS (regular season): Attempts—18 (December 7, 2003, vs. Jacksonville); yards)—41 (September 21, 2003, vs. Kanas City); and rushing touchdowns—0.

Year Team	G	GS	RUSHING Att.	Yds.	Avg.	TD	RECEIVING No.	Yds.	Avg.	TD	KICKOFF RETURNS No.	Yds.	Avg.	TD	TOTALS TD	2pt.	Pts.	Fum.
2003—Houston NFL	14	1	38	102	2.7	0	2	25	12.5	0	8	142	17.8	0	0	0	0	2

H

HOLLOWAY, JABARI — TE — TEXANS

PERSONAL: Born December 18, 1978, in Atlanta, Ga. ... 6-2/260. ... Full name: Jabari Jelani Holloway.
HIGH SCHOOL: Sandy Creek (Tyrone, Ga.).
COLLEGE: Notre Dame.
TRANSACTIONS/CAREER NOTES: Selected by New England Patriots in fourth round (119th pick overall) of 2001 NFL draft. ... Signed by Patriots (July 13, 2001). ... On physically unable to perform list with hamstring injury (July 23-August 28, 2001). ... On injured reserve with hamstring injury (August 28, 2001-entire season). ... Claimed on waivers by Houston Texans (August 26, 2002). ... Released by Texans (September 6, 2002). ... Re-signed by Texans to practice squad (September 10, 2002). ... Activated (October 18, 2002). ... Re-signed by Texans (March 21, 2003). ... Granted free agency (March 3, 2004). ... Re-signed by Texans (March 23, 2004).
SINGLE GAME HIGHS (regular season): Receptions—2 (October 12, 2003, vs. Tennessee); yards—40 (October 12, 2003, vs. Tennessee); and touchdown receptions—0.

			RECEIVING				TOTALS			
Year Team	G	GS	No.	Yds.	Avg.	TD	TD	2pt.	Pts.	Fum.
2002—Houston NFL	11	8	7	73	10.4	0	0	0	0	0
2003—Houston NFL	15	9	8	84	10.5	0	0	0	0	0
Pro totals (2 years)	26	17	15	157	10.5	0	0	0	0	0

HOLMAN, RASHAD — CB — 49ERS

PERSONAL: Born January 17, 1978, in Louisville, Ky. ... 5-11/191.
HIGH SCHOOL: Male (Louisville, Ky.).
COLLEGE: Louisville.
TRANSACTIONS/CAREER NOTES: Selected by San Francisco 49ers in sixth round (179th pick overall) of 2001 NFL draft. ... Signed by 49ers (July 24, 2001).

			TOTALS			INTERCEPTIONS			
Year Team	G	GS	Tk.	Ast.	Sks.	No.	Yds.	Avg.	TD
2001—San Francisco NFL	16	1	42	4	0.0	1	19	19.0	0
2002—San Francisco NFL	16	0	19	0	0.0	1	1	1.0	0
2003—San Francisco NFL	14	0	14	2	0.0	0	0	0.0	0
Pro totals (3 years)	46	1	75	6	0.0	2	20	10.0	0

HOLMES, EARL — LB — LIONS

PERSONAL: Born April 28, 1973, in Tallahassee, Fla. ... 6-2/242. ... Full name: Earl L. Holmes.
HIGH SCHOOL: Florida A&M University (Tallahassee, Fla.).
COLLEGE: Florida A&M.
TRANSACTIONS/CAREER NOTES: Selected by Pittsburgh Steelers in fourth round (126th pick overall) of 1996 NFL draft. ... Signed by Steelers (July 16, 1996). ... Granted unconditional free agency (March 1, 2002). ... Signed by Cleveland Browns (April 5, 2002). ... Released by Browns (February 27, 2003). ... Signed by Detroit Lions (April 9, 2003).
CHAMPIONSHIP GAME EXPERIENCE: Played in AFC championship game (1997 and 2001 seasons).

			TOTALS			INTERCEPTIONS			
Year Team	G	GS	Tk.	Ast.	Sks.	No.	Yds.	Avg.	TD
1996—Pittsburgh NFL	3	1	9	1	1.0	0	0	0.0	0
1997—Pittsburgh NFL	16	16	67	29	4.0	0	0	0.0	0
1998—Pittsburgh NFL	14	14	55	25	1.5	1	36	36.0	0
1999—Pittsburgh NFL	16	16	89	26	0.0	0	0	0.0	0
2000—Pittsburgh NFL	16	16	87	41	1.0	0	0	0.0	0
2001—Pittsburgh NFL	16	16	85	33	2.0	0	0	0.0	0
2002—Cleveland NFL	16	15	96	32	0.0	0	0	0.0	0
2003—Detroit NFL	16	13	68	29	2.0	0	0	0.0	0
Pro totals (8 years)	113	107	556	216	11.5	1	36	36.0	0

HOLMES, KENNY — DE

PERSONAL: Born October 24, 1973, in Vero Beach, Fla. ... 6-4/265. ... Full name: Kenneth Holmes.
HIGH SCHOOL: Vero Beach (Fla.).
COLLEGE: Miami (Fla.).
TRANSACTIONS/CAREER NOTES: Selected by Houston Oilers in first round (18th pick overall) of 1997 NFL draft. ... Oilers franchise moved to Tennessee for 1997 season. ... Signed by Oilers (July 18, 1997). ... Oilers franchise renamed Tennessee Titans for 1999 season (December 26, 1998). ... Granted unconditional free agency (March 2, 2001). ... Signed by New York Giants (March 14, 2001). ... On injured reserve with knee injury (November 19, 2003-remainder of season). ... Granted unconditional free agency (March 3, 2004).
CHAMPIONSHIP GAME EXPERIENCE: Played in AFC championship game (1999 season). ... Played in Super Bowl 34 (1999 season).

			TOTALS			INTERCEPTIONS			
Year Team	G	GS	Tk.	Ast.	Sks.	No.	Yds.	Avg.	TD
1997—Tennessee NFL	16	5	28	5	7.0	0	0	0.0	0
1998—Tennessee NFL	14	11	22	11	2.5	0	0	0.0	0
1999—Tennessee NFL	14	7	13	6	4.0	2	17	8.5	0
2000—Tennessee NFL	14	13	32	5	8.0	0	0	0.0	0
2001—New York Giants NFL	16	16	38	18	3.5	0	0	0.0	0
2002—New York Giants NFL	15	15	32	15	8.0	0	0	0.0	0
2003—New York Giants NFL	9	9	18	7	5.5	0	0	0.0	0
Pro totals (7 years)	98	76	183	67	38.5	2	17	8.5	0

HOLMES, PRIEST — RB — CHIEFS

PERSONAL: Born October 7, 1973, in Fort Smith, Ark. ... 5-9/213. ... Full name: Priest Anthony Holmes.
HIGH SCHOOL: Marshall (Texas).
COLLEGE: Texas.
TRANSACTIONS/CAREER NOTES: Signed as non-drafted free agent by Baltimore Ravens (April 25, 1997). ... Granted free agency (February 11, 2000). ... Re-signed by Ravens (June 9, 2000). ... Granted unconditional free agency (March 2, 2001). ... Signed by Kansas City Chiefs (April 1, 2001).
CHAMPIONSHIP GAME EXPERIENCE: Played in AFC championship game (2000 season). ... Member of Super Bowl championship team (2000 season).
HONORS: Played in Pro Bowl (2001 and 2003 seasons). ... Named to play in Pro Bowl (2002 season); replaced by Travis Henry due to injury. ... Named running back on the THE SPORTING NEWS NFL All-Pro team (2002-2003).
RECORDS: Holds NFL single-season record for most touchdowns—27 (2003).
SINGLE GAME HIGHS (regular season): Attempts—36 (November 22, 1998, vs. Cincinnati); yards—227 (November 22, 1998, vs. Cincinnati); and rushing touchdowns—4 (September 8, 2002, vs. Cleveland).
STATISTICAL PLATEAUS: 100-yard rushing games: 1998 (4), 1999 (2), 2000 (1), 2001 (7), 2002 (9), 2003 (3). Total: 26. 100-yard receiving games: 2001 (2), 2002 (1), 2003 (1). Total: 4.
MISCELLANEOUS: Holds Kansas City Chiefs all-time record for most touchdowns (61).

			RUSHING				RECEIVING				TOTALS			
Year Team	G	GS	Att.	Yds.	Avg.	TD	No.	Yds.	Avg.	TD	TD	2pt.	Pts.	Fum.
1997—Baltimore NFL	7	0	0	0	0.0	0	0	0	0.0	0	0	0	0	0
1998—Baltimore NFL	16	13	233	1008	4.3	7	43	260	6.0	0	7	0	42	3
1999—Baltimore NFL	9	4	89	506	5.7	1	13	104	8.0	1	2	0	12	0
2000—Baltimore NFL	16	2	137	588	4.3	2	32	221	6.9	0	2	0	12	2
2001—Kansas City NFL	16	16	327	*1555	4.8	8	62	614	9.9	2	10	0	60	4
2002—Kansas City NFL	14	14	313	1615	5.2	*21	70	672	9.6	3	*24	0	*144	1
2003—Kansas City NFL	16	16	320	1420	4.4	*27	74	690	9.3	0	*27	0	§162	1
Pro totals (7 years)	94	65	1419	6692	4.7	66	294	2561	8.7	6	72	0	432	11

HOLSEY, BERNARD — DE/DT

PERSONAL: Born December 10, 1973, in Rome, Ga. ... 6-2/286.
HIGH SCHOOL: Coosa (Rome, Ga.).
COLLEGE: Duke.
TRANSACTIONS/CAREER NOTES: Signed as non-drafted free agent by New York Giants (April 26, 1996). ... Granted free agency (February 12, 1999). ... Re-signed by Giants (June 2, 1999). ... Granted unconditional free agency (February 11, 2000). ... Signed by Indianapolis Colts (March 15, 2000). ... Released by Colts (August 20, 2001). ... Signed by New England Patriots (July 25, 2002). ... Granted unconditional free agency (February 28, 2003). ... Signed by Washington Redskins (July 25, 2003). ... Granted unconditional free agency (March 3, 2004).

			TOTALS		
Year Team	G	GS	Tk.	Ast.	Sks.
1996—New York Giants NFL	16	0	10	2	0.0
1997—New York Giants NFL	16	4	10	7	3.5
1998—New York Giants NFL	16	0	4	4	0.0
1999—New York Giants NFL	16	0	15	5	0.0
2000—Indianapolis NFL	16	13	28	14	2.0
2002—New England NFL	8	0	3	2	1.0
2003—Washington NFL	16	16	27	4	2.5
Pro totals (7 years)	104	33	97	38	9.0

HOLT, TERRENCE — S — LIONS

PERSONAL: Born March 5, 1980, in Greensboro, N.C. ... 6-2/208. ... Brother of Torry Holt, wide receiver, St. Louis Rams.
HIGH SCHOOL: Eastern Guilford (Gibsonville, N.C.).
COLLEGE: North Carolina State.
TRANSACTIONS/CAREER NOTES: Selected by Detroit Lions in fifth round (137th pick overall) of 2003 NFL draft. ... Signed by Lions (July 10, 2003).

			TOTALS			INTERCEPTIONS				KICKOFF RETURNS				TOTALS			
Year Team	G	GS	Tk.	Ast.	Sks.	No.	Yds.	Avg.	TD	No.	Yds.	Avg.	TD	TD	2pt.	Pts.	Fum.
2003—Detroit NFL	11	2	19	4	0.0	3	42	14.0	0	0	0	0.0	0	0	0	0	1

HOLT, TORRY — WR — RAMS

PERSONAL: Born June 5, 1976, in Greensboro, N.C. ... 6-0/190. ... Full name: Torry Jabar Holt. ... Brother of Terrence Holt, safety, Detroit Lions.
HIGH SCHOOL: Eastern Guilford (Gibsonville, N.C.).
COLLEGE: North Carolina State.
TRANSACTIONS/CAREER NOTES: Selected by St. Louis Rams in first round (sixth pick overall) of 1999 NFL draft. ... Signed by Rams (June 5, 1999).
CHAMPIONSHIP GAME EXPERIENCE: Played in NFC championship game (1999 and 2001 seasons). ... Member of Super Bowl championship team (1999 season). ... Played in Super Bowl 36 (2001 season).
HONORS: Named wide receiver on THE SPORTING NEWS college All-America first team (1998). ... Named wide receiver on THE SPORTING NEWS NFL All-Pro team (2003). ... Played in Pro Bowl (2000-2003 seasons).
SINGLE GAME HIGHS (regular season): Receptions—12 (September 28, 2003, vs. Arizona); yards—203 (December 30, 2001, vs. Indianapolis); and touchdown receptions—2 (October 19, 2003, vs. Green Bay).

STATISTICAL PLATEAUS: 100-yard receiving games: 1999 (2), 2000 (8), 2001 (3), 2002 (4), 2003 (10). Total: 27.

			RUSHING				RECEIVING				TOTALS			
Year Team	G	GS	Att.	Yds.	Avg.	TD	No.	Yds.	Avg.	TD	TD	2pt.	Pts.	Fum.
1999—St. Louis NFL	16	15	3	25	8.3	0	52	788	15.2	6	6	0	36	4
2000—St. Louis NFL	16	15	2	7	3.5	0	82	*1635	*19.9	6	6	0	36	2
2001—St. Louis NFL	16	14	2	0	0.0	0	81	1363	16.8	7	7	0	42	2
2002—St. Louis NFL	16	11	2	18	9.0	0	91	1302	14.3	4	4	0	24	1
2003—St. Louis NFL	16	15	1	5	5.0	0	*117	*1696	14.5	12	12	0	72	1
Pro totals (5 years)	80	70	10	55	5.5	0	423	6784	16.0	35	35	0	210	10

HOOD, RODERICK — CB — EAGLES

PERSONAL: Born October 3, 1981, in Columbus, Ga. ... 5-11/196.
HIGH SCHOOL: Carver (Columbus, Ga.).
COLLEGE: Auburn.
TRANSACTIONS/CAREER NOTES: Signed as non-drafted free agent by Philadelphia Eagles (April 28, 2003).
CHAMPIONSHIP GAME EXPERIENCE: Played in NFC championship game (2003 season).

			TOTALS			INTERCEPTIONS			
Year Team	G	GS	Tk.	Ast.	Sks.	No.	Yds.	Avg.	TD
2003—Philadelphia NFL	14	0	5	0	0.0	1	5	5.0	0

HOOVER, BRAD — FB — PANTHERS

PERSONAL: Born November 11, 1976, in High Point, N.C. ... 6-0/242. ... Full name: Bradley R. Hoover.
HIGH SCHOOL: Ledford (Thomasville, N.C.).
COLLEGE: Western Carolina.
TRANSACTIONS/CAREER NOTES: Signed as non-drafted free agent by Carolina Panthers (April 17, 2000).
CHAMPIONSHIP GAME EXPERIENCE: Played in NFC championship game (2003 season). ... Played in Super Bowl 38 (2003 season).
SINGLE GAME HIGHS (regular season): Attempts—24 (November 27, 2000, vs. Green Bay); yards—117 (November 27, 2000, vs. Green Bay); and rushing touchdowns—1 (November 27, 2000, vs. Green Bay).
STATISTICAL PLATEAUS: 100-yard rushing games: 2000 (1). Total: 1.

			RUSHING				RECEIVING				TOTALS			
Year Team	G	GS	Att.	Yds.	Avg.	TD	No.	Yds.	Avg.	TD	TD	2pt.	Pts.	Fum.
2000—Carolina NFL	16	4	89	290	3.3	1	15	112	7.5	0	1	0	6	1
2001—Carolina NFL	16	7	17	71	4.2	0	26	185	7.1	0	0	0	0	1
2002—Carolina NFL	16	10	31	129	4.2	0	17	187	11.0	2	2	0	12	1
2003—Carolina NFL	16	9	6	21	3.5	0	12	72	6.0	1	1	0	6	1
Pro totals (4 years)	64	30	143	511	3.6	1	70	556	7.9	3	4	0	24	4

HOPE, CHRIS — S — STEELERS

PERSONAL: Born September 29, 1980, in Rock Hill, S.C. ... 6-0/214.
HIGH SCHOOL: Rock Hill (S.C.).
COLLEGE: Florida State.
TRANSACTIONS/CAREER NOTES: Selected by Pittsburgh Steelers in third round (94th pick overall) of 2002 NFL draft. ... Signed by Steelers (July 12, 2002).
HONORS: Named free safety on THE SPORTING NEWS college All-America second team (2000).

			TOTALS			INTERCEPTIONS			
Year Team	G	GS	Tk.	Ast.	Sks.	No.	Yds.	Avg.	TD
2002—Pittsburgh NFL	14	0	12	0	0.0	0	0	0.0	0
2003—Pittsburgh NFL	16	0	11	2	0.0	0	0	0.0	0
Pro totals (2 years)	30	0	23	2	0.0	0	0	0.0	0

HOPKINS, BRAD — T — TITANS

PERSONAL: Born September 5, 1970, in Columbia, S.C. ... 6-3/305. ... Full name: Bradley D. Hopkins.
HIGH SCHOOL: Moline (Ill.).
COLLEGE: Illinois.
TRANSACTIONS/CAREER NOTES: Selected by Houston Oilers in first round (13th pick overall) of 1993 NFL draft. ... Signed by Oilers (August 10, 1993). ... Granted unconditional free agency (February 14, 1997). ... Re-signed by Oilers (March 10, 1997). ... Oilers franchise moved to Tennessee for 1997 season. ... Oilers franchise renamed Tennessee Titans for 1999 season (December 26, 1998).
PLAYING EXPERIENCE: Houston NFL, 1993-1996; Tennessee NFL, 1997-2003. ... Games/Games started: 1993 (16/11), 1994 (16/15), 1995 (16/16), 1996 (16/16), 1997 (16/16), 1998 (13/13), 1999 (16/16), 2000 (15/15), 2001 (14/14), 2002 (14/14), 2003 (16/16). Total: 168/162.
CHAMPIONSHIP GAME EXPERIENCE: Played in AFC championship game (1999 and 2002 seasons). ... Played in Super Bowl 34 (1999 season).
HONORS: Played in Pro Bowl (2000 and 2003 seasons).

HORN, JOE — WR — SAINTS

PERSONAL: Born January 16, 1972, in Tupelo, Miss. ... 6-1/206. ... Full name: Joseph Horn.
HIGH SCHOOL: Douglas Bird (Fayetteville, N.C.).
JUNIOR COLLEGE: Itawamba J.C.
COLLEGE: None.

TRANSACTIONS/CAREER NOTES: Signed by Memphis Mad Dogs of CFL (March 25, 1995). ... Selected by Kansas City Chiefs in fifth round (135th pick overall) of 1996 NFL draft. ... Signed by Chiefs (June 25, 1996). ... Granted free agency (February 12, 1999). ... Re-signed by Chiefs (June 16, 1999). ... Granted unconditional free agency (February 11, 2000). ... Signed by New Orleans Saints (February 13, 2000).
HONORS: Played in Pro Bowl (2000 and 2002 seasons). ... Named to play in Pro Bowl (2001 season); replaced by Torry Holt due to injury.
SINGLE GAME HIGHS (regular season): Receptions—13 (December 2, 2001, vs. Carolina); yards—180 (November 5, 2000, vs. San Francisco); and touchdown receptions—4 (December 14, 2003, vs. New York Giants).
STATISTICAL PLATEAUS: 100-yard receiving games: 2000 (5), 2001 (4), 2002 (6), 2003 (4). Total: 19.

			RUSHING				RECEIVING				KICKOFF RETURNS				TOTALS			
Year Team	G	GS	Att.	Yds.	Avg.	TD	No.	Yds.	Avg.	TD	No.	Yds.	Avg.	TD	TD	2pt.	Pts.	Fum.
1995—Memphis CFL	17	17	...	...	0.0	...	71	1415	19.9	5	2	17	8.5	0	5	0	30	0
1996—Kansas City NFL	9	0	1	8	8.0	0	2	30	15.0	0	0	0	0.0	0	0	0	0	0
1997—Kansas City NFL	8	0	0	0	0.0	0	2	65	32.5	0	0	0	0.0	0	0	0	0	0
1998—Kansas City NFL	16	1	1	0	0.0	0	14	198	14.1	1	11	233	21.2	0	1	0	6	2
1999—Kansas City NFL	16	1	2	15	7.5	0	35	586	16.7	6	9	165	18.3	0	6	0	36	0
2000—New Orleans NFL	16	16	6	10	1.7	0	94	1340	14.3	8	0	0	0.0	0	8	0	48	1
2001—New Orleans NFL	16	16	1	4	4.0	0	83	1265	15.2	9	0	0	0.0	0	9	0	54	1
2002—New Orleans NFL	16	16	1	2	2.0	0	88	1312	14.9	7	0	0	0.0	0	7	1	44	1
2003—New Orleans NFL	15	14	2	15	7.5	0	78	973	12.5	10	0	0	0.0	0	10	0	60	2
CFL totals (1 year)	17	17	...	...	0.0	...	71	1415	19.9	5	2	17	8.5	0	5	0	30	0
NFL totals (8 years)	112	64	14	54	3.9	0	396	5769	14.6	41	20	398	19.9	0	41	1	248	7
Pro totals (9 years)	129	81	...	...	3.9	...	467	7184	15.4	46	22	415	18.9	0	46	1	278	7

HOUSE, KEVIN — CB — CHARGERS

PERSONAL: Born January 9, 1979, in St. Louis, Mo. ... 6-0/185. ... Full name: Kevin N. House. ... Son of Kevin House, wide receiver with Tampa Bay Buccaneers (1980-86) and Los Angeles Rams: (1986-87).
HIGH SCHOOL: Chamberlain (Tampa).
COLLEGE: South Carolina.
TRANSACTIONS/CAREER NOTES: Signed as non-drafted free agent by New Orleans Saints (April 23, 2002). ... Released by Saints (September 1, 2002). ... Re-signed by Saints to practice squad (September 2, 2002). ... Signed by San Diego Chargers off Saints practice squad (October 3, 2002). ... Re-signed by Chargers (March 25, 2003). ... Re-signed by Chargers (May 13, 2004).

			TOTALS			INTERCEPTIONS			
Year Team	G	GS	Tk.	Ast.	Sks.	No.	Yds.	Avg.	TD
2002—San Diego NFL	1	0	0	0	0.0	0	0	0.0	0
2003—San Diego NFL	15	0	3	0	0.0	0	0	0.0	0
Pro totals (2 years)	16	0	3	0	0.0	0	0	0.0	0

HOUSER, KEVIN — C/LS — SAINTS

PERSONAL: Born August 23, 1977, in Westlake, Ohio. ... 6-2/250. ... Full name: Kevin J. Houser.
HIGH SCHOOL: Westlake (Ohio).
COLLEGE: Ohio State.
TRANSACTIONS/CAREER NOTES: Selected by New Orleans Saints in seventh round (228th pick overall) of 2000 NFL draft. ... Signed by Saints (June 20, 2000).
PLAYING EXPERIENCE: New Orleans NFL, 2000-2003. ... Games/Games started: 2000 (16/0), 2001 (16/0), 2002 (16/0), 2003 (16/0). Total: 64/0.

HOUSHMANDZADEH, T.J. — WR — BENGALS

PERSONAL: Born September 26, 1977, in Victorville, Calif. ... 6-1/197. ... Full name: Touraj Houshmandzadeh.
HIGH SCHOOL: Barstow (Calif.).
JUNIOR COLLEGE: Cerritos (Calif.).
COLLEGE: Oregon State.
TRANSACTIONS/CAREER NOTES: Selected by Cincinnati Bengals in seventh round (204th pick overall) of 2001 NFL draft. ... Signed by Bengals (July 18, 2001). ... Granted free agency (March 3, 2004). ... Re-signed by Bengals (April 14, 2004).
SINGLE GAME HIGHS (regular season): Receptions—9 (December 30, 2001, vs. Pittsburgh); yards—98 (December 30, 2001, vs. Pittsburgh); and touchdown receptions—1 (December 1, 2002, vs. Baltimore).

			RECEIVING				PUNT RETURNS				KICKOFF RETURNS				TOTALS			
Year Team	G	GS	No.	Yds.	Avg.	TD	No.	Yds.	Avg.	TD	No.	Yds.	Avg.	TD	TD	2pt.	Pts.	Fum.
2001—Cincinnati NFL	12	1	21	228	10.9	0	12	163	13.6	0	10	185	18.5	0	0	0	0	3
2002—Cincinnati NFL	16	5	41	492	12.0	1	24	117	4.9	0	13	288	22.2	0	1	0	6	3
2003—Cincinnati NFL	2	0	0	0	0.0	0	0	0	0.0	0	0	0	0.0	0	0	0	0	0
Pro totals (3 years)	30	6	62	720	11.6	1	36	280	7.8	0	23	473	20.6	0	1	0	6	6

HOVAN, CHRIS — DT — VIKINGS

PERSONAL: Born May 12, 1978, in Rocky River, Ohio. ... 6-2/296. ... Full name: Christopher James Hovan.
HIGH SCHOOL: St. Ignatius (Cleveland).
COLLEGE: Boston College.
TRANSACTIONS/CAREER NOTES: Selected by Minnesota Vikings in first round (25th pick overall) of 2000 NFL draft. ... Signed by Vikings (July 24, 2000).
CHAMPIONSHIP GAME EXPERIENCE: Played in NFC championship game (2000 season).
HONORS: Named defensive end on THE SPORTING NEWS college All-America third team (1999).

Year Team	G	GS	TOTALS Tk.	Ast.	Sks.
2000—Minnesota NFL	16	13	43	5	2.0
2001—Minnesota NFL	16	16	30	15	6.0
2002—Minnesota NFL	16	16	38	14	5.5
2003—Minnesota NFL	16	16	19	8	2.0
Pro totals (4 years)	64	61	130	42	15.5

HOWARD, BOBBIE LB

PERSONAL: Born June 14, 1977, in Rand, W.Va. ... 5-10/232. ... Full name: Bobbie Allen Howard.
HIGH SCHOOL: DuPont (Belle, W.Va.).
COLLEGE: Notre Dame.
TRANSACTIONS/CAREER NOTES: Signed as non-drafted free agent by Tampa Bay Buccaneers (April 19, 1999). ... Released by Buccaneers (September 5,1999). ... Re-signed by Buccaneers (January 25, 2000). ... Assigned by Buccaneers to Frankfurt Galaxy in 2000 NFL Europe enhancement allocation program (February 18, 2000). ... Released by Buccaneers (August 27, 2000). ... Signed by Chicago Bears to practice squad (December 6, 2000). ... Activated (December 22, 2000); did not play. ... Waived by Bears (October 1, 2003).

Year Team	G	GS	TOTALS Tk.	Ast.	Sks.	INTERCEPTIONS No.	Yds.	Avg.	TD
2001—Chicago NFL	16	0	0	0	0.0	0	0	0.0	0
2002—Chicago NFL	16	9	38	11	0.5	1	9	9.0	0
2003—Chicago NFL	3	0	2	1	0.0	0	0	0.0	0
Pro totals (3 years)	35	9	40	12	0.5	1	9	9.0	0

HOWARD, DARREN DE SAINTS

PERSONAL: Born November 19, 1976, in St. Petersburg, Fla. ... 6-3/281.
HIGH SCHOOL: Boca Ciega (Fla.).
COLLEGE: Kansas State.
TRANSACTIONS/CAREER NOTES: Selected by New Orleans Saints in second round (33rd pick overall) of 2000 NFL draft. ... Signed by Saints (July 17, 2000). ... Designated by Saints as franchise player (February 24, 2004). ... Re-signed by Saints (May 4, 2004).

Year Team	G	GS	TOTALS Tk.	Ast.	Sks.	INTERCEPTIONS No.	Yds.	Avg.	TD
2000—New Orleans NFL	16	16	37	15	11.0	1	46	46.0	0
2001—New Orleans NFL	16	16	36	18	6.0	1	37	37.0	0
2002—New Orleans NFL	16	16	35	13	8.0	0	0	0.0	0
2003—New Orleans NFL	8	8	27	2	5.0	0	0	0.0	0
Pro totals (4 years)	56	56	135	48	30.0	2	83	41.5	0

HOWARD, REGGIE CB DOLPHINS

PERSONAL: Born May 17, 1977, in Memphis, Tenn. ... 6-0/190. ... Full name: Reginald Clement Howard.
HIGH SCHOOL: Kirby (Memphis,Tenn.).
COLLEGE: Memphis.
TRANSACTIONS/CAREER NOTES: Signed as non-drafted free agent by Carolina Panthers (April 17, 2000). ... Released by Panthers (August 29, 2000). ... Signed by New Orleans Saints to practice squad (September 1, 2000). ... Activated (October 22, 2000). ... Claimed on waivers by Panthers (October 25, 2000). ... Granted free agency (February 28, 2003). ... Re-signed by Panthers (May 2, 2003). ... Granted unconditional free agency (March 3, 2004). ... Signed by Miami Dolphins (March 5, 2004).
CHAMPIONSHIP GAME EXPERIENCE: Played in NFC championship game (2003 season). ... Played in Super Bowl 38 (2003 season).

Year Team	G	GS	TOTALS Tk.	Ast.	Sks.	INTERCEPTIONS No.	Yds.	Avg.	TD
2000—New Orleans NFL	1	0	0	0	0.0	0	0	0.0	0
—Carolina NFL	1	0	0	0	0.0	0	0	0.0	0
2001—Carolina NFL	11	0	15	0	1.0	1	16	16.0	0
2002—Carolina NFL	14	14	75	9	1.0	2	19	9.5	0
2003—Carolina NFL	15	15	52	10	0.5	2	2	1.0	0
Pro totals (4 years)	42	29	142	19	2.5	5	37	7.4	0

HOWELL, JOHN S BUCCANEERS

PERSONAL: Born April 28, 1978, in North Platte, Neb. ... 5-11/210. ... Full name: John Thomas Howell.
HIGH SCHOOL: Mullen (Neb.).
COLLEGE: Colorado State.
TRANSACTIONS/CAREER NOTES: Selected by Tampa Bay Buccaneers in fourth round (117th pick overall) of 2001 NFL draft. ... Signed by Buccaneers (July 25, 2001). ... On injured reserve with hamstring injury (November 11, 2003-remainder of season). ... Granted free agency (March 3, 2004). ... Re-signed by Buccaneers (April 15, 2004).
CHAMPIONSHIP GAME EXPERIENCE: Played in NFC championship game (2002 season). ... Member of Super Bowl championship team (2002 season).

Year Team	G	GS	TOTALS Tk.	Ast.	Sks.	INTERCEPTIONS No.	Yds.	Avg.	TD
2001—Tampa Bay NFL	14	1	16	8	0.0	0	0	0.0	0
2002—Tampa Bay NFL	16	1	14	1	0.0	0	0	0.0	0
2003—Tampa Bay NFL	8	0	3	0	0.0	0	0	0.0	0
Pro totals (3 years)	38	2	33	9	0.0	0	0	0.0	0

HOWRY, KEENAN WR VIKINGS

PERSONAL: Born June 17, 1981, in Los Angeles, Calif. ... 5-10/172. ... Full name: Keenan Rashaun Howry.
HIGH SCHOOL: Los Alamitos (Calif.).
COLLEGE: Oregon.
TRANSACTIONS/CAREER NOTES: Selected by Minnesota Vikings in seventh round (221st pick overall) of 2003 NFL draft. ... Signed by Vikings (July 21, 2003).
SINGLE GAME HIGHS (regular season): Receptions—2 (October 26, 2003, vs. New York Giants); yards—15 (October 26, 2003, vs. New York Giants); and touchdown receptions—0.

			RUSHING				RECEIVING				PUNT RETURNS				KICKOFF RETURNS				TOTALS		
Year Team	G	GS	Att.	Yds.	Avg.	TD	No.	Yds.	Avg.	TD	No.	Yds.	Avg.	TD	No.	Yds.	Avg.	TD	TD	2pt.	Pts.
2003—Min. NFL	16	1	0	0	0.0	0	2	15	7.5	0	35	247	7.1	0	12	271	22.6	0	0	0	0

HUARD, BROCK QB SEAHAWKS

PERSONAL: Born April 15, 1976, in Seattle, Wash. ... 6-4/232. ... Brother of Damon Huard, quarterback with Miami Dolphins and New England Patriots (1997-2003).
HIGH SCHOOL: Puyallup (Wash.).
COLLEGE: Washington.
TRANSACTIONS/CAREER NOTES: Selected after junior season by Seattle Seahawks in third round (77th pick overall) of 1999 NFL draft. ... Signed by Seahawks (July 29, 1999). ... Inactive for all 16 games (1999). ... Granted free agency (March 1, 2002). ... Re-signed by Seahawks (April 19, 2002). ... Traded by Seahawks to Indianapolis Colts for fifth-round pick (DL Rocky Bernard) in 2002 draft (April 19, 2002). ... Released by Colts (February 27, 2004). ... Signed by Seahawks (April 21, 2004).
CHAMPIONSHIP GAME EXPERIENCE: Member of Colts for AFC championship game (2003 season); did not play.
SINGLE GAME HIGHS (regular season): Attempts—34 (October 8, 2000, vs. Carolina); completions—19 (October 15, 2000, vs. Indianapolis); yards—226 (October 15, 2000, vs. Indianapolis); and touchdown passes—3 (October 15, 2000, vs. Indianapolis).
MISCELLANEOUS: Regular-season record as starting NFL quarterback: 0-4.

			PASSING									RUSHING				TOTALS		
Year Team	G	GS	Att.	Cmp.	Pct.	Yds.	TD	Int.	Avg.	Skd.	Rat.	Att.	Yds.	Avg.	TD	TD	2pt.	Pts.
1999—Seattle NFL									Did not play.									
2000—Seattle NFL	5	4	87	49	56.3	540	3	2	6.21	13	76.8	5	29	5.8	0	0	0	0
2001—Seattle NFL	1	0	17	9	52.9	127	1	0	7.47	1	96.9	1	11	11.0	0	0	0	0
2002—Indianapolis NFL									Did not play.									
2003—Indianapolis NFL	2	0	3	2	66.7	22	0	0	7.33	1	88.2	3	8	2.7	0	0	0	0
Pro totals (3 years)	8	4	107	60	56.1	689	4	2	6.44	15	80.3	9	48	5.3	0	0	0	0

HUARD, DAMON QB

PERSONAL: Born July 9, 1973, in Yakima, Wash. ... 6-3/215. ... Brother of Brock Huard, quarterback, Seattle Seahawks.
HIGH SCHOOL: Puyallup (Wash.).
COLLEGE: Washington.
TRANSACTIONS/CAREER NOTES: Signed as non-drafted free agent by Cincinnati Bengals (April 23, 1996). ... Released by Bengals (August 19, 1996). ... Signed by Miami Dolphins (April 24, 1997). ... Released by Dolphins (August 24, 1997). ... Re-signed by Dolphins to practice squad (August 26, 1997). ... Activated (September 6, 1997); did not play. ... Assigned by Dolphins to Frankfurt Galaxy in 1998 NFL Europe enhancement allocation program (February 18, 1998). ... Released by Dolphins (March 19, 2001). ... Signed by New England Patriots (April 2, 2001). ... Granted unconditional free agency (March 3, 2004).
CHAMPIONSHIP GAME EXPERIENCE: Played in AFC championship game (2001 season). ... Member of Super Bowl championship team (2001 season); inactive. ... Member of Patriots for AFC championship game (2003 season); did not play. ... Member of Patriots for Super Bowl 38 (2003 season); did not play.
SINGLE GAME HIGHS (regular season): Attempts—42 (October 17, 1999, vs. New England); completions—24 (October 17, 1999, vs. New England); yards—240 (October 17, 1999, vs. New England); and touchdown passes—2 (November 21, 1999, vs. New England).
MISCELLANEOUS: Regular-season record as starting NFL quarterback: 5-1 (.833).

			PASSING									RUSHING				TOTALS		
Year Team	G	GS	Att.	Cmp.	Pct.	Yds.	TD	Int.	Avg.	Skd.	Rat.	Att.	Yds.	Avg.	TD	TD	2pt.	Pts.
1997—Miami NFL									Did not play.									
1998—Miami NFL	2	0	9	6	66.7	85	0	1	9.44	1	57.4	0	0	0.0	0	0	0	0
1999—Miami NFL	16	5	216	125	57.9	1288	8	4	5.96	28	79.8	28	124	4.4	0	0	0	0
2000—Miami NFL	16	1	63	39	61.9	318	1	3	5.05	4	60.2	0	0	0.0	0	0	0	0
2002—New England NFL	2	0	0	0	0.0	0	0	0	0.00	0	.0	1	4	4.0	0	0	0	0
2003—New England NFL	2	0	1	0	0.0	0	0	0	0.00	0	39.6	1	-1	-1.0	0	0	0	0
Pro totals (5 years)	38	6	289	170	58.8	1691	9	8	5.85	33	74.3	30	127	4.2	0	0	0	0

HUFF, ORLANDO LB

PERSONAL: Born August 14, 1978, in Mobile, Ala. ... 6-2/250.
HIGH SCHOOL: Upland (Calif.).
JUNIOR COLLEGE: Eastern Arizona Junior College.
COLLEGE: Fresno State.
TRANSACTIONS/CAREER NOTES: Selected by Seattle Seahawks in fourth round (104th pick overall) of 2001 NFL draft. ... Signed by Seahawks (July 9, 2001). ... Granted free agency (March 3, 2004).

			TOTALS			INTERCEPTIONS			
Year Team	G	GS	Tk.	Ast.	Sks.	No.	Yds.	Avg.	TD
2001—Seattle NFL	12	0	0	0	0.0	0	0	0.0	0
2002—Seattle NFL	16	7	38	13	0.0	1	0	0.0	0
2003—Seattle NFL	11	2	16	4	1.0	0	0	0.0	0
Pro totals (3 years)	39	9	54	17	1.0	1	0	0.0	0

H

HULSEY, COREY — G/T — RAIDERS

PERSONAL: Born July 26, 1977, in Lula, Ga. ... 6-4/325. ... Full name: Corey Spear Hulsey.
HIGH SCHOOL: North Hall (Lula, Ga.).
COLLEGE: Clemson.
TRANSACTIONS/CAREER NOTES: Signed as non-drafted free agent by Buffalo Bills (April 19, 1999). ... Released by Bills (August 30, 1999). ... Re-signed by Bills (April 27, 2000). ... Released by Bills (August 27, 2000). ... Re-signed by Bills to practice squad (August 28, 2000). ... Released by Bills (September 1, 2002). ... Signed by Oakland Raiders (January 7, 2003). ... Waived by Raiders (August 26, 2003). ... Re-signed by Raiders (November 19, 2003).
PLAYING EXPERIENCE: Buffalo NFL, 2001; Oakland NFL, 2003. ... Games/Games started: 2001 (16/12), 2003 (4/0). Total: 20/12.

HUMPHREY, DEON — LB — JAGUARS

PERSONAL: Born May 7, 1976, in Clewiston, Fla. ... 6-3/240. ... Full name: Deon Morie Humphrey.
HIGH SCHOOL: Lake Worth (Fla.).
COLLEGE: Florida State.
TRANSACTIONS/CAREER NOTES: Signed as non-drafted free agent by Green Bay Packers (April 19, 1999). ... Released by Packers (September 5, 1999). ... Re-signed by Packers to practice squad (December 1, 1999). ... Released by Packers (December 12, 1999). ... Selected by Amsterdam Admirals in NFL Europe draft (February 12, 2000). ... Signed by San Diego Chargers (June 28, 2000). ... Claimed on waivers by Carolina Panthers (August 28, 2000). ... Released by Panthers (September 30, 2000). ... Signed by Chargers to practice squad (October 4, 2000). ... Activated (October 24, 2000). ... Released by Chargers (August 31, 2002). ... Signed by Jacksonville Jaguars (October 15, 2003). ... On injured reserve with knee injury (December 17, 2003-remainder of season).

			TOTALS			INTERCEPTIONS			
Year Team	**G**	**GS**	**Tk.**	**Ast.**	**Sks.**	**No.**	**Yds.**	**Avg.**	**TD**
2000—Carolina NFL	3	0	0	0	0.0	0	0	0.0	0
—San Diego NFL	7	0	0	0	0.0	0	0	0.0	0
2001—San Diego NFL	11	0	0	0	0.0	0	0	0.0	0
2003—Jacksonville NFL	8	0	0	0	0.0	0	0	0.0	0
Pro totals (3 years)	29	0	0	0	0.0	0	0	0.0	0

HUNT, CLETIDUS — DT — PACKERS

PERSONAL: Born January 2, 1976, in Memphis, Tenn. ... 6-4/305. ... Full name: Cletidus Marquell Hunt.
HIGH SCHOOL: Whitehaven (Memphis, Tenn.).
JUNIOR COLLEGE: Northwest Mississippi Community College.
COLLEGE: Kentucky State.
TRANSACTIONS/CAREER NOTES: Selected by Green Bay Packers in third round (94th pick overall) of NFL draft. ... Signed by Packers (July 26, 1999). ... On suspended list for violating league substance abuse policy (July 20-October 14, 2001). ... Granted free agency (March 1, 2002). ... Re-signed by Packers (April 24, 2002). ... Designated by Packers as franchise player (February 20, 2003). ... Re-signed by Packers (March 5, 2003).

			TOTALS		
Year Team	**G**	**GS**	**Tk.**	**Ast.**	**Sks.**
1999—Green Bay NFL	11	1	10	10	0.5
2000—Green Bay NFL	16	11	18	10	5.0
2001—Green Bay NFL	12	4	15	10	0.0
2002—Green Bay NFL	14	14	31	5	5.5
2003—Green Bay NFL	16	16	27	9	4.0
Pro totals (5 years)	69	46	101	44	15.0

HUNTER, PETE — CB — COWBOYS

PERSONAL: Born May 25, 1980, in Atlantic City, N.J. ... 6-2/212. ... Full name: Ralph Hunter.
HIGH SCHOOL: Atlantic City (N.J.).
COLLEGE: Virginia Union.
TRANSACTIONS/CAREER NOTES: Selected by Dallas Cowboys in fifth round (168th pick overall) of 2002 NFL draft. ... Signed by Cowboys (July 25, 2002).

			TOTALS			INTERCEPTIONS			
Year Team	**G**	**GS**	**Tk.**	**Ast.**	**Sks.**	**No.**	**Yds.**	**Avg.**	**TD**
2002—Dallas NFL	11	2	18	2	0.0	1	16	16.0	0
2003—Dallas NFL	16	1	19	2	0.0	1	0	0.0	0
Pro totals (2 years)	27	3	37	4	0.0	2	16	8.0	0

HUTCHINSON, CHAD — QB — COWBOYS

PERSONAL: Born February 21, 1977, in Boulder, Colo. ... 6-5/237. ... Full name: Chad Martin Hutchinson.
HIGH SCHOOL: Torrey Pines (Encinitas, Calif.).
COLLEGE: Stanford.
TRANSACTIONS/CAREER NOTES: Signed as non-drafted free agent by Dallas Cowboys (January 26, 2002). ... Assigned by Cowboys to Rhein Fire in 2004 NFL Europe enhancement allocation program (February 9, 2004).
SINGLE GAME HIGHS (regular season): Attempts—40 (December 15, 2002, vs. New York Giants); completions—22 (November 3, 2002, vs. Detroit); yards—301 (November 24, 2002, vs. Jacksonville); and touchdown passes—2 (November 28, 2002, vs. Washington).
STATISTICAL PLATEAUS: 300-yard passing games: 2002 (1). Total: 1.
MISCELLANEOUS: Regular-season record as starting NFL quarterback: 2-7 (.222).

Year Team	G	GS	PASSING Att.	Cmp.	Pct.	Yds.	TD	Int.	Avg.	Skd.	Rat.	RUSHING Att.	Yds.	Avg.	TD	TOTALS TD	2pt.	Pts.
2002—Dallas NFL	9	9	250	127	50.8	1555	7	8	6.22	34	66.3	18	74	4.1	0	0	0	0
2003—Dallas NFL	1	0	2	1	50.0	8	0	0	4.00	0	60.4	2	-3	-1.5	0	0	0	0
Pro totals (2 years)	10	9	252	128	50.8	1563	7	8	6.20	34	66.3	20	71	3.6	0	0	0	0

HUTCHINSON, STEVE G SEAHAWKS

PERSONAL: Born November 1, 1977, in Fort Lauderdale, Fla. ... 6-5/313.
HIGH SCHOOL: Coral Springs (Fla.).
COLLEGE: Michigan.
TRANSACTIONS/CAREER NOTES: Selected by Seattle Seahawks in first round (17th pick overall) of 2001 NFL draft. ... Signed by Seahawks (July 25, 2001). ... On injured reserve with broken leg (November 12, 2002-remainder of season).
PLAYING EXPERIENCE: Seattle NFL, 2001-2003. ... Games/Games started: 2001 (16/16), 2002 (4/4), 2003 (16/16). Total: 36/36.
HONORS: Named guard on THE SPORTING NEWS college All-America first team (2000). ... Named guard on THE SPORTING NEWS NFL All-Pro team (2003). ... Played in Pro Bowl (2003 season).

IOANE, JUNIOR DT TEXANS

PERSONAL: Born July 21, 1977, in American Samoa. ... 6-4/320. ... Full name: Junior Burton Ioane.
HIGH SCHOOL: North Sanpete (Mount Pleasant, Utah).
JUNIOR COLLEGE: Snow College (Utah).
COLLEGE: Arizona State.
TRANSACTIONS/CAREER NOTES: Selected by Oakland Raiders in fourth round (107th pick overall) of 2000 NFL draft. ... Signed by Raiders (June 1, 2000). ... Inactive for all 16 games (2000). ... Claimed on waivers by Houston Texans (September 1, 2003).
CHAMPIONSHIP GAME EXPERIENCE: Played in AFC championship game (2002 season). ... Played in Super Bowl 37 (2002 season).

Year Team	G	GS	TOTALS Tk.	Ast.	Sks.
2001—Oakland NFL	3	0	0	0	0.0
2002—Oakland NFL	6	0	2	1	1.0
2003—Houston NFL	13	4	19	10	0.5
Pro totals (3 years)	22	4	21	11	1.5

IRONS, GRANT DE RAIDERS

PERSONAL: Born July 7, 1979, in Middleburg Heights, Ohio. ... 6-5/265. ... Full name: Grant Michael Irons. ... Son of Gerald Irons, linebacker with Oakland Raiders (1970-1975) and Cleveland Browns (1976-1979).
HIGH SCHOOL: Woodlands (Texas).
COLLEGE: Notre Dame.
TRANSACTIONS/CAREER NOTES: Signed as non-drafted free agent by Buffalo Bills (April 26, 2002). ... Released by Bills (August 31, 2003). ... Signed by Oakland Raiders (December 18, 2003).

Year Team	G	GS	TOTALS Tk.	Ast.	Sks.
2002—Buffalo NFL	15	0	5	3	2.5
2003—Oakland NFL	1	0	0	0	0.0
Pro totals (2 years)	16	0	5	3	2.5

IRVIN, KEN CB VIKINGS

PERSONAL: Born July 11, 1972, in Rome, Ga. ... 5-11/182. ... Full name: Kenneth Irvin.
HIGH SCHOOL: Pepperell (Lindale, Ga.).
COLLEGE: Memphis.
TRANSACTIONS/CAREER NOTES: Selected by Buffalo Bills in fourth round (109th pick overall) of 1995 NFL draft. ... Signed by Bills (July 10, 1995). ... Granted free agency (February 13, 1998). ... Re-signed by Bills (April 17, 1998). ... Granted unconditional free agency (February 12, 1999). ... Re-signed by Bills (March 17, 1999). ... On injured reserve with foot injury (December 23, 1999-remainder of season). ... Released by Bills (February 28, 2002). ... Signed by New Orleans Saints (April 24, 2002). ... Granted unconditional free agency (February 28, 2003). ... Signed by Minnesota Vikings (March 20, 2003).

Year Team	G	GS	TOTALS Tk.	Ast.	Sks.	INTERCEPTIONS No.	Yds.	Avg.	TD
1995—Buffalo NFL	16	3	18	2	0.0	0	0	0.0	0
1996—Buffalo NFL	16	1	17	4	2.0	0	0	0.0	0
1997—Buffalo NFL	16	0	5	0	0.0	2	28	14.0	0
1998—Buffalo NFL	16	16	46	5	0.0	1	43	43.0	0
1999—Buffalo NFL	14	14	40	5	0.0	1	1	1.0	0
2000—Buffalo NFL	16	16	29	2	0.0	2	1	0.5	0
2001—Buffalo NFL	14	4	33	3	0.0	1	0	0.0	0
2002—New Orleans NFL	16	9	58	4	0.0	2	10	5.0	0
2003—Minnesota NFL	16	8	45	10	0.0	1	1	1.0	0
Pro totals (9 years)	140	71	291	35	2.0	10	84	8.4	0

ISOM, JASEN FB 49ERS

PERSONAL: Born January 7, 1977, in Wheatley Heights, N.Y. ... 6-1/243.
HIGH SCHOOL: Half Hollow Hills (Wheatley Heights, N.Y.).
COLLEGE: Western Illinois.

TRANSACTIONS/CAREER NOTES: Signed as non-drafted free agent by San Francisco 49ers to practice squad (April 27, 2001). ... Waived by 49ers (September 1, 2001). ... Re-signed by 49ers (January 15, 2002). ... Waived by 49ers (August 30, 2002). ... Re-signed by 49ers to practice squad (October 16, 2002) ... Activated (January 30, 2003). ... Waived by 49ers (August 31, 2003). ... Re-signed by 49ers to practice squad (September 1, 2003). ... Activated (October 25, 2003). ... Waived by 49ers (October 27, 2003). ... Re-signed by 49ers to practice squad (October 29, 2003). ... Activated (December 10, 2003).

			RUSHING				TOTALS			
Year Team	G	GS	Att.	Yds.	Avg.	TD	TD	2pt.	Pts.	Fum.
2003—San Francisco NFL	2	0	0	0	0.0	0	0	0	0	0

ISRAEL, RON CB BRONCOS

PERSONAL: Born January 5, 1978, in Voorhees, N.J. ... 6-0/212.
HIGH SCHOOL: Haddon Heights (N.J.).
COLLEGE: Notre Dame.
TRANSACTIONS/CAREER NOTES: Signed as non-drafted free agent by Washington Redskins (April 24, 2002). ... Released by Redskins (August 26, 2002). ... Signed by Minnesota Vikings (April 7, 2003). ... Released by Vikings (August 31, 2003). ... Re-signed by Vikings (September 9, 2003). ... Released by Vikings (September 22, 2003). ... Signed by Cleveland Browns to practice squad (September 24, 2003). ... Released by Browns (September 30, 2003). ... Re-signed by Browns to practice squad (December 3, 2003). ... Activated (December 10, 2003). ... Released by Browns (December 23, 2003). ... Signed by Denver Broncos (December 31, 2003).

			TOTALS			INTERCEPTIONS			
Year Team	G	GS	Tk.	Ast.	Sks.	No.	Yds.	Avg.	TD
2003—Minnesota NFL	1	0	0	0	0.0	0	0	0.0	0

IVY, COREY CB BUCCANEERS

PERSONAL: Born March 29, 1977, in St. Louis, Mo. ... 5-8/183. ... Full name: Corey Terrell Ivy.
HIGH SCHOOL: Moore (Oklahoma).
JUNIOR COLLEGE: Northeastern Oklahoma.
COLLEGE: Oklahoma.
TRANSACTIONS/CAREER NOTES: Signed as non-drafted free agent by New England Patriots (May 13, 1999). ... Released by Patriots (September 5, 1999). ... Re-signed by Patriots to practice squad (December 29, 1999). ... Signed by Cleveland Browns (July 12, 2000). ... Released by Browns (August 27, 2000). ... Signed by Tampa Bay Buccaneers (June 4, 2001). ... Released by Buccaneers (September 2, 2001). ... Re-signed by Buccaneers to practice squad (September 3, 2001). ... Activated (November 10, 2001). ... Released by Buccaneers (December 4, 2001). ... Re-signed by Buccaneers to practice squad (December 5, 2001). ... Assigned by Buccaneers to Rhein Fire in 2002 NFL Europe enhancement allocation program (February 12, 2002).
CHAMPIONSHIP GAME EXPERIENCE: Played in NFC championship game (2002 season). ... Member of Super Bowl championship team (2002 season).

			TOTALS			INTERCEPTIONS			
Year Team	G	GS	Tk.	Ast.	Sks.	No.	Yds.	Avg.	TD
2001—Tampa Bay NFL	1	0	3	2	0.0	0	0	0.0	0
2002—Tampa Bay NFL	16	0	0	0	0.0	0	0	0.0	0
2003—Tampa Bay NFL	16	2	18	0	0.0	0	0	0.0	0
Pro totals (3 years)	33	2	21	2	0.0	0	0	0.0	0

IWUOMA, CHIDI CB STEELERS

PERSONAL: Born February 19, 1978, in Los Angeles, Calif. ... 5-8/184.
HIGH SCHOOL: Pasadena (Calif.).
COLLEGE: California.
TRANSACTIONS/CAREER NOTES: Signed as non-drafted free agent by Detroit Lions (April 27, 2000). ... Released by Lions (September 2, 2001). ... Re-signed by Lions to practice squad (September 4, 2001). ... Activated (September 8, 2001). ... Released by Lions (September 1, 2002). ... Signed by Pittsburgh Steelers (September 11, 2002). ... Granted free agency (March 3, 2004). ... Re-signed by Steelers (April 28, 2004).

			TOTALS			INTERCEPTIONS			
Year Team	G	GS	Tk.	Ast.	Sks.	No.	Yds.	Avg.	TD
2001—Detroit NFL	13	1	5	0	0.0	0	0	0.0	0
2002—Pittsburgh NFL	13	0	0	1	0.0	0	0	0.0	0
2003—Pittsburgh NFL	15	0	0	0	0.0	0	0	0.0	0
Pro totals (3 years)	41	1	5	1	0.0	0	0	0.0	0

IZZO, LARRY LB PATRIOTS

PERSONAL: Born September 26, 1974, in Fort Belvoir, Va. ... 5-10/228. ... Full name: Lawrence Alexander Izzo.
HIGH SCHOOL: McCullough (Houston).
COLLEGE: Rice.
TRANSACTIONS/CAREER NOTES: Signed as non-drafted free agent by Miami Dolphins (April 25, 1996). ... On injured reserve with foot injury (August 18, 1997-entire season). ... Granted free agency (February 12, 1999). ... Re-signed by Dolphins (March 31, 1999). ... Granted unconditional free agency (March 2, 2001). ... Signed by New England Patriots (March 6, 2001).
CHAMPIONSHIP GAME EXPERIENCE: Played in AFC championship game (2001 and 2003 seasons). ... Member of Super Bowl championship team (2001 and 2003 seasons).
HONORS: Played in Pro Bowl (2000 and 2002 seasons).

			TOTALS			INTERCEPTIONS			
Year Team	G	GS	Tk.	Ast.	Sks.	No.	Yds.	Avg.	TD
1996—Miami NFL	16	0	1	0	0.0	0	0	0.0	0

Year Team	G	GS	TOTALS Tk.	Ast.	Sks.	INTERCEPTIONS No.	Yds.	Avg.	TD
1997—Miami NFL					Did not play.				
1998—Miami NFL	13	0	0	0	0.0	0	0	0.0	0
1999—Miami NFL	16	0	0	0	0.0	0	0	0.0	0
2000—Miami NFL	16	0	4	0	0.0	0	0	0.0	0
2001—New England NFL	16	0	1	1	0.0	0	0	0.0	0
2002—New England NFL	15	0	1	0	0.0	0	0	0.0	0
2003—New England NFL	16	0	5	0	0.0	1	0	0.0	0
Pro totals (7 years)	108	0	12	1	0.0	1	0	0.0	0

J

JACKSON, ALONZO LB STEELERS

PERSONAL: Born September 15, 1980, in Americus, Ga. ... 6-4/262.
HIGH SCHOOL: Americus (Ga.).
COLLEGE: Florida State.
TRANSACTIONS/CAREER NOTES: Selected by Pittsburgh Steelers in second round (59th pick overall) of 2003 NFL draft. ... Signed by Steelers (July 25, 2003).

Year Team	G	GS	TOTALS Tk.	Ast.	Sks.	INTERCEPTIONS No.	Yds.	Avg.	TD
2003—Pittsburgh NFL	2	0	0	0	0.0	0	0	0.0	0

JACKSON, CHRIS WR

PERSONAL: Born February 26, 1975, in Bristol, Pa. ... 6-2/205.
HIGH SCHOOL: Mater Dei (Santa Ana, Calif.).
COLLEGE: Washington State.
TRANSACTIONS/CAREER NOTES: Signed as non-drafted free agent by Seattle Seahawks (April 21, 1998). ... Released by Seahawks (August 24, 1998). ... Signed by Tampa Bay Buccaneers to practice squad (September 1, 1998). ... Released by Buccaneers (October 21, 1998). ... Signed by Seahawks (March 23, 1999). ... Released by Seahawks (September 6, 1999). ... Signed by Tennessee Titans to practice squad (October 8, 2000). ... Activated (November 4, 2000). ... On injured reserve with back injury (December 1, 2000-remainder of season). ... Released by Titans (February 28, 2001). ... Signed by Green Bay Packers (August 1, 2002). ... Released by Packers (September 1, 2002). ... Re-signed by Packers (September 29, 2002). ... Released by Packers (October 1, 2002).

Year Team	G	GS	RECEIVING No.	Yds.	Avg.	TD	TOTALS TD	2pt.	Pts.	Fum.
2000—Tennessee NFL	1	0	0	0	0.0	0	0	0	0	0
2002—Green Bay NFL	1	0	0	0	0.0	0	0	0	0	0
2003—Green Bay NFL	1	0	0	0	0.0	0	0	0	0	0
Pro totals (3 years)	3	0	0	0	0.0	0	0	0	0	0

JACKSON, DARRELL WR SEAHAWKS

PERSONAL: Born December 6, 1978, in Dayton, Ohio. ... 6-0/201. ... Full name: Darrell Lamont Jackson.
HIGH SCHOOL: Tampa Catholic.
COLLEGE: Florida.
TRANSACTIONS/CAREER NOTES: Selected after junior season by Seattle Seahawks in third round (80th pick overall) of 2000 NFL draft. ... Signed by Seahawks (July 19, 2000). ... Granted free agency (February 28, 2003). ... Re-signed by Seahawks (April 25, 2003). ... Granted unconditional free agency (March 3, 2004). ... Re-signed by Seahawks (March 9, 2004).
SINGLE GAME HIGHS (regular season): Receptions—10 (September 15, 2002, vs. Arizona); yards—174 (September 15, 2002, vs. Arizona); and touchdown receptions—2 (November 30, 2003, vs. Cleveland).
STATISTICAL PLATEAUS: 100-yard receiving games: 2001 (5), 2002 (2), 2003 (3). Total: 10.

Year Team	G	GS	RUSHING Att.	Yds.	Avg.	TD	RECEIVING No.	Yds.	Avg.	TD	PUNT RETURNS No.	Yds.	Avg.	TD	TOTALS TD	2pt.	Pts.	Fum.
2000—Seattle NFL	16	10	1	-1	-1.0	0	53	713	13.5	6	0	0	0.0	0	6	0	36	2
2001—Seattle NFL	16	16	1	9	9.0	0	70	1081	15.4	8	0	0	0.0	0	8	0	48	0
2002—Seattle NFL	13	13	3	3	1.0	0	62	877	14.1	4	4	32	8.0	0	4	0	24	3
2003—Seattle NFL	16	16	0	0	0.0	0	68	1137	16.7	9	0	0	0.0	0	9	0	54	1
Pro totals (4 years)	61	55	5	11	2.2	0	253	3808	15.1	27	4	32	8.0	0	27	0	162	6

JACKSON, DEXTER S CARDINALS

PERSONAL: Born July 28, 1977, in Quincy, Fla. ... 6-0/205. ... Full name: Dexter Lamar Jackson.
HIGH SCHOOL: James A. Shanks (Quincy, Fla.).
COLLEGE: Florida State.
TRANSACTIONS/CAREER NOTES: Selected by Tampa Bay Buccaneers in fourth round (113th pick overall) of 1999 NFL draft. ... Signed by Buccaneers (July 29, 1999). ... Granted free agency (March 1, 2002). ... Re-signed by Buccaneers (April 26, 2002). ... Granted unconditional free agency (February 28, 2003). ... Signed by Arizona Cardinals (March 12, 2003).
CHAMPIONSHIP GAME EXPERIENCE: Played in NFC championship game (1999 and 2002 seasons). ... Member of Super Bowl championship team (2002 season).
HONORS: Named Most Valuable Player of Super Bowl 37 (2002 season).

Year Team	G	GS	TOTALS Tk.	Ast.	Sks.	INTERCEPTIONS No.	Yds.	Avg.	TD
1999—Tampa Bay NFL	12	0	0	0	0.0	0	0	0.0	0
2000—Tampa Bay NFL	13	0	18	2	0.0	0	0	0.0	0

Year Team	G	GS	TOTALS Tk.	Ast.	Sks.	INTERCEPTIONS No.	Yds.	Avg.	TD
2001—Tampa Bay NFL	15	15	54	11	2.5	4	42	10.5	0
2002—Tampa Bay NFL	16	16	56	15	0.0	3	101	33.7	0
2003—Arizona NFL	16	16	73	13	0.0	6	122	20.3	0
Pro totals (5 years)	72	47	201	41	2.5	13	265	20.4	0

JACKSON, FRISMAN — WR — BROWNS

PERSONAL: Born June 12, 1979, in Chicago, Ill. ... 6-3/215.
HIGH SCHOOL: Morgan Park (Chicago).
COLLEGE: Western Illinois.
TRANSACTIONS/CAREER NOTES: Signed as non-drafted free agent by Cleveland Browns (April 26, 2002).
SINGLE GAME HIGHS (regular season): Receptions—1 (December 28, 2003, vs. Cincinnati); yards—19 (December 28, 2003, vs. Cincinnati); and touchdown receptions—0.

Year Team	G	GS	RECEIVING No.	Yds.	Avg.	TD	KICKOFF RETURNS No.	Yds.	Avg.	TD	TOTALS TD	2pt.	Pts.	Fum.
2002—Cleveland NFL	7	0	1	6	6.0	0	3	58	19.3	0	0	0	0	0
2003—Cleveland NFL	5	0	2	29	14.5	0	0	0	0.0	0	0	0	0	0
Pro totals (2 years)	12	0	3	35	11.7	0	3	58	19.3	0	0	0	0	0

JACKSON, GRADY — DT — PACKERS

PERSONAL: Born January 21, 1973, in Greensboro, Ala. ... 6-2/330.
HIGH SCHOOL: Greensboro (Ala.) East.
JUNIOR COLLEGE: Hinds Community College (Miss.).
COLLEGE: Knoxville.
TRANSACTIONS/CAREER NOTES: Selected by Oakland Raiders in sixth round (193rd pick overall) of 1997 NFL draft. ... Signed by Raiders (July 18, 1997). ... Granted unconditional free agency (March 1, 2002). ... Signed by New Orleans Saints (April 11, 2002). ... Suspended one game for conduct detrimental to team (October 28, 2003). ... Claimed on waivers by Green Bay Packers (November 4, 2003).
CHAMPIONSHIP GAME EXPERIENCE: Played in AFC championship game (2000 season).

Year Team	G	GS	TOTALS Tk.	Ast.	Sks.
1997—Oakland NFL	5	0	4	2	0.0
1998—Oakland NFL	15	1	29	10	3.0
1999—Oakland NFL	15	0	25	9	4.0
2000—Oakland NFL	16	15	51	17	8.0
2001—Oakland NFL	16	16	52	17	4.0
2002—New Orleans NFL	15	15	31	12	5.5
2003—New Orleans NFL	7	6	20	5	3.5
—Green Bay NFL	8	1	16	7	2.5
Pro totals (7 years)	97	54	228	79	30.5

JACKSON, JAMES — RB — BROWNS

PERSONAL: Born August 4, 1976, in Belle Glade, Fla. ... 5-10/215. ... Full name: James Shurrate Jackson.
HIGH SCHOOL: Glades Central (Belle Glade, Fla.).
COLLEGE: Miami (Fla.).
TRANSACTIONS/CAREER NOTES: Selected by Cleveland Browns in third round (65th pick overall) of 2001 NFL draft. ... Signed by Browns (July 23, 2001). ... On injured reserve with ankle injury (December 20, 2001-remainder of season). ... On injured reserve with knee injury (December 9, 2003-remainder of season).
SINGLE GAME HIGHS (regular season): Attempts—31 (September 23, 2001, vs. Detroit); yards—124 (September 23, 2001, vs. Detroit); and rushing touchdowns—2 (November 16, 2003, vs. Arizona).
STATISTICAL PLATEAUS: 100-yard rushing games: 2001 (1). Total: 1.

Year Team	G	GS	RUSHING Att.	Yds.	Avg.	TD	RECEIVING No.	Yds.	Avg.	TD	KICKOFF RETURNS No.	Yds.	Avg.	TD	TOTALS TD	2pt.	Pts.	Fum.
2001—Cleveland NFL	11	10	195	554	2.8	2	7	56	8.0	0	0	0	0.0	0	2	0	12	1
2002—Cleveland NFL	15	0	12	54	4.5	0	3	9	3.0	0	1	13	13.0	0	0	0	0	0
2003—Cleveland NFL	12	6	102	382	3.7	3	14	114	8.1	0	1	68	68.0	0	3	0	18	3
Pro totals (3 years)	38	16	309	990	3.2	5	24	179	7.5	0	2	81	40.5	0	5	0	30	4

JACKSON, JARIOUS — QB — BRONCOS

PERSONAL: Born May 3, 1977, in Tupelo, Miss. ... 6-0/228. ... Full name: Jarious K. Jackson.
HIGH SCHOOL: Tupelo (Miss.).
COLLEGE: Notre Dame.
TRANSACTIONS/CAREER NOTES: Selected by Denver Broncos in seventh round (214th pick overall) of 2000 NFL draft. ... Signed by Broncos (July 20, 2000). ... Assigned by Broncos to Bracelona Dragons in 2001 NFL Europe enhancement allocation program (February 19, 2001). ... Granted free agency (February 28, 2003). ... Re-signed by Broncos (April 18, 2003).
SINGLE GAME HIGHS (regular season): Attempts—12 (December 16, 2001, vs. Kansas City); completions—7 (December 16, 2001, vs. Kansas City); yards—73 (December 16, 2001, vs. Kansas City); and touchdown passes—0.
MISCELLANEOUS: Regular-season record as starting NFL quarterback: 0-1 (.000).

Year Team	G	GS	PASSING Att.	Cmp.	Pct.	Yds.	TD	Int.	Avg.	Skd.	Rat.	RUSHING Att.	Yds.	Avg.	TD	TOTALS TD	2pt.	Pts.
2000—Denver NFL	2	0	1	0	0.0	0	0	0	0.00	1	39.6	1	-1	-1.0	0	0	0	0
2001—Denver NFL	1	0	12	7	58.3	73	0	0	6.08	1	76.0	5	7	1.4	0	0	0	0
2002—Denver NFL	1	0	0	0	0.0	0	0	0	0.00	0	0.0	0	0	0.0	0	0	0	0
2003—Denver NFL	1	1	9	4	44.4	41	0	1	4.56	0	18.5	1	9	9.0	0	0	0	0
Pro totals (4 years)	5	1	22	11	50.0	114	0	1	5.18	2	46.4	7	15	2.1	0	0	0	0

JACKSON, NATE — WR

PERSONAL: Born June 4, 1979, in San Jose, Calif. ... 6-3/223.
HIGH SCHOOL: Pioneer High.
COLLEGE: Menlo.
TRANSACTIONS/CAREER NOTES: Signed as non-drafted free agent by San Francisco 49ers (April 23, 2002). ... Waived by 49ers (August 21, 2002). ... Re-signed by 49ers (January 27, 2003). ... Traded by 49ers to Denver Broncos for a conditional draft pick in 2004 (August 12, 2003). ... Released by Broncos (August 31, 2003). ... Re-signed by Broncos to practice squad (September 1, 2003). ... Released by Broncos (April 14, 2004).

Year Team	G	GS	RECEIVING No.	Yds.	Avg.	TD	TOTALS TD	2pt.	Pts.	Fum.
2003—Denver NFL	1	0	0	0	0.0	0	0	0	0	0

JACKSON, RAY — RB — TITANS

PERSONAL: Born August 1, 1978, in Indianapolis, Ind. ... 6-1/223. ... Full name: Raymond F. Jackson.
HIGH SCHOOL: Central (Lawrence, Ind.).
COLLEGE: Cincinnati.
TRANSACTIONS/CAREER NOTES: Signed as non-drafted free agent by Cincinnati Bengals (March 13, 2003). ... Released by Bengals (August 31, 2003). ... Re-signed by Bengals to practice squad (September 1, 2003). ... Released by Bengals (September 30, 2003). ... Signed by Tennessee Titans to practice squad (November 18, 2003). ... Activated (December 24, 2003). ... Assigned by Titans to Berlin Thunder in 2004 NFL Europe enhancement allocation program (February 9, 2004).

Year Team	G	GS	RUSHING Att.	Yds.	Avg.	TD	KICKOFF RETURNS No.	Yds.	Avg.	TD	TOTALS TD	2pt.	Pts.	Fum.
2003—Tennessee NFL	1	0	0	0	0.0	0	3	77	25.7	0	0	0	0	0

JACKSON, TERRY — FB — 49ERS

PERSONAL: Born January 10, 1976, in Gainesville, Fla. ... 6-0/232. ... Full name: Terrance Bernard Jackson. ... Brother of Willie Jackson Jr., wide receiver, Denver Broncos.
HIGH SCHOOL: P.K. Yonge (Gainesville, Fla.).
COLLEGE: Florida.
TRANSACTIONS/CAREER NOTES: Selected by San Francisco 49ers in fifth round (157th pick overall) of 1999 NFL draft. ... Signed by 49ers (July 26, 1999). ... Granted free agency (March 1, 2002). ... Re-signed by 49ers (July 22, 2002). ... On injured reserve with knee injury (October 16, 2002-remainder of season).
SINGLE GAME HIGHS (regular season): Attempts—5 (December 2, 2001, vs. Buffalo); yards—37 (December 2, 2001, vs. Buffalo); and rushing touchdowns—1 (January 6, 2002, vs. New Orleans).

Year Team	G	GS	RUSHING Att.	Yds.	Avg.	TD	RECEIVING No.	Yds.	Avg.	TD	KICKOFF RETURNS No.	Yds.	Avg.	TD	TOTALS TD	2pt.	Pts.	Fum.
1999—San Francisco NFL	16	0	15	75	5.0	0	3	6	2.0	0	0	0	0.0	0	0	0	0	1
2000—San Francisco NFL	15	1	5	6	1.2	1	5	48	9.6	1	1	9	9.0	0	2	1	14	0
2001—San Francisco NFL	16	1	22	138	6.3	1	12	91	7.6	2	0	0	0.0	0	3	0	18	1
2002—San Francisco NFL	5	0	0	0	0.0	0	0	0	0.0	0	4	67	16.8	0	0	0	0	0
2003—San Francisco NFL	16	0	0	0	0.0	0	0	0	0.0	0	0	0	0.0	0	0	0	0	0
Pro totals (5 years)	68	2	42	219	5.2	2	20	145	7.3	3	5	76	15.2	0	5	1	32	2

JACKSON, TYOKA — DT — RAMS

PERSONAL: Born November 22, 1971, in Washington, DC. ... 6-2/280. ... Name pronounced: tie-OH-kah.
HIGH SCHOOL: Bishop McNamara (Forestville, Md.).
COLLEGE: Penn State.
TRANSACTIONS/CAREER NOTES: Signed as non-drafted free agent by Atlanta Falcons (May 2, 1994). ... Released by Falcons (August 29, 1994). ... Re-signed by Falcons to practice squad (August 30, 1994). ... Signed by Miami Dolphins off Falcons practice squad (November 16, 1994). ... Released by Dolphins (August 27, 1995). ... Signed by Tampa Bay Buccaneers (December 27, 1995). ... Granted free agency (February 13, 1998). ... Re-signed by Buccaneers (June 22, 1998). ... Granted unconditional free agency (March 2, 2001). ... Signed by St. Louis Rams (May 1, 2001). ... Granted unconditional free agency (February 28, 2003). ... Re-signed by Rams (March 17, 2003).
CHAMPIONSHIP GAME EXPERIENCE: Member of Buccaneers for NFC championship game (1999 season); inactive. ... Played in NFC championship game (2001 season). ... Played in Super Bowl 36 (2001 season).

Year Team	G	GS	TOTALS Tk.	Ast.	Sks.	INTERCEPTIONS No.	Yds.	Avg.	TD
1994—Miami NFL	1	0	0	0	0.0	0	0	0.0	0
1995—			Did not play.						
1996—Tampa Bay NFL	13	2	9	2	0.0	0	0	0.0	0
1997—Tampa Bay NFL	12	0	5	2	2.5	0	0	0.0	0
1998—Tampa Bay NFL	16	12	21	6	3.0	0	0	0.0	0
1999—Tampa Bay NFL	6	1	5	2	1.0	0	0	0.0	0
2000—Tampa Bay NFL	16	1	4	3	2.0	0	0	0.0	0

Year Team	G	GS	TOTALS Tk.	Ast.	Sks.	INTERCEPTIONS No.	Yds.	Avg.	TD
2001—St. Louis NFL	16	0	12	7	3.0	0	0	0.0	0
2002—St. Louis NFL	16	0	14	3	3.5	0	0	0.0	0
2003—St. Louis NFL	16	3	19	4	5.5	1	11	11.0	0
Pro totals (9 years)	112	19	89	29	20.5	1	11	11.0	0

JACKSON, WILLIE — WR — BRONCOS

PERSONAL: Born August 16, 1971, in Gainesville, Fla. ... 6-1/212. ... Full name: Willie Bernard Jackson Jr. ... Brother of Terry Jackson, running back, San Francisco 49ers.
HIGH SCHOOL: P.K. Yonge (Gainesville, Fla.).
COLLEGE: Florida.
TRANSACTIONS/CAREER NOTES: Selected by Dallas Cowboys in fourth round (109th pick overall) of 1994 NFL draft. ... Signed by Cowboys (July 16, 1994). ... Inactive for 16 games (1994). ... Selected by Jacksonville Jaguars from Cowboys in NFL expansion draft (February 15, 1995). ... Granted free agency (February 14, 1997). ... Re-signed by Jaguars (March 26, 1997). ... Released by Jaguars (August 30, 1998). ... Signed by Cincinnati Bengals (September 10, 1998). ... Granted unconditional free agency (February 11, 2000). ... Signed by New Orleans Saints (April 28, 2000) ... Granted unconditional free agency (March 2, 2001). ... Re-signed by Saints (April 24, 2001). ... Granted unconditional free agency (March 1, 2002). ... Signed by Atlanta Falcons (July 12, 2002). ... Released by Falcons (October 28, 2002). ... Signed by Washington Redskins (October 31, 2002). ... Released by Redskins (December 12, 2002). ... Signed by Denver Broncos (March 12, 2004).
CHAMPIONSHIP GAME EXPERIENCE: Member of Cowboys for NFC championship game (1994 season); inactive. ... Played in AFC championship game (1996 season).
SINGLE GAME HIGHS (regular season): Receptions—11 (November 11, 2001, vs. San Francisco); yards—167 (November 11, 2001, vs. San Francisco); and touchdown receptions—2 (November 19, 2000, vs. Oakland).
STATISTICAL PLATEAUS: 100-yard receiving games: 1995 (1), 1996 (1), 2001 (3). Total: 5.

Year Team	G	GS	RECEIVING No.	Yds.	Avg.	TD	KICKOFF RETURNS No.	Yds.	Avg.	TD	TOTALS TD	2pt.	Pts.	Fum.
1994—Dallas NFL								Did not play.						
1995—Jacksonville NFL	14	10	53	589	11.1	5	19	404	21.3	0	5	1	32	2
1996—Jacksonville NFL	16	2	33	486	14.7	3	7	149	21.3	0	3	1	20	0
1997—Jacksonville NFL	16	1	17	206	12.1	2	32	653	20.4	0	2	1	14	1
1998—Cincinnati NFL	8	0	7	165	23.6	0	0	0	0.0	0	0	0	0	0
1999—Cincinnati NFL	16	2	31	369	11.9	2	6	179	29.8	0	2	1	14	1
2000—New Orleans NFL	15	7	37	523	14.1	6	0	0	0.0	0	6	0	36	2
2001—New Orleans NFL	16	16	81	1046	12.9	5	0	0	0.0	0	5	1	32	0
2002—Atlanta NFL	7	1	18	199	11.1	0	0	0	0.0	0	0	0	0	1
—Washington NFL	5	0	7	58	8.3	1	3	47	15.7	0	1	0	6	1
2003—								Did not play.						
Pro totals (8 years)	113	39	284	3641	12.8	24	67	1432	21.4	0	24	5	154	8

JACOBS, TAYLOR — WR — REDSKINS

PERSONAL: Born May 30, 1981, in Tallahassee, Fla. ... 6-0/198. ... Full name: Taylor Houser Jacobs.
HIGH SCHOOL: Florida A&M (Tallahassee, Fla.).
COLLEGE: Florida.
TRANSACTIONS/CAREER NOTES: Selected by Washington Redskins in second round (44th pick overall) of 2003 NFL draft. ... Signed by Redskins (July 28, 2003).
SINGLE GAME HIGHS (regular season): Receptions—1 (November 30, 2003, vs. New Orleans); yards—19 (November 2, 2003, vs. Dallas); and touchdown receptions—1 (November 2, 2003, vs. Dallas).

Year Team	G	GS	RUSHING Att.	Yds.	Avg.	TD	RECEIVING No.	Yds.	Avg.	TD	TOTALS TD	2pt.	Pts.	Fum.
2003—Washington NFL	8	0	0	0	0.0	0	3	37	12.3	1	1	0	6	0

JACOX, KENDYL — C/G — SAINTS

PERSONAL: Born June 10, 1975, in Dallas, Texas. ... 6-2/330. ... Full name: Kendyl LaMarc Jacox. ... Name pronounced: JAY-cox.
HIGH SCHOOL: Carter (Dallas).
COLLEGE: Kansas State.
TRANSACTIONS/CAREER NOTES: Signed as non-drafted free agent by San Diego Chargers (April 20, 1998). ... On injured reserve with knee injury (December 4, 1999-remainder of season). ... Granted free agency (March 2, 2001). ... Re-signed by Chargers (April 10, 2001). ... Granted unconditional free agency (March 1, 2002). ... Signed by New Orleans Saints (May 28, 2002).
PLAYING EXPERIENCE: San Diego NFL, 1998-2001; New Orleans NFL, 2002-2003. ... Games/Games started: 1998 (16/6), 1999 (10/5), 2000 (15/3), 2001 (16/16), 2002 (16/16), 2003 (12/11). Total: 85/57.

JAMES, BRADIE — LB — COWBOYS

PERSONAL: Born January 17, 1981, in Monroe, La. ... 6-2/243. ... Full name: Bradie Gene James.
HIGH SCHOOL: West Monroe (Monroe, La.).
COLLEGE: Louisiana State.
TRANSACTIONS/CAREER NOTES: Selected by Dallas Cowboys in fourth round (103rd pick overall) of 2003 NFL draft. ... Signed by Cowboys (July 26, 2003).

Year Team	G	GS	TOTALS Tk.	Ast.	Sks.	INTERCEPTIONS No.	Yds.	Avg.	TD
2003—Dallas NFL	14	0	3	0	0.0	0	0	0.0	0

JAMES, EDGERRIN — RB — COLTS

PERSONAL: Born August 1, 1978, in Immokalee, Fla. ... 6-0/214. ... Full name: Edgerrin Tyree James. ... Name pronounced: EDGE-rin.
HIGH SCHOOL: Immokalee (Fla.).
COLLEGE: Miami (Fla.).
TRANSACTIONS/CAREER NOTES: Selected after junior season by Indianapolis Colts in first round (fourth pick overall) of 1999 NFL draft. ... Signed by Colts (August 12, 1999). ... On injured reserve with knee injury (November 21, 2001-remainder of season).
CHAMPIONSHIP GAME EXPERIENCE: Played in AFC championship game (2003 season).
HONORS: Named NFL Rookie of the Year by THE SPORTING NEWS (1999). ... Named running back on THE SPORTING NEWS NFL All-Pro team (1999 and 2000). ... Played in Pro Bowl (1999 and 2000 seasons).
SINGLE GAME HIGHS (regular season): Attempts—38 (October 15, 2000, vs. Seattle); yards—219 (October 15, 2000, vs. Seattle); and rushing touchdowns—3 (November 16, 2003, vs. New York Jets).
STATISTICAL PLATEAUS: 100-yard rushing games: 1999 (10), 2000 (9), 2001 (5), 2002 (2), 2003 (6). Total: 32.
MISCELLANEOUS: Holds Indianapolis Colts all-time record for most yards rushing (6,172).

			RUSHING				RECEIVING				TOTALS			
Year Team	**G**	**GS**	**Att.**	**Yds.**	**Avg.**	**TD**	**No.**	**Yds.**	**Avg.**	**TD**	**TD**	**2pt.**	**Pts.**	**Fum.**
1999—Indianapolis NFL	16	16	*369	*1553	4.2	▲13	62	586	9.5	4	†17	0	102	8
2000—Indianapolis NFL	16	16	387	*1709	4.4	13	63	594	9.4	5	§18	1	110	5
2001—Indianapolis NFL	6	6	151	662	4.4	3	24	193	8.0	0	3	1	20	3
2002—Indianapolis NFL	14	14	277	989	3.6	2	61	354	5.8	1	3	1	20	4
2003—Indianapolis NFL	13	13	310	1259	4.1	11	51	292	5.7	0	11	0	66	5
Pro totals (5 years)	65	65	1494	6172	4.1	42	261	2019	7.7	10	52	3	318	25

JAMES, JENO — G — DOLPHINS

PERSONAL: Born January 12, 1977, in Montgomery, Ala. ... 6-3/310. ... Full name: Jenorris James.
HIGH SCHOOL: Sidney Lanier (Montgomery, Ala.).
COLLEGE: Auburn.
TRANSACTIONS/CAREER NOTES: Selected by Carolina Panthers in sixth round (182nd pick overall) of 2000 NFL draft. ... Signed by Panthers (June 19, 2000). ... Granted free agency (February 28, 2003). ... Re-signed by Panthers (June 3, 2003). ... Granted unconditional free agency (March 3, 2004). ... Signed by Miami Dolphins (March 5, 2004).
PLAYING EXPERIENCE: Carolina NFL, 2000-2003. ... Games/Games started: 2000 (16/4), 2001 (14/6), 2002 (9/2), 2003 (16/16). Total: 55/28.
CHAMPIONSHIP GAME EXPERIENCE: Played in NFC championship game (2003 season). ... Played in Super Bowl 38 (2003 season).

JAMES, TORY — CB — BENGALS

PERSONAL: Born May 18, 1973, in New Orleans, La. ... 6-2/186. ... Full name: Tory Steven James.
HIGH SCHOOL: Archbishop Shaw (Marrero, La.).
COLLEGE: Louisiana State.
TRANSACTIONS/CAREER NOTES: Selected by Denver Broncos in second round (44th pick overall) of 1996 NFL draft. ... Signed by Broncos (July 22, 1996). ... On injured reserve with knee injury (August 18, 1997-entire season). ... Granted unconditional free agency (February 11, 2000). ... Signed by Oakland Raiders (February 28, 2000). ... Released by Raiders (February 27, 2003). ... Signed by Cincinnati Bengals (March 10, 2003).
CHAMPIONSHIP GAME EXPERIENCE: Played in AFC championship game (1998, 2000 and 2002 seasons). ... Member of Super Bowl championship team (1998 season). ... Played in Super Bowl 37 (2002 season).

			TOTALS			INTERCEPTIONS			
Year Team	**G**	**GS**	**Tk.**	**Ast.**	**Sks.**	**No.**	**Yds.**	**Avg.**	**TD**
1996—Denver NFL	16	2	22	1	0.0	2	15	7.5	0
1997—Denver NFL					Did not play.				
1998—Denver NFL	16	0	10	1	0.0	0	0	0.0	0
1999—Denver NFL	16	4	32	1	0.0	5	59	11.8	0
2000—Oakland NFL	16	1	26	3	0.0	2	25	12.5	0
2001—Oakland NFL	16	2	33	3	0.0	5	72	14.4	0
2002—Oakland NFL	14	13	41	4	0.0	4	35	8.8	0
2003—Cincinnati NFL	16	16	57	6	1.0	4	56	14.0	0
Pro totals (7 years)	110	38	221	19	1.0	22	262	11.9	0

JAMESON, MICHAEL — CB — BROWNS

PERSONAL: Born July 14, 1979, in Killeen, Texas. ... 5-11/205.
HIGH SCHOOL: Ellison (Killeen, Texas).
COLLEGE: Texas A&M.
TRANSACTIONS/CAREER NOTES: Selected by Cleveland Browns in sixth round (165th pick overall) of 2001 NFL draft. ... Signed by Browns (May 24, 2001). ... On injured reserve with ankle injury (August 27, 2001-entire season). ... Released by Browns (September 1, 2002). ... Re-signed by Browns to practice squad (September 4, 2002). ... Activated (October 9, 2002).

			TOTALS			INTERCEPTIONS			
Year Team	**G**	**GS**	**Tk.**	**Ast.**	**Sks.**	**No.**	**Yds.**	**Avg.**	**TD**
2002—Cleveland NFL	11	1	8	2	1.0	1	0	0.0	0
2003—Cleveland NFL	15	0	2	1	0.0	0	0	0.0	0
Pro totals (2 years)	26	1	10	3	1.0	1	0	0.0	0

J

JAMMER, QUENTIN — CB — CHARGERS

PERSONAL: Born June 19, 1979, in Matagorda County, Texas. ... 6-0/204. ... Full name: Quentin T. Jammer.
HIGH SCHOOL: Angleton (Texas).
COLLEGE: Texas.
TRANSACTIONS/CAREER NOTES: Selected by San Diego Chargers in first round (fifth pick overall) of 2002 NFL draft. ... Signed by Chargers (September 11, 2002).
HONORS: Named cornerback on THE SPORTING NEWS college All-America first team (2001).

			TOTALS			INTERCEPTIONS			
Year Team	G	GS	Tk.	Ast.	Sks.	No.	Yds.	Avg.	TD
2002—San Diego NFL	14	4	56	8	0.0	0	0	0.0	0
2003—San Diego NFL	16	16	57	14	0.0	4	6	1.5	0
Pro totals (2 years)	30	20	113	22	0.0	4	6	1.5	0

JANIKOWSKI, SEBASTIAN — K — RAIDERS

PERSONAL: Born March 3, 1978, in Walbrzych, Poland. ... 6-2/255.
HIGH SCHOOL: Seabreeze (Daytona, Fla.).
COLLEGE: Florida State.
TRANSACTIONS/CAREER NOTES: Selected after junior season by Oakland Raiders in first round (17th pick overall) of 2000 NFL draft. ... Signed by Raiders (July 20, 2000).
CHAMPIONSHIP GAME EXPERIENCE: Played in AFC championship game (2000 and 2002 seasons). ... Played in Super Bowl 37 (2002 season).
HONORS: Named kicker on THE SPORTING NEWS college All-America first team (1998 and 1999). ... Lou Groza Award winner (1998 and 1999).
RECORDS: Shares NFL record for most field goals made, one quarter (4), vs. Chicago (October 5, 2003, second quarter).

		FIELD GOALS							TOTALS		
Year Team	G	1-29	30-39	40-49	50+	Tot.	Pct.	Lg.	XPM	XPA	Pts.
2000—Oakland NFL	14	7-7	6-7	8-14	1-4	22-32	68.8	▲54	46	46	112
2001—Oakland NFL	15	7-7	9-10	6-9	1-2	23-28	82.1	52	§42	▲42	111
2002—Oakland NFL	16	10-11	7-8	7-12	2-2	26-33	78.8	51	50	50	128
2003—Oakland NFL	16	6-6	6-6	9-10	1-3	22-25	88.0	55	28	29	94
Pro totals (4 years)	61	30-31	28-31	30-45	5-11	93-118	78.8	55	166	167	445

JANSEN, JON — T — REDSKINS

PERSONAL: Born January 28, 1976, in Clawson, Mich. ... 6-6/305. ... Full name: Jonathan Ward Jansen.
HIGH SCHOOL: Clawson (Mich.).
COLLEGE: Michigan.
TRANSACTIONS/CAREER NOTES: Selected by Washington Redskins in second round (37th pick overall) of 1999 NFL draft. ... Signed by Redskins (July 9, 1999).
PLAYING EXPERIENCE: Washington NFL, 1999-2003. ... Games/Games started: 1999 (16/16), 2000 (16/16), 2001 (16/16), 2002 (16/16), 2003 (16/16). Total: 80/80.

JASPER, ED — DT — FALCONS

PERSONAL: Born January 18, 1973, in Tyler, Texas. ... 6-2/293. ... Full name: Edward Vidal Jasper.
HIGH SCHOOL: Troup (Texas).
COLLEGE: Texas A&M.
TRANSACTIONS/CAREER NOTES: Selected by Philadelphia Eagles in sixth round (198th pick overall) of 1997 NFL draft. ... Signed by Eagles (July 16, 1997). ... Released by Eagles (August 30, 1998). ... Re-signed by Eagles (September 17, 1998). ... Released by Eagles (October 23, 1998). ... Re-signed by Eagles (December 9, 1998). ... Released by Eagles (February 12, 1999). ... Signed by Atlanta Falcons (March 5, 1999).

			TOTALS		
Year Team	G	GS	Tk.	Ast.	Sks.
1997—Philadelphia NFL	10	1	5	3	1.0
1998—Philadelphia NFL	7	0	11	2	0.0
1999—Atlanta NFL	13	0	23	5	0.0
2000—Atlanta NFL	15	15	30	12	3.5
2001—Atlanta NFL	16	1	20	5	3.5
2002—Atlanta NFL	16	16	29	6	2.0
2003—Atlanta NFL	14	14	35	6	3.0
Pro totals (7 years)	91	47	153	39	13.0

JEFFERSON, SHAWN — WR

PERSONAL: Born February 22, 1969, in Jacksonville, Fla. ... 5-11/185. ... Full name: Vanchi LaShawn Jefferson.
HIGH SCHOOL: Raines (Jacksonville).
COLLEGE: Central Florida.
TRANSACTIONS/CAREER NOTES: Selected by Houston Oilers in ninth round (240th pick overall) of 1991 NFL draft. ... Signed by Oilers (July 15, 1991). ... Traded by Oilers with first-round pick (DE Chris Mims) in 1992 draft to San Diego Chargers for DL Lee Williams (August 22, 1991). ... Granted free agency (March 1, 1993). ... Re-signed by Chargers (July 15, 1993). ... Granted free agency (February 17, 1994). ... Re-signed by Chargers (May 2, 1994). ... Released by Chargers (February 29, 1996). ... Signed by New England Patriots (March 14, 1996). ... Granted unconditional free agency (February 11, 2000). ... Signed by Atlanta Falcons (February 12, 2000). ... Waived by Falcons (February 21,

2003). ... Signed by Detroit Lions (May 25, 2003). ... On injured reserve with knee injury (November 11, 2003-remainder of season). ... Granted unconditional free agency (March 3, 2004).

CHAMPIONSHIP GAME EXPERIENCE: Played in AFC championship game (1994 and 1996 seasons). ... Played in Super Bowl 29 (1994 season) and Super Bowl 31 (1996 season).

SINGLE GAME HIGHS (regular season): Receptions—9 (November 10, 2002, vs. Pittsburgh); yards—148 (September 3, 2000, vs. San Francisco); and touchdown receptions—2 (October 31, 1999, vs. Arizona).

STATISTICAL PLATEAUS: 100-yard receiving games: 1995 (1), 1997 (1), 1998 (2), 1999 (1), 2000 (2), 2002 (1). Total: 8.

			RUSHING				RECEIVING				TOTALS			
Year Team	**G**	**GS**	**Att.**	**Yds.**	**Avg.**	**TD**	**No.**	**Yds.**	**Avg.**	**TD**	**TD**	**2pt.**	**Pts.**	**Fum.**
1991—San Diego NFL	16	3	1	27	27.0	0	12	125	10.4	1	1	0	6	0
1992—San Diego NFL	16	1	0	0	0.0	0	29	377	13.0	2	2	0	12	0
1993—San Diego NFL	16	4	5	53	10.6	0	30	391	13.0	2	2	0	12	0
1994—San Diego NFL	16	16	3	40	13.3	0	43	627	14.6	3	3	0	18	0
1995—San Diego NFL	16	15	2	1	0.5	0	48	621	12.9	2	2	0	12	0
1996—New England NFL	15	15	1	6	6.0	0	50	771	15.4	4	4	0	24	2
1997—New England NFL	16	14	0	0	0.0	0	54	841	15.6	2	2	0	12	2
1998—New England NFL	16	16	1	15	15.0	0	34	771	*22.7	2	2	0	12	0
1999—New England NFL	16	16	0	0	0.0	0	40	698	§17.5	6	6	0	36	0
2000—Atlanta NFL	16	14	1	1	1.0	0	60	822	13.7	2	2	0	12	1
2001—Atlanta NFL	16	6	0	0	0.0	0	37	539	14.6	2	2	1	14	0
2002—Atlanta NFL	13	7	0	0	0.0	0	27	394	14.6	1	1	0	6	0
2003—Detroit NFL	7	3	1	3	3.0	0	6	46	7.7	0	0	0	0	0
Pro totals (13 years)	195	130	15	146	9.7	0	470	7023	14.9	29	29	1	176	5

JENKINS, COREY LB DOLPHINS

PERSONAL: Born August 25, 1976, in Columbia, S.C. ... 6-0/222.

HIGH SCHOOL: Dreher (Columbia, S.C.).

JUNIOR COLLEGE: Garden City (Kan.) Community College.

COLLEGE: South Carolina.

TRANSACTIONS/CAREER NOTES: Selected by Miami Dolphins in sixth round (181st pick overall) of 2003 NFL draft. ... Signed by Dolphins (June 9, 2003).

MISCELLANEOUS: Selected by Boston Red Sox organization in first round (24th pick overall) of free-agent draft (June 1, 1995).

			TOTALS			INTERCEPTIONS			
Year Team	**G**	**GS**	**Tk.**	**Ast.**	**Sks.**	**No.**	**Yds.**	**Avg.**	**TD**
2003—Miami NFL	16	0	1	0	0.0	0	0	0.0	0

JENKINS, KERRY G BUCCANEERS

PERSONAL: Born September 6, 1973, in Tuscaloosa, Ala. ... 6-5/305.

HIGH SCHOOL: Holt (Ala.).

COLLEGE: Troy State.

TRANSACTIONS/CAREER NOTES: Signed as non-drafted free agent by Chicago Bears (April 25, 1997). ... Released by Bears (August 24, 1997). ... Re-signed by Bears to practice squad (August 27, 1997). ... Signed by New York Jets off Bears practice squad (December 3, 1997). ... Granted free agency (March 2, 2001). ... Re-signed by Jets (May 30, 2001). ... Granted unconditional free agency (March 1, 2002). ... Signed by Tampa Bay Buccaneers (March 6, 2002).

PLAYING EXPERIENCE: New York Jets NFL, 1997-2001; Tampa Bay NFL, 2002-2003. ... Games/Games started: 1997 (2/2), 1998 (16/0), 1999 (16/16), 2000 (16/16), 2001 (16/16), 2002 (15/15), 2003 (16/11). Total: 97/76.

CHAMPIONSHIP GAME EXPERIENCE: Played in AFC championship game (1998 season). ... Played in NFC championship game (2002 season). ... Member of Super Bowl championship team (2002 season).

JENKINS, KRIS DT PANTHERS

PERSONAL: Born August 3, 1979, in Ypsilanti, Mich. ... 6-4/315. ... Full name: Kristopher Rudy-Charles Jenkins.

HIGH SCHOOL: Belleville (Ypsilanti, Mich.).

COLLEGE: Maryland.

TRANSACTIONS/CAREER NOTES: Selected by Carolina Panthers in second round (44th pick overall) of 2001 NFL draft. ... Signed by Panthers (July 13, 2001).

CHAMPIONSHIP GAME EXPERIENCE: Played in NFC championship game (2003 season). ... Played in Super Bowl 38 (2003 season).

HONORS: Named defensive tackle on THE SPORTING NEWS NFL All-Pro team (2003). ... Played in Pro Bowl (2002 and 2003 seasons).

			TOTALS		
Year Team	**G**	**GS**	**Tk.**	**Ast.**	**Sks.**
2001—Carolina NFL	16	11	27	7	2.0
2002—Carolina NFL	16	16	36	8	7.0
2003—Carolina NFL	16	16	39	7	5.0
Pro totals (3 years)	48	43	102	22	14.0

JENKINS, RONNEY RB SAINTS

PERSONAL: Born May 25, 1977, in Los Angeles, Calif. ... 5-11/185. ... Full name: Ronney Gene Jenkins.

HIGH SCHOOL: Point Hueneme (Oxnard, Calif.).

COLLEGE: Northern Arizona.

TRANSACTIONS/CAREER NOTES: Signed as non-drafted free agent by San Diego Chargers (April 17, 2000). ... Granted free agency (February 28, 2003). ... Signed by Oakland Raiders (March 17, 2003). ... Released by Raiders (November 4, 2003). ... Signed by New Orleans Saints (January 27, 2004).
SINGLE GAME HIGHS (regular season): Attempts—3 (October 29, 2000, vs. Oakland); yards—6 (October 1, 2000, vs. St. Louis); and rushing touchdowns—0.

			KICKOFF RETURNS				TOTALS			
Year Team	**G**	**GS**	**No.**	**Yds.**	**Avg.**	**TD**	**TD**	**2pt.**	**Pts.**	**Fum.**
2000—San Diego NFL	16	0	§67	1531	22.9	▲1	1	0	6	3
2001—San Diego NFL	16	0	§58	*1541	*26.6	†2	2	0	12	1
2002—San Diego NFL	13	0	40	925	23.1	0	0	0	0	0
2003—Oakland NFL	7	0	25	553	22.1	0	0	0	0	0
Pro totals (4 years)	52	0	190	4550	23.9	3	3	0	18	4

JENNINGS, BRIAN — TE/LS — 49ERS

PERSONAL: Born October 14, 1976, in Mesa, Ariz. ... 6-5/245. ... Full name: Brian Lewis Jennings.
HIGH SCHOOL: Red Mountain (Mesa, Ariz.).
COLLEGE: Arizona State.
TRANSACTIONS/CAREER NOTES: Selected by San Francisco 49ers in seventh round (230th pick overall) of 2000 NFL draft. ... Signed by 49ers (July 10, 2000). ... Granted free agency (February 28, 2003). ... Re-signed by 49ers (April 24, 2003). ... Granted unconditional free agency (March 3, 2004). ... Re-signed by 49ers (March 4, 2004).
PLAYING EXPERIENCE: San Francisco NFL, 2000-2003. ... Games/Games started: 2000 (16/0), 2001 (16/0), 2002 (16/0), 2003 (16/0). Total: 64/0.

JENNINGS, JONAS — T — BILLS

PERSONAL: Born November 21, 1977, in College Park, Ga. ... 6-3/325.
HIGH SCHOOL: Tri-Cities (East Point, Ga.).
COLLEGE: Georgia.
TRANSACTIONS/CAREER NOTES: Selected by Buffalo Bills in third round (95th pick overall) of 2001 NFL draft. ... Signed by Bills (June 22, 2001). ... On injured reserve with toe injury (December 3, 2003-remainder of season).
PLAYING EXPERIENCE: Buffalo NFL, 2001-2003. ... Games/Games started: 2001 (12/12), 2002 (15/15), 2003 (11/11). Total: 38/38.

JERMAN, GREG — T — DOLPHINS

PERSONAL: Born January 24, 1979, in Hyannis, Mass. ... 6-5/300. ... Full name: Gregory Stephen Jerman.
HIGH SCHOOL: Franklin (El Paso, Texas).
COLLEGE: Baylor.
TRANSACTIONS/CAREER NOTES: Signed as non-drafted free agent by Miami Dolphins (April 25, 2002). ... Released by Dolphins (August 31, 2003). ... Re-signed by Dolphins to practice squad (September 1, 2003). ... Activated (September 6, 2003).
PLAYING EXPERIENCE: Miami NFL, 2002-2003. ... Games/Games started: 2002 (2/0), 2003 (8/1). Total: 10/1.

JERVEY, TRAVIS — RB

PERSONAL: Born May 5, 1972, in Columbia, S.C. ... 6-0/222. ... Full name: Travis Richard Jervey.
HIGH SCHOOL: Wando (Mount Pleasant, S.C.).
COLLEGE: Citadel.
TRANSACTIONS/CAREER NOTES: Selected by Green Bay Packers in fifth round (170th pick overall) of 1995 NFL draft. ... Signed by Packers (May 23, 1995). ... Granted free agency (February 13, 1998). ... Re-signed by Packers (June 16, 1998). ... On injured reserve with knee and ankle injuries (November 11, 1998-remainder of season). ... Granted unconditional free agency (February 12, 1999). ... Signed by San Francisco 49ers (March 22, 1999). ... On physically unable to perform list with ankle injury (July 27-August 26, 1999). ... On suspended list for violating league substance abuse policy (October 21-November 26, 1999). ... On injured reserve with broken collarbone (October 30, 2000-remainder of season). ... Released by 49ers (March 19, 2001). ... Signed by Atlanta Falcons (May 1, 2001). ... Granted unconditional free agency (March 1, 2002). ... Re-signed by Falcons (April 9, 2002). ... On injured reserve with knee injury (October 22, 2002-remainder of season). ... Granted unconditional free agency (February 28, 2003). ... Re-signed by Falcons (March 7, 2003). ... On injured reserve with neck injury (December 23, 2003-remainder of season). ... Granted unconditional free agency (March 3, 2004).
CHAMPIONSHIP GAME EXPERIENCE: Played in NFC championship game (1995-97 seasons). ... Member of Super Bowl championship team (1996 season). ... Played in Super Bowl 32 (1997 season).
HONORS: Played in Pro Bowl (1997 season).
SINGLE GAME HIGHS (regular season): Attempts—29 (October 25, 1998, vs. Baltimore); yards—95 (November 1, 1998, vs. San Francisco); and rushing touchdowns—1 (January 3, 2000, vs. Atlanta).

			RUSHING				RECEIVING				KICKOFF RETURNS				TOTALS			
Year Team	**G**	**GS**	**Att.**	**Yds.**	**Avg.**	**TD**	**No.**	**Yds.**	**Avg.**	**TD**	**No.**	**Yds.**	**Avg.**	**TD**	**TD**	**2pt.**	**Pts.**	**Fum.**
1995—Green Bay NFL	16	0	0	0	0.0	0	0	0	0.0	0	8	165	20.6	0	0	0	0	0
1996—Green Bay NFL	16	0	26	106	4.1	0	0	0	0.0	0	1	17	17.0	0	0	0	0	4
1997—Green Bay NFL	16	0	0	0	0.0	0	0	0	0.0	0	0	0	0.0	0	0	0	0	0
1998—Green Bay NFL	8	5	83	325	3.9	1	9	33	3.7	0	0	0	0.0	0	1	0	6	0
1999—San Francisco NFL	8	0	6	49	8.2	1	1	2	2.0	0	8	191	23.9	0	1	0	6	0
2000—San Francisco NFL	8	0	1	0	0.0	0	0	0	0.0	0	8	209	26.1	0	0	0	0	0
2001—Atlanta NFL	16	0	3	6	2.0	0	0	0	0.0	0	0	0	0.0	0	0	0	0	0
2002—Atlanta NFL	6	0	10	17	1.7	0	0	0	0.0	0	4	143	35.7	0	0	0	0	1
2003—Atlanta NFL	15	0	0	0	0.0	0	0	0	0.0	0	7	118	16.9	0	0	0	0	1
Pro totals (9 years)	109	5	129	503	3.9	2	10	35	3.5	0	36	843	23.4	0	2	0	12	6

ETT, JOHN P

PERSONAL: Born November 11, 1968, in Richmond, Va. ... 6-0/197.
HIGH SCHOOL: Northumberland (Heathsville, Va.).
COLLEGE: East Carolina.
TRANSACTIONS/CAREER NOTES: Signed as non-drafted free agent by Minnesota Vikings (June 22, 1992). ... Released by Vikings (August 25, 1992). ... Signed by Dallas Cowboys (March 10, 1993). ... Granted unconditional free agency (February 16, 1996). ... Re-signed by Cowboys (April 15, 1996). ... Granted unconditional free agency (February 14, 1997). ... Signed by Detroit Lions (March 7, 1997). ... Granted unconditional free agency (February 11, 2000). ... Re-signed by Lions (February 21, 2000). ... On injured reserve with calf injury (October 29, 2003-remainder of season). ... Granted unconditional free agency (March 3, 2004).
CHAMPIONSHIP GAME EXPERIENCE: Played in NFC championship game (1993-1995 seasons). ... Member of Super Bowl championship team (1993 and 1995 seasons).

		PUNTING					
Year Team	**G**	**No.**	**Yds.**	**Avg.**	**Net avg.**	**In. 20**	**Blk.**
1993—Dallas NFL	16	56	2342	41.8	37.7	22	0
1994—Dallas NFL	16	70	2935	41.9	35.3	26	0
1995—Dallas NFL	16	53	2166	40.9	34.5	17	0
1996—Dallas NFL	16	74	3150	42.6	36.7	22	0
1997—Detroit NFL	16	84	3576	42.6	35.6	24	†2
1998—Detroit NFL	14	66	2892	43.8	36.0	17	0
1999—Detroit NFL	16	86	3637	42.3	34.8	27	0
2000—Detroit NFL	16	‡93	‡4044	43.5	34.8	‡33	†2
2001—Detroit NFL	13	58	2512	43.3	35.5	16	0
2002—Detroit NFL	16	91	3838	42.2	38.0	29	0
2003—Detroit NFL	4	25	995	39.8	35.6	8	0
Pro totals (11 years)	159	756	32087	42.4	35.9	241	4

IMOH, ADE CB REDSKINS

PERSONAL: Born April 18, 1980, in Los Angeles, Calif. ... 6-1/190.
HIGH SCHOOL: El Camino Real (Canoga Park, Calif.).
COLLEGE: Utah State.
TRANSACTIONS/CAREER NOTES: Signed as non-drafted free agent by Washington Redskins (May 2, 2003).

			TOTALS			INTERCEPTIONS			
Year Team	**G**	**GS**	**Tk.**	**Ast.**	**Sks.**	**No.**	**Yds.**	**Avg.**	**TD**
2003—Washington NFL	16	0	5	1	0.0	0	0	0.0	0

OHNSON, AL C COWBOYS

PERSONAL: Born January 27, 1979, in Brussels, Wis. ... 6-3/305. ... Cousin of Ben Johnson, offensive tackle, Detroit Lions.
HIGH SCHOOL: Southern Door (Brussels, Wis.).
COLLEGE: Wisconsin.
TRANSACTIONS/CAREER NOTES: Selected by Dallas Cowboys in second round (38th pick overall) of 2003 NFL draft. ... Signed by Cowboys (July 25, 2003). ... On injured reserve with knee injury (August 26, 2003-entire season).
PLAYING EXPERIENCE: Dallas NFL, 2003. ... Games/Games started: Total: 0/0.

JOHNSON, ALBERT WR TEXANS

PERSONAL: Born November 11, 1977, in Houston, Texas. ... 5-9/190. ... Full name: Albert Johnson III. ... Son of Albert Johnson Jr., defensive back with Houston Oilers (1972-78).
HIGH SCHOOL: Willowridge (Houston).
COLLEGE: Southern Methodist.
TRANSACTIONS/CAREER NOTES: Signed as non-drafted free agent by Miami Dolphins (January 11, 2001). ... On injured reserve with knee injury (August 9, 2001-entire season). ... On injured reserve with knee injury (October 1, 2002-remainder of season). ... Granted free agency (February 28, 2003). ... Signed by New York Jets (April 14, 2003). ... Waived by Jets (September 9, 2003). ... Signed by Houston Texans to practice squad (December 16, 2003). ... Assigned by Texans to Cologne Centurions in 2004 NFL Europe enhancement allocation program (February 9, 2004).

			RECEIVING				PUNT RETURNS				KICKOFF RETURNS				TOTALS			
Year Team	**G**	**GS**	**No.**	**Yds.**	**Avg.**	**TD**	**No.**	**Yds.**	**Avg.**	**TD**	**No.**	**Yds.**	**Avg.**	**TD**	**TD**	**2pt.**	**Pts.**	**Fum.**
2000—Winnipeg CFL	...	...	50	778	15.6	3	79	665	8.4	0	61	1505	24.7	1	0	0	0	0
2002—Miami NFL	4	0	0	0	0.0	0	8	69	8.6	0	12	330	27.5	0	0	0	0	1
2003—New York Jets NFL	1	0	0	0	0.0	0	0	0	0.0	0	2	50	25.0	0	0	0	0	0
CFL totals (1 year)	...	...	50	778	15.6	3	79	665	8.4	0	61	1505	24.7	1	0	0	0	0
NFL totals (2 years)	5	0	0	0	0.0	0	8	69	8.6	0	14	380	27.1	0	0	0	0	1
Pro totals (3 years)	...	...	50	778	15.6	3	87	734	8.4	0	75	1885	25.1	1	0	0	0	1

OHNSON, ANDRE WR TEXANS

PERSONAL: Born July 11, 1981, in Miami, Fla. ... 6-2/221. ... Full name: Andre Lamont Johnson.
HIGH SCHOOL: Senior (Miami).
COLLEGE: Miami (Fla.).
TRANSACTIONS/CAREER NOTES: Selected after junior season by Houston Texans in first round (third pick overall) of 2003 NFL draft. ... Signed by Texans (July 22, 2003).

SINGLE GAME HIGHS (regular season): Receptions—8 (September 28, 2003, vs. Jacksonville); yards—122 (November 16, 2003, vs. Buffalo); and touchdown receptions—2 (September 21, 2003, vs. Kansas City).
STATISTICAL PLATEAUS: 100-yard receiving games: 2003 (3). Total: 3.

			RUSHING				RECEIVING				KICKOFF RETURNS				TOTALS			
Year Team	G	GS	Att.	Yds.	Avg.	TD	No.	Yds.	Avg.	TD	No.	Yds.	Avg.	TD	TD	2pt.	Pts.	Fum.
2003—Houston NFL	16	16	5	-10	-2.0	0	66	976	14.8	4	0	0	0.0	0	4	0	24	0

JOHNSON, BETHEL WR PATRIOTS

PERSONAL: Born February 11, 1979, in Corsicana, Texas. ... 5-11/200.
HIGH SCHOOL: Corsicana (Texas).
COLLEGE: Texas A&M.
TRANSACTIONS/CAREER NOTES: Selected by New England Patriots in second round (45th pick overall) of 2003 NFL draft. ... Signed by Patriots (July 21, 2003).
CHAMPIONSHIP GAME EXPERIENCE: Played in AFC championship game (2003 season). ... Member of Super Bowl championship team (2003 season).
SINGLE GAME HIGHS (regular season): Receptions—5 (November 23, 2003, vs. Houston); yards—65 (November 23, 2003, vs. Houston); and touchdown receptions—1 (December 27, 2003, vs. Buffalo).

			RUSHING				RECEIVING				PUNT RETURNS				KICKOFF RETURNS				TOTALS		
Year Team	G	GS	Att.	Yds.	Avg.	TD	No.	Yds.	Avg.	TD	No.	Yds.	Avg.	TD	No.	Yds.	Avg.	TD	TD	2pt.	Pts.
2003—N.E. NFL	15	5	1	-12	-12.0	0	16	209	13.1	2	1	2	2.0	0	30	847	§28.2	1	3	0	18

JOHNSON, BRAD QB BUCCANEERS

PERSONAL: Born September 13, 1968, in Marietta, Ga. ... 6-5/226. ... Full name: James Bradley Johnson.
HIGH SCHOOL: Charles D. Owen (Black Mountain, N.C.).
COLLEGE: Florida State.
TRANSACTIONS/CAREER NOTES: Selected by Minnesota Vikings in ninth round (227th pick overall) of 1992 NFL draft. ... Signed by Vikings (July 17, 1992). ... Active for one game (1992); did not play. ... Inactive for all 16 games (1993). ... Granted free agency (February 17, 1995). ... Assigned by Vikings to London Monarchs in 1995 World League enhancement allocation program (February 20, 1995). ... Re-signed by Vikings (March 27, 1995). ... On injured reserve with neck injury (December 5, 1997-remainder of season). ... Traded by Vikings to Washington Redskins for first- (QB Daunte Culpepper) and third-round (traded to Pittsburgh) picks in 1999 draft and second-round pick (DE Michael Boireau) in 2000 draft (February 15, 1999). ... Granted unconditional free agency (March 2, 2001). ... Signed by Tampa Bay Buccaneers (March 6, 2001).
CHAMPIONSHIP GAME EXPERIENCE: Member of Vikings for NFC championship game (1998 season); did not play. ... Played in NFC championship game (2002 season). ... Member of Super Bowl championship team (2002 season).
HONORS: Played in Pro Bowl (1999 and 2002 seasons).
SINGLE GAME HIGHS (regular season): Attempts—61 (September 14, 2003, vs. Carolina); completions—40 (November 18, 2001, vs. Chicago); yards—471 (December 26, 1999, vs. San Francisco); and touchdown passes—5 (November 3, 2002, vs. Minnesota).
STATISTICAL PLATEAUS: 300-yard passing games: 1997 (2), 1998 (1), 1999 (4), 2001 (2), 2002 (1), 2003 (4). Total: 14.
MISCELLANEOUS: Regular-season record as starting NFL quarterback: 58-37 (.611). ... Postseason record as starting NFL quarterback: 4-3 (.571).

			PASSING									RUSHING				TOTALS		
Year Team	G	GS	Att.	Cmp.	Pct.	Yds.	TD	Int.	Avg.	Skd.	Rat.	Att.	Yds.	Avg.	TD	TD	2pt.	Pts.
1992—Minnesota NFL						Did not play.												
1993—Minnesota NFL						Did not play.												
1994—Minnesota NFL	4	0	37	22	59.5	150	0	0	4.05	1	68.5	2	-2	-1.0	0	0	0	0
1995—Minnesota NFL	5	0	36	25	69.4	272	0	2	7.56	2	68.3	9	-9	-1.0	0	0	0	0
1996—Minnesota NFL	12	8	311	195	62.7	2258	17	10	7.26	15	89.4	34	90	2.6	1	1	0	6
1997—Minnesota NFL	13	13	452	275	60.8	3036	20	12	6.72	26	84.5	35	139	4.0	0	1	2	10
1998—Minnesota NFL	4	2	101	65	64.4	747	7	5	7.40	4	89.0	12	15	1.3	0	0	0	0
1999—Washington NFL	16	16	519	316	60.9	4005	24	13	7.72	29	90.0	26	31	1.2	2	2	0	12
2000—Washington NFL	12	11	365	228	62.5	2505	11	15	6.86	20	75.7	22	58	2.6	1	1	0	6
2001—Tampa Bay NFL	16	16	559	340	60.8	3406	13	11	6.09	44	77.7	39	120	3.1	3	3	0	18
2002—Tampa Bay NFL	13	13	451	281	62.3	3049	22	6	6.76	21	‡92.9	13	30	2.3	0	0	0	0
2003—Tampa Bay NFL	16	16	*570	‡354	62.1	3811	26	21	6.69	20	81.5	25	33	1.3	0	0	0	0
Pro totals (10 years)	111	95	3401	2101	61.8	23239	140	95	6.83	182	84.1	217	505	2.3	7	8	2	52

JOHNSON, BRYAN FB BEARS

PERSONAL: Born January 18, 1978, in Los Angeles, Calif. ... 6-1/245.
HIGH SCHOOL: Highland (Pocatello, Idaho).
COLLEGE: Boise State.
TRANSACTIONS/CAREER NOTES: Signed as non-drafted free agent by Washington Redskins (April 18, 2000). ... Released by Redskins (August 27, 2000). ... Re-signed by Redskins to practice squad (August 28, 2000). ... Activated (December 18, 2000). ... Re-signed by Redskins (April 29, 2003). ... Traded by Redskins to Chicago Bears for sixth-round pick (OT Jim Molinaro) in 2004 draft (March 29, 2004).
SINGLE GAME HIGHS (regular season): Attempts—1 (September 28, 2003, vs. New England); yards—4 (September 28, 2003, vs. New England); and rushing touchdowns—0.

			RUSHING				RECEIVING				TOTALS			
Year Team	G	GS	Att.	Yds.	Avg.	TD	No.	Yds.	Avg.	TD	TD	2pt.	Pts.	Fum.
2000—Washington NFL	1	0	0	0	0.0	0	0	0	0.0	0	0	0	0	0
2001—Washington NFL	16	1	0	0	0.0	0	9	129	14.3	0	0	0	0	0
2002—Washington NFL	16	12	1	0	0.0	0	15	114	7.6	0	0	0	0	0
2003—Washington NFL	16	11	2	5	2.5	0	9	71	7.9	0	0	0	0	0
Pro totals (4 years)	49	24	3	5	1.7	0	33	314	9.5	0	0	0	0	0

JOHNSON, BRYANT — WR — CARDINALS

PERSONAL: Born March 7, 1981, in Baltimore, Md. ... 6-2/214. ... Full name: Bryant Andrew Johnson.
HIGH SCHOOL: Baltimore City College (Baltimore).
COLLEGE: Penn State.
TRANSACTIONS/CAREER NOTES: Selected by Arizona Cardinals in first round (17th pick overall) of 2003 NFL draft. ... Signed by Cardinals (July 28, 2003).
SINGLE GAME HIGHS (regular season): Receptions—7 (September 14, 2003, vs. Seattle); yards—86 (September 21, 2003, vs. Green Bay); and touchdown receptions—1 (November 9, 2003, vs. Pittsburgh).

			RECEIVING				PUNT RETURNS				TOTALS			
Year Team	G	GS	No.	Yds.	Avg.	TD	No.	Yds.	Avg.	TD	TD	2pt.	Pts.	Fum.
2003—Arizona NFL	15	8	35	438	12.5	1	1	3	3.0	0	1	0	6	1

JOHNSON, CHAD — WR — BENGALS

PERSONAL: Born January 9, 1978, in Miami, Fla. ... 6-1/192.
HIGH SCHOOL: Miami Beach (Fla.).
JUNIOR COLLEGE: Santa Monica College (Calif.).
COLLEGE: Oregon State.
TRANSACTIONS/CAREER NOTES: Selected by Cincinnati Bengals in second round (36th pick overall) of 2001 NFL draft. ... Signed by Bengals (July 18, 2001).
HONORS: Played in Pro Bowl (2003 season).
SINGLE GAME HIGHS (regular season): Receptions—10 (November 23, 2003, vs. San Diego); yards—152 (November 24, 2002, vs. Pittsburgh); and touchdown receptions—3 (November 23, 2003, vs. San Diego).
STATISTICAL PLATEAUS: 100-yard receiving games: 2002 (5), 2003 (5). Total: 10.

			RECEIVING				TOTALS			
Year Team	G	GS	No.	Yds.	Avg.	TD	TD	2pt.	Pts.	Fum.
2001—Cincinnati NFL	12	3	28	329	11.8	1	1	0	6	0
2002—Cincinnati NFL	16	14	69	1166	16.9	5	5	0	30	0
2003—Cincinnati NFL	16	14	90	§1355	15.1	10	10	0	60	0
Pro totals (3 years)	44	31	187	2850	15.2	16	16	0	96	0

JOHNSON, DARRIUS — CB/S

PERSONAL: Born May 18, 1973, in Terrell, Texas. ... 5-9/185.
HIGH SCHOOL: Terrell (Texas).
COLLEGE: Oklahoma.
TRANSACTIONS/CAREER NOTES: Selected by Denver Broncos in fourth round (122nd pick overall) of 1996 NFL draft. ... Signed by Broncos (July 17, 1996). ... Released by Broncos (March 8, 2000). ... On suspended list for violating league substance abuse policy (March 9, 2000). ... Signed by Kansas City Chiefs (April 28, 2003). ... Released by Chiefs (August 26, 2003). ... Re-signed by Chiefs (October 1, 2003). ... On injured reserve with knee injury (October 18, 2003-remainder of season). ... Granted unconditional free agency (March 3, 2004).
CHAMPIONSHIP GAME EXPERIENCE: Played in AFC championship game (1997 and 1998 seasons). ... Member of Super Bowl championship team (1997 and 1998 seasons).

			TOTALS			INTERCEPTIONS			
Year Team	G	GS	Tk.	Ast.	Sks.	No.	Yds.	Avg.	TD
1996—Denver NFL	13	0	11	0	0.0	0	0	0.0	0
1997—Denver NFL	16	0	10	3	0.0	0	0	0.0	0
1998—Denver NFL	16	2	26	4	1.0	2	79	39.5	0
1999—Denver NFL	16	2	25	5	0.0	0	0	0.0	0
2003—Kansas City NFL	2	0	0	0	0.0	0	0	0.0	0
Pro totals (5 years)	63	4	72	12	1.0	2	79	39.5	0

JOHNSON, DENNIS — DE — CARDINALS

PERSONAL: Born December 4, 1979, in Danville, Ky. ... 6-5/269. ... Full name: Dennis Alan Johnson.
HIGH SCHOOL: Harrodburg (Ky.).
COLLEGE: Kentucky.
TRANSACTIONS/CAREER NOTES: Selected after junior season by Arizona Cardinals in third round (98th pick overall) of 2002 NFL draft. ... Signed by Cardinals (June 12, 2002).

			TOTALS		
Year Team	G	GS	Tk.	Ast.	Sks.
2002—Arizona NFL	13	0	10	6	0.0
2003—Arizona NFL	15	10	27	16	3.0
Pro totals (2 years)	28	10	37	22	3.0

JOHNSON, DIRK — P — EAGLES

PERSONAL: Born June 1, 1975, in Hoxie, Kan. ... 6-0/205. ... Full name: Dirk R. Johnson.
HIGH SCHOOL: Montrose (Colo.).
COLLEGE: Northern Colorado.
TRANSACTIONS/CAREER NOTES: Signed as non-drafted free agent by San Diego Chargers (May 4, 2001). ... Released by Chargers (August 27, 2001). ... Signed by New Orleans Saints (February 18, 2002). ... Assigned by Saints to Rhein Fire in 2002 NFL Europe enhancement allo-

cation program (February 18, 2002). ... Released by Saints (September 1, 2002). ... Re-signed by Saints (September 6, 2002). ... Released by Saints (September 9, 2002). ... Signed by Philadelphia Eagles (February 10, 2003).
CHAMPIONSHIP GAME EXPERIENCE: Played in NFC championship game (2003 season).

		PUNTING					
Year Team	G	No.	Yds.	Avg.	Net avg.	In. 20	Blk.
2002—New Orleans NFL	1	8	307	38.4	34.8	1	0
2003—Philadelphia NFL	16	79	3207	40.6	34.6	27	0
Pro totals (2 years)	17	87	3514	40.4	34.6	28	0

JOHNSON, DOUG QB JAGUARS

PERSONAL: Born October 27, 1977, in Gainesville, Fla. ... 6-2/225.
HIGH SCHOOL: Buchholz (Gainesville, Fla.).
COLLEGE: Florida.
TRANSACTIONS/CAREER NOTES: Signed as non-drafted free agent by Atlanta Falcons (April 17, 2000). ... Granted unconditional free agency (March 3, 2004). ... Signed by Jacksonville Jaguars (April 28, 2004).
SINGLE GAME HIGHS (regular season): Attempts—40 (October 5, 2003, vs. Minnesota); completions—28 (October 5, 2003, vs. Minnesota); yards—352 (October 5, 2003, vs.Minnesota); and touchdown passes—2 (November 23, 2003, vs. Tennessee).
STATISTICAL PLATEAUS: 300-yard passing games: 2003 (1). Total: 1.
MISCELLANEOUS: Regular-season record as starting NFL quarterback: 2-9 (.182).

			PASSING									RUSHING				TOTALS		
Year Team	G	GS	Att.	Cmp.	Pct.	Yds.	TD	Int.	Avg.	Skd.	Rat.	Att.	Yds.	Avg.	TD	TD	2pt.	Pts.
2000—Atlanta NFL	5	2	67	36	53.7	406	2	3	6.06	13	63.4	3	11	3.7	0	0	0	0
2001—Atlanta NFL	3	0	5	3	60.0	23	1	0	4.60	2	110.8	5	12	2.4	0	0	0	0
2002—Atlanta NFL	6	1	57	37	64.9	448	2	3	7.86	3	78.7	8	16	2.0	1	1	0	6
2003—Atlanta NFL	10	8	243	136	56.0	1655	8	12	6.81	19	67.5	14	21	1.5	1	1	0	6
Pro totals (4 years)	24	11	372	212	57.0	2532	13	18	6.81	37	69.4	30	60	2.0	2	2	0	12

JOHNSON, EDDIE P VIKINGS

PERSONAL: Born March 2, 1981, in Newport Beach, Calif. ... 6-3/236.
HIGH SCHOOL: Newport Harbor (Newport Beach, Calif.).
JUNIOR COLLEGE: Orange Coast College (Calif.).
COLLEGE: Idaho State.
TRANSACTIONS/CAREER NOTES: Selected by Minnesota Vikings in sixth round (180th pick overall) of 2003 NFL draft. ... Signed by Vikings (July 24, 2003).

		PUNTING					
Year Team	G	No.	Yds.	Avg.	Net avg.	In. 20	Blk.
2003—Minnesota NFL	14	56	2191	39.1	32.6	12	1

JOHNSON, ELLIS DT FALCONS

PERSONAL: Born October 30, 1973, in Wildwood, Fla. ... 6-2/288. ... Full name: Ellis Bernard Johnson.
HIGH SCHOOL: Wildwood (Fla.).
COLLEGE: Florida.
TRANSACTIONS/CAREER NOTES: Selected by Indianapolis Colts in first round (15th pick overall) of 1995 NFL draft. ... Signed by Colts (June 7, 1995). ... On physically unable to perform list with knee injury (July 27-August 20, 2001). ... Released by Colts (August 28, 2002). ... Signed by Atlanta Falcons (September 1, 2002).
CHAMPIONSHIP GAME EXPERIENCE: Played in AFC championship game (1995 season).

			TOTALS			INTERCEPTIONS			
Year Team	G	GS	Tk.	Ast.	Sks.	No.	Yds.	Avg.	TD
1995—Indianapolis NFL	16	2	15	3	4.5	0	0	0.0	0
1996—Indianapolis NFL	12	6	14	8	0.0	0	0	0.0	0
1997—Indianapolis NFL	15	15	38	18	4.5	1	18	18.0	0
1998—Indianapolis NFL	16	16	38	17	8.0	0	0	0.0	0
1999—Indianapolis NFL	16	16	34	12	7.5	0	0	0.0	0
2000—Indianapolis NFL	13	13	29	11	5.0	1	-1	-1.0	0
2001—Indianapolis NFL	16	16	20	14	3.5	0	0	0.0	0
2002—Atlanta NFL	16	2	24	3	7.0	0	0	0.0	0
2003—Atlanta NFL	16	3	34	8	8.0	0	0	0.0	0
Pro totals (9 years)	136	89	246	94	48.0	2	17	8.5	0

JOHNSON, ERIC S/LB FALCONS

PERSONAL: Born April 30, 1976, in Carson, Calif. ... 6-0/220.
HIGH SCHOOL: Alhambra (Arizona).
COLLEGE: Nebraska.
TRANSACTIONS/CAREER NOTES: Signed as non-drafted free agent by Oakland Raiders (March 23, 2000). ... On injured reserve with broken leg (November 7, 2001-remainder of season). ... Granted unconditional free agency (March 3, 2004). ... Signed by Atlanta Falcons (March 9, 2004).
CHAMPIONSHIP GAME EXPERIENCE: Played in AFC championship game (2002 season). ... Played in Super Bowl 37 (2002 season).

Year Team	G	GS	TOTALS Tk.	Ast.	Sks.	INTERCEPTIONS No.	Yds.	Avg.	TD
2000—Oakland NFL	16	0	3	0	0.0	0	0	0.0	0
2001—Oakland NFL	7	0	0	0	0.0	0	0	0.0	0
2002—Oakland NFL	16	0	0	0	0.0	0	0	0.0	0
2003—Oakland NFL	16	2	7	2	0.0	1	3	3.0	0
Pro totals (4 years)	55	2	10	2	0.0	1	3	3.0	0

J

JOHNSON, ERIC TE 49ERS

PERSONAL: Born September 15, 1979, in Needham, Mass. ... 6-3/256.
HIGH SCHOOL: Needham (Mass.).
COLLEGE: Yale.
TRANSACTIONS/CAREER NOTES: Selected by San Francisco 49ers in seventh round (224th pick overall) of 2001 NFL draft. ... Signed by 49ers (July 24, 2001). ... Inactive for seven games (2003). ... On injured reserve with collarbone injury (October 25, 2003-remainder of season).
SINGLE GAME HIGHS (regular season): Receptions—8 (December 15, 2002, vs. Green Bay); yards—69 (September 15, 2002, vs. Denver); and touchdown receptions—1 (December 16, 2001, vs. Miami).

Year Team	G	GS	RECEIVING No.	Yds.	Avg.	TD	TOTALS TD	2pt.	Pts.	Fum.
2001—San Francisco NFL	16	14	40	362	9.1	3	3	1	20	1
2002—San Francisco NFL	12	10	36	321	8.9	0	0	0	0	0
2003—San Francisco NFL					Did not play.					
Pro totals (2 years)	28	24	76	683	9.0	3	3	1	20	1

JOHNSON, JARRET DE RAVENS

PERSONAL: Born August 14, 1981, in Homestead, Fla. ... 6-3/285.
HIGH SCHOOL: Chiefland (Fla.).
COLLEGE: Alabama.
TRANSACTIONS/CAREER NOTES: Selected by Baltimore Ravens in fourth round (109th pick overall) of 2003 NFL draft.

Year Team	G	GS	TOTALS Tk.	Ast.	Sks.
2003—Baltimore NFL	15	1	8	3	0.0

JOHNSON, JEREMI FB BENGALS

PERSONAL: Born September 4, 1980, in Louisville, Ky. ... 5-11/265.
HIGH SCHOOL: Ballard (Louisville, Ky.).
COLLEGE: Western Kentucky.
TRANSACTIONS/CAREER NOTES: Selected by Cincinnati Bengals in fourth round (118th pick overall) of 2003 NFL draft. ... Signed by Bengals (July 27, 2003).
SINGLE GAME HIGHS (regular season): Attempts—5 (November 9, 2003, vs. Houston); yards—17 (November 23, 2003, vs. San Diego); and rushing touchdowns—1 (November 9, 2003, vs. Houston).

Year Team	G	GS	RUSHING Att.	Yds.	Avg.	TD	RECEIVING No.	Yds.	Avg.	TD	KICKOFF RETURNS No.	Yds.	Avg.	TD	TOTALS TD	2pt.	Pts.	Fum.
2003—Cincinnati NFL	16	13	15	41	2.7	1	15	82	5.5	1	1	16	16.0	0	2	0	12	0

JOHNSON, JOE DE PACKERS

PERSONAL: Born July 11, 1972, in Cleveland, Ohio. ... 6-4/275. ... Full name: Joe T. Johnson.
HIGH SCHOOL: Jennings (Mo.).
COLLEGE: Louisville.
TRANSACTIONS/CAREER NOTES: Selected after junior season by New Orleans Saints in first round (13th pick overall) of 1994 NFL draft. ... Signed by Saints (June 7, 1994). ... Designated by Saints as franchise player (February 13, 1998). ... Re-signed by Saints (September 2, 1998). ... On injured reserve with knee injury (August 31, 1999-entire season). ... Granted unconditional free agency (March 1, 2002). ... Signed by Green Bay Packers (March 21, 2002). ... On injured reserve with arm injury (October 9, 2002-remainder of season). ... On injured reserve with quadricep injury (October 15, 2003-remainder of season).
HONORS: Played in Pro Bowl (1998 and 2000 seasons).

Year Team	G	GS	TOTALS Tk.	Ast.	Sks.
1994—New Orleans NFL	15	14	36	10	1.0
1995—New Orleans NFL	14	14	36	14	5.5
1996—New Orleans NFL	13	13	50	10	7.5
1997—New Orleans NFL	16	16	39	7	8.5
1998—New Orleans NFL	16	16	54	16	7.0
1999—New Orleans NFL			Did not play.		
2000—New Orleans NFL	16	15	38	10	12.0
2001—New Orleans NFL	16	16	53	11	9.0
2002—Green Bay NFL	5	5	6	4	2.0
2003—Green Bay NFL	6	6	6	0	0.0
Pro totals (9 years)	117	115	318	82	52.5

JOHNSON, KEVIN — WR — RAVENS

PERSONAL: Born July 15, 1976, in Trenton, N.J. ... 5-11/195. ... Full name: Kevin L. Johnson.
HIGH SCHOOL: Hamilton West (Trenton, N.J.).
COLLEGE: Syracuse.
TRANSACTIONS/CAREER NOTES: Selected by Cleveland Browns in second round (32nd pick overall) of 1999 NFL draft. ... Signed by Browns (July 22, 1999). ... Claimed on waivers by Jacksonville Jaguars (November 12, 2003). ... Traded by Jaguars to Baltimore Ravens for fourth-round pick (WR Ernest Wilford) in 2004 draft (April 25, 2004).
SINGLE GAME HIGHS (regular season): Receptions—11 (September 21, 2003, vs. San Francisco); yards—153 (October 14, 2001, vs. Cincinnati); and touchdown receptions—2 (December 2, 2001, vs. Tennessee).
STATISTICAL PLATEAUS: 100-yard receiving games: 1999 (2), 2000 (1), 2001 (2), 2003 (1). Total: 6.

			RUSHING				RECEIVING				PUNT RETURNS				TOTALS			
Year Team	G	GS	Att.	Yds.	Avg.	TD	No.	Yds.	Avg.	TD	No.	Yds.	Avg.	TD	TD	2pt.	Pts.	Fum.
1999—Cleveland NFL	16	16	1	-6	-6.0	0	66	986	14.9	8	19	128	6.7	0	8	0	48	1
2000—Cleveland NFL	16	16	0	0	0.0	0	57	669	11.7	0	0	0	0.0	0	0	0	0	0
2001—Cleveland NFL	16	16	0	0	0.0	0	84	1097	13.1	9	14	117	8.4	0	9	0	54	2
2002—Cleveland NFL	16	15	0	0	0.0	0	67	703	10.5	4	0	0	0.0	0	4	0	24	0
2003—Cleveland NFL	9	8	0	0	0.0	0	41	381	9.3	2	0	0	0.0	0	2	0	12	0
—Jacksonville NFL	6	1	0	0	0.0	0	17	253	14.9	1	0	0	0.0	0	1	0	6	0
Pro totals (5 years)	79	72	1	-6	-6.0	0	332	4089	12.3	24	33	245	7.4	0	24	0	144	3

J

JOHNSON, KEYSHAWN — WR — COWBOYS

PERSONAL: Born July 22, 1972, in Los Angeles, Calif. ... 6-4/212.
HIGH SCHOOL: Dorsey (Los Angeles).
JUNIOR COLLEGE: West Los Angeles College.
COLLEGE: Southern California.
TRANSACTIONS/CAREER NOTES: Selected by New York Jets in first round (first pick overall) of 1996 NFL draft. ... Signed by Jets (August 6, 1996). ... Traded by Jets to Tampa Bay Buccaneers for two first-round picks (LB John Abraham and TE Anthony Becht) in 2000 draft (April 12, 2000). ... Traded by Buccaneers to Dallas Cowboys for WR Joey Galloway (March 19, 2004).
CHAMPIONSHIP GAME EXPERIENCE: Played in AFC championship game (1998 season). ... Played in NFC championship game (2002 season). ... Member of Super Bowl championship team (2002 season).
HONORS: Named wide receiver on THE SPORTING NEWS college All-America first team (1995). ... Played in Pro Bowl (1998, 1999 and 2001 seasons). ... Named co-Outstanding Player of Pro Bowl (1998 season).
SINGLE GAME HIGHS (regular season): Receptions—12 (November 18, 2001, vs. Chicago); yards—194 (September 12, 1999, vs. New England); and touchdown receptions—2 (November 3, 2002, vs. Minnesota).
STATISTICAL PLATEAUS: 100-yard receiving games: 1997 (1), 1998 (4), 1999 (2), 2000 (2), 2001 (4), 2002 (3), 2003 (2). Total: 18.

			RECEIVING				TOTALS			
Year Team	G	GS	No.	Yds.	Avg.	TD	TD	2pt.	Pts.	Fum.
1996—New York Jets NFL	14	11	63	844	13.4	8	8	1	50	0
1997—New York Jets NFL	16	16	70	963	13.8	5	5	0	30	0
1998—New York Jets NFL	16	16	83	1131	13.6	▲10	11	0	66	0
1999—New York Jets NFL	16	16	89	1170	13.1	8	8	0	48	0
2000—Tampa Bay NFL	16	16	71	874	12.3	8	8	0	48	2
2001—Tampa Bay NFL	15	15	‡106	1266	11.9	1	1	0	6	2
2002—Tampa Bay NFL	16	16	76	1088	14.3	5	5	∞2	34	0
2003—Tampa Bay NFL	10	10	45	600	13.3	3	3	0	18	0
Pro totals (8 years)	119	116	603	7936	13.2	48	49	3	300	4

JOHNSON, LARRY — RB — CHIEFS

PERSONAL: Born November 19, 1979, in State College, Pa. ... 6-1/228. ... Full name: Larry Alphonso Johnson.
HIGH SCHOOL: State College (Pa.).
COLLEGE: Penn State.
TRANSACTIONS/CAREER NOTES: Selected by Kansas City Chiefs in first round (27th pick overall) of 2003 NFL draft. ... Signed by Chiefs (July 17, 2003).
SINGLE GAME HIGHS (regular season): Attempts—7 (December 28, 2003, vs. Chicago); yards—26 (December 28, 2003, vs. Chicago); and rushing touchdowns—1 (December 28, 2003, vs. Chicago).

			RUSHING				RECEIVING				TOTALS			
Year Team	G	GS	Att.	Yds.	Avg.	TD	No.	Yds.	Avg.	TD	TD	2pt.	Pts.	Fum.
2003—Kansas City NFL	6	0	20	85	4.3	1	1	2	2.0	0	1	0	6	0

JOHNSON, LEON — RB/KR — CHARGERS

PERSONAL: Born July 13, 1974, in Morganton, N.C. ... 6-0/222. ... Full name: William Leon Johnson.
HIGH SCHOOL: Freedom (Morganton, N.C.).
COLLEGE: North Carolina.
TRANSACTIONS/CAREER NOTES: Selected by New York Jets in fourth round (104th pick overall) of 1997 NFL draft. ... Signed by Jets (July 17, 1997). ... On injured reserve with rib injury (December 16, 1998-remainder of season). ... On injured reserve with knee injury (September 13, 1999-remainder of season). ... Granted free agency (February 11, 2000). ... Re-signed by Jets (May 8, 2000). ... Released by Jets (June 27, 2000). ... Re-signed by Jets (November 28, 2000). ... Released by Jets (February 19, 2001). ... Signed by Chicago Bears (October 9, 2001). ... Granted unconditional free agency (February 28, 2003). ... Signed by St. Louis Rams (March 22, 2003). ... Released by Rams (August 24, 2003). ... Signed by San Diego Chargers (August 26, 2003). ... Granted unconditional free agency (March 3, 2004). ... Re-signed by Chargers (March 16, 2004).

SINGLE GAME HIGHS (regular season): Attempts—16 (December 22, 2002, vs. Carolina); yards—56 (December 15, 2002, vs. New York Jets); and rushing touchdowns—2 (September 20, 1998, vs Indianapolis).

			RUSHING				RECEIVING				PUNT RETURNS				KICKOFF RETURNS				TOTALS		
Year Team	G	GS	Att.	Yds.	Avg.	TD	No.	Yds.	Avg.	TD	No.	Yds.	Avg.	TD	No.	Yds.	Avg.	TD	TD	2pt.	Pts.
1997—NYJ NFL	16	1	48	158	3.3	2	16	142	8.9	0	§51	*619	12.1	1	12	319	26.6	▲1	4	0	24
1998—NYJ NFL	12	2	41	185	4.5	2	13	222	17.1	2	29	203	7.0	0	16	366	22.9	0	4	0	24
1999—NYJ NFL	1	0	1	2	2.0	0	0	0	0.0	0	1	6	6.0	0	2	31	15.5	0	0	0	0
2000—NYJ NFL	3	0	0	0	0.0	0	0	0	0.0	0	10	62	6.2	0	6	117	19.5	0	0	0	0
2001—Chi. NFL	12	0	20	99	5.0	4	1	0	0.0	0	28	255	9.1	0	14	286	20.4	0	4	0	24
2002—Chi. NFL	16	4	103	329	3.2	1	16	125	7.8	0	28	288	10.3	0	21	418	19.9	0	1	0	6
2003—S.D. NFL	14	0	4	26	6.5	0	0	0	0.0	0	24	184	7.7	0	50	1151	23.0	0	0	0	0
Pro totals (7 years)	74	7	217	799	3.7	9	46	489	10.6	2	171	1617	9.5	1	121	2688	22.2	1	13	0	78

JOHNSON, PATRICK WR BENGALS

PERSONAL: Born August 10, 1976, in Gainesville, Ga. ... 5-10/196. ... Full name: Patrick Jevon Johnson.

HIGH SCHOOL: Redlands (Calif.).

COLLEGE: Oregon.

TRANSACTIONS/CAREER NOTES: Selected by Baltimore Ravens in second round (42nd pick overall) of 1998 NFL draft. ... Signed by Ravens (June 24, 1998). ... Granted free agency (March 2, 2001). ... Signed by Jacksonville Jaguars (March 18, 2002). ... Granted unconditional free agency (February 28, 2003). ... Signed by Washington Redskins (March 11, 2003). ... Granted unconditional free agency (March 3, 2004). ... Signed by Cincinnati Bengals (March 19, 2004).

CHAMPIONSHIP GAME EXPERIENCE: Played in AFC championship game (2000 season). ... Member of Super Bowl championship team (2000 season).

HONORS: Named kick returner on THE SPORTING NEWS college All-America second team (1997).

SINGLE GAME HIGHS (regular season): Receptions—9 (January 2, 2000, vs. New England); yards—114 (January 2, 2000, vs. New England); and touchdown receptions—1 (November 16, 2003, vs. Carolina).

STATISTICAL PLATEAUS: 100-yard receiving games: 1999 (1). Total: 1.

			RECEIVING				PUNT RETURNS				KICKOFF RETURNS				TOTALS			
Year Team	G	GS	No.	Yds.	Avg.	TD	No.	Yds.	Avg.	TD	No.	Yds.	Avg.	TD	TD	2pt.	Pts.	Fum.
1998—Baltimore NFL	13	0	12	159	13.3	1	1	6	6.0	0	16	399	24.9	▲1	2	0	12	1
1999—Baltimore NFL	10	6	29	526	18.1	3	0	0	0.0	0	0	0	0.0	0	3	0	18	1
2000—Baltimore NFL	12	9	12	156	13.0	2	0	0	0.0	0	0	0	0.0	0	2	0	12	0
2001—Baltimore NFL	4	0	5	57	11.4	1	0	0	0.0	0	2	39	19.5	0	1	0	6	1
2002—Jacksonville NFL	9	6	9	187	20.8	2	0	0	0.0	0	0	0	0.0	0	2	0	12	0
2003—Washington NFL	16	2	15	170	11.3	1	3	17	5.7	0	13	310	23.8	0	1	0	6	2
Pro totals (6 years)	64	23	82	1255	15.3	10	4	23	5.8	0	31	748	24.1	1	11	0	66	5

JOHNSON, RAYLEE DE BRONCOS

PERSONAL: Born June 1, 1970, in Chicago, Ill. ... 6-3/272. ... Full name: Raylee Terrell Johnson.

HIGH SCHOOL: Fordyce (Ark.).

COLLEGE: Arkansas.

TRANSACTIONS/CAREER NOTES: Selected by San Diego Chargers in fourth round (95th pick overall) of 1993 NFL draft. ... Signed by Chargers (July 15, 1993). ... Granted unconditional free agency (February 14, 1997). ... Re-signed by Chargers (March 11, 1997). ... On injured reserve with knee injury (August 22, 2000-entire season). ... On injured reserve with foot injury (November 29, 2003-remainder of season). ... Released by Chargers (March 2, 2004). ... Signed by Denver Broncos (March 22, 2004).

CHAMPIONSHIP GAME EXPERIENCE: Played in AFC championship game (1994 season). ... Played in Super Bowl 29 (1994 season).

			TOTALS		
Year Team	G	GS	Tk.	Ast.	Sks.
1993—San Diego NFL	9	0	0	1	0.0
1994—San Diego NFL	15	0	4	2	1.5
1995—San Diego NFL	16	1	14	1	3.0
1996—San Diego NFL	16	1	15	3	3.0
1997—San Diego NFL	16	0	16	3	2.5
1998—San Diego NFL	16	3	23	6	5.5
1999—San Diego NFL	16	16	33	8	10.5
2000—San Diego NFL	Did not play.				
2001—San Diego NFL	16	16	28	10	9.5
2002—San Diego NFL	16	16	32	8	6.5
2003—San Diego NFL	9	1	12	1	4.0
Pro totals (10 years)	145	54	177	43	46.0

JOHNSON, RIALL LB CARDINALS

PERSONAL: Born April 20, 1978, in Lynnwood, Wash. ... 6-3/243. ... Brother of Teyo Johnson, wide receiver/tight end, Oakland Raiders.

HIGH SCHOOL: Mariner (Wash.).

COLLEGE: Stanford.

TRANSACTIONS/CAREER NOTES: Selected by Cincinnati Bengals in sixth round (168th pick overall) of 2001 NFL draft. ... Signed by Bengals (July 11, 2001). ... Released by Bengals (October 27, 2001). ... Re-signed by Bengals (October 30, 2001). ... Granted free agency (March 3, 2004). ... Signed by Arizona Cardinals (April 3, 2004).

			TOTALS			INTERCEPTIONS			
Year Team	G	GS	Tk.	Ast.	Sks.	No.	Yds.	Avg.	TD
2001—Cincinnati NFL	7	0	0	0	0.0	0	0	0.0	0
2002—Cincinnati NFL	12	0	0	0	0.0	0	0	0.0	0
2003—Cincinnati NFL	13	1	2	6	0.0	0	0	0.0	0
Pro totals (3 years)	32	1	2	6	0.0	0	0	0.0	0

JOHNSON, ROB QB

PERSONAL: Born March 18, 1973, in Newport Beach, Calif. ... 6-4/204. ... Full name: Rob Garland Johnson. ... Brother of Bret Johnson, quarterback with Toronto Argonauts of CFL (1993).

HIGH SCHOOL: El Toro (Calif.).

COLLEGE: Southern California.

TRANSACTIONS/CAREER NOTES: Selected by Jacksonville Jaguars in fourth round (99th pick overall) of 1995 NFL draft. ... Signed by Jaguars (June 1, 1995). ... Traded by Jaguars to Buffalo Bills for first- (RB Fred Taylor) and fourth-round (RB Tavian Banks) picks in 1998 draft (February 13, 1998). ... Released by Bills (February 28, 2002). ... Signed by Tampa Bay Buccaneers (March 10, 2002). ... Granted unconditional free agency (February 28, 2003). ... Signed by Washington Redskins (March 11, 2003). ... Released by Redskins (October 22, 2003). ... Signed by Oakland Raiders (November 4, 2003). ... Granted unconditional free agency (March 3, 2004).

CHAMPIONSHIP GAME EXPERIENCE: Member of Jaguars for AFC championship game (1996 season); did not play. ... Member of Buccaneers for NFC championship game (2002 season); did not play. ... Member of Super Bowl championship team (2002 season); did not play.

SINGLE GAME HIGHS (regular season): Attempts—47 (October 15, 2000, vs. San Diego); completions—29 (October 15, 2000, vs. San Diego); yards—321 (October 15, 2000, vs. San Diego); and touchdown passes—3 (September 10, 2000, vs. Green Bay).

STATISTICAL PLATEAUS: 300-yard passing games: 2000 (1), 2001 (1). Total: 2.

MISCELLANEOUS: Selected by Minnesota Twins organization in 16th round of free-agent draft (June 4, 1991); did not sign. ... Regular-season record as starting NFL quarterback: 12-17 (.414). ... Postseason record as starting NFL quarterback: 0-1.

			PASSING										RUSHING				TOTALS		
Year Team	**G**	**GS**	**Att.**	**Cmp.**	**Pct.**	**Yds.**	**TD**	**Int.**	**Avg.**	**Skd.**	**Rat.**	**Att.**	**Yds.**	**Avg.**	**TD**	**TD**	**2pt.**	**Pts.**
1995—Jacksonville NFL	1	0	7	3	42.9	24	0	1	3.43	1	12.5	3	17	5.7	0	0	0	0
1996—Jacksonville NFL	2	0	0	0	0.0	0	0	0	0.00	0	0.0	0	0	0.0	0	0	0	0
1997—Jacksonville NFL	5	1	28	22	78.6	344	2	2	12.29	6	111.9	10	34	3.4	1	1	0	6
1998—Buffalo NFL	8	6	107	67	62.6	910	8	3	8.50	29	102.9	24	123	5.1	1	1	0	6
1999—Buffalo NFL	2	1	34	25	73.5	298	2	0	8.76	1	119.5	8	61	7.6	0	0	0	0
2000—Buffalo NFL	12	11	306	175	57.2	2125	12	7	6.94	49	82.2	42	307	7.3	1	1	0	6
2001—Buffalo NFL	8	8	216	134	62.0	1465	5	7	6.78	31	76.3	36	241	6.7	1	1	0	6
2002—Tampa Bay NFL	6	2	88	57	64.8	536	1	2	6.09	19	75.8	14	73	5.2	0	0	0	0
2003—Washington NFL	2	0	7	5	71.4	39	0	0	5.57	3	84.8	1	6	6.0	0	0	0	0
—Oakland NFL	2	0	13	6	46.2	54	0	1	4.15	1	25.8	2	15	7.5	0	0	0	0
Pro totals (9 years)	48	29	806	494	61.3	5795	30	23	7.19	140	83.6	140	877	6.3	4	4	0	24

JOHNSON, ROBERT TE BEARS

PERSONAL: Born June 20, 1980, in Montgomery, Ala. ... 6-6/270.

HIGH SCHOOL: Jefferson Davis (Montgomery, Ala.).

COLLEGE: Auburn.

TRANSACTIONS/CAREER NOTES: Signed as non-drafted free agent by Atlanta Falcons (April 28, 2003). ... Claimed on waivers by Chicago Bears (May 13, 2003). ... On physically unable to perform list with foot injury (July 25-November 10, 2003). ... On injured reserve with foot injury (November 28, 2003-remainder of season).

			RECEIVING				TOTALS			
Year Team	**G**	**GS**	**No.**	**Yds.**	**Avg.**	**TD**	**TD**	**2pt.**	**Pts.**	**Fum.**
2003—Chicago NFL	1	0	0	0	0.0	0	0	0	0	0

JOHNSON, RON WR RAVENS

PERSONAL: Born May 23, 1980, in Detroit, Mich. ... 6-2/225.

HIGH SCHOOL: Martin Luther King (Detroit).

COLLEGE: Minnesota.

TRANSACTIONS/CAREER NOTES: Selected by Baltimore Ravens in fourth round (123rd pick overall) of 2002 NFL draft. ... Signed by Ravens (July 26, 2002).

SINGLE GAME HIGHS (regular season): Receptions—3 (October 27, 2002, vs. Pittsburgh); yards—37 (October 20, 2002, vs. Jacksonville); and touchdown receptions—1 (September 8, 2002, vs. Carolina).

			RECEIVING				KICKOFF RETURNS				TOTALS			
Year Team	**G**	**GS**	**No.**	**Yds.**	**Avg.**	**TD**	**No.**	**Yds.**	**Avg.**	**TD**	**TD**	**2pt.**	**Pts.**	**Fum.**
2002—Baltimore NFL	16	4	10	114	11.4	1	2	21	10.5	0	2	0	12	0
2003—Baltimore NFL	6	0	1	12	12.0	0	0	0	0.0	0	0	0	0	0
Pro totals (2 years)	22	4	11	126	11.5	1	2	21	10.5	0	2	0	12	0

JOHNSON, RON DE EAGLES

PERSONAL: Born October 23, 1979, in York, Pa. ... 6-5/255.

HIGH SCHOOL: York Catholic (York, Pa.).

COLLEGE: Shippensburg (Pa.).

TRANSACTIONS/CAREER NOTES: Signed as non-drafted free agent by Philadelphia Eagles (April 28, 2003). ... Waived by Eagles (August 31, 2003). ... Re-signed by Eagles to practice squad (September 1, 2003). ... Activated (October 8, 2003).

CHAMPIONSHIP GAME EXPERIENCE: Member of Eagles for NFC championship game (2003 season); inactive.

			TOTALS		
Year Team	**G**	**GS**	**Tk.**	**Ast.**	**Sks.**
2003—Philadelphia NFL	3	0	0	0	0.0

J

JOHNSON, RUDI — RB — BENGALS

PERSONAL: Born October 1, 1979, in Petersburg, Va. ... 5-10/220. ... Full name: Rudi Ali Johnson.
HIGH SCHOOL: Thomas Dale (Ettrick, Va.).
JUNIOR COLLEGE: Butler County Community College (Kan.).
COLLEGE: Auburn.
TRANSACTIONS/CAREER NOTES: Selected by Cincinnati Bengals in fourth round (100th pick overall) of 2001 NFL draft. ... Signed by Bengals (July 17, 2001). ... Granted free agency (March 3, 2004). ... Re-signed by Bengals (May 11, 2004).
HONORS: Named running back on THE SPORTING NEWS college All-America second team (2000).
SINGLE GAME HIGHS (regular season): Attempts—43 (November 9, 2003, vs. Houston); yards—182 (November 9, 2003, vs. Houston); and rushing touchdowns—2 (December 28, 2003, vs. Cleveland).
STATISTICAL PLATEAUS: 100-yard rushing games: 2003 (4). Total: 4.

			RUSHING				RECEIVING				KICKOFF RETURNS				TOTALS			
Year Team	G	GS	Att.	Yds.	Avg.	TD	No.	Yds.	Avg.	TD	No.	Yds.	Avg.	TD	TD	2pt.	Pts.	Fum.
2001—Cincinnati NFL	2	0	0	0	0.0	0	0	0	0.0	0	4	79	19.8	0	0	0	0	0
2002—Cincinnati NFL	7	0	17	67	3.9	0	6	34	5.7	0	13	277	21.3	0	0	0	0	0
2003—Cincinnati NFL	13	5	215	957	4.5	9	21	146	7.0	0	2	23	11.5	0	9	0	54	0
Pro totals (3 years)	22	5	232	1024	4.4	9	27	180	6.7	0	19	379	19.9	0	9	0	54	0

JOHNSON, TED — LB — PATRIOTS

PERSONAL: Born December 4, 1972, in Alameda, Calif. ... 6-4/253. ... Full name: Ted Curtis Johnson.
HIGH SCHOOL: Carlsbad (Calif.).
COLLEGE: Colorado.
TRANSACTIONS/CAREER NOTES: Selected by New England Patriots in second round (57th pick overall) of 1995 NFL draft. ... Signed by Patriots (July 18, 1995). ... On injured reserve with biceps injury (December 11, 1998-remainder of season).
CHAMPIONSHIP GAME EXPERIENCE: Played in AFC championship game (1996, 2001 and 2003 seasons). ... Played in Super Bowl 31 (1996 season). ... Member of Super Bowl championship team (2001 and 2003 seasons).
HONORS: Named linebacker on THE SPORTING NEWS college All-America second team (1994).

			TOTALS			INTERCEPTIONS			
Year Team	G	GS	Tk.	Ast.	Sks.	No.	Yds.	Avg.	TD
1995—New England NFL	12	12	41	28	0.5	0	0	0.0	0
1996—New England NFL	16	16	87	28	0.0	1	0	0.0	0
1997—New England NFL	16	16	95	32	4.0	0	0	0.0	0
1998—New England NFL	13	13	64	33	2.0	0	0	0.0	0
1999—New England NFL	5	5	25	13	2.0	0	0	0.0	0
2000—New England NFL	13	11	51	22	0.5	0	0	0.0	0
2001—New England NFL	12	5	33	13	0.0	0	0	0.0	0
2002—New England NFL	14	11	63	33	1.5	0	0	0.0	0
2003—New England NFL	8	2	15	6	0.0	0	0	0.0	0
Pro totals (9 years)	109	91	474	208	10.5	1	0	0.0	0

JOHNSON, TEYO — TE — RAIDERS

PERSONAL: Born November 29, 1981, in San Diego, Calif. ... 6-5/260. ... Brother of Riall Johnson, linebacker, Arizona Cardinals.
HIGH SCHOOL: Mira Mesa (San Diego).
COLLEGE: Stanford.
TRANSACTIONS/CAREER NOTES: Selected after sophomore season by Oakland Raiders in second round (63rd pick overall) of 2003 NFL draft. ... Signed by Raiders (July 24, 2003).
SINGLE GAME HIGHS (regular season): Receptions—3 (November 9, 2003, vs. New York Jets); yards—30 (November 9, 2003, vs. New York Jets); and touchdown receptions—1 (October 12, 2003, vs. Cleveland).

			RECEIVING				TOTALS			
Year Team	G	GS	No.	Yds.	Avg.	TD	TD	2pt.	Pts.	Fum.
2003—Oakland NFL	16	5	14	128	9.1	1	1	0	6	0

JOHNSON, TIM — LB — RAIDERS

PERSONAL: Born February 7, 1978, in Birmingham, Ala. ... 6-0/240.
HIGH SCHOOL: Fairfield (Ala.).
JUNIOR COLLEGE: East Mississippi Junior College.
COLLEGE: Youngstown State.
TRANSACTIONS/CAREER NOTES: Signed as non-drafted free agent by Baltimore Ravens (April 27, 2001). ... Released by Ravens (September 1, 2001). ... Re-signed by Ravens (September 5, 2001). ... Released by Ravens (September 10, 2001). ... Signed by Chicago Bears to practice squad (September 27, 2001). ... Released by Bears (October 30, 2001). ... Re-signed by Bears to practice squad (November 8, 2001). ... Assigned by Bears to Rhein Fire in 2002 NFL Europe enhancement allocation program (February 18, 2002). ... Released by Bears (September 1, 2002). ... Signed by Oakland Raiders to practice squad (September 3, 2002). ... Released by Raiders (September 18, 2002). ... Re-signed by Raiders to practice squad (September 24, 2002). ... Released by Raiders (October 9, 2002). ... Re-signed by Raiders to practice squad (October 31, 2002). ... Activated (November 24, 2002).
CHAMPIONSHIP GAME EXPERIENCE: Played in AFC championship game (2002 season). ... Played in Super Bowl 37 (2002 season).

			TOTALS			INTERCEPTIONS			
Year Team	G	GS	Tk.	Ast.	Sks.	No.	Yds.	Avg.	TD
2001—Baltimore NFL			Did not play.						
2002—Oakland NFL	6	0	0	0	0.0	0	0	0.0	0
2003—Oakland NFL	12	4	27	5	0.0	0	0	0.0	0
Pro totals (2 years)	18	4	27	5	0.0	0	0	0.0	0

JOHNSON, TODD — SS — BEARS

PERSONAL: Born December 18, 1978, in Sarasota, Fla. ... 6-1/206. ... Full name: Todd Edward Johnson.
HIGH SCHOOL: Riverview (Sarasota, Fla.).
COLLEGE: Florida.
TRANSACTIONS/CAREER NOTES: Selected by Chicago Bears in fourth round (100th pick overall) of 2003 NFL draft. ... Signed by Bears (July 9, 2003). ... On injured reserve with jaw injury (September 9, 2003-entire season).

		INTERCEPTIONS			
Year Team	**G**	**No.**	**Yds.**	**Avg.**	**TD**
2003—Chicago NFL			Did not play.		

JOHNSTONE, LANCE — DE — VIKINGS

PERSONAL: Born June 11, 1973, in Philadelphia, Pa. ... 6-4/250.
HIGH SCHOOL: Germantown (Philadelphia).
COLLEGE: Temple.
TRANSACTIONS/CAREER NOTES: Selected by Oakland Raiders in second round (57th pick overall) of 1996 NFL draft. ... Signed by Raiders for 1996 season. ... Granted unconditional free agency (March 2, 2001). ... Signed by Minnesota Vikings (March 30, 2001). ... Granted unconditional free agency (March 1, 2002). ... Re-signed by Vikings (March 28, 2002). ... Granted unconditional free agency (February 28, 2003). ... Re-signed by Vikings (March 20, 2003).
CHAMPIONSHIP GAME EXPERIENCE: Played in AFC championship game (2000 season).

			TOTALS			INTERCEPTIONS			
Year Team	**G**	**GS**	**Tk.**	**Ast.**	**Sks.**	**No.**	**Yds.**	**Avg.**	**TD**
1996—Oakland NFL	16	10	26	6	1.0	0	0	0.0	0
1997—Oakland NFL	14	6	20	11	3.5	0	0	0.0	0
1998—Oakland NFL	16	15	48	6	11.0	0	0	0.0	0
1999—Oakland NFL	16	16	45	7	10.0	1	0	0.0	0
2000—Oakland NFL	14	9	22	10	3.5	0	0	0.0	0
2001—Minnesota NFL	16	5	29	9	5.5	0	0	0.0	0
2002—Minnesota NFL	16	16	41	10	7.0	0	0	0.0	0
2003—Minnesota NFL	16	0	22	7	10.0	1	33	33.0	1
Pro totals (8 years)	124	77	253	66	51.5	2	33	16.5	1

JOLLEY, DOUG — TE — RAIDERS

PERSONAL: Born January 2, 1979, in Sandy, Utah. ... 6-4/250.
HIGH SCHOOL: Dixie (St. George, Utah).
COLLEGE: Brigham Young.
TRANSACTIONS/CAREER NOTES: Selected by Oakland Raiders in second round (55th pick overall) of 2002 NFL draft. ... Signed by Raiders (July 23, 2002).
CHAMPIONSHIP GAME EXPERIENCE: Played in AFC championship game (2002 season). ... Played in Super Bowl 37 (2002 season).
SINGLE GAME HIGHS (regular season): Receptions—7 (September 28, 2003, vs. San Diego); yards—104 (December 8, 2002, vs. San Diego); and touchdown receptions—1 (September 28, 2003, vs. San Diego).
STATISTICAL PLATEAUS: 100-yard receiving games: 2002 (1). Total: 1.

			RECEIVING				TOTALS			
Year Team	**G**	**GS**	**No.**	**Yds.**	**Avg.**	**TD**	**TD**	**2pt.**	**Pts.**	**Fum.**
2002—Oakland NFL	16	4	32	409	12.8	2	2	0	12	0
2003—Oakland NFL	15	10	31	250	8.1	1	1	0	6	0
Pro totals (2 years)	31	14	63	659	10.5	3	3	0	18	0

JONES, DHANI — LB — EAGLES

PERSONAL: Born February 22, 1978, in San Diego, Calif. ... 6-1/240. ... Full name: Dhani Makalani Jones.
HIGH SCHOOL: Winston Churchill (Potomac, Md.).
COLLEGE: Michigan.
TRANSACTIONS/CAREER NOTES: Selected by New York Giants in sixth round (177th pick overall) of 2000 NFL draft. ... Signed by Giants (July 18, 2000). ... On injured reserve with knee injury (August 20, 2000-entire season). ... Granted free agency (February 28, 2003). ... Re-signed by Giants (April 28, 2003). ... Granted unconditional free agency (March 3, 2004). ... Signed by Philadelphia Eagles (March 9, 2004).

			TOTALS			INTERCEPTIONS			
Year Team	**G**	**GS**	**Tk.**	**Ast.**	**Sks.**	**No.**	**Yds.**	**Avg.**	**TD**
2000—New York Giants NFL				Did not play.					
2001—New York Giants NFL	16	0	9	2	0.0	1	14	14.0	0
2002—New York Giants NFL	15	14	60	22	0.0	1	1	1.0	0
2003—New York Giants NFL	16	16	92	26	3.0	0	0	0.0	0
Pro totals (3 years)	47	30	161	50	3.0	2	15	7.5	0

JONES, FRED — LB — CHIEFS

PERSONAL: Born October 18, 1977, in Subic Bay, Philippines. ... 6-2/247. ... Full name: Fred Allen Jones.
HIGH SCHOOL: St. Augustine (San Diego).
COLLEGE: Colorado.
TRANSACTIONS/CAREER NOTES: Signed as non-drafted free agent by Buffalo Bills (April 23, 2000). ... Released by Bills (September 3, 2002). ... Selected by Frankfurt Galaxy in 2003 NFL Europe draft (February 5, 2003). ... Signed by Kansas City Chiefs (June 19, 2003).

Year Team	G	GS	TOTALS Tk.	Ast.	Sks.	INTERCEPTIONS No.	Yds.	Avg.	TD
2000—Buffalo NFL	15	0	5	2	1.0	0	0	0.0	0
2001—Buffalo NFL	16	0	0	1	0.5	0	0	0.0	0
2002—			Did not play.						
2003—Kansas City NFL	11	0	0	1	0.0	0	0	0.0	0
Pro totals (3 years)	42	0	5	4	1.5	0	0	0.0	0

JONES, FREDDIE TE CARDINALS

PERSONAL: Born September 16, 1974, in Cheverly, Md. ... 6-4/260. ... Full name: Freddie Ray Jones Jr.
HIGH SCHOOL: McKinley (Landover, Md.).
COLLEGE: North Carolina.
TRANSACTIONS/CAREER NOTES: Selected by San Diego Chargers in second round (45th pick overall) of 1997 NFL draft. ... Signed by Chargers (May 21, 1997). ... On injured reserve with leg injury (December 12, 1997-remainder of season). ... Granted free agency (February 11, 2000). ... Re-signed by Chargers (April 29, 2000). ... Released by Chargers (February 27, 2002). ... Signed by Arizona Cardinals (March 18, 2002).
SINGLE GAME HIGHS (regular season): Receptions—10 (October 29, 2000, vs. Oakland); yards—111 (October 29, 2000, vs. Oakland); and touchdown receptions—2 (November 26, 2000, vs. Kansas City).
STATISTICAL PLATEAUS: 100-yard receiving games: 2000 (1). Total: 1.

Year Team	G	GS	RECEIVING No.	Yds.	Avg.	TD	TOTALS TD	2pt.	Pts.	Fum.
1997—San Diego NFL	13	8	41	505	12.3	2	2	0	12	0
1998—San Diego NFL	16	16	57	602	10.6	3	3	1	20	1
1999—San Diego NFL	16	16	56	670	12.0	2	2	0	12	0
2000—San Diego NFL	16	16	71	766	10.8	5	5	0	30	3
2001—San Diego NFL	14	9	35	388	11.1	4	4	0	24	0
2002—Arizona NFL	16	16	44	358	8.1	1	1	0	6	0
2003—Arizona NFL	16	16	55	517	9.4	3	3	0	18	0
Pro totals (7 years)	107	97	359	3806	10.6	20	20	1	122	4

JONES, JOHN TE DOLPHINS

PERSONAL: Born April 4, 1975, in Cleveland, Ohio. ... 6-4/255.
HIGH SCHOOL: Glen Mills (Concordville, Pa.).
COLLEGE: Indiana University (Pa.).
TRANSACTIONS/CAREER NOTES: Signed as non-drafted free agent by Baltimore Ravens (April 28, 2000). ... On injured reserve with ankle injury (January 3, 2000-remainder of season). ... Granted free agency (February 28, 2003). ... Re-signed by Ravens (April 29, 2003). ... Granted unconditional free agency (March 3, 2004). ... Signed by Miami Dolphins (March 29, 2004).
SINGLE GAME HIGHS (regular season): Receptions—2 (October 27, 2002, vs. Pittsburgh); yards—24 (October 27, 2002, vs. Pittsburgh); and touchdown receptions—1 (October 27, 2002, vs. Pittsburgh).

Year Team	G	GS	RECEIVING No.	Yds.	Avg.	TD	TOTALS TD	2pt.	Pts.	Fum.
2000—Baltimore NFL	8	0	0	0	0.0	0	0	0	0	0
2001—Baltimore NFL	15	2	2	13	6.5	0	0	0	0	0
2002—Baltimore NFL	15	4	6	47	7.8	1	1	0	6	0
2003—Baltimore NFL	11	0	0	0	0.0	0	0	0	0	0
Pro totals (4 years)	49	6	8	60	7.5	1	1	0	6	0

JONES, LEVI T BENGALS

PERSONAL: Born August 24, 1979, in Eloy, Ariz. ... 6-5/310. ... Full name: Levi J. Jones.
HIGH SCHOOL: Santa Cruz (Eloy, Ariz.).
COLLEGE: Arizona State.
TRANSACTIONS/CAREER NOTES: Selected by Cincinnati Bengals in first round (10th pick overall) of 2002 NFL draft. ... Signed by Bengals (July 25, 2002).
PLAYING EXPERIENCE: Cincinnati NFL, 2002-2003. ... Games/Games started: 2002 (16/14), 2003 (16/16). Total: 32/30.

JONES, MARVIN LB

PERSONAL: Born June 28, 1972, in Miami, Fla. ... 6-2/244. ... Full name: Marvin Maurice Jones.
HIGH SCHOOL: Miami Northwestern.
COLLEGE: Florida State.
TRANSACTIONS/CAREER NOTES: Selected after junior season by New York Jets in first round (fourth pick overall) of 1993 NFL draft. ... Signed by Jets (August 5, 1993). ... On injured reserve with hip injury (November 16, 1993-remainder of season). ... On injured reserve with knee injury (July 29, 1998-entire season). ... Released by Jets (February 26, 2002). ... Re-signed by Jets (March 6, 2002). ... Released by Jets (March 3, 2004).
HONORS: Butkus Award winner (1992). ... Named College Football Player of the Year by THE SPORTING NEWS (1992). ... Named linebacker on THE SPORTING NEWS college All-America first team (1992).

Year Team	G	GS	TOTALS Tk.	Ast.	Sks.	INTERCEPTIONS No.	Yds.	Avg.	TD
1993—New York Jets NFL	9	0	22	8	0.0	0	0	0.0	0
1994—New York Jets NFL	15	11	60	26	0.5	0	0	0.0	0
1995—New York Jets NFL	10	10	59	33	1.5	0	0	0.0	0
1996—New York Jets NFL	12	12	75	28	1.0	0	0	0.0	0
1997—New York Jets NFL	16	16	87	40	3.0	0	0	0.0	0

Year	Team	G	GS	TOTALS Tk.	Ast.	Sks.	INTERCEPTIONS No.	Yds.	Avg.	TD
1998—New York Jets NFL				Did not play.						
1999—New York Jets NFL		16	16	69	23	1.0	1	15	15.0	0
2000—New York Jets NFL		16	16	102	33	1.0	0	0	0.0	0
2001—New York Jets NFL		16	16	94	38	1.0	3	27	9.0	0
2002—New York Jets NFL		16	16	77	32	0.0	1	0	0.0	0
2003—New York Jets NFL		16	16	72	43	0.0	0	0	0.0	0
Pro totals (10 years)		142	129	717	304	9.0	5	42	8.4	0

JONES, RUSHEN — CB — VIKINGS

PERSONAL: Born August 4, 1980... 5-10/194.
HIGH SCHOOL: Whitehaven (Memphis, Tenn.).
COLLEGE: Vanderbilt.
TRANSACTIONS/CAREER NOTES: Signed as non-drafted free agent by Minnesota Vikings (May 2, 2003).

Year	Team	G	GS	TOTALS Tk.	Ast.	Sks.	INTERCEPTIONS No.	Yds.	Avg.	TD
2003—Minnesota NFL		11	0	0	0	0.0	0	0	0.0	0

JONES, TEBUCKY — S — SAINTS

PERSONAL: Born October 6, 1974, in New Britain, Conn. ... 6-2/218. ... Full name: Tebucky Shermaine Jones.
HIGH SCHOOL: New Britain (Conn.).
COLLEGE: Syracuse.
TRANSACTIONS/CAREER NOTES: Selected by New England Patriots in first round (22nd pick overall) of 1998 NFL draft. ... Signed by Patriots (July 18, 1998). ... On injured reserve with knee injury (December 31, 1999-remainder of season). ... Designated by Patriots as franchise player (February 20, 2003). ... Traded by Patriots to New Orleans Saints for third- (traded to Miami) and seventh-round picks (DE Tully Banta-Cain) in 2003 draft and fourth-round pick (CB Dexter Reid) in 2004 draft (April 14, 2003).
CHAMPIONSHIP GAME EXPERIENCE: Played in AFC championship game (2001 season). ... Member of Super Bowl championship team (2001 season).

Year	Team	G	GS	TOTALS Tk.	Ast.	Sks.	INTERCEPTIONS No.	Yds.	Avg.	TD
1998—New England NFL		16	0	10	3	0.0	0	0	0.0	0
1999—New England NFL		12	2	12	0	0.0	0	0	0.0	0
2000—New England NFL		15	9	42	13	0.0	2	20	10.0	0
2001—New England NFL		16	12	41	16	1.0	1	-4	-4.0	0
2002—New England NFL		14	12	38	12	1.5	1	0	0.0	0
2003—New Orleans NFL		15	15	51	18	0.0	1	2	2.0	0
Pro totals (6 years)		88	50	194	62	2.5	5	18	3.6	0

JONES, TERRY — TE — RAVENS

PERSONAL: Born December 3, 1979, in Tuscaloosa, Ala. ... 6-3/265. ... Full name: Terry Jones Jr.
HIGH SCHOOL: Central (Tuscaloosa, Ala.).
COLLEGE: Alabama.
TRANSACTIONS/CAREER NOTES: Selected by Baltimore Ravens in fifth round (155th pick overall) of 2002 NFL draft. ... Signed by Ravens (July 26, 2002).
SINGLE GAME HIGHS (regular season): Receptions—3 (September 7, 2003, vs. Pittsburgh); yards—35 (December 15, 2002, vs. Houston); and touchdown receptions—1 (December 21, 2003, vs. Cleveland).

Year	Team	G	GS	RECEIVING No.	Yds.	Avg.	TD	TOTALS TD	2pt.	Pts.	Fum.
2002—Baltimore NFL		14	6	11	106	9.6	1	1	0	6	0
2003—Baltimore NFL		16	13	19	159	8.4	3	3	0	18	0
Pro totals (2 years)		30	19	30	265	8.8	4	4	0	24	0

JONES, THOMAS — RB — BEARS

PERSONAL: Born August 19, 1978, in Big Stone Gap, Va. ... 5-10/220. ... Full name: Thomas Quinn Jones. ... Brother of Julius Jones, running back, Dallas Cowboys.
HIGH SCHOOL: Powell Valley (Big Stone Gap, Va.).
COLLEGE: Virginia.
TRANSACTIONS/CAREER NOTES: Selected by Arizona Cardinals in first round (seventh pick overall) of 2000 NFL draft. ... Signed by Cardinals (July 21, 2000). ... On injured reserve with hand injury (November 26, 2002-remainder of season). ... Traded by Cardinals to Tampa Bay Buccaneers for WR Marquise Walker (June 13, 2003). ... Granted unconditional free agency (March 3, 2004). ... Signed by Chicago Bears (March 3, 2004).
HONORS: Named running back on THE SPORTING NEWS college All-America first team (1999).
SINGLE GAME HIGHS (regular season): Attempts—34 (December 14, 2003, vs. Houston); yards—173 (September 15, 2002, vs. Seattle); and rushing touchdowns—1 (December 14, 2003, vs. Houston).
STATISTICAL PLATEAUS: 100-yard rushing games: 2002 (1), 2003 (2). Total: 3.

Year	Team	G	GS	RUSHING Att.	Yds.	Avg.	TD	RECEIVING No.	Yds.	Avg.	TD	KICKOFF RETURNS No.	Yds.	Avg.	TD	TOTALS TD	2pt.	Pts.	Fum.
2000—Arizona NFL		14	4	112	373	3.3	2	32	208	6.5	0	0	0	0.0	0	2	0	12	4
2001—Arizona NFL		16	2	112	380	3.4	5	21	151	7.2	0	0	0	0.0	0	5	0	30	2

Year Team	G	GS	RUSHING Att.	Yds.	Avg.	TD	RECEIVING No.	Yds.	Avg.	TD	KICKOFF RETURNS No.	Yds.	Avg.	TD	TOTALS TD	2pt.	Pts.	Fum.
2002—Arizona NFL	9	9	138	511	3.7	2	20	113	5.7	0	0	0	0.0	0	2	0	12	3
2003—Tampa Bay NFL	16	3	137	627	4.6	3	24	180	7.5	0	17	271	15.9	0	3	0	18	4
Pro totals (4 years)	55	18	499	1891	3.8	12	97	652	6.7	0	17	271	15.9	0	12	0	72	13

JONES, WALTER — T — SEAHAWKS

PERSONAL: Born January 19, 1974, in Aliceville, Ala. ... 6-5/308.
HIGH SCHOOL: Aliceville (Ala.).
JUNIOR COLLEGE: Holmes Junior College (Miss.).
COLLEGE: Florida State.
TRANSACTIONS/CAREER NOTES: Selected by Seattle Seahawks in first round (sixth pick overall) of 1997 NFL draft. ... Signed by Seahawks (August 6, 1997). ... Granted free agency (March 1, 2002). ... Re-signed by Seahawks (September 16, 2002). ... Designated by Seahawks as franchise player (February 20, 2003). ... Re-signed by Seahawks (September 2, 2003). ... Designated by Seahawks as franchise player (February 24, 2004).
PLAYING EXPERIENCE: Seattle NFL, 1997-2003. ... Games/Games started: 1997 (12/12), 1998 (16/16), 1999 (16/16), 2000 (16/16), 2001 (16/16), 2002 (14/14), 2003 (16/16). Total: 106/106.
HONORS: Played in Pro Bowl (1999, 2001 and 2003 seasons). ... Named to play in Pro Bowl (2002 season); replaced by Chris Samuels due to injury.

JOPPRU, BEN — TE — TEXANS

PERSONAL: Born January 5, 1980, in Wayzata, Minn. ... 6-4/272. ... Full name: Benjamin Paul Joppru.
HIGH SCHOOL: Minnetonka (Wayzata, Minn.).
COLLEGE: Michigan.
TRANSACTIONS/CAREER NOTES: Selected by Houston Texans in second round (41st pick overall) of 2003 NFL draft. ... Signed by Texans (July 25, 2003). ... On injured reserve with groin injury (August 31, 2003-entire season).

Year Team	G	GS	RECEIVING No.	Yds.	Avg.	TD	TOTALS TD	2pt.	Pts.	Fum.
2003—Houston NFL				Did not play.						

JORDAN, JAMES — WR — 49ERS

PERSONAL: Born June 11, 1978, in Los Angeles, Calif. ... 6-2/225. ... Full name: James Robert Jordan III.
HIGH SCHOOL: Bonnabel (New Orleans).
COLLEGE: Louisiana Tech.
TRANSACTIONS/CAREER NOTES: Signed as non-drafted free agent by San Francisco 49ers (April 27, 2001). ... Released by 49ers (August 28, 2001). ... Re-signed by 49ers (August 31, 2001). ... Released by 49ers (September 2, 2001). ... Re-signed by 49ers (January 23, 2002). ... Released by 49ers (September 1, 2002). ... Re-signed by 49ers to practice squad (September 2, 2002). ... Activated (October 14, 2002). ... Released by 49ers (November 12, 2002). ... Re-signed by 49ers to practice squad (November 13, 2002). ... Activated (November 25, 2002). ... Released by 49ers (December 3, 2002). ... Re-signed by 49ers to practice squad (December 4, 2002). ... Waived by 49ers (August 31, 2003). ... Re-signed by 49ers to practice squad (October 29, 2003). ... Activated (December 24, 2003).

Year Team	G	GS	RECEIVING No.	Yds.	Avg.	TD	TOTALS TD	2pt.	Pts.	Fum.
2002—San Francisco NFL	6	0	0	0	0.0	0	0	0	0	0
2003—San Francisco NFL	1	0	0	0	0.0	0	0	0	0	0
Pro totals (2 years)	7	0	0	0	0.0	0	0	0	0	0

JORDAN, LAMONT — RB/KR — JETS

PERSONAL: Born November 11, 1978, in Forestville, Md. ... 5-10/230.
HIGH SCHOOL: Suitland (Forestville, Md.).
COLLEGE: Maryland.
TRANSACTIONS/CAREER NOTES: Selected by New York Jets in second round (49th pick overall) of 2001 NFL draft. ... Signed by Jets (July 25, 2001).
HONORS: Named running back on THE SPORTING NEWS college All-America third team (1999).
SINGLE GAME HIGHS (regular season): Attempts—13 (November 24, 2002, vs. Buffalo); yards—107 (November 3, 2002, vs. San Diego); and rushing touchdowns—1 (November 9, 2003, vs. Oakland).
STATISTICAL PLATEAUS: 100-yard rushing games: 2002 (1). Total: 1.

Year Team	G	GS	RUSHING Att.	Yds.	Avg.	TD	RECEIVING No.	Yds.	Avg.	TD	KICKOFF RETURNS No.	Yds.	Avg.	TD	TOTALS TD	2pt.	Pts.	Fum.
2001—New York Jets NFL	16	0	39	292	7.5	1	7	44	6.3	1	3	62	20.7	0	2	0	12	0
2002—New York Jets NFL	14	0	84	316	3.8	3	17	160	9.4	0	5	112	22.4	0	3	0	18	4
2003—New York Jets NFL	16	0	46	190	4.1	4	11	101	9.2	0	11	209	19.0	0	4	0	24	0
Pro totals (3 years)	46	0	169	798	4.7	8	35	305	8.7	1	19	383	20.2	0	9	0	54	4

JORDAN, LEANDER — T/G — CHARGERS

PERSONAL: Born September 15, 1977, in Pittsburgh, Pa. ... 6-4/322. ... Full name: Leander James Jordan.
HIGH SCHOOL: Garfield (Pittsburgh), then Peabody (Pittsburgh), then Brashear (Pittsburgh).
COLLEGE: Indiana University (Pa.).

TRANSACTIONS/CAREER NOTES: Selected by Carolina Panthers in third round (82nd pick overall) of 2000 NFL draft. ... Signed by Panthers (June 8, 2000). ... Inactive for all 16 games (2000). ... Released by Panthers (September 1, 2002). ... Signed by Jacksonville Jaguars (October 15, 2002). ... Granted free agency (February 28, 2003). ... Re-signed by Jaguars (June 3, 2003). ... Granted unconditional free agency (March 3, 2004). ... Signed by San Diego Chargers (March 4, 2004).
PLAYING EXPERIENCE: Carolina NFL, 2001; Jacksonville NFL, 2003. ... Games/Games started: 2001 (13/5), 2003 (6/0). Total: 19/5.

JOSEPH, WILLIAM — DT — GIANTS

PERSONAL: Born September 3, 1979, in Miami, Fla. ... 6-5/315. ... Brother of Carlos Joseph, offensive tackle, San Diego Chargers.
HIGH SCHOOL: Edison (Miami).
COLLEGE: Miami (Fla.).
TRANSACTIONS/CAREER NOTES: Selected by New York Giants in first round (25th pick overall) of 2003 NFL draft. ... Signed by Giants (August 5, 2003).

			TOTALS		
Year Team	G	GS	Tk.	Ast.	Sks.
2003—New York Giants NFL	14	0	5	2	1.0

JOYCE, DELVIN — RB — GIANTS

PERSONAL: Born September 21, 1978, in Martinsville, Va. ... 5-7/195.
HIGH SCHOOL: Fieldale-Collinsville (Va.).
COLLEGE: James Madison.
TRANSACTIONS/CAREER NOTES: Signed as non-drafted free agent by New York Giants (January 15, 2002).
SINGLE GAME HIGHS (regular season): Attempts—4 (December 14, 2003, vs. Houston); yards—21 (December 14, 2003, vs. New Orleans); and rushing touchdowns—0.

			RUSHING				RECEIVING				PUNT RETURNS				KICKOFF RETURNS				TOTALS		
Year Team	G	GS	Att.	Yds.	Avg.	TD	No.	Yds.	Avg.	TD	No.	Yds.	Avg.	TD	No.	Yds.	Avg.	TD	TD	2pt.	Pts.
2002—NYG NFL	12	0	2	2	1.0	0	1	5	5.0	0	25	210	8.4	0	33	776	23.5	0	0	0	0
2003—NYG NFL	16	0	11	39	3.5	0	3	7	2.3	0	2	9	4.5	0	15	309	20.6	0	0	0	0
Pro totals (2 years)	28	0	13	41	3.2	0	4	12	3.0	0	27	219	8.1	0	48	1085	22.6	0	0	0	0

JOYCE, MATT — T — LIONS

PERSONAL: Born March 30, 1972, in St. Petersburg, Fla. ... 6-7/300.
HIGH SCHOOL: New York Military Academy (Cornwall Hudson, N.Y.).
COLLEGE: Richmond.
TRANSACTIONS/CAREER NOTES: Signed as non-drafted free agent by Dallas Cowboys (May 2, 1994). ... Claimed on waivers by Cincinnati Bengals (August 28, 1994); released after failing physical. ... Signed by Cowboys to practice squad (September 5, 1994). ... Granted free agency after 1994 season. ... Signed by Seattle Seahawks (March 1, 1995). ... Released by Seahawks (August 25, 1996). ... Signed by Arizona Cardinals (December 3, 1996). ... Assigned by Cardinals to Scottish Claymores in 1997 World League enhancement allocation program (February 19, 1997). ... Granted free agency (February 12, 1999). ... Re-signed by Cardinals (April 1, 1999). ... Granted unconditional free agency (February 11, 2000). ... Re-signed by Cardinals (February 21, 2000). ... Released by Cardinals (March 16, 2001). ... Signed by Detroit Lions (April 26, 2001). ... On physically unable to perform list with shoulder injury (July 24-August 12, 2001). ... Granted unconditional free agency (March 1, 2002). ... Re-signed by Lions (March 14, 2002).
PLAYING EXPERIENCE: Seattle NFL, 1995; Arizona NFL, 1996-2000; Detroit NFL, 2001-2003. ... Games/Games started: 1995 (16/13), 1996 (2/0), 1997 (9/6), 1998 (11/0), 1999 (15/15), 2000 (13/13), 2001 (16/12), 2002 (15/6), 2003 (13/3). Total: 110/68.

JUE, BHAWOH — CB/S — PACKERS

PERSONAL: Born May 24, 1979, in Monrovia, Liberia. ... 6-0/200. ... Full name: Bhawoh Papi Jue.
HIGH SCHOOL: Chantilly (Va.).
COLLEGE: Penn State.
TRANSACTIONS/CAREER NOTES: Selected by Green Bay Packers in third round (71st pick overall) of 2001 NFL draft. ... Signed by Packers (July 11, 2001). ... On injured reserve with hamstring injury (October 12, 2002-remainder of season). ... Granted free agency (March 3, 2004). ... Re-signed by Packers (April 23, 2004).

			TOTALS			INTERCEPTIONS			
Year Team	G	GS	Tk.	Ast.	Sks.	No.	Yds.	Avg.	TD
2001—Green Bay NFL	15	7	31	12	0.0	2	35	17.5	0
2002—Green Bay NFL	4	0	0	0	0.0	0	0	0.0	0
2003—Green Bay NFL	16	0	23	0	1.5	0	0	0.0	0
Pro totals (3 years)	35	7	54	12	1.5	2	35	17.5	0

JUNE, CATO — LB — COLTS

PERSONAL: Born November 18, 1979, in Riverside, Calif. ... 6-0/227.
HIGH SCHOOL: Anacostia (Washington, D.C.).
COLLEGE: Michigan.
TRANSACTIONS/CAREER NOTES: Selected by Indianapolis Colts in sixth round (198th pick overall) of 2003 NFL draft. ... Signed by Colts (July 24, 2003).
CHAMPIONSHIP GAME EXPERIENCE: Member of Colts for AFC championship game (2003 season); inactive.

Year Team	G	GS	TOTALS Tk.	Ast.	Sks.	INTERCEPTIONS No.	Yds.	Avg.	TD
2003—Indianapolis NFL	11	0	1	0	0.0	0	0	0.0	0

JUREVICIUS, JOE — WR — BUCCANEERS

PERSONAL: Born December 23, 1974, in Cleveland, Ohio. ... 6-5/230. ... Full name: Joe Michael Jurevicius. ... Name pronounced: jur-uh-VISH-us.
HIGH SCHOOL: Lake Catholic (Mentor, Ohio).
COLLEGE: Penn State.
TRANSACTIONS/CAREER NOTES: Selected by New York Giants in second round (55th pick overall) of 1998 NFL draft. ... Signed by Giants (July 28, 1998). ... Granted free agency (March 2, 2001). ... Re-signed by Giants for 2001 season. ... Granted unconditional free agency (March 1, 2002). ... Signed by Tampa Bay Buccaneers (April 9, 2002). ... On injured reserve with knee injury (December 2, 2003-remainder of season).
CHAMPIONSHIP GAME EXPERIENCE: Played in NFC championship game (2000 and 2002 seasons). ... Played in Super Bowl 35 (2000 season). ... Member of Super Bowl championship team (2002 season).
SINGLE GAME HIGHS (regular season): Receptions—8 (December 8, 2002, vs. Atlanta); yards—100 (December 8, 2002, vs. Atlanta); and touchdown receptions—2 (September 8, 2003, vs. Philadelphia).
STATISTICAL PLATEAUS: 100-yard receiving games: 2002 (1). Total: 1.

Year Team	G	GS	RECEIVING No.	Yds.	Avg.	TD	TOTALS TD	2pt.	Pts.	Fum.
1998—New York Giants NFL	14	1	9	146	16.2	0	0	0	0	0
1999—New York Giants NFL	16	1	18	318	17.7	1	1	0	6	1
2000—New York Giants NFL	14	3	24	272	11.3	1	1	0	6	1
2001—New York Giants NFL	14	9	51	706	13.8	3	3	0	18	0
2002—Tampa Bay NFL	15	3	37	423	11.4	4	4	0	24	1
2003—Tampa Bay NFL	5	2	12	118	9.8	2	2	0	12	0
Pro totals (6 years)	78	19	151	1983	13.1	11	11	0	66	3

K

KACYVENSKI, ISAIAH — LB — SEAHAWKS

PERSONAL: Born October 3, 1977, in Syracuse, N.Y. ... 6-1/252. ... Name pronounced: kaz-uh-VEN-skee.
HIGH SCHOOL: Union Endicott (N.Y.).
COLLEGE: Harvard.
TRANSACTIONS/CAREER NOTES: Selected by Seattle Seahawks in fourth round (119th pick overall) of 2000 NFL draft. ... Signed by Seahawks (June 9, 2000). ... On injured reserve with ankle injury (December 4, 2002-remainder of season). ... Granted free agency (February 28, 2003). ... Re-signed by Seahawks (March 28, 2003). ... Granted unconditional free agency (March 3, 2004). ... Re-signed by Seahawks (March 10, 2004).

Year Team	G	GS	TOTALS Tk.	Ast.	Sks.	INTERCEPTIONS No.	Yds.	Avg.	TD
2000—Seattle NFL	16	0	10	3	0.0	1	0	0.0	0
2001—Seattle NFL	16	0	9	2	0.0	1	22	22.0	0
2002—Seattle NFL	9	9	52	20	0.0	1	27	27.0	0
2003—Seattle NFL	14	0	2	4	0.0	0	0	0.0	0
Pro totals (4 years)	55	9	73	29	0.0	3	49	16.3	0

KAESVIHARN, KEVIN — S — BENGALS

PERSONAL: Born August 29, 1976, in Paramount, Calif. ... 6-1/194. ... Full name: Kevin Robert Kaesviharn.
HIGH SCHOOL: Lakeville (Minn.).
COLLEGE: Augustana (S.D.).
TRANSACTIONS/CAREER NOTES: Signed as non-drafted free agent by Green Bay Packers (April 25, 2001). ... Released by Packers (August 27, 2001). ... Signed by Cincinnati Bengals to practice squad (October 23, 2001). ... Activated (October 27, 2001). ... Released by Bengals (October 30, 2001). ... Re-signed by Bengals to practice squad (October 31, 2001). ... Activated (November 10, 2001). ... Granted free agency (March 3, 2004). ... Re-signed by Bengals (April 12, 2004).

Year Team	G	GS	TOTALS Tk.	Ast.	Sks.	INTERCEPTIONS No.	Yds.	Avg.	TD
2001—Cincinnati NFL	10	3	22	3	0.0	3	41	13.7	0
2002—Cincinnati NFL	16	6	43	7	0.0	2	17	8.5	0
2003—Cincinnati NFL	16	7	42	9	1.0	1	10	10.0	0
Pro totals (3 years)	42	16	107	19	1.0	6	68	11.3	0

KALU, N.D. — DE — EAGLES

PERSONAL: Born August 3, 1975, in Baltimore, Md. ... 6-3/265. ... Full name: Ndukwe Dike Kalu. ... Name pronounced: EN-doo-kway ka-LOO.
HIGH SCHOOL: John Marshall (San Antonio).
COLLEGE: Rice.
TRANSACTIONS/CAREER NOTES: Selected by Philadelphia Eagles in fifth round (152nd pick overall) of 1997 NFL draft. ... Signed by Eagles (July 15, 1997). ... Released by Eagles (August 25, 1998). ... Signed by Washington Redskins (August 30, 1998). ... Granted free agency (February 11, 2000). ... Re-signed by Redskins (May 18, 2000). ... Granted unconditional free agency (March 2, 2001). ... Signed by Eagles (March 12, 2001).
CHAMPIONSHIP GAME EXPERIENCE: Played in NFC championship game (2001-2003 seasons).

Year Team	G	GS	TOTALS Tk.	Ast.	Sks.	INTERCEPTIONS No.	Yds.	Avg.	TD
1997—Philadelphia NFL	3	0	0	1	0.0	0	0	0.0	0

Year Team	G	GS	TOTALS Tk.	Ast.	Sks.	INTERCEPTIONS No.	Yds.	Avg.	TD
1998—Washington NFL	13	1	7	7	3.0	0	0	0.0	0
1999—Washington NFL	12	0	11	3	3.5	0	0	0.0	0
2000—Washington NFL	15	0	4	3	1.0	0	0	0.0	0
2001—Philadelphia NFL	14	1	12	1	3.0	0	0	0.0	0
2002—Philadelphia NFL	16	0	18	5	8.0	0	0	0.0	0
2003—Philadelphia NFL	16	16	39	8	5.5	1	15	15.0	1
Pro totals (7 years)	89	18	91	28	24.0	1	15	15.0	1

KAMPMAN, AARON — DE/DT — PACKERS

PERSONAL: Born November 30, 1979, in Cedar Rapids, Iowa. ... 6-4/286.
HIGH SCHOOL: Aplington-Parkersburg (Parkersburg, Iowa).
COLLEGE: Iowa.
TRANSACTIONS/CAREER NOTES: Selected by Green Bay Packers in fifth round (156th pick overall) of 2002 NFL draft. ... Signed by Packers (July 25, 2002).

Year Team	G	GS	TOTALS Tk.	Ast.	Sks.	INTERCEPTIONS No.	Yds.	Avg.	TD
2002—Green Bay NFL	12	6	11	12	0.5	0	0	0.0	0
2003—Green Bay NFL	12	10	19	11	2.0	0	0	0.0	0
Pro totals (2 years)	24	16	30	23	2.5	0	0	0.0	0

K

KANELL, DANNY — QB — BRONCOS

PERSONAL: Born November 21, 1973, in Fort Lauderdale, Fla. ... 6-3/218. ... Name pronounced: KA-nell.
HIGH SCHOOL: Westminster Academy (Fort Lauderdale, Fla.).
COLLEGE: Florida State.
TRANSACTIONS/CAREER NOTES: Selected by New York Giants in fourth round (130th pick overall) of 1996 NFL draft. ... Signed by Giants (July 18, 1996). ... Released by Giants (February 19, 1999). ... Signed by Atlanta Falcons (March 19, 1999). ... On injured reserve with knee injury (December 22, 1999-remainder of season). ... Granted unconditional free agency (March 2, 2001). ... Signed by Denver Broncos (June 3, 2003). ... Waived by Broncos (September 1, 2003). ... Re-signed by Broncos (September 17, 2003).
SINGLE GAME HIGHS (regular season): Attempts—45 (September 21, 1998, vs. Dallas); completions—26 (November 5, 2000, vs. Tampa Bay); yards—259 (October 18, 1998, vs. Arizona); and touchdown passes—3 (October 18, 1998, vs. Arizona).
MISCELLANEOUS: Selected by Milwaukee Brewers organization in 19th round of free-agent baseball draft (June 1, 1992); did not sign. ... Selected by New York Yankees organization in 25th round of free-agent baseball draft (June 1, 1995); did not sign. ... Regular-season record as starting NFL quarterback: 10-13-1 (.438). ... Postseason record as starting NFL quarterback: 0-1.

Year Team	G	GS	PASSING Att.	Cmp.	Pct.	Yds.	TD	Int.	Avg.	Skd.	Rat.	RUSHING Att.	Yds.	Avg.	TD	TOTALS TD	2pt.	Pts.
1996—New York Giants NFL	4	0	60	23	38.3	227	1	1	3.78	7	48.4	7	6	0.9	0	0	0	0
1997—New York Giants NFL	16	10	294	156	53.1	1740	11	9	5.92	19	70.7	15	2	0.1	0	0	0	0
1998—New York Giants NFL	10	10	299	160	53.5	1603	11	10	5.36	22	67.3	15	36	2.4	0	0	0	0
1999—Atlanta NFL	3	1	84	42	50.0	593	4	4	7.06	5	69.2	0	0	0.0	0	0	0	0
2000—Atlanta NFL	5	1	116	57	49.1	524	2	5	4.52	8	49.6	1	0	0.0	0	0	0	0
2003—Denver NFL	5	2	103	53	51.5	442	2	5	4.29	2	49.1	6	5	0.8	0	0	0	0
Pro totals (6 years)	43	24	956	491	51.4	5129	31	34	5.37	63	63.2	44	49	1.1	0	0	0	0

KASAY, JOHN — K — PANTHERS

PERSONAL: Born October 27, 1969, in Athens, Ga. ... 5-10/198. ... Full name: John David Kasay. ... Name pronounced: CASEY.
HIGH SCHOOL: Clarke Central (Athens, Ga.).
COLLEGE: Georgia.
TRANSACTIONS/CAREER NOTES: Selected by Seattle Seahawks in fourth round (98th pick overall) of 1991 NFL draft. ... Signed by Seahawks (July 19, 1991). ... Granted free agency (February 17, 1994). ... Re-signed by Seahawks (July 19, 1994). ... Granted unconditional free agency (February 17, 1995). ... Signed by Carolina Panthers (February 20, 1995). ... On injured reserve with knee injury (December 14, 1999-remainder of season). ... On injured reserve with knee injury (August 14, 2000-entire season). ... On injured reserve with hernia (September 21, 2002-remainder of season).
CHAMPIONSHIP GAME EXPERIENCE: Played in NFC championship game (1996 and 2003 seasons). ... Played in Super Bowl 38 (2003 season).
HONORS: Played in Pro Bowl (1996 season).
POST SEASON RECORDS: Shares NFL postseason single-game record for most field goals made—5 (January 3, 2004, vs. Dallas).

Year Team	G	FIELD GOALS 1-29	30-39	40-49	50+	Tot.	Pct.	Lg.	TOTALS XPM	XPA	Pts.
1991—Seattle NFL	16	6-7	11-14	6-7	2-3	25-31	80.6	54	27	28	102
1992—Seattle NFL	16	4-5	8-11	2-6	0-0	14-22	63.6	43	14	14	56
1993—Seattle NFL	16	6-6	10-11	4-6	3-5	23-28	82.1	55	29	29	98
1994—Seattle NFL	16	2-2	11-11	6-9	1-2	20-24	83.3	50	25	26	85
1995—Carolina NFL	16	6-6	10-14	9-12	1-1	26-33	78.8	52	27	28	105
1996—Carolina NFL	16	16-16	11-12	7-10	3-7	*37-*45	82.2	53	34	35	*145
1997—Carolina NFL	16	7-8	8-8	4-4	3-6	22-26	84.6	54	25	25	91
1998—Carolina NFL	16	5-5	4-5	6-9	4-7	19-26	73.1	56	35	37	92
1999—Carolina NFL	13	9-9	6-6	5-6	2-4	22-25	88.0	52	33	33	99
2000—Carolina NFL					Did not play.						
2001—Carolina NFL	16	10-10	4-4	7-9	2-5	23-28	82.1	52	22	23	91
2002—Carolina NFL	2	2-2	0-0	0-2	0-1	2-5	40.0	27	5	5	11
2003—Carolina NFL	16	13-13	6-8	11-13	2-4	32-38	84.2	53	29	30	125
Pro totals (12 years)	175	86-89	89-104	67-93	23-45	265-331	80.1	56	305	313	1100

KASPER, KEVIN — WR — CARDINALS

PERSONAL: Born December 23, 1977, in Hinsdale, Ill. ... 6-1/197.
HIGH SCHOOL: Hinsdale South (Burr Ridge, Ill.).
COLLEGE: Iowa.
TRANSACTIONS/CAREER NOTES: Selected by Denver Broncos in sixth round (190th pick overall) of 2001 NFL draft. ... Signed by Broncos (May 17, 2001). ... Claimed on waivers by Seattle Seahawks (October 30, 2002). ... Claimed on waivers by Arizona Cardinals (November 23, 2002). ... Granted free agency (March 3, 2004). ... Re-signed by Cardinals (May 7, 2004).
SINGLE GAME HIGHS (regular season): Receptions—4 (December 29, 2002, vs. Denver); yards—54 (December 15, 2002, vs. St. Louis); and touchdown receptions—2 (December 21, 2002, vs. San Francisco).

			RUSHING				RECEIVING				KICKOFF RETURNS				TOTALS			
Year Team	G	GS	Att.	Yds.	Avg.	TD	No.	Yds.	Avg.	TD	No.	Yds.	Avg.	TD	TD	2pt.	Pts.	Fum.
2001—Denver NFL	10	5	3	19	6.3	0	8	84	10.5	0	14	372	26.6	0	0	0	0	0
2002—Denver NFL	4	0	0	0	0.0	0	0	0	0.0	0	15	393	26.2	0	0	0	0	1
—Arizona NFL	6	4	3	19	6.3	0	15	180	12.0	3	32	722	22.6	0	3	0	18	0
—Seattle NFL	3	0	0	0	0.0	0	0	0	0.0	0	8	185	23.1	0	0	0	0	0
2003—Arizona NFL	7	0	1	-4	-4.0	0	1	23	23.0	0	5	136	27.2	0	0	0	0	0
Pro totals (3 years)	30	9	7	34	4.9	0	24	287	12.0	3	74	1808	24.4	0	3	0	18	1

KASSELL, BRAD — LB — TITANS

PERSONAL: Born January 7, 1980, in Llano, Texas. ... 6-3/242.
HIGH SCHOOL: Llano (Texas).
COLLEGE: North Texas.
TRANSACTIONS/CAREER NOTES: Signed as non-drafted free agent by Tennessee Titans (April 22, 2002). ... Released by Titans (September 1, 2002). ... Re-signed by Titans to practice squad (September 3, 2002). ... Activated (November 1, 2002).
CHAMPIONSHIP GAME EXPERIENCE: Played in AFC championship game (2002 season).

			TOTALS			INTERCEPTIONS			
Year Team	G	GS	Tk.	Ast.	Sks.	No.	Yds.	Avg.	TD
2002—Tennessee NFL	9	0	0	0	0.0	0	0	0.0	0
2003—Tennessee NFL	16	4	23	4	0.0	0	0	0.0	0
Pro totals (2 years)	25	4	23	4	0.0	0	0	0.0	0

KEARSE, JEVON — DE — EAGLES

PERSONAL: Born September 3, 1976, in Fort Myers, Fla. ... 6-4/255. ... Name pronounced: juh-VAUGHN CURSE.
HIGH SCHOOL: North Fort Myers (Fla.).
COLLEGE: Florida.
TRANSACTIONS/CAREER NOTES: Selected after junior season by Tennessee Titans in first round (16th pick overall) of 1999 NFL draft. ... Signed by Titans (July 27, 1999). ... Granted unconditional free agency (March 3, 2004). ... Signed by Philadelphia Eagles (March 3, 2004).
CHAMPIONSHIP GAME EXPERIENCE: Played in AFC championship game (1999 and 2002 seasons). ... Played in Super Bowl 34 (1999 season).
HONORS: Named outside linebacker on THE SPORTING NEWS college All-America second team (1998). ... Named defensive end on THE SPORTING NEWS NFL All-Pro team (1999). ... Played in Pro Bowl (1999-2001 seasons).
RECORDS: Holds NFL rookie-season record for most sacks—14.5 (1999).

			TOTALS			INTERCEPTIONS			
Year Team	G	GS	Tk.	Ast.	Sks.	No.	Yds.	Avg.	TD
1999—Tennessee NFL	16	16	48	9	§14.5	0	0	0.0	0
2000—Tennessee NFL	16	16	37	16	11.5	0	0	0.0	0
2001—Tennessee NFL	16	16	25	11	10.0	0	0	0.0	0
2002—Tennessee NFL	4	1	3	1	2.0	0	0	0.0	0
2003—Tennessee NFL	14	14	29	13	9.5	1	0	0.0	0
Pro totals (5 years)	66	63	142	50	47.5	1	0	0.0	0

KEATHLEY, MICHAEL — G — BEARS

PERSONAL: Born March 9, 1978, in Arlington, Texas. ... 6-4/296.
HIGH SCHOOL: Glen Rose (Texas).
COLLEGE: Texas Christian.
TRANSACTIONS/CAREER NOTES: Signed as non-drafted free agent by San Diego Chargers (April 27, 2001). ... Claimed on waivers by Houston Texans (August 27, 2003). ... Released by Texans (October 14, 2003). ... Signed by Chargers (October 21, 2003). ... Released by Chargers (March 2, 2004). ... Signed by Chicago Bears (March 25, 2004).
PLAYING EXPERIENCE: San Diego NFL, 2001-2003. ... Games/Games started: 2001 (16/0), 2002 (12/2), 2003 (8/2). Total: 36/4.

KEITH, JOHN — S

PERSONAL: Born February 4, 1977, in Newnan, Ga. ... 6-0/207. ... Full name: John Martin Keith.
HIGH SCHOOL: East Coweta (Ga.).
COLLEGE: Furman.
TRANSACTIONS/CAREER NOTES: Selected by San Francisco 49ers in fourth round (108th pick overall) of 2000 NFL draft. ... Signed by 49ers (July 16, 2000). ... On injured reserve with broken arm (October 10, 2000-remainder of season). ... On injured reserve with knee injury (September 12, 2001-remainder of season). ... On physically unable to perform list with knee injury (July 22-23, 2002). ... Released by 49ers (August 27, 2002). ... Re-signed by 49ers to practice squad (September 2, 2002). ... Activated (November 6, 2002). ... Granted free agency

(February 28, 2003). ... Re-signed by 49ers (March 28, 2003). ... Waived by 49ers (August 31, 2003). ... Re-signed by 49ers to practice squad (September 1, 2003). ... Activated (October 28, 2003). ... Granted unconditional free agency (March 3, 2004).

			TOTALS			INTERCEPTIONS			
Year Team	G	GS	Tk.	Ast.	Sks.	No.	Yds.	Avg.	TD
2000—San Francisco NFL	6	3	13	5	1.0	1	0	0.0	0
2001—San Francisco NFL	1	0	0	0	0.0	0	0	0.0	0
2002—San Francisco NFL	8	3	11	5	0.0	0	0	0.0	0
2003—San Francisco NFL	8	2	9	4	0.0	0	0	0.0	0
Pro totals (4 years)	23	8	33	14	1.0	1	0	0.0	0

KELLY, BRIAN — CB — BUCCANEERS

PERSONAL: Born January 14, 1976, in Las Vegas, Nev. ... 5-11/193.
HIGH SCHOOL: Overland (Aurora, Colo.).
COLLEGE: Southern California.
TRANSACTIONS/CAREER NOTES: Selected by Tampa Bay Buccaneers in second round (45th pick overall) of 1998 NFL draft. ... Signed by Buccaneers (July 19, 1998). ... Granted free agency (March 2, 2001). ... Re-signed by Buccaneers (March 18, 2001). ... Granted unconditional free agency (March 1, 2002). ... Re-signed by Buccaneers (March 19, 2002). ... On injured reserve with pectoral injury (October 21, 2003-remainder of season).
CHAMPIONSHIP GAME EXPERIENCE: Played in NFC championship game (1999 and 2002 seasons). ... Member of Super Bowl championship team (2002 season).

			TOTALS			INTERCEPTIONS			
Year Team	G	GS	Tk.	Ast.	Sks.	No.	Yds.	Avg.	TD
1998—Tampa Bay NFL	16	3	25	2	0.0	1	4	4.0	0
1999—Tampa Bay NFL	16	3	29	5	0.0	1	26	26.0	0
2000—Tampa Bay NFL	16	3	44	4	0.0	1	9	9.0	1
2001—Tampa Bay NFL	16	11	40	10	1.5	0	0	0.0	0
2002—Tampa Bay NFL	16	16	58	8	1.0	†8	68	8.5	0
2003—Tampa Bay NFL	5	5	13	2	0.0	1	0	0.0	0
Pro totals (6 years)	85	41	209	31	2.5	12	107	8.9	1

K

KELLY, ERIC — CB — VIKINGS

PERSONAL: Born January 15, 1977, in Milwaukee, Wis. ... 5-10/201.
HIGH SCHOOL: Bay (Panama, Fla.).
COLLEGE: Kentucky.
TRANSACTIONS/CAREER NOTES: Selected by Minnesota Vikings in third round (64th pick overall) of 2001 NFL draft. ... Signed by Vikings (July 26, 2001). ... Granted free agency (March 3, 2004). ... Re-signed by Vikings (April 13, 2004).

			TOTALS			INTERCEPTIONS			
Year Team	G	GS	Tk.	Ast.	Sks.	No.	Yds.	Avg.	TD
2001—Minnesota NFL	16	11	59	15	0.0	2	-7	-3.5	0
2002—Minnesota NFL	16	12	59	5	0.0	1	0	0.0	0
2003—Minnesota NFL	16	0	5	0	0.0	0	40	0.0	0
Pro totals (3 years)	48	23	123	20	0.0	3	33	11.0	0

KELLY, LEWIS — G — VIKINGS

PERSONAL: Born April 21, 1977, in Lithonia, Ga. ... 6-4/306.
HIGH SCHOOL: Henderson (Lithonia, Ga.).
COLLEGE: South Carolina State.
TRANSACTIONS/CAREER NOTES: Selected by Minnesota Vikings in seventh round (248th pick overall) of 2000 NFL draft. ... Signed by Vikings (April 27, 2000). ... On injured reserve with knee injury (August 22, 2000-entire season). ... On injured reserve with abdominal injury (December 16, 2002-remainder of season).
PLAYING EXPERIENCE: Minnesota NFL, 2001-2003. ... Games/Games started: 2001 (4/0), 2002 (7/5), 2003 (6/0). Total: 17/5.

KELLY, REGGIE — TE — BENGALS

PERSONAL: Born February 22, 1977, in Aberdeen, Miss. ... 6-4/255. ... Full name: Reginald Kuta Kelly.
HIGH SCHOOL: Aberdeen (Miss.).
COLLEGE: Mississippi State.
TRANSACTIONS/CAREER NOTES: Selected by Atlanta Falcons in second round (42nd pick overall) of 1999 NFL draft. ... Signed by Falcons (June 25, 1999). ... Granted unconditional free agency (February 28, 2003). ... Signed by Cincinnati Bengals (March 13, 2003).
SINGLE GAME HIGHS (regular season): Receptions—4 (December 24, 2000, vs. Kansas City); yards—83 (September 24, 2000, vs. St. Louis); and touchdown receptions—1 (September 28, 2003, vs. Cleveland).

			RECEIVING				TOTALS			
Year Team	G	GS	No.	Yds.	Avg.	TD	TD	2pt.	Pts.	Fum.
1999—Atlanta NFL	16	2	8	146	18.3	0	0	0	0	0
2000—Atlanta NFL	16	16	31	340	11.0	2	2	0	12	1
2001—Atlanta NFL	14	13	16	142	8.9	0	0	0	0	0
2002—Atlanta NFL	16	16	14	162	11.6	0	0	0	0	0
2003—Cincinnati NFL	12	11	13	81	6.2	1	1	0	6	0
Pro totals (5 years)	74	58	82	871	10.6	3	3	0	18	1

KELSAY, CHRIS — DE — BILLS

PERSONAL: Born October 31, 1979, in Auburn, Neb. ... 6-4/275.
HIGH SCHOOL: Auburn (Neb.).
COLLEGE: Nebraska.
TRANSACTIONS/CAREER NOTES: Selected by Buffalo Bills in second round (48th pick overall) of 2003 NFL draft. ... Signed by Bills (July 23, 2003).

			TOTALS		
Year Team	**G**	**GS**	**Tk.**	**Ast.**	**Sks.**
2003—Buffalo NFL	16	0	12	7	0.0

KEMOEATU, MAAKE — DT — RAVENS

PERSONAL: Born January 10, 1979, in Tonga. ... 6-5/335. ... Full name: Maake Tu'Amelie Kemoeatu.
HIGH SCHOOL: Kahuku (Hawaii).
COLLEGE: Utah.
TRANSACTIONS/CAREER NOTES: Signed as non-drafted free agent by Baltimore Ravens (April 26, 2002).

			TOTALS		
Year Team	**G**	**GS**	**Tk.**	**Ast.**	**Sks.**
2002—Baltimore NFL	16	1	11	4	2.0
2003—Baltimore NFL	15	1	8	2	1.0
Pro totals (2 years)	31	2	19	6	3.0

K

KENDALL, PETE — C — CARDINALS

PERSONAL: Born July 9, 1973, in Quincy, Mass. ... 6-5/279. ... Full name: Peter Marcus Kendall.
HIGH SCHOOL: Archbishop Williams (Weymouth, Mass.).
COLLEGE: Boston College.
TRANSACTIONS/CAREER NOTES: Selected by Seattle Seahawks in first round (21st pick overall) of 1996 NFL draft. ... Signed by Seahawks (July 21, 1996). ... Granted unconditional free agency (March 2, 2001). ... Signed by Arizona Cardinals (March 12, 2001). ... On injured reserve with foot injury (December 26, 2001-remainder of season). ... On injured reserve with ankle injury (December 27, 2002-remainder of season).
PLAYING EXPERIENCE: Seattle NFL, 1996-2000; Arizona NFL, 2001-2003. ... Games/Games started: 1996 (12/11), 1997 (16/16), 1998 (16/16), 1999 (16/16), 2000 (16/16), 2001 (11/11), 2002 (12/12), 2003 (13/13). Total: 112/111.

KENNEDY, JIMMY — DT — RAMS

PERSONAL: Born November 15, 1979, in Yonkers, N.Y. ... 6-4/320. ... Full name: Jimmy Wayne Kennedy.
HIGH SCHOOL: Roosevelt (Yonkers, N.Y.).
COLLEGE: Penn State.
TRANSACTIONS/CAREER NOTES: Selected by St. Louis Rams in first round (12th pick overall) of 2003 NFL draft. ... Signed by Rams (July 28, 2003).

			TOTALS		
Year Team	**G**	**GS**	**Tk.**	**Ast.**	**Sks.**
2003—St. Louis NFL	13	0	1	1	0.0

KENNEDY, KENOY — S — BRONCOS

PERSONAL: Born November 15, 1977, in Dallas, Texas. ... 6-1/215. ... Full name: Kenoy Wayne Kennedy.
HIGH SCHOOL: Terrell (Texas).
COLLEGE: Arkansas.
TRANSACTIONS/CAREER NOTES: Selected by Denver Broncos in second round (45th pick overall) of 2000 NFL draft. ... Signed by Broncos (June 1, 2000).

			TOTALS			INTERCEPTIONS			
Year Team	**G**	**GS**	**Tk.**	**Ast.**	**Sks.**	**No.**	**Yds.**	**Avg.**	**TD**
2000—Denver NFL	13	0	5	2	0.0	1	0	0.0	0
2001—Denver NFL	16	16	50	19	2.0	1	6	6.0	0
2002—Denver NFL	15	15	53	14	0.0	0	0	0.0	0
2003—Denver NFL	13	12	41	14	1.0	1	0	0.0	0
Pro totals (4 years)	57	43	149	49	3.0	3	6	2.0	0

KENNEDY, LINCOLN — T

PERSONAL: Born February 12, 1971, in York, Pa. ... 6-6/335. ... Full name: Tamerlane Lincoln Kennedy.
HIGH SCHOOL: Samuel F.B. Morse (San Diego).
COLLEGE: Washington.
TRANSACTIONS/CAREER NOTES: Selected by Atlanta Falcons in first round (ninth pick overall) of 1993 NFL draft. ... Signed by Falcons (August 2, 1993). ... Granted free agency (February 16, 1996). ... Re-signed by Falcons (May 13, 1996). ... Traded by Falcons to Oakland Raiders for fifth-round pick (traded to Washington) in 1997 draft (May 13, 1996).
PLAYING EXPERIENCE: Atlanta NFL, 1993-1995; Oakland NFL, 1996-2003. ... Games/Games started: 1993 (16/16), 1994 (16/2), 1995 (16/4), 1996 (16/16), 1997 (16/16), 1998 (16/16), 1999 (15/15), 2000 (16/16), 2001 (15/15), 2002 (15/15), 2003 (12/10). Total: 169/141.

CHAMPIONSHIP GAME EXPERIENCE: Played in AFC championship game (2000 and 2002 seasons). ... Played in Super Bowl 37 (2002 season).
HONORS: Named offensive tackle on THE SPORTING NEWS college All-America first team (1992). ... Played in Pro Bowl (2000-2002 seasons).

KENNISON, EDDIE — WR — CHIEFS

PERSONAL: Born January 20, 1973, in Lake Charles, La. ... 6-1/201. ... Full name: Eddie Joseph Kennison III.
HIGH SCHOOL: Washington-Marion (Lake Charles, La.).
COLLEGE: Louisiana State.
TRANSACTIONS/CAREER NOTES: Selected after junior season by St. Louis Rams in first round (18th pick overall) of 1996 NFL draft. ... Signed by Rams (July 27, 1996). ... Traded by Rams to New Orleans Saints for second-round pick (DB Dre' Bly) in 1999 draft (February 18, 1999). ... Traded by Saints to Chicago Bears for fifth-round pick (traded to Indianapolis) in 2000 draft (February 21, 2000). ... Granted unconditional free agency (March 2, 2001). ... Signed by Denver Broncos (April 5, 2001). ... Released by Broncos (November 14, 2001). ... Signed by Kansas City Chiefs (December 3, 2001).
SINGLE GAME HIGHS (regular season): Receptions—8 (November 10, 2002, vs. San Francisco); yards—226 (December 15, 1996, vs. Atlanta); and touchdown receptions—3 (December 15, 1996, vs. Atlanta).
STATISTICAL PLATEAUS: 100-yard receiving games: 1996 (2), 1999 (1), 2000 (1), 2001 (1), 2002 (2), 2003 (1). Total: 8.

			RUSHING				RECEIVING				PUNT RETURNS				KICKOFF RETURNS				TOTALS		
Year Team	G	GS	Att.	Yds.	Avg.	TD	No.	Yds.	Avg.	TD	No.	Yds.	Avg.	TD	No.	Yds.	Avg.	TD	TD	2pt.	Pts.
1996—StL. NFL	15	14	0	0	0.0	0	54	924	17.1	9	29	423	14.6	2	23	454	19.7	0	11	0	66
1997—StL. NFL	14	9	3	13	4.3	0	25	404	16.2	0	34	247	7.3	0	1	14	14.0	0	0	0	0
1998—StL. NFL	16	13	2	9	4.5	0	17	234	13.8	1	40	415	10.4	1	0	0	0.0	0	2	0	12
1999—N.O. NFL	16	16	3	20	6.7	0	61	835	13.7	4	35	258	7.4	0	0	0	0.0	0	4	1	26
2000—Chi. NFL	16	10	3	72	24.0	0	55	549	10.0	2	0	0	0.0	0	0	0	0.0	0	2	0	12
2001—Den. NFL	8	6	3	9	3.0	0	15	169	11.3	1	0	0	0.0	0	0	0	0.0	0	1	0	6
—K.C. NFL	5	1	2	13	6.5	0	16	322	20.1	0	0	0	0.0	0	0	0	0.0	0	0	1	2
2002—K.C. NFL	16	14	7	58	8.3	0	53	906	17.1	2	0	0	0.0	0	0	0	0.0	0	2	0	12
2003—K.C. NFL	16	16	2	9	4.5	0	56	853	15.2	5	3	70	23.3	0	0	0	0.0	0	5	0	30
Pro totals (8 years)	122	99	25	203	8.1	0	352	5196	14.8	24	141	1413	10.0	3	24	468	19.5	0	27	2	166

KENT, RASHOD — TE

PERSONAL: Born June 7, 1980, in Fairmont, W.Va. ... 6-6/275.
HIGH SCHOOL: Fairmont (W.Va.).
COLLEGE: Rutgers.
TRANSACTIONS/CAREER NOTES: Signed as non-drafted free agent by Houston Texans (April 28, 2002). ... Waived by Texans (September 1, 2002). ... Re-signed by Texans to practice squad (September 3, 2002). ... Waived by Texans (September 10, 2002). ... Re-signed by Texans (October 4, 2002). ... On injured reserve with calf injury (October 7, 2002-remainder of season). ... Assigned by Texans to Scottish Claymores in 2003 NFL Europe enhancement allocation program (January 29, 2003). ... Released by Texans (November 9, 2003). ... Re-signed by Texans to practice squad (November 11, 2003). ... Activated (December 8, 2003). ... Released by Texans (April 27, 2004).

			RECEIVING				TOTALS			
Year Team	G	GS	No.	Yds.	Avg.	TD	TD	2pt.	Pts.	Fum.
2003—Houston NFL	7	4	0	0	0.0	0	0	0	0	0

KERNEY, PATRICK — DE — FALCONS

PERSONAL: Born December 30, 1976, in Trenton, N.J. ... 6-5/273. ... Full name: Patrick Manning Kerney.
HIGH SCHOOL: Taft Prep (Watertown, Conn.).
COLLEGE: Virginia.
TRANSACTIONS/CAREER NOTES: Selected by Atlanta Falcons in first round (30th pick overall) of 1999 NFL draft. ... Signed by Falcons (June 25, 1999).
HONORS: Named defensive end on THE SPORTING NEWS college All-America second team (1998).

			TOTALS			INTERCEPTIONS			
Year Team	G	GS	Tk.	Ast.	Sks.	No.	Yds.	Avg.	TD
1999—Atlanta NFL	16	2	19	6	2.5	0	0	0.0	0
2000—Atlanta NFL	16	16	30	15	2.5	1	8	8.0	0
2001—Atlanta NFL	16	16	39	10	12.0	0	0	0.0	0
2002—Atlanta NFL	16	16	45	13	10.5	0	0	0.0	0
2003—Atlanta NFL	16	16	34	12	6.5	0	0	0.0	0
Pro totals (5 years)	80	66	167	56	34.0	1	8	8.0	0

KIEL, TERRENCE — S — CHARGERS

PERSONAL: Born November 24, 1980, in Lufkin, Texas. ... 5-11/207. ... Full name: Terrence Dewayne Kiel.
HIGH SCHOOL: Lufkin (Texas).
COLLEGE: Texas A&M.
TRANSACTIONS/CAREER NOTES: Selected by San Diego Chargers in second round (62nd pick overall) of 2003 NFL draft. ... Signed by Chargers (July 25, 2003).

			TOTALS			INTERCEPTIONS			
Year Team	G	GS	Tk.	Ast.	Sks.	No.	Yds.	Avg.	TD
2003—San Diego NFL	16	7	52	7	0.0	2	15	7.5	0

KINCHEN, BRIAN TE/LS

PERSONAL: Born August 6, 1965, in Baton Rouge, La. ... 6-2/240. ... Full name: Brian Douglas Kinchen. ... Brother of Todd Kinchen, wide receiver/kick returner with four NFL teams (1992-98).

HIGH SCHOOL: University (Baton Rouge, La.).

COLLEGE: Louisiana State.

TRANSACTIONS/CAREER NOTES: Selected by Miami Dolphins in 12th round (320th pick overall) of 1988 NFL draft. ... Signed by Dolphins (June 6, 1988). ... On injured reserve with hamstring injury (October 4, 1990-remainder of season). ... Granted unconditional free agency (February 1, 1991). ... Signed by Green Bay Packers (April 1, 1991). ... Released by Packers (August 26, 1991). ... Signed by Cleveland Browns (September 13, 1991). ... Granted unconditional free agency (February 1-April 1, 1992). ... Re-signed by Browns for 1992 season. ... Granted unconditional free agency (February 17, 1994). ... Re-signed by Browns (March 4, 1994). ... Granted unconditional free agency (February 16, 1996). ... Browns franchise moved to Baltimore and renamed Ravens for 1996 season (March 11, 1996). ... Re-signed by Ravens (April 3, 1996). ... Granted unconditional free agency (February 12, 1999). ... Signed by Carolina Panthers (March 8, 1999). ... Released by Panthers (March 5, 2001). ... Signed by New England Patriots (December 17, 2003). ... Granted unconditional free agency (March 3, 2004).

PLAYING EXPERIENCE: Miami NFL, 1988-1990; Cleveland NFL, 1991-1995; Baltimore NFL, 1996-1998; Carolina NFL, 1999-2000; New England NFL, 2003. ... Games/Games started: 1988 (16/0), 1989 (16/0), 1990 (4/0), 1991 (14/0), 1992 (16/0), 1993 (16/15), 1994 (16/11), 1995 (13/12), 1996 (16/16), 1997 (16/7), 1998 (16/5), 1999 (16/0), 2000 (16/0), 2003 (2/0). Total: 193/66.

CHAMPIONSHIP GAME EXPERIENCE: Played in AFC championship game (2003 season). ... Member of Super Bowl championship team (2003 season).

SINGLE GAME HIGHS (regular season): Receptions—9 (November 24, 1996, vs. Jacksonville); yards—87 (December 15, 1996, vs. Carolina); and touchdown receptions—1 (December 12, 1999, vs. Green Bay).

K

KING, ANDRE WR BROWNS

PERSONAL: Born November 26, 1973, in Kingston, Jamaica. ... 5-11/195.

HIGH SCHOOL: Stranahan (Fla.).

COLLEGE: Miami (Fla.).

TRANSACTIONS/CAREER NOTES: Selected by Cleveland Browns in seventh round (245th pick overall) of 2001 NFL draft. ... Signed by Browns (July 18, 2001). ... Granted free agency (March 3, 2004). ... Re-signed by Browns (April 15, 2004).

SINGLE GAME HIGHS (regular season): Receptions—4 (December 16, 2001, vs. Jacksonville); yards—61 (December 30, 2001, vs. Tennessee); and touchdown receptions—0.

			RECEIVING				KICKOFF RETURNS				TOTALS			
Year Team	G	GS	No.	Yds.	Avg.	TD	No.	Yds.	Avg.	TD	TD	2pt.	Pts.	Fum.
2001—Cleveland NFL	7	0	11	149	13.5	0	14	279	19.9	0	0	0	0	1
2002—Cleveland NFL	11	1	5	41	8.2	0	8	155	19.4	0	0	0	0	0
2003—Cleveland NFL	15	0	9	88	9.8	0	9	172	19.1	0	1	0	6	0
Pro totals (3 years)	33	1	25	278	11.1	0	31	606	19.5	0	1	0	6	1

KING, ANDY G RAMS

PERSONAL: Born November 9, 1978, in Lincoln, Ill. ... 6-4/310. ... Full name: Andrew Joel King.

HIGH SCHOOL: Lincoln (Ill.).

COLLEGE: Illinois State.

TRANSACTIONS/CAREER NOTES: Signed as non-drafted free agent by St. Louis Rams (April 22, 2002). ... Released by Rams (September 1, 2002). ... Re-signed by Rams to practice squad (September 3, 2002). ... Activated (October 14, 2002). ... Released by Rams (November 19, 2002). ... Re-signed by Rams to practice squad (November 20, 2002). ... Activated (November 26, 2002). ... Released by Rams (October 27, 2003). ... Re-signed by Rams to practice squad (October 28, 2003). ... Activated (December 11, 2003).

PLAYING EXPERIENCE: St. Louis NFL, 2002-2003. ... Games/Games started: 2002 (5/0), 2003 (1/0). Total: 6/0.

KING, KENNY DE CARDINALS

PERSONAL: Born April 23, 1981, in Daphne, Ala. ... 6-3/285.

HIGH SCHOOL: Daphne (Ala.).

COLLEGE: Alabama.

TRANSACTIONS/CAREER NOTES: Selected by Arizona Cardinals in fifth round (141st pick overall) of 2003 NFL draft. ... Signed by Cardinals (June 9, 2003).

			TOTALS		
Year Team	G	GS	Tk.	Ast.	Sks.
2003—Arizona NFL	11	1	13	4	2.0

KING, LAMAR DE BUCCANEERS

PERSONAL: Born August 10, 1975, in Boston, Mass. ... 6-3/305.

HIGH SCHOOL: Chesapeake (Md.).

JUNIOR COLLEGE: Montgomery College (Md.).

COLLEGE: Saginaw Valley State (Mich.).

TRANSACTIONS/CAREER NOTES: Selected by Seattle Seahawks in first round (22nd pick overall) of 1999 NFL draft. ... Signed by Seahawks (August 12, 1999). ... On injured reserve with calf injury (January 4, 2001-remainder of season). ... On injured reserve with knee injury (December 13, 2002-remainder of season). ... On physically unable to perform list with knee injury (August 31-October 31, 2003). ... Granted unconditional free agency (March 3, 2004). ... Signed by Tampa Bay Buccaneers (May 13, 2004).

			TOTALS		
Year Team	G	GS	Tk.	Ast.	Sks.
1999—Seattle NFL	14	0	9	3	2.0

Year Team	G	GS	TOTALS Tk.	Ast.	Sks.
2000—Seattle NFL	14	14	42	6	6.0
2001—Seattle NFL	8	8	14	9	0.0
2002—Seattle NFL	12	12	17	9	1.0
2003—Seattle NFL	9	3	12	4	3.0
Pro totals (5 years)	57	37	94	31	12.0

KING, SHAUN QB CARDINALS

PERSONAL: Born May 29, 1977, in St. Petersburg, Fla. ... 6-1/215. ... Full name: Shaun Earl King.
HIGH SCHOOL: Gibbs (St. Petersburg, Fla.).
COLLEGE: Tulane.
TRANSACTIONS/CAREER NOTES: Selected by Tampa Bay Buccaneers in second round (50th pick overall) of 1999 NFL draft. ... Signed by Buccaneers (August 1, 1999). ... Granted unconditional free agency (February 28, 2003). ... Re-signed by Buccaneers (April 4, 2003). ... Granted unconditional free agency (March 3, 2004). ... Signed by Arizona Cardinals (March 6, 2004).
CHAMPIONSHIP GAME EXPERIENCE: Played in NFC championship game (1999 season). ... Member of Buccaneers for NFC championship game (2002 season); inactive. ... Member of Super Bowl championship team (2002 season); inactive.
SINGLE GAME HIGHS (regular season): Attempts—42 (December 24, 2000, vs. Green Bay); completions—26 (October 9, 2000, vs. Minnesota); passing yards—297 (December 12, 1999, vs. Detroit); and touchdown passes—4 (October 29, 2000, vs. Minnesota).
MISCELLANEOUS: Regular-season record as starting NFL quarterback: 14-8 (.636). ... Postseason record as starting NFL quarterback: 1-2 (.333).

			PASSING									RUSHING				TOTALS		
Year Team	G	GS	Att.	Cmp.	Pct.	Yds.	TD	Int.	Avg.	Skd.	Rat.	Att.	Yds.	Avg.	TD	TD	2pt.	Pts.
1999—Tampa Bay NFL	6	5	146	89	61.0	875	7	4	5.99	11	82.4	18	38	2.1	0	0	0	0
2000—Tampa Bay NFL	16	16	428	233	54.4	2769	18	13	6.47	37	75.8	73	353	4.8	5	5	1	32
2001—Tampa Bay NFL	3	0	31	21	67.7	210	0	1	6.77	3	73.3	5	-12	-2.4	0	0	1	2
2002—Tampa Bay NFL	3	1	27	10	37.0	80	0	1	2.96	1	30.0	4	25	6.3	0	0	0	0
2003—Tampa Bay NFL	3	0	22	15	68.2	130	1	1	5.91	3	79.7	4	20	5.0	0	0	0	0
Pro totals (5 years)	31	22	654	368	56.3	4064	26	20	6.21	55	75.4	104	424	4.1	5	5	2	34

KINGSBURY, KLIFF QB PATRIOTS

PERSONAL: Born August 9, 1979, in San Antonio. ... 6-4/231.
HIGH SCHOOL: New Braunfels (Texas).
COLLEGE: Texas Tech.
TRANSACTIONS/CAREER NOTES: Selected by New England Patriots in sixth round (201st pick overall) of 2003 NFL draft. ... Signed by Patriots (July 21, 2003). ... On injured reserve with arm injury (August 26, 2003-entire season).

			PASSING									RUSHING				TOTALS		
Year Team	G	GS	Att.	Cmp.	Pct.	Yds.	TD	Int.	Avg.	Skd.	Rat.	Att.	Yds.	Avg.	TD	TD	2pt.	Pts.
2003—New England NFL	Did not play.																	

KINNEY, ERRON TE TITANS

PERSONAL: Born July 28, 1977, in Richmond, Va. ... 6-5/275. ... Full name: Erron Quincy Kinney.
HIGH SCHOOL: Patrick Henry (Ashland, Va.).
COLLEGE: Florida.
TRANSACTIONS/CAREER NOTES: Selected by Tennessee Titans in third round (68th pick overall) of 2000 NFL draft. ... Signed by Titans (July 17, 2000). ... Granted free agency (February 28, 2003). ... Re-signed by Titans (May 12, 2003).
CHAMPIONSHIP GAME EXPERIENCE: Played in AFC championship game (2002 season).
SINGLE GAME HIGHS (regular season): Receptions—7 (October 7, 2001, vs. Baltimore); yards—75 (October 7, 2001, vs. Baltimore); and touchdown receptions—1 (December 21, 2003, vs. Houston).

			RECEIVING				KICKOFF RETURNS				TOTALS			
Year Team	G	GS	No.	Yds.	Avg.	TD	No.	Yds.	Avg.	TD	TD	2pt.	Pts.	Fum.
2000—Tennessee NFL	16	10	19	197	10.4	1	0	0	0.0	0	1	0	6	1
2001—Tennessee NFL	13	12	25	263	10.5	1	1	14	14.0	0	1	0	6	0
2002—Tennessee NFL	15	7	13	173	13.3	0	3	41	13.7	0	0	0	0	0
2003—Tennessee NFL	16	16	41	381	9.3	3	3	37	12.3	0	4	0	24	1
Pro totals (4 years)	60	45	98	1014	10.3	5	7	92	13.1	0	6	0	36	2

KIRCUS, DAVID WR LIONS

PERSONAL: Born February 19, 1980, in Imlay City, Mich. ... 6-1/185.
HIGH SCHOOL: Imlay City (Mich.).
COLLEGE: Grand Valley State.
TRANSACTIONS/CAREER NOTES: Selected by Detroit Lions in sixth round (175th pick overall) of 2003 NFL draft. ... Signed by Lions (July 17, 2003). ... Released by Lions (August 31, 2003). ... Re-signed by Lions to practice squad (September 1, 2003). ... Activated (November 18, 2003).
SINGLE GAME HIGHS (regular season): Receptions—1 (December 28, 2003, vs. St. Louis); yards—19 (December 28, 2003, vs. St. Louis); and touchdown receptions—0.

			RECEIVING				PUNT RETURNS				KICKOFF RETURNS				TOTALS			
Year Team	G	GS	No.	Yds.	Avg.	TD	No.	Yds.	Avg.	TD	No.	Yds.	Avg.	TD	TD	2pt.	Pts.	Fum.
2003—Detroit NFL	5	2	3	53	17.7	0	0	0	0.0	0	0	0	0.0	0	0	0	0	0

KIRSCHKE, TRAVIS DT STEELERS

PERSONAL: Born September 6, 1974, in Fullerton, Calif. ... 6-3/292.
HIGH SCHOOL: Esperanza (Anaheim, Calif.).
COLLEGE: UCLA.
TRANSACTIONS/CAREER NOTES: Signed as non-drafted free agent by Detroit Lions (April 24, 1997). ... Inactive for three games (1998). ... On injured reserve with abdominal injury (September 24, 1998-remainder of season). ... Granted free agency (February 11, 2000). ... Re-signed by Lions (April 25, 2000). ... Granted unconditional free agency (March 1, 2002). ... Re-signed by Lions (April 2, 2002). ... Granted unconditional free agency (February 28, 2003). ... Signed by San Francisco 49ers (April 8, 2003). ... Granted unconditional free agency (March 3, 2004). ... Signed by Pittsburgh Steelers (March 11, 2004).

			TOTALS		
Year Team	G	GS	Tk.	Ast.	Sks.
1997—Detroit NFL	3	0	0	1	0.0
1999—Detroit NFL	15	7	12	8	2.0
2000—Detroit NFL	13	0	4	8	0.5
2001—Detroit NFL	16	2	11	8	0.0
2002—Detroit NFL	15	1	14	5	0.0
2003—San Francisco NFL	15	15	33	10	1.5
Pro totals (6 years)	77	25	74	40	4.0

KITNA, JON QB BENGALS

PERSONAL: Born September 21, 1972, in Tacoma, Wash. ... 6-2/220.
HIGH SCHOOL: Lincoln (Tacoma, Wash.).
COLLEGE: Central Washington.
TRANSACTIONS/CAREER NOTES: Signed as non-drafted free agent by Seattle Seahawks (April 25, 1996) ... Released by Seahawks (August 19, 1996) ... Re-signed by Seahawks to practice squad (August 20, 1996). ... Assigned by Seahawks to Barcelona Dragons in 1997 World League enhancement allocation program (April 7, 1997). ... Granted free agency (February 11, 2000). ... Re-signed by Seahawks (March 15, 2000). ... Granted unconditional free agency (March 2, 2001). ... Signed by Cincinnati Bengals (March 8, 2001).
SINGLE GAME HIGHS (regular season): Attempts—68 (December 30, 2001, vs. Pittsburgh); completions—35 (December 30, 2001, vs. Pittsburgh); yards—411 (December 30, 2001, vs. Pittsburgh); and touchdown passes—4 (November 23, 2003, vs. San Diego).
STATISTICAL PLATEAUS: 300-yard passing games: 2001 (3), 2002 (1), 2003 (1). Total: 5.
MISCELLANEOUS: Regular-season record as starting NFL quarterback: 34-42 (.447). ... Postseason record as starting NFL quarterback: 0-1.

			PASSING									RUSHING				TOTALS		
Year Team	G	GS	Att.	Cmp.	Pct.	Yds.	TD	Int.	Avg.	Skd.	Rat.	Att.	Yds.	Avg.	TD	TD	2pt.	Pts.
1997—Seattle NFL	3	1	45	31	68.9	371	1	2	8.24	3	82.7	10	9	0.9	1	1	0	6
1998—Seattle NFL	6	5	172	98	57.0	1177	7	8	6.84	11	72.3	20	67	3.4	1	1	0	6
1999—Seattle NFL	15	15	495	270	54.5	3346	23	16	6.76	32	77.7	35	56	1.6	0	0	0	0
2000—Seattle NFL	15	12	418	259	62.0	2658	18	19	6.36	33	75.6	48	127	2.6	1	1	0	6
2001—Cincinnati NFL	16	15	*581	313	53.9	3216	12	22	5.54	25	61.1	27	73	2.7	1	1	0	6
2002—Cincinnati NFL	14	12	473	294	62.2	3178	16	16	6.72	24	79.1	24	57	2.4	4	4	0	24
2003—Cincinnati NFL	16	16	520	324	62.3	3591	26	15	6.91	37	87.4	38	113	3.0	0	0	0	0
Pro totals (7 years)	85	76	2704	1589	58.8	17537	103	98	6.49	165	75.7	202	502	2.5	8	8	0	48

KITTNER, KURT QB GIANTS

PERSONAL: Born January 23, 1980, in Schaumburg, Ill. ... 6-2/221.
HIGH SCHOOL: Schaumburg (Ill.).
COLLEGE: Illinois.
TRANSACTIONS/CAREER NOTES: Selected by Atlanta Falcons in fifth round (158th pick overall) of 2002 NFL draft. ... Signed by Falcons (July 25, 2002). ... Claimed on waivers by Cincinnati Bengals (April 30, 2004). ... Claimed on waivers by New York Giants (May 20, 2004).
SINGLE GAME HIGHS (regular season): Attempts—29 (October 19, 2003, vs. New Orleans); completions—11 (November 2, 2003, vs. Philadelphia); yards—115 (October 19, 2003, vs. New Orleans); and touchdown passes—1 (November 9, 2003, vs. New York Giants).
MISCELLANEOUS: Regular-season record as starting NFL quarterback: 1-3 (.250).

			PASSING									RUSHING				TOTALS		
Year Team	G	GS	Att.	Cmp.	Pct.	Yds.	TD	Int.	Avg.	Skd.	Rat.	Att.	Yds.	Avg.	TD	TD	2pt.	Pts.
2003—Atlanta NFL	7	4	114	44	38.6	391	2	6	3.43	5	32.5	8	13	1.6	0	0	0	0

KLECKO, DAN DT PATRIOTS

PERSONAL: Born January 12, 1981, in Colts Neck, N.J. ... 5-11/283. ... Son of Joe Klecko, defensive tackle with New York Jets (1977-87) and Indianapolis Colts (1988).
HIGH SCHOOL: Marlboro (N.J.).
COLLEGE: Temple.
TRANSACTIONS/CAREER NOTES: Selected by New England Patriots in fourth round (117th pick overall) of 2003 NFL draft. ... Signed by Patriots (July 15, 2003).
CHAMPIONSHIP GAME EXPERIENCE: Member of Patriots for AFC championship game (2003 season); inactive. ... Member of Patriots for Super Bowl 38 (2003 season); inactive.

			TOTALS		
Year Team	G	GS	Tk.	Ast.	Sks.
2003—New England NFL	13	1	12	5	1.5

KLEINSASSER, JIM — TE — VIKINGS

PERSONAL: Born January 31, 1977, in Carrington, N.D. ... 6-3/272.
HIGH SCHOOL: Carrington (N.D.).
COLLEGE: North Dakota.
TRANSACTIONS/CAREER NOTES: Selected by Minnesota Vikings in second round (44th pick overall) of 1999 NFL draft. ... Signed by Vikings (August 1, 1999). ... Designated by Vikings as franchise player (February 20, 2003). ... Re-signed by Vikings (March 23, 2003).
CHAMPIONSHIP GAME EXPERIENCE: Played in NFC championship game (2000 season).
SINGLE GAME HIGHS (regular season): Receptions—10 (November 30, 2003, vs. St. Louis); yards—79 (November 30, 2003, vs. St. Louis); and touchdown receptions—2 (September 14, 2003, vs. Chicago). ... Attempts—5 (October 21, 2001, vs. Green Bay); yards—20 (October 21, 2001, vs. Green Bay); and rushing touchdowns—1 (October 21, 2001, vs. Green Bay); receptions—8 (September 30, 2001, vs. Tampa Bay); yards—64 (November 3, 2002, vs. Tampa Bay); and touchdown receptions—1 (October 13, 2002, vs. Detroit).

			RUSHING				RECEIVING				TOTALS			
Year Team	G	GS	Att.	Yds.	Avg.	TD	No.	Yds.	Avg.	TD	TD	2pt.	Pts.	Fum.
1999—Minnesota NFL	13	7	0	0	0.0	0	6	13	2.2	0	0	0	0	2
2000—Minnesota NFL	14	8	12	43	3.6	0	10	98	9.8	0	0	0	0	0
2001—Minnesota NFL	11	11	23	72	3.1	1	24	184	7.7	0	1	0	6	2
2002—Minnesota NFL	14	12	6	17	2.8	0	37	393	10.6	1	1	0	6	0
2003—Minnesota NFL	16	16	2	15	7.5	0	46	401	8.7	4	4	0	24	0
Pro totals (5 years)	68	54	43	147	3.4	1	123	1089	8.9	5	6	0	36	4

KLEMM, ADRIAN — T — PATRIOTS

PERSONAL: Born May 21, 1977, in Inglewood, Calif. ... 6-3/312. ... Full name: Adrian William Klemm.
HIGH SCHOOL: St. Monica (Santa Monica, Calif.).
COLLEGE: Hawaii.
TRANSACTIONS/CAREER NOTES: Selected by New England Patriots in second round (46th pick overall) of 2000 NFL draft. ... Signed by Patriots (July 12, 2000). ... On non-football injured list with knee injury (August 27-November 1, 2000). ... On injured reserve with leg injury (November 2, 2001-remainder of season). ... On injured reserve with knee injury (October 18, 2003-remainder of season).
PLAYING EXPERIENCE: New England NFL, 2000-2003. ... Games/Games started: 2000 (5/4), 2002 (16/3), 2003 (3/3). Total: 24/10.

KNIGHT, BRYAN — LB — BEARS

PERSONAL: Born January 22, 1979, in Buffalo, N.Y. ... 6-2/238. ... Full name: Bryan Jerome Knight.
HIGH SCHOOL: St. Joseph (Buffalo).
COLLEGE: Pittsburgh.
TRANSACTIONS/CAREER NOTES: Selected by Chicago Bears in fifth round (165th pick overall) of 2002 NFL draft. ... Signed by Bears (July 25, 2002).

			TOTALS			INTERCEPTIONS			
Year Team	G	GS	Tk.	Ast.	Sks.	No.	Yds.	Avg.	TD
2002—Chicago NFL	15	0	10	2	1.5	0	0	0.0	0
2003—Chicago NFL	16	2	11	9	0.0	0	0	0.0	0
Pro totals (2 years)	31	2	21	11	1.5	0	0	0.0	0

KNIGHT, ROGER — LB — SAINTS

PERSONAL: Born October 11, 1978, in Queens Village, N.Y. ... 6-0/245. ... Full name: Roger Oliver Knight.
HIGH SCHOOL: Brooklyn Tech (N.Y.).
COLLEGE: Wisconsin.
TRANSACTIONS/CAREER NOTES: Selected by Pittsburgh Steelers in sixth round (182nd pick overall) of 2001 NFL draft. ... Signed by Steelers (June 6, 2001). ... Released by Steelers (August 31, 2001). ... Signed by New Orleans Saints (December 4, 2001). ... On injured reserve with knee injury (December 12, 2001-remainder of season).

			TOTALS			INTERCEPTIONS			
Year Team	G	GS	Tk.	Ast.	Sks.	No.	Yds.	Avg.	TD
2001—New Orleans NFL	1	0	0	0	0.0	0	0	0.0	0
2002—New Orleans NFL	16	0	3	3	0.0	0	0	0.0	0
2003—New Orleans NFL	16	2	15	4	0.0	0	0	0.0	0
Pro totals (3 years)	33	2	18	7	0.0	0	0	0.0	0

KNIGHT, SAMMY — S — DOLPHINS

PERSONAL: Born September 10, 1975, in Fontana, Calif. ... 6-0/215.
HIGH SCHOOL: Rubidoux (Riverside, Calif.).
COLLEGE: Southern California.
TRANSACTIONS/CAREER NOTES: Signed as non-drafted free agent by New Orleans Saints (April 25, 1997). ... Granted unconditional free agency (February 28, 2003). ... Signed by Miami Dolphins (May 13, 2003).
HONORS: Played in Pro Bowl (2001 season).

			TOTALS			INTERCEPTIONS			
Year Team	G	GS	Tk.	Ast.	Sks.	No.	Yds.	Avg.	TD
1997—New Orleans NFL	16	12	67	17	0.0	5	75	15.0	0
1998—New Orleans NFL	14	13	62	13	0.0	6	171	28.5	2
1999—New Orleans NFL	16	16	75	27	0.0	1	0	0.0	0
2000—New Orleans NFL	16	16	74	26	2.0	5	68	13.6	‡2

Year Team	G	GS	TOTALS Tk.	Ast.	Sks.	INTERCEPTIONS No.	Yds.	Avg.	TD
2001—New Orleans NFL	16	16	80	18	1.0	6	114	19.0	0
2002—New Orleans NFL	16	16	82	25	2.0	5	36	7.2	0
2003—Miami NFL	16	16	66	32	0.0	3	98	32.7	0
Pro totals (7 years)	110	105	506	158	5.0	31	562	18.1	4

KNIGHT, TOM — CB — BUCCANEERS

PERSONAL: Born December 29, 1974, in Marlton, N.J. ... 6-0/202. ... Full name: Thomas Lorenzo Knight.
HIGH SCHOOL: Cherokee (Marlton, N.J.).
COLLEGE: Iowa.
TRANSACTIONS/CAREER NOTES: Selected by Arizona Cardinals in first round (ninth pick overall) of 1997 NFL draft. ... Signed by Cardinals (July 16, 1997). ... On injured reserve with hamstring injury (January 3, 2002-remainder of season). ... Granted unconditional free agency (March 1, 2002). ... Signed by New England Patriots (April 4, 2002). ... Released by Patriots (September 9, 2002). ... Signed by Baltimore Ravens (December 5, 2002). ... Granted unconditional free agency (March 3, 2004). ... Signed by Tampa Bay Buccaneers (March 15, 2004).

Year Team	G	GS	TOTALS Tk.	Ast.	Sks.	INTERCEPTIONS No.	Yds.	Avg.	TD
1997—Arizona NFL	15	14	41	6	0.0	0	0	0.0	0
1998—Arizona NFL	8	5	30	3	1.0	0	0	0.0	0
1999—Arizona NFL	16	11	57	8	0.0	2	16	8.0	0
2000—Arizona NFL	16	15	48	8	1.0	0	0	0.0	0
2001—Arizona NFL	8	8	27	4	0.0	1	43	43.0	0
2003—Baltimore NFL	10	1	15	0	0.5	0	0	0.0	0
Pro totals (6 years)	73	54	218	29	2.5	3	59	19.7	0

KNORR, MICAH — P — BRONCOS

PERSONAL: Born January 9, 1975, in Orange, Calif. ... 6-2/199.
HIGH SCHOOL: Orange (Calif.).
COLLEGE: Utah State.
TRANSACTIONS/CAREER NOTES: Signed as non-drafted free agent by Dallas Cowboys (April 18, 2000). ... Released by Cowboys (October 22, 2002). ... Signed by Denver Broncos (October 29, 2002).

Year Team	G	PUNTING No.	Yds.	Avg.	Net avg.	In. 20	Blk.
2000—Dallas NFL	14	58	2485	42.8	35.7	12	0
2001—Dallas NFL	16	78	3135	40.2	31.1	25	*3
2002—Dallas NFL	7	47	1928	41.0	35.1	11	0
—Denver NFL	8	24	906	37.8	34.1	8	0
2003—Denver NFL	16	68	2937	43.2	32.2	14	§2
Pro totals (4 years)	61	275	11391	41.4	33.3	70	5

KONRAD, ROB — FB — DOLPHINS

PERSONAL: Born November 12, 1976, in Rochester, N.Y. ... 6-3/255. ... Full name: Robert L. Konrad.
HIGH SCHOOL: St. John's (Andover, Mass.).
COLLEGE: Syracuse.
TRANSACTIONS/CAREER NOTES: Selected by Miami Dolphins in second round (43rd pick overall) of 1999 NFL draft. ... Signed by Dolphins (July 27, 1999). ... On injured reserve with rib injury (January 12, 2002-remainder of 2001 playoffs). ... Granted unconditional free agency (February 28, 2003). ... Re-signed by Dolphins (March 1, 2003).
SINGLE GAME HIGHS (regular season): Attempts—7 (September 3, 2000, vs. Seattle); yards—19 (December 10, 2001, vs. Indianapolis); and rushing touchdowns—1 (December 10, 2001, vs. Indianapolis).

Year Team	G	GS	RUSHING Att.	Yds.	Avg.	TD	RECEIVING No.	Yds.	Avg.	TD	TOTALS TD	2pt.	Pts.	Fum.
1999—Miami NFL	15	9	9	16	1.8	0	34	251	7.4	1	1	0	6	3
2000—Miami NFL	15	13	15	39	2.6	0	14	83	5.9	0	0	0	0	0
2001—Miami NFL	12	9	5	22	4.4	1	5	52	10.4	1	2	0	12	0
2002—Miami NFL	16	12	3	2	0.7	0	34	233	6.9	3	3	0	18	2
2003—Miami NFL	14	12	4	17	4.3	0	16	166	10.4	0	0	0	0	0
Pro totals (5 years)	72	55	36	96	2.7	1	103	785	7.6	5	6	0	36	5

KOOISTRA, SCOTT — T — BENGALS

PERSONAL: Born October 14, 1980, in Madison, Wis. ... 6-6/320. ... Full name: Daniel Scott Kooistra.
HIGH SCHOOL: Cary (N.C.).
COLLEGE: North Carolina State.
TRANSACTIONS/CAREER NOTES: Selected by Cincinnati Bengals in seventh round (215th pick overall) of 2003 NFL draft.
PLAYING EXPERIENCE: Cincinnati NFL, 2003. ... Games/Games started: 2003 (8/0). Total: 8/0.

KOPPEN, DANIEL — C — PATRIOTS

PERSONAL: Born September 12, 1979, in Dubuque, Iowa. ... 6-2/296.
HIGH SCHOOL: Whitehall (Pa.).
COLLEGE: Boston College.

TRANSACTIONS/CAREER NOTES: Selected by New England Patriots in fifth round (164th pick overall) of 2003 NFL draft. ... Signed by Patriots (July 21, 2003).
PLAYING EXPERIENCE: New England NFL, 2003. ... Games/Games started: 2003 (16/15). Total: 16/15.
CHAMPIONSHIP GAME EXPERIENCE: Played in AFC championship game (2003 season). ... Member of Super Bowl championship team (2003 season).

KOSIER, KYLE — T — 49ERS

PERSONAL: Born January 27, 1978, in Peoria, Ariz. ... 6-5/293. ... Full name: Kyle Blaine Kosier.
HIGH SCHOOL: Cactus (Peoria, Ariz.).
COLLEGE: Arizona State.
TRANSACTIONS/CAREER NOTES: Selected by San Francisco 49ers in seventh round (248th pick overall) of 2002 NFL draft. ... Signed by 49ers (July 21, 2002).
PLAYING EXPERIENCE: San Francisco NFL, 2002-2003. ... Games/Games started: 2002 (15/1), 2003 (16/12). Total: 31/13.

KOZLOWSKI, BRIAN — TE — REDSKINS

PERSONAL: Born October 4, 1970, in Rochester, N.Y. ... 6-3/250. ... Full name: Brian Scott Kozlowski.
HIGH SCHOOL: Webster (N.Y.).
COLLEGE: Connecticut.
TRANSACTIONS/CAREER NOTES: Signed as non-drafted free agent by New York Giants (May 1, 1993). ... Released by Giants (August 16, 1993). ... Re-signed by Giants to practice squad (December 8, 1993). ... Granted unconditional free agency (February 14, 1997). ... Signed by Atlanta Falcons (March 21, 1997). ... Granted unconditional free agency (February 13, 1998). ... Re-signed by Falcons (March 4, 1998). ... Granted unconditional free agency (March 2, 2001). ... Re-signed by Falcons (April 5, 2001). ... Granted unconditional free agency (March 1, 2002). ... Re-signed by Falcons (April 3, 2002). ... Granted unconditional free agency (February 28, 2003). ... Re-signed by Falcons (March 17, 2003). ... Granted unconditional free agency (March 3, 2004). ... Signed by Washington Redskins (April 13, 2004).
CHAMPIONSHIP GAME EXPERIENCE: Played in NFC championship game (1998 season). ... Played in Super Bowl 33 (1998 season).
SINGLE GAME HIGHS (regular season): Receptions—4 (September 23, 2001, vs. Carolina); yards—86 (September 23, 2001, vs. Carolina); and touchdown receptions—1 (November 11, 2001, vs. Dallas).

			RECEIVING				KICKOFF RETURNS				TOTALS			
Year Team	**G**	**GS**	**No.**	**Yds.**	**Avg.**	**TD**	**No.**	**Yds.**	**Avg.**	**TD**	**TD**	**2pt.**	**Pts.**	**Fum.**
1993—New York Giants NFL	Did not play.													
1994—New York Giants NFL	16	3	1	5	5.0	0	2	21	10.5	0	0	0	0	0
1995—New York Giants NFL	16	0	2	17	8.5	0	5	75	15.0	0	0	0	0	1
1996—New York Giants NFL	5	0	1	4	4.0	1	1	16	16.0	0	1	0	6	0
1997—Atlanta NFL	16	5	7	99	14.1	1	2	49	24.5	0	1	0	6	0
1998—Atlanta NFL	16	4	10	103	10.3	1	1	12	12.0	0	1	0	6	0
1999—Atlanta NFL	16	3	11	122	11.1	2	2	19	9.5	0	2	0	12	1
2000—Atlanta NFL	16	3	15	151	10.1	2	7	77	11.0	0	2	0	12	0
2001—Atlanta NFL	16	0	15	270	18.0	1	3	35	11.7	0	1	0	6	0
2002—Atlanta NFL	16	2	6	59	9.8	0	2	35	17.5	0	0	0	0	0
2003—Atlanta NFL	16	9	10	87	8.7	0	3	27	9.0	0	0	0	0	1
Pro totals (10 years)	149	29	78	917	11.8	8	28	366	13.1	0	8	0	48	3

KRAMER, JORDAN — LB — TITANS

PERSONAL: Born December 7, 1979, in Parma, Idaho. ... 6-1/230. ... Son of Jerry Kramer, guard, Green Bay Packers (1958-68).
HIGH SCHOOL: Parma (Idaho).
COLLEGE: Idaho.
TRANSACTIONS/CAREER NOTES: Signed as non-drafted free agent by San Diego Chargers (May 2, 2003). ... Waived by Chargers (August 31, 2003). ... Signed by Tennessee Titans to practice squad (October 1, 2003). ... Activated (November 13, 2003). ... Waived by Titans (November 18, 2003). ... Re-signed by Titans to practice squad (November 26, 2003). ... Activated (December 5, 2003).

			TOTALS			INTERCEPTIONS			
Year Team	**G**	**GS**	**Tk.**	**Ast.**	**Sks.**	**No.**	**Yds.**	**Avg.**	**TD**
2003—Tennessee NFL	2	0	0	0	0.0	0	0	0.0	0

KREIDER, DAN — FB — STEELERS

PERSONAL: Born March 11, 1977, in Lancaster, Pa. ... 5-11/246.
HIGH SCHOOL: Manheim Central (Pa.).
COLLEGE: New Hampshire.
TRANSACTIONS/CAREER NOTES: Signed as non-drafted free agent by Pittsburgh Steelers (April 21, 2000). ... On physically unable to perform list with calf injury (July 20-September 2, 2001). ... Granted free agency (February 28, 2003). ... Re-signed by Steelers (April 20, 2003). ... Granted unconditional free agency (March 3, 2004). ... Re-signed by Steelers (March 3, 2004).
CHAMPIONSHIP GAME EXPERIENCE: Played in AFC championship game (2001 season).
SINGLE GAME HIGHS (regular season): Attempts—3 (September 21, 2003, vs. Cincinnati); yards—24 (December 3, 2000, vs. Oakland); and rushing touchdowns—1 (December 7, 2003, vs. Oakland).

			RUSHING				RECEIVING				KICKOFF RETURNS				TOTALS			
Year Team	**G**	**GS**	**Att.**	**Yds.**	**Avg.**	**TD**	**No.**	**Yds.**	**Avg.**	**TD**	**No.**	**Yds.**	**Avg.**	**TD**	**TD**	**2pt.**	**Pts.**	**Fum.**
2000—Pittsburgh NFL	10	7	2	24	12.0	0	5	42	8.4	0	1	0	0.0	0	0	0	0	0
2001—Pittsburgh NFL	13	1	7	29	4.1	1	2	5	2.5	0	0	0	0.0	0	1	0	6	0
2002—Pittsburgh NFL	16	13	6	16	2.7	0	18	122	6.8	1	1	18	18.0	0	1	1	8	1
2003—Pittsburgh NFL	16	12	7	29	4.1	1	9	107	11.9	0	3	29	9.7	0	1	0	6	0
Pro totals (4 years)	55	33	22	98	4.5	2	34	276	8.1	1	5	47	9.4	0	3	1	20	1

KREUTZ, OLIN — C — BEARS

PERSONAL: Born June 9, 1977, in Honolulu, Hawaii. ... 6-2/292.
HIGH SCHOOL: St. Louis (Honolulu).
COLLEGE: Washington.
TRANSACTIONS/CAREER NOTES: Selected after junior season by Chicago Bears in third round (64th pick overall) of 1998 NFL draft. ... Signed by Bears (July 20, 1998). ... On injured reserve with knee injury (November 21, 2000-remainder of season). ... Granted free agency (March 2, 2001). ... Re-signed by Bears (April 18, 2001). ... Granted unconditional free agency (March 1, 2002). ... Re-signed by Bears (March 4, 2002).
PLAYING EXPERIENCE: Chicago NFL, 1998-2003. ... Games/Games started: 1998 (9/1), 1999 (16/16), 2000 (7/7), 2001 (16/16), 2002 (15/15), 2003 (16/16). Total: 79/71.
HONORS: Named center on THE SPORTING NEWS college All-America first team (1997). ... Played in Pro Bowl (2001 and 2002 seasons). ... Named to play in Pro Bowl (2003 season); replaced by Mike Flanagan due to injury.

KRIEWALDT, CLINT — LB — STEELERS

PERSONAL: Born March 17, 1976, in Shiocton, Wis. ... 6-1/242.
HIGH SCHOOL: Shiocton (Wis.).
COLLEGE: Wisconsin-Stevens Point.
TRANSACTIONS/CAREER NOTES: Selected by Detroit Lions in sixth round (177th pick overall) of 1999 NFL draft. ... Signed by Lions (July 22, 1999). ... Granted free agency (March 1, 2002). ... Re-signed by Lions (April 16, 2002). ... Granted unconditional free agency (February 28, 2003). ... Signed by Pittsburgh Steelers (March 5, 2003).

			TOTALS			INTERCEPTIONS			
Year Team	G	GS	Tk.	Ast.	Sks.	No.	Yds.	Avg.	TD
1999—Detroit NFL	12	0	2	0	0.0	1	2	2.0	0
2000—Detroit NFL	13	1	4	1	0.0	0	0	0.0	0
2001—Detroit NFL	14	1	11	10	0.0	0	0	0.0	0
2002—Detroit NFL	10	0	5	6	0.0	0	0	0.0	0
2003—Pittsburgh NFL	15	0	1	0	0.0	0	0	0.0	0
Pro totals (5 years)	64	2	23	17	0.0	1	2	2.0	0

KUEHL, RYAN — DT — GIANTS

PERSONAL: Born January 18, 1972, in Washington, D.C. ... 6-5/290. ... Full name: Ryan Philip Kuehl.
HIGH SCHOOL: Walt Whitman (Bethesda, Md.).
COLLEGE: Virginia.
TRANSACTIONS/CAREER NOTES: Signed as non-drafted free agent by San Francisco 49ers (April 26, 1995). ... Released by 49ers (August 19, 1995). ... Re-signed by Redskins to practice squad (August 26, 1995). ... Signed by Washington Redskins (February 16, 1996). ... Released by Redskins (August 25, 1996). ... Re-signed by Redskins to practice squad (August 26, 1996). ... Activated (October 19, 1996). ... Released by Redskins (November 6, 1996). ... Re-signed by Redskins to practice squad (November 7, 1996). ... Activated (November 11, 1996). ... Released by Redskins (August 23, 1997). ... Re-signed by Redskins (September 9, 1997). ... Released by Redskins (August 30, 1998). ... Signed by Cleveland Browns (February 11, 1999). ... Granted unconditional free agency (February 28, 2003). ... Signed by New York Giants (March 6, 2003). ... On injured reserve with elbow injury (August 31, 2003-entire season).

			TOTALS		
Year Team	G	GS	Tk.	Ast.	Sks.
1996—Washington NFL	2	0	1	0	0.0
1997—Washington NFL	12	5	9	3	0.0
1999—Cleveland NFL	16	0	0	0	0.0
2000—Cleveland NFL	16	0	0	0	0.0
2001—Cleveland NFL	16	0	0	0	0.0
2002—Cleveland NFL	16	0	0	0	0.0
2003—New York Giants NFL	Did not play.				
Pro totals (6 years)	78	5	10	3	0.0

KYLE, JASON — LB — PANTHERS

PERSONAL: Born May 12, 1972, in Tempe, Ariz. ... 6-3/242. ... Full name: Jason C. Kyle.
HIGH SCHOOL: McClintock (Tempe, Ariz.).
COLLEGE: Arizona State.
TRANSACTIONS/CAREER NOTES: Selected by Seattle Seahawks in fourth round (126th pick overall) of 1995 NFL draft. ... Signed by Seahawks (July 16, 1995). ... On injured reserve with shoulder injury (August 18, 1997-entire season). ... Granted free agency (February 13, 1998). ... Re-signed by Seahawks (April 16, 1998). ... Selected by Cleveland Browns from Seahawks in NFL expansion draft (February 9, 1999). ... On physically unable to perform list with knee injury (August 26, 1999-entire season). ... Released by Browns (August 27, 2000). ... Signed by St. Louis Rams (October 5, 2000). ... Released by Rams (October 16, 2000). ... Re-signed by Rams (October 24, 2000). ... Released by Rams (October 27, 2000). ... Signed by San Francisco 49ers (October 30, 2000). ... Granted unconditional free agency (March 2, 2001). ... Signed by Carolina Panthers (March 5, 2001). ... Granted unconditional free agency (March 3, 2004). ... Re-signed by Panthers (March 11, 2004).
CHAMPIONSHIP GAME EXPERIENCE: Played in NFC championship game (2003 season). ... Played in Super Bowl 38 (2003 season).

			TOTALS			INTERCEPTIONS			
Year Team	G	GS	Tk.	Ast.	Sks.	No.	Yds.	Avg.	TD
1995—Seattle NFL	16	0	0	0	0.0	0	0	0.0	0
1996—Seattle NFL	16	0	1	0	0.0	0	0	0.0	0
1998—Seattle NFL	16	0	0	0	0.0	0	0	0.0	0
1999—Cleveland NFL	Did not play.								
2000—San Francisco NFL	2	0	2	0	0.0	0	0	0.0	0
2001—Carolina NFL	16	0	0	0	0.0	0	0	0.0	0
2002—Carolina NFL	16	0	1	1	0.0	0	0	0.0	0
2003—Carolina NFL	16	0	0	0	0.0	0	0	0.0	0
Pro totals (7 years)	98	0	4	1	0.0	0	0	0.0	0

LACINA, CORBIN G

PERSONAL: Born November 2, 1970, in Mankato, Minn. ... 6-4/302.
HIGH SCHOOL: Cretin-Derham Hall (St. Paul, Minn.).
COLLEGE: Augustana (S.D.).
TRANSACTIONS/CAREER NOTES: Selected by Buffalo Bills in sixth round (167th pick overall) of 1993 NFL draft. ... Signed by Bills (July 12, 1993). ... Released by Bills (August 30, 1993). ... Re-signed by Bills to practice squad (September 1, 1993). ... Activated (December 30, 1993); did not play. ... On injured reserve with foot injury (December 22, 1994-remainder of season). ... On injured reserve with groin injury (November 30, 1996-remainder of season). ... Granted free agency (February 14, 1997). ... Re-signed by Bills (June 12, 1997). ... Granted unconditional free agency (February 13, 1998). ... Signed by Carolina Panthers (February 26, 1998). ... Released by Panthers (June 16, 1999). ... Signed by Minnesota Vikings (June 18, 1999). ... Granted unconditional free agency (March 2, 2001). ... Re-signed by Vikings (June 19, 2001). ... Granted unconditional free agency (February 28, 2003). ... Signed by Buffalo Bills (August 19, 2003). ... Released by Bills (August 28, 2003). ... Signed by Chicago Bears (September 2, 2003). ... Granted unconditional free agency (March 3, 2004).
PLAYING EXPERIENCE: Buffalo NFL, 1994-1997; Carolina NFL, 1998; Minnesota NFL, 1999-2002; Chicago NFL, 2003. ... Games/Games started: 1994 (11/10), 1995 (16/3), 1996 (12/2), 1997 (16/13), 1998 (10/10), 1999 (13/0), 2000 (15/15), 2001 (11/10), 2002 (16/16), 2003 (8/1). Total: 128/80.
CHAMPIONSHIP GAME EXPERIENCE: Member of Bills for AFC championship game (1993 season); inactive. ... Member of Bills for Super Bowl 28 (1993 season); inactive. ... Played in NFC championship game (2000 season).

LAFAVOR, TRON DT BEARS

PERSONAL: Born November 27, 1979, in Fort Lauderdale, Fla. ... 6-2/290.
HIGH SCHOOL: Dillard (Fort Lauderdale, Fla.).
COLLEGE: Florida.
TRANSACTIONS/CAREER NOTES: Selected by Chicago Bears in fifth round (171st pick overall) of 2003 NFL draft. ... Signed by Bears (July 23, 2003).

			TOTALS		
Year Team	G	GS	Tk.	Ast.	Sks.
2003—Chicago NFL	4	0	1	1	0.0

LAFLEUR, BILL P 49ERS

PERSONAL: Born February 25, 1976, in Superior, Neb. ... 6-0/204. ... Full name: William Lafleur.
HIGH SCHOOL: Norfolk Catholic (Norfolk, Neb.).
COLLEGE: Nebraska.
TRANSACTIONS/CAREER NOTES: Signed as non-drafted free agent by New Orleans Saints (April 18, 2000). ... Released by Saints (August 22, 2000). ... Re-signed by Saints (February 20, 2001). ... Released by Saints (September 1, 2001). ... Signed by San Diego Chargers (June 28, 2002). ... Released by Chargers (September 1, 2002). ... Re-signed by Chargers to practice squad (September 3, 2002). ... Signed by San Francisco 49ers off Chargers practice squad (November 27, 2002). ... Re-signed by 49ers (March 10, 2003).

		PUNTING					
Year Team	G	No.	Yds.	Avg.	Net avg.	In. 20	Blk.
2002—San Francisco NFL	5	22	805	36.6	30.8	5	1
2003—San Francisco NFL	16	68	2629	38.7	33.5	17	1
Pro totals (2 years)	21	90	3434	38.2	32.8	22	2

LANDETA, SEAN P RAMS

PERSONAL: Born January 6, 1962, in Baltimore, Md. ... 6-0/215. ... Full name: Sean Edward Landeta.
HIGH SCHOOL: Loch Raven (Baltimore).
COLLEGE: Towson.
TRANSACTIONS/CAREER NOTES: Selected by Philadelphia Stars in 14th round (161st pick overall) of 1983 USFL draft. ... Signed by Stars (January 24, 1983). ... Stars franchise moved to Baltimore (November 1, 1984). ... Granted free agency (August 1, 1985). ... Signed by New York Giants (August 5, 1985). ... On injured reserve with back injury (September 7, 1988-remainder of season). ... Granted free agency (February 1, 1990). ... Re-signed by Giants (July 23, 1990). ... On injured reserve with knee injury (November 25, 1992-remainder of season). ... Granted unconditional free agency (March 1, 1993). ... Re-signed by Giants (March 18, 1993). ... Released by Giants (November 9, 1993). ... Signed by Los Angeles Rams (November 12, 1993). ... Granted unconditional free agency (February 17, 1994). ... Re-signed by Rams (May 10, 1994). ... Granted unconditional free agency (February 17, 1995). ... Rams franchise moved to St. Louis (April 12, 1995). ... Re-signed by Rams (May 8, 1995). ... Released by Rams (March 18, 1997). ... Signed by Tampa Bay Buccaneers (October 9, 1997). ... Granted unconditional free agency (February 13, 1998). ... Signed by Green Packers (February 26, 1998). ... Granted unconditional free agency (February 12, 1999). ... Signed by Philadelphia Eagles (February 26, 1999). ... Granted unconditional free agency (March 1, 2002). ... Re-signed by Eagles (March 21, 2002). ... On injured reserve with calf injury (December 3, 2002-remainder of season). ... Granted unconditional free agency (February 28, 2003). ... Signed by Rams (March 18, 2003). ... Granted unconditional free agency (March 3, 2004). ... Re-signed by Rams (March 4, 2004).
CHAMPIONSHIP GAME EXPERIENCE: Played in USFL championship game (1983-1985 seasons). ... Played in NFC championship game (1986, 1990 and 2001 seasons). ... Member of Super Bowl championship team (1986 and 1990 seasons).
HONORS: Named punter on THE SPORTING NEWS USFL All-Star team (1983 and 1984). ... Named punter on THE SPORTING NEWS NFL All-Pro team (1986, 1989 and 1990). ... Played in Pro Bowl (1986 and 1990 seasons).
RECORDS: Holds NFL career record for most punts—1,327.

		PUNTING					
Year Team	G	No.	Yds.	Avg.	Net avg.	In. 20	Blk.
1983—Philadelphia USFL	18	86	3601	41.9	36.5	31	0
1984—Philadelphia USFL	18	53	2171	41.0	*38.1	18	0
1985—Baltimore USFL	18	65	2718	41.8	33.2	18	0
—New York Giants NFL	16	81	3472	42.9	36.3	20	0
1986—New York Giants NFL	16	79	3539	‡44.8	‡37.1	24	0

Year Team	G	PUNTING No.	Yds.	Avg.	Net avg.	In. 20	Blk.
1987—New York Giants NFL	12	65	2773	42.7	31.0	13	1
1988—New York Giants NFL	1	6	222	37.0	35.7	1	0
1989—New York Giants NFL	16	70	3019	43.1	*37.7	19	0
1990—New York Giants NFL	16	75	3306	‡44.1	37.2	†24	0
1991—New York Giants NFL	15	64	2768	43.3	35.2	16	0
1992—New York Giants NFL	11	53	2317	43.7	31.5	13	*2
1993—New York Giants NFL	8	33	1390	42.1	35.0	11	1
—Los Angeles Rams NFL	8	42	1825	43.5	32.8	7	0
1994—Los Angeles Rams NFL	16	78	3494	*44.8	34.2	23	0
1995—St. Louis NFL	16	83	3679	‡44.3	36.7	23	0
1996—St. Louis NFL	16	78	3491	44.8	36.1	23	0
1997—Tampa Bay NFL	10	54	2274	42.1	34.1	15	1
1998—Green Bay NFL	16	65	2788	42.9	37.1	30	0
1999—Philadelphia NFL	16	*107	‡4524	42.3	35.1	21	1
2000—Philadelphia NFL	16	86	3635	42.3	36.0	23	0
2001—Philadelphia NFL	16	‡97	4221	43.5	36.4	26	0
2002—Philadelphia NFL	12	52	2229	42.9	34.6	19	0
2003—St. Louis NFL	16	59	2525	42.8	32.9	14	0
USFL totals (3 years)	54	204	8490	41.6	35.9	67	0
NFL totals (19 years)	269	1327	57491	43.3	35.4	365	6
Pro totals (21 years)	323	1531	65981	43.1	...	432	6

LANG, KENARD — DE — BROWNS

PERSONAL: Born January 31, 1975, in Orlando, Fla. ... 6-3/280. ... Full name: Kenard Dushun Lang.
HIGH SCHOOL: Maynard Evans (Orlando).
COLLEGE: Miami (Fla.).
TRANSACTIONS/CAREER NOTES: Selected by Washington Redskins in first round (17th pick overall) of 1997 NFL draft. ... Signed by Redskins (July 28, 1997). ... Granted unconditional free agency (March 1, 2002). ... Signed by Cleveland Browns (March 5, 2002).

Year Team	G	GS	TOTALS Tk.	Ast.	Sks.	INTERCEPTIONS No.	Yds.	Avg.	TD
1997—Washington NFL	11	11	26	9	1.5	0	0	0.0	0
1998—Washington NFL	16	16	46	8	7.0	0	0	0.0	0
1999—Washington NFL	16	9	34	3	6.0	0	0	0.0	0
2000—Washington NFL	16	0	16	0	3.0	0	0	0.0	0
2001—Washington NFL	16	16	52	15	4.0	1	14	14.0	0
2002—Cleveland NFL	15	14	33	13	5.5	1	71	71.0	0
2003—Cleveland NFL	15	15	47	13	8.0	1	0	0.0	0
Pro totals (7 years)	105	81	254	61	35.0	3	85	28.3	0

LASSITER, KWAMIE — S — CHARGERS

PERSONAL: Born December 3, 1969, in Newport News, Va. ... 6-0/207.
HIGH SCHOOL: Menchville (Newport News, Va.).
JUNIOR COLLEGE: Butler County Community College (Kan.).
COLLEGE: Kansas.
TRANSACTIONS/CAREER NOTES: Signed as non-drafted free agent by Arizona Cardinals (April 28, 1995). ... On injured reserve with ankle injury (October 5, 1995-remainder of season). ... Granted free agency (February 13, 1998). ... Re-signed by Cardinals (May 21, 1998). ... Granted unconditional free agency (February 12, 1999). ... Re-signed by Cardinals (March 9, 1999). ... Granted free agency (March 1, 2002). ... Re-signed by Cardinals (May 1, 2002). ... Granted unconditional free agency (February 28, 2003). ... Signed by San Diego Chargers (June 9, 2003). ... On injured reserve with knee injury (November 19, 2003-remainder of season).

Year Team	G	GS	TOTALS Tk.	Ast.	Sks.	INTERCEPTIONS No.	Yds.	Avg.	TD
1995—Arizona NFL	5	0	5	2	0.0	0	0	0.0	0
1996—Arizona NFL	14	0	13	3	0.0	1	20	20.0	0
1997—Arizona NFL	16	1	24	15	3.0	1	10	10.0	0
1998—Arizona NFL	16	6	40	15	0.0	‡8	80	10.0	0
1999—Arizona NFL	16	16	69	34	0.0	2	110	55.0	1
2000—Arizona NFL	16	16	63	31	0.0	1	11	11.0	0
2001—Arizona NFL	16	16	83	28	1.0	9	80	8.9	0
2002—Arizona NFL	16	16	59	29	0.0	2	7	3.5	0
2003—San Diego NFL	10	10	51	8	0.0	1	38	38.0	1
Pro totals (9 years)	125	81	407	165	4.0	25	356	14.2	2

LAW, TY — CB — PATRIOTS

PERSONAL: Born February 10, 1974, in Aliquippa, Pa. ... 5-11/200. ... Full name: Tajuan Law.
HIGH SCHOOL: Aliquippa (Pa.).
COLLEGE: Michigan.
TRANSACTIONS/CAREER NOTES: Selected after junior season by New England Patriots in first round (23rd pick overall) of 1995 NFL draft. ... Signed by Patriots (July 20, 1995). ... On injured reserve with hand injury (December 29, 1999-remainder of season).
CHAMPIONSHIP GAME EXPERIENCE: Played in AFC championship game (1996, 2001 and 2003 seasons). ... Played in Super Bowl 31 (1996 season). ... Member of Super Bowl championship team (2001 and 2003 seasons).
HONORS: Named cornerback on THE SPORTING NEWS NFL All-Pro team (1998). ... Played in Pro Bowl (1998, 2001-2003 seasons). ... Named co-Outstanding Player of Pro Bowl (1998 season).

Year Team	G	GS	TOTALS Tk.	Ast.	Sks.	INTERCEPTIONS No.	Yds.	Avg.	TD
1995—New England NFL	14	7	40	7	1.0	3	47	15.7	0
1996—New England NFL	13	12	56	6	0.0	3	45	15.0	1
1997—New England NFL	16	16	69	8	0.5	3	70	23.3	0
1998—New England NFL	16	16	60	10	0.0	*9	133	14.8	1
1999—New England NFL	13	13	50	9	0.5	2	20	10.0	1
2000—New England NFL	15	15	58	16	0.0	2	32	16.0	0
2001—New England NFL	16	16	60	10	1.0	3	91	30.3	†2
2002—New England NFL	16	16	60	17	1.0	4	33	8.3	0
2003—New England NFL	15	15	61	13	0.0	6	112	18.7	1
Pro totals (9 years)	134	126	514	96	4.0	35	583	16.7	6

LAYNE, GEORGE FB FALCONS

PERSONAL: Born October 9, 1978, in Alvin, Texas. ... 5-11/250.
HIGH SCHOOL: Alvin (Texas).
COLLEGE: Texas Christian.
TRANSACTIONS/CAREER NOTES: Selected after junior season by Kansas City Chiefs in fourth round (108th pick overall) of 2001 NFL draft. ... Signed by Chiefs (July 23, 2001). ... Released by Chiefs (September 2, 2001). ... Re-signed by Chiefs to practice squad (September 4, 2001). ... Signed by Atlanta Falcons off Chiefs practice squad (October 2, 2001). ... Released by Falcons (September 1, 2002). ... Signed by Falcons (November 12, 2002). ... Released by Falcons (September 2, 2003). ... Signed by Carolina Panthers to practice squad (September 10, 2003). ... Released by Panthers (October 1, 2003). ... Signed by Atlanta Falcons (November 26, 2003). ... On injured reserve with knee injury (December 16, 2003-remainder of season).
SINGLE GAME HIGHS (regular season): Attempts—1 (December 14, 2003, vs. Indianapolis); yards—15 (December 14, 2003, vs. Indianapolis); and rushing touchdowns—0.

Year Team	G	GS	RUSHING Att.	Yds.	Avg.	TD	RECEIVING No.	Yds.	Avg.	TD	TOTALS TD	2pt.	Pts.	Fum.
2001—Atlanta NFL	2	0	0	0	0.0	0	0	0	0.0	0	0	0	0	0
2002—Atlanta NFL	2	0	1	5	5.0	0	2	11	5.5	0	0	0	0	1
2003—Atlanta NFL	3	0	1	15	15.0	0	1	3	3.0	0	0	0	0	0
Pro totals (3 years)	7	0	2	20	10.0	0	3	14	4.7	0	0	0	0	1

LEACH, MIKE TE/LS BRONCOS

PERSONAL: Born October 18, 1976, in Jefferson Township, N.J. ... 6-2/245.
HIGH SCHOOL: Jefferson Township (N.J.).
COLLEGE: William & Mary.
TRANSACTIONS/CAREER NOTES: Signed as non-drafted free agent by Tennessee Titans (April 20, 2000). ... Released by Titans (October 16, 2001). ... Signed by Chicago Bears (January 10, 2001). ... Released by Bears (August 26, 2002). ... Signed by Denver Broncos (November 4, 2002).
PLAYING EXPERIENCE: Tennessee NFL, 2000-2001; Denver NFL, 2002-2003. ... Games/Games started: 2000 (15/0), 2001 (4/0), 2002 (8/0), 2003 (16/0). Total: 43/0.

LEBER, BEN LB CHARGERS

PERSONAL: Born December 7, 1978, in Vermillion, S.D. ... 6-3/244.
HIGH SCHOOL: Vermillion (S.D.).
COLLEGE: Kansas State.
TRANSACTIONS/CAREER NOTES: Selected by San Diego Chargers in third round (71st pick overall) of 2002 NFL draft. ... Signed by Chargers (July 22, 2002).

Year Team	G	GS	TOTALS Tk.	Ast.	Sks.	INTERCEPTIONS No.	Yds.	Avg.	TD
2002—San Diego NFL	16	14	40	9	5.0	0	0	0.0	0
2003—San Diego NFL	16	16	69	11	3.0	0	0	0.0	0
Pro totals (2 years)	32	30	109	20	8.0	0	0	0.0	0

LEBLANC, CLARENCE S

PERSONAL: Born March 26, 1977, in River Ridge, La. ... 6-3/210.
HIGH SCHOOL: John Curtis (La.).
COLLEGE: Louisiana State.
TRANSACTIONS/CAREER NOTES: Signed as non-drafted free agent by New York Giants (February 16, 2001). ... Assigned by Giants to Rhein Fire in 2001 NFL Europe enhancement allocation program (2001). ... Waived by Giants (September 2, 2001). ... Re-signed by Giants to practice squad (September 3, 2001). ... Activated (October 2, 2001). ... Inactive for four games (2001). ... Claimed on waivers by New York Jets (October 26, 2001). ... Claimed on waivers by New York Giants (December 31, 2001). ... On injured reserve with leg injury (August 17, 2002-entire season). ... On physically unable to perform list with leg injury (July 26-August 10, 2003). ... Waived by Giants (August 31, 2003). ... Re-signed by Giants (November 19, 2003). ... Released by Giants (May 20, 2004).

Year Team	G	GS	TOTALS Tk.	Ast.	Sks.	INTERCEPTIONS No.	Yds.	Avg.	TD
2003—New York Giants NFL	4	0	0	0	0.0	0	0	0.0	0

L

LECHLER, SHANE — P — RAIDERS

PERSONAL: Born August 7, 1976, in Sealy, Texas. ... 6-2/225. ... Full name: Edward Shane Lechler.
HIGH SCHOOL: East Bernard (Texas).
COLLEGE: Texas A&M.
TRANSACTIONS/CAREER NOTES: Selected by Oakland Raiders in fifth round (142nd pick overall) of 2000 NFL draft. ... Signed by Raiders (July 22, 2000).
CHAMPIONSHIP GAME EXPERIENCE: Played in AFC championship game (2000 and 2002 seasons). ... Played in Super Bowl 37 (2002 season).
HONORS: Named punter on THE SPORTING NEWS college All-America second team (1997). ... Named punter on THE SPORTING NEWS college All-America first team (1998). ... Named punter on THE SPORTING NEWS NFL All-Pro team (2000). ... Named punter on THE SPORTING NEWS college All-America third team (1999). ... Played in Pro Bowl (2001 season).

		PUNTING					
Year Team	**G**	**No.**	**Yds.**	**Avg.**	**Net avg.**	**In. 20**	**Blk.**
2000—Oakland NFL	16	65	2984	45.9	*38.0	24	▲1
2001—Oakland NFL	16	73	3375	§46.2	35.6	23	1
2002—Oakland NFL	14	53	2251	42.5	32.7	18	0
2003—Oakland NFL	16	96	*4503	*46.9	37.2	27	0
Pro totals (4 years)	62	287	13113	45.7	36.1	92	2

LEDFORD, DWAYNE — C — 49ERS

PERSONAL: Born November 2, 1976, in Morgantown, N.C. ... 6-4/300. ... Full name: Billy Dwayne Ledford.
HIGH SCHOOL: McDowell (N.C.).
COLLEGE: East Carolina.
TRANSACTIONS/CAREER NOTES: Signed as non-drafted free agent by San Francisco 49ers (April 23, 1999). ... Released by 49ers (September 4, 1999). ... Re-signed by 49ers to practice squad (September 7, 1999). ... Activated (December 29, 1999); did not play. ... Released by 49ers (September 15, 2000). ... Signed by Jacksonville Jaguars to practice squad (November 15, 2000). ... Activated (December 19, 2000); did not play. ... Released by Jaguars (September 2, 2001). ... Signed by Carolina Panthers (October 23, 2001). ... Released by Panthers (November 6, 2001). ... Signed by Philadelphia Eagles (January 29, 2002). ... Released by Eagles (August 27, 2002). ... Selected by Rhein Fire in 2003 NFL Europe draft (February 5, 2003). ... Signed by San Francisco 49ers (June 18, 2003). ... On injured reserve with ankle injury (November 26, 2003-remainder of season).
PLAYING EXPERIENCE: San Francisco NFL, 2000-2003. ... Games/Games started: 2000 (1/0), 2003 (8/1). Total: 9/1.

LEE, CHARLES — WR — BUCCANEERS

PERSONAL: Born November 19, 1977, in Miami, Fla. ... 6-2/210.
HIGH SCHOOL: Homestead (Fla.).
COLLEGE: Central Florida.
TRANSACTIONS/CAREER NOTES: Selected by Green Bay Packers in seventh round (242nd pick overall) of 2000 NFL draft. ... Signed by Packers (June 21, 2000). ... Released by Packers (September 1, 2002). ... Signed by Tampa Bay Buccaneers (October 1, 2002). ... Granted free agency (February 28, 2003). ... Re-signed by Buccaneers (May 22, 2003).
SINGLE GAME HIGHS (regular season): Receptions—10 (December 20, 2003, vs. Atlanta); yards—95 (December 14, 2003, vs. Houston); and touchdown receptions—1 (December 20, 2003, vs. Atlanta).

			RUSHING				RECEIVING				TOTALS			
Year Team	**G**	**GS**	**Att.**	**Yds.**	**Avg.**	**TD**	**No.**	**Yds.**	**Avg.**	**TD**	**TD**	**2pt.**	**Pts.**	**Fum.**
2000—Green Bay NFL	15	1	0	0	0.0	0	10	134	13.4	0	0	0	0	0
2001—Green Bay NFL	7	0	0	0	0.0	0	3	32	10.7	1	1	0	6	0
2002—Tampa Bay NFL	1	0	0	0	0.0	0	0	0	0.0	0	0	0	0	0
2003—Tampa Bay NFL	8	5	2	14	7.0	0	33	432	13.1	2	2	0	12	0
Pro totals (4 years)	31	6	2	14	7.0	0	46	598	13.0	3	3	0	18	0

LEE, DONALD — TE — DOLPHINS

PERSONAL: Born August 31, 1980, in Maben, Miss. ... 6-3/255. ... Full name: Donald Tywon Lee.
HIGH SCHOOL: Maben (Miss.).
COLLEGE: Mississippi State.
TRANSACTIONS/CAREER NOTES: Selected by Miami Dolphins in fifth round (156th pick overall) of 2003 NFL draft. ... Signed by Dolphins (June 16, 2003).
SINGLE GAME HIGHS (regular season): Receptions—2 (December 28, 2003, vs. New York Jets); yards—48 (November 2, 2003, vs. Indianapolis); and touchdown receptions—1 (November 9, 2003, vs.Tennessee).

			RECEIVING				TOTALS			
Year Team	**G**	**GS**	**No.**	**Yds.**	**Avg.**	**TD**	**TD**	**2pt.**	**Pts.**	**Fum.**
2003—Miami NFL	16	5	7	110	15.7	1	1	0	6	0

LEFTWICH, BYRON — QB — JAGUARS

PERSONAL: Born January 14, 1980, in Washington, DC. ... 6-5/245. ... Full name: Byron A. Leftwich.
HIGH SCHOOL: H.D. Woodson (Washington, D.C.).
COLLEGE: Marshall.
TRANSACTIONS/CAREER NOTES: Selected by Jacksonville Jaguars in first round (seventh pick overall) of 2003 NFL draft. ... Signed by Jaguars (August 13, 2003).

SINGLE GAME HIGHS (regular season): Attempts—42 (October 12, 2003, vs. Miami); completions—24 (October 12, 2003, vs. Miami); yards—336 (October 5, 2003, vs. San Diego); and touchdown passes—2 (November 30, 2003, vs. Tampa Bay).
STATISTICAL PLATEAUS: 300-yard passing games: 2003 (1). Total: 1.
MISCELLANEOUS: Regular-season record as starting NFL quarterback: 5-8 (.385).

			PASSING									RUSHING				TOTALS		
Year Team	G	GS	Att.	Cmp.	Pct.	Yds.	TD	Int.	Avg.	Skd.	Rat.	Att.	Yds.	Avg.	TD	TD	2pt.	Pts.
2003—Jacksonville NFL	15	13	418	239	57.2	2819	14	16	6.74	19	73.0	25	108	4.3	2	2	0	12

LEGREE, LANCE DT

PERSONAL: Born December 22, 1977, in Charleston, S.C. ... 6-1/300.
HIGH SCHOOL: St. Stephens (S.C.).
COLLEGE: Notre Dame.
TRANSACTIONS/CAREER NOTES: Signed as non-drafted free agent by New York Giants (April 27, 2001). ... Granted free agency (March 3, 2004).

			TOTALS		
Year Team	G	GS	Tk.	Ast.	Sks.
2001—New York Giants NFL	13	2	15	4	0.0
2002—New York Giants NFL	15	10	18	12	0.0
2003—New York Giants NFL	16	2	15	5	2.0
Pro totals (3 years)	44	14	48	21	2.0

LEHAN, MICHAEL CB BROWNS

PERSONAL: Born November 25, 1979, in Hopkins, Minn. ... 6-0/190.
HIGH SCHOOL: Hopkins (Minn.).
COLLEGE: Minnesota.
TRANSACTIONS/CAREER NOTES: Selected by Cleveland Browns in fifth round (152nd pick overall) of 2003 NFL draft. ... Signed by Browns (August 1, 2003).

			TOTALS			INTERCEPTIONS			
Year Team	G	GS	Tk.	Ast.	Sks.	No.	Yds.	Avg.	TD
2003—Cleveland NFL	12	2	14	2	0.0	0	0	0.0	0

LEHR, MATT C COWBOYS

PERSONAL: Born April 25, 1979, in Jacksonville, Fla. ... 6-2/304. ... Full name: Matthew Steven Lehr.
HIGH SCHOOL: Woodbridge (Va.).
COLLEGE: Virginia Tech.
TRANSACTIONS/CAREER NOTES: Selected by Dallas Cowboys in fifth round (137th pick overall) of 2001 NFL draft. ... Signed by Cowboys (July 21, 2001). ... Granted free agency (March 3, 2004). ... Re-signed by Cowboys (April 14, 2004).
PLAYING EXPERIENCE: Dallas NFL, 2001-2003. ... Games/Games started: 2001 (8/0), 2002 (12/4), 2003 (16/16). Total: 36/20.

LELIE, ASHLEY WR BRONCOS

PERSONAL: Born February 16, 1980, in Bellflower, Calif. ... 6-3/200.
HIGH SCHOOL: Radford (Honolulu, Hawaii).
COLLEGE: Hawaii.
TRANSACTIONS/CAREER NOTES: Selected after junior season by Denver Broncos in first round (19th pick overall) of 2002 NFL draft. ... Signed by Broncos (July 25, 2002).
HONORS: Named wide receiver on THE SPORTING NEWS college All-America third team (2001).
SINGLE GAME HIGHS (regular season): Receptions—8 (November 11, 2002, vs. Oakland); yards—115 (December 21, 2003, vs. Indianapolis); and touchdown receptions—1 (September 28, 2003, vs. Detroit).
STATISTICAL PLATEAUS: 100-yard receiving games: 2002 (1), 2003 (2). Total: 3.

			RUSHING				RECEIVING				TOTALS			
Year Team	G	GS	Att.	Yds.	Avg.	TD	No.	Yds.	Avg.	TD	TD	2pt.	Pts.	Fum.
2002—Denver NFL	16	1	4	40	10.0	0	35	525	15.0	2	2	0	12	0
2003—Denver NFL	16	10	8	43	5.4	0	37	628	17.0	2	2	0	12	0
Pro totals (2 years)	32	11	12	83	6.9	0	72	1153	16.0	4	4	0	24	0

LENON, PARIS LB PACKERS

PERSONAL: Born November 26, 1977, in Lynchburg, Va. ... 6-2/240. ... Full name: Paris Michael Lenon.
HIGH SCHOOL: Heritage (Lynchburg, Va.).
COLLEGE: Richmond.
TRANSACTIONS/CAREER NOTES: Signed as non-drafted free agent by Carolina Panthers (April 26, 2000). ... Released by Panthers (June 9, 2000). ... Signed by Green Bay Packers (April 26, 2001). ... Released by Packers (July 24, 2001). ... Signed by Seattle Seahawks (August 16, 2001). ... Released by Seahawks (August 27, 2001). ... Signed by Packers to practice squad (December 27, 2001). ... Assigned by Packers to Amsterdam Admirals in 2002 NFL Europe enhancement allocation program (February 12, 2002). ... Granted free agency (March 3, 2004). ... Re-signed by Packers (April 22, 2004).

Year	Team	G	GS	TOTALS Tk.	Ast.	Sks.	INTERCEPTIONS No.	Yds.	Avg.	TD
2002—Green Bay NFL		16	0	3	0	0.0	0	0	0.0	0
2003—Green Bay NFL		16	0	4	4	0.0	0	0	0.0	0
Pro totals (2 years)		32	0	7	4	0.0	0	0	0.0	0

LEONARD, MATT — DT — JAGUARS

PERSONAL: Born November 7, 1979, in Agua Dulce, Calif. ... 6-3/301. ... Full name: Molia Matthew Leonard.

HIGH SCHOOL: Palmdale (Calif.).

COLLEGE: Stanford.

TRANSACTIONS/CAREER NOTES: Signed as non-drafted free agent by Jacksonville Jaguars (April 28, 2003). ... Waived by Jaguars (September 16, 2003). ... Re-signed by Jaguars to practice squad (September 18, 2003). ... Activated (October 30, 2003).

Year	Team	G	GS	TOTALS Tk.	Ast.	Sks.
2003—Jacksonville NFL		4	0	0	2	0.0

LEPSIS, MATT — T — BRONCOS

PERSONAL: Born January 13, 1974, in Conroe, Texas. ... 6-4/290. ... Full name: Matthew Lepsis.

HIGH SCHOOL: Frisco (Texas).

COLLEGE: Colorado.

TRANSACTIONS/CAREER NOTES: Signed as non-drafted free agent by Denver Broncos (April 22, 1997). ... On non-football injury list with knee injury (July 16, 1997-entire season). ... Assigned by Broncos to Barcelona Dragons in 1998 NFL Europe enhancement allocation program (February 18, 1998). ... Granted free agency (March 2, 2001). ... Re-signed by Broncos (March 21, 2001).

PLAYING EXPERIENCE: Denver NFL, 1997-2003. ... Games/Games started: 1998 (16/0), 1999 (16/16), 2000 (16/16), 2001 (16/16), 2002 (16/15), 2003 (16/16), Total: 96/79.

CHAMPIONSHIP GAME EXPERIENCE: Played in AFC championship game (1998 season). ... Member of Super Bowl championship team (1998 season).

LEVELS, DWAYNE — LB — BENGALS

PERSONAL: Born May 9, 1979, in Richardson, Texas. ... 6-2/248.

HIGH SCHOOL: Richardson (Texas).

COLLEGE: Oklahoma State.

TRANSACTIONS/CAREER NOTES: Signed as non-drafted free agent by Cincinnati Bengals (April 23, 2002). ... Waived by Bengals (September 1, 2002). ... Re-signed by Bengals to practice squad (September 2, 2002). ... Activated (December 23, 2002). ... Inactive for one game (2002). ... On injured reserve with knee injury (December 9, 2003-remainder of season).

Year	Team	G	GS	TOTALS Tk.	Ast.	Sks.	INTERCEPTIONS No.	Yds.	Avg.	TD
2003—Cincinnati NFL		13	1	5	5	0.0	0	0	0.0	0

LEVENS, DORSEY — RB

PERSONAL: Born May 21, 1970, in Syracuse, N.Y. ... 6-1/230. ... Full name: Herbert Dorsey Levens.

HIGH SCHOOL: Nottingham (Syracuse, N.Y.).

COLLEGE: Georgia Tech.

TRANSACTIONS/CAREER NOTES: Selected by Green Bay Packers in fifth round (149th pick overall) of 1994 NFL draft. ... Signed by Packers (June 9, 1994). ... Granted free agency (February 14, 1997). ... Re-signed by Packers (June 20, 1997). ... Designated by Packers as franchise player (February 13, 1998). ... Re-signed by Packers (August 30, 1998). ... Released by Packers (February 28, 2002). ... Signed by Philadelphia Eagles (July 11, 2002). ... Granted unconditional free agency (February 28, 2003). ... Signed by New York Giants (April 7, 2003). ... Released by Giants (February 25, 2004).

CHAMPIONSHIP GAME EXPERIENCE: Played in NFC championship game (1995-97 and 2002 seasons). ... Member of Super Bowl championship team (1996 season). ... Played in Super Bowl 32 (1997 season).

HONORS: Played in Pro Bowl (1997 season).

SINGLE GAME HIGHS (regular season): Attempts—33 (November 23, 1997, vs. Dallas); yards—190 (November 23, 1997, vs. Dallas); and rushing touchdowns—4 (January 2, 2000, vs. Arizona).

STATISTICAL PLATEAUS: 100-yard rushing games: 1997 (6), 1998 (1), 1999 (3). Total: 10.

Year	Team	G	GS	RUSHING Att.	Yds.	Avg.	TD	RECEIVING No.	Yds.	Avg.	TD	KICKOFF RETURNS No.	Yds.	Avg.	TD	TOTALS TD	2pt.	Pts.	Fum.
1994—Green Bay NFL		14	0	5	15	3.0	0	1	9	9.0	0	2	31	15.5	0	0	0	0	0
1995—Green Bay NFL		15	12	36	120	3.3	3	48	434	9.0	4	0	0	0.0	0	7	0	42	0
1996—Green Bay NFL		16	1	121	566	4.7	5	31	226	7.3	5	5	84	16.8	0	10	0	60	2
1997—Green Bay NFL		16	16	329	1435	4.4	7	53	370	7.0	5	0	0	0.0	0	12	1	74	5
1998—Green Bay NFL		7	4	115	378	3.3	1	27	162	6.0	0	0	0	0.0	0	1	0	6	0
1999—Green Bay NFL		14	14	279	1034	3.7	9	71	573	8.1	1	0	0	0.0	0	10	0	60	5
2000—Green Bay NFL		5	5	77	224	2.9	3	16	146	9.1	0	0	0	0.0	0	3	0	18	0
2001—Green Bay NFL		15	1	44	165	3.8	0	24	159	6.6	1	14	362	25.9	0	1	0	6	0
2002—Philadelphia NFL		16	0	75	411	5.5	1	19	124	6.5	1	1	24	24.0	0	2	0	12	1
2003—New York Giants NFL		11	0	68	197	2.9	3	5	39	7.8	0	0	0	0.0	0	3	0	18	0
Pro totals (10 years)		129	53	1149	4545	4.0	32	295	2242	7.6	17	22	501	22.8	0	49	1	296	13

LEVERETTE, OTIS — DE — CHARGERS

PERSONAL: Born May 31, 1978, in Americus, Ga. ... 6-6/278. ... Full name: Otis Catrell Leverette.
HIGH SCHOOL: Americus (Ga.).
JUNIOR COLLEGE: Middle Georgia College.
COLLEGE: Alabama-Birmingham.
TRANSACTIONS/CAREER NOTES: Selected by Miami Dolphins in sixth round (187th pick overall) of 2001 NFL draft. ... Signed by Dolphins (July 12, 2001). ... Claimed on waivers by Washington Redskins (September 3, 2001). ... Claimed on waivers by San Diego Chargers (November 19, 2002). ... Granted free agency (March 3, 2004). ... Re-signed by Chargers (May 13, 2004).

			TOTALS			INTERCEPTIONS			
Year Team	G	GS	Tk.	Ast.	Sks.	No.	Yds.	Avg.	TD
2001—Washington NFL	4	0	0	0	0.0	1	1	1.0	0
2002—Washington NFL	1	0	1	0	0.0	0	0	0.0	0
2003—San Diego NFL	7	0	17	6	1.0	0	0	0.0	0
Pro totals (3 years)	12	0	18	6	1.0	1	1	1.0	0

LEWIS, CHAD — TE — EAGLES

PERSONAL: Born October 5, 1971, in Fort Dix, N.J. ... 6-6/252. ... Full name: Chad Wayne Lewis.
HIGH SCHOOL: Orem (Utah).
COLLEGE: Brigham Young.
TRANSACTIONS/CAREER NOTES: Signed as non-drafted free agent by Philadelphia Eagles (April 23, 1997). ... Released by Eagles (September 15, 1998). ... Signed by St. Louis Rams (December 9, 1998). ... Inactive for three games with Rams (1998). ... Claimed on waivers by Eagles (November 16, 1999). ... Granted free agency (February 11, 2000). ... Re-signed by Eagles (March 17, 2000).
CHAMPIONSHIP GAME EXPERIENCE: Played in NFC championship game (2001-2003 seasons).
HONORS: Played in Pro Bowl (2000-2002 seasons).
SINGLE GAME HIGHS (regular season): Receptions—9 (December 24, 2000, vs. Cincinnati); yards—100 (December 10, 2000, vs. Cleveland); and touchdown receptions—2 (December 30, 2001, vs. New York Giants).
STATISTICAL PLATEAUS: 100-yard receiving games: 2000 (1). Total: 1.

			RECEIVING				TOTALS			
Year Team	G	GS	No.	Yds.	Avg.	TD	TD	2pt.	Pts.	Fum.
1997—Philadelphia NFL	16	3	12	94	7.8	4	4	0	24	0
1998—Philadelphia NFL	2	0	0	0	0.0	0	0	0	0	0
1999—St. Louis NFL	6	0	1	12	12.0	0	0	0	0	0
—Philadelphia NFL	6	4	7	76	10.9	3	3	0	18	0
2000—Philadelphia NFL	16	16	69	735	10.7	3	3	0	18	0
2001—Philadelphia NFL	15	15	41	422	10.3	6	6	0	36	2
2002—Philadelphia NFL	16	16	42	398	9.5	3	3	∞2	22	2
2003—Philadelphia NFL	16	14	23	293	12.7	1	1	0	6	0
Pro totals (7 years)	93	68	195	2030	10.4	20	20	2	124	4

LEWIS, DAMIONE — DT — RAMS

PERSONAL: Born March 1, 1978, in Sulphur Springs, Texas. ... 6-2/301. ... Full name: Damione Ramon Lewis.
HIGH SCHOOL: Sulphur Springs (Texas).
COLLEGE: Miami (Fla.).
TRANSACTIONS/CAREER NOTES: Selected by St. Louis Rams in first round (12th pick overall) of 2001 NFL draft. ... Signed by Rams (July 27, 2001). ... On injured reserve with foot injury (November 20, 2001-remainder of season).
HONORS: Named defensive tackle on THE SPORTING NEWS college All-America third team (2000).

			TOTALS			INTERCEPTIONS			
Year Team	G	GS	Tk.	Ast.	Sks.	No.	Yds.	Avg.	TD
2001—St. Louis NFL	9	3	9	1	0.0	0	0	0.0	0
2002—St. Louis NFL	16	2	14	6	4.0	0	0	0.0	0
2003—St. Louis NFL	12	7	12	4	0.5	0	0	0.0	0
Pro totals (3 years)	37	12	35	11	4.5	0	0	0.0	0

LEWIS, D.D. — LB — SEAHAWKS

PERSONAL: Born January 8, 1979, in Bremerhaven, Germany. ... 6-1/241. ... Full name: De'Andre De'Wayne Lewis.
HIGH SCHOOL: Aldine (Houston).
COLLEGE: Texas.
TRANSACTIONS/CAREER NOTES: Signed as non-drafted free agent by Seattle Seahawks (April 30, 2002).

			TOTALS			INTERCEPTIONS			
Year Team	G	GS	Tk.	Ast.	Sks.	No.	Yds.	Avg.	TD
2002—Seattle NFL	16	0	15	2	0.0	0	0	0.0	0
2003—Seattle NFL	15	6	38	18	0.0	0	0	0.0	0
Pro totals (2 years)	31	6	53	20	0.0	0	0	0.0	0

LEWIS, DERRICK — WR — SAINTS

PERSONAL: Born October 30, 1975, in New Orleans, La. ... 6-2/185. ... Full name: Derrick Lamont Lewis.
HIGH SCHOOL: Joseph S. Clark (New Orleans).
JUNIOR COLLEGE: Sacramento City College.

COLLEGE: San Diego State.

TRANSACTIONS/CAREER NOTES: Signed as non-drafted free agent by New Orleans Saints (April 23, 2002). ... Released by Saints (August 26, 2002). ... Re-signed by Saints to practice squad (September 2, 2002). ... Released by Saints (September 11, 2002). ... Re-signed by Saints to practice squad (September 18, 2002). ... Activated (December 22, 2002). ... Waived by Saints (September 24, 2003). ... Re-signed by Saints to practice squad (September 25, 2003). ... Activated (November 26, 2003). ... Assigned by Saints to Frankfurt Galaxy in 2004 NFL Europe enhancement allocation program (February 9, 2004).

SINGLE GAME HIGHS (regular season): Receptions—1 (November 30, 2003, vs. Washington); yards—7 (November 30, 2003, vs. Washington); and touchdown receptions—0.

			RECEIVING				TOTALS			
Year Team	**G**	**GS**	**No.**	**Yds.**	**Avg.**	**TD**	**TD**	**2pt.**	**Pts.**	**Fum.**
2002—New Orleans NFL	2	0	0	0	0.0	0	0	0	0	0
2003—New Orleans NFL	3	0	1	7	7.0	0	0	0	0	0
Pro totals (2 years)	5	0	1	7	7.0	0	0	0	0	0

LEWIS, GREG — WR — EAGLES

PERSONAL: Born February 12, 1980, in Chicago, Ill. ... 6-0/180. ... Full name: Gregory Alan Lewis Jr.

HIGH SCHOOL: Rich South (Matteson, Ill.).

COLLEGE: Illinois.

TRANSACTIONS/CAREER NOTES: Signed as non-drafted free agent by Philadelphia Eagles (April 28, 2003).

CHAMPIONSHIP GAME EXPERIENCE: Played in NFC championship game (2003 season).

SINGLE GAME HIGHS (regular season): Receptions—1 (December 27, 2003, vs. Washington); yards—25 (December 27, 2003, vs. Washington); and touchdown receptions—0.

			RECEIVING				TOTALS			
Year Team	**G**	**GS**	**No.**	**Yds.**	**Avg.**	**TD**	**TD**	**2pt.**	**Pts.**	**Fum.**
2003—Philadelphia NFL	11	0	6	95	15.8	0	0	0	0	0

LEWIS, JAMAL — RB — RAVENS

PERSONAL: Born August 29, 1979, in Atlanta, Ga. ... 5-11/240. ... Full name: Jamal Lafitte Lewis.

HIGH SCHOOL: Douglass (Atlanta).

COLLEGE: Tennessee.

TRANSACTIONS/CAREER NOTES: Selected after junior season by Baltimore Ravens in first round (fifth pick overall) of 2000 NFL draft. ... Signed by Ravens (July 24, 2000). ... On injured reserve with knee injury (August 28, 2001-entire season). ... On suspended list for violating league substance abuse policy (November 17, 2001).

CHAMPIONSHIP GAME EXPERIENCE: Played in AFC championship game (2000 season). ... Member of Super Bowl championship team (2000 season).

HONORS: Named College Football Freshman of the Year by THE SPORTING NEWS (1997). ... Named running back on THE SPORTING NEWS NFL All-Pro team (2003). ... Played in Pro Bowl (2003 season).

RECORDS: Holds NFL record for most yards rushing in a game—295 (September 14, 2003, vs. Cleveland).

SINGLE GAME HIGHS (regular season): Attempts—32 (October 26, 2003, vs. Denver); yards—295 (September 14, 2003, vs. Cleveland); and rushing touchdowns—3 (December 7, 2003, vs. Cincinnati).

STATISTICAL PLATEAUS: 100-yard rushing games: 2000 (5), 2002 (5), 2003 (12). Total: 22. 100-yard receiving games: 2002 (1). Total: 1.

MISCELLANEOUS: Holds Baltimore Ravens all-time records for most yards rushing (4,757), most rushing touchdowns (26) and most touchdowns (27).

			RUSHING				RECEIVING				TOTALS			
Year Team	**G**	**GS**	**Att.**	**Yds.**	**Avg.**	**TD**	**No.**	**Yds.**	**Avg.**	**TD**	**TD**	**2pt.**	**Pts.**	**Fum.**
2000—Baltimore NFL	16	13	309	1364	4.4	6	27	296	11.0	0	6	1	38	6
2001—Baltimore NFL							Did not play.							
2002—Baltimore NFL	16	15	308	1327	4.3	6	47	442	9.4	1	7	0	42	8
2003—Baltimore NFL	16	16	387	*2066	5.3	14	26	205	7.9	0	14	0	84	8
Pro totals (3 years)	48	44	1004	4757	4.7	26	100	943	9.4	1	27	1	164	22

LEWIS, JERMAINE — WR/KR — JAGUARS

PERSONAL: Born October 16, 1974, in Lanham, Md. ... 5-7/183. ... Full name: Jermaine Edward Lewis.

HIGH SCHOOL: Eleanor Roosevelt (Greenbelt, Md.).

COLLEGE: Maryland.

TRANSACTIONS/CAREER NOTES: Selected by Baltimore Ravens in fifth round (153rd pick overall) of 1996 NFL draft. ... Signed by Ravens (July 18, 1996). ... Selected by Houston Texans from Ravens in NFL expansion draft (February 18, 2002). ... Released by Texans (February 20, 2003). ... Signed by Jacksonville Jaguars (March 20, 2003). ... On injured reserve with knee injury (September 16, 2003-remainder of season).

CHAMPIONSHIP GAME EXPERIENCE: Played in AFC championship game (2000 season). ... Member of Super Bowl championship team (2000 season).

HONORS: Named punt returner on THE SPORTING NEWS NFL All-Pro team (1998 and 2001). ... Played in Pro Bowl (1998 and 2001 seasons).

RECORDS: Shares NFL single-game records for most touchdowns by punt returns—2; (December 24, 2000, Baltimore vs. New York Jets, and December 7, 1997, Baltimore vs. Seattle) and most touchdowns by combined kick return—2 (December 7, 1997, vs. Seattle and also on December 24, 2000, vs. New York Jets).

SINGLE GAME HIGHS (regular season): Receptions—8 (September 21, 1997, vs. Tennessee); yards—124 (September 21, 1997, vs. Tennessee); and touchdown receptions—2 (December 5, 1999, vs. Tennessee).

STATISTICAL PLATEAUS: 100-yard receiving games: 1997 (2), 1998 (2). Total: 4.

			RUSHING				RECEIVING				PUNT RETURNS				KICKOFF RETURNS				TOTALS		
Year Team	**G**	**GS**	**Att.**	**Yds.**	**Avg.**	**TD**	**No.**	**Yds.**	**Avg.**	**TD**	**No.**	**Yds.**	**Avg.**	**TD**	**No.**	**Yds.**	**Avg.**	**TD**	**TD**	**2pt.**	**Pts.**
1996—Bal. NFL	16	1	1	-3	-3.0	0	5	78	15.6	1	36	339	9.4	0	41	883	21.5	0	1	0	6
1997—Bal. NFL	14	7	3	35	11.7	0	42	648	15.4	6	28	437	*15.6	2	41	905	22.1	0	8	0	48
1998—Bal. NFL	13	13	5	20	4.0	0	41	784	19.1	6	32	405	12.7	†2	6	145	24.2	0	8	0	48
1999—Bal. NFL	15	6	5	11	2.2	0	25	281	11.2	2	*57	452	7.9	0	8	158	19.8	0	2	0	12

Year	Team	G	GS	RUSHING Att.	Yds.	Avg.	TD	RECEIVING No.	Yds.	Avg.	TD	PUNT RETURNS No.	Yds.	Avg.	TD	KICKOFF RETURNS No.	Yds.	Avg.	TD	TOTALS TD	2pt.	Pts.
2000	—Bal. NFL	15	1	3	38	12.7	0	19	161	8.5	1	36	578	*16.1	†2	1	23	23.0	0	3	0	18
2001	—Bal. NFL	15	2	9	33	3.7	0	4	32	8.0	0	*42	*519	12.4	0	42	1039	24.7	0	0	0	0
2002	—Hou. NFL	12	1	3	8	2.7	0	2	41	20.5	0	36	280	7.8	0	46	961	20.9	0	0	0	0
2003	—Jac. NFL	2	0	1	6	6.0	0	4	100	25.0	1	5	45	9.0	0	6	111	18.5	0	1	0	6
Pro totals (8 years)		102	31	30	148	4.9	0	142	2125	15.0	17	272	3055	11.2	6	191	4225	22.1	0	23	0	138

LEWIS, KEVIN LB GIANTS

PERSONAL: Born October 6, 1978, in Orlando, Fla. ... 6-1/235.
HIGH SCHOOL: Jones (Orlando, Fla.).
COLLEGE: Duke.
TRANSACTIONS/CAREER NOTES: Signed by New York Giants as non-drafted free agent (April 20, 2000). ... Released by Giants (September 2, 2001). ... Re-signed by Giants to practice squad (September 3, 2001). ... Activated (November 4, 2001). ... Granted free agency (February 28, 2003). ... Re-signed by Giants (March 6, 2003).
CHAMPIONSHIP GAME EXPERIENCE: Member of Giants for Super Bowl 35 (2000 season); inactive.

Year	Team	G	GS	TOTALS Tk.	Ast.	Sks.	INTERCEPTIONS No.	Yds.	Avg.	TD
2000	—New York Giants NFL	6	0	1	0	0.0	0	0	0.0	0
2001	—New York Giants NFL	9	0	0	0	0.0	0	0	0.0	0
2002	—New York Giants NFL	15	2	10	3	1.0	0	0	0.0	0
2003	—New York Giants NFL	16	0	1	2	0.0	0	0	0.0	0
Pro totals (4 years)		46	2	12	5	1.0	0	0	0.0	0

LEWIS, MICHAEL WR SAINTS

PERSONAL: Born November 14, 1971, in New Orleans, La. ... 5-8/165. ... Full name: Michael Lee Lewis.
HIGH SCHOOL: Grace King (Metairie, La.).
TRANSACTIONS/CAREER NOTES: Signed as non-drafted free agent by Philadelphia Eagles (July 14, 2000). ... Released by Eagles (August 21, 2000). ... Signed by New Orleans Saints (January 9, 2001). ... Assigned by Saints to Rhein Fire in 2001 NFL Europe enhancement allocation program (February 17, 2001). ... Released by Saints (October 30, 2001). ... Re-signed by Saints (December 21, 2001).
HONORS: Played in Pro Bowl (2002 season). ... Named kick returner on the THE SPORTING NEWS NFL All-Pro team (2002).
RECORDS: Holds NFL single-season record for most combined kick returns—114 (2002); and most yards from combined kick returns—2,432 (2002).
SINGLE GAME HIGHS (regular season): Receptions—4 (November 16, 2003, vs. Atlanta); yards—114 (November 24, 2002, vs. Cleveland); and touchdown receptions—1 (November 2, 2003, vs. Tampa Bay).
STATISTICAL PLATEAUS: 100-yard receiving games: 2002 (1). Total: 1.

Year	Team	G	GS	RECEIVING No.	Yds.	Avg.	TD	PUNT RETURNS No.	Yds.	Avg.	TD	KICKOFF RETURNS No.	Yds.	Avg.	TD	TOTALS TD	2pt.	Pts.	Fum.
2001	—New Orleans NFL	8	0	0	0	0.0	0	14	81	5.8	0	32	762	23.8	0	0	0	0	6
2002	—New Orleans NFL	16	0	8	200	25.0	0	44	*625	14.2	1	*70	*1807	25.8	†2	3	0	18	6
2003	—New Orleans NFL	13	1	12	226	18.8	1	30	275	9.2	0	45	1068	23.7	0	1	0	6	2
Pro totals (3 years)		37	1	20	426	21.3	1	88	981	11.1	1	147	3637	24.7	2	4	0	24	14

LEWIS, MICHAEL S EAGLES

PERSONAL: Born April 29, 1980, in Houston, Texas. ... 6-1/211.
HIGH SCHOOL: Lamar Consolidated (Richmond, Texas).
COLLEGE: Colorado.
TRANSACTIONS/CAREER NOTES: Selected by Philadelphia Eagles in second round (58th pick overall) of 2002 NFL draft. ... Signed by Eagles (June 25, 2002).
CHAMPIONSHIP GAME EXPERIENCE: Played in NFC championship game (2002 and 2003 seasons).
HONORS: Named safety on THE SPORTING NEWS college All-America third team (2001).

Year	Team	G	GS	TOTALS Tk.	Ast.	Sks.	INTERCEPTIONS No.	Yds.	Avg.	TD
2002	—Philadelphia NFL	14	4	33	5	1.0	1	0	0.0	0
2003	—Philadelphia NFL	16	16	67	19	2.0	3	31	10.3	0
Pro totals (2 years)		30	20	100	24	3.0	4	31	7.8	0

LEWIS, MO LB

PERSONAL: Born October 21, 1969, in Atlanta, Ga. ... 6-3/258. ... Full name: Morris C. Lewis.
HIGH SCHOOL: J.C. Murphy (Atlanta).
COLLEGE: Georgia.
TRANSACTIONS/CAREER NOTES: Selected by New York Jets in third round (62nd pick overall) of 1991 NFL draft. ... Signed by Jets (July 18, 1991). ... Designated by Jets as franchise player (February 11, 2000). ... Released by Jets (March 1, 2004).
CHAMPIONSHIP GAME EXPERIENCE: Played in AFC championship game (1998 season).
HONORS: Played in Pro Bowl (1998-2000 seasons).

Year	Team	G	GS	TOTALS Tk.	Ast.	Sks.	INTERCEPTIONS No.	Yds.	Avg.	TD
1991	—New York Jets NFL	16	16	48	28	2.0	0	0	0.0	0
1992	—New York Jets NFL	16	16	105	40	1.0	1	1	1.0	0
1993	—New York Jets NFL	16	16	95	63	4.0	2	4	2.0	0

L

Year	Team	G	GS	TOTALS Tk.	Ast.	Sks.	INTERCEPTIONS No.	Yds.	Avg.	TD
1994	New York Jets NFL	16	16	103	27	6.0	4	106	26.5	2
1995	New York Jets NFL	16	16	82	29	5.0	2	22	11.0	▲1
1996	New York Jets NFL	9	9	32	11	0.5	0	0	0.0	0
1997	New York Jets NFL	16	16	45	27	8.0	1	43	43.0	1
1998	New York Jets NFL	16	16	67	14	7.0	1	11	11.0	0
1999	New York Jets NFL	16	16	58	31	5.5	0	0	0.0	0
2000	New York Jets NFL	16	16	65	23	10.0	1	23	23.0	0
2001	New York Jets NFL	16	16	77	31	3.0	1	17	17.0	0
2002	New York Jets NFL	16	16	68	14	0.5	1	14	14.0	0
2003	New York Jets NFL	15	15	34	14	0.0	0	0	0.0	0
Pro totals (13 years)		200	200	879	352	52.5	14	241	17.2	4

LEWIS, RAY — LB — RAVENS

PERSONAL: Born May 15, 1975, in Bartow, Fla. ... 6-1/245. ... Full name: Ray Anthony Lewis.
HIGH SCHOOL: Kathleen (Lakeland, Fla.).
COLLEGE: Miami (Fla.).
TRANSACTIONS/CAREER NOTES: Selected after junior season by Baltimore Ravens in first round (26th pick overall) of 1996 NFL draft. ... Signed by Ravens (July 15, 1996). ... On injured reserve with shoulder injury (November 26, 2002-remainder of season).
CHAMPIONSHIP GAME EXPERIENCE: Played in AFC championship game (2000 season). ... Member of Super Bowl championship team (2000 season).
HONORS: Named linebacker on THE SPORTING NEWS college All-America second team (1995). ... Played in Pro Bowl (1997, 1998, 2000, 2001 and 2003 seasons). ... Named linebacker on THE SPORTING NEWS NFL All-Pro team (1998-2001 and 2003). ... Named to play in Pro Bowl (1999 season); replaced by Junior Seau due to personal reasons. ... Named Most Valuable Player of Super Bowl 35 (2000 season).
MISCELLANEOUS: Shares Baltimore Ravens all-time record for most interceptions (20).

Year	Team	G	GS	TOTALS Tk.	Ast.	Sks.	INTERCEPTIONS No.	Yds.	Avg.	TD
1996	Baltimore NFL	14	13	95	15	2.5	1	0	0.0	0
1997	Baltimore NFL	16	16	*156	28	4.0	1	18	18.0	0
1998	Baltimore NFL	14	14	101	19	3.0	2	25	12.5	0
1999	Baltimore NFL	16	16	*131	37	3.5	3	97	32.3	0
2000	Baltimore NFL	16	16	107	30	3.0	2	1	0.5	0
2001	Baltimore NFL	16	16	*114	48	3.5	3	115	38.3	0
2002	Baltimore NFL	5	5	43	15	0.0	2	4	2.0	0
2003	Baltimore NFL	16	16	121	42	1.5	6	99	16.5	1
Pro totals (8 years)		113	112	868	234	21.0	20	359	18.0	1

L

LIDDIARD, BRODY — TE/LS — VIKINGS

PERSONAL: Born June 12, 1977, in Salt Lake City, Utah. ... 6-4/240. ... Full name: Jon Brody Liddiard.
HIGH SCHOOL: Torrey Pines (San Diego).
COLLEGE: Colorado.
TRANSACTIONS/CAREER NOTES: Signed as non-drafted free agent by Minnesota Vikings (April 25, 2000). ... Released by Vikings (August 14, 2000). ... Signed by New York Giants (August 20, 2000). ... Released by Giants (September 4, 2000). ... Re-signed by Giants to practice squad (September 5, 2000). ... Activated (September 9, 2000). ... Released by Giants (September 12, 2000). ... Signed by Miami Dolphins (November 23, 2000). ... Released by Dolphins (July 11, 2001). ... Signed by Minnesota Vikings (July 23, 2001). ... Granted free agency (February 28, 2003). ... Re-signed by Vikings (February 28, 2003).
PLAYING EXPERIENCE: Miami NFL, 2000; Minnesota NFL, 2001-2003. ... Games/Games started: 2000 (5/0), 2001 (16/0), 2002 (16/0), 2003 (16/0). Total: 53/0.

LIGHT, MATT — T — PATRIOTS

PERSONAL: Born June 23, 1978, in Greenville, Ohio. ... 6-4/305. ... Full name: Matthew Charles Light.
HIGH SCHOOL: Greenville (Ohio).
COLLEGE: Purdue.
TRANSACTIONS/CAREER NOTES: Selected by New England Patriots in second round (48th pick overall) of 2001 NFL draft. ... Signed by Patriots (July 22, 2001).
PLAYING EXPERIENCE: New England NFL, 2001-2003. ... Games/Games started: 2001 (14/12), 2002 (16/16), 2003 (16/16). Total: 46/44.
CHAMPIONSHIP GAME EXPERIENCE: Played in AFC championship game (2001 and 2003 seasons). ... Member of Super Bowl championship team (2001 and 2003 seasons).
HONORS: Named offensive tackle on THE SPORTING NEWS college All-America third team (2000).

LINDELL, RIAN — K — BILLS

PERSONAL: Born January 20, 1977, in Vancouver, Wash. ... 6-3/235. ... Full name: Rian David Lindell.
HIGH SCHOOL: Mountain View (Vancouver, Wash.).
COLLEGE: Washington State.
TRANSACTIONS/CAREER NOTES: Signed as non-drafted free agent by Seattle Seahawks (September 26, 2000). ... Granted free agency (February 28, 2003). ... Signed by Buffalo Bills (March 24, 2003).

Year	Team	G	FIELD GOALS 1-29	30-39	40-49	50+	Tot.	Pct.	Lg.	TOTALS XPM	XPA	Pts.
2000	Seattle NFL	12	4-5	1-1	7-8	3-3	15-17	88.2	52	25	25	70
2001	Seattle NFL	16	7-8	4-5	6-14	3-5	20-32	62.5	54	33	33	93

Year Team	G	FIELD GOALS 1-29	30-39	40-49	50+	Tot.	Pct.	Lg.	TOTALS XPM	XPA	Pts.
2002—Seattle NFL	16	10-10	8-10	4-5	1-4	23-29	79.3	52	38	38	107
2003—Buffalo NFL	16	11-12	3-3	3-7	0-2	17-24	70.8	44	24	24	75
Pro totals (4 years)	60	32-35	16-19	20-34	7-14	75-102	73.5	54	120	120	345

LINDSAY, EVERETT G

PERSONAL: Born September 18, 1970, in Burlington, Iowa. ... 6-4/305. ... Full name: Everett Eric Lindsay.
HIGH SCHOOL: Millbrook (Raleigh, N.C.).
COLLEGE: Mississippi.
TRANSACTIONS/CAREER NOTES: Selected by Minnesota Vikings in fifth round (133rd pick overall) of 1993 NFL draft. ... Signed by Vikings (July 14, 1993). ... On injured reserve with shoulder injury (December 22, 1993-remainder of season). ... On injured reserve with shoulder injury (August 23, 1994-entire season). ... On physically unable to perform list with knee injury (July 22-August 20, 1996). ... On non-football injury list with knee injury (August 20, 1996-entire season). ... Assigned by Vikings to Barcelona Dragons in 1997 World League enhancement allocation program (February 19, 1997). ... Granted unconditional free agency (February 13, 1998). ... Re-signed by Vikings (February 17, 1998). ... Traded by Vikings to Baltimore Ravens for sixth-round pick (DE Talance Sawyer) in 1999 draft (April 17, 1999). ... Granted free agency (February 11, 2000). ... Signed by Cleveland Browns (February 15, 2000). ... Traded by Browns to Vikings for future draft pick (August 14, 2001). ... Granted unconditional free agency (March 3, 2004).
PLAYING EXPERIENCE: Minnesota NFL, 1993-1998; Baltimore NFL, 1999; Cleveland NFL, 2000; Minnesota NFL, 2001-2003. ... Games/Games started: 1993 (12/12), 1995 (16/0), 1997 (16/3), 1998 (16/3), 1999 (16/16), 2000 (16/16), 2001 (16/8), 2002 (16/5), 2003 (12/0). Total: 136/63.
CHAMPIONSHIP GAME EXPERIENCE: Played in NFC championship game (1998 season).
HONORS: Named offensive tackle on THE SPORTING NEWS college All-America second team (1992).

LITTLE, EARL S BROWNS

PERSONAL: Born March 10, 1973, in Miami, Fla. ... 6-1/200. ... Full name: Earl Jerome Little.
HIGH SCHOOL: North Miami.
COLLEGE: Miami (Fla.).
TRANSACTIONS/CAREER NOTES: Signed as non-drafted free agent by Miami Dolphins (April 24, 1997). ... Released by Dolphins (August 24, 1997). ... Re-signed by Dolphins to practice squad (August 26, 1997). ... Released by Dolphins (August 29, 1997). ... Signed by New Orleans Saints to practice squad (October 1, 1997). ... Claimed on waivers by Cleveland Browns (October 25, 1999). ... Granted unconditional free agency (February 28, 2003). ... Re-signed by Browns (March 13, 2003).

Year Team	G	GS	TOTALS Tk.	Ast.	Sks.	INTERCEPTIONS No.	Yds.	Avg.	TD
1998—New Orleans NFL	16	0	0	0	0.0	0	0	0.0	0
1999—New Orleans NFL	1	0	0	0	0.0	0	0	0.0	0
—Cleveland NFL	9	0	5	0	0.0	1	0	0.0	0
2000—Cleveland NFL	16	0	24	2	0.0	1	7	7.0	0
2001—Cleveland NFL	16	16	65	17	1.0	5	33	6.6	0
2002—Cleveland NFL	13	9	42	19	0.0	4	17	4.3	0
2003—Cleveland NFL	16	16	42	18	0.0	6	41	6.8	0
Pro totals (6 years)	87	41	178	56	1.0	17	98	5.8	0

LITTLE, LEONARD DE RAMS

PERSONAL: Born October 19, 1974, in Asheville, N.C. ... 6-3/261. ... Full name: Leonard Antonio Little.
HIGH SCHOOL: Asheville (N.C.).
JUNIOR COLLEGE: Coffeyville (Kan.) Community College.
COLLEGE: Tennessee.
TRANSACTIONS/CAREER NOTES: Selected by St. Louis Rams in third round (65th pick overall) of 1998 NFL draft. ... Signed by Rams (July 2, 1998). ... On non-football injury list for personal reasons (November 17, 1998-November 16, 1999). ... On suspended list for violating league substance abuse policy (July 16-November 9, 1999). ... Granted free agency (March 2, 2001). ... Re-signed by Rams (April 20, 2001). ... Granted unconditional free agency (March 1, 2002). ... Re-signed by Rams (March 3, 2002).
CHAMPIONSHIP GAME EXPERIENCE: Played in NFC championship game (1999 and 2001 seasons). ... Member of Super Bowl championship team (1999 season). ... Played in Super Bowl 36 (2001 season).
HONORS: Played in Pro Bowl (2003 season).

Year Team	G	GS	TOTALS Tk.	Ast.	Sks.
1998—St. Louis NFL	6	0	1	1	0.5
1999—St. Louis NFL	6	0	1	0	0.0
2000—St. Louis NFL	14	0	13	4	5.0
2001—St. Louis NFL	13	0	23	3	14.5
2002—St. Louis NFL	16	15	37	7	12.0
2003—St. Louis NFL	12	12	41	6	12.5
Pro totals (6 years)	67	27	116	21	44.5

LITTLETON, JODY LB LIONS

PERSONAL: Born October 23, 1974, in Denver, Colo. ... 6-1/235.
HIGH SCHOOL: Brighton (Colo.).
COLLEGE: Baylor.
TRANSACTIONS/CAREER NOTES: Signed as non-drafted free agent by Atlanta Falcons (April 27, 1998). ... Released by Falcons (July 2, 1998). ... Signed by New York Giants (May 14, 2001). ... Released by Giants (August 27, 2001). ... Re-signed by Giants (January 15, 2002). ...

Assigned by Giants to Frankfurt Galaxy in 2002 NFL Europe enhancement allocation program (February 12, 2002). ... Released by Giants (August 26, 2002). ... Signed by Chicago Bears (October 17, 2002). ... Released by Bears (October 30, 2002). ... Signed by Detroit Lions to practice squad (December 19, 2002). ... Assigned by Lions to Frankfurt Galaxy in 2003 NFL Europe enhancement allocation program (January 28, 2003). ... Released by Lions (August 31, 2003). ... Re-signed by Lions (December 8, 2003).

			TOTALS			INTERCEPTIONS			
Year Team	G	GS	Tk.	Ast.	Sks.	No.	Yds.	Avg.	TD
2002—Chicago NFL	2	0	0	0	0.0	0	0	0.0	0
2003—Detroit NFL	3	0	0	0	0.0	0	0	0.0	0
Pro totals (2 years)	5	0	0	0	0.0	0	0	0.0	0

LIWIENSKI, CHRIS G VIKINGS

PERSONAL: Born August 2, 1975, in Sterling Heights, Mich. ... 6-5/325. ... Name pronounced: Loo-win-ski.
HIGH SCHOOL: Stevenson (Sterling Heights, Mich.).
COLLEGE: Indiana.
TRANSACTIONS/CAREER NOTES: Selected by Detroit Lions in seventh round (207th pick overall) of 1998 NFL draft. ... Signed by Lions (July 15, 1998). ... Released by Lions (August 24, 1998). ... Signed by Minnesota Vikings to practice squad (August 31, 1998). ... Activated (November 18, 1998). ... Released by Vikings (September 9, 1999). ... Re-signed by Vikings to practice squad (September 10, 1999). ... Activated (December 10, 1999); did not play.
PLAYING EXPERIENCE: Minnesota NFL, 1998-2003. ... Games/Games started: 1998 (1/0), 2000 (14/1), 2001 (16/16), 2002 (16/16), 2003 (16/16). Total: 63/49.
CHAMPIONSHIP GAME EXPERIENCE: Member of Vikings for NFC championship game (1998 season); inactive. ... Played in NFC championship game (2000 season).

LLOYD, BRANDON WR 49ERS

PERSONAL: Born July 5, 1981, in Kansas City, Mo. ... 6-0/184. ... Full name: Brandon Matthew Lloyd.
HIGH SCHOOL: Blue Springs (Mo.).
COLLEGE: Illinois.
TRANSACTIONS/CAREER NOTES: Selected after junior season by San Francisco 49ers in fourth round (124th pick overall) of 2003 NFL draft. ... Signed by 49ers (July 25, 2003).
SINGLE GAME HIGHS (regular season): Receptions—3 (December 27, 2003, vs. Seattle); yards—63 (December 27, 2003, vs. Seattle); and touchdown receptions—1 (December 21, 2003, vs. Philadelphia).

			RUSHING				RECEIVING				PUNT RETURNS				KICKOFF RETURNS				TOTALS		
Year Team	G	GS	Att.	Yds.	Avg.	TD	No.	Yds.	Avg.	TD	No.	Yds.	Avg.	TD	No.	Yds.	Avg.	TD	TD	2pt.	Pts.
2003—S.F. NFL	16	1	0	0	0.0	0	14	212	15.1	2	0	0	0.0	0	2	32	16.0	0	2	1	14

LOCKETT, KEVIN WR

PERSONAL: Born September 8, 1974, in Tulsa, Okla. ... 6-0/186.
HIGH SCHOOL: Washington (Okla.).
COLLEGE: Kansas State.
TRANSACTIONS/CAREER NOTES: Selected by Kansas City Chiefs in second round (47th pick overall) of 1997 NFL draft. ... Signed by Chiefs (July 25, 1997). ... Granted free agency (February 11, 2000). ... Re-signed by Chiefs (May 3, 2000) ... Granted unconditional free agency (March 2, 2001). ... Signed by Washington Redskins (April 9, 2001). ... Claimed on waivers by Jacksonville Jaguars (November 3, 2002). ... Granted unconditional free agency (February 28, 2003). ... Re-signed by Jaguars (March 5, 2003). ... Released by Jaguars (August 26, 2003). ... Signed by New York Jets (November 13, 2003). ... Granted unconditional free agency (March 3, 2004).
SINGLE GAME HIGHS (regular season): Receptions—7 (November 5, 2000, vs. Oakland); yards—77 (October 29, 2000, vs. Seattle); and touchdown receptions—1 (December 15, 2002, vs. Cincinnati).

			RECEIVING				PUNT RETURNS				TOTALS			
Year Team	G	GS	No.	Yds.	Avg.	TD	No.	Yds.	Avg.	TD	TD	2pt.	Pts.	Fum.
1997—Kansas City NFL	9	0	1	35	35.0	0	0	0	0.0	0	0	0	0	0
1998—Kansas City NFL	13	3	19	281	14.8	0	7	36	5.1	0	0	0	0	2
1999—Kansas City NFL	16	1	34	426	12.5	2	1	10	10.0	0	2	0	12	0
2000—Kansas City NFL	16	2	33	422	12.8	2	26	208	8.0	0	2	0	12	3
2001—Washington NFL	16	0	22	293	13.3	0	5	14	2.8	0	0	0	0	1
2002—Washington NFL	6	2	11	129	11.7	2	0	0	0.0	0	2	0	12	1
—Jacksonville NFL	7	2	5	76	15.2	2	0	0	0.0	0	2	0	12	0
2003—New York Jets NFL	3	0	5	76	15.2	0	0	0	0.0	0	0	0	0	0
Pro totals (7 years)	86	10	130	1738	13.4	8	39	268	6.9	0	8	0	48	7

LOGAN, MIKE S STEELERS

PERSONAL: Born September 15, 1974, in Pittsburgh, Pa. ... 6-0/212. ... Full name: Michael V. Logan.
HIGH SCHOOL: McKeesport (Pa.).
COLLEGE: West Virginia.
TRANSACTIONS/CAREER NOTES: Selected by Jacksonville Jaguars in second round (50th pick overall) of 1997 NFL draft. ... Signed by Jaguars (May 23, 1997). ... On injured reserve with ankle injury (September 20, 1999-remainder of season). ... Granted free agency (February 11, 2000). ... Re-signed by Jaguars (March 10, 2000). ... Granted unconditional free agency (March 2, 2001). ... Signed by Pittsburgh Steelers (March 24, 2001). ... On injured reserve with knee injury (January 6, 2003-remainder of 2002 playoffs). ... Granted unconditional free agency (March 3, 2004). ... Re-signed by Steelers (March 22, 2004).
CHAMPIONSHIP GAME EXPERIENCE: Played in AFC championship game (2001 season).

			TOTALS			INTERCEPTIONS				PUNT RETURNS				KICKOFF RETURNS				TOTALS			
Year Team	G	GS	Tk.	Ast.	Sks.	No.	Yds.	Avg.	TD	No.	Yds.	Avg.	TD	No.	Yds.	Avg.	TD	TD	2pt.	Pts.	Fum.
1997—Jac. NFL	11	0	5	0	0.0	0	0	0.0	0	0	0	0.0	0	10	236	23.6	0	0	0	0	0
1998—Jac. NFL	15	0	13	5	0.0	0	0	0.0	0	2	26	13.0	0	18	414	23.0	0	0	0	0	1
1999—Jac. NFL	2	0	0	1	0.0	0	0	0.0	0	1	7	7.0	0	1	25	25.0	0	0	0	0	0
2000—Jac. NFL	15	11	48	6	1.0	2	14	7.0	0	0	0	0.0	0	0	0	0.0	0	0	0	0	0

Year	Team	G	GS	TOTALS Tk.	Ast.	Sks.	INTERCEPTIONS No.	Yds.	Avg.	TD	PUNT RETURNS No.	Yds.	Avg.	TD	KICKOFF RETURNS No.	Yds.	Avg.	TD	TOTALS TD	2pt.	Pts.	Fum.
2001—Pit. NFL		16	1	20	3	2.0	2	2	1.0	0	0	0	0.0	0	1	9	9.0	0	0	0	0	0
2002—Pit. NFL		14	0	29	7	0.5	1	46	46.0	0	0	0	0.0	0	0	0	0.0	0	0	0	0	0
2003—Pit. NFL		16	15	70	23	1.0	0	0	0.0	0	0	0	0.0	0	0	0	0.0	0	0	0	0	0
Pro totals (7 years)		89	27	185	45	4.5	5	62	12.4	0	3	33	11.0	0	30	684	22.8	0	0	0	0	1

LONG, RIEN — DT — TITANS

PERSONAL: Born August 7, 1981, in Los Angeles, Calif. ... 6-6/300. ... Full name: Rien M. Long.
HIGH SCHOOL: Anacortes (Wash.).
COLLEGE: Washington State.
TRANSACTIONS/CAREER NOTES: Selected after junior season by Tennessee Titans in fourth round (126th pick overall) of 2003 NFL draft. ... Signed by Titans (July 16, 2003).

Year	Team	G	GS	TOTALS Tk.	Ast.	Sks.
2003—Tennessee NFL		8	0	2	1	1.0

LONGWELL, RYAN — K — PACKERS

PERSONAL: Born August 16, 1974, in Seattle, Wash. ... 6-0/199. ... Full name: Ryan Walker Longwell.
HIGH SCHOOL: Bend (Ore.).
COLLEGE: California.
TRANSACTIONS/CAREER NOTES: Signed as non-drafted free agent by San Francisco 49ers (April 28, 1997). ... Claimed on waivers by Green Bay Packers (July 10, 1997).
CHAMPIONSHIP GAME EXPERIENCE: Played in NFC championship game (1997 season). ... Played in Super Bowl 32 (1997 season).

Year	Team	G	FIELD GOALS 1-29	30-39	40-49	50+	Tot.	Pct.	Lg.	TOTALS XPM	XPA	Pts.
1997—Green Bay NFL		16	11-12	10-13	2-4	1-1	24-30	80.0	50	*48	*48	120
1998—Green Bay NFL		16	7-7	13-15	9-10	0-1	29-33	87.9	45	41	43	128
1999—Green Bay NFL		16	8-9	8-9	8-10	1-2	25-30	83.3	50	38	38	113
2000—Green Bay NFL		16	7-8	10-10	13-15	3-5	‡33-‡38	86.8	52	32	32	131
2001—Green Bay NFL		16	3-4	9-10	7-14	1-3	20-31	64.5	54	44	45	104
2002—Green Bay NFL		16	9-10	12-13	7-10	0-1	28-34	82.4	49	‡44	‡44	128
2003—Green Bay NFL		16	5-5	11-11	6-9	1-1	23-26	88.5	50	‡51	‡51	120
Pro totals (7 years)		112	50-55	73-81	52-72	7-14	182-222	82.0	54	298	301	844

LOOKER, DANE — WR — RAMS

PERSONAL: Born April 5, 1976, in Puyallup, Wash. ... 6-0/194.
HIGH SCHOOL: Puyallup (Wash.).
COLLEGE: Washington.
TRANSACTIONS/CAREER NOTES: Signed as non-drafted free agent by St. Louis Rams (April 17, 2000). ... Traded by Rams to New England Patriots for undisclosed draft pick (August 7, 2000). ... Inactive for 10 games (2000). ... On injured reserve with leg injury (November 16, 2000-remainder of season). ... Released by Patriots (July 31, 2001). ... Signed by Rams (August 7, 2001). ... Released by Rams (August 27, 2001). ... Re-signed by Rams (February 12, 2002). ... Assigned by Rams to Berlin Thunder in 2002 NFL Europe enhancement allocation program (February 12, 2002). ... Released by Rams (September 1, 2002). ... Re-signed by Rams to practice squad (September 9, 2002). ... Activated (December 12, 2002).
SINGLE GAME HIGHS (regular season): Receptions—5 (September 14, 2003, vs. San Francisco); yards—50 (December 8, 2003, vs. Cleveland); and touchdown receptions—1 (October 19, 2003, vs. Green Bay).

Year	Team	G	GS	RECEIVING No.	Yds.	Avg.	TD	PUNT RETURNS No.	Yds.	Avg.	TD	TOTALS TD	2pt.	Pts.	Fum.
2002—St. Louis NFL		3	0	0	0	0.0	0	0	0	0.0	0	0	0	0	0
2003—St. Louis NFL		16	2	47	495	10.5	3	2	47	23.5	0	3	0	18	1
Pro totals (2 years)		19	2	47	495	10.5	3	2	47	23.5	0	3	0	18	1

LOPIENSKI, TOM — FB — COLTS

PERSONAL: Born June 12, 1979, in Parkersburg, W.Va. ... 6-0/246.
COLLEGE: Notre Dame.
TRANSACTIONS/CAREER NOTES: Signed as non-drafted free agent by Indianapolis Colts (May 5, 2003). ... Waived by Colts (August 31, 2003). ... Re-signed by Colts (December 2, 2003).
CHAMPIONSHIP GAME EXPERIENCE: Played in AFC championship game (2003 season).

Year	Team	G	GS	RUSHING Att.	Yds.	Avg.	TD	TOTALS TD	2pt.	Pts.	Fum.
2003—Indianapolis NFL		4	0	0	0	0.0	0	0	0	0	0

LOTT, ANDRE — CB — REDSKINS

PERSONAL: Born May 31, 1979, in Memphis, Tenn. ... 5-10/196. ... Full name: Andre Marquette Lott.
HIGH SCHOOL: Melrose (Memphis, Tenn.).
COLLEGE: Tennessee.

TRANSACTIONS/CAREER NOTES: Selected by Washington Redskins in fifth round (159th pick overall) of 2002 NFL draft. ... Signed by Redskins (July 12, 2002).

Year Team	G	GS	TOTALS Tk.	Ast.	Sks.	INTERCEPTIONS No.	Yds.	Avg.	TD
2002—Washington NFL	16	0	4	0	1.0	0	0	0.0	0
2003—Washington NFL	11	0	4	2	0.0	0	0	0.0	0
Pro totals (2 years)	27	0	8	2	1.0	0	0	0.0	0

LOVE, CLARENCE — CB — RAIDERS

PERSONAL: Born June 16, 1976, in Jackson, Mich. ... 5-10/180. ... Full name: Clarence Eugene Love.
HIGH SCHOOL: Jackson (Mich.).
COLLEGE: Toledo.
TRANSACTIONS/CAREER NOTES: Selected by Philadelphia Eagles in fourth round (116th pick overall) of 1998 NFL draft. ... Signed by Eagles (July 14, 1998). ... Assigned by Eagles to Frankfurt Galaxy in 1999 NFL Europe enhancement allocation program (February 22, 1999). ... Released by Eagles (September 5, 1999). ... Signed by Jacksonville Jaguars to practice squad (September 21, 1999). ... Released by Jaguars (November 23, 1999). ... Signed by Baltimore Ravens to practice squad (December 15, 1999). ... Activated (December 31, 1999); did not play. ... Released by Ravens (June 13, 2001). ... Signed by Oakland Raiders (February 11, 2002).
CHAMPIONSHIP GAME EXPERIENCE: Member of Ravens for AFC Championship game (2000 season); inactive. ... Member of Super Bowl championship team (2000 season); inactive. ... Played in AFC championship game (2002 season). ... Played in Super Bowl 37 (2002 season).

Year Team	G	GS	TOTALS Tk.	Ast.	Sks.	INTERCEPTIONS No.	Yds.	Avg.	TD
1998—Philadelphia NFL	6	0	2	1	0.0	0	0	0.0	0
2000—Baltimore NFL	1	0	0	0	0.0	0	0	0.0	0
2002—Oakland NFL	11	3	13	1	0.0	0	0	0.0	0
2003—Oakland NFL	13	0	2	0	0.0	0	0	0.0	0
Pro totals (4 years)	31	3	17	2	0.0	0	0	0.0	0

LOVELADY, JOSH — G — LIONS

L

PERSONAL: Born January 28, 1978, in Fort Hood, Texas. ... 6-3/330.
HIGH SCHOOL: Tidehaven (Midfield, Texas).
COLLEGE: Houston.
TRANSACTIONS/CAREER NOTES: Signed as non-drafted free agent by Detroit Lions (June 12, 2001). ... Released by Lions (September 2, 2001). ... Re-signed by Lions to practice squad (September 4, 2001). ... Activated (October 31, 2001); did not play. ... Assigned by Lions to Scottish Claymores in 2002 NFL Europe enhancement allocation program (February 12, 2002). ... Released by Lions (September 1, 2002). ... Re-signed by Lions to practice squad (September 2, 2002). ... Activated (December 3, 2002). ... Re-signed by Lions (March 25, 2003).
PLAYING EXPERIENCE: Detroit NFL, 2002-2003. ... Games/Games started: 2002 (3/0), 2003 (12/0). Total: 15/0.

LOVERNE, DAVID — G — LIONS

PERSONAL: Born May 22, 1976, in Concord, Calif. ... 6-3/303. ... Name pronounced: LAH-vern.
HIGH SCHOOL: De La Salle (Concord, Calif.).
COLLEGE: San Jose State.
TRANSACTIONS/CAREER NOTES: Selected by New York Jets in third round (90th pick overall) of 1999 NFL draft. ... Signed by Jets (July 1, 1999). ... Inactive for all 16 games (1999). ... Granted free agency (March 1, 2002). ... Re-signed by Jets (April 6, 2002). ... Traded by Jets with undisclosed draft pick to Washington Redskins for undisclosed draft pick (April 6, 2002). ... Traded by Redskins with fourth-round pick (DB DeJuan Groce) in 2003 draft to St. Louis Rams for RB Trung Canidate (February 28, 2003). ... Granted unconditional free agency (March 3, 2004). ... Signed by Detroit Lions (March 23, 2004).
PLAYING EXPERIENCE: New York Jets NFL, 2000-2001; Washington NFL, 2002; St. Louis NFL, 2003. ... Games/Games started: 2000 (16/0), 2001 (16/0), 2002 (15/11), 2003 (1/0). Total: 48/11.

LOWE, OMARE — CB — JETS

PERSONAL: Born April 20, 1978, in Seattle, Wash. ... 6-1/196.
HIGH SCHOOL: Tacoma (Wash.).
COLLEGE: Washington.
TRANSACTIONS/CAREER NOTES: Selected by Miami Dolphins in fifth round (161st pick overall) of 2002 NFL draft. ... Signed by Dolphins (July 25, 2002). ... Waived by Dolphins (August 31, 2003). ... Signed by Tennessee Titans to practice squad (September 3, 2003). ... Released by Titans (September 19, 2003). ... Signed by New York Jets to practice squad (October 15, 2003). ... Activated (November 11, 2003).

Year Team	G	GS	TOTALS Tk.	Ast.	Sks.	INTERCEPTIONS No.	Yds.	Avg.	TD
2002—Miami NFL	1	0	0	0	0.0	0	0	0.0	0
2003—New York Jets NFL	2	0	0	0	0.0	0	0	0.0	0
Pro totals (2 years)	3	0	0	0	0.0	0	0	0.0	0

LOYD, JEREMY — LB — RAMS

PERSONAL: Born July 30, 1980, in Pittsburg, Texas. ... 6-2/235.
HIGH SCHOOL: Pittsburg (Texas).
JUNIOR COLLEGE: Tyler (Texas).
COLLEGE: Iowa State.

TRANSACTIONS/CAREER NOTES: Signed as non-drafted free agent by Cleveland Browns (May 2, 2003). ... Released by Browns (August 31, 2003). ... Signed by St. Louis Rams to practice squad (September 9, 2003). ... Activated (September 15, 2003). ... Released by Rams (October 27, 2003). ... Re-signed by Rams to practice squad (October 28, 2003). ... Activated (November 25, 2003).

			TOTALS			INTERCEPTIONS			
Year Team	**G**	**GS**	**Tk.**	**Ast.**	**Sks.**	**No.**	**Yds.**	**Avg.**	**TD**
2003—St. Louis NFL	10	0	0	0	0.0	0	0	0.0	0

LUCAS, JUSTIN — S — CARDINALS

PERSONAL: Born July 15, 1976, in Victoria, Texas. ... 5-10/211.
HIGH SCHOOL: Stroman (Victoria, Texas).
COLLEGE: Abilene Christian.
TRANSACTIONS/CAREER NOTES: Signed as non-drafted free agent by Arizona Cardinals (April 23, 1999). ... Released by Cardinals (September 5, 1999). ... Re-signed by Cardinals to practice squad (September 7, 1999). ... Activated (October 17, 1999). ... Released by Cardinals (October 19, 1999). ... Re-signed by Cardinals to practice squad (October 20, 1999). ... Activated (December 31, 1999). ... Granted free agency (February 28, 2003). ... Re-signed by Cardinals (April 3, 2003). ... On injured reserve with ankle injury (December 20, 2003-remainder of season). ... Granted unconditional free agency (March 3, 2004). ... Re-signed by Cardinals (March 26, 2004).

			TOTALS			INTERCEPTIONS			
Year Team	**G**	**GS**	**Tk.**	**Ast.**	**Sks.**	**No.**	**Yds.**	**Avg.**	**TD**
1999—Arizona NFL	2	0	0	0	0.0	0	0	0.0	0
2000—Arizona NFL	16	0	12	8	0.0	0	0	0.0	0
2001—Arizona NFL	13	4	26	5	0.0	0	0	0.0	0
2002—Arizona NFL	16	4	27	9	0.0	2	80	40.0	2
2003—Arizona NFL	11	0	20	2	0.0	0	0	0.0	0
Pro totals (5 years)	58	8	85	24	0.0	2	80	40.0	2

LUCAS, KEN — CB — SEAHAWKS

PERSONAL: Born January 23, 1979, in Cleveland, Miss. ... 6-0/205.
HIGH SCHOOL: East Side (Cleveland, Miss.).
COLLEGE: Mississippi.
TRANSACTIONS/CAREER NOTES: Selected by Seattle Seahawks in second round (40th pick overall) of 2001 NFL draft. ... Signed by Seahawks (July 26, 2001).

			TOTALS			INTERCEPTIONS			
Year Team	**G**	**GS**	**Tk.**	**Ast.**	**Sks.**	**No.**	**Yds.**	**Avg.**	**TD**
2001—Seattle NFL	16	8	42	5	0.0	1	0	0.0	0
2002—Seattle NFL	16	16	71	11	0.0	3	67	22.3	0
2003—Seattle NFL	14	7	52	10	0.0	1	27	27.0	0
Pro totals (3 years)	46	31	165	26	0.0	5	94	18.8	0

LUCHEY, NICK — FB — PACKERS

PERSONAL: Born March 30, 1977, in Royal Oak, Mich. ... 6-2/270. ... Full name: James Nicolas Luchey. ... Formerly known as Nick Williams.
HIGH SCHOOL: Harrison (Farmington Hills, Mich.).
COLLEGE: Miami (Fla.).
TRANSACTIONS/CAREER NOTES: Selected by Cincinnati Bengals in fifth round (135th pick overall) of 1999 NFL draft. ... Signed by Bengals (May 19, 1999). ... On physically unable to perform list with knee injury (July 22-November 27, 2001). ... Granted free agency (March 1, 2002). ... Re-signed by Bengals (April 23, 2002). ... Granted unconditional free agency (February 28, 2003). ... Signed by Green Bay Packers (March 11, 2003).
SINGLE GAME HIGHS (regular season): Attempts—12 (December 22, 2002, vs. New Orleans); yards—59 (December 22, 2002, vs. New Orleans); and rushing touchdowns—2 (December 22, 2002, vs. New Orleans).

			RUSHING				RECEIVING				KICKOFF RETURNS				TOTALS			
Year Team	**G**	**GS**	**Att.**	**Yds.**	**Avg.**	**TD**	**No.**	**Yds.**	**Avg.**	**TD**	**No.**	**Yds.**	**Avg.**	**TD**	**TD**	**2pt.**	**Pts.**	**Fum.**
1999—Cincinnati NFL	11	0	10	30	3.0	0	10	96	9.6	0	8	109	13.6	0	0	0	0	1
2000—Cincinnati NFL	14	4	10	54	5.4	0	7	84	12.0	0	2	12	6.0	0	0	0	0	2
2001—Cincinnati NFL	4	2	0	0	0.0	0	0	0	0.0	0	0	0	0.0	0	0	0	0	0
2002—Cincinnati NFL	16	3	12	59	4.9	2	7	46	6.6	0	3	40	13.3	0	2	0	12	0
2003—Green Bay NFL	11	2	1	3	3.0	0	1	12	12.0	0	2	21	10.5	0	0	0	0	0
Pro totals (5 years)	56	11	33	146	4.4	2	25	238	9.5	0	15	182	12.1	0	2	0	12	3

LUCIER, WAYNE — C — GIANTS

PERSONAL: Born December 5, 1979, in Amesbury, Mass. ... 6-3/300. ... Name pronounced: loo-SEAR.
HIGH SCHOOL: St. John's (Salem, N.H.).
COLLEGE: Colorado.
TRANSACTIONS/CAREER NOTES: Selected by New York Giants in seventh round (249th pick overall) of 2003 NFL draft. ... Signed by Giants (July 16, 2003). ... On injured reserve with knee injury (December 2, 2003-remainder of season).
PLAYING EXPERIENCE: New York Giants NFL, 2003. ... Games/Games started: 2003 (12/11). Total: 12/11.

LUZAR, CHRIS — TE — JAGUARS

PERSONAL: Born February 12, 1979, in Newport News, Va. ... 6-7/262. ... Full name: Christopher Myers Luzar.
HIGH SCHOOL: Lafayette (Williamsburg, Va.).
COLLEGE: Virginia.
TRANSACTIONS/CAREER NOTES: Selected by Jacksonville Jaguars in fourth round (118th pick overall) of 2002 NFL draft. ... Signed by Jaguars (June 19, 2002).

SINGLE GAME HIGHS (regular season): Receptions—1 (December 14, 2003, vs. New England); yards—21 (December 14, 2003, vs. New England); and touchdown receptions—0.

			RECEIVING				TOTALS			
Year Team	G	GS	No.	Yds.	Avg.	TD	TD	2pt.	Pts.	Fum.
2002—Jacksonville NFL	12	0	1	5	5.0	0	0	0	0	0
2003—Jacksonville NFL	11	1	3	30	10.0	0	0	0	0	0
Pro totals (2 years)	23	1	4	35	8.8	0	0	0	0	0

LYLE, RICK DE

PERSONAL: Born February 26, 1971, in Monroe, La. ... 6-5/285. ... Full name: Rick James Earl Lyle.
HIGH SCHOOL: Hickman Mills (Kansas City, Mo.).
COLLEGE: Missouri.
TRANSACTIONS/CAREER NOTES: Signed as non-drafted free agent by Cleveland Browns (May 2, 1994). ... On injured reserve with back injury (September 2, 1995-entire season). ... Browns franchise moved to Baltimore and renamed Ravens for 1996 season (March 11, 1996). ... Granted unconditional free agency (February 14, 1997). ... Signed by New York Jets (March 24, 1997). ... Granted unconditional free agency (March 2, 2001). ... Re-signed by Jets (May 14, 2001). ... Granted unconditional free agency (March 1, 2002). ... Signed by New England Patriots (March 12, 2002). ... Granted unconditional free agency (February 28, 2003). ... Re-signed by Patriots (March 5, 2003). ... Granted unconditional free agency (March 3, 2004).
CHAMPIONSHIP GAME EXPERIENCE: Played in AFC championship game (1998 season). ... Member of Patriots for AFC championship game (2003 season); inactive. ... Member of Patriots for Super Bowl 38 (2003 season); inactive.

			TOTALS		
Year Team	G	GS	Tk.	Ast.	Sks.
1994—Cleveland NFL	3	0	2	0	0.0
1995—Cleveland NFL		Did not play.			
1996—Baltimore NFL	11	3	6	1	1.0
1997—New York Jets NFL	16	16	30	12	3.0
1998—New York Jets NFL	16	16	29	12	1.5
1999—New York Jets NFL	16	16	27	18	1.0
2000—New York Jets NFL	14	14	40	8	1.0
2001—New York Jets NFL	16	3	27	13	3.5
2002—New England NFL	13	2	13	7	0.0
2003—New England NFL	8	1	6	3	0.0
Pro totals (9 years)	113	71	180	74	11.0

LYMAN, DUSTIN TE BEARS

PERSONAL: Born August 5, 1976, in Boulder, Colo. ... 6-4/245.
HIGH SCHOOL: Fairview (Boulder, Colo.).
COLLEGE: Wake Forest.
TRANSACTIONS/CAREER NOTES: Selected by Chicago Bears in third round (87th pick overall) of 2000 NFL draft. ... Signed by Bears (June 15, 2000). ... On injured reserve with knee injury (December 10, 2002-remainder of season). ... On injured reserve with spleen injury (December 15, 2003-remainder of season).
SINGLE GAME HIGHS (regular season): Receptions—7 (December 1, 2002, vs. Green Bay); yards—58 (December 1, 2002, vs. Green Bay); and touchdown receptions—2 (December 1, 2002, vs. Green Bay).

			RECEIVING				TOTALS			
Year Team	G	GS	No.	Yds.	Avg.	TD	TD	2pt.	Pts.	Fum.
2000—Chicago NFL	14	7	1	4	4.0	0	0	0	0	0
2001—Chicago NFL	4	0	0	0	0.0	0	0	0	0	0
2002—Chicago NFL	12	3	14	121	8.6	2	2	0	12	0
2003—Chicago NFL	9	1	11	80	7.3	0	0	0	0	0
Pro totals (4 years)	39	11	26	205	7.9	2	2	0	12	0

LYNCH, JOHN S BRONCOS

PERSONAL: Born September 25, 1971, in Hinsdale, Ill. ... 6-2/220. ... Full name: John Terrence Lynch. ... Son of John Lynch, linebacker with Pittsburgh Steelers (1969).
HIGH SCHOOL: Torrey Pines (Encinitas, Calif.).
COLLEGE: Stanford.
TRANSACTIONS/CAREER NOTES: Selected by Tampa Bay Buccaneers in third round (82nd pick overall) of 1993 NFL draft. ... Signed by Buccaneers (June 1, 1993). ... On injured reserve with knee injury (December 12, 1995-remainder of season). ... Granted free agency (February 16, 1996). ... Re-signed by Buccaneers (July 13, 1996). ... Released by Buccaneers (March 11, 2004). ... Signed by Denver Broncos (March 22, 2004).
CHAMPIONSHIP GAME EXPERIENCE: Played in NFC championship game (1999 and 2002 seasons). ... Member of Super Bowl championship team (2002 season).
HONORS: Played in Pro Bowl (1997 and 1999-2002 seasons). ... Named safety on THE SPORTING NEWS NFL All-Pro team (1999 and 2000).

			TOTALS			INTERCEPTIONS			
Year Team	G	GS	Tk.	Ast.	Sks.	No.	Yds.	Avg.	TD
1993—Tampa Bay NFL	15	4	8	5	0.0	0	0	0.0	0
1994—Tampa Bay NFL	16	0	11	4	0.0	0	0	0.0	0
1995—Tampa Bay NFL	9	6	27	10	0.0	3	3	1.0	0
1996—Tampa Bay NFL	16	14	74	29	1.0	3	26	8.7	0
1997—Tampa Bay NFL	16	16	75	34	0.0	2	28	14.0	0
1998—Tampa Bay NFL	15	15	50	35	2.0	2	29	14.5	0
1999—Tampa Bay NFL	16	16	81	36	0.5	2	32	16.0	0
2000—Tampa Bay NFL	16	16	56	29	1.0	3	43	14.3	0

Year Team	G	GS	Tk.	Ast.	Sks.	No.	Yds.	Avg.	TD
2001—Tampa Bay NFL	16	16	62	25	1.0	3	21	7.0	0
2002—Tampa Bay NFL	15	15	41	23	0.0	3	0	0.0	0
2003—Tampa Bay NFL	14	14	50	22	0.5	2	18	9.0	0
Pro totals (11 years)	164	132	535	252	6.0	23	200	8.7	0

LYON, BILLY — DE/DT — VIKINGS

PERSONAL: Born December 10, 1973, in Ashland, Ky. ... 6-5/304. ... Full name: William Morton Lyon.
HIGH SCHOOL: Lloyd (Erlanger, Ky.).
COLLEGE: Marshall.
TRANSACTIONS/CAREER NOTES: Signed as non-drafted free agent by Kansas City Chiefs (April 28, 1997). ... Released by Chiefs (August 15, 1997). ... Signed by Green Bay Packers to practice squad (November 20, 1997) ... Granted unconditional free agency (February 28, 2003). ... Signed by Minnesota Vikings (March 4, 2003).

			TOTALS			INTERCEPTIONS			
Year Team	G	GS	Tk.	Ast.	Sks.	No.	Yds.	Avg.	TD
1998—Green Bay NFL	4	0	4	2	1.0	0	0	0.0	0
1999—Green Bay NFL	16	4	9	10	2.0	1	0	0.0	0
2000—Green Bay NFL	11	1	7	4	1.0	0	0	0.0	0
2001—Green Bay NFL	12	0	13	6	2.0	0	0	0.0	0
2002—Green Bay NFL	16	2	11	4	2.0	0	0	0.0	0
2003—Minnesota NFL	13	0	4	1	0.0	0	0	0.0	0
Pro totals (6 years)	72	7	48	27	8.0	1	0	0.0	0

MACHADO, J.P. — C

PERSONAL: Born January 6, 1976, in Monmouth, Ill. ... 6-4/300.
HIGH SCHOOL: Monmouth (Ill.).
COLLEGE: Illinois.
TRANSACTIONS/CAREER NOTES: Selected by New York Jets in sixth round (197th pick overall) of 1999 NFL draft. ... Signed by Jets (July 27, 1999). ... Granted unconditional free agency (March 3, 2004).
PLAYING EXPERIENCE: New York Jets NFL, 1999-2003. ... Games/Games started: 1999 (5/0), 2000 (16/0), 2001 (16/3), 2002 (16/12), 2003 (16/0). Total: 69/15.

MACK, STACEY — RB

PERSONAL: Born June 26, 1975, in Orlando, Fla. ... 6-1/241. ... Full name: Stacey Lamar Mack.
HIGH SCHOOL: Boone (Orlando, Fla.).
JUNIOR COLLEGE: Southwest Mississippi College.
COLLEGE: Temple.
TRANSACTIONS/CAREER NOTES: Signed as non-drafted free agent by Jacksonville Jaguars (April 22, 1999). ... On injured reserve with finger injury (October 12, 2000-remainder of season). ... Granted free agency (March 1, 2002). ... Re-signed by Jaguars (March 1, 2002). ... Granted unconditional free agency (February 28, 2003). ... Signed by Houston Texans (April 9, 2003). ... On injured reserve with toe injury (November 26, 2003-remainder of season). ... Granted unconditional free agency (March 3, 2004).
CHAMPIONSHIP GAME EXPERIENCE: Member of Jaguars for AFC championship game (1999 season); inactive.
SINGLE GAME HIGHS (regular season): Attempts—28 (December 16, 2001, vs. Cleveland); yards—125 (December 30, 2001, vs. Kansas City); and rushing touchdowns—3 (September 29, 2002, vs. New York Jets).
STATISTICAL PLATEAUS: 100-yard rushing games: 2001 (3). Total: 3.

			RUSHING				RECEIVING				KICKOFF RETURNS				TOTALS			
Year Team	G	GS	Att.	Yds.	Avg.	TD	No.	Yds.	Avg.	TD	No.	Yds.	Avg.	TD	TD	2pt.	Pts.	Fum.
1999—Jacksonville NFL	12	0	7	40	5.7	0	0	0	0.0	0	6	112	18.7	0	0	0	0	0
2000—Jacksonville NFL	6	2	54	145	2.7	1	0	0	0.0	0	6	104	17.3	0	1	0	6	3
2001—Jacksonville NFL	16	11	213	877	4.1	9	23	165	7.2	1	2	49	24.5	0	10	0	60	3
2002—Jacksonville NFL	16	0	98	436	4.4	9	11	79	7.2	0	12	234	19.5	0	9	0	54	0
2003—Houston NFL	8	5	93	253	2.7	4	9	55	6.1	0	0	0	0.0	0	4	0	24	2
Pro totals (5 years)	58	18	465	1751	3.8	23	43	299	7.0	1	26	499	19.2	0	24	0	144	8

M

MACKENZIE, MALAEFOU — FB — PATRIOTS

PERSONAL: Born July 24, 1979, in Apia, Samoa. ... 5-10/238.
HIGH SCHOOL: Capistrano Valley (Mission Viejo, Calif.).
COLLEGE: Southern California.
TRANSACTIONS/CAREER NOTES: Selected by Jacksonville Jaguars in seventh round (218th pick overall) of 2003 NFL draft. ... Signed by Jaguars (July 25, 2003). ... Waived by Jaguars (September 16, 2003). ... Signed by New England Patriots (February 6, 2004).

			RUSHING				TOTALS			
Year Team	G	GS	Att.	Yds.	Avg.	TD	TD	2pt.	Pts.	Fum.
2003—Jacksonville NFL	1	0	0	0	0.0	0	0	0	0	0

MACKLIN, DAVID — CB — CARDINALS

PERSONAL: Born July 14, 1978, in Newport News, Va. ... 5-9/196. ... Full name: David Thurman Macklin.
HIGH SCHOOL: Menchville (Newport News, Va.).
COLLEGE: Penn State.

TRANSACTIONS/CAREER NOTES: Selected by Indianapolis Colts in third round (91st pick overall) of 2000 NFL draft. ... Signed by Colts (July 13, 2000). ... Granted free agency (February 28, 2003). ... Re-signed by Colts (April 15, 2003). ... Granted unconditional free agency (March 3, 2004). ... Signed by Arizona Cardinals (March 10, 2004).
CHAMPIONSHIP GAME EXPERIENCE: Played in AFC championship game (2003 season).

			TOTALS			INTERCEPTIONS			
Year Team	**G**	**GS**	**Tk.**	**Ast.**	**Sks.**	**No.**	**Yds.**	**Avg.**	**TD**
2000—Indianapolis NFL	16	2	23	4	0.0	2	35	17.5	0
2001—Indianapolis NFL	16	16	53	9	0.5	3	15	5.0	0
2002—Indianapolis NFL	16	15	47	9	0.0	1	30	30.0	0
2003—Indianapolis NFL	16	4	27	5	0.0	1	0	0.0	0
Pro totals (4 years)	64	37	150	27	0.5	7	80	11.4	0

MADDOX, NICK — RB — BROWNS

PERSONAL: Born December 11, 1980, in Shelby, N.C. ... 5-11/209.
HIGH SCHOOL: A.L. Brown (Kannapolis, N.C.).
COLLEGE: Florida State.
TRANSACTIONS/CAREER NOTES: Signed as non-drafted free agent by San Diego Chargers (May 2, 2003). ... Waived by Chargers (August 26, 2003). ... Signed by Buffalo Bills to practice squad (September 24, 2003). ... Released by Bills (November 19, 2003). ... Signed by Cleveland Browns (December 11, 2003).

			RUSHING				KICKOFF RETURNS				TOTALS			
Year Team	**G**	**GS**	**Att.**	**Yds.**	**Avg.**	**TD**	**No.**	**Yds.**	**Avg.**	**TD**	**TD**	**2pt.**	**Pts.**	**Fum.**
2003—Cleveland NFL	1	0	0	0	0.0	0	3	58	19.3	0	0	0	0	1

MADDOX, TOMMY — QB — STEELERS

PERSONAL: Born September 2, 1971, in Shreveport, La. ... 6-4/220. ... Full name: Thomas Alfred Maddox.
HIGH SCHOOL: L.D. Bell (Hurst, Texas).
COLLEGE: UCLA.
TRANSACTIONS/CAREER NOTES: Selected after sophomore season by Denver Broncos in first round (25th pick overall) of 1992 NFL draft. ... Signed by Broncos (July 22, 1992). ... Traded by Broncos to Los Angeles Rams for fourth-round pick (LB Ken Brown) in 1995 draft (August 27, 1994). ... Granted free agency (February 17, 1995). ... Rams franchise moved to St. Louis (April 12, 1995). ... Re-signed by Rams (July 7, 1995). ... Released by Rams (August 27, 1995). ... Signed by New York Giants (August 30, 1995). ... Released by Giants (August 19, 1996). ... Signed by Atlanta Falcons (April 19, 1997). ... Released by Falcons (August 18, 1997). ... Signed by New Jersey Red Dogs of Arena League (November 9, 1999). ... Signed by Pittsburgh Steelers (June 12, 2001).
CHAMPIONSHIP GAME EXPERIENCE: Member of Steelers for AFC championship game (2001 season); did not play.
SINGLE GAME HIGHS (regular season): Attempts—57 (December 8, 2002, vs. Houston); completions—31 September 28, 2003, vs. Tennessee); yards—473 (November 10, 2002 vs. Atlanta); and touchdown passes—4 (November 10, 2002, vs. Atlanta).
STATISTICAL PLATEAUS: 300-yard passing games: 2002 (2), 2003 (4). Total: 6.
MISCELLANEOUS: Regular-season record as starting NFL quarterback: 13-17-1 (.435). ... Postseason record as starting NFL quarterback: 1-1 (.500).

			PASSING									RUSHING				TOTALS		
Year Team	**G**	**GS**	**Att.**	**Cmp.**	**Pct.**	**Yds.**	**TD**	**Int.**	**Avg.**	**Skd.**	**Rat.**	**Att.**	**Yds.**	**Avg.**	**TD**	**TD**	**2pt.**	**Pts.**
1992—Denver NFL	13	4	121	66	54.5	757	5	9	6.26	10	56.4	9	20	2.2	0	0	0	0
1993—Denver NFL	16	0	1	1	100.0	1	1	0	1.00	0	118.8	2	-2	-1.0	0	0	0	0
1994—L.A. NFL	5	0	19	10	52.6	141	0	2	7.42	0	37.3	1	1	1.0	0	0	0	0
1995—New York Giants NFL	16	0	23	6	26.1	49	0	3	2.13	2	0.0	1	4	4.0	0	0	0	0
1996—							Did not play.											
1997—							Did not play.											
1998—							Did not play.											
1999—							Did not play.											
2000—							Did not play.											
2001—Pittsburgh NFL	5	0	9	7	77.8	154	1	1	17.11	1	116.2	6	9	1.5	1	1	0	6
2002—Pittsburgh NFL	15	11	377	234	62.1	2836	20	16	7.52	26	85.2	19	43	2.3	0	0	0	0
2003—Pittsburgh NFL	16	16	519	298	57.4	3414	18	§17	6.58	41	75.3	13	12	0.9	0	0	0	0
Pro totals (7 years)	86	31	1069	622	58.2	7352	45	48	6.88	80	74.5	51	87	1.7	1	1	0	6

MADISE, ADRIAN — WR — BRONCOS

PERSONAL: Born March 23, 1980, in Lancaster, Texas. ... 5-11/215. ... Full name: Adrian James Madise.
HIGH SCHOOL: Lancaster (Texas).
JUNIOR COLLEGE: Middle Georgia Junior College.
COLLEGE: Texas Christian.
TRANSACTIONS/CAREER NOTES: Selected by Denver Broncos in fifth round (158th pick overall) of 2003 NFL draft. ... Signed by Broncos (June 16, 2003).
SINGLE GAME HIGHS (regular season): Receptions—1 (December 28, 2003, vs. Green Bay); yards—5 (December 28, 2003, vs. Green Bay); and touchdown receptions—0.

			RECEIVING				KICKOFF RETURNS				TOTALS			
Year Team	**G**	**GS**	**No.**	**Yds.**	**Avg.**	**TD**	**No.**	**Yds.**	**Avg.**	**TD**	**TD**	**2pt.**	**Pts.**	**Fum.**
2003—Denver NFL	11	0	2	10	5.0	0	5	137	27.4	0	0	0	0	1

MADISON, SAM — CB — DOLPHINS

PERSONAL: Born April 23, 1974, in Thomasville, Ga. ... 5-11/185. ... Full name: Samuel A. Madison Jr.
HIGH SCHOOL: Florida A&M High (Monticello, Fla.).
COLLEGE: Louisville.

TRANSACTIONS/CAREER NOTES: Selected by Miami Dolphins in second round (44th pick overall) of 1997 NFL draft. ... Signed by Dolphins (June 16, 1997).
HONORS: Named cornerback on THE SPORTING NEWS NFL All-Pro team (1999 and 2000). ... Played in Pro Bowl (1999, 2000 and 2002 seasons). ... Named to play in Pro Bowl (2001 season); replaced by Ryan McNeil due to injury.

			TOTALS			INTERCEPTIONS			
Year Team	**G**	**GS**	**Tk.**	**Ast.**	**Sks.**	**No.**	**Yds.**	**Avg.**	**TD**
1997—Miami NFL	14	3	16	5	0.0	1	21	21.0	0
1998—Miami NFL	16	16	31	13	1.0	8	114	14.3	0
1999—Miami NFL	16	16	38	8	0.0	†7	164	23.4	1
2000—Miami NFL	16	16	29	10	0.0	5	80	16.0	0
2001—Miami NFL	13	13	18	7	0.0	2	0	0.0	0
2002—Miami NFL	16	16	24	10	0.0	3	15	5.0	0
2003—Miami NFL	16	16	47	3	0.0	3	82	27.3	1
Pro totals (7 years)	107	96	203	56	1.0	29	476	16.4	2

MAESE, JOE — C/LS — RAVENS

PERSONAL: Born December 2, 1978, in Morenci, Ariz. ... 6-0/241.
HIGH SCHOOL: Cortez (Ariz.).
JUNIOR COLLEGE: Phoenix College.
COLLEGE: New Mexico.
TRANSACTIONS/CAREER NOTES: Selected by Baltimore Ravens in sixth round (194th pick overall) in 2001 NFL draft. ... Signed by Ravens (June 14, 2001). ... On injured reserve with knee injury (January 3, 2002-remainder of season). ... Granted free agency (March 3, 2004).
PLAYING EXPERIENCE: Baltimore NFL, 2001-2003. ... Games/Games started: 2001 (15/0), 2002 (16/0), 2003 (16/0). Total: 47/0.

MAHAN, SEAN — G — BUCCANEERS

PERSONAL: Born May 28, 1980, in Tulsa, Okla. ... 6-3/301. ... Full name: Sean Christopher Mahan.
HIGH SCHOOL: Jenks (Okla.).
COLLEGE: Notre Dame.
TRANSACTIONS/CAREER NOTES: Selected by Tampa Bay Buccaneers in fifth round (168th pick overall) of 2003 NFL draft. ... Signed by Buccaneers (July 18, 2003).
PLAYING EXPERIENCE: Tampa Bay NFL, 2003. ... Games/Games started: 2003 (9/0). Total: 9/0.

MAHE, RENO — RB — EAGLES

PERSONAL: Born June 3, 1980, in Los Angeles, Calif. ... 5-10/195. ... Full name: Sateki Reno Mahe Jr.
HIGH SCHOOL: Brighton (Salt Lake City, Utah).
JUNIOR COLLEGE: Dixie (Utah).
COLLEGE: Brigham Young.
TRANSACTIONS/CAREER NOTES: Signed as non-drafted free agent by Philadelphia Eagles (April 28, 2003).
CHAMPIONSHIP GAME EXPERIENCE: Played in NFC championship game (2003 sesaon).

			RUSHING				RECEIVING				PUNT RETURNS				TOTALS			
Year Team	**G**	**GS**	**Att.**	**Yds.**	**Avg.**	**TD**	**No.**	**Yds.**	**Avg.**	**TD**	**No.**	**Yds.**	**Avg.**	**TD**	**TD**	**2pt.**	**Pts.**	**Fum.**
2003—Philadelphia NFL	2	0	0	0	0.0	0	1	5	5.0	0	6	55	9.2	0	0	0	0	0

M

MALLARD, WESLY — LB — GIANTS

PERSONAL: Born November 21, 1978, in Hinesville, Ga. ... 6-1/230.
HIGH SCHOOL: Hardaway (Columbus, Ga.).
COLLEGE: Oregon.
TRANSACTIONS/CAREER NOTES: Selected by New York Giants in sixth round (188th pick overall) of 2002 NFL draft. ... Signed by Giants (July 12, 2002). ... On injured reserve with knee injury (December 24, 2003-remainder of season).

			TOTALS			INTERCEPTIONS			
Year Team	**G**	**GS**	**Tk.**	**Ast.**	**Sks.**	**No.**	**Yds.**	**Avg.**	**TD**
2002—New York Giants NFL	15	0	0	1	0.0	0	0	0.0	0
2003—New York Giants NFL	15	0	1	0	0.0	0	0	0.0	0
Pro totals (2 years)	30	0	1	1	0.0	0	0	0.0	0

MANGUM, KRIS — TE — PANTHERS

PERSONAL: Born August 15, 1973, in Magee, Miss. ... 6-4/249. ... Full name: Kris Thomas Mangum. ... Son of John Mangum, defensive tackle with Boston Patriots (1966 and 1967) of AFL; and brother of John Mangum, cornerback with Chicago Bears (1990-98).
HIGH SCHOOL: Magee (Miss.).
COLLEGE: Mississippi.
TRANSACTIONS/CAREER NOTES: Selected by Carolina Panthers in seventh round (228th pick overall) of 1997 NFL draft. ... Signed by Panthers (May 20, 1997). ... Released by Panthers (September 2, 1997). ... Re-signed by Panthers to practice squad (September 4, 1997). ... Activated (December 5, 1997). ... Granted unconditional free agency (March 3, 2004). ... Re-signed by Panthers (March 4, 2004).
CHAMPIONSHIP GAME EXPERIENCE: Played in NFC championship game (2003 season). ... Played in Super Bowl 38 (2003 season).
SINGLE GAME HIGHS (regular season): Receptions—4 (October 19, 2003, vs. Tennessee); yards—56 (December 20, 1997, vs. St. Louis); and touchdown receptions—1 (December 9, 2001, vs. Buffalo).

Year Team	G	GS	RECEIVING No.	Yds.	Avg.	TD	TOTALS TD	2pt.	Pts.	Fum.
1997—Carolina NFL	2	1	4	56	14.0	0	0	0	0	0
1998—Carolina NFL	6	0	1	5	5.0	0	0	0	0	0
1999—Carolina NFL	11	0	1	6	6.0	0	0	0	0	0
2000—Carolina NFL	15	6	19	215	11.3	1	1	0	6	0
2001—Carolina NFL	16	10	15	89	5.9	2	2	0	12	0
2002—Carolina NFL	16	8	16	159	9.9	0	0	0	0	0
2003—Carolina NFL	16	11	17	199	11.7	0	0	0	0	0
Pro totals (7 years)	82	36	73	729	10.0	3	3	0	18	0

MANNELLY, PATRICK — T/LS — BEARS

PERSONAL: Born April 18, 1975, in Atlanta, Ga. ... 6-5/265. ... Full name: James Patrick Mannelly.
HIGH SCHOOL: Marist (Atlanta).
COLLEGE: Duke.
TRANSACTIONS/CAREER NOTES: Selected by Chicago Bears in sixth round (189th pick overall) of 1998 NFL draft. ... Signed by Bears (June 11, 1998).
PLAYING EXPERIENCE: Chicago NFL, 1998-2003. ... Games/Games started: 1998 (16/0), 1999 (16/0), 2000 (16/0), 2001 (15/0), 2002 (14/0), 2003 (16/0). Total: 93/0.

MANNING, PEYTON — QB — COLTS

PERSONAL: Born March 24, 1976, in New Orleans, La. ... 6-5/230. ... Full name: Peyton Williams Manning. ... Son of Archie Manning, quarterback with New Orleans Saints (1971-82), Houston Oilers (1982-83) and Minnesota Vikings (1983-84). ... Brother of Eli Manning, quarterback, New York Giants.
HIGH SCHOOL: Isidore Newman (New Orleans).
COLLEGE: Tennessee.
TRANSACTIONS/CAREER NOTES: Selected by Indianapolis Colts in first round (first pick overall) of 1998 NFL draft. ... Signed by Colts (July 28, 1998). ... Designated by Colts as franchise player (February 24, 2004). ... Re-signed by Colts (March 2, 2004).
CHAMPIONSHIP GAME EXPERIENCE: Played in AFC championship game (2003 season).
HONORS: Davey O'Brien Award winner (1997). ... Named quarterback on THE SPORTING NEWS college All-America second team (1997). ... Named quarterback on THE SPORTING NEWS NFL All-Pro team (2003). ... Played in Pro Bowl (1999, 2000, 2002 and 2003 seasons). ... Named NFL Player of the Year by THE SPORTING NEWS (2003).
RECORDS: Holds NFL rookie-season records for most passes attempted—575 (1998); most passes completed—326 (1998); and most yards passing—3,739 (1998).
SINGLE GAME HIGHS (regular season): Attempts—54 (October 8, 2000, vs. New England); completions—37 (November 3, 2002, vs. Tennessee); yards—440 (September 25, 2000, vs. Jacksonville); and touchdown passes—6 (September 28, 2003, vs. New Orleans).
STATISTICAL PLATEAUS: 300-yard passing games: 1998 (4), 1999 (2), 2000 (5), 2001 (5), 2002 (4), 2003 (4). Total: 24.
MISCELLANEOUS: Regular-season record as starting NFL quarterback: 54-42 (.563). ... Postseason record as starting NFL quarterback: 2-4 (.333).

Year Team	G	GS	PASSING Att.	Cmp.	Pct.	Yds.	TD	Int.	Avg.	Skd.	Rat.	RUSHING Att.	Yds.	Avg.	TD	TOTALS TD	2pt.	Pts.
1998—Indianapolis NFL	16	16	*575	§326	56.7	§3739	26	*28	6.50	22	71.2	15	62	4.1	0	0	0	0
1999—Indianapolis NFL	16	16	533	§331	§62.1	§4135	§26	15	§7.76	14	§90.7	35	73	2.1	2	2	0	12
2000—Indianapolis NFL	16	16	571	*357	62.5	*4413	†33	15	7.73	20	94.7	37	116	3.1	1	1	0	6
2001—Indianapolis NFL	16	16	547	343	62.7	§4131	26	23	7.55	29	84.1	35	157	4.5	4	4	0	24
2002—Indianapolis NFL	16	16	591	392	66.3	4200	27	§19	7.11	23	88.8	38	148	3.9	2	2	0	12
2003—Indianapolis NFL	16	16	§566	*379	*67.0	*4267	§29	10	7.54	18	99.0	28	26	0.9	0	0	0	0
Pro totals (6 years)	96	96	3383	2128	62.9	24885	167	110	7.36	126	88.1	188	582	3.1	9	9	0	54

MANNING, RICKY — CB — PANTHERS

PERSONAL: Born November 18, 1980, in Fresno, Calif. ... 5-9/185. ... Full name: Ricky Manning Jr.
HIGH SCHOOL: Edison (Fresno, Calif.).
COLLEGE: UCLA.
TRANSACTIONS/CAREER NOTES: Selected by Carolina Panthers in third round (82nd pick overall) of 2003 NFL draft. ... Signed by Panthers (June 3, 2003).
CHAMPIONSHIP GAME EXPERIENCE: Played in NFC championship game (2003 season). ... Played in Super Bowl 38 (2003 season).
MISCELLANEOUS: Selected by Minnesota Twins organization in 22nd round of free-agent draft (1999).

Year Team	G	GS	TOTALS Tk.	Ast.	Sks.	INTERCEPTIONS No.	Yds.	Avg.	TD
2003—Carolina NFL	16	7	48	6	0.0	3	33	11.0	1

MANUEL, MARQUAND — S — BENGALS

PERSONAL: Born July 11, 1979, in Miami, Fla. ... 6-0/209. ... Full name: Marquand Alexander Manuel.
HIGH SCHOOL: Miami Senior (Fla.).
COLLEGE: Florida.
TRANSACTIONS/CAREER NOTES: Selected by Cincinnati Bengals in sixth round (181st pick overall) of 2002 NFL draft. ... Signed by Bengals (May 13, 2002).

Year Team	G	GS	TOTALS Tk.	Ast.	Sks.	INTERCEPTIONS No.	Yds.	Avg.	TD
2002—Cincinnati NFL	15	8	26	8	0.0	0	0	0.0	0
2003—Cincinnati NFL	13	1	9	2	0.0	0	0	0.0	0
Pro totals (2 years)	28	9	35	10	0.0	0	0	0.0	0

MANUMALEUNA, BRANDON — TE — RAMS

PERSONAL: Born January 4, 1980, in Torrance, Calif. ... 6-2/288. ... Full name: Brandon Michael Manumaleuna.
HIGH SCHOOL: Narbonne (Calif.).
COLLEGE: Arizona.
TRANSACTIONS/CAREER NOTES: Selected by St. Louis Rams in fourth round (129th pick overall) of 2001 NFL draft. ... Signed by Rams (June 21, 2001). ... Granted free agency (March 3, 2004). ... Tendered offer sheet by Carolina Panthers (March 4, 2004). ... Offer matched by Rams (March 11, 2004).
CHAMPIONSHIP GAME EXPERIENCE: Played in NFC championship game (2001 season). ... Played in Super Bowl 36 (2001 season).
SINGLE GAME HIGHS (regular season): Receptions—4 (October 19, 2003, vs. Green Bay); yards—56 (October 13, 2003, vs. Atlanta); and touchdown receptions—1 (December 28, 2003, vs. Detroit).

			RECEIVING				TOTALS			
Year Team	G	GS	No.	Yds.	Avg.	TD	TD	2pt.	Pts.	Fum.
2001—St. Louis NFL	16	0	1	1	1.0	1	1	0	6	0
2002—St. Louis NFL	16	10	8	106	13.3	1	1	0	6	0
2003—St. Louis NFL	16	15	29	238	8.2	2	2	0	12	0
Pro totals (3 years)	48	25	38	345	9.1	4	4	0	24	0

MANUWAI, VINCE — G — JAGUARS

PERSONAL: Born July 12, 1980, in Honolulu, Hawaii. ... 6-2/312. ... Full name: Vincent Manuwai.
HIGH SCHOOL: Farrington (Honolulu, Hawaii).
COLLEGE: Hawaii.
TRANSACTIONS/CAREER NOTES: Selected by Jacksonville Jaguars in third round (72nd pick overall) of 2003 NFL draft. ... Signed by Jaguars (July 25, 2003).
PLAYING EXPERIENCE: Jacksonville NFL, 2003. ... Games/Games started: 2003 (15/14). Total: 15/14.

MARE, OLINDO — K — DOLPHINS

PERSONAL: Born June 6, 1973, in Hollywood, Fla. ... 5-10/190. ... Full name: Olindo Franco Mare. ... Name pronounced: o-LEND-o MAR-ray.
HIGH SCHOOL: Cooper City (Fla.).
JUNIOR COLLEGE: Valencia Community College (Fla.).
COLLEGE: Syracuse.
TRANSACTIONS/CAREER NOTES: Signed as non-drafted free agent by New York Giants (May 2, 1996). ... Released by Giants (August 25, 1996). ... Re-signed by Giants to practice squad (August 27, 1996). ... Granted free agency after 1996 season. ... Signed by Miami Dolphins (February 27, 1997). ... Granted free agency (February 11, 2000). ... Re-signed by Dolphins (June 15, 2000). ... Granted unconditional free agency (March 2, 2001). ... Re-signed by Dolphins (March 2, 2001).
HONORS: Named kicker on THE SPORTING NEWS NFL All-Pro team (1999). ... Played in Pro Bowl (1999 season).
RECORDS: Shares NFL single-season record for most field goals made—39 (1999).

		FIELD GOALS							TOTALS		
Year Team	G	1-29	30-39	40-49	50+	Tot.	Pct.	Lg.	XPM	XPA	Pts.
1996—New York Giants NFL				Did not play.							
1997—Miami NFL	16	16-17	8-10	3-6	1-3	28-36	77.8	50	33	33	117
1998—Miami NFL	16	12-13	5-5	5-7	0-2	22-27	81.5	48	33	34	99
1999—Miami NFL	16	10-10	17-17	9-14	3-5	*39-*46	84.8	54	27	27	144
2000—Miami NFL	16	7-8	9-10	12-13	0-0	28-31	90.3	49	33	34	117
2001—Miami NFL	16	9-9	8-8	2-4	0-0	19-21	90.5	46	39	40	96
2002—Miami NFL	16	13-14	2-3	7-11	2-3	24-31	77.4	53	42	43	114
2003—Miami NFL	16	9-9	3-6	6-8	4-6	22-29	75.9	52	33	34	99
Pro totals (7 years)	112	76-80	52-59	44-63	10-19	182-221	82.4	54	240	245	786

MARION, BROCK — S — LIONS

PERSONAL: Born June 11, 1970, in Bakersfield, Calif. ... 5-11/200. ... Full name: Brock Elliot Marion.
HIGH SCHOOL: West (Bakersfield, Calif.).
COLLEGE: Nevada.
TRANSACTIONS/CAREER NOTES: Selected by Dallas Cowboys in seventh round (196th overall) of 1993 NFL draft. ... Signed by Cowboys (July 14, 1993). ... Granted free agency (February 16, 1996). ... Re-signed by Cowboys (May 2, 1996). ... Granted unconditional free agency (February 14, 1997). ... Re-signed by Cowboys (April 7, 1997). ... Granted unconditional free agency (February 13, 1998). ... Signed by Miami Dolphins (March 3, 1998). ... Granted unconditional free agency (March 2, 2001). ... Re-signed by Dolphins (June 9, 2001). ... Released by Dolphins (February 28, 2002). ... Re-signed by Dolphins (March 10, 2002). ... Released by Dolphins (March 2, 2004). ... Signed by Detroit Lions (March 25, 2004).
CHAMPIONSHIP GAME EXPERIENCE: Played in NFC championship game (1993-1995 seasons). ... Member of Super Bowl championship team (1993 and 1995 seasons).
HONORS: Played in Pro Bowl (2000, 2002 and 2003 seasons).

			TOTALS			INTERCEPTIONS				KICKOFF RETURNS				TOTALS			
Year Team	G	GS	Tk.	Ast.	Sks.	No.	Yds.	Avg.	TD	No.	Yds.	Avg.	TD	TD	2pt.	Pts.	Fum.
1993—Dallas NFL	15	0	11	5	0.0	1	2	2.0	0	0	0	0.0	0	0	0	0	0
1994—Dallas NFL	14	1	22	4	1.0	1	11	11.0	0	2	39	19.5	0	0	0	0	0
1995—Dallas NFL	16	16	64	16	0.0	6	40	6.7	1	1	16	16.0	0	1	0	6	0
1996—Dallas NFL	10	10	41	10	0.0	0	0	0.0	0	3	68	22.7	0	0	0	0	1
1997—Dallas NFL	16	16	100	17	0.0	0	0	0.0	0	10	311	31.1	0	0	0	0	0
1998—Miami NFL	16	16	71	27	0.0	0	0	0.0	0	6	109	18.2	0	0	0	0	0
1999—Miami NFL	16	16	53	33	1.0	2	30	15.0	0	*62	*1524	24.6	0	0	0	0	2

Year	Team	G	GS	TOTALS Tk.	Ast.	Sks.	INTERCEPTIONS No.	Yds.	Avg.	TD	KICKOFF RETURNS No.	Yds.	Avg.	TD	TOTALS TD	2pt.	Pts.	Fum.
2000—Miami NFL		16	16	72	24	0.0	5	72	14.4	0	22	513	23.3	0	0	0	0	0
2001—Miami NFL		15	15	55	24	0.0	5	*227	45.4	†2	17	371	21.8	0	2	0	12	1
2002—Miami NFL		16	16	64	29	0.0	5	99	19.8	0	0	0	0.0	0	0	0	0	0
2003—Miami NFL		16	16	57	24	0.0	3	3	1.0	0	0	0	0.0	0	0	0	0	0
Pro totals (11 years)		166	138	610	213	2.0	28	484	17.3	3	123	2951	24.0	0	3	0	18	4

MARLER, SETH K JAGUARS

PERSONAL: Born March 27, 1981, in Atlanta, Ga. ... 6-1/200. ... Full name: Michael Seth Marler.
HIGH SCHOOL: Parkview (Lilburn, Ga.).
COLLEGE: Tulane.
TRANSACTIONS/CAREER NOTES: Signed as non-drafted free agent by Jacksonville Jaguars (April 28, 2003).

Year	Team	G	FIELD GOALS 1-29	30-39	40-49	50+	Tot.	Pct.	Lg.	TOTALS XPM	XPA	Pts.
2003—Jacksonville NFL		16	10-11	4-8	5-12	1-2	20-33	60.6	53	30	30	90

MARSHALL, LEMAR LB REDSKINS

PERSONAL: Born December 17, 1976, in Cincinnati, Ohio. ... 6-2/227.
HIGH SCHOOL: St. Xavier (Cincinnati).
COLLEGE: Michigan State.
TRANSACTIONS/CAREER NOTES: Signed as non-drafted free agent by Tampa Bay Buccaneers (April 19, 1999). ... Released by Buccaneers (September 6, 1999). ... Re-signed by Eagles (January 12, 2000). ... Claimed on waivers by Buccaneers (August 22, 2000). ... Released by Buccaneers (August 28, 2000). ... Re-signed by Buccaneers to practice squad (November 22, 2000). ... Released by Buccaneers (December 14, 2000). ... Signed by Denver Broncos (January 29, 2001). ... Released by Broncos (September 1, 2001). ... Signed by Washington Redskins (December 26, 2001).

Year	Team	G	GS	TOTALS Tk.	Ast.	Sks.	INTERCEPTIONS No.	Yds.	Avg.	TD
2002—Washington NFL		16	0	3	0	0.0	0	0	0.0	0
2003—Washington NFL		12	0	2	0	0.5	0	0	0.0	0
Pro totals (2 years)		28	0	5	0	0.5	0	0	0.0	0

MARSHALL, TORRANCE LB PACKERS

PERSONAL: Born June 12, 1977, in Miami, Fla. ... 6-2/255.
HIGH SCHOOL: Sunset (Miami).
JUNIOR COLLEGE: Kemper Military Junior College (Mo.), then Miami-Dade Community College.
COLLEGE: Oklahoma.
TRANSACTIONS/CAREER NOTES: Selected by Green Bay Packers in third round (72nd pick overall) of 2001 NFL draft. ... Signed by Packers (July 24, 2001). ... On suspended list for violating league substance abuse policy (September 7-30, 2003). ... Granted free agency (March 3, 2004). ... Re-signed by Packers (April 21, 2004).
HONORS: Named linebacker on THE SPORTING NEWS college All-America third team (2000).

Year	Team	G	GS	TOTALS Tk.	Ast.	Sks.	INTERCEPTIONS No.	Yds.	Avg.	TD
2001—Green Bay NFL		14	1	9	3	0.0	0	0	0.0	0
2002—Green Bay NFL		16	0	2	1	0.0	0	0	0.0	0
2003—Green Bay NFL		12	1	11	3	1.0	0	0	0.0	0
Pro totals (3 years)		42	2	22	7	1.0	0	0	0.0	0

MARTIN, CECIL FB

PERSONAL: Born July 8, 1975, in Chicago, Ill. ... 6-0/235.
HIGH SCHOOL: Evanston (Ill.).
COLLEGE: Wisconsin.
TRANSACTIONS/CAREER NOTES: Selected by Philadelphia Eagles in sixth round (172nd pick overall) of 1999 NFL draft. ... Signed by Eagles (July 25, 1999). ... Granted free agency (March 1, 2002). ... Re-signed by Eagles (April 26, 2002). ... Granted unconditional free agency (February 28, 2003). ... Signed by Oakland Raiders (March 19, 2003). ... Released by Raiders (August 31, 2003). ... Signed by Tampa Bay Buccaneers (October 14, 2003). ... Released by Buccaneers (October 29, 2003). ... Re-signed by Buccaneers (December 16, 2003). ... Released by Buccaneers (April 1, 2004).
CHAMPIONSHIP GAME EXPERIENCE: Played in NFC championship game (2001 and 2002 seasons).
SINGLE GAME HIGHS (regular season): Attempts—5 (September 30, 2001, vs. Dallas); yards—28 (December 24, 2000, vs. Cincinnati); and rushing touchdowns—0.

Year	Team	G	GS	RUSHING Att.	Yds.	Avg.	TD	RECEIVING No.	Yds.	Avg.	TD	TOTALS TD	2pt.	Pts.	Fum.
1999—Philadelphia NFL		12	5	3	3	1.0	0	11	22	2.0	0	0	0	0	0
2000—Philadelphia NFL		16	9	13	77	5.9	0	31	219	7.1	0	0	0	0	1
2001—Philadelphia NFL		16	15	9	27	3.0	0	24	124	5.2	2	2	0	12	0
2002—Philadelphia NFL		16	9	1	-4	-4.0	0	15	126	8.4	0	0	0	0	1
2003—Tampa Bay NFL		1	0	0	0	0.0	0	0	0	0.0	0	0	0	0	0
Pro totals (5 years)		61	38	26	103	4.0	0	81	491	6.1	2	2	0	12	2

MARTIN, CURTIS — RB — JETS

PERSONAL: Born May 1, 1973, in Pittsburgh, Pa. ... 5-11/205.
HIGH SCHOOL: Taylor-Allderdice (Pittsburgh).
COLLEGE: Pittsburgh.
TRANSACTIONS/CAREER NOTES: Selected after junior season by New England Patriots in third round (74th pick overall) of 1995 NFL draft. ... Signed by Patriots (July 18, 1995). ... Granted free agency (February 13, 1998). ... Tendered offer sheet by New York Jets (March 20, 1998). ... Patriots declined to match offer (March 25, 1998).
CHAMPIONSHIP GAME EXPERIENCE: Played in AFC championship game (1996 and 1998 seasons). ... Played in Super Bowl 31 (1996 season).
HONORS: Named NFL Rookie of the Year by THE SPORTING NEWS (1995). ... Played in Pro Bowl (1995, 1996, 1998 and 2001 seasons). ... Named running back on THE SPORTING NEWS NFL All-Pro team (2001).
SINGLE GAME HIGHS (regular season): Attempts—40 (September 14, 1997, vs. New York Jets); yards—203 (December 3, 2000, vs. Indianapolis); and rushing touchdowns—3 (November 11, 2001, vs. Kansas City).
STATISTICAL PLATEAUS: 100-yard rushing games: 1995 (9), 1996 (2), 1997 (3), 1998 (8), 1999 (6), 2000 (3), 2001 (7), 2002 (5), 2003 (4). Total: 47.

			RUSHING				RECEIVING				TOTALS			
Year Team	G	GS	Att.	Yds.	Avg.	TD	No.	Yds.	Avg.	TD	TD	2pt.	Pts.	Fum.
1995—New England NFL	16	15	§368	§1487	4.0	14	30	261	8.7	1	15	1	92	5
1996—New England NFL	16	15	316	1152	3.6	§14	46	333	7.2	3	§17	1	104	4
1997—New England NFL	13	13	274	1160	4.2	4	41	296	7.2	1	5	0	30	3
1998—New York Jets NFL	15	15	369	1287	3.5	8	43	365	8.5	1	9	0	54	5
1999—New York Jets NFL	16	16	367	1464	4.0	5	45	259	5.8	0	5	0	30	2
2000—New York Jets NFL	16	16	316	1204	3.8	9	70	508	7.3	2	11	0	66	2
2001—New York Jets NFL	16	16	333	1513	4.5	10	53	320	6.0	0	10	0	60	2
2002—New York Jets NFL	16	16	261	1094	4.2	7	49	362	7.4	0	7	1	44	0
2003—New York Jets NFL	16	16	323	1308	4.0	2	42	262	6.2	0	2	0	12	2
Pro totals (9 years)	140	138	2927	11669	4.0	73	419	2966	7.1	8	81	3	492	25

MARTIN, DAVID — TE — PACKERS

PERSONAL: Born March 13, 1979, in Fort Campbell, Ky. ... 6-4/260. ... Full name: David Earl Martin.
HIGH SCHOOL: Norview (Norfolk, Va.).
COLLEGE: Tennessee.
TRANSACTIONS/CAREER NOTES: Selected by Green Bay Packers in sixth round (198th pick overall) of 2001 NFL draft. ... Signed by Packers (June 15, 2001). ... Granted free agency (March 3, 2004). ... Re-signed with Packers (April 20, 2004).
SINGLE GAME HIGHS (regular season): Receptions—3 (October 20, 2002, vs. Washington); yards—33 (October 7, 2001, vs. Tampa Bay); and touchdown receptions—1 (December 22, 2003, vs. Oakland).

			RECEIVING				TOTALS			
Year Team	G	GS	No.	Yds.	Avg.	TD	TD	2pt.	Pts.	Fum.
2001—Green Bay NFL	14	1	13	144	11.1	1	1	0	6	0
2002—Green Bay NFL	8	2	8	33	4.1	1	1	0	6	0
2003—Green Bay NFL	16	3	13	79	6.1	2	2	0	12	0
Pro totals (3 years)	38	6	34	256	7.5	4	4	0	24	0

MARTIN, JAMAR — FB — COWBOYS

PERSONAL: Born April 12, 1980... 5-11/256.
HIGH SCHOOL: McKinley (Canton, Ohio).
COLLEGE: Ohio State.
TRANSACTIONS/CAREER NOTES: Selected by Dallas Cowboys in fourth round (129th pick overall) of 2002 NFL draft. ... Signed by Cowboys (July 25, 2002). ... On injured reserve with knee injury (August 27, 2002-remainder of season).
SINGLE GAME HIGHS (regular season): Attempts—1 (December 28, 2003, vs. New Orleans); yards—3 (November 2, 2003, vs. Washington); and rushing touchdowns—0.

			RUSHING				RECEIVING				TOTALS			
Year Team	G	GS	Att.	Yds.	Avg.	TD	No.	Yds.	Avg.	TD	TD	2pt.	Pts.	Fum.
2003—Dallas NFL	14	1	4	7	1.8	0	2	9	4.5	0	0	0	0	0

MARTIN, STEVE — DT — VIKINGS

PERSONAL: Born May 31, 1974, in St. Paul, Minn. ... 6-4/292. ... Full name: Steven Albert Martin.
HIGH SCHOOL: Jefferson City (Mo.).
COLLEGE: Missouri.
TRANSACTIONS/CAREER NOTES: Selected by Indianapolis Colts in fifth round (151st pick overall) of 1996 NFL draft. ... Signed by Colts (July 5, 1996). ... Claimed on waivers by Philadelphia Eagles (October 23, 1998). ... Granted free agency (February 12, 1999). ... Re-signed by Eagles (April 9, 1999). ... Granted unconditional free agency (February 11, 2000). ... Signed by Kansas City Chiefs (February 24, 2000). ... Released by Chiefs (September 1, 2001). ... Signed by New York Jets (September 3, 2001). ... Granted unconditional free agency (March 1, 2002). ... Signed by New England Patriots (April 3, 2002). ... Released by Patriots (December 19, 2002). ... Signed by Green Bay Packers (July 22, 2003). ... Released by Packers (August 31, 2003). ... Signed by Houston Texans (September 15, 2003). ... Granted unconditional free agency (March 3, 2004). ... Signed by Minnesota Vikings (March 6, 2004).

			TOTALS		
Year Team	G	GS	Tk.	Ast.	Sks.
1996—Indianapolis NFL	14	5	25	11	1.0
1997—Indianapolis NFL	12	0	9	7	0.0

Year	Team	G	GS	TOTALS Tk.	Ast.	Sks.
1998	—Indianapolis NFL	4	0	2	0	0.0
	—Philadelphia NFL	9	3	21	7	1.0
1999	—Philadelphia NFL	16	15	26	17	2.0
2000	—Kansas City NFL	16	0	8	5	0.0
2001	—New York Jets NFL	16	15	40	18	2.5
2002	—New England NFL	14	6	13	4	0.0
2003	—Houston NFL	14	8	45	17	1.0
Pro totals (8 years)		115	52	189	86	7.5

MARTIN, TEE — QB — RAIDERS

PERSONAL: Born July 25, 1978, in Mobile, Ala. ... 6-2/225. ... Full name: Tamaurice Nigel Martin.
HIGH SCHOOL: Williamson (Mobile, Ala.).
COLLEGE: Tennessee.
TRANSACTIONS/CAREER NOTES: Selected by Pittsburgh Steelers in fifth round (163rd pick overall) of 2000 NFL draft. ... Signed by Steelers (July 16, 2000). ... Inactive for 13 games (2000). ... Assigned by Steelers to Rhein Fire in 2002 NFL Europe enhancement allocation program (February 12, 2002). ... Released by Steelers (September 1, 2002). ... Signed by Philadelphia Eagles to practice squad (November 27, 2002). ... Signed by Oakland Raiders off Eagles practice squad (February 18, 2003). ... Waived by Raiders (August 26, 2003). ... Re-signed by Raiders to practice squad (September 2, 2003). ... Activated (November 5, 2003). ... Granted free agency (March 3, 2004). ... Re-signed by Raiders (March 9, 2004).
CHAMPIONSHIP GAME EXPERIENCE: Played in AFC championship game (2001 season).
SINGLE GAME HIGHS (regular season): Attempts—11 (December 28, 2003, vs. San Diego); completions—4 (December 22, 2003, vs. Green Bay); yards—55 (December 22, 2003, vs. Green Bay); and touchdown passes—0.

Year	Team	G	GS	PASSING Att.	Cmp.	Pct.	Yds.	TD	Int.	Avg.	Skd.	Rat.	RUSHING Att.	Yds.	Avg.	TD	TOTALS TD	2pt.	Pts.
2000	—Pittsburgh NFL	Did not play.																	
2001	—Pittsburgh NFL	1	0	0	0	0.0	0	0	0	0.00	0	0.0	1	8	8.0	0	0	0	0
2003	—Oakland NFL	2	0	16	6	37.5	69	0	1	4.31	1	25.3	5	28	5.6	0	0	0	0
Pro totals (2 years)		3	0	16	6	37.5	69	0	1	4.31	1	25.3	6	36	6.0	0	0	0	0

MARTIN, TERRANCE — DE — TEXANS

PERSONAL: Born July 6, 1979, in Toano, Va. ... 6-2/290.
HIGH SCHOOL: Lafayette (Toano, Va.).
COLLEGE: North Carolina State.
TRANSACTIONS/CAREER NOTES: Signed as non-drafted free agent by Houston Texans (May 12, 2003).

Year	Team	G	GS	TOTALS Tk.	Ast.	Sks.
2003	—Houston NFL	12	1	3	3	0.0

M

MASLOWSKI, MIKE — LB — CHIEFS

PERSONAL: Born July 11, 1974, in Thorp, Wis. ... 6-1/243. ... Full name: Michael John Maslowski.
HIGH SCHOOL: Thorp (Wis.).
COLLEGE: Wisconsin-La Crosse.
TRANSACTIONS/CAREER NOTES: Signed as non-drafted free agent by San Diego Chargers (April 21, 1997). ... Released by Chargers (August 1997). ... Played for San Jose Sabercats of Arena League (1998). ... Signed by Kansas City Chiefs (January 12, 1999). ... Assigned by Chiefs to Barcelona Dragons in 1999 NFL Europe enhancement allocation program (February 22, 1999). ... On injured reserve with knee injury (December 22, 2001-remainder of season). ... Granted free agency (March 1, 2002). ... Tendered offer sheet by New England Patriots (March 7, 2002). ... Offer matched by Chiefs (March 14, 2002).

Year	Team	G	GS	TOTALS Tk.	Ast.	Sks.	INTERCEPTIONS No.	Yds.	Avg.	TD
1999	—Kansas City NFL	15	0	0	0	0.0	0	0	0.0	0
2000	—Kansas City NFL	16	5	29	12	2.0	0	0	0.0	0
2001	—Kansas City NFL	8	0	5	1	1.0	0	0	0.0	0
2002	—Kansas City NFL	16	16	94	32	1.0	3	28	9.3	0
2003	—Kansas City NFL	10	10	46	14	0.0	0	0	0.0	0
Pro totals (5 years)		65	31	174	59	4.0	3	28	9.3	0

MASON, DERRICK — WR — TITANS

PERSONAL: Born January 17, 1974, in Detroit, Mich. ... 5-10/190. ... Full name: Derrick James Mason.
HIGH SCHOOL: Mumford (Detroit).
COLLEGE: Michigan State.
TRANSACTIONS/CAREER NOTES: Selected by Houston Oilers in fourth round (98th pick overall) of 1997 NFL draft. ... Oilers franchise moved to Tennessee for 1997 season. ... Signed by Oilers (July 19, 1997). ... Oilers franchise renamed Tennessee Titans for 1999 season (December 26, 1998). ... Granted free agency (February 11, 2000). ... Re-signed by Titans (June 1, 2000). ... Granted unconditional free agency (March 2, 2001). ... Re-signed by Titans (March 2, 2001).
CHAMPIONSHIP GAME EXPERIENCE: Played in AFC championship game (1999 and 2002 seasons). ... Played in Super Bowl 34 (1999 season).
HONORS: Named kick returner on THE SPORTING NEWS NFL All-Pro team (2000). ... Played in Pro Bowl (2000 and 2003 seasons).
RECORDS: Holds NFL single-season record for most combined net yards—2,690 (2000).

SINGLE GAME HIGHS (regular season): Receptions—12 (December 1, 2002, vs. New York Giants); yards—186 (January 6, 2002, vs. Cincinnati); and touchdown receptions—3 (October 12, 2003, vs. Houston).
STATISTICAL PLATEAUS: 100-yard receiving games: 2000 (1), 2001 (4), 2002 (3), 2003 (3). Total: 11.

			RUSHING				RECEIVING				PUNT RETURNS				KICKOFF RETURNS				TOTALS		
Year Team	G	GS	Att.	Yds.	Avg.	TD	No.	Yds.	Avg.	TD	No.	Yds.	Avg.	TD	No.	Yds.	Avg.	TD	TD	2pt.	Pts.
1997—Ten. NFL	16	2	1	-7	-7.0	0	14	186	13.3	0	13	95	7.3	0	26	551	21.2	0	0	0	0
1998—Ten. NFL	16	0	0	0	0.0	0	25	333	13.3	3	31	228	7.4	0	8	154	19.3	0	3	0	18
1999—Ten. NFL	13	0	0	0	0.0	0	8	89	11.1	0	26	225	8.7	1	41	805	19.6	0	1	0	6
2000—Ten. NFL	16	12	1	1	1.0	0	63	895	14.2	5	*51	*662	13.0	1	42	1132	§27.0	0	6	0	36
2001—Ten. NFL	15	15	0	0	0.0	0	73	1128	15.5	9	20	128	6.4	0	34	748	22.0	1	10	1	62
2002—Ten. NFL	14	14	0	0	0.0	0	79	1012	12.8	5	9	60	6.7	0	0	0	0.0	0	5	0	30
2003—Ten. NFL	16	16	3	11	3.7	0	95	1303	13.7	8	8	99	12.4	0	5	106	21.2	0	8	0	48
Pro totals (7 years)	106	59	5	5	1.0	0	357	4946	13.9	30	158	1497	9.5	2	156	3496	22.4	1	33	1	200

MASSEY, CHRIS — RB — RAMS

PERSONAL: Born August 21, 1979, in Charleston, W.Va. ... 6-0/245. ... Full name: Christopher Todd Massey.
HIGH SCHOOL: East Bank (W.Va.).
COLLEGE: Marshall.
TRANSACTIONS/CAREER NOTES: Selected by St. Louis Rams in seventh round (243rd pick overall) of 2002 NFL draft. ... Signed by Rams (June 28, 2002).
SINGLE GAME HIGHS (regular season): Attempts—1 (September 28, 2003, vs. Arizona); yards—-1 (September 28, 2003, vs. Arizona); and rushing touchdowns—0.

			RUSHING				TOTALS			
Year Team	G	GS	Att.	Yds.	Avg.	TD	TD	2pt.	Pts.	Fum.
2002—St. Louis NFL	16	1	0	0	0.0	0	0	0	0	0
2003—St. Louis NFL	16	0	1	-1	-1.0	0	0	0	0	0
Pro totals (2 years)	32	1	1	-1	-1.0	0	0	0	0	0

MATHEWS, JASON — T — TITANS

PERSONAL: Born February 9, 1971, in Orange, Texas. ... 6-5/285. ... Full name: Samuel Jason Mathews.
HIGH SCHOOL: Bridge City (Texas).
COLLEGE: Texas A&M.
TRANSACTIONS/CAREER NOTES: Selected by Indianapolis Colts in third round (67th pick overall) of 1994 NFL draft. ... Signed by Colts (July 23, 1994). ... Granted free agency (February 14, 1997). ... Re-signed by Colts (April 30, 1997). ... Granted unconditional free agency (February 13, 1998). ... Signed by Tampa Bay Buccaneers (May 7, 1998). ... Released by Buccaneers (August 30, 1998). ... Signed by Tennessee Oilers (September 1, 1998). ... Oilers franchise renamed Tennessee Titans for 1999 season (December 26, 1998).
PLAYING EXPERIENCE: Indianapolis NFL, 1994-1997; Tennessee NFL, 1998-2003. ... Games/Games started: 1994 (10/0), 1995 (16/16), 1996 (16/15), 1997 (16/0), 1998 (3/0), 1999 (3/0), 2000 (16/1), 2001 (16/2), 2002 (16/2), 2003 (15/0). Total: 127/36.
CHAMPIONSHIP GAME EXPERIENCE: Played in AFC championship game (1995, 1999 and 2002 seasons). ... Member of Titans for Super Bowl 34 (1999 season); did not play.

MATHIS, KEVIN — CB — FALCONS

PERSONAL: Born April 29, 1974, in Gainesville, Texas. ... 5-9/185.
HIGH SCHOOL: Gainesville (Texas).
COLLEGE: Texas A&M-Commerce.
TRANSACTIONS/CAREER NOTES: Signed as non-drafted free agent by Dallas Cowboys (April 24, 1997). ... Granted free agency (February 11, 2000). ... Re-signed by Cowboys (April 26, 2000). ... Traded by Cowboys to New Orleans Saints for LB Chris Bordano (April 26, 2000). ... Granted unconditional free agency (March 2, 2001). ... Re-signed by Saints (March 2, 2001). ... Released by Saints (July 24, 2002). ... Signed by Atlanta Falcons (September 17, 2002). ... Granted unconditional free agency (February 28, 2003). ... Re-signed by Falcons (March 31, 2003).

			TOTALS			INTERCEPTIONS				PUNT RETURNS				KICKOFF RETURNS				TOTALS			
Year Team	G	GS	Tk.	Ast.	Sks.	No.	Yds.	Avg.	TD	No.	Yds.	Avg.	TD	No.	Yds.	Avg.	TD	TD	2pt.	Pts.	Fum.
1997—Dal. NFL	16	3	15	1	0.0	0	0	0.0	0	11	91	8.3	0	0	0	0.0	0	0	0	0	2
1998—Dal. NFL	13	4	28	4	1.0	2	0	0.0	0	2	3	1.5	0	25	621	24.8	0	0	0	0	2
1999—Dal. NFL	8	4	11	3	0.0	0	0	0.0	0	0	0	0.0	0	18	408	22.7	0	0	0	0	1
2000—N.O. NFL	16	16	58	15	0.0	1	0	0.0	0	1	5	5.0	0	8	187	23.4	0	0	0	0	1
2001—N.O. NFL	14	13	63	14	1.0	2	34	17.0	0	0	0	0.0	0	0	0	0.0	0	0	0	0	0
2002—Atl. NFL	11	0	15	1	0.0	3	21	7.0	0	0	0	0.0	0	0	0	0.0	0	0	0	0	0
2003—Atl. NFL	14	2	29	4	1.0	1	32	32.0	1	0	0	0.0	0	0	0	0.0	0	1	0	6	0
Pro totals (7 years)	92	42	219	42	3.0	9	87	9.7	1	14	99	7.1	0	51	1216	23.8	0	1	0	6	6

MATHIS, RASHEAN — S — JAGUARS

PERSONAL: Born August 27, 1980, in Jacksonville, Fla. ... 6-1/200.
HIGH SCHOOL: Englewood (Jacksonville, Fla.).
COLLEGE: Bethune-Cookman.
TRANSACTIONS/CAREER NOTES: Selected by Jacksonville Jaguars in second round (39th pick overall) of 2003 NFL draft. ... Signed by Jaguars (July 25, 2003).

			TOTALS			INTERCEPTIONS				PUNT RETURNS				KICKOFF RETURNS				TOTALS			
Year Team	G	GS	Tk.	Ast.	Sks.	No.	Yds.	Avg.	TD	No.	Yds.	Avg.	TD	No.	Yds.	Avg.	TD	TD	2pt.	Pts.	Fum.
2003—Jac. NFL	16	16	68	10	0.0	2	0	0.0	0	2	7	3.5	0	1	7	7.0	0	0	0	0	0

MATHIS, ROBERT DE COLTS

PERSONAL: Born February 26, 1981, in Atlanta, Ga. ... 6-2/235.
HIGH SCHOOL: McNair (Atlanta).
COLLEGE: Alabama A&M.
TRANSACTIONS/CAREER NOTES: Selected by Indianapolis Colts in fifth round (138th pick overall) of 2003 NFL draft. ... Signed by Colts (July 24, 2003).
CHAMPIONSHIP GAME EXPERIENCE: Played in AFC championship game (2003 season).

			TOTALS		
Year Team	**G**	**GS**	**Tk.**	**Ast.**	**Sks.**
2003—Indianapolis NFL	16	0	7	1	3.5

MATTOS, GRANT WR CHARGERS

PERSONAL: Born March 12, 1981, in Mountain View, Calif. ... 6-2/220.
HIGH SCHOOL: St. Francis (Mountain View, Calif.).
COLLEGE: Southern California.
TRANSACTIONS/CAREER NOTES: Signed as non-drafted free agent by San Diego Chargers (May 2, 2003). ... Released by Chargers (August 31, 2003). ... Re-signed by Chargers to practice squad (September 2, 2003). ... Activated (September 17, 2003). ... Waived by Chargers (October 4, 2003). ... Re-signed by Chargers to practice squad (October 7, 2003). ... Activated (November 26, 2003).

			RECEIVING				TOTALS			
Year Team	**G**	**GS**	**No.**	**Yds.**	**Avg.**	**TD**	**TD**	**2pt.**	**Pts.**	**Fum.**
2003—San Diego NFL	6	0	0	0	0.0	0	0	0	0	0

MAWAE, KEVIN C JETS

PERSONAL: Born January 23, 1971, in Savannah, Ga. ... 6-4/289. ... Full name: Kevin James Mawae. ... Name pronounced: ma-WHY.
HIGH SCHOOL: Leesville (La.).
COLLEGE: Louisiana State.
TRANSACTIONS/CAREER NOTES: Selected by Seattle Seahawks in second round (36th pick overall) of 1994 NFL draft. ... Signed by Seahawks (July 21, 1994). ... Granted free agency (February 14, 1997). ... Re-signed by Seahawks (May 5, 1997). ... Granted unconditional free agency (February 13, 1998). ... Signed by New York Jets (February 19, 1998).
PLAYING EXPERIENCE: Seattle NFL, 1994-1997; New York Jets NFL, 1998-2003. ... Games/Games started: 1994 (14/11), 1995 (16/16), 1996 (16/16), 1997 (16/16), 1998 (16/16), 1999 (16/16), 2000 (16/16), 2001 (16/16), 2002 (16/16), 2003 (16/16). Total: 158/155.
CHAMPIONSHIP GAME EXPERIENCE: Played in AFC championship game (1998 season).
HONORS: Named center on THE SPORTING NEWS NFL All-Pro team (1999, 2001 and 2002). ... Played in Pro Bowl (1999-2003 seasons).

M

MAYBERRY, JERMANE G/T EAGLES

PERSONAL: Born August 29, 1973, in Floresville, Texas. ... 6-4/325. ... Full name: Jermane Timothy Mayberry.
HIGH SCHOOL: Floresville (Texas).
JUNIOR COLLEGE: Navarro College (Texas).
COLLEGE: Texas A&M-Kingsville.
TRANSACTIONS/CAREER NOTES: Selected by Philadelphia Eagles in first round (25th pick overall) of 1996 NFL draft. ... Signed by Eagles (June 13, 1996). ... On injured reserve with elbow injury (October 27, 2003-remainder of season).
PLAYING EXPERIENCE: Philadelphia NFL, 1996-2003. ... Games/Games started: 1996 (3/1), 1997 (16/16), 1998 (15/10), 1999 (13/5), 2000 (16/16), 2001 (16/15), 2002 (16/16), 2003 (5/5). Total: 100/84.
CHAMPIONSHIP GAME EXPERIENCE: Played in NFC championship game (2001 and 2002 seasons).
HONORS: Played in Pro Bowl (2002 season).

MAYER, SHAWN S PATRIOTS

PERSONAL: Born March 4, 1979, in Hillsborough, N.J. ... 6-0/202. ... Full name: Shawn Arron Mayer.
HIGH SCHOOL: Hillsborough (N.J.).
COLLEGE: Penn State.
TRANSACTIONS/CAREER NOTES: Signed as non-drafted free agent by New England Patriots (May 2, 2003). ... Released by Patriots (August 31, 2003). ... Re-signed by Patriots to practice squad (September 1, 2003). ... Activated (October 18, 2003). ... Waived by Patriots (November 7, 2003). ... Re-signed by Patriots to practice squad (November 10, 2003). ... Activated (November 22, 2003).
CHAMPIONSHIP GAME EXPERIENCE: Played in AFC championship game (2003 season). ... Member of Super Bowl championship team (2003 season).

			TOTALS			INTERCEPTIONS			
Year Team	**G**	**GS**	**Tk.**	**Ast.**	**Sks.**	**No.**	**Yds.**	**Avg.**	**TD**
2003—New England NFL	9	0	3	0	0.0	0	0	0.0	0

MAYNARD, BRAD P BEARS

PERSONAL: Born February 9, 1974, in Tipton, Ind. ... 6-1/186. ... Full name: Bradley Alan Maynard.
HIGH SCHOOL: Sheridan (Ind.).
COLLEGE: Ball State.
TRANSACTIONS/CAREER NOTES: Selected by New York Giants in third round (95th pick overall) of 1997 NFL draft. ... Signed by Giants (July 19, 1997). ... Granted free agency (February 11, 2000). ... Re-signed by Giants (June 8, 2000). ... Granted unconditional free agency (March 2, 2001). ... Signed by Chicago Bears (March 3, 2001).

CHAMPIONSHIP GAME EXPERIENCE: Played in NFC championship game (2000 season). ... Played in Super Bowl 35 (2000 season).
HONORS: Named punter on THE SPORTING NEWS college All-America second team (1996).

		PUNTING					
Year Team	**G**	**No.**	**Yds.**	**Avg.**	**Net avg.**	**In. 20**	**Blk.**
1997—New York Giants NFL	16	*111	*4531	40.8	34.6	*33	1
1998—New York Giants NFL	16	101	*4566	45.2	37.8	∞33	0
1999—New York Giants NFL	16	89	3651	41.0	35.1	‡31	0
2000—New York Giants NFL	16	79	3210	40.6	33.7	26	1
2001—Chicago NFL	16	87	3709	42.6	37.0	*36	0
2002—Chicago NFL	16	87	3679	42.3	37.4	26	0
2003—Chicago NFL	16	79	3258	41.2	34.6	23	2
Pro totals (7 years)	112	633	26604	42.0	35.8	208	4

MAYS, LEE — WR — STEELERS

PERSONAL: Born September 18, 1978, in Houston, Texas. ... 6-2/200.
HIGH SCHOOL: Westfield (Houston).
COLLEGE: Texas-El Paso.
TRANSACTIONS/CAREER NOTES: Selected by Pittsburgh Steelers in sixth round (202nd pick overall) of 2002 NFL draft. ... Signed by Steelers (July 18, 2002).
SINGLE GAME HIGHS (regular season): Receptions—1 (December 14, 2003, vs. New York Jets); yards—9 (September 28, 2003, vs. Tennessee); and touchdown receptions—0.

			RUSHING				RECEIVING				KICKOFF RETURNS				TOTALS			
Year Team	**G**	**GS**	**Att.**	**Yds.**	**Avg.**	**TD**	**No.**	**Yds.**	**Avg.**	**TD**	**No.**	**Yds.**	**Avg.**	**TD**	**TD**	**2pt.**	**Pts.**	**Fum.**
2002—Pittsburgh NFL	16	0	0	0	0.0	0	0	0	0.0	0	32	671	21.0	0	0	0	0	0
2003—Pittsburgh NFL	16	0	0	0	0.0	0	2	17	8.5	0	4	79	19.8	0	0	0	0	0
Pro totals (2 years)	32	0	0	0	0.0	0	2	17	8.5	0	36	750	20.8	0	0	0	0	0

MCADDLEY, JASON — WR — CARDINALS

PERSONAL: Born July 28, 1979, in Brooklyn, N.Y. ... 6-2/200.
HIGH SCHOOL: Oak Ridge (Tenn.).
COLLEGE: Alabama.
TRANSACTIONS/CAREER NOTES: Selected by Arizona Cardinals in fifth round (149th pick overall) of 2002 NFL draft. ... Signed by Cardinals (June 5, 2002). ... On injured reserve with hamstring injury (November 26, 2003-remainder of season).
SINGLE GAME HIGHS (regular season): Receptions—5 (December 8, 2002, vs. Detroit); yards—113 (November 10, 2002, vs. Seattle); and touchdown receptions—1 (November 17, 2002, vs. Philadelphia).
STATISTICAL PLATEAUS: 100-yard receiving games: 2002 (1). Total: 1.

			RUSHING				RECEIVING				KICKOFF RETURNS				TOTALS			
Year Team	**G**	**GS**	**Att.**	**Yds.**	**Avg.**	**TD**	**No.**	**Yds.**	**Avg.**	**TD**	**No.**	**Yds.**	**Avg.**	**TD**	**TD**	**2pt.**	**Pts.**	**Fum.**
2002—Arizona NFL	9	8	0	0	0.0	0	25	362	14.5	1	2	45	22.5	0	1	0	6	0
2003—Arizona NFL	2	0	0	0	0.0	0	4	53	13.3	0	0	0	0.0	0	0	0	0	0
Pro totals (2 years)	11	8	0	0	0.0	0	29	415	14.3	1	2	45	22.5	0	1	0	6	0

MCAFEE, FRED — RB

PERSONAL: Born June 20, 1968, in Philadelphia, Miss. ... 5-10/193. ... Full name: Fred Lee McAfee.
HIGH SCHOOL: Philadelphia (Miss.).
COLLEGE: Mississippi College.
TRANSACTIONS/CAREER NOTES: Selected by New Orleans Saints in sixth round (154th pick overall) of 1991 NFL draft. ... Signed by Saints (July 14, 1991). ... Released by Saints (August 26, 1991). ... Re-signed by Saints to practice squad (August 28, 1991). ... Activated (October 18, 1991). ... On injured reserve with shoulder injury (December 15, 1992-remainder of season). ... Granted free agency (February 17, 1994). ... Signed by Arizona Cardinals (August 2, 1994). ... Released by Cardinals (October 31, 1994). ... Signed by Pittsburgh Steelers (November 9, 1994). ... Granted unconditional free agency (February 16, 1996). ... Re-signed by Steelers (April 12, 1996). ... Granted unconditional free agency (February 12, 1999). ... Signed by Kansas City Chiefs (July 30, 1999). ... Released by Chiefs (August 31, 1999). ... Signed by Tampa Bay Buccaneers (December 28, 1999). ... Granted unconditional free agency (February 11, 2000). ... Signed by Saints (October 2, 2000). ... Granted unconditional free agency (March 2, 2001). ... Re-signed by Saints (June 6, 2001). ... Granted unconditional free agency (February 28, 2003). ... Re-signed by Saints (March 19, 2003). ... Granted unconditional free agency (March 3, 2004).
CHAMPIONSHIP GAME EXPERIENCE: Played in AFC championship game (1994, 1995 and 1997 seasons). ... Played in Super Bowl 30 (1995 season). ... Played in NFC championship game (1999 season).
HONORS: Played in Pro Bowl (2002 season).
SINGLE GAME HIGHS (regular season): Attempts—28 (November 24, 1991, vs. Atlanta); yards—138 (November 24, 1991, vs. Atlanta); and rushing touchdowns—1 (September 10, 1995, vs. Houston).
STATISTICAL PLATEAUS: 100-yard rushing games: 1991 (1). Total: 1.

			RUSHING				RECEIVING				KICKOFF RETURNS				TOTALS			
Year Team	**G**	**GS**	**Att.**	**Yds.**	**Avg.**	**TD**	**No.**	**Yds.**	**Avg.**	**TD**	**No.**	**Yds.**	**Avg.**	**TD**	**TD**	**2pt.**	**Pts.**	**Fum.**
1991—New Orleans NFL	9	0	109	494	4.5	2	1	8	8.0	0	1	14	14.0	0	2	0	12	2
1992—New Orleans NFL	14	1	39	114	2.9	1	1	16	16.0	0	19	393	20.7	0	1	0	6	0
1993—New Orleans NFL	15	4	51	160	3.1	1	1	3	3.0	0	28	580	20.7	0	1	0	6	3
1994—Arizona NFL	7	0	2	-5	-2.5	1	1	4	4.0	0	7	113	16.1	0	1	0	6	1
—Pittsburgh NFL	6	0	16	56	3.5	1	0	0	0.0	0	0	0	0.0	0	1	0	6	0
1995—Pittsburgh NFL	16	1	39	156	4.0	1	15	88	5.9	0	5	56	11.2	0	1	0	6	0
1996—Pittsburgh NFL	14	0	7	17	2.4	0	5	21	4.2	0	0	0	0.0	0	0	0	0	0
1997—Pittsburgh NFL	14	0	13	41	3.2	0	2	44	22.0	0	0	0	0.0	0	0	0	0	1
1998—Pittsburgh NFL	14	0	18	111	6.2	0	9	27	3.0	0	1	10	10.0	0	1	0	6	0
1999—Tampa Bay NFL	1	0	0	0	0.0	0	0	0	0.0	0	0	0	0.0	0	0	0	0	0

Year Team	G	GS	RUSHING Att.	Yds.	Avg.	TD	RECEIVING No.	Yds.	Avg.	TD	KICKOFF RETURNS No.	Yds.	Avg.	TD	TOTALS TD	2pt.	Pts.	Fum.
2000—New Orleans NFL	12	0	2	37	18.5	0	0	0	0.0	0	10	251	25.1	0	0	0	0	0
2001—New Orleans NFL	16	0	1	2	2.0	0	0	0	0.0	0	6	144	24.0	0	0	0	0	0
2002—New Orleans NFL	11	0	1	11	11.0	0	0	0	0.0	0	2	69	34.5	0	0	0	0	0
2003—New Orleans NFL	14	0	1	13	13.0	0	0	0	0.0	0	9	140	15.6	0	0	0	0	1
Pro totals (13 years)	163	6	299	1207	4.0	7	35	211	6.0	0	88	1770	20.1	0	8	0	48	8

MCALISTER, CHRIS — CB — RAVENS

PERSONAL: Born June 14, 1977, in Pasadena, Calif. ... 6-1/206. ... Full name: Christopher James McAlister. ... Son of James McAlister, running back with Philadelphia Eagles (1975 and 1976) and New England Patriots (1978).
HIGH SCHOOL: Pasadena (Calif.).
JUNIOR COLLEGE: Mt. San Antonio College (Calif.).
COLLEGE: Arizona.
TRANSACTIONS/CAREER NOTES: Selected by Baltimore Ravens in first round (10th pick overall) of 1999 NFL draft. ... Signed by Ravens (July 23, 1999). ... Designated by Ravens as franchise player (February 20, 2003). ... Designated by Ravens as franchise player (February 24, 2004).
CHAMPIONSHIP GAME EXPERIENCE: Played in AFC championship game (2000 season). ... Member of Super Bowl championship team (2000 season).
HONORS: Named cornerback on THE SPORTING NEWS college All-America third team (1997). ... Named cornerback on THE SPORTING NEWS college All-America first team (1998). ... Played in Pro Bowl (2003 season).

Year Team	G	GS	TOTALS Tk.	Ast.	Sks.	INTERCEPTIONS No.	Yds.	Avg.	TD	PUNT RETURNS No.	Yds.	Avg.	TD	TOTALS TD	2pt.	Pts.	Fum.
1999—Baltimore NFL	16	12	45	2	0.0	5	28	5.6	0	0	0	0.0	0	0	0	0	0
2000—Baltimore NFL	16	16	35	6	0.0	4	*165	41.2	1	0	0	0.0	0	1	0	6	0
2001—Baltimore NFL	16	16	63	8	0.0	1	0	0.0	0	5	44	8.8	0	0	0	0	0
2002—Baltimore NFL	13	12	48	5	0.0	1	0	0.0	0	17	122	7.2	0	1	0	6	2
2003—Baltimore NFL	15	15	33	10	0.0	3	93	31.0	1	0	0	0.0	0	1	0	6	0
Pro totals (5 years)	76	71	224	31	0.0	14	286	20.4	2	22	166	7.5	0	3	0	18	2

MCALLISTER, DEUCE — RB — SAINTS

PERSONAL: Born December 27, 1978, in Lena, Miss. ... 6-1/221. ... Full name: Dulymus James McAllister.
HIGH SCHOOL: Morton (Miss.).
COLLEGE: Mississippi.
TRANSACTIONS/CAREER NOTES: Selected by New Orleans Saints in first round (23rd pick overall) of 2001 NFL draft. ... Signed by Saints (August 4, 2001).
HONORS: Played in Pro Bowl (2002 season). ... Named to play in Pro Bowl (2003 season); replaced by Shaun Alexander due to injury.
SINGLE GAME HIGHS (regular season): Attempts—32 (December 8, 2002, vs. Baltimore); yards—184 (November 23, 2003, vs. Philadelphia); and rushing touchdowns—3 (December 8, 2002, vs. Baltimore).
STATISTICAL PLATEAUS: 100-yard rushing games: 2002 (8), 2003 (9). Total: 17.

Year Team	G	GS	RUSHING Att.	Yds.	Avg.	TD	RECEIVING No.	Yds.	Avg.	TD	PUNT RETURNS No.	Yds.	Avg.	TD	KICKOFF RETURNS No.	Yds.	Avg.	TD	TOTALS TD	2pt.	Pts.
2001—N.O. NFL	16	4	16	91	5.7	1	15	166	11.1	1	4	24	6.0	0	45	1091	24.2	0	2	0	12
2002—N.O. NFL	15	15	‡325	‡1388	4.3	13	47	352	7.5	3	0	0	0.0	0	0	0	0.0	0	16	0	96
2003—N.O. NFL	16	16	351	1641	4.7	8	69	516	7.5	0	0	0	0.0	0	0	0	0.0	0	8	0	48
Pro totals (3 years)	47	35	692	3120	4.5	22	131	1034	7.9	4	4	24	6.0	0	45	1091	24.2	0	26	0	156

MCBRIDE, TOD — CB — FALCONS

PERSONAL: Born January 26, 1976, in Los Angeles, Calif. ... 6-1/208. ... Full name: Tod Anthony McBride.
HIGH SCHOOL: Walnut (Calif.).
COLLEGE: UCLA.
TRANSACTIONS/CAREER NOTES: Signed as non-drafted free agent by Seattle Seahawks (April 23, 1999). ... Claimed on waivers by Green Bay Packers (June 23, 1999). ... Granted free agency (March 1, 2002). ... Re-signed by Packers (April 24, 2002). ... Granted unconditional free agency (February 28, 2003). ... Signed by Atlanta Falcons (March 24, 2003).

Year Team	G	GS	TOTALS Tk.	Ast.	Sks.	INTERCEPTIONS No.	Yds.	Avg.	TD
1999—Green Bay NFL	15	0	4	1	0.0	0	0	0.0	0
2000—Green Bay NFL	15	6	43	11	0.0	2	43	21.5	0
2001—Green Bay NFL	16	0	29	7	2.0	0	0	0.0	0
2002—Green Bay NFL	15	4	35	7	0.0	1	0	0.0	0
2003—Atlanta NFL	12	9	26	1	0.0	3	44	14.7	1
Pro totals (5 years)	73	19	137	27	2.0	6	87	14.5	1

MCBURROWS, GERALD — S

PERSONAL: Born October 7, 1973, in Detroit, Mich. ... 5-11/208. ... Full name: Gerald Lance McBurrows.
HIGH SCHOOL: Martin Luther King (Detroit).
COLLEGE: Kansas.
TRANSACTIONS/CAREER NOTES: Selected by St. Louis Rams in seventh round (214th pick overall) of 1995 NFL draft. ... Signed by Rams (June 16, 1995). ... On injured reserve with knee injury (October 29, 1997-remainder of season). ... Granted free agency (February 13, 1998). ... Re-signed by Rams (April 24, 1998). ... On injured reserve with knee injury (November 17, 1998-remainder of season). ... Granted unconditional free agency (February 12, 1999). ... Signed by Atlanta Falcons (March 2, 1999). ... Granted unconditional free agency (March 2, 2001). ... Re-signed by Falcons (March 21, 2001). ... Granted unconditional free agency (March 3, 2004).

Year	Team	G	GS	TOTALS Tk.	Ast.	Sks.	INTERCEPTIONS No.	Yds.	Avg.	TD
1995	St. Louis NFL	14	3	23	4	1.0	0	0	0.0	0
1996	St. Louis NFL	16	7	55	7	0.0	1	3	3.0	0
1997	St. Louis NFL	8	3	16	3	0.0	0	0	0.0	0
1998	St. Louis NFL	10	0	3	0	0.0	0	0	0.0	0
1999	Atlanta NFL	16	4	28	12	1.0	2	64	32.0	0
2000	Atlanta NFL	16	4	29	7	2.0	0	0	0.0	0
2001	Atlanta NFL	14	8	41	6	0.0	0	0	0.0	0
2002	Atlanta NFL	15	14	39	10	0.5	2	36	18.0	0
2003	Atlanta NFL	13	2	12	1	0.0	0	0	0.0	0
Pro totals (9 years)		122	45	246	50	4.5	5	103	20.6	0

MCCADAM, KEVIN — S — FALCONS

PERSONAL: Born March 6, 1979, in La Mesa, Calif. ... 6-1/219. ... Full name: Kevin Edward McCadam.

HIGH SCHOOL: El Capitan (Calif.).

JUNIOR COLLEGE: Grossmont College.

COLLEGE: Virginia Tech.

TRANSACTIONS/CAREER NOTES: Selected by Atlanta Falcons in fifth round (148th pick overall) of 2002 NFL draft. ... Signed by Falcons (June 19, 2002).

Year	Team	G	GS	TOTALS Tk.	Ast.	Sks.	INTERCEPTIONS No.	Yds.	Avg.	TD
2002	Atlanta NFL	11	1	3	0	0.0	0	0	0.0	0
2003	Atlanta NFL	12	3	12	1	1.0	0	0	0.0	0
Pro totals (2 years)		23	4	15	1	1.0	0	0	0.0	0

MCCAFFREY, ED — WR

PERSONAL: Born August 17, 1968, in Waynesboro, Pa. ... 6-5/215. ... Full name: Edward McCaffrey.

HIGH SCHOOL: Allentown (Pa.) Central Catholic.

COLLEGE: Stanford.

TRANSACTIONS/CAREER NOTES: Selected by New York Giants in third round (83rd pick overall) of 1991 NFL draft. ... Signed by Giants (July 23, 1991). ... Granted free agency (February 17, 1994). ... Signed by San Francisco 49ers (July 24, 1994). ... Granted unconditional free agency (February 17, 1995). ... Signed by Denver Broncos (March 7, 1995). ... On injured reserve with leg injury (September 12, 2001-remainder of season). ... Announced retirement (March 2, 2004).

CHAMPIONSHIP GAME EXPERIENCE: Played in NFC championship game (1994 season). ... Member of Super Bowl championship team (1994, 1997 and 1998 seasons). ... Played in AFC championship game (1997 and 1998 seasons).

HONORS: Named wide receiver on THE SPORTING NEWS college All-America second team (1990). ... Played in Pro Bowl (1998 season).

SINGLE GAME HIGHS (regular season): Receptions—10 (November 19, 2000, vs. San Diego); yards—148 (November 19, 2000, vs. San Diego); and touchdown receptions—3 (September 13, 1999, vs. Miami).

STATISTICAL PLATEAUS: 100-yard receiving games: 1992 (1), 1997 (1), 1998 (4), 1999 (4), 2000 (5), 2002 (4). Total: 19.

Year	Team	G	GS	RECEIVING No.	Yds.	Avg.	TD	TOTALS TD	2pt.	Pts.	Fum.
1991	New York Giants NFL	16	0	16	146	9.1	0	0	0	0	0
1992	New York Giants NFL	16	3	49	610	12.4	5	5	0	30	2
1993	New York Giants NFL	16	1	27	335	12.4	2	2	0	12	0
1994	San Francisco NFL	16	0	11	131	11.9	2	2	0	12	0
1995	Denver NFL	16	5	39	477	12.2	2	2	1	14	1
1996	Denver NFL	15	15	48	553	11.5	7	7	0	42	0
1997	Denver NFL	15	15	45	590	13.1	8	8	0	48	0
1998	Denver NFL	15	15	64	1053	16.5	▲10	10	1	62	1
1999	Denver NFL	15	15	71	1018	14.3	7	7	0	42	0
2000	Denver NFL	16	16	101	1317	13.0	9	9	1	56	0
2001	Denver NFL	1	1	6	94	15.7	1	1	0	6	0
2002	Denver NFL	16	16	69	903	13.1	2	2	0	12	1
2003	Denver NFL	12	7	19	195	10.3	0	0	0	0	0
Pro totals (13 years)		185	109	565	7422	13.1	55	55	3	336	5

MCCANTS, DARNERIEN — WR — REDSKINS

PERSONAL: Born August 1, 1977, in Odenton, Md. ... 6-3/214. ... Full name: Damerien McCants.

HIGH SCHOOL: Arundel (Md.).

COLLEGE: Delaware State.

TRANSACTIONS/CAREER NOTES: Selected by Washington Redskins in fifth round (154th pick overall) of 2001 NFL draft. ... Signed by Redskins (July 25, 2001). ... Granted free agency (March 3, 2004). ... Re-signed by Redskins (March 30, 2004).

SINGLE GAME HIGHS (regular season): Receptions—6 (December 29, 2002, vs. Dallas); yards—79 (October 5, 2003, vs. Philadelphia); and touchdown receptions—1 (December 7, 2003, vs. New York Giants).

Year	Team	G	GS	RECEIVING No.	Yds.	Avg.	TD	TOTALS TD	2pt.	Pts.	Fum.
2002	Washington NFL	9	1	21	256	12.2	2	2	0	12	1
2003	Washington NFL	15	1	27	360	13.3	6	6	2	40	0
Pro totals (2 years)		24	2	48	616	12.8	8	8	2	52	1

M

MCCARDELL, KEENAN — WR — BUCCANEERS

PERSONAL: Born January 6, 1970, in Houston, Texas. ... 6-1/191. ... Full name: Keenan Wayne McCardell. ... Name pronounced: mc-CAR-dell.

HIGH SCHOOL: Waltrip (Houston).

COLLEGE: UNLV.

TRANSACTIONS/CAREER NOTES: Selected by Washington Redskins in 12th round (326th pick overall) of 1991 NFL draft. ... Signed by Redskins for 1991 season. ... On injured reserve with knee injury (August 20, 1991-entire season). ... Granted unconditional free agency (February 1, 1992). ... Signed by Cleveland Browns (March 24, 1992). ... Released by Browns (September 1, 1992). ... Re-signed by Browns to practice squad (September 3, 1992). ... Activated (October 6, 1992). ... Released by Browns (October 13, 1992). ... Re-signed by Browns to practice squad (October 14, 1992). ... Activated (November 14, 1992). ... Released by Browns (November 19, 1992). ... Re-signed by Browns to practice squad (November 20, 1992). ... Activated (December 26, 1992). ... Released by Browns (September 22, 1993). ... Signed by Chicago Bears to practice squad (November 2, 1993). ... Signed by Browns off Bears practice squad (November 24, 1993). ... Granted free agency (February 17, 1994). ... Re-signed by Browns (March 4, 1994). ... Granted unconditional free agency (February 16, 1996). ... Signed by Jacksonville Jaguars (March 2, 1996). ... Released by Jaguars (June 3, 2002). ... Signed by Tampa Bay Buccaneers (June 8, 2002).

CHAMPIONSHIP GAME EXPERIENCE: Played in AFC championship game (1996 and 1999 seasons). ... Played in NFC championship game (2002 season). ... Member of Super Bowl championship team (2002 season).

HONORS: Played in Pro Bowl (1996 and 2003 seasons).

SINGLE GAME HIGHS (regular season): Receptions—16 (October 20, 1996, vs. St. Louis); yards—232 (October 20, 1996, vs. St. Louis); and touchdown receptions—2 (October 6, 2003, vs. Indianapolis).

STATISTICAL PLATEAUS: 100-yard receiving games: 1995 (1), 1996 (3), 1997 (4), 1998 (2), 1999 (3), 2000 (5), 2001 (2), 2002 (2), 2003 (4). Total: 26.

			RECEIVING				TOTALS			
Year Team	G	GS	No.	Yds.	Avg.	TD	TD	2pt.	Pts.	Fum.
1991—Washington NFL					Did not play.					
1992—Cleveland NFL	2	0	1	8	8.0	0	0	0	0	0
1993—Cleveland NFL	6	3	13	234	18.0	4	4	0	24	0
1994—Cleveland NFL	13	3	10	182	18.2	0	0	0	0	0
1995—Cleveland NFL	16	5	56	709	12.7	4	4	0	24	0
1996—Jacksonville NFL	16	15	85	1129	13.3	3	3	2	22	1
1997—Jacksonville NFL	16	16	85	1164	13.7	5	5	0	30	0
1998—Jacksonville NFL	15	15	64	892	13.9	6	6	1	38	0
1999—Jacksonville NFL	16	15	78	891	11.4	5	5	1	32	1
2000—Jacksonville NFL	16	16	94	1207	12.8	5	5	0	30	3
2001—Jacksonville NFL	16	16	93	1110	11.9	6	6	1	38	1
2002—Tampa Bay NFL	14	14	61	670	11.0	6	6	0	36	1
2003—Tampa Bay NFL	16	16	84	1174	14.0	8	9	0	54	1
Pro totals (12 years)	162	134	724	9370	12.9	52	53	5	328	8

MCCAREINS, JUSTIN — WR — JETS

PERSONAL: Born December 11, 1978, in Evanston, Ill. ... 6-2/215.

HIGH SCHOOL: Naperville (Ill.) North.

COLLEGE: Northern Illinois.

TRANSACTIONS/CAREER NOTES: Selected by Tennessee Titans in fourth round (124th pick overall) of 2001 NFL draft. ... Signed by Titans (July 9, 2001). ... Traded by Titans to New York Jets for second-round pick (DE Travis LaBoy) in 2004 draft (March 5, 2004).

CHAMPIONSHIP GAME EXPERIENCE: Played in AFC championship game (2002 season).

SINGLE GAME HIGHS (regular season): Receptions—5 (December 1, 2003, vs. New York Jets); yards—92 (December 1, 2003, vs. New York Jets); and touchdown receptions—1 (December 14, 2003, vs. Buffalo).

			RECEIVING				PUNT RETURNS				KICKOFF RETURNS				TOTALS			
Year Team	G	GS	No.	Yds.	Avg.	TD	No.	Yds.	Avg.	TD	No.	Yds.	Avg.	TD	TD	2pt.	Pts.	Fum.
2001—Tennessee NFL	4	1	3	88	29.3	0	2	29	14.5	0	4	70	17.5	0	0	0	0	0
2002—Tennessee NFL	16	1	19	301	15.8	2	6	44	7.3	0	13	300	23.1	0	2	0	12	0
2003—Tennessee NFL	16	10	47	813	§17.3	7	29	330	11.4	1	13	256	19.7	0	8	0	48	2
Pro totals (3 years)	36	12	69	1202	17.4	9	37	403	10.9	1	30	626	20.9	0	10	0	60	2

MCCLAIN, JIMMY — LB — JAGUARS

PERSONAL: Born July 23, 1980, in Enterprise, Ala. ... 6-0/231.

HIGH SCHOOL: Enterprise (Ala.).

COLLEGE: Troy State.

TRANSACTIONS/CAREER NOTES: Signed as non-drafted free agent by Houston Texans (April 25, 2002). ... Waived by Texans (September 2, 2003). ... Re-signed by Texans (September 10, 2003). ... Released by Texans (November 17, 2003). ... Signed by Jacksonville Jaguars (January 27, 2004). ... Assigned by Jaguars to Scottish Claymores in 2004 NFL Europe enhancement allocation program (February 9, 2004).

			TOTALS			INTERCEPTIONS			
Year Team	G	GS	Tk.	Ast.	Sks.	No.	Yds.	Avg.	TD
2002—Houston NFL	15	0	1	1	0.0	0	0	0.0	0
2003—Houston NFL	9	0	0	0	0.0	0	0	0.0	0
Pro totals (2 years)	24	0	1	1	0.0	0	0	0.0	0

MCCLEON, DEXTER — CB — CHIEFS

PERSONAL: Born October 9, 1973, in Meridian, Miss. ... 5-10/195. ... Full name: Dexter Keith McCleon.

HIGH SCHOOL: Meridian (Miss.).

COLLEGE: Clemson.

TRANSACTIONS/CAREER NOTES: Selected by St. Louis Rams in second round (40th pick overall) of 1997 NFL draft. ... Signed by Rams (July 3, 1997). ... Granted free agency (February 11, 2000). ... Re-signed by Rams (June 13, 2000). ... Released by Rams (February 27, 2003). ... Signed by Kansas City Chiefs (March 5, 2003).
CHAMPIONSHIP GAME EXPERIENCE: Played in NFC championship game (1999 and 2001 seasons). ... Member of Super Bowl championship team (1999 season). ... Played in Super Bowl 36 (2001 season).
MISCELLANEOUS: Selected by Minnesota Twins organization in 13th round of free-agent baseball draft (June 3, 1992); did not sign.

			TOTALS			INTERCEPTIONS			
Year Team	**G**	**GS**	**Tk.**	**Ast.**	**Sks.**	**No.**	**Yds.**	**Avg.**	**TD**
1997—St. Louis NFL	16	1	13	0	1.0	1	0	0.0	0
1998—St. Louis NFL	15	6	28	1	0.0	2	29	14.5	0
1999—St. Louis NFL	15	15	41	4	1.5	4	17	4.3	0
2000—St. Louis NFL	16	16	49	5	2.0	8	28	3.5	0
2001—St. Louis NFL	16	16	59	6	0.0	4	66	16.5	0
2002—St. Louis NFL	13	4	17	4	0.0	1	0	0.0	0
2003—Kansas City NFL	16	16	55	5	0.0	6	-3	-0.5	0
Pro totals (7 years)	107	74	262	25	4.5	26	137	5.3	0

MCCLURE, TODD — C — FALCONS

PERSONAL: Born February 16, 1977, in Baton Rouge, La. ... 6-1/286.
HIGH SCHOOL: Central (Baton Rouge, La.).
COLLEGE: Louisiana State.
TRANSACTIONS/CAREER NOTES: Selected by Atlanta Falcons in seventh round (237th pick overall) of 1999 NFL draft. ... Signed by Falcons (June 25, 1999). ... On injured reserve with knee injury (August 30, 1999-entire season). ... Granted free agency (March 1, 2002). ... Re-signed by Falcons (May 28, 2002). ... Granted unconditional free agency (February 28, 2003). ... Re-signed by Falcons (April 16, 2003).
PLAYING EXPERIENCE: Atlanta NFL, 1999-2003. ... Games/Games started: 2000 (9/7), 2001 (15/15), 2002 (16/16), 2003 (16/16), Total: 56/54.

MCCOLLUM, ANDY — G — RAMS

PERSONAL: Born June 2, 1970, in Akron, Ohio. ... 6-4/300. ... Full name: Andrew Jon McCollum. ... Name pronounced: Mc-COL-umn.
HIGH SCHOOL: Revere (Richfield, Ohio).
COLLEGE: Toledo.
TRANSACTIONS/CAREER NOTES: Played with Milwaukee Mustangs of Arena League (1994). ... Signed as non-drafted free agent by Cleveland Browns (June 1994). ... Released by Browns (August 28, 1994). ... Re-signed by Browns to practice squad (August 30, 1994). ... Signed by New Orleans Saints off Browns practice squad (November 15, 1994). ... Inactive for five games (1994). ... Assigned by Saints to Barcelona Dragons in 1995 World League enhancement allocation program (February 20, 1995). ... Granted unconditional free agency (February 12, 1999). ... Signed by St. Louis Rams (April 13, 1999). ... Granted unconditional free agency (February 11, 2000). ... Re-signed by Rams (February 22, 2000). ... Granted unconditional free agency (February 28, 2003). ... Re-signed by Rams (April 4, 2003).
PLAYING EXPERIENCE: New Orleans NFL, 1995-1998; St. Louis NFL, 1999-2003. ... Games/Games started: 1995 (11/9), 1996 (16/16), 1997 (16/16), 1998 (16/5), 1999 (16/2), 2000 (16/16), 2001 (16/16), 2002 (16/16), 2003 (16/16). Total: 139/112.
CHAMPIONSHIP GAME EXPERIENCE: Played in NFC championship game (1999 and 2001 seasons). ... Member of Super Bowl championship team (1999 season). ... Played in Super Bowl 36 (2001 season).

M

MCCORD, QUENTIN — WR

PERSONAL: Born June 26, 1978, in LaGrange, Ga. ... 5-10/188.
HIGH SCHOOL: La Grange (Ga.).
COLLEGE: Kentucky.
TRANSACTIONS/CAREER NOTES: Selected by Atlanta Falcons in seventh round (236th pick overall) of 2001 NFL draft. ... Signed by Falcons (June 20, 2001). ... Released by Falcons (September 1, 2002). ... Re-signed by Falcons to practice squad (September 3, 2002). ... Activated (October 28, 2002). ... Waived by Falcons (November 17, 2003).
SINGLE GAME HIGHS (regular season): Receptions—7 (December 22, 2002, vs. Detroit); yards—182 (December 22, 2002, vs. Detroit); and touchdown receptions—1 (December 22, 2002, vs. Detroit).
STATISTICAL PLATEAUS: 100-yard receiving games: 2002 (1). Total: 1.

			RUSHING				RECEIVING				TOTALS			
Year Team	**G**	**GS**	**Att.**	**Yds.**	**Avg.**	**TD**	**No.**	**Yds.**	**Avg.**	**TD**	**TD**	**2pt.**	**Pts.**	**Fum.**
2001—Atlanta NFL	7	0	2	11	5.5	0	3	53	17.7	0	0	0	0	0
2002—Atlanta NFL	9	0	0	0	0.0	0	11	253	23.0	1	1	0	6	0
2003—Atlanta NFL	9	2	2	2	1.0	0	9	121	13.4	0	0	0	0	0
Pro totals (3 years)	25	2	4	13	3.3	0	23	427	18.6	1	1	0	6	0

MCCOWN, JOSH — QB — CARDINALS

PERSONAL: Born July 4, 1979, in Jacksonville, Texas. ... 6-4/212. ... Full name: Joshua McCown. ... Brother of Luke McCown, quarterback, Cleveland Browns.
HIGH SCHOOL: Jacksonville (Texas).
COLLEGE: Sam Houston State.
TRANSACTIONS/CAREER NOTES: Selected by Arizona Cardinals in third round (81st pick overall) of 2002 NFL draft. ... Signed by Cardinals (July 25, 2002).
SINGLE GAME HIGHS (regular season): Attempts—40 (December 3, 2003, vs. Seattle); completions—25 (December 3, 2003, vs. Seattle); yards—274 (December 3, 2003, vs. Seattle); and touchdown passes—2 (December 28, 2003, vs. Minnesota).
MISCELLANEOUS: Regular-season record as starting NFL quarterback: 1-2 (.333).

Year Team	G	GS	PASSING Att.	Cmp.	Pct.	Yds.	TD	Int.	Avg.	Skd.	Rat.	RUSHING Att.	Yds.	Avg.	TD	TOTALS TD	2pt.	Pts.
2002—Arizona NFL	2	0	18	7	38.9	66	0	2	3.67	5	10.2	1	20	20.0	0	0	0	0
2003—Arizona NFL	10	3	166	95	57.2	1018	5	6	6.13	25	70.3	28	158	5.6	1	1	0	6
Pro totals (2 years)	12	3	184	102	55.4	1084	5	8	5.89	30	63.8	29	178	6.1	1	1	0	6

MCCRARY, FRED — FB — PATRIOTS

PERSONAL: Born September 19, 1972, in Naples, Fla. ... 6-0/247. ... Full name: Freddy Demetrius McCrary.
HIGH SCHOOL: Naples (Fla.).
COLLEGE: Mississippi State.
TRANSACTIONS/CAREER NOTES: Selected by Philadelphia Eagles in sixth round (208th pick overall) of 1995 NFL draft. ... Signed by Eagles (June 27, 1995). ... Released by Eagles (August 25, 1996). ... Signed by New Orleans Saints (March 5, 1997). ... Released by Saints (August 24, 1998). ... Signed by San Diego Chargers (March 26, 1999). ... Granted free agency (February 11, 2000). ... Re-signed by Chargers (May 22, 2000). ... Released by Chargers (February 25, 2003). ... Signed by New England Patriots (March 24, 2003). ... Released by Patriots (October 4, 2003). ... Re-signed by Patriots (October 7, 2003). ... On injured reserve with leg injury (November 20, 2003-remainder of season).
SINGLE GAME HIGHS (regular season): Attempts—5 (September 24, 2000, vs. Seattle); yards—13 (November 23, 1997, vs. Atlanta); and rushing touchdowns—1 (September 10, 1995, vs. Arizona).

Year Team	G	GS	RUSHING Att.	Yds.	Avg.	TD	RECEIVING No.	Yds.	Avg.	TD	TOTALS TD	2pt.	Pts.	Fum.
1995—Philadelphia NFL	13	4	3	1	0.3	1	9	60	6.7	0	1	0	6	0
1996—					Did not play.									
1997—New Orleans NFL	7	0	8	15	1.9	0	4	17	4.3	0	0	0	0	0
1998—					Did not play.									
1999—San Diego NFL	16	14	0	0	0.0	0	37	201	5.4	1	1	0	6	0
2000—San Diego NFL	15	12	7	8	1.1	0	18	141	7.8	2	2	0	12	1
2001—San Diego NFL	16	12	2	3	1.5	0	13	71	5.5	0	0	0	0	0
2002—San Diego NFL	16	16	2	1	0.5	0	22	96	4.4	3	3	0	18	1
2003—New England NFL	6	3	3	3	1.0	0	2	12	6.0	0	0	0	0	0
Pro totals (7 years)	89	61	25	31	1.2	1	105	598	5.7	6	7	0	42	2

MCCREE, MARLON — S — TEXANS

PERSONAL: Born March 17, 1977, in Orlando, Fla. ... 5-11/196. ... Full name: Marlon Tarron McCree.
HIGH SCHOOL: Atlantic (Daytona, Fla.).
COLLEGE: Kentucky.
TRANSACTIONS/CAREER NOTES: Selected by Jacksonville Jaguars in seventh round (233rd pick overall) of 2001 NFL draft. ... Signed by Jaguars (May 30, 2001). ... Waived by Jaguars (September 16, 2003). ... Claimed on waivers by Houston Texans (September 17, 2003). ... Granted free agency (March 3, 2004). ... Re-signed by Texans (April 30, 2004).

Year Team	G	GS	TOTALS Tk.	Ast.	Sks.	INTERCEPTIONS No.	Yds.	Avg.	TD
2001—Jacksonville NFL	13	11	33	13	1.0	1	10	10.0	0
2002—Jacksonville NFL	16	16	56	15	1.0	6	129	21.5	0
2003—Jacksonville NFL	2	0	1	1	0.0	0	0	0.0	0
—Houston NFL	13	11	34	16	0.0	1	95	95.0	1
Pro totals (3 years)	44	38	124	45	2.0	8	234	29.3	1

MCCULLOUGH, SULTAN — RB — REDSKINS

PERSONAL: Born February 12, 1980, in Pasadena, Calif. ... 6-0/197.
HIGH SCHOOL: Muir (Pasadena, Calif.).
COLLEGE: Southern California.
TRANSACTIONS/CAREER NOTES: Signed as non-drafted free agent by Washington Redskins (May 2, 2003).
SINGLE GAME HIGHS (regular season): Attempts—1 (November 2, 2003, vs. Dallas); yards—9 (November 2, 2003, vs. Dallas); and rushing touchdowns—0.

Year Team	G	GS	RUSHING Att.	Yds.	Avg.	TD	RECEIVING No.	Yds.	Avg.	TD	TOTALS TD	2pt.	Pts.	Fum.
2003—Washington NFL	1	0	1	9	9.0	0	3	13	4.3	0	0	0	0	0

MCCUTCHEON, DAYLON — CB — BROWNS

PERSONAL: Born December 9, 1976, in Los Angeles, Calif. ... 5-10/190. ... Name pronounced: mc-CUTCH-in. ... Son of Lawrence McCutcheon, Director of Scouting, St. Louis Rams, and former running back with four NFL teams (1972-81).
HIGH SCHOOL: Bishop Amat (La Puente, Calif.).
COLLEGE: Southern California.
TRANSACTIONS/CAREER NOTES: Selected by Cleveland Browns in third round (62nd pick overall) of 1999 NFL draft. ... Signed by Browns (July 22, 1999). ... Granted free agency (March 1, 2002). ... Re-signed by Browns (June 11, 2002).
HONORS: Named cornerback on THE SPORTING NEWS college All-America second team (1998).

Year Team	G	GS	TOTALS Tk.	Ast.	Sks.	INTERCEPTIONS No.	Yds.	Avg.	TD
1999—Cleveland NFL	16	15	74	5	1.0	1	12	12.0	0
2000—Cleveland NFL	15	15	56	3	4.0	1	20	20.0	0
2001—Cleveland NFL	16	15	67	6	2.0	4	62	15.5	1

Year	Team	G	GS	TOTALS Tk.	Ast.	Sks.	INTERCEPTIONS No.	Yds.	Avg.	TD
2002—Cleveland NFL		13	11	40	2	0.0	1	24	24.0	0
2003—Cleveland NFL		15	14	43	5	0.0	1	75	75.0	1
Pro totals (5 years)		75	70	280	21	7.0	8	193	24.1	2

MCDANIEL, EMMANUEL CB

PERSONAL: Born July 27, 1972, in Griffin, Ga. ... 5-9/180.

HIGH SCHOOL: Jonesboro (Ga.).

COLLEGE: East Carolina.

TRANSACTIONS/CAREER NOTES: Selected by Carolina Panthers in fourth round (111th pick overall) of 1996 NFL draft. ... Signed by Panthers (July 20, 1996). ... Released by Panthers (August 26, 1997). ... Signed by Indianapolis Colts (November 27, 1997). ... Released by Colts (August 24, 1998). ... Re-signed by Colts (September 3, 1998). ... Inactive for one game with Colts (1998). ... Released by Colts (September 9, 1998). ... Signed by Miami Dolphins (October 8, 1998). ... Inactive for one game with Dolphins (1998). ... Released by Dolphins (October 14, 1998). ... Re-signed by Dolphins to practice squad (October 15, 1998). ... Activated (January 7, 1999). ... Claimed on waivers by New York Giants (September 1, 1999). ... Released by Giants (September 5, 1999). ... Re-signed by Giants to practice squad (September 6, 1999). ... Activated (November 15, 1999). ... Granted free agency (March 2, 2001). ... Re-signed by Giants (April 19, 2001). ... Granted unconditional free agency (March 1, 2002). ... Signed by Cleveland Browns (June 14, 2002). ... Released by Browns (August 27, 2002). ... Signed by Panthers (August 28, 2002). ... Released by Panthers (August 25, 2003). ... Signed by Arizona Cardinals (August 30, 2003). ... Granted unconditional free agency (March 3, 2004).

CHAMPIONSHIP GAME EXPERIENCE: Member of Panthers for NFC championship game (1996 season); inactive. ... Played in NFC championship game (2000 season). ... Played in Super Bowl 35 (2000 season).

Year	Team	G	GS	TOTALS Tk.	Ast.	Sks.	INTERCEPTIONS No.	Yds.	Avg.	TD
1996—Carolina NFL		2	0	0	1	0.0	0	0	0.0	0
1997—Indianapolis NFL		3	0	0	0	0.0	0	0	0.0	0
1999—New York Giants NFL		7	2	18	1	0.0	0	0	0.0	0
2000—New York Giants NFL		16	3	37	3	1.0	6	30	5.0	0
2001—New York Giants NFL		16	0	10	2	0.0	0	0	0.0	0
2002—Carolina NFL		16	5	23	5	0.0	2	13	6.5	0
2003—Arizona NFL		15	0	22	1	0.0	0	0	0.0	0
Pro totals (7 years)		75	10	110	13	1.0	8	43	5.4	0

MCDERMOTT, SEAN TE/LS PATRIOTS

PERSONAL: Born December 5, 1976, in Lufkin, Texas. ... 6-4/250.

HIGH SCHOOL: Fort Worth Arlington Heights (Texas).

COLLEGE: Kansas.

TRANSACTIONS/CAREER NOTES: Signed as non-drafted free agent by Tampa Bay Buccaneers (June 4, 2001). ... Selected by Houston Texans from Buccaneers in NFL expansion draft (February 18, 2002). ... Re-signed by Texans (March 24, 2003). ... Released by Texans (June 18, 2003). ... Signed by Miami Dolphins (August 10, 2003). ... Waived by Dolphins (October 14, 2003). ... Signed by New England Patriots (December 10, 2003). ... On injured reserve with shoulder injury (December 17, 2003-remainder of season).

PLAYING EXPERIENCE: Tampa Bay NFL, 2001; Houston NFL, 2002; Miami NFL, 2003; New England NFL, 2003. ... Games/Games started: 2001 (16/0), 2002 (16/0), 2003 (6/0). Total: 38/0.

M

MCDONALD, SHAUN WR RAMS

PERSONAL: Born June 13, 1981, in Phoenix, Ariz. ... 5-10/183. ... Full name: Shaun Terrance McDonald.

HIGH SCHOOL: Shadow Mountain (Phoenix).

COLLEGE: Arizona State.

TRANSACTIONS/CAREER NOTES: Selected after junior season by St. Louis Rams in fourth round (106th pick overall) of 2003 NFL draft. ... Signed by Rams (July 18, 2003).

SINGLE GAME HIGHS (regular season): Receptions—6 (September 7, 2003, vs. New York Giants); yards—September 7, 2003, vs. New York Giants); and touchdown receptions—0.

Year	Team	G	GS	RUSHING Att.	Yds.	Avg.	TD	RECEIVING No.	Yds.	Avg.	TD	TOTALS TD	2pt.	Pts.	Fum.
2003—St. Louis NFL		8	1	2	7	3.5	0	10	62	6.2	0	0	0	0	1

MCDOUGLE, JEROME DE EAGLES

PERSONAL: Born December 15, 1978, in Pompano Beach, Fla. ... 6-2/264. ... Full name: Jerome McDougle Jr. ... Brother of Stockar McDougle, offensive tackle, Detroit Lions.

HIGH SCHOOL: Ely (Pompano Beach, Fla.).

JUNIOR COLLEGE: Hinds Community College (Miss.).

COLLEGE: Miami (Fla.).

TRANSACTIONS/CAREER NOTES: Selected by Philadelphia Eagles in first round (15th pick overall) of 2003 NFL draft. ... Signed by Eagles (July 31, 2003).

CHAMPIONSHIP GAME EXPERIENCE: Played in NFC championship game (2003 sesaon).

Year	Team	G	GS	TOTALS Tk.	Ast.	Sks.	INTERCEPTIONS No.	Yds.	Avg.	TD
2003—Philadelphia NFL		8	0	6	4	0.0	0	0	0.0	0

MCDOUGLE, STOCKAR — T — LIONS

PERSONAL: Born January 11, 1977, in Fort Lauderdale, Fla. ... 6-6/335. ... Brother of Jerome McDougle, defensive end, Philadelphia Eagles.
HIGH SCHOOL: Deerfield Beach (Fla.).
JUNIOR COLLEGE: Navarro College (Texas).
COLLEGE: Oklahoma.
TRANSACTIONS/CAREER NOTES: Selected by Detroit Lions in first round (20th pick overall) of 2000 NFL draft. ... Signed by Lions (July 15, 2000).
PLAYING EXPERIENCE: Detroit NFL, 2000-2003. ... Games/Games started: 2000 (8/8), 2001 (9/3), 2002 (12/11), 2003 (16/16). Total: 45/38.

MCFARLAND, ANTHONY — DT — BUCCANEERS

PERSONAL: Born December 18, 1977, in Winnsboro, La. ... 6-0/300. ... Full name: Anthony Darelle McFarland.
HIGH SCHOOL: Winnsboro (La.).
COLLEGE: Louisiana State.
TRANSACTIONS/CAREER NOTES: Selected by Tampa Bay Buccaneers in first round (15th pick overall) of 1999 NFL draft. ... Signed by Buccaneers (August 3, 1999). ... On injured reserve with foot injury (December 17, 2002-remainder of season).
CHAMPIONSHIP GAME EXPERIENCE: Played in NFC championship game (1999 season).
HONORS: Named defensive tackle on THE SPORTING NEWS college All-America second team (1998).

			TOTALS			INTERCEPTIONS			
Year Team	G	GS	Tk.	Ast.	Sks.	No.	Yds.	Avg.	TD
1999—Tampa Bay NFL	14	0	9	5	1.0	0	0	0.0	0
2000—Tampa Bay NFL	16	16	31	19	6.5	0	0	0.0	0
2001—Tampa Bay NFL	14	14	24	17	3.5	0	0	0.0	0
2002—Tampa Bay NFL	10	10	12	8	1.5	0	0	0.0	0
2003—Tampa Bay NFL	16	16	38	12	2.5	1	0	0.0	0
Pro totals (5 years)	70	56	114	61	15.0	1	0	0.0	0

MCGARRAHAN, SCOTT — S

PERSONAL: Born February 12, 1974, in Arlington, Texas. ... 6-1/200. ... Full name: John Scott McGarrahan. ... Name pronounced: ma-GAIR-a-han.
HIGH SCHOOL: Lamar (Arlington, Texas).
COLLEGE: New Mexico.
TRANSACTIONS/CAREER NOTES: Selected by Green Bay Packers in sixth round (156th pick overall) of 1998 NFL draft. ... Signed by Packers (July 17, 1998). ... On injured reserve with hamstring injury (December 29, 1999-remainder of season). ... Granted free agency (March 2, 2001). ... Re-signed by Packers (May 8, 2001). ... Released by Packers (September 1, 2001). ... Signed by Miami Dolphins (September 5, 2001). ... Granted unconditional free agency (March 1, 2002). ... Re-signed by Dolphins (March 21, 2002). ... Traded by Dolphins to Packers for 2006 conditional seventh-round pick (August 25, 2003). ... Released by Packers (August 31, 2003). ... Signed by Tennessee Titans (September 2, 2003). ... Granted unconditional free agency (March 3, 2004).

			TOTALS			INTERCEPTIONS			
Year Team	G	GS	Tk.	Ast.	Sks.	No.	Yds.	Avg.	TD
1998—Green Bay NFL	15	0	8	3	0.0	0	0	0.0	0
1999—Green Bay NFL	13	0	2	0	0.0	0	0	0.0	0
2000—Green Bay NFL	16	0	8	1	0.5	0	0	0.0	0
2001—Miami NFL	16	0	0	0	0.0	0	0	0.0	0
2002—Miami NFL	14	0	1	1	1.0	0	0	0.0	0
2003—Tennessee NFL	16	2	20	7	1.0	0	0	0.0	0
Pro totals (6 years)	90	2	39	12	2.5	0	0	0.0	0

MCGEE, TERRENCE — CB — BILLS

PERSONAL: Born October 14, 1980, in Athens, Texas. ... 5-9/195.
HIGH SCHOOL: Athens (Texas).
COLLEGE: Northwestern State.
TRANSACTIONS/CAREER NOTES: Selected by Buffalo Bills in fourth round (111th pick overall) of 2003 NFL draft. ... Signed by Bills (July 23, 2003).

			INTERCEPTIONS				PUNT RETURNS				KICKOFF RETURNS				TOTALS			
Year Team	G	GS	No.	Yds.	Avg.	TD	No.	Yds.	Avg.	TD	No.	Yds.	Avg.	TD	TD	2pt.	Pts.	Fum.
2003—Buffalo NFL	14	2	2	5	2.5	0	0	0	0.0	0	8	160	20.0	0	0	0	0	0

MCGEE, TONY — TE

PERSONAL: Born April 21, 1971, in Terre Haute, Ind. ... 6-4/241.
HIGH SCHOOL: Terre Haute (Ind.) South.
COLLEGE: Michigan.
TRANSACTIONS/CAREER NOTES: Selected by Cincinnati Bengals in second round (37th pick overall) of 1993 NFL draft. ... Signed by Bengals (July 20, 1993). ... Granted free agency (February 16, 1996). ... Re-signed by Bengals for 1996 season. ... On injured reserve with broken ankle (December 14, 2000-remainder of season). ... On injured reserve with ankle injury (December 3, 2001-remainder of season). ... Released by Bengals (April 25, 2002). ... Signed by Dallas Cowboys (April 28, 2002). ... Released by Cowboys (August 31, 2003). ... Signed by Tampa Bay Buccaneers (September 1, 2003). ... Released by Buccaneers (September 5, 2003). ... Re-signed by Cowboys (October 7, 2003). ... Released by Cowboys (October 18, 2003). ... Signed by New York Giants (December 2, 2003). ... Granted unconditional free agency (March 3, 2004).

SINGLE GAME HIGHS (regular season): Receptions—8 (December 22, 1996, vs. Indianapolis); yards—118 (September 3, 1995, vs. Indianapolis); and touchdown receptions—2 (November 9, 1997, vs. Indianapolis).
STATISTICAL PLATEAUS: 100-yard receiving games: 1993 (1), 1995 (2). Total: 3.

			RECEIVING				TOTALS			
Year Team	**G**	**GS**	**No.**	**Yds.**	**Avg.**	**TD**	**TD**	**2pt.**	**Pts.**	**Fum.**
1993—Cincinnati NFL	15	15	44	525	11.9	0	0	0	0	1
1994—Cincinnati NFL	16	16	40	492	12.3	1	1	0	6	0
1995—Cincinnati NFL	16	16	55	754	13.7	4	4	0	24	2
1996—Cincinnati NFL	16	16	38	446	11.7	4	4	0	24	0
1997—Cincinnati NFL	16	16	34	414	12.2	6	6	1	38	0
1998—Cincinnati NFL	16	16	22	363	16.5	1	1	0	6	0
1999—Cincinnati NFL	16	16	26	344	13.2	2	2	0	12	0
2000—Cincinnati NFL	14	14	26	309	11.9	1	1	0	6	0
2001—Cincinnati NFL	11	9	14	148	10.6	1	1	0	6	0
2002—Dallas NFL	16	16	23	294	12.8	1	1	0	6	0
2003—Dallas NFL	1	0	0	0	0.0	0	0	0	0	0
—New York Giants NFL	3	0	0	0	0.0	0	0	0	0	0
Pro totals (11 years)	156	150	322	4089	12.7	21	21	1	128	3

MCGINEST, WILLIE — DE — PATRIOTS

PERSONAL: Born December 11, 1971, in Long Beach, Calif. ... 6-5/270. ... Full name: William Lee McGinest Jr.
HIGH SCHOOL: Polytechnic (Pasadena, Calif.).
COLLEGE: Southern California.
TRANSACTIONS/CAREER NOTES: Selected by New England Patriots in first round (fourth pick overall) of 1994 NFL draft. ... Signed by Patriots (May 17, 1994). ... Granted unconditional free agency (February 13, 1998). ... Re-signed by Patriots (February 12, 1998).
CHAMPIONSHIP GAME EXPERIENCE: Played in AFC championship game (1996, 2001 and 2003 seasons). ... Played in Super Bowl 31 (1996 season). ... Member of Super Bowl championship team (2001 and 2003 seasons).
HONORS: Played in Pro Bowl (2003 season).

			TOTALS			INTERCEPTIONS			
Year Team	**G**	**GS**	**Tk.**	**Ast.**	**Sks.**	**No.**	**Yds.**	**Avg.**	**TD**
1994—New England NFL	16	7	29	14	4.5	0	0	0.0	0
1995—New England NFL	16	16	70	18	11.0	0	0	0.0	0
1996—New England NFL	16	16	49	18	9.5	1	46	46.0	1
1997—New England NFL	11	11	25	10	2.0	0	0	0.0	0
1998—New England NFL	9	8	21	8	3.5	0	0	0.0	0
1999—New England NFL	16	16	51	25	9.0	0	0	0.0	0
2000—New England NFL	14	14	45	18	6.0	0	0	0.0	0
2001—New England NFL	11	5	25	8	6.0	0	0	0.0	0
2002—New England NFL	16	10	42	21	5.5	1	2	2.0	0
2003—New England NFL	14	11	46	21	5.5	1	15	15.0	1
Pro totals (10 years)	139	114	403	161	62.5	3	63	21.0	2

M

MCGLOCKTON, CHESTER — DT

PERSONAL: Born September 16, 1969, in Whiteville, N.C. ... 6-3/334.
HIGH SCHOOL: Whiteville (N.C.).
COLLEGE: Clemson.
TRANSACTIONS/CAREER NOTES: Selected after junior season by Los Angeles Raiders in first round (16th pick overall) of 1992 NFL draft. ... Signed by Raiders for 1992 season. ... On injured reserve (January 11, 1994-remainder of 1993 playoffs). ... Raiders franchise moved to Oakland (July 21, 1995). ... Designated by Raiders as franchise player (February 12, 1998). ... Tendered offer sheet by Kansas City Chiefs (April 10, 1998). ... Raiders declined to match offer (April 17, 1998). ... Released by Chiefs (February 28, 2001). ... Signed by Denver Broncos (April 10, 2001). ... Waived by Broncos (February 25, 2003). ... Signed by New York Jets (July 15, 2003). ... Granted unconditional free agency (March 3, 2004).
HONORS: Named defensive tackle on THE SPORTING NEWS NFL All-Pro team (1994). ... Played in Pro Bowl (1994-1997 seasons).

			TOTALS			INTERCEPTIONS			
Year Team	**G**	**GS**	**Tk.**	**Ast.**	**Sks.**	**No.**	**Yds.**	**Avg.**	**TD**
1992—Los Angeles Raiders NFL	10	0	18	0	3.0	0	0	0.0	0
1993—Los Angeles Raiders NFL	16	16	63	15	7.0	1	19	19.0	0
1994—Los Angeles Raiders NFL	16	16	48	14	9.5	0	0	0.0	0
1995—Oakland NFL	16	16	47	8	7.5	0	0	0.0	0
1996—Oakland NFL	16	16	59	4	8.0	0	0	0.0	0
1997—Oakland NFL	16	16	54	10	4.5	0	0	0.0	0
1998—Kansas City NFL	10	9	23	4	1.0	0	0	0.0	0
1999—Kansas City NFL	16	16	30	12	1.5	1	30	30.0	0
2000—Kansas City NFL	15	15	34	6	4.5	0	0	0.0	0
2001—Denver NFL	16	16	34	5	1.0	2	17	8.5	0
2002—Denver NFL	16	15	32	5	2.5	0	0	0.0	0
2003—New York Jets NFL	16	0	24	7	1.0	0	0	0.0	0
Pro totals (12 years)	179	151	466	90	51.0	4	66	16.5	0

MCGRAW, JON — S — JETS

PERSONAL: Born April 2, 1979, in Manhattan, Kan. ... 6-3/206.
HIGH SCHOOL: Riley County (Manhattan, Kan.).
COLLEGE: Kansas State.

TRANSACTIONS/CAREER NOTES: Selected by New York Jets in second round (57th pick overall) of 2002 NFL draft. ... Signed by Jets (July 26, 2002). ... On injured reserve with shoulder injury (November 17, 2003-remainder of season).

			TOTALS			INTERCEPTIONS			
Year Team	G	GS	Tk.	Ast.	Sks.	No.	Yds.	Avg.	TD
2002—New York Jets NFL	15	1	20	8	0.0	1	0	0.0	0
2003—New York Jets NFL	6	6	19	11	0.0	0	0	0.0	0
Pro totals (2 years)	21	7	39	19	0.0	1	0	0.0	0

MCINTOSH, DAMION T DOLPHINS

PERSONAL: Born March 25, 1977, in Kingston, Jamaica. ... 6-4/325. ... Full name: Damion Alexis McIntosh.
HIGH SCHOOL: McArthur (Hollywood, Fla.).
COLLEGE: Kansas State.
TRANSACTIONS/CAREER NOTES: Selected by San Diego Chargers in third round (83rd pick overall) of 2000 NFL draft. ... Signed by Chargers (July 20, 2000). ... Granted free agency (February 28, 2003). ... Re-signed by Chargers (April 16, 2003). ... Granted unconditional free agency (March 3, 2004). ... Signed by Miami Dolphins (March 16, 2004).
PLAYING EXPERIENCE: San Diego NFL, 2000-2003. ... Games/Games started: 2000 (3/0), 2001 (15/14), 2002 (10/10), 2003 (13/13). Total: 41/37.

MCKENZIE, KAREEM T JETS

PERSONAL: Born May 24, 1979, in Willingboro, N.J. ... 6-6/327. ... Full name: Kareem Michael McKenzie.
HIGH SCHOOL: Willingboro (N.J.).
COLLEGE: Penn State.
TRANSACTIONS/CAREER NOTES: Selected by New York Jets in third round (79th pick overall) of 2001 NFL draft. ... Signed by Jets (July 25, 2001). ... Granted free agency (March 3, 2004). ... Re-signed by Jets (May 10, 2004).
PLAYING EXPERIENCE: New York Jets NFL, 2001-2003. ... Games/Games started: 2001 (8/0), 2002 (16/16), 2003 (16/16). Total: 40/32.

MCKENZIE, KEITH DE BILLS

PERSONAL: Born October 17, 1973, in Detroit, Mich. ... 6-3/267. ... Full name: Keith Derrick McKenzie.
HIGH SCHOOL: Highland Park (Mich.).
COLLEGE: Ball State.
TRANSACTIONS/CAREER NOTES: Selected by Green Bay Packers in seventh round (252nd pick overall) of 1996 NFL draft. ... Signed by Packers (July 15, 1996). ... Granted free agency (February 12, 1999). ... Re-signed by Packers (June 1, 1999). ... Granted unconditional free agency (February 11, 2000). ... Signed by Cleveland Browns (February 24, 2000). ... On injured reserve with ankle injury (November 9, 2001-remainder of season). ... Granted unconditional free agency (March 1, 2002). ... Signed by Chicago Bears (May 30, 2002). ... Released by Bears (October 16, 2002). ... Signed by Packers (Novemebr 20, 2002). ... Released by Packers (January 1, 2003). ... Signed by Buffalo Bills (February 25, 2003). ... Granted unconditional free agency (March 3, 2004). ... Re-signed by Bills (March 24, 2004).
CHAMPIONSHIP GAME EXPERIENCE: Member of Super Bowl championship team (1996 season). ... Played in NFC championship game (1996 and 1997 seasons). ... Played in Super Bowl 32 (1997 season).

M

			TOTALS			INTERCEPTIONS			
Year Team	G	GS	Tk.	Ast.	Sks.	No.	Yds.	Avg.	TD
1996—Green Bay NFL	10	0	3	3	1.0	0	0	0.0	0
1997—Green Bay NFL	16	0	2	1	1.5	0	0	0.0	0
1998—Green Bay NFL	16	0	19	9	8.0	1	33	33.0	1
1999—Green Bay NFL	16	2	21	11	8.0	0	0	0.0	0
2000—Cleveland NFL	16	16	50	8	8.0	0	0	0.0	0
2001—Cleveland NFL	7	6	12	2	3.0	0	0	0.0	0
2002—Chicago NFL	4	3	4	0	0.0	0	0	0.0	0
—Green Bay NFL	4	0	3	2	0.0	0	0	0.0	0
2003—Buffalo NFL	6	0	3	3	0.0	0	0	0.0	0
Pro totals (8 years)	95	27	117	39	29.5	1	33	33.0	1

MCKENZIE, MIKE CB PACKERS

PERSONAL: Born April 26, 1976, in Miami, Fla. ... 6-0/194. ... Full name: Michael Terrance McKenzie.
HIGH SCHOOL: Norland (Miami).
COLLEGE: Memphis.
TRANSACTIONS/CAREER NOTES: Selected after junior season by Green Bay Packers in third round (87th pick overall) of 1999 NFL draft. ... Signed by Packers (July 8, 1999).

			TOTALS			INTERCEPTIONS			
Year Team	G	GS	Tk.	Ast.	Sks.	No.	Yds.	Avg.	TD
1999—Green Bay NFL	16	16	53	12	0.0	6	4	0.7	0
2000—Green Bay NFL	10	8	30	3	0.0	1	26	26.0	0
2001—Green Bay NFL	16	16	54	10	0.0	2	38	19.0	1
2002—Green Bay NFL	13	13	47	19	1.0	2	0	0.0	0
2003—Green Bay NFL	14	14	52	6	0.0	4	98	24.5	1
Pro totals (5 years)	69	67	236	50	1.0	15	166	11.1	2

MCKIE, JASON FB BEARS

PERSONAL: Born May 22, 1980, in Gulf Breeze, Fla. ... 5-11/231.
HIGH SCHOOL: Gulf Breeze (Fla.).
COLLEGE: Temple.

TRANSACTIONS/CAREER NOTES: Signed as non-drafted free agent by Philadelphia Eagles (April 23, 2002). ... Released by Eagles (September 1, 2002). ... Re-signed by Eagles to practice squad (September 3, 2002). ... Released by Eagles (September 17, 2002). ... Re-signed by Eagles to practice squad (September 25, 2002). ... Signed by Dallas Cowboys off Eagles practice squad (December 7, 2002). ... Released by Cowboys (August 17, 2003). ... Signed by Chicago Bears (August 19, 2003). ... Waived by Bears (August 31, 2003). ... Re-signed by Bears to practice squad (September 1, 2003). ... Activated (November 21, 2003).

			RUSHING				TOTALS			
Year Team	G	GS	Att.	Yds.	Avg.	TD	TD	2pt.	Pts.	Fum.
2002—Dallas NFL	1	1	0	0	0.0	0	0	0	0	0
2003—Chicago NFL	6	0	0	0	0.0	0	0	0	0	0
Pro totals (2 years)	7	1	0	0	0.0	0	0	0	0	0

MCKINLEY, ALVIN DT BROWNS

PERSONAL: Born June 9, 1978, in Kosciusko, Miss. ... 6-3/310. ... Full name: Alvin Jerome McKinley.
HIGH SCHOOL: Weir (Miss.).
JUNIOR COLLEGE: Holmes Junior College (Miss.).
COLLEGE: Mississippi State.
TRANSACTIONS/CAREER NOTES: Selected by Carolina Panthers in fourth round (120th pick overall) of 2000 NFL draft. ... Signed by Panthers (June 21, 2000). ... Claimed on waivers by Cleveland Browns (August 29, 2001). ... Released by Browns (September 1, 2001). ... Re-signed by Browns to practice squad (September 3, 2001). ... Activated (October 9, 2001). ... Granted free agency (February 28, 2003). ... Re-signed by Browns (March 7, 2003). ... On injured reserve with knee injury (November 12, 2003-remainder of season).

			TOTALS		
Year Team	G	GS	Tk.	Ast.	Sks.
2000—Carolina NFL	7	0	9	0	0.0
2001—Cleveland NFL	7	0	6	6	0.0
2002—Cleveland NFL	13	0	7	4	0.0
2003—Cleveland NFL	9	0	9	14	0.0
Pro totals (4 years)	36	0	31	24	0.0

MCKINNEY, SETH C DOLPHINS

PERSONAL: Born June 12, 1979, in Buffalo, Texas. ... 6-3/305.
HIGH SCHOOL: Westlake (Austin, Texas).
JUNIOR COLLEGE: Lackawanna Junior College (Pa.).
COLLEGE: Texas A&M.
TRANSACTIONS/CAREER NOTES: Selected by Miami Dolphins in third round (90th pick overall) of 2002 NFL draft. ... Signed by Dolphins (July 28, 2002).
PLAYING EXPERIENCE: Miami NFL, 2002-2003. ... Games/Games started: 2002 (16/2), 2003 (16/3). Total: 32/5.
HONORS: Named center on THE SPORTING NEWS college All-America second team (2001).

MCKINNEY, STEVE C TEXANS

PERSONAL: Born October 15, 1975, in Galveston, Texas. ... 6-4/295. ... Full name: Stephen Michael McKinney.
HIGH SCHOOL: Clear Lake (Houston).
COLLEGE: Texas A&M.
TRANSACTIONS/CAREER NOTES: Selected by Indianapolis Colts in fourth round (93rd pick overall) of 1998 NFL draft. ... Signed by Colts (July 23, 1998). ... Granted free agency (March 2, 2001). ... Re-signed by Colts (May 9, 2001). ... Granted unconditional free agency (March 1, 2002). ... Signed by Houston Texans (March 6, 2002).
PLAYING EXPERIENCE: Indianapolis NFL, 1998-2001; Houston NFL, 2002-2003. ... Games/Games started: 1998 (16/16), 1999 (15/14), 2000 (16/16), 2001 (14/14), 2002 (16/16), 2003 (16/16). Total: 93/92.

M

MCKINNIE, BRYANT T VIKINGS

PERSONAL: Born September 23, 1979, in Woodbury, N.J. ... 6-8/346. ... Full name: Bryant Douglas McKinnie.
HIGH SCHOOL: Woodbury (N.J.).
JUNIOR COLLEGE: Lackawanna Junior College (Pa.).
COLLEGE: Miami (Fla.).
TRANSACTIONS/CAREER NOTES: Selected by Minnesota Vikings in first round (seventh pick overall) of 2002 NFL draft. ... Signed by Vikings (November 2, 2002).
PLAYING EXPERIENCE: Minnesota NFL, 2002-2003. ... Games/Games started: 2002 (8/7), 2003 (16/16). Total: 24/23.
HONORS: Named offensive tackle on THE SPORTING NEWS college All-America first team (2001). ... Outland Trophy winner (2001).

MCKINNON, RONALD LB CARDINALS

PERSONAL: Born September 20, 1973, in Fort Rucker, Ala. ... 6-0/245.
HIGH SCHOOL: Elba (Ala.).
COLLEGE: North Alabama.
TRANSACTIONS/CAREER NOTES: Signed as non-drafted free agent by Arizona Cardinals (April 23, 1996). ... Granted free agency (February 12, 1999). ... Re-signed by Cardinals (June 14, 1999). ... Granted unconditional free agency (February 11, 2000). ... Re-signed by Cardinals (February 24, 2000).
HONORS: Harlon Hill Trophy winner (1995).

Year Team	G	GS	TOTALS Tk.	Ast.	Sks.	INTERCEPTIONS No.	Yds.	Avg.	TD
1996—Arizona NFL	16	0	6	1	0.0	0	0	0.0	0
1997—Arizona NFL	16	16	61	36	1.0	3	40	13.3	0
1998—Arizona NFL	13	13	66	29	2.0	5	25	5.0	0
1999—Arizona NFL	16	16	94	47	1.0	1	0	0.0	0
2000—Arizona NFL	16	16	119	38	4.0	0	0	0.0	0
2001—Arizona NFL	16	16	98	49	2.0	1	24	24.0	1
2002—Arizona NFL	16	16	67	41	0.0	0	0	0.0	0
2003—Arizona NFL	16	16	80	25	2.0	0	0	0.0	0
Pro totals (8 years)	125	109	591	266	12.0	10	89	8.9	1

MCKNIGHT, JAMES WR GIANTS

PERSONAL: Born June 17, 1972, in Orlando, Fla. ... 6-1/198.

HIGH SCHOOL: Apopka (Fla.).

COLLEGE: Liberty.

TRANSACTIONS/CAREER NOTES: Signed as non-drafted free agent by Seattle Seahawks (April 29, 1994). ... Released by Seahawks (August 28, 1994). ... Re-signed by Seahawks to practice squad (August 29, 1994). ... Activated (November 19, 1994). ... Granted unconditional free agency (February 13, 1998). ... Re-signed by Seahawks (February 17, 1998). ... Traded by Seahawks to Dallas Cowboys for third-round pick (WR Darrell Jackson) in 2000 draft (June 24, 1999). ... On injured reserve with knee injury (August 27, 1999-entire season). ... Granted unconditional free agency (March 2, 2001). ... Signed by Miami Dolphins (March 16, 2001). ... Released by Dolphins (March 2, 2004). ... Signed by New York Giants (May 20, 2004).

SINGLE GAME HIGHS (regular season): Receptions—9 (November 18, 2001, vs. New York Jets); yards—164 (November 12, 2000, vs. Cincinnati); and touchdown receptions—1 (November 23, 2003, vs. Washington).

STATISTICAL PLATEAUS: 100-yard receiving games: 1997 (1), 1998 (1), 2000 (3), 2002 (1). Total: 6.

Year Team	G	GS	RUSHING Att.	Yds.	Avg.	TD	RECEIVING No.	Yds.	Avg.	TD	TOTALS TD	2pt.	Pts.	Fum.
1994—Seattle NFL	2	0	0	0	0.0	0	1	25	25.0	1	1	0	6	0
1995—Seattle NFL	16	0	0	0	0.0	0	6	91	15.2	0	0	0	0	1
1996—Seattle NFL	16	0	0	0	0.0	0	1	73	73.0	0	0	0	0	0
1997—Seattle NFL	12	6	0	0	0.0	0	34	637	*18.7	6	6	0	36	1
1998—Seattle NFL	14	3	0	0	0.0	0	21	346	16.5	2	2	0	12	0
1999—Dallas NFL					Did not play.									
2000—Dallas NFL	16	15	0	0	0.0	0	52	926	17.8	2	2	0	12	1
2001—Miami NFL	16	15	6	39	6.5	0	55	684	12.4	3	3	1	20	3
2002—Miami NFL	15	9	7	58	8.3	0	29	528	18.2	2	2	0	12	2
2003—Miami NFL	15	1	2	75	37.5	1	23	285	12.4	2	3	0	18	1
Pro totals (9 years)	122	49	15	172	11.5	1	222	3595	16.2	18	19	1	116	9

MCLEOD, KEVIN FB

PERSONAL: Born October 17, 1974, in Montego Bay, Jamaica. ... 6-0/250. ... Full name: Kevin Aston McLeod.

HIGH SCHOOL: Clarkston (Ga.).

COLLEGE: Auburn.

TRANSACTIONS/CAREER NOTES: Selected by Jacksonville Jaguars in sixth round (182nd pick overall) of 1998 NFL draft. ... Signed by Jaguars (May 19, 1998). ... Released by Jaguars (August 26, 1998). ... Signed by Tampa Bay Buccaneers to practice squad (October 27, 1998). ... Released by Buccaneers (September 5, 1999). ... Re-signed by Buccaneers to practice squad (September 6, 1999). ... Activated (October 9, 1999). ... On non-football injury list (August 27, 2000-remainder of season). ... Released by Buccaneers (September 20, 2000). ... Signed by Atlanta Falcons (January 25, 2001). ... Assigned by Falcons to Frankfurt Galaxy in 2001 NFL Europe enhancement allocation program (February 7, 2001). ... Released by Falcons (September 2, 2001). ... Signed by Green Bay Packers (February 5, 2002). ... Released by Packers (July 24, 2002). ... Signed by Cleveland Browns (August 5, 2002). ... Released by Browns (September 1, 2002). ... Re-signed by Browns (August 4, 2003). ... Released by Browns (September 24, 2003).

CHAMPIONSHIP GAME EXPERIENCE: Played in NFC championship game (1999 season).

Year Team	G	GS	RUSHING Att.	Yds.	Avg.	TD	TOTALS TD	2pt.	Pts.	Fum.
1998—Tampa Bay NFL					Did not play.					
1999—Tampa Bay NFL	7	0	0	0	0.0	0	1	0	6	0
2003—Cleveland NFL	1	1	0	0	0.0	0	0	0	0	0
Pro totals (2 years)	8	1	0	0	0.0	0	1	0	6	0

MCMAHON, MIKE QB LIONS

PERSONAL: Born February 8, 1979, in Pittsburgh, Pa. ... 6-2/208. ... Full name: Michael Edward McMahon.

HIGH SCHOOL: North Allegheny (Pa.).

COLLEGE: Rutgers.

TRANSACTIONS/CAREER NOTES: Selected by Detroit Lions in fifth round (149th pick overall) of 2001 NFL draft. ... Signed by Lions (June 7, 2001). ... Granted free agency (March 3, 2004). ... Re-signed by Lions (March 31, 2004).

SINGLE GAME HIGHS (regular season): Attempts—44 (December 29, 2002, vs. Minnesota); completions—19 (December 29, 2002, vs. Minnesota); yards—293 (December 29, 2002, vs. Minnesota); and touchdown passes—3 (December 29, 2002, vs. Minnesota).

MISCELLANEOUS: Regular-season record as starting NFL quarterback: 1-6 (.143).

Year Team	G	GS	PASSING Att.	Cmp.	Pct.	Yds.	TD	Int.	Avg.	Skd.	Rat.	RUSHING Att.	Yds.	Avg.	TD	TOTALS TD	2pt.	Pts.
2001—Detroit NFL	8	3	115	53	46.1	671	3	1	5.83	21	69.9	27	145	5.4	1	1	1	8
2002—Detroit NFL	8	4	147	62	42.2	874	7	9	5.95	12	52.4	14	96	6.9	3	3	0	18
2003—Detroit NFL	3	0	31	9	29.0	87	0	2	2.81	2	12.7	5	32	6.4	0	0	0	0
Pro totals (3 years)	19	7	293	124	42.3	1632	10	12	5.57	35	54.9	46	273	5.9	4	4	1	26

MCMICHAEL, RANDY — TE — DOLPHINS

PERSONAL: Born June 28, 1979, in Griffin, Ga. ... 6-3/250.
HIGH SCHOOL: Peach County (Fort Valley, Ga.).
COLLEGE: Georgia.
TRANSACTIONS/CAREER NOTES: Selected by Miami Dolphins in fourth round (114th pick overall) of 2002 NFL draft. ... Signed by Dolphins (July 25, 2002).
SINGLE GAME HIGHS (regular season): Receptions—8 (October 19, 2003, vs. New England); yards—102 (October 19, 2003, vs. New England); and touchdown receptions—1 (October 27, 2003, vs. San Diego).
STATISTICAL PLATEAUS: 100-yard receiving games: 2003 (1). Total: 1.

			RECEIVING				TOTALS			
Year Team	G	GS	No.	Yds.	Avg.	TD	TD	2pt.	Pts.	Fum.
2002—Miami NFL	16	16	39	485	12.4	4	4	0	24	1
2003—Miami NFL	16	16	49	598	12.2	2	3	0	18	0
Pro totals (2 years)	32	32	88	1083	12.3	6	7	0	42	1

MCMILLON, TODD — CB — BEARS

PERSONAL: Born September 26, 1974, in Bellflower, Calif. ... 5-11/188.
HIGH SCHOOL: Cerritus (Bellflower, Calif.).
COLLEGE: Northern Arizona.
TRANSACTIONS/CAREER NOTES: Signed as non-drafted free agent by Chicago Bears (February 16, 2000). ... Released by Bears (August 22, 2000). ... Re-signed by Bears to practice squad (August 29, 2000). ... Activated (November 15, 2000). ... Assigned by Bears to Frankfurt Galaxy in 2001 NFL Europe enhancement allocation program (February 19, 2001). ... Released by Bears (September 3, 2001). ... Re-signed by Bears to practice squad (September 5, 2001). ... Activated (November 13, 2001). ... On injured reserve with thumb injury (November 19, 2002-remainder of season). ... Granted free agency (February 28, 2003). ... Re-signed by Bears (April 22, 2003).

			TOTALS			INTERCEPTIONS			
Year Team	G	GS	Tk.	Ast.	Sks.	No.	Yds.	Avg.	TD
2000—Chicago NFL	3	0	3	0	0.0	0	0	0.0	0
2001—Chicago NFL	8	0	1	0	0.0	0	0	0.0	0
2002—Chicago NFL	10	1	22	2	0.0	0	0	0.0	0
2003—Chicago NFL	13	0	3	0	0.0	0	0	0.0	0
Pro totals (4 years)	34	1	29	2	0.0	0	0	0.0	0

MCMULLEN, BILLY — WR — EAGLES

PERSONAL: Born March 8, 1980, in Richmond, Va. ... 6-4/210. ... Full name: Wilbur Anthony McMullen Jr.
HIGH SCHOOL: Henrico (Richmond, Va.).
COLLEGE: Virginia.
TRANSACTIONS/CAREER NOTES: Selected by Philadelphia Eagles in third round (95th pick overall) of 2003 NFL draft. ... Signed by Eagles (July 24, 2003).
CHAMPIONSHIP GAME EXPERIENCE: Member of Eagles for NFC championship game (2003 season); inactive.
SINGLE GAME HIGHS (regular season): Receptions—1 (October 5, 2003, vs. Washington); yards—2 (October 5, 2003, vs. Washington); and touchdown receptions—0.

			RUSHING				RECEIVING				TOTALS			
Year Team	G	GS	Att.	Yds.	Avg.	TD	No.	Yds.	Avg.	TD	TD	2pt.	Pts.	Fum.
2003—Philadelphia NFL	5	0	0	0	0.0	0	1	2	2.0	0	0	0	0	0

MCNABB, DONOVAN — QB — EAGLES

PERSONAL: Born November 25, 1976, in Chicago, Ill. ... 6-2/240. ... Full name: Donovan Jamal McNabb.
HIGH SCHOOL: Mount Carmel (Ill.).
COLLEGE: Syracuse.
TRANSACTIONS/CAREER NOTES: Selected by Philadelphia Eagles in first round (second pick overall) of 1999 NFL draft. ... Signed by Eagles (July 30, 1999).
CHAMPIONSHIP GAME EXPERIENCE: Played in NFC championship game (2001-2003 seasons).
HONORS: Played in Pro Bowl (2000-2002 seasons). ... Named to play in Pro Bowl (2003 season); replaced by Marc Bulger due to injury.
SINGLE GAME HIGHS (regular season): Attempts—55 (November 12, 2000, vs. Pittsburgh); completions—32 (September 9, 2001, vs. St. Louis); passing yards—390 (December 10, 2000, vs. Cleveland); and touchdown passes—4 (November 17, 2002, vs. Arizona).
STATISTICAL PLATEAUS: 100-yard rushing games: 2000 (1), 2002 (2). Total: 3. 300-yard passing games: 2000 (2), 2001 (1), 2003 (2). Total: 5.
MISCELLANEOUS: Regular-season record as starting NFL quarterback: 43-21 (.672). ... Postseason record as starting NFL quarterback: 5-4 (.556).

			PASSING									RUSHING				TOTALS		
Year Team	G	GS	Att.	Cmp.	Pct.	Yds.	TD	Int.	Avg.	Skd.	Rat.	Att.	Yds.	Avg.	TD	TD	2pt.	Pts.
1999—Philadelphia NFL	12	6	216	106	49.1	948	8	7	4.39	28	60.1	47	313	6.7	0	0	1	2
2000—Philadelphia NFL	16	16	569	330	58.0	3365	21	13	5.91	45	77.8	86	629	7.3	6	6	0	36
2001—Philadelphia NFL	16	16	493	285	57.8	3233	25	12	6.56	39	84.3	82	482	5.9	2	2	0	12
2002—Philadelphia NFL	10	10	361	211	58.4	2289	17	6	6.34	28	86.0	63	460	7.3	6	6	0	36
2003—Philadelphia NFL	16	16	478	275	57.5	3216	16	11	6.73	‡43	79.6	71	355	5.0	3	3	0	18
Pro totals (5 years)	70	64	2117	1207	57.0	13051	87	49	6.16	183	79.3	349	2239	6.4	17	17	1	104

MCNAIR, STEVE QB TITANS

PERSONAL: Born February 14, 1973, in Mt. Olive, Miss. ... 6-2/235. ... Full name: Steve LaTreal McNair.
HIGH SCHOOL: Mount Olive (Miss.).
COLLEGE: Alcorn State.
TRANSACTIONS/CAREER NOTES: Selected by Houston Oilers in first round (third pick overall) of 1995 NFL draft. ... Signed by Oilers (July 25, 1995). ... Oilers franchise moved to Tennessee for 1997 season. ... Oilers franchise renamed Tennessee Titans for 1999 season (December 26, 1998).
CHAMPIONSHIP GAME EXPERIENCE: Played in AFC championship game (1999 and 2002 seasons). ... Played in Super Bowl 34 (1999 season).
HONORS: Walter Payton Award winner (1994). ... Named to play in Pro Bowl (2000 season); replaced by Elvis Grbac due to injury. ... Played in Pro Bowl (2003 season).
SINGLE GAME HIGHS (regular season): Attempts—49 (December 20, 1998, vs. Green Bay); completions—32 (September 29, 2002, vs. Oakland); yards—421 (October 12, 2003, vs. Houston); and touchdown passes—5 (December 26, 1999, vs. Jacksonville).
STATISTICAL PLATEAUS: 300-yard passing games: 1996 (1), 1999 (1), 2001 (2), 2002 (2), 2003 (2). Total: 8.
MISCELLANEOUS: Regular-season record as starting NFL quarterback: 69-40 (.633). ... Postseason record as starting NFL quarterback: 5-4 (.556).

			PASSING									RUSHING				TOTALS		
Year Team	G	GS	Att.	Cmp.	Pct.	Yds.	TD	Int.	Avg.	Skd.	Rat.	Att.	Yds.	Avg.	TD	TD	2pt.	Pts.
1995—Houston NFL	4	2	80	41	51.3	569	3	1	7.11	6	81.7	11	38	3.5	0	0	0	0
1996—Houston NFL	9	4	143	88	61.5	1197	6	4	8.37	9	90.6	31	169	5.5	2	2	0	12
1997—Tennessee NFL	16	16	415	216	52.0	2665	14	13	6.42	31	70.4	101	674	*6.7	8	8	0	48
1998—Tennessee NFL	16	16	492	289	58.7	3228	15	10	6.56	33	80.1	77	559	7.3	4	4	0	24
1999—Tennessee NFL	11	11	331	187	56.5	2179	12	8	6.58	16	78.6	72	337	4.7	8	8	0	48
2000—Tennessee NFL	16	15	396	248	62.6	2847	15	13	7.19	24	83.2	72	403	5.6	0	0	0	0
2001—Tennessee NFL	15	15	431	264	61.3	3350	21	12	§7.77	37	90.2	75	414	5.5	5	5	0	30
2002—Tennessee NFL	16	16	492	301	61.2	3387	22	15	6.88	21	84.0	82	440	5.4	3	3	1	20
2003—Tennessee NFL	14	14	400	250	62.5	3215	24	7	*8.04	19	*100.4	38	138	3.6	4	4	1	26
Pro totals (9 years)	117	109	3180	1884	59.2	22637	132	83	7.12	196	84.1	559	3172	5.7	34	34	2	208

MCNEIL, RYAN CB

PERSONAL: Born October 4, 1970, in Fort Pierce, Fla. ... 6-2/210. ... Full name: Ryan Darrell McNeil.
HIGH SCHOOL: Westwood Christian (Miami).
COLLEGE: Miami (Fla.).
TRANSACTIONS/CAREER NOTES: Selected by Detroit Lions in second round (33rd pick overall) of 1993 NFL draft. ... Signed by Lions (August 25, 1993). ... Granted unconditional free agency (February 14, 1997). ... Signed by St. Louis Rams (July 7, 1997). ... Designated by Rams as franchise player (February 13, 1998). ... Re-signed by Rams (August 31, 1998). ... Granted unconditional free agency (February 12, 1999). ... Signed by Cleveland Browns (August 1, 1999). ... Granted unconditional free agency (February 11, 2000). ... Signed by Dallas Cowboys (March 2, 2000). ... Released by Cowboys (February 28, 2001). ... Signed by San Diego Chargers (March 6, 2001). ... Waived by Chargers (August 12, 2003). ... Signed by Denver Broncos (November 11, 2003). ... Granted unconditional free agency (March 3, 2004).
HONORS: Named defensive back on THE SPORTING NEWS college All-America second team (1992). ... Played in Pro Bowl (2001 season).

			TOTALS			INTERCEPTIONS			
Year Team	G	GS	Tk.	Ast.	Sks.	No.	Yds.	Avg.	TD
1993—Detroit NFL	16	2	29	4	0.0	2	19	9.5	0
1994—Detroit NFL	14	13	51	7	0.0	1	14	14.0	0
1995—Detroit NFL	16	16	69	17	0.0	2	26	13.0	0
1996—Detroit NFL	16	16	68	18	0.0	5	14	2.8	0
1997—St. Louis NFL	16	16	62	9	0.0	*9	127	14.1	1
1998—St. Louis NFL	16	12	43	5	0.0	1	37	37.0	1
1999—Cleveland NFL	16	14	64	17	1.0	0	0	0.0	0
2000—Dallas NFL	16	16	68	9	0.0	2	4	2.0	0
2001—San Diego NFL	16	16	64	12	0.0	8	55	6.9	0
2002—San Diego NFL	15	15	72	7	0.0	1	16	16.0	0
2003—Denver NFL	4	0	1	0	0.0	0	0	0.0	0
Pro totals (11 years)	161	136	591	105	1.0	31	312	10.1	2

MCQUARTERS, R.W. CB BEARS

PERSONAL: Born December 21, 1976, in Tulsa, Okla. ... 5-10/198. ... Full name: Robert William McQuarters II.
HIGH SCHOOL: Washington (Okla.).
COLLEGE: Oklahoma State.
TRANSACTIONS/CAREER NOTES: Selected after junior season by San Francisco 49ers in first round (28th pick overall) of 1998 NFL draft. ... Signed by 49ers (July 28, 1998). ... On injured reserve with shoulder injury (November 30, 1999-remainder of season). ... Traded by 49ers to Chicago Bears for sixth-round pick (WR Cedrick Wilson) in 2001 draft (June 5, 2000).

			TOTALS			INTERCEPTIONS				PUNT RETURNS				KICKOFF RETURNS				TOTALS			
Year Team	G	GS	Tk.	Ast.	Sks.	No.	Yds.	Avg.	TD	No.	Yds.	Avg.	TD	No.	Yds.	Avg.	TD	TD	2pt.	Pts.	Fum.
1998—S.F. NFL	16	7	45	4	0.0	0	0	0.0	0	*47	406	8.6	1	17	339	19.9	0	1	0	6	4
1999—S.F. NFL	11	4	25	3	0.0	1	25	25.0	0	18	90	5.0	0	26	568	21.8	0	0	0	0	1
2000—Chi. NFL	15	2	22	7	1.0	1	61	61.0	1	0	0	0.0	0	0	0	0.0	0	1	0	6	0
2001—Chi. NFL	16	16	65	14	1.0	3	47	15.7	0	12	96	8.0	0	0	0	0.0	0	1	0	6	0
2002—Chi. NFL	9	9	35	8	0.0	1	33	33.0	0	0	0	0.0	0	0	0	0.0	0	0	0	0	0
2003—Chi. NFL	16	6	38	8	0.0	2	72	36.0	0	37	452	12.2	1	0	0	0.0	0	1	0	6	1
Pro totals (6 years)	83	44	230	44	2.0	8	238	29.8	1	114	1044	9.2	2	43	907	21.1	0	4	0	24	6

MEADOWS, ADAM — T — PANTHERS

PERSONAL: Born January 25, 1974, in Powder Springs, Ga. ... 6-5/290. ... Full name: Adam Jonathon Meadows.

HIGH SCHOOL: McEachern (Powder Springs, Ga.).

COLLEGE: Georgia.

TRANSACTIONS/CAREER NOTES: Selected by Indianapolis Colts in second round (48th pick overall) of 1997 NFL draft. ... Signed by Colts (July 8, 1997). ... Granted free agency (February 11, 2000). ... Re-signed by Colts (March 1, 2000). ... On injured reserve with shoulder injury (December 24, 2003-remainder of season). ... Released by Colts (February 27, 2004). ... Signed by Carolina Panthers (March 8, 2004).

PLAYING EXPERIENCE: Indianapolis NFL, 1997-2003. ... Games/Games started: 1997 (16/16), 1998 (14/14), 1999 (16/16), 2000 (16/16), 2001 (15/15), 2002 (14/14), 2003 (12/5). Total: 103/96.

MEESTER, BRAD — C — JAGUARS

PERSONAL: Born March 23, 1977, in Iowa Falls, Iowa. ... 6-3/300. ... Full name: Brad Ley Meester.

HIGH SCHOOL: Aplington-Parkersburg (Aplington, Iowa).

COLLEGE: Northern Iowa.

TRANSACTIONS/CAREER NOTES: Selected by Jacksonville Jaguars in second round (60th pick overall) of 2000 NFL draft. ... Signed by Jaguars (May 16, 2000).

PLAYING EXPERIENCE: Jacksonville NFL, 2000-2003. ... Games/Games started: 2000 (16/16), 2001 (16/16), 2002 (16/16), 2003 (16/16). Total: 64/64.

MEIER, ROB — DT — JAGUARS

PERSONAL: Born August 29, 1977, in Vancouver, BC. ... 6-5/293. ... Full name: Robert Jack Daniel Meier.

HIGH SCHOOL: Sentinel (West Vancouver, B.C.).

COLLEGE: Washington State.

TRANSACTIONS/CAREER NOTES: Selected by Jacksonville Jaguars in seventh round (241st pick overall) of 2000 NFL draft. ... Signed by Jaguars (May 17, 2000).

			TOTALS		
Year Team	**G**	**GS**	**Tk.**	**Ast.**	**Sks.**
2000—Jacksonville NFL	16	0	10	1	0.5
2001—Jacksonville NFL	16	0	12	3	0.0
2002—Jacksonville NFL	16	7	20	3	2.0
2003—Jacksonville NFL	16	0	20	5	1.5
Pro totals (4 years)	64	7	62	12	4.0

MEIER, SHAD — TE — TITANS

PERSONAL: Born June 7, 1978, in St. Louis, Mo. ... 6-4/255.

HIGH SCHOOL: Pittsburgh (Kan.).

COLLEGE: Kansas State.

TRANSACTIONS/CAREER NOTES: Selected by Tennessee Titans in third round (90th pick overall) of 2001 NFL draft. ... Signed by Titans (July 24, 2001). ... Granted free agency (March 3, 2004). ... Re-signed by Titans (April 14, 2004).

CHAMPIONSHIP GAME EXPERIENCE: Played in AFC championship game (2002 season).

SINGLE GAME HIGHS (regular season): Receptions—4 (September 21, 2003, vs. New Orleans); yards—53 (September 21, 2003, vs. New Orleans); and touchdown receptions—1 (November 10, 2002, vs. Houston).

			RECEIVING				TOTALS			
Year Team	**G**	**GS**	**No.**	**Yds.**	**Avg.**	**TD**	**TD**	**2pt.**	**Pts.**	**Fum.**
2001—Tennessee NFL	11	1	3	31	10.3	0	0	0	0	0
2002—Tennessee NFL	12	0	1	17	17.0	1	1	0	6	0
2003—Tennessee NFL	15	6	13	159	12.2	0	0	0	0	1
Pro totals (3 years)	38	7	17	207	12.2	1	1	0	6	1

MERRITT, AHMAD — WR — BEARS

PERSONAL: Born February 5, 1977, in Chicago, Ill. ... 5-10/195.

HIGH SCHOOL: St. Rita (Chicago).

COLLEGE: Wisconsin.

TRANSACTIONS/CAREER NOTES: Signed as non-drafted free agent by Chicago Bears (May 22, 2000). ... Released by Bears (August 22, 2000). ... Re-signed by Bears to practice squad (December 6, 2000). ... Assigned by Bears to Berlin Thunder in 2001 NFL Europe enhancement allocation program (February 19, 2001). ... Released by Bears (September 2, 2001). ... Re-signed by Bears to practice squad (September 3, 2001).

SINGLE GAME HIGHS (regular season): Receptions—4 (December 29, 2002, vs. Tampa Bay); yards—30 (November 3, 2002, vs. Philadelphia); and touchdown receptions—0.

			RUSHING				RECEIVING				PUNT RETURNS				KICKOFF RETURNS				TOTALS		
Year Team	**G**	**GS**	**Att.**	**Yds.**	**Avg.**	**TD**	**No.**	**Yds.**	**Avg.**	**TD**	**No.**	**Yds.**	**Avg.**	**TD**	**No.**	**Yds.**	**Avg.**	**TD**	**TD**	**2pt.**	**Pts.**
2001—Chi. NFL	2	0	0	0	0.0	0	2	20	10.0	0	0	0	0.0	0	0	0	0.0	0	0	0	0
2002—Chi. NFL	12	3	1	5	5.0	0	14	100	7.1	0	10	71	7.1	0	45	1029	22.9	0	0	0	0
2003—Chi. NFL	15	1	0	0	0.0	0	3	50	16.7	0	0	0	0.0	0	20	405	20.3	0	0	0	0
Pro totals (3 years)	29	4	1	5	5.0	0	19	170	8.9	0	10	71	7.1	0	65	1434	22.1	0	0	0	0

METCALF, TERRENCE — G/T — BEARS

PERSONAL: Born January 28, 1978, in Clarksdale, Miss. ... 6-3/325. ... Full name: Terrence Orlando Metcalf.
HIGH SCHOOL: Clarksdale (Miss.).
COLLEGE: Mississippi.
TRANSACTIONS/CAREER NOTES: Selected by Chicago Bears in third round (93rd pick overall) of 2002 NFL draft. ... Signed by Bears (July 12, 2002).
PLAYING EXPERIENCE: Chicago NFL, 2002-2003. ... Games/Games started: 2002 (5/0), 2003 (9/2). Total: 14/2.
HONORS: Named guard on THE SPORTING NEWS college All-America second team (1999). ... Named offensive tackle on THE SPORTING NEWS college All-America third team (2001).

MICKENS, RAY — CB — JETS

PERSONAL: Born January 4, 1973, in Frankfurt, Germany. ... 5-8/180.
HIGH SCHOOL: Andress (El Paso, Texas).
COLLEGE: Texas A&M.
TRANSACTIONS/CAREER NOTES: Selected by New York Jets in third round (62nd pick overall) of 1996 NFL draft. ... Signed by Jets (July 13, 1996). ... Granted free agency (February 12, 1999). ... Re-signed by Jets (April 9, 1999).
CHAMPIONSHIP GAME EXPERIENCE: Played in AFC championship game (1998 season).
HONORS: Named defensive back on THE SPORTING NEWS college All-America second team (1995).

			TOTALS			INTERCEPTIONS			
Year Team	**G**	**GS**	**Tk.**	**Ast.**	**Sks.**	**No.**	**Yds.**	**Avg.**	**TD**
1996—New York Jets NFL	15	10	37	7	0.0	0	0	0.0	0
1997—New York Jets NFL	16	0	25	1	1.0	4	2	0.5	0
1998—New York Jets NFL	16	4	30	4	0.0	3	10	3.3	0
1999—New York Jets NFL	15	5	34	7	2.0	2	2	1.0	0
2000—New York Jets NFL	16	0	19	3	0.0	0	0	0.0	0
2001—New York Jets NFL	16	4	52	10	1.0	0	0	0.0	0
2002—New York Jets NFL	16	1	29	7	2.0	0	0	0.0	0
2003—New York Jets NFL	16	14	54	9	0.0	2	16	8.0	0
Pro totals (8 years)	126	38	280	48	6.0	11	30	2.7	0

MIDDLEBROOKS, WILLIE — CB — BRONCOS

PERSONAL: Born February 12, 1979, in Miami, Fla. ... 6-1/200.
HIGH SCHOOL: Homestead (Fla.).
COLLEGE: Minnesota.
TRANSACTIONS/CAREER NOTES: Selected after junior season by Denver Broncos in first round (24th pick overall) of 2001 NFL draft. ... Signed by Broncos (July 27, 2001).

			TOTALS			INTERCEPTIONS			
Year Team	**G**	**GS**	**Tk.**	**Ast.**	**Sks.**	**No.**	**Yds.**	**Avg.**	**TD**
2001—Denver NFL	8	0	1	0	0.0	0	0	0.0	0
2002—Denver NFL	15	0	0	0	0.0	0	0	0.0	0
2003—Denver NFL	16	0	5	1	0.0	0	0	0.0	0
Pro totals (3 years)	39	0	6	1	0.0	0	0	0.0	0

M

MIDDLETON, FRANK — G — RAIDERS

PERSONAL: Born October 25, 1974, in Beaumont, Texas. ... 6-4/330. ... Full name: Frank Middleton Jr.
HIGH SCHOOL: West Brook (Beaumont, Texas).
JUNIOR COLLEGE: Fort Scott (Kan.) Community College.
COLLEGE: Arizona.
TRANSACTIONS/CAREER NOTES: Selected by Tampa Bay Buccaneers in third round (63rd pick overall) of 1997 NFL draft. ... Signed by Buccaneers (July 20, 1997). ... Granted free agency (February 11, 2000). ... Re-signed by Buccanners (May 2, 2000). ... Granted unconditional free agency (March 2, 2001). ... Signed by Oakland Raiders (April 26, 2001). ... On injured reserve with quadriceps injury (December 17, 2003-remainder of season).
PLAYING EXPERIENCE: Tampa Bay NFL, 1997-2000; Oakland NFL, 2001-2003. ... Games/Games started: 1997 (15/2), 1998 (16/16), 1999 (16/16), 2000 (16/16), 2001 (13/12), 2002 (16/16), 2003 (10/8). Total: 102/86.
CHAMPIONSHIP GAME EXPERIENCE: Played in NFC championship game (1999 season). ... Played in AFC championship game (2002 season). ... Played in Super Bowl 37 (2002 season).

MIKELL, QUINTIN — S — EAGLES

PERSONAL: Born September 16, 1980, in New Orleans, La. ... 5-10/206.
HIGH SCHOOL: Willamette (Eugene, Oreg.).
COLLEGE: Boise State.
TRANSACTIONS/CAREER NOTES: Signed as non-drafted free agent by Philadelphia Eagles (April 28, 2003).
CHAMPIONSHIP GAME EXPERIENCE: Played in NFC championship game (2003 season).

			TOTALS			INTERCEPTIONS			
Year Team	**G**	**GS**	**Tk.**	**Ast.**	**Sks.**	**No.**	**Yds.**	**Avg.**	**TD**
2003—Philadelphia NFL	16	0	2	0	0.0	0	0	0.0	0

MILI, ITULA TE SEAHAWKS

PERSONAL: Born April 20, 1973, in Kahuku, Hawaii. ... 6-4/260. ... Name pronounced: EE-too-la MEE-lee.
HIGH SCHOOL: Kahuku (Hawaii).
COLLEGE: Brigham Young.
TRANSACTIONS/CAREER NOTES: Selected by Seattle Seahawks in sixth round (174th pick overall) of 1997 NFL draft. ... Signed by Seahawks (June 11, 1997). ... On physically unable to perform list with knee injury (August 18, 1997-entire season). ... On injured reserve with knee injury (December 25, 1998-remainder of season). ... Granted free agency (March 2, 2001). ... Re-signed by Seahawks (April 13, 2001). ... Granted unconditional free agency (March 1, 2002). ... Re-signed by Seahawks (March 14, 2002).
SINGLE GAME HIGHS (regular season): Receptions—7 (December 29, 2002, vs. San Diego); yards—119 (December 29, 2002, vs. San Diego); and touchdown receptions—2 (October 26. 2003, vs. Cincinnati).
STATISTICAL PLATEAUS: 100-yard receiving games: 2002 (1). Total: 1.

			RECEIVING				TOTALS			
Year Team	G	GS	No.	Yds.	Avg.	TD	TD	2pt.	Pts.	Fum.
1997—Seattle NFL					Did not play.					
1998—Seattle NFL	7	0	1	20	20.0	0	0	0	0	0
1999—Seattle NFL	16	1	5	28	5.6	1	1	0	6	1
2000—Seattle NFL	16	6	28	288	10.3	3	3	0	18	1
2001—Seattle NFL	16	5	8	98	12.3	2	2	0	12	0
2002—Seattle NFL	16	12	43	508	11.8	2	2	0	12	1
2003—Seattle NFL	16	12	46	492	10.7	4	4	0	24	0
Pro totals (6 years)	87	36	131	1434	10.9	12	12	0	72	3

MILLER, BILLY TE TEXANS

PERSONAL: Born April 24, 1977, in Los Angeles, Calif. ... 6-3/230. ... Full name: Billy RoShawn Miller.
HIGH SCHOOL: Westlake (Westlake Village, Calif.).
COLLEGE: Southern California.
TRANSACTIONS/CAREER NOTES: Selected by Denver Broncos in seventh round (218th pick overall) of 1999 NFL draft. ... Signed by Broncos (July 20, 1999). ... Released by Broncos (September 5, 1999). ... Re-signed by Broncos to practice squad (September 6, 1999). ... Activated (October 19, 1999). ... Released by Broncos (September 2, 2001). ... Signed by Houston Texans (February 8, 2002). ... Granted free agency (February 28, 2003). ... Re-signed by Texans (June 19, 2003).
SINGLE GAME HIGHS (regular season): Receptions—8 (December 15, 2002, vs. Baltimore); yards—78 (October 27, 2002, vs. Jacksonville); and touchdown receptions—1 (November 23, 2003, vs. New England).
MISCELLANEOUS: Holds Houston Texans all-time records for most receptions (91).

			RECEIVING				TOTALS			
Year Team	G	GS	No.	Yds.	Avg.	TD	TD	2pt.	Pts.	Fum.
1999—Denver NFL	10	0	5	59	11.8	0	0	0	0	0
2000—Denver NFL	12	0	1	7	7.0	0	0	0	0	0
2002—Houston NFL	16	7	51	613	12.0	3	3	0	18	0
2003—Houston NFL	16	6	40	355	8.9	3	3	0	18	0
Pro totals (4 years)	54	13	97	1034	10.7	6	6	0	36	0

M

MILLER, FRED T TITANS

PERSONAL: Born February 6, 1973, in Houston, Texas. ... 6-7/320. ... Full name: Fred J. Miller Jr.
HIGH SCHOOL: Aldine Eisenhower (Houston).
COLLEGE: Baylor.
TRANSACTIONS/CAREER NOTES: Selected by St. Louis Rams in fifth round (141st pick overall) of 1996 NFL draft. ... Signed by Rams (July 15, 1996). ... Granted free agency (February 12, 1999). ... Re-signed by Rams (May 24, 1999). ... Granted unconditional free agency (February 11, 2000). ... Signed by Tennessee Titans (February 16, 2000).
PLAYING EXPERIENCE: St. Louis NFL, 1996-1999; Tennessee NFL, 2000-2003. ... Games/Games started: 1996 (14/0), 1997 (15/7), 1998 (15/15), 1999 (16/16), 2000 (16/16), 2001 (16/16), 2002 (16/16), 2003 (16/16). Total: 124/102.
CHAMPIONSHIP GAME EXPERIENCE: Played in NFC championship game (1999 season). ... Member of Super Bowl championship team (1999 season). ... Played in AFC championship game (2002 season).

MILLER, JOSH P PATRIOTS

PERSONAL: Born July 14, 1970, in Queens, N.Y. ... 6-4/225.
HIGH SCHOOL: East Brunswick (N.J.).
JUNIOR COLLEGE: Scottsdale (Ariz.) Community College.
COLLEGE: Arizona.
TRANSACTIONS/CAREER NOTES: Signed as non-drafted free agent by Green Bay Packers (April 1993). ... Released by Packers before 1993 season. ... Signed by Baltimore Stallions of CFL (June 1994). ... Signed by Seattle Seahawks (May 29, 1996). ... Released by Seahawks (August 13, 1996). ... Signed by Pittsburgh Steelers (August 15, 1996). ... On injured reserve with shoulder injury (December 20, 2002-remainder of season). ... Released by Steelers (March 6, 2004). ... Signed by New England Patriots (March 15, 2004).
CHAMPIONSHIP GAME EXPERIENCE: Played in Grey Cup, CFL championship game (1994). ... Played in AFC championship game (1997 and 2001 seasons).
HONORS: Named punter on the Sporting News college All-America first team (1992).

		PUNTING					
Year Team	G	No.	Yds.	Avg.	Net avg.	In. 20	Blk.
1994—Baltimore CFL	18	117	5024	42.9	36.9	...	...
1995—Baltimore CFL	18	118	5629	47.7	42.2	...	...
1996—Pittsburgh NFL	12	55	2256	41.0	33.6	18	0
1997—Pittsburgh NFL	16	64	2729	42.6	35.0	17	0

Year	Team	G	PUNTING No.	Yds.	Avg.	Net avg.	In. 20	Blk.
1998	—Pittsburgh NFL	16	81	3530	43.6	36.8	*34	0
1999	—Pittsburgh NFL	16	84	3795	45.2	38.1	27	0
2000	—Pittsburgh NFL	16	90	3944	43.8	37.5	*34	▲1
2001	—Pittsburgh NFL	16	59	2505	42.5	34.9	23	1
2002	—Pittsburgh NFL	14	55	2267	41.2	32.5	14	1
2003	—Pittsburgh NFL	16	84	3521	41.9	36.0	27	1
CFL totals (2 years)		36	235	10653	45.3	39.6	...	...
NFL totals (8 years)		122	572	24547	42.9	35.9	194	4
Pro totals (10 years)		158	807	35200	43.6	...	...	...

MILLOY, LAWYER — S — BILLS

PERSONAL: Born November 14, 1973, in St. Louis, Mo. ... 6-0/210.
HIGH SCHOOL: Lincoln (Tacoma, Wash.).
COLLEGE: Washington.
TRANSACTIONS/CAREER NOTES: Selected after junior season by New England Patriots in second round (36th pick overall) of 1996 NFL draft. ... Signed by Patriots (June 5, 1996). ... Released by Patriots (September 2, 2003). ... Signed by Buffalo Bills (September 4, 2003).
CHAMPIONSHIP GAME EXPERIENCE: Played in AFC championship game (1996 and 2001 seasons). ... Played in Super Bowl 31 (1996 season). ... Member of Super Bowl championship team (2001 season).
HONORS: Named defensive back on THE SPORTING NEWS college All-America first team (1995). ... Played in Pro Bowl (1998, 1999, 2001 and 2002 seasons). ... Named safety on THE SPORTING NEWS NFL All-Pro team (1999).

Year	Team	G	GS	TOTALS Tk.	Ast.	Sks.	INTERCEPTIONS No.	Yds.	Avg.	TD
1996	—New England NFL	16	10	54	30	1.0	2	14	7.0	0
1997	—New England NFL	16	16	82	30	0.0	3	15	5.0	0
1998	—New England NFL	16	16	79	41	1.0	6	54	9.0	1
1999	—New England NFL	16	16	91	29	2.0	4	17	4.3	0
2000	—New England NFL	16	16	90	31	0.0	2	2	1.0	0
2001	—New England NFL	16	16	77	36	3.0	2	21	10.5	0
2002	—New England NFL	16	16	61	30	0.0	0	0	0.0	0
2003	—Buffalo NFL	16	16	70	35	3.0	0	0	0.0	0
Pro totals (8 years)		128	122	604	262	10.0	19	123	6.5	1

MINOR, TRAVIS — RB — DOLPHINS

PERSONAL: Born June 30, 1979, in New Orleans, La. ... 5-10/205. ... Full name: Travis D. Minor.
HIGH SCHOOL: Catholic (Baton, La.).
COLLEGE: Florida State.
TRANSACTIONS/CAREER NOTES: Selected by Miami Dolphins in third round (85th pick overall) of 2001 NFL draft. ... Signed by Dolphins (July 23, 2001). ... Granted free agency (March 3, 2004). ... Re-signed by Dolphins (April 21, 2004).
SINGLE GAME HIGHS (regular season): Attempts—11 (September 8, 2002, vs. Detroit); yards—71 (November 11, 2001, vs. Indianapolis); and rushing touchdowns—1 (December 15, 2003, vs. Philadelphia).

Year	Team	G	GS	RUSHING Att.	Yds.	Avg.	TD	RECEIVING No.	Yds.	Avg.	TD	KICKOFF RETURNS No.	Yds.	Avg.	TD	TOTALS TD	2pt.	Pts.	Fum.
2001	—Miami NFL	16	0	59	281	4.8	2	29	263	9.1	1	0	0	0.0	0	4	0	24	0
2002	—Miami NFL	16	0	44	180	4.1	2	0	0	0.0	0	46	1071	23.3	0	2	0	12	0
2003	—Miami NFL	16	0	41	193	4.7	1	4	13	3.3	0	34	727	21.4	0	1	0	6	0
Pro totals (3 years)		48	0	144	654	4.5	5	33	276	8.4	1	80	1798	22.5	0	7	0	42	0

MINTER, MIKE — S — PANTHERS

PERSONAL: Born January 15, 1974, in Cleveland, Ohio. ... 5-10/188. ... Full name: Michael Christopher Minter.
HIGH SCHOOL: Lawton (Okla.).
COLLEGE: Nebraska.
TRANSACTIONS/CAREER NOTES: Selected by Carolina Panthers in second round (56th pick overall) of 1997 NFL draft. ... Signed by Panthers (June 12, 1997). ... Granted unconditional free agency (March 2, 2001). ... Re-signed by Panthers (March 3, 2001).
CHAMPIONSHIP GAME EXPERIENCE: Played in NFC championship game (2003 season). ... Played in Super Bowl 38 (2003 season).

Year	Team	G	GS	TOTALS Tk.	Ast.	Sks.	INTERCEPTIONS No.	Yds.	Avg.	TD
1997	—Carolina NFL	16	11	53	16	3.5	0	0	0.0	0
1998	—Carolina NFL	6	4	19	7	0.0	1	7	7.0	0
1999	—Carolina NFL	16	16	63	20	1.0	3	69	23.0	0
2000	—Carolina NFL	16	16	86	30	2.0	2	38	19.0	1
2001	—Carolina NFL	14	14	64	14	0.0	2	32	16.0	0
2002	—Carolina NFL	16	16	62	20	1.0	4	125	31.2	1
2003	—Carolina NFL	16	16	71	18	0.0	3	100	33.3	†2
Pro totals (7 years)		100	93	418	125	7.5	15	371	24.7	4

MIRER, RICK — QB — LIONS

PERSONAL: Born March 19, 1970, in Elkhart, Ind. ... 6-3/210. ... Full name: Rick F. Mirer.
HIGH SCHOOL: Goshen (Ind.).
COLLEGE: Notre Dame.

TRANSACTIONS/CAREER NOTES: Selected by Seattle Seahawks in first round (second pick overall) of 1993 NFL draft. ... Signed by Seahawks (August 2, 1993). ... On injured reserve with thumb injury (December 20, 1994-remainder of season). ... Traded by Seahawks with fourth-round pick (RB Darnell Autry) in 1997 draft to Chicago Bears for first-round pick (traded to Atlanta) in 1997 draft (February 18, 1997). ... Released by Bears (August 30, 1998). ... Signed by Green Bay Packers (September 2, 1998). ... Active for four games (1998); did not play. ... Traded by Packers to New York Jets for fourth-round pick (traded to San Francisco) in 2000 draft (August 20, 1999). ... Released by Jets (February 2, 2000). ... Signed by San Francisco 49ers (June 13, 2000). ... Granted unconditional free agency (March 2, 2001). ... Re-signed by 49ers (June 5, 2001). ... Released by 49ers (September 4, 2001). ... Re-signed by 49ers (October 31, 2001). ... Granted unconditional free agency (March 1, 2002). ... Signed by Oakland Raiders (March 24, 2002). ... Granted unconditional free agency (February 28, 2003). ... Re-signed by Raiders (March 19, 2003). ... Granted unconditional free agency (March 3, 2004). ... Signed by Detroit Lions (April 5, 2004).
CHAMPIONSHIP GAME EXPERIENCE: Member of Raiders for AFC championship game (2002 season); inactive. ... Member of Raiders for Super Bowl 37 (2002 season); inactive.
SINGLE GAME HIGHS (regular season): Attempts—43 (October 24, 1993, vs. New England); completions—25 (October 3, 1993, vs. San Diego); yards—287 (December 5, 1993, vs. Kansas City); and touchdown passes—3 (September 11, 1994, vs. Los Angeles Raiders).
MISCELLANEOUS: Regular-season record as starting NFL quarterback: 24-44 (.353).

			PASSING										RUSHING				TOTALS		
Year Team	**G**	**GS**	**Att.**	**Cmp.**	**Pct.**	**Yds.**	**TD**	**Int.**	**Avg.**	**Skd.**	**Rat.**	**Att.**	**Yds.**	**Avg.**	**TD**	**TD**	**2pt.**	**Pts.**
1993—Seattle NFL	16	16	486	274	56.4	2833	12	17	5.83	*47	67.0	68	343	5.0	3	3	0	18
1994—Seattle NFL	13	13	381	195	51.2	2151	11	7	5.65	27	70.2	34	153	4.5	0	0	0	0
1995—Seattle NFL	15	13	391	209	53.5	2564	13	§20	6.56	42	63.7	43	193	4.5	1	1	0	6
1996—Seattle NFL	11	9	265	136	51.3	1546	5	12	5.83	22	56.6	33	191	5.8	2	2	0	12
1997—Chicago NFL	7	3	103	53	51.5	420	0	6	4.08	16	37.7	20	78	3.9	1	1	1	8
1998—Green Bay NFL	Did not play.																	
1999—New York Jets NFL	8	6	176	95	54.0	1062	5	9	6.03	22	60.4	21	89	4.2	1	1	0	6
2000—San Francisco NFL	3	0	20	10	50.0	126	1	0	6.30	1	86.7	3	0	0.0	0	0	0	0
2001—San Francisco NFL	Did not play.																	
2002—Oakland NFL	Did not play.																	
2003—Oakland NFL	9	8	221	116	52.5	1267	3	5	5.73	22	64.8	20	83	4.2	1	1	0	6
Pro totals (8 years)	82	68	2043	1088	53.3	11969	50	76	5.86	199	63.5	242	1130	4.7	9	9	1	56

MITCHELL, ANTHONY — S — JAGUARS

PERSONAL: Born December 13, 1974, in Youngstown, Ohio. ... 6-1/198. ... Full name: Anthony Maurice Mitchell.
HIGH SCHOOL: West Lake (Atlanta, Ga.).
COLLEGE: Tuskegee.
TRANSACTIONS/CAREER NOTES: Signed as non-drafted free agent by Jacksonville Jaguars (April 26, 1999). ... Released by Jaguars (September 1, 1999). ... Signed by Baltimore Ravens to practice squad (September 7, 1999). ... Activated (December 7, 1999). ... Traded by Ravens to Jaguars for a 2004 conditional draft choice (August 26, 2003).
CHAMPIONSHIP GAME EXPERIENCE: Member of Super Bowl championship team (2000 season).

			TOTALS			INTERCEPTIONS			
Year Team	**G**	**GS**	**Tk.**	**Ast.**	**Sks.**	**No.**	**Yds.**	**Avg.**	**TD**
2000—Baltimore NFL	16	0	0	1	0.0	0	0	0.0	0
2001—Baltimore NFL	16	0	5	2	0.0	0	0	0.0	0
2002—Baltimore NFL	16	6	20	14	0.0	3	62	20.7	0
2003—Jacksonville NFL	16	1	8	2	0.0	0	0	0.0	0
Pro totals (4 years)	64	7	33	19	0.0	3	62	20.7	0

MITCHELL, BRANDON — DE — SEAHAWKS

PERSONAL: Born June 19, 1975, in Abbeville, La. ... 6-3/290. ... Full name: Brandon Pete Mitchell.
HIGH SCHOOL: Abbeville (La.).
COLLEGE: Texas A&M.
TRANSACTIONS/CAREER NOTES: Selected by New England Patriots in second round (59th pick overall) of 1997 NFL draft. ... Signed by Patriots (June 6, 1997). ... On injured reserve with ankle injury (October 30, 1998-remainder of season). ... Granted free agency (February 11, 2000). ... Re-signed by Patriots (July 16, 2000). ... On injured reserve with leg injury (December 6, 2000-remainder of season). ... Granted unconditional free agency (March 2, 2001). ... Re-signed by Patriots (April 16, 2001). ... Granted unconditional free agency (March 1, 2002). ... Signed by Seattle Seahawks (April 10, 2002). ... On injured reserve with calf injury (October 30, 2002-remainder of season).
CHAMPIONSHIP GAME EXPERIENCE: Played in AFC championship game (2001 season). ... Member of Super Bowl championship team (2001 season).

			TOTALS		
Year Team	**G**	**GS**	**Tk.**	**Ast.**	**Sks.**
1997—New England NFL	11	0	6	3	0.0
1998—New England NFL	7	1	14	7	2.0
1999—New England NFL	16	16	23	25	3.0
2000—New England NFL	11	9	13	16	0.0
2001—New England NFL	16	11	26	17	1.0
2002—Seattle NFL	5	2	5	3	1.0
2003—Seattle NFL	14	6	20	4	3.0
Pro totals (7 years)	80	45	107	75	10.0

MITCHELL, BRIAN — RB/KR

PERSONAL: Born August 18, 1968, in Fort Polk, La. ... 5-11/225. ... Full name: Brian Keith Mitchell.
HIGH SCHOOL: Plaquemine (La.).
COLLEGE: Louisiana-Lafayette.
TRANSACTIONS/CAREER NOTES: Selected by Washington Redskins in fifth round (130th pick overall) of 1990 NFL draft. ... Signed by Redskins (July 22, 1990). ... Granted free agency (February 1, 1992). ... Re-signed by Redskins for 1992 season. ... Granted unconditional

free agency (February 17, 1994). ... Re-signed by Redskins (May 24, 1994). ... Granted free agency (February 17, 1995). ... Re-signed by Redskins (March 27, 1995). ... Granted unconditional free agency (February 13, 1998). ... Re-signed by Redskins (February 12, 1998). ... Released by Redskins (June 1, 2000). ... Signed by Philadelphia Eagles (June 9, 2000). ... Granted unconditional free agency (March 1, 2002). ... Re-signed by Eagles (March 27, 2002). ... Granted unconditional free agency (February 28, 2003). ... Signed by New York Giants (March 3, 2003). ... Released by Giants (February 25, 2004).

CHAMPIONSHIP GAME EXPERIENCE: Played in NFC championship game (1991, 2001 and 2002 seasons). ... Member of Super Bowl championship team (1991 season).

HONORS: Named punt returner on THE SPORTING NEWS NFL All-Pro team (1995). ... Played in Pro Bowl (1995 season).

RECORDS: Holds NFL career records for most total yards—23,330; most punt returns—463; most combined kick returns—1,070; most yards by combined kick returns—19,013; most yards gained by punt return—4,999; most kickoff returns—607; most yards gained by kick return—14,014; and most touchdowns by combined kick returns—13. ... Holds NFL career record for most fair catches—231. ... Holds NFL single-season record for most fair catches—33 (2000).

SINGLE GAME HIGHS (regular season): Attempts—21 (September 6, 1993, vs. Dallas); yards—116 (September 6, 1993, vs. Dallas); and rushing touchdowns—2 (September 6, 1993, vs. Dallas).

STATISTICAL PLATEAUS: 100-yard rushing games: 1993 (1), 2000 (1). Total: 2.

			RUSHING				RECEIVING				PUNT RETURNS				KICKOFF RETURNS				TOTALS		
Year Team	G	GS	Att.	Yds.	Avg.	TD	No.	Yds.	Avg.	TD	No.	Yds.	Avg.	TD	No.	Yds.	Avg.	TD	TD	2pt.	Pts.
1990—Was. NFL	15	0	15	81	5.4	1	2	5	2.5	0	12	107	8.9	0	18	365	20.3	0	1	0	6
1991—Was. NFL	16	0	3	14	4.7	0	0	0	0.0	0	45	*600	13.3	*2	29	583	20.1	0	2	0	12
1992—Was. NFL	16	0	6	70	11.7	0	3	30	10.0	0	29	271	9.3	1	23	492	21.4	0	1	0	6
1993—Was. NFL	16	4	63	246	3.9	3	20	157	7.9	0	29	193	6.7	0	33	678	20.5	0	3	0	18
1994—Was. NFL	16	7	78	311	4.0	0	26	236	9.1	1	32	‡452	*14.1	†2	58	1478	25.5	0	3	1	20
1995—Was. NFL	16	1	46	301	6.5	1	38	324	8.5	1	25	315	12.6	†1	55	1408	‡25.6	0	3	0	18
1996—Was. NFL	16	2	39	193	4.9	0	32	286	8.9	0	23	258	11.2	0	56	1258	22.5	0	0	0	0
1997—Was. NFL	16	1	23	107	4.7	1	36	438	12.2	1	38	442	11.6	∞1	47	1094	23.3	1	4	0	24
1998—Was. NFL	16	0	39	208	5.3	2	44	306	7.0	0	44	‡506	11.5	0	59	1337	22.7	1	3	0	18
1999—Was. NFL	16	0	40	220	5.5	1	31	305	9.8	0	40	332	8.3	0	43	893	20.8	0	1	0	6
2000—Phi. NFL	16	1	25	187	7.5	2	13	89	6.8	1	32	335	10.5	1	47	1124	23.9	1	5	0	30
2001—Phi. NFL	16	0	7	9	1.3	0	6	122	20.3	0	39	‡467	12.0	0	41	1025	25.0	1	1	0	6
2002—Phi. NFL	16	0	0	0	0.0	0	0	0	0.0	0	46	567	12.3	1	43	1162	27.0	0	1	0	6
2003—NYG NFL	16	0	4	20	5.0	1	4	38	9.5	0	29	154	5.3	0	55	1117	20.3	0	1	0	6
Pro totals (14 years)	223	16	388	1967	5.1	12	255	2336	9.2	4	463	4999	10.8	9	607	14014	23.1	4	29	1	176

MITCHELL, DONALD CB COWBOYS

PERSONAL: Born December 14, 1976, in Beaumont, Texas. ... 5-10/182. ... Full name: Donald Roosevelt Mitchell.

HIGH SCHOOL: Central (Beaumont, Texas).

COLLEGE: Southern Methodist.

TRANSACTIONS/CAREER NOTES: Selected by Tennessee Titans in fourth round (117th pick overall) of 1999 NFL draft. ... Signed by Titans (July 27, 1999). ... On injured reserve with knee injury (August 22, 2000-entire season). ... Granted unconditional free agency (February 28, 2003). ... Signed by Dallas Cowboys (March 20, 2003). ... On injured reserve with ankle injury (August 31, 2003-entire season).

CHAMPIONSHIP GAME EXPERIENCE: Played in AFC championship game (1999 and 2002 seasons). ... Played in Super Bowl 34 (1999 season).

			TOTALS			INTERCEPTIONS			
Year Team	G	GS	Tk.	Ast.	Sks.	No.	Yds.	Avg.	TD
1999—Tennessee NFL	16	0	7	1	0.0	1	42	42.0	1
2001—Tennessee NFL	12	3	22	4	0.0	0	0	0.0	0
2002—Tennessee NFL	16	10	39	10	0.0	1	-2	-2.0	0
2003—Dallas NFL	Did not play.								
Pro totals (3 years)	44	13	68	15	0.0	2	40	20.0	1

MITCHELL, FREDDIE WR EAGLES

PERSONAL: Born November 28, 1978, in Lakeland, Fla. ... 5-11/184. ... Full name: Freddie Lee Mitchell II.

HIGH SCHOOL: Kathleen (Lakeland, Fla.).

COLLEGE: UCLA.

TRANSACTIONS/CAREER NOTES: Selected after junior season by Philadelphia Eagles in first round (25th pick overall) of 2001 NFL draft. ... Signed by Eagles (July 26, 2001).

CHAMPIONSHIP GAME EXPERIENCE: Played in NFC championship game (2001-2003 seasons).

HONORS: Named wide receiver on THE SPORTING NEWS college All-America first team (2000).

SINGLE GAME HIGHS (regular season): Receptions—4 (December 27, 2003, vs. Washington); yards—62 (November 4, 2001, vs. Arizona); and touchdown receptions—1 (December 27, 2003, vs. Washington).

			RECEIVING				TOTALS			
Year Team	G	GS	No.	Yds.	Avg.	TD	TD	2pt.	Pts.	Fum.
2001—Philadelphia NFL	15	1	21	283	13.5	1	1	0	6	0
2002—Philadelphia NFL	16	1	12	105	8.8	0	0	0	0	1
2003—Philadelphia NFL	16	6	35	498	14.2	2	2	0	12	0
Pro totals (3 years)	47	8	68	886	13.0	3	3	0	18	1

MITCHELL, JEFF C PANTHERS

PERSONAL: Born January 29, 1974, in Dallas, Texas. ... 6-4/300. ... Full name: Jeffrey Clay Mitchell. ... Brother of Clint Mitchell, defensive end, Denver Broncos.

HIGH SCHOOL: Countryside (Clearwater, Fla.).

COLLEGE: Florida.

TRANSACTIONS/CAREER NOTES: Selected by Baltimore Ravens in fifth round (134th pick overall) of 1997 NFL draft. ... Signed by Ravens (July 10, 1997). ... On injured reserve with knee injury (August 18, 1997-entire season). ... Granted free agency (February 11, 2000). ... Re-signed by Ravens (April 17, 2000) ... Granted unconditional free agency (March 2, 2001). ... Signed by Carolina Panthers (March 12, 2001).
PLAYING EXPERIENCE: Baltimore NFL, 1998-2000; Carolina NFL, 2001-2003. ... Games/Games started: 1998 (11/10), 1999 (16/16), 2000 (14/14), 2001 (15/15), 2002 (16/16), 2003 (15/15). Total: 87/86.
CHAMPIONSHIP GAME EXPERIENCE: Played in AFC championship game (2000 and 2003 seasons). ... Member of Super Bowl championship team (2000 season). ... Played in Super Bowl 38 (2003 season).

MITCHELL, KAWIKA — LB — CHIEFS

PERSONAL: Born October 10, 1979, in Winter Springs, Fla. ... 6-0/253.
HIGH SCHOOL: Lake Howell (Casselberry, Fla.).
COLLEGE: South Florida.
TRANSACTIONS/CAREER NOTES: Selected by Kansas City Chiefs in second round (47th pick overall) of 2003 NFL draft. ... Signed by Chiefs (July 14, 2003).

			TOTALS			INTERCEPTIONS			
Year Team	G	GS	Tk.	Ast.	Sks.	No.	Yds.	Avg.	TD
2003—Kansas City NFL	12	6	14	3	0.0	1	3	3.0	0

MITCHELL, KEITH — LB

PERSONAL: Born July 24, 1974, in Garland, Texas. ... 6-2/236. ... Full name: Clarence Marquis Mitchell.
HIGH SCHOOL: Lakeview (Garland, Texas).
COLLEGE: Texas A&M.
TRANSACTIONS/CAREER NOTES: Signed as non-drafted free agent by New Orleans Saints (April 25, 1997). ... Released by Saints (June 4, 2002). ... Signed by Houston Texans (July 20, 2002). ... Granted unconditional free agency (February 28, 2003). ... Signed by Jacksonville Jaguars (March 14, 2003). ... Released by Jaguars (November 27, 2003).
HONORS: Named outside linebacker on THE SPORTING NEWS college All-America second team (1996). ... Played in Pro Bowl (2000 season).

			TOTALS			INTERCEPTIONS			
Year Team	G	GS	Tk.	Ast.	Sks.	No.	Yds.	Avg.	TD
1997—New Orleans NFL	16	2	20	4	4.0	0	0	0.0	0
1998—New Orleans NFL	16	15	42	24	2.5	0	0	0.0	0
1999—New Orleans NFL	16	16	76	28	3.5	3	22	7.3	0
2000—New Orleans NFL	16	16	60	25	6.5	1	40	40.0	1
2001—New Orleans NFL	15	14	63	27	2.0	0	0	0.0	0
2002—Houston NFL	11	7	21	7	1.0	0	0	0.0	0
2003—Jacksonville NFL	3	2	4	2	0.0	0	0	0.0	0
Pro totals (7 years)	93	72	286	117	19.5	4	62	15.5	1

MITCHELL, KEVIN — LB — REDSKINS

PERSONAL: Born January 1, 1971, in Harrisburg, Pa. ... 6-1/258. ... Full name: Kevin Danyelle Mitchell.
HIGH SCHOOL: Harrisburg (Pa.).
COLLEGE: Syracuse.
TRANSACTIONS/CAREER NOTES: Selected by San Francisco 49ers in second round (53rd pick overall) of 1994 NFL draft. ... Signed by 49ers (July 20, 1994). ... Granted free agency (February 14, 1997). ... Re-signed by 49ers (April 24, 1997). ... Granted free agency (February 13, 1998). ... Signed by New Orleans Saints (February 19, 1998). ... Granted unconditional free agency (February 11, 2000). ... Signed by Washington Redskins (February 29, 2000). ... Granted unconditional free agency (March 2, 2001). ... Re-signed by Redskins (March 29, 2001). ... On injured reserve with ankle injury (December 26, 2001-remainder of season). ... Granted unconditional free agency (February 28, 2003). ... Re-signed by Redskins (April 24, 2003). ... Granted unconditional free agency (March 3, 2004). ... Re-signed by Redskins (March 4, 2004).
CHAMPIONSHIP GAME EXPERIENCE: Played in NFC championship game (1994 and 1997 seasons). ... Member of Super Bowl championship team (1994 season).
HONORS: Named defensive lineman on THE SPORTING NEWS college All-America second team (1992 and 1993).

			TOTALS			INTERCEPTIONS			
Year Team	G	GS	Tk.	Ast.	Sks.	No.	Yds.	Avg.	TD
1994—San Francisco NFL	16	0	6	0	0.0	0	0	0.0	0
1995—San Francisco NFL	15	0	4	0	0.0	0	0	0.0	0
1996—San Francisco NFL	12	3	15	1	1.0	0	0	0.0	0
1997—San Francisco NFL	16	0	4	2	0.0	0	0	0.0	0
1998—New Orleans NFL	8	8	31	25	2.5	0	0	0.0	0
1999—New Orleans NFL	16	1	14	1	0.0	0	0	0.0	0
2000—Washington NFL	16	0	4	0	1.0	1	0	0.0	0
2001—Washington NFL	13	13	69	13	2.0	0	0	0.0	0
2002—Washington NFL	16	3	20	4	0.0	1	7	7.0	0
2003—Washington NFL	16	0	3	0	0.0	0	0	0.0	0
Pro totals (10 years)	144	28	170	46	6.5	2	7	3.5	0

MITCHELL, QASIM — G — BEARS

PERSONAL: Born December 3, 1979, in Jacksonville, N.C. ... 6-6/355.
COLLEGE: North Carolina A&T.
TRANSACTIONS/CAREER NOTES: Signed as non-drafted free agent by Cleveland Browns (April 26, 2002) ... On injured reserve with lung injury (August 27, 2002-entire season). ... Re-signed by Browns to practice squad (September 1, 2003). ... Claimed on waivers by Chicago

Bears (September 16, 2003). ... Signed by Bears to practice squad (September 17, 2003). ... Activated (November 14, 2003). ... On injured reserve with broken fibia (December 23, 2003-remainder of season).
PLAYING EXPERIENCE: Chicago NFL, 2003. ... Games/Games started: 2003 (2/2). Total: 2/2.

MIXON, KENNY DE VIKINGS

PERSONAL: Born May 31, 1975, in Sun Valley, Calif. ... 6-4/271. ... Full name: Kenneth Jermaine Mixon.
HIGH SCHOOL: Pineville (La.).
COLLEGE: Louisiana State.
TRANSACTIONS/CAREER NOTES: Selected by Miami Dolphins in second round (49th pick overall) of 1998 NFL draft. ... Signed by Dolphins (July 21, 1998). ... Granted unconditional free agency (March 1, 2002). ... Signed by Minnesota Vikings (March 10, 2002).

			TOTALS			INTERCEPTIONS			
Year Team	**G**	**GS**	**Tk.**	**Ast.**	**Sks.**	**No.**	**Yds.**	**Avg.**	**TD**
1998—Miami NFL	16	16	22	13	2.0	0	0	0.0	0
1999—Miami NFL	11	2	4	6	0.0	0	0	0.0	0
2000—Miami NFL	16	16	25	19	2.5	0	0	0.0	0
2001—Miami NFL	16	16	26	18	2.0	1	56	56.0	1
2002—Minnesota NFL	16	16	45	26	4.5	1	6	6.0	0
2003—Minnesota NFL	16	16	45	8	5.0	0	0	0.0	0
Pro totals (6 years)	91	82	167	90	16.0	2	62	31.0	1

MOBLEY, JOHN LB BRONCOS

PERSONAL: Born October 10, 1973, in Chester, Pa. ... 6-1/236. ... Full name: John Ulysses Mobley.
HIGH SCHOOL: Chichester (Marcus Hook, Pa.).
COLLEGE: Kutztown.
TRANSACTIONS/CAREER NOTES: Selected by Denver Broncos in first round (15th pick overall) of 1996 NFL draft. ... Signed by Broncos (July 23, 1996). ... On injured reserve with knee injury (September 22, 1999-remainder of season). ... Granted unconditional free agency (March 2, 2001). ... Re-signed by Broncos (March 2, 2001). ... On injured reserve with neck injury (November 6, 2003-remainder of season).
CHAMPIONSHIP GAME EXPERIENCE: Played in AFC championship game (1997 and 1998 seasons). ... Member of Super Bowl championship team (1997 and 1998 seasons).
HONORS: Named outside linebacker on THE SPORTING NEWS NFL All-Pro team (1997).

			TOTALS			INTERCEPTIONS			
Year Team	**G**	**GS**	**Tk.**	**Ast.**	**Sks.**	**No.**	**Yds.**	**Avg.**	**TD**
1996—Denver NFL	16	16	49	12	1.5	1	8	8.0	0
1997—Denver NFL	16	16	96	36	4.0	1	13	13.0	1
1998—Denver NFL	16	15	93	19	1.0	1	-2	-2.0	0
1999—Denver NFL	2	2	7	3	0.0	0	0	0.0	0
2000—Denver NFL	15	14	69	16	2.0	1	9	9.0	0
2001—Denver NFL	16	16	76	13	1.0	1	17	17.0	0
2002—Denver NFL	16	16	70	27	1.0	0	0	0.0	0
2003—Denver NFL	8	7	19	3	0.0	0	0	0.0	0
Pro totals (8 years)	105	102	479	129	10.5	5	45	9.0	1

MOHR, CHRIS P FALCONS

PERSONAL: Born May 11, 1966, in Atlanta, Ga. ... 6-5/215. ... Full name: Christopher Garrett Mohr.
HIGH SCHOOL: Briarwood Academy (Warrenton, Ga.).
COLLEGE: Alabama.
TRANSACTIONS/CAREER NOTES: Selected by Tampa Bay Buccaneers in sixth round (146th pick overall) of 1989 NFL draft. ... Signed by Buccaneers (July 15, 1989). ... Released by Buccaneers (September 2, 1990). ... Signed by WLAF (January 31, 1991). ... Selected by Montreal Machine in first round (eighth punter) of 1991 WLAF positional draft. ... Signed by Buffalo Bills (June 6, 1991). ... Granted unconditional free agency (February 17, 1994). ... Re-signed by Bills (March 3, 1994). ... Granted unconditional free agency (February 14, 1997). ... Re-signed by Bills (March 4, 1997). ... Released by Bills (February 22, 2001). ... Signed by Atlanta Falcons (March 13, 2001). ... Re-signed by Falcons (March 13, 2003).
CHAMPIONSHIP GAME EXPERIENCE: Played in AFC championship game (1991-1993 seasons). ... Played in Super Bowl 26 (1991 season), Super Bowl 27 (1992 season) and Super Bowl 28 (1993 season).
HONORS: Named punter on All-World League team (1991).

		PUNTING					
Year Team	**G**	**No.**	**Yds.**	**Avg.**	**Net avg.**	**In. 20**	**Blk.**
1989—Tampa Bay NFL	16	∞84	3311	39.4	32.1	10	2
1990—			Did not play.				
1991—Buffalo NFL	16	54	2085	38.6	36.1	12	0
1992—Buffalo NFL	15	60	2531	42.2	36.7	12	0
1993—Buffalo NFL	16	74	2991	40.4	36.0	19	0
1994—Buffalo NFL	16	67	2799	41.8	36.0	13	0
1995—Buffalo NFL	16	86	3473	40.4	36.2	23	0
1996—Buffalo NFL	16	§101	§4194	41.5	36.5	§27	0
1997—Buffalo NFL	16	90	3764	41.8	36.0	24	1
1998—Buffalo NFL	16	69	2882	41.8	33.2	18	0
1999—Buffalo NFL	16	73	2840	38.9	33.9	20	0
2000—Buffalo NFL	16	95	3661	38.5	31.4	19	▲1
2001—Atlanta NFL	16	69	2680	38.8	36.1	25	0
2002—Atlanta NFL	16	67	2804	41.9	*38.7	21	0
2003—Atlanta NFL	16	87	3473	39.9	36.0	19	0
Pro totals (14 years)	223	1076	43488	40.4	35.2	262	4

MOLDEN, ALEX CB

PERSONAL: Born August 4, 1973, in Detroit, Mich. ... 5-10/190. ... Full name: Alex M. Molden.
HIGH SCHOOL: Sierra (Colorado Springs, Colo.).
COLLEGE: Oregon.
TRANSACTIONS/CAREER NOTES: Selected by New Orleans Saints in first round (11th pick overall) of 1996 NFL draft. ... Signed by Saints (July 21, 1996). ... Granted unconditional free agency (March 2, 2001). ... Signed by San Diego Chargers (March 7, 2001). ... On injured reserve with ankle injury (December 14, 2001-remainder of season). ... Released by Chargers (February 27, 2003). ... Signed by Washington Redskins (May 2, 2003). ... Waived by Redskins (August 26, 2003). ... Signed by Detroit Lions (September 8, 2003). ... Released by Lions (October 7, 2003).
HONORS: Named defensive back on THE SPORTING NEWS college All-America second team (1995).

			TOTALS			INTERCEPTIONS			
Year Team	G	GS	Tk.	Ast.	Sks.	No.	Yds.	Avg.	TD
1996—New Orleans NFL	14	2	17	4	2.0	2	2	1.0	0
1997—New Orleans NFL	16	15	57	11	4.0	0	0	0.0	0
1998—New Orleans NFL	16	15	54	8	0.0	2	35	17.5	0
1999—New Orleans NFL	13	0	13	2	0.0	1	2	2.0	0
2000—New Orleans NFL	15	6	24	9	0.0	3	24	8.0	0
2001—San Diego NFL	6	3	18	1	0.0	1	0	0.0	0
2002—San Diego NFL	16	16	68	11	2.0	3	9	3.0	0
2003—Detroit NFL	2	0	1	0	0.0	0	0	0.0	0
Pro totals (8 years)	98	57	252	46	8.0	12	72	6.0	0

MONK, QUINCY LB GIANTS

PERSONAL: Born January 30, 1979, in Jacksonville, N.C. ... 6-3/250. ... Full name: Quincy Omar Monk.
HIGH SCHOOL: White Oak (Jacksonville, N.C.).
COLLEGE: North Carolina.
TRANSACTIONS/CAREER NOTES: Selected by New York Giants in seventh round (245th pick overall) of 2002 NFL draft.

			TOTALS			INTERCEPTIONS			
Year Team	G	GS	Tk.	Ast.	Sks.	No.	Yds.	Avg.	TD
2002—New York Giants NFL	9	0	1	0	0.0	0	0	0.0	0
2003—New York Giants NFL	4	0	0	0	0.0	0	0	0.0	0
Pro totals (2 years)	13	0	1	0	0.0	0	0	0.0	0

MOORE, BRANDON LB 49ERS

PERSONAL: Born January 16, 1979, in East Meadow, N.Y. ... 6-1/242. ... Full name: Brandon T. Moore. ... Brother of Rob Moore, wide receiver with New York Jets (1990-95) and Arizona Cardinals (1996-2001).
HIGH SCHOOL: Baldwin (N.Y.).
COLLEGE: Oklahoma.
TRANSACTIONS/CAREER NOTES: Signed as non-drafted free agent by San Francisco 49ers (April 26, 2002). ... Released by 49ers (September 2, 2002). ... Signed by New England Patriots to practice squad (September 3, 2002). ... Signed by 49ers off Patriots practice squad (September 24, 2002).

			TOTALS			INTERCEPTIONS			
Year Team	G	GS	Tk.	Ast.	Sks.	No.	Yds.	Avg.	TD
2002—San Francisco NFL	13	2	7	1	0.0	0	0	0.0	0
2003—San Francisco NFL	15	1	3	0	0.0	0	0	0.0	0
Pro totals (2 years)	28	3	10	1	0.0	0	0	0.0	0

M

MOORE, BRANDON G JETS

PERSONAL: Born June 3, 1980, in Gary, Ind. ... 6-3/295.
HIGH SCHOOL: West Side (Gary, Ind.).
COLLEGE: Illinois.
TRANSACTIONS/CAREER NOTES: Signed as non-drafted free agent by New York Jets (April 26, 2002). ... Waived by Jets (August 26, 2002). ... Re-signed by Jets to practice squad (December 26, 2002). ... Assigned by Jets to Scottish Claymores in 2003 NFL Europe enhancement allocation program (January 28, 2003). ... Activated (October 23, 2003).
PLAYING EXPERIENCE: New York Jets NFL, 2003. ... Games/Games started: 2003 (3/1). Total: 3/1.

MOORE, DAVE TE BUCCANEERS

PERSONAL: Born November 11, 1969, in Morristown, N.J. ... 6-2/250. ... Full name: David Edward Moore.
HIGH SCHOOL: Roxbury (Succasunna, N.J.).
COLLEGE: Pittsburgh.
TRANSACTIONS/CAREER NOTES: Selected by Miami Dolphins in seventh round (191st pick overall) of 1992 NFL draft. ... Signed by Dolphins (July 15, 1992). ... Released by Dolphins (August 31, 1992). ... Re-signed by Dolphins to practice squad (September 1, 1992). ... Released by Dolphins (September 16, 1992). ... Re-signed by Dolphins to practice squad (October 21, 1992). ... Activated (October 24, 1992). ... Released by Dolphins (October 28, 1992). ... Re-signed by Dolphins to practice squad (October 28, 1992). ... Released by Dolphins (November 18, 1992). ... Signed by Tampa Bay Buccaneers to practice squad (November 24, 1992). ... Activated (December 4, 1992). ... Granted free agency (February 16, 1996). ... Re-signed by Buccaneers (May 31, 1996). ... Granted unconditional free agency (February 14, 1997). ... Re-signed by Buccaneers (February 18, 1997). ... Granted unconditional free agency (February 11, 2000). ... Re-signed by Buccaneers (March 20, 2000). ... Released by Buccaneers (February 27, 2002). ... Signed by Buffalo Bills (March 11, 2002). ... Released by Bills (March 3, 2004). ... Signed by Buccaneers (March 3, 2004).

CHAMPIONSHIP GAME EXPERIENCE: Played in NFC championship game (1999 season).
SINGLE GAME HIGHS (regular season): Receptions—6 (November 2, 1997, vs. Indianapolis); yards—62 (November 3, 1996, vs. Chicago); and touchdown receptions—1 (November 30, 2003, vs. New York Giants).

			RECEIVING				TOTALS			
Year Team	G	GS	No.	Yds.	Avg.	TD	TD	2pt.	Pts.	Fum.
1992—Miami NFL	1	0	0	0	0.0	0	0	0	0	0
—Tampa Bay NFL	4	2	1	10	10.0	0	0	0	0	0
1993—Tampa Bay NFL	15	1	4	47	11.8	1	1	0	6	0
1994—Tampa Bay NFL	15	5	4	57	14.3	0	0	0	0	0
1995—Tampa Bay NFL	16	8	13	102	7.8	0	0	0	0	0
1996—Tampa Bay NFL	16	8	27	237	8.8	3	3	0	18	0
1997—Tampa Bay NFL	16	7	19	217	11.4	4	4	0	24	0
1998—Tampa Bay NFL	16	16	24	255	10.6	4	4	0	24	1
1999—Tampa Bay NFL	16	16	23	276	12.0	5	5	0	30	0
2000—Tampa Bay NFL	16	16	29	288	9.9	3	3	0	18	0
2001—Tampa Bay NFL	16	16	35	285	8.1	4	4	0	24	0
2002—Buffalo NFL	14	5	16	141	8.8	2	2	0	12	0
2003—Buffalo NFL	15	6	7	82	11.7	2	2	0	12	1
Pro totals (12 years)	176	106	202	1997	9.9	28	28	0	168	2

MOORE, EDDIE — LB — DOLPHINS

PERSONAL: Born July 5, 1980, in South Pittsburg, Tenn. ... 237. ... Full name: Eddie Deon Moore.
HIGH SCHOOL: Pittsburg (Tenn.).
COLLEGE: Tennessee.
TRANSACTIONS/CAREER NOTES: Selected by Miami Dolphins in second round (49th pick overall) of 2003 NFL draft. ... Signed by Dolphins (July 24, 2003). ... On injured reserve with foot injury (August 29, 2003-entire season).

			TOTALS		
Year Team	G	GS	Tk.	Ast.	Sks.
2003—Miami NFL			Did not play.		

MOORE, LARRY — C — BENGALS

PERSONAL: Born June 1, 1975, in San Diego, Calif. ... 6-2/309. ... Full name: Larry Maceo Moore.
HIGH SCHOOL: Monte Vista (Spring Valley, Calif.).
JUNIOR COLLEGE: Grossmont College (Calif.).
COLLEGE: Brigham Young.
TRANSACTIONS/CAREER NOTES: Signed as non-drafted free agent by Seattle Seahawks (April 25, 1997). ... Released by Seahawks (August 17, 1997). ... Signed by Washington Redskins to practice squad (August 26, 1997). ... Released by Redskins (September 3, 1997). ... Signed by Indianapolis Colts (January 29, 1998). ... Granted free agency (March 2, 2001). ... Re-signed by Colts (April 21, 2001). ... Granted unconditional free agency (March 1, 2002). ... Signed by Redskins (March 13, 2002). ... On injured reserve with foot injury (December 9, 2003-remainder of season). ... Released by Redskins (April 23, 2004). ... Signed by Cincinnati Bengals (April 30, 2004).
PLAYING EXPERIENCE: Indianapolis NFL, 1998-2001; Washington NFL, 2002-2003. ... Games/Games started: 1998 (6/5), 1999 (16/16), 2000 (16/16), 2001 (16/11), 2002 (16/16), 2003 (9/8). Total: 79/72.

M

MOORE, MICHAEL — G — FALCONS

PERSONAL: Born November 1, 1976, in Fayette, Ala. ... 6-2/318.
HIGH SCHOOL: Fayette (Ark.) County.
COLLEGE: Troy State.
TRANSACTIONS/CAREER NOTES: Selected by Washington Redskins in fourth round (129th pick overall) of 2000 NFL draft. ... Signed by Redskins (June 5, 2000). ... Released by Redskins (September 2, 2001). ... Signed by Denver Broncos (December 24, 2001). ... Released by Broncos (September 1, 2002). ... Re-signed by Broncos (October 23, 2002). ... Released by Broncos (October 28, 2002). ... Re-signed by Broncos (December 4, 2002). ... Released by Broncos (December 10, 2002). ... Signed by Atlanta Falcons (January 17, 2003). ... Waived by Falcons (August 30, 2003). ... Re-signed by Falcons (November 4, 2003).
PLAYING EXPERIENCE: Washington NFL, 2000; Atlanta NFL, 2003. ... Games/Games started: 2000 (5/1), 2003 (2/0). Total: 7/1.

MOORE, RASHAD — DT — SEAHAWKS

PERSONAL: Born March 16, 1979, in Huntsville, Ala. ... 6-3/324. ... Full name: Glenn Rashad Moore.
HIGH SCHOOL: Johnson (Huntsville, Ala.).
COLLEGE: Tennessee.
TRANSACTIONS/CAREER NOTES: Selected by Seattle Seahawks in sixth round (183rd pick overall) of 2003 NFL draft. ... Signed by Seahawks (July 16, 2003).

			TOTALS		
Year Team	G	GS	Tk.	Ast.	Sks.
2003—Seattle NFL	13	6	20	10	1.0

MOOREHEAD, AARON — WR — COLTS

PERSONAL: Born November 5, 1980, in Aurora, Colo. ... 6-3/200.
COLLEGE: Illinois.
TRANSACTIONS/CAREER NOTES: Signed as non-drafted free agent by Indianapolis Colts (May 5, 2003).

CHAMPIONSHIP GAME EXPERIENCE: Member of Colts for AFC championship game (2003 season); inactive.
SINGLE GAME HIGHS (regular season): Receptions—5 (November 23, 2003, vs. Buffalo); yards—71(November 23, 2003, vs. Buffalo); and touchdown receptions—0.

			RECEIVING				TOTALS			
Year Team	G	GS	No.	Yds.	Avg.	TD	TD	2pt.	Pts.	Fum.
2003—Indianapolis NFL	7	0	7	101	14.4	0	0	0	0	1

MOOREHEAD, KINDAL DT PANTHERS

PERSONAL: Born October 14, 1978, in Memphis, Tenn. ... 6-2/285.
HIGH SCHOOL: Melrose (Memphis, Tenn.).
COLLEGE: Alabama.
TRANSACTIONS/CAREER NOTES: Selected by Carolina Panthers in fifth round (145th pick overall) of 2003 NFL draft. ... Signed by Panthers (July 26, 2003).
CHAMPIONSHIP GAME EXPERIENCE: Member of Panthers for NFC championship game (2003 season); inactive. ... Member of Panthers for Super Bowl 38 (2003 season); inactive.

			TOTALS		
Year Team	G	GS	Tk.	Ast.	Sks.
2003—Carolina NFL	14	0	6	4	0.0

MOORMAN, BRIAN P BILLS

PERSONAL: Born February 5, 1976, in Wichita, Kan. ... 6-0/175.
HIGH SCHOOL: Segdwick (Kan.).
COLLEGE: Pittsburg State.
TRANSACTIONS/CAREER NOTES: Signed as non-drafted free agent by Seattle Seahawks (February 24, 1999). ... Released by Seahawks (August 30, 1999). ... Re-signed by Seahawks (February 17, 2000). ... Assigned by Seahawks to Berlin Thunder in 2000 NFL Europe enhancement allocation program (February 18, 2000). ... Released by Seahawks (August 27, 2000). ... Signed by Buffalo Bills (July 20, 2001).

		PUNTING					
Year Team	G	No.	Yds.	Avg.	Net avg.	In. 20	Blk.
2001—Buffalo NFL	16	80	3262	40.8	33.8	16	0
2002—Buffalo NFL	16	66	2844	43.1	36.0	18	1
2003—Buffalo NFL	16	85	3788	44.6	37.1	20	0
Pro totals (3 years)	48	231	9894	42.8	35.6	54	1

MORAN, SEAN DE RAMS

PERSONAL: Born June 5, 1973, in Denver, Colo. ... 6-4/275. ... Full name: Sean Farrell Moran.
HIGH SCHOOL: Overland (Aurora, Colo.).
COLLEGE: Colorado State.
TRANSACTIONS/CAREER NOTES: Selected by Buffalo Bills in fourth round (120th pick overall) of 1996 NFL draft. ... Signed by Bills (July 9, 1996). ... Granted free agency (February 12, 1999). ... Re-signed by Bills (April 1, 1999). ... Granted unconditional free agency (February 11, 2000). ... Signed by St. Louis Rams (March 15, 2000). ... Granted unconditional free agency (March 1, 2002). ... Signed by San Francisco 49ers (April 4, 2002). ... Released by 49ers (February 26, 2004). ... Signed by Rams (March 25, 2004).
CHAMPIONSHIP GAME EXPERIENCE: Played in NFC championship game (2001 season). ... Played in Super Bowl 36 (2001 season).

			TOTALS			INTERCEPTIONS			
Year Team	G	GS	Tk.	Ast.	Sks.	No.	Yds.	Avg.	TD
1996—Buffalo NFL	16	0	4	1	0.0	0	0	0.0	0
1997—Buffalo NFL	16	7	24	13	4.5	2	12	6.0	0
1998—Buffalo NFL	9	2	0	0	0.0	0	0	0.0	0
1999—Buffalo NFL	16	0	7	4	0.5	0	0	0.0	0
2000—St. Louis NFL	15	3	6	3	2.0	0	0	0.0	0
2001—St. Louis NFL	16	1	11	5	2.0	0	0	0.0	0
2002—San Francisco NFL	16	0	6	3	0.0	0	0	0.0	0
2003—San Francisco NFL	16	0	11	3	1.5	0	0	0.0	0
Pro totals (8 years)	120	13	69	32	10.5	2	12	6.0	0

MORENO, ZEKE LB CHARGERS

PERSONAL: Born October 10, 1978, in Chula Vista, Calif. ... 6-2/246. ... Full name: Ezekiel Aaron Moreno.
HIGH SCHOOL: Castle Park (Chula Vista, Calif.).
COLLEGE: Southern California.
TRANSACTIONS/CAREER NOTES: Selected by San Diego Chargers in fifth round (139th pick overall) of 2001 NFL draft. ... Signed by Chargers (July 19, 2001). ... Granted free agency (March 3, 2004). ... Re-signed by Chargers (May 13, 2004).

			TOTALS			INTERCEPTIONS			
Year Team	G	GS	Tk.	Ast.	Sks.	No.	Yds.	Avg.	TD
2001—San Diego NFL	16	0	5	1	1.0	0	0	0.0	0
2002—San Diego NFL	16	3	28	4	0.0	1	8	8.0	0
2003—San Diego NFL	16	13	78	17	2.0	0	0	0.0	0
Pro totals (3 years)	48	16	111	22	3.0	1	8	8.0	0

MOREY, SEAN — WR — EAGLES

PERSONAL: Born February 26, 1976, in Marshfield, Mass. ... 5-11/200. ... Full name: Sean Joseph Morey.
HIGH SCHOOL: Marshfield (Mass.).
COLLEGE: Brown.
TRANSACTIONS/CAREER NOTES: Selected by New England Patriots in seventh round (241st pick overall) of 1999 NFL draft. ... Signed by Patriots (June 10, 1999). ... Released by Patriots (September 15, 1999). ... Re-signed by Patriots to practice squad (September 16, 1999). ... Activated (December 7, 1999). ... Assigned by Patriots to Barcelona Dragons in 2000 NFL Europe enhancement allocation program (February 18, 2000). ... Released by Patriots (August 27, 2000). ... Re-signed by Patriots to practice squad (October 18, 2000). ... Released by Patriots (December 6, 2000). ... Signed by Patriots (January 3, 2001). ... Assigned by Patriots to Barcelona Dragons in 2001 NFL Europe enhancement allocation program (February 19, 2001). ... Released by Patriots (September 2, 2001). ... Signed by Philadelphia Eagles (January 8, 2002). ... Released by Eagles (September 1, 2002). ... Re-signed by Eagles and assigned to NFL Europe (January 30, 2003).
CHAMPIONSHIP GAME EXPERIENCE: Played in NFC championship game (2001 and 2003 seasons).

			RECEIVING				KICKOFF RETURNS				TOTALS			
Year Team	G	GS	No.	Yds.	Avg.	TD	No.	Yds.	Avg.	TD	TD	2pt.	Pts.	Fum.
1999—New England NFL	2	0	0	0	0.0	0	0	0	0.0	0	0	0	0	0
2003—Philadelphia NFL	16	0	0	0	0.0	0	7	93	13.3	0	0	0	0	1
Pro totals (2 years)	18	0	0	0	0.0	0	7	93	13.3	0	0	0	0	1

MORGAN, DAN — LB — PANTHERS

PERSONAL: Born December 19, 1978, in Coral Springs, Fla. ... 6-2/233. ... Full name: Daniel Thomas Morgan Jr.
HIGH SCHOOL: Taravella (Coral Springs, Fla.).
COLLEGE: Miami (Fla.).
TRANSACTIONS/CAREER NOTES: Selected by Carolina Panthers in first round (11th pick overall) of 2001 NFL draft. ... Signed by Panthers (July 21, 2001). ... On injured reserve with shoulder injury (December 12, 2002-remainder of season). ... Inactive for five games (2003) due to concussion and hamstring injuries.
CHAMPIONSHIP GAME EXPERIENCE: Played in NFC championship game (2003 season). ... Played in Super Bowl 38 (2003 season).
HONORS: Named linebacker on THE SPORTING NEWS college All-America first team (2000). ... Butkus Award winner (2000). ... Bronko Nagurski Award winner (2000).

			TOTALS			INTERCEPTIONS			
Year Team	G	GS	Tk.	Ast.	Sks.	No.	Yds.	Avg.	TD
2001—Carolina NFL	11	11	45	22	1.0	1	10	10.0	0
2002—Carolina NFL	8	8	39	15	1.0	2	26	13.0	0
2003—Carolina NFL	11	11	46	20	0.0	0	0	0.0	0
Pro totals (3 years)	30	30	130	57	2.0	3	36	12.0	0

MORGAN, DWAYNE — T — FALCONS

M

PERSONAL: Born May 3, 1974, in Griffin, Ga. ... 6-4/300.
COLLEGE: Clemson.
TRANSACTIONS/CAREER NOTES: Signed as non-drafted free agent by Atlanta Falcons (February 5, 2003). ... Waived by Falcons (August 30, 2003). ... Re-signed by Falcons to practice squad (September 2, 2003). ... Activated (November 3, 2003). ... On injured reserve with knee injury (December 9, 2003-remainder of season).
PLAYING EXPERIENCE: Atlanta NFL, 2003. ... Games/Games started: 2003 (5/0). Total: 5/0.

MORGAN, QUINCY — WR — BROWNS

PERSONAL: Born September 23, 1977, in Garland, Texas. ... 6-1/210.
HIGH SCHOOL: South Garland (Texas).
COLLEGE: Kansas State.
TRANSACTIONS/CAREER NOTES: Selected by Cleveland Browns in second round (33rd pick overall) of 2001 NFL draft. ... Signed by Browns (July 23, 2001).
HONORS: Named wide receiver on THE SPORTING NEWS college All-America third team (2000).
SINGLE GAME HIGHS (regular season): Receptions—9 (September 8, 2002, vs. Kansas City); yards—151 (September 8, 2002, vs. Kansas City); and touchdown receptions—2 (December 8, 2002, vs. Jacksonville).
STATISTICAL PLATEAUS: 100-yard receiving games: 2002 (2), 2003 (1). Total: 3.

			RUSHING				RECEIVING				KICKOFF RETURNS				TOTALS			
Year Team	G	GS	Att.	Yds.	Avg.	TD	No.	Yds.	Avg.	TD	No.	Yds.	Avg.	TD	TD	2pt.	Pts.	Fum.
2001—Cleveland NFL	16	10	2	27	13.5	0	30	432	14.4	2	7	175	25.0	0	2	0	12	3
2002—Cleveland NFL	16	16	3	7	2.3	0	56	964	*17.2	7	0	0	0.0	0	7	1	44	2
2003—Cleveland NFL	16	15	3	-4	-1.3	0	38	516	13.6	3	2	67	33.5	0	3	0	18	0
Pro totals (3 years)	48	41	8	30	3.8	0	124	1912	15.4	12	9	242	26.9	0	12	1	74	5

MORRIS, ARIC — S

PERSONAL: Born July 22, 1977, in Winston-Salem, N.C. ... 5-10/210.
HIGH SCHOOL: Berkley (Mich.).
COLLEGE: Michigan State.
TRANSACTIONS/CAREER NOTES: Selected by Tennessee Titans in fifth round (135th pick overall) of 2000 NFL draft. ... Signed by Titans (July 5, 2000). ... Released by Titans (March 23, 2003). ... Signed by New England Patriots (May 9, 2003). ... Released by Patriots (October 7, 2003).
CHAMPIONSHIP GAME EXPERIENCE: Played in AFC championship game (2002 season).

Year Team	G	GS	TOTALS Tk.	Ast.	Sks.	INTERCEPTIONS No.	Yds.	Avg.	TD
2000—Tennessee NFL	15	0	1	0	0.0	0	0	0.0	0
2001—Tennessee NFL	16	10	33	14	1.5	0	0	0.0	0
2002—Tennessee NFL	16	0	7	2	0.0	0	0	0.0	0
2003—New England NFL	4	0	0	0	0.0	1	33	33.0	0
Pro totals (4 years)	51	10	41	16	1.5	1	33	33.0	0

MORRIS, MAURICE RB SEAHAWKS

PERSONAL: Born December 1, 1979, in Chester, S.C. ... 5-11/202. ... Full name: Maurice Autora Morris.
HIGH SCHOOL: Chester (S.C.).
JUNIOR COLLEGE: Fresno City College.
COLLEGE: Oregon.
TRANSACTIONS/CAREER NOTES: Selected by Seattle Seahawks in second round (54th pick overall) of 2002 NFL draft. ... Signed by Seahawks (July 25, 2002).
SINGLE GAME HIGHS (regular season): Attempts—15 (November 10, 2002, vs. Arizona); yards—72 (November 10, 2002, vs. Arizona); and rushing touchdowns—0.

Year Team	G	GS	RUSHING Att.	Yds.	Avg.	TD	RECEIVING No.	Yds.	Avg.	TD	KICKOFF RETURNS No.	Yds.	Avg.	TD	TOTALS TD	2pt.	Pts.	Fum.
2002—Seattle NFL	11	0	32	153	4.8	0	3	25	8.3	0	34	821	24.1	1	1	0	6	1
2003—Seattle NFL	16	1	38	239	6.3	0	4	32	8.0	1	47	1007	21.4	0	1	0	6	2
Pro totals (2 years)	27	1	70	392	5.6	0	7	57	8.1	1	81	1828	22.6	1	2	0	12	3

MORRIS, ROB LB COLTS

PERSONAL: Born January 18, 1975, in Nampa, Idaho. ... 6-2/243. ... Full name: Robert Samuel Morris.
HIGH SCHOOL: Nampa (Idaho).
COLLEGE: Brigham Young.
TRANSACTIONS/CAREER NOTES: Selected by Indianapolis Colts in first round (28th pick overall) of 2000 NFL draft. ... Signed by Colts (July 26, 2000). ... On injured reserve with knee injury (October 25, 2000-remainder of season).
CHAMPIONSHIP GAME EXPERIENCE: Played in AFC championship game (2003 season).
HONORS: Named linebacker on THE SPORTING NEWS college All-America second team (1999).

Year Team	G	GS	TOTALS Tk.	Ast.	Sks.	INTERCEPTIONS No.	Yds.	Avg.	TD
2000—Indianapolis NFL	7	0	8	3	0.0	0	0	0.0	0
2001—Indianapolis NFL	14	14	84	30	1.0	0	0	0.0	0
2002—Indianapolis NFL	16	16	76	24	3.0	0	0	0.0	0
2003—Indianapolis NFL	16	16	58	25	0.0	0	0	0.0	0
Pro totals (4 years)	53	46	226	82	4.0	0	0	0.0	0

MORRIS, SAMMY RB DOLPHINS

M

PERSONAL: Born March 23, 1977, in San Antonio, Texas. ... 6-0/220. ... Full name: Samuel Morris III.
HIGH SCHOOL: John Jay (San Antonio).
COLLEGE: Texas Tech.
TRANSACTIONS/CAREER NOTES: Selected by Buffalo Bills in fifth round (156th pick overall) of 2000 NFL draft. ... Signed by Bills (June 21, 2000). ... Granted free agency (February 28, 2003). ... Re-signed by Bills (April 17, 2003). ... Granted unconditional free agency (March 3, 2004). ... Signed by Miami Dolphins (March 12, 2004).
SINGLE GAME HIGHS (regular season): Attempts—19 (October 29, 2000, vs. New York Jets); yards—60 (October 15, 2000, vs. San Diego); and rushing touchdowns—1 (November 23, 2003, vs. Indianapolis).

Year Team	G	GS	RUSHING Att.	Yds.	Avg.	TD	RECEIVING No.	Yds.	Avg.	TD	KICKOFF RETURNS No.	Yds.	Avg.	TD	TOTALS TD	2pt.	Pts.	Fum.
2000—Buffalo NFL	12	8	93	341	3.7	5	37	268	7.2	1	1	17	17.0	0	6	0	36	2
2001—Buffalo NFL	16	1	20	72	3.6	0	7	36	5.1	0	0	0	0.0	0	0	0	0	1
2002—Buffalo NFL	16	0	2	5	2.5	0	3	48	16.0	0	1	0	0.0	0	0	0	0	0
2003—Buffalo NFL	9	0	19	70	3.7	1	14	100	7.1	0	6	146	24.3	0	1	0	6	0
Pro totals (4 years)	53	9	134	488	3.6	6	61	452	7.4	1	8	163	20.4	0	7	0	42	3

MORROW, HAROLD FB RAVENS

PERSONAL: Born February 24, 1973, in Maplesville, Ala. ... 5-11/232. ... Full name: Harold Morrow Jr.
HIGH SCHOOL: Maplesville (Ala.).
COLLEGE: Auburn.
TRANSACTIONS/CAREER NOTES: Signed as non-drafted free agent by Dallas Cowboys (April 25, 1996). ... Claimed on waivers by Minnesota Vikings (August 26, 1996). ... Granted free agency (February 12, 1999). ... Re-signed by Vikings (April 23, 1999). ... Granted unconditional free agency (February 11, 2000). ... Re-signed by Vikings (March 7, 2000). ... Granted unconditional free agency (March 1, 2002). ... Re-signed by Vikings (March 6, 2002). ... Released by Vikings (February 27, 2003). ... Signed by Baltimore Ravens (March 6, 2003).
CHAMPIONSHIP GAME EXPERIENCE: Played in NFC championship game (1998 and 2000 seasons).
SINGLE GAME HIGHS (regular season): Attempts—5 (January 7, 2002, vs. Baltimore); yards—24 (December 30, 2001, vs. Green Bay); and rushing touchdowns—0.

Year Team	G	GS	RUSHING Att.	Yds.	Avg.	TD	TOTALS TD	2pt.	Pts.	Fum.
1996—Minnesota NFL	8	0	0	0	0.0	0	0	0	0	0

Year Team	G	GS	RUSHING Att.	Yds.	Avg.	TD	TOTALS TD	2pt.	Pts.	Fum.
1997—Minnesota NFL	16	0	0	0	0.0	0	0	0	0	0
1998—Minnesota NFL	11	0	3	7	2.3	0	0	0	0	0
1999—Minnesota NFL	16	0	2	1	0.5	0	0	0	0	0
2000—Minnesota NFL	16	0	0	0	0.0	0	0	0	0	0
2001—Minnesota NFL	16	2	12	67	5.6	0	0	0	0	1
2002—Minnesota NFL	16	0	0	0	0.0	0	0	0	0	0
2003—Baltimore NFL	14	0	0	0	0.0	0	0	0	0	0
Pro totals (8 years)	113	2	17	75	4.4	0	0	0	0	1

MORTON, CHAD — RB/KR — REDSKINS

PERSONAL: Born April 4, 1977, in Torrance, Calif. ... 5-8/203. ... Brother of Johnnie Morton, wide receiver, Kansas City Chiefs; and half brother of Michael Morton, running back with Tampa Bay Buccaneers (1982-84), Washington Redskins (1985) and Seattle Seahawks (1987).

HIGH SCHOOL: South Torrance (Calif.).

COLLEGE: Southern California.

TRANSACTIONS/CAREER NOTES: Selected by New Orleans Saints in fifth round (166th pick overall) of 2000 NFL draft. ... Signed by Saints (July 11, 2000). ... Traded by Saints to New York Jets for CB Earthwind Moreland and sixth-round pick (TE John Gilmore) in 2002 draft (August 23, 2001). ... Granted free agency (February 28, 2003). ... Tendered offer sheet by Washington Redskins (March 6, 2003). ... Jets ruled not to have matched offer sheet by arbitrator (April 7, 2003).

RECORDS: Shares NFL single-game record for most kickoff return touchdowns—2 (September 8, 2002, New York Jets at Buffalo).

SINGLE GAME HIGHS (regular season): Attempts—13 (December 7, 2003, vs. New York Giants); yards—56 (December 7, 2003, vs. New York Giants); and rushing touchdowns—0.

Year Team	G	GS	RUSHING Att.	Yds.	Avg.	TD	RECEIVING No.	Yds.	Avg.	TD	PUNT RETURNS No.	Yds.	Avg.	TD	KICKOFF RETURNS No.	Yds.	Avg.	TD	TOTALS TD	2pt.	Pts.
2000—N.O. NFL	16	3	36	136	3.8	0	30	213	7.1	0	30	278	9.3	0	44	1029	23.4	0	0	0	0
2001—NYJ NFL	9	0	0	0	0.0	0	0	0	0.0	0	13	113	8.7	0	12	247	20.6	0	0	0	0
2002—NYJ NFL	16	0	4	8	2.0	0	3	19	6.3	0	4	51	12.8	0	58	§1509	26.0	†2	2	0	12
2003—Was. NFL	15	2	48	216	4.5	0	15	187	12.5	1	19	188	9.9	0	44	1029	23.4	1	2	0	12
Pro totals (4 years)	56	5	88	360	4.1	0	48	419	8.7	1	66	630	9.5	0	158	3814	24.1	3	4	0	24

MORTON, JOHNNIE — WR — CHIEFS

PERSONAL: Born October 7, 1971, in Inglewood, Calif. ... 6-0/190. ... Full name: Johnnie James Morton. ... Brother of Chad Morton, running back, Washington Redskins.

HIGH SCHOOL: South Torrance (Calif.).

COLLEGE: Southern California.

TRANSACTIONS/CAREER NOTES: Selected by Detroit Lions in first round (21st pick overall) of 1994 NFL draft. ... Signed by Lions (July 18, 1994). ... Released by Lions (March 14, 2002). ... Signed by Kansas City Chiefs (March 29, 2002).

HONORS: Named wide receiver on THE SPORTING NEWS college All-America first team (1993).

SINGLE GAME HIGHS (regular season): Receptions—10 (January 2, 2000, vs. Minnesota); yards—174 (September 22, 1996, vs. Chicago); and touchdown receptions—2 (January 2, 2000, vs. Minnesota).

STATISTICAL PLATEAUS: 100-yard receiving games: 1995 (1), 1996 (2), 1997 (3), 1998 (3), 1999 (5), 2001 (4), 2003 (1). Total: 19.

Year Team	G	GS	RUSHING Att.	Yds.	Avg.	TD	RECEIVING No.	Yds.	Avg.	TD	KICKOFF RETURNS No.	Yds.	Avg.	TD	TOTALS TD	2pt.	Pts.	Fum.
1994—Detroit NFL	14	0	0	0	0.0	0	3	39	13.0	1	4	143	35.7	1	2	0	12	1
1995—Detroit NFL	16	13	3	33	11.0	0	44	590	13.4	8	18	390	21.7	0	8	0	48	1
1996—Detroit NFL	16	15	9	35	3.9	0	55	714	13.0	6	0	0	0.0	0	6	0	36	1
1997—Detroit NFL	16	16	3	33	11.0	0	80	1057	13.2	6	0	0	0.0	0	6	0	36	2
1998—Detroit NFL	16	16	1	11	11.0	0	69	1028	14.9	2	0	0	0.0	0	2	0	12	0
1999—Detroit NFL	16	12	0	0	0.0	0	80	1129	14.1	5	1	22	22.0	0	5	0	30	0
2000—Detroit NFL	16	16	4	25	6.3	0	61	788	12.9	3	0	0	0.0	0	3	1	20	1
2001—Detroit NFL	16	16	1	6	6.0	0	77	1154	15.0	4	1	4	4.0	0	4	0	24	1
2002—Kansas City NFL	14	14	10	124	12.4	0	29	397	13.7	1	0	0	0.0	0	1	0	6	0
2003—Kansas City NFL	16	16	8	94	11.8	0	50	740	14.8	4	0	0	0.0	0	4	0	24	0
Pro totals (10 years)	156	134	39	361	9.3	0	548	7636	13.9	40	24	559	23.3	1	41	1	248	7

MOSES, J.J. — WR — TEXANS

PERSONAL: Born September 12, 1979, in Waterloo, Iowa. ... 5-6/178. ... Full name: Jerry James Moses Jr.

HIGH SCHOOL: Waterloo (Iowa).

COLLEGE: Iowa State.

TRANSACTIONS/CAREER NOTES: Signed as non-drafted free agent by Kansas City Chiefs (April 26, 2001). ... Released by Chiefs (August 27, 2001). ... Signed by Green Bay Packers to practice squad (September 26, 2001). ... Released by Packers (October 3, 2001). ... Signed by Chiefs to practice squad (November 21, 2001). ... Assigned by Chiefs to Scottish Claymores in 2002 NFL Europe enhancement allocation program (February 12, 2002). ... Released by Chiefs (September 1, 2002). ... Signed by Packers to practice squad (November 13, 2002). ... Released by Packers (November 28, 2002). ... Re-signed by Packers to practice squad (December 2, 2002). ... Activated (December 15, 2002). ... Released by Packers (December 24, 2002). ... Signed by Houston Texans (February 2, 2003).

Year Team	G	GS	RECEIVING No.	Yds.	Avg.	TD	PUNT RETURNS No.	Yds.	Avg.	TD	KICKOFF RETURNS No.	Yds.	Avg.	TD	TOTALS TD	2pt.	Pts.	Fum.
2002—Green Bay NFL	2	0	0	0	0.0	0	5	12	2.4	0	4	69	17.3	0	0	0	0	1
2003—Houston NFL	15	0	0	0	0.0	0	36	244	6.8	0	§58	1355	23.4	0	0	0	0	0
Pro totals (2 years)	17	0	0	0	0.0	0	41	256	6.2	0	62	1424	23.0	0	0	0	0	1

MOSS, RANDY — WR — VIKINGS

PERSONAL: Born February 13, 1977, in Rand, W.Va. ... 6-4/200. ... Half brother of Eric Moss, offensive lineman with Minnesota Vikings (1997-99).
HIGH SCHOOL: DuPont (Belle, W.Va.).
COLLEGE: Marshall.
TRANSACTIONS/CAREER NOTES: Selected after sophomore season by Minnesota Vikings in first round (21st pick overall) of 1998 NFL draft. ... Signed by Minnesota Vikings (July 26, 1998).
CHAMPIONSHIP GAME EXPERIENCE: Played in NFC championship game (1998 and 2000 seasons).
HONORS: Fred Biletnikoff Award winner (1997). ... Named wide receiver on THE SPORTING NEWS college All-America first team (1997). ... Named NFL Rookie of the Year by THE SPORTING NEWS (1998). ... Named wide receiver on THE SPORTING NEWS NFL All-Pro team (1998 and 2000). ... Played in Pro Bowl (1998 and 1999 seasons). ... Named Outstanding Player of Pro Bowl (1999). ... Named to play in Pro Bowl (2000 season); replaced by Joe Horn due to injury. ... Named to play in Pro Bowl (2002 season); replaced by Donald Driver due to injury. ... Named to play in Pro Bowl (2003 season); replaced by Laveranues Coles due to injury.
RECORDS: Holds NFL rookie-season record for most receiving touchdowns—17 (1998).
SINGLE GAME HIGHS (regular season): Receptions—12 (November 14, 1999, vs. Chicago); yards—204 (November 14, 1999, vs. Chicago); and touchdown receptions—3 (September 28, 2003, vs. San Francisco).
STATISTICAL PLATEAUS: 100-yard receiving games: 1998 (4), 1999 (7), 2000 (8), 2001 (4), 2002 (7), 2003 (8). Total: 38.

			RECEIVING				PUNT RETURNS				TOTALS			
Year Team	G	GS	No.	Yds.	Avg.	TD	No.	Yds.	Avg.	TD	TD	2pt.	Pts.	Fum.
1998—Minnesota NFL	16	11	69	1313	‡19.0	*17	1	0	0.0	0	‡17	†2	106	2
1999—Minnesota NFL	16	16	80	‡1413	17.7	11	17	162	9.5	∞1	12	0	72	3
2000—Minnesota NFL	16	16	77	1437	18.7	*15	0	0	0.0	0	15	1	92	2
2001—Minnesota NFL	16	16	82	1233	15.0	10	0	0	0.0	0	10	0	60	0
2002—Minnesota NFL	16	16	‡106	‡1347	12.7	7	0	0	0.0	0	7	0	42	1
2003—Minnesota NFL	16	16	111	1632	14.7	*17	0	0	0.0	0	17	0	102	1
Pro totals (6 years)	96	91	525	8375	16.0	77	18	162	9.0	1	78	3	474	9

MOSS, SANTANA — WR — JETS

PERSONAL: Born June 1, 1979, in Miami, Fla. ... 5-10/185. ... Full name: Santana Terrell Moss.
HIGH SCHOOL: Carol City (Miami).
COLLEGE: Miami (Fla.).
TRANSACTIONS/CAREER NOTES: Selected by New York Jets in first round (16th pick overall) of 2001 NFL draft. ... Signed by Jets (July 28, 2001).
HONORS: Named kick returner on THE SPORTING NEWS college All-America first team (2000). ... Named punt returner on the THE SPORTING NEWS NFL All-Pro team (2002).
SINGLE GAME HIGHS (regular season): Receptions—10 (November 2, 2003, vs. New York Giants); yards—146 (November 9, 2003, vs. Oakland); and touchdown receptions—3 (November 2, 2003, vs. New York Giants).
STATISTICAL PLATEAUS: 100-yard receiving games: 2002 (1), 2003 (4). Total: 5.

			RECEIVING				PUNT RETURNS				TOTALS			
Year Team	G	GS	No.	Yds.	Avg.	TD	No.	Yds.	Avg.	TD	TD	2pt.	Pts.	Fum.
2001—New York Jets NFL	5	0	2	40	20.0	0	6	82	13.7	0	0	0	0	0
2002—New York Jets NFL	15	1	30	433	14.4	4	25	§413	§16.5	†2	6	0	36	2
2003—New York Jets NFL	16	12	74	1105	14.9	10	30	332	11.1	0	10	0	60	4
Pro totals (3 years)	36	13	106	1578	14.9	14	61	827	13.6	2	16	0	96	6

MOULDS, ERIC — WR — BILLS

PERSONAL: Born July 17, 1973, in Lucedale, Miss. ... 6-2/210. ... Full name: Eric Shannon Moulds.
HIGH SCHOOL: George County (Lucedale, Miss.).
COLLEGE: Mississippi State.
TRANSACTIONS/CAREER NOTES: Selected by Buffalo Bills in first round (24th pick overall) of 1996 NFL draft. ... Signed by Bills (July 16, 1996).
HONORS: Played in Pro Bowl (1998, 2000-2002 seasons).
POST SEASON RECORDS: Holds NFL postseason single-game record for most yards receiving—240 (January 2, 1999, vs. Miami).
SINGLE GAME HIGHS (regular season): Receptions—12 (October 22, 2000, vs. Minnesota); yards—196 (November 25, 2001, vs. Miami); and touchdown receptions—2 (December 8, 2002, vs. New England).
STATISTICAL PLATEAUS: 100-yard receiving games: 1998 (4), 1999 (3), 2000 (7), 2001 (2), 2002 (5), 2003 (2). Total: 23.

			RUSHING				RECEIVING				KICKOFF RETURNS				TOTALS			
Year Team	G	GS	Att.	Yds.	Avg.	TD	No.	Yds.	Avg.	TD	No.	Yds.	Avg.	TD	TD	2pt.	Pts.	Fum.
1996—Buffalo NFL	16	5	12	44	3.7	0	20	279	14.0	2	52	1205	23.2	▲1	3	0	18	1
1997—Buffalo NFL	16	8	4	59	14.8	0	29	294	10.1	0	43	921	21.4	0	0	1	2	3
1998—Buffalo NFL	16	15	0	0	0.0	0	67	§1368	20.4	9	0	0	0.0	0	9	0	54	0
1999—Buffalo NFL	14	14	1	1	1.0	0	65	994	15.3	7	0	0	0.0	0	7	0	42	1
2000—Buffalo NFL	16	16	2	24	12.0	0	94	1326	14.1	5	0	0	0.0	0	5	0	30	1
2001—Buffalo NFL	16	16	3	3	1.0	0	67	904	13.5	5	0	0	0.0	0	5	1	32	1
2002—Buffalo NFL	16	15	1	7	7.0	0	100	1292	12.9	10	0	0	0.0	0	10	0	60	1
2003—Buffalo NFL	13	13	0	0	0.0	0	64	780	12.2	1	0	0	0.0	0	1	0	6	0
Pro totals (8 years)	123	102	23	138	6.0	0	506	7237	14.3	39	95	2126	22.4	1	40	2	244	8

MUGHELLI, OVIE — FB — RAVENS

PERSONAL: Born June 10, 1980, in Boston, Mass. ... 6-1/260.
HIGH SCHOOL: Porter-Gaud (Charleston, S.C.).
COLLEGE: Wake Forest.

TRANSACTIONS/CAREER NOTES: Selected by Baltimore Ravens in fourth round (134th pick overall) of 2003 NFL draft.

			RUSHING				RECEIVING				TOTALS			
Year Team	G	GS	Att.	Yds.	Avg.	TD	No.	Yds.	Avg.	TD	TD	2pt.	Pts.	Fum.
2003—Baltimore NFL	6	0	0	0	0.0	0	0	0	0.0	0	0	0	0	0

MUHAMMAD, MUHSIN WR PANTHERS

PERSONAL: Born May 5, 1973, in Lansing, Mich. ... 6-2/217. ... Full name: Muhsin Muhammad II. ... Name pronounced: moo-SIN moo-HAH-med.
HIGH SCHOOL: Waverly (Lansing, Mich.).
COLLEGE: Michigan State.
TRANSACTIONS/CAREER NOTES: Selected by Carolina Panthers in second round (43rd pick overall) of 1996 NFL draft. ... Signed by Panthers (July 23, 1996).
CHAMPIONSHIP GAME EXPERIENCE: Played in NFC championship game (1996 and 2003 seasons). ... Played in Super Bowl 38 (2003 season).
HONORS: Played in Pro Bowl (1999 season).
POST SEASON RECORDS: Holds Super Bowl record for longest pass completion (from Jake Delhomme)—85 yards (February 1, 2004, vs. New England).
SINGLE GAME HIGHS (regular season): Receptions—11 (November 27, 2000, vs. Green Bay); yards—192 (September 13, 1998, vs. New Orleans); and touchdown receptions—3 (December 18, 1999, vs. San Francisco).
STATISTICAL PLATEAUS: 100-yard receiving games: 1998 (3), 1999 (5), 2000 (5), 2001 (2), 2002 (3), 2003 (1). Total: 19.
MISCELLANEOUS: Holds Carolina Panthers all-time records for most receiving yards (6,346) and most receptions (485).

			RUSHING				RECEIVING				TOTALS			
Year Team	G	GS	Att.	Yds.	Avg.	TD	No.	Yds.	Avg.	TD	TD	2pt.	Pts.	Fum.
1996—Carolina NFL	9	5	1	-1	-1.0	0	25	407	16.3	1	1	0	6	0
1997—Carolina NFL	13	5	0	0	0.0	0	27	317	11.7	0	0	1	2	0
1998—Carolina NFL	16	16	0	0	0.0	0	68	941	13.8	6	6	1	38	2
1999—Carolina NFL	15	15	0	0	0.0	0	‡96	1253	13.1	8	8	0	48	1
2000—Carolina NFL	16	16	2	12	6.0	0	†102	1183	11.6	6	6	0	36	1
2001—Carolina NFL	11	11	0	0	0.0	0	50	585	11.7	1	1	0	6	2
2002—Carolina NFL	14	14	3	40	13.3	0	63	823	13.1	3	3	0	18	0
2003—Carolina NFL	15	15	2	-2	-1.0	0	54	837	15.5	3	3	0	18	3
Pro totals (8 years)	109	97	8	49	6.1	0	485	6346	13.1	28	28	2	172	9

MULITALO, EDWIN G RAVENS

PERSONAL: Born September 1, 1974, in Daly City, Calif. ... 6-3/345. ... Full name: Edwin Moliki Mulitalo. ... Name pronounced: moo-lih-TAHL-oh.
HIGH SCHOOL: Jefferson (Daly City, Calif.).
JUNIOR COLLEGE: Ricks College (Idaho).
COLLEGE: Arizona.
TRANSACTIONS/CAREER NOTES: Selected by Baltimore Ravens in fourth round (129th pick overall) of 1999 NFL draft. ... Signed by Ravens (July 29, 1999). ... Granted free agency (March 1, 2002). ... Re-signed by Ravens (June 17, 2002).
PLAYING EXPERIENCE: Baltimore NFL, 1999-2003. ... Games/Games started: 1999 (10/8), 2000 (16/16), 2001 (14/14), 2002 (16/15), 2003 (15/15). Total: 71/68.
CHAMPIONSHIP GAME EXPERIENCE: Played in AFC championship game (2000 season). ... Member of Super Bowl championship team (2000 season).

M

MUNGRO, JAMES RB COLTS

PERSONAL: Born February 13, 1978, in East Stroudsburg, Pa. ... 5-9/214. ... Full name: James Alevia Mungro II.
HIGH SCHOOL: East Stroudsburg (Pa.).
COLLEGE: Syracuse.
TRANSACTIONS/CAREER NOTES: Signed as non-drafted free agent by Detroit Lions (April 26, 2002). ... Claimed on waivers by Indianapolis Colts (September 3, 2002). ... On injured reserve with toe injury (December 2, 2003-remainder of season).
SINGLE GAME HIGHS (regular season): Attempts—28 (November 10, 2002, vs. Philadelphia); yards—114 (November 10, 2002, vs. Philadelphia); and rushing touchdowns—2 (December 15, 2002, vs. Cleveland).
STATISTICAL PLATEAUS: 100-yard rushing games: 2002 (1). Total: 1.

			RUSHING				RECEIVING				TOTALS			
Year Team	G	GS	Att.	Yds.	Avg.	TD	No.	Yds.	Avg.	TD	TD	2pt.	Pts.	Fum.
2002—Indianapolis NFL	9	1	97	336	3.5	8	13	81	6.2	0	8	0	48	3
2003—Indianapolis NFL	7	0	24	60	2.5	2	1	-4	-4.0	0	2	1	14	0
Pro totals (2 years)	16	1	121	396	3.3	10	14	77	5.5	0	10	1	62	3

MURPHY, MATT TE TEXANS

PERSONAL: Born February 23, 1980, in New Haven, Mich. ... 6-5/260.
HIGH SCHOOL: New Haven (Mich.).
COLLEGE: Maryland.
TRANSACTIONS/CAREER NOTES: Selected by Detroit Lions in seventh round (252nd pick overall) of 2002 NFL draft. ... Signed by Lions (July 18, 2002). ... Released by Lions (August 31, 2003). ... Re-signed by Lions to practice squad (September 1, 2003). ... Signed by Houston Texans off Lions practice squad (December 10, 2003).
SINGLE GAME HIGHS (regular season): Receptions—1 (December 29, 2002, vs. Minnesota); yards—8 (December 29, 2002, vs. Minnesota); and touchdown receptions—0.

Year Team	G	GS	RECEIVING No.	Yds.	Avg.	TD	TOTALS TD	2pt.	Pts.	Fum.
2002—Detroit NFL	3	0	1	8	8.0	0	0	0	0	0
2003—Houston NFL	1	0	0	0	0.0	0	0	0	0	0
Pro totals (2 years)	4	0	1	8	8.0	0	0	0	0	0

MURPHY, ROB C 49ERS

PERSONAL: Born January 18, 1977, in Buffalo, N.Y. ... 6-5/310. ... Full name: Robert Donald Murphy.

HIGH SCHOOL: Moeller (Cincinnati).

COLLEGE: Ohio State.

TRANSACTIONS/CAREER NOTES: Signed as non-drafted free agent by Cincinnati Bengals (July 9, 1999). ... Released by Bengals (August 30, 1999). ... Signed by Kansas City Chiefs (January 11, 2000). ... Allocated by Chiefs to Frankfurt Galaxy in 2000 NFL Europe enhancement allocation program (February 18, 2000). ... Released by Chiefs (September 18, 2000). ... Signed by Indianapolis Colts (April 22, 2001). ... Released by Colts (September 1, 2001). ... Re-signed by Colts to practice squad (September 3, 2001). ... Activated (March 23, 2003). ... Released by Colts (July 25, 2003). ... Signed by San Francisco 49ers (August 1, 2003). ... Waived by 49ers (August 31, 2003). ... Re-signed by 49ers (November 26, 2003).

PLAYING EXPERIENCE: Indianapolis NFL, 2002; San Francisco NFL, 2003. ... Games/Games started: 2002 (9/0), 2003 (2/0). Total: 11/0.

MURRELL, ADRIAN RB

PERSONAL: Born October 16, 1970, in Fayetteville, N.C. ... 5-11/211. ... Full name: Adrian Bryan Murrell.

HIGH SCHOOL: Leilehua (Wahiawa, Hawaii).

COLLEGE: West Virginia.

TRANSACTIONS/CAREER NOTES: Selected by New York Jets in fifth round (120th pick overall) of 1993 NFL draft. ... Signed by Jets (July 22, 1993). ... Granted free agency (February 16, 1996). ... Re-signed by Jets (April 21, 1996). ... Traded by Jets with seventh-round pick (DE Jomo Cousins) in 1998 draft to Arizona Cardinals for third-round pick (traded to St. Louis) in 1998 draft (April 7, 1998). ... Granted unconditional free agency (February 11, 2000). ... Signed by Washington Redskins (March 22, 2000). ... Granted unconditional free agency (March 2, 2001). ... Signed by Carolina Panthers (May 3, 2001). ... Released by Panthers (June 7, 2001). ... Signed by Dallas Cowboys (August 13, 2003). ... Released by Cowboys (August 31, 2003). ... Re-signed by Cowboys (October 29, 2003). ... Released by Cowboys (November 21, 2003).

SINGLE GAME HIGHS (regular season): Attempts—40 (September 28, 1997, vs. Cincinnati); yards—199 (October 27, 1996, vs. Arizona); and rushing touchdowns—2 (November 10, 1996, vs. New England).

STATISTICAL PLATEAUS: 100-yard rushing games: 1995 (1), 1996 (5), 1997 (3), 1998 (3). Total: 12.

Year Team	G	GS	RUSHING Att.	Yds.	Avg.	TD	RECEIVING No.	Yds.	Avg.	TD	KICKOFF RETURNS No.	Yds.	Avg.	TD	TOTALS TD	2pt.	Pts.	Fum.
1993—New York Jets NFL	16	0	34	157	4.6	1	5	12	2.4	0	23	342	14.9	0	1	0	6	4
1994—New York Jets NFL	10	1	33	160	4.8	0	7	76	10.9	0	14	268	19.1	0	0	0	0	1
1995—New York Jets NFL	15	9	192	795	4.1	1	71	465	6.5	2	1	5	5.0	0	3	0	18	2
1996—New York Jets NFL	16	16	301	1249	4.1	6	17	81	4.8	1	0	0	0.0	0	7	0	42	6
1997—New York Jets NFL	16	15	300	1086	3.6	7	27	106	3.9	0	0	0	0.0	0	7	0	42	4
1998—Arizona NFL	15	14	274	1042	3.8	8	18	169	9.4	2	0	0	0.0	0	10	0	60	6
1999—Arizona NFL	16	12	193	553	2.9	0	49	335	6.8	0	0	0	0.0	0	0	0	0	4
2000—Washington NFL	15	0	20	50	2.5	0	16	93	5.8	0	12	214	17.8	0	0	0	0	1
2003—Dallas NFL	3	0	28	107	3.8	0	4	32	8.0	0	0	0	0.0	0	0	0	0	0
Pro totals (9 years)	122	67	1375	5199	3.8	23	214	1369	6.4	5	50	829	16.6	0	28	0	168	28

M

MUSTARD, CHAD TE BROWNS

PERSONAL: Born October 8, 1977, in Central City, Neb. ... 6-6/288.

HIGH SCHOOL: Scotus Central Catholic (Neb.).

COLLEGE: North Dakota.

TRANSACTIONS/CAREER NOTES: Signed as non-drafted free agent by Cleveland Browns (January 8, 2003). ... Assigned by Browns to 2003 NFL Europe enhancement allocation program (February 5, 2003). ... Waived by Browns (August 31, 2003). ... Re-signed by Browns to practice squad (October 1, 2003). ... Activated (October 11, 2003). ... Released by Browns (November 4, 2003). ... Re-signed by Browns to practice squad (November 5, 2003). ... Activated (November 12, 2003).

SINGLE GAME HIGHS (regular season): Receptions—2 (November 23, 2003, vs. Pittsburgh); yards—17 (November 16, 2003, vs. Arizona); and touchdown receptions—0.

Year Team	G	GS	RECEIVING No.	Yds.	Avg.	TD	TOTALS TD	2pt.	Pts.	Fum.
2003—Cleveland NFL	10	0	4	29	7.3	0	0	0	0	0

MYERS, LEONARD CB

PERSONAL: Born December 18, 1978, in Fort Lauderdale, Fla. ... 5-10/196. ... Full name: Leonard Bernard Myers.

HIGH SCHOOL: Dillard (Fort Lauderdale, Fla.).

COLLEGE: Miami (Fla.).

TRANSACTIONS/CAREER NOTES: Selected by New England Patriots in sixth round (200th pick overall) of 2001 NFL draft. ... Signed by Patriots (July 2, 2001). ... On physically unable to perform list with groin injury (September 1-November 10, 2002). ... Released by Patriots (August 31, 2003). ... Signed by New York Jets to practice squad (September 18, 2003). ... Activated (September 30, 2003). ... Reached injury settlement with Jets (October 15, 2003). ... Signed by Detroit Lions to practice squad (November 11, 2003). ... Activated (December 13, 2003). ... Granted free agency (March 3, 2004).

CHAMPIONSHIP GAME EXPERIENCE: Member of Patriots for AFC championship game (2001 season); inactive. ... Member of Super Bowl championship team (2001 season); inactive.

Year Team	G	GS	TOTALS Tk.	Ast.	Sks.	INTERCEPTIONS No.	Yds.	Avg.	TD
2001—New England NFL	7	0	3	2	0.0	0	0	0.0	0
2002—New England NFL	8	1	11	1	0.0	0	0	0.0	0
2003—New York Jets NFL	1	0	2	0	0.0	0	0	0.0	0
—Detroit NFL	1	0	0	0	0.0	0	0	0.0	0
Pro totals (3 years)	17	1	16	3	0.0	0	0	0.0	0

MYERS, MICHAEL — DT — BROWNS

PERSONAL: Born January 20, 1976, in Vicksburg, Miss. ... 6-2/292.
HIGH SCHOOL: Vicksburg (Miss.).
JUNIOR COLLEGE: Hinds Community College (Miss.).
COLLEGE: Alabama.
TRANSACTIONS/CAREER NOTES: Selected by Dallas Cowboys in fourth round (100th pick overall) of 1998 NFL draft. ... Signed by Cowboys (July 10, 1998). ... Granted free agency (March 2, 2001). ... Re-signed by Cowboys (May 3, 2001). ... Granted unconditional free agency (March 1, 2002). ... Re-signed by Cowboys (April 19, 2002). ... Granted unconditional free agency (February 28, 2003). ... Re-signed by Cowboys (May 1, 2003). ... Released by Cowboys (October 7, 2003). ... Signed by Cleveland Browns (November 12, 2003). ... Granted unconditional free agency (March 3, 2004). ... Re-signed by Browns (March 18, 2004).
HONORS: Named defensive tackle on THE SPORTING NEWS college All-America first team (1996).

Year Team	G	GS	TOTALS Tk.	Ast.	Sks.
1998—Dallas NFL	16	1	10	5	3.0
1999—Dallas NFL	6	0	4	4	0.0
2000—Dallas NFL	13	7	28	7	0.0
2001—Dallas NFL	16	16	37	18	3.5
2002—Dallas NFL	16	0	22	13	1.0
2003—Dallas NFL	1	1	0	1	0.0
—Cleveland NFL	7	1	8	6	3.0
Pro totals (6 years)	75	26	109	54	10.5

MYLES, REGGIE — CB — BENGALS

PERSONAL: Born October 10, 1979, in Pascagoula, Miss. ... 5-11/185.
HIGH SCHOOL: Pascagoula (Miss.).
COLLEGE: Alabama.
TRANSACTIONS/CAREER NOTES: Signed as non-drafted free agent by Cincinnati Bengals (April 23, 2002). ... Released by Bengals (September 1, 2002). ... Re-signed by Bengals to practice squad (September 2, 2002). ... Activated (November 2, 2002).

Year Team	G	GS	TOTALS Tk.	Ast.	Sks.	INTERCEPTIONS No.	Yds.	Avg.	TD
2002—Cincinnati NFL	9	0	4	0	0.0	0	0	0.0	0
2003—Cincinnati NFL	16	0	4	0	0.0	0	0	0.0	0
Pro totals (2 years)	25	0	8	0	0.0	0	0	0.0	0

NAEOLE, CHRIS — G — JAGUARS

PERSONAL: Born December 25, 1974, in Kailua, Hawaii. ... 6-3/317. ... Full name: Chris Kealoha Naeole. ... Name pronounced: NAY-oh-lee.
HIGH SCHOOL: Kahuka (Kaaava, Hawaii).
COLLEGE: Colorado.
TRANSACTIONS/CAREER NOTES: Selected by New Orleans Saints in first round (10th pick overall) of 1997 NFL draft. ... Signed by Saints (July 17, 1997). ... On injured reserve with ankle injury (October 17, 1997-remainder of season). ... Granted unconditional free agency (March 1, 2002). ... Signed by Jacksonville Jaguars (April 5, 2002).
PLAYING EXPERIENCE: New Orleans NFL, 1997-2001; Jacksonville NFL, 2002-2003. ... Games/Games started: 1997 (4/0), 1998 (16/16), 1999 (15/15), 2000 (16/16), 2001 (16/16), 2002 (16/16), 2003 (16/16). Total: 99/95.
HONORS: Named guard on THE SPORTING NEWS college All-America second team (1996).

N

NAILS, JAMIE — G

PERSONAL: Born June 3, 1977, in Baxley, Ga. ... 6-6/335. ... Full name: Jamie Marcellus Nails.
HIGH SCHOOL: Appling County (Baxley, Ga.).
COLLEGE: Florida A&M.
TRANSACTIONS/CAREER NOTES: Selected by Buffalo Bills in fourth round (120th pick overall) of 1997 NFL draft. ... Signed by Bills (July 2, 1997). ... Granted free agency (February 11, 2000). ... Re-signed by Bills (April 28, 2000) ... Granted unconditional free agency (March 2, 2001). ... Signed by Miami Dolphins (August 15, 2001). ... Released by Dolphins (September 2, 2001). ... Re-signed by Dolphins (March 5, 2002). ... On injured reserve with Achilles' injury (December 17, 2002-remainder of season). ... Granted unconditional free agency (March 3, 2004).
PLAYING EXPERIENCE: Buffalo NFL, 1997-2000; Miami NFL, 2002-2003. ... Games/Games started: 1997 (2/0), 1998 (15/3), 1999 (16/3), 2000 (16/16), 2002 (14/14), 2003 (15/15). Total: 78/51.

NALEN, TOM — C — BRONCOS

PERSONAL: Born May 13, 1971, in Foxboro, Mass. ... 6-3/286. ... Full name: Thomas Andrew Nalen.
HIGH SCHOOL: Foxboro (Mass.).
COLLEGE: Boston College.

TRANSACTIONS/CAREER NOTES: Selected by Denver Broncos in seventh round (218th pick overall) of 1994 NFL draft. ... Signed by Broncos (July 15, 1994). ... Released by Broncos (September 2, 1994). ... Re-signed by Broncos to practice squad (September 6, 1994). ... Activated (October 7, 1994). ... On injured reserve with knee injury (October 23, 2002-remainder of season).

PLAYING EXPERIENCE: Denver NFL, 1994-2003. ... Games/Games started: 1994 (7/1), 1995 (15/15), 1996 (16/16), 1997 (16/16), 1998 (16/16), 1999 (16/16), 2000 (16/16), 2001 (16/16), 2002 (7/7), 2003 (16/16). Total: 141/135.

CHAMPIONSHIP GAME EXPERIENCE: Played in AFC championship game (1997 and 1998 seasons). ... Member of Super Bowl championship team (1997 and 1998 seasons).

HONORS: Played in Pro Bowl (1997-1999 and 2003 seasons). ... Named center on THE SPORTING NEWS NFL All-Pro team (1999 and 2000). ... Named to play in Pro Bowl (2000 season); replaced by Tim Ruddy due to injury.

NALL, CRAIG — QB — PACKERS

PERSONAL: Born April 21, 1979, in Alexandria, La. ... 6-3/230. ... Full name: Craig Matthew Nall.
HIGH SCHOOL: Alexandria (La.).
COLLEGE: Northwestern State.
TRANSACTIONS/CAREER NOTES: Selected by Green Bay Packers in fifth round (164th pick overall) of 2002 NFL draft. ... Signed by Packers (July 22, 2002). ... Assigned by Packers to NFL Europe in 2003 enhancement allocation program (February 26, 2003).

			PASSING									RUSHING				TOTALS		
Year Team	G	GS	Att.	Cmp.	Pct.	Yds.	TD	Int.	Avg.	Skd.	Rat.	Att.	Yds.	Avg.	TD	TD	2pt.	Pts.
2003—Green Bay NFL	1	0	0	0	0.0	0	0	0	0.00	0	0.0	2	-2	-1.0	0	0	0	0

NATTIEL, MICHAEL — LB — VIKINGS

PERSONAL: Born November 8, 1980, in Gainesville, Fla. ... 6-0/227. ... Full name: Michael Dondrill Nattiel.
HIGH SCHOOL: Newberry (Archer, Fla.).
COLLEGE: Florida.
TRANSACTIONS/CAREER NOTES: Selected by Minnesota Vikings in sixth round (190th pick overall) of 2003 NFL draft. ... Signed by Vikings (July 15, 2003).

			TOTALS			INTERCEPTIONS			
Year Team	G	GS	Tk.	Ast.	Sks.	No.	Yds.	Avg.	TD
2003—Minnesota NFL	16	0	15	2	0.0	1	80	80.0	1

NAVIES, HANNIBAL — LB — PACKERS

PERSONAL: Born July 19, 1977, in Chicago, Ill. ... 6-3/247. ... Full name: Hannibal Carter Navies. ... Name pronounced: NAY-vees.
HIGH SCHOOL: St. Patrick (Chicago), then Berkeley (Oakland).
COLLEGE: Colorado.
TRANSACTIONS/CAREER NOTES: Selected by Carolina Panthers in fourth round (100th pick overall) of 1999 NFL draft. ... Signed by Panthers (July 21, 1999). ... On injured reserve with broken arm (October 23, 2001-remainder of season). ... Granted free agency (March 1, 2002). ... Re-signed by Panthers (May 10, 2002). ... Granted unconditional free agency (February 28, 2003). ... Signed by Green Bay Packers (March 19, 2003).

			TOTALS			INTERCEPTIONS			
Year Team	G	GS	Tk.	Ast.	Sks.	No.	Yds.	Avg.	TD
1999—Carolina NFL	9	0	3	0	0.0	0	0	0.0	0
2000—Carolina NFL	13	1	19	1	2.0	1	0	0.0	0
2001—Carolina NFL	5	5	17	4	0.0	0	0	0.0	0
2002—Carolina NFL	12	9	21	11	0.0	0	0	0.0	0
2003—Green Bay NFL	16	16	69	17	1.0	0	0	0.0	0
Pro totals (5 years)	55	31	129	33	3.0	1	0	0.0	0

NEAD, SPENCER — FB — RAMS

PERSONAL: Born November 3, 1977, in Tacoma, Wash. ... 6-4/259.
HIGH SCHOOL: Teton (Tetonia, Idaho).
JUNIOR COLLEGE: Ricks College (Idaho).
COLLEGE: Brigham Young.
TRANSACTIONS/CAREER NOTES: Selected by New England Patriots in seventh round (234th pick overall) of 2003 NFL draft. ... Signed by Patriots (July 21, 2003). ... Released by Patriots (August 20, 2003). ... Signed by St. Louis Rams (August 25, 2003). ... Released by Rams (September 15, 2003). ... Re-signed by Rams to practice squad (September 17, 2003). ... Released by Rams (September 30, 2003). ... Re-signed by Rams to practice squad (October 2, 2003). ... Activated (October 11, 2003). ... Released by Rams (December 9, 2003). ... Re-signed by Rams to practice squad (December 11, 2003).
SINGLE GAME HIGHS (regular season): Receptions—1 (November 2, 2003, vs. San Francisco); yards—6 (November 2, 2003, vs. San Francisco); and touchdown receptions—0.

			RECEIVING				KICKOFF RETURNS				TOTALS			
Year Team	G	GS	No.	Yds.	Avg.	TD	No.	Yds.	Avg.	TD	TD	2pt.	Pts.	Fum.
2003—St. Louis NFL	10	0	1	6	6.0	0	2	27	13.5	0	0	0	0	1

NEAL, LORENZO — FB — CHARGERS

PERSONAL: Born December 27, 1970, in Hanford, Calif. ... 5-11/245. ... Full name: Lorenzo LaVonne Neal.
HIGH SCHOOL: Lemoore (Calif.).
COLLEGE: Fresno State.

TRANSACTIONS/CAREER NOTES: Selected by New Orleans Saints in fourth round (89th pick overall) of 1993 NFL draft. ... Signed by Saints (July 15, 1993). ... On injured reserve with ankle injury (September 15, 1993-remainder of season). ... Granted free agency (February 16, 1996). ... Re-signed by Saints (July 1, 1996). ... Granted unconditional free agency (February 14, 1997). ... Signed by New York Jets (March 31, 1997). ... Traded by Jets to Tampa Bay Buccaneers for fifth-round pick (TE Blake Spence) in 1998 draft (March 12, 1998). ... Released by Buccaneers (February 11, 1999). ... Signed by Tennessee Titans (March 2, 1999). ... Released by Titans (March 1, 2001). ... Signed by Cincinnati Bengals (May 7, 2001). ... Granted unconditional free agency (February 28, 2003). ... Signed by San Diego Chargers (February 28, 2003).

CHAMPIONSHIP GAME EXPERIENCE: Played in AFC championship game (1999 season). ... Played in Super Bowl 34 (1999 season).

HONORS: Played in Pro Bowl (2002 season).

SINGLE GAME HIGHS (regular season): Attempts—14 (October 9, 1994, vs. Chicago); yards—89 (September 5, 1993, vs. Houston); and rushing touchdowns—1 (September 28, 2003, vs. Oakland).

			RUSHING				RECEIVING				KICKOFF RETURNS				TOTALS			
Year Team	**G**	**GS**	**Att.**	**Yds.**	**Avg.**	**TD**	**No.**	**Yds.**	**Avg.**	**TD**	**No.**	**Yds.**	**Avg.**	**TD**	**TD**	**2pt.**	**Pts.**	**Fum.**
1993—New Orleans NFL	2	2	21	175	8.3	1	0	0	0.0	0	0	0	0.0	0	1	0	6	1
1994—New Orleans NFL	16	7	30	90	3.0	1	2	9	4.5	0	1	17	17.0	0	1	0	6	1
1995—New Orleans NFL	16	7	5	3	0.6	0	12	123	10.3	1	2	28	14.0	0	1	0	6	2
1996—New Orleans NFL	16	11	21	58	2.8	1	31	194	6.3	1	0	0	0.0	0	2	0	12	1
1997—New York Jets NFL	16	10	10	28	2.8	0	8	40	5.0	1	2	22	11.0	0	1	0	6	0
1998—Tampa Bay NFL	16	1	5	25	5.0	0	5	14	2.8	1	0	0	0.0	0	1	0	6	0
1999—Tennessee NFL	16	14	2	1	0.5	1	7	27	3.9	2	2	15	7.5	0	3	0	18	0
2000—Tennessee NFL	16	5	1	-2	-2.0	0	9	31	3.4	2	1	15	15.0	0	2	0	12	0
2001—Cincinnati NFL	16	10	5	10	2.0	0	19	101	5.3	1	0	0	0.0	0	1	0	6	0
2002—Cincinnati NFL	16	8	9	31	3.4	0	21	133	6.3	1	5	52	10.4	0	1	0	6	0
2003—San Diego NFL	16	15	18	40	2.2	1	16	62	3.9	0	1	1	1.0	0	1	0	6	0
Pro totals (11 years)	162	90	127	459	3.6	5	130	734	5.6	10	14	150	10.7	0	15	0	90	5

NECE, RYAN — LB — BUCCANEERS

PERSONAL: Born February 24, 1979, in San Bernardino, Calif. ... 6-3/224. ... Full name: Ryan Clint Nece. ... Son of Ronnie Lott, Hall of Fame safety with San Francisco 49ers (1981-90), Los Angeles Raiders (1991-92) and New York Jets (1993-94).

HIGH SCHOOL: Pacific (San Bernardino, Calif.).

COLLEGE: UCLA.

TRANSACTIONS/CAREER NOTES: Signed as non-drafted free agent by Tampa Bay Buccaneers (April 22, 2002). ... On injured reserve with knee injury (October 29, 2002-remainder of season).

			TOTALS			INTERCEPTIONS			
Year Team	**G**	**GS**	**Tk.**	**Ast.**	**Sks.**	**No.**	**Yds.**	**Avg.**	**TD**
2002—Tampa Bay NFL	8	0	1	1	0.0	0	0	0.0	0
2003—Tampa Bay NFL	15	10	44	11	0.0	1	2	2.0	0
Pro totals (2 years)	23	10	45	12	0.0	1	2	2.0	0

NED, LARRY — RB — VIKINGS

PERSONAL: Born August 23, 1978, in Eunice, La. ... 5-11/217. ... Full name: Larry Lee Ned Jr.

HIGH SCHOOL: Rancho Verde (Calif.).

COLLEGE: San Diego State.

TRANSACTIONS/CAREER NOTES: Selected by Oakland Raiders in sixth round (197th pick overall) of 2002 NFL draft. ... Signed by Raiders (July 25, 2002). ... Released by Raiders (August 26, 2002). ... Signed by San Diego Chargers to practice squad (September 3, 2002). ... Released by Chargers (November 26, 2002). ... Signed by Minnesota Vikings to practice squad (December 10, 2002). ... Released by Vikings (August 31, 2003). ... Re-signed by Vikings to practice squad (September 1, 2003). ... Activated (December 9, 2003).

			RUSHING				RECEIVING				TOTALS			
Year Team	**G**	**GS**	**Att.**	**Yds.**	**Avg.**	**TD**	**No.**	**Yds.**	**Avg.**	**TD**	**TD**	**2pt.**	**Pts.**	**Fum.**
2003—Minnesota NFL	3	0	0	0	0.0	0	0	0	0.0	0	0	0	0	0

NEDNEY, JOE — K — TITANS

PERSONAL: Born March 22, 1973, in San Jose, Calif. ... 6-5/225. ... Full name: Joseph Thomas Nedney. ... Name pronounced: NED-nee.

HIGH SCHOOL: Santa Teresa (San Jose, Calif.).

COLLEGE: San Jose State.

TRANSACTIONS/CAREER NOTES: Signed as non-drafted free agent by Green Bay Packers (April 1995). ... Released by Packers (August 27, 1995). ... Signed by Oakland Raiders to practice squad (August 29, 1995). ... Released by Raiders (September 6, 1995). ... Signed by Miami Dolphins to practice squad (September 21, 1995). ... Claimed on waivers by New York Jets (August 12, 1997). ... Released by Jets (August 25, 1997). ... Signed by Dolphins (October 3, 1997). ... Released by Dolphins (October 6, 1997). ... Signed by Arizona Cardinals (October 15, 1997). ... On injured reserve with knee injury (December 1, 1998-remainder of season). ... Released by Cardinals (February 12, 1999). ... Re-signed by Cardinals (March 31, 1999). ... Claimed on waivers by Baltimore Ravens (October 6, 1999). ... Inactive for four games with Ravens (1999). ... Released by Ravens (November 9, 1999). ... Signed by Raiders (December 14, 1999). ... Released by Raiders (August 27, 2000). ... Signed by Denver Broncos (September 12, 2000). ... Released by Broncos (October 2, 2000). ... Signed by Carolina Panthers (October 3, 2000). ... Granted unconditional free agency (March 2, 2001). ... Signed by Tennessee Titans (March 9, 2001). ... On injured reserve with ACL injury (September 11, 2003-remainder of season).

CHAMPIONSHIP GAME EXPERIENCE: Played in AFC championship game (2002 season).

		FIELD GOALS							TOTALS		
Year Team	**G**	**1-29**	**30-39**	**40-49**	**50+**	**Tot.**	**Pct.**	**Lg.**	**XPM**	**XPA**	**Pts.**
1995—Miami NFL				Did not play.							
1996—Miami NFL	16	8-8	7-11	3-8	0-2	18-29	62.1	44	35	36	89
1997—Arizona NFL	10	4-4	4-4	3-7	0-2	11-17	64.7	45	19	19	52
1998—Arizona NFL	12	6-6	1-1	5-8	1-4	13-19	68.4	53	30	30	69
1999—Arizona NFL	1	0-0	0-0	0-0	0-0	0-0	0.0	0	0	0	0

Year Team	G	FIELD GOALS 1-29	30-39	40-49	50+	Tot.	Pct.	Lg.	TOTALS XPM	XPA	Pts.
—Oakland NFL	3	2-2	2-2	0-1	1-2	5-7	71.4	52	13	13	28
2000—Denver NFL	3	6-6	1-1	1-2	0-1	8-10	80.0	43	4	4	28
—Carolina NFL	12	11-11	6-7	7-8	2-2	26-28	92.9	52	20	20	98
2001—Tennessee NFL	16	6-6	5-5	8-15	1-2	20-28	71.4	51	34	35	94
2002—Tennessee NFL	16	9-9	10-12	5-8	1-2	25-31	80.6	53	36	36	111
2003—Tennessee NFL	1	0-0	0-0	0-0	1-1	1-1	100.0	50	0	1	3
Pro totals (8 years)	90	52-52	36-43	32-57	7-18	127-170	74.7	53	191	194	572

NEIL, DAN — G — BRONCOS

PERSONAL: Born October 21, 1973, in Houston, Texas. ... 6-2/285. ... Full name: Daniel Neil.
HIGH SCHOOL: Cypress Creek (Houston).
COLLEGE: Texas.
TRANSACTIONS/CAREER NOTES: Selected by Denver Broncos in third round (67th pick overall) of 1997 NFL draft. ... Signed by Broncos (July 17, 1997). ... Granted free agency (February 11, 2000). ... Re-signed by Broncos (April 28, 2000) ... Granted unconditional free agency (March 2, 2001). ... Re-signed by Broncos (March 2, 2001).
PLAYING EXPERIENCE: Denver NFL, 1997-2003. ... Games/Games started: 1997 (3/0), 1998 (16/16), 1999 (15/15), 2000 (16/16), 2001 (15/15), 2002 (16/16), 2003 (14/14). Total: 95/92.
CHAMPIONSHIP GAME EXPERIENCE: Member of Broncos for AFC championship game (1997 season); inactive. ... Member of Super Bowl championship team (1997 season); inactive. ... Played in AFC championship game (1998 season). ... Member of Super Bowl championship team (1998 season).
HONORS: Named guard on THE SPORTING NEWS college All-America first team (1996).

NELSON, BRUCE — G — PANTHERS

PERSONAL: Born May 12, 1979, in Emmetsburg, Iowa. ... 6-5/301.
HIGH SCHOOL: Emmetsburg (Iowa).
COLLEGE: Iowa.
TRANSACTIONS/CAREER NOTES: Selected by Carolina Panthers in second round (50th pick overall) of 2003 NFL draft. ... Signed by Panthers (July 28, 2003).
PLAYING EXPERIENCE: Carolina NFL, 2003. ... Games/Games started: 2003 (14/1). Total: 14/1.
CHAMPIONSHIP GAME EXPERIENCE: Played in NFC championship game (2003 season). ... Played in Super Bowl 38 (2003 season).

NELSON, JIM — LB — COLTS

PERSONAL: Born April 16, 1975, in Riverside, Calif. ... 6-1/234. ... Full name: James Robert Nelson.
HIGH SCHOOL: McDonough (Waldorf, Md.).
COLLEGE: Penn State.
TRANSACTIONS/CAREER NOTES: Signed as non-drafted free agent by San Francisco 49ers (April 24, 1998). ... Claimed on waivers by Green Bay Packers (July 20, 1998). ... Released by Packers (August 25, 1998). ... Re-signed by Packers to practice squad (September 14, 1998). ... Activated (December 29, 1998); did not play. ... Claimed on waivers by Minnesota Vikings (August 28, 2000). ... Granted free agency (March 1, 2002). ... Re-signed by Vikings (April 23, 2002). ... Granted unconditional free agency (February 28, 2003). ... Signed by Indianapolis Colts (March 22, 2003). ... Granted unconditional free agency (March 3, 2004). ... Re-signed by Colts (March 11, 2004).
CHAMPIONSHIP GAME EXPERIENCE: Played in NFC championship game (2000 season). ... Played in AFC championship game (2003 season).

Year Team	G	GS	TOTALS Tk.	Ast.	Sks.	INTERCEPTIONS No.	Yds.	Avg.	TD
1998—Green Bay NFL				Did not play.					
1999—Green Bay NFL	16	0	7	1	0.0	1	0	0.0	0
2000—Minnesota NFL	16	0	3	3	0.0	0	0	0.0	0
2001—Minnesota NFL	16	2	21	16	0.0	0	0	0.0	0
2002—Minnesota NFL	16	2	7	2	0.0	0	0	0.0	0
2003—Indianapolis NFL	7	0	12	1	0.0	2	22	11.0	0
Pro totals (5 years)	71	4	50	23	0.0	3	22	7.3	0

NELSON, RHETT — CB — VIKINGS

PERSONAL: Born February 16, 1980, in Minneapolis, Minn. ... 6-0/200.
COLLEGE: Colorado State.
TRANSACTIONS/CAREER NOTES: Signed as non-drafted free agent by Arizona Cardinals (April 28, 2003). ... Released by Cardinals (August 30, 2003). ... Signed by Minnesota Vikings to practice squad (September 9, 2003). ... Activated (November 12, 2003).

Year Team	G	GS	TOTALS Tk.	Ast.	Sks.	INTERCEPTIONS No.	Yds.	Avg.	TD
2003—Minnesota NFL	3	0	0	0	0.0	0	0	0.0	0

NESBIT, JAMAR — G/C — SAINTS

PERSONAL: Born December 17, 1976, in Heidelberg, Germany. ... 6-4/329. ... Full name: Jamar Kendric Nesbit.
HIGH SCHOOL: Summerville (S.C.).
COLLEGE: South Carolina.

TRANSACTIONS/CAREER NOTES: Signed as non-drafted free agent by Carolina Panthers (April 18, 1999). ... Granted free agency (March 1, 2002). ... Re-signed by Panthers (June 21, 2002). ... Granted unconditional free agency (February 28, 2003). ... Signed by Jacksonville Jaguars (May 5, 2003). ... Granted unconditional free agency (March 3, 2004). ... Signed by New Orleans Saints (March 25, 2004).
PLAYING EXPERIENCE: Carolina NFL, 1999-2002; Jacksonville NFL, 2003. ... Games/Games started: 1999 (7/0), 2000 (16/16), 2001 (16/16), 2002 (14/13), 2003 (16/2). Total: 69/47.

NEUFELD, RYAN — TE — BILLS

PERSONAL: Born November 22, 1975, in Morgan Hill, Calif. ... 6-4/250. ... Full name: Ryan Matthew Neufeld.
HIGH SCHOOL: Live Oak (Morgan Hill, Calif.).
COLLEGE: UCLA.
TRANSACTIONS/CAREER NOTES: Signed as non-drafted free agent by Dallas Cowboys (April 23, 1999). ... Released by Cowboys (September 5, 1999). ... Re-signed by Cowboys to practice squad (September 6, 1999). ... Activated (October 27, 1999). ... Assigned by Cowboys to Rhein Fire in 2000 NFL Europe enhancement allocation program (February 18, 2000). ... Released by Cowboys (August 27, 2000). ... Signed by Miami Dolphins to practice squad (August 30, 2000). ... Released by Dolphins (September 5, 2000). ... Signed by Jacksonville Jaguars to practice squad (September 13, 2000). ... Activated (October 12, 2000). ... Released by Jaguars (October 21, 2000). ... Re-signed by Jaguars (October 24, 2000). ... Released by Jaguars (August 25, 2001). ... Signed by Seattle Seahawks (January 23, 2002). ... Released by Seahawks (August 25, 2002). ... Signed by Buffalo Bills (January 22, 2003).
SINGLE GAME HIGHS (regular season): Receptions—1 (November 30, 2003, vs. New York Giants); yards—25 (October 19, 2003, vs. Washington); and touchdown receptions—0.

			RECEIVING				TOTALS			
Year Team	G	GS	No.	Yds.	Avg.	TD	TD	2pt.	Pts.	Fum.
1999—Dallas NFL	6	0	0	0	0.0	0	0	0	0	0
2000—Jacksonville NFL	2	0	0	0	0.0	0	0	0	0	0
2003—Buffalo NFL	16	1	3	41	13.7	0	0	0	0	0
Pro totals (3 years)	24	1	3	41	13.7	0	0	0	0	0

NEWBERRY, JEREMY — C — 49ERS

PERSONAL: Born March 23, 1976, in Antioch, Calif. ... 6-5/310. ... Full name: Jeremy David Newberry.
HIGH SCHOOL: Antioch (Calif.).
COLLEGE: California.
TRANSACTIONS/CAREER NOTES: Selected by after junior season San Francisco 49ers in second round (58th pick overall) of 1998 NFL draft. ... Signed by San Francisco 49ers (July 18, 1998). ... On physically unable to perform list with knee injury (July 17-November 7, 1998). ... Active for one game (1998); did not play. ... Granted unconditional free agency (March 1, 2002). ... Re-signed by 49ers (March 12, 2002).
PLAYING EXPERIENCE: San Francisco NFL, 1999-2003. ... Games/Games started: 1999 (16/16), 2000 (16/16), 2001 (15/15), 2002 (16/16), 2003 (16/16). Total: 79/79.
HONORS: Played in Pro Bowl (2001 and 2002 seasons).

NEWMAN, KEITH — LB

PERSONAL: Born January 19, 1977, in Tampa, Fla. ... 6-2/248. ... Full name: Keith Anthony Newman.
HIGH SCHOOL: Thomas Jefferson (Tampa).
COLLEGE: North Carolina.
TRANSACTIONS/CAREER NOTES: Selected by Buffalo Bills in fourth round (119th pick overall) of 1999 NFL draft. ... Signed by Bills (July 27, 1999). ... Granted free agency (March 1, 2002). ... Re-signed by Bills (May 21, 2002). ... Granted unconditional free agency (February 28, 2003). ... Signed by Atlanta Falcons (March 17, 2003). ... On suspended list for violation of league substance abuse policy (August 30-October 5, 2003). ... Released by Falcons (April 27, 2004).

			TOTALS			INTERCEPTIONS			
Year Team	G	GS	Tk.	Ast.	Sks.	No.	Yds.	Avg.	TD
1999—Buffalo NFL	3	0	0	1	0.0	0	0	0.0	0
2000—Buffalo NFL	16	16	44	18	8.0	0	0	0.0	0
2001—Buffalo NFL	16	16	62	21	3.5	0	0	0.0	0
2002—Buffalo NFL	16	10	21	13	3.0	0	0	0.0	0
2003—Atlanta NFL	12	11	35	6	2.0	1	29	29.0	0
Pro totals (5 years)	63	53	162	59	16.5	1	29	29.0	0

N

NEWMAN, TERENCE — CB — COWBOYS

PERSONAL: Born September 4, 1978, in Salina, Kan. ... 5-11/188.
HIGH SCHOOL: Central (Salina, Kan.).
COLLEGE: Kansas State.
TRANSACTIONS/CAREER NOTES: Selected by Dallas Cowboys in first round (fifth pick overall) of 2003 NFL draft. ... Signed by Cowboys (July 24, 2003).

			TOTALS			INTERCEPTIONS			
Year Team	G	GS	Tk.	Ast.	Sks.	No.	Yds.	Avg.	TD
2003—Dallas NFL	16	16	66	10	1.0	4	23	5.8	0

NEWSON, KENDALL — WR — DOLPHINS

PERSONAL: Born March 5, 1980, in Decatur, Ga. ... 6-1/197. ... Full name: Kendall Montrae Newson.
HIGH SCHOOL: Columbia (Decatur, Ga.).
COLLEGE: Middle Tennessee State.

TRANSACTIONS/CAREER NOTES: Selected by Jacksonville Jaguars in seventh round (222nd pick overall) of 2002 NFL draft. ... Signed by Jaguars (June 12, 2002). ... Released by Jaguars (August 25, 2002). ... Signed by Tennessee Titans to practice squad (September 3, 2002). ... Released by Titans (September 10, 2002). ... Selected by Rhein Fire in 2003 NFL Europe draft (February 5, 2003). ... Signed by Miami Dolphins (February 27, 2003). ... Released by Dolphins (August 31, 2003). ... Re-signed by Dolphins to practice squad (September 1, 2003). ... Activated (November 7, 2003). ... Waived by Dolphins (December 20, 2003). ... Re-signed by Dolphins (December 24, 2003).
SINGLE GAME HIGHS (regular season): Receptions—2 (November 9, 2003, vs. Tennesee); yards—55 (November 9, 2003, vs. Tennessee); and touchdown receptions—0.

			RECEIVING				TOTALS			
Year Team	G	GS	No.	Yds.	Avg.	TD	TD	2pt.	Pts.	Fum.
2003—Miami NFL	6	0	2	55	27.5	0	0	0	0	1

NEWTON, JIM — T — COLTS

PERSONAL: Born October 13, 1978, in Omaha, Neb. ... 6-9/297.
COLLEGE: Utah State.
TRANSACTIONS/CAREER NOTES: Signed as non-drafted free agent by Indianapolis Colts (May 5, 2003). ... Released by Colts (August 31, 2003). ... Re-signed by Colts to practice squad (October 11, 2003). ... Waived by Colts (October 14, 2003). ... Re-signed by Colts to practice squad (October 25, 2003). ... Waived by Colts (November 5, 2003). ... Re-signed by Colts (November 7, 2003). ... Waived by Colts (November 10, 2003). ... Re-signed by Colts (February 4, 2004).
PLAYING EXPERIENCE: Indianapolis NFL, 2003. ... Games/Games started: 2003 (3/0). Total: 3/0.

NGUYEN, DAT — LB — COWBOYS

PERSONAL: Born September 25, 1975, in Saigon, Vietnam. ... 5-11/243. ... Name pronounced: WIN.
HIGH SCHOOL: Rockport-Fulton (Rockport, Texas).
COLLEGE: Texas A&M.
TRANSACTIONS/CAREER NOTES: Selected by Dallas Cowboys in third round (85th pick overall) of 1999 NFL draft. ... Signed by Cowboys (July 26, 1999). ... Granted free agency (March 1, 2002). ... Re-signed by Cowboys (April 16, 2002).
HONORS: Lombardi Award winner (1998). ... Named inside linebacker on THE SPORTING NEWS college All-America first team (1998).

			TOTALS			INTERCEPTIONS			
Year Team	G	GS	Tk.	Ast.	Sks.	No.	Yds.	Avg.	TD
1999—Dallas NFL	16	0	26	5	1.0	1	6	6.0	0
2000—Dallas NFL	10	5	42	6	0.0	2	31	15.5	0
2001—Dallas NFL	16	16	91	22	0.0	0	0	0.0	0
2002—Dallas NFL	8	8	42	10	1.0	0	0	0.0	0
2003—Dallas NFL	16	16	90	31	2.0	0	0	0.0	0
Pro totals (5 years)	66	45	291	74	4.0	3	37	12.3	0

NICKEY, DONNIE — S — TITANS

PERSONAL: Born April 25, 1980, in Akron, Ohio. ... 6-2/215.
HIGH SCHOOL: Jonathan Alder (Plain City, Ohio).
COLLEGE: Ohio State.
TRANSACTIONS/CAREER NOTES: Selected by Tennessee Titans in fifth round (154th pick overall) of 2003 NFL draft. ... Signed by Titans (July 16, 2003).

			TOTALS			INTERCEPTIONS			
Year Team	G	GS	Tk.	Ast.	Sks.	No.	Yds.	Avg.	TD
2003—Tennessee NFL	12	0	0	0	0.0	0	0	0.0	0

NKWENTI, MATHIAS — T

PERSONAL: Born May 11, 1978, in Yaounde, Cameroon. ... 6-3/300. ... Full name: Mathias Fru Nkwenti.
HIGH SCHOOL: Thomas S. Wootton (Rockville, Md.).
COLLEGE: Temple.
TRANSACTIONS/CAREER NOTES: Selected by Pittsburgh Steelers in fourth round (111th pick overall) of 2001 NFL draft. ... Signed by Steelers (May 21, 2001). ... On injured reserve with back injury (October 22, 2003-remainder of season). ... Granted free agency (March 3, 2004).
PLAYING EXPERIENCE: Pittsburgh NFL, 2001-2003. ... Games/Games started: 2001 (1/0), 2003 (1/0). Total: 2/0.
CHAMPIONSHIP GAME EXPERIENCE: Member of Steelers for AFC championship game (2001 season); inactive.

NORMAN, DENNIS — C/T — SEAHAWKS

PERSONAL: Born January 26, 1980, in Philadelphia, Pa. ... 6-5/312.
HIGH SCHOOL: Cherokee (N.J.).
COLLEGE: Princeton.
TRANSACTIONS/CAREER NOTES: Selected by Seattle Seahawks in seventh round (222nd pick overall) of NFL draft. ... Signed by Seahawks (July 11, 2001). ... Granted free agency (March 3, 2004). ... Re-signed by Seahawks (April 4, 2004).
PLAYING EXPERIENCE: Seattle NFL, 2003. ... Games/Games started: 2003 (1/0). Total: 1/0.

NORMAN, JOSH — TE — CHARGERS

PERSONAL: Born July 27, 1980, in Midland, Texas. ... 6-2/236.
HIGH SCHOOL: Robert E. Lee (Midland, Texas).
COLLEGE: Oklahoma.

TRANSACTIONS/CAREER NOTES: Signed as non-drafted free agent by San Diego Chargers (April 26, 2002). ... Granted free agency (March 3, 2004). ... Re-signed by Chargers (May 13, 2004).
SINGLE GAME HIGHS (regular season): Receptions—4 (September 7, 2003, vs. Kansas City); yards—64 (September 7, 2003, vs. Kansas City); and touchdown receptions—1 (September 7, 2003, vs. Kansas City).

			RECEIVING				TOTALS			
Year Team	**G**	**GS**	**No.**	**Yds.**	**Avg.**	**TD**	**TD**	**2pt.**	**Pts.**	**Fum.**
2002—San Diego NFL	11	1	16	201	12.6	1	1	0	6	0
2003—San Diego NFL	7	1	6	72	12.0	1	1	0	6	0
Pro totals (2 years)	18	2	22	273	12.4	2	2	0	12	0

NORRIS, MORAN — FB — TEXANS

PERSONAL: Born June 16, 1978, in Houston, Texas. ... 6-1/250. ... Full name: Torrance Moran Norris.
HIGH SCHOOL: James Madison (Houston).
COLLEGE: Kansas.
TRANSACTIONS/CAREER NOTES: Selected by New Orleans Saints in fourth round (115th pick overall) of 2001 NFL draft. ... Signed by Saints (July 27, 2001). ... Claimed on waivers by Houston Texans (September 18, 2002). ... Granted free agency (March 3, 2004). ... Re-signed by Texans (April 19, 2004).

			RUSHING				RECEIVING				KICKOFF RETURNS				TOTALS			
Year Team	**G**	**GS**	**Att.**	**Yds.**	**Avg.**	**TD**	**No.**	**Yds.**	**Avg.**	**TD**	**No.**	**Yds.**	**Avg.**	**TD**	**TD**	**2pt.**	**Pts.**	**Fum.**
2001—New Orleans NFL	5	0	0	0	0.0	0	0	0	0.0	0	0	0	0.0	0	0	0	0	0
2002—Houston NFL	13	0	0	0	0.0	0	0	0	0.0	0	2	11	5.5	0	0	0	0	0
2003—Houston NFL	16	9	0	0	0.0	0	7	40	5.7	0	5	71	14.2	0	0	0	0	0
Pro totals (3 years)	34	9	0	0	0.0	0	7	40	5.7	0	7	82	11.7	0	0	0	0	0

NORTHCUTT, DENNIS — WR — BROWNS

PERSONAL: Born December 22, 1977, in Los Angeles, Calif. ... 5-11/175.
HIGH SCHOOL: Dorsey (Los Angeles).
COLLEGE: Arizona.
TRANSACTIONS/CAREER NOTES: Selected by Cleveland Browns in second round (32nd pick overall) of 2000 NFL draft. ... Signed by Browns (July 19, 2000). ... On non-football injury list with shoulder injury (July 23-September 30, 2001).
HONORS: Named wide receiver on THE SPORTING NEWS college All-America second team (1999).
SINGLE GAME HIGHS (regular season): Receptions—8 (October 6, 2002, vs. Baltimore); yards—165 (October 6, 2002, vs. Baltimore); and touchdown receptions—2 (October 6, 2002, vs. Baltimore).
STATISTICAL PLATEAUS: 100-yard receiving games: 2002 (1), 2003 (1). Total: 2.

			RECEIVING				PUNT RETURNS				TOTALS			
Year Team	**G**	**GS**	**No.**	**Yds.**	**Avg.**	**TD**	**No.**	**Yds.**	**Avg.**	**TD**	**TD**	**2pt.**	**Pts.**	**Fum.**
2000—Cleveland NFL	15	8	39	422	10.8	0	27	289	10.7	0	0	0	0	1
2001—Cleveland NFL	12	7	18	211	11.7	0	15	86	5.7	0	0	0	0	3
2002—Cleveland NFL	13	0	38	601	15.8	5	25	367	14.7	†2	8	1	50	2
2003—Cleveland NFL	15	6	62	729	11.8	2	36	295	8.2	0	2	0	12	2
Pro totals (4 years)	55	21	157	1963	12.5	7	103	1037	10.1	2	10	1	62	8

NWOKORIE, CHUKIE — DE — PACKERS

PERSONAL: Born July 10, 1975, in Tuskegee, Ala. ... 6-3/288. ... Full name: Chijioke Obinna Nwokorie. ... Name pronounced: CHEW-key wuh-CORE-e.
HIGH SCHOOL: Lafayette-Jefferson (Lafayette, Ind.).
COLLEGE: Purdue.
TRANSACTIONS/CAREER NOTES: Signed as non-drafted free agent by Indianapolis Colts (April 20, 1999). ... Released by Colts (October 25, 2000). ... Re-signed by Colts to practice squad (October 26, 2000). ... Activated (December 22, 2000). ... Granted free agency (March 1, 2002). ... Re-signed by Colts (May 21, 2002). ... On physically unable to perform list with back injury (August 26-November 6, 2002). ... Granted unconditional free agency (February 28, 2003). ... Signed by Green Bay Packers (April 8, 2003).

			TOTALS		
Year Team	**G**	**GS**	**Tk.**	**Ast.**	**Sks.**
1999—Indianapolis NFL	1	0	0	0	0.0
2000—Indianapolis NFL	1	0	0	0	0.0
2001—Indianapolis NFL	16	5	32	9	5.0
2002—Indianapolis NFL	3	0	1	1	0.0
2003—Green Bay NFL	14	0	16	2	2.5
Pro totals (5 years)	35	5	49	12	7.5

OBEN, ROMAN — T — BUCCANEERS

PERSONAL: Born October 9, 1972, in Cameroon, West Africa. ... 6-4/305. ... Name pronounced: OH-bin.
HIGH SCHOOL: Gonzaga (Washington, D.C.), then Fork Union (Va.) Military Academy.
COLLEGE: Louisville.
TRANSACTIONS/CAREER NOTES: Selected by New York Giants in third round (66th pick overall) of 1996 NFL draft. ... Signed by Giants (July 20, 1996). ... Granted free agency (February 12, 1999). ... Re-signed by Giants (July 28, 1999). ... Granted unconditional free agency (February 11, 2000). ... Signed by Cleveland Browns (March 9, 2000). ... Released by Browns (February 25, 2002). ... Signed by Tampa Bay Buccaneers (May 20, 2002). ... Granted unconditional free agency (February 28, 2003). ... Re-signed by Buccaneers (March 31, 2003).
PLAYING EXPERIENCE: New York Giants NFL, 1996-1999; Cleveland NFL, 2000-2001; Tampa Bay NFL, 2002-2003. ... Games/Games started: 1996 (2/0), 1997 (16/16), 1998 (16/16), 1999 (16/16), 2000 (16/16), 2001 (16/14), 2002 (16/16), 2003 (15/13). Total: 113/107.

CHAMPIONSHIP GAME EXPERIENCE: Played in NFC championship game (2002 season). ... Member of Super Bowl championship team (2002 season).

ODOM, JOE — LB — BEARS

PERSONAL: Born December 14, 1979, in Bethalto, Ill. ... 6-1/238. ... Full name: Joe Edward Odom.
HIGH SCHOOL: Civic Memorial (Bethalto, Ill.).
COLLEGE: Purdue.
TRANSACTIONS/CAREER NOTES: Selected by Chicago Bears in sixth round (191st pick overall) of 2003 NFL draft. ... Signed by Bears (June 9, 2003). ... On injured reserve with groin injury (November 21, 2003-remainder of season).

			TOTALS			INTERCEPTIONS			
Year Team	G	GS	Tk.	Ast.	Sks.	No.	Yds.	Avg.	TD
2003—Chicago NFL	10	3	14	6	0.0	0	0	0.0	0

O'DONNELL, NEIL — QB

PERSONAL: Born July 3, 1966, in Morristown, N.J. ... 6-3/228. ... Full name: Neil Kennedy O'Donnell.
HIGH SCHOOL: Madison-Boro (Madison, N.J.).
COLLEGE: Maryland.
TRANSACTIONS/CAREER NOTES: Selected by Pittsburgh Steelers in third round (70th pick overall) of 1990 NFL draft. ... Signed by Steelers (August 8, 1990). ... Active for three games (1990); did not play. ... Granted free agency (March 1, 1993). ... Tendered offer sheet by Tampa Bay Buccaneers (April 2, 1993). ... Offer matched by Steelers (April 12, 1993). ... Granted unconditional free agency (February 16, 1996). ... Signed by New York Jets (February 29, 1996). ... Released by Jets (June 24, 1998). ... Signed by Cincinnati Bengals (July 7, 1998). ... On injured reserve with hand injury (December 9, 1998-remainder of season). ... Released by Bengals (April 19, 1999). ... Signed by Tennessee Titans (July 23, 1999). ... Granted unconditional free agency (February 11, 2000). ... Re-signed by Titans (April 25, 2000). ... Released by Titans (February 20, 2003). ... Re-signed by Titans (June 24, 2003). ... Released by Titans (August 31, 2003). ... Re-signed by Titans (December 18, 2003). ... Granted unconditional free agency (March 3, 2004).
CHAMPIONSHIP GAME EXPERIENCE: Played in AFC championship game (1994, 1995 and 1999 seasons). ... Played in Super Bowl 30 (1995 season). ... Member of Titans for Super Bowl 34 (1999 season); did not play. ... Member of Titans for AFC championship game (2002); did not play.
HONORS: Played in Pro Bowl (1992 season).
RECORDS: Holds NFL career record for lowest interception percentage—2.11.
POST SEASON RECORDS: Holds NFL postseason single-game record for most passes attempted without an interception—54 (January 15, 1995, vs. San Diego).
SINGLE GAME HIGHS (regular season): Attempts—55 (December 24, 1995, vs. Green Bay); completions—34 (November 5, 1995, vs. Chicago); yards—377 (November 19, 1995, vs. Cincinnati); and touchdown passes—5 (August 31, 1997, vs. Seattle).
STATISTICAL PLATEAUS: 300-yard passing games: 1991 (1), 1993 (1), 1995 (4), 1996 (2), 1997 (1), 1998 (1), 1999 (2). Total: 12.
MISCELLANEOUS: Regular-season record as starting NFL quarterback: 55-45 (.550). ... Postseason record as starting NFL quarterback: 3-4 (.429).

			PASSING									RUSHING				TOTALS		
Year Team	G	GS	Att.	Cmp.	Pct.	Yds.	TD	Int.	Avg.	Skd.	Rat.	Att.	Yds.	Avg.	TD	TD	2pt.	Pts.
1990—Pittsburgh NFL			Did not play.															
1991—Pittsburgh NFL	12	8	286	156	54.5	1963	11	7	6.86	30	78.8	18	82	4.6	1	1	0	6
1992—Pittsburgh NFL	12	12	313	185	59.1	2283	13	9	7.29	27	83.6	27	5	0.2	1	1	0	6
1993—Pittsburgh NFL	16	15	486	270	55.6	3208	14	7	6.60	41	79.5	26	111	4.3	0	0	0	0
1994—Pittsburgh NFL	14	14	370	212	57.3	2443	13	9	6.60	35	78.9	31	80	2.6	1	1	0	6
1995—Pittsburgh NFL	12	12	416	246	59.1	2970	17	7	7.14	15	87.7	24	45	1.9	0	0	0	0
1996—New York Jets NFL	6	6	188	110	58.5	1147	4	7	6.10	18	67.8	6	30	5.0	0	0	0	0
1997—New York Jets NFL	15	14	460	259	56.3	2796	17	7	6.08	45	80.3	32	36	1.1	1	1	0	6
1998—Cincinnati NFL	13	11	343	212	§61.8	2216	15	4	6.46	30	90.2	13	34	2.6	0	0	0	0
1999—Tennessee NFL	8	5	195	116	59.5	1382	10	5	7.09	9	87.6	19	1	0.1	0	0	0	0
2000—Tennessee NFL	5	1	64	36	56.3	530	2	3	8.28	3	74.3	9	-2	-0.2	0	0	0	0
2001—Tennessee NFL	5	1	76	42	55.3	496	2	2	6.53	6	73.1	6	28	4.7	0	0	0	0
2002—Tennessee NFL	4	0	5	3	60.0	24	0	0	4.80	0	72.1	3	-3	-1.0	0	0	0	0
2003—Tennessee NFL	1	1	27	18	66.7	232	2	1	8.59	0	102.7	1	-1	-1.0	0	0	0	0
Pro totals (13 years)	123	100	3229	1865	57.8	21690	120	68	6.72	259	81.8	215	446	2.1	4	4	0	24

O'DWYER, MATT — G — BUCCANEERS

PERSONAL: Born September 1, 1972, in Lincolnshire, Ill. ... 6-5/305. ... Full name: Matthew Phillip O'Dwyer.
HIGH SCHOOL: Adlai E. Stevenson (Prairie View, Ill.).
COLLEGE: Northwestern.
TRANSACTIONS/CAREER NOTES: Selected by New York Jets in second round (33rd pick overall) of 1995 NFL draft. ... Signed by Jets (July 20, 1995). ... Granted unconditional free agency (February 12, 1999). ... Signed by Cincinnati Bengals (June 19, 1999). ... Suspended two games by NFL for involvement in bar fight (March 14, 2000). ... On injured reserve with broken ankle (November 20, 2000-remainder of season). ... Granted unconditional free agency (March 2, 2001). ... Re-signed by Bengals (March 2, 2001). ... On injured reserve with foot injury (December 9, 2003-remainder of season). ... Granted unconditional free agency (March 3, 2004). ... Signed by Tampa Bay Buccaneers (March 9, 2004).
PLAYING EXPERIENCE: New York Jets NFL, 1995-1998; Cincinnati NFL, 1999-2003. ... Games/Games started: 1995 (12/2), 1996 (16/16), 1997 (16/16), 1998 (16/16), 1999 (16/16), 2000 (10/10), 2001 (12/12), 2002 (16/16), 2003 (4/1). Total: 118/105.
CHAMPIONSHIP GAME EXPERIENCE: Played in AFC championship game (1998 season).

O

OFFORD, WILLIE — S — VIKINGS

PERSONAL: Born December 22, 1978, in Palatka, Fla. ... 6-1/216.
HIGH SCHOOL: Palatka (Fla.).
COLLEGE: South Carolina.

TRANSACTIONS/CAREER NOTES: Selected by Minnesota Vikings in third round (70th pick overall) of 2002 NFL draft. ... Signed by Vikings (July 25, 2002).

Year Team	G	GS	TOTALS Tk.	Ast.	Sks.	INTERCEPTIONS No.	Yds.	Avg.	TD
2002—Minnesota NFL	12	6	23	4	0.0	1	6	6.0	0
2003—Minnesota NFL	16	0	4	0	0.0	0	0	0.0	0
Pro totals (2 years)	28	6	27	4	0.0	1	6	6.0	0

OGBOGU, ERIC — DE — COWBOYS

PERSONAL: Born July 18, 1975, in Irvington, N.Y. ... 6-4/270. ... Name pronounced: a-BAH-goo.
HIGH SCHOOL: Archbishop Stepinac (White Plains, N.Y.).
COLLEGE: Maryland.
TRANSACTIONS/CAREER NOTES: Selected by New York Jets in sixth round (163rd pick overall) of 1998 NFL draft. ... Signed by Jets (July 2, 1998). ... On injured reserve with shoulder injury (August 7, 2000-entire season). ... Granted unconditional free agency (March 1, 2002). ... Signed by Cincinnati Bengals (April 29, 2002). ... Released by Bengals (May 27, 2003). ... Signed by Dallas Cowboys (August 11, 2003).
CHAMPIONSHIP GAME EXPERIENCE: Played in AFC championship game (1998 season).

Year Team	G	GS	TOTALS Tk.	Ast.	Sks.
1998—New York Jets NFL	12	0	5	3	0.0
1999—New York Jets NFL	14	0	9	4	1.0
2000—New York Jets NFL			Did not play.		
2001—New York Jets NFL	15	0	15	3	0.0
2002—Cincinnati NFL	12	0	1	2	0.0
2003—Dallas NFL	16	3	24	9	3.5
Pro totals (5 years)	69	3	54	21	4.5

OGDEN, JONATHAN — T — RAVENS

PERSONAL: Born July 31, 1974, in Washington, DC. ... 6-9/340. ... Full name: Jonathan Phillip Ogden. ... Brother of Marques Ogden, offensive tackle, Jacksonville Jaguars.
HIGH SCHOOL: St. Alban's (Washington, D.C.).
COLLEGE: UCLA.
TRANSACTIONS/CAREER NOTES: Selected by Baltimore Ravens in first round (fourth pick overall) of 1996 NFL draft. ... Signed by Ravens (July 15, 1996).
PLAYING EXPERIENCE: Baltimore NFL, 1996-2003. ... Games/Games started: 1996 (16/16), 1997 (16/16), 1998 (13/13), 1999 (16/16), 2000 (15/15), 2001 (16/16), 2002 (16/16), 2003 (16/16). Total: 124/124.
CHAMPIONSHIP GAME EXPERIENCE: Played in AFC championship game (2000 season). ... Member of Super Bowl championship team (2000 season).
HONORS: Outland Trophy winner (1995). ... Named offensive lineman on THE SPORTING NEWS college All-America first team (1995). ... Named offensive tackle on the THE SPORTING NEWS NFL All-Pro team (1997 and 2000-2003). ... Played in Pro Bowl (1997-2003 seasons).

OGUNLEYE, ADEWALE — DE — DOLPHINS

PERSONAL: Born August 9, 1977, in Brooklyn, N.Y. ... 6-4/260.
HIGH SCHOOL: Tottenville (Staten Island, N.Y.).
COLLEGE: Indiana.
TRANSACTIONS/CAREER NOTES: Signed as non-drafted free agent by Miami Dolphins (April 25, 2000). ... On non-football injury list with knee injury (August 22, 2000-entire season). ... Signed by Dolphins (July 24, 2003). ... Granted free agency (March 3, 2004).
HONORS: Played in Pro Bowl (2003 season).

Year Team	G	GS	TOTALS Tk.	Ast.	Sks.
2001—Miami NFL	7	0	1	2	0.5
2002—Miami NFL	16	16	33	12	9.5
2003—Miami NFL	16	16	43	21	§15.0
Pro totals (3 years)	39	32	77	35	25.0

O

OHALETE, IFEANYI — CB/S — REDSKINS

PERSONAL: Born May 22, 1979, in Springfield, Ill. ... 6-2/222.
HIGH SCHOOL: Los Alamitos (Calif.).
COLLEGE: Southern California.
TRANSACTIONS/CAREER NOTES: Signed as non-drafted free agent by Washington Redskins (April 25, 2001). ... On injured reserve with knee and ankle injuries (December 23, 2003-remainder of season). ... Granted free agency (March 3, 2004). ... Re-signed by Redskins (May 12, 2004).

Year Team	G	GS	TOTALS Tk.	Ast.	Sks.	INTERCEPTIONS No.	Yds.	Avg.	TD
2001—Washington NFL	16	0	0	0	0.0	1	12	12.0	0
2002—Washington NFL	16	10	44	15	1.0	3	109	36.3	1
2003—Washington NFL	15	14	73	22	0.0	3	60	20.0	0
Pro totals (3 years)	47	24	117	37	1.0	7	181	25.9	1

O'HARA, SHAUN — G/C — GIANTS

PERSONAL: Born June 23, 1977, in Chicago, Ill. ... 6-3/306.
HIGH SCHOOL: Hillsborough (N.J.).
COLLEGE: Rutgers.
TRANSACTIONS/CAREER NOTES: Signed as non-drafted free agent by Cleveland Browns (April 17, 2000). ... Granted free agency (February 28, 2003). ... Re-signed by Browns (June 6, 2003). ... Granted unconditional free agency (March 3, 2004). ... Signed by New York Giants (March 6, 2004).
PLAYING EXPERIENCE: Cleveland NFL, 2000-2003. ... Games/Games started: 2000 (9/4), 2001 (16/4), 2002 (16/16), 2003 (14/14). Total: 55/38.

OKANLAWON, TONY — CB — CHARGERS

PERSONAL: Born March 4, 1979, in Lagos, Nigeria. ... 5-11/187.
HIGH SCHOOL: Dematha (Baltimore, Md.).
COLLEGE: Maryland.
TRANSACTIONS/CAREER NOTES: Signed as non-drafted free agent by San Diego Chargers (April 24, 2002). ... On injured reserve with knee injury (September 20, 2002-remainder of season). ... Released by Chargers (August 31, 2003). ... Re-signed by Chargers (November 19, 2003).

			TOTALS			INTERCEPTIONS			
Year Team	**G**	**GS**	**Tk.**	**Ast.**	**Sks.**	**No.**	**Yds.**	**Avg.**	**TD**
2003—San Diego NFL	1	0	0	0	0.0	0	0	0.0	0

OKEAFOR, CHIKE — DE — SEAHAWKS

PERSONAL: Born March 27, 1976, in Grand Rapids, Mich. ... 6-4/265. ... Full name: Chikeze Russell Okeafor. ... Name pronounced: chee-KAY oh-KEY-fer.
HIGH SCHOOL: West Lafayette (Ind.).
COLLEGE: Purdue.
TRANSACTIONS/CAREER NOTES: Selected by San Francisco 49ers in third round (89th pick overall) of 1999 NFL draft. ... Signed by 49ers (July 27, 1999). ... On non-football injury list with back injury (July 27-September 5, 1999). ... Granted free agency (March 1, 2002). ... Re-signed by 49ers (April 20, 2002). ... Granted unconditional free agency (February 28, 2003). ... Signed by Seattle Seahawks (April 4, 2003).

			TOTALS			INTERCEPTIONS			
Year Team	**G**	**GS**	**Tk.**	**Ast.**	**Sks.**	**No.**	**Yds.**	**Avg.**	**TD**
1999—San Francisco NFL	12	0	10	0	1.0	0	0	0.0	0
2000—San Francisco NFL	15	0	22	9	2.0	0	0	0.0	0
2001—San Francisco NFL	14	3	23	10	2.5	0	0	0.0	0
2002—San Francisco NFL	16	16	32	11	6.0	0	0	0.0	0
2003—Seattle NFL	16	16	33	14	8.0	1	18	18.0	0
Pro totals (5 years)	73	35	120	44	19.5	1	18	18.0	0

OKOBI, CHUKKY — C/G — STEELERS

PERSONAL: Born October 18, 1978, in Pittsburgh, Pa. ... 6-1/310. ... Full name: Chukwunweze Sonume Okobi.
HIGH SCHOOL: Trinity Prawling (N.Y.).
COLLEGE: Purdue.
TRANSACTIONS/CAREER NOTES: Selected by Pittsburgh Steelers in fifth round (146th pick overall) of 2001 NFL draft. ... Signed by Steelers (May 17, 2001). ... On physically unable to perform list with leg injury (July 20-August 14, 2001). ... Granted free agency (March 3, 2004). ... Re-signed by Steelers (March 16, 2004).
PLAYING EXPERIENCE: Pittsburgh NFL, 2001-2003. ... Games/Games started: 2001 (1/0), 2002 (13/5), 2003 (16/0). Total: 30/5.
CHAMPIONSHIP GAME EXPERIENCE: Member of Steelers for AFC championship game (2001 season); inactive.

OLSON, BENJI — G — TITANS

PERSONAL: Born June 5, 1975, in Bremerton, Wash. ... 6-4/320. ... Full name: Benji Dempsey Olson.
HIGH SCHOOL: South Kitsap (Port Orchard, Wash.).
COLLEGE: Washington.
TRANSACTIONS/CAREER NOTES: Selected after junior season by Tennessee Oilers in fifth round (139th pick overall) of 1998 NFL draft. ... Signed by Oilers (June 29, 1998). ... Oilers franchise renamed Tennessee Titans for 1999 season (December 26, 1998). ... Granted free agency (March 2, 2001). ... Re-signed by Titans (July 25, 2001).
PLAYING EXPERIENCE: Tennessee NFL, 1998-2003. ... Games/Games started: 1998 (13/1), 1999 (16/16), 2000 (16/16), 2001 (16/16), 2002 (16/16), 2003 (16/16). Total: 93/81.
CHAMPIONSHIP GAME EXPERIENCE: Played in AFC championship game (1999 and 2002 seasons). ... Played in Super Bowl 34 (1999 season).
HONORS: Named guard on THE SPORTING NEWS college All-America first team (1996).

O'NEAL, DELTHA — CB — BENGALS

PERSONAL: Born January 30, 1977, in Palo Alto, Calif. ... 5-10/196. ... Full name: Deltha Lee O'Neal III.
HIGH SCHOOL: West (Milpitas, Calif.).
COLLEGE: California.

TRANSACTIONS/CAREER NOTES: Selected by Denver Broncos in first round (15th pick overall) of 2000 NFL draft. ... Signed by Broncos (July 21, 2000). ... Traded by Broncos with first-round pick (RB Chris Perry) and fourth-round pick (DE Robert Geathers) in 2004 draft to Cincinnati Bengals for first-round pick (LB D.J. Williams) in 2004 draft (April 9, 2004).
HONORS: Named kick returner on THE SPORTING NEWS college All-America first team (1999). ... Named cornerback on THE SPORTING NEWS college All-America second team (1999). ... Played in Pro Bowl (2001 season).

			TOTALS			INTERCEPTIONS				PUNT RETURNS				KICKOFF RETURNS				TOTALS			
Year Team	G	GS	Tk.	Ast.	Sks.	No.	Yds.	Avg.	TD	No.	Yds.	Avg.	TD	No.	Yds.	Avg.	TD	TD	2pt.	Pts.	Fum.
2000—Den. NFL	16	0	3	0	0.0	0	0	0.0	0	34	354	10.4	0	46	1102	24.0	▲1	1	0	6	6
2001—Den. NFL	16	16	63	7	0.0	9	115	12.8	0	31	405	13.1	1	0	0	0.0	0	1	0	6	2
2002—Den. NFL	16	14	59	10	0.0	5	70	14.0	▲2	30	251	8.4	0	1	15	15.0	0	2	0	12	2
2003—Den. NFL	13	6	19	3	0.0	1	6	6.0	0	33	315	9.5	1	8	128	16.0	0	1	0	6	2
Pro totals (4 years)	61	36	144	20	0.0	15	191	12.7	2	128	1325	10.4	2	55	1245	22.6	1	5	0	30	12

O'NEIL, KEITH — LB — COWBOYS

PERSONAL: Born August 26, 1980, in Rochester, Mich. ... 6-0/230.
HIGH SCHOOL: Sweet Home (Amherst, N.Y.).
COLLEGE: Northern Arizona.
TRANSACTIONS/CAREER NOTES: Signed as non-drafted free agent by Dallas Cowboys (May 1, 2003).

			TOTALS			INTERCEPTIONS			
Year Team	G	GS	Tk.	Ast.	Sks.	No.	Yds.	Avg.	TD
2003—Dallas NFL	15	0	0	0	0.0	0	0	0.0	0

ORR, SHANTEE — LB — TEXANS

PERSONAL: Born May 28, 1981, in Detroit, Mich. ... 6-0/250. ... Full name: Shantee DeShJuan Orr.
HIGH SCHOOL: Denby (Detroit, Mich.).
COLLEGE: Michigan.
TRANSACTIONS/CAREER NOTES: Signed as non-drafted free agent by Green Bay Packers (May 2, 2003). ... Claimed on waivers by Houston Texans (July 30, 2003). ... Waived by Texans (August 31, 2003). ... Re-signed by Texans to practice squad (September 1, 2003). ... Activated (November 16, 2003). ... On injured reserve with fibula injury (December 22, 2003-remainder of season).

			TOTALS			INTERCEPTIONS			
Year Team	G	GS	Tk.	Ast.	Sks.	No.	Yds.	Avg.	TD
2003—Houston NFL	6	0	3	3	2.0	0	0	0.0	0

OSGOOD, KASSIM — WR — CHARGERS

PERSONAL: Born May 20, 1980, in Boston, Mass. ... 6-5/209.
HIGH SCHOOL: North Salinas.
COLLEGE: San Diego State.
TRANSACTIONS/CAREER NOTES: Signed as non-drafted free agent by San Diego Chargers (May 2, 2003).
SINGLE GAME HIGHS (regular season): Receptions—4 (December 21, 2003, vs. Pittsburgh); yards—102 (December 21, 2003, vs. Pittsburgh); and touchdown receptions—1 (December 21, 2003, vs. Pittsburgh).
STATISTICAL PLATEAUS: 100-yard receiving games: 2003 (1). Total: 1.

			RECEIVING				TOTALS			
Year Team	G	GS	No.	Yds.	Avg.	TD	TD	2pt.	Pts.	Fum.
2003—San Diego NFL	16	2	13	278	21.4	2	2	0	12	0

OSIKA, CRAIG — G/C — BROWNS

PERSONAL: Born December 4, 1979, in Hobart, Ind. ... 6-3/293.
HIGH SCHOOL: Hobart (Ind.).
COLLEGE: Indiana.
TRANSACTIONS/CAREER NOTES: Signed as non-drafted free agent by San Diego Chargers (April 26, 2002). ... Released by Chargers (September 1, 2002). ... Re-signed by Chargers to practice squad (September 3, 2002). ... Signed by San Francisco 49ers off Chargers practice squad (September 25, 2002). ... Assigned by 49ers to Amsterdam Admirals in 2003 NFL Europe enhancement allocation program (February 4, 2003). ... Waived by 49ers (August 31, 2003). ... Signed by Cleveland Browns (September 17, 2003). ... Released by Browns (September 28, 2003). ... Re-signed by Browns to practice squad (September 30, 2003). ... Activated (October 17, 2003). ... Waived by Browns (November 11, 2003). ... Re-signed by Browns to practice squad (November 13, 2003). ... Activated (December 3, 2003).
PLAYING EXPERIENCE: San Francisco NFL, 2002; Cleveland NFL, 2003. ... Games/Games started: 2002 (1/0), 2003 (1/0). Total: 2/0.

OVERSTREET, WILL — LB — FALCONS

PERSONAL: Born October 7, 1979, in Jackson, Miss. ... 6-2/259. ... Full name: William Sparkman Overstreet.
HIGH SCHOOL: Jackson (Miss.) Prep.
COLLEGE: Tennessee.
TRANSACTIONS/CAREER NOTES: Selected by Atlanta Falcons in third round (80th pick overall) of 2002 NFL draft. ... Signed by Falcons (July 22, 2002). ... On injured reserve with shoulder injury (October 14, 2002-remainder of season).

			TOTALS			INTERCEPTIONS			
Year Team	G	GS	Tk.	Ast.	Sks.	No.	Yds.	Avg.	TD
2002—Atlanta NFL	2	0	2	0	0.0	0	0	0.0	0
2003—Atlanta NFL	4	2	4	2	0.0	0	0	0.0	0
Pro totals (2 years)	6	2	6	2	0.0	0	0	0.0	0

OWENS, JOHN — TE — LIONS

PERSONAL: Born January 10, 1980, in Washington, DC. ... 6-3/266. ... Full name: John Wesley Owens.
HIGH SCHOOL: DeMatha (Hyattsville, Md.).
COLLEGE: Notre Dame.
TRANSACTIONS/CAREER NOTES: Selected by Detroit Lions in fifth round (138th pick overall) of 2002 NFL draft. ... Signed by Lions (July 22, 2002).
SINGLE GAME HIGHS (regular season): Receptions—2 (October 20, 2002, vs. Chicago); yards—19 (October 20, 2002, vs. Chicago); and touchdown receptions—0.

			RECEIVING				TOTALS			
Year Team	G	GS	No.	Yds.	Avg.	TD	TD	2pt.	Pts.	Fum.
2002—Detroit NFL	15	8	5	49	9.8	0	0	0	0	0
2003—Detroit NFL	7	1	0	0	0.0	0	0	0	0	0
Pro totals (2 years)	22	9	5	49	9.8	0	0	0	0	0

OWENS, TERRELL — WR — EAGLES

PERSONAL: Born December 7, 1973, in Alexander City, Ala. ... 6-3/226. ... Full name: Terrell Eldorado Owens. ... Name pronounced: TARE-el.
HIGH SCHOOL: Benjamin Russell (Alexander City, Ala.).
COLLEGE: Chattanooga.
TRANSACTIONS/CAREER NOTES: Selected by San Francisco 49ers in third round (89th pick overall) of 1996 NFL draft. ... Signed by 49ers (July 18, 1996). ... On physically unable to perform list with foot injury (July 17-August 11, 1997). ... Designated by 49ers as franchise player (February 12, 1999). ... Re-signed by 49ers (June 4, 1999). ... On injured reserve with fractured collarbone (December 24, 2003-remainder of season). ... Traded by 49ers to Baltimore Ravens for a 2004 second-round draft choice (March 4, 2004). ... Traded by Ravens to Philadelphia Eagles as part of a three-way trade involving the San Francisco 49ers (March 16, 2004). The Ravens received a fifth-round draft choice from the Eagles as well as the 2004 second-round pick they sent to San Francisco in the March 4 trade. The 49ers received DE Brandon Whiting from Philadelphia.
CHAMPIONSHIP GAME EXPERIENCE: Played in NFC championship game (1997 season).
HONORS: Played in Pro Bowl (2000-2003 seasons). ... Named wide receiver on THE SPORTING NEWS NFL All-Pro team (2001 and 2002).
RECORDS: Holds NFL record for most receptions in a game—20 (December 17, 2000, vs. Chicago).
POST SEASON RECORDS: Holds NFL single-game and career record for two-point conversions—2 (January 5, 2003 vs. New York Giants).
SINGLE GAME HIGHS (regular season): Receptions—20 (December 17, 2000, vs. Chicago); yards—283 (December 17, 2000, vs. Chicago); and touchdown receptions—3 (October 14, 2001, vs. Atlanta).
STATISTICAL PLATEAUS: 100-yard receiving games: 1996 (1), 1998 (2), 1999 (2), 2000 (5), 2001 (6), 2002 (5), 2003 (4). Total: 25.

			RUSHING				RECEIVING				TOTALS			
Year Team	G	GS	Att.	Yds.	Avg.	TD	No.	Yds.	Avg.	TD	TD	2pt.	Pts.	Fum.
1996—San Francisco NFL	16	10	0	0	0.0	0	35	520	14.9	4	4	0	24	1
1997—San Francisco NFL	16	15	0	0	0.0	0	60	936	15.6	8	8	0	48	1
1998—San Francisco NFL	16	10	4	53	13.3	1	67	1097	16.4	14	15	1	92	1
1999—San Francisco NFL	14	14	0	0	0.0	0	60	754	12.6	4	4	0	24	1
2000—San Francisco NFL	14	13	3	11	3.7	0	97	1451	15.0	13	13	1	80	3
2001—San Francisco NFL	16	16	4	21	5.3	0	93	1412	15.2	*16	16	0	96	0
2002—San Francisco NFL	14	14	7	79	11.3	1	100	1300	13.0	*13	14	0	84	0
2003—San Francisco NFL	15	15	3	-2	-0.7	0	80	1102	13.8	9	9	0	54	0
Pro totals (8 years)	121	107	21	162	7.7	2	592	8572	14.5	81	83	2	502	7

PACE, CALVIN — DE — CARDINALS

PERSONAL: Born October 28, 1980, in Detroit, Mich. ... 6-4/262.
HIGH SCHOOL: Lithia Springs (Douglasville, Ga.).
COLLEGE: Wake Forest.
TRANSACTIONS/CAREER NOTES: Selected by Arizona Cardinals in first round (18th pick overall) of 2003 NFL draft. ... Signed by Cardinals (July 27, 2003).

			TOTALS		
Year Team	G	GS	Tk.	Ast.	Sks.
2003—Arizona NFL	16	16	25	7	1.0

PACE, ORLANDO — T — RAMS

PERSONAL: Born November 4, 1975, in Sandusky, Ohio. ... 6-7/325. ... Full name: Orlando Lamar Pace.
HIGH SCHOOL: Sandusky (Ohio).
COLLEGE: Ohio State.
TRANSACTIONS/CAREER NOTES: Selected after junior season by St. Louis Rams in first round (first pick overall) of 1997 NFL draft. ... Signed by Rams (August 16, 1997). ... Designated by Rams as franchise player (February 20, 2003). ... Re-signed by Rams (August 26, 2003). ... Designated by Rams as franchise player (February 24, 2004).
PLAYING EXPERIENCE: St. Louis NFL, 1997-2003. ... Games/Games started: 1997 (13/9), 1998 (16/16), 1999 (16/16), 2000 (16/16), 2001 (16/16), 2002 (10/10), 2003 (16/16). Total: 103/99.
CHAMPIONSHIP GAME EXPERIENCE: Played in NFC championship game (1999 and 2001 seasons). ... Member of Super Bowl championship team (1999 season). ... Played in Super Bowl 36 (2001 season).
HONORS: Lombardi Award winner (1995 and 1996). ... Named offensive tackle on THE SPORTING NEWS college All-America first team (1995 and 1996). ... Outland Trophy winner (1996). ... Named offensive tackle on THE SPORTING NEWS NFL All-Pro team (1999-2001 and 2003). ... Played in Pro Bowl (1999, 2000 and 2003 seasons). ... Named to play in Pro Bowl (2001 season); replaced by Tra Thomas due to injury. ... Named to play in Pro Bowl (2002 season); replaced by Jon Runyan due to injury.

PAGE, SOLOMON G/T

PERSONAL: Born February 27, 1976, in Pittsburgh, Pa. ... 6-4/325.
HIGH SCHOOL: Brashear (Pittsburgh).
COLLEGE: West Virginia.
TRANSACTIONS/CAREER NOTES: Selected after junior season by Dallas Cowboys in second round (55th pick overall) of 1999 NFL draft. ... Signed by Cowboys (July 28, 1999). ... On injured reserve with knee injury (December 24, 2001-remainder of season). ... Granted unconditional free agency (February 28, 2003). ... Signed by San Diego Chargers (June 4, 2003). ... Granted unconditional free agency (March 3, 2004).
PLAYING EXPERIENCE: Dallas NFL, 1999-2002; San Diego NFL, 2003. ... Games/Games started: 1999 (14/6), 2000 (16/16), 2001 (14/14), 2002 (15/15), 2003 (8/7). Total: 67/58.

PAGEL, DEREK S JETS

PERSONAL: Born October 24, 1979, in Plainfield, Iowa. ... 6-1/208.
HIGH SCHOOL: Nashua-Plainfield (Plainfield, Iowa).
COLLEGE: Iowa.
TRANSACTIONS/CAREER NOTES: Selected by New York Jets in fifth round (140th pick overall) of 2003 NFL draft. ... Signed by Jets (July 14, 2003).

			TOTALS			INTERCEPTIONS			
Year Team	G	GS	Tk.	Ast.	Sks.	No.	Yds.	Avg.	TD
2003—New York Jets NFL	14	0	0	1	0.0	0	0	0.0	0

PALEPOI, ANTON DE SEAHAWKS

PERSONAL: Born November 19, 1978, in American Samoa. ... 6-3/283. ... Full name: Anton Charles Palepoi.
HIGH SCHOOL: Hunter (Salt Lake City, Utah).
JUNIOR COLLEGE: Dixie College (Utah).
COLLEGE: UNLV.
TRANSACTIONS/CAREER NOTES: Selected by Seattle Seahawks in second round (60th pick overall) of 2002 NFL draft. ... Signed by Seahawks (July 25, 2002).

			TOTALS		
Year Team	G	GS	Tk.	Ast.	Sks.
2002—Seattle NFL	13	1	10	7	1.0
2003—Seattle NFL	7	0	1	2	0.0
Pro totals (2 years)	20	1	11	9	1.0

PALMER, JESSE QB GIANTS

PERSONAL: Born October 5, 1978, in Toronto, ON. ... 6-2/225. ... Full name: Jesse James Palmer.
HIGH SCHOOL: St. Pius X (Ottawa).
COLLEGE: Florida.
TRANSACTIONS/CAREER NOTES: Selected by New York Giants in fourth round (125th pick overall) of 2001 NFL draft. ... Signed by Giants (July 26, 2001). ... Inactive for all 16 games (2001). ... Granted free agency (March 3, 2004). ... Re-signed by Giants (April 16, 2004).
SINGLE GAME HIGHS (regular season): Attempts—44 (December 28, 2003, vs. Carolina); completions—18 (December 28, 2003, vs. Carolina); yards—190 (December 21, 2003, vs. Dallas); and touchdown passes—2 (December 28, 2003, vs. Carolina)..
MISCELLANEOUS: Regular-season record as starting NFL quarterback: 0-3 (.000).

			PASSING									RUSHING				TOTALS		
Year Team	G	GS	Att.	Cmp.	Pct.	Yds.	TD	Int.	Avg.	Skd.	Rat.	Att.	Yds.	Avg.	TD	TD	2pt.	Pts.
2001—New York Giants NFL								Did not play.										
2002—New York Giants NFL	2	0	4	3	75.0	30	0	0	7.50	0	95.8	1	-3	-3.0	0	0	0	0
2003—New York Giants NFL	6	3	116	60	51.7	532	3	4	4.59	16	58.5	4	23	5.8	0	0	0	0
Pro totals (2 years)	8	3	120	63	52.5	562	3	4	4.68	16	59.8	5	20	4.0	0	0	0	0

PARKER, ERIC WR CHARGERS

PERSONAL: Born April 14, 1979, in Shorewood, Ill. ... 6-0/180. ... Full name: Eric Samuel Parker.
HIGH SCHOOL: Joliet Township (Shorewood, Ill.).
COLLEGE: Tennessee.
TRANSACTIONS/CAREER NOTES: Signed as non-drafted free agent by Houston Texans (April 25, 2002). ... Released by Texans (July 13, 2002). ... Signed by San Diego Chargers (July 23, 2002). ... Released by Chargers (September 1, 2002). ... Re-signed by Chargers to practice squad (September 3, 2002). ... Activated (September 26, 2002). ... Released by Chargers (October 12, 2002). ... Re-signed by Chargers (October 15, 2002). ... On injured reserve with shoulder injury (November 5, 2003-remainder of season).
SINGLE GAME HIGHS (regular season): Receptions—7 (December 8, 2002, vs. Oakland); yards—96 (December 8, 2002, vs. Oakland); and touchdown receptions—1 (October 5, 2003, vs. Jacksonville).

P

			RUSHING				RECEIVING				PUNT RETURNS				TOTALS			
Year Team	G	GS	Att.	Yds.	Avg.	TD	No.	Yds.	Avg.	TD	No.	Yds.	Avg.	TD	TD	2pt.	Pts.	Fum.
2002—San Diego NFL	9	2	0	0	0.0	0	17	268	15.8	1	0	0	0.0	0	1	0	6	0
2003—San Diego NFL	8	4	3	21	7.0	0	18	244	13.6	3	23	207	9.0	0	3	0	18	1
Pro totals (2 years)	17	6	3	21	7.0	0	35	512	14.6	4	23	207	9.0	0	4	0	24	1

PARKER, RIDDICK — DE

PERSONAL: Born November 20, 1972, in Emporia, Va. ... 6-3/295.
HIGH SCHOOL: Southampton (Courtland, Va.).
COLLEGE: North Carolina.
TRANSACTIONS/CAREER NOTES: Signed as non-drafted free agent by San Diego Chargers (April 28, 1995). ... Released by Chargers (August 22, 1995). ... Signed by Seattle Seahawks (July 8, 1996). ... Released by Seahawks (August 24, 1996). ... Re-signed by Seahawks to practice squad (August 26, 1996). ... Granted free agency (February 11, 2000). ... Re-signed by Seahawks (May 12, 2000). ... Granted unconditional free agency (March 2, 2001). ... Signed by New England Patriots (June 5, 2001). ... Granted unconditional free agency (March 1, 2002). ... Signed by New York Jets (April 22, 2002). ... Released by Jets (July 17, 2002). ... Signed by Patriots (July 26, 2002). ... Released by Patriots (September 1, 2002). ... Signed by Baltimore Ravens (October 15, 2002). ... Granted unconditional free agency (February 28, 2003). ... Re-signed by Ravens (March 11, 2003). ... Granted unconditional free agency (March 3, 2004).
CHAMPIONSHIP GAME EXPERIENCE: Played in AFC championship game (2001 season). ... Member of Super Bowl championship team (2001 season); did not play.

			TOTALS		
Year Team	**G**	**GS**	**Tk.**	**Ast.**	**Sks.**
1997—Seattle NFL	12	0	2	1	0.0
1998—Seattle NFL	8	0	5	2	1.0
1999—Seattle NFL	16	3	15	9	2.0
2000—Seattle NFL	16	16	32	16	0.0
2001—New England NFL	13	0	7	3	1.0
2002—Baltimore NFL	11	0	15	4	1.0
2003—Baltimore NFL	6	1	5	3	0.0
Pro totals (7 years)	82	20	81	38	5.0

PARKER, VAUGHN — T

PERSONAL: Born June 5, 1971, in Buffalo, N.Y. ... 6-3/300. ... Full name: Vaughn Antoine Parker.
HIGH SCHOOL: Saint Joseph's Collegiate Institute (Buffalo).
COLLEGE: UCLA.
TRANSACTIONS/CAREER NOTES: Selected by San Diego Chargers in second round (63rd pick overall) of 1994 NFL draft. ... Signed by Chargers (July 12, 1994). ... Granted free agency (February 14, 1997). ... Re-signed by Chargers (June 6, 1997). ... On injured reserve with leg injury (December 12, 1998-remainder of season). ... Granted unconditional free agency (February 11, 2000). ... Re-signed by Chargers (February 11, 2000). ... On injured reserve with knee injury (September 24, 2003-remainder of season). ... Released by Chargers (March 2, 2004).
PLAYING EXPERIENCE: San Diego NFL, 1994-2003. ... Games/Games started: 1994 (6/0), 1995 (15/7), 1996 (16/16), 1997 (16/16), 1998 (6/6), 1999 (15/15), 2000 (16/16), 2001 (16/16), 2002 (12/12), 2003 (3/3). Total: 121/107.
CHAMPIONSHIP GAME EXPERIENCE: Played in AFC championship game (1994 season). ... Played in Super Bowl 29 (1994 season).

PARRELLA, JOHN — DT — RAIDERS

PERSONAL: Born November 22, 1969, in Topeka, Kan. ... 6-3/300. ... Full name: John Lorin Parrella.
HIGH SCHOOL: Grand Island (Neb.) Central Catholic.
COLLEGE: Nebraska.
TRANSACTIONS/CAREER NOTES: Selected by Buffalo Bills in second round (55th pick overall) of 1993 NFL draft. ... Signed by Bills (July 12, 1993). ... Released by Bills (August 28, 1994). ... Signed by San Diego Chargers (September 12, 1994). ... Granted free agency (February 16, 1996). ... Re-signed by Chargers (June 14, 1996). ... Granted unconditional free agency (March 1, 2002). ... Signed by Oakland Raiders (March 7, 2002). ... On injured reserve with groin injury (December 10, 2003-remainder of season).
CHAMPIONSHIP GAME EXPERIENCE: Member of Bills for AFC championship game (1993 season); inactive. ... Member of Bills for Super Bowl 28 (1993 season); inactive. ... Played in AFC championship game (1994 and 2002 seasons). ... Played in Super Bowl 29 (1994 season). ... Played in Super Bowl 37 (2002 season).

			TOTALS		
Year Team	**G**	**GS**	**Tk.**	**Ast.**	**Sks.**
1993—Buffalo NFL	10	0	1	1	1.0
1994—San Diego NFL	13	1	4	3	1.0
1995—San Diego NFL	16	1	9	4	2.0
1996—San Diego NFL	16	9	31	7	2.0
1997—San Diego NFL	16	16	32	7	3.5
1998—San Diego NFL	16	16	30	7	1.5
1999—San Diego NFL	16	16	45	9	5.5
2000—San Diego NFL	16	16	54	11	7.0
2001—San Diego NFL	16	16	61	6	2.0
2002—Oakland NFL	16	15	36	8	1.0
2003—Oakland NFL	5	5	14	4	0.0
Pro totals (11 years)	156	111	317	67	26.5

PARRISH, TONY — S — 49ERS

PERSONAL: Born November 23, 1975, in Los Angeles, Calif. ... 6-0/210.
HIGH SCHOOL: Marina (Huntington Beach, Calif.).
COLLEGE: Washington.
TRANSACTIONS/CAREER NOTES: Selected by Chicago Bears in second round (35th pick overall) of 1998 NFL draft. ... Signed by Bears (July 20, 1998). ... Granted unconditional free agency (March 1, 2002). ... Signed by San Francisco 49ers (April 4, 2002).

Year Team	G	GS	TOTALS Tk.	Ast.	Sks.	INTERCEPTIONS No.	Yds.	Avg.	TD
1998—Chicago NFL	16	16	65	13	1.0	1	8	8.0	0
1999—Chicago NFL	16	16	87	13	0.0	1	41	41.0	0
2000—Chicago NFL	16	16	63	20	2.0	3	81	27.0	1
2001—Chicago NFL	16	16	56	11	1.0	3	36	12.0	0
2002—San Francisco NFL	16	16	63	9	0.0	7	204	29.1	0
2003—San Francisco NFL	16	16	51	15	0.5	†9	202	22.4	0
Pro totals (6 years)	96	96	385	81	4.5	24	572	23.8	1

PASS, PATRICK FB PATRIOTS

PERSONAL: Born December 31, 1977, in Scottsdale, Ga. ... 5-10/217. ... Full name: Patrick D. Pass.

HIGH SCHOOL: Tucker (Ga.).

COLLEGE: Georgia.

TRANSACTIONS/CAREER NOTES: Selected by New England Patriots in seventh round (239th pick overall) of 2000 NFL draft. ... Signed by Patriots (June 29, 2000). ... Released by Patriots (August 27, 2000). ... Re-signed by Patriots to practice squad (August 29, 2000). ... Activated (September 16, 2000). ... Granted free agency (February 28, 2003). ... Re-signed by Patriots (May 22, 2003). ... Released by Patriots (August 31, 2003). ... Re-signed by Patriots (September 22, 2003). ... Granted unconditional free agency (March 3, 2004). ... Re-signed by Patriots (March 16, 2004).

CHAMPIONSHIP GAME EXPERIENCE: Played in AFC championship game (2001 and 2003 seasons). ... Member of Super Bowl championship team (2001 and 2003 seasons).

SINGLE GAME HIGHS (regular season): Attempts—12 (November 19, 2000, vs. Cincinnati); yards—39 (November 19, 2000, vs. Cincinnati); and rushing touchdowns—0.

MISCELLANEOUS: Selected by Florida Marlins organization in 44th round of free-agent draft (June 4, 1996).

Year Team	G	GS	RUSHING Att.	Yds.	Avg.	TD	RECEIVING No.	Yds.	Avg.	TD	KICKOFF RETURNS No.	Yds.	Avg.	TD	TOTALS TD	2pt.	Pts.	Fum.
2000—New England NFL	5	2	18	58	3.2	0	4	17	4.3	0	0	0	0.0	0	0	0	0	0
2001—New England NFL	16	0	1	7	7.0	0	6	66	11.0	1	10	222	22.2	0	1	0	6	0
2002—New England NFL	15	0	4	27	6.8	0	0	0	0.0	0	7	123	17.6	0	0	0	0	0
2003—New England NFL	13	1	6	27	4.5	0	4	21	5.3	0	11	254	23.1	0	0	0	0	0
Pro totals (4 years)	49	3	29	119	4.1	0	14	104	7.4	1	28	599	21.4	0	1	0	6	0

PATHON, JEROME WR SAINTS

PERSONAL: Born December 16, 1975, in Cape Town, South Africa. ... 6-0/182. ... Name pronounced: PAY-thin.

HIGH SCHOOL: Carson Graham Secondary School (North Vancouver).

COLLEGE: Washington.

TRANSACTIONS/CAREER NOTES: Selected by Indianapolis Colts in second round (32nd pick overall) of 1998 NFL draft. ... Signed by Colts (July 26, 1998). ... On injured reserve with foot injury (November 19, 2001-remainder of season). ... Granted unconditional free agency (March 1, 2002). ... Signed by New Orleans Saints (April 15, 2002).

HONORS: Named wide receiver on THE SPORTING NEWS college All-America second team (1997).

SINGLE GAME HIGHS (regular season): Receptions—9 (September 23, 2001, vs. Buffalo); yards—168 (September 23, 2001, vs. Buffalo); and touchdown receptions—1 (December 21, 2003, vs. Jacksonville).

STATISTICAL PLATEAUS: 100-yard receiving games: 2001 (1). Total: 1.

Year Team	G	GS	RECEIVING No.	Yds.	Avg.	TD	TOTALS TD	2pt.	Pts.	Fum.
1998—Indianapolis NFL	16	15	50	511	10.2	1	1	0	6	0
1999—Indianapolis NFL	12	2	14	163	11.6	0	0	0	0	0
2000—Indianapolis NFL	16	10	50	646	12.9	3	3	0	18	0
2001—Indianapolis NFL	4	3	24	330	13.8	2	2	0	12	0
2002—New Orleans NFL	14	13	43	523	12.2	4	4	0	24	0
2003—New Orleans NFL	16	12	44	578	13.1	4	4	0	24	1
Pro totals (6 years)	78	55	225	2751	12.2	14	14	0	84	1

PATTEN, DAVID WR PATRIOTS

PERSONAL: Born August 19, 1974, in Hopkins, S.C. ... 5-10/190.

HIGH SCHOOL: Lower Richland (Hopkins, S.C.).

COLLEGE: Western Carolina.

TRANSACTIONS/CAREER NOTES: Played for Albany Firebirds of Arena League (1996). ... Signed as non-drafted free agent by New York Giants (March 24, 1997). ... Released by Giants (August 24, 1997). ... Re-signed by Giants to practice squad (August 25, 1997). ... Activated (August 27, 1997). ... On injured reserve with knee injury (December 16, 1998-remainder of season). ... Granted free agency (February 11, 2000). ... Signed by Cleveland Browns (March 16, 2000). ... Granted unconditional free agency (March 2, 2001). ... Signed by New England Patriots (April 2, 2001). ... On injured reserve with knee injury (November 7, 2003-remainder of season).

CHAMPIONSHIP GAME EXPERIENCE: Played in AFC championship game (2001 season). ... Member of Super Bowl championship team (2001 season).

SINGLE GAME HIGHS (regular season): Receptions—7 (September 29, 2002, vs. San Diego); yards—117 (October 21, 2001, vs. Indianapolis); and touchdown receptions—2 (October 6, 2002, vs. Miami).

STATISTICAL PLATEAUS: 100-yard receiving games: 2000 (2), 2001 (1), 2002 (2). Total: 5.

Year Team	G	GS	RECEIVING No.	Yds.	Avg.	TD	KICKOFF RETURNS No.	Yds.	Avg.	TD	TOTALS TD	2pt.	Pts.	Fum.
1997—New York Giants NFL	16	3	13	226	17.4	2	8	123	15.4	0	2	0	12	2
1998—New York Giants NFL	12	0	11	119	10.8	1	43	928	21.6	1	2	0	12	0
1999—New York Giants NFL	16	0	9	115	12.8	0	33	673	20.4	0	0	0	0	0
2000—Cleveland NFL	14	11	38	546	14.4	1	22	469	21.3	0	1	0	6	2

Year	Team	G	GS	RECEIVING No.	Yds.	Avg.	TD	KICKOFF RETURNS No.	Yds.	Avg.	TD	TOTALS TD	2pt.	Pts.	Fum.
2001—New England NFL		16	14	51	749	14.7	4	2	44	22.0	0	5	0	30	1
2002—New England NFL		16	14	61	824	13.5	5	0	0	0.0	0	5	0	30	0
2003—New England NFL		6	5	9	140	15.6	0	0	0	0.0	0	0	0	0	0
Pro totals (7 years)		96	47	192	2719	14.2	13	108	2237	20.7	1	15	0	90	5

PAXTON, LONIE — C/LS — PATRIOTS

PERSONAL: Born March 13, 1978, in Anaheim, Calif. ... 6-2/260. ... Full name: Leonidas E. Paxton.
HIGH SCHOOL: Centennial (Carona, Calif.).
COLLEGE: Sacramento State.
TRANSACTIONS/CAREER NOTES: Signed as non-drafted free agent by New England Patriots (April 19, 2000). ... Granted free agency (February 28, 2003). ... Re-signed by Patriots (February 28, 2003). ... On injured reserve with leg injury (December 10, 2003-remainder of season).
PLAYING EXPERIENCE: New England NFL, 2000-2003. ... Games/Games started: 2000 (16/0), 2001 (16/0), 2002 (16/0), 2003 (13/0). Total: 61/0.
CHAMPIONSHIP GAME EXPERIENCE: Played in AFC championship game (2001 season). ... Member of Super Bowl championship team (2001 season).

PAYNE, SETH — DT — TEXANS

PERSONAL: Born February 12, 1975, in Clifton Springs, N.Y. ... 6-4/303. ... Full name: Seth Copeland Payne.
HIGH SCHOOL: Victor (N.Y.) Central.
COLLEGE: Cornell.
TRANSACTIONS/CAREER NOTES: Selected by Jacksonville Jaguars in fourth round (114th pick overall) of 1997 NFL draft. ... Signed by Jaguars (May 23, 1997). ... On injured reserve with shoulder injury (November 17, 1998-remainder of season). ... Selected by Houston Texans from Jaguars in NFL expansion draft (February 18, 2002). ... On injured reserve with knee injury (September 15, 2003-remainder of season).
CHAMPIONSHIP GAME EXPERIENCE: Played in AFC championship game (1999 season).

Year	Team	G	GS	TOTALS Tk.	Ast.	Sks.
1997—Jacksonville NFL		12	5	12	2	0.0
1998—Jacksonville NFL		6	1	7	4	0.0
1999—Jacksonville NFL		16	16	13	11	1.5
2000—Jacksonville NFL		16	14	22	11	2.0
2001—Jacksonville NFL		16	16	41	14	5.0
2002—Houston NFL		16	16	54	11	1.0
2003—Houston NFL		2	2	6	3	1.0
Pro totals (7 years)		84	70	155	56	10.5

PEARSON, MIKE — T — JAGUARS

PERSONAL: Born August 22, 1980, in Tampa, Fla. ... 6-7/297. ... Full name: Michael Wayne Pearson.
HIGH SCHOOL: Armwood (Seffner, Fla.).
COLLEGE: Florida.
TRANSACTIONS/CAREER NOTES: Selected after junior season by Jacksonville Jaguars in second round (40th pick overall) of 2002 NFL draft. ... Signed by Jaguars (July 24, 2002).
PLAYING EXPERIENCE: Jacksonville NFL, 2002-2003. ... Games/Games started: 2002 (16/11), 2003 (16/16). Total: 32/27.
HONORS: Named offensive tackle on THE SPORTING NEWS college All-America first team (2001).

PEDERSON, DOUG — QB — PACKERS

PERSONAL: Born January 31, 1968, in Bellingham, Wash. ... 6-3/220. ... Full name: Douglas Irvin Pederson.
HIGH SCHOOL: Ferndale (Wash.).
COLLEGE: Louisiana-Monroe.
TRANSACTIONS/CAREER NOTES: Signed as non-drafted free agent by Miami Dolphins (April 30, 1991). ... Released by Dolphins (August 16, 1991). ... Selected by New York/New Jersey Knights in fifth round (49th pick overall) of 1992 World League draft. ... Re-signed by Dolphins (June 1, 1992). ... Released by Dolphins (August 31, 1992). ... Re-signed by Dolphins to practice squad (September 1, 1992). ... Released by Dolphins (October 7, 1992). ... Re-signed by Dolphins (March 3, 1993). ... Released by Dolphins (August 30, 1993). ... Re-signed by Dolphins to practice squad (August 31, 1993). ... Activated (October 22, 1993). ... Released by Dolphins (December 15, 1993). ... Re-signed by Dolphins (April 15, 1994). ... Inactive for all 16 games (1994). ... Selected by Carolina Panthers from Dolphins in NFL expansion draft (February 15, 1995). ... Released by Panthers (May 22, 1995). ... Signed by Dolphins (July 11, 1995). ... Released by Dolphins (August 21, 1995). ... Re-signed by Dolphins (October 10, 1995). ... Inactive for two games with Dolphins (1995). ... Released by Dolphins (October 25, 1995). ... Signed by Green Bay Packers (November 22, 1995). ... Inactive for five games with Packers (1995). ... Granted unconditional free agency (February 14, 1997). ... Re-signed by Packers (February 20, 1997). ... Granted unconditional free agency (February 12, 1999). ... Signed by Philadelphia Eagles (February 17, 1999). ... Released by Eagles (August 27, 2000). ... Signed by Cleveland Browns (September 1, 2000). ... Released by Browns (February 22, 2001). ... Signed by Packers (March 13, 2001). ... Granted unconditional free agency (March 1, 2002). ... Re-signed by Packers (April 2, 2002). ... Granted unconditional free agency (February 28, 2003). ... Re-signed by Packers (April 29, 2003). ... Granted unconditional free agency (March 3, 2004). ... Re-signed by Packers (April 28, 2004).
CHAMPIONSHIP GAME EXPERIENCE: Member of Packers for NFC championship game (1995-97 seasons); inactive. ... Member of Super Bowl championship team (1996 season); inactive. ... Member of Packers for Super Bowl 32 (1997 season); inactive.
SINGLE GAME HIGHS (regular season): Attempts—40 (December 10, 2000, vs. Philadelphia); completions—29 (December 10, 2000, vs. Philadelphia); yards—309 (December 10, 2000, vs. Philadelphia); and touchdown passes—2 (October 17, 1999, vs. Chicago).

STATISTICAL PLATEAUS: 300-yard passing games: 2000 (1). Total: 1.
MISCELLANEOUS: Regular-season record as starting NFL quarterback: 3-14 (.176).

Year Team	G	GS	PASSING Att.	Cmp.	Pct.	Yds.	TD	Int.	Avg.	Skd.	Rat.	RUSHING Att.	Yds.	Avg.	TD	TOTALS TD	2pt.	Pts.
1993—Miami NFL	7	0	8	4	50.0	41	0	0	5.13	1	65.1	2	-1	-0.5	0	0	0	0
1994—Miami NFL	Did not play.																	
1995—Miami NFL	Did not play.																	
—Green Bay NFL	Did not play.																	
1996—Green Bay NFL	1	0	0	0	0.0	0	0	0	0.00	0	0.0	0	0	0.0	0	0	0	0
1997—Green Bay NFL	1	0	0	0	0.0	0	0	0	0.00	0	0.0	3	-4	-1.3	0	0	0	0
1998—Green Bay NFL	12	0	24	14	58.3	128	2	0	5.33	1	100.7	8	-4	-0.5	0	0	0	0
1999—Philadelphia NFL	16	9	227	119	52.4	1276	7	9	5.62	20	62.9	20	33	1.7	0	0	0	0
2000—Cleveland NFL	11	8	210	117	55.7	1047	2	8	4.99	17	56.6	18	68	3.8	0	0	0	0
2001—Green Bay NFL	16	0	0	0	0.0	0	0	0	0.00	0	0.0	1	-1	-1.0	0	0	0	0
2002—Green Bay NFL	16	0	28	19	67.9	134	1	0	4.79	1	90.5	1	-1	-1.0	0	0	0	0
2003—Green Bay NFL	16	0	2	2	100.0	16	0	0	8.00	0	100.0	6	-5	-0.8	0	0	0	0
Pro totals (9 years)	96	17	499	275	55.1	2642	12	17	5.29	40	63.9	59	85	1.4	0	0	0	0

PEEK, ANTWAN — LB — TEXANS

PERSONAL: Born October 29, 1979, in Cincinnati, Ohio. ... 6-1/230.
HIGH SCHOOL: Woodward (Cincinnati).
COLLEGE: Cincinnati.
TRANSACTIONS/CAREER NOTES: Selected by Houston Texans in third round (67th pick overall) of 2003 NFL draft. ... Signed by Texans (July 23, 2003).

Year Team	G	GS	TOTALS Tk.	Ast.	Sks.	INTERCEPTIONS No.	Yds.	Avg.	TD
2003—Houston NFL	10	4	19	4	1.0	0	0	0.0	0

PEELLE, JUSTIN — TE — CHARGERS

PERSONAL: Born March 15, 1979, in Fresno, Calif. ... 6-4/255. ... Full name: Justin Morris Peelle.
HIGH SCHOOL: Dublin (Calif.).
COLLEGE: Oregon.
TRANSACTIONS/CAREER NOTES: Selected by San Diego Chargers in fourth round (103rd pick overall) of 2002 NFL draft. ... Signed by Chargers (July 18, 2002).
SINGLE GAME HIGHS (regular season): Receptions—4 (September 21, 2003, vs. Baltimore); yards—29 (December 21, 2003, vs. Pittsburgh); and touchdown receptions—1 (September 28, 2003, vs. Oakland).

Year Team	G	GS	RECEIVING No.	Yds.	Avg.	TD	TOTALS TD	2pt.	Pts.	Fum.
2002—San Diego NFL	15	2	3	15	5.0	0	0	0	0	0
2003—San Diego NFL	15	9	16	133	8.3	1	1	0	6	0
Pro totals (2 years)	30	11	19	148	7.8	1	1	0	6	0

PEETE, RODNEY — QB — PANTHERS

PERSONAL: Born March 16, 1966, in Mesa, Ariz. ... 6-0/230. ... Son of Willie Peete, former running backs coach and scout with Chicago Bears.
HIGH SCHOOL: Sahuaro (Tucson, Ariz.), then Shawnee Mission South (Overland Park, Kan.).
COLLEGE: Southern California.
TRANSACTIONS/CAREER NOTES: Selected by Detroit Lions in sixth round (141st pick overall) of 1989 NFL draft. ... Signed by Lions (July 13, 1989). ... On injured reserve with Achilles' tendon injury (October 30, 1991-remainder of season). ... Granted free agency (February 1, 1992). ... Re-signed by Lions (July 30, 1992). ... Granted unconditional free agency (February 17, 1994). ... Signed by Dallas Cowboys (May 4, 1994). ... Granted unconditional free agency (February 17, 1995). ... Signed by Philadelphia Eagles (April 22, 1995). ... Granted unconditional free agency (February 16, 1996). ... Re-signed by Eagles (March 14, 1996). ... On injured reserve with knee injury (October 3, 1996-remainder of season). ... Granted unconditional free agency (February 14, 1997). ... Re-signed by Eagles (April 1, 1997). ... Traded by Eagles to Washington Redskins for sixth-round pick (C John Romero) in 2000 draft (April 28, 1999). ... Released by Redskins (April 18, 2000). ... Signed by Oakland Raiders (July 13, 2000). ... Released by Raiders (September 2, 2001). ... Re-signed by Raiders (September 29, 2001). ... Granted unconditional free agency (March 1, 2002). ... Signed by Carolina Panthers (March 28, 2002). ... Granted unconditional free agency (February 28, 2003). ... Re-signed by Panthers (March 5, 2003).
CHAMPIONSHIP GAME EXPERIENCE: Member of Cowboys for NFC championship game (1994 season); did not play. ... Member of Raiders for AFC Championship game (2000 season); inactive. ... Member of Panthers for NFC championship game (2003 season); did not play. ... Member of Panthers for Super Bowl 38 (2003 season); did not play.
HONORS: Named quarterback on THE SPORTING NEWS college All-America second team (1988).
SINGLE GAME HIGHS (regular season): Attempts—45 (October 8, 1995, vs. Washington); completions—30 (October 8, 1995, vs. Washington); yards—323 (September 27, 1992, vs. Tampa Bay); and touchdown passes—4 (December 16, 1990, vs. Chicago).
STATISTICAL PLATEAUS: 300-yard passing games: 1990 (1), 1992 (1), 2002 (3). Total: 5.
MISCELLANEOUS: Selected by Toronto Blue Jays organization in 30th round of free-agent baseball draft (June 4, 1984); did not sign. ... Selected by Oakland Athletics organization in 14th round of free-agent baseball draft (June 1, 1988); did not sign. ... Selected by Athletics organization in 13th round of free-agent baseball draft (June 5, 1989); did not sign. ... Regular-season record as starting NFL quarterback: 45-42 (.517). ... Postseason record as starting NFL quarterback: 1-1 (.500).

P

Year Team	G	GS	PASSING Att.	Cmp.	Pct.	Yds.	TD	Int.	Avg.	Skd.	Rat.	RUSHING Att.	Yds.	Avg.	TD	TOTALS TD	2pt.	Pts.
1989—Detroit NFL	8	8	195	103	52.8	1479	5	9	7.58	27	67.0	33	148	4.5	4	4	0	24
1990—Detroit NFL	11	11	271	142	52.4	1974	13	8	7.28	27	79.8	47	363	7.7	6	6	0	36
1991—Detroit NFL	8	8	194	116	59.8	1339	5	9	6.90	11	69.9	25	125	5.0	2	2	0	12
1992—Detroit NFL	10	10	213	123	57.7	1702	9	9	7.99	28	80.0	21	83	4.0	0	0	0	0

Year	Team	G	GS	PASSING Att.	Cmp.	Pct.	Yds.	TD	Int.	Avg.	Skd.	Rat.	RUSHING Att.	Yds.	Avg.	TD	TOTALS TD	2pt.	Pts.
1993—Detroit NFL		10	10	252	157	62.3	1670	6	14	6.63	34	66.4	45	165	3.7	1	1	0	6
1994—Dallas NFL		7	1	56	33	58.9	470	4	1	8.39	4	102.5	9	-2	-0.2	0	0	0	0
1995—Philadelphia NFL		15	12	375	215	57.3	2326	8	14	6.20	33	67.3	32	147	4.6	1	1	0	6
1996—Philadelphia NFL		5	5	134	80	59.7	992	3	5	7.40	11	74.6	20	31	1.6	1	1	0	6
1997—Philadelphia NFL		5	3	118	68	57.6	869	4	4	7.36	17	78.0	8	37	4.6	0	0	0	0
1998—Philadelphia NFL		5	4	129	71	55.0	758	2	4	5.88	16	64.7	5	30	6.0	1	1	0	6
1999—Washington NFL		3	0	17	8	47.1	107	2	1	6.29	2	82.2	2	-1	-0.5	0	0	0	0
2000—Oakland NFL										Did not play.									
2001—Oakland NFL		1	0	0	0	0.0	0	0	0	0.00	0	0.0	0	0	0.0	0	0	0	0
2002—Carolina NFL		14	14	381	223	58.5	2630	15	14	6.90	31	77.4	22	14	0.6	0	0	0	0
2003—Carolina NFL		1	1	10	4	40.0	19	0	0	1.90	3	47.9	0	0	0.0	0	0	0	0
Pro totals (14 years)		103	87	2345	1343	57.3	16335	76	92	6.97	244	73.3	269	1140	4.2	16	16	0	96

PEKO, TUPE — C/G — COLTS

PERSONAL: Born September 19, 1978, in Whittier, Calif. ... 6-4/305. ... Full name: Siitupe Peko.
HIGH SCHOOL: La Serna (Calif.).
JUNIOR COLLEGE: Cerritos College (Calif.).
COLLEGE: Michigan State.
TRANSACTIONS/CAREER NOTES: Selected by New York Jets in seventh round (217th pick overall) in 2001 NFL draft. ... Signed by Jets (June 22, 2001). ... Released by Jets (September 2, 2001). ... Re-signed by Jets to practice squad (September 3, 2001). ... Released by Jets (September 26, 2001). ... Signed by Seattle Seahawks to practice squad (October 16, 2001). ... Released by Seahawks (September 2, 2002). ... Signed by Indianapolis Colts to practice squad (September 3, 2002). ... Activated (October 5, 2002).
PLAYING EXPERIENCE: Indianapolis NFL, 2003. ... Games/Games started: 2003 (16/1). Total: 16/1.
CHAMPIONSHIP GAME EXPERIENCE: Played in AFC championship game (2003 season).

PENNINGTON, CHAD — QB — JETS

PERSONAL: Born June 26, 1976, in Knoxville, Tenn. ... 6-3/225. ... Full name: James Chad Pennington.
HIGH SCHOOL: Webb (Knoxville, Tenn.).
COLLEGE: Marshall.
TRANSACTIONS/CAREER NOTES: Selected by New York Jets in first round (18th pick overall) of 2000 NFL draft. ... Signed by Jets (July 13, 2000).
HONORS: Named quarterback on THE SPORTING NEWS college All-America third team (1999).
SINGLE GAME HIGHS (regular season): Attempts—45 (November 2, 2003, vs. New York Giants); completions—28 (November 3, 2002, vs. San Diego); yards—324 (October 20, 2002, vs. Minnesota); and touchdown passes—4 (November 2, 2003, vs. New York Giants).
STATISTICAL PLATEAUS: 300-yard passing games: 2002 (1). Total: 1.
MISCELLANEOUS: Regular-season record as starting NFL quarterback: 12-9 (.571). ... Postseason record as starting NFL quarterback: 1-1 (.500).

Year	Team	G	GS	PASSING Att.	Cmp.	Pct.	Yds.	TD	Int.	Avg.	Skd.	Rat.	RUSHING Att.	Yds.	Avg.	TD	TOTALS TD	2pt.	Pts.
2000—New York Jets NFL		2	0	5	2	40.0	67	1	0	13.40	1	127.1	1	0	0.0	0	0	0	0
2001—New York Jets NFL		2	0	20	10	50.0	92	1	0	4.60	1	79.6	1	11	11.0	0	0	0	0
2002—New York Jets NFL		15	12	399	275	*68.9	3120	22	6	7.82	22	*104.2	29	49	1.7	2	2	0	12
2003—New York Jets NFL		10	9	297	189	63.6	2139	13	12	7.20	25	82.9	21	42	2.0	2	2	0	12
Pro totals (4 years)		29	21	721	476	66.0	5418	37	18	7.51	49	95.1	52	102	2.0	4	4	0	24

PEPPERS, JULIUS — DE — PANTHERS

PERSONAL: Born January 18, 1980, in Wilson, N.C. ... 6-6/283. ... Full name: Julius Frazier Peppers.
HIGH SCHOOL: Southern Nash (Bailey, N.C.).
COLLEGE: North Carolina.
TRANSACTIONS/CAREER NOTES: Selected after junior season by Carolina Panthers in first round (second pick overall) of 2002 NFL draft. ... Signed by Panthers (July 22, 2002). ... On suspended list for violating league substance abuse policy (December 4, 2002-remainder of season).
CHAMPIONSHIP GAME EXPERIENCE: Played in NFC championship game (2003 season). ... Played in Super Bowl 38 (2003 season).
HONORS: Lombardi Award winner (2001). ... Named defensive end on THE SPORTING NEWS college All-America first team (2001).

Year	Team	G	GS	TOTALS Tk.	Ast.	Sks.	INTERCEPTIONS No.	Yds.	Avg.	TD
2002—Carolina NFL		12	12	29	7	12.0	1	21	21.0	0
2003—Carolina NFL		16	16	39	7	7.0	0	0	0.0	0
Pro totals (2 years)		28	28	68	14	19.0	1	21	21.0	0

PERRY, TODD — G

PERSONAL: Born November 28, 1970, in Elizabethtown, Ky. ... 6-5/310. ... Full name: Todd Joseph Perry.
HIGH SCHOOL: North Hardin (Radcliff, Ky.).
COLLEGE: Kentucky.
TRANSACTIONS/CAREER NOTES: Selected by Chicago Bears in fourth round (97th pick overall) of 1993 NFL draft. ... Signed by Bears (June 16, 1993). ... On injured reserve with back injury (December 19, 1997-remainder of season). ... Granted unconditional free agency (February 11, 2000). ... Re-signed by Bears (May 4, 2000). ... Granted unconditional free agency (March 2, 2001). ... Signed by Miami Dolphins (March 3, 2001). ... Released by Dolphins (March 3, 2004).

PLAYING EXPERIENCE: Chicago NFL, 1993-2000; Miami NFL, 2001-2003. ... Games/Games started: 1993 (13/3), 1994 (15/4), 1995 (15/15), 1996 (16/16), 1997 (11/11), 1998 (16/16), 1999 (16/16), 2000 (16/16), 2001 (16/16), 2002 (16/16), 2003 (15/15). Total: 165/144.

PERRYMAN, RAY — S — JAGUARS

PERSONAL: Born November 27, 1978, in Phoenix, Ariz. ... 6-0/204. ... Full name: Raymond Perryman.
HIGH SCHOOL: South Mountain (Phoenix).
COLLEGE: Northern Arizona.
TRANSACTIONS/CAREER NOTES: Selected by Oakland Raiders in fifth round (158th pick overall) of 2001 NFL draft. ... Signed by Raiders (July 21, 2001). ... Released by Raiders (September 2, 2001). ... Re-signed by Raiders to practice squad (September 4, 2001). ... Activated (January 17, 2002). ... Assigned by Raiders to Amsterdam Admirals in 2002 NFL Europe enhancement allocation program (February 12, 2002). ... Released by Raiders (September 1, 2002). ... Signed by Baltimore Ravens to practice squad (November 19, 2002). ... Activated (November 27, 2002). ... Re-signed by Ravens (March 23, 2003). ... Waived by Ravens (August 25, 2003). ... Signed by Jacksonville Jaguars to practice squad (October 30, 2003). ... Activated (November 27, 2003).

			TOTALS			INTERCEPTIONS			
Year Team	G	GS	Tk.	Ast.	Sks.	No.	Yds.	Avg.	TD
2002—Baltimore NFL	2	0	0	0	0.0	0	0	0.0	0
2003—Jacksonville NFL	4	0	0	0	0.0	0	0	0.0	0
Pro totals (2 years)	6	0	0	0	0.0	0	0	0.0	0

PETERS, SCOTT — C/G — GIANTS

PERSONAL: Born November 23, 1978, in Arcadia, Calif. ... 6-3/300. ... Full name: Scott Thomas Peters.
HIGH SCHOOL: Amador Valley (Pleasanton, Calif.).
COLLEGE: Arizona State.
TRANSACTIONS/CAREER NOTES: Selected by Philadelphia Eagles in fourth round (124th pick overall) of 2002 NFL draft. ... Signed by Eagles (June 19, 2002). ... Released by Eagles (August 31, 2003). ... Signed by New York Giants (November 15, 2003).
PLAYING EXPERIENCE: New York Giants NFL, 2003. ... Games/Games started: 2003 (7/4). Total: 7/4.
CHAMPIONSHIP GAME EXPERIENCE: Member of Eagles for NFC championship game (2002 season); inactive.

PETERSON, ADRIAN — RB — BEARS

PERSONAL: Born July 1, 1979, in Gainesville, Fla. ... 5-10/210.
HIGH SCHOOL: Sante Fe (Alachua, Fla.).
COLLEGE: Georgia Southern.
TRANSACTIONS/CAREER NOTES: Selected by Chicago Bears in sixth round (199th pick overall) of 2002 NFL draft. ... Signed by Bears (July 25, 2002). ... On injured reserve with ankle injury (November 14, 2003-remainder of season).
SINGLE GAME HIGHS (regular season): Attempts—16 (October 19, 2003, vs. Seattle); yards—55 (October 19, 2003, vs. Seattle); and rushing touchdowns—1 (December 15, 2002, vs. New York Jets).

			RUSHING				RECEIVING				KICKOFF RETURNS				TOTALS			
Year Team	G	GS	Att.	Yds.	Avg.	TD	No.	Yds.	Avg.	TD	No.	Yds.	Avg.	TD	TD	2pt.	Pts.	Fum.
2002—Chicago NFL	9	0	19	101	5.3	1	3	18	6.0	0	2	37	18.5	0	1	0	6	0
2003—Chicago NFL	6	1	22	70	3.2	0	1	5	5.0	0	0	0	0.0	0	0	0	0	0
Pro totals (2 years)	15	1	41	171	4.2	1	4	23	5.8	0	2	37	18.5	0	1	0	6	0

PETERSON, JULIAN — LB — 49ERS

PERSONAL: Born July 28, 1978, in Temple Hills, Md. ... 6-3/235. ... Full name: Julian Thomas Peterson.
HIGH SCHOOL: Crossland (Temple Hills, Md.).
JUNIOR COLLEGE: Valley Forge Junior College (Pa.).
COLLEGE: Michigan State.
TRANSACTIONS/CAREER NOTES: Selected by San Francisco 49ers in first round (16th pick overall) of 2000 NFL draft. ... Signed by 49ers (July 27, 2000). ... Designated by 49ers as franchise player (February 24, 2004).
HONORS: Named linebacker on THE SPORTING NEWS NFL All-Pro team (2003). ... Played in Pro Bowl (2002 and 2003 seasons).

			TOTALS			INTERCEPTIONS			
Year Team	G	GS	Tk.	Ast.	Sks.	No.	Yds.	Avg.	TD
2000—San Francisco NFL	13	7	29	17	4.0	2	33	16.5	0
2001—San Francisco NFL	14	14	37	15	3.0	0	0	0.0	0
2002—San Francisco NFL	16	16	78	18	2.0	1	2	2.0	0
2003—San Francisco NFL	16	16	69	26	7.0	2	31	15.5	0
Pro totals (4 years)	59	53	213	76	16.0	5	66	13.2	0

PETERSON, KENNY — DT/DE — PACKERS

PERSONAL: Born November 21, 1978, in Canton, Ohio. ... 6-3/300.
HIGH SCHOOL: McKinley (Canton, Ohio).
COLLEGE: Ohio State.
TRANSACTIONS/CAREER NOTES: Selected by Green Bay Packers in third round (79th pick overall) of 2003 NFL draft. ... Signed by Packers (July 19, 2003).

			TOTALS		
Year Team	G	GS	Tk.	Ast.	Sks.
2003—Green Bay NFL	9	0	5	3	0.0

PETERSON, MIKE LB JAGUARS

PERSONAL: Born June 17, 1976, in Gainesville, Fla. ... 6-1/230. ... Full name: Porter Michael Peterson.
HIGH SCHOOL: Santa Fe (Alachua, Fla.).
COLLEGE: Florida.
TRANSACTIONS/CAREER NOTES: Selected by Indianapolis Colts in second round (36th pick overall) of 1999 NFL draft. ... Signed by Colts (July 28, 1999). ... Granted unconditional free agency (February 28, 2003). ... Signed by Jacksonville Jaguars (March 13, 2003).
HONORS: Named outside linebacker on THE SPORTING NEWS college All-America first team (1998).

			TOTALS			INTERCEPTIONS			
Year Team	G	GS	Tk.	Ast.	Sks.	No.	Yds.	Avg.	TD
1999—Indianapolis NFL	16	13	71	21	3.0	0	0	0.0	0
2000—Indianapolis NFL	16	16	103	55	0.0	2	8	4.0	0
2001—Indianapolis NFL	9	9	46	19	1.5	2	18	9.0	0
2002—Indianapolis NFL	16	16	103	33	0.0	3	96	32.0	0
2003—Jacksonville NFL	16	16	73	29	1.0	3	8	2.7	0
Pro totals (5 years)	73	70	396	157	5.5	10	130	13.0	0

PETERSON, TODD K 49ERS

PERSONAL: Born February 4, 1970, in Washington, DC. ... 5-10/177. ... Full name: Joseph Todd Peterson.
HIGH SCHOOL: Valdosta (Ga.) State.
COLLEGE: Georgia.
TRANSACTIONS/CAREER NOTES: Selected by New York Giants in seventh round (177th pick overall) of 1993 NFL draft. ... Signed by Giants (July 19, 1993). ... Released by Giants (August 24, 1993). ... Signed by New England Patriots to practice squad (November 30, 1993). ... Released by Patriots (December 6, 1993). ... Signed by Atlanta Falcons (May 3, 1994). ... Released by Falcons (August 29, 1994). ... Signed by Arizona Cardinals (October 12, 1994). ... Released by Cardinals (October 24, 1994). ... Signed by Seattle Seahawks (January 17, 1995). ... Granted free agency (February 13, 1998). ... Re-signed by Seahawks for 1998 season. ... Granted unconditional free agency (February 12, 1999). ... Re-signed by Seahawks (March 2, 1999). ... Released by Seahawks (August 27, 2000). ... Signed by Kansas City Chiefs (October 11, 2000). ... Granted unconditional free agency (March 1, 2002). ... Signed by Pittsburgh Steelers (March 25, 2002). ... On injured reserve with rib injury (November 19, 2002-remainder of season). ... Released by Steelers (February 27, 2003). ... Signed by San Francisco 49ers (October 28, 2003). ... Granted unconditional free agency (March 3, 2004). ... Re-signed by 49ers (March 23, 2004).

		FIELD GOALS							TOTALS		
Year Team	G	1-29	30-39	40-49	50+	Tot.	Pct.	Lg.	XPM	XPA	Pts.
1993—New England NFL				Did not play.							
1994—Arizona NFL	2	1-1	1-1	0-2	0-0	2-4	50.0	35	4	4	10
1995—Seattle NFL	16	6-6	9-10	8-10	0-2	23-28	82.1	49	§40	§40	109
1996—Seattle NFL	16	11-13	7-7	8-11	2-3	28-34	82.4	54	27	27	111
1997—Seattle NFL	16	9-9	7-10	5-7	1-2	22-28	78.6	52	37	37	103
1998—Seattle NFL	16	7-7	4-5	5-5	3-7	19-24	79.2	51	41	41	98
1999—Seattle NFL	16	11-11	8-11	14-16	1-2	34-40	85.0	51	32	32	134
2000—Kansas City NFL	11	6-6	7-9	2-5	0-0	15-20	75.0	42	25	25	70
2001—Kansas City NFL	16	9-11	9-10	8-12	1-2	27-35	77.1	51	27	28	108
2002—Pittsburgh NFL	10	3-4	6-10	3-7	0-0	12-21	57.1	46	25	26	61
2003—San Francisco NFL	8	5-7	3-3	4-4	0-1	12-15	80.0	48	22	23	58
Pro totals (10 years)	127	68-75	61-76	57-79	8-19	194-249	77.9	54	280	283	862

PETERSON, WILLIAM CB GIANTS

PERSONAL: Born June 15, 1979, in Uniontown, Pa. ... 6-0/200. ... Full name: William James Peterson Jr.
HIGH SCHOOL: Laurel Highlands (Pa.).
COLLEGE: Western Illinois.
TRANSACTIONS/CAREER NOTES: Selected by New York Giants in third round (78th pick overall) of 2001 NFL draft. ... Signed by Giants (July 26, 2001). ... On injured reserve with back injury (November 11, 2003-remainder of season). ... Granted free agency (March 3, 2004). ... Re-signed by Giants (March 15, 2004).

			TOTALS			INTERCEPTIONS			
Year Team	G	GS	Tk.	Ast.	Sks.	No.	Yds.	Avg.	TD
2001—New York Giants NFL	16	5	47	5	0.0	1	0	0.0	0
2002—New York Giants NFL	12	12	36	4	0.0	2	1	0.5	0
2003—New York Giants NFL	5	5	24	6	0.0	0	0	0.0	0
Pro totals (3 years)	33	22	107	15	0.0	3	1	0.3	0

PETITGOUT, LUKE T GIANTS

PERSONAL: Born June 16, 1976, in Milford, Del. ... 6-6/310. ... Full name: Lucas George Petitgout. ... Name pronounced: pet-ee-GOO.
HIGH SCHOOL: Sussex Central (Georgetown, Del.).
COLLEGE: Notre Dame.
TRANSACTIONS/CAREER NOTES: Selected by New York Giants in first round (19th pick overall) of 1999 NFL draft. ... Signed by Giants (July 29, 1999). ... Granted unconditional free agency (February 28, 2003). ... Re-signed by Giants (February 28, 2003). ... On injured reserve with back injury (December 17, 2003-remainder of season).
PLAYING EXPERIENCE: New York Giants NFL, 1999-2003. ... Games/Games started: 1999 (15/8), 2000 (16/16), 2001 (16/16), 2002 (16/16), 2003 (10/10). Total: 73/66.
CHAMPIONSHIP GAME EXPERIENCE: Played in NFC championship game (2000 season). ... Played in Super Bowl 35 (2000 season).

PHIFER, ROMAN — LB — PATRIOTS

PERSONAL: Born March 5, 1968, in Plattsburgh, N.Y. ... 6-2/248. ... Full name: Roman Zubinsky Phifer.
HIGH SCHOOL: South Mecklenburg (Charlotte).
COLLEGE: UCLA.
TRANSACTIONS/CAREER NOTES: Selected by Los Angeles Rams in second round (31st pick overall) of 1991 NFL draft. ... Signed by Rams (July 19, 1991). ... On injured reserve with broken leg (November 26, 1991-remainder of season). ... Granted unconditional free agency (February 17, 1995). ... Re-signed by Rams (March 22, 1995). ... Rams franchise moved to St. Louis (April 12, 1995). ... Granted unconditional free agency (February 12, 1999). ... Signed by New York Jets (March 9, 1999). ... Released by Jets (February 22, 2001). ... Signed by New England Patriots (August 3, 2001). ... Granted unconditional free agency (March 1, 2002). ... Re-signed by Patriots (June 21, 2002).
CHAMPIONSHIP GAME EXPERIENCE: Played in AFC championship game (2001 and 2003 seasons). ... Member of Super Bowl championship team (2001 and 2003 seasons).

			TOTALS			INTERCEPTIONS			
Year Team	G	GS	Tk.	Ast.	Sks.	No.	Yds.	Avg.	TD
1991—Los Angeles Rams NFL	12	5	21	3	2.0	0	0	0.0	0
1992—Los Angeles Rams NFL	16	14	51	15	0.0	1	3	3.0	0
1993—Los Angeles Rams NFL	16	16	96	21	0.0	0	0	0.0	0
1994—Los Angeles Rams NFL	16	15	79	17	1.5	2	7	3.5	0
1995—St. Louis NFL	16	16	87	28	3.0	3	52	17.3	0
1996—St. Louis NFL	15	15	104	18	1.5	0	0	0.0	0
1997—St. Louis NFL	16	15	57	18	2.0	0	0	0.0	0
1998—St. Louis NFL	13	13	57	14	6.5	1	41	41.0	0
1999—New York Jets NFL	16	12	36	14	4.5	2	20	10.0	0
2000—New York Jets NFL	16	10	32	13	4.0	0	0	0.0	0
2001—New England NFL	16	16	71	21	2.0	1	14	14.0	0
2002—New England NFL	14	14	69	40	0.5	0	0	0.0	0
2003—New England NFL	16	15	67	33	0.0	0	0	0.0	0
Pro totals (13 years)	198	176	827	255	27.5	10	137	13.7	0

PHILLIPS, JERMAINE — S — BUCCANEERS

PERSONAL: Born March 27, 1979, in Roswell, Ga. ... 6-1/214.
HIGH SCHOOL: Roswell (Ga.).
COLLEGE: Georgia.
TRANSACTIONS/CAREER NOTES: Selected by Tampa Bay Buccaneers in fifth round (157th pick overall) of 2002 NFL draft. ... Signed by Buccaneers (July 22, 2002).
CHAMPIONSHIP GAME EXPERIENCE: Played in NFC championship game (2002 season). ... Member of Super Bowl championship team (2002 season).

			TOTALS			INTERCEPTIONS			
Year Team	G	GS	Tk.	Ast.	Sks.	No.	Yds.	Avg.	TD
2002—Tampa Bay NFL	16	0	0	1	0.0	0	0	0.0	0
2003—Tampa Bay NFL	14	8	30	9	0.0	1	41	41.0	0
Pro totals (2 years)	30	8	30	10	0.0	1	41	41.0	0

PICKETT, RYAN — DT — RAMS

PERSONAL: Born October 8, 1979, in Zephyrhills, Fla. ... 6-2/310.
HIGH SCHOOL: Zephyrhills (Fla.).
COLLEGE: Ohio State.
TRANSACTIONS/CAREER NOTES: Selected after junior season by St. Louis Rams in first round (29th pick overall) of 2001 NFL draft. ... Signed by Rams (July 29, 2001).
CHAMPIONSHIP GAME EXPERIENCE: Played in NFC championship game (2001 season). ... Played in Super Bowl 36 (2001 season).

			TOTALS		
Year Team	G	GS	Tk.	Ast.	Sks.
2001—St. Louis NFL	11	0	10	9	0.5
2002—St. Louis NFL	16	14	45	22	0.5
2003—St. Louis NFL	16	13	30	12	1.0
Pro totals (3 years)	43	27	85	43	2.0

PIERCE, ANTONIO — LB — REDSKINS

PERSONAL: Born October 26, 1978, in Ontario, Calif. ... 6-1/240.
HIGH SCHOOL: Paramount (Calif.).
JUNIOR COLLEGE: Mount San Antonio College (Calif.).
COLLEGE: Arizona.
TRANSACTIONS/CAREER NOTES: Signed as non-drafted free agent by Washington Redskins (April 25, 2001). ... Granted free agency (March 3, 2004). ... Re-signed by Redskins (April 22, 2004).

			TOTALS			INTERCEPTIONS			
Year Team	G	GS	Tk.	Ast.	Sks.	No.	Yds.	Avg.	TD
2001—Washington NFL	16	7	42	8	1.0	1	0	0.0	0
2002—Washington NFL	8	1	8	4	0.0	0	0	0.0	0
2003—Washington NFL	15	0	6	0	0.0	0	0	0.0	0
Pro totals (3 years)	39	8	56	12	1.0	1	0	0.0	0

PIERCE, TERRY LB BRONCOS

PERSONAL: Born June 21, 1981, in Fort Worth, Texas. ... 6-1/251.
HIGH SCHOOL: Western Hills (Fort Worth, Texas).
COLLEGE: Kansas State.
TRANSACTIONS/CAREER NOTES: Selected after junior season by Denver Broncos in second round (51st pick overall) of 2003 NFL draft. ... Signed by Broncos (July 24, 2003). ... On injured reserve with pectoral injury (November 18, 2003-remainder of season).

			TOTALS			INTERCEPTIONS			
Year Team	**G**	**GS**	**Tk.**	**Ast.**	**Sks.**	**No.**	**Yds.**	**Avg.**	**TD**
2003—Denver NFL	3	0	1	1	0.0	0	0	0.0	0

PIERSON, SHURRON DE/LB RAIDERS

PERSONAL: Born May 31, 1982, in Inverness, Fla. ... 6-2/250. ... Full name: Shurron Torian Pierson.
HIGH SCHOOL: Wildwood (Fla.).
COLLEGE: South Florida.
TRANSACTIONS/CAREER NOTES: Selected after junior season by Oakland Raiders in fourth round (129th pick overall) of 2003 NFL draft. ... Signed by Raiders (July 24, 2003). ... Waived by Raiders (August 31, 2003). ... Re-signed by Raiders to practice squad (September 2, 2003). ... Activated (November 12, 2003). ... Assigned by Raiders in 2004 NFL Europe enhancement allocation program (February 9, 2004).

			TOTALS		
Year Team	**G**	**GS**	**Tk.**	**Ast.**	**Sks.**
2003—Oakland NFL	6	0	0	0	0.0

PILLER, ZACH G TITANS

PERSONAL: Born May 2, 1976, in St. Petersburg, Fla. ... 6-5/321. ... Full name: Zachary Paul Piller.
HIGH SCHOOL: Lincoln (Tallahassee, Fla.).
COLLEGE: Florida.
TRANSACTIONS/CAREER NOTES: Selected by Tennessee Titans in third round (81st pick overall) of 1999 NFL draft. ... Signed by Titans (July 22, 1999). ... Granted unconditional free agency (February 28, 2003). ... Re-signed by Titans (March 3, 2003).
PLAYING EXPERIENCE: Tennessee NFL, 1999-2003. ... Games/Games started: 1999 (8/0), 2000 (16/0), 2001 (14/9), 2002 (13/13), 2003 (16/16). Total: 67/38.
CHAMPIONSHIP GAME EXPERIENCE: Member of Titans for AFC championship game (1999 season); inactive. ... Member of Titans for Super Bowl 34 (1999 season); inactive. ... Played in AFC championship game (2002 season).

PINKNEY, CLEVELAND DT BUCCANEERS

PERSONAL: Born September 14, 1977, in Sumter, S.C. ... 6-1/300. ... Full name: Cleveland Pinkney III.
HIGH SCHOOL: Sumter (S.C.).
JUNIOR COLLEGE: Copiah-Lincoln (Wesson, Miss.).
COLLEGE: South Carolina.
TRANSACTIONS/CAREER NOTES: Signed as non-drafted free agent by Tampa Bay Buccaneers (April 14, 2003). ... Released by Buccaneers (November 14, 2003). ... Re-signed by Buccaneers to practice squad (November 14, 2003). ... Activated (December 13, 2003).

			TOTALS		
Year Team	**G**	**GS**	**Tk.**	**Ast.**	**Sks.**
2003—Tampa Bay NFL	4	0	3	2	1.0

PINKSTON, TODD WR EAGLES

PERSONAL: Born April 23, 1977, in Forest, Miss. ... 6-2/174.
HIGH SCHOOL: Forest (Miss.).
COLLEGE: Southern Mississippi.
TRANSACTIONS/CAREER NOTES: Selected by Philadelphia Eagles in second round (36th pick overall) of 2000 NFL draft. ... Signed by Eagles (July 16, 2000).
CHAMPIONSHIP GAME EXPERIENCE: Played in NFC championship game (2001-2003 seasons).
SINGLE GAME HIGHS (regular season): Receptions—7 (December 8, 2002, vs. Seattle); yards—121 (December 21, 2003, vs. San Francisco); and touchdown receptions—2 (September 22, 2002, vs. Dallas).
STATISTICAL PLATEAUS: 100-yard receiving games: 2003 (1). Total: 1.

			RECEIVING				TOTALS			
Year Team	**G**	**GS**	**No.**	**Yds.**	**Avg.**	**TD**	**TD**	**2pt.**	**Pts.**	**Fum.**
2000—Philadelphia NFL	16	1	10	181	18.1	0	0	0	0	0
2001—Philadelphia NFL	15	15	42	586	14.0	4	4	0	24	0
2002—Philadelphia NFL	15	15	60	798	13.3	7	7	0	42	2
2003—Philadelphia NFL	16	15	36	575	16.0	2	2	0	12	1
Pro totals (4 years)	62	46	148	2140	14.5	13	13	0	78	3

PINNER, ARTOSE RB LIONS

PERSONAL: Born January 5, 1978, in Hopkinsville, Ky. ... 5-10/229. ... Full name: Artose Deonce Pinner.
HIGH SCHOOL: Hopkinsville (Ky.).
COLLEGE: Kentucky.

TRANSACTIONS/CAREER NOTES: Selected by Detroit Lions in fourth round (99th pick overall) of 2003 NFL draft. ... Signed by Lions (July 21, 2003). ... On non-football injury list with leg injury (July 23-November 23, 2003). ... Activated (November 24, 2003).
SINGLE GAME HIGHS (regular season): Attempts—18 (December 28, 2003, vs. St. Louis); yards—51 (December 28, 2003, vs. St. Louis); and rushing touchdowns—0.

			RUSHING				RECEIVING				TOTALS			
Year Team	**G**	**GS**	**Att.**	**Yds.**	**Avg.**	**TD**	**No.**	**Yds.**	**Avg.**	**TD**	**TD**	**2pt.**	**Pts.**	**Fum.**
2003—Detroit NFL	3	2	39	99	2.5	0	5	40	8.0	0	0	0	0	0

PINNOCK, ANDREW — FB — CHARGERS

PERSONAL: Born March 12, 1980, in Hartford, Conn. ... 5-10/260.
HIGH SCHOOL: Bloomfield (Conn.).
COLLEGE: South Carolina.
TRANSACTIONS/CAREER NOTES: Selected by San Diego Chargers in seventh round (229th pick overall) of 2003 NFL draft. ... Signed by Chargers (June 19, 2003).

			RUSHING				RECEIVING				TOTALS			
Year Team	**G**	**GS**	**Att.**	**Yds.**	**Avg.**	**TD**	**No.**	**Yds.**	**Avg.**	**TD**	**TD**	**2pt.**	**Pts.**	**Fum.**
2003—San Diego NFL	16	0	0	0	0.0	0	0	0	0.0	0	0	0	0	0

PITTMAN, BRYAN — C/LS — TEXANS

PERSONAL: Born January 20, 1977, in Tacoma, Wash. ... 6-4/255.
HIGH SCHOOL: Thomas Jefferson (Federal Way, Wa.).
JUNIOR COLLEGE: Walla Walla (Wash.).
COLLEGE: Washington.
TRANSACTIONS/CAREER NOTES: Signed as non-drafted free agent by Cleveland Browns (April 9, 2003). ... Released by Browns (May 19, 2003). ... Re-signed by Browns (July 25, 2003). ... Waived by Browns (August 28, 2003). ... Signed by Houston Texans to practice squad (September 1, 2003). ... Activated (September 7, 2003).
PLAYING EXPERIENCE: Houston NFL, 2003. ... Games/Games started: 2003 (16/0). Total: 16/0.

PITTMAN, KAVIKA — DE — PANTHERS

PERSONAL: Born October 9, 1974, in Frankfurt, Germany. ... 6-6/273. ... Name pronounced: kuh-VEE-kuh.
HIGH SCHOOL: Leesville (La.).
COLLEGE: McNeese State.
TRANSACTIONS/CAREER NOTES: Selected by Dallas Cowboys in second round (37th pick overall) of 1996 NFL draft. ... Signed by Cowboys (July 16, 1996). ... Granted unconditional free agency (February 11, 2000). ... Signed by Denver Broncos (February 22, 2000). ... On injured reserve with calf injury (December 19, 2001-remainder of season). ... Waived by Broncos (February 25, 2003). ... Signed by Carolina Panthers (May 22, 2003). ... On injured reserve with knee injury (September 18, 2003-remainder of season). ... Granted unconditional free agency (March 3, 2004). ... Re-signed by Panthers (March 22, 2004).

			TOTALS		
Year Team	**G**	**GS**	**Tk.**	**Ast.**	**Sks.**
1996—Dallas NFL	15	0	2	0	0.0
1997—Dallas NFL	15	0	4	1	1.0
1998—Dallas NFL	15	15	37	4	6.0
1999—Dallas NFL	16	16	33	10	3.0
2000—Denver NFL	15	15	26	2	7.0
2001—Denver NFL	14	14	28	6	1.0
2002—Denver NFL	16	15	29	9	0.0
2003—Carolina NFL	2	0	0	0	0.0
Pro totals (8 years)	108	75	159	32	18.0

PITTMAN, MICHAEL — RB — BUCCANEERS

PERSONAL: Born August 14, 1975, in New Orleans, La. ... 6-0/218.
HIGH SCHOOL: Mira Mesa (San Diego).
COLLEGE: Fresno State.
TRANSACTIONS/CAREER NOTES: Selected by Arizona Cardinals in fourth round (95th pick overall) of 1998 NFL draft. ... Signed by Cardinals (May 20, 1998). ... Granted free agency (March 2, 2001). ... Re-signed by Cardinals (May 11, 2001). ... On suspended list (September 9-23, 2001). ... Granted unconditional free agency (March 1, 2002). ... Signed by Tampa Bay Buccaneers (March 25, 2002).
CHAMPIONSHIP GAME EXPERIENCE: Played in NFC championship game (2002 season). ... Member of Super Bowl championship team (2002 season).
SINGLE GAME HIGHS (regular season): Attempts—30 (October 26, 2003, vs. Dallas); yards—133 (November 14, 1999, vs. Detroit); and rushing touchdowns—1 (December 15, 2002, vs. Detroit).
STATISTICAL PLATEAUS: 100-yard rushing games: 1999 (1), 2000 (1), 2003 (2). Total: 4.

			RUSHING				RECEIVING				PUNT RETURNS				KICKOFF RETURNS				TOTALS		
Year Team	**G**	**GS**	**Att.**	**Yds.**	**Avg.**	**TD**	**No.**	**Yds.**	**Avg.**	**TD**	**No.**	**Yds.**	**Avg.**	**TD**	**No.**	**Yds.**	**Avg.**	**TD**	**TD**	**2pt.**	**Pts.**
1998—Ari. NFL	15	0	29	91	3.1	0	0	0	0.0	0	0	0	0.0	0	4	84	21.0	0	0	0	0
1999—Ari. NFL	10	2	64	289	4.5	2	16	196	12.3	0	4	16	4.0	0	2	31	15.5	0	2	0	12
2000—Ari. NFL	16	12	184	719	3.9	4	73	579	7.9	2	0	0	0.0	0	0	0	0.0	0	6	0	36
2001—Ari. NFL	15	14	241	846	3.5	5	42	264	6.3	0	0	0	0.0	0	6	161	26.8	0	5	0	30
2002—T.B. NFL	16	15	204	718	3.5	1	59	477	8.1	0	0	0	0.0	0	0	0	0.0	0	1	0	6
2003—T.B. NFL	16	13	187	751	4.0	0	75	597	8.0	2	0	0	0.0	0	0	0	0.0	0	2	0	12
Pro totals (6 years)	88	56	909	3414	3.8	12	265	2113	8.0	4	4	16	4.0	0	12	276	23.0	0	16	0	96

PITTS, CHESTER G/T TEXANS

PERSONAL: Born June 26, 1979, in Inglewood, Calif. ... 6-4/320. ... Full name: Chester Morise Pitts II.
HIGH SCHOOL: California Academy for Math and Science (Los Angeles).
COLLEGE: San Diego State.
TRANSACTIONS/CAREER NOTES: Selected by Houston Texans in second round (50th pick overall) of 2002 NFL draft. ... Signed by Texans (July 16, 2002).
PLAYING EXPERIENCE: Houston NFL, 2002-2003. ... Games/Games started: 2002 (16/16), 2003 (16/16). Total: 32/32.

PLAYER, SCOTT P CARDINALS

PERSONAL: Born December 17, 1969, in St. Augustine, Fla. ... 6-1/213.
HIGH SCHOOL: St. Augustine (Fla.).
JUNIOR COLLEGE: Florida Community College.
COLLEGE: Florida State.
TRANSACTIONS/CAREER NOTES: Played with Birmingham Barracudas of CFL (1995). ... Granted free agency (March 7, 1996). ... Signed as non-drafted free agent by Arizona Cardinals (April 23, 1996). ... Released by Cardinals (August 19, 1996). ... Signed by New York Giants (February 14, 1997). ... Assigned by Giants to Frankfurt Galaxy in 1997 World League enhancement allocation program (February 18, 1997). ... Released by Giants (August 24, 1997). ... Signed by New York Jets to practice squad (August 26, 1997). ... Released by Jets (August 28, 1997). ... Re-signed by Cardinals (March 3, 1998). ... Granted free agency (March 2, 2001). ... Re-signed by Cardinals (July 13, 2001).
HONORS: Played in Pro Bowl (2000 season).

		PUNTING					
Year Team	**G**	**No.**	**Yds.**	**Avg.**	**Net avg.**	**In. 20**	**Blk.**
1995—Birmingham CFL	18	143	6247	43.7	36.5	...	...
1996—		Did not play.					
1998—Arizona NFL	16	81	3378	41.7	35.9	12	∞1
1999—Arizona NFL	16	94	3948	42.0	36.7	18	0
2000—Arizona NFL	16	65	2871	44.2	37.3	17	0
2001—Arizona NFL	12	67	2779	41.5	33.8	17	0
2002—Arizona NFL	16	88	3864	43.9	35.0	28	1
2003—Arizona NFL	16	82	3511	42.8	34.4	19	1
CFL totals (1 year)	18	143	6247	43.7	36.5	...	...
NFL totals (6 years)	92	477	20351	42.7	35.5	111	3
Pro totals (7 years)	110	620	26598	42.9	...	...	...

PLEASANT, ANTHONY DE

PERSONAL: Born January 27, 1968, in Century, Fla. ... 6-5/280. ... Full name: Anthony Devon Pleasant.
HIGH SCHOOL: Century (Fla.).
COLLEGE: Tennessee State.
TRANSACTIONS/CAREER NOTES: Selected by Cleveland Browns in third round (73rd pick overall) of 1990 NFL draft. ... Signed by Browns (July 22, 1990). ... Browns franchise moved to Baltimore and renamed Ravens for 1996 season (March 11, 1996). ... Granted unconditional free agency (February 14, 1997). ... Signed by Atlanta Falcons (June 21, 1997). ... Released by Falcons (February 11, 1998). ... Signed by New York Jets (March 12, 1998). ... Granted unconditional free agency (February 11, 2000). ... Signed by San Francisco 49ers (July 19, 2000). ... Granted unconditional free agency (March 2, 2001). ... Signed by New England Patriots (March 22, 2001). ... Granted unconditional free agency (March 3, 2004).
CHAMPIONSHIP GAME EXPERIENCE: Played in AFC championship game (1998 and 2001 seasons). ... Member of Super Bowl championship team (2001 season). ... Member of Patriots for AFC championship game (2003 season); inactive. ... Member of Patriots for Super Bowl 38 (2003 season); inactive.

			TOTALS			INTERCEPTIONS			
Year Team	**G**	**GS**	**Tk.**	**Ast.**	**Sks.**	**No.**	**Yds.**	**Avg.**	**TD**
1990—Cleveland NFL	16	7	38	12	3.5	0	0	0.0	0
1991—Cleveland NFL	16	7	12	9	2.5	0	0	0.0	0
1992—Cleveland NFL	16	14	35	16	4.0	0	0	0.0	0
1993—Cleveland NFL	16	13	43	23	11.0	0	0	0.0	0
1994—Cleveland NFL	14	14	44	14	4.5	0	0	0.0	0
1995—Cleveland NFL	16	16	41	10	8.0	0	0	0.0	0
1996—Baltimore NFL	12	12	22	3	4.0	0	0	0.0	0
1997—Atlanta NFL	11	0	9	1	0.5	0	0	0.0	0
1998—New York Jets NFL	16	15	34	12	6.0	0	0	0.0	0
1999—New York Jets NFL	16	16	41	11	2.0	0	0	0.0	0
2000—San Francisco NFL	16	16	17	5	2.0	0	0	0.0	0
2001—New England NFL	16	16	35	8	6.0	2	0	0.0	0
2002—New England NFL	14	11	20	15	3.0	0	0	0.0	0
2003—New England NFL	7	0	1	0	1.0	0	0	0.0	0
Pro totals (14 years)	202	157	392	139	58.0	2	0	0.0	0

PLUMMER, AHMED CB 49ERS

PERSONAL: Born March 26, 1976, in Wyoming, Ohio. ... 6-0/191. ... Full name: Ahmed Kamil Plummer.
HIGH SCHOOL: Wyoming (Ohio).
COLLEGE: Ohio State.
TRANSACTIONS/CAREER NOTES: Selected by San Francisco 49ers in first round (24th pick overall) of 2000 NFL draft. ... Signed by 49ers (July 15, 2000). ... Granted unconditional free agency (March 3, 2004). ... Re-signed by 49ers (March 5, 2004).

Year Team	G	GS	TOTALS Tk.	Ast.	Sks.	INTERCEPTIONS No.	Yds.	Avg.	TD
2000—San Francisco NFL	16	15	66	9	0.0	0	0	0.0	0
2001—San Francisco NFL	15	15	58	6	0.0	7	45	6.4	0
2002—San Francisco NFL	15	15	52	11	0.0	1	0	0.0	0
2003—San Francisco NFL	15	15	59	8	0.0	4	85	21.3	1
Pro totals (4 years)	61	60	235	34	0.0	12	130	10.8	1

PLUMMER, JAKE QB BRONCOS

PERSONAL: Born December 19, 1974, in Boise, Idaho. ... 6-2/212. ... Full name: Jason Steven Plummer.

HIGH SCHOOL: Capital (Boise, Idaho).

COLLEGE: Arizona State.

TRANSACTIONS/CAREER NOTES: Selected by Arizona Cardinals in second round (42nd pick overall) of 1997 NFL draft. ... Signed by Cardinals (July 14, 1997). ... Granted unconditional free agency (February 28, 2003). ... Signed by Denver Broncos (March 5, 2003).

HONORS: Named quarterback on THE SPORTING NEWS college All-America second team (1996).

SINGLE GAME HIGHS (regular season): Attempts—57 (January 2, 2000, vs. Green Bay); completions—35 (January 2, 2000, vs. Green Bay); yards—465 (November 15, 1998, vs. Dallas); and touchdown passes—4 (November 18, 2001, vs. Detroit).

STATISTICAL PLATEAUS: 300-yard passing games: 1997 (2), 1998 (2), 1999 (1), 2000 (1), 2001 (1). Total: 7.

MISCELLANEOUS: Regular-season record as starting NFL quarterback: 39-54 (.419). ... Postseason record as starting NFL quarterback: 1-2 (.333).

Year Team	G	GS	PASSING Att.	Cmp.	Pct.	Yds.	TD	Int.	Avg.	Skd.	Rat.	RUSHING Att.	Yds.	Avg.	TD	TOTALS TD	2pt.	Pts.
1997—Arizona NFL	10	9	296	157	53.0	2203	15	15	7.44	‡52	73.1	39	216	5.5	2	2	1	14
1998—Arizona NFL	16	16	547	324	59.2	3737	17	20	6.83	†49	75.0	51	217	4.3	4	4	0	24
1999—Arizona NFL	12	11	381	201	52.8	2111	9	*24	5.54	27	50.8	39	121	3.1	2	2	0	12
2000—Arizona NFL	14	14	475	270	56.8	2946	13	‡21	6.20	22	66.0	37	183	4.9	0	0	0	0
2001—Arizona NFL	16	16	525	304	57.9	3653	18	14	6.96	29	79.6	35	163	4.7	0	0	1	2
2002—Arizona NFL	16	16	530	284	53.6	2972	18	20	5.61	36	65.7	46	283	6.2	2	2	0	12
2003—Denver NFL	11	11	302	189	62.6	2182	15	7	7.23	14	91.2	37	205	5.5	3	3	0	18
Pro totals (7 years)	95	93	3056	1729	56.6	19804	105	121	6.48	229	71.2	284	1388	4.9	13	13	2	82

POCHMAN, OWEN K

PERSONAL: Born August 2, 1977, in Renton, Wash. ... 6-0/180.

HIGH SCHOOL: Mercer Island (Wash.).

COLLEGE: Brigham Young.

TRANSACTIONS/CAREER NOTES: Selected by New England Patriots in seventh round (216th pick overall) of 2001 NFL draft. ... Signed by Patriots (July 13, 2001). ... Claimed on waivers by New York Giants (September 3, 2001). ... On injured reserve with knee injury (September 3, 2002-entire season). ... Re-signed by Giants (March 23, 2003). ... Claimed on waivers by Green Bay Packers (June 16, 2003). ... Waived by Packers (July 16, 2003). ... Signed by St. Louis Rams (July 22, 2003). ... Released by Rams (August 25, 2003). ... Signed by San Francisco 49ers (September 16, 2003). ... Waived by 49ers (October 28, 2003).

Year Team	G	FIELD GOALS 1-29	30-39	40-49	50+	Tot.	Pct.	Lg.	TOTALS XPM	XPA	Pts.
2001—New York Giants NFL	10	0-0	0-0	0-0	0-2	0-2	0.0	0	0	0	0
2003—San Francisco NFL	6	1-1	3-8	4-5	0-1	8-15	53.3	48	9	10	33
Pro totals (2 years)	16	1-1	3-8	4-5	0-3	8-17	47.1	48	9	10	33

POLAMALU, TROY S STEELERS

PERSONAL: Born April 19, 1981, in Garden Grove, Calif. ... 5-10/213. ... Full name: Troy Aumua Polamalu.

HIGH SCHOOL: Douglas (Winston, Ore.).

COLLEGE: Southern California.

TRANSACTIONS/CAREER NOTES: Selected by Pittsburgh Steelers in first round (16th pick overall) of 2003 NFL draft. ... Signed by Steelers (July 28, 2003).

Year Team	G	GS	TOTALS Tk.	Ast.	Sks.	INTERCEPTIONS No.	Yds.	Avg.	TD
2003—Pittsburgh NFL	16	0	17	6	2.0	0	0	0.0	0

POLK, CARLOS LB CHARGERS

PERSONAL: Born February 22, 1977, in Memphis, Tenn. ... 6-2/250. ... Full name: Carlos Devonn Polk.

HIGH SCHOOL: Guilford (Rockford, Ill.).

COLLEGE: Nebraska.

TRANSACTIONS/CAREER NOTES: Selected by San Diego Chargers in fourth round (112th pick overall) of 2001 NFL draft. ... Signed by Chargers (June 20, 2001). ... On injured reserve with shoulder injury (November 14, 2001-remainder of season). ... Granted free agency (March 3, 2004). ... Re-signed by Chargers (April 27, 2004).

HONORS: Named linebacker on THE SPORTING NEWS college All-America third team (2000).

Year Team	G	GS	TOTALS Tk.	Ast.	Sks.	INTERCEPTIONS No.	Yds.	Avg.	TD
2001—San Diego NFL	6	0	0	0	0.0	0	0	0.0	0
2002—San Diego NFL	15	0	3	1	1.0	0	0	0.0	0
2003—San Diego NFL	16	0	5	1	0.0	0	0	0.0	0
Pro totals (3 years)	37	0	8	2	1.0	0	0	0.0	0

POLK, DASHON — LB — TEXANS

PERSONAL: Born March 13, 1977, in Pacoima, Calif. ... 6-2/242. ... Full name: DaShon Lamor Polk.
HIGH SCHOOL: Taft (Woodlands Hills, Calif.).
COLLEGE: Arizona.
TRANSACTIONS/CAREER NOTES: Selected by Buffalo Bills in seventh round (251st pick overall) of 2000 NFL draft. ... Signed by Bills (June 22, 2000). ... Granted free agency (February 28, 2003). ... Re-signed by Bills (April 10, 2003). ... Granted unconditional free agency (March 3, 2004). ... Signed by Houston Texans (March 16, 2004).

			TOTALS			INTERCEPTIONS			
Year Team	G	GS	Tk.	Ast.	Sks.	No.	Yds.	Avg.	TD
2000—Buffalo NFL	5	0	0	0	0.0	0	0	0.0	0
2001—Buffalo NFL	16	1	13	6	0.0	0	0	0.0	0
2002—Buffalo NFL	16	0	8	10	0.0	0	0	0.0	0
2003—Buffalo NFL	16	0	1	3	0.0	0	0	0.0	0
Pro totals (4 years)	53	1	22	19	0.0	0	0	0.0	0

POLLARD, MARCUS — TE — COLTS

PERSONAL: Born February 8, 1972, in Valley, Ala. ... 6-3/247. ... Full name: Marcus LaJuan Pollard.
HIGH SCHOOL: Valley (Ala.).
JUNIOR COLLEGE: Seward County Community College, Kan. (did not play football).
COLLEGE: Bradley.
TRANSACTIONS/CAREER NOTES: Signed as non-drafted free agent by Indianapolis Colts (January 24, 1995). ... Released by Colts (August 22, 1995). ... Re-signed by Colts to practice squad (August 28, 1995). ... Activated (October 10, 1995). ... Granted free agency (February 13, 1998). ... Tendered offer sheet by Philadelphia Eagles (March 4, 1998). ... Offer matched by Colts (March 9, 1998). ... Designated by Colts as franchise player (February 22, 2001).
CHAMPIONSHIP GAME EXPERIENCE: Played in AFC championship game (1995 and 2003 seasons).
SINGLE GAME HIGHS (regular season): Receptions—7 (November 3, 2002, vs. Tennessee); yards—216 (November 18, 2001, vs. New Orleans); and touchdown receptions—2 (October 10, 1999, vs. Miami).
STATISTICAL PLATEAUS: 100-yard receiving games: 2001 (2). Total: 2.

			RECEIVING				TOTALS			
Year Team	G	GS	No.	Yds.	Avg.	TD	TD	2pt.	Pts.	Fum.
1995—Indianapolis NFL	8	0	0	0	0.0	0	0	0	0	0
1996—Indianapolis NFL	16	4	6	86	14.3	1	1	0	6	0
1997—Indianapolis NFL	16	6	10	116	11.6	0	0	1	2	0
1998—Indianapolis NFL	16	11	24	309	12.9	4	4	†2	28	0
1999—Indianapolis NFL	16	10	34	374	11.0	4	4	0	24	2
2000—Indianapolis NFL	16	14	30	439	14.6	3	3	1	20	0
2001—Indianapolis NFL	16	16	47	739	15.7	8	8	0	48	0
2002—Indianapolis NFL	15	15	43	478	11.1	6	6	1	38	1
2003—Indianapolis NFL	14	13	40	541	13.5	3	3	0	18	1
Pro totals (9 years)	133	89	234	3082	13.2	29	29	5	184	4

POLLEY, TOMMY — LB — RAMS

PERSONAL: Born January 18, 1978, in Baltimore, Md. ... 6-3/240.
HIGH SCHOOL: Dunbar (Baltimore).
COLLEGE: Florida State.
TRANSACTIONS/CAREER NOTES: Selected by St. Louis Rams in second round (42nd pick overall) of 2001 NFL draft. ... Signed by Rams (July 23, 2001).
CHAMPIONSHIP GAME EXPERIENCE: Played in NFC championship game (2001 season). ... Played in Super Bowl 36 (2001 season).
HONORS: Named linebacker on THE SPORTING NEWS college All-America third team (2000).

			TOTALS			INTERCEPTIONS			
Year Team	G	GS	Tk.	Ast.	Sks.	No.	Yds.	Avg.	TD
2001—St. Louis NFL	16	11	61	17	0.0	0	0	0.0	0
2002—St. Louis NFL	12	11	42	15	0.0	0	0	0.0	0
2003—St. Louis NFL	14	14	58	12	0.0	4	32	8.0	0
Pro totals (3 years)	42	36	161	44	0.0	4	32	8.0	0

PONDER, WILLIE — WR — GIANTS

PERSONAL: Born February 14, 1980, in Tulsa, Okla. ... 6-0/205. ... Full name: Willie Columbus Ponder Jr.
HIGH SCHOOL: Central (Tulsa, Okla.).
JUNIOR COLLEGE: Coffeyville (Kan).
COLLEGE: Southeast Missouri State.
TRANSACTIONS/CAREER NOTES: Selected by New York Giants in sixth round (199th pick overall) of 2003 NFL draft. ... Signed by Giants (June 12, 2003).
SINGLE GAME HIGHS (regular season): Receptions—2 (December 28, 2003, vs. Carolina); yards—18 (December 28, 2003, vs. Carolina); and touchdown receptions—0.

			RECEIVING				TOTALS			
Year Team	G	GS	No.	Yds.	Avg.	TD	TD	2pt.	Pts.	Fum.
2003—New York Giants NFL	4	0	7	35	5.0	0	0	0	0	0

PONTBRIAND, RYAN C/LS BROWNS

PERSONAL: Born October 1, 1979, in Houston, Texas. ... 6-2/255. ... Full name: Ryan David Pontbriand. ... Name pronounced: pownt-bree-AWND.
HIGH SCHOOL: W.P. Clements (Sugar Land, Texas).
COLLEGE: Rice.
TRANSACTIONS/CAREER NOTES: Selected by Cleveland Browns in fifth round (142nd pick overall) of 2003 NFL draft. ... Signed by Browns (July 27, 2003).
PLAYING EXPERIENCE: Cleveland NFL, 2003. ... Games/Games started: 2003 (16/0). Total: 16/0.

POOLE, NATHAN WR CARDINALS

PERSONAL: Born February 1, 1977, in Danville, Va. ... 6-2/210.
HIGH SCHOOL: George Washington (Danville, Va.).
COLLEGE: Marshall.
TRANSACTIONS/CAREER NOTES: Signed as non-drafted free agent by Arizona Cardinals (April 23, 2001). ... Released by Cardinals (September 1, 2001). ... Re-signed by Cardinals to practice squad (December 3, 2001). ... Released by Cardinals (August 26, 2002). ... Re-signed by Cardinals to practice squad (October 30, 2002). ... Activated (November 6, 2002). ... Granted free agency (March 3, 2003). ... Re-signed by Cardinals (April 2, 2003). ... Waived by Cardinals (August 30, 2003). ... Re-signed by Cardinals (September 12, 2003).
SINGLE GAME HIGHS (regular season): Receptions—6 (December 8, 2002, vs. Detroit); yards—86 (December 28, 2003, vs. Minnesota); and touchdown receptions—1 (December 28, 2003, vs. Minnesota).

			RECEIVING				TOTALS			
Year Team	G	GS	No.	Yds.	Avg.	TD	TD	2pt.	Pts.	Fum.
2002—Arizona NFL	5	1	13	108	8.3	1	1	0	6	0
2003—Arizona NFL	15	1	13	177	13.6	1	1	0	6	0
Pro totals (2 years)	20	2	26	285	11.0	2	2	0	12	0

POOLE, TYRONE CB PATRIOTS

PERSONAL: Born February 3, 1972, in LaGrange, Ga. ... 5-8/188.
HIGH SCHOOL: La Grange (Ga.).
COLLEGE: Fort Valley (Ga.) State.
TRANSACTIONS/CAREER NOTES: Selected by Carolina Panthers in first round (22nd pick overall) of 1995 NFL draft. ... Signed by Panthers (July 15, 1995). ... Traded by Panthers to Indianapolis Colts for second-round pick (OT Chris Terry) in 1999 draft (July 22, 1998). ... Released by Colts (March 1, 2001). ... Signed by Denver Broncos (May 22, 2001). ... On reserve/left squad list (August 9, 2001-February 27, 2002). ... Granted unconditional free agency (February 28, 2003). ... Signed by New England Patriots (March 4, 2003).
CHAMPIONSHIP GAME EXPERIENCE: Played in NFC championship game (1996 season). ... Played in AFC championship game (2003 season). ... Member of Super Bowl championship team (2003 season).

			TOTALS			INTERCEPTIONS				PUNT RETURNS				TOTALS			
Year Team	G	GS	Tk.	Ast.	Sks.	No.	Yds.	Avg.	TD	No.	Yds.	Avg.	TD	TD	2pt.	Pts.	Fum.
1995—Carolina NFL	16	13	59	9	2.0	2	8	4.0	0	0	0	0.0	0	0	0	0	0
1996—Carolina NFL	15	15	57	11	0.0	1	35	35.0	0	3	26	8.7	0	0	0	0	0
1997—Carolina NFL	16	16	48	4	1.0	2	0	0.0	0	26	191	7.3	0	0	0	0	3
1998—Indianapolis NFL	15	15	52	9	0.0	1	0	0.0	0	12	107	8.9	0	0	0	0	0
1999—Indianapolis NFL	15	14	34	5	1.0	3	85	28.3	0	0	0	0.0	0	0	0	0	0
2000—Indianapolis NFL	15	12	38	12	0.0	1	1	1.0	0	0	0	0.0	0	0	0	0	0
2002—Denver NFL	16	4	41	10	1.0	0	0	0.0	0	4	24	6.0	0	0	0	0	1
2003—New England NFL	16	16	47	12	0.0	6	81	13.5	0	11	75	6.8	0	0	0	0	1
Pro totals (8 years)	124	105	376	72	5.0	16	210	13.1	0	56	423	7.6	0	0	0	0	5

POPE, MONSANTO DT BRONCOS

PERSONAL: Born January 27, 1978, in Norfolk, Va. ... 6-3/300.
HIGH SCHOOL: Hopewell (Va.).
COLLEGE: Virginia.
TRANSACTIONS/CAREER NOTES: Selected by Denver Broncos in seventh round (231st pick overall) of 2002 NFL draft. ... Signed by Broncos (June 14, 2002).

			TOTALS		
Year Team	G	GS	Tk.	Ast.	Sks.
2002—Denver NFL	14	1	15	3	4.0
2003—Denver NFL	16	5	13	5	1.0
Pro totals (2 years)	30	6	28	8	5.0

PORCHER, ROBERT DE LIONS

PERSONAL: Born July 30, 1969, in Wando, S.C. ... 6-3/266. ... Full name: Robert Porcher III. ... Name pronounced: por-SHAY.
HIGH SCHOOL: Cainhoy (Huger, S.C.).
COLLEGE: South Carolina State.
TRANSACTIONS/CAREER NOTES: Selected by Detroit Lions in first round (26th pick overall) of 1992 NFL draft. ... Signed by Lions (July 25, 1992). ... Granted unconditional free agency (February 16, 1996). ... Re-signed by Lions (March 29, 1996). ... Granted unconditional free agency (February 14, 1997). ... Re-signed by Lions (March 4, 1997). ... Designated by Lions as franchise player (February 10, 2000). ... Re-signed by Lions (August 8, 2000).
HONORS: Played in Pro Bowl (1999 and 2001 seasons).
MISCELLANEOUS: Holds Detroit Lions all-time record for most sacks (95.5).

Year Team	G	GS	TOTALS Tk.	Ast.	Sks.	INTERCEPTIONS No.	Yds.	Avg.	TD
1992—Detroit NFL	16	1	11	10	1.0	0	0	0.0	0
1993—Detroit NFL	16	4	37	10	8.5	0	0	0.0	0
1994—Detroit NFL	15	15	47	22	3.0	0	0	0.0	0
1995—Detroit NFL	16	16	29	22	5.0	0	0	0.0	0
1996—Detroit NFL	16	16	45	21	10.0	0	0	0.0	0
1997—Detroit NFL	16	15	40	32	12.5	1	5	5.0	0
1998—Detroit NFL	16	16	41	21	11.5	0	0	0.0	0
1999—Detroit NFL	15	14	32	16	15.0	0	0	0.0	0
2000—Detroit NFL	16	16	30	6	8.0	0	0	0.0	0
2001—Detroit NFL	16	16	45	7	11.0	0	0	0.0	0
2002—Detroit NFL	15	15	30	15	5.5	0	0	0.0	0
2003—Detroit NFL	14	14	25	9	4.5	0	0	0.0	0
Pro totals (12 years)	187	158	412	191	95.5	1	5	5.0	0

PORTER, ALVIN CB BENGALS

PERSONAL: Born May 10, 1977, in Shreveport, La. ... 5-11/175. ... Full name: Alvin Guy Porter.
HIGH SCHOOL: Adamson (Dallas).
COLLEGE: Oklahoma State.
TRANSACTIONS/CAREER NOTES: Signed as non-drafted free agent by Baltimore Ravens (April 27, 2001). ... Released by Ravens (October 6, 2003). ... Signed by Cincinnati Bengals (January 16, 2004).

Year Team	G	GS	TOTALS Tk.	Ast.	Sks.	INTERCEPTIONS No.	Yds.	Avg.	TD
2001—Baltimore NFL	16	0	5	0	0.0	1	-3	-3.0	0
2002—Baltimore NFL	16	5	27	5	0.0	0	0	0.0	0
2003—Baltimore NFL	1	0	0	0	0.0	0	0	0.0	0
Pro totals (3 years)	33	5	32	5	0.0	1	-3	-3.0	0

PORTER, JERRY WR RAIDERS

PERSONAL: Born July 14, 1978, in Washington, DC. ... 6-2/220.
HIGH SCHOOL: Coolidge (Washington, D.C.).
COLLEGE: West Virginia.
TRANSACTIONS/CAREER NOTES: Selected by Oakland Raiders in second round (47th pick overall) of 2000 NFL draft. ... Signed by Raiders (July 22, 2000).
CHAMPIONSHIP GAME EXPERIENCE: Played in AFC championship game (2000 and 2002 seasons). ... Played in Super Bowl 37 (2002 season).
SINGLE GAME HIGHS (regular season): Receptions—7 (November 23, 2003, vs. Kansas City); yards—117 (October 6, 2002, vs. Buffalo); and touchdown receptions—2 (November 24, 2002, vs. Arizona).
STATISTICAL PLATEAUS: 100-yard receiving games: 2002 (1). Total: 1.

Year Team	G	GS	RUSHING Att.	Yds.	Avg.	TD	RECEIVING No.	Yds.	Avg.	TD	TOTALS TD	2pt.	Pts.	Fum.
2000—Oakland NFL	12	0	0	0	0.0	0	1	6	6.0	0	0	0	0	0
2001—Oakland NFL	15	1	2	13	6.5	0	19	220	11.6	0	0	0	0	0
2002—Oakland NFL	16	13	4	6	1.5	0	51	688	13.5	9	9	2	58	0
2003—Oakland NFL	10	1	1	10	10.0	0	28	361	12.9	1	1	0	6	1
Pro totals (4 years)	53	15	7	29	4.1	0	99	1275	12.9	10	10	2	64	1

PORTER, JOEY LB STEELERS

PERSONAL: Born March 22, 1977, in Bakersfield, Calif. ... 6-2/250. ... Full name: Joey Eugene Porter.
HIGH SCHOOL: Foothills (Calif.).
COLLEGE: Colorado State.
TRANSACTIONS/CAREER NOTES: Selected by Pittsburgh Steelers in third round (73rd pick overall) of 1999 NFL draft. ... Signed by Steelers (July 30, 1999). ... Granted free agency (March 1, 2002). ... Re-signed by Steelers (April 29, 2002).
CHAMPIONSHIP GAME EXPERIENCE: Played in AFC championship game (2001 season).
HONORS: Played in Pro Bowl (2002 season). ... Named linebacker on the THE SPORTING NEWS NFL All-Pro team (2002).

Year Team	G	GS	TOTALS Tk.	Ast.	Sks.	INTERCEPTIONS No.	Yds.	Avg.	TD
1999—Pittsburgh NFL	16	0	10	0	2.0	0	0	0.0	0
2000—Pittsburgh NFL	16	16	41	18	10.5	1	0	0.0	0
2001—Pittsburgh NFL	15	15	47	14	9.0	0	0	0.0	0
2002—Pittsburgh NFL	16	16	61	28	9.0	4	153	38.2	0
2003—Pittsburgh NFL	14	14	50	16	5.0	0	0	0.0	0
Pro totals (5 years)	77	61	209	76	35.5	5	153	30.6	0

PORTIS, CLINTON RB REDSKINS

PERSONAL: Born September 1, 1981, in Laurel, Miss. ... 5-11/205. ... Full name: Clinton Earl Portis.
HIGH SCHOOL: Gainesville (Fla.).
COLLEGE: Miami (Fla.).

TRANSACTIONS/CAREER NOTES: Selected after junior season by Denver Broncos in second round (51st pick overall) of 2002 NFL draft. ... Signed by Broncos (July 25, 2002). ... Traded by Broncos to Washington Redskins for CB Champ Bailey and a second-round pick (RB Tatum Bell) in 2004 NFL draft (March 4, 2004).
HONORS: Named NFL Rookie of the Year by THE SPORTING NEWS (2002). ... Played in Pro Bowl (2003 season).
SINGLE GAME HIGHS (regular season): Attempts—38 (December 14, 2003, vs. Cleveland); yards—228 (December 29, 2002, vs. Arizona); and rushing touchdowns—5 (December 7, 2003, vs. Kansas City).
STATISTICAL PLATEAUS: 100-yard rushing games: 2002 (8), 2003 (10). Total: 18.

			RUSHING				RECEIVING				TOTALS			
Year Team	**G**	**GS**	**Att.**	**Yds.**	**Avg.**	**TD**	**No.**	**Yds.**	**Avg.**	**TD**	**TD**	**2pt.**	**Pts.**	**Fum.**
2002—Denver NFL	16	12	273	1508	§5.5	15	33	364	11.0	2	17	0	102	5
2003—Denver NFL	13	13	290	1591	*5.5	14	38	314	8.3	0	14	1	86	3
Pro totals (2 years)	29	25	563	3099	5.5	29	71	678	9.5	2	31	1	188	8

POSEY, JEFF LB BILLS

PERSONAL: Born August 14, 1975, in Bassfield, Miss. ... 6-4/241.
HIGH SCHOOL: Greenville (Miss.).
JUNIOR COLLEGE: Pearl River Community College (Miss.).
COLLEGE: Southern Mississippi.
TRANSACTIONS/CAREER NOTES: Signed as non-drafted free agent by San Francisco 49ers (May 2, 1997) ... Released by 49ers (August 19, 1997). ... Re-signed by 49ers to practice squad (August 25, 1997). ... Granted free agency (March 2, 2001). ... Signed by Philadelphia Eagles (June 18, 2001). ... Released by Eagles (August 31, 2001). ... Signed by Carolina Panthers (October 23, 2001). ... Claimed on waivers by Jacksonville Jaguars (November 21, 2001). ... Granted unconditional free agency (March 1, 2002). ... Signed by Houston Texans (April 19, 2002). ... Granted unconditional free agency (February 28, 2003). ... Signed by Buffalo Bills (February 28, 2003).

			TOTALS			INTERCEPTIONS			
Year Team	**G**	**GS**	**Tk.**	**Ast.**	**Sks.**	**No.**	**Yds.**	**Avg.**	**TD**
1998—San Francisco NFL	16	0	7	2	0.5	0	0	0.0	0
1999—San Francisco NFL	16	6	10	5	2.0	0	0	0.0	0
2000—San Francisco NFL	16	8	22	11	0.5	0	0	0.0	0
2001—Carolina NFL	4	0	2	0	0.0	0	0	0.0	0
—Jacksonville NFL	7	5	5	1	0.0	0	0	0.0	0
2002—Houston NFL	16	9	45	15	8.0	1	0	0.0	0
2003—Buffalo NFL	16	16	38	26	5.5	0	0	0.0	0
Pro totals (6 years)	91	44	129	60	16.5	1	0	0.0	0

POTEAT, HANK CB PANTHERS

PERSONAL: Born August 30, 1977, in Harrisburg, Pa. ... 5-9/192. ... Full name: Henry Major Poteat II.
HIGH SCHOOL: Harrisburg (Pa.).
COLLEGE: Pittsburgh.
TRANSACTIONS/CAREER NOTES: Selected by Pittsburgh Steelers in third round (77th pick overall) of 2000 NFL draft. ... Signed by Steelers (July 21, 2000). ... Granted free agency (February 28, 2003). ... Re-signed by Steelers (April 21, 2003). ... Released by Steelers (August 31, 2003). ... Signed by Tampa Bay Buccaneers (October 21, 2003). ... Released by Buccaneers (November 12, 2003). ... Signed by Carolina Panthers (December 30, 2003).
CHAMPIONSHIP GAME EXPERIENCE: Member of Steelers for AFC championship game (2001 season); inactive.

			TOTALS			INTERCEPTIONS				PUNT RETURNS				KICKOFF RETURNS				TOTALS			
Year Team	**G**	**GS**	**Tk.**	**Ast.**	**Sks.**	**No.**	**Yds.**	**Avg.**	**TD**	**No.**	**Yds.**	**Avg.**	**TD**	**No.**	**Yds.**	**Avg.**	**TD**	**TD**	**2pt.**	**Pts.**	**Fum.**
2000—Pit. NFL	15	0	0	0	0.0	0	0	0.0	0	36	467	13.0	1	24	465	19.4	0	1	0	6	3
2001—Pit. NFL	13	0	1	0	0.0	0	0	0.0	0	36	292	8.1	0	16	250	15.6	0	0	0	0	4
2002—Pit. NFL	13	0	8	0	0.0	0	0	0.0	0	4	29	7.3	0	5	103	20.6	0	0	0	0	1
2003—T.B. NFL	1	0	0	0	0.0	0	0	0.0	0	0	0	0.0	0	0	0	0.0	0	0	0	0	0
Pro totals (4 years)	42	0	9	0	0.0	0	0	0.0	0	76	788	10.4	1	45	818	18.2	0	1	0	6	8

POWELL, CARL DE BENGALS

PERSONAL: Born January 4, 1974, in Detroit, Mich. ... 6-2/285. ... Full name: Carl Demetris Powell.
HIGH SCHOOL: Northern (Detroit).
JUNIOR COLLEGE: Grand Rapids (Mich.) Community College.
COLLEGE: Louisville.
TRANSACTIONS/CAREER NOTES: Selected by Indianapolis Colts in fifth round (156th pick overall) of 1997 NFL draft. ... Signed by Colts (July 3, 1997). ... Released by Colts (August 28, 1998). ... Selected by Rhein Fire in 1999 NFL Europe draft (February 23, 1999). ... Signed by Baltimore Ravens (July 21, 2000). ... Released by Ravens (November 13, 2000). ... Signed by Chicago Bears (March 5, 2001). ... Granted unconditional free agency (March 1, 2002). ... Signed by Washington Redskins (March 28, 2002). ... Granted unconditional free agency (February 28, 2003). ... Signed by Cincinnati Bengals (March 2, 2003).

			TOTALS		
Year Team	**G**	**GS**	**Tk.**	**Ast.**	**Sks.**
1997—Indianapolis NFL	11	0	3	0	0.0
2000—Baltimore NFL	2	0	0	0	0.0
2001—Chicago NFL	16	0	8	1	0.0
2002—Washington NFL	15	4	21	10	3.0
2003—Cincinnati NFL	16	3	10	10	0.5
Pro totals (5 years)	60	7	42	21	3.5

POWELL, JEMEEL CB COWBOYS

PERSONAL: Born August 29, 1980, in Los Angeles, Calif. ... 6-0/186.
COLLEGE: California.
TRANSACTIONS/CAREER NOTES: Signed as non-drafted free agent by Detroit Lions (May 2, 2003). ... Claimed on waivers by Dallas Cowboys (September 1, 2003).

			TOTALS			INTERCEPTIONS			
Year Team	G	GS	Tk.	Ast.	Sks.	No.	Yds.	Avg.	TD
2003—Dallas NFL	3	0	0	0	0.0	0	0	0.0	0

PRICE, MARCUS T BILLS

PERSONAL: Born March 3, 1972, in Port Arthur, Texas. ... 6-4/310. ... Full name: Marcus Raymond Price.
HIGH SCHOOL: Lincoln (Port Arthur, Texas).
COLLEGE: Louisiana State.
TRANSACTIONS/CAREER NOTES: Selected by Jacksonville Jaguars in sixth round (172nd pick overall) of 1995 NFL draft. ... Signed by Jaguars (June 1, 1995). ... On injured reserve with ankle injury (August 19, 1995-entire season). ... Released by Jaguars (August 25, 1996). ... Signed by Denver Broncos to practice squad (December 3, 1996). ... Released by Broncos (December 30, 1996). ... Signed by Jaguars (January 31, 1997). ... Released by Jaguars (August 19, 1997). ... Re-signed by Jaguars to practice squad (October 28, 1997). ... Signed by San Diego Chargers off Jaguars practice squad (November 26, 1997). ... Released by Chargers (September 21, 1999). ... Signed by New Orleans Saints (March 23, 2000). ... Released by Saints (December 3, 2000). ... Re-signed by Saints (December 5, 2000). ... Granted unconditional free agency (March 1, 2002). ... Signed by Buffalo Bills (March 13, 2002).
PLAYING EXPERIENCE: San Diego NFL, 1997-1998; New Orleans NFL, 2000-2001; Buffalo NFL, 2002-2003. ... Games/Games started: 1997 (2/0), 1998 (10/0), 2000 (7/0), 2001 (12/0), 2002 (16/3), 2003 (16/4). Total: 63/7.

PRICE, PEERLESS WR FALCONS

PERSONAL: Born October 27, 1976, in Dayton, Ohio. ... 5-11/190. ... Full name: Peerless LeCross Price.
HIGH SCHOOL: Meadowdale (Dayton, Ohio).
COLLEGE: Tennessee.
TRANSACTIONS/CAREER NOTES: Selected by Buffalo Bills in second round (53rd pick overall) of 1999 NFL draft. ... Signed by Bills (July 30, 1999). ... Designated by Bills as franchise player (February 19, 2003). ... Traded by Bills to Atlanta Falcons for first-round pick (RB Willis McGahee) in 2003 draft (March 7, 2003).
SINGLE GAME HIGHS (regular season): Receptions—13 (September 15, 2002, vs. Minnesota); yards—185 (September 15, 2002, vs. Minnesota); and touchdown receptions—2 (December 1, 2002, vs. Miami).
STATISTICAL PLATEAUS: 100-yard receiving games: 1999 (1), 2000 (1), 2001 (3), 2002 (5), 2003 (1). Total: 11.

			RUSHING				RECEIVING				PUNT RETURNS				KICKOFF RETURNS				TOTALS		
Year Team	G	GS	Att.	Yds.	Avg.	TD	No.	Yds.	Avg.	TD	No.	Yds.	Avg.	TD	No.	Yds.	Avg.	TD	TD	2pt.	Pts.
1999—Buf. NFL	16	4	1	-7	-7.0	0	31	393	12.7	3	1	16	16.0	0	1	27	27.0	0	3	0	18
2000—Buf. NFL	16	16	2	32	16.0	0	52	762	14.7	3	5	27	5.4	0	0	0	0.0	0	3	0	18
2001—Buf. NFL	16	16	6	97	16.2	0	55	895	16.3	7	19	110	5.8	0	0	0	0.0	0	7	0	42
2002—Buf. NFL	16	16	3	-13	-4.3	0	94	1252	13.3	9	0	0	0.0	0	0	0	0.0	0	9	0	5
2003—Atl. NFL	16	15	2	3	1.5	0	64	838	13.1	3	0	0	0.0	0	0	0	0.0	0	3	0	18
Pro totals (5 years)	80	67	14	112	8.0	0	296	4140	14.0	25	25	153	6.1	0	1	27	27.0	0	25	0	150

PRIOLEAU, PIERSON S BILLS

PERSONAL: Born August 6, 1977, in Charleston, S.C. ... 5-11/188. ... Full name: Pierson Olin Prioleau. ... Name pronounced: pray-LOW.
HIGH SCHOOL: Macedonia (Saint Stephens, S.C.).
COLLEGE: Virginia Tech.
TRANSACTIONS/CAREER NOTES: Selected by San Francisco 49ers in fourth round (110th pick overall) of 1999 NFL draft. ... Signed by 49ers (July 27, 1999). ... Released by 49ers (September 2, 2001). ... Signed by Buffalo Bills (November 7, 2001). ... Granted free agency (March 1, 2002). ... Re-signed by Bills (April 16, 2002).
HONORS: Named strong safety on THE SPORTING NEWS college All-America third team (1997).

			TOTALS			INTERCEPTIONS			
Year Team	G	GS	Tk.	Ast.	Sks.	No.	Yds.	Avg.	TD
1999—San Francisco NFL	14	5	32	8	0.0	0	0	0.0	0
2000—San Francisco NFL	13	5	36	10	0.0	1	13	13.0	0
2001—Buffalo NFL	6	2	23	8	1.0	0	0	0.0	0
2002—Buffalo NFL	16	16	64	22	1.0	0	0	0.0	0
2003—Buffalo NFL	16	6	21	12	0.5	0	0	0.0	0
Pro totals (5 years)	65	34	176	60	2.5	1	13	13.0	0

PRITCHETT, KELVIN DT LIONS

PERSONAL: Born October 24, 1969, in Atlanta, Ga. ... 6-3/322. ... Full name: Kelvin Bratodd Pritchett.
HIGH SCHOOL: Therrell (Atlanta).
COLLEGE: Mississippi.
TRANSACTIONS/CAREER NOTES: Selected by Dallas Cowboys in first round (20th pick overall) of 1991 NFL draft. ... Rights traded by Cowboys to Detroit Lions for second- (LB Dixon Edwards), third- (G James Richards) and fourth-round (DE Tony Hill) picks in 1991 draft (April 21, 1991). ... Granted free agency (February 17, 1994). ... Re-signed by Lions (August 12, 1994). ... Granted unconditional free agency (February 17, 1995). ... Signed by Jacksonville Jaguars (March 11, 1995). ... On injured reserve with knee injury (November 4, 1997-remainder of season). ... Granted unconditional free agency (February 12, 1999). ... Signed by Lions (April 22, 1999). ... Granted unconditional free agency (February 11, 2000). ... Re-signed by Lions (May 12, 2000). ... Granted unconditional free agency (March 2, 2001). ... Re-signed by

P

Lions (July 11, 2001). ... Granted unconditional free agency (March 1, 2002). ... Re-signed by Lions (March 26, 2002). ... Granted unconditional free agency (February 28, 2003). ... Re-signed by Lions (March 13, 2003). ... Granted unconditional free agency (March 3, 2004). ... Re-signed by Lions (March 4, 2004).

CHAMPIONSHIP GAME EXPERIENCE: Played in NFC championship game (1991 season). ... Played in AFC championship game (1996 season).

			TOTALS			INTERCEPTIONS			
Year Team	**G**	**GS**	**Tk.**	**Ast.**	**Sks.**	**No.**	**Yds.**	**Avg.**	**TD**
1991—Detroit NFL	16	0	20	6	1.5	0	0	0.0	0
1992—Detroit NFL	16	15	38	21	6.5	0	0	0.0	0
1993—Detroit NFL	16	5	33	9	4.0	0	0	0.0	0
1994—Detroit NFL	16	15	41	33	5.5	0	0	0.0	0
1995—Jacksonville NFL	16	16	41	22	1.5	0	0	0.0	0
1996—Jacksonville NFL	13	4	16	7	2.0	0	0	0.0	0
1997—Jacksonville NFL	8	5	20	12	3.0	0	0	0.0	0
1998—Jacksonville NFL	15	9	25	8	3.0	0	0	0.0	0
1999—Detroit NFL	16	2	16	4	1.0	0	0	0.0	0
2000—Detroit NFL	15	0	8	8	2.5	1	78	78.0	0
2001—Detroit NFL	16	1	10	7	0.0	0	0	0.0	0
2002—Detroit NFL	16	3	28	14	0.0	0	0	0.0	0
2003—Detroit NFL	13	0	8	1	0.0	0	0	0.0	0
Pro totals (13 years)	192	75	304	152	30.5	1	78	78.0	0

PRITCHETT, STANLEY — FB

PERSONAL: Born December 22, 1973, in Atlanta, Ga. ... 6-2/250. ... Full name: Stanley Jerome Pritchett.

HIGH SCHOOL: Frederick Douglass (College Park, Ga.).

COLLEGE: South Carolina.

TRANSACTIONS/CAREER NOTES: Selected by Miami Dolphins in fourth round (118th pick overall) of 1996 NFL draft. ... Signed by Dolphins (July 10, 1996). ... Granted free agency (February 12, 1999). ... Re-signed by Dolphins (April 13, 1999). ... Granted unconditional free agency (February 11, 2000). ... Signed by Philadelphia Eagles (March 9, 2000). ... Released by Eagles (September 2, 2001). ... Signed by Chicago Bears (October 17, 2001). ... Granted unconditional free agency (February 28, 2003). ... Re-signed by Bears (March 1, 2003). ... Granted unconditional free agency (March 3, 2004). ... Re-signed by Bears (March 3, 2004). ... Released by Bears (May 6, 2004).

SINGLE GAME HIGHS (regular season): Attempts—17 (December 12, 1999, vs. New York Jets); yards—68 (December 12, 1999, vs. New York Jets); and rushing touchdowns—1 (October 19, 2003, vs. Seattle).

			RUSHING				RECEIVING				TOTALS			
Year Team	**G**	**GS**	**Att.**	**Yds.**	**Avg.**	**TD**	**No.**	**Yds.**	**Avg.**	**TD**	**TD**	**2pt.**	**Pts.**	**Fum.**
1996—Miami NFL	16	16	7	27	3.9	0	33	354	10.7	2	2	0	12	3
1997—Miami NFL	6	5	3	7	2.3	0	5	35	7.0	0	0	0	0	0
1998—Miami NFL	16	12	6	19	3.2	1	17	97	5.7	0	1	0	6	0
1999—Miami NFL	14	7	47	158	3.4	1	43	312	7.3	4	5	0	30	0
2000—Philadelphia NFL	16	2	58	225	3.9	1	25	193	7.7	0	1	0	6	1
2001—Chicago NFL	7	0	0	0	0.0	0	0	0	0.0	0	0	0	0	0
2002—Chicago NFL	16	2	1	2	2.0	0	19	165	8.7	1	1	0	6	0
2003—Chicago NFL	16	11	21	93	4.4	2	18	83	4.6	0	2	0	12	0
Pro totals (8 years)	107	55	143	531	3.7	5	160	1239	7.7	7	12	0	72	4

PROEHL, RICKY — WR — PANTHERS

PERSONAL: Born March 7, 1968, in Bronx, N.Y. ... 6-0/190. ... Full name: Richard Scott Proehl.

HIGH SCHOOL: Hillsborough (Belle Mead, N.J.).

COLLEGE: Wake Forest.

TRANSACTIONS/CAREER NOTES: Selected by Phoenix Cardinals in third round (58th pick overall) of 1990 NFL draft. ... Signed by Cardinals (July 23, 1990). ... Granted free agency (March 1, 1993). ... Tendered offer sheet by New England Patriots (April 13, 1993). ... Offer matched by Cardinals (April 19, 1993). ... Cardinals franchise renamed Arizona Cardinals for 1994 season. ... Traded by Cardinals to Seattle Seahawks for fourth-round pick (traded to New York Jets) in 1995 draft (April 3, 1995). ... Released by Seahawks (March 7, 1997). ... Signed by Chicago Bears (April 10, 1997). ... Granted unconditional free agency (February 13, 1998). ... Signed by St. Louis Rams (February 25, 1998). ... Granted unconditional free agency (March 1, 2002). ... Re-signed by Rams (April 9, 2002). ... Granted unconditional free agency (February 28, 2003). ... Signed by Carolina Panthers (March 17, 2003). ... Granted unconditional free agency (March 3, 2004). ... Re-signed by Panthers (May 1, 2004).

CHAMPIONSHIP GAME EXPERIENCE: Played in NFC championship game (1999, 2001 and 2003 seasons). ... Member of Super Bowl championship team (1999 season). ... Played in Super Bowl 36 (2001 season) and Super Bowl 38 (2003 season).

SINGLE GAME HIGHS (regular season): Receptions—11 (November 16, 1997, vs. New York Jets); yards—164 (November 27, 1997, vs. Detroit); and touchdown receptions—2 (January 6, 2002, vs. Atlanta).

STATISTICAL PLATEAUS: 100-yard receiving games: 1990 (2), 1991 (1), 1992 (3), 1993 (1), 1997 (3), 1998 (1), 2001 (1), 2003 (1). Total: 13.

			RUSHING				RECEIVING				TOTALS			
Year Team	**G**	**GS**	**Att.**	**Yds.**	**Avg.**	**TD**	**No.**	**Yds.**	**Avg.**	**TD**	**TD**	**2pt.**	**Pts.**	**Fum.**
1990—Phoenix NFL	16	2	1	4	4.0	0	56	802	14.3	4	4	0	24	0
1991—Phoenix NFL	16	16	3	21	7.0	0	55	766	13.9	2	2	0	12	0
1992—Phoenix NFL	16	15	3	23	7.7	0	60	744	12.4	3	3	0	18	5
1993—Phoenix NFL	16	16	8	47	5.9	0	65	877	13.5	7	7	0	42	1
1994—Arizona NFL	16	16	0	0	0.0	0	51	651	12.8	5	5	0	30	2
1995—Seattle NFL	8	0	0	0	0.0	0	5	29	5.8	0	0	0	0	0
1996—Seattle NFL	16	7	0	0	0.0	0	23	309	13.4	2	2	0	12	0
1997—Chicago NFL	15	10	0	0	0.0	0	58	753	13.0	7	7	1	44	2
1998—St. Louis NFL	16	11	1	14	14.0	0	60	771	12.9	3	3	1	20	0
1999—St. Louis NFL	15	2	0	0	0.0	0	33	349	10.6	0	0	0	0	0
2000—St. Louis NFL	12	4	0	0	0.0	0	31	441	14.2	4	4	0	24	0
2001—St. Louis NFL	16	3	1	5	5.0	0	40	563	14.1	5	5	1	32	0
2002—St. Louis NFL	16	2	0	0	0.0	0	43	466	10.8	4	4	0	24	0
2003—Carolina NFL	16	2	0	0	0.0	0	27	389	14.4	4	4	0	24	0
Pro totals (14 years)	210	106	17	114	6.7	0	607	7910	13.0	50	50	3	306	10

Q

PRYCE, TREVOR DE BRONCOS

PERSONAL: Born August 3, 1975, in Brooklyn, N.Y. ... 6-5/295.
HIGH SCHOOL: Lake Howell (Casselberry, Fla.).
COLLEGE: Clemson.
TRANSACTIONS/CAREER NOTES: Selected by Denver Broncos in first round (28th pick overall) of 1997 NFL draft. ... Signed by Broncos (July 24, 1997).
CHAMPIONSHIP GAME EXPERIENCE: Played in AFC championship game (1997 and 1998 seasons). ... Member of Super Bowl championship team (1997 and 1998 seasons).
HONORS: Played in Pro Bowl (1999, 2000 and 2002 seasons). ... Named to play in Pro Bowl (2001 season); replaced by Gary Walker due to injury.

			TOTALS			INTERCEPTIONS			
Year Team	**G**	**GS**	**Tk.**	**Ast.**	**Sks.**	**No.**	**Yds.**	**Avg.**	**TD**
1997—Denver NFL	8	3	16	8	2.0	0	0	0.0	0
1998—Denver NFL	16	15	31	12	8.5	1	1	1.0	0
1999—Denver NFL	15	15	33	13	13.0	1	0	0.0	0
2000—Denver NFL	16	16	34	12	12.0	0	0	0.0	0
2001—Denver NFL	16	16	34	7	7.0	0	0	0.0	0
2002—Denver NFL	16	16	40	6	9.0	0	0	0.0	0
2003—Denver NFL	16	16	27	9	8.5	0	0	0.0	0
Pro totals (7 years)	103	97	215	67	60.0	2	1	0.5	0

PUCILLO, MIKE G BILLS

PERSONAL: Born July 14, 1979, in Cleveland, Ohio. ... 6-4/311. ... Full name: Michael Pucillo.
HIGH SCHOOL: Brandon (Fla.).
COLLEGE: Auburn.
TRANSACTIONS/CAREER NOTES: Selected by Buffalo Bills in seventh round (215th pick overall) of 2002 NFL draft. ... Signed by Bills (July 17, 2002).
PLAYING EXPERIENCE: Buffalo NFL, 2003. ... Games/Games started: 2003 (13/12). Total: 13/12.

PUTZIER, JEB TE BRONCOS

PERSONAL: Born January 20, 1979, in Eagle, Idaho. ... 6-4/256.
HIGH SCHOOL: Eagle (Idaho).
COLLEGE: Boise State.
TRANSACTIONS/CAREER NOTES: Selected by Denver Broncos in sixth round (191st pick overall) of 2002 NFL draft. ... Signed by Broncos (June 14, 2002).
SINGLE GAME HIGHS (regular season): Receptions—4 (December 28, 2003, vs. Green Bay); yards—34 (December 28, 2003, vs. Green Bay); and touchdown receptions—0.

			RECEIVING				TOTALS			
Year Team	**G**	**GS**	**No.**	**Yds.**	**Avg.**	**TD**	**TD**	**2pt.**	**Pts.**	**Fum.**
2002—Denver NFL	3	1	0	0	0.0	0	0	0	0	0
2003—Denver NFL	4	0	4	34	8.5	0	0	0	0	0
Pro totals (2 years)	7	1	4	34	8.5	0	0	0	0	0

PYATT, BRAD WR COLTS

PERSONAL: Born April 16, 1980, in Arvada, Colo. ... 5-11/195.
COLLEGE: Northern Colorado.
TRANSACTIONS/CAREER NOTES: Signed as non-drafted free agent by Indianapolis Colts (July 23, 2003). ... On injured reserve with concussion (November 9, 2003-remainder of season). ... Granted free agency (March 3, 2004). ... Re-signed by Colts (March 12, 2004).

			RECEIVING				PUNT RETURNS				KICKOFF RETURNS				TOTALS			
Year Team	**G**	**GS**	**No.**	**Yds.**	**Avg.**	**TD**	**No.**	**Yds.**	**Avg.**	**TD**	**No.**	**Yds.**	**Avg.**	**TD**	**TD**	**2pt.**	**Pts.**	**Fum.**
2003—Indianapolis NFL	8	0	1	2	2.0	0	12	110	9.2	0	19	544	28.6	0	0	0	0	2

QUARLES, SHELTON LB BUCCANEERS

PERSONAL: Born September 11, 1971, in Nashville, Tenn. ... 6-1/225. ... Full name: Shelton Eugene Quarles.
HIGH SCHOOL: Whites Creek (Tenn.).
COLLEGE: Vanderbilt.
TRANSACTIONS/CAREER NOTES: Signed as non-drafted free agent by Miami Dolphins (April 29, 1994). ... Released by Dolphins (August 15, 1994). ... Signed by B.C. Lions of CFL (December 1, 1994). ... Granted free agency (February 16, 1997). ... Signed by Tampa Bay Buccaneers (March 21, 1997). ... Granted unconditional free agency (February 28, 2003). ... Re-signed by Buccaneers (March 7, 2003).
CHAMPIONSHIP GAME EXPERIENCE: Played in NFC championship game (1999 and 2002 seasons). ... Member of Super Bowl championship team (2002 season).
HONORS: Played in Pro Bowl (2002).

			TOTALS			INTERCEPTIONS			
Year Team	**G**	**GS**	**Tk.**	**Ast.**	**Sks.**	**No.**	**Yds.**	**Avg.**	**TD**
1997—Tampa Bay NFL	16	0	1	3	0.0	0	0	0.0	0
1998—Tampa Bay NFL	16	0	9	3	1.0	0	0	0.0	0
1999—Tampa Bay NFL	16	14	23	12	0.0	0	0	0.0	0
2000—Tampa Bay NFL	14	13	35	15	2.0	1	5	5.0	0

Year Team	G	GS	TOTALS Tk.	Ast.	Sks.	INTERCEPTIONS No.	Yds.	Avg.	TD
2001—Tampa Bay NFL	16	16	28	16	2.0	1	98	98.0	1
2002—Tampa Bay NFL	16	16	74	39	1.0	2	29	14.5	1
2003—Tampa Bay NFL	11	11	57	23	0.0	0	0	0.0	0
Pro totals (7 years)	105	70	227	111	6.0	4	132	33.0	2

R

QUINN, JONATHAN — QB — BEARS

PERSONAL: Born February 27, 1975, in Turlock, Calif. ... 6-6/243. ... Full name: Jonathan Ryan Quinn.
HIGH SCHOOL: McGavock (Nashville).
COLLEGE: Tulane, then Middle Tennessee State.
TRANSACTIONS/CAREER NOTES: Selected by Jacksonville Jaguars in third round (86th pick overall) of 1998 NFL draft. ... Signed by Jaguars (May 19, 1998). ... Active for one game (1999); did not play. ... Assigned by Jaguars to Berlin Thunder in 2001 NFL Europe enhancement allocation program (February 19, 2001). ... Granted unconditional free agency (March 1, 2002). ... Signed by Kansas City Chiefs (May 1, 2002). ... Granted unconditional free agency (March 3, 2004). ... Signed by Chicago Bears (March 3, 2004).
CHAMPIONSHIP GAME EXPERIENCE: Member of Jaguars for AFC championship game (1999 season); inactive.
SINGLE GAME HIGHS (regular season): Attempts—31 (November 18, 2001, vs. Pittsburgh); completions—17 (November 18, 2001, vs. Pittsburgh); yards—225 (November 18, 2001, vs. Pittsburgh); and touchdown passes—1 (September 30, 2001, vs. Cleveland).
MISCELLANEOUS: Regular-season record as starting NFL quarterback: 1-2 (.333).

			PASSING									RUSHING				TOTALS		
Year Team	G	GS	Att.	Cmp.	Pct.	Yds.	TD	Int.	Avg.	Skd.	Rat.	Att.	Yds.	Avg.	TD	TD	2pt.	Pts.
1998—Jacksonville NFL	4	2	64	34	53.1	387	2	3	6.05	9	62.4	11	77	7.0	1	1	0	6
1999—Jacksonville NFL								Did not play.										
2000—Jacksonville NFL	2	0	0	0	0.0	0	0	0	0.00	0	0.0	2	-2	-1.0	0	0	0	0
2001—Jacksonville NFL	6	1	61	32	52.5	361	1	1	5.92	6	69.1	8	42	5.3	0	0	0	0
2002—Kansas City NFL	1	0	0	0	0.0	0	0	0	0.00	0	0.0	1	-1	-1.0	0	0	0	0
2003—Kansas City NFL								Did not play.										
Pro totals (4 years)	13	3	125	66	52.8	748	3	4	5.98	15	65.7	22	116	5.3	1	1	0	6

QUINN, MIKE — QB — BRONCOS

PERSONAL: Born April 15, 1974, in Houston. ... 6-4/216. ... Full name: Michael Patrick Quinn.
HIGH SCHOOL: Robert E. Lee (Houston).
COLLEGE: Stephen F. Austin.
TRANSACTIONS/CAREER NOTES: Signed as non-drafted free agent by Pittsburgh Steelers (April 21, 1997). ... Assigned by Steelers to Rhein Fire in 1998 NFL Europe enhancement allocation program (February 18, 1998). ... Claimed on waivers by Indianapolis Colts (August 31, 1998). ... Inactive for one game with Colts (1998). ... Claimed on waivers by Dallas Cowboys (September 9, 1998). ... Active for two games (1999); did not play. ... Granted free agency (February 11, 2000). ... Resigned by Cowboys (April 11, 2000) ... Released by Cowboys (May 4, 2000). ... Signed by Miami Dolphins (May 23, 2000). ... Released by Dolphins (November 10, 2000). ... Re-signed by Dolphins (November 13, 2000). ... Granted unconditional free agency (March 2, 2001). ... Re-signed by Dolphins (March 14, 2001). ... Released by Dolphins (September 2, 2001). ... Signed by Houston Texans (December 29, 2001). ... Granted unconditional free agency (February 28, 2003). ... Re-signed by Texans (March 18, 2003). ... Granted unconditional free agency (March 3, 2004). ... Signed by Denver Broncos (March 10, 2004).
CHAMPIONSHIP GAME EXPERIENCE: Member of Steelers for AFC championship game (1997 season); inactive.
SINGLE GAME HIGHS (regular season): Attempts—2 (November 9, 1997, vs. Baltimore); completions—1 (November 2, 1998, vs. Philadelphia); yards—10 (November 2, 1998, vs. Philadelphia); and touchdown passes—0.

			PASSING									RUSHING				TOTALS		
Year Team	G	GS	Att.	Cmp.	Pct.	Yds.	TD	Int.	Avg.	Skd.	Rat.	Att.	Yds.	Avg.	TD	TD	2pt.	Pts.
1997—Pittsburgh NFL	1	0	2	1	50.0	10	0	0	5.00	0	64.6	0	0	0.0	0	0	0	0
1998—Dallas NFL	3	0	1	1	100.0	10	0	0	10.00	0	108.3	5	-6	-1.2	0	0	0	0
1999—Dallas NFL								Did not play.										
2000—Miami NFL	1	0	0	0	0.0	0	0	0	0.00	0	0.0	0	0	0.0	0	0	0	0
2003—Houston NFL								Did not play.										
Pro totals (3 years)	5	0	3	2	66.7	20	0	0	6.67	0	85.4	5	-6	-1.2	0	0	0	0

RABACH, CASEY — G/C — RAVENS

PERSONAL: Born September 24, 1977, in Sturgeon Bay, Wis. ... 6-4/301.
HIGH SCHOOL: Sturgeon Bay (Wis.).
COLLEGE: Wisconsin.
TRANSACTIONS/CAREER NOTES: Selected by Baltimore Ravens in third round (92nd pick overall) of 2001 NFL draft. ... Signed by Ravens (July 21, 2001). ... Active for two games (2001); did not play. ... Granted free agency (March 3, 2004). ... Re-signed by Ravens (March 5, 2004).
PLAYING EXPERIENCE: Baltimore NFL, 2001-2003. ... Games/Games started: 2002 (12/5), 2003 (14/2), Total: 26/7.

RACKERS, NEIL — K — CARDINALS

PERSONAL: Born August 16, 1976, in St. Louis, Mo. ... 6-0/205. ... Full name: Neil W. Rackers.
HIGH SCHOOL: Aquinas-Mercy (Florissant, Mo.).
COLLEGE: Illinois.
TRANSACTIONS/CAREER NOTES: Selected by Cincinnati Bengals in sixth round (169th pick overall) of 2000 NFL draft. ... Signed by Bengals (July 21, 2000). ... Granted free agency (February 28, 2003). ... Re-signed by Bengals (April 15, 2003). ... Waived by Bengals (September 1, 2003). ... Signed by Arizona Cardinals (November 11, 2003).

Year Team	G	FIELD GOALS 1-29	30-39	40-49	50+	Tot.	Pct.	Lg.	TOTALS XPM	XPA	Pts.
2000—Cincinnati NFL	16	5-5	5-9	2-7	0-0	12-21	57.1	45	21	21	57
2001—Cincinnati NFL	16	4-6	8-11	4-9	1-2	17-28	60.7	52	23	24	74
2002—Cincinnati NFL	16	7-7	3-3	3-5	2-3	15-18	83.3	54	30	32	75
2003—Arizona NFL	7	5-5	1-4	3-3	0-0	9-12	75.0	49	8	8	35
Pro totals (4 years)	55	21-23	17-27	12-24	3-5	53-79	67.1	54	82	85	241

RACKLEY, DEREK — TE/LS — FALCONS

PERSONAL: Born July 18, 1977, in Apple Valley, Minn. ... 6-4/250.
HIGH SCHOOL: Apple Valley (Minn.).
COLLEGE: Minnesota.
TRANSACTIONS/CAREER NOTES: Signed as non-drafted free agent by Atlanta Falcons (April 17, 2000). ... Granted free agency (February 28, 2003). ... Re-signed by Falcons (March 25, 2003).
PLAYING EXPERIENCE: Atlanta NFL, 2000-2003. ... Games/Games started: 2000 (16/0), 2001 (16/0), 2002 (16/0), 2003 (16/1). Total: 64/1.
SINGLE GAME HIGHS (regular season): Receptions—1 (December 30, 2001, vs. Miami); yards—1 (December 30, 2001, vs. Miami); and touchdown receptions—1 (December 30, 2001, vs. Miami).

RAGONE, DAVE — QB — TEXANS

PERSONAL: Born October 3, 1979, in Middleburg Heights, Ohio. ... 6-3/245.
HIGH SCHOOL: St. Igantius (Middleburg Heights, Ohio).
COLLEGE: Louisville.
TRANSACTIONS/CAREER NOTES: Selected by Houston Texans in third round (88th pick overall) of 2003 NFL draft. ... Signed by Texans (July 25, 2003).
SINGLE GAME HIGHS (regular season): Attempts—23 (December 7, 2003, vs. Jacksonville); completions—11 (December 7, 2003, vs. Jacksonville); yards—71 (December 7, 2003, vs. Jacksonville); and touchdown passes—0.
MISCELLANEOUS: Regular-season record as starting NFL quarterback: 0-2 (.000).

Year Team	G	GS	PASSING Att.	Cmp.	Pct.	Yds.	TD	Int.	Avg.	Skd.	Rat.	RUSHING Att.	Yds.	Avg.	TD	TOTALS TD	2pt.	Pts.
2003—Houston NFL	2	2	40	20	50.0	135	0	1	3.38	8	47.4	6	51	8.5	0	0	0	0

RAINER, WALI — LB — LIONS

PERSONAL: Born April 19, 1977, in Rockingham, N.C. ... 6-2/247. ... Full name: Wali Rashid Rainer.
HIGH SCHOOL: West Charlotte (N.C.).
COLLEGE: Virginia.
TRANSACTIONS/CAREER NOTES: Selected by Cleveland Browns in fourth round (124th pick overall) of 1999 NFL draft. ... Signed by Browns (July 22, 1999). ... Granted free agency (March 1, 2002). ... Re-signed by Browns (April 20, 2002). ... Traded by Browns with third-round pick (traded to Washington) in 2002 draft to Jacksonville Jaguars for third-round pick (C Melvin Fowler) in 2002 draft (April 20, 2002). ... Granted unconditional free agency (February 28, 2003). ... Signed by Detroit Lions (April 7, 2003).

Year Team	G	GS	TOTALS Tk.	Ast.	Sks.	INTERCEPTIONS No.	Yds.	Avg.	TD
1999—Cleveland NFL	16	15	108	29	1.0	0	0	0.0	0
2000—Cleveland NFL	16	16	86	33	1.0	1	5	5.0	0
2001—Cleveland NFL	14	14	50	28	1.0	0	0	0.0	0
2002—Jacksonville NFL	16	14	66	20	1.0	0	0	0.0	0
2003—Detroit NFL	16	0	8	3	0.0	0	0	0.0	0
Pro totals (5 years)	78	59	318	113	4.0	1	5	5.0	0

RAIOLA, DOMINIC — C — LIONS

PERSONAL: Born December 30, 1978, in Honolulu, Hawaii. ... 6-1/295.
HIGH SCHOOL: St. Louis (Honolulu, Hawaii).
COLLEGE: Nebraska.
TRANSACTIONS/CAREER NOTES: Selected by Detroit Lions in second round (50th pick overall) of 2001 NFL draft. ... Signed by Lions (July 23, 2001).
PLAYING EXPERIENCE: Detroit NFL, 2001-2003. ... Games/Games started: 2001 (16/0), 2002 (16/16), 2003 (16/16). Total: 48/32.
HONORS: Named center on THE SPORTING NEWS college All-America second team (2000).

RAMSEY, PATRICK — QB — REDSKINS

PERSONAL: Born February 14, 1979, in Ruston, La. ... 6-2/217. ... Full name: Patrick Allen Ramsey.
HIGH SCHOOL: Ruston (La.).
COLLEGE: Tulane.
TRANSACTIONS/CAREER NOTES: Selected by Washington Redskins in first round (32nd pick overall) of 2002 NFL draft. ... Signed by Redskins (August 7, 2002). ... On injured reserve with foot injury (December 8, 2003-remainder of season).
SINGLE GAME HIGHS (regular season): Attempts—50 (October 5, 2003, vs. Philadelphia); completions—25 (October 5, 2003, vs. Philadelphia); yards—356 (September 14, 2003, vs. Atlanta); and touchdown passes—3 (December 15, 2002, vs. Philadelphia).
STATISTICAL PLATEAUS: 300-yard passing games: 2002 (1), 2003 (2). Total: 3.
MISCELLANEOUS: Regular-season record as starting NFL quarterback: 6-10 (.375).

Year	Team	G	GS	PASSING Att.	Cmp.	Pct.	Yds.	TD	Int.	Avg.	Skd.	Rat.	RUSHING Att.	Yds.	Avg.	TD	TOTALS TD	2pt.	Pts.
2002—Washington NFL		10	5	227	117	51.5	1539	9	8	6.78	18	71.8	13	-1	-0.1	1	1	0	6
2003—Washington NFL		11	11	337	179	53.1	2166	14	9	6.43	30	75.8	15	62	4.1	1	1	0	6
Pro totals (2 years)		21	16	564	296	52.5	3705	23	17	6.57	48	74.2	28	61	2.2	2	2	0	12

RANDALL, GREG T 49ERS

PERSONAL: Born June 23, 1978, in Galveston, Texas. ... 6-5/322.
HIGH SCHOOL: La Marque (Texas).
JUNIOR COLLEGE: Coffeyville (Kan.) Community College.
COLLEGE: Michigan State.
TRANSACTIONS/CAREER NOTES: Selected by New England Patriots in fourth round (127th pick overall) of 2000 NFL draft. ... Signed by Patriots (July 12, 2000). ... Traded by Patriots to Houston Texans for fifth-round pick (traded to Tennessee) in 2003 draft (March 6, 2003). ... Granted unconditional free agency (March 3, 2004). ... Signed by San Francisco 49ers (April 20, 2004).
PLAYING EXPERIENCE: New England NFL, 2000-2002; Houston NFL, 2003. ... Games/Games started: 2000 (12/4), 2001 (16/16), 2002 (7/3), 2003 (16/16). Total: 51/39.
CHAMPIONSHIP GAME EXPERIENCE: Played in AFC championship game (2001 season). ... Member of Super Bowl championship team (2001 season).

R

RANDLE, JOHN DT SEAHAWKS

PERSONAL: Born December 12, 1967, in Hearne, Texas. ... 6-1/290. ... Brother of Ervin Randle, linebacker with Tampa Bay Buccaneers (1985-90) and Kansas City Chiefs (1991 and 1992).
HIGH SCHOOL: Hearne (Texas).
JUNIOR COLLEGE: Trinity Valley Community College (Texas).
COLLEGE: Texas A&M-Kingsville.
TRANSACTIONS/CAREER NOTES: Signed as non-drafted free agent by Minnesota Vikings (May 4, 1990). ... Designated by Vikings as transition player (January 15, 1994). ... Designated by Vikings as transition player (February 13, 1998). ... Tendered offer sheet by Miami Dolphins (February 16, 1998). ... Offer matched by Vikings (February 18, 1998). ... Released by Vikings (March 1, 2001). ... Signed by Seattle Seahawks (March 3, 2001).
CHAMPIONSHIP GAME EXPERIENCE: Played in NFC championship game (1998 and 2000 seasons).
HONORS: Played in Pro Bowl (1993-1998 and 2001 seasons). ... Named defensive tackle on THE SPORTING NEWS NFL All-Pro team (1994-1998).

Year	Team	G	GS	TOTALS Tk.	Ast.	Sks.	INTERCEPTIONS No.	Yds.	Avg.	TD
1990—Minnesota NFL		16	0	12	9	1.0	0	0	0.0	0
1991—Minnesota NFL		16	8	32	26	9.5	0	0	0.0	0
1992—Minnesota NFL		16	14	45	11	11.5	0	0	0.0	0
1993—Minnesota NFL		16	16	54	5	12.5	0	0	0.0	0
1994—Minnesota NFL		16	16	30	12	∞13.5	0	0	0.0	0
1995—Minnesota NFL		16	16	33	11	10.5	0	0	0.0	0
1996—Minnesota NFL		16	16	35	11	11.5	0	0	0.0	0
1997—Minnesota NFL		16	16	47	11	*15.5	0	0	0.0	0
1998—Minnesota NFL		16	16	27	14	10.5	0	0	0.0	0
1999—Minnesota NFL		16	16	29	9	10.0	1	1	1.0	0
2000—Minnesota NFL		16	16	25	1	8.0	0	0	0.0	0
2001—Seattle NFL		15	14	26	9	11.0	0	0	0.0	0
2002—Seattle NFL		12	12	13	2	7.0	0	0	0.0	0
2003—Seattle NFL		16	9	12	5	5.5	0	0	0.0	0
Pro totals (14 years)		219	185	420	136	137.5	1	1	1.0	0

RANDLE EL, ANTWAAN WR STEELERS

PERSONAL: Born August 17, 1979, in Riverdale, Ill. ... 5-10/186.
HIGH SCHOOL: Thornton (Riverdale, Ill.).
COLLEGE: Indiana.
TRANSACTIONS/CAREER NOTES: Selected by Pittsburgh Steelers in second round (62nd pick overall) of 2002 NFL draft. ... Signed by Steelers (July 23, 2002).
POST SEASON RECORDS: Shares NFL career and single-game record for most punt returns for touchdown—1 (January 5, 2003 vs. Cleveland).
SINGLE GAME HIGHS (regular season): Receptions—8 (December 8, 2002, vs. Houston); yards—88 (December 8, 2002, vs. Houston); and touchdown receptions—1 (November 17, 2003, vs. San Francisco).

Year	Team	G	GS	RUSHING Att.	Yds.	Avg.	TD	RECEIVING No.	Yds.	Avg.	TD	PUNT RETURNS No.	Yds.	Avg.	TD	KICKOFF RETURNS No.	Yds.	Avg.	TD	TOTALS TD	2pt.	Pts.
2002—Pit. NFL		16	0	19	134	7.1	0	47	489	10.4	2	§37	257	6.9	0	32	733	22.9	1	3	0	18
2003—Pit. NFL		16	1	15	75	5.0	0	37	364	9.8	1	†45	§542	12.0	†2	24	466	19.4	0	3	0	18
Pro totals (2 years)		32	1	34	209	6.1	0	84	853	10.2	3	82	799	9.7	2	56	1199	21.4	1	6	0	36

RANSOM, DERRICK DT

PERSONAL: Born September 13, 1976, in Indianapolis, Ind. ... 6-3/306. ... Full name: Derrick Wayne Ransom Jr.
HIGH SCHOOL: Lawrence Central (Indianapolis).
COLLEGE: Cincinnati.
TRANSACTIONS/CAREER NOTES: Selected by Kansas City Chiefs in sixth round (181st pick overall) of 1998 NFL draft. ... Signed by Chiefs (June 3, 1998). ... Granted free agency (March 2, 2001). ... Re-signed by Chiefs (April 3, 2001). ... Granted unconditional free agency (March

1, 2002). ... Re-signed by Chiefs (April 3, 2002). ... Released by Chiefs (August 31, 2003). ... Signed by Arizona Cardinals (September 16, 2003). ... Granted unconditional free agency (March 3, 2004).

			TOTALS		
Year Team	G	GS	Tk.	Ast.	Sks.
1998—Kansas City NFL	7	0	1	0	0.0
1999—Kansas City NFL	10	0	1	0	1.0
2000—Kansas City NFL	10	0	2	0	0.0
2001—Kansas City NFL	16	16	41	13	3.0
2002—Kansas City NFL	13	10	20	5	0.0
2003—Arizona NFL	5	0	1	2	0.0
Pro totals (6 years)	61	26	66	20	4.0

R

RASBY, WALTER TE REDSKINS

PERSONAL: Born September 7, 1972, in Washington, DC. ... 6-3/252. ... Full name: Walter Herbert Rasby.
HIGH SCHOOL: Washington (N.C.).
COLLEGE: Wake Forest.
TRANSACTIONS/CAREER NOTES: Signed as non-drafted free agent by Pittsburgh Steelers (April 29, 1994). ... Released by Steelers (August 27, 1995). ... Signed by Carolina Panthers (October 17, 1995). ... Granted free agency (February 14, 1997). ... Re-signed by Panthers (June 3, 1997). ... On injured reserve with knee injury (December 10, 1997-remainder of season). ... Granted unconditional free agency (February 13, 1998). ... Signed by Detroit Lions (April 13, 1998). ... Granted unconditional free agency (March 2, 2001). ... Signed by Washington Redskins (April 10, 2001). ... Released by Redskins (February 26, 2003). ... Signed by New Orleans Saints (May 14, 2003). ... Granted unconditional free agency (March 3, 2004). ... Signed by Redskins (March 10, 2004).
CHAMPIONSHIP GAME EXPERIENCE: Played in AFC championship game (1994 season). ... Played in NFC championship game (1996 season).
SINGLE GAME HIGHS (regular season): Receptions—5 (October 4, 1998, vs. Chicago); yards—45 (January 6, 2002, vs. Arizona); and touchdown receptions—1 (January 6, 2002, vs. Arizona).

			RECEIVING				TOTALS			
Year Team	G	GS	No.	Yds.	Avg.	TD	TD	2pt.	Pts.	Fum.
1994—Pittsburgh NFL	2	0	0	0	0.0	0	0	0	0	0
1995—Carolina NFL	9	2	5	47	9.4	0	0	1	2	0
1996—Carolina NFL	16	1	0	0	0.0	0	0	0	0	0
1997—Carolina NFL	14	2	1	1	1.0	0	0	0	0	0
1998—Detroit NFL	16	16	15	119	7.9	1	1	0	6	0
1999—Detroit NFL	16	6	3	19	6.3	1	1	0	6	0
2000—Detroit NFL	16	8	10	78	7.8	1	1	0	6	0
2001—Washington NFL	16	11	10	128	12.8	2	2	0	12	0
2002—Washington NFL	13	9	9	85	9.4	0	0	0	0	0
2003—New Orleans NFL	16	7	6	55	9.2	0	0	0	0	0
Pro totals (10 years)	134	62	59	532	9.0	5	5	1	32	0

RASHEED, SALEEM LB 49ERS

PERSONAL: Born June 15, 1981, in Birmingham, Ala. ... 6-2/229.
HIGH SCHOOL: Shades Valley (Birmingham, Ala.).
COLLEGE: Alabama.
TRANSACTIONS/CAREER NOTES: Selected after junior season by San Francisco in third round (69th pick overall) of 2002 NFL draft. ... Signed by 49ers (July 21, 2002).

			TOTALS			INTERCEPTIONS			
Year Team	G	GS	Tk.	Ast.	Sks.	No.	Yds.	Avg.	TD
2002—San Francisco NFL	6	0	6	0	1.0	0	0	0.0	0
2003—San Francisco NFL	16	1	3	3	0.0	0	0	0.0	0
Pro totals (2 years)	22	1	9	3	1.0	0	0	0.0	0

RASMUSSEN, KEMP DE PANTHERS

PERSONAL: Born May 25, 1979, in Rochester, Mich. ... 6-3/255. ... Full name: Kemp Alan Rasmussen.
HIGH SCHOOL: Lampeer West (Hadley, Mich.).
COLLEGE: Indiana.
TRANSACTIONS/CAREER NOTES: Signed as non-drafted free agent by Carolina Panthers (April 29, 2002).
CHAMPIONSHIP GAME EXPERIENCE: Played in NFC championship game (2003 season). ... Played in Super Bowl 38 (2003 season).

			TOTALS		
Year Team	G	GS	Tk.	Ast.	Sks.
2002—Carolina NFL	10	0	2	1	0.0
2003—Carolina NFL	13	0	4	0	1.0
Pro totals (2 years)	23	0	6	1	1.0

RATTAY, TIM QB 49ERS

PERSONAL: Born March 15, 1977, in Elyria, Ohio. ... 6-0/200.
HIGH SCHOOL: Phoenix (Ariz.) Christian.
JUNIOR COLLEGE: Scottsdale (Ariz.) Community College.
COLLEGE: Louisiana Tech.

TRANSACTIONS/CAREER NOTES: Selected by San Francisco 49ers in seventh round (212th pick overall) of 2000 NFL draft. ... Signed by 49ers (July 16, 2000). ... Granted free agency (February 28, 2003). ... Re-signed by 49ers (April 7, 2003).

SINGLE GAME HIGHS (regular season): Attempts—30 (November 23, 2003, vs. Green Bay); completions—21 (November 17, 2003, vs. Pittsburgh); yards—254 (November 17, 2003, vs. Pittsburgh); and touchdown passes—3 (November 2, 2003, vs. St. Louis).

MISCELLANEOUS: Regular-season record as starting NFL quarterback: 2-1 (.667).

			PASSING									RUSHING				TOTALS		
Year Team	**G**	**GS**	**Att.**	**Cmp.**	**Pct.**	**Yds.**	**TD**	**Int.**	**Avg.**	**Skd.**	**Rat.**	**Att.**	**Yds.**	**Avg.**	**TD**	**TD**	**2pt.**	**Pts.**
2000—San Francisco NFL	1	0	1	1	100.0	-4	0	0	-4.00	0	79.2	2	-1	-0.5	0	0	0	0
2001—San Francisco NFL	3	0	2	2	100.0	21	0	0	10.50	0	110.4	5	-3	-0.6	0	0	0	0
2002—San Francisco NFL	4	0	43	26	60.5	232	2	0	5.40	5	90.5	5	0	0.0	0	0	0	0
2003—San Francisco NFL	11	3	118	73	61.9	856	7	2	7.25	7	96.6	8	0	0.0	0	0	0	0
Pro totals (4 years)	19	3	164	102	62.2	1105	9	2	6.74	12	95.2	20	-4	-0.2	0	0	0	0

RAYBURN, SAM — DT — EAGLES

PERSONAL: Born October 20, 1980, in Chickasha, Okla. ... 6-3/303. ... Full name: Sam Branson Rayburn.

HIGH SCHOOL: Chickasha (Okla.).

COLLEGE: Tulsa.

TRANSACTIONS/CAREER NOTES: Signed as non-drafted free agent by Philadelphia Eagles (April 28, 2003).

CHAMPIONSHIP GAME EXPERIENCE: Played in NFC championship game (2003 season).

			TOTALS		
Year Team	**G**	**GS**	**Tk.**	**Ast.**	**Sks.**
2003—Philadelphia NFL	10	0	9	0	2.0

RAYMER, CORY — C — REDSKINS

PERSONAL: Born March 3, 1973, in Fond du Lac, Wis. ... 6-3/300.

HIGH SCHOOL: Goodrich (Fond du Lac, Wis.).

COLLEGE: Wisconsin.

TRANSACTIONS/CAREER NOTES: Selected by Washington Redskins in second round (37th pick overall) of 1995 NFL draft. ... Signed by Redskins (July 24, 1995). ... On injured reserve with back injury (November 25, 1996-remainder of season). ... Granted unconditional free agency (February 12, 1999). ... Re-signed by Redskins (March 16, 1999). ... Granted unconditional free agency (February 11, 2000). ... Re-signed by Redskins (February 26, 2000). ... On injured reserve with knee injury (September 28, 2000-remainder of season). ... Granted unconditional free agency (March 1, 2002). ... Signed by San Diego Chargers (March 8, 2002). ... On injured reserve with Achilles injury (September 26, 2002-remainder of season). ... Released by Chargers (March 2, 2004). ... Signed by Washington Redskins (March 11, 2004).

PLAYING EXPERIENCE: Washington NFL, 1995-2001; San Diego NFL, 2002-2003. ... Games/Games started: 1995 (3/2), 1996 (6/5), 1997 (6/3), 1998 (16/16), 1999 (16/16), 2001 (16/16), 2002 (3/3), 2003 (15/8), Total: 81/69.

HONORS: Named offensive lineman on THE SPORTING NEWS college All-America first team (1994).

REAGOR, MONTAE — DT — COLTS

PERSONAL: Born June 29, 1977, in Waxahachie, Texas. ... 6-3/285. ... Full name: Willie Montae Reagor. ... Name pronounced: MON-tay RAY-ger.

HIGH SCHOOL: Waxahachie (Texas).

COLLEGE: Texas Tech.

TRANSACTIONS/CAREER NOTES: Selected by Denver Broncos in second round (58th pick overall) of 1999 NFL draft. ... Signed by Broncos (July 13, 1999). ... Granted unconditional free agency (February 28, 2003). ... Signed by Indianapolis Colts (March 3, 2003).

CHAMPIONSHIP GAME EXPERIENCE: Played in AFC championship game (2003 season).

HONORS: Named defensive end on THE SPORTING NEWS college All-America second team (1997). ... Named defensive end on THE SPORTING NEWS college All-America first team (1998).

			TOTALS			INTERCEPTIONS			
Year Team	**G**	**GS**	**Tk.**	**Ast.**	**Sks.**	**No.**	**Yds.**	**Avg.**	**TD**
1999—Denver NFL	9	0	9	1	0.0	0	0	0.0	0
2000—Denver NFL	13	0	8	1	2.0	0	0	0.0	0
2001—Denver NFL	8	0	4	0	1.0	0	0	0.0	0
2002—Denver NFL	15	1	12	8	1.0	1	31	31.0	0
2003—Indianapolis NFL	13	12	18	8	0.5	0	0	0.0	0
Pro totals (5 years)	58	13	51	18	4.5	1	31	31.0	0

REDDING, CORY — DE — LIONS

PERSONAL: Born November 15, 1980, in Houston, Texas. ... 6-4/285. ... Full name: Cory B. Redding.

HIGH SCHOOL: North Shore (Houston).

COLLEGE: Texas.

TRANSACTIONS/CAREER NOTES: Selected by Detroit Lions in third round (66th pick overall) of 2003 NFL draft. ... Signed by Lions (July 22, 2003).

			TOTALS			INTERCEPTIONS			
Year Team	**G**	**GS**	**Tk.**	**Ast.**	**Sks.**	**No.**	**Yds.**	**Avg.**	**TD**
2003—Detroit NFL	9	0	6	1	0.0	0	0	0.0	0

REDMAN, CHRIS — QB

PERSONAL: Born July 7, 1977, in Louisville, Ky. ... 6-3/223.
HIGH SCHOOL: Male (Louisville, Ky.).
COLLEGE: Louisville.
TRANSACTIONS/CAREER NOTES: Selected by Baltimore Ravens in third round (75th pick overall) of 2000 NFL draft. ... Signed by Ravens (July 24, 2000). ... Inactive for 14 games (2001). ... Granted free agency (February 28, 2003). ... Re-signed by Ravens (May 20, 2003). ... Granted unconditional free agency (March 3, 2004).
CHAMPIONSHIP GAME EXPERIENCE: Member of Ravens for AFC Championship game (2000 season); inactive. ... Member of Super Bowl championship team (2000 season); inactive.
SINGLE GAME HIGHS (regular season): Attempts—38 (September 15, 2002, vs. Tampa Bay); completions—20 (September 8, 2002, vs.Carolina); yards—218 (September 8, 2002, vs. Carolina); and touchdown passes—2 (October 20, 2002, vs. Jacksonville).
MISCELLANEOUS: Regular-season record as starting NFL quarterback: 3-3 (.500).

			PASSING									RUSHING				TOTALS		
Year Team	G	GS	Att.	Cmp.	Pct.	Yds.	TD	Int.	Avg.	Skd.	Rat.	Att.	Yds.	Avg.	TD	TD	2pt.	Pts.
2000—Baltimore NFL	2	0	3	2	66.7	19	0	0	6.33	0	84.0	1	0	0.0	0	0	0	0
2001—Baltimore NFL								Did not play.										
2002—Baltimore NFL	6	6	182	97	53.3	1034	7	3	5.68	11	76.1	10	8	0.8	0	0	0	0
2003—Baltimore NFL	2	0	13	7	53.8	58	0	2	4.46	6	26.0	2	4	2.0	0	0	0	0
Pro totals (3 years)	10	6	198	106	53.5	1111	7	5	5.61	17	71.3	13	12	0.9	0	0	0	0

REDMOND, JIMMY — WR — JAGUARS

PERSONAL: Born August 18, 1977, in Kansas City, Mo. ... 6-0/190. ... Full name: James Louis Redmond III.
HIGH SCHOOL: South (Blue Springs, Mo.).
COLLEGE: McNeese State.
TRANSACTIONS/CAREER NOTES: Signed as non-drafted free agent by Tennessee Titans (April 27, 2001). ... Released by Titans (August 26, 2001). ... Signed by Jacksonville Jaguars to practice squad (December 11, 2001). ... Assigned by Jaguars to Frankfurt Galaxy in 2002 NFL Europe enhancement allocation program (February 12, 2002). ... Re-signed by Jaguars (March 24, 2003). ... Released by Jaguars (August 31, 2003). ... Re-signed by Jaguars (September 9, 2003).
SINGLE GAME HIGHS (regular season): Receptions—1 (September 28, 2003, vs. Houston); yards—29 (September 14, 2003, vs. Buffalo); and touchdown receptions—0.

			RECEIVING				KICKOFF RETURNS				TOTALS			
Year Team	G	GS	No.	Yds.	Avg.	TD	No.	Yds.	Avg.	TD	TD	2pt.	Pts.	Fum.
2002—Jacksonville NFL	14	0	0	0	0.0	0	1	32	32.0	0	0	0	0	0
2003—Jacksonville NFL	12	0	3	67	22.3	0	1	21	21.0	0	0	0	0	0
Pro totals (2 years)	26	0	3	67	22.3	0	2	53	26.5	0	0	0	0	0

REDMOND, J.R. — RB — RAIDERS

PERSONAL: Born September 28, 1977, in Los Angeles, Calif. ... 5-11/215. ... Full name: Joseph Robert Redmond.
HIGH SCHOOL: Carson (Calif.).
COLLEGE: Arizona State.
TRANSACTIONS/CAREER NOTES: Selected by New England Patriots in third round (76th pick overall) of 2000 NFL draft. ... Signed by Patriots (July 23, 2000). ... Released by Patriots (August 24, 2003). ... Signed by Oakland Raiders (November 19, 2003).
CHAMPIONSHIP GAME EXPERIENCE: Played in AFC championship game (2001 season). ... Member of Super Bowl championship team (2001 season).
SINGLE GAME HIGHS (regular season): Attempts—24 (November 5, 2000, vs. Buffalo); yards—97 (October 22, 2000, vs. Indianapolis); and rushing touchdowns—1 (November 5, 2000 vs. Buffalo).

			RUSHING				RECEIVING				TOTALS			
Year Team	G	GS	Att.	Yds.	Avg.	TD	No.	Yds.	Avg.	TD	TD	2pt.	Pts.	Fum.
2000—New England NFL	12	5	125	406	3.2	1	20	126	6.3	2	3	0	18	2
2001—New England NFL	12	0	35	119	3.4	0	13	132	10.2	0	0	0	0	0
2002—New England NFL	9	0	4	2	0.5	0	2	5	2.5	0	0	0	0	0
2003—Oakland NFL	1	0	9	30	3.3	0	1	6	6.0	0	0	0	0	0
Pro totals (4 years)	34	5	173	557	3.2	1	36	269	7.5	2	3	0	18	2

REED, ED — S — RAVENS

PERSONAL: Born September 11, 1978, in St. Rose, La. ... 5-11/200. ... Full name: Edward Earl Reed.
HIGH SCHOOL: Destrehan (St. Rose, La.).
COLLEGE: Miami (Fla.).
TRANSACTIONS/CAREER NOTES: Selected by Baltimore Ravens in first round (24th pick overall) of 2002 NFL draft. ... Signed by Ravens (August 3, 2002).
HONORS: Named free safety on THE SPORTING NEWS college All-America first team (2001). ... Named safety on THE SPORTING NEWS NFL All-Pro team (2003). ... Played in Pro Bowl (2003 season).

			TOTALS			INTERCEPTIONS				PUNT RETURNS				TOTALS			
Year Team	G	GS	Tk.	Ast.	Sks.	No.	Yds.	Avg.	TD	No.	Yds.	Avg.	TD	TD	2pt.	Pts.	Fum.
2002—Baltimore NFL	16	16	67	13	1.0	5	167	33.4	0	0	0	0.0	0	1	0	6	1
2003—Baltimore NFL	16	15	58	12	1.0	▲7	132	18.9	1	5	33	6.6	0	3	0	18	1
Pro totals (2 years)	32	31	125	25	2.0	12	299	24.9	1	5	33	6.6	0	4	0	24	2

REED, JAMES — DT

PERSONAL: Born February 3, 1977, in Saginaw, Mich. ... 6-0/286. ... Full name: James Reed Jr.
HIGH SCHOOL: Saginaw (Mich.).
COLLEGE: Iowa State.
TRANSACTIONS/CAREER NOTES: Selected by New York Jets in seventh round (206th pick overall) of 2001 NFL draft. ... Signed by Jets (June 28, 2001). ... Granted free agency (March 3, 2004).

			TOTALS		
Year Team	G	GS	Tk.	Ast.	Sks.
2001—New York Jets NFL	16	2	19	9	1.0
2002—New York Jets NFL	16	0	12	4	0.0
2003—New York Jets NFL	16	0	18	13	1.0
Pro totals (3 years)	48	2	49	26	2.0

REED, JEFF — K — STEELERS

PERSONAL: Born April 9, 1979, in Charlotte, N.C. ... 5-11/226. ... Full name: Jeffrey Montgomery Reed.
HIGH SCHOOL: East Mecklenburg (Charlotte, N.C.).
COLLEGE: North Carolina.
TRANSACTIONS/CAREER NOTES: Signed as non-drafted free agent by New Orleans Saints (April 23, 2002). ... Released by Saints (August 26, 2002). ... Signed by Pittsburgh Steelers (November 19, 2002).

		FIELD GOALS							TOTALS		
Year Team	G	1-29	30-39	40-49	50+	Tot.	Pct.	Lg.	XPM	XPA	Pts.
2002—Pittsburgh NFL	6	5-5	5-5	6-7	1-2	17-19	89.5	50	10	11	61
2003—Pittsburgh NFL	16	9-12	6-7	7-12	1-1	23-32	71.9	51	31	32	100
Pro totals (2 years)	22	14-17	11-12	13-19	2-3	40-51	78.4	51	41	43	161

REED, JOSH — WR — BILLS

PERSONAL: Born May 1, 1980, in Lafayette, La. ... 5-10/208. ... Full name: Joshua Blake Reed.
HIGH SCHOOL: Rayne (La.).
COLLEGE: Louisiana State.
TRANSACTIONS/CAREER NOTES: Selected after junior season by Buffalo Bills in second round (36th pick overall) of 2002 NFL draft. ... Signed by Bills (July 25, 2002).
HONORS: Named wide receiver on THE SPORTING NEWS college All-America first team (2001). ... Fred Biletnikoff Award winner (2001).
SINGLE GAME HIGHS (regular season): Receptions—8 (October 26, 2003, vs. Kansas City); yards—110 (September 15, 2002, vs. Minnesota); and touchdown receptions—1 (December 7, 2003, vs. New York Jets).
STATISTICAL PLATEAUS: 100-yard receiving games: 2002 (1), 2003 (1). Total: 2.

			RUSHING				RECEIVING				PUNT RETURNS				KICKOFF RETURNS				TOTALS		
Year Team	G	GS	Att.	Yds.	Avg.	TD	No.	Yds.	Avg.	TD	No.	Yds.	Avg.	TD	No.	Yds.	Avg.	TD	TD	2pt.	Pts.
2002—Buf. NFL	16	2	0	0	0.0	0	37	509	13.8	2	0	0	0.0	0	0	0	0.0	0	2	0	12
2003—Buf. NFL	16	16	3	38	12.7	0	58	588	10.1	2	0	0	0.0	0	0	0	0.0	0	2	0	12
Pro totals (2 years)	32	18	3	38	12.7	0	95	1097	11.5	4	0	0	0.0	0	0	0	0.0	0	4	0	24

REESE, ALLEN — DT

PERSONAL: Born October 10, 1980, in Bartow, Fla. ... 5-10/294. ... Full name: Allen Barnard Reese.
HIGH SCHOOL: Aburndale (Fla.).
JUNIOR COLLEGE: Hutchinson (Kan.).
COLLEGE: Kansas State.
TRANSACTIONS/CAREER NOTES: Signed as non-drafted free agent by Kansas City Chiefs (April 29, 2003). ... Released by Chiefs (September 16, 2003). ... Re-signed by Chiefs to practice squad (October 1, 2003). ... Released by Chiefs (October 15, 2003).

			TOTALS		
Year Team	G	GS	Tk.	Ast.	Sks.
2003—Kansas City NFL	2	0	0	0	0.0

REESE, IKE — LB — EAGLES

PERSONAL: Born October 16, 1973, in Jacksonville, N.C. ... 6-2/222. ... Full name: Isaiah Reese.
HIGH SCHOOL: Woodward (Cincinnati), then Aiken (Cincinnati).
COLLEGE: Michigan State.
TRANSACTIONS/CAREER NOTES: Selected by Philadelphia Eagles in fifth round (142nd pick overall) of 1998 NFL draft. ... Signed by Eagles (July 14, 1998). ... Granted free agency (March 2, 2001). ... Re-signed by Eagles (March 20, 2001).
CHAMPIONSHIP GAME EXPERIENCE: Member of Eagles for NFC championship game (2001 season); inactive. ... Played in NFC championship game (2002 and 2003 seasons).

			TOTALS			INTERCEPTIONS			
Year Team	G	GS	Tk.	Ast.	Sks.	No.	Yds.	Avg.	TD
1998—Philadelphia NFL	16	0	3	1	0.0	0	0	0.0	0
1999—Philadelphia NFL	16	0	15	6	3.0	0	0	0.0	0
2000—Philadelphia NFL	16	0	4	1	0.0	0	0	0.0	0
2001—Philadelphia NFL	16	0	13	5	0.0	0	0	0.0	0
2002—Philadelphia NFL	16	3	42	7	1.5	0	0	0.0	0
2003—Philadelphia NFL	16	1	25	1	1.0	0	0	0.0	0
Pro totals (6 years)	96	4	102	21	5.5	0	0	0.0	0

REESE, IZELL — S — BILLS

PERSONAL: Born May 7, 1974, in Dothan, Ala. ... 6-2/195.
HIGH SCHOOL: Northview (Dothan, Ala.).
COLLEGE: Alabama-Birmingham.
TRANSACTIONS/CAREER NOTES: Selected by Dallas Cowboys in sixth round (188th pick overall) of 1998 NFL draft. ... Signed by Cowboys (July 15, 1998). ... On injured reserve with neck injury (November 19, 1999-remainder of season). ... Granted free agency (March 2, 2001). ... Re-signed by Cowboys (April 30, 2001). ... Granted unconditional free agency (March 1, 2002). ... Signed by Denver Broncos (April 1, 2002). ... Granted unconditional free agency (February 28, 2003). ... Signed by Buffalo Bills (March 21, 2003). ... On injured reserve with calf injury (December 17, 2003-remainder of season).

			TOTALS			INTERCEPTIONS			
Year Team	**G**	**GS**	**Tk.**	**Ast.**	**Sks.**	**No.**	**Yds.**	**Avg.**	**TD**
1998—Dallas NFL	16	0	4	0	0.0	1	6	6.0	0
1999—Dallas NFL	8	4	17	5	0.0	3	28	9.3	0
2000—Dallas NFL	16	7	32	15	0.0	2	60	30.0	0
2001—Dallas NFL	16	4	24	1	3.0	1	42	42.0	0
2002—Denver NFL	15	15	41	10	0.5	0	0	0.0	0
2003—Buffalo NFL	13	9	23	10	0.0	0	0	0.0	0
Pro totals (6 years)	84	39	141	41	3.5	7	136	19.4	0

R

REHBERG, SCOTT — T — 49ERS

PERSONAL: Born November 17, 1973, in Kalamazoo, Mich. ... 6-8/325. ... Full name: Scott Joseph Rehberg. ... Name pronounced: RAY-berg.
HIGH SCHOOL: Central (Kalamazoo, Mich.).
COLLEGE: Central Michigan.
TRANSACTIONS/CAREER NOTES: Selected by New England Patriots in seventh round (230th pick overall) of 1997 NFL draft. ... Signed by Patriots (June 19, 1997). ... Selected by Cleveland Browns from Patriots in NFL expansion draft (February 9, 1999). ... Granted free agency (February 11, 2000). ... Signed by Cincinnati Bengals (March 2, 2000). ... Released by Bengals (April 1, 2004). ... Signed by San Francisco 49ers (April 12, 2004).
PLAYING EXPERIENCE: New England NFL, 1997-1998; Cleveland NFL, 1999; Cincinnati NFL, 2000-2003. ... Games/Games started: 1997 (6/0), 1998 (2/0), 1999 (15/13), 2000 (10/6), 2001 (15/4), 2002 (16/3), 2003 (16/1). Total: 80/27.

REID, GABE — TE — BEARS

PERSONAL: Born May 28, 1977, in American Samoa. ... 6-4/260.
HIGH SCHOOL: Leone H.S.
COLLEGE: Brigham Young.
TRANSACTIONS/CAREER NOTES: Signed as non-drafted free agent by New York Jets (May 5, 2003). ... Released by Jets (August 31, 2003). ... Signed by Tennessee Titans to practice squad (September 10, 2003). ... Released by Titans (November 11, 2003). ... Re-signed by Titans to practice squad (November 18, 2003). ... Signed by Chicago Bears off Titans practice squad (November 28, 2003). ... Activated (December 1, 2003).

			RECEIVING				TOTALS			
Year Team	**G**	**GS**	**No.**	**Yds.**	**Avg.**	**TD**	**TD**	**2pt.**	**Pts.**	**Fum.**
2003—Chicago NFL	1	0	0	0	0.0	0	0	0	0	0

REYNOLDS, JAMAL — DE — PACKERS

PERSONAL: Born February 20, 1979, in Augusta, Ga. ... 6-3/260.
HIGH SCHOOL: Aiken (S.C.).
COLLEGE: Florida State.
TRANSACTIONS/CAREER NOTES: Selected by Green Bay Packers in first round (10th pick overall) of 2001 NFL draft. ... Signed by Packers (July 25, 2001).
HONORS: Named defensive end on THE SPORTING NEWS college All-America first team (2000). ... Lombardi Trophy winner (2000).

			TOTALS		
Year Team	**G**	**GS**	**Tk.**	**Ast.**	**Sks.**
2001—Green Bay NFL	6	0	4	0	2.0
2002—Green Bay NFL	7	0	5	3	1.0
2003—Green Bay NFL	5	0	3	1	0.0
Pro totals (3 years)	18	0	12	4	3.0

REYNOLDS, JOFFREY — RB — BROWNS

PERSONAL: Born November 26, 1979, in Tyler, Texas. ... 5-10/221. ... Full name: Joffrey Roy Reynolds.
HIGH SCHOOL: Lee (Tyler, Texas).
COLLEGE: Houston.
TRANSACTIONS/CAREER NOTES: Signed as non-drafted free agent by St. Louis Rams (May 1, 2003). ... Released by Rams (August 31, 2003). ... Re-signed by Rams to practice squad (September 1, 2003). ... Activated (October 11, 2003). ... Released by Rams (November 6, 2003). ... Signed by Cleveland Browns (January 2, 2004). ... Assigned by Browns to Rhein Fire in 2004 NFL Europe enhancement allocation program (February 9, 2004).

			RUSHING				KICKOFF RETURNS				TOTALS			
Year Team	**G**	**GS**	**Att.**	**Yds.**	**Avg.**	**TD**	**No.**	**Yds.**	**Avg.**	**TD**	**TD**	**2pt.**	**Pts.**	**Fum.**
2003—St. Louis NFL	4	0	0	0	0.0	0	6	109	18.2	0	0	0	0	0

RHINEHART, COBY — CB — CARDINALS

PERSONAL: Born February 7, 1977, in Dallas, Texas. ... 5-11/198. ... Full name: Jacoby M. Rhinehart.
HIGH SCHOOL: Tyler Street Christian Academy (Dallas).
COLLEGE: Southern Methodist.
TRANSACTIONS/CAREER NOTES: Selected by Arizona Cardinals in sixth round (190th pick overall) of 1999 NFL draft. ... Signed by Cardinals (June 18, 1999). ... On injured reserve with knee injury (August 22, 2000-entire season). ... Granted free agency (March 1, 2002). ... Re-signed by Cardinals (May 2, 2002). ... Granted unconditional free agency (February 28, 2003). ... Re-signed by Cardinals (March 20, 2003).

			TOTALS			INTERCEPTIONS			
Year Team	**G**	**GS**	**Tk.**	**Ast.**	**Sks.**	**No.**	**Yds.**	**Avg.**	**TD**
1999—Arizona NFL	16	0	2	0	0.0	0	0	0.0	0
2001—Arizona NFL	13	0	5	2	0.0	0	0	0.0	0
2002—Arizona NFL	16	2	15	1	0.0	1	0	0.0	0
2003—Arizona NFL	16	2	15	1	0.0	1	5	5.0	0
Pro totals (4 years)	61	4	37	4	0.0	2	5	2.5	0

RHODES, DOMINIC — RB — COLTS

PERSONAL: Born January 17, 1979, in Waco, Texas. ... 5-9/203. ... Full name: Dominic Dondrell Rhodes.
HIGH SCHOOL: Cooper (Texas).
JUNIOR COLLEGE: Tyler Junior College.
COLLEGE: Midwestern State.
TRANSACTIONS/CAREER NOTES: Signed as non-drafted free agent by Indianapolis Colts (April 22, 2001). ... On injured reserve with knee injury (August 26, 2002-entire season).
CHAMPIONSHIP GAME EXPERIENCE: Played in AFC championship game (2003 season).
SINGLE GAME HIGHS (regular season): Attempts—34 (November 4, 2001, vs. Buffalo); yards—177 (December 16, 2001, vs. Atlanta); and rushing touchdowns—2 (December 16, 2001, vs. Atlanta).
STATISTICAL PLATEAUS: 100-yard rushing games: 2001 (5). Total: 5.

			RUSHING				RECEIVING				KICKOFF RETURNS				TOTALS			
Year Team	**G**	**GS**	**Att.**	**Yds.**	**Avg.**	**TD**	**No.**	**Yds.**	**Avg.**	**TD**	**No.**	**Yds.**	**Avg.**	**TD**	**TD**	**2pt.**	**Pts.**	**Fum.**
2001—Indianapolis NFL	15	10	233	1104	4.7	9	34	224	6.6	0	14	356	25.4	1	10	0	60	6
2002—Indianapolis NFL								Did not play.										
2003—Indianapolis NFL	11	0	37	157	4.2	0	6	62	10.3	1	16	411	25.7	0	1	0	6	0
Pro totals (1 year)	26	10	270	1261	4.7	9	40	286	7.2	1	30	767	25.6	1	11	0	66	6

RICARD, ALAN — FB — RAVENS

PERSONAL: Born January 17, 1977, in Independence, La. ... 5-11/237.
HIGH SCHOOL: Amite (La.).
COLLEGE: Louisiana-Monroe.
TRANSACTIONS/CAREER NOTES: Signed as non-drafted free agent by Dallas Cowboys (April 30, 1999). ... Released by Cowboys (August 4, 1999). ... Signed by Baltimore Ravens (July 21, 2000). ... Released by Ravens (August 26, 2000). ... Re-signed by Ravens to practice squad (August 29, 2000).
SINGLE GAME HIGHS (regular season): Attempts—4 (December 21, 2003, vs. Cleveland); yards—36 (September 14, 2003, vs. Cleveland); and rushing touchdowns—1 (December 29, 2002, vs. Pittsburgh).

			RUSHING				RECEIVING				TOTALS			
Year Team	**G**	**GS**	**Att.**	**Yds.**	**Avg.**	**TD**	**No.**	**Yds.**	**Avg.**	**TD**	**TD**	**2pt.**	**Pts.**	**Fum.**
2001—Baltimore NFL	5	0	0	0	0.0	0	0	0	0.0	0	0	0	0	0
2002—Baltimore NFL	16	8	14	58	4.1	2	10	60	6.0	0	3	0	18	0
2003—Baltimore NFL	16	13	19	79	4.2	0	9	62	6.9	0	1	0	6	0
Pro totals (3 years)	37	21	33	137	4.2	2	19	122	6.4	0	4	0	24	0

RICE, JERRY — WR — RAIDERS

PERSONAL: Born October 13, 1962, in Crawford, Miss. ... 6-2/200. ... Full name: Jerry Lee Rice.
HIGH SCHOOL: Crawford MS Moor (Crawford, Miss.).
COLLEGE: Mississippi Valley State.
TRANSACTIONS/CAREER NOTES: Selected by Birmingham Stallions in first round (first pick overall) of 1985 USFL draft. ... Selected by San Francisco 49ers in first round (16th pick overall) of 1985 NFL draft. ... Signed by 49ers (July 23, 1985). ... Granted free agency (February 1, 1992). ... Re-signed by 49ers (August 25, 1992). ... On injured reserve with knee injury (December 23, 1997-remainder of season). ... Released by 49ers (June 4, 2001). ... Signed by Oakland Raiders (June 5, 2001).
CHAMPIONSHIP GAME EXPERIENCE: Played in NFC championship game (1988-1990 and 1992-1994 seasons). ... Member of Super Bowl championship team (1988, 1989 and 1994 seasons). ... Played in AFC championship game (2002 season). ... Played in Super Bowl 37 (2002 season).
HONORS: Named wide receiver on THE SPORTING NEWS college All-America first team (1984). ... Named wide receiver on THE SPORTING NEWS NFL All-Pro team (1986-1996). ... Played in Pro Bowl (1986, 1987, 1989-1993, 1995, 1998 and 2002 seasons). ... Named NFL Player of the Year by THE SPORTING NEWS (1987 and 1990). ... Named Most Valuable Player of Super Bowl 23 (1988 season). ... Named to play in Pro Bowl (1988 season); replaced by J.T. Smith due to injury. ... Named to play in Pro Bowl (1994 season); replaced by Herman Moore due to injury. ... Named Outstanding Player of Pro Bowl (1995 season). ... Named to play in Pro Bowl (1996 season); replaced by Irving Fryar due to injury.
RECORDS: Holds NFL career records for most touchdowns—205; most touchdown receptions—194; most receiving yards—22,466; most pass receptions—1,519; most seasons with 1,000 or more yards receiving—14; most games with 100 or more yards receiving—75; most consecutive games with one or more reception—273 (December 9, 1985-present); most consecutive games with one or more touchdown reception—13 (December 19, 1986-December 27, 1987); and most seasons with 50 or more receptions—17. ... Holds NFL single-season record for most yards receiving—1,848 (1995); and most touchdown receptions—22 (1987). ... Shares NFL single-game record for most touchdown receptions—5 (October 14, 1990, at Atlanta).

POST SEASON RECORDS: Holds Super Bowl career records for most points—48; most touchdowns—8; most touchdown receptions—8; most receptions—33; most combined yards—604; and most yards receiving—589. ... Holds Super Bowl single-game records for most touchdowns receptions—3 (January 28, 1990, vs. Denver and January 29, 1995, vs. San Diego); and most yards receiving—215 (January 22, 1989, vs. Cincinnati). ... Shares Super Bowl single-game records for most points—18; most touchdowns—3 (January 28, 1990, vs. Denver and January 29, 1995, vs. San Diego); and most receptions—11 (January 22, 1989, vs. Cincinnati). ... Holds NFL postseason career records for most touchdown receptions—22; most receptions—151; most yards receiving—2,245; and most games with 100 or more yards receiving—8; most points by a non-kicker—132. ... Holds NFL postseason record for most consecutive games with one or more receptions—28 (1985-present). ... Shares NFL postseason career record for most consecutive games with 100 or more yards receiving—3 (1988-89). ... Shares NFL postseason single-game record for most touchdown receptions—3 (January 28, 1990, vs. Denver; January 1, 1989, vs. Minnesota; and January 29, 1995, vs. San Diego).

SINGLE GAME HIGHS (regular season): Receptions—16 (November 20, 1994, vs. Los Angeles Rams); yards—289 (December 18, 1995, vs. Minnesota); and touchdown receptions—5 (October 14, 1990, vs. Atlanta).

STATISTICAL PLATEAUS: 100-yard receiving games: 1985 (2), 1986 (6), 1987 (4), 1988 (5), 1989 (8), 1990 (7), 1991 (4), 1992 (3), 1993 (5), 1994 (5), 1995 (9), 1996 (3), 1998 (3), 1999 (2), 2001 (2), 2002 (5), 2003 (2). Total: 75.

MISCELLANEOUS: Active NFL leader for career receptions (1,519), receiving yards (22,466), touchdown receptions (194) and touchdowns (205). ... Holds San Francisco 49ers all-time records for most yards receiving (19,247), most touchdowns (187), most receptions (1,281) and most touchdown receptions (176).

			RUSHING				RECEIVING				TOTALS			
Year Team	**G**	**GS**	**Att.**	**Yds.**	**Avg.**	**TD**	**No.**	**Yds.**	**Avg.**	**TD**	**TD**	**2pt.**	**Pts.**	**Fum.**
1985—San Francisco NFL	16	4	6	26	4.3	1	49	927	18.9	3	4	0	24	1
1986—San Francisco NFL	16	15	10	72	7.2	1	‡86	*1570	18.3	*15	16	0	96	2
1987—San Francisco NFL	12	12	8	51	6.4	1	65	1078	16.6	*22	*23	0	*138	2
1988—San Francisco NFL	16	16	13	107	8.2	1	64	1306	20.4	9	10	0	60	2
1989—San Francisco NFL	16	16	5	33	6.6	0	82	*1483	18.1	*17	17	0	102	0
1990—San Francisco NFL	16	16	2	0	0.0	0	*100	*1502	15.0	*13	13	0	78	1
1991—San Francisco NFL	16	16	1	2	2.0	0	80	1206	15.1	*14	14	0	84	1
1992—San Francisco NFL	16	16	9	58	6.4	1	84	1201	14.3	10	11	0	66	2
1993—San Francisco NFL	16	16	3	69	23.0	1	98	*1503	15.3	†15	*16	0	96	3
1994—San Francisco NFL	16	16	7	93	13.3	2	112	*1499	13.4	13	15	1	92	1
1995—San Francisco NFL	16	16	5	36	7.2	1	122	*1848	15.1	15	17	1	104	3
1996—San Francisco NFL	16	16	11	77	7.0	1	*108	1254	11.6	8	9	0	54	0
1997—San Francisco NFL	2	1	1	-10	-10.0	0	7	78	11.1	1	1	0	6	0
1998—San Francisco NFL	16	16	0	0	0.0	0	82	1157	14.1	9	9	†2	58	2
1999—San Francisco NFL	16	16	2	13	6.5	0	67	830	12.4	5	5	0	30	0
2000—San Francisco NFL	16	16	1	-2	-2.0	0	75	805	10.7	7	7	0	42	3
2001—Oakland NFL	16	15	0	0	0.0	0	83	1139	13.7	9	9	0	54	1
2002—Oakland NFL	16	16	3	20	6.7	0	92	1211	13.2	7	7	0	42	1
2003—Oakland NFL	16	15	0	0	0.0	0	63	869	13.8	2	2	0	12	2
Pro totals (19 years)	286	270	87	645	7.4	10	1519	22466	14.8	194	205	4	1238	27

RICE, SIMEON — DE — BUCCANEERS

PERSONAL: Born February 24, 1974, in Chicago, Ill. ... 6-5/268. ... Name pronounced: simm-ee-ON.

HIGH SCHOOL: Mount Carmel (Chicago).

COLLEGE: Illinois.

TRANSACTIONS/CAREER NOTES: Selected by Arizona Cardinals in first round (third pick overall) of 1996 NFL draft. ... Signed by Cardinals (August 19, 1996). ... Designated by Cardinals as franchise player (February 11, 2000). ... Re-signed by Cardinals (September 7, 2000). ... Granted unconditional free agency (March 2, 2001). ... Signed by Tampa Bay Buccaneers (March 23, 2001).

CHAMPIONSHIP GAME EXPERIENCE: Played in NFC championship game (2002 season). ... Member of Super Bowl championship team (2002 season).

HONORS: Played in Pro Bowl (1999 and 2002 seasons). ... Named linebacker on THE SPORTING NEWS college All-America second team (1995). ... Named defensive end of THE SPORTING NFL All-Pro team (2002, 2003). ... Named to play in Pro Bowl (2003 season); replaced by Kabeer Gbaja-Biamila due to disciplinary problems.

			TOTALS			INTERCEPTIONS			
Year Team	**G**	**GS**	**Tk.**	**Ast.**	**Sks.**	**No.**	**Yds.**	**Avg.**	**TD**
1996—Arizona NFL	16	15	42	10	12.5	0	0	0.0	0
1997—Arizona NFL	16	15	33	14	5.0	1	0	0.0	0
1998—Arizona NFL	16	16	34	5	10.0	0	0	0.0	0
1999—Arizona NFL	16	16	38	11	16.5	0	0	0.0	0
2000—Arizona NFL	15	11	30	3	7.5	0	0	0.0	0
2001—Tampa Bay NFL	16	16	39	5	11.0	0	0	0.0	0
2002—Tampa Bay NFL	16	16	41	9	‡15.5	1	30	30.0	0
2003—Tampa Bay NFL	16	16	45	5	15.0	2	12	6.0	0
Pro totals (8 years)	127	121	302	62	93.0	4	42	10.5	0

RICHARD, KRIS — CB — SEAHAWKS

PERSONAL: Born October 28, 1978, in Los Angeles, Calif. ... 5-11/190.

HIGH SCHOOL: Serra (Gardena, Calif.).

COLLEGE: Southern California.

TRANSACTIONS/CAREER NOTES: Selected by Seattle Seahawks in third round (85th pick overall) of 2002 NFL draft. ... Signed by Seahawks (July 25, 2002). ... On injured reserve with hernia (December 17, 2002-remainder of season).

			TOTALS			INTERCEPTIONS				PUNT RETURNS				TOTALS			
Year Team	**G**	**GS**	**Tk.**	**Ast.**	**Sks.**	**No.**	**Yds.**	**Avg.**	**TD**	**No.**	**Yds.**	**Avg.**	**TD**	**TD**	**2pt.**	**Pts.**	**Fum.**
2002—Seattle NFL	7	0	3	0	0.0	0	0	0.0	0	0	0	0.0	0	0	0	0	0
2003—Seattle NFL	15	1	9	2	1.0	0	0	0.0	0	1	0	0.0	0	0	0	0	1
Pro totals (2 years)	22	1	12	2	1.0	0	0	0.0	0	1	0	0.0	0	0	0	0	1

RICHARDSON, KYLE — P — BENGALS

PERSONAL: Born March 2, 1973, in Farmington, Mo. ... 6-2/210. ... Full name: Kyle Davis Richardson.
HIGH SCHOOL: Farmington (Mo.).
COLLEGE: Arkansas State.
TRANSACTIONS/CAREER NOTES: Played for Rhein Fire of World League (1996). ... Signed as non-drafted free agent by Miami Dolphins (September 3, 1997). ... Released by Dolphins (September 8, 1997). ... Re-signed by Dolphins (September 18, 1997). ... Released by Dolphins (October 7, 1997). ... Signed by Seattle Seahawks (November 12, 1997). ... Released by Seahawks (November 25, 1997). ... Signed by Baltimore Ravens (March 25, 1998). ... Granted free agency (March 2, 2001). ... Re-signed by Ravens for 2001 season. ... Granted unconditional free agency (March 1, 2002). ... Signed by Minnesota Vikings (April 21, 2002). ... Granted unconditional free agency (February 28, 2003). ... Signed by Philadelphia Eagles (May 12, 2003). ... Released by Eagles (August 24, 2003). ... Signed by Cincinnati Bengals (October 7, 2003).
CHAMPIONSHIP GAME EXPERIENCE: Played in AFC championship game (2000 season). ... Member of Super Bowl championship team (2000 season).

		PUNTING					
Year Team	**G**	**No.**	**Yds.**	**Avg.**	**Net avg.**	**In. 20**	**Blk.**
1997—Miami NFL	3	11	480	43.6	33.1	0	0
—Seattle NFL	2	8	324	40.5	23.8	2	†2
1998—Baltimore NFL	16	90	3948	43.9	38.3	25	*2
1999—Baltimore NFL	16	103	4355	42.3	35.5	*39	1
2000—Baltimore NFL	16	86	3457	40.2	33.9	*35	0
2001—Baltimore NFL	16	85	3309	38.9	33.6	§29	§2
2002—Minnesota NFL	16	62	2474	39.9	35.3	21	1
2003—Cincinnati NFL	11	49	1961	40.0	33.5	9	0
Pro totals (7 years)	96	494	20308	41.1	34.9	160	8

RICHARDSON, TONY — FB — CHIEFS

PERSONAL: Born December 17, 1971, in Frankfurt, Germany. ... 6-1/232. ... Full name: Antonio Richardson.
HIGH SCHOOL: Daleville (Ala.).
COLLEGE: Auburn.
TRANSACTIONS/CAREER NOTES: Signed as non-drafted free agent by Dallas Cowboys (April 28, 1994). ... Released by Cowboys (August 28, 1994). ... Re-signed by Cowboys to practice squad (August 30, 1994). ... Granted free agency after 1994 season. ... Signed by Kansas City Chiefs (February 28, 1995). ... On injured reserve with wrist injury (December 11, 1996-remainder of season). ... On injured reserve with shoulder injury (December 17, 2002-remainder of season).
HONORS: Played in Pro Bowl (2003 season).
SINGLE GAME HIGHS (regular season): Attempts—23 (December 17, 2000, vs. Denver); yards—156 (December 17, 2000, vs. Denver); and rushing touchdowns—2 (November 4, 2001, vs. San Diego).
STATISTICAL PLATEAUS: 100-yard rushing games: 2000 (1). Total: 1.

			RUSHING				RECEIVING				TOTALS			
Year Team	**G**	**GS**	**Att.**	**Yds.**	**Avg.**	**TD**	**No.**	**Yds.**	**Avg.**	**TD**	**TD**	**2pt.**	**Pts.**	**Fum.**
1995—Kansas City NFL	14	1	8	18	2.3	0	0	0	0.0	0	0	0	0	0
1996—Kansas City NFL	13	0	4	10	2.5	0	2	18	9.0	1	1	0	6	0
1997—Kansas City NFL	14	0	2	11	5.5	0	3	6	2.0	3	3	0	18	0
1998—Kansas City NFL	14	1	20	45	2.3	2	2	13	6.5	0	2	0	12	0
1999—Kansas City NFL	16	16	84	387	4.6	1	24	141	5.9	0	1	0	6	1
2000—Kansas City NFL	16	16	147	697	4.7	3	58	468	8.1	3	6	0	36	3
2001—Kansas City NFL	14	7	66	191	2.9	7	30	265	8.8	0	7	0	42	0
2002—Kansas City NFL	14	12	22	81	3.7	2	18	125	6.9	1	3	0	18	1
2003—Kansas City NFL	16	10	24	60	2.5	0	12	76	6.3	0	0	0	0	0
Pro totals (9 years)	131	63	377	1500	4.0	15	149	1112	7.5	8	23	0	138	5

RICHEY, WADE — K — RAVENS

PERSONAL: Born May 19, 1976, in Lafayette, La. ... 6-3/205. ... Full name: Wade Edward Richey.
HIGH SCHOOL: Carencro (Lafayette, La.).
COLLEGE: Louisiana State.
TRANSACTIONS/CAREER NOTES: Signed as non-drafted free agent by Seattle Seahawks (April 21, 1998). ... Claimed on waivers by San Francisco 49ers (August 26, 1998). ... Granted free agency (March 2, 2001). ... Tendered offer sheet by San Diego Chargers (April 13, 2001). ... 49ers declined to match offer (April 18, 2001). ... Released by Chargers (December 2, 2002). ... Signed by Baltimore Ravens (August 20, 2003). ... Granted unconditional free agency (March 3, 2004). ... Re-signed by Ravens (March 16, 2004).

		FIELD GOALS							TOTALS		
Year Team	**G**	**1-29**	**30-39**	**40-49**	**50+**	**Tot.**	**Pct.**	**Lg.**	**XPM**	**XPA**	**Pts.**
1998—San Francisco NFL	16	9-10	3-4	6-13	0-0	18-27	66.7	46	49	51	103
1999—San Francisco NFL	16	8-8	7-8	5-6	1-1	21-23	*91.3	52	30	31	93
2000—San Francisco NFL	16	6-7	6-8	3-6	0-1	15-22	68.2	47	43	∞45	88
2001—San Diego NFL	16	13-15	4-7	3-7	1-3	21-32	65.6	51	26	26	89
2002—San Diego NFL	12	0-0	0-0	0-0	0-0	0-0	0.0	0	0	0	0
2003—Baltimore NFL	15	0-0	0-0	0-0	1-2	1-2	50.0	§56	0	0	3
Pro totals (6 years)	91	36-40	20-27	17-32	3-7	76-106	71.7	56	148	153	376

RICKS, MIKHAEL — TE — LIONS

PERSONAL: Born November 14, 1974, in Galveston, Texas. ... 6-5/260. ... Full name: Mikhael Roy Ricks. ... Name pronounced: Michael.
HIGH SCHOOL: Anahuac (Texas).
COLLEGE: Stephen F. Austin.

TRANSACTIONS/CAREER NOTES: Selected by San Diego Chargers in second round (59th pick overall) of 1998 NFL draft. ... Signed by Chargers (July 23, 1998). ... Released by Chargers (October 3, 2000). ... Signed by Kansas City Chiefs (October 11, 2000). ... Granted unconditional free agency (March 1, 2002). ... Signed by Detroit Lions (April 17, 2002). ... Granted unconditional free agency (February 28, 2003). ... Re-signed by Lions (March 7, 2003).
SINGLE GAME HIGHS (regular season): Receptions—6 (October 24, 1999,vs. Green Bay); yards—86 (September 19, 1999, vs. Cincinnati); and touchdown receptions—1 (October 26, 2003, vs. Chicago).

			RECEIVING				TOTALS			
Year Team	G	GS	No.	Yds.	Avg.	TD	TD	2pt.	Pts.	Fum.
1998—San Diego NFL	16	9	30	450	15.0	2	2	0	12	1
1999—San Diego NFL	16	15	40	429	10.7	0	0	1	2	0
2000—San Diego NFL	3	1	3	35	11.7	0	0	0	0	0
—Kansas City NFL	1	0	0	0	0.0	0	0	0	0	0
2001—Kansas City NFL	16	0	18	252	14.0	1	1	0	8	0
2002—Detroit NFL	14	12	27	339	12.6	3	3	0	18	0
2003—Detroit NFL	16	6	37	434	11.7	2	2	0	12	0
Pro totals (6 years)	82	43	155	1939	12.5	8	8	1	52	1

R

RIEMERSMA, JAY TE STEELERS

PERSONAL: Born May 17, 1973, in Evansville, Ind. ... 6-5/255. ... Full name: Allen Jay Riemersma. ... Name pronounced: REEM-urz-muh.
HIGH SCHOOL: Zeeland (Mich.).
COLLEGE: Michigan.
TRANSACTIONS/CAREER NOTES: Selected by Buffalo Bills in seventh round (244th pick overall) of 1996 NFL draft. ... Signed by Bills (July 9, 1996). ... Released by Bills (August 25, 1996). ... Re-signed by Bills to practice squad (August 26, 1996). ... Activated (October 15, 1996); did not play. ... Granted free agency (February 12, 1999). ... Re-signed by Bills (April 26, 1999). ... Granted unconditional free agency (February 11, 2000). ... Re-signed by Bills (February 15, 2000). ... On physically unable to perform list with hamstring injury (July 25-28, 2002). ... Released by Bills (February 27, 2003). ... Signed by Pittsburgh Steelers (March 19, 2003).
SINGLE GAME HIGHS (regular season): Receptions—8 (December 30, 2001, vs. New York Jets); yards—86 (November 7, 1999, vs. Washington); and touchdown receptions—2 (September 10, 2000, vs. Green Bay).

			RECEIVING				TOTALS			
Year Team	G	GS	No.	Yds.	Avg.	TD	TD	2pt.	Pts.	Fum.
1996—Buffalo NFL					Did not play.					
1997—Buffalo NFL	16	8	26	208	8.0	2	2	1	14	1
1998—Buffalo NFL	16	4	25	288	11.5	6	6	0	36	0
1999—Buffalo NFL	14	11	37	496	13.4	4	4	0	24	0
2000—Buffalo NFL	12	12	31	372	12.0	5	5	0	30	1
2001—Buffalo NFL	16	15	53	590	11.1	3	3	0	18	0
2002—Buffalo NFL	16	15	32	350	10.9	0	0	0	0	0
2003—Pittsburgh NFL	11	7	10	138	13.8	1	1	0	6	0
Pro totals (7 years)	101	72	214	2442	11.4	21	21	1	128	2

RILEY, KARON LB FALCONS

PERSONAL: Born August 23, 1978, in Detroit, Mich. ... 6-2/268.
HIGH SCHOOL: Martin Luther King (Detroit).
COLLEGE: Minnesota.
TRANSACTIONS/CAREER NOTES: Selected by Chicago Bears in fourth round (103rd pick overall) of 2001 NFL draft. ... Signed by Bears (June 18, 2001). ... Released by Bears (September 1, 2002). ... Signed by Atlanta Falcons to practice squad (September 3, 2002). ... Activated (October 14, 2002). ... Released by Falcons (November 12, 2002). ... Re-signed by Falcons to practice squad (November 13, 2002). ... Activated (November 25, 2002). ... Granted free agency (March 3, 2004). ... Re-signed by Falcons (March 25, 2004).
HONORS: Named defensive end on THE SPORTING NEWS college All-America third team (2000).

			TOTALS			INTERCEPTIONS			
Year Team	G	GS	Tk.	Ast.	Sks.	No.	Yds.	Avg.	TD
2001—Chicago NFL	5	0	1	0	0.0	0	0	0.0	0
2002—Atlanta NFL	3	0	0	0	0.0	0	0	0.0	0
2003—Atlanta NFL	16	0	6	4	0.0	0	0	0.0	0
Pro totals (3 years)	24	0	7	4	0.0	0	0	0.0	0

RILEY, VICTOR T SAINTS

PERSONAL: Born November 4, 1974, in Lexington, S.C. ... 6-5/328. ... Full name: Victor Allan Riley.
HIGH SCHOOL: Swansea (S.C.).
COLLEGE: Auburn.
TRANSACTIONS/CAREER NOTES: Selected by Kansas City Chiefs in first round (27th pick overall) of 1998 NFL draft. ... Signed by Chiefs (July 2, 1998). ... Granted unconditional free agency (March 1, 2002). ... Signed by New Orleans Saints (April 4, 2002).
PLAYING EXPERIENCE: Kansas City NFL, 1998-2001; New Orleans NFL, 2002-2003. ... Games/Games started: 1998 (16/15), 1999 (16/16), 2000 (16/16), 2001 (7/5), 2002 (14/2), 2003 (16/16). Total: 85/70.

RITCHIE, JON FB EAGLES

PERSONAL: Born September 4, 1974, in Mechanicsburg, Pa. ... 6-2/250.
HIGH SCHOOL: Cumberland Valley (Mechanicsburg, Pa.).
COLLEGE: Stanford.
TRANSACTIONS/CAREER NOTES: Selected by Oakland Raiders in third round (63rd pick overall) of 1998 NFL draft. ... Signed by Raiders (July 18, 1998). ... Granted unconditional free agency (February 28, 2003). ... Signed by Philadelphia Eagles (March 7, 2003).

CHAMPIONSHIP GAME EXPERIENCE: Played in AFC championship game (2000, 2002 and 2003 seasons). ... Played in Super Bowl 37 (2002 season).

SINGLE GAME HIGHS (regular season): Attempts—2 (September 12, 1999, vs. Green Bay); yards—14 (November 15, 1998, vs. Seattle); and rushing touchdowns—0.

			RUSHING				RECEIVING				TOTALS			
Year Team	**G**	**GS**	**Att.**	**Yds.**	**Avg.**	**TD**	**No.**	**Yds.**	**Avg.**	**TD**	**TD**	**2pt.**	**Pts.**	**Fum.**
1998—Oakland NFL	15	10	9	23	2.6	0	29	225	7.8	0	0	0	0	2
1999—Oakland NFL	16	14	5	12	2.4	0	45	408	9.1	1	1	0	6	0
2000—Oakland NFL	13	12	0	0	0.0	0	26	173	6.7	0	0	0	0	0
2001—Oakland NFL	15	10	0	0	0.0	0	19	154	8.1	2	2	0	12	0
2002—Oakland NFL	16	2	0	0	0.0	0	10	66	6.6	1	1	0	6	1
2003—Philadelphia NFL	16	7	1	1	1.0	0	17	86	5.1	3	3	0	18	0
Pro totals (6 years)	91	55	15	36	2.4	0	146	1112	7.6	7	7	0	42	3

R

RIVERA, MARCO G PACKERS

PERSONAL: Born April 26, 1972, in Brooklyn, N.Y. ... 6-4/310. ... Full name: Marco Anthony Rivera.

HIGH SCHOOL: Elmont (N.Y.) Memorial.

COLLEGE: Penn State.

TRANSACTIONS/CAREER NOTES: Selected by Green Bay Packers in sixth round (208th pick overall) of 1996 NFL draft. ... Signed by Packers (July 15, 1996). ... Inactive for all 16 games (1996). ... Assigned by Packers to Scottish Claymores in 1997 World League enhancement allocation program (February 19, 1997). ... Granted free agency (February 12, 1999). ... Re-signed by Packers (March 24, 1999).

PLAYING EXPERIENCE: Green Bay NFL, 1997-2003. ... Games/Games started: 1997 (14/0), 1998 (15/15), 1999 (16/16), 2000 (16/16), 2001 (16/16), 2002 (16/16), 2003 (16/16). Total: 109/95.

CHAMPIONSHIP GAME EXPERIENCE: Member of Packers for NFC championship game (1996 season); inactive. ... Member of Super Bowl championship team (1996 season); inactive. ... Played in NFC championship game (1997 season). ... Played in Super Bowl 32 (1997 season).

HONORS: Played in Pro Bowl (2002 and 2003 seasons).

RIVERS, MARCELLUS TE GIANTS

PERSONAL: Born October 26, 1978, in Oklahoma City, Okla. ... 6-4/250.

HIGH SCHOOL: Douglass (Oklahoma City, Okla.).

COLLEGE: Oklahoma State.

TRANSACTIONS/CAREER NOTES: Signed as non-drafted free agent by New York Giants (April 27, 2001). ... Granted free agency (March 3, 2004). ... Re-signed by Giants (April 19, 2004).

SINGLE GAME HIGHS (regular season): Receptions—4 (October 19, 2003, vs. Philadelphia); yards—49 (October 12, 2003, vs. New England); and touchdown receptions—1 (October 6, 2002, vs. Dallas).

			RECEIVING				TOTALS			
Year Team	**G**	**GS**	**No.**	**Yds.**	**Avg.**	**TD**	**TD**	**2pt.**	**Pts.**	**Fum.**
2001—New York Giants NFL	16	0	3	11	3.7	2	2	0	12	0
2002—New York Giants NFL	15	0	2	25	12.5	1	1	1	8	0
2003—New York Giants NFL	12	6	17	155	9.1	0	0	0	0	0
Pro totals (3 years)	43	6	22	191	8.7	3	3	1	20	0

ROAF, WILLIE T CHIEFS

PERSONAL: Born April 18, 1970, in Pine Bluff, Ark. ... 6-5/320. ... Full name: William Layton Roaf.

HIGH SCHOOL: Pine Bluff (Ark.).

COLLEGE: Louisiana Tech.

TRANSACTIONS/CAREER NOTES: Selected by New Orleans Saints in first round (eighth pick overall) of 1993 NFL draft. ... Signed by Saints (July 15, 1993). ... Designated by Saints as transition player (February 15, 1994). ... On injured reserve with knee injury (November 28, 2001-remainder of season). ... Traded by Saints to Kansas City Chiefs for third-round pick (traded to New England) in 2003 draft (March 26, 2002).

PLAYING EXPERIENCE: New Orleans NFL, 1993-2001; Kansas City NFL, 2002-2003. ... Games/Games started: 1993 (16/16), 1994 (16/16), 1995 (16/16), 1996 (13/13), 1997 (16/16), 1998 (15/15), 1999 (16/16), 2000 (16/16), 2001 (7/7), 2002 (16/16), 2003 (16/16). Total: 163/163.

HONORS: Named offensive tackle on THE SPORTING NEWS college All-America second team (1992). ... Named offensive tackle on THE SPORTING NEWS NFL All-Pro team (1994-1996). ... Played in Pro Bowl (1994-1997, 1999, 2000 and 2002 seasons). ... Named to play in Pro Bowl (1998 season); replaced by Bob Whitfield due to injury. ... Named to play in Pro Bowl (2003 season); replaced by Brad Hopkins due to injury.

ROBBINS, BARRET C RAIDERS

PERSONAL: Born August 26, 1973, in Houston, Texas. ... 6-3/320.

HIGH SCHOOL: Sharpstown (Houston).

COLLEGE: Texas Christian.

TRANSACTIONS/CAREER NOTES: Selected by Los Angeles Raiders in second round (49th pick overall) of 1995 NFL draft. ... Signed by Raiders (June 20, 1995). ... Raiders franchise moved to Oakland (July 21, 1995). ... On injured reserve with knee injury (September 26, 2001-remainder of season).

PLAYING EXPERIENCE: Oakland NFL, 1995-2003. ... Games/Games started: 1995 (16/0), 1996 (14/14), 1997 (16/16), 1998 (16/16), 1999 (16/16), 2000 (16/16), 2001 (2/2), 2002 (16/16), 2003 (9/9). Total: 121/105.

CHAMPIONSHIP GAME EXPERIENCE: Played in AFC championship game (2000 and 2002 seasons). ... Member of Raiders for Super Bowl 37 (2002 season); inactive.

HONORS: Named to play in Pro Bowl (2002 season); replaced by Damien Woody due to injury.

ROBBINS, FRED — DT — GIANTS

PERSONAL: Born March 25, 1977, in Pensacola, Fla. ... 6-4/306. ... Full name: Fredrick Robbins.
HIGH SCHOOL: Tate (Gonzalez, Fla.).
COLLEGE: Wake Forest.
TRANSACTIONS/CAREER NOTES: Selected by Minnesota Vikings in second round (55th pick overall) of 2000 NFL draft. ... Signed by Vikings (July 21, 2000). ... Granted unconditional free agency (March 3, 2004). ... Signed by New York Giants (March 5, 2004).
CHAMPIONSHIP GAME EXPERIENCE: Member of Vikings for NFC championship game (2000 season); inactive.

			TOTALS		
Year Team	G	GS	Tk.	Ast.	Sks.
2000—Minnesota NFL	8	0	1	2	1.0
2001—Minnesota NFL	16	12	17	10	2.0
2002—Minnesota NFL	16	15	19	14	0.0
2003—Minnesota NFL	16	12	21	8	0.5
Pro totals (4 years)	56	39	58	34	3.5

R

ROBERTS, TERRELL — CB — BENGALS

PERSONAL: Born April 7, 1981, in Berkeley, Calif. ... 5-10/197.
HIGH SCHOOL: El Cerrito High School.
COLLEGE: Oregon State.
TRANSACTIONS/CAREER NOTES: Signed as non-drafted free agent by Cincinnati Bengals (May 2, 2003).

			TOTALS			INTERCEPTIONS				KICKOFF RETURNS				TOTALS			
Year Team	G	GS	Tk.	Ast.	Sks.	No.	Yds.	Avg.	TD	No.	Yds.	Avg.	TD	TD	2pt.	Pts.	Fum.
2003—Cincinnati NFL	12	0	13	3	1.0	1	6	6.0	0	7	128	18.3	0	0	0	0	0

ROBERTSON, DEWAYNE — DT — JETS

PERSONAL: Born October 16, 1981, in Memphis, Tenn. ... 6-1/317.
HIGH SCHOOL: Melrose (Memphis, Tenn.).
COLLEGE: Kentucky.
TRANSACTIONS/CAREER NOTES: Selected after junior season by New York Jets in first round (fourth pick overall) of 2003 NFL draft. ... Signed by Jets (July 20, 2003).

			TOTALS		
Year Team	G	GS	Tk.	Ast.	Sks.
2003—New York Jets NFL	16	16	34	9	1.5

ROBERTSON, JAMAL — RB — 49ERS

PERSONAL: Born January 10, 1977, in Washington, DC. ... 5-10/210.
HIGH SCHOOL: Stebbins (Dayton, Ohio).
COLLEGE: Ohio Northern.
TRANSACTIONS/CAREER NOTES: Signed by Calgary Stampeders of CFL (June 7, 2001). ... Released by Stampeders (June 23, 2001). ... Re-signed by Stampeders to practice squad (June 24, 2001). ... Signed as non-drafted free agent by San Francisco 49ers (January 23, 2002). ... Assigned by 49ers to Rhein Fire in 2002 NFL Europe enhancement allocation program (February 12, 2002). ... On injured reserve with hamstring injury (December 30, 2002-remainder of season).
SINGLE GAME HIGHS (regular season): Attempts—8 (December 7, 2003, vs. Arizona); yards—46 (December 7, 2003, vs. Arizona); and rushing touchdowns—0.

			RUSHING				KICKOFF RETURNS				TOTALS			
Year Team	G	GS	Att.	Yds.	Avg.	TD	No.	Yds.	Avg.	TD	TD	2pt.	Pts.	Fum.
2002—San Francisco NFL	6	0	0	0	0.0	0	11	242	22.0	0	0	0	0	0
2003—San Francisco NFL	9	0	32	136	4.3	0	0	0	0.0	0	0	0	0	0
Pro totals (2 years)	15	0	32	136	4.3	0	11	242	22.0	0	0	0	0	0

ROBINSON, BRYAN — DT — BEARS

PERSONAL: Born June 22, 1974, in Toledo, Ohio. ... 6-4/305. ... Full name: Bryan Keith Robinson.
HIGH SCHOOL: Woodward (Cincinnati).
JUNIOR COLLEGE: College of the Desert (Palm Desert, Calif.).
COLLEGE: Fresno State.
TRANSACTIONS/CAREER NOTES: Signed as non-drafted free agent by St. Louis Rams (April 29, 1997). ... Claimed on waivers by Chicago Bears (August 31, 1998). ... Granted free agency (February 11, 2000). ... Re-signed by Bears (April 19, 2000). ... Designated by Bears as transition player (February 22, 2001).

			TOTALS		
Year Team	G	GS	Tk.	Ast.	Sks.
1997—St. Louis NFL	11	0	10	0	1.0
1998—Chicago NFL	11	5	11	7	0.5
1999—Chicago NFL	16	16	38	4	5.0
2000—Chicago NFL	16	16	42	9	4.5
2001—Chicago NFL	16	16	38	10	4.5
2002—Chicago NFL	15	13	28	6	1.0
2003—Chicago NFL	16	16	23	6	1.0
Pro totals (7 years)	101	82	190	42	17.5

ROBINSON, DAMIEN S SEAHAWKS

PERSONAL: Born December 23, 1973, in Dallas, Texas. ... 6-2/223. ... Full name: Damien Dion Robinson.
HIGH SCHOOL: Hillcrest (Dallas).
COLLEGE: Iowa.
TRANSACTIONS/CAREER NOTES: Selected by Philadelphia Eagles in fourth round (119th pick overall) of 1997 NFL draft. ... Signed by Eagles (June 4, 1997). ... Released by Eagles (August 25, 1997). ... Re-signed by Eagles to practice squad (August 27, 1997). ... Signed by Tampa Bay Buccaneers off Eagles practice squad (September 17, 1997). ... Inactive for 13 games (1997). ... On injured reserve with arm injury (October 27, 1998-remainder of season). ... Granted free agency (February 11, 2000). ... Re-signed by Buccaneers (May 15, 2000). ... Granted unconditional free agency (March 2, 2001). ... Signed by New York Jets (April 25, 2001). ... Released by Jets (February 20, 2003). ... Signed by Seattle Seahawks (March 11, 2003).
CHAMPIONSHIP GAME EXPERIENCE: Played in NFC championship game (1999 season).

			TOTALS			INTERCEPTIONS			
Year Team	G	GS	Tk.	Ast.	Sks.	No.	Yds.	Avg.	TD
1998—Tampa Bay NFL	7	0	6	6	0.0	0	0	0.0	0
1999—Tampa Bay NFL	16	16	50	22	0.5	2	36	18.0	0
2000—Tampa Bay NFL	16	16	51	20	0.0	6	1	0.2	0
2001—New York Jets NFL	14	14	38	18	0.0	2	58	29.0	0
2002—New York Jets NFL	15	15	55	18	0.0	2	12	6.0	0
2003—Seattle NFL	15	4	26	4	0.0	1	26	26.0	0
Pro totals (6 years)	83	65	226	88	0.5	13	133	10.2	0

ROBINSON, JEFF TE/LS COWBOYS

PERSONAL: Born February 20, 1970, in Spokane, Wash. ... 6-4/264. ... Full name: Jeffrey William Robinson.
HIGH SCHOOL: Joel E. Ferris (Spokane, Wash.).
COLLEGE: Idaho.
TRANSACTIONS/CAREER NOTES: Selected by Denver Broncos in fourth round (98th pick overall) of 1993 NFL draft. ... Signed by Broncos (July 13, 1993). ... Granted free agency (February 16, 1996). ... Re-signed by Broncos (March 28, 1996). ... Granted unconditional free agency (February 14, 1997). ... Signed by St. Louis Rams (March 14, 1997). ... Granted unconditional free agency (March 1, 2002). ... Signed by Dallas Cowboys (March 5, 2002). ... On injured reserve with knee injury (August 27, 2002-entire season).
CHAMPIONSHIP GAME EXPERIENCE: Played in NFC championship game (1999 and 2001 seasons). ... Member of Super Bowl championship team (1999 season). ... Played in Super Bowl 36 (2001 season).
SINGLE GAME HIGHS (regular season): Receptions—2 (November 18, 2001, vs. New England); yards—34 (December 10, 2000, vs. Minnesota); and touchdown receptions—1 (December 7, 2003, vs. Philadelphia).
MISCELLANEOUS: Played defensive line (1993-98).

			RECEIVING				TOTALS			
Year Team	G	GS	No.	Yds.	Avg.	TD	TD	2pt.	Pts.	Fum.
1993—Denver NFL	16	0	0	0	0.0	0	0	0	0	1
1994—Denver NFL	16	0	0	0	0.0	0	0	0	0	0
1995—Denver NFL	16	0	0	0	0.0	0	0	0	0	0
1996—Denver NFL	16	0	0	0	0.0	0	0	0	0	0
1997—St. Louis NFL	16	0	0	0	0.0	0	0	0	0	0
1998—St. Louis NFL	16	0	1	4	4.0	1	1	0	6	0
1999—St. Louis NFL	16	9	6	76	12.7	2	2	0	12	0
2000—St. Louis NFL	16	2	5	52	10.4	0	0	0	0	0
2001—St. Louis NFL	16	6	11	108	9.8	1	1	0	6	0
2002—Dallas NFL	Did not play.									
2003—Dallas NFL	16	0	2	8	4.0	2	2	0	12	0
Pro totals (10 years)	160	17	25	248	9.9	6	6	0	36	1

ROBINSON, KOREN WR SEAHAWKS

PERSONAL: Born March 19, 1980, in Belmont, N.C. ... 6-1/205.
HIGH SCHOOL: South Point (N.C.).
COLLEGE: North Carolina State.
TRANSACTIONS/CAREER NOTES: Selected after sophomore season by Seattle Seahawks in first round (ninth pick overall) of 2001 NFL draft. ... Signed by Seahawks (July 27, 2001).
SINGLE GAME HIGHS (regular season): Receptions—9 (December 29, 2002, vs. San Diego); yards—168 (November 24, 2002, vs. Kansas City); and touchdown receptions—1 (December 27, 2003, vs. San Francisco).
STATISTICAL PLATEAUS: 100-yard receiving games: 2002 (5), 2003 (1). Total: 6.

			RUSHING				RECEIVING				TOTALS			
Year Team	G	GS	Att.	Yds.	Avg.	TD	No.	Yds.	Avg.	TD	TD	2pt.	Pts.	Fum.
2001—Seattle NFL	16	13	4	13	3.3	0	39	536	13.7	1	1	0	6	2
2002—Seattle NFL	16	16	8	56	7.0	0	78	1240	15.9	5	5	0	30	2
2003—Seattle NFL	15	15	4	15	3.8	0	65	896	13.8	4	5	0	30	1
Pro totals (3 years)	47	44	16	84	5.3	0	182	2672	14.7	10	11	0	66	5

ROBINSON, MARCUS WR VIKINGS

PERSONAL: Born February 27, 1975, in Ft. Valley, Ga. ... 6-3/215.
HIGH SCHOOL: Peach County (Fort Valley, Ga.).
COLLEGE: South Carolina.
TRANSACTIONS/CAREER NOTES: Selected by Chicago Bears in fourth round (108th pick overall) of 1997 NFL draft. ... Signed by Bears (July 11, 1997). ... Inactive for four games (1997). ... On injured reserve with thumb injury (September 24, 1997-remainder of season). ... Assigned

by Bears to Rhein Fire in 1998 NFL Europe enhancement allocation program (February 18, 1998). ... On injured reserve with back injury (December 4, 2000-remainder of season). ... On injured reserve with knee injury (October 23, 2001-remainder of season). ... Released by Bears (April 16, 2003). ... Signed by Baltimore Ravens (May 1, 2003). ... Granted unconditional free agency (March 3, 2004). ... Signed by Minnesota Vikings (March 8, 2004).

SINGLE GAME HIGHS (regular season): Receptions—11 (December 19, 1999, vs. Detroit); yards—170 (December 19, 1999, vs. Detroit); and touchdown receptions—4 (November 23, 2003, vs. Seattle).

STATISTICAL PLATEAUS: 100-yard receiving games: 1999 (5), 2000 (1), 2001 (1), 2003 (2). Total: 9.

			RECEIVING				TOTALS			
Year Team	**G**	**GS**	**No.**	**Yds.**	**Avg.**	**TD**	**TD**	**2pt.**	**Pts.**	**Fum.**
1997—Chicago NFL				Did not play.						
1998—Chicago NFL	3	0	4	44	11.0	1	1	0	6	0
1999—Chicago NFL	16	11	84	1400	16.7	9	9	0	54	0
2000—Chicago NFL	11	11	55	738	13.4	5	5	0	30	1
2001—Chicago NFL	5	4	23	269	11.7	2	2	0	12	0
2002—Chicago NFL	16	2	21	244	11.6	3	3	0	18	0
2003—Baltimore NFL	15	5	31	451	14.5	6	6	0	36	0
Pro totals (6 years)	66	33	218	3146	14.4	26	26	0	156	1

R

ROBINSON, TERRENCE — LB — FALCONS

PERSONAL: Born March 12, 1980, in Tyler, Texas. ... 6-0/240.

HIGH SCHOOL: John Tyler (Tyler, Texas).

COLLEGE: Oklahoma State.

TRANSACTIONS/CAREER NOTES: Signed as non-drafted free agent by Pittsburgh Steelers (May 2, 2003). ... Released by Steelers (August 31, 2003). ... Signed by Atlanta Falcons to practice squad (October 15, 2003). ... Activated (December 23, 2003). ... Assigned by Falcons to Rhein Fire in 2004 NFL Europe enhancement allocation program (February 9, 2004).

			TOTALS			INTERCEPTIONS			
Year Team	**G**	**GS**	**Tk.**	**Ast.**	**Sks.**	**No.**	**Yds.**	**Avg.**	**TD**
2003—Atlanta NFL	1	0	0	0	0.0	0	0	0.0	0

ROBINSON, TRAVARIS — S/CB — BUCCANEERS

PERSONAL: Born September 1, 1981, in Miami, Fla. ... 5-10/193. ... Full name: Travaris Jerod Robinson.

HIGH SCHOOL: Coral Park (Miami, Fla.).

COLLEGE: Auburn.

TRANSACTIONS/CAREER NOTES: Signed as non-drafted free agent by Atlanta Falcons (April 28, 2003). ... Claimed on waivers by Tampa Bay Buccaneers (October 7, 2003).

			TOTALS			INTERCEPTIONS			
Year Team	**G**	**GS**	**Tk.**	**Ast.**	**Sks.**	**No.**	**Yds.**	**Avg.**	**TD**
2003—Atlanta NFL	5	1	11	0	0.0	0	0	0.0	0
—Tampa Bay NFL	4	0	0	0	0.0	1	6	6.0	0
Pro totals (1 year)	9	1	11	0	0.0	1	6	6.0	0

RODGERS, DERRICK — LB — SAINTS

PERSONAL: Born October 14, 1971, in Memphis, Tenn. ... 6-1/230. ... Full name: Derrick Andre Rodgers.

HIGH SCHOOL: St. Augustine (New Orleans).

JUNIOR COLLEGE: Riverside (Calif.) Community College.

COLLEGE: Arizona State.

TRANSACTIONS/CAREER NOTES: Selected by Miami Dolphins in third round (92nd pick overall) of 1997 NFL draft. ... Signed by Dolphins (July 8, 1997). ... Granted free agency (February 11, 2000). ... Re-signed by Dolphins (April 28, 2000). ... Granted unconditional free agency (March 2, 2001). ... Re-signed by Dolphins (March 3, 2001). ... On injured reserve with shoulder injury (December 27, 2001-remainder of season). ... Traded by Dolphins to New Orleans Saints for seventh-round pick (traded to Atlanta) in 2004 draft (May 27, 2003). ... On suspended list for violating league personal conduct policy (August 31-September 8, 2003). ... Granted unconditional free agency (March 3, 2004). ... Re-signed by Saints (March 3, 2004).

			TOTALS			INTERCEPTIONS			
Year Team	**G**	**GS**	**Tk.**	**Ast.**	**Sks.**	**No.**	**Yds.**	**Avg.**	**TD**
1997—Miami NFL	15	14	56	24	5.0	0	0	0.0	0
1998—Miami NFL	16	16	26	21	2.5	0	0	0.0	0
1999—Miami NFL	16	15	21	15	0.0	1	5	5.0	0
2000—Miami NFL	16	14	52	23	0.5	0	0	0.0	0
2001—Miami NFL	14	14	40	26	1.0	0	0	0.0	0
2002—Miami NFL	16	15	45	29	0.0	2	28	14.0	0
2003—New Orleans NFL	15	15	56	18	0.0	1	40	40.0	1
Pro totals (7 years)	108	103	296	156	9.0	4	73	18.3	1

ROEHL, JEFF — T — GIANTS

PERSONAL: Born May 18, 1980, in Evergreen Park, Ill. ... 6-4/300.

COLLEGE: Northwestern.

TRANSACTIONS/CAREER NOTES: Signed as non-drafted free agent by New York Giants (May 2, 2003).

PLAYING EXPERIENCE: New York Giants NFL, 2003. ... Games/Games started: 2003 (12/2). Total: 12/2.

ROGERS, CHARLES WR LIONS

PERSONAL: Born May 23, 1981, in Saginaw, Mich. ... 6-2/202.
HIGH SCHOOL: Saginaw (Mich.).
COLLEGE: Michigan State.
TRANSACTIONS/CAREER NOTES: Selected after junior season by Detroit Lions in first round (second pick overall) of 2003 NFL draft. ... Signed by Lions (July 23, 2003). ... On injured reserve with collarbone injury (December 2, 2003-remainder of season).
SINGLE GAME HIGHS (regular season): Receptions—6 (September 21, 2003, vs. Minnesota); yards—62 (September 28, 2003, vs. Denver); and touchdown receptions—2 (September 7, 2003, vs. Arizona).

			RUSHING				RECEIVING				PUNT RETURNS				TOTALS			
Year Team	G	GS	Att.	Yds.	Avg.	TD	No.	Yds.	Avg.	TD	No.	Yds.	Avg.	TD	TD	2pt.	Pts.	Fum.
2003—Detroit NFL	5	5	2	17	8.5	0	22	243	11.0	3	0	0	0.0	0	3	0	18	0

ROGERS, CHARLIE RB/KR

PERSONAL: Born June 19, 1976, in Cliffwood, N.J. ... 5-9/180. ... Full name: John Edward Rogers.
HIGH SCHOOL: Matawan Regional (Aberdeen, N.J.).
COLLEGE: Georgia Tech.
TRANSACTIONS/CAREER NOTES: Selected by Seattle Seahawks in fifth round (152nd pick overall) of 1999 NFL draft. ... Signed by Seahawks (July 29, 1999). ... Selected by Houston Texans from Seahawks in NFL expansion draft (February 18, 2002). ... Granted free agency (March 1, 2002). ... Re-signed by Texans (April 17, 2002). ... Traded by Texans to Buffalo Bills for LB Jay Foreman (April 17, 2002). ... Granted unconditional free agency (February 28, 2003). ... Signed by Miami Dolphins (April 11, 2003). ... Released by Dolphins (November 8, 2003). ... Re-signed by Dolphins (November 25, 2003). ... Granted unconditional free agency (March 3, 2004).

			PUNT RETURNS				KICKOFF RETURNS				TOTALS			
Year Team	G	GS	No.	Yds.	Avg.	TD	No.	Yds.	Avg.	TD	TD	2pt.	Pts.	Fum.
1999—Seattle NFL	12	0	22	318	*14.5	1	18	465	25.8	0	1	0	6	3
2000—Seattle NFL	15	0	26	363	14.0	0	66	§1629	24.7	▲1	1	0	6	5
2001—Seattle NFL	13	0	25	244	9.8	0	50	1120	22.4	0	0	0	0	2
2002—Buffalo NFL	16	0	26	137	5.3	0	§64	1280	20.0	1	1	0	6	1
2003—Miami NFL	11	0	21	186	8.9	0	19	383	20.2	0	0	0	0	2
Pro totals (5 years)	67	0	120	1248	10.4	1	217	4877	22.5	2	3	0	18	13

ROGERS, NICK LB VIKINGS

PERSONAL: Born May 31, 1979, in East Point, Ga. ... 6-2/250. ... Full name: Nicholas Quixote Rogers.
HIGH SCHOOL: St. Pius X (East Point, Ga.).
COLLEGE: Georgia Tech.
TRANSACTIONS/CAREER NOTES: Selected by Minnesota Vikings in sixth round (177th pick overall) of 2002 NFL draft. ... Signed by Vikings (July 16, 2002).

			TOTALS			INTERCEPTIONS			
Year Team	G	GS	Tk.	Ast.	Sks.	No.	Yds.	Avg.	TD
2002—Minnesota NFL	16	11	33	9	2.0	0	0	0.0	0
2003—Minnesota NFL	16	5	11	2	0.0	0	0	0.0	0
Pro totals (2 years)	32	16	44	11	2.0	0	0	0.0	0

ROGERS, SAM LB

PERSONAL: Born May 30, 1970, in Pontiac, Mich. ... 6-3/245. ... Full name: Sammy Lee Rogers.
HIGH SCHOOL: Saint Mary's Preparatory (Orchard Lake, Mich.).
JUNIOR COLLEGE: West Hills College (Calif.), then West Los Angeles College.
COLLEGE: Colorado.
TRANSACTIONS/CAREER NOTES: Selected by Buffalo Bills in second round (64th pick overall) of 1994 NFL draft. ... Signed by Bills (July 12, 1994). ... Granted free agency (February 14, 1997). ... Re-signed by Bills (June 12, 1997). ... Granted unconditional free agency (February 13, 1998). ... Re-signed by Bills (February 15, 1998). ... Released by Bills (March 1, 2001). ... Signed by San Diego Chargers (May 23, 2001). ... Released by Chargers (June 6, 2002). ... Signed by Atlanta Falcons (August 12, 2002). ... Granted unconditional free agency (February 28, 2003). ... Re-signed by Falcons (May 13, 2003). ... On injured reserve with knee injury (October 15, 2003-remainder of season). ... Released by Falcons (March 1, 2004).

			TOTALS			INTERCEPTIONS			
Year Team	G	GS	Tk.	Ast.	Sks.	No.	Yds.	Avg.	TD
1994—Buffalo NFL	14	0	0	0	0.0	0	0	0.0	0
1995—Buffalo NFL	16	8	32	13	2.0	0	0	0.0	0
1996—Buffalo NFL	14	14	38	20	3.5	0	0	0.0	0
1997—Buffalo NFL	15	15	39	14	3.5	0	0	0.0	0
1998—Buffalo NFL	15	15	39	19	4.5	0	0	0.0	0
1999—Buffalo NFL	16	16	52	16	3.0	1	24	24.0	0
2000—Buffalo NFL	11	11	28	12	5.0	1	10	10.0	0
2001—San Diego NFL	15	0	4	0	1.0	0	0	0.0	0
2002—Atlanta NFL	15	13	32	9	6.5	0	0	0.0	0
2003—Atlanta NFL	2	2	3	0	1.0	0	0	0.0	0
Pro totals (10 years)	133	94	267	103	30.0	2	34	17.0	0

ROGERS, SHAUN — DT — LIONS

PERSONAL: Born March 12, 1979, in Houston, Texas. ... 6-4/357.
HIGH SCHOOL: LaPorte (Texas).
COLLEGE: Texas.
TRANSACTIONS/CAREER NOTES: Selected by Detroit Lions in second round (61st pick overall) of 2001 NFL draft. ... Signed by Lions (July 23, 2001). ... On physically unable to perfrom list with ankle injury (July 24-August 6, 2001). ... On physically unable to perform list with thumb injury (July 25-August 19, 2002).

			TOTALS		
Year Team	G	GS	Tk.	Ast.	Sks.
2001—Detroit NFL	16	16	62	19	3.0
2002—Detroit NFL	14	12	26	22	2.5
2003—Detroit NFL	16	16	41	17	4.0
Pro totals (3 years)	46	44	129	58	9.5

ROGERS, TYRONE — DE

PERSONAL: Born March 9, 1974, in Montgomery, Ala. ... 6-5/280.
HIGH SCHOOL: Robert E. Lee (Montgomery, Ala.).
COLLEGE: Alabama State.
TRANSACTIONS/CAREER NOTES: Signed as non-drafted free agent by Cleveland Browns (April 23, 1999). ... Released by Browns (September 5, 1999). ... Re-signed by Browns to practice squad (September 6, 1999). ... Activated (November 23, 1999). ... Granted unconditional free agency (March 3, 2004).

			TOTALS		
Year Team	G	GS	Tk.	Ast.	Sks.
1999—Cleveland NFL	3	0	3	0	0.0
2000—Cleveland NFL	16	0	9	4	2.0
2001—Cleveland NFL	16	10	31	9	6.0
2002—Cleveland NFL	14	5	19	7	3.0
2003—Cleveland NFL	8	3	9	4	1.0
Pro totals (5 years)	57	18	71	24	12.0

ROLLE, SAMARI — CB — TITANS

PERSONAL: Born August 10, 1976, in Miami, Fla. ... 6-0/175. ... Full name: Samari Toure Rolle. ... Name pronounced: suh-MARI ROLL.
HIGH SCHOOL: Miami Beach.
COLLEGE: Florida State.
TRANSACTIONS/CAREER NOTES: Selected by Tennessee Oilers in second round (46th pick overall) of 1998 NFL draft. ... Signed by Oilers (July 24, 1998). ... Oilers franchise renamed Tennessee Titans for 1999 season (December 26, 1998). ... Granted free agency (March 2, 2001). ... Re-signed by Titans (July 28, 2001). ... On physically unable to perform list with knee injury (July 28-August 14, 2001).
CHAMPIONSHIP GAME EXPERIENCE: Played in AFC championship game (1999 and 2002 seasons). ... Played in Super Bowl 34 (1999 season).
HONORS: Named cornerback on THE SPORTING NEWS NFL All-Pro team (2000). ... Played in Pro Bowl (2000 season).

			TOTALS			INTERCEPTIONS			
Year Team	G	GS	Tk.	Ast.	Sks.	No.	Yds.	Avg.	TD
1998—Tennessee NFL	15	1	22	3	2.0	0	0	0.0	0
1999—Tennessee NFL	16	16	59	10	3.0	4	65	16.3	0
2000—Tennessee NFL	15	15	35	4	1.5	▲7	140	20.0	1
2001—Tennessee NFL	14	14	51	5	2.0	3	3	1.0	0
2002—Tennessee NFL	16	16	39	9	0.0	2	0	0.0	0
2003—Tennessee NFL	13	13	23	8	0.0	6	141	23.5	0
Pro totals (6 years)	89	75	229	39	8.5	22	349	15.9	1

ROMAN, MARK — S — PACKERS

PERSONAL: Born March 26, 1977, in New Iberia, La. ... 5-11/200. ... Full name: Mark Emery Roman.
HIGH SCHOOL: New Iberia (La.).
COLLEGE: Louisiana State.
TRANSACTIONS/CAREER NOTES: Selected by Cincinnati Bengals in second round (34th pick overall) of 2000 NFL draft. ... Signed by Bengals (August 7, 2000). ... On injured reserve with finger injury (December 20, 2001-remainder of season). ... On injured reserve with knee injury (December 23, 2002-remainder of season). ... Granted unconditional free agency (March 3, 2004). ... Signed by Green Bay Packers (March 24, 2004).

			TOTALS			INTERCEPTIONS			
Year Team	G	GS	Tk.	Ast.	Sks.	No.	Yds.	Avg.	TD
2000—Cincinnati NFL	8	2	15	1	0.0	0	0	0.0	0
2001—Cincinnati NFL	13	8	44	7	2.0	1	0	0.0	0
2002—Cincinnati NFL	13	1	23	7	0.0	0	0	0.0	0
2003—Cincinnati NFL	16	16	55	19	0.5	1	1	1.0	0
Pro totals (4 years)	50	27	137	34	2.5	2	1	0.5	0

ROMANOWSKI, BILL — LB

R

PERSONAL: Born April 2, 1966, in Vernon, Conn. ... 6-4/245. ... Full name: William Thomas Romanowski.
HIGH SCHOOL: Rockville (Vernon, Conn.).
COLLEGE: Boston College.
TRANSACTIONS/CAREER NOTES: Selected by San Francisco 49ers in third round (80th pick overall) of 1988 NFL draft. ... Signed by 49ers (July 15, 1988). ... Granted free agency (February 1, 1991). ... Re-signed by 49ers (July 17, 1991). ... Granted unconditional free agency (March 1, 1993). ... Re-signed by 49ers (March 23, 1993). ... Traded by 49ers to Philadelphia Eagles for third-(traded to Los Angeles Rams) and sixth-round (traded to Green Bay) picks in 1994 draft (April 24, 1994). ... Granted unconditional free agency (February 16, 1996). ... Signed by Denver Broncos (February 23, 1996). ... Released by Broncos (February 21, 2002). ... Signed by Oakland Raiders (February 27, 2002). ... On injured reserve with concussion (October 23, 2003-remainder of season). ... Released by Raiders (March 2, 2004).
CHAMPIONSHIP GAME EXPERIENCE: Played in NFC championship game (1988-1990, 1992 and 1993 seasons). ... Member of Super Bowl championship team (1988, 1989, 1997 and 1998 seasons). ... Played in AFC championship game (1997, 1998 and 2002 seasons). ... Played in Super Bowl 37 (2002 season).
HONORS: Played in Pro Bowl (1996 and 1998 seasons).

			TOTALS			INTERCEPTIONS			
Year Team	**G**	**GS**	**Tk.**	**Ast.**	**Sks.**	**No.**	**Yds.**	**Avg.**	**TD**
1988—San Francisco NFL	16	8	38	15	0.0	0	0	0.0	0
1989—San Francisco NFL	16	4	47	6	1.0	1	13	13.0	0
1990—San Francisco NFL	16	16	68	11	1.0	0	0	0.0	0
1991—San Francisco NFL	16	16	67	9	1.0	1	7	7.0	0
1992—San Francisco NFL	16	16	65	15	1.0	0	0	0.0	0
1993—San Francisco NFL	16	16	81	23	3.0	0	0	0.0	0
1994—Philadelphia NFL	16	15	49	17	2.5	2	8	4.0	0
1995—Philadelphia NFL	16	16	50	13	1.0	2	5	2.5	0
1996—Denver NFL	16	16	56	21	3.0	3	1	0.3	0
1997—Denver NFL	16	16	56	14	2.0	1	7	7.0	0
1998—Denver NFL	16	16	55	17	7.5	2	22	11.0	0
1999—Denver NFL	16	16	55	18	0.0	3	35	11.7	1
2000—Denver NFL	16	16	62	10	3.5	2	0	0.0	0
2001—Denver NFL	16	16	55	14	7.0	0	0	0.0	0
2002—Oakland NFL	16	16	65	26	4.0	1	0	0.0	0
2003—Oakland NFL	3	3	16	4	2.0	0	0	0.0	0
Pro totals (16 years)	243	222	885	233	39.5	18	98	5.4	1

ROMERO, DARIO — DT — DOLPHINS

PERSONAL: Born April 13, 1978, in Spokane, Wash. ... 6-3/305.
HIGH SCHOOL: Lewis and Clark (Spokane, Wash.).
COLLEGE: Eastern Washington.
TRANSACTIONS/CAREER NOTES: Signed as non-drafted free agent by Edmonton Eskimos of the CFL (2001). ... Signed by Miami Dolphins (February 27, 2002). ... Inactive for 16 games (2002).

			TOTALS		
Year Team	**G**	**GS**	**Tk.**	**Ast.**	**Sks.**
2003—Miami NFL	8	1	3	2	0.0

ROSENFELS, SAGE — QB — DOLPHINS

PERSONAL: Born March 6, 1978, in Maquoketa, Iowa. ... 6-4/222.
HIGH SCHOOL: Maquoketa (Iowa).
COLLEGE: Iowa State.
TRANSACTIONS/CAREER NOTES: Selected by Washington Redskins in fourth round (109th pick overall) of 2001 NFL draft. ... Signed by Redskins (July 26, 2001). ... Traded by Redskins to Miami Dolphins for undisclosed pick in 2003 draft (August 22, 2002). ... Granted free agency (March 3, 2004). ... Re-signed by Dolphins (April 20, 2004).
SINGLE GAME HIGHS (regular season): Attempts—6 (November 9, 2003, vs. Tennessee); completions—4 (November 9, 2003, vs. Tennessee); yards—50 (November 9, 2003, vs. Tennessee); and touchdown passes—1 (November 9, 2003, vs. Tennessee).

			PASSING									RUSHING				TOTALS		
Year Team	**G**	**GS**	**Att.**	**Cmp.**	**Pct.**	**Yds.**	**TD**	**Int.**	**Avg.**	**Skd.**	**Rat.**	**Att.**	**Yds.**	**Avg.**	**TD**	**TD**	**2pt.**	**Pts.**
2002—Miami NFL	4	0	3	0	0.0	0	0	0	0.00	0	39.6	2	-9	-4.5	0	0	0	0
2003—Miami NFL	2	0	6	4	66.7	50	1	0	8.33	0	131.9	1	-1	-1.0	0	0	0	0
Pro totals (2 years)	6	0	9	4	44.4	50	1	0	5.56	0	99.3	3	-10	-3.3	0	0	0	0

ROSENTHAL, MIKE — T — VIKINGS

PERSONAL: Born June 10, 1977, in Pittsburgh, Pa. ... 6-7/310. ... Full name: Michael Paul Rosenthal.
HIGH SCHOOL: Penn (Mishawaka, Ind.).
COLLEGE: Notre Dame.
TRANSACTIONS/CAREER NOTES: Selected by New York Giants in fifth round (149th pick overall) of 1999 NFL draft. ... Signed by Giants (July 26, 1999). ... Granted free agency (March 1, 2002). ... Re-signed by Giants (April 24, 2002). ... Granted unconditional free agency (February 28, 2003). ... Signed by Minnesota Vikings (March 20, 2003).
PLAYING EXPERIENCE: New York Giants NFL, 1999-2002; Minnesota NFL, 2003. ... Games/Games started: 1999 (9/7), 2000 (8/2), 2001 (7/0), 2002 (16/16), 2003 (16/16). Total: 56/41.
CHAMPIONSHIP GAME EXPERIENCE: Played in NFC championship game (2000 season). ... Played in Super Bowl 35 (2000 season).

ROSS, ADRIAN LB BENGALS

PERSONAL: Born February 19, 1975, in Santa Clara, Calif. ... 6-2/245. ... Full name: Adrian Lamont Ross.
HIGH SCHOOL: Elk Grove (Calif.).
COLLEGE: Colorado State.
TRANSACTIONS/CAREER NOTES: Signed as non-drafted free agent by Cincinnati Bengals (April 21, 1998). ... Granted free agency (March 2, 2001). ... Re-signed by Bengals (May 1, 2001). ... On injured reserve with knee injury (December 22, 2003-remainder of season).

			TOTALS			INTERCEPTIONS			
Year Team	G	GS	Tk.	Ast.	Sks.	No.	Yds.	Avg.	TD
1998—Cincinnati NFL	14	1	11	2	0.0	1	11	11.0	0
1999—Cincinnati NFL	16	10	15	3	1.0	0	0	0.0	0
2000—Cincinnati NFL	13	4	31	2	1.0	0	0	0.0	0
2001—Cincinnati NFL	16	1	4	5	1.0	0	0	0.0	0
2002—Cincinnati NFL	16	6	17	3	0.0	0	0	0.0	0
2003—Cincinnati NFL	15	12	33	21	0.0	0	0	0.0	0
Pro totals (6 years)	90	34	111	36	3.0	1	11	11.0	0

R

ROSS, DEREK CB FALCONS

PERSONAL: Born January 5, 1980, in Rock Hill, S.C. ... 5-10/197.
HIGH SCHOOL: Northwestern (Rock Hill, S.C.).
COLLEGE: Ohio State.
TRANSACTIONS/CAREER NOTES: Selected after junior season by Dallas Cowboys in third round (75th pick overall) of 2002 NFL draft. ... Signed by Cowboys (July 26, 2002). ... Claimed on waivers by Atlanta Falcons (December 3, 2003).

			TOTALS			INTERCEPTIONS				KICKOFF RETURNS				TOTALS			
Year Team	G	GS	Tk.	Ast.	Sks.	No.	Yds.	Avg.	TD	No.	Yds.	Avg.	TD	TD	2pt.	Pts.	Fum.
2002—Dallas NFL	14	9	51	5	0.0	5	17	3.4	0	0	0	0.0	0	0	0	0	0
2003—Dallas NFL	8	0	2	1	0.0	1	0	0.0	0	18	434	24.1	0	0	0	0	2
—Atlanta NFL	2	0	2	0	0.0	0	0	0.0	0	0	0	0.0	0	0	0	0	0
Pro totals (2 years)	24	9	55	6	0.0	6	17	2.8	0	18	434	24.1	0	0	0	0	2

ROSS, MICAH WR CHARGERS

PERSONAL: Born January 13, 1976, in Jacksonville, Fla. ... 6-2/221. ... Full name: Micah David Ross.
HIGH SCHOOL: Andrew Jackson (Fla.).
COLLEGE: Jacksonville.
TRANSACTIONS/CAREER NOTES: Signed as non-drafted free agent by Jacksonville Jaguars (August 17, 2001). ... Released by Jaguars (August 28, 2001). ... Re-signed by Jaguars to practice squad (October 31, 2001). ... Activated (December 8, 2001). ... Re-signed by Jaguars (March 24, 2003). ... Waived by Jaguars (October 3, 2003). ... Signed by San Diego Chargers (November 5, 2003).

			RECEIVING				TOTALS			
Year Team	G	GS	No.	Yds.	Avg.	TD	TD	2pt.	Pts.	Fum.
2001—Jacksonville NFL	5	0	0	0	0.0	0	0	0	0	1
2002—Jacksonville NFL	16	0	0	0	0.0	0	0	0	0	0
2003—Jacksonville NFL	1	0	0	0	0.0	0	0	0	0	0
—San Diego NFL	6	0	0	0	0.0	0	0	0	0	0
Pro totals (3 years)	28	0	0	0	0.0	0	0	0	0	1

ROSS, OLIVER G STEELERS

PERSONAL: Born September 27, 1974, in Culver City, Calif. ... 6-5/317.
HIGH SCHOOL: Washington (Los Angeles).
JUNIOR COLLEGE: Southwestern College (Calif.).
COLLEGE: Iowa State.
TRANSACTIONS/CAREER NOTES: Selected by Dallas Cowboys in fifth round (138th pick overall) of 1998 NFL draft. ... Signed by Cowboys (July 16, 1998). ... Assigned by Cowboys to Rhein Fire in 1999 NFL Europe enhancement allocation program (February 22, 1999). ... Released by Cowboys (September 5, 1999). ... Signed by Philadelphia Eagles to practice squad (September 8, 1999). ... Activated (September 14, 1999); did not play. ... Assigned by Eagles to Amsterdam Admirals in 2000 NFL Europe enhancement allocation program (February 18, 2000). ... Released by Eagles (August 27, 2000). ... Signed by Chicago Bears to practice squad (September 4, 2000). ... Released by Bears (September 7, 2000). ... Signed by Steelers to practice squad (November 22, 2000). ... Activated (December 13, 2000). ... Granted free agency (March 1, 2002). ... Tendered offer sheet by Cleveland Browns (March 13, 2002). ... Offer matched by Steelers (March 15, 2002).
PLAYING EXPERIENCE: Dallas NFL, 1998; Philadelphia NFL, 1999; Pittsburgh NFL, 2001-2003. ... Games/Games started: 1998 (2/0), 2001 (16/7), 2002 (16/1), 2003 (16/11), Total: 50/19.
CHAMPIONSHIP GAME EXPERIENCE: Played in AFC championship game (2001 season).

ROSSUM, ALLEN CB FALCONS

PERSONAL: Born October 22, 1975, in Dallas, Texas. ... 5-8/178.
HIGH SCHOOL: Skyline (Dallas).
COLLEGE: Notre Dame.
TRANSACTIONS/CAREER NOTES: Selected by Philadelphia Eagles in third round (85th pick overall) of 1998 NFL draft. ... Signed by Eagles (July 14, 1998). ... Traded by Eagles to Green Bay Packers for fifth-round pick (TE Tony Stewart) in 2001 draft (August 21, 2000). ... Granted free agency (March 2, 2001). ... Re-signed by Packers (April 23, 2001). ... Granted unconditional free agency (March 1, 2002). ... Signed by Atlanta Falcons (March 13, 2002).

Year	Team	G	GS	PUNT RETURNS No.	Yds.	Avg.	TD	KICKOFF RETURNS No.	Yds.	Avg.	TD	TOTALS TD	2pt.	Pts.	Fum.
1998—Philadelphia NFL		15	2	22	187	8.5	0	44	1080	24.5	0	0	0	0	4
1999—Philadelphia NFL		16	0	28	250	8.9	0	54	1347	24.9	1	1	0	6	6
2000—Green Bay NFL		16	0	29	248	8.6	0	50	1288	25.8	1	1	0	6	4
2001—Green Bay NFL		6	0	11	109	9.9	∞1	23	431	18.7	0	1	0	6	0
2002—Atlanta NFL		14	0	24	288	12.0	0	53	1164	22.0	1	1	0	6	1
2003—Atlanta NFL		16	0	39	*545	14.0	1	62	1291	20.8	0	1	0	6	3
Pro totals (6 years)		83	2	153	1627	10.6	2	286	6601	23.1	3	5	0	30	18

ROUEN, TOM — P — SEAHAWKS

R

PERSONAL: Born June 9, 1968, in Hinsdale, Ill. ... 6-3/225. ... Full name: Thomas Francis Rouen Jr. ... Name pronounced: RUIN.
HIGH SCHOOL: Heritage (Littleton, Colo.).
COLLEGE: Colorado.
TRANSACTIONS/CAREER NOTES: Signed as non-drafted free agent by New York Giants (April 29, 1991). ... Released by Giants (August 19, 1991). ... Selected by Ohio Glory in fourth round (44th pick overall) of 1992 World League draft. ... Signed by Los Angeles Rams (July 1992). ... Released by Rams (August 24, 1992). ... Signed by Denver Broncos (April 29, 1993). ... Granted unconditional free agency (February 14, 1997). ... Re-signed by Broncos (March 6, 1997). ... Granted unconditional free agency (February 11, 2000). ... Re-signed by Broncos (February 24, 2000). ... Released by Broncos (October 29, 2002). ... Signed by Giants (November 1, 2002). ... Released by Giants (November 19, 2002). ... Signed by Pittsburgh Steelers (December 20, 2002). ... Granted unconditional free agency (February 28, 2003). ... Signed by Seattle Seahawks (July 22, 2003) ... Granted unconditional free agency (March 3, 2004). ... Re-signed by Seahawks (March 18, 2004).
CHAMPIONSHIP GAME EXPERIENCE: Played in AFC championship game (1997 and 1998 seasons). ... Member of Super Bowl championship team (1997 and 1998 seasons).
HONORS: Named punter on THE SPORTING NEWS college All-America second team (1989).

Year	Team	G	PUNTING No.	Yds.	Avg.	Net avg.	In. 20	Blk.
1993—Denver NFL		16	67	3017	45.0	37.1	17	1
1994—Denver NFL		16	76	3258	42.9	*37.1	23	0
1995—Denver NFL		16	52	2192	42.2	37.6	22	1
1996—Denver NFL		16	65	2714	41.8	36.2	16	0
1997—Denver NFL		16	60	2598	43.3	38.1	22	0
1998—Denver NFL		16	66	3097	46.9	37.6	14	1
1999—Denver NFL		16	84	3908	*46.5	35.6	19	0
2000—Denver NFL		16	61	2455	40.2	32.3	18	▲1
2001—Denver NFL		16	81	3668	45.3	36.5	25	1
2002—Denver NFL		8	29	1239	42.7	31.7	6	2
—New York Giants NFL		2	8	333	41.6	33.0	1	0
—Pittsburgh NFL		2	7	316	45.1	38.7	1	0
2003—Seattle NFL		16	67	2762	41.2	37.1	29	2
Pro totals (11 years)		172	723	31557	43.6	36.3	213	9

ROYAL, ROBERT — TE — REDSKINS

PERSONAL: Born May 15, 1979, in New Orleans, La. ... 6-4/257. ... Full name: Robert Shelton Royal Jr.
HIGH SCHOOL: Karr (New Orleans).
COLLEGE: Louisiana State.
TRANSACTIONS/CAREER NOTES: Selected by Washington Redskins in fifth round (160th pick overall) of 2002 NFL draft. ... Signed by Redskins (July 22, 2002). ... On injured reserve with ankle injury (September 1, 2002-entire season). ... On injured reserve with hip injury (October 14, 2003-remainder of season).
SINGLE GAME HIGHS (regular season): Receptions—2 (October 5, 2003, vs. Philadelphia); yards—24 (September 4, 2003, vs. New York Jets); and touchdown receptions—0.

Year	Team	G	GS	RECEIVING No.	Yds.	Avg.	TD	TOTALS TD	2pt.	Pts.	Fum.
2003—Washington NFL		6	6	5	48	9.6	0	0	0	0	1

ROYALS, MARK — P

PERSONAL: Born June 22, 1965, in Hampton, Va. ... 6-5/225. ... Full name: Mark Alan Royals.
HIGH SCHOOL: Mathews (Va.).
JUNIOR COLLEGE: Chowan College (N.C.).
COLLEGE: Appalachian State.
TRANSACTIONS/CAREER NOTES: Signed as non-drafted free agent by Dallas Cowboys (June 6, 1986). ... Released by Cowboys (August 8, 1986). ... Signed as replacement player by St. Louis Cardinals (September 30, 1987). ... Released by Cardinals (October 7, 1987). ... Signed as replacement player by Philadelphia Eagles (October 14, 1987). ... Released by Eagles (November 1987). ... Signed by Cardinals (December 12, 1987). ... Released by Cardinals (July 27, 1988). ... Signed by Miami Dolphins (May 2, 1989). ... Released by Dolphins (August 28, 1989). ... Signed by Tampa Bay Buccaneers (April 24, 1990). ... Granted unconditional free agency (February 1, 1992). ... Signed by Pittsburgh Steelers (March 15, 1992). ... Granted unconditional free agency (February 17, 1995). ... Signed by Detroit Lions (April 26, 1995). ... Granted free agency (February 16, 1996). ... Re-signed by Lions (June 19, 1996). ... Granted unconditional free agency (February 14, 1997). ... Signed by New Orleans Saints (April 25, 1997). ... Released by Saints (June 29, 1999). ... Signed by Buccaneers (August 4, 1999). ... Granted unconditional free agency (February 11, 2000). ... Re-signed by Buccaneers (March 24, 2000). ... Released by Buccaneers (February 26, 2002). ... Signed by Miami Dolphins (April 14, 2002). ... Granted unconditional free agency (February 28, 2003). ... Re-signed by Dolphins (March 4, 2003). ... Released by Dolphins (September 29, 2003). ... Signed by Jacksonville Jaguars (October 10, 2003). ... Granted unconditional free agency (March 3, 2004).
CHAMPIONSHIP GAME EXPERIENCE: Played in AFC championship game (1994 season). ... Played in NFC championship game (1999 season).

Year Team	G	PUNTING No.	Yds.	Avg.	Net avg.	In. 20	Blk.
1987—St. Louis NFL	1	6	222	37.0	0.0	2	0
—Philadelphia NFL	1	5	209	41.8	0.0	1	0
1988—			Did not play.				
1989—			Did not play.				
1990—Tampa Bay NFL	16	72	2902	40.3	34.0	8	0
1991—Tampa Bay NFL	16	84	3389	40.3	32.2	22	0
1992—Pittsburgh NFL	16	73	3119	42.7	35.6	22	1
1993—Pittsburgh NFL	16	89	3781	42.5	34.2	§28	0
1994—Pittsburgh NFL	16	§97	3849	39.7	35.7	†35	0
1995—Detroit NFL	16	57	2393	42.0	31.0	15	2
1996—Detroit NFL	16	69	3020	43.8	33.3	11	1
1997—New Orleans NFL	16	88	4038	*45.9	34.9	21	0
1998—New Orleans NFL	16	88	4017	‡45.6	36.0	26	0
1999—Tampa Bay NFL	16	90	3882	43.1	37.4	23	0
2000—Tampa Bay NFL	16	85	3551	41.8	35.1	17	0
2001—Tampa Bay NFL	16	83	3382	40.7	34.2	26	0
2002—Miami NFL	16	69	2772	40.2	34.5	15	0
2003—Miami NFL	3	16	643	40.2	36.3	5	0
—Jacksonville NFL	11	45	1852	41.2	34.8	9	0
Pro totals (15 years)	224	1116	47021	42.1	34.5	286	4

R

ROYE, ORPHEUS — DT/DE — BROWNS

PERSONAL: Born January 21, 1973, in Miami, Fla. ... 6-4/320. ... Full name: Orpheus Michael Roye. ... Name pronounced: OR-fee-us ROY.
HIGH SCHOOL: Miami Springs.
JUNIOR COLLEGE: Jones County Junior College (Miss.).
COLLEGE: Florida State.
TRANSACTIONS/CAREER NOTES: Selected by Pittsburgh Steelers in sixth round (200th pick overall) of 1996 NFL draft. ... Signed by Steelers (July 16, 1996). ... Granted free agency (February 12, 1999). ... Re-signed by Steelers (April 23, 1999). ... Granted unconditional free agency (February 11, 2000). ... Signed by Cleveland Browns (February 12, 2000). ... On injured reserve with knee injury (December 11, 2001-remainder of season).
CHAMPIONSHIP GAME EXPERIENCE: Played in AFC championship game (1997 season).

Year Team	G	GS	TOTALS Tk.	Ast.	Sks.	INTERCEPTIONS No.	Yds.	Avg.	TD
1996—Pittsburgh NFL	13	1	1	2	0.0	0	0	0.0	0
1997—Pittsburgh NFL	16	0	3	1	1.0	0	0	0.0	0
1998—Pittsburgh NFL	16	9	29	13	3.5	0	0	0.0	0
1999—Pittsburgh NFL	16	16	41	17	4.5	1	2	2.0	0
2000—Cleveland NFL	16	16	42	13	2.0	0	0	0.0	0
2001—Cleveland NFL	12	10	18	7	0.0	1	0	0.0	0
2002—Cleveland NFL	16	16	38	17	0.5	0	0	0.0	0
2003—Cleveland NFL	16	15	42	15	1.5	0	0	0.0	0
Pro totals (8 years)	121	83	214	85	13.0	2	2	1.0	0

RUCKER, MIKE — DE — PANTHERS

PERSONAL: Born February 28, 1975, in St. Joseph, Mo. ... 6-5/275. ... Full name: Michael Dean Rucker.
HIGH SCHOOL: Benton (St. Joseph, Mo.).
COLLEGE: Nebraska.
TRANSACTIONS/CAREER NOTES: Selected by Carolina Panthers in second round (38th pick overall) of 1999 NFL draft. ... Signed by Panthers (July 13, 1999).
CHAMPIONSHIP GAME EXPERIENCE: Played in NFC championship game (2003 season). ... Played in Super Bowl 38 (2003 season).
HONORS: Played in Pro Bowl (2003 season).

Year Team	G	GS	TOTALS Tk.	Ast.	Sks.
1999—Carolina NFL	16	0	24	6	3.0
2000—Carolina NFL	16	1	33	6	2.5
2001—Carolina NFL	16	16	44	12	9.0
2002—Carolina NFL	16	15	58	10	10.0
2003—Carolina NFL	14	14	48	11	12.0
Pro totals (5 years)	78	46	207	45	36.5

RUDD, DWAYNE — LB — RAIDERS

PERSONAL: Born February 3, 1976, in Batesville, Miss. ... 6-2/235. ... Full name: Dwayne Dupree Rudd.
HIGH SCHOOL: South Panola (Batesville, Miss.).
COLLEGE: Alabama.
TRANSACTIONS/CAREER NOTES: Selected by Minnesota Vikings in first round (20th pick overall) of 1997 NFL draft. ... Signed by Vikings (July 18, 1997). ... Granted unconditional free agency (March 2, 2001). ... Signed by Cleveland Browns (March 3, 2001). ... Released by Browns (February 26, 2003). ... Signed by Tampa Bay Buccaneers (April 8, 2003). ... Released by Buccaneers (March 2, 2004). ... Signed by Oakland Raiders (March 13, 2004).
CHAMPIONSHIP GAME EXPERIENCE: Played in NFC championship game (1998 and 2000 seasons).
RECORDS: Shares NFL single-season records for most touchdowns by fumble recovery—2 (1998); most touchdowns by recovery of opponents' fumbles—2 (1998).

Year Team	G	GS	TOTALS Tk.	Ast.	Sks.	INTERCEPTIONS No.	Yds.	Avg.	TD
1997—Minnesota NFL	16	2	31	15	5.0	0	0	0.0	0
1998—Minnesota NFL	15	15	79	14	2.0	0	0	0.0	0
1999—Minnesota NFL	16	16	88	29	3.0	0	0	0.0	0
2000—Minnesota NFL	14	13	52	17	0.0	0	0	0.0	0
2001—Cleveland NFL	16	16	69	27	0.5	1	0	0.0	0
2002—Cleveland NFL	16	15	50	12	1.0	0	0	0.0	0
2003—Tampa Bay NFL	16	2	7	4	0.0	0	0	0.0	0
Pro totals (7 years)	109	79	376	118	11.5	1	0	0.0	0

R

RUDDY, TIM — C

PERSONAL: Born April 27, 1972, in Scranton, Pa. ... 6-3/295. ... Full name: Timothy Daniel Ruddy.
HIGH SCHOOL: Dunmore (Pa.).
COLLEGE: Notre Dame.
TRANSACTIONS/CAREER NOTES: Selected by Miami Dolphins in second round (65th pick overall) of 1994 NFL draft. ... Signed by Dolphins (July 18, 1994). ... Granted unconditional free agency (February 11, 2000). ... Re-signed by Dolphins (February 24, 2000). ... Released by Dolphins (March 3, 2004).
PLAYING EXPERIENCE: Miami NFL, 1994-2003. ... Games/Games started: 1994 (16/0), 1995 (16/16), 1996 (16/16), 1997 (15/15), 1998 (16/16), 1999 (16/16), 2000 (16/16), 2001 (15/15), 2002 (16/16), 2003 (14/14). Total: 156/140.
HONORS: Played in Pro Bowl (2000 season).

RUEGAMER, GREY — G/C — PACKERS

PERSONAL: Born June 11, 1976, in Las Vegas, Nev. ... 6-4/310. ... Full name: Christopher Grey Ruegamer.
HIGH SCHOOL: Bishop Gorman (Las Vegas, Nev.).
COLLEGE: Arizona State.
TRANSACTIONS/CAREER NOTES: Selected by Miami Dolphins in third round (72nd pick overall) of 1999 NFL draft. ... Signed by Dolphins (July 27, 1999). ... Active for one game (1999); did not play. ... Released by Dolphins (August 27, 2000). ... Signed by Pittsburgh Steelers to practice squad (August 29, 2000). ... Signed by New England Patriots off Steelers practice squad (November 16, 2000). ... Granted free agency (March 1, 2002). ... Re-signed by Patriots (April 19, 2002). ... Granted unconditional free agency (February 28, 2003). ... Signed by Green Bay Packers (April 8, 2003).
PLAYING EXPERIENCE: Miami NFL, 1999; New England NFL, 2000-2002; Green Bay NFL, 2003. ... Games/Games started: 2000 (6/0), 2001 (14/1), 2002 (13/2), 2003 (15/0), Total: 48/3.
CHAMPIONSHIP GAME EXPERIENCE: Played in AFC championship game (2001 season). ... Member of Super Bowl championship team (2001 season).

RUFF, ORLANDO — LB — SAINTS

PERSONAL: Born September 28, 1976, in Charleston, S.C. ... 6-3/250. ... Full name: Orlando Bernarda Ruff.
HIGH SCHOOL: Fairfield Central (Winnsboro, S.C.).
COLLEGE: Furman.
TRANSACTIONS/CAREER NOTES: Signed as non-drafted free agent by San Diego Chargers (April 20, 1999). ... Granted free agency (March 1, 2002). ... Re-signed by Chargers (April 3, 2002). ... Granted unconditional free agency (February 28, 2003). ... Signed by New Orleans Saints (March 3, 2003).

Year Team	G	GS	TOTALS Tk.	Ast.	Sks.	INTERCEPTIONS No.	Yds.	Avg.	TD
1999—San Diego NFL	14	0	5	2	0.0	0	0	0.0	0
2000—San Diego NFL	16	14	54	14	0.0	1	18	18.0	0
2001—San Diego NFL	16	15	59	15	1.0	0	0	0.0	0
2002—San Diego NFL	16	0	4	0	0.0	0	0	0.0	0
2003—New Orleans NFL	16	9	47	19	0.0	1	7	7.0	0
Pro totals (5 years)	78	38	169	50	1.0	2	25	12.5	0

RUMPH, MIKE — CB — 49ERS

PERSONAL: Born November 8, 1979, in Boynton Beach, Fla. ... 6-2/205. ... Full name: Michael Jamaine Rumph.
HIGH SCHOOL: Atlantic (Delray Beach, Fla.).
COLLEGE: Miami (Fla.).
TRANSACTIONS/CAREER NOTES: Selected by San Francisco 49ers in first round (27th pick overall) of 2002 NFL draft. ... Signed by 49ers (July 23, 2002).

Year Team	G	GS	TOTALS Tk.	Ast.	Sks.	INTERCEPTIONS No.	Yds.	Avg.	TD
2002—San Francisco NFL	16	1	36	5	0.0	0	0	0.0	0
2003—San Francisco NFL	15	13	53	9	2.0	3	19	6.3	0
Pro totals (2 years)	31	14	89	14	2.0	3	19	6.3	0

RUNYAN, JON — T — EAGLES

PERSONAL: Born November 27, 1973, in Flint, Mich. ... 6-7/330. ... Full name: Jon Daniel Runyan.
HIGH SCHOOL: Carman-Ainsworth (Flint, Mich.).
COLLEGE: Michigan.

TRANSACTIONS/CAREER NOTES: Selected after junior season by Houston Oilers in fourth round (109th pick overall) of 1996 NFL draft. ... Signed by Oilers (July 20, 1996). ... Oilers franchise moved to Tennessee for 1997 season. ... Oilers franchise renamed Tennessee Titans for 1999 season (December 26, 1998). ... Granted free agency (February 12, 1999). ... Re-signed by Titans (June 23, 1999). ... Granted unconditional free agency (February 11, 2000). ... Signed by Philadelphia Eagles (February 14, 2000).

PLAYING EXPERIENCE: Houston NFL, 1996; Tennessee NFL, 1997-1999; Philadelphia NFL, 2000-2003. ... Games/Games started: 1996 (10/0), 1997 (16/16), 1998 (16/16), 1999 (16/16), 2000 (16/16), 2001 (16/16), 2002 (16/16), 2003 (16/16). Total: 122/112.

CHAMPIONSHIP GAME EXPERIENCE: Played in AFC championship game (1999 season). ... Played in Super Bowl 34 (1999 season). ... Played in NFC championship game (2001-2003 seasons).

HONORS: Named offensive lineman on THE SPORTING NEWS college All-America second team (1995). ... Played in Pro Bowl (2002 season).

RUSSELL, BRIAN — S — VIKINGS

PERSONAL: Born February 5, 1978, in West Covina, Calif. ... 6-2/204. ... Full name: Brian William Russell.

HIGH SCHOOL: Bishop Amat (West Covina, Calif.).

COLLEGE: San Diego State.

TRANSACTIONS/CAREER NOTES: Signed as non-drafted free by Minnesota Vikings (April 23, 2001). ... Released by Vikings (September 1, 2001). ... Re-signed by Vikings to practice squad (September 3, 2001). ... Activated (February 12, 2002).

			TOTALS			INTERCEPTIONS			
Year Team	G	GS	Tk.	Ast.	Sks.	No.	Yds.	Avg.	TD
2002—Minnesota NFL	16	2	10	4	0.0	1	18	18.0	0
2003—Minnesota NFL	16	16	72	15	1.0	†9	185	20.6	0
Pro totals (2 years)	32	18	82	19	1.0	10	203	20.3	0

RUSSELL, CLIFF — WR — REDSKINS

PERSONAL: Born February 8, 1979, in Ewa Beach, Hawaii. ... 5-11/193. ... Full name: Clifford Russell.

HIGH SCHOOL: Campbell (Ewa Beach, Hawaii).

COLLEGE: Utah.

TRANSACTIONS/CAREER NOTES: Selected by Washington Redskins in third round (87th pick overall) of 2002 NFL draft. ... Signed by Redskins (July 23, 2002).

SINGLE GAME HIGHS (regular season): Receptions—2 (December 27, 2003, vs. Philadelphia); yards—10 (December 27, 2003, vs. Philadelphia); and touchdown receptions—0.

			RUSHING				RECEIVING				TOTALS			
Year Team	G	GS	Att.	Yds.	Avg.	TD	No.	Yds.	Avg.	TD	TD	2pt.	Pts.	Fum.
2003—Washington NFL	3	0	0	0	0.0	0	2	10	5.0	0	0	0	0	0

RUSSELL, DARRELL — DT — BUCCANEERS

PERSONAL: Born May 27, 1976, in Pensacola, Fla. ... 6-5/325.

HIGH SCHOOL: St. Augustine (San Diego).

COLLEGE: Southern California.

TRANSACTIONS/CAREER NOTES: Selected by Oakland Raiders in first round (second pick overall) of 1997 NFL draft. ... Signed by Raiders (July 23, 1997). ... On suspended list for violating league substance abuse policy (September 9-October 14, 2001). ... On suspended list for violating league substance abuse policy (December 29, 2001-June 2003). ... Waived by Raiders (October 27, 2003). ... Signed by Washington Redskins (October 30, 2003). ... Granted unconditional free agency (March 3, 2004). ... Signed by Tampa Bay Buccaneers (March 30, 2004).

HONORS: Played in Pro Bowl (1998 and 1999 seasons). ... Named defensive tackle on THE SPORTING NEWS NFL All-Pro team (1999).

			TOTALS			INTERCEPTIONS			
Year Team	G	GS	Tk.	Ast.	Sks.	No.	Yds.	Avg.	TD
1997—Oakland NFL	16	10	35	9	3.5	0	0	0.0	0
1998—Oakland NFL	16	16	56	8	10.0	0	0	0.0	0
1999—Oakland NFL	16	16	34	11	9.5	0	0	0.0	0
2000—Oakland NFL	16	16	25	9	3.0	0	0	0.0	0
2001—Oakland NFL	11	7	32	10	2.5	1	0	0.0	0
2002—Oakland NFL			Did not play.						
2003—Washington NFL	8	0	3	3	0.0	0	0	0.0	0
Pro totals (6 years)	83	65	185	50	28.5	1	0	0.0	0

RUSSELL, TWAN — LB

PERSONAL: Born April 25, 1974, in Fort Lauderdale, Fla. ... 6-1/230. ... Full name: Twan Sanchez Russell.

HIGH SCHOOL: St. Thomas Aquinas (Fort Lauderdale, Fla.).

COLLEGE: Miami (Fla.).

TRANSACTIONS/CAREER NOTES: Selected by Washington Redskins in fifth round (148th pick overall) of 1997 NFL draft. ... Signed by Redskins (May 9, 1997). ... On injured reserve with foot and knee injuries (September 23, 1998-remainder of season). ... On injured reserve with knee injury (November 16, 1999-remainder of season). ... Granted free agency (February 11, 2000). ... Signed by Miami Dolphins (March 23, 2000). ... Granted unconditional free agency (March 2, 2001). ... Re-signed by Dolphins (March 6, 2001). ... On injured reserve with knee injury (November 13, 2002-remainder of season). ... Released by Dolphins (February 26, 2003). ... Signed by Atlanta Falcons (March 24, 2003). ... Granted unconditional free agency (March 3, 2004).

			TOTALS			INTERCEPTIONS			
Year Team	G	GS	Tk.	Ast.	Sks.	No.	Yds.	Avg.	TD
1997—Washington NFL	15	0	3	0	0.0	0	0	0.0	0
1998—Washington NFL	3	0	0	0	0.0	0	0	0.0	0
1999—Washington NFL	9	0	2	0	0.0	0	0	0.0	0

Year Team	G	GS	TOTALS Tk.	Ast.	Sks.	INTERCEPTIONS No.	Yds.	Avg.	TD
2000—Miami NFL	16	2	3	0	0.0	0	0	0.0	0
2001—Miami NFL	16	2	4	6	0.0	0	0	0.0	0
2002—Miami NFL	3	0	0	0	0.0	0	0	0.0	0
2003—Atlanta NFL	16	0	1	0	0.0	0	0	0.0	0
Pro totals (7 years)	78	4	13	6	0.0	0	0	0.0	0

RUTLEDGE, JOHNNY LB BRONCOS

PERSONAL: Born January 4, 1977, in Belle Glade, Fla. ... 6-3/239. ... Full name: Johnny Boykins Rutledge III.
HIGH SCHOOL: Glades Central (Belle Glade, Fla.).
COLLEGE: Florida.
TRANSACTIONS/CAREER NOTES: Selected by Arizona Cardinals in second round (51st pick overall) of 1999 NFL draft. ... Signed by Cardinals (July 29, 1999). ... Granted unconditional free agency (February 28, 2003). ... Signed by Baltimore Ravens (August 7, 2003). ... Released by Ravens (August 30, 2003). ... Signed by Denver Broncos (November 12, 2003). ... Granted unconditional free agency (March 3, 2004). ... Re-signed by Broncos (May 11, 2004).

Year Team	G	GS	TOTALS Tk.	Ast.	Sks.	INTERCEPTIONS No.	Yds.	Avg.	TD
1999—Arizona NFL	6	0	1	1	0.0	0	0	0.0	0
2000—Arizona NFL	11	3	16	7	0.0	0	0	0.0	0
2001—Arizona NFL	14	0	1	0	0.0	0	0	0.0	0
2002—Arizona NFL	9	0	0	0	0.0	0	0	0.0	0
2003—Denver NFL	6	0	0	0	0.0	0	0	0.0	0
Pro totals (5 years)	46	3	18	8	0.0	0	0	0.0	0

SALAAM, EPHRAIM T JAGUARS

PERSONAL: Born June 19, 1976, in Chicago, Ill. ... 6-7/295. ... Full name: Ephraim Mateen Salaam. ... Name pronounced: EFF-rum sah-LAHM.
HIGH SCHOOL: Florin (Sacramento).
COLLEGE: San Diego State.
TRANSACTIONS/CAREER NOTES: Selected by Atlanta Falcons in seventh round (199th pick overall) of 1998 NFL draft. ... Signed by Falcons (June 3, 1998). ... Granted free agency (March 2, 2001). ... Re-signed by Falcons (April 6, 2001). ... Granted unconditional free agency (March 1, 2002). ... Signed by Denver Broncos (April 15, 2002). ... Waived by Broncos (March 2, 2004). ... Signed by Jacksonville Jaguars (March 26, 2004).
PLAYING EXPERIENCE: Atlanta NFL, 1998-2001; Denver NFL, 2002-2003. ... Games/Games started: 1998 (16/16), 1999 (16/16), 2000 (14/10), 2001 (14/13), 2002 (16/16), 2003 (14/14). Total: 90/85.
CHAMPIONSHIP GAME EXPERIENCE: Played in NFC championship game (1998 season). ... Played in Super Bowl 33 (1998 season).

SALAVE'A, JOE DT REDSKINS

PERSONAL: Born March 23, 1975, in Leone, American Samoa. ... 6-3/305. ... Full name: Joe Fagaone Salave'a. ... Name pronounced: sala-VAY-uh.
HIGH SCHOOL: Oceanside (Calif.).
COLLEGE: Arizona.
TRANSACTIONS/CAREER NOTES: Selected by Tennessee Oilers in fourth round (107th pick overall) of 1998 NFL draft. ... Signed by Oilers (June 30, 1998). ... Oilers franchise renamed Tennessee Titans for 1999 season (December 26, 1998). ... Granted free agency (March 2, 2001). ... Re-signed by Titans (April 25, 2001). ... Granted unconditional free agency (March 1, 2002). ... Re-signed by Titans (May 9, 2002). ... Released by Titans (August 31, 2002). ... Signed by Baltimore Ravens (January 6, 2003). ... Released by Ravens (August 31, 2003). ... Signed by San Diego Chargers (October 15, 2003). ... Granted unconditional free agency (March 3, 2004). ... Signed by Washington Redskins (March 26, 2004).
CHAMPIONSHIP GAME EXPERIENCE: Played in AFC championship game (1999 season). ... Played in Super Bowl 34 (1999 season).
HONORS: Named defensive tackle on THE SPORTING NEWS college All-America third team (1997).

Year Team	G	GS	TOTALS Tk.	Ast.	Sks.
1998—Tennessee NFL	13	0	8	1	1.0
1999—Tennessee NFL	10	0	5	1	0.0
2000—Tennessee NFL	15	1	16	4	4.0
2001—Tennessee NFL	11	0	4	5	0.0
2003—San Diego NFL	9	1	2	3	0.0
Pro totals (5 years)	58	2	35	14	5.0

SAMUEL, ASANTE CB PATRIOTS

PERSONAL: Born January 6, 1981, in Fort Lauderdale, Fla. ... 5-10/185.
HIGH SCHOOL: Boyd Anderson (Lauderdale Lake, Fla.).
COLLEGE: Central Florida.
TRANSACTIONS/CAREER NOTES: Selected by New England Patriots in fourth round (120th pick overall) of 2003 NFL draft. ... Signed by Patriots (July 15, 2003).
CHAMPIONSHIP GAME EXPERIENCE: Played in AFC championship game (2003 season). ... Member of Super Bowl championship team (2003 season).

Year Team	G	GS	TOTALS Tk.	Ast.	Sks.	INTERCEPTIONS No.	Yds.	Avg.	TD
2003—New England NFL	16	1	27	5	0.0	2	55	27.5	1

SAMUELS, CHRIS — T — REDSKINS

PERSONAL: Born July 28, 1977, in Mobile, Ala. ... 6-5/310.
HIGH SCHOOL: Shaw (Mobile, Ala.).
COLLEGE: Alabama.
TRANSACTIONS/CAREER NOTES: Selected by Washington Redskins in first round (third pick overall) of 2000 NFL draft. ... Signed by Redskins (July 18, 2000).
PLAYING EXPERIENCE: Washington NFL, 2000-2003. ... Games/Games started: 2000 (16/16), 2001 (16/16), 2002 (15/15), 2003 (13/13). Total: 60/60.
HONORS: Outland Trophy winner (1999). ... Named offensive tackle on THE SPORTING NEWS college All-America first team (1999). ... Played in Pro Bowl (2001 and 2002 seasons).

SANDERS, DARNELL — TE — BROWNS

PERSONAL: Born March 16, 1979, in Cleveland, Ohio. ... 6-6/270.
HIGH SCHOOL: Warrensville Heights (Ohio).
COLLEGE: Ohio State.
TRANSACTIONS/CAREER NOTES: Selected after junior season by Cleveland Browns in fourth round (122nd pick overall) of 2002 NFL draft. ... Signed by Browns (July 8, 2002).
SINGLE GAME HIGHS (regular season): Receptions—3 (November 30, 2003, vs. Seattle); yards—23 (November 9, 2003, vs. Kansas City); and touchdown receptions—1 (October 19, 2003, vs. San Diego).

			RECEIVING				TOTALS			
Year Team	G	GS	No.	Yds.	Avg.	TD	TD	2pt.	Pts.	Fum.
2002—Cleveland NFL	10	3	3	23	7.7	1	1	0	6	0
2003—Cleveland NFL	16	12	15	95	6.3	1	1	0	6	1
Pro totals (2 years)	26	15	18	118	6.6	2	2	0	12	1

S

SANDERS, FRANK — WR

PERSONAL: Born February 17, 1973, in Fort Lauderdale, Fla. ... 6-2/215. ... Full name: Frank Vondel Sanders.
HIGH SCHOOL: Dillard (Fort Lauderdale, Fla.).
COLLEGE: Auburn.
TRANSACTIONS/CAREER NOTES: Selected by Arizona Cardinals in second round (47th pick overall) of 1995 NFL draft. ... Signed by Cardinals (July 17, 1995). ... Granted free agency (February 13, 1998). ... Re-signed by Cardinals (March 13, 1998). ... On injured reserve with foot injury (December 27, 2002-remainder of season). ... Granted unconditional free agency (February 28, 2003). ... Signed by Baltimore Ravens (April 16, 2003). ... Released by Ravens (April 27, 2004).
HONORS: Named wide receiver on THE SPORTING NEWS college All-America second team (1994).
SINGLE GAME HIGHS (regular season): Receptions—13 (January 2, 2000, vs. Green Bay); yards—190 (November 15, 1998, vs. Dallas); and touchdown receptions—2 (October 8, 2000, vs. Cleveland).
STATISTICAL PLATEAUS: 100-yard receiving games: 1995 (2), 1997 (2), 1998 (5), 1999 (2), 2001 (1). Total: 12.

			RECEIVING				TOTALS			
Year Team	G	GS	No.	Yds.	Avg.	TD	TD	2pt.	Pts.	Fum.
1995—Arizona NFL	16	15	52	883	17.0	2	2	2	16	0
1996—Arizona NFL	16	16	69	813	11.8	4	4	0	24	1
1997—Arizona NFL	16	16	75	1017	13.6	4	4	1	26	3
1998—Arizona NFL	16	16	‡89	1145	12.9	3	3	0	18	3
1999—Arizona NFL	16	16	79	954	12.1	1	1	0	6	2
2000—Arizona NFL	16	16	54	749	13.9	6	6	0	36	0
2001—Arizona NFL	15	13	41	618	15.1	2	2	0	12	1
2002—Arizona NFL	12	12	34	400	11.8	2	2	1	14	0
2003—Baltimore NFL	13	0	14	170	12.1	0	0	0	0	0
Pro totals (9 years)	136	120	507	6749	13.3	24	24	4	152	10

SANDERS, LEWIS — CB/S — JAGUARS

PERSONAL: Born June 22, 1978, in Staten Island, N.Y. ... 6-1/210. ... Full name: Lewis Lindell Sanders.
HIGH SCHOOL: St. Peter's (Staten Island, N.Y.).
COLLEGE: Maryland.
TRANSACTIONS/CAREER NOTES: Selected after junior season by Cleveland Browns in fourth round (95th pick overall) of 2000 NFL draft. ... Signed by Browns (June 3, 2000). ... On injured reserve with leg injury (August 27, 2001-entire season). ... Granted free agency (February 28, 2003). ... Re-signed by Browns (March 25, 2003). ... On injured reserve with groin injury (December 9, 2003-remainder of season). ... Granted unconditional free agency (March 3, 2004). ... Signed by Jacksonville Jaguars (March 9, 2004).
HONORS: Named cornerback on THE SPORTING NEWS college All-America third team (1999).

			TOTALS			INTERCEPTIONS			
Year Team	G	GS	Tk.	Ast.	Sks.	No.	Yds.	Avg.	TD
2000—Cleveland NFL	11	2	9	6	0.0	1	0	0.0	0
2002—Cleveland NFL	16	2	26	1	1.0	1	25	25.0	0
2003—Cleveland NFL	9	1	4	3	0.0	0	0	0.0	0
Pro totals (3 years)	36	5	39	10	1.0	2	25	12.5	0

SANDERSON, SCOTT — T

PERSONAL: Born July 25, 1974, in Walnut Creek, Calif. ... 6-6/295. ... Full name: Scott Michael Sanderson.
HIGH SCHOOL: Clayton Valley (Concord, Calif.).
COLLEGE: Washington State.

TRANSACTIONS/CAREER NOTES: Selected by Houston Oilers in third round (81st pick overall) of 1997 NFL draft. ... Oilers franchise moved to Tennessee for 1997 season. ... Signed by Oilers (July 17, 1997). ... Oilers franchise renamed Tennessee Titans for 1999 season (December 26, 1998). ... On injured reserve with back injury (October 9, 1999-remainder of season). ... Granted free agency (February 11, 2000). ... Re-signed by Titans (March 24, 2000). ... Granted unconditional free agency (March 2, 2001). ... Signed by Cleveland Browns (July 29, 2001). ... Released by Browns (September 3, 2001). ... Signed by New Orleans Saints (November 28, 2001). ... Granted unconditional free agency (February 28, 2003). ... Re-signed by Saints (April 1, 2003). ... Released by Saints (August 31, 2003). ... Signed by Chicago Bears (September 9, 2003). ... Released by Bears (November 10, 2003).

PLAYING EXPERIENCE: Tennessee NFL, 1997-2000; New Orleans NFL, 2002; Chicago NFL, 2003. ... Games/Games started: 1997 (10/0), 1998 (16/3), 1999 (3/3), 2000 (9/0), 2002 (6/0), 2003 (1/0). Total: 45/6.

HONORS: Named offensive tackle on THE SPORTING NEWS college All-America first team (1996).

SANDS, TERDELL — DT — RAIDERS

PERSONAL: Born October 31, 1979, in Chattanooga, Tenn. ... 6-7/337. ... Full name: Terdell Duane Sands.

HIGH SCHOOL: Howard (Chattanooga, Tenn.).

COLLEGE: Chattanooga.

TRANSACTIONS/CAREER NOTES: Selected by Kansas City Chiefs in seventh round (243rd pick overall) of 2001 NFL draft. ... Signed by Chiefs (July 19, 2001). ... On non-football injury list with foot injury (August 28, 2001-remainder of season). ... Assigned by Chiefs to Berlin Thunder in 2002 NFL Europe enhancement allocation program (February 12, 2002). ... Released by Chiefs (September 7, 2002). ... Re-signed by Chiefs to practice squad (September 10, 2002). ... Released by Chiefs (September 17, 2002). ... Signed by Green Bay Packers to practice squad (November 20, 2002). ... Waived by Packers (August 26, 2003). ... Re-signed by Packers to practice squad (September 2, 2003). ... Released by Packers (September 16, 2003). ... Re-signed by Packers to practice squad (October 1, 2003). ... Activated (October 15, 2003). ... Claimed on waivers by Oakland Raiders (November 12, 2003).

S

			TOTALS		
Year Team	**G**	**GS**	**Tk.**	**Ast.**	**Sks.**
2003—Green Bay NFL	1	0	1	0	0.0
—Oakland NFL	3	1	2	1	0.0
Pro totals (1 year)	4	1	3	1	0.0

SANTIAGO, O.J. — TE — BRONCOS

PERSONAL: Born April 4, 1974, in Whitby, ON. ... 6-7/265. ... Full name: Otis Jason Santiago.

HIGH SCHOOL: St. Michael's (Toronto).

COLLEGE: Kent State.

TRANSACTIONS/CAREER NOTES: Selected by Atlanta Falcons in third round (70th pick overall) of 1997 NFL draft. ... Signed by Falcons (July 11, 1997). ... On injured reserved with leg injury (November 20, 1997-remainder of season). ... Granted free agency (February 11, 2000). ... Re-signed by Falcons (June 5, 2000). ... Traded by Falcons to Dallas Cowboys for fourth round pick (LB Matt Stewart) in 2001 draft and seventh-round pick (WR Michael Coleman) in 2002 draft (August 27, 2000). ... Claimed on waivers by Cleveland Browns (November 22, 2000). ... Granted unconditional free agency (March 2, 2001). ... Re-signed by Browns (March 26, 2001). ... Granted unconditional free agency (March 1, 2002). ... Signed by Minnesota Vikings (July 15, 2002). ... Released by Vikings (August 27, 2002). ... Signed by Oakland Raiders (March 8, 2003). ... Granted unconditional free agency (March 3, 2004). ... Signed by Denver Broncos (April 15, 2004).

CHAMPIONSHIP GAME EXPERIENCE: Played in NFC championship game (1998 season). ... Played in Super Bowl 33 (1998 season).

SINGLE GAME HIGHS (regular season): Reception—5 (September 14, 1997, vs. Oakland); yards—65 (December 27, 1998, vs. Miami); and touchdown receptions—2 (December 27, 1998, vs. Miami).

			RECEIVING				TOTALS			
Year Team	**G**	**GS**	**No.**	**Yds.**	**Avg.**	**TD**	**TD**	**2pt.**	**Pts.**	**Fum.**
1997—Atlanta NFL	11	11	17	217	12.8	2	2	0	12	1
1998—Atlanta NFL	16	16	27	428	15.9	5	5	0	30	1
1999—Atlanta NFL	14	14	15	174	11.6	0	0	0	0	0
2000—Dallas NFL	11	0	0	0	0.0	0	0	0	0	0
2001—Cleveland NFL	14	12	17	153	9.0	2	2	0	12	0
2002—				Did not play.						
2003—Oakland NFL	12	7	5	69	13.8	0	0	0	0	0
Pro totals (6 years)	78	60	81	1041	12.9	9	9	0	54	2

SAPE, LAUVALE — DT — BILLS

PERSONAL: Born August 29, 1980, in American Samoa. ... 6-1/296.

HIGH SCHOOL: Leilehua (Hawaii).

COLLEGE: Utah.

TRANSACTIONS/CAREER NOTES: Selected by Buffalo Bills in sixth round (187th pick overall) of 2003 NFL draft. ... Signed by Bills (July 11, 2003).

			TOTALS		
Year Team	**G**	**GS**	**Tk.**	**Ast.**	**Sks.**
2003—Buffalo NFL	1	0	0	0	0.0

SAPP, CECIL — RB — BRONCOS

PERSONAL: Born December 12, 1978, in Miami, Fla. ... 5-11/229.

HIGH SCHOOL: Palmetto (Miami, Fla.).

COLLEGE: Colorado State.

TRANSACTIONS/CAREER NOTES: Signed as non-drafted free agent by Denver Broncos (April 28, 2003). ... Waived by Broncos (August 31, 2003). ... Re-signed by Broncos to practice squad (September 1, 2003). ... Activated (December 26, 2003).

SINGLE GAME HIGHS (regular season): Attempts—12 (December 28, 2003, vs. Green Bay); yards—31 (December 28, 2003, vs. Green Bay); and rushing touchdowns—0.

Year	Team	G	GS	RUSHING Att.	Yds.	Avg.	TD	TOTALS TD	2pt.	Pts.	Fum.
2003—Denver NFL		1	0	12	31	2.6	0	0	0	0	0

SAPP, GEROME — S — RAVENS

PERSONAL: Born February 8, 1981, in Houston, Texas. ... 6-1/216. ... Full name: Gerome Daren Sapp.
HIGH SCHOOL: Lamar (Houston).
COLLEGE: Notre Dame.
TRANSACTIONS/CAREER NOTES: Selected by Baltimore Ravens in sixth round (182nd pick overall) of 2003 NFL draft.

Year	Team	G	GS	TOTALS Tk.	Ast.	Sks.	INTERCEPTIONS No.	Yds.	Avg.	TD
2003—Baltimore NFL		14	0	0	0	0.0	0	0	0.0	0

SAPP, WARREN — DT — RAIDERS

PERSONAL: Born December 19, 1972, in Orlando, Fla. ... 6-2/303. ... Full name: Warren Carlos Sapp.
HIGH SCHOOL: Apopka (Fla.).
COLLEGE: Miami (Fla.).
TRANSACTIONS/CAREER NOTES: Selected after junior season by Tampa Bay Buccaneers in first round (12th pick overall) of 1995 NFL draft. ... Signed by Buccaneers (April 27, 1995). ... Granted unconditional free agency (March 3, 2004). ... Signed by Oakland Raiders (March 21, 2004).
CHAMPIONSHIP GAME EXPERIENCE: Played in NFC championship game (1999 and 2002 seasons). ... Member of Super Bowl championship team (2002 season).
HONORS: Lombardi Award winner (1994). ... Bronko Nagurski Award winner (1994). ... Named defensive lineman on THE SPORTING NEWS college All-America first team (1994). ... Played in Pro Bowl (1997-2000 seasons). ... Named defensive tackle on THE SPORTING NEWS NFL All-Pro team (1999-2002). ... Named to play in Pro Bowl (2001 season); replaced by Ted Washington due to injury. ... Named to play in Pro Bowl (2002 season); replaced by Kris Jenkins due to injury. ... Named to play in Pro Bowl (2003 season); replaced by Corey Simon due to injury.

Year	Team	G	GS	TOTALS Tk.	Ast.	Sks.	INTERCEPTIONS No.	Yds.	Avg.	TD
1995—Tampa Bay NFL		16	8	17	10	3.0	1	5	5.0	1
1996—Tampa Bay NFL		15	14	41	10	9.0	0	0	0.0	0
1997—Tampa Bay NFL		15	15	47	11	10.5	0	0	0.0	0
1998—Tampa Bay NFL		16	16	28	17	7.0	0	0	0.0	0
1999—Tampa Bay NFL		15	15	27	14	12.5	0	0	0.0	0
2000—Tampa Bay NFL		16	15	43	9	16.5	0	0	0.0	0
2001—Tampa Bay NFL		16	16	28	8	6.0	0	0	0.0	0
2002—Tampa Bay NFL		16	16	40	7	7.5	2	0	0.0	0
2003—Tampa Bay NFL		15	15	37	7	5.0	0	0	0.0	0
Pro totals (9 years)		140	130	308	93	77.0	3	5	1.7	1

SATURDAY, JEFF — C — COLTS

PERSONAL: Born June 8, 1975, in Atlanta, Ga. ... 6-2/292. ... Full name: Jeffrey Bryant Saturday.
HIGH SCHOOL: Shamrock (Tucker, Ga.).
COLLEGE: North Carolina.
TRANSACTIONS/CAREER NOTES: Signed as non-drafted free agent by Baltimore Ravens (April 27, 1998). ... Released by Ravens (June 12, 1998). ... Signed by Indianapolis Colts (January 7, 1999). ... Granted free agency (March 1, 2002). ... Re-signed by Colts (April 3, 2002). ... Granted unconditional free agency (February 28, 2003). ... Re-signed by Colts (February 28, 2003).
PLAYING EXPERIENCE: Indianapolis NFL, 1999-2003. ... Games/Games started: 1999 (13/2), 2000 (16/16), 2001 (16/16), 2002 (16/16), 2003 (16/16). Total: 77/66.
CHAMPIONSHIP GAME EXPERIENCE: Played in AFC championship game (2003 season).

SAUERBRUN, TODD — P — PANTHERS

PERSONAL: Born January 4, 1973, in Setauket, N.Y. ... 5-10/211. ... Name pronounced: SOUR-brun.
HIGH SCHOOL: Ward Melville (Setauket, N.Y.).
COLLEGE: West Virginia.
TRANSACTIONS/CAREER NOTES: Selected by Chicago Bears in second round (56th pick overall) of 1995 NFL draft. ... Signed by Bears (July 20, 1995). ... Granted free agency (February 13, 1998). ... Re-signed by Bears (May 19, 1998). ... On injured reserve with knee injury (September 23, 1998-remainder of season). ... Granted unconditional free agency (February 11, 2000). ... Signed by Kansas City Chiefs (March 27, 2000). ... Released by Chiefs (March 13, 2001). ... Signed by Carolina Panthers (April 24, 2001). ... Designated by Panthers as franchise player (February 19, 2003). ... Re-signed by Panthers (April 25, 2003).
CHAMPIONSHIP GAME EXPERIENCE: Played in NFC championship game (2003 season). ... Played in Super Bowl 38 (2003 season).
HONORS: Named punter on THE SPORTING NEWS college All-America first team (1994). ... Named punter on THE SPORTING NEWS NFL All-Pro team (2001-2003). ... Played in Pro Bowl (2001-2003 seasons).

Year	Team	G	PUNTING No.	Yds.	Avg.	Net avg.	In. 20	Blk.
1995—Chicago NFL		15	55	2080	37.8	31.1	16	0
1996—Chicago NFL		16	78	3491	44.8	34.9	15	0
1997—Chicago NFL		16	95	4059	42.7	32.8	26	0
1998—Chicago NFL		3	15	741	49.4	42.1	6	0
1999—Chicago NFL		16	85	3478	40.9	35.4	20	0

S

Year Team	G	PUNTING No.	Yds.	Avg.	Net avg.	In. 20	Blk.
2000—Kansas City NFL	16	82	3656	44.6	35.8	28	0
2001—Carolina NFL	16	93	*4419	*47.5	*38.9	35	1
2002—Carolina NFL	16	‡104	*4735	*45.5	37.5	‡31	1
2003—Carolina NFL	16	77	3433	‡44.6	35.6	22	*3
Pro totals (9 years)	130	684	30092	44.0	35.7	199	5

SAWYER, TALANCE — DE

PERSONAL: Born June 14, 1976, in Bastrop, La. ... 6-2/270.
HIGH SCHOOL: Bastrop (La.).
COLLEGE: UNLV.
TRANSACTIONS/CAREER NOTES: Selected by Minnesota Vikings in sixth round (185th pick overall) of 1999 NFL draft. ... Signed by Vikings (June 4, 1999). ... Granted free agency (March 1, 2002). ... Re-signed by Vikings (April 22, 2002). ... On injured reserve with knee and ankle injuries (October 29, 2002-remainder of season). ... Granted unconditional free agency (February 28, 2003). ... Re-signed by Vikings (October 9, 2003). ... Released by Vikings (February 24, 2004).
CHAMPIONSHIP GAME EXPERIENCE: Played in NFC championship game (2000 season).

S

Year Team	G	GS	TOTALS Tk.	Ast.	Sks.	INTERCEPTIONS No.	Yds.	Avg.	TD
1999—Minnesota NFL	2	0	0	0	0.0	0	0	0.0	0
2000—Minnesota NFL	16	16	27	10	6.0	0	0	0.0	0
2001—Minnesota NFL	16	16	35	22	5.0	1	2	2.0	0
2002—Minnesota NFL	2	0	1	0	0.0	0	0	0.0	0
2003—Minnesota NFL	3	0	0	1	0.0	0	0	0.0	0
Pro totals (5 years)	39	32	63	33	11.0	1	2	2.0	0

SCHIFINO, JAKE — WR — TITANS

PERSONAL: Born November 15, 1979, in Pittsburgh, Pa. ... 6-1/201. ... Full name: Vernon Martin Schifino.
HIGH SCHOOL: Penn Hills (Pa.).
COLLEGE: Akron.
TRANSACTIONS/CAREER NOTES: Selected by Tennessee Titans in fifth round (151st pick overall) of 2002 NFL draft. ... Signed by Titans (July 19, 2002). ... On injured reserve with hamstring injury (August 22, 2002-entire season).

Year Team	G	GS	RECEIVING No.	Yds.	Avg.	TD	KICKOFF RETURNS No.	Yds.	Avg.	TD	TOTALS TD	2pt.	Pts.	Fum.
2003—Tennessee NFL	13	0	0	0	0.0	0	35	703	20.1	0	0	0	0	0

SCHLESINGER, CORY — FB — LIONS

PERSONAL: Born June 23, 1972, in Columbus, Neb. ... 6-0/247.
HIGH SCHOOL: Columbus (Neb.).
COLLEGE: Nebraska.
TRANSACTIONS/CAREER NOTES: Selected by Detroit Lions in sixth round (192nd pick overall) of 1995 NFL draft. ... Signed by Lions (July 19, 1995). ... Granted unconditional free agency (March 2, 2001). ... Re-signed by Lions (March 2, 2001).
SINGLE GAME HIGHS (regular season): Attempts—10 (September 12, 1999, vs. Seattle); yards—50 (September 12, 1999, vs. Seattle); and rushing touchdowns—1 (September 22, 2002, vs. Green Bay).

Year Team	G	GS	RUSHING Att.	Yds.	Avg.	TD	RECEIVING No.	Yds.	Avg.	TD	TOTALS TD	2pt.	Pts.	Fum.
1995—Detroit NFL	16	2	1	1	1.0	0	1	2	2.0	0	0	0	0	0
1996—Detroit NFL	16	1	0	0	0.0	0	0	0	0.0	0	0	0	0	0
1997—Detroit NFL	16	2	7	11	1.6	0	5	69	13.8	1	1	0	6	0
1998—Detroit NFL	15	2	5	17	3.4	0	3	16	5.3	1	1	0	6	0
1999—Detroit NFL	16	11	43	124	2.9	0	21	151	7.2	1	1	0	6	4
2000—Detroit NFL	16	8	1	3	3.0	0	12	73	6.1	0	0	0	0	0
2001—Detroit NFL	16	13	47	154	3.3	3	60	466	7.8	0	3	0	18	1
2002—Detroit NFL	16	14	49	139	2.8	2	35	263	7.5	0	2	0	12	2
2003—Detroit NFL	16	10	9	16	1.8	0	34	247	7.3	2	2	0	12	0
Pro totals (9 years)	143	63	162	465	2.9	5	171	1287	7.5	5	10	0	60	7

SCHNECK, MIKE — C/LS — STEELERS

PERSONAL: Born August 4, 1977, in Whitefish Bay, Wis. ... 6-0/246. ... Full name: Mike Louis Schneck.
HIGH SCHOOL: Whitefish Bay (Wis.).
COLLEGE: Wisconsin.
TRANSACTIONS/CAREER NOTES: Signed as non-drafted free agent by Pittsburgh Steelers (April 23, 1999); contract voided by NFL because he did not meet eligibility requirements. ... Re-signed by Steelers (July 12, 1999). ... Granted free agency (March 1, 2002). ... Re-signed by Steelers (April 23, 2002). ... Granted unconditional free agency (March 3, 2004). ... Re-signed by Steelers (March 30, 2004).
PLAYING EXPERIENCE: Pittsburgh NFL, 1999-2003. ... Games/Games started: 1999 (16/0), 2000 (16/0), 2001 (16/0), 2002 (12/0), 2003 (16/0). Total: 76/0.
CHAMPIONSHIP GAME EXPERIENCE: Played in AFC championship game (2001 season).

SCHOBEL, AARON — DE — BILLS

PERSONAL: Born September 1, 1977, in Columbus, Texas. ... 6-4/262. ... Brother of Matt Schobel, tight end, Cincinnati Bengals.
HIGH SCHOOL: Columbus (Texas).
COLLEGE: Texas Christian.
TRANSACTIONS/CAREER NOTES: Selected by Buffalo Bills in second round (46th pick overall) of 2001 NFL draft. ... Signed by Bills (July 26, 2001).
HONORS: Named defensive end on THE SPORTING NEWS college All-America second team (2000).

			TOTALS			INTERCEPTIONS			
Year Team	**G**	**GS**	**Tk.**	**Ast.**	**Sks.**	**No.**	**Yds.**	**Avg.**	**TD**
2001—Buffalo NFL	16	11	31	11	6.5	0	0	0.0	0
2002—Buffalo NFL	16	16	34	18	8.5	0	0	0.0	0
2003—Buffalo NFL	16	16	38	22	11.5	1	6	6.0	0
Pro totals (3 years)	48	43	103	51	26.5	1	6	6.0	0

SCHOBEL, MATT — TE — BENGALS

PERSONAL: Born November 4, 1978, in Columbus, Texas. ... 6-5/257. ... Full name: Matthew Thomas Schobel. ... Brother of Aaron Schobel, defensive end, Buffalo Bills.
HIGH SCHOOL: Columbus (Texas).
COLLEGE: Texas Christian.
TRANSACTIONS/CAREER NOTES: Selected by Cincinnati Bengals in third round (67th pick overall) of 2002 NFL draft. ... Signed by Bengals (May 10, 2002).
SINGLE GAME HIGHS (regular season): Receptions—4 (December 28, 2003, vs. Cleveland); yards—97 (September 7, 2003, vs. Denver); and touchdown receptions—1 (November 30, 2003, vs. Pittsburgh).

			RECEIVING				TOTALS			
Year Team	**G**	**GS**	**No.**	**Yds.**	**Avg.**	**TD**	**TD**	**2pt.**	**Pts.**	**Fum.**
2002—Cincinnati NFL	16	10	27	212	7.9	2	2	0	12	0
2003—Cincinnati NFL	15	1	24	332	13.8	2	2	0	12	2
Pro totals (2 years)	31	11	51	544	10.7	4	4	0	24	2

SCHROEDER, BILL — WR

PERSONAL: Born January 9, 1971, in Eau Claire, Wis. ... 6-3/200. ... Full name: William Fredrich Schroeder. ... Name pronounced: SHRAY-der.
HIGH SCHOOL: Sheboygan (Wis.) South.
COLLEGE: Wisconsin-La Crosse.
TRANSACTIONS/CAREER NOTES: Selected by Green Bay Packers in sixth round (181st pick overall) of 1994 NFL draft. ... Signed by Packers (May 10, 1994). ... Released by Packers (August 28, 1994). ... Re-signed by Packers to practice squad (August 30, 1994). ... Activated (December 29, 1994). ... Traded by Packers with TE Jeff Wilner to New England Patriots for C Mike Arthur (August 11, 1995). ... On injured reserve with foot injury (August 27, 1995-entire season). ... Released by Patriots (August 14, 1996). ... Signed by Packers to practice squad (August 28, 1996). ... Assigned by Packers to Rhein Fire in 1997 World League enhancement allocation program (February 19, 1997). ... On injured reserve with broken collarbone (December 9, 1998-remainder of season). ... Granted unconditional free agency (March 1, 2002). ... Signed by Detroit Lions (March 14, 2002). ... Released by Lions (March 2, 2004).
CHAMPIONSHIP GAME EXPERIENCE: Member of Packers for NFC championship game (1997 season); inactive. ... Member of Packers for Super Bowl 32 (1997 season); inactive.
SINGLE GAME HIGHS (regular season): Receptions—8 (December 17, 2000, vs. Minnesota); yards—158 (October 10, 1999, vs. Tampa Bay); and touchdown receptions—2 (November 17, 2002, vs. New York Jets).
STATISTICAL PLATEAUS: 100-yard receiving games: 1998 (1), 1999 (1), 2000 (3), 2001 (5), 2002 (1). Total: 11.

			RECEIVING				PUNT RETURNS				KICKOFF RETURNS				TOTALS			
Year Team	**G**	**GS**	**No.**	**Yds.**	**Avg.**	**TD**	**No.**	**Yds.**	**Avg.**	**TD**	**No.**	**Yds.**	**Avg.**	**TD**	**TD**	**2pt.**	**Pts.**	**Fum.**
1994—Green Bay NFL							Did not play.											
1995—New England NFL							Did not play.											
1996—Green Bay NFL							Did not play.											
1997—Green Bay NFL	15	1	2	15	7.5	1	33	342	10.4	0	24	562	23.4	0	1	0	6	4
1998—Green Bay NFL	13	3	31	452	14.6	1	2	5	2.5	0	0	0	0.0	0	1	0	6	1
1999—Green Bay NFL	16	16	74	1051	14.2	5	0	0	0.0	0	1	10	10.0	0	5	0	30	3
2000—Green Bay NFL	16	16	65	999	15.4	4	0	0	0.0	0	0	0	0.0	0	4	0	24	1
2001—Green Bay NFL	14	14	53	918	‡17.3	9	0	0	0.0	0	0	0	0.0	0	9	0	54	1
2002—Detroit NFL	14	13	36	595	16.5	5	0	0	0.0	0	0	0	0.0	0	5	1	32	0
2003—Detroit NFL	16	13	36	397	11.0	2	0	0	0.0	0	0	0	0.0	0	2	0	12	0
Pro totals (7 years)	104	76	297	4427	14.9	27	35	347	9.9	0	25	572	22.9	0	27	1	164	10

SCHULTERS, LANCE — S — TITANS

PERSONAL: Born May 27, 1975, in Guyana. ... 6-2/202.
HIGH SCHOOL: Canarsie (Brooklyn, N.Y.).
JUNIOR COLLEGE: Nassau Community College (N.Y.).
COLLEGE: Hofstra.
TRANSACTIONS/CAREER NOTES: Selected by San Francisco 49ers in fourth round (119th pick overall) of 1998 NFL draft. ... Signed by 49ers (July 18, 1998). ... On injured reserve with knee injury (December 21, 2000-remainder of season). ... Granted free agency (March 2, 2001). ... Re-signed by 49ers (March 2, 2001). ... On physically unable to perform list with knee injury (July 29-August 6, 2001). ... Granted unconditional free agency (March 1, 2002). ... Signed by Tennessee Titans (April 11, 2002).
CHAMPIONSHIP GAME EXPERIENCE: Played in AFC championship game (2002 season).
HONORS: Played in Pro Bowl (1999 season).

Year Team	G	GS	TOTALS Tk.	Ast.	Sks.	INTERCEPTIONS No.	Yds.	Avg.	TD
1998—San Francisco NFL	15	0	12	3	0.0	0	0	0.0	0
1999—San Francisco NFL	13	13	53	9	0.0	6	127	21.2	1
2000—San Francisco NFL	12	12	61	30	0.5	0	0	0.0	0
2001—San Francisco NFL	16	16	52	9	1.0	3	0	0.0	0
2002—Tennessee NFL	16	16	71	13	2.0	6	56	9.3	0
2003—Tennessee NFL	16	16	65	20	1.0	0	0	0.0	0
Pro totals (6 years)	88	73	314	84	4.5	15	183	12.2	1

SCIFRES, MIKE — P — CHARGERS

PERSONAL: Born October 8, 1980, in Metairie, La. ... 6-2/236. ... Full name: Michael Scifres.
HIGH SCHOOL: Destrehan (Norco, La.).
COLLEGE: Western Illinois.
TRANSACTIONS/CAREER NOTES: Selected by San Diego Chargers in fifth round (149th pick overall) of 2003 NFL draft. ... Signed by Chargers (July 19, 2003).

Year Team	G	PUNTING No.	Yds.	Avg.	Net avg.	In. 20	Blk.
2003—San Diego NFL	6	0	0	0.0	0.0	0	0

SCIOLI, BRAD — DE — COLTS

PERSONAL: Born September 6, 1976, in Bridgeport, Pa. ... 6-3/280. ... Full name: Brad Elliott Scioli. ... Name pronounced: SHE-o-lee.
HIGH SCHOOL: Upper Merion (King of Prussia, Pa.).
COLLEGE: Penn State.
TRANSACTIONS/CAREER NOTES: Selected by Indianapolis Colts in fifth round (138th pick overall) of 1999 NFL draft. ... Signed by Colts (July 22, 1999). ... Granted free agency (March 1, 2002). ... Re-signed by Colts (April 16, 2002). ... Granted unconditional free agency (February 28, 2003). ... Re-signed by Colts (March 9, 2003).
CHAMPIONSHIP GAME EXPERIENCE: Played in AFC championship game (2003 season).

Year Team	G	GS	TOTALS Tk.	Ast.	Sks.
1999—Indianapolis NFL	10	0	1	0	0.0
2000—Indianapolis NFL	16	2	7	3	2.0
2001—Indianapolis NFL	13	12	22	10	4.0
2002—Indianapolis NFL	16	13	39	11	7.0
2003—Indianapolis NFL	16	0	10	2	0.0
Pro totals (5 years)	71	27	79	26	13.0

SCIULLO, STEVE — G — COLTS

PERSONAL: Born August 27, 1980, in Pittsburgh, Pa. ... 6-5/330. ... Full name: Steven William Sciullo.
HIGH SCHOOL: Shaler Area (Pittsburgh).
COLLEGE: Marshall.
TRANSACTIONS/CAREER NOTES: Selected by Indianapolis Colts in fourth round (122nd pick overall) of 2003 NFL draft. ... Signed by Colts (July 25, 2003).
PLAYING EXPERIENCE: Indianapolis NFL, 2003. ... Games/Games started: 2003 (13/13). Total: 13/13.
CHAMPIONSHIP GAME EXPERIENCE: Played in AFC championship game (2003 season).

SCOBEY, JOSH — RB — CARDINALS

PERSONAL: Born December 11, 1979, in Oklahoma City, Okla. ... 6-0/222.
HIGH SCHOOL: Del City (Oklahoma City, Okla.).
JUNIOR COLLEGE: Northeastern A&M Community College (Okla.).
COLLEGE: Kansas State.
TRANSACTIONS/CAREER NOTES: Selected by Arizona Cardinals in sixth round (185th pick overall) of 2002 NFL draft. ... Signed by Cardinals (May 31, 2002). ... On injured reserve with thumb injury (September 1, 2002-remainder of season).

Year Team	G	GS	RUSHING Att.	Yds.	Avg.	TD	RECEIVING No.	Yds.	Avg.	TD	KICKOFF RETURNS No.	Yds.	Avg.	TD	TOTALS TD	2pt.	Pts.	Fum.
2003—Arizona NFL	15	0	0	0	0.0	0	1	9	9.0	0	*73	*1684	23.1	1	1	0	6	0

SCOTT, BART — LB — RAVENS

PERSONAL: Born August 18, 1980, in Detroit, Mich. ... 6-2/235. ... Full name: Bart Edward Scott.
HIGH SCHOOL: Southeastern (Detroit).
COLLEGE: Southern Illinois.
TRANSACTIONS/CAREER NOTES: Signed as non-drafted free agent by Baltimore Ravens (April 25, 2002).

Year Team	G	GS	TOTALS Tk.	Ast.	Sks.	INTERCEPTIONS No.	Yds.	Avg.	TD
2002—Baltimore NFL	16	0	2	2	0.0	1	0	0.0	0
2003—Baltimore NFL	16	0	7	0	0.0	0	0	0.0	0
Pro totals (2 years)	32	0	9	2	0.0	1	0	0.0	0

SCOTT, BRYAN — CB — FALCONS

PERSONAL: Born April 13, 1981, in Washington, DC. ... 6-1/219. ... Full name: Bryan Anderson Scott.
HIGH SCHOOL: Central Bucks (Pa.).
COLLEGE: Penn State.
TRANSACTIONS/CAREER NOTES: Selected by Atlanta Falcons in second round (55th pick overall) of 2003 NFL draft. ... Signed by Falcons (July 10, 2003).

			TOTALS			INTERCEPTIONS			
Year Team	G	GS	Tk.	Ast.	Sks.	No.	Yds.	Avg.	TD
2003—Atlanta NFL	15	7	49	7	0.0	2	3	1.5	0

SCOTT, CAREY — S/CB

PERSONAL: Born August 11, 1978, in Savannah, Ga. ... 5-11/214.
HIGH SCHOOL: Beach (Ga.).
COLLEGE: Kentucky State.
TRANSACTIONS/CAREER NOTES: Selected by Minnesota Vikings in sixth round (189th pick overall) of 2001 NFL draft. ... Signed by Vikings (July 30, 2001). ... On injured reserve with stomach injury (September 2, 2001-entire season). ... Released by Vikings (September 1, 2002). ... Re-signed by Vikings to practice squad (September 3, 2002). ... Released by Vikings (October 15, 2002). ... Signed by Oakland Raiders to practice squad (October 30, 2002). ... Released by Raiders (December 14, 2002). ... Signed by Vikings (December 16, 2002). ... Released by Vikings (August 31, 2003). ... Signed by Raiders to practice squad (October 30, 2003). ... Activated (November 19, 2003). ... Released by Raiders (December 13, 2003).

			TOTALS			INTERCEPTIONS			
Year Team	G	GS	Tk.	Ast.	Sks.	No.	Yds.	Avg.	TD
2001—Minnesota NFL			Did not play.						
2002—Oakland NFL	1	0	0	0	0.0	0	0	0.0	0
—Minnesota NFL	1	0	0	0	0.0	0	0	0.0	0
2003—Oakland NFL	5	0	0	0	0.0	0	0	0.0	0
Pro totals (2 years)	7	0	0	0	0.0	0	0	0.0	0

S

SCOTT, CHAD — CB — STEELERS

PERSONAL: Born September 6, 1974, in Capitol Heights, Md. ... 6-1/205. ... Full name: Chad Oliver Scott.
HIGH SCHOOL: Suitland (Forestville, Md.).
COLLEGE: Maryland.
TRANSACTIONS/CAREER NOTES: Selected by Pittsburgh Steelers in first round (24th pick overall) of 1997 NFL draft. ... Signed by Steelers (July 16, 1997). ... On injured reserve with knee injury (July 20, 1998-remainder of season). ... On injured reserve with hand injury (December 2, 2003-remainder of season).
CHAMPIONSHIP GAME EXPERIENCE: Played in AFC championship game (1997 and 2001 seasons).

			TOTALS			INTERCEPTIONS			
Year Team	G	GS	Tk.	Ast.	Sks.	No.	Yds.	Avg.	TD
1997—Pittsburgh NFL	13	9	45	2	0.0	2	-4	-2.0	0
1998—Pittsburgh NFL			Did not play.						
1999—Pittsburgh NFL	13	12	49	1	0.0	1	16	16.0	0
2000—Pittsburgh NFL	16	16	64	6	0.0	5	49	9.8	0
2001—Pittsburgh NFL	15	15	71	9	0.0	5	204	40.8	†2
2002—Pittsburgh NFL	15	15	64	17	0.0	2	30	15.0	1
2003—Pittsburgh NFL	12	12	44	12	0.0	3	50	16.7	1
Pro totals (6 years)	84	79	337	47	0.0	18	345	19.2	4

SCOTT, DEQUINCY — DT — CHARGERS

PERSONAL: Born March 5, 1978, in La Place, La. ... 6-1/280.
HIGH SCHOOL: East St. John (LaPlace, La.).
COLLEGE: Southern Mississippi.
TRANSACTIONS/CAREER NOTES: Signed as non-drafted free agent by San Diego Chargers (April 24, 2001). ... Released by Chargers (September 2, 2001). ... Re-signed by Chargers to practice squad (September 3, 2001).

			TOTALS		
Year Team	G	GS	Tk.	Ast.	Sks.
2002—San Diego NFL	10	0	8	0	2.0
2003—San Diego NFL	16	0	14	4	6.5
Pro totals (2 years)	26	0	22	4	8.5

SCOTT, IAN — DT — BEARS

PERSONAL: Born November 8, 1981, in Greenville, S.C. ... 6-2/315. ... Full name: Josef Ian Scott.
HIGH SCHOOL: Gainesville (Fla.).
COLLEGE: Florida.
TRANSACTIONS/CAREER NOTES: Selected after junior season by Chicago Bears in fourth round (116th pick overall) of 2003 NFL draft. ... Signed by Bears (July 24, 2003).

			TOTALS		
Year Team	G	GS	Tk.	Ast.	Sks.
2003—Chicago NFL	6	0	2	0	0.0

SCOTT, LYNN — S — COWBOYS

PERSONAL: Born June 23, 1977, in Turpin, Okla. ... 6-0/221.
HIGH SCHOOL: Turpin (Okla.).
COLLEGE: Northwestern Oklahoma State.
TRANSACTIONS/CAREER NOTES: Signed as non-drafted free agent by Dallas Cowboys (April 27, 2001). ... Re-signed by Cowboys (March 13, 2003). ... Granted free agency (March 3, 2004). ... Re-signed by Cowboys (April 15, 2004).

			TOTALS			INTERCEPTIONS			
Year Team	**G**	**GS**	**Tk.**	**Ast.**	**Sks.**	**No.**	**Yds.**	**Avg.**	**TD**
2001—Dallas NFL	14	0	2	0	0.0	0	0	0.0	0
2002—Dallas NFL	14	0	6	4	0.0	0	0	0.0	0
2003—Dallas NFL	16	0	3	0	0.0	0	0	0.0	0
Pro totals (3 years)	44	0	11	4	0.0	0	0	0.0	0

SEARS, COREY — DE — TEXANS

PERSONAL: Born April 15, 1973, in San Antonio, Texas. ... 6-3/319. ... Full name: Corey Alexander Sears.
HIGH SCHOOL: Judson (Converse, Texas).
JUNIOR COLLEGE: Navarro College (Texas).
COLLEGE: Mississippi State.
TRANSACTIONS/CAREER NOTES: Signed as non-drafted free agent by Baltimore Ravens (April 29, 1996). ... On injured reserve with knee injury (August 20-November 6, 1996). ... Released by Ravens (November 6, 1996). ... Signed by St. Louis Rams (April 24, 1998). ... Claimed on waivers by San Francisco 49ers (August 26, 1998). ... Released by 49ers (August 28, 1998). ... Signed by Rams to practice squad (September 1, 1998). ... Activated (November 30, 1998). ... Claimed on waivers by Arizona Cardinals (September 6, 1999). ... Released by Cardinals (February 19, 2001). ... Signed by Houston Texans (February 8, 2002). ... Granted unconditional free agency (February 28, 2003). ... Re-signed by Texans (March 11, 2003). ... Granted unconditional free agency (March 3, 2004). ... Re-signed by Texans (March 22, 2004).

			TOTALS		
Year Team	**G**	**GS**	**Tk.**	**Ast.**	**Sks.**
1998—St. Louis NFL	4	0	4	0	0.0
1999—Arizona NFL	9	1	6	2	0.0
2000—Arizona NFL	8	2	9	9	0.0
2002—Houston NFL	16	0	13	8	1.0
2003—Houston NFL	16	12	26	11	1.0
Pro totals (5 years)	53	15	58	30	2.0

SEAU, JUNIOR — LB — DOLPHINS

PERSONAL: Born January 19, 1969, in San Diego, Calif. ... 6-3/250. ... Full name: Tiaina Seau Jr. ... Name pronounced: SAY-ow.
HIGH SCHOOL: Oceanside (Calif.).
COLLEGE: Southern California.
TRANSACTIONS/CAREER NOTES: Selected after junior season by San Diego Chargers in first round (fifth pick overall) of 1990 NFL draft. ... Signed by Chargers (August 27, 1990). ... Traded by Chargers to Miami Dolphins for fifth-round pick (RB Michael Turner) in 2004 draft (April 16, 2003).
CHAMPIONSHIP GAME EXPERIENCE: Played in AFC championship game (1994 season). ... Played in Super Bowl 29 (1994 season).
HONORS: Named linebacker on THE SPORTING NEWS college All-America first team (1989). ... Played in Pro Bowl (1991-2001 seasons). ... Named inside linebacker on THE SPORTING NEWS NFL All-Pro team (1992-1996, 1998 and 2000). ... Named to play in Pro Bowl (2002 season); replaced by Jason Gildon due to injury.

			TOTALS			INTERCEPTIONS			
Year Team	**G**	**GS**	**Tk.**	**Ast.**	**Sks.**	**No.**	**Yds.**	**Avg.**	**TD**
1990—San Diego NFL	16	15	61	24	1.0	0	0	0.0	0
1991—San Diego NFL	16	16	111	18	7.0	0	0	0.0	0
1992—San Diego NFL	15	15	79	23	4.5	2	51	25.5	0
1993—San Diego NFL	16	16	§108	21	0.0	2	58	29.0	0
1994—San Diego NFL	16	16	*124	31	5.5	0	0	0.0	0
1995—San Diego NFL	16	16	111	19	2.0	2	5	2.5	0
1996—San Diego NFL	15	15	110	28	7.0	2	18	9.0	0
1997—San Diego NFL	15	15	84	13	7.0	2	33	16.5	0
1998—San Diego NFL	16	16	92	23	3.5	0	0	0.0	0
1999—San Diego NFL	14	14	75	24	3.5	1	16	16.0	0
2000—San Diego NFL	16	16	103	20	3.5	2	2	1.0	0
2001—San Diego NFL	16	16	84	11	1.0	1	2	2.0	0
2002—San Diego NFL	13	13	60	24	1.5	1	25	25.0	0
2003—Miami NFL	15	15	66	30	3.0	0	0	0.0	0
Pro totals (14 years)	215	214	1268	309	50.0	15	210	14.0	0

SEHORN, JASON — S/CB

PERSONAL: Born April 15, 1971, in Sacramento, Calif. ... 6-2/213.
HIGH SCHOOL: Mt. Shasta (Calif.).
JUNIOR COLLEGE: Shasta College (Calif.).
COLLEGE: Southern California.
TRANSACTIONS/CAREER NOTES: Selected by New York Giants in second round (59th pick overall) of 1994 NFL draft. ... Signed by Giants (July 17, 1994). ... Granted free agency (February 14, 1997). ... Re-signed by Giants (August 9, 1997). ... On injured reserve with knee injury (August 25, 1998-entire season). ... Granted unconditional free agency (March 2, 2001). ... Re-signed by Giants (March 2, 2001). ... On injured

reserve with knee injury (January 2, 2002-remainder of season). ... Released by Giants (March 7, 2003). ... Signed by St. Louis Rams (May 19, 2003). ... Granted unconditional free agency (March 3, 2004).

CHAMPIONSHIP GAME EXPERIENCE: Played in NFC championship game (2000 season). ... Played in Super Bowl 35 (2000 season).

			TOTALS			INTERCEPTIONS			
Year Team	G	GS	Tk.	Ast.	Sks.	No.	Yds.	Avg.	TD
1994—New York Giants NFL	8	0	1	0	0.0	0	0	0.0	0
1995—New York Giants NFL	14	0	4	2	0.0	0	0	0.0	0
1996—New York Giants NFL	16	15	83	14	3.0	5	61	12.2	1
1997—New York Giants NFL	16	16	75	11	1.5	6	74	12.3	1
1998—New York Giants NFL			Did not play.						
1999—New York Giants NFL	10	10	37	8	0.0	1	-4	-4.0	0
2000—New York Giants NFL	14	14	60	13	0.0	2	32	16.0	0
2001—New York Giants NFL	13	13	57	6	1.0	3	34	11.3	1
2002—New York Giants NFL	16	5	43	4	0.0	2	31	15.5	1
2003—St. Louis NFL	10	3	14	4	0.0	0	0	0.0	0
Pro totals (9 years)	117	76	374	62	5.5	19	228	12.0	4

SEIDMAN, MIKE — TE — PANTHERS

PERSONAL: Born February 11, 1981, in Westlake, Calif. ... 6-4/261. ... Full name: Michael H. Seidman.

HIGH SCHOOL: Westlake (Calif.).

COLLEGE: UCLA.

TRANSACTIONS/CAREER NOTES: Selected by Carolina Panthers in third round (76th pick overall) of 2003 NFL draft. ... Signed by Panthers (July 26, 2003). ... On injured reserve with knee injury (December 2, 2003-remainder of season).

SINGLE GAME HIGHS (regular season): Receptions—2 (October 5, 2003, vs. New Orleans); yards—24 (October 5, 2003, vs. New Orleans); and touchdown receptions—0.

			RECEIVING				KICKOFF RETURNS				TOTALS			
Year Team	G	GS	No.	Yds.	Avg.	TD	No.	Yds.	Avg.	TD	TD	2pt.	Pts.	Fum.
2003—Carolina NFL	12	5	5	35	7.0	0	2	24	12.0	0	0	0	0	0

S

SERWANGA, KATO — CB

PERSONAL: Born July 23, 1976, in Kampala, Uganda. ... 6-0/205. ... Name pronounced: kah-TOE ser-WAN-guh. ... Twin brother of Wasswa Serwanga, cornerback, with San Francisco 49ers (1999) and Minnesota Vikings (2000 and 2001).

HIGH SCHOOL: Sacramento (Calif.).

COLLEGE: California.

TRANSACTIONS/CAREER NOTES: Signed as non-drafted free agent by New England Patriots (April 24, 1998). ... Released by Patriots (August 30, 1998). ... Re-signed by Patriots to practice squad (August 31, 1998). ... Activated (December 12, 1998); did not play. ... Assigned by Patriots to Scottish Claymores in 2001 NFL Europe enhancement allocation program (February 19, 2001). ... Released by Patriots (September 2, 2001). ... Signed by Washington Redskins (October 16, 2001). ... Granted free agency (March 1, 2002). ... Re-signed by Redskins (April 11, 2002). ... On injured reserve with knee injury (September 1-November 27, 2002). ... Released by Redskins (November 27, 2002). ... Signed by Giants (December 4, 2002). ... Granted unconditional free agency (February 28, 2003). ... Re-signed by Giants (March 3, 2003). ... Granted unconditional free agency (March 3, 2004).

			TOTALS			INTERCEPTIONS			
Year Team	G	GS	Tk.	Ast.	Sks.	No.	Yds.	Avg.	TD
1998—New England NFL			Did not play.						
1999—New England NFL	16	3	37	7	1.0	3	2	0.7	0
2000—New England NFL	15	0	20	3	2.0	0	0	0.0	0
2001—Washington NFL	11	0	0	0	0.0	0	0	0.0	0
2002—New York Giants NFL	3	0	2	0	0.0	0	0	0.0	0
2003—New York Giants NFL	13	0	6	2	0.0	0	0	0.0	0
Pro totals (5 years)	58	3	65	12	3.0	3	2	0.7	0

SEUBERT, RICH — G — GIANTS

PERSONAL: Born March 30, 1979, in Rozellville, Wis. ... 6-5/305.

HIGH SCHOOL: Marsfield Columbus (Stratford, Wis.).

COLLEGE: Western Illinois.

TRANSACTIONS/CAREER NOTES: Signed as non-drafted free agent by New York Giants (April 27, 2001). ... On injured reserve with leg injury (October 21, 2003-remainder of season).

PLAYING EXPERIENCE: New York Giants NFL, 2001-2003. ... Games/Games started: 2001 (2/0), 2002 (16/16), 2003 (6/6). Total: 24/22.

SEYMOUR, RICHARD — DT — PATRIOTS

PERSONAL: Born October 6, 1979, in Gadsden, S.C. ... 6-6/310.

HIGH SCHOOL: Lower Richland (S.C.).

COLLEGE: Georgia.

TRANSACTIONS/CAREER NOTES: Selected by New England Patriots in first round (sixth pick overall) of 2001 NFL draft. ... Signed by Patriots (July 24, 2001).

CHAMPIONSHIP GAME EXPERIENCE: Played in AFC championship game (2001 and 2003 seasons). ... Member of Super Bowl championship team (2001 and 2003 seasons).

HONORS: Named defensive tackle on THE SPORTING NEWS college All-America second team (2000). ... Named defensive tackle on THE SPORTING NEWS NFL All-Pro team (2003). ... Played in Pro Bowl (2002 and 2003 seasons).

Year Team	G	GS	TOTALS Tk.	Ast.	Sks.	INTERCEPTIONS No.	Yds.	Avg.	TD
2001—New England NFL	13	10	25	20	3.0	0	0	0.0	0
2002—New England NFL	16	16	33	23	5.5	1	6	6.0	0
2003—New England NFL	15	14	34	22	8.0	0	0	0.0	0
Pro totals (3 years)	44	40	92	65	16.5	1	6	6.0	0

SHABAZZ, SIDDEEQ S FALCONS

PERSONAL: Born February 5, 1981, in Frankfurt, Germany. ... 5-11/200. ... Full name: Siddeeq Muneer Shabazz.
HIGH SCHOOL: Gadsden (Anthony, N.M.).
COLLEGE: New Mexico State.
TRANSACTIONS/CAREER NOTES: Selected by Oakland Raiders in seventh round (246th pick overall) of 2003 NFL draft. ... Signed by Raiders (July 24, 2003). ... Claimed on waivers by Atlanta Falcons (October 2, 2003).

Year Team	G	GS	TOTALS Tk.	Ast.	Sks.	INTERCEPTIONS No.	Yds.	Avg.	TD
2003—Oakland NFL	4	0	0	0	0.0	0	0	0.0	0
—Atlanta NFL	7	0	1	0	0.0	0	0	0.0	0
Pro totals (1 year)	11	0	1	0	0.0	0	0	0.0	0

S

SHAFFER, KEVIN T FALCONS

PERSONAL: Born March 2, 1980, in Salisbury, Md. ... 6-5/290.
HIGH SCHOOL: Conestoga (Md.).
COLLEGE: Tulsa.
TRANSACTIONS/CAREER NOTES: Selected by Atlanta Falcons in seventh round (244th pick overall) of 2002 NFL draft. ... Signed by Falcons (June 14, 2002).
PLAYING EXPERIENCE: Atlanta NFL, 2002-2003. ... Games/Games started: 2002 (6/0), 2003 (16/8). Total: 22/8.

SHANLE, SCOTT LB COWBOYS

PERSONAL: Born November 23, 1979, in Genoa, Neb. ... 6-2/245.
HIGH SCHOOL: St. Edward (Neb.).
COLLEGE: Nebraska.
TRANSACTIONS/CAREER NOTES: Selected by St. Louis Rams in seventh round (251st pick overall) of 2003 NFL draft. ... Signed by Rams (July 23, 2003). ... On suspended list for violating league substance abuse policy (September 26-October 27, 2003). ... Claimed on waivers by Dallas Cowboys (December 10, 2003).

Year Team	G	GS	TOTALS Tk.	Ast.	Sks.	INTERCEPTIONS No.	Yds.	Avg.	TD
2003—St. Louis NFL	5	0	0	0	0.0	0	0	0.0	0

SHARPE, MONTIQUE DT CHIEFS

PERSONAL: Born March 10, 1980, in Washington, DC. ... 6-2/296.
HIGH SCHOOL: Dunbar (Washington, D.C.).
COLLEGE: Wake Forest.
TRANSACTIONS/CAREER NOTES: Selected by Kansas City Chiefs in seventh round (230th pick overall) of 2003 NFL draft. ... Signed by Chiefs (July 20, 2003). ... On non-football injury list with knee injury (August 26, 2003-October 20, 2003). ... Assigned by Chiefs to Berlin Thunder in 2004 NFL Europe enhancement allocation program (February 9, 2004).

Year Team	G	GS	TOTALS Tk.	Ast.	Sks.
2003—Kansas City NFL	5	0	4	0	1.0

SHARPE, SHANNON TE

PERSONAL: Born June 26, 1968, in Chicago, Ill. ... 6-2/228. ... Brother of Sterling Sharpe, wide receiver with Green Bay Packers (1988-94).
HIGH SCHOOL: Glennville (Ga.).
COLLEGE: Savannah State.
TRANSACTIONS/CAREER NOTES: Selected by Denver Broncos in seventh round (192nd pick overall) of 1990 NFL draft. ... Signed by Broncos (July 1990). ... Granted free agency (February 1, 1992). ... Re-signed by Broncos (July 31, 1992). ... Designated by Broncos as transition player (February 15, 1994). ... On injured reserve with broken collarbone (November 30, 1999-remainder of season). ... Granted unconditional free agency (February 11, 2000). ... Signed by Baltimore Ravens (February 16, 2000). ... Released by Ravens (February 27, 2002). ... Signed by Broncos (April 12, 2002). ... Announced retirement (May 17, 2004).
CHAMPIONSHIP GAME EXPERIENCE: Played in AFC championship game (1991, 1997, 1998 and 2000 seasons). ... Member of Super Bowl championship team (1997, 1998 and 2000 seasons).
HONORS: Played in Pro Bowl (1992, 1993, 1995-1997 and 2001 seasons). ... Named tight end on THE SPORTING NEWS NFL All-Pro team (1993 and 1996-1998). ... Named to play in Pro Bowl (1994 season); replaced by Eric Green due to injury. ... Named to play in Pro Bowl (1998 season); replaced by Frank Wycheck due to injury.
POST SEASON RECORDS: Shares NFL postseason single-game record for most receptions—13 (January 9, 1994, vs. Los Angeles Raiders).
SINGLE GAME HIGHS (regular season): Receptions—13 (October 6, 1996, vs. San Diego); yards—214 (October 20, 2002, vs. Kansas City); and touchdown receptions—3 (November 16, 2003, vs. San Diego).

STATISTICAL PLATEAUS: 100-yard receiving games: 1992 (2), 1993 (2), 1994 (1), 1995 (2), 1996 (3), 1997 (4), 2000 (2), 2002 (2), 2003 (1). Total: 19.
MISCELLANEOUS: Holds Denver Broncos all-time records for most receptions (675) and most receiving touchdowns (55).

			RECEIVING				TOTALS			
Year Team	**G**	**GS**	**No.**	**Yds.**	**Avg.**	**TD**	**TD**	**2pt.**	**Pts.**	**Fum.**
1990—Denver NFL	16	2	7	99	14.1	1	1	0	6	1
1991—Denver NFL	16	9	22	322	14.6	1	1	0	6	0
1992—Denver NFL	16	11	53	640	12.1	2	2	0	12	1
1993—Denver NFL	16	12	81	995	12.3	§9	9	0	54	1
1994—Denver NFL	15	13	87	1010	11.6	4	4	2	28	1
1995—Denver NFL	13	12	63	756	12.0	4	4	0	24	1
1996—Denver NFL	15	15	80	1062	13.3	10	10	0	60	1
1997—Denver NFL	16	16	72	1107	15.4	3	3	1	20	1
1998—Denver NFL	16	16	64	768	12.0	▲10	10	0	60	0
1999—Denver NFL	5	5	23	224	9.7	0	0	0	0	0
2000—Baltimore NFL	16	15	67	810	12.1	5	5	0	30	0
2001—Baltimore NFL	16	15	73	811	11.1	2	2	0	12	1
2002—Denver NFL	13	13	61	686	11.2	3	3	0	18	0
2003—Denver NFL	15	15	62	770	12.4	8	8	0	48	0
Pro totals (14 years)	204	169	815	10060	12.3	62	62	3	378	8

SHARPER, DARREN S PACKERS

PERSONAL: Born November 3, 1975, in Richmond, Va. ... 6-2/210. ... Full name: Darren Mallory Sharper. ... Brother of Jamie Sharper, linebacker, Houston Texans.
HIGH SCHOOL: Hermitage (Richmond, Va.).
COLLEGE: William & Mary.
TRANSACTIONS/CAREER NOTES: Selected by Green Bay Packers in second round (60th pick overall) of 1997 NFL draft. ... Signed by Packers (July 11, 1997).
CHAMPIONSHIP GAME EXPERIENCE: Played in NFC championship game (1997 season). ... Played in Super Bowl 32 (1997 season).
HONORS: Named safety on THE SPORTING NEWS NFL All-Pro team (2000 and 2002). ... Played in Pro Bowl (2000 and 2002 seasons).

			TOTALS			INTERCEPTIONS				PUNT RETURNS				TOTALS			
Year Team	**G**	**GS**	**Tk.**	**Ast.**	**Sks.**	**No.**	**Yds.**	**Avg.**	**TD**	**No.**	**Yds.**	**Avg.**	**TD**	**TD**	**2pt.**	**Pts.**	**Fum.**
1997—Green Bay NFL	14	0	12	1	0.0	2	70	35.0	∞2	7	32	4.6	0	3	0	18	1
1998—Green Bay NFL	16	16	53	20	0.0	0	0	0.0	0	0	0	0.0	0	0	0	0	0
1999—Green Bay NFL	16	16	84	29	1.0	3	12	4.0	0	0	0	0.0	0	0	0	0	0
2000—Green Bay NFL	16	16	72	20	1.0	*9	109	12.1	0	0	0	0.0	0	0	0	0	0
2001—Green Bay NFL	16	16	71	24	2.0	6	78	13.0	0	1	18	18.0	0	0	0	0	1
2002—Green Bay NFL	13	13	51	17	0.0	7	*233	33.3	1	1	0	0.0	0	1	0	6	0
2003—Green Bay NFL	15	15	71	13	2.0	5	78	15.6	0	0	0	0.0	0	0	0	0	0
Pro totals (7 years)	106	92	414	124	6.0	32	580	18.1	3	9	50	5.6	0	4	0	24	2

SHARPER, JAMIE LB TEXANS

PERSONAL: Born November 23, 1974, in Richmond, Va. ... 6-3/240. ... Full name: Harry Jamie Sharper Jr. ... Brother of Darren Sharper, safety, Green Bay Packers.
HIGH SCHOOL: Hermitage (Richmond, Va.).
COLLEGE: Virginia.
TRANSACTIONS/CAREER NOTES: Selected by Baltimore Ravens in second round (34th pick overall) of 1997 NFL draft. ... Signed by Ravens (July 23, 1997). ... Granted free agency (February 11, 2000). ... Re-signed by Ravens (June 16, 2000). ... Granted unconditional free agency (March 2, 2001). ... Re-signed by Ravens (April 3, 2001). ... Selected by Houston Texans from Ravens in NFL expansion draft (February 18, 2002).
CHAMPIONSHIP GAME EXPERIENCE: Played in AFC championship game (2000 season). ... Member of Super Bowl championship team (2000 season).
MISCELLANEOUS: Holds Houston Texans all-time record for most sacks (9.5).

			TOTALS			INTERCEPTIONS			
Year Team	**G**	**GS**	**Tk.**	**Ast.**	**Sks.**	**No.**	**Yds.**	**Avg.**	**TD**
1997—Baltimore NFL	16	15	52	14	3.0	1	4	4.0	0
1998—Baltimore NFL	16	16	45	9	1.0	0	0	0.0	0
1999—Baltimore NFL	16	16	69	17	4.0	0	0	0.0	0
2000—Baltimore NFL	16	16	59	13	0.0	1	45	45.0	0
2001—Baltimore NFL	16	16	77	31	6.0	0	0	0.0	0
2002—Houston NFL	16	16	95	42	5.5	0	0	0.0	0
2003—Houston NFL	16	16	107	59	4.0	0	0	0.0	0
Pro totals (7 years)	112	111	504	185	23.5	2	49	24.5	0

SHAW, BOBBY WR BILLS

PERSONAL: Born April 23, 1975, in San Francisco, Calif. ... 6-1/185.
HIGH SCHOOL: Galileo (San Francisco).
COLLEGE: California.
TRANSACTIONS/CAREER NOTES: Selected by Seattle Seahawks in sixth round (169th pick overall) of 1998 NFL draft. ... Signed by Seahawks (June 5, 1998). ... Released by Seahawks (August 30, 1998). ... Re-signed by Seahawks to practice squad (August 31, 1998). ... Activated (November 4, 1998); did not play. ... Released by Seahawks (November 18, 1998). ... Signed by Pittsburgh Steelers (November 20, 1998). ... Granted free agency (March 2, 2001). ... Re-signed by Steelers (March 2, 2001). ... Granted unconditional free agency (March 1, 2002). ...

Signed by Jacksonville Jaguars (April 3, 2002). ... Granted unconditional free agency (February 28, 2003). ... Signed by Buffalo Bills (March 17, 2003).
CHAMPIONSHIP GAME EXPERIENCE: Played in AFC championship game (2001 season).
HONORS: Named wide receiver on THE SPORTING NEWS college All-America first team (1997).
SINGLE GAME HIGHS (regular season): Receptions—8 (September 28, 2003, vs. Philadelphia); yards—131 (January 2, 2000, vs. Tennessee); and touchdown receptions—1 (December 14, 2003, vs. Tennessee).
STATISTICAL PLATEAUS: 100-yard receiving games: 1999 (1), 2001 (1). Total: 2.

			RUSHING				RECEIVING				PUNT RETURNS				KICKOFF RETURNS				TOTALS		
Year Team	G	GS	Att.	Yds.	Avg.	TD	No.	Yds.	Avg.	TD	No.	Yds.	Avg.	TD	No.	Yds.	Avg.	TD	TD	2pt.	Pts.
1998—Sea. NFL	Did not play.																				
1999—Pit. NFL	15	1	0	0	0.0	0	28	387	13.8	3	4	53	13.3	0	0	0	0.0	0	3	0	18
2000—Pit. NFL	16	0	0	0	0.0	0	40	672	16.8	4	2	17	8.5	0	0	-8	0.0	0	4	0	24
2001—Pit. NFL	16	0	0	0	0.0	0	24	409	17.0	2	4	45	11.3	0	1	2	2.0	0	2	0	12
2002—Jac. NFL	16	10	0	0	0.0	0	44	525	11.9	1	25	310	12.4	1	3	53	17.7	0	2	0	12
2003—Buf. NFL	16	7	0	0	0.0	0	56	732	13.1	4	0	0	0.0	0	0	0	0.0	0	4	0	24
Pro totals (5 years)	79	18	0	0	0.0	0	192	2725	14.2	14	35	425	12.1	1	4	47	11.8	0	15	0	90

SHAW, TERRANCE — CB — PANTHERS

PERSONAL: Born January 11, 1973, in Marshall, Texas. ... 6-0/200. ... Full name: Terrance Bernard Shaw.
HIGH SCHOOL: Marshall (Texas).
COLLEGE: Stephen F. Austin.
TRANSACTIONS/CAREER NOTES: Selected by San Diego Chargers in second round (34th pick overall) of 1995 NFL draft. ... Signed by Chargers (June 15, 1995). ... Released by Chargers (March 21, 2000). ... Signed by Miami Dolphins (June 13, 2000). ... Granted unconditional free agency (March 2, 2001). ... Signed by New England Patriots (March 22, 2001). ... Released by Patriots (February 25, 2002). ... Signed by Oakland Raiders (March 21, 2002). ... Granted unconditional free agency (March 3, 2004). ... Signed by Carolina Panthers (April 22, 2004).
CHAMPIONSHIP GAME EXPERIENCE: Played in AFC championship game (2001 and 2002 seasons). ... Member of Super Bowl championship team (2001 season). ... Played in Super Bowl 37 (2002 season).

			TOTALS			INTERCEPTIONS			
Year Team	G	GS	Tk.	Ast.	Sks.	No.	Yds.	Avg.	TD
1995—San Diego NFL	16	14	53	5	0.0	1	31	31.0	0
1996—San Diego NFL	16	16	72	13	0.0	3	78	26.0	0
1997—San Diego NFL	16	16	66	5	0.0	1	11	11.0	0
1998—San Diego NFL	13	13	35	5	0.0	2	0	0.0	0
1999—San Diego NFL	8	8	21	3	0.0	0	0	0.0	0
2000—Miami NFL	11	3	15	3	0.0	1	0	0.0	0
2001—New England NFL	13	2	19	2	0.0	0	0	0.0	0
2002—Oakland NFL	16	7	30	4	0.0	2	-2	-1.0	0
2003—Oakland NFL	16	8	52	12	0.0	0	0	0.0	0
Pro totals (9 years)	125	87	363	52	0.0	10	118	11.8	0

SHEA, AARON — TE — BROWNS

PERSONAL: Born December 5, 1976, in Ottawa, Ill. ... 6-3/255. ... Full name: Aaron T. Shea.
HIGH SCHOOL: Ottawa (Ill.).
COLLEGE: Michigan.
TRANSACTIONS/CAREER NOTES: Selected by Cleveland Browns in fourth round (110th pick overall) of 2000 NFL draft. ... Signed by Browns (July 13, 2000). ... On injured reserve with shoulder injury (December 27, 2001-remainder of season). ... On injured reserve with ankle injury (November 19, 2002-remainder of season). ... Granted free agency (February 28, 2003). ... Re-signed by Browns (April 25, 2003). ... On injured reserve with arm injury (October 7, 2003-remainder of season).
SINGLE GAME HIGHS (regular season): Receptions—6 (December 2, 2001, vs. Tennessee); yards—76 (October 15, 2000, vs. Denver); and touchdown receptions—1 (November 12, 2000, vs. New England).

			RECEIVING				TOTALS			
Year Team	G	GS	No.	Yds.	Avg.	TD	TD	2pt.	Pts.	Fum.
2000—Cleveland NFL	15	8	30	302	10.1	2	2	0	12	1
2001—Cleveland NFL	12	5	14	86	6.1	0	0	0	0	0
2002—Cleveland NFL	7	3	7	49	7.0	0	0	0	0	0
2003—Cleveland NFL	4	2	2	9	4.5	0	0	0	0	0
Pro totals (4 years)	38	18	53	446	8.4	2	2	0	12	1

SHELTON, DAIMON — FB — BILLS

PERSONAL: Born September 15, 1972, in Duarte, Calif. ... 262.
HIGH SCHOOL: Duarte (Calif.).
JUNIOR COLLEGE: Fresno (Calif.) City College.
COLLEGE: Cal State Sacramento.
TRANSACTIONS/CAREER NOTES: Selected by Jacksonville Jaguars in sixth round (184th pick overall) of 1997 NFL draft. ... Signed by Jaguars (May 23, 1997). ... Granted free agency (February 11, 2000). ... Re-signed by Jaguars (March 21, 2000). ... Granted unconditional free agency (March 2, 2001). ... Signed by Chicago Bears (May 23, 2001). ... Granted unconditional free agency (March 1, 2002). ... Re-signed by Bears (April 2, 2002). ... On suspended list for violating league substance abuse policy (September 1-27, 2002). ... Waived by Bears (August 31, 2003). ... Signed by Buffalo Bills (January 28, 2004).
CHAMPIONSHIP GAME EXPERIENCE: Played in AFC championship game (1999 season).
SINGLE GAME HIGHS (regular season): Attempts—13 (October 18, 1998, vs. Buffalo); yards —44 (October 18, 1998, vs. Buffalo); and rushing touchdowns—1 (November 1, 1998, vs. Baltimore).

Year Team	G	GS	RUSHING Att.	Yds.	Avg.	TD	RECEIVING No.	Yds.	Avg.	TD	TOTALS TD	2pt.	Pts.	Fum.
1997—Jacksonville NFL	13	0	6	4	0.7	0	0	0	0.0	0	0	0	0	1
1998—Jacksonville NFL	14	8	30	95	3.2	1	10	79	7.9	0	1	0	6	0
1999—Jacksonville NFL	16	9	1	2	2.0	0	12	87	7.3	0	0	0	0	0
2000—Jacksonville NFL	16	9	2	3	1.5	0	4	48	12.0	0	0	0	0	0
2001—Chicago NFL	16	9	0	0	0.0	0	12	76	6.3	1	1	0	6	2
2002—Chicago NFL	12	8	0	0	0.0	0	7	34	4.9	0	0	0	0	0
2003—Chicago NFL	Did not play.													
Pro totals (6 years)	87	43	39	104	2.7	1	45	324	7.2	1	2	0	12	3

SHELTON, L.J. — T — CARDINALS

PERSONAL: Born March 21, 1976, in Rochester Hills, Mich. ... 6-6/335. ... Full name: Lonnie Jewel Shelton. ... Son of Lonnie Shelton, forward with New York Knicks (1976-77 and 1977-78), Seattle SuperSonics (1978-79 through 1982-83) and Cleveland Cavaliers (1983-84 through 1985-86).

HIGH SCHOOL: Rochester (Rochester Hills, Mich.).

COLLEGE: Eastern Michigan.

TRANSACTIONS/CAREER NOTES: Selected by Arizona Cardinals in first round (21st pick overall) of 1999 NFL draft. ... Signed by Cardinals (September 24, 1999).

PLAYING EXPERIENCE: Arizona NFL, 1999-2003. ... Games/Games started: 1999 (9/7), 2000 (14/14), 2001 (16/16), 2002 (16/16), 2003 (15/15). Total: 70/68.

S

SHEPHERD, EDELL — WR — BUCCANEERS

PERSONAL: Born May 18, 1980, in Los Angeles, Calif. ... 6-1/175. ... Full name: Edell Eugene Shepherd.

HIGH SCHOOL: Dorsey H.S. (Los Angeles).

JUNIOR COLLEGE: West Los Angeles College.

COLLEGE: San Jose State.

TRANSACTIONS/CAREER NOTES: Signed as non-drafted free agent by Chicago Bears (April 22, 2002). ... Waived by Bears (October 1, 2002). ... Re-signed by Bears to practice squad (October 15, 2002). ... Assigned by Bears to Scottish Claymores in 2003 NFL Europe enhancement allocation program (February 4, 2003). ... Waived by Bears (August 29, 2003). ... Signed by Tampa Bay Buccaneers to practice squad (September 2, 2003). ... Activated (December 6, 2003).

Year Team	G	GS	RECEIVING No.	Yds.	Avg.	TD	TOTALS TD	2pt.	Pts.	Fum.
2003—Tampa Bay NFL	2	0	4	38	9.5	0	0	0	0	0

SHEPHERD, JACOBY — CB/S — RAIDERS

PERSONAL: Born August 31, 1979, in Lufkin, Texas. ... 6-2/204. ... Full name: Jacoby Lamar Shepherd.

HIGH SCHOOL: Lufkin (Texas).

JUNIOR COLLEGE: Tyler (Texas) Junior College, then Cloud County Community College, Kan. (did not.

COLLEGE: Oklahoma State.

TRANSACTIONS/CAREER NOTES: Selected after junior season by St. Louis Rams in second round (62nd pick overall) of 2000 NFL draft. ... Signed by Rams (July 17, 2000). ... On injured reserve with quadriceps injury (November 27, 2001-remainder of season). ... Traded by Rams to Houston Texans for conditional seventh-round pick in 2003 draft (March 29, 2002). ... Released by Texans (September 1, 2002). ... Signed by Green Bay Packers (January 1, 2003). ... Released by Packers (August 26, 2003). ... Signed by New York Jets (August 30, 2003). ... Waived by Jets (September 30, 2003). ... Signed by Detroit Lions (October 29, 2003). ... Released by Lions (November 24, 2003). ... Signed by Oakland Raiders (April 12, 2004).

Year Team	G	GS	TOTALS Tk.	Ast.	Sks.	INTERCEPTIONS No.	Yds.	Avg.	TD
2000—St. Louis NFL	14	1	14	1	0.0	1	0	0.0	0
2001—St. Louis NFL	7	0	0	0	0.0	0	0	0.0	0
2003—New York Jets NFL	4	0	0	0	0.0	0	0	0.0	0
—Detroit NFL	4	0	0	0	0.0	0	0	0.0	0
Pro totals (3 years)	29	1	14	1	0.0	1	0	0.0	0

SHEPPARD, LITO — CB — EAGLES

PERSONAL: Born April 8, 1981, in Jacksonville, Fla. ... 5-10/194. ... Full name: Lito Decorian Sheppard.

HIGH SCHOOL: Raines (Jacksonville).

COLLEGE: Florida.

TRANSACTIONS/CAREER NOTES: Selected after junior season by Philadelphia Eagles in first round (26th pick overall) of 2002 NFL draft. ... Signed by Eagles (July 24, 2002).

CHAMPIONSHIP GAME EXPERIENCE: Member of Eagles for NFC championship game (2002 season); inactive. ... Played in NFC championship game (2003 season).

HONORS: Named cornerback on THE SPORTING NEWS college All-America second team (2000 and 2001).

Year Team	G	GS	TOTALS Tk.	Ast.	Sks.	INTERCEPTIONS No.	Yds.	Avg.	TD	PUNT RETURNS No.	Yds.	Avg.	TD	KICKOFF RETURNS No.	Yds.	Avg.	TD	TOTALS TD	2pt.	Pts.	Fum.
2002—Phi. NFL	12	0	5	2	0.0	0	0	0.0	0	0	0	0.0	0	0	0	0.0	0	0	0	0	0
2003—Phi. NFL	16	9	44	6	0.0	1	34	34.0	0	4	15	3.8	0	0	0	0.0	0	0	0	0	0
Pro totals (2 years)	28	9	49	8	0.0	1	34	34.0	0	4	15	3.8	0	0	0	0.0	0	0	0	0	0

SHIANCOE, VISANTHE — TE — GIANTS

PERSONAL: Born June 18, 1980, in Laurel, Md. ... 6-4/250. ... Full name: Vishante Shiancoe.
HIGH SCHOOL: Blair (Laurel, Md.).
COLLEGE: Morgan State.
TRANSACTIONS/CAREER NOTES: Selected by New York Giants in third round (91st pick overall) of 2003 NFL draft. ... Signed by Giants (July 24, 2003).
SINGLE GAME HIGHS (regular season): Receptions—3 (December 21, 2003, vs. Dallas); yards—20 (December 21, 2003, vs. Dallas); and touchdown receptions—1 (December 28, 2003, vs. Carolina).

			RECEIVING				TOTALS			
Year Team	G	GS	No.	Yds.	Avg.	TD	TD	2pt.	Pts.	Fum.
2003—New York Giants NFL	16	7	10	56	5.6	2	2	0	12	0

SHIELDS, WILL — G — CHIEFS

PERSONAL: Born September 15, 1971, in Fort Riley, Kan. ... 6-3/315. ... Full name: Will Herthie Shields.
HIGH SCHOOL: Lawton (Okla.).
COLLEGE: Nebraska.
TRANSACTIONS/CAREER NOTES: Selected by Kansas City Chiefs in the third round (74th pick overall) of 1993 NFL draft. ... Signed by Chiefs (May 3, 1993). ... Designated by Chiefs as franchise player (February 11, 2000).
PLAYING EXPERIENCE: Kansas City NFL, 1993-2003. ... Games/Games started: 1993 (16/15), 1994 (16/16), 1995 (16/16), 1996 (16/16), 1997 (16/16), 1998 (16/16), 1999 (16/16), 2000 (16/16), 2001 (16/16), 2002 (16/16), 2003 (16/16). Total: 176/175.
CHAMPIONSHIP GAME EXPERIENCE: Played in AFC championship game (1993 season).
HONORS: Named guard on THE SPORTING NEWS college All-America second team (1991). ... Named guard on THE SPORTING NEWS college All-America first team (1992). ... Named guard on THE SPORTING NEWS NFL All-Pro team (1999, 2002 and 2003). ... Played in Pro Bowl (1995-2003 seasons).

S

SHIPP, MARCEL — RB — CARDINALS

PERSONAL: Born August 8, 1978, in Paterson, N.J. ... 5-11/230.
HIGH SCHOOL: Milford (Conn.), then Passaic (N.J.).
COLLEGE: Massachusetts.
TRANSACTIONS/CAREER NOTES: Signed as non-drafted free agent by Arizona Cardinals (April 23, 2001).
SINGLE GAME HIGHS (regular season): Attempts—35 (October 26, 2003, vs. San Francisco); yards—165 (October 26, 2003, vs. San Francisco); and rushing touchdowns—2 (December 15, 2002, vs. St. Louis).
STATISTICAL PLATEAUS: 100-yard rushing games: 2002 (1), 2003 (2). Total: 3.

			RUSHING				RECEIVING				KICKOFF RETURNS				TOTALS			
Year Team	G	GS	Att.	Yds.	Avg.	TD	No.	Yds.	Avg.	TD	No.	Yds.	Avg.	TD	TD	2pt.	Pts.	Fum.
2001—Arizona NFL	11	0	0	0	0.0	0	0	0	0.0	0	6	118	19.7	0	0	0	0	0
2002—Arizona NFL	15	6	188	834	4.4	6	38	413	10.9	3	6	120	20.0	0	9	0	54	4
2003—Arizona NFL	16	11	228	830	3.6	0	30	184	6.1	0	0	0	0.0	0	0	0	0	3
Pro totals (3 years)	42	17	416	1664	4.0	6	68	597	8.8	3	12	238	19.8	0	9	0	54	7

SHOCKEY, JEREMY — TE — GIANTS

PERSONAL: Born August 18, 1980, in Ada, Okla. ... 6-5/253. ... Full name: Jeremy Charles Shockey.
HIGH SCHOOL: Ada (Okla.).
JUNIOR COLLEGE: Northeastern A&M Community College (Okla.).
COLLEGE: Miami (Fla.).
TRANSACTIONS/CAREER NOTES: Selected after junior season by New York Giants in first round (14th pick overall) of 2002 NFL draft. ... Signed by Giants (July 29, 2002).
HONORS: Played in Pro Bowl (2002 season). ... Named to play in Pro Bowl (2003 season); replaced by Bubba Franks due to injury.
SINGLE GAME HIGHS (regular season): Receptions—11 (October 5, 2003, vs. Miami); yards—116 (December 22, 2002, vs. Indianapolis); and touchdown receptions—1 (October 19, 2003, vs. Philadelphia).
STATISTICAL PLATEAUS: 100-yard receiving games: 2002 (2), 2003 (1). Total: 3.

			RECEIVING				TOTALS			
Year Team	G	GS	No.	Yds.	Avg.	TD	TD	2pt.	Pts.	Fum.
2002—New York Giants NFL	15	14	74	894	12.1	2	2	0	12	3
2003—New York Giants NFL	9	9	48	535	11.1	2	2	0	12	1
Pro totals (2 years)	24	23	122	1429	11.7	4	4	0	24	4

SHORT, BRANDON — LB — PANTHERS

PERSONAL: Born July 11, 1977, in McKeesport, Pa. ... 6-3/253. ... Full name: Brandon Darnell Short.
HIGH SCHOOL: McKeesport (Pa.).
COLLEGE: Penn State.
TRANSACTIONS/CAREER NOTES: Selected by New York Giants in fourth round (105th pick overall) of 2000 NFL draft. ... Signed by Giants (July 25, 2000). ... Granted free agency (February 28, 2003). ... Granted unconditional free agency (March 3, 2004). ... Signed by Carolina Panthers (March 24, 2004).
CHAMPIONSHIP GAME EXPERIENCE: Played in NFC championship game (2000 season). ... Played in Super Bowl 35 (2000 season).
HONORS: Named linebacker on THE SPORTING NEWS college All-America second team (1999).

Year Team	G	GS	TOTALS Tk.	Ast.	Sks.	INTERCEPTIONS No.	Yds.	Avg.	TD
2000—New York Giants NFL	11	0	3	0	0.0	0	0	0.0	0
2001—New York Giants NFL	16	16	45	15	1.0	1	21	21.0	0
2002—New York Giants NFL	16	15	62	25	3.0	1	32	32.0	0
2003—New York Giants NFL	16	12	49	26	3.0	0	0	0.0	0
Pro totals (4 years)	59	43	159	66	7.0	2	53	26.5	0

SIDNEY, DAINON CB LIONS

PERSONAL: Born May 30, 1975, in Atlanta, Ga. ... 6-0/197. ... Full name: Dainon Tarquinius Sidney. ... Name pronounced: DAY-nun.
HIGH SCHOOL: Riverdale (Ga.).
COLLEGE: Alabama-Birmingham.
TRANSACTIONS/CAREER NOTES: Selected by Tennessee Oilers in third round (77th pick overall) of 1998 NFL draft. ... Signed by Oilers (July 21, 1998). ... Oilers franchise renamed Tennessee Titans for 1999 season (December 26, 1998). ... Granted free agency (March 2, 2001). ... On injured reserve with knee injury (September 26, 2001-remainder of season). ... Granted unconditional free agency (March 1, 2002). ... Re-signed by Titans (March 12, 2002). ... Granted unconditional free agency (February 28, 2003). ... Signed by Buffalo Bills (April 10, 2003). ... Granted unconditional free agency (March 3, 2004). ... Signed by Detroit Lions (March 3, 2004).
CHAMPIONSHIP GAME EXPERIENCE: Played in AFC championship game (1999 and 2002 seasons). ... Played in Super Bowl 34 (1999 season).

Year Team	G	GS	TOTALS Tk.	Ast.	Sks.	INTERCEPTIONS No.	Yds.	Avg.	TD
1998—Tennessee NFL	16	1	15	1	0.0	0	0	0.0	0
1999—Tennessee NFL	16	2	33	5	0.0	3	12	4.0	0
2000—Tennessee NFL	11	2	16	3	0.0	3	19	6.3	0
2001—Tennessee NFL	1	1	0	0	0.0	0	0	0.0	0
2002—Tennessee NFL	4	0	0	0	0.0	0	0	0.0	0
2003—Buffalo NFL	2	0	2	0	0.0	0	0	0.0	0
Pro totals (6 years)	50	6	66	9	0.0	6	31	5.2	0

S

SIMMONS, ANTHONY LB SEAHAWKS

PERSONAL: Born June 20, 1976, in Spartanburg, S.C. ... 6-0/240.
HIGH SCHOOL: Spartanburg (S.C.).
COLLEGE: Clemson.
TRANSACTIONS/CAREER NOTES: Selected after junior season by Seattle Seahawks in first round (15th pick overall) of 1998 NFL draft. ... Signed by Seahawks (July 18, 1998). ... Granted unconditional free agency (February 28, 2003). ... Re-signed by Seahawks (March 4, 2003).
HONORS: Named inside linebacker on THE SPORTING NEWS college All-America first team (1996 and 1997).

Year Team	G	GS	TOTALS Tk.	Ast.	Sks.	INTERCEPTIONS No.	Yds.	Avg.	TD
1998—Seattle NFL	12	4	31	10	0.0	1	36	36.0	1
1999—Seattle NFL	16	16	57	35	0.0	0	0	0.0	0
2000—Seattle NFL	16	16	§119	28	4.0	2	15	7.5	0
2001—Seattle NFL	16	16	103	20	2.0	0	0	0.0	0
2002—Seattle NFL	7	7	35	11	1.0	2	19	9.5	0
2003—Seattle NFL	13	13	80	20	3.0	3	38	12.7	0
Pro totals (6 years)	80	72	425	124	10.0	8	108	13.5	1

SIMMONS, BRIAN LB BENGALS

PERSONAL: Born June 21, 1975, in New Bern, N.C. ... 6-3/244. ... Full name: Brian Eugene Simmons.
HIGH SCHOOL: New Bern (N.C.).
COLLEGE: North Carolina.
TRANSACTIONS/CAREER NOTES: Selected by Cincinnati Bengals in first round (17th pick overall) of 1998 NFL draft. ... Signed by Bengals (July 27, 1998). ... On injured reserve with knee injury (November 9, 2000-remainder of season).
HONORS: Named outside linebacker on THE SPORTING NEWS college All-America second team (1996). ... Named outside linebacker on THE SPORTING NEWS college All-America third team (1997).

Year Team	G	GS	TOTALS Tk.	Ast.	Sks.	INTERCEPTIONS No.	Yds.	Avg.	TD
1998—Cincinnati NFL	14	12	62	16	3.0	1	18	18.0	0
1999—Cincinnati NFL	16	16	90	20	3.0	0	0	0.0	0
2000—Cincinnati NFL	1	1	7	2	1.0	0	0	0.0	0
2001—Cincinnati NFL	16	16	52	32	6.5	1	5	5.0	0
2002—Cincinnati NFL	16	15	65	21	3.0	1	51	51.0	1
2003—Cincinnati NFL	16	16	73	30	1.5	2	14	7.0	0
Pro totals (6 years)	79	76	349	121	18.0	5	88	17.6	1

SIMMONS, JASON CB TEXANS

PERSONAL: Born March 30, 1976, in Inglewood, Calif. ... 5-9/198. ... Full name: Jason Lawrence Simmons.
HIGH SCHOOL: Leuzinger (Lawndale, Calif.).
COLLEGE: Arizona State.
TRANSACTIONS/CAREER NOTES: Selected by Pittsburgh Steelers in fifth round (137th pick overall) of 1998 NFL draft. ... Signed by Steelers (July 14, 1998). ... Granted free agency (March 2, 2001). ... Re-signed by Steelers (April 26, 2001). ... Granted unconditional free agency

(March 1, 2002). ... Signed by Houston Texans (April 8, 2002). ... Granted unconditional free agency (February 28, 2003). ... Re-signed by Texans (March 21, 2003). ... Granted unconditional free agency (March 3, 2004). ... Re-signed by Texans (March 11, 2004).
CHAMPIONSHIP GAME EXPERIENCE: Played in AFC championship game (2001 season).

			TOTALS			INTERCEPTIONS			
Year Team	**G**	**GS**	**Tk.**	**Ast.**	**Sks.**	**No.**	**Yds.**	**Avg.**	**TD**
1998—Pittsburgh NFL	6	0	7	1	0.0	0	0	0.0	0
1999—Pittsburgh NFL	16	0	3	1	0.0	0	0	0.0	0
2000—Pittsburgh NFL	15	0	12	1	0.0	0	0	0.0	0
2001—Pittsburgh NFL	12	0	4	1	0.0	0	0	0.0	0
2002—Houston NFL	15	0	7	1	1.0	0	0	0.0	0
2003—Houston NFL	16	2	18	4	0.0	0	0	0.0	0
Pro totals (6 years)	80	2	51	9	1.0	0	0	0.0	0

SIMMONS, KENDALL — G — STEELERS

PERSONAL: Born March 11, 1979, in Ripley, Miss. ... 6-3/313. ... Full name: Henry Alexander Kendall Simmons.
HIGH SCHOOL: Ripley (Miss.).
COLLEGE: Auburn.
TRANSACTIONS/CAREER NOTES: Selected by Pittsburgh Steelers in first round (30th pick overall) of 2002 NFL draft. ... Signed by Steelers (July 26, 2002).
PLAYING EXPERIENCE: Pittsburgh NFL, 2002-2003. ... Games/Games started: 2002 (14/14), 2003 (16/16). Total: 30/30.

S

SIMMONS, SAM — WR — DOLPHINS

PERSONAL: Born November 25, 1979, in Kansas City, Kan. ... 5-9/200. ... Full name: Samuel Leeland Simmons.
HIGH SCHOOL: F.L. Schlagle (Kansas City, Kan.).
COLLEGE: Northwestern.
TRANSACTIONS/CAREER NOTES: Selected by Miami Dolphins in fifth round (170th pick overall) of 2002 NFL draft. ... Signed by Dolphins (July 25, 2002). ... Released by Dolphins (August 25, 2002). ... Re-signed by Dolphins to practice squad (September 2, 2002). ... On injured reserve with ankle injury (November 25, 2003-remainder of season).

			RUSHING				RECEIVING				PUNT RETURNS				KICKOFF RETURNS				TOTALS		
Year Team	**G**	**GS**	**Att.**	**Yds.**	**Avg.**	**TD**	**No.**	**Yds.**	**Avg.**	**TD**	**No.**	**Yds.**	**Avg.**	**TD**	**No.**	**Yds.**	**Avg.**	**TD**	**TD**	**2pt.**	**Pts.**
2003—Mia. NFL	11	0	0	0	0.0	0	0	0	0.0	0	8	100	12.5	0	3	64	21.3	0	0	0	0

SIMON, COREY — DT — EAGLES

PERSONAL: Born March 2, 1977, in Boynton Beach, Fla. ... 6-2/293.
HIGH SCHOOL: Ely (Pompano Beach, Fla.).
COLLEGE: Florida State.
TRANSACTIONS/CAREER NOTES: Selected by Philadelphia Eagles in first round (sixth pick overall) of 2000 NFL draft. ... Signed by Eagles (July 28, 2000).
CHAMPIONSHIP GAME EXPERIENCE: Played in NFC championship game (2001-2003 seasons).
HONORS: Named defensive tackle on THE SPORTING NEWS college All-America first team (1999). ... Played in Pro Bowl (2003 season).

			TOTALS		
Year Team	**G**	**GS**	**Tk.**	**Ast.**	**Sks.**
2000—Philadelphia NFL	16	16	38	13	9.5
2001—Philadelphia NFL	16	16	39	11	7.5
2002—Philadelphia NFL	14	14	32	7	2.0
2003—Philadelphia NFL	16	16	32	8	7.5
Pro totals (4 years)	62	62	141	39	26.5

SIMON, JOHN — RB — REDSKINS

PERSONAL: Born December 11, 1978, in Baton Rouge, La. ... 5-11/202. ... Full name: John Ray Simon Jr.
HIGH SCHOOL: Lab (Baton Rouge, La.).
COLLEGE: Louisiana Tech.
TRANSACTIONS/CAREER NOTES: Signed as non-drafted free agent by Tennessee Titans (April 22, 2002). ... Waived by Titans (August 31, 2003). ... Signed by Washington Redskins (November 4, 2003). ... Released by Redskins (November 28, 2003). ... Re-signed by Redskins (December 2, 2003).
CHAMPIONSHIP GAME EXPERIENCE: Played in AFC championship game (2002 season).
SINGLE GAME HIGHS (regular season): Attempts—4 (September 29, 2002, vs. Oakland); yards—11 (September 29, 2002, vs. Oakland); and rushing touchdowns—1 (September 29, 2002, vs. Oakland).

			RUSHING				RECEIVING				PUNT RETURNS				KICKOFF RETURNS				TOTALS		
Year Team	**G**	**GS**	**Att.**	**Yds.**	**Avg.**	**TD**	**No.**	**Yds.**	**Avg.**	**TD**	**No.**	**Yds.**	**Avg.**	**TD**	**No.**	**Yds.**	**Avg.**	**TD**	**TD**	**2pt.**	**Pts.**
2002—Ten. NFL	12	0	9	18	2.0	1	16	167	10.4	3	13	113	8.7	0	20	371	18.6	0	4	0	24
2003—Was. NFL	4	0	3	9	3.0	0	3	21	7.0	0	0	0	0.0	0	1	21	21.0	0	0	0	0
Pro totals (2 years)	16	0	12	27	2.3	1	19	188	9.9	3	13	113	8.7	0	21	392	18.7	0	4	0	24

SIMONEAU, MARK — LB — EAGLES

PERSONAL: Born January 16, 1977, in Phillipsburg, Kan. ... 6-0/234.
HIGH SCHOOL: Smith Center (Kan.).
COLLEGE: Kansas State.

TRANSACTIONS/CAREER NOTES: Selected by Atlanta Falcons in third round (67th pick overall) of 2000 NFL draft. ... Signed by Falcons (May 17, 2000). ... Granted free agency (February 28, 2003). ... Traded by Falcons to Philadelphia Eagles for sixth-round pick (DB Waine Bacon) in 2003 draft and fourth-round pick (traded to Indianapolis) in 2004 draft (March 4, 2003).
CHAMPIONSHIP GAME EXPERIENCE: Played in NFC championship game (2003 season).
HONORS: Named linebacker on THE SPORTING NEWS college All-America first team (1999).

			TOTALS			INTERCEPTIONS			
Year Team	G	GS	Tk.	Ast.	Sks.	No.	Yds.	Avg.	TD
2000—Atlanta NFL	14	4	36	11	0.5	0	0	0.0	0
2001—Atlanta NFL	16	5	25	6	0.0	0	0	0.0	0
2002—Atlanta NFL	15	0	6	1	0.0	0	0	0.0	0
2003—Philadelphia NFL	16	16	79	22	2.0	0	0	0.0	0
Pro totals (4 years)	61	25	146	40	2.5	0	0	0.0	0

SIMONTON, KEN — RB — BILLS

PERSONAL: Born June 7, 1979, in Pittsburg, Calif. ... 5-8/191.
HIGH SCHOOL: Pittsburg (Calif.).
COLLEGE: Oregon State.
TRANSACTIONS/CAREER NOTES: Signed as non-drafted free agent by Buffalo Bills (January 24, 2003).
SINGLE GAME HIGHS (regular season): Attempts—2 (September 28, 2003, vs. Philadelphia); yards—4 (September 28, 2003, vs. Philadelphia),

			RUSHING				TOTALS			
Year Team	G	GS	Att.	Yds.	Avg.	TD	TD	2pt.	Pts.	Fum.
2003—Buffalo NFL	2	0	2	4	2.0	0	0	0	0	0

S

SIMS, BARRY — T — RAIDERS

PERSONAL: Born December 1, 1974, in Park City, Utah. ... 6-5/300.
HIGH SCHOOL: Park City (Utah).
JUNIOR COLLEGE: Dixie College (Utah).
COLLEGE: Utah.
TRANSACTIONS/CAREER NOTES: Selected by Scottish Claymores in 1999 NFL Europe draft (February 23, 1999). ... Signed as non-drafted free agent by Oakland Raiders (July, 1999).
PLAYING EXPERIENCE: Oakland NFL, 1999-2003. ... Games/Games started: 1999 (16/10), 2000 (16/8), 2001 (15/15), 2002 (15/15), 2003 (16/16). Total: 78/64.
CHAMPIONSHIP GAME EXPERIENCE: Played in AFC championship game (2000 and 2002 seasons). ... Played in Super Bowl 37 (2002 season).

SIMS, RYAN — DT — CHIEFS

PERSONAL: Born May 4, 1980, in Spartanburg, S.C. ... 6-4/315. ... Full name: Ryan O'Neal Sims.
HIGH SCHOOL: Paul M. Dorman (Spartanburg, S.C.).
COLLEGE: North Carolina.
TRANSACTIONS/CAREER NOTES: Selected by Kansas City Chiefs in first round (sixth pick overall) of 2002 NFL draft. ... Signed by Chiefs (August 28, 2002). ... On injured reserve with elbow injury (October 17, 2002-remainder of season).

			TOTALS			INTERCEPTIONS			
Year Team	G	GS	Tk.	Ast.	Sks.	No.	Yds.	Avg.	TD
2002—Kansas City NFL	6	2	5	1	0.0	0	0	0.0	0
2003—Kansas City NFL	16	16	35	4	3.0	1	8	8.0	0
Pro totals (2 years)	22	18	40	5	3.0	1	8	8.0	0

SINGLETON, ALSHERMOND — LB — COWBOYS

PERSONAL: Born August 7, 1975, in Newark, N.J. ... 6-2/228. ... Full name: Alshermond Glendale Singleton.
HIGH SCHOOL: Irvington (N.J.).
COLLEGE: Temple.
TRANSACTIONS/CAREER NOTES: Selected by Tampa Bay Buccaneers in fourth round (128th pick overall) of 1997 NFL draft. ... Signed by Buccaneers (July 17, 1997). ... Granted unconditional free agency (February 28, 2003). ... Signed by Dallas Cowboys (March 13, 2003).
CHAMPIONSHIP GAME EXPERIENCE: Member of Buccaneers for NFC championship game (1999 season); inactive. ... Played in NFC championship game (2002 season). ... Member of Super Bowl championship team (2002 season).

			TOTALS			INTERCEPTIONS			
Year Team	G	GS	Tk.	Ast.	Sks.	No.	Yds.	Avg.	TD
1997—Tampa Bay NFL	12	0	0	0	0.0	0	0	0.0	0
1998—Tampa Bay NFL	15	0	11	4	0.0	0	0	0.0	0
1999—Tampa Bay NFL	15	0	13	8	0.5	1	7	7.0	0
2000—Tampa Bay NFL	13	1	16	6	0.0	0	0	0.0	0
2001—Tampa Bay NFL	16	0	17	4	1.0	0	0	0.0	0
2002—Tampa Bay NFL	16	14	40	18	1.0	1	0	0.0	0
2003—Dallas NFL	16	15	32	9	1.0	2	42	21.0	1
Pro totals (7 years)	103	30	129	49	3.5	4	49	12.3	1

SIRMON, PETER — LB — TITANS

PERSONAL: Born February 18, 1977, in Walla Walla, Wash. ... 6-2/237. ... Full name: Peter Anton Sirmon.
HIGH SCHOOL: Walla Walla (Wash.).
COLLEGE: Oregon.
TRANSACTIONS/CAREER NOTES: Selected by Tennessee Titans in fourth round (128th pick overall) of 2000 NFL draft. ... Signed by Titans (July 11, 2000). ... Granted free agency (February 28, 2003). ... Re-signed by Titans (April 17, 2003).
CHAMPIONSHIP GAME EXPERIENCE: Played in AFC championship game (2002 season).

			TOTALS			INTERCEPTIONS			
Year Team	G	GS	Tk.	Ast.	Sks.	No.	Yds.	Avg.	TD
2000—Tennessee NFL	5	0	0	0	0.0	0	0	0.0	0
2001—Tennessee NFL	16	0	0	0	0.0	0	0	0.0	0
2002—Tennessee NFL	16	11	72	21	2.0	3	88	29.3	1
2003—Tennessee NFL	14	14	63	23	0.0	0	0	0.0	0
Pro totals (4 years)	51	25	135	44	2.0	3	88	29.3	1

SLAUGHTER, CHAD — T — RAIDERS

PERSONAL: Born June 4, 1978, in Dallas, Texas. ... 6-8/340.
HIGH SCHOOL: Kimball (Dallas).
COLLEGE: Alcorn State.
TRANSACTIONS/CAREER NOTES: Signed as non-drafted free agent by Dallas Cowboys (April 18, 2000). ... Claimed on waivers by New York Jets (August 22, 2000). ... Inactive for 16 games (2000). ... Claimed on waivers by Cowboys (August, 2001). ... Released by Cowboys (2001). ... Signed by Oakland Raiders to practice squad (February 7, 2002). ... Activated (February 24, 2002). ... Inactive for 16 games (2002). ... Granted restricted free agency (March 3, 2004). ... Re-signed by Raiders (March 19, 2004).
PLAYING EXPERIENCE: Oakland NFL, 2003. ... Games/Games started: 2003 (6/1). Total: 6/1.

SLAUGHTER, T.J. — LB — RAVENS

PERSONAL: Born February 20, 1977, in Birmingham, Ala. ... 6-0/234. ... Full name: Tavaris Jermell Slaughter.
HIGH SCHOOL: John Carroll (Birmingham, Ala.).
COLLEGE: Southern Mississippi.
TRANSACTIONS/CAREER NOTES: Selected by Jacksonville Jaguars in third round (92nd pick overall) of 2000 NFL draft. ... Signed by Jaguars (May 16, 2000). ... On suspended list for violating league substance abuse policy (September 6-October 7, 2002). ... On injured reserve with knee injury (December 8, 2001-remainder of season). ... Granted free agency (February 28, 2003). ... Re-signed by Jaguars (May 15, 2003). ... Released by Jaguars (October 28, 2003). ... Signed by Green Bay Packers (November 11, 2003). ... Released by Packers (December 9, 2003). ... Signed by Baltimore Ravens (December 17, 2003).

			TOTALS			INTERCEPTIONS			
Year Team	G	GS	Tk.	Ast.	Sks.	No.	Yds.	Avg.	TD
2000—Jacksonville NFL	16	7	38	16	0.0	0	0	0.0	0
2001—Jacksonville NFL	9	8	41	13	1.0	0	0	0.0	0
2002—Jacksonville NFL	11	11	39	20	0.0	0	0	0.0	0
2003—Jacksonville NFL	6	3	16	3	1.0	0	0	0.0	0
—Green Bay NFL	1	0	0	0	0.0	0	0	0.0	0
—Baltimore NFL	1	0	0	0	0.0	0	0	0.0	0
Pro totals (4 years)	44	29	134	52	2.0	0	0	0.0	0

SLECHTA, JEREMY — DT — TEXANS

PERSONAL: Born May 12, 1980, in LaVista, Neb. ... 6-6/285.
HIGH SCHOOL: Papillion-LaVista (LaVista, Neb.).
COLLEGE: Nebraska.
TRANSACTIONS/CAREER NOTES: Signed as non-drafted free agent by Philadelphia Eagles (April 23, 2002). ... Released by Eagles (September 1, 2002). ... Re-signed by Eagles to practice squad (September 3, 2002). ... Activated (September 26, 2002). ... Released by Eagles (August 31, 2003). ... Signed by Houston Texans (December 3, 2003).
CHAMPIONSHIP GAME EXPERIENCE: Played in NFC championship game (2002 season).

			TOTALS		
Year Team	G	GS	Tk.	Ast.	Sks.
2002—Philadelphia NFL	13	0	2	2	0.0
2003—Houston NFL	2	0	2	0	0.0
Pro totals (2 years)	15	0	4	2	0.0

SLOAN, DAVID — TE

PERSONAL: Born June 8, 1972, in Fresno, Calif. ... 6-6/260. ... Full name: David Lyle Sloan.
HIGH SCHOOL: Sierra Joint Union (Tollhouse, Calif.).
JUNIOR COLLEGE: Fresno (Calif.) City College.
COLLEGE: New Mexico.
TRANSACTIONS/CAREER NOTES: Selected by Detroit Lions in third round (70th pick overall) of 1995 NFL draft. ... Signed by Lions (July 20, 1995). ... Granted free agency (February 13, 1998). ... Re-signed by Lions (June 10, 1998). ... On physically unable to perform list with knee injury (August 25-October 23, 1998). ... Granted unconditional free agency (February 12, 1999). ... Re-signed by Lions (March 24, 1999). ... Granted unconditional free agency (March 1, 2002). ... Signed by New Orleans Saints (April 3, 2002). ... Released by Saints (August 31, 2003). ... Re-signed by Saints (December 3, 2003). ... Granted unconditional free agency (March 3, 2004).

HONORS: Played in Pro Bowl (1999 season).
SINGLE GAME HIGHS (regular season): Receptions—7 (November 14, 1999, vs. Arizona); yards—88 (November 14, 1999, vs. Arizona); and touchdown receptions—2 (December 23, 2001, vs. Pittsburgh).

			RECEIVING				TOTALS			
Year Team	G	GS	No.	Yds.	Avg.	TD	TD	2pt.	Pts.	Fum.
1995—Detroit NFL	16	7	17	184	10.8	1	1	0	6	0
1996—Detroit NFL	4	4	7	51	7.3	0	0	0	0	0
1997—Detroit NFL	14	12	29	264	9.1	0	0	0	0	0
1998—Detroit NFL	10	2	11	146	13.3	1	1	0	6	0
1999—Detroit NFL	16	15	47	591	12.6	4	4	0	24	0
2000—Detroit NFL	15	10	32	379	11.8	2	2	0	12	0
2001—Detroit NFL	15	15	37	409	11.1	7	7	0	42	0
2002—New Orleans NFL	16	14	12	127	10.6	0	0	0	0	0
2003—New Orleans NFL	4	0	0	0	0.0	0	0	0	0	0
Pro totals (9 years)	110	79	192	2151	11.2	15	15	0	90	0

SMART, ROD — RB — PANTHERS

PERSONAL: Born January 9, 1977, in Lakeland, Fla. ... 5-11/201.
HIGH SCHOOL: Lakeland (Fla.).
COLLEGE: Western Kentucky.
TRANSACTIONS/CAREER NOTES: Signed as non-drafted free agent by San Diego Chargers (May 19, 2000). ... Released by Chargers (June 9, 2000). ... Signed by Philadelphia Eagles to practice squad (October 2, 2001). ... Activated (November 19, 2001). ... On injured reserve with foot injury (January 8, 2002-remainder of season). ... Claimed on waivers by Carolina Panthers (September 2, 2002). ... Granted free agency (March 3, 2004). ... Re-signed by Panthers (March 17, 2004).
CHAMPIONSHIP GAME EXPERIENCE: Played in NFC championship game (2003 season). ... Played in Super Bowl 38 (2003 season).
SINGLE GAME HIGHS (regular season): Attempts—9 (December 21, 2003, vs. Detroit); yards—24 (December 21, 2003, vs. Detroit); and rushing touchdowns—0.

			RUSHING				RECEIVING				KICKOFF RETURNS				TOTALS			
Year Team	G	GS	Att.	Yds.	Avg.	TD	No.	Yds.	Avg.	TD	No.	Yds.	Avg.	TD	TD	2pt.	Pts.	Fum.
2001—Philadelphia NFL	6	0	2	6	3.0	0	0	0	0.0	0	0	0	0.0	0	0	0	0	0
2002—Carolina NFL	16	0	1	2	2.0	0	0	0	0.0	0	0	0	0.0	0	0	0	0	0
2003—Carolina NFL	16	0	20	49	2.5	0	3	11	3.7	0	41	947	23.1	1	1	0	6	2
Pro totals (3 years)	38	0	23	57	2.5	0	3	11	3.7	0	41	947	23.1	1	1	0	6	2

SMITH, AARON — DE — STEELERS

PERSONAL: Born April 9, 1976, in Colorado Springs, Colo. ... 6-5/300. ... Full name: Aaron Douglas Smith.
HIGH SCHOOL: Sierra (Colorado Springs, Colo.).
COLLEGE: Northern Colorado.
TRANSACTIONS/CAREER NOTES: Selected by Pittsburgh Steelers in fourth round (109th pick overall) of 1999 NFL draft. ... Signed by Steelers (August 3, 1999). ... Granted free agency (March 1, 2002). ... Re-signed by Steelers (July 25, 2002).
CHAMPIONSHIP GAME EXPERIENCE: Played in AFC championship game (2001 season).

			TOTALS		
Year Team	G	GS	Tk.	Ast.	Sks.
1999—Pittsburgh NFL	6	0	1	1	0.0
2000—Pittsburgh NFL	16	15	27	15	4.0
2001—Pittsburgh NFL	16	16	23	6	8.0
2002—Pittsburgh NFL	16	16	53	17	5.5
2003—Pittsburgh NFL	16	16	36	9	2.0
Pro totals (5 years)	70	63	140	48	19.5

SMITH, ANTOWAIN — RB

PERSONAL: Born March 14, 1972, in Millbrook, Ala. ... 6-2/232. ... Full name: Antowain Drurell Smith. ... Name pronounced: AN-twan.
HIGH SCHOOL: Elmore (Ala.).
JUNIOR COLLEGE: East Mississippi Junior College.
COLLEGE: Houston.
TRANSACTIONS/CAREER NOTES: Selected by Buffalo Bills in first round (23rd pick overall) of 1997 NFL draft. ... Signed by Bills (July 11, 1997). ... Released by Bills (May 18, 2001). ... Signed by New England Patriots (June 7, 2001). ... Granted unconditional free agency (March 1, 2002). ... Re-signed by Patriots (March 1, 2002). ... Granted unconditional free agency (March 3, 2004).
CHAMPIONSHIP GAME EXPERIENCE: Played in AFC championship game (2001 and 2003 seasons). ... Member of Super Bowl championship team (2001 and 2003 seasons).
SINGLE GAME HIGHS (regular season): Attempts—31 (October 11, 1998, vs. Indianapolis); yards—156 (December 22, 2001, vs. Miami); and rushing touchdowns—3 (December 23, 2000, vs. Seattle).
STATISTICAL PLATEAUS: 100-yard rushing games: 1997 (1), 1998 (3), 1999 (2), 2000 (1), 2001 (4), 2002 (1), 2003 (1). Total: 13.

			RUSHING				RECEIVING				TOTALS			
Year Team	G	GS	Att.	Yds.	Avg.	TD	No.	Yds.	Avg.	TD	TD	2pt.	Pts.	Fum.
1997—Buffalo NFL	16	0	194	840	4.3	8	28	177	6.3	0	8	0	48	4
1998—Buffalo NFL	16	14	300	1124	3.7	8	5	11	2.2	0	8	0	48	5
1999—Buffalo NFL	14	11	165	614	3.7	6	2	32	16.0	0	6	0	36	4
2000—Buffalo NFL	11	3	101	354	3.5	4	3	20	6.7	0	4	0	24	1
2001—New England NFL	16	15	287	1157	4.0	12	19	192	10.1	1	13	0	78	4
2002—New England NFL	16	15	252	982	3.9	6	31	243	7.8	2	8	1	50	2
2003—New England NFL	13	6	182	642	3.5	3	14	92	6.6	0	3	0	18	1
Pro totals (7 years)	102	64	1481	5713	3.9	47	102	767	7.5	3	50	1	302	21

SMITH, BRADY — DE — FALCONS

PERSONAL: Born June 5, 1973, in Royal Oak, Mich. ... 6-5/274. ... Full name: Brady McKay Smith. ... Son of Steve Smith, offensive tackle with four NFL teams (1966-74).

HIGH SCHOOL: Barrington (Ill.).

COLLEGE: Colorado State.

TRANSACTIONS/CAREER NOTES: Selected by New Orleans Saints in third round (70th pick overall) of 1996 NFL draft. ... Signed by Saints (July 12, 1996). ... Granted free agency (February 12, 1999). ... Re-signed by Saints (April 14, 1999). ... Granted unconditional free agency (February 11, 2000). ... Signed by Atlanta Falcons (February 19, 2000).

			TOTALS		
Year Team	**G**	**GS**	**Tk.**	**Ast.**	**Sks.**
1996—New Orleans NFL	16	4	15	2	2.0
1997—New Orleans NFL	16	2	22	8	5.0
1998—New Orleans NFL	14	5	10	2	0.0
1999—New Orleans NFL	16	16	26	7	6.0
2000—Atlanta NFL	15	14	29	5	4.5
2001—Atlanta NFL	15	15	26	8	8.0
2002—Atlanta NFL	14	14	26	13	6.5
2003—Atlanta NFL	16	14	24	1	4.0
Pro totals (8 years)	122	84	178	46	36.0

SMITH, BRENT — G/T — JETS

PERSONAL: Born November 21, 1973, in Dallas, Texas. ... 6-5/305. ... Full name: Gary Brent Smith.

HIGH SCHOOL: Pontotoc (Miss.).

COLLEGE: Mississippi State.

TRANSACTIONS/CAREER NOTES: Selected by Miami Dolphins in third round (96th pick overall) of 1997 NFL draft. ... Signed by Dolphins (July 8, 1997). ... Active for two games (1997); did not play. ... Granted free agency (February 11, 2000). ... Re-signed by Dolphins (June 9, 2000). ... On injured reserve with knee injury (July 28, 2001-entire season). ... On injured reserve with knee injury (August 27, 2002-entire season). ... Granted unconditional free agency (February 28, 2003). ... Signed by New York Jets (May 6, 2003). ... Granted unconditional free agency (March 3, 2004). ... Re-signed by Jets (March 5, 2004).

PLAYING EXPERIENCE: Miami NFL, 1998-2000; New York Jets NFL, 2003. ... Games/Games started: 1998 (8/7), 1999 (13/4), 2000 (16/2), 2003 (16/16). Total: 53/29.

SMITH, BRUCE — DE

PERSONAL: Born June 18, 1963, in Norfolk, Va. ... 6-4/262. ... Full name: Bruce Bernard Smith.

HIGH SCHOOL: Booker T. Washington (Norfolk, Va.).

COLLEGE: Virginia Tech.

TRANSACTIONS/CAREER NOTES: Selected by Baltimore Stars in 1985 USFL territorial draft. ... Signed by Buffalo Bills (February 28, 1985). ... Selected officially by Bills in first round (first pick overall) of 1985 NFL draft. ... On non-football injury list with substance abuse problem (September 2-28, 1988). ... Granted free agency (February 1, 1989). ... Tendered offer sheet by Denver Broncos (March 23, 1989). ... Offer matched by Bills (March 29, 1989). ... On injured reserve with knee injury (October 12-November 30, 1991). ... Released by Bills (February 10, 2000). ... Signed by Washington Redskins (February 14, 2000). ... Released by Redskins (February 24, 2004).

CHAMPIONSHIP GAME EXPERIENCE: Played in AFC championship game (1988 and 1990-1993 seasons). ... Played in Super Bowl 25 (1990 season), Super Bowl 26 (1991 season), Super Bowl 27 (1992 season) and Super Bowl 28 (1993 season).

HONORS: Named defensive lineman on THE SPORTING NEWS college All-America second team (1983 and 1984). ... Outland Trophy winner (1984). ... Named defensive end on THE SPORTING NEWS NFL All-Pro team (1987, 1988, 1990 and 1992-1997). ... Played in Pro Bowl (1987-1990, 1994, 1995, 1997 and 1998 seasons). ... Named Outstanding Player of Pro Bowl (1987 season). ... Named to play in Pro Bowl (1992 season); replaced by Howie Long due to injury. ... Named to play in Pro Bowl (1993 season); replaced by Sean Jones due to injury. ... Named to play in Pro Bowl (1996 season); replaced by Willie McGinest due to injury.

RECORDS: Holds NFL career record for most sacks (200).

POST SEASON RECORDS: Shares Super Bowl single-game record for most safeties—1 (January 27, 1991, vs. New York Giants). ... Holds NFL postseason career record for most sacks—14.5. ... Shares NFL postseason single-game record for most safeties—1 (January 27, 1991, vs. New York Giants).

MISCELLANEOUS: Active NFL leader for career sacks (200). ... Holds Buffalo Bills all-time record for most sacks (171).

			TOTALS			INTERCEPTIONS			
Year Team	**G**	**GS**	**Tk.**	**Ast.**	**Sks.**	**No.**	**Yds.**	**Avg.**	**TD**
1985—Buffalo NFL	16	13	32	16	6.5	0	0	0.0	0
1986—Buffalo NFL	16	15	36	27	15.0	0	0	0.0	0
1987—Buffalo NFL	12	12	60	18	12.0	0	0	0.0	0
1988—Buffalo NFL	12	12	39	17	11.0	0	0	0.0	0
1989—Buffalo NFL	16	16	66	22	13.0	0	0	0.0	0
1990—Buffalo NFL	16	16	82	19	19.0	0	0	0.0	0
1991—Buffalo NFL	5	5	13	5	1.5	0	0	0.0	0
1992—Buffalo NFL	15	15	66	23	14.0	0	0	0.0	0
1993—Buffalo NFL	16	16	87	21	14.0	1	0	0.0	0
1994—Buffalo NFL	15	15	57	24	10.0	1	0	0.0	0
1995—Buffalo NFL	15	15	52	22	10.5	0	0	0.0	0
1996—Buffalo NFL	16	16	69	21	▲13.5	0	0	0.0	0
1997—Buffalo NFL	16	16	49	16	§14.0	0	0	0.0	0
1998—Buffalo NFL	15	15	35	15	10.0	0	0	0.0	0
1999—Buffalo NFL	16	16	30	15	7.0	0	0	0.0	0
2000—Washington NFL	16	16	50	8	10.0	0	0	0.0	0
2001—Washington NFL	14	14	31	11	5.0	0	0	0.0	0
2002—Washington NFL	16	16	37	12	9.0	0	0	0.0	0
2003—Washington NFL	16	8	17	5	5.0	0	0	0.0	0
Pro totals (19 years)	279	267	908	317	200.0	2	0	0.0	0

SMITH, CLIFTON LB REDSKINS

PERSONAL: Born July 21, 1980, in Freeport, N.Y. ... 6-3/255.
HIGH SCHOOL: Freeport (N.Y.).
COLLEGE: Syracuse.
TRANSACTIONS/CAREER NOTES: Signed as non-drafted free agent by Washington Redskins (May 2, 2003). ... Waived by Redskins (August 31, 2003). ... Re-signed by Redskins to practice squad (September 2, 2003). ... Activated (December 10, 2003).

			TOTALS			INTERCEPTIONS			
Year Team	G	GS	Tk.	Ast.	Sks.	No.	Yds.	Avg.	TD
2003—Washington NFL	1	0	0	1	0.0	0	0	0.0	0

SMITH, COREY DE BUCCANEERS

PERSONAL: Born November 2, 1979, in Richmond, Va. ... 6-2/250. ... Full name: Corey Dominique Smith.
HIGH SCHOOL: John Marshall (Richmond, Va.).
COLLEGE: North Carolina State.
TRANSACTIONS/CAREER NOTES: Signed as non-drafted free agent by Tampa Bay Buccaneers (April 22, 2002). ... On injured reserve with knee injury (November 28, 2002-remainder of season). ... Released by Buccaneers (August 31, 2003). ... Re-signed by Buccaneers to practice squad (December 9, 2003). ... Activated (December 22, 2003). ... Assigned by Buccaneers to Berlin Thunder in 2004 NFL Europe enhancement allocation program (February 9, 2004).

			TOTALS		
Year Team	G	GS	Tk.	Ast.	Sks.
2002—Tampa Bay NFL	6	0	1	0	1.0
2003—Tampa Bay NFL	1	0	0	0	0.0
Pro totals (2 years)	7	0	1	0	1.0

S

SMITH, DARRIN LB SAINTS

PERSONAL: Born April 15, 1970, in Miami, Fla. ... 6-1/236. ... Full name: Darrin Andrew Smith.
HIGH SCHOOL: Miami Norland.
COLLEGE: Miami (Fla.).
TRANSACTIONS/CAREER NOTES: Selected by Dallas Cowboys in second round (54th pick overall) of 1993 NFL draft. ... Signed by Cowboys (July 21, 1993). ... On reserve/did not report list (July 20-October 14, 1995). ... Granted free agency (February 16, 1996). ... Re-signed by Cowboys (June 17, 1996). ... Granted unconditional free agency (February 14, 1997). ... Signed by Philadelphia Eagles (April 19, 1997). ... On injured reserve with ankle injury (November 19, 1997-remainder of season). ... Granted unconditional free agency (February 13, 1998). ... Signed by Seattle Seahawks (February 19, 1998). ... Released by Seahawks (February 10, 2000). ... Signed by New Orleans Saints (July 16, 2000). ... Granted unconditional free agency (March 2, 2001). ... Re-signed by Saints (April 10, 2001).
CHAMPIONSHIP GAME EXPERIENCE: Played in NFC championship game (1993 and 1995 seasons). ... Member of Super Bowl championship team (1993 and 1995 seasons).

			TOTALS			INTERCEPTIONS			
Year Team	G	GS	Tk.	Ast.	Sks.	No.	Yds.	Avg.	TD
1993—Dallas NFL	16	13	49	44	1.0	0	0	0.0	0
1994—Dallas NFL	16	16	46	21	4.0	2	13	6.5	1
1995—Dallas NFL	9	9	40	6	3.0	0	0	0.0	0
1996—Dallas NFL	16	16	54	27	1.0	0	0	0.0	0
1997—Philadelphia NFL	7	7	9	4	1.0	0	0	0.0	0
1998—Seattle NFL	13	12	59	21	5.0	3	56	18.7	▲2
1999—Seattle NFL	15	15	65	25	1.0	1	0	0.0	0
2000—New Orleans NFL	16	11	61	30	2.0	2	56	28.0	1
2001—New Orleans NFL	16	16	49	17	1.5	0	0	0.0	0
2002—New Orleans NFL	15	15	63	33	3.5	2	21	10.5	0
2003—New Orleans NFL	14	10	44	16	1.0	1	9	9.0	0
Pro totals (11 years)	153	140	539	244	24.0	11	155	14.1	4

SMITH, DEREK LB 49ERS

PERSONAL: Born January 18, 1975, in American Fork, Utah. ... 6-2/245. ... Full name: Derek Mecham Smith.
HIGH SCHOOL: American Fork (Utah).
JUNIOR COLLEGE: Snow College (Utah).
COLLEGE: Arizona State.
TRANSACTIONS/CAREER NOTES: Selected by Washington Redskins in third round (80th pick overall) of 1997 NFL draft. ... Signed by Redskins (July 11, 1997). ... Granted free agency (February 11, 2000). ... Re-signed by Redskins (April 11, 2000). ... Granted unconditional free agency (March 2, 2001). ... Signed by San Francisco 49ers (March 23, 2001).

			TOTALS			INTERCEPTIONS			
Year Team	G	GS	Tk.	Ast.	Sks.	No.	Yds.	Avg.	TD
1997—Washington NFL	16	16	59	28	2.0	0	0	0.0	0
1998—Washington NFL	16	15	78	25	0.5	0	0	0.0	0
1999—Washington NFL	16	16	66	28	1.0	1	0	0.0	0
2000—Washington NFL	16	14	71	17	1.0	0	0	0.0	0
2001—San Francisco NFL	14	14	78	30	3.0	1	0	0.0	0
2002—San Francisco NFL	16	16	83	29	1.0	0	0	0.0	0
2003—San Francisco NFL	16	16	85	27	3.5	0	0	0.0	0
Pro totals (7 years)	110	107	520	184	12.0	2	0	0.0	0

SMITH, DETRON — RB

PERSONAL: Born February 25, 1974, in Dallas, Texas. ... 5-10/229. ... Full name: Detron Negil Smith. ... Name pronounced: DEE-tron.
HIGH SCHOOL: Lake Highlands (Dallas).
COLLEGE: Texas A&M.
TRANSACTIONS/CAREER NOTES: Selected by Denver Broncos in third round (65th pick overall) of 1996 NFL draft. ... Signed by Broncos (July 20, 1996). ... Released by Broncos (February 27, 2002). ... Signed by Jacksonville Jaguars (April 8, 2002). ... Released by Jaguars (September 1, 2002). ... Signed by Indianapolis Colts (September 3, 2002). ... Re-signed by Colts (March 4, 2003). ... On injured reserve with knee injury (December 2, 2003-remainder of season). ... Released by Colts (February 27, 2004).
CHAMPIONSHIP GAME EXPERIENCE: Played in AFC championship game (1997 and 1998 seasons). ... Member of Super Bowl championship team (1997 and 1998 seasons).
HONORS: Played in Pro Bowl (1999 season).
SINGLE GAME HIGHS (regular season): Attempts—2 (December 21, 1997, vs. San Diego); yards—11 (December 21, 1997, vs. San Diego); and rushing touchdowns—0.

			RUSHING				TOTALS			
Year Team	**G**	**GS**	**Att.**	**Yds.**	**Avg.**	**TD**	**TD**	**2pt.**	**Pts.**	**Fum.**
1996—Denver NFL	13	0	0	0	0.0	0	0	0	0	0
1997—Denver NFL	16	0	4	10	2.5	0	1	0	6	0
1998—Denver NFL	15	2	0	0	0.0	0	0	0	0	0
1999—Denver NFL	16	0	1	7	7.0	0	0	0	0	0
2000—Denver NFL	16	0	0	0	0.0	0	1	0	6	0
2001—Denver NFL	15	0	0	0	0.0	0	0	0	0	0
2002—Indianapolis NFL	11	2	0	0	0.0	0	0	0	0	0
2003—Indianapolis NFL	11	0	0	0	0.0	0	0	0	0	0
Pro totals (8 years)	113	4	5	17	3.4	0	2	0	12	0

SMITH, DWIGHT — S — BUCCANEERS

PERSONAL: Born August 13, 1978, in Detroit, Mich. ... 5-10/201.
HIGH SCHOOL: Central (Detroit).
COLLEGE: Akron.
TRANSACTIONS/CAREER NOTES: Selected by Tampa Bay Buccaneers in third round (84th pick overall) of 2001 NFL draft. ... Signed by Buccaneers (July 17, 2001).
CHAMPIONSHIP GAME EXPERIENCE: Played in NFC championship game (2002 season). ... Member of Super Bowl championship team (2002 season).
HONORS: Named cornerback on THE SPORTING NEWS college All-America third team (2000).
POST SEASON RECORDS: Holds single-game Super Bowl record for most interceptions returned for touchdown—2 (January 26, 2003, vs. Oakland). ... Shares NFL single-game record for most interceptions returned for touchdown—2 (January 26, 2003, vs. Oakland).

			TOTALS			INTERCEPTIONS				KICKOFF RETURNS				TOTALS			
Year Team	**G**	**GS**	**Tk.**	**Ast.**	**Sks.**	**No.**	**Yds.**	**Avg.**	**TD**	**No.**	**Yds.**	**Avg.**	**TD**	**TD**	**2pt.**	**Pts.**	**Fum.**
2001—Tampa Bay NFL	15	0	4	1	0.0	0	0	0.0	0	16	355	22.2	0	0	0	0	2
2002—Tampa Bay NFL	16	2	24	2	0.0	4	39	9.8	0	4	93	23.2	0	0	0	0	1
2003—Tampa Bay NFL	16	16	55	12	0.0	5	3	0.6	0	0	0	0.0	0	0	0	0	0
Pro totals (3 years)	47	18	83	15	0.0	9	42	4.7	0	20	448	22.4	0	0	0	0	3

SMITH, EMMITT — RB — CARDINALS

PERSONAL: Born May 15, 1969, in Pensacola, Fla. ... 5-10/221. ... Full name: Emmitt J. Smith III.
HIGH SCHOOL: Escambia (Pensacola, Fla.).
COLLEGE: Florida.
TRANSACTIONS/CAREER NOTES: Selected after junior season by Dallas Cowboys in first round (17th pick overall) of 1990 NFL draft. ... Signed by Cowboys (September 4, 1990). ... Granted roster exemption (September 4-8, 1990). ... Granted free agency (March 1, 1993). ... Re-signed by Cowboys (September 16, 1993). ... Released by Cowboys (February 27, 2003). ... Signed by Arizona Cardinals (March 26, 2003).
CHAMPIONSHIP GAME EXPERIENCE: Played in NFC championship game (1992-1995 seasons). ... Member of Super Bowl championship team (1992, 1993 and 1995 seasons).
HONORS: Named running back on THE SPORTING NEWS college All-America first team (1989). ... Played in Pro Bowl (1990-1992, 1995, 1998 and 1999 seasons). ... Named running back on THE SPORTING NEWS NFL All-Pro team (1992-1995). ... Named NFL Player of the Year by THE SPORTING NEWS (1993). ... Named Most Valuable Player of Super Bowl 28 (1993 season). ... Named to play in Pro Bowl (1993 season); replaced by Rodney Hampton due to injury. ... Named Sportsman of the Year by THE SPORTING NEWS (1994). ... Named to play in Pro Bowl (1994 season); replaced by Ricky Watters due to injury.
RECORDS: Holds NFL career record for most rushing attempts—4,142; most yards rushing—17,418; most rushing touchdowns—155; most consecutive seasons with 1,000 or more yards rushing—11 (1991-2001); and most seasons with 1,000 or more yards rushing—11 (1991-2001).
POST SEASON RECORDS: Holds NFL postseason career record for most rushing touchdowns—19. ... Holds NFL postseason career record for most yards rushing—1,586. ... Shares NFL postseason career record for most games with 100 or more yards rushing—7. ... Holds Super Bowl career record for most rushing touchdowns—5.
SINGLE GAME HIGHS (regular season): Attempts—35 (November 7, 1994, vs. New York Giants); yards—237 (October 31, 1993, vs. Philadelphia); and rushing touchdowns—4 (September 4, 1995, vs. New York Giants).
STATISTICAL PLATEAUS: 100-yard rushing games: 1990 (3), 1991 (8), 1992 (7), 1993 (7), 1994 (6), 1995 (11), 1996 (4), 1997 (2), 1998 (7), 1999 (9), 2000 (6), 2001 (4), 2002 (2). Total: 76. 100-yard receiving games: 1990 (1), 1993 (1). Total: 2.
MISCELLANEOUS: Active NFL leader for career rushing yards (17,418) and rushing touchdowns (155). ... Holds Dallas Cowboys all-time records for most yards rushing (17,162), most touchdowns (164) and most rushing touchdowns (153).

			RUSHING				RECEIVING				TOTALS			
Year Team	**G**	**GS**	**Att.**	**Yds.**	**Avg.**	**TD**	**No.**	**Yds.**	**Avg.**	**TD**	**TD**	**2pt.**	**Pts.**	**Fum.**
1990—Dallas NFL	16	15	241	937	3.9	11	24	228	9.5	0	11	0	66	7
1991—Dallas NFL	16	16	*365	*1563	4.3	12	49	258	5.3	1	13	0	78	8

Year Team	G	GS	RUSHING Att.	Yds.	Avg.	TD	RECEIVING No.	Yds.	Avg.	TD	TOTALS TD	2pt.	Pts.	Fum.
1992—Dallas NFL	16	16	‡373	*1713	4.6	*18	59	335	5.7	1	*19	0	114	4
1993—Dallas NFL	14	13	283	*1486	*5.3	9	57	414	7.3	1	10	0	60	4
1994—Dallas NFL	15	15	*368	1484	4.0	*21	50	341	6.8	1	*22	0	132	1
1995—Dallas NFL	16	16	*377	*1773	4.7	*25	62	375	6.0	0	*25	0	*150	7
1996—Dallas NFL	15	15	327	1204	3.7	12	47	249	5.3	3	15	0	90	5
1997—Dallas NFL	16	16	261	1074	4.1	4	40	234	5.9	0	4	1	26	1
1998—Dallas NFL	16	16	319	1332	4.2	13	27	175	6.5	2	15	0	90	3
1999—Dallas NFL	15	15	‡329	1397	4.2	11	27	119	4.4	2	13	0	78	5
2000—Dallas NFL	16	16	294	1203	4.1	9	11	79	7.2	0	9	0	54	6
2001—Dallas NFL	14	14	261	1021	3.9	3	17	116	6.8	0	3	0	18	1
2002—Dallas NFL	16	16	254	975	3.8	5	16	89	5.6	0	5	0	30	3
2003—Arizona NFL	10	5	90	256	2.8	2	14	107	7.6	0	2	0	12	2
Pro totals (14 years)	211	204	4142	17418	4.2	155	500	3119	6.2	11	166	1	998	57

SMITH, HUNTER — P — COLTS

PERSONAL: Born August 9, 1977, in Sherman, Texas. ... 6-2/209. ... Full name: Hunter Dwight Smith.
HIGH SCHOOL: Sherman (Texas).
COLLEGE: Notre Dame.
TRANSACTIONS/CAREER NOTES: Selected by Indianapolis Colts in seventh round (210th pick overall) of 1999 NFL draft. ... Signed by Colts (July 22, 1999). ... Granted free agency (March 1, 2002). ... Re-signed by Colts (May 21, 2002). ... Granted unconditional free agency (February 28, 2003). ... Re-signed by Colts (March 16, 2003).
CHAMPIONSHIP GAME EXPERIENCE: Played in AFC championship game (2003 season).

Year Team	G	PUNTING No.	Yds.	Avg.	Net avg.	In. 20	Blk.
1999—Indianapolis NFL	16	58	2467	42.5	30.6	16	†2
2000—Indianapolis NFL	16	65	2906	44.7	36.4	20	0
2001—Indianapolis NFL	16	68	3023	44.5	33.8	12	0
2002—Indianapolis NFL	16	66	2672	40.5	34.9	26	1
2003—Indianapolis NFL	16	62	2617	42.2	35.5	20	1
Pro totals (5 years)	80	319	13685	42.9	34.3	94	4

SMITH, JIMMY — WR — JAGUARS

PERSONAL: Born February 9, 1969, in Detroit, Mich. ... 6-1/213. ... Full name: Jimmy Lee Smith Jr.
HIGH SCHOOL: Callaway (Jackson, Miss.).
COLLEGE: Jackson State.
TRANSACTIONS/CAREER NOTES: Selected by Dallas Cowboys in second round (36th pick overall) of 1992 NFL draft. ... Signed by Cowboys (April 26, 1992). ... On injured reserve with fibula injury (September 2-October 7, 1992); on practice squad (September 28-October 7, 1992). ... On non-football injury list with appendicitis (September 2, 1993-entire season). ... Released by Cowboys (July 11, 1994). ... Signed by Philadelphia Eagles (July 19, 1994). ... Released by Eagles (August 29, 1994). ... Signed by Jacksonville Jaguars (February 28, 1995). ... Granted free agency (February 16, 1996). ... Re-signed by Jaguars (May 28, 1996). ... On reserve/did not report list (July 25-September 1, 2002). ... On suspended list for violating league substance abuse policy (August 31-September 29, 2003).
CHAMPIONSHIP GAME EXPERIENCE: Played in NFC championship game (1992 season). ... Member of Super Bowl championship team (1992 season). ... Played in AFC championship game (1996 and 1999 seasons).
HONORS: Played in Pro Bowl (1997-2000 seasons). ... Named to play in Pro Bowl (2001 season); replaced by Hines Ward due to injury.
SINGLE GAME HIGHS (regular season): Receptions—15 (September 10, 2000, vs. Baltimore); yards—291 (September 10, 2000, vs. Baltimore); and touchdown receptions—3 (September 10, 2000, vs. Baltimore).
STATISTICAL PLATEAUS: 100-yard receiving games: 1996 (4), 1997 (6), 1998 (5), 1999 (9), 2000 (5), 2001 (6), 2002 (2), 2003 (2). Total: 39.
MISCELLANEOUS: Holds Jacksonville Jaguars all-time record for most receptions (718), most yards receiving (10,092), most touchdowns (57) and most touchdown receptions (55).

Year Team	G	GS	RECEIVING No.	Yds.	Avg.	TD	KICKOFF RETURNS No.	Yds.	Avg.	TD	TOTALS TD	2pt.	Pts.	Fum.
1992—Dallas NFL	7	0	0	0	0.0	0	0	0	0.0	0	0	0	0	0
1993—Dallas NFL						Did not play.								
1994—						Did not play.								
1995—Jacksonville NFL	16	4	22	288	13.1	3	24	540	22.5	1	5	0	30	2
1996—Jacksonville NFL	16	9	83	§1244	15.0	7	2	49	24.5	0	7	0	42	1
1997—Jacksonville NFL	16	16	82	1324	16.1	4	0	0	0.0	0	4	0	24	1
1998—Jacksonville NFL	16	15	78	1182	15.2	8	0	0	0.0	0	8	0	48	2
1999—Jacksonville NFL	16	16	*116	1636	14.1	6	0	0	0.0	0	6	1	38	1
2000—Jacksonville NFL	15	14	91	1213	13.3	8	0	0	0.0	0	8	0	48	1
2001—Jacksonville NFL	16	16	112	1373	12.3	8	0	0	0.0	0	8	0	48	1
2002—Jacksonville NFL	16	16	80	1027	12.8	7	0	0	0.0	0	7	1	44	0
2003—Jacksonville NFL	12	12	54	805	14.9	4	0	0	0.0	0	4	0	24	1
Pro totals (10 years)	146	118	718	10092	14.1	55	26	589	22.7	1	57	2	346	10

SMITH, JUSTIN — DE — BENGALS

PERSONAL: Born September 30, 1979, in Jefferson City, Mo. ... 6-4/270.
HIGH SCHOOL: Jefferson City (Mo.).
COLLEGE: Missouri.
TRANSACTIONS/CAREER NOTES: Selected after junior season by Cincinnati Bengals in first round (fourth pick overall) of 2001 NFL draft. ... Signed by Bengals (September 8, 2001).

HONORS: Named defensive end on THE SPORTING NEWS college All-America third team (2000).

Year Team	G	GS	TOTALS Tk.	Ast.	Sks.	INTERCEPTIONS No.	Yds.	Avg.	TD
2001—Cincinnati NFL	15	11	41	13	8.5	2	28	14.0	0
2002—Cincinnati NFL	16	16	48	13	6.5	0	0	0.0	0
2003—Cincinnati NFL	16	16	41	19	5.0	0	0	0.0	0
Pro totals (3 years)	47	43	130	45	20.0	2	28	14.0	0

SMITH, JUSTIN LB RAMS

PERSONAL: Born June 5, 1979, in Indianapolis, Ind. ... 6-0/218. ... Full name: Justin Curtis Smith.
HIGH SCHOOL: Warren Central (Ind.).
COLLEGE: Indiana.
TRANSACTIONS/CAREER NOTES: Signed as non-drafted free agent by Tampa Bay Buccaneers (April 22, 2002). ... Released by Buccaneers (August 31, 2003). ... Re-signed by Buccaneers to practice squad (September 2, 2003). ... Activated (October 7, 2003). ... Released by Buccaneers (October 14, 2003). ... Re-signed by Buccaneers to practice squad (October 14, 2003). ... Activated (November 14, 2003). ... Waived by Buccaneers (December 6, 2003). ... Re-signed by Buccaneers to practice squad (December 9, 2003). ... Signed by Rams off Buccaneers practice squad (December 11. 2003).

Year Team	G	GS	TOTALS Tk.	Ast.	Sks.
2003—Tampa Bay NFL	2	0	0	0	0.0
—St. Louis NFL	3	0	0	0	0.0
Pro totals (1 year)	5	0	0	0	0.0

S

SMITH, KENNY DT/DE SAINTS

PERSONAL: Born September 8, 1977, in Meridian, Miss. ... 6-4/295.
HIGH SCHOOL: Meridian (Miss.).
COLLEGE: Alabama.
TRANSACTIONS/CAREER NOTES: Selected by New Orleans Saints in third round (81st pick overall) of 2001 NFL draft. ... Signed by Saints (July 28, 2001). ... Granted free agency (March 3, 2004). ... Re-signed by Saints (April 29, 2004).

Year Team	G	GS	TOTALS Tk.	Ast.	Sks.
2001—New Orleans NFL	6	0	7	1	0.0
2002—New Orleans NFL	9	1	17	2	3.5
2003—New Orleans NFL	15	9	32	10	1.0
Pro totals (3 years)	30	10	56	13	4.5

SMITH, LAMAR RB SAINTS

PERSONAL: Born November 29, 1970, in Ft. Wayne, Ind. ... 5-11/230.
HIGH SCHOOL: South Side (Fort Wayne, Ind.).
COLLEGE: Houston.
TRANSACTIONS/CAREER NOTES: Selected by Seattle Seahawks in third round (73rd pick overall) of 1994 NFL draft. ... Signed by Seahawks (July 19, 1994). ... On non-football injury list with back injury (December 13, 1994-remainder of season). ... Granted free agency (February 14, 1997). ... Re-signed by Seahawks (February 1997). ... Granted unconditional free agency (February 13, 1998). ... Signed by New Orleans Saints (February 28, 1998). ... Released by Saints (February 24, 2000). ... Signed by Miami Dolphins (March 15, 2000). ... Granted unconditional free agency (March 1, 2002). ... Signed by Carolina Panthers (March 25, 2002). ... On injured reserve with shoulder injury (December 18, 2002-remainder of season). ... Released by Panthers (March 5, 2003). ... Signed by Green Bay Packers (June 2, 2003). ... Waived by Packers (August 31, 2003). ... Signed by Saints (November 26, 2003). ... Granted unconditional free agency (March 3, 2004). ... Re-signed by Saints (March 11, 2004).
SINGLE GAME HIGHS (regular season): Attempts—33 (November 17, 1996, vs. Detroit); yards—158 (January 6, 2002, vs. Buffalo); and rushing touchdowns—2 (September 29, 2002, vs. Green Bay).
STATISTICAL PLATEAUS: 100-yard rushing games: 1996 (1), 1998 (1), 2000 (4), 2001 (3), 2002 (1). Total: 10.

Year Team	G	GS	RUSHING Att.	Yds.	Avg.	TD	RECEIVING No.	Yds.	Avg.	TD	TOTALS TD	2pt.	Pts.	Fum.
1994—Seattle NFL	2	0	2	-1	-0.5	0	0	0	0.0	0	0	0	0	0
1995—Seattle NFL	12	0	36	215	6.0	0	1	10	10.0	0	0	0	0	1
1996—Seattle NFL	16	2	153	680	4.4	8	9	58	6.4	0	8	*3	54	4
1997—Seattle NFL	12	2	91	392	4.3	2	23	183	8.0	0	2	1	14	0
1998—New Orleans NFL	14	9	138	457	3.3	1	24	249	10.4	2	3	0	18	4
1999—New Orleans NFL	13	2	60	205	3.4	0	20	151	7.6	1	1	0	6	1
2000—Miami NFL	15	15	309	1139	3.7	14	31	201	6.5	2	16	0	96	3
2001—Miami NFL	16	16	313	968	3.1	6	30	234	7.8	2	8	0	48	6
2002—Carolina NFL	11	11	209	737	3.5	7	20	167	8.4	0	7	0	42	2
2003—New Orleans NFL	4	0	11	61	5.5	0	1	2	2.0	0	0	0	0	0
Pro totals (10 years)	115	57	1322	4853	3.7	38	159	1255	7.9	7	45	4	278	21

SMITH, LARRY DT PACKERS

PERSONAL: Born December 4, 1974, in Kingsland, Ga. ... 6-5/310. ... Full name: Larry Smith Jr.
HIGH SCHOOL: Charlton County (Folkston, Ga.), then Valley Forge (Pa.).
COLLEGE: Florida State.

TRANSACTIONS/CAREER NOTES: Selected after junior season by Jacksonville Jaguars in second round (56th pick overall) of 1999 NFL draft. ... Signed by Jaguars (April 26, 1999). ... Granted unconditional free agency (February 28, 2003). ... Re-signed by Jaguars (May 2, 2003). ... Released by Jaguars (August 13, 2003). ... Signed by Green Bay Packers (August 18, 2003). ... Released by Packers (September 1, 2003). ... Re-signed by Packers (October 9, 2003). ... Granted unconditional free agency (March 3, 2004). ... Re-signed by Packers (March 29, 2004).
CHAMPIONSHIP GAME EXPERIENCE: Played in AFC championship game (1999 season).

			TOTALS		
Year Team	**G**	**GS**	**Tk.**	**Ast.**	**Sks.**
1999—Jacksonville NFL	15	0	11	1	3.0
2000—Jacksonville NFL	14	4	15	5	0.0
2001—Jacksonville NFL	7	0	3	0	0.0
2002—Jacksonville NFL	15	3	15	3	1.0
2003—Green Bay NFL	10	0	9	6	1.5
Pro totals (5 years)	61	7	53	15	5.5

SMITH, L.J. TE EAGLES

PERSONAL: Born May 13, 1980, in Highland Park, N.J. ... 6-3/258. ... Full name: John Smith.
HIGH SCHOOL: Highland Park (N.J.).
COLLEGE: Rutgers.
TRANSACTIONS/CAREER NOTES: Selected by Philadelphia Eagles in second round (61st pick overall) of 2003 NFL draft. ... Signed by Eagles (July 24, 2003).
CHAMPIONSHIP GAME EXPERIENCE: Played in NFC championship game (2003 season).
SINGLE GAME HIGHS (regular season): Receptions—6 (November 2, 2003, vs. Atlanta); yards—97 (November 2, 2003, vs. Atlanta); and touchdown receptions—1 (December 7, 2003, vs. Dallas).

			RECEIVING				TOTALS			
Year Team	**G**	**GS**	**No.**	**Yds.**	**Avg.**	**TD**	**TD**	**2pt.**	**Pts.**	**Fum.**
2003—Philadelphia NFL	15	5	27	321	11.9	1	1	0	6	1

SMITH, MARVEL T STEELERS

PERSONAL: Born August 6, 1978, in Oakland, Calif. ... 6-5/310. ... Full name: Marvel Amos Smith.
HIGH SCHOOL: Skyline (Oakland).
COLLEGE: Arizona State.
TRANSACTIONS/CAREER NOTES: Selected after junior season by Pittsburgh Steelers in second round (38th pick overall) of 2000 NFL draft. ... Signed by Steelers (July 16, 2000). ... On injured reserve with neck injury (December 23, 2003-remainder of season).
PLAYING EXPERIENCE: Pittsburgh NFL, 2000-2003. ... Games/Games started: 2000 (12/9), 2001 (16/16), 2002 (16/16), 2003 (6/6). Total: 50/47.
CHAMPIONSHIP GAME EXPERIENCE: Played in AFC championship game (2001 season).
HONORS: Named offensive tackle on THE SPORTING NEWS college All-America third team (1999).

SMITH, MUSA RB RAVENS

PERSONAL: Born May 31, 1982, in Elliottsburg, Pa. ... 6-0/232.
HIGH SCHOOL: West Perry (Pa.).
COLLEGE: Georgia.
TRANSACTIONS/CAREER NOTES: Selected after junior season by Baltimore Ravens in third round (77th pick overall) of 2003 NFL draft.
SINGLE GAME HIGHS (regular season): Attempts—5 (November 30, 2003, vs. San Francisco); yards—21 (December 21, 2003, vs. Cleveland); and rushing touchdowns—1 (December 21, 2003, vs. Cleveland).

			RUSHING				RECEIVING				KICKOFF RETURNS				TOTALS			
Year Team	**G**	**GS**	**Att.**	**Yds.**	**Avg.**	**TD**	**No.**	**Yds.**	**Avg.**	**TD**	**No.**	**Yds.**	**Avg.**	**TD**	**TD**	**2pt.**	**Pts.**	**Fum.**
2003—Baltimore NFL	11	0	9	31	3.4	2	0	0	0.0	0	2	17	8.5	0	2	0	12	1

SMITH, OMAR C GIANTS

PERSONAL: Born September 8, 1977, in Spanish Town, Jamaica. ... 6-2/295. ... Full name: Omar Dave Smith.
HIGH SCHOOL: Nova (Davie, Fla.).
COLLEGE: Kentucky.
TRANSACTIONS/CAREER NOTES: Signed as non-drafted free agent by St. Louis Rams (April 25, 2001). ... Released by Rams (August 27, 2001). ... Signed by New York Giants (January 15, 2002). ... Released by Giants (October 3, 2002). ... Re-signed by Giants to practice squad (October 7, 2002). ... Activated (October 31, 2002). ... Waived by Giants (August 31, 2003). ... Re-signed by Giants to practice squad (September 1, 2003). ... Activated (October 21, 2003). ... Waived by Giants (November 15, 2003). ... Re-signed by Giants to practice squad (November 17, 2003). ... Activated (December 2, 2003).
PLAYING EXPERIENCE: New York Giants NFL, 2002-2003. ... Games/Games started: 2002 (7/0), 2003 (4/0). Total: 11/0.

SMITH, ONTERRIO RB VIKINGS

PERSONAL: Born December 8, 1980, in Sacramento, Calif. ... 5-10/214. ... Full name: Onterrio Raymond Smith.
HIGH SCHOOL: Grant (Sacramento).
COLLEGE: Oregon.
TRANSACTIONS/CAREER NOTES: Selected after junior season by Minnesota Vikings in fourth round (105th pick overall) of 2003 NFL draft. ... Signed by Vikings (July 27, 2003).

SINGLE GAME HIGHS (regular season): Attempts—27 (December 14, 2003, vs. Chicago); yards—148 (December 14, 2003, vs. Chicago); and rushing touchdowns—3 (December 20, 2003, vs. Kansas City).
STATISTICAL PLATEAUS: 100-yard rushing games: 2003 (2). Total: 2.

			RUSHING				RECEIVING				KICKOFF RETURNS				TOTALS			
Year Team	G	GS	Att.	Yds.	Avg.	TD	No.	Yds.	Avg.	TD	No.	Yds.	Avg.	TD	TD	2pt.	Pts.	Fum.
2003—Minnesota NFL	15	3	107	579	‡5.4	5	15	129	8.6	0	27	588	21.8	0	5	1	32	1

SMITH, OTIS — CB — PATRIOTS

PERSONAL: Born October 22, 1965, in New Orleans, La. ... 5-11/198. ... Full name: Otis Smith III.
HIGH SCHOOL: East Jefferson (Metairie, La.).
JUNIOR COLLEGE: Taft (Calif.) College.
COLLEGE: Missouri.
TRANSACTIONS/CAREER NOTES: Signed as non-drafted free agent by Philadelphia Eagles (April 25, 1990). ... On physically unable to perform list with appendectomy (August 2, 1990-entire season). ... Granted free agency (February 1, 1992). ... Re-signed by Eagles (August 11, 1992). ... Granted unconditional free agency (February 17, 1994). ... Re-signed by Eagles (April 25, 1994). ... Released by Eagles (March 22, 1995). ... Signed by New York Jets (April 13, 1995). ... Released by Jets (September 24, 1996). ... Signed by New England Patriots (October 9, 1996). ... Granted unconditional free agency (February 14, 1997). ... Re-signed by Jets (May 20, 1997). ... Granted unconditional free agency (February 13, 1998). ... Re-signed by Jets (April 9, 1998). ... On injured reserve with broken collarbone (October 5, 1999-remainder of season). ... Released by Jets (August 20, 2000). ... Signed by Patriots (August 23, 2000). ... On injured reserve with shoulder injury (December 19, 2002-remainder of season). ... Released by Patriots (August 18, 2003). ... Signed by Detroit Lions (September 2, 2003). ... Granted unconditional free agency (March 3, 2004). ... Signed by New England Patriots (April 13, 2004).
CHAMPIONSHIP GAME EXPERIENCE: Played in AFC championship game (1996, 1998 and 2001 seasons). ... Played in Super Bowl 31 (1996 season). ... Member of Super Bowl championship team (2001 season).

S

			TOTALS			INTERCEPTIONS			
Year Team	G	GS	Tk.	Ast.	Sks.	No.	Yds.	Avg.	TD
1990—Philadelphia NFL				Did not play.					
1991—Philadelphia NFL	15	1	7	3	0.0	2	74	37.0	∞1
1992—Philadelphia NFL	16	1	16	8	0.0	1	0	0.0	0
1993—Philadelphia NFL	15	0	3	2	0.0	1	0	0.0	0
1994—Philadelphia NFL	16	2	19	1	1.0	0	0	0.0	0
1995—New York Jets NFL	11	10	34	7	0.0	6	101	16.8	▲1
1996—New York Jets NFL	2	0	0	0	0.0	0	0	0.0	0
—New England NFL	11	6	26	5	1.0	2	20	10.0	0
1997—New York Jets NFL	16	16	57	13	0.0	6	158	26.3	†3
1998—New York Jets NFL	16	16	57	13	0.0	2	34	17.0	0
1999—New York Jets NFL	1	1	3	0	0.0	0	0	0.0	0
2000—New England NFL	16	14	59	10	0.0	1	56	56.0	0
2001—New England NFL	15	15	50	7	2.0	5	181	36.2	†2
2002—New England NFL	14	13	44	7	0.0	2	21	10.5	0
2003—Detroit NFL	16	13	47	10	1.5	1	0	0.0	0
Pro totals (13 years)	180	108	422	86	5.5	29	645	22.2	7

SMITH, PAUL — RB — LIONS

PERSONAL: Born January 31, 1978, in El Paso, Texas. ... 5-11/234.
HIGH SCHOOL: Andress (El Paso, Texas).
COLLEGE: Texas-El Paso.
TRANSACTIONS/CAREER NOTES: Selected by San Francisco 49ers in fifth round (132nd pick overall) of 2000 NFL draft. ... Signed by 49ers (July 21, 2000). ... Released by 49ers (August 31, 2003). ... Signed by Detroit Lions (November 11, 2003).
SINGLE GAME HIGHS (regular season): Attempts—13 (December 8, 2002, vs. Dallas); yards—40 (December 8, 2002, vs. Dallas); and rushing touchdowns—1 (December 2, 2001, vs. Buffalo).

			RUSHING				RECEIVING				KICKOFF RETURNS				TOTALS			
Year Team	G	GS	Att.	Yds.	Avg.	TD	No.	Yds.	Avg.	TD	No.	Yds.	Avg.	TD	TD	2pt.	Pts.	Fum.
2000—San Francisco NFL	10	0	18	72	4.0	0	2	55	27.5	0	9	167	18.6	0	0	0	0	2
2001—San Francisco NFL	15	0	4	27	6.8	1	0	0	0.0	0	3	37	12.3	0	1	0	6	1
2002—San Francisco NFL	11	0	18	90	5.0	0	5	33	6.6	0	7	107	15.3	0	0	0	0	0
2003—Detroit NFL	7	0	2	5	2.5	0	5	45	9.0	0	0	0	0.0	0	0	0	0	0
Pro totals (4 years)	43	0	42	194	4.6	1	12	133	11.1	0	19	311	16.4	0	1	0	6	3

SMITH, RAONALL — LB — VIKINGS

PERSONAL: Born October 22, 1978, in Mesa, Ariz. ... 6-2/241. ... Full name: Raonall Aarrig Smith.
HIGH SCHOOL: Peninsula (Gig Harbor, Wash.).
COLLEGE: Washington State.
TRANSACTIONS/CAREER NOTES: Selected by Minnesota Vikings in second round (38th pick overall) of 2002 NFL draft. ... Signed by Vikings (July 26, 2002). ... On injured reserve with shoulder injury (September 11, 2002-remainder of season).

			TOTALS			INTERCEPTIONS			
Year Team	G	GS	Tk.	Ast.	Sks.	No.	Yds.	Avg.	TD
2003—Minnesota NFL	7	0	0	0	0.0	0	0	0.0	0

SMITH, ROBAIRE — DT/DE — TEXANS

PERSONAL: Born November 15, 1977, in Flint, Mich. ... 6-4/310. ... Full name: Robaire Freddick Smith. ... Brother of Fernando Smith, defensive end, with four NFL teams (1994-2000).
HIGH SCHOOL: Flint (Mich.).
COLLEGE: Michigan State.

TRANSACTIONS/CAREER NOTES: Selected by Tennessee Titans in sixth round (197th pick overall) of 2000 NFL draft. ... Signed by Titans (July 5, 2000). ... Granted free agency (February 28, 2003). ... Re-signed by Titans (May 8, 2003). ... Granted unconditional free agency (March 3, 2004). ... Signed by Houston Texans (March 4, 2004).

CHAMPIONSHIP GAME EXPERIENCE: Played in AFC championship game (2002 season).

HONORS: Named defensive end on THE SPORTING NEWS college All-America second team (1999).

			TOTALS		
Year Team	G	GS	Tk.	Ast.	Sks.
2000—Tennessee NFL	7	0	5	1	2.5
2001—Tennessee NFL	10	0	5	2	2.0
2002—Tennessee NFL	16	2	25	9	2.5
2003—Tennessee NFL	16	15	20	15	4.5
Pro totals (4 years)	49	17	55	27	11.5

SMITH, ROD — WR — BRONCOS

PERSONAL: Born May 15, 1970, in Texarkana, Ark. ... 6-0/200.

HIGH SCHOOL: Texarkana (Ark.).

COLLEGE: Missouri Southern State.

TRANSACTIONS/CAREER NOTES: Signed as non-drafted free agent by Denver Broncos (March 23, 1995).

CHAMPIONSHIP GAME EXPERIENCE: Played in AFC championship game (1997 and 1998 seasons). ... Member of Super Bowl championship team (1997 and 1998 seasons).

HONORS: Played in Pro Bowl (2000 season). ... Named to play in Pro Bowl (2001 season); replaced by Troy Brown due to injury.

SINGLE GAME HIGHS (regular season): Receptions—14 (September 23, 2001, vs. Arizona); yards—187 (November 19, 2000, vs. San Diego); and touchdown receptions—3 (October 15, 2000, vs. Cleveland).

STATISTICAL PLATEAUS: 100-yard receiving games: 1997 (6), 1998 (4), 1999 (3), 2000 (8), 2001 (5), 2003 (1). Total: 27.

MISCELLANEOUS: Holds Denver Broncos all-time record for most yards receiving (8,628).

			RUSHING				RECEIVING				PUNT RETURNS				KICKOFF RETURNS				TOTALS		
Year Team	G	GS	Att.	Yds.	Avg.	TD	No.	Yds.	Avg.	TD	No.	Yds.	Avg.	TD	No.	Yds.	Avg.	TD	TD	2pt.	Pts.
1995—Den. NFL	16	1	0	0	0.0	0	6	152	25.3	1	0	0	0.0	0	4	54	13.5	0	1	0	6
1996—Den. NFL	10	1	1	1	1.0	0	16	237	14.8	2	23	283	12.3	0	1	29	29.0	0	2	0	12
1997—Den. NFL	16	16	5	16	3.2	0	70	1180	16.9	▲12	1	12	12.0	0	0	0	0.0	0	12	0	72
1998—Den. NFL	16	16	6	63	10.5	0	86	1222	14.2	6	0	0	0.0	0	0	0	0.0	0	7	0	42
1999—Den. NFL	15	15	0	0	0.0	0	79	1020	12.9	4	0	0	0.0	0	1	10	10.0	0	4	0	24
2000—Den. NFL	16	16	6	99	16.5	1	100	§1602	16.0	8	0	0	0.0	0	0	0	0.0	0	9	0	54
2001—Den. NFL	15	14	3	27	9.0	0	*113	1343	11.9	11	0	0	0.0	0	0	0	0.0	0	11	1	68
2002—Den. NFL	16	16	6	9	1.5	0	89	1027	11.5	5	0	0	0.0	0	0	0	0.0	0	5	0	30
2003—Den. NFL	15	15	10	98	9.8	0	74	845	11.4	3	6	127	21.2	1	0	0	0.0	0	4	0	24
Pro totals (9 years)	135	110	37	313	8.5	1	633	8628	13.6	52	30	422	14.1	1	6	93	15.5	0	55	1	332

SMITH, SHAUN — DT — COWBOYS

PERSONAL: Born August 19, 1981, in Brooklyn, N.Y. ... 6-2/320.

HIGH SCHOOL: Wichita Heights (Wichita, Kan.).

COLLEGE: South Carolina.

TRANSACTIONS/CAREER NOTES: Signed as non-drafted free agent by Dallas Cowboys (May 1, 2003). ... Released by Cowboys (August 31, 2003). ... Re-signed by Cowboys to practice squad (September 1, 2003). ... Activated (January 5, 2004).

			TOTALS		
Year Team	G	GS	Tk.	Ast.	Sks.
2003—Dallas NFL	1	0	0	0	0.0

SMITH, STEVE — WR/PR — PANTHERS

PERSONAL: Born May 12, 1979, in Los Angeles, Calif. ... 5-9/179. ... Full name: Stevonne Smith.

HIGH SCHOOL: University (Los Angeles).

JUNIOR COLLEGE: Santa Monica Junior College.

COLLEGE: Utah.

TRANSACTIONS/CAREER NOTES: Selected by Carolina Panthers in third round (74th pick overall) of 2001 NFL draft. ... Signed by Panthers (June 19, 2001).

CHAMPIONSHIP GAME EXPERIENCE: Played in NFC championship game (2003 season). ... Played in Super Bowl 38 (2003 season).

HONORS: Named kick returner on THE SPORTING NEWS NFL All-Pro team (2001). ... Played in Pro Bowl (2001 season).

RECORDS: Shares NFL single-game records for most touchdowns by punt returns—2; and most touchdowns by combined kick return—2 (December 8, 2002, vs. Cincinnati).

SINGLE GAME HIGHS (regular season): Receptions—10 (October 19, 2003, vs. Tennessee); yards—151 (October 19, 2003, vs. Tennessee); and touchdown receptions—1 (December 21, 2003, vs. Detroit).

STATISTICAL PLATEAUS: 100-yard receiving games: 2002 (2), 2003 (3). Total: 5.

			RECEIVING				PUNT RETURNS				KICKOFF RETURNS				TOTALS			
Year Team	G	GS	No.	Yds.	Avg.	TD	No.	Yds.	Avg.	TD	No.	Yds.	Avg.	TD	TD	2pt.	Pts.	Fum.
2001—Carolina NFL	15	1	10	154	15.4	0	34	364	10.7	†1	56	1431	‡25.6	†2	3	0	18	8
2002—Carolina NFL	15	13	54	872	16.1	3	*55	470	8.5	†2	26	571	22.0	0	5	0	30	5
2003—Carolina NFL	16	11	88	1110	12.6	7	‡44	439	10.0	1	11	309	28.1	0	8	0	48	5
Pro totals (3 years)	46	25	152	2136	14.1	10	133	1273	9.6	4	93	2311	24.8	2	16	0	96	18

SMITH, TERRELLE FB BROWNS

PERSONAL: Born March 12, 1978, in West Covina, Calif. ... 6-0/246. ... Full name: Terrelle Vernon Smith.
HIGH SCHOOL: Canyon Springs (Moreno Valley, Calif.).
COLLEGE: Arizona State.
TRANSACTIONS/CAREER NOTES: Selected by New Orleans Saints in fourth round (96th pick overall) of 2000 NFL draft. ... Signed by Saints (July 11, 2000). ... Granted free agency (February 28, 2003). ... Re-signed by Saints (April 22, 2003). ... Granted unconditional free agency (March 3, 2004). ... Signed by Cleveland Browns (March 11, 2004).
SINGLE GAME HIGHS (regular season): Attempts—6 (December 10, 2000, vs. San Francisco); yards—42 (November 19, 2000, vs. Oakland); and rushing touchdowns—0.

			RUSHING				RECEIVING				TOTALS			
Year Team	G	GS	Att.	Yds.	Avg.	TD	No.	Yds.	Avg.	TD	TD	2pt.	Pts.	Fum.
2000—New Orleans NFL	14	9	29	131	4.5	0	12	65	5.4	0	0	0	0	1
2001—New Orleans NFL	14	9	5	8	1.6	0	4	30	7.5	2	2	0	12	1
2002—New Orleans NFL	16	8	5	11	2.2	0	9	30	3.3	0	0	0	0	1
2003—New Orleans NFL	15	10	0	0	0.0	0	6	28	4.7	0	0	0	0	0
Pro totals (4 years)	59	36	39	150	3.8	0	31	153	4.9	2	2	0	12	3

SMITH, TRAVIAN LB RAIDERS

PERSONAL: Born August 26, 1975, in Shepherd, Texas. ... 6-4/240.
HIGH SCHOOL: Tatum (Texas).
COLLEGE: Oklahoma.
TRANSACTIONS/CAREER NOTES: Selected by Oakland Raiders in fifth round (152nd pick overall) of 1998 NFL draft. ... Signed by Raiders (July 6, 1998). ... Released by Raiders (August 26, 1998). ... Re-signed by Raiders to practice squad (August 31, 1998). ... Activated (December 15, 1998). ... On injured reserve with knee injury (November 19, 2003-remainder of season).
CHAMPIONSHIP GAME EXPERIENCE: Played in AFC championship game (2000 and 2002 seasons). ... Played in Super Bowl 37 (2002 season).

			TOTALS			INTERCEPTIONS			
Year Team	G	GS	Tk.	Ast.	Sks.	No.	Yds.	Avg.	TD
1998—Oakland NFL	2	0	0	0	0.0	0	0	0.0	0
1999—Oakland NFL	16	1	6	1	0.0	0	0	0.0	0
2000—Oakland NFL	16	0	2	0	0.0	0	0	0.0	0
2001—Oakland NFL	16	2	14	11	2.5	1	9	9.0	0
2002—Oakland NFL	16	2	23	7	5.0	0	0	0.0	0
2003—Oakland NFL	10	7	50	10	1.0	0	0	0.0	0
Pro totals (6 years)	76	12	95	29	8.5	1	9	9.0	0

SMITH, TRENT TE RAVENS

PERSONAL: Born September 15, 1979, in Norman, Okla. ... 6-5/243.
HIGH SCHOOL: Clinton (Okla.).
COLLEGE: Oklahoma.
TRANSACTIONS/CAREER NOTES: Selected by Baltimore Ravens in seventh round (223rd pick overall) of 2003 NFL draft. ... Signed by Ravens (July 25, 2003). ... On injured reserve with leg injury (August 25, 2003-entire season).

			RECEIVING				TOTALS			
Year Team	G	GS	No.	Yds.	Avg.	TD	TD	2pt.	Pts.	Fum.
2003—Baltimore NFL	Did not play.									

SMITH, WADE T DOLPHINS

PERSONAL: Born April 26, 1981, in Dallas, Texas. ... 6-4/300.
HIGH SCHOOL: Lake Highlands (Dallas).
COLLEGE: Memphis.
TRANSACTIONS/CAREER NOTES: Selected by Miami Dolphins in third round (78th pick overall) of 2003 NFL draft.
PLAYING EXPERIENCE: Miami NFL, 2003. ... Games/Games started: 2003 (16/16). Total: 16/16.

SMITH, ZURIEL WR COWBOYS

PERSONAL: Born January 15, 1980, in Richmond, Va. ... 5-11/166.
HIGH SCHOOL: Altee (Mechanicsville, Va.).
COLLEGE: Hampton.
TRANSACTIONS/CAREER NOTES: Selected by Dallas Cowboys in sixth round (186th pick overall) of 2003 NFL draft. ... Signed by Cowboys (July 22, 2003).
SINGLE GAME HIGHS (regular season): Receptions—2 (November 16, 2003, vs. New England); yards—38 (November 16, 2003, vs. New England); and touchdown receptions—0.

			RECEIVING				PUNT RETURNS				KICKOFF RETURNS				TOTALS			
Year Team	G	GS	No.	Yds.	Avg.	TD	No.	Yds.	Avg.	TD	No.	Yds.	Avg.	TD	TD	2pt.	Pts.	Fum.
2003—Dallas NFL	9	0	3	46	15.3	0	30	212	7.1	0	23	495	21.5	0	0	0	0	3

SMOOT, FRED CB REDSKINS

PERSONAL: Born April 17, 1979, in Jackson, Miss. ... 5-11/174. ... Full name: Fredrick D. Smoot.
HIGH SCHOOL: Provine (Jackson, Miss.).
JUNIOR COLLEGE: Hinds Community College (Miss.).
COLLEGE: Mississippi State.

TRANSACTIONS/CAREER NOTES: Selected by Washington Redskins in second round (45th pick overall) of 2001 NFL draft. ... Signed by Redskins (July 31, 2001).
HONORS: Named cornerback on THE SPORTING NEWS college All-America first team (2000).

Year Team	G	GS	TOTALS Tk.	Ast.	Sks.	INTERCEPTIONS No.	Yds.	Avg.	TD
2001—Washington NFL	14	13	30	3	0.0	5	36	7.2	0
2002—Washington NFL	16	16	49	12	0.0	4	12	3.0	0
2003—Washington NFL	15	15	49	8	0.0	4	35	8.8	0
Pro totals (3 years)	45	44	128	23	0.0	13	83	6.4	0

SNOW, JUSTIN — TE — COLTS

PERSONAL: Born December 21, 1976, in Fort Worth, Texas. ... 6-3/240.
HIGH SCHOOL: Cooper (Abilene, Texas.).
COLLEGE: Baylor.
TRANSACTIONS/CAREER NOTES: Signed as non-drafted free agent by Indianapolis Colts (April 20, 2000).
CHAMPIONSHIP GAME EXPERIENCE: Played in AFC championship game (2003 season).

Year Team	G	GS	RECEIVING No.	Yds.	Avg.	TD	TOTALS TD	2pt.	Pts.	Fum.
2000—Indianapolis NFL	16	0	0	0	0.0	0	0	0	0	0
2001—Indianapolis NFL	16	0	0	0	0.0	0	0	0	0	0
2002—Indianapolis NFL	16	0	0	0	0.0	0	0	0	0	0
2003—Indianapolis NFL	16	0	0	0	0.0	0	0	0	0	0
Pro totals (4 years)	64	0	0	0	0.0	0	0	0	0	0

S

SOBIESKI, BEN — T — BILLS

PERSONAL: Born May 3, 1979, in Mahtomedi, Minn. ... 6-5/315.
HIGH SCHOOL: Mahtomedi (Minn.).
COLLEGE: Iowa.
TRANSACTIONS/CAREER NOTES: Selected by Buffalo Bills in fifth round (151st pick overall) of 2003 NFL draft. ... Signed by Bills (June 19, 2003).
PLAYING EXPERIENCE: Buffalo NFL, 2003. ... Games/Games started: 2003 (1/0). Total: 1/0.

SORENSEN, NICK — S — JAGUARS

PERSONAL: Born July 31, 1978, in Winter Haven, Fla. ... 6-2/205. ... Full name: Nicholas Carl Sorensen.
HIGH SCHOOL: George C. Marshall (Vienna, Va.).
COLLEGE: Virginia Tech.
TRANSACTIONS/CAREER NOTES: Signed as non-drafted free agent by Miami Dolphins (April 26, 2001). ... Released by Dolphins (August 26, 2001). ... Signed by St. Louis Rams to practice squad (October 16, 2001). ... Activated (November 16, 2001). ... Released by Rams (November 24, 2001). ... Re-signed by Rams (November 27, 2001). ... Released by Rams (August 31, 2003). ... Signed by Jacksonville Jaguars (September 16, 2003).
CHAMPIONSHIP GAME EXPERIENCE: Played in NFC championship game (2001 season). ... Played in Super Bowl 36 (2001 season).

Year Team	G	GS	TOTALS Tk.	Ast.	Sks.	INTERCEPTIONS No.	Yds.	Avg.	TD
2001—St. Louis NFL	7	0	1	0	0.0	0	0	0.0	0
2002—St. Louis NFL	16	0	1	0	0.0	0	0	0.0	0
2003—Jacksonville NFL	14	0	0	0	0.0	0	0	0.0	0
Pro totals (3 years)	37	0	2	0	0.0	0	0	0.0	0

SOWELL, JERALD — FB — JETS

PERSONAL: Born January 21, 1974, in Elyria, Ohio. ... 6-0/237. ... Full name: Jerald Monye Sowell.
HIGH SCHOOL: Baker (La.).
COLLEGE: Tulane.
TRANSACTIONS/CAREER NOTES: Selected by Green Bay Packers in seventh round (231st pick overall) of 1997 NFL draft. ... Signed by Packers (July 10, 1997). ... Claimed on waivers by New York Jets (August 25, 1997). ... Granted free agency (February 11, 2000). ... Re-signed by Jets (April 25, 2000). ... Granted unconditional free agency (February 28, 2003). ... Re-signed by Jets (March 3, 2003).
CHAMPIONSHIP GAME EXPERIENCE: Member of Jets for AFC championship game (1998 season); inactive.
SINGLE GAME HIGHS (regular season): Attempts—14 (November 8, 1998, vs. Buffalo); yards—82 (September 20, 1998, vs. Indianapolis); and rushing touchdowns—0.

Year Team	G	GS	RUSHING Att.	Yds.	Avg.	TD	RECEIVING No.	Yds.	Avg.	TD	TOTALS TD	2pt.	Pts.	Fum.
1997—New York Jets NFL	9	0	7	35	5.0	0	1	8	8.0	0	0	0	0	0
1998—New York Jets NFL	16	2	40	164	4.1	0	10	59	5.9	0	0	0	0	2
1999—New York Jets NFL	16	0	3	5	1.7	0	0	0	0.0	0	0	0	0	0
2000—New York Jets NFL	16	0	2	0	0.0	0	6	84	14.0	0	0	0	0	0
2001—New York Jets NFL	16	0	4	9	2.3	0	1	19	19.0	0	0	0	0	0
2002—New York Jets NFL	16	0	1	0	0.0	0	9	85	9.4	1	1	0	6	0
2003—New York Jets NFL	16	16	1	2	2.0	0	47	436	9.3	1	1	0	6	0
Pro totals (7 years)	105	18	58	215	3.7	0	74	691	9.3	2	2	0	12	2

SPEARMAN, ARMEGIS — LB — PACKERS

PERSONAL: Born April 5, 1978, in Oxford, Miss. ... 6-2/251.
HIGH SCHOOL: Bruce (Miss.).
COLLEGE: Mississippi.
TRANSACTIONS/CAREER NOTES: Signed as non-drafted free agent by Cincinnati Bengals (April 27, 2000). ... On injured reserve with torn pectoral muscle (September 2, 2001-remainder of season). ... On injured reserve with ankle injury (November 1, 2002-remainder of season). ... Granted free agency (February 28, 2003). ... Tendered offer sheet by Green Bay Packers (March 10, 2003). ... Offer matched by Bengals (March 17, 2003). ... Waived by Bengals (August 31, 2003). ... Signed by Houston Texans (September 2, 2003). ... Waived by Texans (September 10, 2003). ... Signed by Green Bay Packers (April 14, 2004).

			TOTALS			INTERCEPTIONS			
Year Team	**G**	**GS**	**Tk.**	**Ast.**	**Sks.**	**No.**	**Yds.**	**Avg.**	**TD**
2000—Cincinnati NFL	15	11	46	24	1.0	0	0	0.0	0
2002—Cincinnati NFL	7	0	0	0	0.0	0	0	0.0	0
2003—Houston NFL	1	0	0	0	0.0	0	0	0.0	0
Pro totals (3 years)	23	11	46	24	1.0	0	0	0.0	0

SPEARS, MARCUS — T — CHIEFS

S

PERSONAL: Born September 28, 1971, in Baton Rouge, La. ... 6-4/320. ... Full name: Marcus DeWayne Spears.
HIGH SCHOOL: Belaire (Baton Rouge, La.).
COLLEGE: Northwestern State.
TRANSACTIONS/CAREER NOTES: Selected by Chicago Bears in second round (39th pick overall) of 1994 NFL draft. ... Signed by Bears (July 16, 1994). ... Inactive for all 16 games (1994). ... Active for five games (1995); did not play. ... Assigned by Bears to Amsterdam Admirals in 1996 World League enhancement allocation program (February 19, 1996). ... Granted unconditional free agency (February 14, 1997). ... Signed by Green Bay Packers (March 12, 1997). ... Released by Packers (August 19, 1997). ... Signed by Kansas City Chiefs (September 16, 1997). ... On injured reserve with hand injury (December 9, 1998-remainder of season). ... Granted unconditional free agency (February 12, 1999). ... Re-signed by Chiefs (February 16, 1999). ... On injured reserve with arm injury (December 15, 2000-remainder of season). ... Granted unconditional free agency (March 1, 2002). ... Re-signed by Chiefs (May 6, 2002).
PLAYING EXPERIENCE: Chicago NFL, 1996; Kansas City NFL, 1997-2003. ... Games/Games started: 1996 (9/0), 1997 (3/0), 1998 (12/0), 1999 (10/2), 2000 (13/0), 2001 (16/16), 2002 (9/0), 2003 (15/0). Total: 87/18.
HONORS: Named offensive lineman on THE SPORTING NEWS college All-America second team (1993).

SPENCER, JIMMY — CB — BRONCOS

PERSONAL: Born March 29, 1969, in Manning, S.C. ... 5-9/188. ... Full name: James Arthur Spencer Jr.
HIGH SCHOOL: Glades Central (Belle Glade, Fla.).
COLLEGE: Florida.
TRANSACTIONS/CAREER NOTES: Selected by Washington Redskins in eighth round (215th pick overall) of 1991 NFL draft. ... Signed by Redskins for 1991 season. ... Released by Redskins (August 26, 1991). ... Signed by New Orleans Saints (April 2, 1992). ... Granted unconditional free agency (February 16, 1996). ... Signed by Cincinnati Bengals (March 21, 1996). ... Released by Bengals (August 25, 1998). ... Signed by San Diego Chargers (September 1, 1998). ... Granted unconditional free agency (February 12, 1999). ... Re-signed by Chargers (April 7, 1999). ... On injured reserve with broken arm (December 20, 1999-remainder of season). ... Released by Chargers (February 10, 2000). ... Signed by Denver Broncos (March 6, 2000). ... Released by Broncos (February 25, 2003). ... Re-signed by Broncos (February 26, 2003). ... Granted unconditional free agency (March 3, 2004). ... Re-signed by Broncos (March 15, 2004).

			TOTALS			INTERCEPTIONS			
Year Team	**G**	**GS**	**Tk.**	**Ast.**	**Sks.**	**No.**	**Yds.**	**Avg.**	**TD**
1992—New Orleans NFL	16	4	37	6	0.0	0	0	0.0	0
1993—New Orleans NFL	16	3	15	5	0.0	0	0	0.0	0
1994—New Orleans NFL	16	16	56	7	0.0	5	24	4.8	0
1995—New Orleans NFL	16	15	59	7	0.0	4	11	2.8	0
1996—Cincinnati NFL	15	14	55	8	0.0	5	48	9.6	0
1997—Cincinnati NFL	16	9	36	2	0.0	1	-2	-2.0	0
1998—San Diego NFL	15	4	29	0	0.0	1	0	0.0	0
1999—San Diego NFL	14	7	40	8	0.0	4	1	0.3	0
2000—Denver NFL	16	6	37	3	1.0	3	102	34.0	2
2001—Denver NFL	16	1	27	1	0.0	3	25	8.3	0
2002—Denver NFL	5	0	4	0	0.0	0	0	0.0	0
2003—Denver NFL	16	2	9	0	0.0	0	0	0.0	0
Pro totals (12 years)	177	81	404	47	1.0	26	209	8.0	2

SPICER, PAUL — DE — JAGUARS

PERSONAL: Born August 18, 1975, in Indianapolis, Ind. ... 6-4/287.
HIGH SCHOOL: Northwestern (Indianapolis).
COLLEGE: Saginaw Valley State (Mich.).
TRANSACTIONS/CAREER NOTES: Signed as non-drafted free agent by Seattle Seahawks (April 20, 1998). ... Released by Seahawks (August 24, 1998). ... Signed by Sasketchewan Roughriders of CFL (September 26, 1998). ... Signed by Detroit Lions (February 24, 1999). ... Released by Lions (September 5, 1999). ... Re-signed by Lions to practice squad (September 7, 1999). ... Activated (October 8, 1999). ... Released by Lions (November 6, 1999). ... Re-signed by Lions to practice squad (November 10, 1999). ... Released by Lions (August 22, 2000). ... Signed by Jacksonville Jaguars to practice squad (August 30, 2000). ... Activated (October 4, 2000). ... Assigned by Jaguars to Frankfurt Galaxy in 2001 NFL Europe enhancement allocation program (February 19, 2001). ... Granted free agency (February 28, 2003). ... Re-signed by Jaguars (April 23, 2003).

Year Team	G	GS	TOTALS Tk.	Ast.	Sks.	INTERCEPTIONS No.	Yds.	Avg.	TD
1998—Saskatchewan CFL	7	...	...	...	4.0	0	0	0.0	0
1999—Detroit NFL	2	0	0	0	0.0	0	0	0.0	0
2000—Jacksonville NFL	3	0	4	1	1.0	0	0	0.0	0
2001—Jacksonville NFL	16	4	23	5	2.0	0	0	0.0	0
2002—Jacksonville NFL	16	4	35	2	4.0	0	0	0.0	0
2003—Jacksonville NFL	16	1	24	8	0.0	1	2	2.0	0
CFL totals (1 year)	7	...	...	...	4.0	0	0	0.0	0
NFL totals (5 years)	53	9	86	16	7.0	1	2	2.0	0
Pro totals (6 years)	60	...	...	...	11.0	1	2	2.0	0

SPIKES, CAMERON G CARDINALS

PERSONAL: Born November 6, 1976, in Madisonville, Texas. ... 6-4/325. ... Full name: Cameron Wade Spikes.
HIGH SCHOOL: Bryan (Texas).
COLLEGE: Texas A&M.
TRANSACTIONS/CAREER NOTES: Selected by St. Louis Rams in fifth round (145th pick overall) of 1999 NFL draft. ... Signed by Rams (July 19, 1999). ... Granted free agency (March 1, 2002). ... Re-signed by Rams (April 17, 2002). ... Claimed on waivers by Houston Texans (August 26, 2002). ... Granted unconditional free agency (February 28, 2003). ... Signed by Arizona Cardinals (March 28, 2003).
PLAYING EXPERIENCE: St. Louis NFL, 1999-2001; Houston NFL, 2002; Arizona NFL, 2003. ... Games/Games started: 1999 (5/0), 2000 (9/0), 2001 (5/0), 2002 (12/5), 2003 (16/16). Total: 47/21.
CHAMPIONSHIP GAME EXPERIENCE: Member of Rams for NFC championship game (1999 and 2001 seasons); inactive. ... Member of Super Bowl championship team (1999 season); inactive. ... Played in Super Bowl 36 (2001 season).

S

SPIKES, TAKEO LB BILLS

PERSONAL: Born December 17, 1976, in Sandersville, Ga. ... 6-2/242. ... Full name: Takeo Gerard Spikes. ... Name pronounced: tuh-KEE-oh.
HIGH SCHOOL: Washington County (Sandersville, Ga.).
COLLEGE: Auburn.
TRANSACTIONS/CAREER NOTES: Selected after junior season by Cincinnati Bengals in first round (13th pick overall) of 1998 NFL draft. ... Signed by Bengals (July 25, 1998). ... Designated by Bengals as transition player (February 20, 2003). ... Tendered offer sheet by Buffalo Bills (March 10, 2003). ... Bengals declined to match offer (March 11, 2003).
HONORS: Named inside linebacker on THE SPORTING NEWS college All-America first team (1997). ... Played in Pro Bowl (2003 season).

Year Team	G	GS	TOTALS Tk.	Ast.	Sks.	INTERCEPTIONS No.	Yds.	Avg.	TD
1998—Cincinnati NFL	16	16	95	17	2.0	0	0	0.0	0
1999—Cincinnati NFL	16	16	82	23	3.0	2	7	3.5	0
2000—Cincinnati NFL	16	16	109	19	2.0	2	12	6.0	0
2001—Cincinnati NFL	15	15	80	29	6.0	1	66	66.0	1
2002—Cincinnati NFL	16	16	81	32	1.5	0	0	0.0	0
2003—Buffalo NFL	16	16	70	56	2.0	2	1	0.5	0
Pro totals (6 years)	95	95	517	176	16.5	7	86	12.3	1

SPIRES, GREG DE BUCCANEERS

PERSONAL: Born August 12, 1974, in Marianna, Fla. ... 6-1/265. ... Full name: Greg Tyrone Spires.
HIGH SCHOOL: Mariner (Cape Coral, Fla.).
COLLEGE: Florida State.
TRANSACTIONS/CAREER NOTES: Selected by New England Patriots in third round (83rd pick overall) of 1998 NFL draft. ... Signed by Patriots (July 16, 1998). ... On injured reserve with knee injury (December 15, 1999-remainder of season). ... Granted free agency (March 2, 2001). ... Re-signed by Patriots (April 30, 2001). ... Claimed on waivers by Cleveland Browns (September 4, 2001). ... Granted unconditional free agency (March 1, 2002). ... Signed by Tampa Bay Buccaneers (March 22, 2002). ... On injured reserve with shoulder injury (December 22, 2003-remainder of season).
CHAMPIONSHIP GAME EXPERIENCE: Played in NFC championship game (2002 season). ... Member of Super Bowl championship team (2002 season).

Year Team	G	GS	TOTALS Tk.	Ast.	Sks.
1998—New England NFL	15	1	18	6	3.0
1999—New England NFL	11	1	6	1	0.5
2000—New England NFL	16	2	12	5	6.0
2001—Cleveland NFL	16	4	23	8	4.0
2002—Tampa Bay NFL	16	16	27	10	3.5
2003—Tampa Bay NFL	15	15	24	12	3.5
Pro totals (6 years)	89	39	110	42	20.5

SPRAGAN, DONNIE LB BRONCOS

PERSONAL: Born July 12, 1976, in Oakland, Calif. ... 6-3/239.
HIGH SCHOOL: Logan (Union City, Calif.).
COLLEGE: Stanford.
TRANSACTIONS/CAREER NOTES: Signed as non-drafted free agent by New Orleans Saints (April 23, 1999). ... On injured reserve with knee injury (September 6, 1999-entire season). ... Released by Saints (August 22, 2000). ... Signed by Green Bay Packers (July 19, 2001). ... Released by Packers (September 1, 2001). ... Signed by Cleveland Browns to practice squad (October 2, 2001). ... Released by Browns (October 31, 2001). ... Signed by Denver Broncos to practice squad (December 11, 2001). ... Granted free agency (March 3, 2004). ... Re-signed by Broncos (2004).

Year Team	G	GS	TOTALS Tk.	Ast.	Sks.	INTERCEPTIONS No.	Yds.	Avg.	TD
2002—Denver NFL	16	0	0	0	0.0	0	0	0.0	0
2003—Denver NFL	16	8	38	8	0.0	0	0	0.0	0
Pro totals (2 years)	32	8	38	8	0.0	0	0	0.0	0

SPRIGGS, MARCUS T/G

PERSONAL: Born May 30, 1974, in Hattiesburg, Miss. ... 6-3/310. ... Full name: Thomas Marcus Spriggs.
HIGH SCHOOL: Byram (Jackson, Miss.).
JUNIOR COLLEGE: Hinds Community College (Miss.).
COLLEGE: Houston.
TRANSACTIONS/CAREER NOTES: Selected by Buffalo Bills in sixth round (185th pick overall) of 1997 NFL draft. ... Signed by Bills (June 13, 1997). ... Granted free agency (February 11, 2000). ... Re-signed by Bills (April 10, 2000). ... Granted unconditional free agency (March 2, 2001). ... Signed by Miami Dolphins (April 19, 2001). ... On injured reserve with knee injury (September 11, 2001-remainder of season) ... Granted unconditional free agency (February 28, 2003). ... Signed by Green Bay Packers (June 3, 2003). ... Granted unconditional free agency (March 3, 2004).
PLAYING EXPERIENCE: Buffalo NFL, 1997-2000; Miami NFL, 2001-2002; Green Bay NFL, 2003. ... Games/Games started: 1997 (2/0), 1998 (1/0), 1999 (11/2), 2000 (16/11), 2001 (1/1), 2002 (16/4), 2003 (2/0). Total: 49/18.

S

SPRINGS, SHAWN CB REDSKINS

PERSONAL: Born March 11, 1975, in Silver Springs, Md. ... 6-0/204. ... Son of Ron Springs, running back with Dallas Cowboys (1979-84) and Tampa Bay Buccaneers (1985 and 1986).
HIGH SCHOOL: Springbrook (Silver Spring, Md.).
COLLEGE: Ohio State.
TRANSACTIONS/CAREER NOTES: Selected by Seattle Seahawks in first round (third pick overall) of 1997 NFL draft. ... Signed by Seahawks (August 4, 1997). ... On suspended list for violating league substance abuse policy (November 27-January 4, 2001). ... Granted unconditional free agency (March 3, 2004). ... Signed by Washington Redskins (March 4, 2004).
HONORS: Named cornerback on THE SPORTING NEWS college All-America second team (1996). ... Played in Pro Bowl (1998 season).

Year Team	G	GS	TOTALS Tk.	Ast.	Sks.	INTERCEPTIONS No.	Yds.	Avg.	TD
1997—Seattle NFL	10	10	34	5	0.0	1	0	0.0	0
1998—Seattle NFL	16	16	61	14	0.0	7	142	20.3	▲2
1999—Seattle NFL	16	16	63	10	0.0	5	77	15.4	0
2000—Seattle NFL	16	16	72	13	0.0	2	8	4.0	0
2001—Seattle NFL	8	7	16	4	0.0	1	0	0.0	0
2002—Seattle NFL	15	15	54	5	0.0	3	0	0.0	0
2003—Seattle NFL	12	8	34	5	1.5	1	8	8.0	0
Pro totals (7 years)	93	88	334	56	1.5	20	235	11.8	2

STAAT, JEREMY DE

PERSONAL: Born October 10, 1976, in Bakersfield, Calif. ... 6-5/300. ... Full name: Jeremy Ray Staat. ... Name pronounced: STOHT.
HIGH SCHOOL: Bakersfield (Calif.).
JUNIOR COLLEGE: Bakersfield (Calif.) College.
COLLEGE: Arizona State.
TRANSACTIONS/CAREER NOTES: Selected by Pittsburgh Steelers in second round (41st pick overall) of 1998 NFL draft. ... Signed by Steelers (June 19, 1998). ... On injured reserve with shoulder injury (December 13, 2000-remainder of season). ... Released by Steelers (February 19, 2001). ... Signed by Seattle Seahawks (April 4, 2001). ... Released by Seahawks (September 2, 2001). ... Signed by Oakland Raiders (February 5, 2002) ... Released by Raiders (August 26, 2002). ... Signed by St. Louis Rams (January 28, 2003). ... Released by Rams (August 29, 2003). ... Re-signed by Rams (November 7, 2003). ... Released by Rams (December 1, 2003).
HONORS: Named defensive tackle on THE SPORTING NEWS college All-America second team (1997).

Year Team	G	GS	TOTALS Tk.	Ast.	Sks.
1998—Pittsburgh NFL	5	0	0	0	0.0
1999—Pittsburgh NFL	16	2	8	3	0.0
2000—Pittsburgh NFL	7	0	4	5	0.0
2003—St. Louis NFL	2	0	0	0	0.0
Pro totals (4 years)	30	2	12	8	0.0

STACKHOUSE, CHARLES FB TEXANS

PERSONAL: Born April 11, 1980, in West Memphis, Ark. ... 6-2/250.
HIGH SCHOOL: West Memphis (Ark.).
COLLEGE: Mississippi.
TRANSACTIONS/CAREER NOTES: Signed as non-drafted free agent by New York Giants (April 26, 2002). ... Released by Giants (August 31, 2003). ... Signed by Minnesota Vikings (September 9, 2003). ... Released by Vikings (May 10, 2004). ... Signed by Houston Texans (May 26, 2004).
SINGLE GAME HIGHS (regular season): Attempts—1 (October 19, 2003, vs. Denver); yards—0; and rushing touchdowns—0.

Year Team	G	GS	RUSHING Att.	Yds.	Avg.	TD	RECEIVING No.	Yds.	Avg.	TD	TOTALS TD	2pt.	Pts.	Fum.
2002—New York Giants NFL	16	2	0	0	0.0	0	13	88	6.8	3	3	0	18	1
2003—Minnesota NFL	14	2	1	0	0.0	0	6	30	5.0	0	0	0	0	0
Pro totals (2 years)	30	4	1	0	0.0	0	19	118	6.2	3	3	0	18	1

STALEY, DUCE — RB — STEELERS

PERSONAL: Born February 27, 1975, in Tampa, Fla. ... 5-11/220. ... Name pronounced: DEUCE.
HIGH SCHOOL: Airport (Columbia, S.C.).
JUNIOR COLLEGE: Itawamba Community College (Miss.).
COLLEGE: South Carolina.
TRANSACTIONS/CAREER NOTES: Selected by Philadelphia Eagles in third round (71st pick overall) of 1997 NFL draft. ... Signed by Eagles (June 12, 1997). ... On injured reserve with foot injury (October 10, 2000-remainder of season). ... On reserve/did not report list (July 29, 2003). ... Activated (August 24, 2003). ... Granted unconditional free agency (March 3, 2004). ... Signed by Pittsburgh Steelers (March 10, 2004).
CHAMPIONSHIP GAME EXPERIENCE: Played in NFC championship game (2001-2003 seasons).
SINGLE GAME HIGHS (regular season): Attempts—31 (November 17, 2002, vs. Arizona); yards—201 (September 3, 2000, vs. Dallas); and rushing touchdowns—2 (December 21, 2003, vs. San Francisco).
STATISTICAL PLATEAUS: 100-yard rushing games: 1998 (1), 1999 (5), 2000 (1), 2001 (2), 2002 (4). Total: 13. 100-yard receiving games: 2001 (1). Total: 1.

			RUSHING				RECEIVING				KICKOFF RETURNS				TOTALS			
Year Team	G	GS	Att.	Yds.	Avg.	TD	No.	Yds.	Avg.	TD	No.	Yds.	Avg.	TD	TD	2pt.	Pts.	Fum.
1997—Philadelphia NFL	16	0	7	29	4.1	0	2	22	11.0	0	47	1139	24.2	0	0	0	0	0
1998—Philadelphia NFL	16	13	258	1065	4.1	5	57	432	7.6	1	1	19	19.0	0	6	0	36	2
1999—Philadelphia NFL	16	16	325	1273	3.9	4	41	294	7.2	2	0	0	0.0	0	6	0	36	5
2000—Philadelphia NFL	5	5	79	344	4.4	1	25	201	8.0	0	0	0	0.0	0	1	0	6	3
2001—Philadelphia NFL	13	10	166	604	3.6	2	63	626	9.9	2	0	0	0.0	0	4	0	24	3
2002—Philadelphia NFL	16	16	269	1029	3.8	5	51	541	10.6	3	0	0	0.0	0	8	1	50	3
2003—Philadelphia NFL	16	4	96	463	4.8	5	36	382	10.6	2	0	0	0.0	0	7	0	42	2
Pro totals (7 years)	98	64	1200	4807	4.0	22	275	2498	9.1	10	48	1158	24.1	0	32	1	194	18

STALLWORTH, DONTE' — WR — SAINTS

PERSONAL: Born November 10, 1980, in Sacramento, Calif. ... 6-0/197. ... Full name: Donte' Lamar Stallworth.
HIGH SCHOOL: Grant (Sacramento, Calif.).
COLLEGE: Tennessee.
TRANSACTIONS/CAREER NOTES: Selected after junior season by New Orleans Saints in first round (13th pick overall) of 2002 NFL draft. ... Signed by Saints (July 29, 2002).
SINGLE GAME HIGHS (regular season): Receptions—8 (September 7, 2003, vs. Seattle); yards—114 (December 28, 2003, vs. Dallas); and touchdown receptions—1 (December 28, 2003, vs. Dallas).
STATISTICAL PLATEAUS: 100-yard receiving games: 2002 (1), 2003 (2). Total: 3.

			RUSHING				RECEIVING				PUNT RETURNS				KICKOFF RETURNS				TOTALS		
Year Team	G	GS	Att.	Yds.	Avg.	TD	No.	Yds.	Avg.	TD	No.	Yds.	Avg.	TD	No.	Yds.	Avg.	TD	TD	2pt.	Pts.
2002—N.O. NFL	13	7	2	2	1.0	0	42	594	14.1	8	0	0	0.0	0	0	0	0.0	0	8	0	48
2003—N.O. NFL	11	3	1	3	3.0	0	25	485	19.4	3	5	44	8.8	0	8	171	21.4	0	3	0	18
Pro totals (2 years)	24	10	3	5	1.7	0	67	1079	16.1	11	5	44	8.8	0	8	171	21.4	0	11	0	66

STAMER, JOSH — LB — BILLS

PERSONAL: Born October 11, 1977, in Sutherland, Iowa. ... 6-2/238.
HIGH SCHOOL: Sutherland (Iowa).
COLLEGE: South Dakota.
TRANSACTIONS/CAREER NOTES: Signed as non-drafted free agent by New York Giants (April 26, 2001). ... Released by Giants (June 28, 2002). ... Signed by Seattle Seahawks (July 23, 2002). ... Released by Seahawks (September 1, 2002). ... Signed by Buffalo Bills (January 21, 2003).

			TOTALS			INTERCEPTIONS			
Year Team	G	GS	Tk.	Ast.	Sks.	No.	Yds.	Avg.	TD
2003—Buffalo NFL	16	0	3	1	0.0	0	0	0.0	0

STANLEY, CHAD — P — TEXANS

PERSONAL: Born January 29, 1976, in Ore City, Texas. ... 6-3/205. ... Full name: Benjamin Chadwick Stanley.
HIGH SCHOOL: Ore City (Texas).
COLLEGE: Stephen F. Austin.
TRANSACTIONS/CAREER NOTES: Signed as non-drafted free agent by San Francisco 49ers (April 23, 1999). ... Released by 49ers (September 1, 2001). ... Signed by Arizona Cardinals (November 6, 2001). ... Released by Cardinals (December 5, 2001). ... Signed by Houston Texans (February 6, 2002). ... Granted free agency (February 28, 2003). ... Re-signed by Texans (June 1, 2003).
RECORDS: Shares NFL single-season record for most punts—114 (2002).

		PUNTING					
Year Team	G	No.	Yds.	Avg.	Net avg.	In. 20	Blk.
1999—San Francisco NFL	16	69	2737	39.7	30.7	20	†2
2000—San Francisco NFL	16	69	2727	39.5	32.2	15	1
2001—Arizona NFL	4	19	751	39.5	34.2	4	0
2002—Houston NFL	16	*114	§4720	41.4	36.8	*36	2
2003—Houston NFL	16	*97	4028	41.5	36.7	*36	0
Pro totals (5 years)	68	368	14963	40.7	34.6	111	5

STARKEY, JASON — C

PERSONAL: Born July 15, 1977, in Barboursville, W.Va. ... 6-4/290.

HIGH SCHOOL: Cabell-Midland (W.Va.).

COLLEGE: Marshall.

TRANSACTIONS/CAREER NOTES: Signed as non-drafted free agent by Arizona Cardinals (June 1, 2000). ... Released by Cardinals (August 27, 2000). ... Re-signed by Cardinals to practice squad (August 28, 2000). ... Activated (September 8, 2000). ... Released by Cardinals (September 11, 2000). ... Re-signed by Cardinals to practice squad (September 13, 2000). ... Granted free agency (February 28, 2003). ... Re-signed by Cardinals (March 20, 2003). ... On injured reserve with shoulder injury (September 30, 2003-remainder of season). ... Granted unconditional free agency (March 3, 2004).

PLAYING EXPERIENCE: Arizona NFL, 2000-2003. ... Games/Games started: 2000 (2/0), 2001 (12/1), 2002 (16/8), 2003 (4/0). Total: 34/9.

STARKS, DUANE — CB — CARDINALS

PERSONAL: Born May 23, 1974, in Miami. ... 5-10/172. ... Full name: Duane Lonell Starks.

HIGH SCHOOL: Miami Beach Senior.

JUNIOR COLLEGE: Holmes Junior College (Miss.).

COLLEGE: Miami (Fla.).

TRANSACTIONS/CAREER NOTES: Selected by Baltimore Ravens in first round (10th pick overall) of 1998 NFL draft. ... Signed by Ravens (August 5, 1998). ... Granted unconditional free agency (March 1, 2002). ... Signed by Arizona Cardinals (March 18, 2002). ... On injured reserve with knee injury (August 27, 2003-entire season).

CHAMPIONSHIP GAME EXPERIENCE: Played in AFC championship game (2000 season). ... Member of Super Bowl championship team (2000 season).

MISCELLANEOUS: Shares Baltimore Ravens all-time record for most interceptions (20).

			TOTALS			INTERCEPTIONS			
Year Team	G	GS	Tk.	Ast.	Sks.	No.	Yds.	Avg.	TD
1998—Baltimore NFL	16	8	49	4	0.0	5	3	0.6	0
1999—Baltimore NFL	16	6	39	3	0.0	5	59	11.8	1
2000—Baltimore NFL	15	15	45	4	0.0	6	125	20.8	0
2001—Baltimore NFL	15	15	54	5	0.0	4	9	2.3	0
2002—Arizona NFL	10	10	47	8	0.0	2	3	1.5	0
2003—Arizona NFL	Did not play.								
Pro totals (5 years)	72	54	234	24	0.0	22	199	9.0	1

ST. CLAIR, JOHN — T — DOLPHINS

PERSONAL: Born July 15, 1977, in Roanoke, Va. ... 6-4/320. ... Full name: John Bradley St. Clair.

HIGH SCHOOL: William Fleming (Roanoke, Va.).

COLLEGE: Virginia.

TRANSACTIONS/CAREER NOTES: Selected by St. Louis Rams in third round (94th pick overall) of 2000 NFL draft. ... Signed by Rams (July 20, 2000). ... Granted free agency (February 28, 2003). ... Re-signed by Rams (April 23, 2003). ... Granted unconditional free agency (March 3, 2004). ... Signed by Miami Dolphins (March 11, 2004).

PLAYING EXPERIENCE: St. Louis NFL, 2000-2003. ... Games/Games started: 2002 (16/16), 2003 (16/0), Total: 32/16.

CHAMPIONSHIP GAME EXPERIENCE: Member of Rams for NFC championship game (2001 season); inactive. ... Member of Rams for Super Bowl 36 (2001 season); inactive.

STECKER, AARON — RB — SAINTS

PERSONAL: Born November 13, 1975, in Green Bay, Wis. ... 5-10/205.

HIGH SCHOOL: Ashwaubenon (Green Bay).

COLLEGE: Western Illinois.

TRANSACTIONS/CAREER NOTES: Signed as non-drafted free agent by Chicago Bears (April 18, 1999). ... Released by Bears (August 30, 1999). ... Signed by Tampa Bay Buccaneers to practice squad (October 20, 1999). ... Granted free agency (February 28, 2003). ... Re-signed by Buccaneers (April 10, 2003). ... Granted unconditional free agency (March 3, 2004). ... Signed by New Orleans Saints (March 4, 2004).

CHAMPIONSHIP GAME EXPERIENCE: Played in NFC championship game (2002 season). ... Member of Super Bowl championship team (2002 season).

SINGLE GAME HIGHS (regular season): Attempts—12 (January 6, 2002, vs. Philadelphia); yards—59 (November 3, 2002, vs. Minnesota); and rushing touchdowns—1 (January 6, 2002, vs. Philadelphia).

			RUSHING				RECEIVING				KICKOFF RETURNS				TOTALS			
Year Team	G	GS	Att.	Yds.	Avg.	TD	No.	Yds.	Avg.	TD	No.	Yds.	Avg.	TD	TD	2pt.	Pts.	Fum.
2000—Tampa Bay NFL	10	0	12	31	2.6	0	1	15	15.0	0	29	663	22.9	0	0	0	0	1
2001—Tampa Bay NFL	13	0	24	72	3.0	1	10	101	10.1	1	9	259	28.8	0	2	0	12	0
2002—Tampa Bay NFL	16	1	28	174	6.2	0	13	69	5.3	0	37	934	25.2	0	0	0	0	3
2003—Tampa Bay NFL	16	1	37	125	3.4	0	9	48	5.3	1	25	520	20.8	0	1	0	6	1
Pro totals (4 years)	55	2	101	402	4.0	1	33	233	7.1	2	100	2376	23.8	0	3	0	18	5

STEELE, GLEN — DT — GIANTS

PERSONAL: Born October 4, 1974, in Ligonier, Ind. ... 6-4/300. ... Full name: James Lendale Steele Jr.

HIGH SCHOOL: West Noble (Ligonier, Ind.).

COLLEGE: Michigan.

TRANSACTIONS/CAREER NOTES: Selected by Cincinnati Bengals in fourth round (105th pick overall) of 1998 NFL draft. ... Signed by Bengals (July 14, 1998). ... On injured reserve with ankle injury (December 15, 1998-remainder of season). ... Granted unconditional free agency (March 3, 2004). ... Signed by New York Giants (May 20, 2004).

Year Team	G	GS	TOTALS Tk.	Ast.	Sks.
1998—Cincinnati NFL	10	0	6	1	0.0
1999—Cincinnati NFL	16	1	13	1	0.0
2000—Cincinnati NFL	16	1	13	4	2.0
2001—Cincinnati NFL	16	1	5	5	1.0
2002—Cincinnati NFL	16	7	15	13	0.0
2003—Cincinnati NFL	16	0	17	4	0.5
Pro totals (6 years)	90	10	69	28	3.5

STEELE, MARKUS — LB — COWBOYS

PERSONAL: Born July 24, 1979, in Cleveland, Ohio. ... 6-3/240.
HIGH SCHOOL: Chanel (New Bedford, Ohio).
JUNIOR COLLEGE: Long Beach City College.
COLLEGE: Southern California.
TRANSACTIONS/CAREER NOTES: Selected by Dallas Cowboys in fourth round (122nd pick overall) of 2001 NFL draft. ... Signed by Cowboys (July 20, 2001). ... Granted free agency (March 3, 2004). ... Re-signed by Cowboys (April 14, 2004).

			TOTALS			INTERCEPTIONS			
Year Team	G	GS	Tk.	Ast.	Sks.	No.	Yds.	Avg.	TD
2001—Dallas NFL	15	10	32	4	0.0	0	0	0.0	0
2002—Dallas NFL	13	2	13	5	0.0	0	0	0.0	0
2003—Dallas NFL	14	0	1	0	0.0	0	0	0.0	0
Pro totals (3 years)	42	12	46	9	0.0	0	0	0.0	0

STEINBACH, ERIC — G — BENGALS

PERSONAL: Born April 4, 1980, in New Lenox, Ill. ... 6-6/297.
HIGH SCHOOL: Providence Catholic (New Lenox, Ill.).
COLLEGE: Iowa.
TRANSACTIONS/CAREER NOTES: Selected by Cincinnati Bengals in second round (33rd pick overall) of 2003 NFL draft. ... Signed by Bengals (July 29, 2003).
PLAYING EXPERIENCE: Cincinnati NFL, 2003. ... Games/Games started: 2003 (15/15). Total: 15/15.

STEUSSIE, TODD — T — BUCCANEERS

PERSONAL: Born December 1, 1970, in Canoga Park, Calif. ... 6-6/308. ... Full name: Todd Edward Steussie. ... Name pronounced: STEW-see.
HIGH SCHOOL: Agoura (Calif.).
COLLEGE: California.
TRANSACTIONS/CAREER NOTES: Selected by Minnesota Vikings in first round (19th pick overall) of 1994 NFL draft. ... Signed by Vikings (July 13, 1994). ... Released by Vikings (March 14, 2001). ... Signed by Carolina Panthers (March 29, 2001). ... Released by Panthers (March 11, 2004). ... Signed by Tampa Bay Buccaneers (March 15, 2004).
PLAYING EXPERIENCE: Minnesota NFL, 1994-2000; Carolina NFL, 2001-2003. ... Games/Games started: 1994 (16/16), 1995 (16/16), 1996 (16/16), 1997 (16/16), 1998 (15/15), 1999 (16/16), 2000 (16/16), 2001 (16/16), 2002 (16/16), 2003 (16/16). Total: 159/159.
CHAMPIONSHIP GAME EXPERIENCE: Played in NFC championship game (1998, 2000 and 2003 seasons). ... Played in Super Bowl 38 (2003 season).
HONORS: Named offensive lineman on THE SPORTING NEWS college All-America second team (1993). ... Played in Pro Bowl (1997 and 1998 seasons).

STEVENS, JERRAMY — TE — SEAHAWKS

PERSONAL: Born November 13, 1979, in Boise, Idaho. ... 6-7/260.
HIGH SCHOOL: River Ridge (Olympia, Wash.).
COLLEGE: Washington.
TRANSACTIONS/CAREER NOTES: Selected after junior season by Seattle Seahawks in first round (28th pick overall) of 2002 NFL draft. ... Signed by Seahawks (July 30, 2002).
SINGLE GAME HIGHS (regular season): Receptions—4 (December 29, 2002, vs. San Diego); yards—70 (December 22, 2002, vs. St. Louis); and touchdown receptions—1 (December 15, 2002, vs. Atlanta).

			RECEIVING				TOTALS			
Year Team	G	GS	No.	Yds.	Avg.	TD	TD	2pt.	Pts.	Fum.
2002—Seattle NFL	12	1	26	252	9.7	3	3	0	18	1
2003—Seattle NFL	16	2	6	72	12.0	0	0	0	0	0
Pro totals (2 years)	28	3	32	324	10.1	3	3	0	18	1

STEVENS, MATT — S

PERSONAL: Born June 14, 1973, in Chapel Hill, N.C. ... 6-0/205. ... Full name: Matthew Brian Stevens.
HIGH SCHOOL: Chapel Hill (N.C.).
COLLEGE: Appalachian State.
TRANSACTIONS/CAREER NOTES: Selected by Buffalo Bills in third round (87th pick overall) of 1996 NFL draft. ... Signed by Bills (July 15, 1996). ... Claimed on waivers by Philadelphia Eagles (August 25, 1997). ... On suspended list for anabolic steroid use (August 27-September 29, 1997). ... Claimed on waivers by Washington Redskins (December 8, 1998). ... Granted free agency (February 12, 1999). ... Re-signed by Redskins (April 23, 1999). ... Granted unconditional free agency (February 11, 2000). ... Re-signed by Redskins (May 12, 2000). ... Claimed

on waivers by New England Patriots (December 20, 2000). ... Granted unconditional free agency (March 2, 2001). ... Re-signed by Patriots (March 16, 2001). ... Selected by Houston Texans from Patriots in NFL expansion draft (February 18, 2002). ... Released by Texans (February 27, 2003). ... Re-signed by Texans (March 21, 2003). ... On injured reserve with knee injury (December 3, 2003-remainder of season). ... Released by Texans (February 24, 2004).

CHAMPIONSHIP GAME EXPERIENCE: Played in AFC championship game (2001 season). ... Member of Super Bowl championship team (2001 season).

			TOTALS			INTERCEPTIONS			
Year Team	**G**	**GS**	**Tk.**	**Ast.**	**Sks.**	**No.**	**Yds.**	**Avg.**	**TD**
1996—Buffalo NFL	13	11	26	7	0.0	2	0	0.0	0
1997—Philadelphia NFL	11	0	10	0	0.0	1	0	0.0	0
1998—Philadelphia NFL	7	1	6	5	0.0	0	0	0.0	0
—Washington NFL	3	0	0	0	0.0	0	0	0.0	0
1999—Washington NFL	15	1	30	6	1.0	6	61	10.2	0
2000—Washington NFL	15	4	26	10	0.0	1	0	0.0	0
—New England NFL	1	0	0	0	0.0	0	0	0.0	0
2001—New England NFL	15	4	24	13	0.0	1	9	9.0	0
2002—Houston NFL	16	16	60	23	0.0	1	0	0.0	0
2003—Houston NFL	12	5	23	7	0.0	1	12	12.0	0
Pro totals (8 years)	108	42	205	71	1.0	13	82	6.3	0

STEVENSON, DOMINIQUE LB BILLS

PERSONAL: Born December 28, 1977, in Gaffney, S.C. ... 6-0/235. ... Full name: Antone Dominique Stevenson.

HIGH SCHOOL: Gaffney (S.C.).

COLLEGE: Tennessee.

TRANSACTIONS/CAREER NOTES: Selected by Buffalo Bills in seventh round (260th pick overall) of 2002 NFL draft.. ... Signed by Bills (July 3, 2002). ... Released by Bills (September 3, 2002). ... Re-signed by Bills to practice squad (September 4, 2002). ... Activated (October 2, 2002).

			TOTALS			INTERCEPTIONS			
Year Team	**G**	**GS**	**Tk.**	**Ast.**	**Sks.**	**No.**	**Yds.**	**Avg.**	**TD**
2002—Buffalo NFL	4	0	0	0	0.0	0	0	0.0	0
2003—Buffalo NFL	16	0	2	0	0.0	0	0	0.0	0
Pro totals (2 years)	20	0	2	0	0.0	0	0	0.0	0

STEWART, DALEROY DT COWBOYS

PERSONAL: Born November 2, 1978, in Vero Beach, Fla. ... 6-4/327. ... Full name: Daleroy Andrew Stewart.

HIGH SCHOOL: Vero Beach (Fla.).

COLLEGE: Southern Mississippi.

TRANSACTIONS/CAREER NOTES: Selected by Dallas Cowboys in sixth round (171st pick overall) in 2001 NFL draft. ... Signed by Cowboys (July 21, 2001). ... On non-football injury list with shoulder injury (August 28, 2001-remainder of season). ... Inactive for 16 games (2002).

			TOTALS		
Year Team	**G**	**GS**	**Tk.**	**Ast.**	**Sks.**
2003—Dallas NFL	15	1	12	5	1.5

STEWART, JAMES RB

PERSONAL: Born December 27, 1971, in Morristown, Tenn. ... 6-1/224. ... Full name: James Ottis Stewart III.

HIGH SCHOOL: Morristown-Hamblen West (Morristown, Tenn.).

COLLEGE: Tennessee.

TRANSACTIONS/CAREER NOTES: Selected by Jacksonville Jaguars in first round (19th pick overall) of 1995 NFL draft. ... Signed by Jaguars (June 1, 1995). ... On injured reserve with knee injury (September 22, 1998-remainder of season). ... Granted unconditional free agency (February 11, 2000). ... Signed by Detroit Lions (February 14, 2000). ... On injured reserve with shoulder injury (September 2, 2003-entire season). ... Released by Lions (March 2, 2004).

CHAMPIONSHIP GAME EXPERIENCE: Played in AFC championship game (1996 and 1999 seasons).

SINGLE GAME HIGHS (regular season): Attempts—37 (December 17, 2000, vs. New York Jets); yards—172 (October 20, 2002, vs. Chicago); and rushing touchdowns—5 (October 12, 1997, vs. Philadelphia).

STATISTICAL PLATEAUS: 100-yard rushing games: 1996 (1), 1997 (1), 1998 (2), 1999 (2), 2000 (3), 2001 (2), 2002 (2). Total: 13.

			RUSHING				RECEIVING				TOTALS			
Year Team	**G**	**GS**	**Att.**	**Yds.**	**Avg.**	**TD**	**No.**	**Yds.**	**Avg.**	**TD**	**TD**	**2pt.**	**Pts.**	**Fum.**
1995—Jacksonville NFL	14	8	137	525	3.8	2	21	190	9.0	1	3	0	18	1
1996—Jacksonville NFL	13	11	190	723	3.8	8	30	177	5.9	2	10	0	60	2
1997—Jacksonville NFL	16	5	136	555	4.1	8	41	336	8.2	1	9	0	54	0
1998—Jacksonville NFL	3	3	53	217	4.1	2	6	42	7.0	1	3	0	18	2
1999—Jacksonville NFL	14	7	249	931	3.7	▲13	21	108	5.1	0	13	0	78	4
2000—Detroit NFL	16	16	‡339	1184	3.5	10	32	287	9.0	1	11	3	72	4
2001—Detroit NFL	11	10	143	685	4.8	1	23	242	10.5	1	2	0	12	0
2002—Detroit NFL	14	9	231	1021	4.4	4	46	333	7.2	2	6	0	36	0
2003—Detroit NFL	Did not play.													
Pro totals (8 years)	101	69	1478	5841	4.0	48	220	1715	7.8	9	57	3	348	13

STEWART, KORDELL QB

PERSONAL: Born October 16, 1972, in New Orleans, La. ... 6-1/218.

HIGH SCHOOL: John Ehret (Marrero, La.).

COLLEGE: Colorado.

TRANSACTIONS/CAREER NOTES: Selected by Pittsburgh Steelers in second round (60th pick overall) of 1995 NFL draft. ... Signed by Steelers (July 17, 1995). ... Released by Steelers (February 26, 2003). ... Signed by Chicago Bears (March 13, 2003). ... Released by Bears (March 1, 2004).

CHAMPIONSHIP GAME EXPERIENCE: Played in AFC championship game (1995, 1997 and 2001 seasons). ... Played in Super Bowl 30 (1995 season).

HONORS: Played in Pro Bowl (2001 season).

SINGLE GAME HIGHS (regular season): Attempts—48 (December 13, 1997, vs. New England); completions—26 (December 13, 1997, vs. New England); yards—333 (December 16, 2001, vs. Baltimore); and touchdown passes—3 (December 30, 2001, vs. Cincinnati).

STATISTICAL PLATEAUS: 100-yard rushing games: 1996 (1), 1998 (1). Total: 2. 300-yard passing games: 1997 (2), 2001 (1). Total: 3.

MISCELLANEOUS: Regular-season record as starting NFL quarterback: 48-34 (.585). ... Postseason record as starting NFL quarterback: 2-2 (.500). ... Started two games at wide receiver (1995). ... Started two games at wide receiver (1996). ... Started one game at wide receiver (1999).

			PASSING								RUSHING				RECEIVING				TOTALS		
Year Team	G	GS	Att.	Cmp.	Pct.	Yds.	TD	Int.	Avg.	Rat.	Att.	Yds.	Avg.	TD	No.	Yds.	Avg.	TD	TD	2pt.	Pts.
1995—Pittsburgh NFL	10	2	7	5	71.4	60	1	0	8.57	136.9	15	86	5.7	1	14	235	16.8	1	2	0	12
1996—Pittsburgh NFL	16	2	30	11	36.7	100	0	2	3.33	18.8	39	171	4.4	5	17	293	17.2	3	8	0	48
1997—Pittsburgh NFL	16	16	440	236	53.6	3020	21	§17	6.86	75.2	88	476	5.4	11	0	0	0.0	0	11	0	66
1998—Pittsburgh NFL	16	16	458	252	55.0	2560	11	18	5.59	62.9	81	406	5.0	2	1	17	17.0	0	2	0	12
1999—Pittsburgh NFL	16	12	275	160	58.2	1464	6	10	5.32	64.9	56	258	4.6	2	9	113	12.6	1	3	0	18
2000—Pittsburgh NFL	16	11	289	151	52.2	1860	11	8	6.44	73.6	78	436	5.6	7	0	0	0.0	0	7	0	42
2001—Pittsburgh NFL	16	16	442	266	60.2	3109	14	11	7.03	81.7	96	537	5.6	5	0	0	0.0	0	5	0	30
2002—Pittsburgh NFL	8	5	166	109	65.7	1155	6	6	6.96	82.8	43	191	4.4	2	0	0	0.0	0	2	0	12
2003—Chicago NFL	9	7	251	126	50.2	1418	7	12	5.65	56.8	59	290	4.9	3	0	0	0.0	0	3	1	20
Pro totals (9 years)	123	87	2358	1316	55.8	14746	77	84	6.25	70.7	555	2851	5.1	38	41	658	16.0	5	43	1	260

STEWART, MATT — LB — FALCONS

PERSONAL: Born August 31, 1979, in Columbus, Ohio. ... 6-3/232.

HIGH SCHOOL: DeSales (Columbus, Ohio).

COLLEGE: Vanderbilt.

TRANSACTIONS/CAREER NOTES: Selected by Atlanta Falcons in fourth round (102nd pick overall) of 2001 NFL draft. ... Signed by Falcons (May 30, 2001). ... Granted free agency (March 3, 2004). ... Re-signed by Falcons (May 20, 2004).

			TOTALS			INTERCEPTIONS			
Year Team	G	GS	Tk.	Ast.	Sks.	No.	Yds.	Avg.	TD
2001—Atlanta NFL	15	0	9	3	0.0	0	0	0.0	0
2002—Atlanta NFL	16	13	48	5	3.0	0	0	0.0	0
2003—Atlanta NFL	16	16	59	17	2.5	0	0	0.0	0
Pro totals (3 years)	47	29	116	25	5.5	0	0	0.0	0

STEWART, QUINCY — LB — JETS

PERSONAL: Born March 27, 1978, in Tyler, Texas. ... 6-1/234. ... Full name: Quincy Jermaine Stewart.

HIGH SCHOOL: John Tyler (Texas).

COLLEGE: Louisiana Tech.

TRANSACTIONS/CAREER NOTES: Signed as non-drafted free agent by San Francisco 49ers (April 25, 2001). ... Granted free agency (February 28, 2003). ... Signed by Denver Broncos (April 2, 2003). ... Released by Broncos (August 26, 2003). ... Signed by New York Jets (September 30, 2003). ... Granted free agency (March 3, 2004). ... Re-signed by Jets (March 22, 2004).

			TOTALS			INTERCEPTIONS			
Year Team	G	GS	Tk.	Ast.	Sks.	No.	Yds.	Avg.	TD
2001—San Francisco NFL	16	0	0	0	0.0	0	0	0.0	0
2002—San Francisco NFL	15	0	3	1	0.0	1	0	0.0	0
2003—New York Jets NFL	12	0	1	0	0.0	0	0	0.0	0
Pro totals (3 years)	43	0	4	1	0.0	1	0	0.0	0

STEWART, TONY — TE — BENGALS

PERSONAL: Born August 9, 1979, in Lohne, Germany. ... 6-5/260. ... Full name: Tony Alexander Stewart.

HIGH SCHOOL: Allentown Central (Pa.).

COLLEGE: Penn State.

TRANSACTIONS/CAREER NOTES: Selected by Philadelphia Eagles in fifth round (147th pick overall) of 2001 NFL draft. ... Signed by Eagles (May 22, 2001). ... Released by Eagles (September 10, 2002). ... Re-signed by Eagles to practice squad (September 12, 2002). ... Signed by Cincinnati Bengals off Eagles practice squad (November 23, 2002). ... Granted free agency (March 3, 2004). ... Re-signed by Bengals (April 16, 2004).

CHAMPIONSHIP GAME EXPERIENCE: Member of Eagles for NFC championship game (2001 season); inactive.

SINGLE GAME HIGHS (regular season): Receptions—5 (October 5, 2003, vs. Buffalo); yards—56 (September 28, 2003, vs. Cleveland); and touchdown receptions—1 (November 29, 2001, vs. Kansas City).

			RECEIVING				TOTALS			
Year Team	G	GS	No.	Yds.	Avg.	TD	TD	2pt.	Pts.	Fum.
2001—Philadelphia NFL	3	1	5	52	10.4	1	1	0	6	0
2002—Cincinnati NFL	3	0	1	6	6.0	0	0	0	0	0
2003—Cincinnati NFL	16	7	21	212	10.1	0	0	0	0	0
Pro totals (3 years)	22	8	27	270	10.0	1	1	0	6	0

STILLS, GARY — DE — CHIEFS

PERSONAL: Born July 11, 1974, in Trenton, N.J. ... 6-2/244.
HIGH SCHOOL: Valley Forge (Pa.) Military Academy.
COLLEGE: West Virginia.
TRANSACTIONS/CAREER NOTES: Selected by Kansas City Chiefs in third round (75th pick overall) of 1999 NFL draft. ... Signed by Chiefs (July 26, 1999). ... Assigned by Chiefs to Frankfurt Galaxy in 2001 NFL Europe enhancement allocation program (February 19, 2001). ... Granted free agency (March 1, 2002). ... Re-signed by Chiefs (April 20, 2002). ... Granted unconditional free agency (February 27, 2003). ... Re-signed by Chiefs (February 27, 2003).
HONORS: Played in Pro Bowl (2003 season).

			TOTALS			INTERCEPTIONS			
Year Team	G	GS	Tk.	Ast.	Sks.	No.	Yds.	Avg.	TD
1999—Kansas City NFL	2	0	0	0	0.0	0	0	0.0	0
2000—Kansas City NFL	11	0	0	0	0.0	0	0	0.0	0
2001—Kansas City NFL	10	0	1	0	0.0	0	0	0.0	0
2002—Kansas City NFL	16	1	18	3	2.0	0	0	0.0	0
2003—Kansas City NFL	16	0	16	0	3.0	0	0	0.0	0
Pro totals (5 years)	55	1	35	3	5.0	0	0	0.0	0

STINCHCOMB, JON — T — SAINTS

S

PERSONAL: Born August 27, 1979, in Lilburn, Ga. ... 6-5/302. ... Full name: Jonathan Stinchcomb. ... Brother of Matt Stinchcomb, offensive lineman, Tampa Bay Buccaneers.
HIGH SCHOOL: Parkview (Lilburn, Ga.).
COLLEGE: Georgia.
TRANSACTIONS/CAREER NOTES: Selected by New Orleans Saints in second round (37th pick overall) of 2003 NFL draft. ... Signed by Saints (July 25, 2003).
PLAYING EXPERIENCE: New Orleans NFL, 2003. ... Games/Games started: 2003 (6/0). Total: 6/0.

STINCHCOMB, MATT — G/T — BUCCANEERS

PERSONAL: Born June 3, 1977, in Lilburn, Ga. ... 6-6/310. ... Full name: Matthew Douglass Stinchcomb. ... Brother of Jon Stinchcomb, offensive tackle, New Orleans Saints.
HIGH SCHOOL: Parkview (Lilburn, Ga.).
COLLEGE: Georgia.
TRANSACTIONS/CAREER NOTES: Selected by Oakland Raiders in first round (18th pick overall) of 1999 NFL draft. ... Signed by Raiders (July 22, 1999). ... Inactive for three games (1999). ... On injured reserve with shoulder injury (October 1, 1999-remainder of season). ... On injured reserve with shoulder injury (November 12, 2003-remainder of season). ... Granted unconditional free agency (March 3, 2004). ... Signed by Tampa Bay Buccaneers (March 5, 2004).
PLAYING EXPERIENCE: Oakland NFL, 1999-2003. ... Games/Games started: 2000 (13/9), 2001 (14/1), 2002 (16/6), 2003 (6/4), Total: 49/20.
CHAMPIONSHIP GAME EXPERIENCE: Member of Raiders for AFC Championship game (2000 season); did not play. ... Played in AFC championship game (2002 season). ... Played in Super Bowl 37 (2002 season).
HONORS: Named offensive tackle on THE SPORTING NEWS college All-America second team (1997 and 1998).

ST. LOUIS, BRAD — TE/LS — BENGALS

PERSONAL: Born August 19, 1976, in Waverly, Mo. ... 6-3/247. ... Full name: Brad Allen St. Louis.
HIGH SCHOOL: Belton (Mo.).
COLLEGE: Southwest Missouri State.
TRANSACTIONS/CAREER NOTES: Selected by Cincinnati Bengals in seventh round (210th pick overall) of 2000 NFL draft. ... Signed by Bengals (July 20, 2000). ... On injured reserve with leg injury (December 5, 2001-remainder of season). ... Granted free agency (February 28, 2003). ... Re-signed by Bengals (March 17, 2003). ... Re-signed by Bengals (December 20, 2003).
PLAYING EXPERIENCE: Cincinnati NFL, 2000-2003. ... Games/Games started: 2000 (16/0), 2001 (11/0), 2002 (16/0), 2003 (16/0). Total: 59/0.

STOKES, BARRY — T/G — GIANTS

PERSONAL: Born December 20, 1973, in Flint, Mich. ... 6-4/310. ... Full name: Barry Wade Stokes.
HIGH SCHOOL: Davison (Mich.).
COLLEGE: Eastern Michigan.
TRANSACTIONS/CAREER NOTES: Signed as non-drafted free agent by Detroit Lions (April 26, 1996). ... Released by Lions (August 14, 1996). ... Signed by Jacksonville Jaguars to practice squad (October 23, 1996). ... Granted free agency after 1996 season. ... Signed by Atlanta Falcons (January 30, 1997). ... Released by Falcons (August 1997). ... Signed by St. Louis Rams to practice squad (August 26, 1997). ... Released by Rams (October 6, 1997). ... Signed by Miami Dolphins to practice squad (November 26, 1997). ... Assigned by Dolphins to Scottish Claymores in 1998 NFL Europe enhancement allocation program (February 18, 1998). ... Released by Dolphins (August 25, 1998). ... Re-signed by Dolphins (November 4, 1998). ... Assigned by Dolphins to Scottish Claymores in 1999 NFL Europe enhancement allocation program (February 22, 1999). ... Released by Dolphins (September 4, 1999). ... Signed by Green Bay Packers (September 8, 1999). ... Released by Packers (September 21, 1999). ... Re-signed by Packers (October 20, 1999). ... Inactive for five games (1999). ... Released by Packers (November 9, 1999). ... Signed by Oakland Raiders (January 2, 2000). ... Released by Raiders (July 21, 2000). ... Signed by Packers (July 22, 2000). ... Released by Packers (September 27, 2000). ... Re-signed by Packers (October 23, 2000). ... Granted unconditional free agency (March 1, 2002). ... Signed by Cleveland Browns (April 1, 2002). ... Granted unconditional free agency (March 3, 2004). ... Signed by New York Giants (March 13, 2004).
PLAYING EXPERIENCE: Miami NFL, 1998; Green Bay NFL, 2000-2001; Cleveland NFL, 2002-2003. ... Games/Games started: 1998 (3/0), 2000 (8/0), 2001 (16/3), 2002 (16/16), 2003 (13/13). Total: 56/32.

STOKES, J.J. — WR — PATRIOTS

PERSONAL: Born October 6, 1972, in San Diego, Calif. ... 6-4/218. ... Full name: Jerel Jamal Stokes.
HIGH SCHOOL: Point Loma (San Diego).
COLLEGE: UCLA.
TRANSACTIONS/CAREER NOTES: Selected by San Francisco 49ers in first round (10th pick overall) of 1995 NFL draft. ... Signed by 49ers (July 27, 1995). ... On injured reserve with wrist injury (October 26, 1996-remainder of season). ... Granted unconditional free agency (February 12, 1999). ... Re-signed by 49ers (March 8, 1999). ... Released by 49ers (June 1, 2003). ... Signed by Jacksonville Jaguars (June 17, 2003). ... Waived by Jaguars (November 12, 2003). ... Signed by New England Patriots (November 18, 2003). ... Waived by Patriots (December 9, 2003). ... Granted unconditional free agency (March 3, 2004). ... Re-signed by Patriots (March 3, 2004).
CHAMPIONSHIP GAME EXPERIENCE: Played in NFC championship game (1997 season). ... Member of Patriots for AFC championship game (2003 season); inactive. ... Member of Patriots for Super Bowl 38 (2003 season); inactive.
HONORS: Named wide receiver on THE SPORTING NEWS college All-America first team (1993).
SINGLE GAME HIGHS (regular season): Receptions—9 (October 18, 1998, vs. Indianapolis); yards—130 (January 3, 2000, vs. Atlanta); and touchdown receptions—2 (December 30, 2001, vs. Dallas).
STATISTICAL PLATEAUS: 100-yard receiving games: 1995 (1), 1998 (2), 1999 (1). Total: 4.

			RECEIVING				TOTALS			
Year Team	G	GS	No.	Yds.	Avg.	TD	TD	2pt.	Pts.	Fum.
1995—San Francisco NFL	12	2	38	517	13.6	4	4	0	24	0
1996—San Francisco NFL	6	6	18	249	13.8	0	0	0	0	0
1997—San Francisco NFL	16	16	58	733	12.6	4	4	0	24	1
1998—San Francisco NFL	16	11	63	770	12.2	8	8	0	48	0
1999—San Francisco NFL	16	4	34	429	12.6	3	3	1	20	1
2000—San Francisco NFL	16	3	30	524	17.5	3	3	1	20	0
2001—San Francisco NFL	16	16	54	585	10.8	7	7	0	42	0
2002—San Francisco NFL	13	8	32	332	10.4	1	1	0	6	0
2003—Jacksonville NFL	5	3	13	116	8.9	0	0	0	0	0
—New England NFL	2	0	2	38	19.0	0	0	0	0	0
Pro totals (9 years)	118	69	342	4293	12.6	30	30	2	184	2

S

STOKLEY, BRANDON — WR — COLTS

PERSONAL: Born June 23, 1976, in Blacksburg, Va. ... 5-11/197.
HIGH SCHOOL: Comeaux (Lafayette, La.).
COLLEGE: Louisiana-Lafayette.
TRANSACTIONS/CAREER NOTES: Selected by Baltimore Ravens in fourth round (105th pick overall) of 1999 NFL draft. ... Signed by Ravens (July 28, 1999). ... On injured reserve with shoulder injury (October 25, 1999-remainder of season). ... Granted free agency (March 1, 2002). ... Re-signed by Ravens (April 16, 2002). ... On injured reserve with foot injury (November 26, 2002-remainder of season). ... Granted unconditional free agency (February 28, 2003). ... Signed by Indianapolis Colts (March 13, 2003).
CHAMPIONSHIP GAME EXPERIENCE: Played in AFC championship game (2000 and 2003 seasons). ... Member of Super Bowl championship team (2000 season).
SINGLE GAME HIGHS (regular season): Receptions—9 (December 28, 2003, vs. Houston); yards—95 (December 14, 2003, vs. Atlanta); and touchdown receptions—2 (December 14, 2003, vs. Atlanta).

			RUSHING				RECEIVING				TOTALS			
Year Team	G	GS	Att.	Yds.	Avg.	TD	No.	Yds.	Avg.	TD	TD	2pt.	Pts.	Fum.
1999—Baltimore NFL	2	0	0	0	0.0	0	1	28	28.0	1	1	0	6	0
2000—Baltimore NFL	7	1	1	6	6.0	0	11	184	16.7	2	2	0	12	0
2001—Baltimore NFL	16	5	1	1	1.0	0	24	344	14.3	2	2	0	12	1
2002—Baltimore NFL	8	5	6	31	5.2	0	24	357	14.9	2	2	0	12	1
2003—Indianapolis NFL	6	3	0	0	0.0	0	22	211	9.6	3	3	0	18	0
Pro totals (5 years)	39	14	8	38	4.8	0	82	1124	13.7	10	10	0	60	2

STONE, JOHN — WR — RAIDERS

PERSONAL: ... 5-11/180.
HIGH SCHOOL: Mainland Regional (N.J.).
COLLEGE: Wake Forest.
TRANSACTIONS/CAREER NOTES: Signed as non-drafted free agent by Indianapolis Colts (April 26, 2002). ... Released by Colts (August 26, 2002). ... Signed by Oakland Raiders (January 13, 2003). ... Waived by Raiders (August 26, 2003). ... Re-signed by Raiders to practice squad (September 2, 2003). ... Activated (December 10, 2003).

			RECEIVING				TOTALS			
Year Team	G	GS	No.	Yds.	Avg.	TD	TD	2pt.	Pts.	Fum.
2003—Oakland NFL	1	0	0	0	0.0	0	0	0	0	0

STONE, RON — G — RAIDERS

PERSONAL: Born July 20, 1971, in Boston, Mass. ... 6-5/325.
HIGH SCHOOL: West Roxbury (Mass.).
COLLEGE: Boston College.
TRANSACTIONS/CAREER NOTES: Selected by Dallas Cowboys in fourth round (96th pick overall) of 1993 NFL draft. ... Signed by Cowboys (July 16, 1993). ... Active for four games with Cowboys (1993); did not play. ... Granted free agency (February 16, 1996). ... Tendered offer sheet by New York Giants (March 1, 1996). ... Cowboys declined to match offer (March 7, 1996). ... Granted unconditional free agency (March 1, 2002). ... Signed by San Francisco 49ers (April 12, 2002). ... Released by 49ers (March 2, 2004). ... Signed by Oakland Raiders (March 8, 2004).

PLAYING EXPERIENCE: Dallas NFL, 1994-1995; New York Giants NFL, 1996-2001; San Francisco NFL, 2002-2003. ... Games/Games started: 1994 (16/0), 1995 (16/1), 1996 (16/16), 1997 (16/16), 1998 (14/14), 1999 (16/16), 2000 (15/15), 2001 (15/15), 2002 (15/15), 2003 (13/13). Total: 152/121.
CHAMPIONSHIP GAME EXPERIENCE: Member of Cowboys for NFC championship game (1993 season); inactive. ... Member of Super Bowl championship team (1993 and 1995 seasons). ... Played in NFC championship game (1994, 1995 and 2000 seasons). ... Played in Super Bowl 35 (2000 season).
HONORS: Played in Pro Bowl (2000-2002 seasons).

STOUTMIRE, OMAR — S — GIANTS

PERSONAL: Born July 9, 1974, in Pensacola, Fla. ... 5-11/205.
HIGH SCHOOL: Polytechnic (Pasadena, Calif.).
COLLEGE: Fresno State.
TRANSACTIONS/CAREER NOTES: Selected by Dallas Cowboys in seventh round (224th pick overall) of 1997 NFL draft. ... Signed by Cowboys (July 14, 1997). ... Claimed on waivers by Cleveland Browns (September 6, 1999). ... Inactive for two games with Browns (1999). ... Released by Browns (September 21, 1999). ... Signed by New York Jets (October 6, 1999). ... Granted free agency (February 11, 2000). ... Re-signed by Jets (April 18, 2000). ... Released by Jets (August 27, 2000). ... Signed by New York Giants (August 30, 2000). ... Granted unconditional free agency (March 2, 2001). ... Re-signed by Giants (May 14, 2001). ... Granted unconditional free agency (February 28, 2003). ... Re-signed by Giants (March 19, 2003).
CHAMPIONSHIP GAME EXPERIENCE: Played in NFC championship game (2000 season). ... Played in Super Bowl 35 (2000 season).

S

			TOTALS			INTERCEPTIONS			
Year Team	**G**	**GS**	**Tk.**	**Ast.**	**Sks.**	**No.**	**Yds.**	**Avg.**	**TD**
1997—Dallas NFL	16	2	38	8	2.0	2	8	4.0	0
1998—Dallas NFL	16	12	36	16	1.0	0	0	0.0	0
1999—New York Jets NFL	12	5	25	4	1.0	2	97	48.5	1
2000—New York Giants NFL	16	0	1	0	0.0	0	0	0.0	0
2001—New York Giants NFL	16	0	2	0	0.0	0	0	0.0	0
2002—New York Giants NFL	16	16	63	18	0.0	0	0	0.0	0
2003—New York Giants NFL	16	16	74	21	1.0	1	34	34.0	0
Pro totals (7 years)	108	51	239	67	5.0	5	139	27.8	1

STOVER, MATT — K — RAVENS

PERSONAL: Born January 27, 1968, in Dallas, Texas. ... 5-11/178. ... Full name: John Matthew Stover.
HIGH SCHOOL: Lake Highlands (Dallas).
COLLEGE: Louisiana Tech.
TRANSACTIONS/CAREER NOTES: Selected by New York Giants in 12th round (329th pick overall) of 1990 NFL draft. ... Signed by Giants (July 23, 1990). ... On injured reserve with leg injury (September 4, 1990-entire season). ... Granted unconditional free agency (February 1, 1991). ... Signed by Cleveland Browns (March 15, 1991). ... Granted free agency (March 1, 1993). ... Re-signed by Browns (July 24, 1993). ... Released by Browns (August 30, 1993). ... Re-signed by Browns (August 31, 1993). ... Granted unconditional free agency (February 17, 1994). ... Re-signed by Browns (March 4, 1994). ... Browns franchise moved to Baltimore and renamed Ravens for 1996 season (March 11, 1996). ... Granted unconditional free agency (March 3, 2004). ... Re-signed by Ravens (March 9, 2004).
CHAMPIONSHIP GAME EXPERIENCE: Played in AFC championship game (2000 season). ... Member of Super Bowl championship team (2000 season).
HONORS: Named kicker on THE SPORTING NEWS NFL All-Pro team (2000). ... Played in Pro Bowl (2000 season).
RECORDS: Holds NFL record for most consecutive games with one or more field goals made—38 (October 31, 1999-December 2, 2001).

		FIELD GOALS							TOTALS		
Year Team	**G**	**1-29**	**30-39**	**40-49**	**50+**	**Tot.**	**Pct.**	**Lg.**	**XPM**	**XPA**	**Pts.**
1990—New York Giants NFL				Did not play.							
1991—Cleveland NFL	16	3-5	8-9	3-6	2-2	16-22	72.7	§55	33	34	81
1992—Cleveland NFL	16	12-12	6-8	2-6	1-3	21-29	72.4	51	29	30	92
1993—Cleveland NFL	16	4-4	5-6	6-8	1-4	16-22	72.7	53	36	36	84
1994—Cleveland NFL	16	8-8	10-11	8-8	0-1	26-28	*92.9	45	32	32	110
1995—Cleveland NFL	16	13-13	9-10	7-9	0-1	29-33	§87.9	47	26	26	113
1996—Baltimore NFL	16	8-8	5-6	5-10	1-1	19-25	76.0	50	34	35	91
1997—Baltimore NFL	16	8-9	12-12	6-11	0-2	26-34	76.5	49	32	32	110
1998—Baltimore NFL	16	6-6	5-5	10-17	0-0	21-28	75.0	48	24	24	87
1999—Baltimore NFL	16	13-13	6-8	7-7	2-5	28-33	84.8	50	32	32	116
2000—Baltimore NFL	16	11-11	12-13	10-12	2-3	*35-*39	89.7	51	30	30	§135
2001—Baltimore NFL	16	16-16	9-10	5-9	0-0	30-35	85.7	49	25	25	115
2002—Baltimore NFL	15	9-9	4-5	7-10	1-1	21-25	84.0	51	33	33	96
2003—Baltimore NFL	16	16-16	6-6	11-14	0-2	33-§38	86.8	49	35	35	134
Pro totals (13 years)	207	127-130	97-109	87-127	10-25	321-391	82.1	55	401	404	1364

STRAHAN, MICHAEL — DE — GIANTS

PERSONAL: Born November 21, 1971, in Houston, Texas. ... 6-5/275. ... Full name: Michael Anthony Strahan. ... Name pronounced: STRAY-han.
HIGH SCHOOL: Westbury (Houston), then Mannheim (West Germany) American.
COLLEGE: Texas Southern.
TRANSACTIONS/CAREER NOTES: Selected by New York Giants in second round (40th pick overall) of 1993 NFL draft. ... Signed by Giants (July 25, 1993). ... On injured reserve with foot injury (January 13, 1994-remainder of playoffs). ... Granted free agency (February 16, 1996). ... Re-signed by Giants (July 8, 1996).
CHAMPIONSHIP GAME EXPERIENCE: Played in NFC championship game (2000 season). ... Played in Super Bowl 35 (2000 season).
HONORS: Named defensive end on THE SPORTING NEWS NFL All-Pro team (1997, 2001 and 2003). ... Played in Pro Bowl (1997-1999 and 2001-2003 seasons).

RECORDS: Holds NFL single-season record for most sacks—22 1/2 (2001).

Year Team	G	GS	TOTALS Tk.	Ast.	Sks.	INTERCEPTIONS No.	Yds.	Avg.	TD
1993—New York Giants NFL	9	0	1	2	1.0	0	0	0.0	0
1994—New York Giants NFL	15	15	27	13	4.5	0	0	0.0	0
1995—New York Giants NFL	15	15	48	10	7.5	2	56	28.0	0
1996—New York Giants NFL	16	16	54	9	5.0	0	0	0.0	0
1997—New York Giants NFL	16	16	49	19	14.0	0	0	0.0	0
1998—New York Giants NFL	16	15	53	14	15.0	1	24	24.0	1
1999—New York Giants NFL	16	16	43	15	5.5	1	44	44.0	1
2000—New York Giants NFL	16	16	51	15	9.5	0	0	0.0	0
2001—New York Giants NFL	16	16	62	11	*22.5	0	0	0.0	0
2002—New York Giants NFL	16	16	57	14	11.0	0	0	0.0	0
2003—New York Giants NFL	16	16	60	15	*18.5	0	0	0.0	0
Pro totals (11 years)	167	157	505	137	114.0	4	124	31.0	2

STREETS, TAI — WR — LIONS

PERSONAL: Born April 20, 1977, in Matteson, Ill. ... 6-3/207.
HIGH SCHOOL: Thornton Township (Harvey, Ill.).
COLLEGE: Michigan.
TRANSACTIONS/CAREER NOTES: Selected by San Francisco 49ers in sixth round (171st pick overall) of 1999 NFL draft. ... Signed by 49ers (July 30, 1999). ... On non-football injury list with Achilles' tendon injury (July 30-November 30, 1999). ... Granted free agency (February 28, 2003). ... Re-signed by 49ers (May 16, 2003). ... Granted unconditional free agency (March 3, 2004). ... Signed by Detroit Lions (March 10, 2004).
SINGLE GAME HIGHS (regular season): Receptions—8 (December 21, 2002, vs. Arizona); yards—90 (December 21, 2002, vs. Arizona); and touchdown receptions—2 (December 30, 2002, vs. St. Louis).

S

Year Team	G	GS	RECEIVING No.	Yds.	Avg.	TD	TOTALS TD	2pt.	Pts.	Fum.
1999—San Francisco NFL	2	0	2	25	12.5	0	0	0	0	0
2000—San Francisco NFL	15	1	19	287	15.1	0	0	0	0	1
2001—San Francisco NFL	16	3	28	345	12.3	1	1	0	6	0
2002—San Francisco NFL	16	14	72	756	10.5	5	5	0	30	1
2003—San Francisco NFL	16	16	47	595	12.7	7	7	0	42	0
Pro totals (5 years)	65	34	168	2008	12.0	13	13	0	78	2

STRICKLAND, DONALD — CB — COLTS

PERSONAL: Born November 24, 1980, in Redwood City, Calif. ... 5-10/187.
HIGH SCHOOL: Archbishop Riordan (San Francisco).
COLLEGE: Colorado.
TRANSACTIONS/CAREER NOTES: Selected by Indianapolis Colts in third round (90th pick overall) of 2003 NFL draft. ... Signed by Colts (July 30, 2003).
CHAMPIONSHIP GAME EXPERIENCE: Played in AFC championship game (2003 season).

Year Team	G	GS	TOTALS Tk.	Ast.	Sks.	INTERCEPTIONS No.	Yds.	Avg.	TD
2003—Indianapolis NFL	11	8	23	13	0.0	2	43	21.5	0

STRONG, MACK — FB — SEAHAWKS

PERSONAL: Born September 11, 1971, in Columbus, Ga. ... 6-0/245.
HIGH SCHOOL: Brookstone (Columbus, Ga.).
COLLEGE: Georgia.
TRANSACTIONS/CAREER NOTES: Signed as non-drafted free agent by Seattle Seahawks (April 28, 1993). ... Released by Seahawks (September 4, 1993). ... Re-signed by Seahawks to practice squad (September 6, 1993). ... Released by Seahawks (February 10, 2000). ... Re-signed by Seahawks (February 14, 2000). ... Granted unconditional free agency (March 1, 2002). ... Re-signed by Seahawks (May 1, 2002). ... Granted unconditional free agency (February 28, 2003). ... Re-signed by Seahawks (April 8, 2003).
SINGLE GAME HIGHS (regular season): Attempts—10 (December 11, 1994, vs. Houston); yards—44 (December 11, 1994, vs. Houston); rushing touchdowns—1 (October 12, 2003, vs. San Francisco).

Year Team	G	GS	RUSHING Att.	Yds.	Avg.	TD	RECEIVING No.	Yds.	Avg.	TD	KICKOFF RETURNS No.	Yds.	Avg.	TD	TOTALS TD	2pt.	Pts.	Fum.
1993—Seattle NFL							Did not play.											
1994—Seattle NFL	8	1	27	114	4.2	2	3	3	1.0	0	0	0	0.0	0	2	0	12	1
1995—Seattle NFL	16	2	8	23	2.9	1	12	117	9.8	3	4	65	16.3	0	4	0	24	2
1996—Seattle NFL	14	8	5	8	1.6	0	9	78	8.7	0	0	0	0.0	0	0	0	0	0
1997—Seattle NFL	16	9	4	8	2.0	0	13	91	7.0	2	1	16	16.0	0	2	0	12	0
1998—Seattle NFL	16	5	15	47	3.1	0	8	48	6.0	2	0	0	0.0	0	2	0	12	2
1999—Seattle NFL	14	1	1	0	0.0	0	1	5	5.0	0	0	0	0.0	0	0	0	0	0
2000—Seattle NFL	16	12	3	9	3.0	0	23	141	6.1	1	1	26	26.0	0	1	0	6	0
2001—Seattle NFL	16	13	17	55	3.2	0	17	141	8.3	0	1	16	16.0	0	0	0	0	0
2002—Seattle NFL	16	12	23	94	4.1	0	22	120	5.5	2	3	54	18.0	0	2	0	12	0
2003—Seattle NFL	16	10	37	174	4.7	1	29	216	7.4	0	3	60	20.0	0	1	0	6	1
Pro totals (10 years)	148	73	140	532	3.8	4	137	960	7.0	10	13	237	18.2	0	14	0	84	6

STROUD, MARCUS DT JAGUARS

PERSONAL: Born June 25, 1978, in Thomasville, Ga. ... 6-6/312.
HIGH SCHOOL: Brooks County (Barney, Ga.).
COLLEGE: Georgia.
TRANSACTIONS/CAREER NOTES: Selected by Jacksonville Jaguars in first round (13th pick overall) of 2001 draft. ... Signed by Jaguars (July 26, 2001).
HONORS: Played in Pro Bowl (2003 season).

			TOTALS		
Year Team	G	GS	Tk.	Ast.	Sks.
2001—Jacksonville NFL	16	0	21	4	0.0
2002—Jacksonville NFL	16	16	41	7	6.5
2003—Jacksonville NFL	16	16	47	18	4.5
Pro totals (3 years)	48	32	109	29	11.0

STRYZINSKI, DAN P

PERSONAL: Born May 15, 1965, in Indianapolis, Ind. ... 6-0/237. ... Full name: Daniel Thomas Stryzinski. ... Name pronounced: stra-ZIN-ski.
HIGH SCHOOL: Lincoln (Vincennes, Ind.).
COLLEGE: Indiana.
TRANSACTIONS/CAREER NOTES: Signed as non-drafted free agent by Indianapolis Colts (July 1988). ... Released by Colts (August 23, 1988). ... Signed by Cleveland Browns (August 25, 1988). ... Released by Browns (August 30, 1988). ... Re-signed by Browns for 1989 season. ... Released by Browns (August 30, 1989). ... Signed by New Orleans Saints to developmental squad (October 11, 1989). ... Granted free agency following 1989 season. ... Signed by Pittsburgh Steelers (March 14, 1990). ... Granted unconditional free agency (February 1, 1992). ... Signed by Tampa Bay Buccaneers (February 21, 1992). ... Granted unconditional free agency (February 17, 1995). ... Signed by Atlanta Falcons (February 20, 1995). ... Granted unconditional free agency (March 2, 2001). ... Signed by Kansas City Chiefs (March 9, 2001). ... Released by Chiefs (February 28, 2003). ... Signed by New York Jets (March 24, 2003). ... Granted unconditional free agency (March 3, 2004).
CHAMPIONSHIP GAME EXPERIENCE: Played in NFC championship game (1998 season). ... Played in Super Bowl 33 (1998 season).

		PUNTING					
Year Team	G	No.	Yds.	Avg.	Net avg.	In. 20	Blk.
1990—Pittsburgh NFL	16	65	2454	37.8	34.1	18	1
1991—Pittsburgh NFL	16	74	2996	40.5	36.2	10	1
1992—Tampa Bay NFL	16	74	3015	40.7	36.2	15	0
1993—Tampa Bay NFL	16	*93	3772	40.6	35.2	24	1
1994—Tampa Bay NFL	16	72	2800	38.9	35.8	20	0
1995—Atlanta NFL	16	67	2759	41.2	36.2	21	0
1996—Atlanta NFL	16	75	3152	42.0	35.5	22	0
1997—Atlanta NFL	16	89	3498	39.3	36.7	20	0
1998—Atlanta NFL	16	74	2963	40.0	36.6	25	0
1999—Atlanta NFL	16	80	3163	39.5	37.1	27	0
2000—Atlanta NFL	16	84	3447	41.0	‡37.9	27	1
2001—Kansas City NFL	16	73	2976	40.8	35.6	27	0
2002—Kansas City NFL	16	64	2422	37.8	31.2	15	1
2003—New York Jets NFL	16	71	2655	37.4	31.3	22	1
Pro totals (14 years)	224	1055	42072	39.9	35.5	293	6

STUBBLEFIELD, DANA DT

PERSONAL: Born November 14, 1970, in Cleves, Ohio. ... 6-2/300. ... Full name: Dana William Stubblefield.
HIGH SCHOOL: Taylor (North Bend, Ohio).
COLLEGE: Kansas.
TRANSACTIONS/CAREER NOTES: Selected by San Francisco 49ers in first round (26th pick overall) of 1993 NFL draft. ... Signed by 49ers (July 14, 1993). ... Granted unconditional free agency (February 13, 1998). ... Signed by Washington Redskins (February 23, 1998). ... Released by Redskins (March 1, 2001). ... Signed by 49ers (April 25, 2001). ... Released by 49ers (February 26, 2003). ... Signed by Oakland Raiders (March 12, 2003). ... Granted unconditional free agency (March 3, 2004).
CHAMPIONSHIP GAME EXPERIENCE: Played in NFC championship game (1993, 1994 and 1997 seasons). ... Member of Super Bowl championship team (1994 season).
HONORS: Played in Pro Bowl (1994, 1995 and 1997 seasons). ... Named defensive tackle on THE SPORTING NEWS NFL All-Pro team (1997).

			TOTALS			INTERCEPTIONS			
Year Team	G	GS	Tk.	Ast.	Sks.	No.	Yds.	Avg.	TD
1993—San Francisco NFL	16	14	55	9	10.5	0	0	0.0	0
1994—San Francisco NFL	14	14	34	4	8.5	0	0	0.0	0
1995—San Francisco NFL	16	16	27	7	4.5	1	12	12.0	0
1996—San Francisco NFL	15	15	26	7	1.0	1	15	15.0	0
1997—San Francisco NFL	16	16	48	13	15.0	0	0	0.0	0
1998—Washington NFL	7	7	26	6	1.5	0	0	0.0	0
1999—Washington NFL	16	16	30	14	3.0	0	0	0.0	0
2000—Washington NFL	15	14	31	9	2.5	0	0	0.0	0
2001—San Francisco NFL	16	16	25	7	4.0	0	0	0.0	0
2002—San Francisco NFL	15	15	29	9	3.0	0	0	0.0	0
2003—Oakland NFL	8	6	12	6	0.0	0	0	0.0	0
Pro totals (11 years)	154	149	343	91	53.5	2	27	13.5	0

STUVAINTS, RUSSELL S STEELERS

PERSONAL: Born August 28, 1980... 6-0/195. ... Full name: Russell Stuvaints Jr.
HIGH SCHOOL: McKeesport (Pa.).
COLLEGE: Youngstown State.
TRANSACTIONS/CAREER NOTES: Signed as non-drafted free agent by Pittsburgh Steelers (May 2, 2003). ... Released by Steelers (August 26, 2003). ... Re-signed by Steelers to practice squad (September 1, 2003). ... Released by Steelers (September 30, 2003). ... Re-signed by Steelers to practice squad (October 7, 2003). ... Released by Steelers (October 21, 2003). ... Re-signed by Steelers to practice squad (October 28, 2003). ... Activated (December 2, 2003).

			TOTALS			INTERCEPTIONS			
Year Team	G	GS	Tk.	Ast.	Sks.	No.	Yds.	Avg.	TD
2003—Pittsburgh NFL	4	0	0	0	0.0	0	0	0.0	0

SUGGS, LEE RB BROWNS

PERSONAL: Born August 11, 1980, in Roanoke, Va. ... 6-0/205. ... Full name: Lee Ernest Suggs Jr.
HIGH SCHOOL: William Fleming (Roanoke, Va.).
COLLEGE: Virginia Tech.
TRANSACTIONS/CAREER NOTES: Selected by Cleveland Browns in fourth round (115th pick overall) of 2003 NFL draft. ... Signed by Browns (August 13, 2003). ... On non-football injury list with shoulder injury (August 31-November 12, 2003).
SINGLE GAME HIGHS (regular season): Attempts—26 (December 28, 2003, vs. Cincinnati); yards—186 (December 28, 2003, vs. Cincinnati); and rushing touchdowns—2 (December 28, 2003, vs. Cincinnati).
STATISTICAL PLATEAUS: 100-yard rushing games: 2003 (1). Total: 1.

			RUSHING				RECEIVING				KICKOFF RETURNS				TOTALS			
Year Team	G	GS	Att.	Yds.	Avg.	TD	No.	Yds.	Avg.	TD	No.	Yds.	Avg.	TD	TD	2pt.	Pts.	Fum.
2003—Cleveland NFL	7	0	56	289	5.2	2	2	0	0.0	0	14	318	22.7	0	2	0	12	2

SUGGS, TERRELL LB RAVENS

PERSONAL: Born October 11, 1982, in Minneapolis, Minn. ... 6-3/260. ... Full name: Terrell Raynonn Suggs.
HIGH SCHOOL: Hamilton (Chandler, Ariz.).
COLLEGE: Arizona State.
TRANSACTIONS/CAREER NOTES: Selected after junior season by Baltimore Ravens in first round (10th pick overall) of 2003 NFL draft. ... Signed by Baltimore Ravens (July 29, 2003).

			TOTALS			INTERCEPTIONS			
Year Team	G	GS	Tk.	Ast.	Sks.	No.	Yds.	Avg.	TD
2003—Baltimore NFL	16	1	19	8	12.0	1	11	11.0	0

SULLIVAN, JOHNATHAN DT SAINTS

PERSONAL: Born January 21, 1981, in Griffin, Ga. ... 6-3/313.
HIGH SCHOOL: Griffin (Ga.).
COLLEGE: Georgia.
TRANSACTIONS/CAREER NOTES: Selected after junior season by New Orleans Saints in first round (sixth pick overall) of 2003 NFL draft. ... Signed by Saints (July 30, 2003).

			TOTALS		
Year Team	G	GS	Tk.	Ast.	Sks.
2003—New Orleans NFL	14	12	26	8	1.0

SULLIVAN, MARQUES T BILLS

PERSONAL: Born February 2, 1978, in Oak Park, Ill. ... 6-5/325.
HIGH SCHOOL: Fenwick (Oak Park, Ill.).
COLLEGE: Illinois.
TRANSACTIONS/CAREER NOTES: Selected by Buffalo Bills in fifth round (144th pick overall) of 2001 NFL draft. ... Signed by Bills (June 11, 2001).
PLAYING EXPERIENCE: Buffalo NFL, 2001-2003. ... Games/Games started: 2001 (10/2), 2002 (16/16), 2003 (6/4). Total: 32/22.

SURTAIN, PATRICK CB DOLPHINS

PERSONAL: Born June 19, 1976, in New Orleans, La. ... 5-11/192. ... Full name: Patrick Frank Surtain. ... Name pronounced: sir-TANE.
HIGH SCHOOL: Edna Karr (New Orleans).
COLLEGE: Southern Mississippi.
TRANSACTIONS/CAREER NOTES: Selected by Miami Dolphins in second round (44th pick overall) of 1998 NFL draft. ... Signed by Dolphins (July 21, 1998).
HONORS: Named cornerback on THE SPORTING NEWS college All-America second team (1997). ... Named to play in Pro Bowl (2002 season); replaced by Sam Madison due to injury. ... Named cornerback on the THE SPORTING NEWS NFL All-Pro team (2002 and 2003). ... Played in Pro Bowl (2003 season).

			TOTALS			INTERCEPTIONS			
Year Team	G	GS	Tk.	Ast.	Sks.	No.	Yds.	Avg.	TD
1998—Miami NFL	16	0	23	5	0.0	2	1	0.5	0

Year Team	G	GS	TOTALS Tk.	Ast.	Sks.	INTERCEPTIONS No.	Yds.	Avg.	TD
1999—Miami NFL	16	6	32	5	2.0	2	28	14.0	0
2000—Miami NFL	16	16	44	9	1.0	5	55	11.0	0
2001—Miami NFL	16	16	43	10	1.0	3	74	24.7	1
2002—Miami NFL	14	14	39	19	1.5	6	79	13.2	1
2003—Miami NFL	15	15	34	19	0.0	▲7	59	8.4	0
Pro totals (6 years)	93	67	215	67	5.5	25	296	11.8	2

SWAYNE, KEVIN — WR — JETS

PERSONAL: Born January 17, 1975, in Riverside, Calif. ... 6-1/191.
HIGH SCHOOL: Banning (Calif.).
COLLEGE: Wayne State (Neb.).
TRANSACTIONS/CAREER NOTES: Signed as non-drafted free agent by Chicago Bears (April 25, 1997). ... Released by Bears prior to 1997 season. ... Signed by Philadelphia Eagles to practice squad (November 17, 1999). ... Granted free agency after 1999 season. ... Signed by San Diego Chargers (February 10, 2000). ... Released by Chargers (August 23, 2000). ... Signed by New York Jets (May 30, 2001).
SINGLE GAME HIGHS (regular season): Receptions—4 (December 16, 2001, vs. Cincinnati); yards—74 (December 16, 2001, vs. Cincinnati); and touchdown receptions—1 (December 1, 2003, vs. Tennessee).

Year Team	G	GS	RECEIVING No.	Yds.	Avg.	TD	KICKOFF RETURNS No.	Yds.	Avg.	TD	TOTALS TD	2pt.	Pts.	Fum.
2001—New York Jets NFL	15	1	13	203	15.6	0	0	0	0.0	0	0	0	0	0
2002—New York Jets NFL	15	0	5	78	15.6	0	1	13	13.0	0	0	0	0	1
2003—New York Jets NFL	15	0	2	29	14.5	1	3	48	16.0	0	1	0	6	0
Pro totals (3 years)	45	1	20	310	15.5	1	4	61	15.3	0	1	0	6	1

SWINEY, ERWIN — CB — PACKERS

PERSONAL: Born October 8, 1978, in Dallas, Texas. ... 6-0/192. ... Full name: Erwin Bernard Swiney.
HIGH SCHOOL: Northeast (Lincoln, Neb.).
COLLEGE: Nebraska.
TRANSACTIONS/CAREER NOTES: Signed as non-drafted free agent by Green Bay Packers (April 25, 2002). ... Released by Packers (September 1, 2002). ... Re-signed by Packers to practice squad (September 3, 2002). ... Released by Packers (September 5, 2002). ... Re-signed by Packers to practice squad (September 10, 2002). ... Activated (October 12, 2002). ... Released by Packers (October 16, 2002). ... Re-signed by Packers to practice squad (October 17, 2002). ... Released by Packers (October 22, 2002). ... Re-signed by Packers to practice squad (October 31, 2002). ... Activated (December 22, 2002). ... Waived by Packers (October 4, 2003). ... Signed by Packers to practice squad (October 11, 2003). ... Activated (December 6, 2003). ... Assigned by Packers to Cologne Centurions in 2004 NFL Europe enhancement allocation program (February 9, 2004).

Year Team	G	GS	TOTALS Tk.	Ast.	Sks.	INTERCEPTIONS No.	Yds.	Avg.	TD
2002—Green Bay NFL	3	0	0	0	0.0	0	0	0.0	0
2003—Green Bay NFL	6	0	2	1	0.0	0	0	0.0	0
Pro totals (2 years)	9	0	2	1	0.0	0	0	0.0	0

SWINTON, REGGIE — WR — LIONS

PERSONAL: Born July 24, 1975, in Little Rock, Ark. ... 6-0/186.
HIGH SCHOOL: Central (Ark.).
COLLEGE: Murray State.
TRANSACTIONS/CAREER NOTES: Signed as non-drafted free agent by Jacksonville Jaguars (April 18, 1998). ... Released by Jaguars (August 25, 1998). ... Signed by Toronto Argonauts of the CFL (February 19, 1999). ... Traded by Argonauts with QB Kerwin Bell to Winnipeg Blue Bombers for Eric Blount and RB Mitch Running (March 1, 1999). ... Released by Blue Bombers (August 16, 1999). ... Signed by Edmonton Eskimos of CFL (September 13, 1999). ... Released by Eskimos (October 12, 1999). ... Signed by Seattle Seahawks (February 24, 2000). ... Released by Seahawks (August 27, 2000). ... Signed by Dallas Cowboys (August 6, 2001). ... Traded by Cowboys to Green Bay Packers for a sixth-round pick (traded to San Francisco) in 2004 draft (September 29, 2003). ... Claimed on waivers by Detroit Lions (October 10, 2003). ... Granted free agency (March 3, 2004). ... Re-signed by Lions (April 19, 2004).
SINGLE GAME HIGHS (regular season): Receptions—5 (December 7, 2003, vs. San Diego); yards—72 (December 23, 2001, vs. Arizona); and touchdown receptions—1 (December 23, 2001, vs. Arizona).

Year Team	G	GS	RECEIVING No.	Yds.	Avg.	TD	PUNT RETURNS No.	Yds.	Avg.	TD	KICKOFF RETURNS No.	Yds.	Avg.	TD	TOTALS TD	2pt.	Pts.	Fum.
1999—Winnipeg CFL	4	...	11	162	14.7	1	7	235	33.6	1	5	18	3.6	0	2	0	12	0
—Toronto CFL	3	...	3	22	7.3	0	9	178	19.8	0	3	33	11.0	0	0	0	0	0
2000—							Did not play.											
2001—Dallas NFL	15	1	7	117	16.7	1	31	414	13.4	†1	56	1327	23.7	0	2	0	12	4
2002—Dallas NFL	14	0	7	63	9.0	0	19	141	7.4	0	28	697	24.9	1	1	0	6	1
2003—Dallas NFL	1	0	0	0	0.0	0	1	0	0.0	0	3	65	21.7	0	0	0	0	0
—Detroit NFL	11	1	9	100	11.1	0	23	318	13.8	1	40	964	24.1	1	2	0	12	4
CFL totals (1 year)	7	...	14	184	13.1	1	16	413	25.8	1	8	51	6.4	0	2	0	12	0
NFL totals (3 years)	41	2	23	280	12.2	1	74	873	11.8	2	127	3053	24.0	2	5	0	30	9
Pro totals (4 years)	48	...	37	464	12.5	2	90	1286	14.3	3	135	3104	23.0	2	7	0	42	9

SYKES, JASHON — LB — BRONCOS

PERSONAL: Born September 25, 1979, in Los Angeles, Calif. ... 6-2/236.
HIGH SCHOOL: Serra (Los Angeles, Calif.).
COLLEGE: Colorado.

TRANSACTIONS/CAREER NOTES: Signed as non-drafted free agent by Denver Broncos (December 31, 2002).

			TOTALS			INTERCEPTIONS			
Year Team	**G**	**GS**	**Tk.**	**Ast.**	**Sks.**	**No.**	**Yds.**	**Avg.**	**TD**
2003—Denver NFL	16	8	38	14	0.0	0	0	0.0	0
—New York Giants NFL					Did not play.				
Pro totals (1 year)	16	8	38	14	0.0	0	0	0.0	0

SZOTT, DAVE G

PERSONAL: Born December 12, 1967, in Passaic, N.J. ... 6-4/289. ... Full name: David Andrew Szott. ... Name pronounced: ZOT.
HIGH SCHOOL: Clifton (N.J.).
COLLEGE: Penn State.
TRANSACTIONS/CAREER NOTES: Selected by Kansas City Chiefs in seventh round (180th pick overall) of 1990 NFL draft. ... Signed by Chiefs (July 25, 1990). ... Granted free agency (March 1, 1993). ... Re-signed by Chiefs for 1993 season. ... On injured reserve with arm injury (December 2, 1998-remainder of season). ... On injured reserve with arm injury (October 11, 2000-remainder of season). ... Granted unconditional free agency (March 2, 2001). ... Signed by Washington Redskins (August 19, 2001). ... Granted unconditional free agency (March 1, 2002). ... Signed by New York Jets (March 21, 2002). ... On physically unable to perform list with knee injury (August 27-November 18, 2002). ... Announced retirement (February 27, 2004).
PLAYING EXPERIENCE: Kansas City NFL, 1990-2000; Washington NFL, 2001; New York Jets NFL, 2002-2003. ... Games/Games started: 1990 (16/11), 1991 (16/16), 1992 (16/16), 1993 (14/13), 1994 (16/16), 1995 (16/16), 1996 (16/16), 1997 (16/16), 1998 (1/1), 1999 (14/14), 2000 (1/1), 2001 (16/16), 2002 (4/4), 2003 (15/15). Total: 177/171.
CHAMPIONSHIP GAME EXPERIENCE: Played in AFC championship game (1993 season).

TAFOYA, JOE DE BEARS

PERSONAL: Born September 6, 1978, in Pittsburg, Calif. ... 6-4/278. ... Full name: Joseph Peter Tafoya.
HIGH SCHOOL: Pittsburgh (Calif.).
COLLEGE: Arizona.
TRANSACTIONS/CAREER NOTES: Selected by Tampa Bay Buccaneers in seventh round (234th pick overall) of 2001 NFL draft. ... Signed by Buccaneers (July 18, 2001). ... Released by Buccaneers (September 2, 2001). ... Signed by Chicago Bears to practice squad (October 9, 2001). ... Activated (October 23, 2001). ... Re-signed by Bears (February 28, 2003). ... Granted free agency (March 3, 2004). ... Re-signed by Bears (April 19, 2004).

			TOTALS		
Year Team	**G**	**GS**	**Tk.**	**Ast.**	**Sks.**
2001—Chicago NFL	5	0	0	0	0.0
2002—Chicago NFL	14	1	5	3	0.5
2003—Chicago NFL	16	0	4	3	0.0
Pro totals (3 years)	35	1	9	6	0.5

T

TAIT, JOHN T BEARS

PERSONAL: Born January 26, 1975, in Phoenix, Ariz. ... 6-6/323.
HIGH SCHOOL: McClintock (Tempe, Ariz.).
COLLEGE: Brigham Young.
TRANSACTIONS/CAREER NOTES: Selected after junior season by Kansas City Chiefs in first round (14th pick overall) of 1999 NFL draft. ... Signed by Chiefs (September 9, 1999). ... Designated by Chiefs as franchise player (February 24, 2004). ... Tendered offer sheet by Chicago Bears (March 6, 2004). ... Chiefs declined to match offer (March 12, 2004).
PLAYING EXPERIENCE: Kansas City NFL, 1999-2003. ... Games/Games started: 1999 (12/3), 2000 (15/15), 2001 (16/16), 2002 (16/16), 2003 (16/16). Total: 75/66.

TANNER, BARRON DT CARDINALS

PERSONAL: Born September 14, 1973, in Athens, Texas. ... 6-3/360. ... Full name: Barron Keith Tanner.
HIGH SCHOOL: Athens (Texas).
COLLEGE: Oklahoma.
TRANSACTIONS/CAREER NOTES: Selected by Miami Dolphins in fifth round (149th pick overall) of 1997 NFL draft. ... Signed by Dolphins (July 8, 1997). ... Traded by Dolphins to Washington Redskins for seventh-round pick (traded to San Francisco) in 2001 draft (September 4, 1999). ... Inactive for all 16 games (1999). ... Granted free agency (February 11, 2000). ... Re-signed by Redskins (June 6, 2000). ... Released by Redskins (August 27, 2000). ... Signed by Arizona Cardinals (November 6, 2000). ... Granted unconditional free agency (February 28, 2003). ... Re-signed by Cardinals (March 5, 2003).

			TOTALS			INTERCEPTIONS			
Year Team	**G**	**GS**	**Tk.**	**Ast.**	**Sks.**	**No.**	**Yds.**	**Avg.**	**TD**
1997—Miami NFL	16	0	16	6	0.0	0	0	0.0	0
1998—Miami NFL	13	0	5	4	0.0	0	0	0.0	0
1999—Washington NFL				Did not play.					
2000—Arizona NFL	4	0	5	0	0.0	0	0	0.0	0
2001—Arizona NFL	16	16	24	13	0.0	0	0	0.0	0
2002—Arizona NFL	15	8	17	9	2.0	1	17	17.0	0
2003—Arizona NFL	14	2	14	4	1.0	0	0	0.0	0
Pro totals (6 years)	78	26	81	36	3.0	1	17	17.0	0

TAUSCHER, MARK — T/G — PACKERS

PERSONAL: Born June 17, 1977, in Marshfield, Wis. ... 6-4/320. ... Full name: Mark Gerald Tauscher.
HIGH SCHOOL: Auburndale (Wis.).
COLLEGE: Wisconsin.
TRANSACTIONS/CAREER NOTES: Selected by Green Bay Packers in seventh round (224th pick overall) of 2000 NFL draft. ... Signed by Packers (June 21, 2000). ... On injured reserve with knee injury (September 18, 2002-remainder of season).
PLAYING EXPERIENCE: Green Bay NFL, 2000-2003. ... Games/Games started: 2000 (16/14), 2001 (16/16), 2002 (2/2), 2003 (16/16). Total: 50/48.

TAYLOR, BEN — LB — BROWNS

PERSONAL: Born August 31, 1978, in Bellaire, Ohio. ... 6-2/245. ... Full name: Benjamin Frazier Taylor.
HIGH SCHOOL: Bellaire (Ohio).
COLLEGE: Virginia Tech.
TRANSACTIONS/CAREER NOTES: Selected by Cleveland Browns in fourth round (111th pick overall) of 2002 NFL draft. ... Signed by Browns (July 19, 2002). ... On injured reserve with hamstring injury (November 25, 2002-remainder of season).
HONORS: Named linebacker on THE SPORTING NEWS college All-America third team (2001).

			TOTALS			INTERCEPTIONS			
Year Team	**G**	**GS**	**Tk.**	**Ast.**	**Sks.**	**No.**	**Yds.**	**Avg.**	**TD**
2002—Cleveland NFL	7	0	1	2	0.0	0	0	0.0	0
2003—Cleveland NFL	13	8	63	16	0.0	1	0	0.0	0
Pro totals (2 years)	20	8	64	18	0.0	1	0	0.0	0

TAYLOR, BOBBY — CB — SEAHAWKS

PERSONAL: Born December 28, 1973, in Houston, Texas. ... 6-3/216. ... Full name: Robert Taylor. ... Son of Robert Taylor, silver medalist in 100-meter dash and member of gold-medal winning 400-meter relay team at 1972 Summer Olympics.
HIGH SCHOOL: Longview (Texas).
COLLEGE: Notre Dame.
TRANSACTIONS/CAREER NOTES: Selected after junior season by Philadelphia Eagles in second round (49th pick overall) of 1995 NFL draft. ... Signed by Eagles (July 19, 1995). ... On injured reserve with knee injury (October 17, 1997-remainder of season). ... Granted free agency (February 13, 1998). ... Re-signed by Eagles (June 11, 1998). ... On injured reserve with fractured jaw (December 28, 1999-remainder of season). ... Granted unconditional free agency (March 3, 2004). ... Signed by Seattle Seahawks (March 25, 2004).
CHAMPIONSHIP GAME EXPERIENCE: Played in NFC championship game (2001-2003 seasons).
HONORS: Named defensive back on THE SPORTING NEWS college All-America first team (1993 and 1994). ... Played in Pro Bowl (2002 season).

			TOTALS			INTERCEPTIONS			
Year Team	**G**	**GS**	**Tk.**	**Ast.**	**Sks.**	**No.**	**Yds.**	**Avg.**	**TD**
1995—Philadelphia NFL	16	12	47	5	0.0	2	52	26.0	0
1996—Philadelphia NFL	16	16	55	7	1.0	3	-1	-0.3	0
1997—Philadelphia NFL	6	5	14	4	2.0	0	0	0.0	0
1998—Philadelphia NFL	11	10	22	9	0.0	0	0	0.0	0
1999—Philadelphia NFL	15	14	39	7	0.0	4	59	14.8	1
2000—Philadelphia NFL	16	15	39	7	0.0	3	64	21.3	0
2001—Philadelphia NFL	16	14	36	3	1.0	1	5	5.0	0
2002—Philadelphia NFL	16	16	47	11	0.0	5	43	8.6	1
2003—Philadelphia NFL	7	7	18	1	0.0	1	2	2.0	0
Pro totals (9 years)	119	109	317	54	4.0	19	224	11.8	2

TAYLOR, CHESTER — RB — RAVENS

PERSONAL: Born September 22, 1979, in River Rouge, Mich. ... 5-11/213. ... Full name: Chester Lamar Taylor.
HIGH SCHOOL: River Rouge (Mich.).
COLLEGE: Toledo.
TRANSACTIONS/CAREER NOTES: Selected by Baltimore Ravens in sixth round (207th pick overall) of 2002 NFL draft. ... Signed by Ravens (July 24, 2002).
SINGLE GAME HIGHS (regular season): Attempts—10 (October 12, 2003, vs. Arizona); yards—47 (September 28, 2003, vs. Kansas City); and rushing touchdowns—1 (November 2, 2003, vs. Jacksonville).

			RUSHING				RECEIVING				KICKOFF RETURNS				TOTALS			
Year Team	**G**	**GS**	**Att.**	**Yds.**	**Avg.**	**TD**	**No.**	**Yds.**	**Avg.**	**TD**	**No.**	**Yds.**	**Avg.**	**TD**	**TD**	**2pt.**	**Pts.**	**Fum.**
2002—Baltimore NFL	15	2	33	122	3.7	0	14	129	9.2	2	10	236	23.6	0	2	1	14	1
2003—Baltimore NFL	16	1	63	276	4.4	2	20	132	6.6	0	23	448	19.5	0	2	0	12	3
Pro totals (2 years)	31	3	96	398	4.1	2	34	261	7.7	2	33	684	20.7	0	4	1	26	4

TAYLOR, FRED — RB — JAGUARS

PERSONAL: Born January 27, 1976, in Pahokee, Fla. ... 6-1/234. ... Full name: Frederick Antwon Taylor.
HIGH SCHOOL: Glades Central (Belle Glade, Fla.).
COLLEGE: Florida.
TRANSACTIONS/CAREER NOTES: Selected by Jacksonville Jaguars in first round (ninth pick overall) of 1998 NFL draft. ... Signed by Jaguars (July 6, 1998).
CHAMPIONSHIP GAME EXPERIENCE: Played in AFC championship game (1999 season).

HONORS: Named running back on THE SPORTING NEWS college All-America third team (1997).
SINGLE GAME HIGHS (regular season): Attempts—34 (December 21, 2003, vs. New Orleans); yards—234 (November 19, 2000, vs. Pittsburgh); and rushing touchdowns—3 (December 3, 2000, vs. Cleveland).
STATISTICAL PLATEAUS: 100-yard rushing games: 1998 (6), 1999 (3), 2000 (9), 2002 (5), 2003 (7). Total: 30.
MISCELLANEOUS: Holds Jacksonville Jaguars all-time records for most yards rushing (6,356) and most rushing touchdowns (46).

			RUSHING				RECEIVING				TOTALS			
Year Team	**G**	**GS**	**Att.**	**Yds.**	**Avg.**	**TD**	**No.**	**Yds.**	**Avg.**	**TD**	**TD**	**2pt.**	**Pts.**	**Fum.**
1998—Jacksonville NFL	15	12	264	1223	4.6	14	44	421	9.6	3	17	0	102	3
1999—Jacksonville NFL	10	9	159	732	4.6	6	10	83	8.3	0	6	0	36	0
2000—Jacksonville NFL	13	13	292	1399	4.8	12	36	240	6.7	2	14	0	84	4
2001—Jacksonville NFL	2	2	30	116	3.9	0	2	13	6.5	0	0	0	0	1
2002—Jacksonville NFL	16	16	287	1314	4.6	8	49	408	8.3	0	8	2	52	3
2003—Jacksonville NFL	16	16	345	1572	4.6	6	48	370	7.7	1	7	0	42	6
Pro totals (6 years)	72	68	1377	6356	4.6	46	189	1535	8.1	6	52	2	316	17

TAYLOR, IKE — CB — STEELERS

PERSONAL: Born May 5, 1980, in New Orleans, La. ... 6-0/195. ... Full name: Ivan Taylor.
HIGH SCHOOL: Abramson (Gretna, La.).
COLLEGE: Louisiana-Lafayette.
TRANSACTIONS/CAREER NOTES: Selected by Pittsburgh Steelers in fourth round (125th pick overall) of 2003 NFL draft. ... Signed by Steelers (May 28, 2003).

			RUSHING				RECEIVING				KICKOFF RETURNS				TOTALS			
Year Team	**G**	**GS**	**Att.**	**Yds.**	**Avg.**	**TD**	**No.**	**Yds.**	**Avg.**	**TD**	**No.**	**Yds.**	**Avg.**	**TD**	**TD**	**2pt.**	**Pts.**	**Fum.**
2003—Pittsburgh NFL	16	1	0	0	0.0	0	0	0	0.0	0	37	831	22.5	0	0	0	0	1

TAYLOR, JASON — DE — DOLPHINS

PERSONAL: Born September 1, 1974, in Pittsburgh, Pa. ... 6-6/255. ... Full name: Jason Paul Taylor.
HIGH SCHOOL: Woodland Hills (Pittsburgh).
COLLEGE: Akron.
TRANSACTIONS/CAREER NOTES: Selected by Miami Dolphins in third round (73rd pick overall) of 1997 NFL draft. ... Signed by Dolphins (July 9, 1997). ... On injured reserve with broken collarbone (December 29, 1998-remainder of playoffs). ... Granted free agency (February 11, 2000). ... Re-signed by Dolphins (April 13, 2000). ... Designated by Dolphins as franchise player (February 22, 2001). ... Re-signed by Dolphins (July 23, 2001).
HONORS: Named defensive end on THE SPORTING NEWS NFL All-Pro team (2000 and 2002). ... Played in Pro Bowl (2000 and 2002 seasons).
MISCELLANEOUS: Holds Miami Dolphins all-time record for most sacks (71).

			TOTALS			INTERCEPTIONS			
Year Team	**G**	**GS**	**Tk.**	**Ast.**	**Sks.**	**No.**	**Yds.**	**Avg.**	**TD**
1997—Miami NFL	13	11	30	12	5.0	0	0	0.0	0
1998—Miami NFL	16	15	34	18	9.0	0	0	0.0	0
1999—Miami NFL	15	15	24	16	2.5	1	0	0.0	0
2000—Miami NFL	16	16	35	28	14.5	1	2	2.0	0
2001—Miami NFL	16	16	48	23	8.5	1	4	4.0	0
2002—Miami NFL	16	16	46	23	*18.5	0	0	0.0	0
2003—Miami NFL	16	16	37	22	13.0	0	0	0.0	0
Pro totals (7 years)	108	105	254	142	71.0	3	6	2.0	0

TAYLOR, SHANNON — LB

PERSONAL: Born February 16, 1975, in Roanoke, Va. ... 6-3/247. ... Full name: Shannon Andre Taylor.
HIGH SCHOOL: Patrick Henry (Roanoke, Va.).
COLLEGE: Virginia.
TRANSACTIONS/CAREER NOTES: Selected by San Diego Chargers in sixth round (184th pick overall) of 2000 NFL draft. ... Signed by Chargers (June 21, 2000). ... Released by Chargers (August 27, 2000). ... Re-signed by Chargers to practice squad (August 29, 2000). ... Activated (October 4, 2000). ... Released by Chargers (August 27, 2001). ... Signed by Baltimore Ravens (September 9, 2001). ... On injured reserve with shoulder injury (January 10, 2002-remainder of season). ... Granted free agency (February 28, 2003). ... Signed by Houston Texans (April 1, 2003). ... Released by Texans (July 30, 2003). ... Signed by Jacksonville Jaguars (September 16, 2003). ... Waived by Jaguars (October 15, 2003).

			TOTALS			INTERCEPTIONS			
Year Team	**G**	**GS**	**Tk.**	**Ast.**	**Sks.**	**No.**	**Yds.**	**Avg.**	**TD**
2000—San Diego NFL	11	0	3	0	0.0	0	0	0.0	0
2001—Baltimore NFL	11	0	3	1	1.0	0	0	0.0	0
2002—Baltimore NFL	16	2	6	3	0.0	0	0	0.0	0
2003—Jacksonville NFL	2	0	0	0	0.0	0	0	0.0	0
Pro totals (4 years)	40	2	12	4	1.0	0	0	0.0	0

TAYLOR, TRAVIS — WR — RAVENS

PERSONAL: Born March 30, 1978, in Fernadina, Fla. ... 6-1/200. ... Full name: Travis Lamont Taylor.
HIGH SCHOOL: Camden County (Ga.), then Jean Ribault (Jacksonville).
COLLEGE: Florida.

T

TRANSACTIONS/CAREER NOTES: Selected after junior season by Baltimore Ravens in first round (10th pick overall) of 2000 NFL draft. ... Signed by Ravens (August 1, 2000). ... On injured reserve with broken clavicle (November 8, 2000-remainder of season).
SINGLE GAME HIGHS (regular season): Receptions—7 (November 10, 2002, vs. Cincinnati); yards—138 (October 19, 2003, vs. Cincinnati); and touchdown receptions—2 (October 19, 2003, vs. Cincinnati).
STATISTICAL PLATEAUS: 100-yard receiving games: 2002 (1), 2003 (1). Total: 2.

			RUSHING				RECEIVING				TOTALS			
Year Team	**G**	**GS**	**Att.**	**Yds.**	**Avg.**	**TD**	**No.**	**Yds.**	**Avg.**	**TD**	**TD**	**2pt.**	**Pts.**	**Fum.**
2000—Baltimore NFL	9	8	2	11	5.5	0	28	276	9.9	3	3	0	18	1
2001—Baltimore NFL	16	13	5	46	9.2	0	42	560	13.3	3	3	0	18	0
2002—Baltimore NFL	16	15	11	105	9.5	0	61	869	14.2	6	6	0	36	0
2003—Baltimore NFL	16	16	11	62	5.6	0	39	632	16.2	3	3	0	18	0
Pro totals (4 years)	57	52	29	224	7.7	0	170	2337	13.7	15	15	0	90	1

TEAGUE, TREY — C — BILLS

PERSONAL: Born December 27, 1974, in Jackson, Tenn. ... 6-5/300. ... Full name: Fred Everette Teague III. ... Name pronounced: TEEG.
HIGH SCHOOL: University (Jackson, Tenn).
COLLEGE: Tennessee.
TRANSACTIONS/CAREER NOTES: Selected by Denver Broncos in seventh round (200th pick overall) of 1998 NFL draft. ... Signed by Broncos (July 23, 1998). ... Inactive for all 16 games (1998). ... On injured reserve with knee injury (September 12, 2000-remainder of season). ... Granted free agency (March 2, 2001). ... Re-signed by Broncos (May 3, 2001). ... Granted unconditional free agency (March 1, 2002). ... Signed by Buffalo Bills (March 27, 2002).
PLAYING EXPERIENCE: Denver NFL, 1999-2001; Buffalo NFL, 2002-2003. ... Games/Games started: 1999 (16/4), 2000 (2/0), 2001 (16/16), 2002 (16/16), 2003 (16/16). Total: 66/52.
CHAMPIONSHIP GAME EXPERIENCE: Member of Broncos for AFC championship game (1998 season); inactive. ... Member of Super Bowl championship team (1998 season); inactive.

TERRELL, DARYL — G/T — REDSKINS

PERSONAL: Born January 25, 1975, in Vossburg, Miss. ... 6-4/317.
HIGH SCHOOL: Heidelberg (Miss.).
JUNIOR COLLEGE: Jones County Junior College (Miss.).
COLLEGE: Southern Mississippi.
TRANSACTIONS/CAREER NOTES: Signed as non-drafted free agent by Baltimore Ravens (June 3, 1997). ... Released by Ravens (July 8, 1997). ... Signed by New Orleans Saints (April 27, 1998). ... Released by Saints (August 24, 1998). ... Re-signed by Saints to practice squad (September 2, 1998). ... Assigned by Saints to Amsterdam Admirals in 1999 NFL Europe enhancement allocation program (February 22, 1999). ... Granted free agency (March 1, 2002). ... Signed by Jacksonville Jaguars (June 5, 2002). ... Released by Jaguars (August 30, 2003). ... Signed by Washington Redskins (December 3, 2003). ... Waived by Redskins (December 5, 2003). ... Re-signed by Redskins (December 9, 2003). ... Granted unconditional free agency (March 3, 2004). ... Re-signed by Redskins (March 24, 2004).
PLAYING EXPERIENCE: New Orleans NFL, 1999-2001; Jacksonville NFL, 2002; Washington NFL, 2003. ... Games/Games started: 1999 (12/1), 2000 (16/0), 2001 (16/10), 2002 (9/0), 2003 (3/0). Total: 56/11.

TERRELL, DAVID — WR — BEARS

PERSONAL: Born March 13, 1979, in Richmond, Va. ... 6-3/215.
HIGH SCHOOL: Huguenot (Richmond, Va.).
COLLEGE: Michigan.
TRANSACTIONS/CAREER NOTES: Selected after junior season by Chicago Bears in first round (eighth pick overall) of 2001 NFL draft. ... Signed by Bears (July 31, 2001). ... On injured reserve with foot injury (November 12, 2002-remainder of season).
HONORS: Named wide receiver on THE SPORTING NEWS college All-America second team (2000).
SINGLE GAME HIGHS (regular season): Receptions—7 (November 2, 2003, vs. San Diego); yards—94 (December 16, 2001, vs. Tampa Bay); and touchdown receptions—2 (October 28, 2001, vs. San Francisco).

			RECEIVING				TOTALS			
Year Team	**G**	**GS**	**No.**	**Yds.**	**Avg.**	**TD**	**TD**	**2pt.**	**Pts.**	**Fum.**
2001—Chicago NFL	16	6	34	415	12.2	4	4	0	24	0
2002—Chicago NFL	5	1	9	127	14.1	3	3	0	18	0
2003—Chicago NFL	16	7	43	361	8.4	1	1	0	6	1
Pro totals (3 years)	37	14	86	903	10.5	8	8	0	48	1

TERRELL, DAVID — S — RAIDERS

PERSONAL: Born July 8, 1975, in Floydada, Texas. ... 6-0/190.
HIGH SCHOOL: Sweetwater (Texas).
COLLEGE: Texas-El Paso.
TRANSACTIONS/CAREER NOTES: Selected by Washington Redskins in seventh round (191st pick overall) of 1998 NFL draft. ... Signed by Redskins (May 13, 1998). ... Released by Redskins (August 25, 1998). ... Selected by Rhein Fire in 1999 NFL Europe draft (February 23, 1999). ... Released by Redskins (September 4, 1999). ... Re-signed by Redskins to practice squad (September 14, 1999). ... Granted free agency (February 28, 2003). ... Re-signed by Redskins (April 22, 2003). ... Granted unconditional free agency (March 3, 2004). ... Signed by Oakland Raiders (May 17, 2004).

			TOTALS			INTERCEPTIONS			
Year Team	**G**	**GS**	**Tk.**	**Ast.**	**Sks.**	**No.**	**Yds.**	**Avg.**	**TD**
2000—Washington NFL	16	0	3	0	0.0	0	0	0.0	0
2001—Washington NFL	16	16	61	10	1.0	2	0	0.0	0
2002—Washington NFL	16	16	48	15	0.0	2	41	20.5	0
2003—Washington NFL	13	1	13	4	0.0	2	21	10.5	0
Pro totals (4 years)	61	33	125	29	1.0	6	62	10.3	0

TERRY, CHRIS — T — SEAHAWKS

PERSONAL: Born August 8, 1975, in Jacksonville, Fla. ... 6-5/295. ... Full name: Christopher Alexander Terry.

HIGH SCHOOL: Jean Ribault (Jacksonville).

COLLEGE: Georgia.

TRANSACTIONS/CAREER NOTES: Selected by Carolina Panthers in second round (34th pick overall) of 1999 NFL draft. ... Signed by Panthers (May 24, 1999). ... Waived by Panthers (November 20, 2002). ... Claimed on waivers by Seattle Seahawks (November 21, 2002).

PLAYING EXPERIENCE: Carolina NFL, 1999-2001; Seattle NFL, 2002; Carolina NFL, 2002; Seattle NFL, 2003. ... Games/Games started: 1999 (16/16), 2000 (16/16), 2001 (15/15), 2002 (10/10), 2003 (12/10). Total: 69/67.

TESTAVERDE, VINNY — QB — JETS

PERSONAL: Born November 13, 1963, in Brooklyn, N.Y. ... 6-5/235. ... Full name: Vincent Frank Testaverde. ... Name pronounced: TESS-tuh-VER-dee.

HIGH SCHOOL: Sewanhaka (Floral Park, N.Y.), then Fork Union (Va.) Military Academy.

COLLEGE: Miami (Fla.).

TRANSACTIONS/CAREER NOTES: Signed by Tampa Bay Buccaneers (April 3, 1987). ... Selected officially by Buccaneers in first round (first pick overall) of 1987 NFL draft. ... On injured reserve with ankle injury (December 20, 1989-remainder of season). ... Granted unconditional free agency (March 1, 1993). ... Signed by Cleveland Browns (March 31, 1993). ... Browns franchise moved to Baltimore and renamed Ravens for 1996 season (March 11, 1996). ... Released by Ravens (June 2, 1998). ... Signed by New York Jets (June 24, 1998). ... Granted free agency (February 12, 1999). ... Re-signed by Jets (March 1, 1999). ... On injured reserve with torn Achilles' tendon (September 13, 1999-remainder of season).

CHAMPIONSHIP GAME EXPERIENCE: Played in AFC championship game (1998 season).

HONORS: Named quarterback on THE SPORTING NEWS college All-America second team (1985). ... Heisman Trophy winner (1986). ... Named College Football Player of the Year by THE SPORTING NEWS (1986). ... Maxwell Award winner (1986). ... Davey O'Brien Award winner (1986). ... Named quarterback on THE SPORTING NEWS college All-America first team (1986). ... Played in Pro Bowl (1996 and 1998 seasons).

SINGLE GAME HIGHS (regular season): Attempts—69 (December 24, 2000, vs. Baltimore); completions—42 (December 6, 1998, vs. Seattle); yards—481 (December 24, 2000, vs. Baltimore); and touchdown passes—5 (October, 23, 2000, vs. Miami).

STATISTICAL PLATEAUS: 100-yard rushing games: 1990 (1). Total: 1. 300-yard passing games: 1987 (1), 1988 (4), 1989 (4), 1990 (1), 1991 (1), 1992 (1), 1993 (1), 1995 (2), 1996 (5), 1997 (3), 1998 (1), 2000 (2), 2003 (1). Total: 27.

MISCELLANEOUS: Regular-season record as starting NFL quarterback: 82-106-1 (.437). ... Postseason record as starting NFL quarterback: 2-3 (.400). ... Holds Tampa Bay Buccaneers all-time records for most yards passing (14,820) and most touchdown passes (77). ... Holds Baltimore Ravens all-time records for most yards passing (7,148) and most touchdown passes (51).

			PASSING									RUSHING				TOTALS		
Year Team	G	GS	Att.	Cmp.	Pct.	Yds.	TD	Int.	Avg.	Skd.	Rat.	Att.	Yds.	Avg.	TD	TD	2pt.	Pts.
1987—Tampa Bay NFL	6	4	165	71	43.0	1081	5	6	6.55	18	60.2	13	50	3.8	1	1	0	6
1988—Tampa Bay NFL	15	15	466	222	47.6	3240	13	*35	6.95	33	48.8	28	138	4.9	1	1	0	6
1989—Tampa Bay NFL	14	14	480	258	53.8	3133	20	†22	6.53	38	68.9	25	139	5.6	0	0	0	0
1990—Tampa Bay NFL	14	13	365	203	55.6	2818	17	∞18	‡7.72	38	75.6	38	280	7.4	1	1	0	6
1991—Tampa Bay NFL	13	12	326	166	50.9	1994	8	15	6.12	‡35	59.0	32	101	3.2	0	0	0	0
1992—Tampa Bay NFL	14	14	358	206	57.5	2554	14	16	7.13	35	74.2	36	197	5.5	2	2	0	12
1993—Cleveland NFL	10	6	230	130	56.5	1797	14	9	‡7.81	17	85.7	18	74	4.1	0	0	0	0
1994—Cleveland NFL	14	13	376	207	55.1	2575	16	18	6.85	12	70.7	21	37	1.8	2	2	0	12
1995—Cleveland NFL	13	12	392	241	61.5	2883	17	10	7.35	17	87.8	18	62	3.4	2	2	0	12
1996—Baltimore NFL	16	16	549	325	59.2	4177	§33	19	7.61	34	88.7	34	188	5.5	2	2	1	14
1997—Baltimore NFL	13	13	470	271	57.7	2971	18	15	6.32	20	75.9	34	138	4.1	0	0	0	0
1998—New York Jets NFL	14	13	421	259	61.5	3256	§29	7	7.73	19	§101.6	24	104	4.3	1	1	0	6
1999—New York Jets NFL	1	1	15	10	66.7	96	1	1	6.40	0	78.7	0	0	0.0	0	0	0	0
2000—New York Jets NFL	16	16	*590	328	55.6	3732	21	*25	6.33	13	69.0	25	32	1.3	0	0	0	0
2001—New York Jets NFL	16	16	441	260	59.0	2752	15	14	6.24	18	75.3	31	25	0.8	0	0	0	0
2002—New York Jets NFL	5	4	83	54	65.1	499	3	3	6.01	9	78.3	2	23	11.5	0	0	0	0
2003—New York Jets NFL	7	7	198	123	62.1	1385	7	2	6.99	6	90.6	6	17	2.8	0	0	0	0
Pro totals (17 years)	201	189	5925	3334	56.3	40943	251	235	6.91	362	75.4	385	1605	4.2	12	12	1	74

THOMAS, ADALIUS — DE — RAVENS

PERSONAL: Born August 18, 1977, in Equality, Ala. ... 6-2/270. ... Full name: Adalius Donquail Thomas.

HIGH SCHOOL: Central Coosa (Equality, Ala.).

COLLEGE: Southern Mississippi.

TRANSACTIONS/CAREER NOTES: Selected by Baltimore Ravens in sixth round (186th pick overall) of 2000 NFL draft. ... Signed by Ravens (July 6, 2000). ... Granted free agency (February 28, 2003). ... Re-signed by Ravens (June 17, 2003). ... On injured reserve with arm injury (December 17, 2003-remainder of season). ... Granted unconditional free agency (March 3, 2004). ... Re-signed by Ravens (March 22, 2004).

CHAMPIONSHIP GAME EXPERIENCE: Played in AFC championship game (2000 season). ... Member of Super Bowl championship team (2000 season); inactive.

HONORS: Named defensive end on THE SPORTING NEWS college All-America second team (1999). ... Named to play in Pro Bowl (2003 season); replaced by Gary Stillis due to injury.

			TOTALS			INTERCEPTIONS			
Year Team	G	GS	Tk.	Ast.	Sks.	No.	Yds.	Avg.	TD
2000—Baltimore NFL	3	0	0	1	0.0	0	0	0.0	0
2001—Baltimore NFL	16	2	22	6	3.5	0	0	0.0	0
2002—Baltimore NFL	16	12	30	11	3.0	2	57	28.5	1
2003—Baltimore NFL	13	11	25	2	4.0	0	0	0.0	0
Pro totals (4 years)	48	25	77	20	10.5	2	57	28.5	1

THOMAS, ANTHONY RB BEARS

PERSONAL: Born November 7, 1977, in Winnfield, La. ... 6-2/228. ... Full name: Anthony Jermaine Thomas.
HIGH SCHOOL: Winnfield (La.).
COLLEGE: Michigan.
TRANSACTIONS/CAREER NOTES: Selected by Chicago Bears in second round (38th pick overall) of 2001 NFL draft. ... Signed by Bears (July 20, 2001). ... On injured reserve with finger injury (December 10, 2002-remainder of season).
HONORS: Named running back to THE SPORTING NEWS college All-America third team (2000).
SINGLE GAME HIGHS (regular season): Attempts—33 (January 6, 2002, vs. Jacksonville); yards—188 (October 21, 2001, vs. Cincinnati); and rushing touchdowns—2 (November 2, 2003, vs. San Diego).
STATISTICAL PLATEAUS: 100-yard rushing games: 2001 (4), 2002 (1), 2003 (4). Total: 9.

			RUSHING				RECEIVING				TOTALS			
Year Team	G	GS	Att.	Yds.	Avg.	TD	No.	Yds.	Avg.	TD	TD	2pt.	Pts.	Fum.
2001—Chicago NFL	14	10	278	1183	4.3	7	22	178	8.1	0	7	1	44	0
2002—Chicago NFL	12	12	214	721	3.4	6	24	163	6.8	0	6	0	36	5
2003—Chicago NFL	13	13	244	1024	4.2	6	9	36	4.0	0	6	0	36	1
Pro totals (3 years)	39	35	736	2928	4.0	19	55	377	6.9	0	19	1	116	6

THOMAS, BRYAN DE JETS

PERSONAL: Born June 7, 1979, in Birmingham, Ala. ... 6-4/266.
HIGH SCHOOL: Minor (Birmingham, Ala.).
COLLEGE: Alabama-Birmingham.
TRANSACTIONS/CAREER NOTES: Selected by New York Jets in first round (22nd pick overall) of 2002 NFL draft. ... Signed by Jets (June 19, 2002).

			TOTALS		
Year Team	G	GS	Tk.	Ast.	Sks.
2002—New York Jets NFL	15	0	5	4	0.5
2003—New York Jets NFL	16	10	26	16	1.0
Pro totals (2 years)	31	10	31	20	1.5

T

THOMAS, FRED CB SAINTS

PERSONAL: Born September 11, 1973, in Bruce, Miss. ... 5-9/184.
HIGH SCHOOL: Bruce (Miss.).
JUNIOR COLLEGE: Northwest Mississippi Community College.
COLLEGE: Tennessee-Martin.
TRANSACTIONS/CAREER NOTES: Selected by Seattle Seahawks in second round (47th pick overall) of 1996 NFL draft. ... Signed by Seahawks (July 19, 1996). ... Granted free agency (February 12, 1999). ... Re-signed by Seahawks (May 27, 1999). ... On injured reserve with broken leg (September 17, 1999-remainder of season). ... Granted unconditional free agency (February 11, 2000). ... Signed by New Orleans Saints (February 14, 2000). ... Granted unconditional free agency (March 3, 2004). ... Re-signed by Saints (March 4, 2004).

			TOTALS			INTERCEPTIONS			
Year Team	G	GS	Tk.	Ast.	Sks.	No.	Yds.	Avg.	TD
1996—Seattle NFL	15	0	4	1	0.0	0	0	0.0	0
1997—Seattle NFL	16	3	24	4	0.0	0	0	0.0	0
1998—Seattle NFL	15	2	32	7	0.0	0	0	0.0	0
1999—Seattle NFL	1	0	0	0	0.0	0	0	0.0	0
2000—New Orleans NFL	11	0	16	0	0.0	0	0	0.0	0
2001—New Orleans NFL	16	16	51	13	0.0	1	0	0.0	0
2002—New Orleans NFL	15	14	69	11	1.0	5	80	16.0	0
2003—New Orleans NFL	16	14	75	11	1.0	4	47	11.8	0
Pro totals (8 years)	105	49	271	47	2.0	10	127	12.7	0

THOMAS, HOLLIS DT EAGLES

PERSONAL: Born January 10, 1974, in Abilene, Texas. ... 6-0/306.
HIGH SCHOOL: Sumner (St. Louis).
COLLEGE: Northern Illinois.
TRANSACTIONS/CAREER NOTES: Signed as non-drafted free agent by Philadelphia Eagles (April 26, 1996). ... On injured reserve with arm/shoulder injury (December 2, 1998-remainder of season). ... On injured reserve with foot injury (December 31, 2001-remainder of season). ... On injured reserve with foot injury (August 27, 2002-remainder of season). ... On injured reserve with biceps injury (October 28, 2003-remainder of season).

			TOTALS		
Year Team	G	GS	Tk.	Ast.	Sks.
1996—Philadelphia NFL	16	5	32	10	1.0
1997—Philadelphia NFL	16	16	39	22	2.5
1998—Philadelphia NFL	12	12	34	8	5.0
1999—Philadelphia NFL	16	16	36	13	1.0
2000—Philadelphia NFL	16	16	46	14	4.0
2001—Philadelphia NFL	14	14	43	9	0.0
2002—Philadelphia NFL			Did not play.		
2003—Philadelphia NFL	7	2	13	6	0.0
Pro totals (7 years)	97	81	243	82	13.5

THOMAS, JASON G

PERSONAL: Born July 10, 1977, in Savannah, Ga. ... 6-3/300.
HIGH SCHOOL: A.E. Beach (Savannah, Ga.).
COLLEGE: Hampton.
TRANSACTIONS/CAREER NOTES: Selected by San Diego Chargers in seventh round (222nd pick overall) of 2000 NFL draft. ... Signed by Chargers (July 19, 2000). ... Released by Chargers (August 27, 2000). ... Re-signed by Chargers to practice squad (August 29, 2000). ... Activated (December 23, 2000); did not play. ... Released by Chargers (September 2, 2001). ... Re-signed by Chargers to practice squad (September 4, 2001). ... Signed by Baltimore Ravens off Chargers practice squad (November 21, 2001); did not play. ... Released by Ravens (September 8, 2003).
PLAYING EXPERIENCE: San Diego NFL, 2000; Baltimore NFL, 2001-2003. ... Games/Games started: 2002 (13/0), 2003 (1/0), Total: 14/0.

THOMAS, JUQUA DE TITANS

PERSONAL: Born May 15, 1978, in Houston, Texas. ... 6-2/250. ... Full name: Juqua Demail Thomas.
HIGH SCHOOL: Aldine (Texas).
JUNIOR COLLEGE: Northeastern Oklahoma.
COLLEGE: Oklahoma State.
TRANSACTIONS/CAREER NOTES: Signed as non-drafted free agent by Tennessee Titans (April 27, 2001). ... Re-signed by Titans (April 2, 2003). ... Granted free agency (March 3, 2004). ... Re-signed by Titans (March 26, 2004).
CHAMPIONSHIP GAME EXPERIENCE: Member of Titans for AFC championship game (2002 season); inactive.

			TOTALS		
Year Team	G	GS	Tk.	Ast.	Sks.
2001—Tennessee NFL	7	0	4	1	0.0
2002—Tennessee NFL	9	0	9	0	1.0
2003—Tennessee NFL	15	0	12	4	4.0
Pro totals (3 years)	31	0	25	5	5.0

THOMAS, KEVIN CB BILLS

PERSONAL: Born July 28, 1978, in Phoenix, Ariz. ... 6-0/182. ... Full name: Marvin Kevin Thomas.
HIGH SCHOOL: Foothill (Calif.).
COLLEGE: UNLV.
TRANSACTIONS/CAREER NOTES: Selected by Buffalo Bills in sixth round (176th pick overall) of 2002 NFL draft. ... Signed by Bills (July 23, 2002).

			TOTALS			INTERCEPTIONS			
Year Team	G	GS	Tk.	Ast.	Sks.	No.	Yds.	Avg.	TD
2002—Buffalo NFL	6	1	8	0	0.0	1	31	31.0	0
2003—Buffalo NFL	16	1	11	5	0.5	0	0	0.0	0
Pro totals (2 years)	22	2	19	5	0.5	1	31	31.0	0

THOMAS, KIWAUKEE CB JAGUARS

PERSONAL: Born June 19, 1977, in Warner Robins, Ga. ... 5-11/192. ... Full name: Kiwaukee Sanchez Thomas. ... Name pronounced: kee-WA-kee.
HIGH SCHOOL: Perry (Ga.).
COLLEGE: Georgia Southern.
TRANSACTIONS/CAREER NOTES: Selected by Jacksonville Jaguars in fifth round (159th pick overall) of 2000 NFL draft. ... Signed by Jaguars (May 25, 2000). ... Granted free agency (February 28, 2003). ... Re-signed by Jaguars (April 23, 2003).

			TOTALS			INTERCEPTIONS			
Year Team	G	GS	Tk.	Ast.	Sks.	No.	Yds.	Avg.	TD
2000—Jacksonville NFL	16	3	17	1	0.0	0	0	0.0	0
2001—Jacksonville NFL	16	5	40	2	3.0	0	0	0.0	0
2002—Jacksonville NFL	16	0	23	2	0.0	0	0	0.0	0
2003—Jacksonville NFL	11	1	10	3	1.0	0	0	0.0	0
Pro totals (4 years)	59	9	90	8	4.0	0	0	0.0	0

THOMAS, RANDY G REDSKINS

PERSONAL: Born January 19, 1976, in East Point, Ga. ... 6-5/306.
HIGH SCHOOL: Tri-Cities (East Point, Ga.).
JUNIOR COLLEGE: Copiah-Lincoln Junior College (Miss.).
COLLEGE: Mississippi State.
TRANSACTIONS/CAREER NOTES: Selected by New York Jets in second round (57th pick overall) of 1999 NFL draft. ... Signed by Jets (July 20, 1999). ... Granted unconditional free agency (February 28, 2003). ... Signed by Washington Redskins (March 1, 2003).
PLAYING EXPERIENCE: New York Jets NFL, 1999-2002; Washington NFL, 2003. ... Games/Games started: 1999 (16/16), 2000 (16/16), 2001 (13/13), 2002 (16/16), 2003 (16/16). Total: 77/77.
HONORS: Named offensive guard on THE SPORTING NEWS college All-America second team (1998).

THOMAS, ROBERT — LB — RAMS

PERSONAL: Born July 17, 1980, in El Centro, Calif. ... 6-1/237. ... Full name: Robert W. Thomas.
HIGH SCHOOL: Imperial (Calif.).
COLLEGE: UCLA.
TRANSACTIONS/CAREER NOTES: Selected by St. Louis Rams in first round (31st pick overall) of 2002 NFL draft. ... Signed by Rams (July 23, 2002).
HONORS: Named linebacker on THE SPORTING NEWS college All-America first team (2001).

			TOTALS			INTERCEPTIONS			
Year Team	**G**	**GS**	**Tk.**	**Ast.**	**Sks.**	**No.**	**Yds.**	**Avg.**	**TD**
2002—St. Louis NFL	16	10	34	3	0.0	0	0	0.0	0
2003—St. Louis NFL	12	9	61	9	2.0	0	0	0.0	0
Pro totals (2 years)	28	19	95	12	2.0	0	0	0.0	0

THOMAS, TRA — T — EAGLES

PERSONAL: Born November 20, 1974, in DeLand, Fla. ... 6-7/349. ... Full name: William Thomas III. ... Name pronounced: TRAY.
HIGH SCHOOL: De Land (Fla.).
COLLEGE: Florida State.
TRANSACTIONS/CAREER NOTES: Selected by Philadelphia Eagles in first round (11th pick overall) of 1998 NFL draft. ... Signed by Eagles (June 19, 1998).
PLAYING EXPERIENCE: Philadelphia NFL, 1998-2003. ... Games/Games started: 1998 (16/16), 1999 (16/15), 2000 (16/16), 2001 (15/15), 2002 (16/16), 2003 (15/15). Total: 94/93.
CHAMPIONSHIP GAME EXPERIENCE: Played in NFC championship game (2001-2003 seasons).
HONORS: Played in Pro Bowl (2001 and 2002 seasons). ... Named offensive tackle on the THE SPORTING NEWS NFL All-Pro team (2002).

THOMAS, ZACH — LB — DOLPHINS

PERSONAL: Born September 1, 1973, in Pampa, Texas. ... 5-11/230. ... Full name: Zach Michael Thomas.
HIGH SCHOOL: White Deer (Texas), then Pampa (Texas).
COLLEGE: Texas Tech.
TRANSACTIONS/CAREER NOTES: Selected by Miami Dolphins in fifth round (154th pick overall) of 1996 NFL draft. ... Signed by Dolphins (July 10, 1996). ... Granted free agency (February 12, 1999). ... Re-signed by Dolphins (February 12, 1999). ... Re-signed by Dolphins (March 29, 2003).
HONORS: Named linebacker on THE SPORTING NEWS college All-America second team (1994). ... Named linebacker on THE SPORTING NEWS college All-America first team (1995). ... Played in Pro Bowl (1999, 2000, 2002 and 2003 seasons). ... Named to play in Pro Bowl (2001 season); replaced by Al Wilson due to injury.

			TOTALS			INTERCEPTIONS			
Year Team	**G**	**GS**	**Tk.**	**Ast.**	**Sks.**	**No.**	**Yds.**	**Avg.**	**TD**
1996—Miami NFL	16	16	120	34	2.0	3	64	21.3	1
1997—Miami NFL	15	15	78	50	0.5	1	10	10.0	0
1998—Miami NFL	16	16	86	51	2.0	3	21	7.0	▲2
1999—Miami NFL	16	16	80	53	1.0	1	0	0.0	0
2000—Miami NFL	11	11	56	43	1.5	1	0	0.0	0
2001—Miami NFL	15	15	96	59	3.0	2	51	25.5	1
2002—Miami NFL	16	16	100	56	0.5	1	7	7.0	0
2003—Miami NFL	15	15	85	68	1.0	3	21	7.0	0
Pro totals (8 years)	120	120	701	414	11.5	15	174	11.6	4

THOMPSON, CHAUN — LB — BROWNS

PERSONAL: Born May 22, 1980, in Mount Pleasant, Texas. ... 6-2/250.
HIGH SCHOOL: Mount Pleasant (Texas).
COLLEGE: West Texas A&M.
TRANSACTIONS/CAREER NOTES: Selected by Cleveland Browns in second round (52nd pick overall) of 2003 NFL draft. ... Signed by Browns (July 30, 2003).

			TOTALS			INTERCEPTIONS			
Year Team	**G**	**GS**	**Tk.**	**Ast.**	**Sks.**	**No.**	**Yds.**	**Avg.**	**TD**
2003—Cleveland NFL	16	0	4	0	0.0	0	0	0.0	0

THOMPSON, DERRIUS — WR — DOLPHINS

PERSONAL: Born July 5, 1977, in Dallas, Texas. ... 6-2/220. ... Full name: Derrius Damon Thompson.
HIGH SCHOOL: Cedar Hill (Texas).
COLLEGE: Baylor.
TRANSACTIONS/CAREER NOTES: Signed as non-drafted free agent by Washington Redskins (April 21, 1999). ... Released by Redskins (September 4, 1999). ... Re-signed by Redskins to practice squad (September 6, 1999). ... Activated (November 16, 1999). ... Released by Redskins (August 27, 2000). ... Re-signed by Redskins to practice squad (August 28, 2000). ... Activated (September 8, 2000). ... Released by Redskins (September 18, 2000). ... Re-signed by Redskins to practice squad (November 16, 2000). ... Activated (December 18, 2000). ... Granted free agency (March 1, 2002). ... Re-signed by Redskins (June 14, 2002). ... Granted unconditional free agency (February 28, 2003). ... Signed by Miami Dolphins (March 8, 2003).

SINGLE GAME HIGHS (regular season): Receptions—7 (December 15, 2002, vs. Philadelphia); yards—122 (December 8, 2002, vs. New York Giants); and touchdown receptions—1 (December 22, 2002, vs. Houston).
STATISTICAL PLATEAUS: 100-yard receiving games: 2002 (1). Total: 1.

			RUSHING				RECEIVING				KICKOFF RETURNS				TOTALS			
Year Team	G	GS	Att.	Yds.	Avg.	TD	No.	Yds.	Avg.	TD	No.	Yds.	Avg.	TD	TD	2pt.	Pts.	Fum.
1999—Washington NFL	1	0	0	0	0.0	0	0	0	0.0	0	0	0	0.0	0	0	0	0	0
2000—Washington NFL	4	0	0	0	0.0	0	0	0	0.0	0	0	0	0.0	0	0	0	0	0
2001—Washington NFL	16	0	0	0	0.0	0	3	52	17.3	1	3	17	5.7	0	1	0	6	0
2002—Washington NFL	16	14	10	77	7.7	0	53	773	14.6	4	6	91	15.2	0	4	0	24	2
2003—Miami NFL	16	12	0	0	0.0	0	26	359	13.8	0	0	0	0.0	0	0	0	0	0
Pro totals (5 years)	53	26	10	77	7.7	0	82	1184	14.4	5	9	108	12.0	0	5	0	30	2

THOMPSON, LAMONT S TITANS

PERSONAL: Born July 30, 1978, in Richmond, Calif. ... 6-1/220. ... Full name: Lamont Darnell Thompson.
HIGH SCHOOL: El Cerrito (Richmond, Calif.).
COLLEGE: Washington State.
TRANSACTIONS/CAREER NOTES: Selected by Cincinnati Bengals in second round (41st pick overall) of 2002 NFL draft. ... Signed by Bengals (July 25, 2002). ... On injured reserve with knee injury (December 12, 2002-remainder of season). ... Released by Bengals (August 31, 2003). ... Signed by Tennessee Titans (September 3, 2003).
HONORS: Named free safety on THE SPORTING NEWS college All-America second team (2001).

			TOTALS			INTERCEPTIONS			
Year Team	G	GS	Tk.	Ast.	Sks.	No.	Yds.	Avg.	TD
2002—Cincinnati NFL	13	0	10	0	0.0	1	4	4.0	0
2003—Tennessee NFL	16	0	4	2	0.0	0	0	0.0	0
Pro totals (2 years)	29	0	14	2	0.0	1	4	4.0	0

THOMPSON, RAY LB CARDINALS

PERSONAL: Born November 21, 1977, in Los Angeles, Calif. ... 6-3/224. ... Full name: Raynoch Joseph Thompson.
HIGH SCHOOL: St. Augustine (New Orleans).
COLLEGE: Tennessee.
TRANSACTIONS/CAREER NOTES: Selected by Arizona Cardinals in second round (41st pick overall) of 2000 NFL draft. ... Signed by Cardinals (June 21, 2000). ... On injured reserve with knee injury (December 15, 2000-remainder of season). ... On suspended list for violating league substance abuse policy (December 2-29, 2003).

			TOTALS			INTERCEPTIONS			
Year Team	G	GS	Tk.	Ast.	Sks.	No.	Yds.	Avg.	TD
2000—Arizona NFL	11	9	30	13	0.0	0	0	0.0	0
2001—Arizona NFL	14	14	62	21	0.5	0	0	0.0	0
2002—Arizona NFL	16	16	73	31	3.0	0	0	0.0	0
2003—Arizona NFL	12	12	54	9	3.0	0	0	0.0	0
Pro totals (4 years)	53	51	219	74	6.5	0	0	0.0	0

THORNTON, DAVID LB COLTS

PERSONAL: Born November 1, 1978, in Goldsboro, N.C. ... 6-2/230. ... Full name: David Dontay Thornton.
HIGH SCHOOL: Goldsboro (N.C.).
COLLEGE: North Carolina.
TRANSACTIONS/CAREER NOTES: Selected by Indianapolis Colts in fourth round (106th pick overall) of 2002 NFL draft. ... Signed by Colts (July 10, 2002).
CHAMPIONSHIP GAME EXPERIENCE: Played in AFC championship game (2003 season).

			TOTALS			INTERCEPTIONS			
Year Team	G	GS	Tk.	Ast.	Sks.	No.	Yds.	Avg.	TD
2002—Indianapolis NFL	15	0	27	6	0.0	0	0	0.0	0
2003—Indianapolis NFL	16	16	108	32	1.0	2	3	1.5	0
Pro totals (2 years)	31	16	135	38	1.0	2	3	1.5	0

THORNTON, JOHN DT BENGALS

PERSONAL: Born October 2, 1976, in Philadelphia, Pa. ... 6-3/297. ... Full name: John Jason Thornton.
HIGH SCHOOL: Scotland (Pa.) School for Veterans' Children.
COLLEGE: West Virginia.
TRANSACTIONS/CAREER NOTES: Selected by Tennessee Titans in second round (52nd pick overall) of 1999 NFL draft. ... Signed by Titans (July 26, 1999). ... On injured reserve with shoulder injury (November 8, 2001-remainder of season). ... Granted free agency (March 1, 2002). ... Re-signed by Titans (March 28, 2002). ... Granted unconditional free agency (February 28, 2003). ... Signed by Cincinnati Bengals (May 5, 2003).
CHAMPIONSHIP GAME EXPERIENCE: Played in AFC championship game (1999 and 2002 seasons). ... Played in Super Bowl 34 (1999 season).

			TOTALS		
Year Team	G	GS	Tk.	Ast.	Sks.
1999—Tennessee NFL	16	3	16	4	4.5
2000—Tennessee NFL	16	16	19	9	4.0
2001—Tennessee NFL	3	0	0	0	0.0
2002—Tennessee NFL	16	16	15	5	2.0
2003—Cincinnati NFL	16	16	19	12	6.0
Pro totals (5 years)	67	51	69	30	16.5

T

THRASH, JAMES — WR — REDSKINS

PERSONAL: Born April 28, 1975, in Denver, Colo. ... 6-0/200.
HIGH SCHOOL: Wewoka (Okla.).
COLLEGE: Missouri Southern State.
TRANSACTIONS/CAREER NOTES: Signed as non-drafted free agent by Philadelphia Eagles (April 22, 1997). ... Released by Eagles (July 8, 1997). ... Signed by Washington Redskins (July 11, 1997). ... On injured reserve with shoulder injury (December 8, 1998-remainder of season). ... Granted free agency (February 11, 2000). ... Re-signed with Redskins (April 21, 2000). ... Granted unconditional free agency (March 2, 2001). ... Signed by Eagles (March 9, 2001). ... Traded by Eagles to Washington Redskins for a fifth-round pick in 2005 draft (March 30, 2004).
CHAMPIONSHIP GAME EXPERIENCE: Played in NFC championship game (2001-2003 seasons).
SINGLE GAME HIGHS (regular season): Receptions—10 (September 23, 2001, vs. Seattle); yards—165 (September 23, 2001, vs. Seattle); and touchdown receptions—2 (November 11, 2001, vs. Minnesota).
STATISTICAL PLATEAUS: 100-yard receiving games: 2000 (2), 2001 (2), 2002 (1). Total: 5.

			RUSHING				RECEIVING				KICKOFF RETURNS				TOTALS			
Year Team	**G**	**GS**	**Att.**	**Yds.**	**Avg.**	**TD**	**No.**	**Yds.**	**Avg.**	**TD**	**No.**	**Yds.**	**Avg.**	**TD**	**TD**	**2pt.**	**Pts.**	**Fum.**
1997—Washington NFL	4	0	0	0	0.0	0	2	24	12.0	0	0	0	0.0	0	0	0	0	0
1998—Washington NFL	10	1	0	0	0.0	0	10	163	16.3	1	6	129	21.5	0	1	0	6	0
1999—Washington NFL	16	0	1	37	37.0	0	3	44	14.7	0	14	355	25.4	1	1	0	6	0
2000—Washington NFL	16	8	10	82	8.2	0	50	653	13.1	2	45	1000	22.2	0	2	0	12	1
2001—Philadelphia NFL	15	15	6	57	9.5	0	63	833	13.2	8	5	101	20.2	0	8	0	48	1
2002—Philadelphia NFL	16	16	18	126	7.0	2	52	635	12.2	6	0	0	0.0	0	8	0	48	1
2003—Philadelphia NFL	16	16	5	52	10.4	0	49	558	11.4	1	34	815	24.0	0	1	0	6	0
Pro totals (7 years)	93	56	40	354	8.9	2	229	2910	12.7	18	104	2400	23.1	1	21	0	126	3

TILLMAN, CHARLES — CB — BEARS

PERSONAL: Born February 23, 1981, in Chicago, Ill. ... 6-1/196.
HIGH SCHOOL: Copperas Cove (Texas).
COLLEGE: Louisiana-Lafayette.
TRANSACTIONS/CAREER NOTES: Selected by Chicago Bears in second round (35th pick overall) of 2003 NFL draft. ... Signed by Bears (July 26, 2003).

			TOTALS			INTERCEPTIONS			
Year Team	**G**	**GS**	**Tk.**	**Ast.**	**Sks.**	**No.**	**Yds.**	**Avg.**	**TD**
2003—Chicago NFL	16	13	74	7	1.0	4	27	6.8	0

TILLMAN, TRAVARES — S

PERSONAL: Born October 8, 1977, in Lyons, Ga. ... 6-1/190. ... Full name: Travares Arastius Tillman.
HIGH SCHOOL: Toombs County (Lyons, Ga.).
COLLEGE: Georgia Tech.
TRANSACTIONS/CAREER NOTES: Selected by Buffalo Bills in second round (58th pick overall) of 2000 NFL draft. ... Signed by Bills (July 20, 2000). ... Released by Bills (September 1, 2002). ... Signed by Houston Texans (January 14, 2003). ... Claimed on waivers by Carolina Panthers (September 18, 2003). ... Granted free agency (March 3, 2004).
CHAMPIONSHIP GAME EXPERIENCE: Member of Panthers for NFC championship game (2003 season); inactive. ... Member of Panthers for Super Bowl 38 (2003 season); inactive.

			TOTALS			INTERCEPTIONS			
Year Team	**G**	**GS**	**Tk.**	**Ast.**	**Sks.**	**No.**	**Yds.**	**Avg.**	**TD**
2000—Buffalo NFL	15	4	19	3	0.0	0	0	0.0	0
2001—Buffalo NFL	13	6	22	11	0.0	1	0	0.0	0
2003—Carolina NFL	7	0	0	0	0.0	0	0	0.0	0
Pro totals (3 years)	35	10	41	14	0.0	1	0	0.0	0

TIMMERMAN, ADAM — G — RAMS

PERSONAL: Born August 14, 1971, in Cherokee, Iowa. ... 6-4/310. ... Full name: Adam Larry Timmerman.
HIGH SCHOOL: Washington (Cherokee, Iowa).
COLLEGE: South Dakota State.
TRANSACTIONS/CAREER NOTES: Selected by Green Bay Packers in seventh round (230th pick overall) of 1995 NFL draft. ... Signed by Packers (June 2, 1995). ... Granted free agency (February 13, 1998). ... Re-signed by Packers (April 15, 1998). ... Granted unconditional free agency (February 12, 1999). ... Signed by St. Louis Rams (February 15, 1999).
PLAYING EXPERIENCE: Green Bay NFL, 1995-1998; St. Louis NFL, 1999-2003. ... Games/Games started: 1995 (13/0), 1996 (16/16), 1997 (16/16), 1998 (16/16), 1999 (16/16), 2000 (16/15), 2001 (16/16), 2002 (16/16), 2003 (16/16). Total: 141/127.
CHAMPIONSHIP GAME EXPERIENCE: Played in NFC championship game (1995-97, 1999 and 2001 seasons). ... Member of Super Bowl championship team (1996 and 1999 seasons). ... Played in Super Bowl 32 (1997 season). ... Played in Super Bowl 36 (2001 season).
HONORS: Played in Pro Bowl (1999 and 2001 seasons).

TINOISAMOA, PISA — LB — RAMS

PERSONAL: Born July 15, 1981, in San Diego, Calif. ... 6-1/235.
HIGH SCHOOL: Vista (Calif.).
COLLEGE: Hawaii.

TRANSACTIONS/CAREER NOTES: Selected by St. Louis Rams in second round (43rd pick overall) of 2003 NFL draft. ... Signed by Rams (July 24, 2004).

Year	Team	G	GS	TOTALS Tk.	Ast.	Sks.	INTERCEPTIONS No.	Yds.	Avg.	TD
2003	St. Louis NFL	16	15	65	13	2.0	3	46	15.3	0

TOBECK, ROBBIE — C/G — SEAHAWKS

PERSONAL: Born March 6, 1970, in Tarpon Springs, Fla. ... 6-4/297. ... Full name: Robert L. Tobeck.
HIGH SCHOOL: New Port Richey (Fla.).
COLLEGE: Washington State.
TRANSACTIONS/CAREER NOTES: Signed as non-drafted free agent by Atlanta Falcons (May 7, 1993). ... Released by Falcons (August 30, 1993). ... Re-signed by Falcons to practice squad (August 31, 1993). ... Activated (January 1, 1994). ... Granted unconditional free agency (February 11, 2000). ... Signed by Seattle Seahawks (March 20, 2000). ... On physically unable to perform list with knee injury (August 20-October 14, 2000).
PLAYING EXPERIENCE: Atlanta NFL, 1994-1999; Seattle NFL, 2000-2003. ... Games/Games started: 1994 (5/0), 1995 (16/16), 1996 (16/16), 1997 (16/15), 1998 (16/16), 1999 (15/15), 2000 (4/0), 2001 (16/16), 2002 (16/16), 2003 (16/16). Total: 136/126.
CHAMPIONSHIP GAME EXPERIENCE: Played in NFC championship game (1998 season). ... Played in Super Bowl 33 (1998 season).

TOEFIELD, LABRANDON — RB — JAGUARS

PERSONAL: Born September 24, 1980, in Independence, La. ... 5-11/232. ... Full name: LaBrandon Cordell Toefield.
HIGH SCHOOL: Independence (La.).
COLLEGE: Louisiana State.
TRANSACTIONS/CAREER NOTES: Selected after junior season by Jacksonville Jaguars in fourth round (132nd pick overall) of 2003 NFL draft. ... Signed by Jaguars (July 24, 2003).
SINGLE GAME HIGHS (regular season): Attempts—10 (December 7, 2003, vs. Houston); yards—54 (December 7, 2003, vs. Houston); and rushing touchdowns—1 (December 28, 2003, vs. Atlanta).

Year	Team	G	GS	RUSHING Att.	Yds.	Avg.	TD	RECEIVING No.	Yds.	Avg.	TD	KICKOFF RETURNS No.	Yds.	Avg.	TD	TOTALS TD	2pt.	Pts.	Fum.
2003	Jacksonville NFL	16	0	53	212	4.0	2	14	105	7.5	1	14	272	19.4	0	3	0	18	0

T

TOLVER, J.R. — WR — DOLPHINS

PERSONAL: Born January 13, 1980, in Long Beach, Calif. ... 6-1/202. ... Full name: Gregory D. Tolver Jr.
HIGH SCHOOL: Mira Mesa (San Diego).
COLLEGE: San Diego State.
TRANSACTIONS/CAREER NOTES: Selected by Miami Dolphins in fifth round (169th pick overall) of 2003 NFL draft. ... Signed by Dolphins (July 26, 2003). ... Inactive for 10 games (2003). ... On injured reserve with knee injury (November 25, 2003-remainder of season).

Year	Team	G	GS	RECEIVING No.	Yds.	Avg.	TD	TOTALS TD	2pt.	Pts.	Fum.
2003	Miami NFL	Did not play.									

TOMLINSON, LADAINIAN — RB — CHARGERS

PERSONAL: Born June 23, 1979, in Rosebud, Texas. ... 5-10/221.
HIGH SCHOOL: Waco University (Texas).
COLLEGE: Texas Christian.
TRANSACTIONS/CAREER NOTES: Selected by San Diego Chargers in first round (fifth pick overall) of 2001 draft. ... Signed by Chargers (August 23, 2001).
HONORS: Named running back on THE SPORTING NEWS college All-America third team (1999). ... Named running back on THE SPORTING NEWS college All-America first team (2000). ... Doak Walker Award winner (2000). ... Played in Pro Bowl (2002 season).
SINGLE GAME HIGHS (regular season): Attempts—39 (October 20, 2002, vs. Oakland); yards—243 (December 28, 2003, vs. Oakland); and rushing touchdowns—3 (December 1, 2002, vs. Denver).
STATISTICAL PLATEAUS: 100-yard rushing games: 2001 (4), 2002 (7), 2003 (6). Total: 17. 100-yard receiving games: 2003 (2). Total: 2.

Year	Team	G	GS	RUSHING Att.	Yds.	Avg.	TD	RECEIVING No.	Yds.	Avg.	TD	TOTALS TD	2pt.	Pts.	Fum.
2001	San Diego NFL	16	16	339	1236	3.6	10	59	367	6.2	0	10	0	60	8
2002	San Diego NFL	16	16	372	1683	4.5	14	79	489	6.2	1	15	0	90	3
2003	San Diego NFL	16	16	313	1645	5.3	13	§100	725	7.3	4	17	0	102	2
Pro totals (3 years)		48	48	1024	4564	4.5	37	238	1581	6.6	5	42	0	252	13

TONGUE, REGGIE — S — JETS

PERSONAL: Born April 11, 1973, in Baltimore, Md. ... 6-0/204. ... Full name: Reginald Clinton Tongue.
HIGH SCHOOL: Lathrop (Fairbanks, Alaska).
COLLEGE: Oregon State.
TRANSACTIONS/CAREER NOTES: Selected by Kansas City Chiefs in second round (58th pick overall) of 1996 NFL draft. ... Signed by Chiefs (July 26, 1996). ... Granted unconditional free agency (February 11, 2000). ... Signed by Seattle Seahawks (February 22, 2000). ... Granted unconditional free agency (March 3, 2004). ... Signed by New York Jets (March 22, 2004).

Year Team	G	GS	TOTALS Tk.	Ast.	Sks.	INTERCEPTIONS No.	Yds.	Avg.	TD
1996—Kansas City NFL	16	0	4	0	0.0	0	0	0.0	0
1997—Kansas City NFL	16	16	67	21	2.5	1	0	0.0	0
1998—Kansas City NFL	15	15	78	20	2.0	0	0	0.0	0
1999—Kansas City NFL	16	16	66	10	2.0	1	80	80.0	1
2000—Seattle NFL	16	6	31	9	0.0	0	0	0.0	0
2001—Seattle NFL	16	16	56	20	1.0	3	67	22.3	1
2002—Seattle NFL	16	16	68	25	0.0	5	118	23.6	1
2003—Seattle NFL	14	14	50	13	2.0	4	11	2.8	0
Pro totals (8 years)	125	99	420	118	9.5	14	276	19.7	3

TOOMER, AMANI — WR — GIANTS

PERSONAL: Born September 8, 1974, in Berkeley, Calif. ... 6-3/208. ... Name pronounced: uh-MAHN-ee.
HIGH SCHOOL: De La Salle Catholic (Concord, Calif.).
COLLEGE: Michigan.
TRANSACTIONS/CAREER NOTES: Selected by New York Giants in second round (34th pick overall) of 1996 NFL draft. ... Signed by Giants (July 21, 1996). ... On injured reserve with knee injury (October 31, 1996-remainder of season). ... Granted free agency (February 12, 1999). ... Re-signed by Giants (July 31, 1999).
CHAMPIONSHIP GAME EXPERIENCE: Played in NFC championship game (2000 season). ... Played in Super Bowl 35 (2000 season).
SINGLE GAME HIGHS (regular season): Receptions—10 (December 22, 2002, vs. Indianapolis); yards—204 (December 22, 2002, vs. Indianapolis); and touchdown receptions—3 (December 22, 2002, vs. Indianapolis).
STATISTICAL PLATEAUS: 100-yard receiving games: 1999 (4), 2000 (5), 2001 (2), 2002 (5), 2003 (3). Total: 19.
MISCELLANEOUS: Holds New York Giants all-time record for most yards receiving (6,366).

Year Team	G	GS	RECEIVING No.	Yds.	Avg.	TD	PUNT RETURNS No.	Yds.	Avg.	TD	KICKOFF RETURNS No.	Yds.	Avg.	TD	TOTALS TD	2pt.	Pts.	Fum.
1996—New York Giants NFL	7	1	1	12	12.0	0	18	298	16.6	2	11	191	17.4	0	2	0	12	1
1997—New York Giants NFL	16	0	16	263	16.4	1	47	455	9.7	∞1	0	0	0.0	0	2	0	12	0
1998—New York Giants NFL	16	0	27	360	13.3	5	35	252	7.2	0	4	66	16.5	0	5	0	30	0
1999—New York Giants NFL	16	16	79	1183	15.0	6	1	14	14.0	0	0	0	0.0	0	6	0	36	0
2000—New York Giants NFL	16	15	78	1094	14.0	7	0	0	0.0	0	0	0	0.0	0	8	0	48	1
2001—New York Giants NFL	16	14	72	1054	14.6	5	8	41	5.1	0	0	0	0.0	0	5	0	30	2
2002—New York Giants NFL	16	16	82	1343	16.4	8	0	0	0.0	0	0	0	0.0	0	8	0	48	0
2003—New York Giants NFL	16	16	63	1057	16.8	5	0	0	0.0	0	0	0	0.0	0	5	0	30	0
Pro totals (8 years)	119	78	418	6366	15.2	37	109	1060	9.7	3	15	257	17.1	0	41	0	246	4

TOWNS, LESTER — LB

PERSONAL: Born August 28, 1977, in Los Angeles, Calif. ... 6-1/252. ... Full name: Lester Towns III.
HIGH SCHOOL: Pasadena (Calif.).
COLLEGE: Washington.
TRANSACTIONS/CAREER NOTES: Selected by Carolina Panthers in seventh round (221st pick overall) of 2000 NFL draft. ... Signed by Panthers (July 14, 2000). ... On injured reserve with foot injury (November 21, 2002-remainder of season). ... Granted free agency (February 28, 2003). ... Re-signed by Panthers (2003). ... Granted unrestricted free agency (March 3, 2004).
CHAMPIONSHIP GAME EXPERIENCE: Played in NFC championship game (2003 season). ... Played in Super Bowl 38 (2003 season).

Year Team	G	GS	TOTALS Tk.	Ast.	Sks.	INTERCEPTIONS No.	Yds.	Avg.	TD
2000—Carolina NFL	16	14	79	14	0.0	0	0	0.0	0
2001—Carolina NFL	16	15	61	25	0.0	1	0	0.0	0
2002—Carolina NFL	8	0	2	1	0.0	0	0	0.0	0
2003—Carolina NFL	15	1	11	4	0.0	0	0	0.0	0
Pro totals (4 years)	55	30	153	44	0.0	1	0	0.0	0

TOWNSEND, DESHEA — CB — STEELERS

PERSONAL: Born September 8, 1975, in Batesville, Miss. ... 5-9/191. ... Full name: Trevor Deshea Townsend.
HIGH SCHOOL: South Panola (Batesville, Miss.).
COLLEGE: Alabama.
TRANSACTIONS/CAREER NOTES: Selected by Pittsburgh Steelers in fourth round (117th pick overall) of 1998 NFL draft. ... Signed by Steelers (July 6, 1998). ... Granted free agency (March 2, 2001). ... Re-signed by Steelers (March 2, 2001). ... Granted unconditional free agency (March 1, 2002). ... Re-signed by Steelers (April 2, 2002).
CHAMPIONSHIP GAME EXPERIENCE: Played in AFC championship game (2001 season).

Year Team	G	GS	TOTALS Tk.	Ast.	Sks.	INTERCEPTIONS No.	Yds.	Avg.	TD
1998—Pittsburgh NFL	12	0	9	2	0.0	0	0	0.0	0
1999—Pittsburgh NFL	16	4	27	4	0.0	0	0	0.0	0
2000—Pittsburgh NFL	16	0	20	5	3.5	0	0	0.0	0
2001—Pittsburgh NFL	16	1	20	4	2.0	2	7	3.5	0
2002—Pittsburgh NFL	16	5	28	6	0.0	3	3	1.0	0
2003—Pittsburgh NFL	16	8	37	6	1.0	3	24	8.0	1
Pro totals (6 years)	92	18	141	27	6.5	8	34	4.3	1

TRAPP, JAMES — S

PERSONAL: Born December 28, 1969, in Greenville, S.C. ... 6-0/195. ... Full name: James Harold Trapp.
HIGH SCHOOL: Lawton (Okla.).
COLLEGE: Clemson.
TRANSACTIONS/CAREER NOTES: Selected by Los Angeles Raiders in third round (72nd pick overall) of 1993 NFL draft. ... Signed by Raiders (July 13, 1993). ... Raiders franchise moved to Oakland (July 21, 1995). ... Granted free agency (February 16, 1996). ... Re-signed by Raiders (March 30, 1996). ... Granted unconditional free agency (February 12, 1999). ... Signed by Baltimore Ravens (April 23, 1999). ... Granted unconditional free agency (February 11, 2000). ... Re-signed by Ravens (March 16, 2000). ... On injured reserve with groin injury (January 16, 2002-remainder of 2001 playoffs). ... Granted unconditional free agency (March 1, 2002). ... Re-signed by Ravens (May 20, 2002). ... Granted unconditional free agency (February 28, 2003). ... Signed by Jacksonville Jaguars (May 5, 2003). ... On injured reserve with ankle injury (October 30, 2003-remainder of season). ... Granted unconditional free agency (March 3, 2004).
CHAMPIONSHIP GAME EXPERIENCE: Played in AFC championship game (2000 season). ... Member of Super Bowl championship team (2000 season).

			TOTALS			INTERCEPTIONS			
Year Team	**G**	**GS**	**Tk.**	**Ast.**	**Sks.**	**No.**	**Yds.**	**Avg.**	**TD**
1993—Los Angeles Raiders NFL	14	2	19	2	0.0	1	7	7.0	0
1994—Los Angeles Raiders NFL	16	2	23	6	1.0	0	0	0.0	0
1995—Oakland NFL	14	2	23	2	0.0	0	0	0.0	0
1996—Oakland NFL	12	4	21	2	0.0	1	23	23.0	0
1997—Oakland NFL	16	16	82	21	0.0	2	24	12.0	0
1998—Oakland NFL	16	0	7	6	0.0	0	0	0.0	0
1999—Baltimore NFL	16	0	1	2	1.0	0	0	0.0	0
2000—Baltimore NFL	16	1	19	2	2.0	0	0	0.0	0
2001—Baltimore NFL	10	4	22	5	1.0	1	15	15.0	0
2002—Baltimore NFL	14	1	23	3	1.0	3	26	8.7	0
2003—Jacksonville NFL	5	0	8	3	0.0	1	4	4.0	0
Pro totals (11 years)	149	32	248	54	6.0	9	99	11.0	0

TRAYLOR, KEITH — DT — PATRIOTS

PERSONAL: Born September 3, 1969, in Little Rock, Ark. ... 6-2/340. ... Full name: Byron Keith Traylor.
HIGH SCHOOL: Malvern (Ark.).
JUNIOR COLLEGE: Coffeyville (Kan.) Community College.
COLLEGE: Central Oklahoma.
TRANSACTIONS/CAREER NOTES: Selected by Denver Broncos in third round (61st pick overall) of 1991 NFL draft. ... Signed by Broncos for 1991 season. ... Released by Broncos (June 7, 1993). ... Signed by Los Angeles Raiders (June 1993). ... Released by Raiders (August 30, 1993). ... Signed by Green Bay Packers (September 14, 1993). ... Released by Packers (November 9, 1993). ... Signed by Kansas City Chiefs (January 7, 1994). ... Released by Chiefs (January 14, 1994). ... Re-signed by Chiefs (May 18, 1994). ... Released by Chiefs (August 28, 1994). ... Re-signed by Chiefs (February 28, 1995). ... Granted unconditional free agency (February 14, 1997). ... Signed by Broncos (March 10, 1997). ... Released by Broncos (March 14, 2001). ... Signed by Chicago Bears (March 24, 2001). ... Granted unconditional free agency (March 3, 2004). ... Signed by New England Patriots (March 31, 2004).
CHAMPIONSHIP GAME EXPERIENCE: Played in AFC championship game (1991, 1997 and 1998 seasons). ... Member of Super Bowl championship team (1997 and 1998 seasons).

			TOTALS			INTERCEPTIONS			
Year Team	**G**	**GS**	**Tk.**	**Ast.**	**Sks.**	**No.**	**Yds.**	**Avg.**	**TD**
1991—Denver NFL	16	2	12	15	0.0	0	0	0.0	0
1992—Denver NFL	16	3	21	18	1.0	0	0	0.0	0
1993—Green Bay NFL	5	0	0	1	0.0	0	0	0.0	0
1994—				Did not play.					
1995—Kansas City NFL	16	0	9	2	1.5	0	0	0.0	0
1996—Kansas City NFL	15	1	21	6	1.0	0	0	0.0	0
1997—Denver NFL	16	16	28	11	2.0	1	62	62.0	1
1998—Denver NFL	15	14	24	8	2.0	0	0	0.0	0
1999—Denver NFL	15	15	25	7	1.5	0	0	0.0	0
2000—Denver NFL	16	16	32	5	1.0	0	0	0.0	0
2001—Chicago NFL	16	15	29	4	2.0	1	67	67.0	0
2002—Chicago NFL	15	15	26	5	1.0	0	0	0.0	0
2003—Chicago NFL	10	10	13	4	0.0	0	0	0.0	0
Pro totals (12 years)	171	107	240	86	13.0	2	129	64.5	1

TREJO, STEPHEN — FB — LIONS

PERSONAL: Born November 20, 1977, in Mesa, Ariz. ... 6-2/254. ... Full name: Stephen Nicholas Trejo.
HIGH SCHOOL: Casa Grande (Ariz.).
COLLEGE: Arizona State.
TRANSACTIONS/CAREER NOTES: Signed as non-drafted free agent by Detroit Lions (April 27, 2001). ... Granted free agency (March 3, 2004). ... Re-signed by Lions (April 23, 2004).
SINGLE GAME HIGHS (regular season): Attempts—1 (September 15, 2002, vs. Carolina); yards—0; and rushing touchdowns—0.

			RUSHING				TOTALS			
Year Team	**G**	**GS**	**Att.**	**Yds.**	**Avg.**	**TD**	**TD**	**2pt.**	**Pts.**	**Fum.**
2001—Detroit NFL	14	0	0	0	0.0	0	0	0	0	0
2002—Detroit NFL	16	0	1	0	0.0	0	0	0	0	0
2003—Detroit NFL	16	0	0	0	0.0	0	0	0	0	0
Pro totals (3 years)	46	0	1	0	0.0	0	0	0	0	0

TREU, ADAM — C/LS — RAIDERS

PERSONAL: Born June 24, 1974, in Lincoln, Neb. ... 6-5/300. ... Name pronounced: TRUE.
HIGH SCHOOL: Pius X (Lincoln, Neb.).
COLLEGE: Nebraska.
TRANSACTIONS/CAREER NOTES: Selected by Oakland Raiders in third round (72nd pick overall) of 1997 NFL draft. ... Signed by Raiders for 1997 season.
PLAYING EXPERIENCE: Oakland NFL, 1997-2003. ... Games/Games started: 1997 (16/0), 1998 (16/0), 1999 (16/0), 2000 (16/0), 2001 (16/14), 2002 (16/0), 2003 (16/4). Total: 112/18.
CHAMPIONSHIP GAME EXPERIENCE: Played in AFC championship game (2000 and 2002 seasons). ... Played in Super Bowl 37 (2002 season).

TRIPPLETT, LARRY — DT — COLTS

PERSONAL: Born January 18, 1979, in Los Angeles, Calif. ... 6-2/300.
HIGH SCHOOL: Westchester (Los Angeles).
COLLEGE: Washington.
TRANSACTIONS/CAREER NOTES: Selected by Indianapolis Colts in second round (42nd pick overall) of 2002 NFL draft. ... Signed by Colts (July 26, 2002).
CHAMPIONSHIP GAME EXPERIENCE: Played in AFC championship game (2003 season).
HONORS: Named defensive tackle on THE SPORTING NEWS college All-America second team (2000). ... Named defensive tackle on THE SPORTING NEWS college All-America third team (2001).

			TOTALS		
Year Team	G	GS	Tk.	Ast.	Sks.
2002—Indianapolis NFL	13	10	18	3	0.0
2003—Indianapolis NFL	16	16	29	18	1.0
Pro totals (2 years)	29	26	47	21	1.0

TROTTER, JEREMIAH — LB — REDSKINS

T

PERSONAL: Born January 20, 1977, in Texarkana, Texas. ... 6-1/262.
HIGH SCHOOL: Hooks (Texas).
COLLEGE: Stephen F. Austin.
TRANSACTIONS/CAREER NOTES: Selected after junior season by Philadelphia Eagles in third round (72nd pick overall) of 1998 NFL draft. ... Signed by Eagles (July 14, 1998). ... Granted free agency (March 2, 2001). ... Re-signed by Eagles (April 27, 2001). ... Designated by Eagles as franchise player (February 21, 2002). ... Granted unconditional free agency (April 5, 2002). ... Signed by Washington Redskins (April 22, 2002). ... On injured reserve with knee injury (December 2, 2002-remainder of season).
CHAMPIONSHIP GAME EXPERIENCE: Played in NFC championship game (2001 season).
HONORS: Played in Pro Bowl (2000 and 2001 seasons).

			TOTALS			INTERCEPTIONS			
Year Team	G	GS	Tk.	Ast.	Sks.	No.	Yds.	Avg.	TD
1998—Philadelphia NFL	8	0	3	0	0.0	0	0	0.0	0
1999—Philadelphia NFL	16	16	91	31	2.5	2	30	15.0	0
2000—Philadelphia NFL	16	16	99	21	3.0	1	27	27.0	1
2001—Philadelphia NFL	16	16	93	22	3.5	2	64	32.0	1
2002—Washington NFL	12	12	58	33	0.0	1	2	2.0	0
2003—Washington NFL	16	16	92	23	1.5	1	21	21.0	0
Pro totals (6 years)	84	76	436	130	10.5	7	144	20.6	2

TRUFANT, MARCUS — CB — SEAHAWKS

PERSONAL: Born December 25, 1980, in Tacoma, Wash. ... 5-11/199. ... Full name: Marcus Lavon Trufant.
HIGH SCHOOL: Wilson (Tacoma, Wash.).
COLLEGE: Washington State.
TRANSACTIONS/CAREER NOTES: Selected by Seattle Seahawks in first round (11th pick overall) of 2003 NFL draft. ... Signed by Seahawks (July 24, 2003).

			TOTALS			INTERCEPTIONS			
Year Team	G	GS	Tk.	Ast.	Sks.	No.	Yds.	Avg.	TD
2003—Seattle NFL	16	16	69	9	0.0	2	21	10.5	0

TRULUCK, R-KAL — DE — CHIEFS

PERSONAL: Born September 30, 1974, in Brooklyn, N.Y. ... 6-4/255. ... Full name: R-Kal K-Quan Truluck.
HIGH SCHOOL: Spring Valley (Rockland County, N.Y.).
COLLEGE: Cortland State.
TRANSACTIONS/CAREER NOTES: Signed as non-drafted free agent by Washington Redskins (April 27, 1997). ... Released by Redskins (August 20, 1997). ... Signed by Saskatchewan Roughriders of CFL (May 1998). ... Signed by St. Louis Rams (April 16, 2001). ... Released by Rams (April 26, 2001). ... Signed by Redskins to practice squad (August 26, 2001). ... Released by Redskins (September 2, 2001). ... Played with Detroit Fury of Arena League (2001-02). ... Signed by Kansas City Chiefs (August 6, 2002). ... Released by Chiefs (September 1, 2002). ... Re-signed by Chiefs to practice squad (September 3, 2002). ... Activated (November 20, 2002).

			TOTALS		
Year Team	G	GS	Tk.	Ast.	Sks.
1998—Saskatchewan CFL	3	...	...	...	4.0

Year Team	G	GS	TOTALS Tk.	Ast.	Sks.
1999—Saskatchewan CFL	18	...	...	...	7.0
2000—Saskatchewan CFL	17	...	...	...	1.0
2002—Kansas City NFL	6	0	6	2	0.5
2003—Kansas City NFL	14	0	10	2	5.0
CFL totals (3 years)	38	...	...	...	12.0
NFL totals (2 years)	20	0	16	4	5.5
Pro totals (5 years)	58	...	...	...	17.5

TUCKER, REX — G — BEARS

PERSONAL: Born December 20, 1976, in Midland, Texas. ... 6-5/315. ... Full name: Rex Truman Tucker. ... Brother of Ryan Tucker, offensive tackle, Cleveland Browns.

HIGH SCHOOL: Robert E. Lee (Midland, Texas).

COLLEGE: Texas A&M.

TRANSACTIONS/CAREER NOTES: Selected in third round by Chicago Bears (66th pick overall) of 1999 NFL draft. ... Signed by Bears (July 21, 1999). ... Granted free agency (March 1, 2002). ... Re-signed by Bears (April 19, 2002). ... On injured reserve with ankle injury (October 9, 2002-remainder of season). ... On injured reserve with ankle injury (August 31, 2003-entire season).

PLAYING EXPERIENCE: Chicago NFL, 1999-2003. ... Games/Games started: 1999 (2/1), 2000 (6/0), 2001 (16/16), 2002 (5/5), Total: 29/22.

TUCKER, ROSS — G — BILLS

PERSONAL: Born March 2, 1979, in Wyomissing, Pa. ... 6-4/316.

HIGH SCHOOL: Wyomissing (Pa.).

COLLEGE: Princeton.

TRANSACTIONS/CAREER NOTES: Singed as non-drafted free agent by Washington Redskins (April 25, 2001). ... Claimed on waivers by Dallas Cowboys (October 23, 2002). ... Claimed on waivers by Buffalo Bills (June 16, 2003).

PLAYING EXPERIENCE: Washington NFL, 2001; Dallas NFL, 2002; Washington NFL, 2002; Buffalo NFL, 2003. ... Games/Games started: 2001 (3/0), 2002 (3/0), 2003 (12/5). Total: 18/5.

TUCKER, RYAN — T — BROWNS

PERSONAL: Born June 12, 1975, in Midland, Texas. ... 6-6/325. ... Full name: Ryan Huey Tucker. ... Brother of Rex Tucker, guard, Chicago Bears.

HIGH SCHOOL: Robert E. Lee (Midland, Texas).

COLLEGE: Texas Christian.

TRANSACTIONS/CAREER NOTES: Selected by St. Louis Rams in fourth round (112th pick overall) of 1997 NFL draft. ... Signed by Rams (July 3, 1997). ... On physically unable to perform list with knee injury (August 19-October 29, 1997). ... Granted free agency (February 11, 2000). ... Tendered offer sheet by Miami Dolphins (February 17, 2000). ... Offer matched by Rams (February 22, 2000). ... Released by Rams (February 28, 2002). ... Signed by Cleveland Browns (March 7, 2002).

PLAYING EXPERIENCE: St. Louis NFL, 1997-2001; Cleveland NFL, 2002-2003. ... Games/Games started: 1997 (7/0), 1998 (5/0), 1999 (16/0), 2000 (16/16), 2001 (15/15), 2002 (14/14), 2003 (16/16). Total: 89/61.

CHAMPIONSHIP GAME EXPERIENCE: Played in NFC championship game (1999 and 2001 seasons). ... Member of Super Bowl championship team (1999 season). ... Played in Super Bowl 36 (2001 season).

TUCKER, TORRIN — G — COWBOYS

PERSONAL: Born December 25, 1979... 6-6/329.

HIGH SCHOOL: Southeast Lauderdale (Meridian, Miss.).

COLLEGE: Southern Mississippi.

TRANSACTIONS/CAREER NOTES: Signed as non-drafted free agent by Dallas Cowboys (May 1, 2003). ... Released by Cowboys (August 31, 2003). ... Re-signed by Cowboys to practice squad (September 1, 2003). ... Activated (October 1, 2003).

PLAYING EXPERIENCE: Dallas NFL, 2003. ... Games/Games started: 2003 (7/1). Total: 7/1.

TUIASOSOPO, MARQUES — QB — RAIDERS

PERSONAL: Born March 22, 1979, in Seattle, Wash. ... 6-1/220.

HIGH SCHOOL: Woodinville (Wash.).

COLLEGE: Washington.

TRANSACTIONS/CAREER NOTES: Selected by Oakland Raiders in second round (59th pick overall) of 2001 NFL draft. ... Signed by Raiders (July 21, 2001). ... On injured reserve with knee injury (November 5, 2003-remainder of season).

CHAMPIONSHIP GAME EXPERIENCE: Member of Raiders for AFC championship game (2002 season); did not play. ... Member of Raiders for Super Bowl 37 (2002 season); did not play.

SINGLE GAME HIGHS (regular season): Attempts—28 (October 20, 2003, vs. Kansas City); completions—16 (October 20, 2003, vs. Kansas City); yards—224 (October 20, 2003, vs. Kansas City); and touchdown passes—0.

MISCELLANEOUS: Regular-season record as starting NFL quarterback: 0-1 (.000).

			PASSING									RUSHING				TOTALS		
Year Team	G	GS	Att.	Cmp.	Pct.	Yds.	TD	Int.	Avg.	Skd.	Rat.	Att.	Yds.	Avg.	TD	TD	2pt.	Pts.
2001—Oakland NFL	1	0	4	3	75.0	34	0	0	8.50	0	100.0	1	1	1.0	0	0	0	0
2002—Oakland NFL	3	0	0	0	0.0	0	0	0	0.00	0	0.0	2	-3	-1.5	0	0	0	0
2003—Oakland NFL	4	1	45	25	55.6	324	0	3	7.20	2	50.6	6	22	3.7	0	0	0	0
Pro totals (3 years)	8	1	49	28	57.1	358	0	3	7.31	2	54.6	9	20	2.2	0	0	0	0

TUMAN, JERAME TE STEELERS

PERSONAL: Born March 24, 1976, in Liberal, Kan. ... 6-4/255. ... Full name: Jerame Dean Tuman. ... Name pronounced: Jeremy TOO-man.
HIGH SCHOOL: Liberal (Kan.).
COLLEGE: Michigan.
TRANSACTIONS/CAREER NOTES: Selected by Pittsburgh Steelers in fifth round (136th pick overall) of 1999 NFL draft. ... Signed by Steelers (July 19, 1999). ... On injured reserve with knee injury (October 27, 1999-remainder of season). ... Granted free agency (March 1, 2002). ... Re-signed by Steelers (April 10, 2002). ... Granted unconditional free agency (February 28, 2003). ... Re-signed by Steelers (February 28, 2003).
CHAMPIONSHIP GAME EXPERIENCE: Played in AFC championship game (2001 season).
HONORS: Named tight end on THE SPORTING NEWS college All-America third team (1997).
SINGLE GAME HIGHS (regular season): Receptions—2 (December 28, 2003, vs. Baltimore); yards—32 (October 21, 2001, vs. Tampa Bay); and touchdown receptions—1 (November 10, 2002, vs. Atlanta).

			RECEIVING				TOTALS			
Year Team	G	GS	No.	Yds.	Avg.	TD	TD	2pt.	Pts.	Fum.
1999—Pittsburgh NFL	7	0	0	0	0.0	0	0	0	0	0
2000—Pittsburgh NFL	16	1	0	0	0.0	0	0	0	0	0
2001—Pittsburgh NFL	16	7	7	96	13.7	1	1	0	6	0
2002—Pittsburgh NFL	13	7	4	63	15.8	1	1	0	6	0
2003—Pittsburgh NFL	16	12	12	113	9.4	0	0	0	0	0
Pro totals (5 years)	68	27	23	272	11.8	2	2	0	12	0

TUPA, TOM P REDSKINS

PERSONAL: Born February 6, 1966, in Cleveland, Ohio. ... 6-4/225. ... Full name: Thomas Joseph Tupa Jr.
HIGH SCHOOL: Brecksville (Broadview Heights, Ohio).
COLLEGE: Ohio State.
TRANSACTIONS/CAREER NOTES: Selected by Phoenix Cardinals in third round (68th pick overall) of 1988 NFL draft. ... Signed by Cardinals (July 12, 1988). ... Granted free agency (February 1, 1991). ... Re-signed by Cardinals (July 17, 1991). ... Granted unconditional free agency (February 1, 1992). ... Signed by Indianapolis Colts (March 31, 1992). ... Released by Colts (August 30, 1993). ... Signed by Cleveland Browns (November 9, 1993). ... Released by Browns (November 24, 1993). ... Re-signed by Browns (March 30, 1994). ... Granted unconditional free agency (February 16, 1996). ... Signed by New England Patriots (March 15, 1996). ... Granted unconditional free agency (February 12, 1999). ... Signed by New York Jets (February 15, 1999). ... Released by Jets (February 25, 2002). ... Signed by Tampa Bay Buccaneers (May 10, 2002). ... Granted unconditional free agency (February 28, 2003). ... Re-signed by Buccaneers (June 17, 2003). ... Granted unconditional free agency (March 3, 2004). ... Signed by Washington Redskins (March 9, 2004).
CHAMPIONSHIP GAME EXPERIENCE: Played in AFC championship game (1996 season). ... Played in Super Bowl 31 (1996 season). ... Played in NFC championship game (2002 season). ... Member of Super Bowl championship team (2002 season).
HONORS: Played in Pro Bowl (1999 season).
STATISTICAL PLATEAUS: 300-yard passing games: 1991 (1). Total: 1.
MISCELLANEOUS: Regular-season starting record as starting NFL quarterback: 4-9 (.308).

		PUNTING					
Year Team	G	No.	Yds.	Avg.	Net avg.	In. 20	Blk.
1988—Phoenix NFL	2	0	0	0.0	0.0	0	0
1989—Phoenix NFL	14	6	280	46.7	39.7	2	0
1990—Phoenix NFL	15	0	0	0.0	0.0	0	0
1991—Phoenix NFL	11	0	0	0.0	0.0	0	0
1992—Indianapolis NFL	3	0	0	0.0	0.0	0	0
1993—Cleveland NFL		Did not play.					
1994—Cleveland NFL	16	80	3211	40.1	35.3	27	0
1995—Cleveland NFL	16	65	2831	43.6	36.2	18	0
1996—New England NFL	16	63	2739	43.5	36.0	14	0
1997—New England NFL	16	78	3569	§45.8	36.1	24	1
1998—New England NFL	16	74	3294	44.5	35.4	13	0
1999—New York Jets NFL	16	81	3659	45.2	38.2	25	0
2000—New York Jets NFL	16	83	3714	44.7	33.2	18	0
2001—New York Jets NFL	15	67	2575	38.4	32.0	21	0
2002—Tampa Bay NFL	16	90	3856	42.8	35.4	30	0
2003—Tampa Bay NFL	16	83	3590	43.3	35.9	26	0
Pro totals (15 years)	204	770	33318	43.3	35.4	218	1

TURK, MATT P DOLPHINS

PERSONAL: Born June 16, 1968, in Greenfield, Wis. ... 6-5/250. ... Brother of Dan Turk, center with five NFL teams (1985-99).
HIGH SCHOOL: Greenfield (Wis.).
COLLEGE: Wisconsin-Whitewater.
TRANSACTIONS/CAREER NOTES: Signed as non-drafted free agent by Green Bay Packers (July 13, 1993). ... Released by Packers (August 4, 1993). ... Signed by Los Angeles Rams (April 1994). ... Released by Rams (August 22, 1994). ... Signed by Washington Redskins (April 5, 1995). ... Traded by Redskins to Miami Dolphins for sventh-round pick (traded to San Francisco) in 2001 draft (March 9, 2000). ... Granted unconditional free agency (March 1, 2002). ... Signed by New York Jets (April 23, 2002). ... Released by Jets (March 7, 2003). ... Signed by Miami Dolphins (September 29, 2003). ... Granted unconditional free agency (March 3, 2004). ... Re-signed by Dolphins (March 23, 2004).
HONORS: Played in Pro Bowl (1996-1998 seasons). ... Named punter on THE SPORTING NEWS NFL All-Pro team (1997).

		PUNTING					
Year Team	G	No.	Yds.	Avg.	Net avg.	In. 20	Blk.
1995—Washington NFL	16	74	3140	42.4	37.7	†29	0
1996—Washington NFL	16	75	3386	*45.1	*39.2	24	0
1997—Washington NFL	16	84	3788	45.1	*39.2	32	1

Year Team	G	PUNTING No.	Yds.	Avg.	Net avg.	In. 20	Blk.
1998—Washington NFL	16	93	4103	44.1	‡39.0	∞33	∞1
1999—Washington NFL	14	62	2564	41.4	35.6	16	0
2000—Miami NFL	16	92	3870	42.1	36.2	25	0
2001—Miami NFL	16	81	3321	41.0	37.6	28	0
2002—New York Jets NFL	16	63	2584	41.0	34.9	13	0
2003—Miami NFL	13	68	2631	38.7	34.5	23	0
Pro totals (9 years)	139	692	29387	42.5	37.3	223	2

TURLEY, KYLE — T — RAMS

PERSONAL: Born September 24, 1975, in Moreno Valley, Calif. ... 6-5/309. ... Full name: Kyle John Turley.
HIGH SCHOOL: Valley View (Moreno Valley, Calif.).
COLLEGE: San Diego State.
TRANSACTIONS/CAREER NOTES: Selected by New Orleans Saints in first round (seventh pick overall) of 1998 NFL draft. ... Signed by Saints (July 23, 1998). ... Traded by Saints to St. Louis Rams for second-round pick (DE Courtney Watson) in 2004 draft (March 21, 2003).
PLAYING EXPERIENCE: New Orleans NFL, 1998-2002; St. Louis NFL, 2003. ... Games/Games started: 1998 (15/15), 1999 (16/16), 2000 (16/16), 2001 (16/16), 2002 (16/16), 2003 (16/16). Total: 95/95.
HONORS: Named offensive tackle on THE SPORTING NEWS college All-America first team (1997).

TURNER, SCOTT — CB — BRONCOS

PERSONAL: Born February 26, 1972, in Richardson, Texas. ... 5-10/190.
HIGH SCHOOL: J.J. Pearce (Richardson, Texas).
COLLEGE: Illinois.
TRANSACTIONS/CAREER NOTES: Selected by Washington Redskins in seventh round (226th pick overall) of 1995 NFL draft. ... Signed by Redskins (July 18, 1995). ... On injured reserve with ankle injury (December 11, 1997-remainder of season). ... Granted free agency (February 13, 1998). ... Re-signed by Redskins (April 30, 1998). ... Claimed on waivers by San Diego Chargers (August 31, 1998). ... Granted unconditional free agency (February 11, 2000). ... Re-signed by Chargers (April 3, 2000). ... Granted unconditional free agency (March 2, 2001). ... Re-signed by Chargers (December 5, 2001). ... Granted unconditional free agency (March 1, 2002). ... Signed by Buffalo Bills (February 4, 2003). ... Released by Buffalo (August 31, 2003). ... Signed by Denver Broncos (October 14, 2003). ... Granted unconditional free agency (March 3, 2004). ... Re-signed by Broncos (March 10, 2004).

			TOTALS			INTERCEPTIONS			
Year Team	G	GS	Tk.	Ast.	Sks.	No.	Yds.	Avg.	TD
1995—Washington NFL	16	0	27	3	1.0	1	0	0.0	0
1996—Washington NFL	16	0	23	2	0.0	2	16	8.0	0
1997—Washington NFL	9	0	0	0	0.0	0	0	0.0	0
1998—San Diego NFL	16	1	7	0	1.0	1	0	0.0	0
1999—San Diego NFL	15	0	6	2	0.0	0	0	0.0	0
2000—San Diego NFL	16	2	8	0	0.0	1	75	75.0	1
2001—San Diego NFL	4	1	1	1	0.0	0	0	0.0	0
2003—Denver NFL	9	0	0	0	0.0	0	0	0.0	0
Pro totals (8 years)	101	4	72	8	2.0	5	91	18.2	1

TYREE, DAVID — WR — GIANTS

PERSONAL: Born January 3, 1980, in Livingston, N.J. ... 6-0/205. ... Full name: David Mikel Tyree.
HIGH SCHOOL: Montclair (N.J.).
COLLEGE: Syracuse.
TRANSACTIONS/CAREER NOTES: Selected by New York Giants in sixth round (211th pick overall) of 2003 NFL draft. ... Signed by Giants (June 13, 2003).
SINGLE GAME HIGHS (regular season): Receptions—5 (November 16, 2003, vs. Philadelphia); yards—106 (November 16, 2003, vs. Philadelphia); and touchdown receptions—0.
STATISTICAL PLATEAUS: 100-yard receiving games: 2003 (1). Total: 1.

			RECEIVING				PUNT RETURNS				TOTALS			
Year Team	G	GS	No.	Yds.	Avg.	TD	No.	Yds.	Avg.	TD	TD	2pt.	Pts.	Fum.
2003—New York Giants NFL	16	3	16	211	13.2	0	0	0	0.0	0	0	0	0	0

ULBRICH, JEFF — LB — 49ERS

PERSONAL: Born February 17, 1977, in San Jose, Calif. ... 6-0/249.
HIGH SCHOOL: Live Oak (Morgan Hill, Calif.).
JUNIOR COLLEGE: Gavilan College (Calif.).
COLLEGE: Hawaii.
TRANSACTIONS/CAREER NOTES: Selected by San Francisco 49ers in third round (86th pick overall) of 2000 NFL draft. ... Signed by 49ers (July 13, 2000). ... On injured reserve with shoulder injury (November 20, 2000-remainder of season).

			TOTALS			INTERCEPTIONS			
Year Team	G	GS	Tk.	Ast.	Sks.	No.	Yds.	Avg.	TD
2000—San Francisco NFL	4	0	0	1	0.0	0	0	0.0	0
2001—San Francisco NFL	14	14	62	24	0.5	0	0	0.0	0
2002—San Francisco NFL	14	13	46	22	1.5	0	0	0.0	0
2003—San Francisco NFL	15	15	53	21	2.5	1	7	7.0	0
Pro totals (4 years)	47	42	161	68	4.5	1	7	7.0	0

ULMER, ARTIE LB FALCONS

PERSONAL: Born July 30, 1973, in Rincon, Ga. ... 6-3/247. ... Full name: Charles Artie Ulmer.
HIGH SCHOOL: Effingham County (Springfield, Ga.).
COLLEGE: Valdosta State.
TRANSACTIONS/CAREER NOTES: Selected by Minnesota Vikings in seventh round (220th pick overall) of 1997 NFL draft. ... On suspended list for violating league substance abuse policy (August 19-September 23, 1997). ... Signed by Vikings (June 17, 1997). ... Assigned by Vikings to Frankfurt Galaxy in 1998 NFL Europe enhancement allocation program (February 18, 1998). ... Released by Vikings (August 24, 1998). ... Signed by Denver Broncos (January 14, 1999). ... On injured reserve with knee injury (November 4, 1999-remainder of season). ... Granted free agency (February 11, 2000). ... Signed by San Francisco 49ers to practice squad (September 14, 2000). ... Activated (September 19, 2000). ... Released by 49ers (February 19, 2001). ... Signed by Atlanta Falcons (April 16, 2001). ... Granted unconditional free agency (March 1, 2002). ... Re-signed by Falcons (March 22, 2002). ... Granted unconditional free agency (February 28, 2003). ... Re-signed by Falcons (April 1, 2003). ... Granted unconditional free agency (March 3, 2004). ... Re-signed by Falcons (March 19, 2004).

			TOTALS			INTERCEPTIONS			
Year Team	**G**	**GS**	**Tk.**	**Ast.**	**Sks.**	**No.**	**Yds.**	**Avg.**	**TD**
1999—Denver NFL	7	0	0	0	0.0	0	0	0.0	0
2000—San Francisco NFL	12	2	6	6	1.0	0	0	0.0	0
2001—Atlanta NFL	15	0	3	1	0.0	0	0	0.0	0
2002—Atlanta NFL	15	0	2	0	0.0	0	0	0.0	0
2003—Atlanta NFL	16	0	4	2	0.0	0	0	0.0	0
Pro totals (5 years)	65	2	15	9	1.0	0	0	0.0	0

UMENYIORA, OSI DE GIANTS

PERSONAL: Born November 16, 1980, in London, England. ... 6-3/280.
HIGH SCHOOL: Auburn (Ala.).
COLLEGE: Troy State.
TRANSACTIONS/CAREER NOTES: Selected by New York Giants in second round (56th pick overall) of 2003 NFL draft. ... Signed by Giants (July 18, 2003).

			TOTALS		
Year Team	**G**	**GS**	**Tk.**	**Ast.**	**Sks.**
2003—New York Giants NFL	13	1	13	7	1.0

UNCK, MASON LB BROWNS

PERSONAL: Born September 7, 1980, in Ogden, Utah. ... 6-3/235. ... Full name: Mason Douglas Unck.
HIGH SCHOOL: Bonneville (Ogden, Utah).
COLLEGE: Arizona State.
TRANSACTIONS/CAREER NOTES: Signed by Cleveland Browns as a non-drafted free agent (May 2, 2003). ... Waived by Browns (August 31, 2003). ... Re-signed by Browns to practice squad (September 1, 2003). ... Activated (November 26, 2003). ... Assigned by Browns to Frankfurt Galaxy in 2004 NFL Europe enhancement allocation program (February 9, 2004).

			TOTALS			INTERCEPTIONS			
Year Team	**G**	**GS**	**Tk.**	**Ast.**	**Sks.**	**No.**	**Yds.**	**Avg.**	**TD**
2003—Cleveland NFL	1	0	0	0	0.0	0	0	0.0	0

U

UPSHAW, REGAN DE REDSKINS

PERSONAL: Born August 12, 1975, in Berrien Springs, Mich. ... 6-4/265. ... Full name: Regan Charles Upshaw.
HIGH SCHOOL: Pittsburg (Calif.).
COLLEGE: California.
TRANSACTIONS/CAREER NOTES: Selected after junior season by Tampa Bay Buccaneers in first round (12th pick overall) of 1996 NFL draft. ... Signed by Buccaneers (July 21, 1996). ... Traded by Buccaneers to Jacksonville Jaguars for sixth-round pick (RB Jameel Cook) in 2001 draft (October 19, 1999). ... Granted unconditional free agency (February 11, 2000). ... Signed by Oakland Raiders (March 1, 2000). ... On physically unable to perform list with knee injury (August 26-November 20, 2002). ... Released by Raiders (February 27, 2003). ... Signed by Washington Redskins (March 1, 2003).
CHAMPIONSHIP GAME EXPERIENCE: Played in AFC championship game (1999, 2000 and 2002 seasons). ... Played in Super Bowl 37 (2002 season).

			TOTALS			INTERCEPTIONS			
Year Team	**G**	**GS**	**Tk.**	**Ast.**	**Sks.**	**No.**	**Yds.**	**Avg.**	**TD**
1996—Tampa Bay NFL	16	15	20	5	4.0	0	0	0.0	0
1997—Tampa Bay NFL	15	15	23	5	7.5	0	0	0.0	0
1998—Tampa Bay NFL	16	16	23	6	7.0	1	26	26.0	0
1999—Tampa Bay NFL	1	0	0	1	0.0	0	0	0.0	0
—Jacksonville NFL	6	0	6	0	0.0	0	0	0.0	0
2000—Oakland NFL	16	7	17	5	6.0	0	0	0.0	0
2001—Oakland NFL	16	15	24	8	7.0	0	0	0.0	0
2002—Oakland NFL	5	1	2	1	2.0	0	0	0.0	0
2003—Washington NFL	16	8	16	5	1.0	0	0	0.0	0
Pro totals (8 years)	107	77	131	36	34.5	1	26	26.0	0

URLACHER, BRIAN LB BEARS

PERSONAL: Born May 25, 1978, in Pasco, Wash. ... 6-4/258. ... Full name: Brian Keith Urlacher.
HIGH SCHOOL: Lovington (N.M.).
COLLEGE: New Mexico.

TRANSACTIONS/CAREER NOTES: Selected by Chicago Bears in first round (ninth pick overall) of 2000 NFL draft. ... Signed by Bears (June 16, 2000).
HONORS: Named strong safety on THE SPORTING NEWS college All-America second team (1999). ... Named NFL Rookie of the Year by THE SPORTING NEWS (2000). ... Played in Pro Bowl (2000-2003 seasons). ... Named linebacker on THE SPORTING NEWS NFL All-Pro team (2001 and 2002).

			TOTALS			INTERCEPTIONS			
Year Team	G	GS	Tk.	Ast.	Sks.	No.	Yds.	Avg.	TD
2000—Chicago NFL	16	14	97	26	8.0	2	19	9.5	0
2001—Chicago NFL	16	16	90	27	6.0	3	60	20.0	0
2002—Chicago NFL	16	16	*116	36	4.5	1	0	0.0	0
2003—Chicago NFL	16	16	86	29	2.5	0	0	0.0	0
Pro totals (4 years)	64	62	389	118	21.0	6	79	13.2	0

VAN BUREN, COURTNEY — T — CHARGERS

PERSONAL: Born February 22, 1980, in St. Louis, Mo. ... 6-5/350.
HIGH SCHOOL: Ladue Horton Watkins (St. Louis).
COLLEGE: Arkansas-Pine Bluff.
TRANSACTIONS/CAREER NOTES: Selected by San Diego Chargers in third round (80th pick overall) of 2003 NFL draft. ... Signed by Chargers (July 17, 2003). ... On injured reserve with knee injury (December 17, 2003-remainder of season).
PLAYING EXPERIENCE: San Diego NFL, 2003. ... Games/Games started: 2003 (8/7). Total: 8/7.

VANDEN BOSCH, KYLE — DE — CARDINALS

PERSONAL: Born November 17, 1978, in Larchwood, Iowa. ... 6-4/263.
HIGH SCHOOL: West Lyon (Larchwood, Iowa).
COLLEGE: Nebraska.
TRANSACTIONS/CAREER NOTES: Selected by Arizona Cardinals in second round (34th pick overall) of 2001 NFL draft. ... Signed by Cardinals (July 12, 2001). ... On injured reserve with knee injury (October 25, 2001-remainder of season). ... On injured reserve with knee injury (August 26, 2003-entire season).

			TOTALS		
Year Team	G	GS	Tk.	Ast.	Sks.
2001—Arizona NFL	3	3	12	1	0.5
2002—Arizona NFL	16	16	37	13	3.5
2003—Arizona NFL			Did not play.		
Pro totals (2 years)	19	19	49	14	4.0

VANDERJAGT, MIKE — K — COLTS

PERSONAL: Born March 24, 1970, in Oakville, ON. ... 6-5/211. ... Name pronounced: vander-JAT.
HIGH SCHOOL: White Oaks (Ont.).
JUNIOR COLLEGE: Allan Hancock College (Calif.).
COLLEGE: West Virginia.
TRANSACTIONS/CAREER NOTES: Signed by Saskatchewan Roughriders of CFL prior to 1993 season. ... Signed by Toronto Argonauts of CFL (February 15, 1994). ... Released by Argonauts (June 13, 1994). ... Signed by Hamilton Tiger-Cats of CFL (June 24, 1994). ... Released by Tiger-Cats (July 11, 1994). ... Re-signed by Argonauts (March 16, 1995). ... Released by Argonauts (June 25, 1995). ... Re-signed by Argonauts of CFL (May 10, 1996). ... Signed as non-drafted free agent by Indianapolis Colts (March 4, 1998).
CHAMPIONSHIP GAME EXPERIENCE: Member of CFL Championship team (1996 and 1997). ... Played in AFC championship game (2003 season).
HONORS: Named Most Outstanding Canadian Player in Grey Cup (1996). ... Named to CFL All-Star team (1997). ... Named kicker on THE SPORTING NEWS NFL All-Pro team (2003). ... Played in Pro Bowl (2003 season).
RECORDS: Holds NFL career record for highest field-goal percentage—87.9. ... Shares NFL single-season record for highest field-goal percentage—100.0 (2003). ... Holds NFL career record for most consecutive field goals made—41 (December 22, 2002 through December 28, 2003 (current)).

		FIELD GOALS							TOTALS		
Year Team	G	1-29	30-39	40-49	50+	Tot.	Pct.	Lg.	XPM	XPA	Pts.
1993—Saskatchewan CFL	2	...-...	...-...	...-...	...-...	0-0	...	0	0	0	0
1994—							Did not play.				
1995—							Did not play.				
1996—Toronto CFL	18	...-...	...-...	...-...	...-...	40-56	71.4	51	59	59	179
1997—Toronto CFL	18	...-...	...-...	...-...	...-...	33-43	76.7	51	77	77	176
1998—Indianapolis NFL	14	9-9	4-4	8-9	6-9	27-31	87.1	53	23	23	104
1999—Indianapolis NFL	16	12-12	11-13	10-11	1-2	34-38	§89.5	53	43	43	*145
2000—Indianapolis NFL	16	7-7	13-13	5-6	0-1	25-27	§92.6	48	46	46	121
2001—Indianapolis NFL	16	7-8	6-6	12-16	3-4	28-34	82.4	52	41	▲42	§125
2002—Indianapolis NFL	16	8-9	6-7	6-12	3-3	23-31	74.2	54	34	34	103
2003—Indianapolis NFL	16	17-17	7-7	12-12	1-1	§37-37	*100.0	50	46	46	157
CFL totals (3 years)	38	...-...	...-...	...-...	...-...	73-99	73.7	51	136	136	355
NFL totals (6 years)	94	60-62	47-50	53-66	14-20	174-198	87.9	54	233	234	755
Pro totals (9 years)	132	...-...	...-...	...-...	...-...	247-297	83.2	54	369	370	1110

V

VAN PELT, ALEX — QB

PERSONAL: Born May 1, 1970, in Pittsburgh, Pa. ... 6-1/220. ... Full name: Gregory Alexander Van Pelt.
HIGH SCHOOL: Grafton (W.Va.), then Winston Churchill (San Antonio).
COLLEGE: Pittsburgh.
TRANSACTIONS/CAREER NOTES: Selected by Pittsburgh Steelers in eighth round (216th pick overall) of 1993 NFL draft. ... Signed by Steelers for 1993 season. ... Released by Steelers (August 30, 1993). ... Signed by Kansas City Chiefs to practice squad (November 3, 1993). ... Activated (November 8, 1993); did not play. ... Released by Chiefs (November 17, 1993). ... Re-signed by Chiefs (May 18, 1994). ... Released by Chiefs (August 23, 1994). ... Signed by Buffalo Bills to practice squad (December 14, 1994). ... Activated (December 17, 1994); did not play. ... Granted unconditional free agency (February 11, 2000). ... Re-signed by Bills (July 31, 2000). ... Granted unconditional free agency (March 2, 2001). ... Re-signed by Bills (March 19, 2001). ... Released by Bills (March 16, 2004).
SINGLE GAME HIGHS (regular season): Attempts—44 (December 16, 2001, vs. New England); completions—28 (November 18, 2001, vs. Seattle); yards—316 (November 18, 2001, vs. Seattle); and touchdown passes—3 (November 25, 2001, vs. Miami).
STATISTICAL PLATEAUS: 300-yard passing games: 2001 (2). Total: 2.
MISCELLANEOUS: Regular season record as starting NFL quarterback: 3-8 (.273).

			PASSING										RUSHING				TOTALS		
Year Team	G	GS	Att.	Cmp.	Pct.	Yds.	TD	Int.	Avg.	Skd.	Rat.		Att.	Yds.	Avg.	TD	TD	2pt.	Pts.
1993—Kansas City NFL								Did not play.											
1994—Buffalo NFL								Did not play.											
1995—Buffalo NFL	1	0	18	10	55.6	106	2	0	5.89	0	110.0		0	0	0.0	0	0	0	0
1996—Buffalo NFL	1	0	5	2	40.0	9	0	0	1.80	0	47.9		3	-5	-1.7	0	0	0	0
1997—Buffalo NFL	6	3	124	60	48.4	684	2	10	5.52	4	37.2		11	33	3.0	1	1	0	6
1998—Buffalo NFL	1	0	0	0	0.0	0	0	0	0.00	0	0.0		1	-1	-1.0	0	0	0	0
1999—Buffalo NFL	2	0	1	1	100.0	9	0	0	9.00	0	104.2		1	-1	-1.0	0	0	0	0
2000—Buffalo NFL	2	0	8	4	50.0	67	0	0	8.38	0	78.6		0	0	0.0	0	0	0	0
2001—Buffalo NFL	12	8	307	178	58.0	2056	12	11	6.70	14	76.4		12	33	2.8	0	0	0	0
2002—Buffalo NFL	2	0	2	2	100.0	5	0	0	2.50	0	79.2		0	0	0.0	0	0	0	0
2003—Buffalo NFL	6	0	12	5	41.7	49	0	3	4.08	1	14.2		4	-6	-1.5	0	0	0	0
Pro totals (9 years)	33	11	477	262	54.9	2985	16	24	6.26	19	64.1		32	53	1.7	1	1	0	6

VAUGHN, DARRICK — CB/KR — TEXANS

PERSONAL: Born October 2, 1978, in Houston, Texas. ... 5-11/193.
HIGH SCHOOL: Aldine Nimitz (Houston).
COLLEGE: Southwest Texas State.
TRANSACTIONS/CAREER NOTES: Selected by Atlanta Falcons in seventh round (211th pick overall) of 2000 NFL draft. ... Signed by Falcons (May 17, 2000). ... Released by Falcons (September 1, 2002). ... Signed by Houston Texans (January 14, 2003). ... Granted free agency (March 3, 2004). ... Re-signed by Texans (April 20, 2004).

			TOTALS			INTERCEPTIONS				KICKOFF RETURNS				TOTALS			
Year Team	G	GS	Tk.	Ast.	Sks.	No.	Yds.	Avg.	TD	No.	Yds.	Avg.	TD	TD	2pt.	Pts.	Fum.
2000—Atlanta NFL	16	0	10	1	0.0	0	0	0.0	0	39	1082	*27.7	*3	3	0	18	1
2001—Atlanta NFL	16	0	20	4	0.0	1	0	0.0	0	*61	‡1491	24.4	1	1	0	6	3
2002—								Did not play.									
2003—Houston NFL	16	0	6	1	0.0	0	0	0.0	0	3	47	15.7	0	0	0	0	0
Pro totals (3 years)	48	0	36	6	0.0	1	0	0.0	0	103	2620	25.4	4	4	0	24	4

VEAL, DEMETRIN — DE — FALCONS

PERSONAL: Born August 11, 1981, in Paramount, Calif. ... 6-2/288. ... Full name: Demetrin Leeotis Veal.
HIGH SCHOOL: Paramount (Calif.).
JUNIOR COLLEGE: Cerritos Junior College (Calif.).
COLLEGE: Tennessee.
TRANSACTIONS/CAREER NOTES: Selected by Atlanta Falcons in seventh round (238th pick overall) of 2003 NFL draft. ... Signed by Falcons (June 18, 2003).

			TOTALS		
Year Team	G	GS	Tk.	Ast.	Sks.
2003—Atlanta NFL	3	0	1	2	0.0

VERBA, ROSS — T — BROWNS

PERSONAL: Born October 31, 1973, in Des Moines, Iowa. ... 6-4/308. ... Full name: Ross Robert Verba.
HIGH SCHOOL: Dowling (West Des Moines, Iowa).
COLLEGE: Iowa.
TRANSACTIONS/CAREER NOTES: Selected by Green Bay Packers in first round (30th pick overall) of 1997 NFL draft. ... Signed by Packers (July 31, 1997). ... Granted unconditional free agency (March 2, 2001). ... Signed by Cleveland Browns (March 23, 2001). ... On physically unable to perform list with back injury (July 23-August 13, 2001). ... On injured reserve with biceps injury (August 31, 2003-entire season).
PLAYING EXPERIENCE: Green Bay NFL, 1997-2000; Cleveland NFL, 2001-03. ... Games/Games started: 1997 (16/11), 1998 (16/16), 1999 (11/10), 2000 (16/16), 2001 (15/15), 2002 (16/16), Total: 90/84.
CHAMPIONSHIP GAME EXPERIENCE: Played in NFC championship game (1997 season). ... Played in Super Bowl 32 (1997 season).

VICK, MICHAEL — QB — FALCONS

PERSONAL: Born June 26, 1980, in Newport News, Va. ... 6-0/215. ... Full name: Michael Dwayne Vick.
HIGH SCHOOL: Warwick (Newport News, Va.).
COLLEGE: Virginia Tech.

TRANSACTIONS/CAREER NOTES: Selected after sophomore season by Atlanta Falcons in first round (first pick overall) of 2001 draft. ... Signed by Falcons (May 9, 2001).
HONORS: Named College Football Freshman of the Year by THE SPORTING NEWS (1999). ... Named quarterback on THE SPORTING NEWS college All-America first team (1999). ... Named to play in Pro Bowl (2002 season); replaced by Brad Johnson due to injury.
SINGLE GAME HIGHS (regular season): Attempts—46 (November 10, 2002, vs. Pittsburgh); completions—24 (November 10, 2002, vs. Pittsburgh); yards—337 (December 22, 2002, vs. Detroit); and touchdown passes—2 (December 28, 2003, vs. Jacksonville).
STATISTICAL PLATEAUS: 100-yard rushing games: 2002 (1), 2003 (1). Total: 2. 300-yard passing games: 2002 (1). Total: 1.
MISCELLANEOUS: Regular-season record as starting NFL quarterback: 12-8-1 (.595). ... Postseason record as starting NFL quarterback: 1-1 (.500).

			PASSING									RUSHING				TOTALS		
Year Team	G	GS	Att.	Cmp.	Pct.	Yds.	TD	Int.	Avg.	Skd.	Rat.	Att.	Yds.	Avg.	TD	TD	2pt.	Pts.
2001—Atlanta NFL	8	2	113	50	44.2	785	2	3	6.95	21	62.7	31	289	9.3	1	1	0	6
2002—Atlanta NFL	15	15	421	231	54.9	2936	16	8	6.97	33	81.6	113	777	*6.9	8	8	0	48
2003—Atlanta NFL	5	4	100	50	50.0	585	4	3	5.85	9	69.0	40	255	6.4	1	1	0	6
Pro totals (3 years)	28	21	634	331	52.2	4306	22	14	6.79	63	76.3	184	1321	7.2	10	10	0	60

VILLARRIAL, CHRIS G BILLS

PERSONAL: Born June 9, 1973, in Hummelstown, Pa. ... 6-3/318. ... Name pronounced: vuh-LAR-ree-uhl.
HIGH SCHOOL: Hershey (Pa.).
COLLEGE: Indiana University (Pa.).
TRANSACTIONS/CAREER NOTES: Selected by Chicago Bears in fifth round (152nd pick overall) of 1996 NFL draft. ... Signed by Bears (July 11, 1996). ... Granted free agency (February 12, 1999). ... Re-signed by Bears (April 16, 1999). ... Granted unconditional free agency (March 3, 2004). ... Signed by Buffalo Bills (March 3, 2004).
PLAYING EXPERIENCE: Chicago NFL, 1996-2003. ... Games/Games started: 1996 (14/8), 1997 (11/11), 1998 (16/16), 1999 (15/15), 2000 (16/15), 2001 (16/16), 2002 (15/15), 2003 (13/13). Total: 116/109.

VINATIERI, ADAM K PATRIOTS

PERSONAL: Born December 28, 1972, in Yankton, S.D. ... 6-0/202. ... Full name: Adam Matthew Vinatieri. ... Name pronounced: VIN-a-TERRY.
HIGH SCHOOL: Rapid City (S.D.) Central.
COLLEGE: South Dakota State.
TRANSACTIONS/CAREER NOTES: Signed by Amsterdam Admirals of World League for 1996 season. ... Signed as non-drafted free agent by New England Patriots (June 28, 1996). ... Granted free agency (February 12, 1999). ... Re-signed by Patriots (March 12, 1999). ... Granted free agency (March 1, 2002). ... Re-signed by Patriots (March 15, 2002).
CHAMPIONSHIP GAME EXPERIENCE: Played in AFC championship game (1996, 2001 and 2003 seasons). ... Played in Super Bowl 31 (1996 season). ... Member of Super Bowl championship team (2001 and 2003 seasons).
POST SEASON RECORDS: Shares NFL postseason single-game record for most field goals made—5 (January 18, 2004, vs. Indianapolis).
HONORS: Played in Pro Bowl (2002 season).

		FIELD GOALS							TOTALS		
Year Team	G	1-29	30-39	40-49	50+	Tot.	Pct.	Lg.	XPM	XPA	Pts.
1996—New England NFL	16	10-11	8-8	8-14	1-2	27-35	77.1	50	39	42	120
1997—New England NFL	16	11-11	7-9	6-8	1-1	25-29	86.2	52	40	40	115
1998—New England NFL	16	11-11	9-14	9-12	2-2	31-39	79.5	55	32	32	125
1999—New England NFL	16	15-15	5-7	5-9	1-2	26-33	78.8	51	29	30	107
2000—New England NFL	16	11-13	8-9	7-8	1-3	27-33	81.8	53	25	25	106
2001—New England NFL	16	9-9	7-8	7-12	1-1	24-30	80.0	54	41	▲42	113
2002—New England NFL	16	6-6	12-12	8-10	1-2	§27-30	*90.0	*57	36	36	117
2003—New England NFL	16	16-17	4-8	5-8	0-1	25-34	73.5	48	37	38	112
Pro totals (8 years)	128	89-93	60-75	55-81	8-14	212-263	80.6	57	279	285	915

VINCENT, KEYDRICK G STEELERS

PERSONAL: Born April 13, 1978, in Bartow, Fla. ... 6-5/330. ... Full name: Keydrick Trepell Vincent.
HIGH SCHOOL: Lake Gibson (Fla.).
COLLEGE: Mississippi.
TRANSACTIONS/CAREER NOTES: Signed as non-drafted free agent by Pittsburgh Steelers (April 23, 2001). ... Re-signed by Steelers (February 19, 2003). ... Granted free agency (March 3, 2004). ... Re-signed by Steelers (April 22, 2004).
PLAYING EXPERIENCE: Pittsburgh NFL, 2001-2003. ... Games/Games started: 2001 (5/1), 2002 (7/1), 2003 (10/9). Total: 22/11.
CHAMPIONSHIP GAME EXPERIENCE: Played in AFC championship game (2001 season).

VINCENT, TROY CB BILLS

PERSONAL: Born June 8, 1971, in Trenton, N.J. ... 6-1/200. ... Full name: Troy D. Vincent.
HIGH SCHOOL: Pennsbury (Fairless Hills, Pa.).
COLLEGE: Wisconsin.
TRANSACTIONS/CAREER NOTES: Selected by Miami Dolphins in first round (seventh pick overall) of 1992 NFL draft. ... Signed by Dolphins (August 8, 1992). ... Designated by Dolphins as transition player (February 25, 1993). ... On injured reserve with knee injury (December 15, 1993-remainder of season). ... Tendered offer sheet by Philadelphia Eagles (February 24, 1996). ... Dolphins declined to match offer (March 3, 1996). ... Granted unconditional free agency (March 3, 2004). ... Signed by Buffalo Bills (March 15, 2004).
CHAMPIONSHIP GAME EXPERIENCE: Played in AFC championship game (1992 season). ... Played in NFC championship game (2001-03 seasons).
HONORS: Named defensive back on THE SPORTING NEWS college All-America first team (1991). ... Played in Pro Bowl (1999, 2000, 2002 and 2003 seasons). ... Named to play in Pro Bowl (2001 season); replaced by Champ Bailey due to injury.

Year Team	G	GS	TOTALS Tk.	Ast.	Sks.	INTERCEPTIONS No.	Yds.	Avg.	TD
1992—Miami NFL	15	14	56	21	0.0	2	47	23.5	0
1993—Miami NFL	13	13	58	10	0.0	2	29	14.5	0
1994—Miami NFL	13	12	41	11	0.0	5	113	22.6	1
1995—Miami NFL	16	16	52	10	0.0	5	95	19.0	▲1
1996—Philadelphia NFL	16	16	45	7	0.0	3	144	*48.0	1
1997—Philadelphia NFL	16	16	50	15	0.0	3	14	4.7	0
1998—Philadelphia NFL	13	13	42	8	1.0	2	29	14.5	0
1999—Philadelphia NFL	14	14	62	20	1.0	†7	91	13.0	0
2000—Philadelphia NFL	16	16	64	13	1.0	5	34	6.8	0
2001—Philadelphia NFL	15	15	58	11	1.5	3	0	0.0	0
2002—Philadelphia NFL	15	15	55	12	0.0	2	1	0.5	0
2003—Philadelphia NFL	13	13	49	8	0.0	3	28	9.3	0
Pro totals (12 years)	175	173	632	146	4.5	42	625	14.9	3

VOLEK, BILLY QB TITANS

PERSONAL: Born April 28, 1976, in Hemet, Calif. ... 6-2/214. ... Full name: John William Volek.
HIGH SCHOOL: Clovis West (Fresno, Calif.).
COLLEGE: Fresno State.
TRANSACTIONS/CAREER NOTES: Signed as non-drafted free agent by Tennessee Titans (April 18, 2000). ... Active for one game (2000); did not play. ... Granted free agency (February 28, 2003). ... Re-signed by Titans (April 9, 2003). ... On injured reserve with spleen injury (December 18, 2003-remainder of season). ... Granted unconditional free agency (March 3, 2004). ... Re-signed by Titans (March 24, 2004).
CHAMPIONSHIP GAME EXPERIENCE: Member of Titans for AFC championship game (2002 season); inactive.
SINGLE GAME HIGHS (regular season): Attempts—41 (December 14, 2003, vs. Buffalo); completions—26 (December 14, 2003, vs. Buffalo); yards—295 (December 14, 2003, vs. Buffalo); and touchdown passes—2 (December 14, 2003, vs. Buffalo).
MISCELLANEOUS: Regular-season record as starting NFL quarterback: 1-0 (1.000).

Year Team	G	GS	PASSING Att.	Cmp.	Pct.	Yds.	TD	Int.	Avg.	Skd.	Rat.	RUSHING Att.	Yds.	Avg.	TD	TOTALS TD	2pt.	Pts.
2000—Tennessee NFL	1	0	0	0	0.0	0	0	0	0.00	0	0.0	0	0	0.0	0	0	0	0
2001—Tennessee NFL	1	0	3	0	0.0	0	0	0	0.00	0	39.6	0	0	0.0	0	0	0	0
2003—Tennessee NFL	7	1	69	44	63.8	545	4	1	7.90	6	101.4	11	4	0.4	1	1	0	6
Pro totals (3 years)	9	1	72	44	61.1	545	4	1	7.57	6	97.3	11	4	0.4	1	1	0	6

VOLLERS, KURT T COWBOYS

PERSONAL: Born April 4, 1979, in San Gabriel, Calif. ... 6-7/317.
HIGH SCHOOL: Servite (Whittier, Calif.).
COLLEGE: Notre Dame.
TRANSACTIONS/CAREER NOTES: Signed as non-drafted free agent by Indianapolis Colts (April 20, 2002). ... Released by Colts (September 1, 2002). ... Re-signed by Colts to practice squad (September 3, 2002). ... Claimed on waivers by Dallas Cowboys (October 23, 2002).
PLAYING EXPERIENCE: Dallas NFL, 2002-2003. ... Games/Games started: 2002 (1/0), 2003 (13/8). Total: 14/8.

VON OELHOFFEN, KIMO DT STEELERS

PERSONAL: Born January 30, 1971, in Kaunakakai, Hawaii. ... 6-4/300. ... Full name: Kimo K. von Oelhoffen. ... Name pronounced: KEE-moe von OHL-hoffen.
HIGH SCHOOL: Molokai (Hoolehua, Hawaii).
JUNIOR COLLEGE: Walla Walla (Wash.) Community College.
COLLEGE: Boise State.
TRANSACTIONS/CAREER NOTES: Selected by Cincinnati Bengals in sixth round (162nd pick overall) of 1994 NFL draft. ... Signed by Bengals (May 9, 1994). ... Granted unconditional free agency (February 11, 2000). ... Signed by Pittsburgh Steelers (February 14, 2000).
CHAMPIONSHIP GAME EXPERIENCE: Played in AFC championship game (2001 season).

Year Team	G	GS	TOTALS Tk.	Ast.	Sks.
1994—Cincinnati NFL	7	0	2	0	0.0
1995—Cincinnati NFL	16	1	7	1	0.0
1996—Cincinnati NFL	11	1	11	4	1.0
1997—Cincinnati NFL	13	13	32	10	0.0
1998—Cincinnati NFL	16	16	36	9	0.0
1999—Cincinnati NFL	16	5	24	2	4.0
2000—Pittsburgh NFL	16	16	29	15	1.0
2001—Pittsburgh NFL	15	15	20	8	4.0
2002—Pittsburgh NFL	16	16	12	10	3.0
2003—Pittsburgh NFL	16	16	27	8	8.0
Pro totals (10 years)	142	99	200	67	21.0

VRABEL, MIKE LB PATRIOTS

PERSONAL: Born August 14, 1975, in Akron, Ohio. ... 6-4/261. ... Full name: Michael George Vrabel.
HIGH SCHOOL: Walsh Jesuit (Cuyahoga Falls, Ohio).
COLLEGE: Ohio State.

TRANSACTIONS/CAREER NOTES: Selected by Pittsburgh Steelers in third round (91st pick overall) of 1997 NFL draft. ... Signed by Steelers (July 15, 1997). ... Granted free agency (February 11, 2000). ... Re-signed by Steelers (April 20, 2000). ... Granted unconditional free agency (March 2, 2001). ... Signed by New England Patriots (March 16, 2001).
CHAMPIONSHIP GAME EXPERIENCE: Played in AFC championship game (1997, 2001 and 2003 seasons). ... Member of Super Bowl championship team (2001 and 2003 seasons).

			TOTALS			INTERCEPTIONS			
Year Team	G	GS	Tk.	Ast.	Sks.	No.	Yds.	Avg.	TD
1997—Pittsburgh NFL	15	0	14	3	1.5	0	0	0.0	0
1998—Pittsburgh NFL	11	0	6	3	2.5	0	0	0.0	0
1999—Pittsburgh NFL	10	0	4	1	2.0	0	0	0.0	0
2000—Pittsburgh NFL	15	0	3	2	1.0	0	0	0.0	0
2001—New England NFL	16	12	37	23	3.0	2	27	13.5	0
2002—New England NFL	16	13	51	24	4.5	1	0	0.0	0
2003—New England NFL	13	9	38	14	9.5	2	18	9.0	0
Pro totals (7 years)	96	34	153	70	24.0	5	45	9.0	0

WADE, BOBBY — WR — BEARS

PERSONAL: Born February 25, 1981, in Orange County, Calif. ... 5-10/193. ... Full name: Robert Louis Wade, Jr.
HIGH SCHOOL: Desert Vista (Phoenix).
COLLEGE: Arizona.
TRANSACTIONS/CAREER NOTES: Selected by Chicago Bears in fifth round (139th pick overall) of 2003 NFL draft. ... Signed by Bears (July 25, 2003).
SINGLE GAME HIGHS (regular season): Receptions—3 (November 1, 2003, vs. San Diego); yards—42 (November 2, 2003, vs. San Diego); and touchdown receptions—0.

			RUSHING				RECEIVING				PUNT RETURNS				KICKOFF RETURNS				TOTALS		
Year Team	G	GS	Att.	Yds.	Avg.	TD	No.	Yds.	Avg.	TD	No.	Yds.	Avg.	TD	No.	Yds.	Avg.	TD	TD	2pt.	Pts.
2003—Chi. NFL	12	1	5	14	2.8	0	12	137	11.4	0	2	9	4.5	0	0	0	0.0	0	0	0	0

WADE, JOHN — C — BUCCANEERS

PERSONAL: Born January 25, 1975, in Harrisonburg, Va. ... 6-5/299. ... Full name: John Robert Wade.
HIGH SCHOOL: Harrisonburg (Va.).
COLLEGE: Marshall.
TRANSACTIONS/CAREER NOTES: Selected by Jacksonville Jaguars in fifth round (148th pick overall) of 1998 NFL draft. ... Signed by Jaguars (June 1, 1998). ... On injured reserve with broken foot (September 27, 2000-remainder of season). ... On physically unable to perform list with foot injury (July 27-September 2, 2001). ... Granted unconditional free agency (March 1, 2002). ... Re-signed by Jaguars (March 13, 2002). ... Granted unconditional free agency (February 28, 2003). ... Signed by Tampa Bay Buccaneers (March 10, 2003).
PLAYING EXPERIENCE: Jacksonville NFL, 1998-2002; Tampa Bay NFL, 2003. ... Games/Games started: 1998 (5/0), 1999 (16/16), 2000 (2/2), 2001 (15/0), 2002 (16/16), 2003 (16/16). Total: 70/50.
CHAMPIONSHIP GAME EXPERIENCE: Played in AFC championship game (1999 season).

WADE, TODD — T — TEXANS

PERSONAL: Born October 30, 1976, in Greenwood, Miss. ... 6-8/315. ... Full name: Todd McLaurin Wade.
HIGH SCHOOL: Jackson (Miss.) Prep.
COLLEGE: Mississippi.
TRANSACTIONS/CAREER NOTES: Selected by Miami Dolphins in second round (53rd pick overall) of 2000 NFL draft. ... Signed by Dolphins (July 24, 2000). ... Granted unconditional free agency (March 3, 2004). ... Signed by Houston Texans (March 4, 2004).
PLAYING EXPERIENCE: Miami NFL, 2000-2003. ... Games/Games started: 2000 (16/16), 2001 (15/15), 2002 (16/16), 2003 (16/16). Total: 63/63.

WAHLE, MIKE — G — PACKERS

PERSONAL: Born March 29, 1977, in Portland, Ore. ... 6-6/307. ... Full name: Michael James Wahle. ... Name pronounced: WALL.
HIGH SCHOOL: Rim of the World (Lake Arrowhead, Calif.).
COLLEGE: Navy.
TRANSACTIONS/CAREER NOTES: Selected by Green Bay Packers in second round of 1998 supplemental draft (July 9, 1998). ... Signed by Packers (August 6, 1998). ... Granted free agency (March 2, 2001). ... Re-signed by Packers (May 31, 2001). ... Granted unconditional free agency (March 1, 2002). ... Re-signed by Packers (March 8, 2002).
PLAYING EXPERIENCE: Green Bay NFL, 1998-2003. ... Games/Games started: 1998 (1/0), 1999 (16/13), 2000 (16/6), 2001 (16/16), 2002 (16/16), 2003 (16/16). Total: 81/67.

WAKEFIELD, FRED — DE — CARDINALS

PERSONAL: Born September 17, 1978, in Tuscola, Ill. ... 6-7/288.
HIGH SCHOOL: Tuscola (Ill.).
COLLEGE: Illinois.
TRANSACTIONS/CAREER NOTES: Signed as non-drafted free agent by Arizona Cardinals (April 23, 2001).

			TOTALS			INTERCEPTIONS			
Year Team	G	GS	Tk.	Ast.	Sks.	No.	Yds.	Avg.	TD
2001—Arizona NFL	16	12	28	6	2.5	1	20	20.0	1

Year Team	G	GS	TOTALS Tk.	Ast.	Sks.	INTERCEPTIONS No.	Yds.	Avg.	TD
2002—Arizona NFL	16	15	21	10	3.0	0	0	0.0	0
2003—Arizona NFL	10	5	21	3	1.0	0	0	0.0	0
Pro totals (3 years)	42	32	70	19	6.5	1	20	20.0	1

WALKER, AARON TE 49ERS

PERSONAL: Born March 14, 1980, in Titusville, Fla. ... 6-6/252. ... Full name: Aaron Scott Walker.
HIGH SCHOOL: Astronaut (Mims, Fla.).
COLLEGE: Florida.
TRANSACTIONS/CAREER NOTES: Selected by San Francisco 49ers in fifth round (161st pick overall) of 2003 NFL draft.
SINGLE GAME HIGHS (regular season): Receptions—1 (December 27, 2003, vs. Seattle); yards—20 (December 27, 2003, vs. Seattle); and touchdown receptions—1 (October 5, 2003, vs. Detroit).

Year Team	G	GS	RECEIVING No.	Yds.	Avg.	TD	TOTALS TD	2pt.	Pts.	Fum.
2003—San Francisco NFL	16	2	8	116	14.5	1	1	0	6	0

WALKER, BRACY S LIONS

PERSONAL: Born October 28, 1970, in Portsmouth, Va. ... 6-0/210. ... Full name: Bracy Wordell Walker.
HIGH SCHOOL: Pine Forest (Fayetteville, N.C.).
COLLEGE: North Carolina.
TRANSACTIONS/CAREER NOTES: Selected by Kansas City Chiefs in fourth round (127th pick overall) of 1994 NFL draft. ... Signed by Chiefs (July 20, 1994). ... Claimed on waivers by Cincinnati Bengals (October 12, 1994). ... Granted free agency (February 14, 1997). ... Re-signed by Bengals (April 18, 1997). ... Claimed on waivers by Miami Dolphins (August 20, 1997). ... On injured reserve with leg injury (December 2, 1997-remainder of season). ... Granted unconditional free agency (February 13, 1998). ... Re-signed by Dolphins (April 27, 1998). ... Released by Dolphins (August 19, 1998). ... Re-signed by Chiefs (November 3, 1998). ... Granted unconditional free agency (February 11, 2000). ... Re-signed by Chiefs (February 24, 2000). ... Granted unconditional free agency (March 2, 2002). ... Signed by Detroit Lions (April 15, 2002). ... On injured reserve with liver injury (December 18, 2002-remainder of season). ... Re-signed by Lions (March 11, 2003). ... Granted unconditional free agency (March 3, 2004). ... Re-signed by Lions (March 5, 2004).
HONORS: Named defensive back on THE SPORTING NEWS college All-America second team (1993).

Year Team	G	GS	TOTALS Tk.	Ast.	Sks.	INTERCEPTIONS No.	Yds.	Avg.	TD
1994—Kansas City NFL	2	0	0	0	0.0	0	0	0.0	0
—Cincinnati NFL	7	0	1	1	0.0	0	0	0.0	0
1995—Cincinnati NFL	14	14	60	25	0.0	4	56	14.0	0
1996—Cincinnati NFL	16	16	57	13	0.0	2	35	17.5	0
1997—Miami NFL	12	0	2	0	0.0	0	0	0.0	0
1998—Kansas City NFL	8	0	1	0	0.0	0	0	0.0	0
1999—Kansas City NFL	16	1	8	0	0.0	0	0	0.0	0
2000—Kansas City NFL	15	0	0	0	0.0	0	0	0.0	0
2001—Kansas City NFL	15	0	1	0	0.0	0	0	0.0	0
2002—Detroit NFL	14	1	24	12	1.0	0	0	0.0	0
2003—Detroit NFL	16	1	27	2	0.0	0	0	0.0	0
Pro totals (10 years)	135	33	181	53	1.0	6	91	15.2	0

WALKER, BRIAN S LIONS

PERSONAL: Born May 31, 1972, in Colorado Springs, Colo. ... 6-1/205.
HIGH SCHOOL: Widefield (Colorado Springs, Colo.).
JUNIOR COLLEGE: Snow College (Utah).
COLLEGE: Washington State.
TRANSACTIONS/CAREER NOTES: Signed as non-drafted free agent by Washington Redskins (May 1, 1996). ... Released by Redskins (October 9, 1997). ... Signed by Miami Dolphins (December 9, 1997). ... Active for two games with Dolphins (1997); did not play. ... Claimed on waivers by Seattle Seahawks (September 6, 1999). ... Released by Seahawks (September 14, 1999). ... Re-signed by Seahawks (September 30, 1999). ... On injured reserve with hamstring injury (January 8, 2000-remainder of playoffs). ... Granted unconditional free agency (February 11, 2000). ... Signed by Dolphins (February 16, 2000). ... Granted unconditional free agency (March 1, 2002). ... Signed by Detroit Lions (March 5, 2002).

W

Year Team	G	GS	TOTALS Tk.	Ast.	Sks.	INTERCEPTIONS No.	Yds.	Avg.	TD
1996—Washington NFL	16	4	29	9	1.0	0	0	0.0	0
1997—Washington NFL	5	0	0	0	0.0	0	0	0.0	0
1998—Miami NFL	16	0	12	3	0.0	4	12	3.0	0
1999—Seattle NFL	5	0	8	1	0.0	1	21	21.0	0
2000—Miami NFL	16	16	60	28	2.0	▲7	80	11.4	0
2001—Miami NFL	13	13	52	25	0.0	1	0	0.0	0
2002—Detroit NFL	10	9	32	12	1.0	0	0	0.0	0
2003—Detroit NFL	16	16	60	20	0.0	2	0	0.0	0
Pro totals (8 years)	97	58	253	98	4.0	15	113	7.5	0

WALKER, DARWIN DT EAGLES

PERSONAL: Born June 15, 1977, in Walterboro, S.C. ... 6-3/294. ... Full name: Darwin Jamar Walker.
HIGH SCHOOL: Walterboro (S.C.).
COLLEGE: Tennessee.

TRANSACTIONS/CAREER NOTES: Selected by Arizona Cardinals in third round (71st pick overall) of 2000 NFL draft. ... Signed by Cardinals (June 19, 2000). ... Claimed on waivers by Philadelphia Eagles (September 12, 2000).
CHAMPIONSHIP GAME EXPERIENCE: Played in NFC championship game (2001-2003 seasons).
HONORS: Named defensive tackle on THE SPORTING NEWS college All-America second team (1999).

			TOTALS		
Year Team	**G**	**GS**	**Tk.**	**Ast.**	**Sks.**
2000—Arizona NFL	1	0	0	0	0.0
2001—Philadelphia NFL	10	0	4	1	1.0
2002—Philadelphia NFL	16	16	29	6	7.5
2003—Philadelphia NFL	16	16	35	7	6.0
Pro totals (4 years)	43	32	68	14	14.5

WALKER, DENARD CB RAIDERS

PERSONAL: Born August 9, 1973, in Dallas, Texas. ... 6-1/198. ... Full name: Denard Antuan Walker.
HIGH SCHOOL: South Garland (Texas), then Harlingen (Texas) Military Institute.
COLLEGE: Louisiana State.
TRANSACTIONS/CAREER NOTES: Selected by Houston Oilers in third round (75th pick overall) of 1997 NFL draft. ... Oilers franchise moved to Tennessee for 1997 season. ... Signed by Oilers (July 18, 1997). ... Oilers franchise renamed Tennessee Titans for 1999 season (December 26, 1998). ... Granted free agency (February 11, 2000). ... Re-signed by Titans (June 3, 2000). ... On suspended list (September 3-5, 2000). ... Granted unconditional free agency (March 2, 2001). ... Signed by Denver Broncos (March 19, 2001). ... Waived by Broncos (February 25, 2003). ... Signed by Minnesota Vikings (March 12, 2003). ... Waived by Vikings (March 30, 2004). ... Signed by Oakland Raiders (April 15, 2004).
CHAMPIONSHIP GAME EXPERIENCE: Played in AFC championship game (1999 season). ... Played in Super Bowl 34 (1999 season).

			TOTALS			INTERCEPTIONS			
Year Team	**G**	**GS**	**Tk.**	**Ast.**	**Sks.**	**No.**	**Yds.**	**Avg.**	**TD**
1997—Tennessee NFL	15	11	56	12	0.0	2	53	26.5	1
1998—Tennessee NFL	16	16	68	15	0.0	2	6	3.0	0
1999—Tennessee NFL	15	14	39	8	0.0	1	27	27.0	0
2000—Tennessee NFL	15	14	44	1	0.0	2	4	2.0	0
2001—Denver NFL	16	15	51	5	0.0	3	60	20.0	1
2002—Denver NFL	16	16	56	8	0.0	1	8	8.0	0
2003—Minnesota NFL	16	8	48	5	0.0	1	0	0.0	0
Pro totals (7 years)	109	94	362	54	0.0	12	158	13.2	2

WALKER, FRANK CB GIANTS

PERSONAL: Born August 6, 1980, in Tuskegee, Ala. ... 5-10/198. ... Full name: Frank Bernard Walker Jr.
HIGH SCHOOL: Booker T. Washington (Tuskegee, Ala.).
COLLEGE: Tuskegee.
TRANSACTIONS/CAREER NOTES: Selected by New York Giants in sixth round (207th pick overall) of 2003 NFL draft. ... Signed by Giants (June 26, 2003).

			TOTALS			INTERCEPTIONS			
Year Team	**G**	**GS**	**Tk.**	**Ast.**	**Sks.**	**No.**	**Yds.**	**Avg.**	**TD**
2003—New York Giants NFL	10	7	30	4	0.0	2	74	37.0	1

WALKER, GARY DE

PERSONAL: Born February 28, 1973, in Royston, Ga. ... 6-2/305. ... Full name: Gary Lamar Walker.
HIGH SCHOOL: Franklin County (Carnesville, Ga.).
JUNIOR COLLEGE: Hinds Community College (Miss.).
COLLEGE: Auburn.
TRANSACTIONS/CAREER NOTES: Selected by Houston Oilers in fifth round (159th pick overall) of 1995 NFL draft. ... Signed by Oilers (July 10, 1995). ... Oilers franchise moved to Tennessee for 1997 season. ... Granted free agency (February 13, 1998). ... Re-signed by Oilers (July 15, 1998). ... Granted unconditional free agency (February 12, 1999). ... Signed by Jacksonville Jaguars (February 15, 1999). ... Selected by Houston Texans from Jaguars in NFL expansion draft (February 18, 2002). ... Released by Texans (March 21, 2004).
CHAMPIONSHIP GAME EXPERIENCE: Played in AFC championship game (1999 season).
HONORS: Played in Pro Bowl (2001 and 2002 seasons).

			TOTALS		
Year Team	**G**	**GS**	**Tk.**	**Ast.**	**Sks.**
1995—Houston NFL	15	9	22	10	2.5
1996—Houston NFL	16	16	30	15	5.5
1997—Tennessee NFL	15	15	31	13	7.0
1998—Tennessee NFL	16	16	31	16	1.0
1999—Jacksonville NFL	16	16	46	8	10.0
2000—Jacksonville NFL	15	14	40	3	5.0
2001—Jacksonville NFL	16	16	35	8	7.5
2002—Houston NFL	16	16	37	15	6.5
2003—Houston NFL	4	4	7	6	0.0
Pro totals (9 years)	129	122	279	94	45.0

WALKER, JAVON WR PACKERS

PERSONAL: Born October 14, 1978, in Galveston, Texas. ... 6-3/220.
HIGH SCHOOL: St. Thomas More (Lafayette, La.).
JUNIOR COLLEGE: Jones Junior College (Miss.).

COLLEGE: Florida State.
TRANSACTIONS/CAREER NOTES: Selected by Green Bay Packers in first round (20th pick overall) of 2002 NFL draft. ... Signed by Packers (July 23, 2002).
SINGLE GAME HIGHS (regular season): Receptions—5 (September 29, 2003, vs. Chicago); yards—124 (December 22, 2003, vs. Oakland); and touchdown receptions—2 (December 22, 2003, vs. Oakland).
STATISTICAL PLATEAUS: 100-yard receiving games: 2003 (1). Total: 1.

			RUSHING				RECEIVING				KICKOFF RETURNS				TOTALS			
Year Team	**G**	**GS**	**Att.**	**Yds.**	**Avg.**	**TD**	**No.**	**Yds.**	**Avg.**	**TD**	**No.**	**Yds.**	**Avg.**	**TD**	**TD**	**2pt.**	**Pts.**	**Fum.**
2002—Green Bay NFL	15	2	1	11	11.0	0	23	319	13.9	1	35	769	22.0	0	1	0	6	1
2003—Green Bay NFL	16	3	2	1	0.5	0	41	716	17.5	9	0	0	0.0	0	9	0	54	1
Pro totals (2 years)	31	5	3	12	4.0	0	64	1035	16.2	10	35	769	22.0	0	10	0	60	2

WALKER, KENYATTA — T — BUCCANEERS

PERSONAL: Born February 1, 1979, in Meridian, Miss. ... 6-5/302. ... Full name: Idrees Kenyatta Walker.
HIGH SCHOOL: Meridian (Miss.).
COLLEGE: Florida.
TRANSACTIONS/CAREER NOTES: Selected after junior season by Tampa Bay Buccaneers in first round (14th pick overall) of 2001 draft. ... Signed by Buccaneers (July 26, 2001). ... On injured reserved with knee injury (December 26, 2003-remainder of season).
PLAYING EXPERIENCE: Tampa Bay NFL, 2001-2003. ... Games/Games started: 2001 (16/16), 2002 (13/13), 2003 (14/14). Total: 43/43.
CHAMPIONSHIP GAME EXPERIENCE: Played in NFC championship game (2002 season). ... Member of Super Bowl championship team (2002 season).

WALKER, LANGSTON — T — RAIDERS

PERSONAL: Born September 3, 1979, in Oakland, Calif. ... 6-8/345.
HIGH SCHOOL: Bishop O'Dowd (Calif.).
COLLEGE: California.
TRANSACTIONS/CAREER NOTES: Selected by Oakland Raiders in second round (53rd pick overall) of 2002 NFL draft. ... Signed by Raiders (July 19, 2002).
PLAYING EXPERIENCE: Oakland NFL, 2002-2003. ... Games/Games started: 2002 (12/2), 2003 (16/8). Total: 28/10.
CHAMPIONSHIP GAME EXPERIENCE: Played in AFC championship game (2002 season). ... Played in Super Bowl 37 (2002 season).

WALKER, RAMON — S — TEXANS

PERSONAL: Born November 8, 1979, in Akron, Ohio. ... 6-0/197. ... Full name: Ramon D. Walker.
HIGH SCHOOL: John R. Buchtel (Akron, Ohio).
COLLEGE: Pittsburgh.
TRANSACTIONS/CAREER NOTES: Selected after junior season by Houston Texans in fifth round (153rd pick overall) of 2002 NFL draft. ... Signed by Texans (July 17, 2002). ... On injured reserve with knee injury (December 24, 2002-remainder of season). ... On injured reserve with knee injury (December 1, 2003-remainder of season).

			TOTALS			INTERCEPTIONS			
Year Team	**G**	**GS**	**Tk.**	**Ast.**	**Sks.**	**No.**	**Yds.**	**Avg.**	**TD**
2002—Houston NFL	9	1	4	0	0.0	0	0	0.0	0
2003—Houston NFL	11	0	0	0	0.0	0	0	0.0	0
Pro totals (2 years)	20	1	4	0	0.0	0	0	0.0	0

WALKER, ROD — DT — PANTHERS

PERSONAL: Born February 4, 1976, in Milton, Fla. ... 6-3/320. ... Full name: Roderick Dion Walker.
HIGH SCHOOL: Milton (Fla.).
COLLEGE: Troy State.
TRANSACTIONS/CAREER NOTES: Signed as non-drafted free agent by Washington Redskins (April 21, 1999). ... Released by Redskins (August 30, 1999). ... Re-signed by Redskins (September 2, 1999). ... Released by Redskins (September 4, 1999). ... Signed by Tennessee Titans to practice squad (October 26, 1999). ... Released by Titans (August 26, 2000). ... Re-signed by Titans to practice squad (August 30, 2000). ... Activated (December 1, 2000); did not play. ... Traded by Titans to Green Bay Packers for seventh-round pick (DE Carlos Hall) in 2002 NFL draft (September 2, 2001). ... On injured reserve with knee injury (November 4, 2003-remainder of season). ... Greanted unconditional free agency (March 3, 2004). ... Signed by Carolina Panthers (March 15, 2004).

			TOTALS		
Year Team	**G**	**GS**	**Tk.**	**Ast.**	**Sks.**
2001—Green Bay NFL	11	0	5	2	0.0
2002—Green Bay NFL	13	5	10	8	0.0
2003—Green Bay NFL	7	1	9	1	0.0
Pro totals (3 years)	31	6	24	11	0.0

W

WALLACE, AL — DE — PANTHERS

PERSONAL: Born March 25, 1974, in Delray Beach, Fla. ... 6-5/258. ... Full name: Alonzo Dwight Wallace.
HIGH SCHOOL: Spanish River (Boca Raton, Fla.).
COLLEGE: Maryland.
TRANSACTIONS/CAREER NOTES: Signed as non-drafted free agent by Jacksonville Jaguars (April 21, 1997). ... Released by Jaguars (August 19, 1997). ... Re-signed by Jaguars to practice squad (August 25, 1997). ... Signed by Philadelphia Eagles off Jaguars practice squad

(December 2, 1997). ... On injured reserve with ankle injury (September 5, 1999-entire season). ... Released by Eagles (August 27, 2000). ... Signed by Chicago Bears (December 20, 2000). ... Released by Bears (August 28, 2001). ... Signed by Miami Dolphins (January 15, 2002). ... Traded by Dolphins with fourth-round pick (DB Colin Branch) in 2003 draft to Carolina Panthers for DE Jay Williams (July 19, 2002).
CHAMPIONSHIP GAME EXPERIENCE: Played in NFC championship game (2003 season). ... Played in Super Bowl 38 (2003 season).

			TOTALS			INTERCEPTIONS			
Year Team	**G**	**GS**	**Tk.**	**Ast.**	**Sks.**	**No.**	**Yds.**	**Avg.**	**TD**
1997—Philadelphia NFL	1	0	0	0	0.0	0	0	0.0	0
1998—Philadelphia NFL	15	0	14	4	6.0	0	0	0.0	0
1999—Philadelphia NFL			Did not play.						
2002—Carolina NFL	16	4	22	4	3.0	0	0	0.0	0
2003—Carolina NFL	16	2	28	8	5.0	2	58	29.0	0
Pro totals (4 years)	48	6	64	16	14.0	2	58	29.0	0

WALLACE, TACO — WR — SEAHAWKS

PERSONAL: Born April 14, 1981, in Harbor City, Calif. ... 6-1/190.
HIGH SCHOOL: Taft (Woodlands Hills, Calif.).
JUNIOR COLLEGE: Mount San Antonio College (Calif.).
COLLEGE: Kansas State.
TRANSACTIONS/CAREER NOTES: Selected by Seattle Seahawks in seventh round (224th pick overall) of 2003 NFL draft. ... Signed by Seahawks (July 9, 2003).

			RECEIVING				TOTALS			
Year Team	**G**	**GS**	**No.**	**Yds.**	**Avg.**	**TD**	**TD**	**2pt.**	**Pts.**	**Fum.**
2003—Seattle NFL	1	0	0	0	0.0	0	0	0	0	0

WALLS, LENNY — CB — BRONCOS

PERSONAL: Born September 26, 1979, in San Francisco, Calif. ... 6-4/192.
HIGH SCHOOL: Galileo (San Francisco).
JUNIOR COLLEGE: City College of San Francisco.
COLLEGE: Boston College.
TRANSACTIONS/CAREER NOTES: Signed as non-drafted free agent by Denver Broncos (April 22, 2002).

			TOTALS			INTERCEPTIONS			
Year Team	**G**	**GS**	**Tk.**	**Ast.**	**Sks.**	**No.**	**Yds.**	**Avg.**	**TD**
2002—Denver NFL	13	0	0	0	0.0	0	0	0.0	0
2003—Denver NFL	16	16	53	5	0.0	1	0	0.0	0
Pro totals (2 years)	29	16	53	5	0.0	1	0	0.0	0

WALLS, RAYMOND — CB — RAVENS

PERSONAL: Born July 24, 1979, in Kentwood, La. ... 5-10/188. ... Full name: Raymond Omoncial Tyshone Walls.
HIGH SCHOOL: Kentwood (La.).
COLLEGE: Southern Mississippi.
TRANSACTIONS/CAREER NOTES: Selected by Indianapolis Colts in fifth round (152nd pick overall) of 2001 NFL draft. ... Signed by Colts (June 13, 2001). ... Released by Colts (September 1, 2001). ... Re-signed by Colts to practice squad (September 3, 2001). ... Activated (October 8, 2001). ... Released by Colts (August 28, 2002). ... Signed by Cleveland Browns to practice squad (September 25, 2002). ... Activated (October 23, 2002). ... Released by Browns (November 14, 2002). ... Re-signed by Browns to practice squad (November 14, 2002). ... Activated (November 26, 2002). ... Waived by Browns (August 4, 2003). ... Signed by Baltimore Ravens (August 20, 2003). ... Granted free agency (March 3, 2004). ... Re-signed by Ravens (April 14, 2004).

			TOTALS			INTERCEPTIONS			
Year Team	**G**	**GS**	**Tk.**	**Ast.**	**Sks.**	**No.**	**Yds.**	**Avg.**	**TD**
2001—Indianapolis NFL	4	0	3	0	0.0	1	0	0.0	0
2002—Cleveland NFL	4	0	0	0	0.0	0	0	0.0	0
2003—Baltimore NFL	10	0	4	0	0.0	0	0	0.0	0
Pro totals (3 years)	18	0	7	0	0.0	1	0	0.0	0

WALLS, WESLEY — TE

PERSONAL: Born March 26, 1966, in Batesville, Miss. ... 6-5/240. ... Full name: Charles Wesley Walls.
HIGH SCHOOL: Pontotoc (Miss.).
COLLEGE: Mississippi.
TRANSACTIONS/CAREER NOTES: Selected by San Francisco 49ers in second round (56th pick overall) of 1989 NFL draft. ... Signed by 49ers (July 26, 1989). ... Granted free agency (February 1, 1992). ... Re-signed by 49ers (July 18, 1992). ... On injured reserve with shoulder injury (September 1, 1992-January 16, 1993). ... On injured reserve with shoulder injury (October 27, 1993-remainder of season). ... Granted unconditional free agency (February 17, 1994). ... Signed by New Orleans Saints (April 27, 1994). ... Granted unconditional free agency (February 16, 1996). ... Signed by Carolina Panthers (February 21, 1996). ... On injured reserve with knee injury (October 31, 2000-remainder of season). ... Released by Panthers (February 26, 2003). ... Signed by Green Bay Packers (August 6, 2003). ... Granted unconditional free agency (March 3, 2004).
CHAMPIONSHIP GAME EXPERIENCE: Played in NFC championship game (1989, 1990 and 1996 seasons). ... Member of Super Bowl championship team (1989 season).
HONORS: Named tight end on THE SPORTING NEWS college All-America second team (1988). ... Played in Pro Bowl (1996-1999 seasons). ... Named to play in Pro Bowl (2001 season); replaced by Byron Chamberlain due to injury.
SINGLE GAME HIGHS (regular season): Receptions—10 (October 7, 2001, vs. San Francisco); yards—147 (September 7, 1997, vs. Atlanta); and touchdown receptions—2 (January 2, 2000, vs. New Orleans).

STATISTICAL PLATEAUS: 100-yard receiving games: 1997 (2), 2000 (1). Total: 3.
MISCELLANEOUS: Holds Carolina Panthers all-time records for most touchdown receptions (44) and most touchdowns (44).

			RECEIVING				TOTALS			
Year Team	**G**	**GS**	**No.**	**Yds.**	**Avg.**	**TD**	**TD**	**2pt.**	**Pts.**	**Fum.**
1989—San Francisco NFL	16	0	4	16	4.0	1	1	0	6	1
1990—San Francisco NFL	16	0	5	27	5.4	0	0	0	0	0
1991—San Francisco NFL	15	0	2	24	12.0	0	0	0	0	0
1992—San Francisco NFL					Did not play.					
1993—San Francisco NFL	6	0	0	0	0.0	0	0	0	0	0
1994—New Orleans NFL	15	7	38	406	10.7	4	4	1	26	0
1995—New Orleans NFL	16	11	57	694	12.2	4	4	1	26	1
1996—Carolina NFL	16	15	61	713	11.7	10	10	0	60	0
1997—Carolina NFL	15	15	58	746	12.9	6	6	0	36	0
1998—Carolina NFL	14	14	49	506	10.3	5	5	0	30	0
1999—Carolina NFL	16	16	63	822	13.0	12	12	0	72	1
2000—Carolina NFL	8	8	31	422	13.6	2	2	0	12	0
2001—Carolina NFL	14	14	43	452	10.5	5	5	0	30	0
2002—Carolina NFL	15	14	19	241	12.7	4	4	0	24	0
2003—Green Bay NFL	14	1	20	222	11.1	1	1	0	6	0
Pro totals (14 years)	196	115	450	5291	11.8	54	54	2	328	3

WALTER, KEN P

PERSONAL: Born August 15, 1972, in Cleveland, Ohio. ... 6-1/207. ... Full name: Kenneth Matthew Walter Jr.
HIGH SCHOOL: Euclid (Ohio).
COLLEGE: Kent State.
TRANSACTIONS/CAREER NOTES: Signed as non-drafted free agent by Carolina Panthers (April 14, 1997). ... Released by Panthers (April 24, 2001). ... Signed by New England Patriots (October 16, 2001). ... Waived by Patriots (December 2, 2003). ... Re-signed by Patriots (December 12, 2004). ... Granted unconditional free agency (March 3, 2004).
CHAMPIONSHIP GAME EXPERIENCE: Played in AFC championship game (2001 and 2003 seasons). ... Member of Super Bowl championship team (2001 and 2003 seasons).

		PUNTING					
Year Team	**G**	**No.**	**Yds.**	**Avg.**	**Net avg.**	**In. 20**	**Blk.**
1997—Carolina NFL	16	85	3604	42.4	36.4	29	0
1998—Carolina NFL	16	77	3131	40.7	38.1	20	0
1999—Carolina NFL	16	65	2562	39.4	36.7	18	0
2000—Carolina NFL	16	64	2459	38.4	33.8	19	†2
2001—New England NFL	11	49	1964	40.1	§38.1	24	0
2002—New England NFL	16	70	2723	38.9	33.3	19	1
2003—New England NFL	15	76	2865	37.7	33.6	25	1
Pro totals (7 years)	106	486	19308	39.7	35.6	154	4

WALTER, KEVIN WR BENGALS

PERSONAL: Born August 4, 1981, in Lake Forest, Ill. ... 6-3/221. ... Full name: Kevin Patrick Walter.
HIGH SCHOOL: Libertyville (Ill.).
COLLEGE: Eastern Michigan.
TRANSACTIONS/CAREER NOTES: Selected by New York Giants in seventh round (255th pick overall) of 2003 NFL draft. ... Signed by Giants (June 16, 2003). ... Claimed on waivers by Cincinnati Bengals (August 26, 2003). ... Waived by Bengals (August 31, 2003). ... Re-signed by Bengals to practice squad (September 1, 2003). ... Activated (October 16, 2003).
SINGLE GAME HIGHS (regular season): Receptions—1 (December 21, 2003, vs. St. Louis); yards—9 (November 23, 2003, vs. San Diego); and touchdown receptions—0.

			RECEIVING				TOTALS			
Year Team	**G**	**GS**	**No.**	**Yds.**	**Avg.**	**TD**	**TD**	**2pt.**	**Pts.**	**Fum.**
2003—Cincinnati NFL	11	0	3	18	6.0	0	0	0	0	0

WALTER, TYSON T COWBOYS

PERSONAL: Born March 17, 1978, in Bainbridge, Ohio. ... 6-4/310.
HIGH SCHOOL: Kenston (Ohio).
COLLEGE: Ohio State.
TRANSACTIONS/CAREER NOTES: Selected by Dallas Cowboys in sixth round (179th pick overall) of 2002 NFL draft. ... Signed by Cowboys (July 24, 2002).
PLAYING EXPERIENCE: Dallas NFL, 2002-2003. ... Games/Games started: 2002 (10/8), 2003 (16/0). Total: 26/8.

WALTERS, MATT DE JETS

PERSONAL: Born August 22, 1979, in Melbourne, Fla. ... 6-5/272. ... Full name: Matthew Jeremy Walters.
HIGH SCHOOL: Eau Galle (Melbourne, Fla.).
COLLEGE: Miami (Fla.).
TRANSACTIONS/CAREER NOTES: Selected by New York Jets in fifth round (150th pick overall) of 2003 NFL draft. ... Signed by Jets (July 20, 2003).

			TOTALS		
Year Team	**G**	**GS**	**Tk.**	**Ast.**	**Sks.**
2003—New York Jets NFL	11	0	5	0	0.0

WALTERS, TROY — WR — COLTS

PERSONAL: Born December 15, 1976, in Bloomington, Ind. ... 5-7/172. ... Full name: Troy M. Walters.
HIGH SCHOOL: A&M Consolidated (College Station, Texas).
COLLEGE: Stanford.
TRANSACTIONS/CAREER NOTES: Selected by Minnesota Vikings in fifth round (165th pick overall) of 2000 NFL draft. ... Signed by Vikings (July 12, 2000). ... Claimed on waivers by Indianapolis Colts (February 24, 2002). ... Re-signed by Colts (January 5, 2003).
CHAMPIONSHIP GAME EXPERIENCE: Played in NFC championship game (2000 season). ... Played in AFC championship game (2003 season).
HONORS: Named wide receiver on THE SPORTING NEWS college All-America first team (1999). ... Fred Biletnikoff Award winner (1999).
SINGLE GAME HIGHS (regular season): Receptions—7 (November 17, 2002, vs. Dallas); yards—91 (November 17, 2002, vs. Dallas); and touchdown receptions—1 (November 30, 2003, vs. New England).

			RUSHING				RECEIVING				PUNT RETURNS				KICKOFF RETURNS				TOTALS		
Year Team	**G**	**GS**	**Att.**	**Yds.**	**Avg.**	**TD**	**No.**	**Yds.**	**Avg.**	**TD**	**No.**	**Yds.**	**Avg.**	**TD**	**No.**	**Yds.**	**Avg.**	**TD**	**TD**	**2pt.**	**Pts.**
2000—Min. NFL	12	0	1	3	3.0	0	1	5	5.0	0	15	217	14.5	0	30	692	23.1	0	0	0	0
2001—Min. NFL	6	0	0	0	0.0	0	0	0	0.0	0	11	69	6.3	0	18	425	23.6	0	0	0	0
2002—Ind. NFL	16	1	2	33	16.5	0	18	207	11.5	0	35	270	7.7	0	53	1150	21.7	0	0	0	0
2003—Ind. NFL	15	4	1	6	6.0	0	36	456	12.7	3	11	105	9.5	0	6	126	21.0	0	3	0	18
Pro totals (4 years)	49	5	4	42	10.5	0	55	668	12.1	3	72	661	9.2	0	107	2393	22.4	0	3	0	18

WALTON, SHANE — S — RAMS

PERSONAL: Born October 9, 1979, in San Diego, Calif. ... 5-11/195. ... Full name: Shane Scott Walton.
HIGH SCHOOL: The Bishop's School (San Diego).
COLLEGE: Notre Dame.
TRANSACTIONS/CAREER NOTES: Selected by St. Louis Rams in fifth round (170th pick overall) of 2003 NFL draft. ... Signed by Rams (July 23, 2003). ... On injured reserve with back injury (October 9, 2003-remainder of season).

			TOTALS			INTERCEPTIONS			
Year Team	**G**	**GS**	**Tk.**	**Ast.**	**Sks.**	**No.**	**Yds.**	**Avg.**	**TD**
2003—St. Louis NFL	4	0	0	0	0.0	0	0	0.0	0

WAND, SETH — T — TEXANS

PERSONAL: Born August 6, 1979, in Springfield, Mo. ... 6-7/327.
HIGH SCHOOL: Springfield Catholic (Springfield, Mo.).
COLLEGE: Northwest Missouri State.
TRANSACTIONS/CAREER NOTES: Selected by Houston Texans in third round (75th pick overall) of 2003 NFL draft. ... Signed by Texans (July 18, 2003).
PLAYING EXPERIENCE: Houston NFL, 2003. ... Games/Games started: 2003 (16/2). Total: 16/2.

WANSLEY, TIM — CB

PERSONAL: Born November 7, 1979, in Buford, Ga. ... 5-8/186.
HIGH SCHOOL: Buford (Ga.).
COLLEGE: Georgia.
TRANSACTIONS/CAREER NOTES: Selected by Tampa Bay Buccaneers in seventh round (233rd pick overall) of 2002 NFL draft. ... Signed by Buccaneers (July 24, 2002). ... On injured reserve with hamstring injury (December 2, 2003-remainder of season). ... Released by Buccaneers (April 28, 2004).
CHAMPIONSHIP GAME EXPERIENCE: Member of Buccaneers for NFC championship game (2002 season); inactive. ... Member of Super Bowl championship team (2002 season); inactive.

			TOTALS			INTERCEPTIONS				PUNT RETURNS				TOTALS			
Year Team	**G**	**GS**	**Tk.**	**Ast.**	**Sks.**	**No.**	**Yds.**	**Avg.**	**TD**	**No.**	**Yds.**	**Avg.**	**TD**	**TD**	**2pt.**	**Pts.**	**Fum.**
2002—Tampa Bay NFL	1	0	0	0	0.0	0	0	0.0	0	0	0	0.0	0	0	0	0	0
2003—Tampa Bay NFL	12	6	49	4	0.0	2	38	19.0	1	8	74	9.3	0	1	0	6	1
Pro totals (2 years)	13	6	49	4	0.0	2	38	19.0	1	8	74	9.3	0	1	0	6	1

WARD, DEDRIC — WR

PERSONAL: Born September 29, 1974, in Cedar Rapids, Iowa. ... 5-9/187. ... Full name: Dedric Lamar Ward. ... Name pronounced: DEE-drick.
HIGH SCHOOL: Washington (Cedar Rapids, Iowa).
COLLEGE: Northern Iowa.
TRANSACTIONS/CAREER NOTES: Selected by New York Jets in third round (88th pick overall) of 1997 NFL draft. ... Signed by Jets (July 17, 1997). ... Granted free agency (February 11, 2000). ... Re-signed by Jets (May 3, 2000). ... Granted unconditional free agency (March 2, 2001). ... Signed by Miami Dolphins (April 18, 2001). ... Released by Dolphins (February 26, 2003). ... Signed by New England Patriots (May 22, 2003). ... Released by Patriots (August 31, 2003). ... Signed by Baltimore Ravens (October 6, 2003). ... Waived by Ravens (November 18, 2003). ... Signed by Patriots (November 20, 2003). ... Granted unconditional free agency (March 3, 2004).
CHAMPIONSHIP GAME EXPERIENCE: Played in AFC championship game (1998 and 2003 seasons). ... Member of Super Bowl championship team (2003 season).
SINGLE GAME HIGHS (regular season): Receptions—8 (December 24, 2000, vs. Baltimore); yards—147 (December 24, 2000, vs. Baltimore); and touchdown receptions—1 (November 30, 2003, vs. Indianapolis).
STATISTICAL PLATEAUS: 100-yard receiving games: 1997 (1), 2000 (3). Total: 4.

Year	Team	G	GS	RECEIVING No.	Yds.	Avg.	TD	PUNT RETURNS No.	Yds.	Avg.	TD	KICKOFF RETURNS No.	Yds.	Avg.	TD	TOTALS TD	2pt.	Pts.	Fum.
1997—New York Jets NFL		11	0	18	212	11.8	1	8	55	6.9	0	2	10	5.0	0	1	0	6	1
1998—New York Jets NFL		16	2	25	477	19.1	4	8	72	9.0	0	3	60	20.0	0	4	0	24	0
1999—New York Jets NFL		16	10	22	325	14.8	3	38	288	7.6	0	0	0	0.0	0	3	0	18	2
2000—New York Jets NFL		16	16	54	801	14.8	3	27	214	7.9	0	0	0	0.0	0	3	0	18	1
2001—Miami NFL		13	1	21	209	10.0	0	9	88	9.8	0	0	0	0.0	0	0	0	0	1
2002—Miami NFL		16	1	19	172	9.1	0	16	169	10.6	0	0	0	0.0	0	0	0	0	1
2003—Baltimore NFL		3	0	0	0	0.0	0	3	26	8.7	0	1	20	20.0	0	0	0	0	0
—New England NFL		4	0	7	106	15.1	1	0	0	0.0	0	0	0	0.0	0	1	0	6	0
Pro totals (7 years)		95	30	166	2302	13.9	12	109	912	8.4	0	6	90	15.0	0	12	0	72	6

WARD, HINES — WR — STEELERS

PERSONAL: Born March 8, 1976, in Forest Park, Ga. ... 6-0/205. ... Full name: Hines Ward Jr.
HIGH SCHOOL: Forest Park (Ga.).
COLLEGE: Georgia.
TRANSACTIONS/CAREER NOTES: Selected by Pittsburgh Steelers in third round (92nd pick overall) of 1998 NFL draft. ... Signed by Steelers (July 20, 1998). ... Granted free agency (March 2, 2001). ... Re-signed by Steelers (July 1, 2001).
CHAMPIONSHIP GAME EXPERIENCE: Played in AFC championship game (2001 season).
HONORS: Played in Pro Bowl (2001-2003 seasons).
SINGLE GAME HIGHS (regular season): Receptions—13 (November 30, 2003, vs. Cincinnati); yards—168 (November 17, 2002, vs. Tennessee); and touchdown receptions—2 (November 9, 2003, vs. Arizona).
STATISTICAL PLATEAUS: 100-yard receiving games: 2001 (2), 2002 (4), 2003 (2). Total: 8.

Year	Team	G	GS	RUSHING Att.	Yds.	Avg.	TD	RECEIVING No.	Yds.	Avg.	TD	TOTALS TD	2pt.	Pts.	Fum.
1998—Pittsburgh NFL		16	0	1	13	13.0	0	15	246	16.4	0	0	0	0	0
1999—Pittsburgh NFL		16	14	2	-2	-1.0	0	61	638	10.5	7	7	†1	44	1
2000—Pittsburgh NFL		16	15	4	53	13.3	0	48	672	14.0	4	4	0	24	2
2001—Pittsburgh NFL		16	16	10	83	8.3	0	94	1003	10.7	4	4	0	24	1
2002—Pittsburgh NFL		16	16	12	142	11.8	0	112	1329	11.9	§12	12	*3	78	1
2003—Pittsburgh NFL		16	16	11	61	5.5	0	95	1163	12.2	10	10	0	60	0
Pro totals (6 years)		96	77	40	350	8.8	0	425	5051	11.9	37	37	4	230	5

WARD, LASHAUN — WR — CHIEFS

PERSONAL: Born September 22, 1980, in Pasadena, Calif. ... 5-11/198. ... Full name: LaShaun Brandon Ward.
HIGH SCHOOL: John Muir (Pasadena, Calif.).
COLLEGE: California.
TRANSACTIONS/CAREER NOTES: Signed as non-drafted free agent by Kansas City Chiefs (April 29, 2003). ... Waived by Chiefs (August 31, 2003). ... Re-signed by Chiefs to practice squad (September 1, 2003). ... Activated (December 10, 2003). ... Assigned by Chiefs to Berlin Thunder in 2004 NFL Europe enhancement allocation program (February 9, 2004).

Year	Team	G	GS	RECEIVING No.	Yds.	Avg.	TD	KICKOFF RETURNS No.	Yds.	Avg.	TD	TOTALS TD	2pt.	Pts.	Fum.
2003—Kansas City NFL		1	0	0	0	0.0	0	1	11	11.0	0	0	0	0	1

WARE, KEVIN — TE — REDSKINS

PERSONAL: Born September 30, 1980... 6-3/259.
HIGH SCHOOL: Klein Oak (Houston, Texas).
COLLEGE: Washington.
TRANSACTIONS/CAREER NOTES: Signed by Washington Redskins as non-drafted free agent (May 2, 2003). ... Waived by Redskins (August 31, 2003). ... Re-signed by Redskins to practice squad (September 2, 2003). ... Activated (September 12, 2003). ... Waived by Redskins (September 15, 2003). ... Re-signed by Redskins to practice squad (September 17, 2003). ... Activated (September 19, 2003). ... Waived by Redskins (September 22, 2003). ... Re-signed by Redskins to practice squad (September 24, 2003). ... Activated (October 31, 2003).
SINGLE GAME HIGHS (regular season): Receptions—2 (December 27, 2003, vs. Philadelphia); yards—11 (December 27, 2003, vs. Philadelphia); and touchdown receptions—0.

Year	Team	G	GS	RECEIVING No.	Yds.	Avg.	TD	TOTALS TD	2pt.	Pts.	Fum.
2003—Washington NFL		11	2	3	17	5.7	0	0	0	0	0

W

WARFIELD, ERIC — CB — CHIEFS

PERSONAL: Born March 3, 1976, in Vicksburg, Miss. ... 6-0/200. ... Full name: Eric Andrew Warfield.
HIGH SCHOOL: Arkansas (Texarkana, Ark.).
COLLEGE: Nebraska.
TRANSACTIONS/CAREER NOTES: Selected by Kansas City Chiefs in seventh round (216th pick overall) of 1998 NFL draft. ... Signed by Chiefs (May 27, 1998). ... Granted unconditional free agency (March 1, 2002). ... Re-signed by Chiefs (March 4, 2002).

Year	Team	G	GS	TOTALS Tk.	Ast.	Sks.	INTERCEPTIONS No.	Yds.	Avg.	TD
1998—Kansas City NFL		12	0	0	0	0.0	0	0	0.0	0
1999—Kansas City NFL		16	1	25	4	0.0	3	0	0.0	0
2000—Kansas City NFL		13	4	19	2	0.0	0	0	0.0	0
2001—Kansas City NFL		16	16	64	6	0.0	4	61	15.3	1

Year Team	G	GS	TOTALS Tk.	Ast.	Sks.	INTERCEPTIONS No.	Yds.	Avg.	TD
2002—Kansas City NFL	16	16	56	8	0.0	4	30	7.5	0
2003—Kansas City NFL	15	15	62	4	1.0	4	39	9.8	0
Pro totals (6 years)	88	52	226	24	1.0	15	130	8.7	1

WARNER, JOSH — C/G — BEARS

PERSONAL: Born May 15, 1979, in Cato, N.Y. ... 6-5/320.
HIGH SCHOOL: Meridian (Cato, N.Y.).
COLLEGE: SUNY-Brockport.
TRANSACTIONS/CAREER NOTES: Signed as non-drafted free agent by New York Giants (April 27, 2001). ... Released by Giants (August 31, 2001). ... Signed by Chicago Bears (January 9, 2002). ... Waived by Bears (August 30, 2002). ... Re-signed by Bears to practice squad (November 20, 2002). ... Activated (December 17, 2002).
PLAYING EXPERIENCE: Chicago NFL, 2003. ... Games/Games started: 2003 (10/0). Total: 10/0.

WARNER, KURT — QB — RAMS

PERSONAL: Born June 22, 1971, in Burlington, Iowa. ... 6-2/220. ... Full name: Kurtis Eugene Warner.
HIGH SCHOOL: Regis (Cedar Rapids, Iowa).
COLLEGE: Northern Iowa.
TRANSACTIONS/CAREER NOTES: Signed as non-drafted free agent by Green Bay Packers (April 28, 1994). ... Released by Packers prior to 1994 season. ... Played for Iowa Barnstormers of Arena Football League (1995-97). ... Signed by St. Louis Rams (December 26, 1997). ... Assigned by Rams to Amsterdam Admirals in 1998 NFL Europe enhancement allocation program (February 18, 1998). ... On injured reserve with hand injury (December 12, 2002-remaider of season).
CHAMPIONSHIP GAME EXPERIENCE: Played in NFC championship game (1999 and 2001 seasons). ... Member of Super Bowl championship team (1999 season). ... Played in Super Bowl 36 (2001 season).
HONORS: Named NFL Player of the Year by THE SPORTING NEWS (1999). ... Named quarterback on THE SPORTING NEWS NFL All-Pro team (1999 and 2001). ... Named Most Valuable Player of Super Bowl 34 (1999 season). ... Played in Pro Bowl (1999 and 2001 seasons). ... Named to play in Pro Bowl (2000 season); replaced by Donovan McNabb due to injury.
RECORDS: Holds NFL career record for highest passer rating—97.2. ... Shares NFL record for most consecutive games with 300 or more yards passing—6 (September 4-October 15, 2000).
POST SEASON RECORDS: Holds Super Bowl single-game record for most yards passing—414 (January 30, 2000, vs. Tennessee).
SINGLE GAME HIGHS (regular season): Attempts—54 (September 7, 2003, vs. New York Giants); completions—35 (September 10, 2000, vs. Seattle); yards—441 (September 4, 2000, vs. Denver); and touchdown passes—5 (October 10, 1999, vs. San Francisco).
STATISTICAL PLATEAUS: 300-yard passing games: 1999 (9), 2000 (8), 2001 (9), 2002 (3), 2003 (1). Total: 30.
MISCELLANEOUS: Regular-season record as starting NFL quarterback: 35-15 (.700). ... Postseason record as starting NFL quarterback: 5-2 (.714).

Year Team	G	GS	PASSING Att.	Cmp.	Pct.	Yds.	TD	Int.	Avg.	Skd.	Rat.	RUSHING Att.	Yds.	Avg.	TD	TOTALS TD	2pt.	Pts.
1998—St. Louis NFL	1	0	11	4	36.4	39	0	0	3.55	0	47.2	0	0	0.0	0	0	0	0
1999—St. Louis NFL	16	16	499	325	*65.1	4353	*41	13	*8.72	29	*109.2	23	92	4.0	1	1	0	6
2000—St. Louis NFL	11	11	347	235	*67.7	3429	21	18	*9.88	20	98.3	18	17	0.9	0	0	0	0
2001—St. Louis NFL	16	16	546	*375	*68.7	*4830	*36	∞22	*8.85	38	*101.4	28	60	2.1	0	0	0	0
2002—St. Louis NFL	7	6	220	144	65.5	1431	3	11	6.50	21	67.4	8	33	4.1	0	0	0	0
2003—St. Louis NFL	2	1	65	38	58.5	365	1	1	5.62	6	72.9	1	0	0.0	0	0	0	0
Pro totals (6 years)	53	50	1688	1121	66.4	14447	102	65	8.56	114	97.2	78	202	2.6	1	1	0	6

WARNER, RON — DE — REDSKINS

PERSONAL: Born September 26, 1975, in Independence, Kan. ... 6-2/270.
HIGH SCHOOL: Independence (Kan.).
JUNIOR COLLEGE: Independence (Kan.) Community College.
COLLEGE: Kansas.
TRANSACTIONS/CAREER NOTES: Selected by New Orleans Saints in seventh round (239th pick overall) of 1998 NFL draft. ... Signed by Saints (July 23, 1998). ... On non-football injury list with knee injury (August 25-November 4, 1998). ... Released by Saints (September 5, 1999). ... Signed by Washington Redskins to practice (September 14, 1999). ... Released by Redskins (November 24, 1999). ... Signed by Chicago Bears to practice squad (December 22, 1999). ... Granted free agency following 1999 season. ... Signed by Buccaneers (March 4, 2001). ... Released by Buccaneers (September 8, 2001). ... Re-signed by Buccaneers to practice squad (September 10, 2001). ... On suspended list (September 1-30, 2002). ... Released by Buccaneers (October 7, 2002). ... Re-signed by Buccaneers (November 28, 2002). ... Released by Buccaneers (October 7, 2003). ... Signed by Redskins (October 21, 2003). ... Waived by Redskins (October 30, 2003). ... Re-signed by Redskins (December 23, 2003).
CHAMPIONSHIP GAME EXPERIENCE: Played in NFC championship game (2002 season). ... Member of Super Bowl championship team (2002 season).
HONORS: Named outside linebacker on THE SPORTING NEWS college All-America second team (1997).

Year Team	G	GS	TOTALS Tk.	Ast.	Sks.
1998—New Orleans NFL	1	0	2	2	0.0
2002—Tampa Bay NFL	4	0	0	0	0.0
2003—Tampa Bay NFL	4	0	0	1	0.0
—Washington NFL	1	0	0	0	0.0
Pro totals (3 years)	10	0	2	3	0.0

W

WARREN, GERARD — DT — BROWNS

PERSONAL: Born July 25, 1978, in Lake City, Fla. ... 6-4/325. ... Full name: Gerard T. Warren.
HIGH SCHOOL: Union City (Raiford, Fla.).
COLLEGE: Florida.
TRANSACTIONS/CAREER NOTES: Selected by Cleveland Browns in first round (third pick overall) of 2001 draft. ... Signed by Browns (August 1, 2001).

			TOTALS		
Year Team	G	GS	Tk.	Ast.	Sks.
2001—Cleveland NFL	15	15	48	13	5.0
2002—Cleveland NFL	16	16	30	10	2.0
2003—Cleveland NFL	16	15	24	8	5.5
Pro totals (3 years)	47	46	102	31	12.5

WARREN, TY — DT/DE — PATRIOTS

PERSONAL: Born February 6, 1981, in Bryan, Texas. ... 6-5/300. ... Full name: Ty'ron Markeith Warren.
HIGH SCHOOL: Bryan (Texas).
COLLEGE: Texas A&M.
TRANSACTIONS/CAREER NOTES: Selected by New England Patriots in first round (13th pick overall) of 2003 NFL draft. ... Signed by Patriots (July 21, 2003).
CHAMPIONSHIP GAME EXPERIENCE: Played in AFC championship game (2003 season). ... Member of Super Bowl championship team (2003 season).

			TOTALS		
Year Team	G	GS	Tk.	Ast.	Sks.
2003—New England NFL	16	4	19	14	1.0

WARRICK, PETER — WR/PR — BENGALS

PERSONAL: Born June 19, 1977, in Bradenton, Fla. ... 5-11/192.
HIGH SCHOOL: Southeast (Bradenton, Fla.).
COLLEGE: Florida State.
TRANSACTIONS/CAREER NOTES: Selected by Cincinnati Bengals in first round (fourth pick overall) of 2000 NFL draft. ... Signed by Bengals (June 4, 2000).
HONORS: Named wide receiver on THE SPORTING NEWS college All-America first team (1998 and 1999).
SINGLE GAME HIGHS (regular season): Receptions—11 (December 7, 2003, vs. Baltimore); yards—114 (November 16, 2003, vs. Kansas City); and touchdown receptions—2 (December 8, 2002, vs. Carolina).
STATISTICAL PLATEAUS: 100-yard receiving games: 2001 (1), 2003 (2). Total: 3.

			RUSHING				RECEIVING				PUNT RETURNS				TOTALS			
Year Team	G	GS	Att.	Yds.	Avg.	TD	No.	Yds.	Avg.	TD	No.	Yds.	Avg.	TD	TD	2pt.	Pts.	Fum.
2000—Cincinnati NFL	16	16	16	148	9.3	2	51	592	11.6	4	7	123	17.6	1	7	0	42	2
2001—Cincinnati NFL	16	14	8	14	1.8	0	70	667	9.5	1	18	116	6.4	0	1	0	6	3
2002—Cincinnati NFL	15	10	8	22	2.8	0	53	606	11.4	6	4	14	3.5	0	6	0	36	2
2003—Cincinnati NFL	15	14	18	157	8.7	0	79	819	10.4	7	25	273	10.9	1	8	0	48	2
Pro totals (4 years)	62	54	50	341	6.8	2	253	2684	10.6	18	54	526	9.7	2	22	0	132	9

WASHINGTON, DEWAYNE — CB — JAGUARS

PERSONAL: Born December 27, 1972, in Durham, N.C. ... 5-11/195. ... Full name: Dewayne Neron Washington.
HIGH SCHOOL: Northern (Durham, N.C.).
COLLEGE: North Carolina State.
TRANSACTIONS/CAREER NOTES: Selected by Minnesota Vikings in first round (18th pick overall) of 1994 NFL draft. ... Signed by Vikings (July 14, 1994). ... Granted unconditional free agency (February 13, 1998). ... Signed by Pittsburgh Steelers (February 25, 1998). ... Released by Steelers (February 27, 2003). ... Signed by Jacksonville Jaguars (March 9, 2004).
CHAMPIONSHIP GAME EXPERIENCE: Played in AFC championship game (2001 season).
HONORS: Was a high school All-America selection by The Sporting News (1989).

			TOTALS			INTERCEPTIONS			
Year Team	G	GS	Tk.	Ast.	Sks.	No.	Yds.	Avg.	TD
1994—Minnesota NFL	16	16	68	7	0.0	3	135	45.0	2
1995—Minnesota NFL	15	14	54	8	0.0	1	25	25.0	0
1996—Minnesota NFL	16	16	69	6	0.0	2	27	13.5	1
1997—Minnesota NFL	16	16	74	10	0.0	4	71	17.8	0
1998—Pittsburgh NFL	16	16	79	14	0.0	5	§178	35.6	▲2
1999—Pittsburgh NFL	16	16	50	2	0.0	4	1	0.3	0
2000—Pittsburgh NFL	16	16	69	9	0.0	5	59	11.8	0
2001—Pittsburgh NFL	16	16	66	11	1.0	1	15	15.0	0
2002—Pittsburgh NFL	16	16	45	9	0.0	3	51	17.0	0
2003—Pittsburgh NFL	16	12	50	5	0.0	1	7	7.0	0
Pro totals (10 years)	159	154	624	81	1.0	29	569	19.6	5

WASHINGTON, KEITH — DE — GIANTS

PERSONAL: Born December 18, 1972, in Dallas, Texas. ... 6-4/285. ... Full name: Keith L. Washington.
HIGH SCHOOL: Wilmer-Hutchins (Dallas).
COLLEGE: Nevada-Las Vegas.

TRANSACTIONS/CAREER NOTES: Signed as non-drafted free agent by Minnesota Vikings (April 9, 1995). ... Released by Vikings (August 27, 1995). ... Re-signed by Vikings to practice squad (August 28, 1995). ... Activated (October 9, 1995); did not play. ... On injured reserve with ankle injury (November 15, 1995-remainder of season). ... Released by Vikings (August 25, 1996). ... Signed by Detroit Lions (August 26, 1996). ... Released by Lions (August 26, 1997). ... Signed by Baltimore Ravens (October 15, 1997). ... Granted free agency (February 13, 1998). ... Re-signed by Ravens (April 14, 1998). ... Granted unconditional free agency (February 11, 2000). ... Re-signed by Ravens (March 31, 2000). ... Released by Ravens (March 13, 2001). ... Signed by Denver Broncos (April 6, 2001). ... Released by Broncos (February 25, 2003). ... Signed by New York Giants (March 28, 2003). ... Granted unconditional free agency (March 3, 2004). ... Re-signed by Giants (March 3, 2004).
CHAMPIONSHIP GAME EXPERIENCE: Played in AFC championship game (2000 season). ... Member of Super Bowl championship team (2000 season).

			TOTALS			INTERCEPTIONS			
Year Team	**G**	**GS**	**Tk.**	**Ast.**	**Sks.**	**No.**	**Yds.**	**Avg.**	**TD**
1996—Detroit NFL	12	0	7	0	0.0	0	0	0.0	0
1997—Baltimore NFL	10	1	14	4	2.0	0	0	0.0	0
1998—Baltimore NFL	16	0	13	2	1.0	0	0	0.0	0
1999—Baltimore NFL	16	0	9	2	1.0	0	0	0.0	0
2000—Baltimore NFL	16	0	11	7	0.0	0	0	0.0	0
2001—Denver NFL	16	16	27	9	4.0	0	0	0.0	0
2002—Denver NFL	10	0	9	0	0.0	1	-2	-2.0	0
2003—New York Giants NFL	14	6	16	8	1.0	0	0	0.0	0
Pro totals (8 years)	110	23	106	32	9.0	1	-2	-2.0	0

WASHINGTON, KELLEY WR BENGALS

PERSONAL: Born August 21, 1979, in Stephens City, Va. ... 6-3/218. ... Full name: James Kelley Washington.
HIGH SCHOOL: Sherando (Stephens City, Va.).
COLLEGE: Tennessee.
TRANSACTIONS/CAREER NOTES: Selected after junior season by Cincinnati Bengals in third round (65th pick overall) of 2003 NFL draft. ... Signed by Bengals (August 3, 2003).
SINGLE GAME HIGHS (regular season): Receptions—5 (November 23, 2003, vs. San Diego); yards—61 (November 23, 2003, vs. San Diego); and touchdown receptions—1 (December 21, 2003, vs. St. Louis).
MISCELLANEOUS: Selected by Florida Marlins organization in 10th round of free-agent draft (June 2, 1997).

			RECEIVING				TOTALS			
Year Team	**G**	**GS**	**No.**	**Yds.**	**Avg.**	**TD**	**TD**	**2pt.**	**Pts.**	**Fum.**
2003—Cincinnati NFL	16	3	22	299	13.6	4	4	0	24	0

WASHINGTON, MARCUS LB REDSKINS

PERSONAL: Born October 17, 1977, in Auburn, Ala. ... 6-3/247. ... Full name: Marcus Cornelius Washington.
HIGH SCHOOL: Auburn (Ala.).
COLLEGE: Auburn.
TRANSACTIONS/CAREER NOTES: Selected by Indianapolis Colts in second round (59th pick overall) of 2000 NFL draft. ... Signed by Colts (July 13, 2000). ... Granted unconditional free agency (March 3, 2004). ... Signed by Washington Redskins (March 5, 2004).
CHAMPIONSHIP GAME EXPERIENCE: Played in AFC championship game (2003 season).

			TOTALS			INTERCEPTIONS			
Year Team	**G**	**GS**	**Tk.**	**Ast.**	**Sks.**	**No.**	**Yds.**	**Avg.**	**TD**
2000—Indianapolis NFL	16	0	6	5	2.0	1	1	1.0	0
2001—Indianapolis NFL	16	16	74	20	8.0	0	0	0.0	0
2002—Indianapolis NFL	15	15	47	19	2.0	1	40	40.0	1
2003—Indianapolis NFL	16	16	55	25	6.0	0	0	0.0	0
Pro totals (4 years)	63	47	182	69	18.0	2	41	20.5	1

WASHINGTON, TED DT RAIDERS

PERSONAL: Born April 13, 1968, in Tampa, Fla. ... 6-5/365. ... Full name: Theodore Washington. ... Son of Ted Washington, linebacker with New York Jets (1973) and Houston Oilers (1974-82).
HIGH SCHOOL: Tampa Bay Vocational Tech Senior.
COLLEGE: Louisville.
TRANSACTIONS/CAREER NOTES: Selected by San Francisco 49ers in first round (25th pick overall) of 1991 NFL draft. ... Signed by 49ers (July 10, 1991). ... Traded by 49ers to Denver Broncos for fifth-round pick (traded to Green Bay) in 1994 draft (April 19, 1994). ... Granted unconditional free agency (February 17, 1995). ... Signed by Buffalo Bills (February 25, 1995). ... Designated by Bills as franchise player (February 13, 1998). ... Free agency status changed from franchise to transitional (February 27, 1998). ... Re-signed by Bills (March 2, 1998). ... Released by Bills (February 22, 2001). ... Signed by Chicago Bears (April 10, 2001). ... On injured reserve with leg injury (November 29, 2002-remainder of season). ... Traded by Bears to New England Patriots for a fourth-round pick (traded to Washington) in 2004 NFL draft (August 19, 2003). ... Granted unconditional free agency (March 3, 2004). ... Signed by Oakland Raiders (March 4, 2004).
CHAMPIONSHIP GAME EXPERIENCE: Played in NFC championship game (1992 and 1993 seasons). ... Played in AFC championship game (2003 season). ... Member of Super Bowl championship team (2003 season).
HONORS: Played in Pro Bowl (1997, 1998, 2000 and 2001 seasons). ... Named defensive tackle on THE SPORTING NEWS NFL All-Pro team (2001).

			TOTALS			INTERCEPTIONS			
Year Team	**G**	**GS**	**Tk.**	**Ast.**	**Sks.**	**No.**	**Yds.**	**Avg.**	**TD**
1991—San Francisco NFL	16	0	20	1	1.0	0	0	0.0	0
1992—San Francisco NFL	16	6	27	8	2.0	0	0	0.0	0
1993—San Francisco NFL	12	12	36	5	3.0	0	0	0.0	0
1994—Denver NFL	15	15	44	12	2.5	1	5	5.0	0
1995—Buffalo NFL	16	15	42	11	2.5	0	0	0.0	0

Year Team	G	GS	TOTALS Tk.	Ast.	Sks.	INTERCEPTIONS No.	Yds.	Avg.	TD
1996—Buffalo NFL	16	16	70	22	3.5	0	0	0.0	0
1997—Buffalo NFL	16	16	63	17	4.0	0	0	0.0	0
1998—Buffalo NFL	16	16	35	15	4.5	1	0	0.0	0
1999—Buffalo NFL	16	16	35	10	2.5	0	0	0.0	0
2000—Buffalo NFL	16	16	37	21	2.5	0	0	0.0	0
2001—Chicago NFL	16	15	26	8	1.5	0	0	0.0	0
2002—Chicago NFL	2	2	4	1	0.0	0	0	0.0	0
2003—New England NFL	10	10	32	8	2.0	0	0	0.0	0
Pro totals (13 years)	183	155	471	139	31.5	2	5	2.5	0

WASHINGTON, TODD — C — TEXANS

PERSONAL: Born September 19, 1976, in Nassawadox, Va. ... 6-3/310. ... Full name: Todd Page Washington.
HIGH SCHOOL: Nandua (Onley, Va.).
COLLEGE: Virginia Tech.
TRANSACTIONS/CAREER NOTES: Selected by Tampa Bay Buccaneers in fourth round (104th pick overall) of 1998 NFL draft. ... Signed by Buccaneers (June 11, 1998). ... Granted free agency (March 2, 2001). ... Re-signed by Buccaneers (March 14, 2001). ... Granted unconditional free agency (March 1, 2002). ... Re-signed by Buccaneers (March 18, 2002). ... Signed by Houston Texans (March 24, 2003). ... Granted unconditional free agency (March 3, 2004). ... Re-signed by Texans (March 4, 2004).
PLAYING EXPERIENCE: Tampa Bay NFL, 1998-2002; Houston NFL, 2003. ... Games/Games started: 1998 (4/0), 1999 (6/0), 2000 (9/0), 2001 (15/1), 2002 (16/2), 2003 (16/14). Total: 66/17.
CHAMPIONSHIP GAME EXPERIENCE: Played in NFC championship game (1999 and 2002 seasons). ... Member of Super Bowl championship team (2002).

WATERS, BRIAN — G — CHIEFS

PERSONAL: Born February 18, 1977, in Waxahachie, Texas. ... 6-3/318. ... Full name: Brian Demond Waters.
HIGH SCHOOL: Waxahachie (Texas).
COLLEGE: North Texas.
TRANSACTIONS/CAREER NOTES: Signed as non-drafted free agent by Dallas Cowboys (April 23, 1999). ... Released by Cowboys (September 5, 1999). ... Signed by Kansas City Chiefs (January 11, 2000).
PLAYING EXPERIENCE: Kansas City NFL, 2000-2003. ... Games/Games started: 2000 (6/0), 2001 (16/8), 2002 (16/16), 2003 (16/16). Total: 54/40.

WATSON, KENNY — RB — BENGALS

PERSONAL: Born March 13, 1978, in Harrisburg, Pa. ... 5-11/214.
HIGH SCHOOL: Harrisburg (Pa.).
COLLEGE: Penn State.
TRANSACTIONS/CAREER NOTES: Signed as non-drafted free agent by Washington Redskins (April 23, 2001). ... Released by Redskins (October 16, 2001). ... Re-signed by Redskins to practice squad (October 18, 2001). ... Waived by Redskins (August 31, 2003). ... Signed by Cincinnati Bengals (September 30, 2003).
SINGLE GAME HIGHS (regular season): Attempts—23 (November 3, 2002, vs. Seattle); yards—110 (December 22, 2002, vs. Houston); and rushing touchdowns—1 (December 29, 2002, vs. Dallas).
STATISTICAL PLATEAUS: 100-yard rushing games: 2002 (2). Total: 2.

Year Team	G	GS	RUSHING Att.	Yds.	Avg.	TD	RECEIVING No.	Yds.	Avg.	TD	KICKOFF RETURNS No.	Yds.	Avg.	TD	TOTALS TD	2pt.	Pts.	Fum.
2002—Washington NFL	16	4	116	534	4.6	1	32	253	7.9	1	23	496	21.6	0	2	0	12	0
2003—Cincinnati NFL	8	0	0	0	0.0	0	0	0	0.0	0	7	113	16.1	0	0	0	0	1
Pro totals (2 years)	24	4	116	534	4.6	1	32	253	7.9	1	30	609	20.3	0	2	0	12	1

WAYNE, NATE — LB — EAGLES

W

PERSONAL: Born January 12, 1975, in Chicago, Ill. ... 6-0/237.
HIGH SCHOOL: Noxubee County (Macon, Miss.).
COLLEGE: Mississippi.
TRANSACTIONS/CAREER NOTES: Selected by Denver Broncos in seventh round (219th pick overall) of 1998 NFL draft. ... Signed by Broncos (June 9, 1998). ... Assigned by Broncos to Barcelona Dragons in 1999 NFL Europe enhancement allocation program (February 22, 1999). ... Released by Broncos (September 19, 1999). ... Re-signed by Broncos to practice squad (September 21, 1999). ... Activated (September 22, 1999). ... Traded by Broncos to Green Bay Packers for conditional future draft pick (August 15, 2000). ... Released by Packers (March 10, 2003). ... Signed by Philadelphia Eagles (March 14, 2003).
CHAMPIONSHIP GAME EXPERIENCE: Member of Broncos for AFC championship game (1998 season); inactive. ... Member of Super Bowl championship team (1998 season); inactive. ... Played in NFC championship game (2003 season).

Year Team	G	GS	TOTALS Tk.	Ast.	Sks.	INTERCEPTIONS No.	Yds.	Avg.	TD
1998—Denver NFL	1	0	0	0	0.0	0	0	0.0	0
1999—Denver NFL	16	0	8	2	2.0	0	0	0.0	0
2000—Green Bay NFL	16	13	75	26	2.0	0	0	0.0	0
2001—Green Bay NFL	12	12	60	26	5.5	3	55	18.3	0
2002—Green Bay NFL	16	15	70	41	2.5	3	32	10.7	0
2003—Philadelphia NFL	16	16	69	21	3.0	1	33	33.0	0
Pro totals (6 years)	77	56	282	116	15.0	7	120	17.1	0

WAYNE, REGGIE WR COLTS

PERSONAL: Born November 17, 1978, in New Orleans, La. ... 6-0/203.
HIGH SCHOOL: Ehret (La.).
COLLEGE: Miami (Fla.).
TRANSACTIONS/CAREER NOTES: Selected by Indianapolis Colts in first round (30th pick overall) of 2001 NFL draft. ... Signed by Colts (July 26, 2001).
CHAMPIONSHIP GAME EXPERIENCE: Played in AFC championship game (2003 season).
SINGLE GAME HIGHS (regular season): Receptions—10 (September 21, 2003, vs. Jacksonville); yards—141 (November 16, 2003, vs. New York Jets); and touchdown receptions—2 (October 26, 2003, vs. Houston).
STATISTICAL PLATEAUS: 100-yard receiving games: 2002 (3), 2003 (2). Total: 5.

			RECEIVING				TOTALS			
Year Team	G	GS	No.	Yds.	Avg.	TD	TD	2pt.	Pts.	Fum.
2001—Indianapolis NFL	13	9	27	345	12.8	0	0	0	0	0
2002—Indianapolis NFL	16	7	49	716	14.6	4	4	0	24	2
2003—Indianapolis NFL	16	16	68	838	12.3	7	7	0	42	0
Pro totals (3 years)	45	32	144	1899	13.2	11	11	0	66	2

WEARY, FRED G TEXANS

PERSONAL: Born September 30, 1977, in Montgomery, Ala. ... 6-4/308. ... Full name: Fred Edward Weary Jr.
HIGH SCHOOL: Robert E. Lee (Montgomery, Ala.).
COLLEGE: Tennessee.
TRANSACTIONS/CAREER NOTES: Selected by Houston Texans in third round (66th pick overall) of 2002 NFL draft. ... Signed by Texans (July 17, 2002).
PLAYING EXPERIENCE: Houston NFL, 2002-2003. ... Games/Games started: 2002 (16/12), 2003 (14/2). Total: 30/14.
HONORS: Named guard on THE SPORTING NEWS college All-America second team (2001).

WEARY, FRED CB

PERSONAL: Born April 12, 1974, in Jacksonville, Fla. ... 5-10/181. ... Full name: Joseph Fredrick Weary.
HIGH SCHOOL: Mandarin (Jacksonville).
COLLEGE: Florida.
TRANSACTIONS/CAREER NOTES: Selected by New Orleans Saints in fourth round (97th pick overall) of 1998 NFL draft. ... Signed by Saints (July 10, 1998). ... On injured reserve with knee injury (November 29, 2000-remainder of season). ... Granted free agency (March 2, 2001). ... Re-signed by Saints (March 30, 2001). ... Granted unconditional free agency (March 1, 2002). ... Signed by Atlanta Falcons (April 9, 2002). ... Granted unconditional free agency (February 28, 2003). ... Signed by San Francisco 49ers (June 18, 2003). ... Waived by 49ers (August 26, 2003). ... Signed by St. Louis Rams (August 31, 2003). ... Granted unconditional free agency (March 3, 2004).
HONORS: Named cornerback on THE SPORTING NEWS college All-America first team (1997).

			TOTALS			INTERCEPTIONS			
Year Team	G	GS	Tk.	Ast.	Sks.	No.	Yds.	Avg.	TD
1998—New Orleans NFL	14	1	28	6	0.0	2	64	32.0	1
1999—New Orleans NFL	16	11	57	8	0.0	2	49	24.5	0
2000—New Orleans NFL	12	12	48	7	2.0	2	27	13.5	0
2001—New Orleans NFL	14	1	14	2	0.0	0	0	0.0	0
2002—Atlanta NFL	16	0	18	2	0.0	1	14	14.0	0
2003—St. Louis NFL	11	0	1	0	0.0	0	0	0.0	0
Pro totals (6 years)	83	25	166	25	2.0	7	154	22.0	1

WEATHERSBY, DENNIS CB BENGALS

PERSONAL: Born June 16, 1980, in Glendora, Calif. ... 6-1/204.
HIGH SCHOOL: Duarte (Calif.).
COLLEGE: Oregon State.
TRANSACTIONS/CAREER NOTES: Selected by Cincinnati Bengals in fourth round (98th pick overall) of 2003 NFL draft. ... Signed by Bengals (July 27, 2003).

			TOTALS			INTERCEPTIONS			
Year Team	G	GS	Tk.	Ast.	Sks.	No.	Yds.	Avg.	TD
2003—Cincinnati NFL	4	0	0	0	0.0	0	0	0.0	0

W

WEAVER, ANTHONY DE RAVENS

PERSONAL: Born July 28, 1980, in Abilene, Texas. ... 6-3/290. ... Full name: Anthony Lee Weaver.
HIGH SCHOOL: Saratoga Springs (N.Y.).
COLLEGE: Notre Dame.
TRANSACTIONS/CAREER NOTES: Selected by Baltimore Ravens in second round (52nd pick overall) of 2002 NFL draft. ... Signed by Ravens (July 27, 2002).

			TOTALS			INTERCEPTIONS			
Year Team	G	GS	Tk.	Ast.	Sks.	No.	Yds.	Avg.	TD
2002—Baltimore NFL	16	16	27	4	3.5	0	0	0.0	0
2003—Baltimore NFL	15	15	27	9	5.0	0	0	0.0	0
Pro totals (2 years)	31	31	54	13	8.5	0	0	0.0	0

WEAVER, JED — TE — BRONCOS

PERSONAL: Born August 11, 1976, in Bend, Ore. ... 6-4/258. ... Full name: Timothy Jed Weaver. ... Cousin of Jeff Weaver, pitcher, New York Yankees.

HIGH SCHOOL: Redmond (Ore.).

COLLEGE: Oregon.

TRANSACTIONS/CAREER NOTES: Selected by Philadelphia Eagles in seventh round (208th pick overall) of 1999 NFL draft. ... Signed by Eagles (July 16, 1999). ... Claimed on waivers by Miami Dolphins (August 23, 2000). ... Granted free agency (March 1, 2002). ... Re-signed by Dolphins (April 1, 2002). ... Granted unconditional free agency (February 28, 2003). ... Signed by San Francisco 49ers (March 11, 2003). ... Granted unconditional free agency (March 3, 2004). ... Signed by Denver Broncos (March 19, 2004).

SINGLE GAME HIGHS (regular season): Receptions—5 (December 24, 2000, vs. New England); yards—76 (December 7, 2003, vs. Arizona); and touchdown receptions—1 (December 27, 2003, vs. Seattle).

			RECEIVING				TOTALS			
Year Team	**G**	**GS**	**No.**	**Yds.**	**Avg.**	**TD**	**TD**	**2pt.**	**Pts.**	**Fum.**
1999—Philadelphia NFL	16	10	11	91	8.3	0	0	1	2	0
2000—Miami NFL	16	0	10	179	17.9	0	0	0	0	1
2001—Miami NFL	16	7	18	215	11.9	2	2	0	12	1
2002—Miami NFL	16	4	6	75	12.5	3	3	0	18	0
2003—San Francisco NFL	16	16	35	437	12.5	1	1	0	6	1
Pro totals (5 years)	80	37	80	997	12.5	6	6	1	38	3

WEBSTER, JASON — CB — FALCONS

PERSONAL: Born September 8, 1977, in Houston, Texas. ... 5-10/187. ... Full name: Jason Richmond Webster.

HIGH SCHOOL: Willowridge (Houston).

COLLEGE: Texas A&M.

TRANSACTIONS/CAREER NOTES: Selected by San Francisco 49ers in second round (48th pick overall) of 2000 NFL draft. ... Signed by 49ers (July 18, 2000). ... On physically unable to perform list with knee injury (July 25-September 7, 2003). ... Granted unconditional free agency (March 3, 2004). ... Signed by Atlanta Falcons (March 5, 2004).

			TOTALS			INTERCEPTIONS			
Year Team	**G**	**GS**	**Tk.**	**Ast.**	**Sks.**	**No.**	**Yds.**	**Avg.**	**TD**
2000—San Francisco NFL	16	10	41	14	0.0	2	78	39.0	1
2001—San Francisco NFL	16	16	69	7	0.5	3	61	20.3	0
2002—San Francisco NFL	16	16	71	14	0.0	1	37	37.0	1
2003—San Francisco NFL	5	2	7	3	0.0	1	17	17.0	0
Pro totals (4 years)	53	44	188	38	0.5	7	193	27.6	2

WEBSTER, NATE — LB — BENGALS

PERSONAL: Born November 29, 1977, in Miami, Fla. ... 6-0/230. ... Full name: Nathaniel Webster Jr.

HIGH SCHOOL: Northwestern (Miami).

COLLEGE: Miami (Fla.).

TRANSACTIONS/CAREER NOTES: Selected after junior season by Tampa Bay Buccaneers in third round (90th pick overall) of 2000 NFL draft. ... Signed by Buccaneers (July 11, 2000). ... Granted free agency (February 28, 2003). ... Re-signed by Buccaneers (April 24, 2003). ... Granted unconditional free agency (March 3, 2004). ... Signed by Cincinnati Bengals (March 4, 2004).

CHAMPIONSHIP GAME EXPERIENCE: Played in NFC championship game (2002 season). ... Member of Super Bowl championship team (2002 season).

HONORS: Named linebacker on THE SPORTING NEWS college All-America second team (1999).

			TOTALS			INTERCEPTIONS			
Year Team	**G**	**GS**	**Tk.**	**Ast.**	**Sks.**	**No.**	**Yds.**	**Avg.**	**TD**
2000—Tampa Bay NFL	16	0	17	3	0.0	0	0	0.0	0
2001—Tampa Bay NFL	16	1	25	11	0.0	0	0	0.0	0
2002—Tampa Bay NFL	16	0	14	9	0.0	0	0	0.0	0
2003—Tampa Bay NFL	15	5	25	26	1.0	0	0	0.0	0
Pro totals (4 years)	63	6	81	49	1.0	0	0	0.0	0

WEINER, TODD — T — FALCONS

PERSONAL: Born September 16, 1975, in Bristol, Pa. ... 6-4/297.

HIGH SCHOOL: Taravella (Coral Springs, Fla.).

COLLEGE: Kansas State.

TRANSACTIONS/CAREER NOTES: Selected by Seattle Seahawks in second round (47th pick overall) of 1998 NFL draft. ... Signed by Seahawks (July 15, 1998). ... Granted unconditional free agency (March 1, 2002). ... Signed by Atlanta Falcons (March 6, 2002).

PLAYING EXPERIENCE: Seattle NFL, 1998-2001; Atlanta NFL, 2002-2003. ... Games/Games started: 1998 (6/0), 1999 (11/1), 2000 (16/6), 2001 (16/13), 2002 (16/15), 2003 (16/16). Total: 81/51.

HONORS: Named offensive tackle on THE SPORTING NEWS college All-America second team (1997).

WEINKE, CHRIS — QB — PANTHERS

PERSONAL: Born July 31, 1972, in St. Paul, Minn. ... 6-4/232.

HIGH SCHOOL: Cretin-Derham (St. Paul, Minn.).

COLLEGE: Florida State.

TRANSACTIONS/CAREER NOTES: Selected by Carolina Panthers in fourth round (106th pick overall) of 2001 NFL draft. ... Signed by Panthers (July 21, 2001). ... Inactive for 16 games (2003).
CHAMPIONSHIP GAME EXPERIENCE: Member of Panthers for NFC championship game (2003 season); inactive. ... Member of Panthers for Super Bowl 38 (2003 season); inactive.
HONORS: Named quarterback on THE SPORTING NEWS college All-America second team (2000). ... Heisman Trophy winner (2000). ... Davey O'Brien Award winner (2000).
SINGLE GAME HIGHS (regular season): Attempts—63 (December 30, 2001, vs. Arizona); completions—36 (December 30, 2001, vs. Arizona); yards—312 (December 23, 2001, vs. St. Louis); and touchdown passes—2 (November 18, 2001, vs. San Francisco).
STATISTICAL PLATEAUS: 300-yard passing games: 2001 (1). Total: 1.
MISCELLANEOUS: Regular-season record as starting NFL quarterback: 1-15 (.063).

			PASSING									RUSHING				TOTALS		
Year Team	G	GS	Att.	Cmp.	Pct.	Yds.	TD	Int.	Avg.	Skd.	Rat.	Att.	Yds.	Avg.	TD	TD	2pt.	Pts.
2001—Carolina NFL	15	15	540	293	54.3	2931	11	19	5.43	26	62.0	37	128	3.5	6	6	0	36
2002—Carolina NFL	6	1	38	17	44.7	180	0	3	4.74	6	26.2	5	9	1.8	0	0	0	0
2003—Carolina NFL			Did not play.															
Pro totals (2 years)	21	16	578	310	53.6	3111	11	22	5.38	32	59.7	42	137	3.3	6	6	0	36

WELBOURN, JOHN — G/T — CHIEFS

PERSONAL: Born March 30, 1976, in Torrance, Calif. ... 6-5/318. ... Full name: John R. Welbourn.
HIGH SCHOOL: Palos Verdes Peninsula (Rolling Hills Estate, Calif.).
COLLEGE: California.
TRANSACTIONS/CAREER NOTES: Selected by Philadelphia Eagles in fourth round (97th pick overall) of 1999 NFL draft. ... Signed by Eagles (July 25, 1999). ... On injured reserve with knee injury (September 13, 1999-remainder of season). ... Traded by Eagles to Kansas City Chiefs for fifth-round pick (RB Thomas Tapeh) in 2004 draft and fifth-round pick in 2005 draft (April 25, 2004).
PLAYING EXPERIENCE: Philadelphia NFL, 1999-2003. ... Games/Games started: 1999 (1/1), 2000 (16/16), 2001 (15/15), 2002 (11/11), 2003 (13/13). Total: 56/56.
CHAMPIONSHIP GAME EXPERIENCE: Played in NFC championship game (2001-2003 seasons).

WELLS, JONATHAN — RB — TEXANS

PERSONAL: Born July 21, 1979, in River Ridge, La. ... 6-1/243.
HIGH SCHOOL: John Curtis (River Ridge, La.).
COLLEGE: Ohio State.
TRANSACTIONS/CAREER NOTES: Selected by Houston Texans in fourth round (99th pick overall) of 2002 NFL draft. ... Signed by Texans (July 19, 2002).
SINGLE GAME HIGHS (regular season): Attempts—24 (November 24, 2002, vs. New York Giants); yards—93 (September 22, 2002, vs. Indianapolis); and rushing touchdowns—1 (December 15, 2002, vs. Baltimore).

			RUSHING				RECEIVING				KICKOFF RETURNS				TOTALS			
Year Team	G	GS	Att.	Yds.	Avg.	TD	No.	Yds.	Avg.	TD	No.	Yds.	Avg.	TD	TD	2pt.	Pts.	Fum.
2002—Houston NFL	16	11	197	529	2.7	3	9	48	5.3	0	0	0	0.0	0	3	0	18	3
2003—Houston NFL	13	0	5	14	2.8	0	2	17	8.5	0	2	24	12.0	0	0	0	0	0
Pro totals (2 years)	29	11	202	543	2.7	3	11	65	5.9	0	2	24	12.0	0	3	0	18	3

WELLS, RAY — LB — TITANS

PERSONAL: Born August 20, 1980, in Oakland, Calif. ... 6-1/234.
HIGH SCHOOL: Mount Miguel (Spring Valley, Calif.).
JUNIOR COLLEGE: Mesa Junior College.
COLLEGE: Arizona.
TRANSACTIONS/CAREER NOTES: Signed as non-drafted free agent by San Francisco 49ers (May 2, 2003). ... Claimed on waivers by Tennessee Titans (September 1, 2003).

			TOTALS			INTERCEPTIONS			
Year Team	G	GS	Tk.	Ast.	Sks.	No.	Yds.	Avg.	TD
2003—Tennessee NFL	16	0	1	0	0.0	0	0	0.0	0

WELLS, REGGIE — T — CARDINALS

PERSONAL: Born November 3, 1980, in Liberty, Pa. ... 6-4/298.
HIGH SCHOOL: South Park (Liberty, Pa.).
COLLEGE: Clarion.
TRANSACTIONS/CAREER NOTES: Selected by Arizona Cardinals in sixth round (177th pick overall) of 2003 NFL draft. ... Signed by Cardinals (June 4, 2003).
PLAYING EXPERIENCE: Arizona NFL, 2003. ... Games/Games started: 2003 (15/1). Total: 15/1.

WESLEY, DANTE — CB — PANTHERS

PERSONAL: Born April 5, 1979, in St. Louis, Mo. ... 6-1/211.
HIGH SCHOOL: Watson Chapel (Pine Bluff, Ark.).
COLLEGE: Arkansas-Pine Bluff.
TRANSACTIONS/CAREER NOTES: Selected by Carolina Panthers in fourth round (100th pick overall) of 2002 NFL draft. ... Signed by Panthers (July 15, 2002).

CHAMPIONSHIP GAME EXPERIENCE: Played in NFC championship game (2003 season). ... Played in Super Bowl 38 (2003 season).

Year Team	G	GS	TOTALS Tk.	Ast.	Sks.	INTERCEPTIONS No.	Yds.	Avg.	TD
2002—Carolina NFL	13	1	15	3	0.0	0	0	0.0	0
2003—Carolina NFL	16	1	7	1	1.0	0	0	0.0	0
Pro totals (2 years)	29	2	22	4	1.0	0	0	0.0	0

WESLEY, GREG — S — CHIEFS

PERSONAL: Born March 19, 1978, in Little Rock, Ark. ... 6-2/206. ... Full name: Gregory Lashon Wesley.
HIGH SCHOOL: England (Ark.).
COLLEGE: Arkansas-Pine Bluff.
TRANSACTIONS/CAREER NOTES: Selected by Kansas City Chiefs in third round (85th pick overall) of 2000 NFL draft. ... Signed by Chiefs (June 6, 2000). ... Granted free agency (February 28, 2003). ... Re-signed by Chiefs (May 16, 2003).

Year Team	G	GS	TOTALS Tk.	Ast.	Sks.	INTERCEPTIONS No.	Yds.	Avg.	TD
2000—Kansas City NFL	16	16	69	16	1.0	2	28	14.0	0
2001—Kansas City NFL	16	16	72	11	2.0	2	44	22.0	0
2002—Kansas City NFL	13	13	54	10	1.0	6	170	28.3	0
2003—Kansas City NFL	16	16	87	15	2.0	6	63	10.5	0
Pro totals (4 years)	61	61	282	52	6.0	16	305	19.1	0

WEST, LYLE — S — CHIEFS

PERSONAL: Born December 20, 1976, in Columbus, Ga. ... 6-0/210.
HIGH SCHOOL: Washington (Fremont, Calif.).
JUNIOR COLLEGE: Chabot College (Calif.).
COLLEGE: San Jose State.
TRANSACTIONS/CAREER NOTES: Selected by New York Giants in sixth round (189th pick overall) of 1999 NFL draft. ... Signed by Giants (July 29, 1999). ... On suspended list for violating league substance abuse policy (November 23-December 20, 1999). ... Released by Giants (May 14, 2001). ... Signed by Kansas City Chiefs (August 1, 2001). ... Released by Chiefs (August 28, 2001). ... Re-signed by Chiefs (February 21, 2002). ... Granted unconditional free agency (March 3, 2004). ... Re-signed by Chiefs (April 1, 2004).
CHAMPIONSHIP GAME EXPERIENCE: Played in NFC championship game (2000 season). ... Played in Super Bowl 35 (2000 season).

Year Team	G	GS	TOTALS Tk.	Ast.	Sks.	INTERCEPTIONS No.	Yds.	Avg.	TD
1999—New York Giants NFL	7	0	0	0	0.0	0	0	0.0	0
2000—New York Giants NFL	16	2	8	0	0.0	0	0	0.0	0
2002—Kansas City NFL	16	0	3	0	0.0	0	0	0.0	0
2003—Kansas City NFL	13	0	3	0	0.0	0	0	0.0	0
Pro totals (4 years)	52	2	14	0	0.0	0	0	0.0	0

WESTBROOK, BRIAN — RB/KR — EAGLES

PERSONAL: Born September 2, 1979, in Washington, DC. ... 5-8/200.
HIGH SCHOOL: DeMantha (Ft. Washington, Md.).
COLLEGE: Villanova.
TRANSACTIONS/CAREER NOTES: Selected by Philadelphia Eagles in third round (91st pick overall) of 2002 NFL draft. ... Signed by Eagles (July 11, 2002). ... On injured reserve with triceps injury (January 7, 2004-remainder of 2003 season).
CHAMPIONSHIP GAME EXPERIENCE: Played in NFC championship game (2002 season).
HONORS: Walter Payton Award winner (2001).
SINGLE GAME HIGHS (regular season): Attempts—15 (October 19, 2003, vs. New York Giants); yards—96 (September 28, 2003, vs. Buffalo); and rushing touchdowns—1 (December 15, 2003, vs. Miami).

Year Team	G	GS	RUSHING Att.	Yds.	Avg.	TD	RECEIVING No.	Yds.	Avg.	TD	PUNT RETURNS No.	Yds.	Avg.	TD	KICKOFF RETURNS No.	Yds.	Avg.	TD	TOTALS TD	2pt.	Pts.
2002—Phi. NFL	15	3	46	193	4.2	0	9	86	9.6	0	0	0	0.0	0	0	0	0.0	0	0	0	0
2003—Phi. NFL	15	8	117	613	5.2	7	37	332	9.0	4	20	306‡	15.3	†2	23	487	21.2	0	13	0	78
Pro totals (2 years)	30	11	163	806	4.9	7	46	418	9.1	4	20	306	15.3	2	23	487	21.2	0	13	0	78

W

WESTMORELAND, ERIC — LB

PERSONAL: Born March 11, 1977, in Jasper, Tenn. ... 6-0/230. ... Full name: Eric Lebron Westmoreland.
HIGH SCHOOL: Marion County (Tenn.).
COLLEGE: Tennessee.
TRANSACTIONS/CAREER NOTES: Selected by Jacksonville Jaguars in third round (73rd pick overall) of 2001 NFL draft. ... Signed by Jaguars (June 4, 2001). ... Waived by Jaguars (October 8, 2003).

Year Team	G	GS	TOTALS Tk.	Ast.	Sks.	INTERCEPTIONS No.	Yds.	Avg.	TD
2001—Jacksonville NFL	11	2	15	4	1.0	0	0	0.0	0
2002—Jacksonville NFL	15	2	21	7	1.0	0	0	0.0	0
2003—Jacksonville NFL	2	0	0	0	0.0	0	0	0.0	0
Pro totals (3 years)	28	4	36	11	2.0	0	0	0.0	0

WHALEN, JAMES — TE — COWBOYS

PERSONAL: Born December 11, 1977, in Portland, Ore. ... 6-2/244. ... Full name: James Patrick Whalen Jr.
HIGH SCHOOL: La Salle (Portland, Ore.).
JUNIOR COLLEGE: Shasta College (Calif.).
COLLEGE: Kentucky.
TRANSACTIONS/CAREER NOTES: Selected by Tampa Bay Buccaneers in fifth round (157th pick overall) of 2000 NFL draft. ... Signed by Buccaneers (July 10, 2000). ... Released by Buccaneers (August 27, 2000). ... Signed by Dallas Cowboys to practice squad (August 30, 2000). ... Activated (December 7, 2000). ... Assigned by Cowboys to Scottish Claymores in 2001 NFL Europe enhancement allocation program (February 12, 2001). ... On injured reserve with Achilles' tendon injury (September 22, 2001-remainder of season). ... Granted free agency (March 3, 2004). ... Re-signed by Cowboys (April 21, 2004).
HONORS: Named tight end on THE SPORTING NEWS college All-America third team (1999).
SINGLE GAME HIGHS (regular season): Receptions—5 (September 29, 2002, vs. St. Louis); yards—38 (September 29, 2002, vs. St. Louis); and touchdown receptions—0.

			RECEIVING				TOTALS			
Year Team	G	GS	No.	Yds.	Avg.	TD	TD	2pt.	Pts.	Fum.
2000—Dallas NFL	3	0	0	0	0.0	0	0	0	0	0
2002—Dallas NFL	16	6	17	152	8.9	0	0	0	0	0
2003—Dallas NFL	7	0	0	0	0.0	0	0	0	0	0
Pro totals (3 years)	26	6	17	152	8.9	0	0	0	0	0

WHEATLEY, TYRONE — RB — RAIDERS

PERSONAL: Born January 19, 1972, in Inkster, Mich. ... 6-0/235.
HIGH SCHOOL: Robichaud (Dearborn Heights, Mich.).
COLLEGE: Michigan.
TRANSACTIONS/CAREER NOTES: Selected by New York Giants in first round (17th pick overall) of 1995 NFL draft. ... Signed by Giants (August 9, 1995). ... Traded by Giants to Miami Dolphins for seventh-round pick (LB O.J. Childress) in 1999 draft (February 12, 1999). ... Released by Dolphins (August 3, 1999). ... Signed by Oakland Raiders (August 4, 1999). ... Granted unconditional free agency (February 28, 2003). ... Re-signed by Raiders (March 25, 2003).
CHAMPIONSHIP GAME EXPERIENCE: Played in AFC championship game (2000 and 2002 seasons). ... Played in Super Bowl 37 (2002 season).
SINGLE GAME HIGHS (regular season): Attempts—32 (November 16, 2003, vs. Minnesota); yards—156 (October 22, 2000, vs. Seattle); and rushing touchdowns—2 (October 7, 2001, vs. Dallas).
STATISTICAL PLATEAUS: 100-yard rushing games: 1997 (1), 1999 (2), 2000 (3), 2003 (1). Total: 7.

			RUSHING				RECEIVING				KICKOFF RETURNS				TOTALS			
Year Team	G	GS	Att.	Yds.	Avg.	TD	No.	Yds.	Avg.	TD	No.	Yds.	Avg.	TD	TD	2pt.	Pts.	Fum.
1995—New York Giants NFL	13	1	78	245	3.1	3	5	27	5.4	0	10	186	18.6	0	3	0	18	2
1996—New York Giants NFL	14	0	112	400	3.6	1	12	51	4.3	2	23	503	21.9	0	3	0	18	6
1997—New York Giants NFL	14	7	152	583	3.8	4	16	140	8.8	0	0	0	0.0	0	4	0	24	3
1998—New York Giants NFL	5	0	14	52	3.7	0	0	0	0.0	0	1	16	16.0	0	0	0	0	0
1999—Oakland NFL	16	9	242	936	3.9	8	21	196	9.3	3	0	0	0.0	0	11	0	66	3
2000—Oakland NFL	14	14	232	1046	4.5	9	20	156	7.8	1	0	0	0.0	0	10	0	60	4
2001—Oakland NFL	11	2	88	276	3.1	5	12	61	5.1	1	0	0	0.0	0	6	0	36	3
2002—Oakland NFL	14	0	108	419	3.9	2	12	71	5.9	0	0	0	0.0	0	2	0	12	1
2003—Oakland NFL	15	5	159	678	4.3	4	12	120	10.0	0	0	0	0.0	0	4	0	24	2
Pro totals (9 years)	116	38	1185	4635	3.9	36	110	822	7.5	7	34	705	20.7	0	43	0	258	24

WHITAKER, RONYELL — CB — BUCCANEERS

PERSONAL: Born March 19, 1979, in Norfolk, Va. ... 5-9/196. ... Full name: Roynell Deshawn Whitaker.
HIGH SCHOOL: Lake Taylor (Norfolk, Va.).
COLLEGE: Virginia Tech.
TRANSACTIONS/CAREER NOTES: Signed as non-drafted free agent by Tampa Bay Buccaneers (April 28, 2003). ... Released by Buccaneers (August 29, 2003). ... Re-signed by Buccaneers to practice squad (October 9, 2003). ... Activated (December 2, 2003).

			TOTALS			INTERCEPTIONS			
Year Team	G	GS	Tk.	Ast.	Sks.	No.	Yds.	Avg.	TD
2003—Tampa Bay NFL	4	1	7	2	0.0	0	0	0.0	0

WHITE, DEWAYNE — DE — BUCCANEERS

PERSONAL: Born October 19, 1979, in Marbury, Ala. ... 6-2/273.
HIGH SCHOOL: Marbury (Ala.).
COLLEGE: Louisville.
TRANSACTIONS/CAREER NOTES: Selected after junior season by Tampa Bay Buccaneers in second round (64th pick overall) of 2003 NFL draft. ... Signed by Buccaneers (July 18, 2003).

			TOTALS			INTERCEPTIONS			
Year Team	G	GS	Tk.	Ast.	Sks.	No.	Yds.	Avg.	TD
2003—Tampa Bay NFL	12	1	3	3	0.0	0	0	0.0	0

WHITE, DEZ — WR — FALCONS

PERSONAL: Born August 23, 1979, in Orange Park, Fla. ... 6-1/215. ... Full name: Edward Dezmon White.
HIGH SCHOOL: Bolles (Orange Park, Fla.).
COLLEGE: Georgia Tech.

TRANSACTIONS/CAREER NOTES: Selected after junior season by Chicago Bears in third round (69th pick overall) of 2000 NFL draft. ... Signed by Bears (July 19, 2000). ... Granted free agency (February 28, 2003). ... Re-signed by Bears (April 25, 2003). ... On injured reserve with knee injury (December 24, 2003-remainder of season). ... Granted unconditional free agency (March 3, 2004). ... Signed by Atlanta Falcons (March 23, 2004).

SINGLE GAME HIGHS (regular season): Receptions—8 (November 24, 2002, vs. Detroit); yards—106 (November 24, 2002, vs. Detroit); and touchdown receptions—2 (December 22, 2002, vs. Carolina).

STATISTICAL PLATEAUS: 100-yard receiving games: 2002 (1). Total: 1.

			RUSHING				RECEIVING				KICKOFF RETURNS				TOTALS			
Year Team	G	GS	Att.	Yds.	Avg.	TD	No.	Yds.	Avg.	TD	No.	Yds.	Avg.	TD	TD	2pt.	Pts.	Fum.
2000—Chicago NFL	15	0	0	0	0.0	0	10	87	8.7	1	0	0	0.0	0	1	0	6	1
2001—Chicago NFL	14	6	0	0	0.0	0	45	428	9.5	0	0	0	0.0	0	0	0	0	0
2002—Chicago NFL	16	14	3	11	3.7	0	51	656	12.9	4	2	47	23.5	0	4	0	24	1
2003—Chicago NFL	15	11	2	13	6.5	0	49	583	11.9	3	0	0	0.0	0	3	0	18	0
Pro totals (4 years)	60	31	5	24	4.8	0	155	1754	11.3	8	2	47	23.5	0	8	0	48	2

WHITE, JAMEL — RB — BUCCANEERS

PERSONAL: Born February 11, 1978, in Los Angeles, Calif. ... 5-9/222.

HIGH SCHOOL: Palmdale (Calif.).

COLLEGE: South Dakota.

TRANSACTIONS/CAREER NOTES: Signed as non-drafted free agent by Indianapolis Colts (April 20, 2000). ... Released by Colts (August 27, 2000). ... Signed by Cleveland Browns (August 29, 2000). ... Granted free agency (February 28, 2003). ... Re-signed by Browns (April 18, 2003). ... Released by Browns (March 5, 2004). ... Signed by Tampa Bay Buccaneers (March 18, 2004).

SINGLE GAME HIGHS (regular season): Attempts—23 (September 30, 2001, vs. Jacksonville); yards—131 (December 23, 2001, vs. Green Bay); and rushing touchdowns—2 (December 30, 2001, vs. Tennessee).

STATISTICAL PLATEAUS: 100-yard rushing games: 2001 (1), 2002 (1), 2003 (1). Total: 3.

			RUSHING				RECEIVING				KICKOFF RETURNS				TOTALS			
Year Team	G	GS	Att.	Yds.	Avg.	TD	No.	Yds.	Avg.	TD	No.	Yds.	Avg.	TD	TD	2pt.	Pts.	Fum.
2000—Cleveland NFL	13	0	47	145	3.1	0	13	100	7.7	0	43	935	21.7	0	0	0	0	0
2001—Cleveland NFL	16	7	126	443	3.5	5	44	418	9.5	1	9	189	21.0	0	6	1	38	1
2002—Cleveland NFL	14	6	106	470	4.4	3	63	452	7.2	0	2	21	10.5	0	3	0	18	0
2003—Cleveland NFL	16	3	70	266	3.8	1	46	303	6.6	1	2	2	1.0	0	2	0	12	1
Pro totals (4 years)	59	16	349	1324	3.8	9	166	1273	7.7	2	56	1147	20.5	0	11	1	68	2

WHITE, TRACY — LB — SEAHAWKS

PERSONAL: Born April 14, 1981, in Charleston, S.C. ... 6-0/230.

COLLEGE: Howard.

TRANSACTIONS/CAREER NOTES: Signed as non-drafted free agent by Seattle Seahawks (May 1, 2003).

			TOTALS			INTERCEPTIONS			
Year Team	G	GS	Tk.	Ast.	Sks.	No.	Yds.	Avg.	TD
2003—Seattle NFL	11	0	0	0	0.0	0	0	0.0	0

WHITEHEAD, WILLIE — DE — SAINTS

PERSONAL: Born January 26, 1973, in Tuskegee, Ala. ... 6-3/285. ... Full name: William Whitehead.

HIGH SCHOOL: Tuskegee (Ala.) Institute.

COLLEGE: Auburn.

TRANSACTIONS/CAREER NOTES: Signed as non-drafted free agent by San Francisco 49ers (April 26, 1995). ... Released by 49ers (July 16, 1995). ... Signed by Baltimore Stallions of CFL (August 1995). ... Signed by Montreal Alouettes of CFL to practice squad (1996). ... Signed by Hamilton Tiger-Cats of CFL (May 14, 1997). ... Signed by Detroit Lions (February 11, 1998). ... Released by Lions (August 25, 1998). ... Signed by New Orleans Saints (January 27, 1999). ... Assigned by Saints to Frankfurt Galaxy in 1999 NFL Europe enhancement allocation program (February 22, 1999). ... Granted free agency (March 1, 2002). ... Re-signed by Saints (April 4, 2002). ... Granted unconditional free agency (February 28, 2003). ... Re-signed by Saints (April 25, 2003).

			TOTALS		
Year Team	G	GS	Tk.	Ast.	Sks.
1995—Baltimore CFL	1	...	...	...	0.0
1996—Montreal CFL	Did not play.				
1997—Hamilton CFL	15	...	...	...	13.0
1998—	Did not play.				
1999—New Orleans NFL	16	3	24	6	7.0
2000—New Orleans NFL	16	2	17	10	5.5
2001—New Orleans NFL	14	0	18	3	2.0
2002—New Orleans NFL	12	10	24	10	3.0
2003—New Orleans NFL	11	10	34	6	5.5
CFL totals (2 years)	16	...	...	...	13.0
NFL totals (5 years)	69	25	117	35	23.0
Pro totals (7 years)	85	...	...	...	36.0

WHITESIDE, KEYON — LB — COLTS

PERSONAL: Born January 31, 1980, in Forest City, N.C. ... 6-0/229. ... Full name: Keyon Shontel Whiteside.

HIGH SCHOOL: Chase (Forest City, N.C.).

COLLEGE: Tennessee.

TRANSACTIONS/CAREER NOTES: Selected by Indianapolis Colts in fifth round (162nd pick overall) of 2003 NFL draft. ... Signed by Colts (July 24, 2003). ... Claimed on waivers by Cincinnati Bengals (September 1, 2003). ... Waived by Bengals (October 22, 2003). ... Signed by Colts (November 18, 2003).
CHAMPIONSHIP GAME EXPERIENCE: Played in AFC championship game (2003 season).

Year Team	G	GS	TOTALS Tk.	Ast.	Sks.	INTERCEPTIONS No.	Yds.	Avg.	TD
2003—Indianapolis NFL	5	0	0	0	0.0	0	0	0.0	0

WHITFIELD, BOB — T — FALCONS

PERSONAL: Born October 18, 1971, in Carson, Calif. ... 6-5/310. ... Full name: Bob Whitfield Jr.
HIGH SCHOOL: Banning (Los Angeles).
COLLEGE: Stanford.
TRANSACTIONS/CAREER NOTES: Selected after junior season by Atlanta Falcons in first round (eighth pick overall) of 1992 NFL draft. ... Signed by Falcons (September 4, 1992). ... Granted roster exemption for one game (September 1992). ... On injured reserve with leg injury (November 3, 2003-remainder of season).
PLAYING EXPERIENCE: Atlanta NFL, 1992-2003. ... Games/Games started: 1992 (11/0), 1993 (16/16), 1994 (16/16), 1995 (16/16), 1996 (16/16), 1997 (16/16), 1998 (16/16), 1999 (16/16), 2000 (15/15), 2001 (16/16), 2002 (16/16), 2003 (8/8). Total: 178/167.
CHAMPIONSHIP GAME EXPERIENCE: Played in NFC championship game (1998 season). ... Played in Super Bowl 33 (1998 season).
HONORS: Named offensive tackle on THE SPORTING NEWS college All-America first team (1991). ... Played in Pro Bowl (1998 season).

WHITING, BRANDON — DE/DT — 49ERS

PERSONAL: Born July 30, 1976, in Santa Rosa, Calif. ... 6-3/285. ... Name pronounced: WHITE-ing.
HIGH SCHOOL: Polytechnic (Pasadena, Calif.).
COLLEGE: California.
TRANSACTIONS/CAREER NOTES: Selected by Philadelphia Eagles in fourth round (112th pick overall) of 1998 NFL draft. ... Signed by Eagles (July 14, 1998). ... Granted free agency (March 2, 2001). ... Re-signed by Eagles (March 20, 2001). ... Traded by Eagles to San Francisco 49ers as part of a three-way trade involving the Baltimore Ravens (March 16, 2004). The Ravens received a fifth-round draft choice from the Eagles as well as a 2004 second-round pick they sent to San Francisco in an earlier trade. The Eagles received WR Terrell Owens from Baltimore.
CHAMPIONSHIP GAME EXPERIENCE: Played in NFC championship game (2001-2003 seasons).

Year Team	G	GS	TOTALS Tk.	Ast.	Sks.	INTERCEPTIONS No.	Yds.	Avg.	TD
1998—Philadelphia NFL	16	5	14	4	1.5	0	0	0.0	0
1999—Philadelphia NFL	13	2	9	7	1.0	1	22	22.0	1
2000—Philadelphia NFL	16	11	23	11	3.5	0	0	0.0	0
2001—Philadelphia NFL	13	12	15	11	2.5	0	0	0.0	0
2002—Philadelphia NFL	16	15	23	16	6.0	0	0	0.0	0
2003—Philadelphia NFL	14	14	32	13	2.0	0	0	0.0	0
Pro totals (6 years)	88	59	116	62	16.5	1	22	22.0	1

WHITLEY, JAMES — CB — PACKERS

PERSONAL: Born May 13, 1979, in Decatur, Ill. ... 5-11/190. ... Full name: James LaVell Whitley.
HIGH SCHOOL: Norview (Va.).
COLLEGE: Michigan.
TRANSACTIONS/CAREER NOTES: Signed by Montreal Alouettes of CFL (2001). ... Signed as non-drafted free agent by St. Louis Rams (February 26, 2002). ... On physically unable to perform list with foot injury (August 26-October 17, 2003). ... Released by Rams (December 2, 2003). ... Signed by Green Bay Packers (December 10, 2003). ... Granted unconditional free agency (March 3, 2004). ... Re-signed by Packers (April 15, 2004).

Year Team	G	GS	TOTALS Tk.	Ast.	Sks.	INTERCEPTIONS No.	Yds.	Avg.	TD
2001—Montreal CFL	14	5	...	...	1.0	2	18	9.0	0
2002—St. Louis NFL	13	1	26	1	3.0	0	0	0.0	0
2003—St. Louis NFL	3	0	3	0	0.0	0	0	0.0	0
—Green Bay NFL	3	0	0	0	0.0	0	0	0.0	0
CFL totals (1 year)	14	5	...	...	1.0	2	18	9.0	0
NFL totals (2 years)	19	1	29	1	3.0	0	0	0.0	0
Pro totals (3 years)	33	6	...	...	4.0	2	18	9.0	0

W

WHITTED, ALVIS — WR — RAIDERS

PERSONAL: Born September 4, 1974, in Durham, N.C. ... 6-0/185. ... Full name: Alvis James Whitted.
HIGH SCHOOL: Orange (Hillsborough, N.C.).
COLLEGE: North Carolina State.
TRANSACTIONS/CAREER NOTES: Selected by Jacksonville Jaguars in seventh round (192nd pick overall) of 1998 NFL draft. ... Signed by Jaguars (May 19, 1998). ... Released by Jaguars (December 4, 2001). ... Signed by Atlanta Falcons (January 10, 2002). ... Released by Falcons (August 31, 2002). ... Signed by Oakland Raiders (September 25, 2002).
CHAMPIONSHIP GAME EXPERIENCE: Played in AFC championship game (1999 and 2002 seasons). ... Played in Super Bowl 37 (2002 season).
SINGLE GAME HIGHS (regular season): Receptions—4 (December 23, 2000, vs. New York Giants); yards—55 (October 29, 2000, vs. Dallas); and touchdown receptions—2 (October 29, 2000, vs. Dallas).

Year	Team	G	GS	RUSHING Att.	Yds.	Avg.	TD	RECEIVING No.	Yds.	Avg.	TD	KICKOFF RETURNS No.	Yds.	Avg.	TD	TOTALS TD	2pt.	Pts.	Fum.
1998—Jacksonville NFL		16	0	3	13	4.3	0	2	61	30.5	0	0	0	0.0	0	1	0	6	0
1999—Jacksonville NFL		14	1	1	9	9.0	0	0	0	0.0	0	8	187	23.4	▲1	1	0	6	0
2000—Jacksonville NFL		16	3	0	0	0.0	0	13	137	10.5	3	4	67	16.8	0	3	0	18	1
2001—Jacksonville NFL		11	0	1	4	4.0	0	2	17	8.5	0	0	0	0.0	0	0	0	0	0
2002—Oakland NFL		9	0	0	0	0.0	0	0	0	0.0	0	4	50	12.5	0	0	0	0	0
2003—Oakland NFL		16	2	6	37	6.2	0	7	106	15.1	1	4	48	12.0	0	1	0	6	0
Pro totals (6 years)		82	6	11	63	5.7	0	24	321	13.4	4	20	352	17.6	1	6	0	36	1

WHITTLE, JASON — G — BUCCANEERS

PERSONAL: Born March 7, 1975, in Springfield, Mo. ... 6-4/305.

HIGH SCHOOL: Camdenton (Mo.).

COLLEGE: Southwest Missouri State.

TRANSACTIONS/CAREER NOTES: Signed as non-drafted free agent by New York Giants (April 24, 1998). ... Released by Giants (August 30, 1998). ... Re-signed by Giants to practice squad (September 1, 1998). ... Activated (December 16, 1998). ... Granted free agency (March 1, 2002). ... Re-signed by Giants (April 24, 2002). ... Granted unconditional free agency (February 28, 2003). ... Signed by Tampa Bay Buccaneers (March 7, 2003).

PLAYING EXPERIENCE: New York Giants NFL, 1998-2002; Tampa Bay NFL, 2003. ... Games/Games started: 1998 (1/0), 1999 (16/1), 2000 (16/2), 2001 (16/2), 2002 (14/14), 2003 (16/5). Total: 79/24.

CHAMPIONSHIP GAME EXPERIENCE: Played in NFC championship game (2000 season). ... Played in Super Bowl 35 (2000 season).

WIEGERT, ZACH — T — TEXANS

PERSONAL: Born August 16, 1972, in Fremont, Neb. ... 6-5/309. ... Full name: Zach Allen Wiegert. ... Name pronounced: WEE-gert.

HIGH SCHOOL: Fremont (Neb.) Bergan.

COLLEGE: Nebraska.

TRANSACTIONS/CAREER NOTES: Selected by St. Louis Rams in second round (38th pick overall) of 1995 NFL draft. ... Signed by Rams (July 18, 1995). ... Granted free agency (February 13, 1998). ... Re-signed by Rams (June 17, 1998). ... Designated by Rams as transition player (February 12, 1999). ... Re-signed by Rams (March 24, 1999). ... Released by Rams (April 28, 1999). ... Signed by Jacksonville Jaguars (May 5, 1999). ... On injured reserve with knee injury (October 25, 2000-remainder of season). ... On injured reserve with knee injury (November 6, 2002-remainder of season). ... Granted unconditional free agency (February 28, 2003). ... Signed by Houston Texans (March 1, 2003).

PLAYING EXPERIENCE: St. Louis NFL, 1995-1998; Jacksonville NFL, 1999-2002; Houston NFL, 2003. ... Games/Games started: 1995 (5/2), 1996 (16/16), 1997 (15/15), 1998 (13/13), 1999 (16/12), 2000 (8/8), 2001 (16/16), 2002 (7/7), 2003 (15/14). Total: 111/103.

CHAMPIONSHIP GAME EXPERIENCE: Played in AFC championship game (1999 season).

HONORS: Outland Trophy Award winner (1994). ... Named offensive lineman on THE SPORTING NEWS college All-America first team (1994).

WIEGMANN, CASEY — C — CHIEFS

PERSONAL: Born July 20, 1973, in Parkersburg, Iowa. ... 6-2/285. ... Name pronounced: WEG-man.

HIGH SCHOOL: Parkersburg (Iowa).

COLLEGE: Iowa.

TRANSACTIONS/CAREER NOTES: Signed as non-drafted free agent by Indianapolis Colts (April 26, 1996). ... Released by Colts (August 25, 1996). ... Re-signed by Colts to practice squad (August 27, 1996). ... Activated (September 10, 1996); did not play. ... Released by Colts (September 22, 1996). ... Re-signed by Colts to practice squad (September 23, 1996). ... Activated (October 15, 1996); did not play. ... Claimed on waivers by New York Jets (October 29, 1996). ... Released by Jets (September 21, 1997). ... Signed by Chicago Bears (September 24, 1997). ... Granted free agency (February 12, 1999). ... Tendered offer sheet by Miami Dolphins (April 5, 1999). ... Offer matched by Bears (April 8, 1999). ... Granted unconditional free agency (March 2, 2001). ... Signed by Kansas City Chiefs (March 15, 2001).

PLAYING EXPERIENCE: Indianapolis NFL, 1996; New York Jets NFL, 1997; Chicago NFL, 1997-2000; Kansas City NFL, 2001-2003. ... Games/Games started: 1997 (1/0), 1998 (16/15), 1999 (16/0), 2000 (16/10), 2001 (15/15), 2002 (16/16), 2003 (16/16), Total: 96/72.

WIGGINS, JERMAINE — TE — VIKINGS

PERSONAL: Born January 18, 1975, in East Boston, Mass. ... 6-2/255.

HIGH SCHOOL: East Boston.

COLLEGE: Georgia.

TRANSACTIONS/CAREER NOTES: Signed by New York Jets as non-drafted free agent (April 19, 1999). ... Released by Jets (August 23, 1999). ... Re-signed by Jets to practice squad (August 28, 1999). ... Claimed on waivers by New England Patriots (November 28, 2000). ... Released by Patriots (May 2, 2002). ... Signed by Indianapolis Colts (May 14, 2002). ... Released by Colts (September 24, 2002). ... Signed by Carolina Panthers (October 8, 2002). ... Granted free agency (February 28, 2003). ... Re-signed by Panthers (May 2, 2003). ... Granted unconditional free agency (March 3, 2004). ... Signed by Minnesota Vikings (March 19, 2004).

CHAMPIONSHIP GAME EXPERIENCE: Played in AFC championship game (2001 and 2003 seasons). ... Member of Super Bowl championship team (2001 and 2003 seasons).

SINGLE GAME HIGHS (regular season): Receptions—5 (December 4, 2000, vs. Kansas City); yards—81 (December 24, 2000, vs. Miami); and touchdown receptions—1 (December 7, 2003, vs. Atlanta).

Year	Team	G	GS	RECEIVING No.	Yds.	Avg.	TD	TOTALS TD	2pt.	Pts.	Fum.
2000—New York Jets NFL		11	0	2	4	2.0	1	1	0	6	0
—New England NFL		4	2	16	203	12.7	1	1	0	6	1
2001—New England NFL		16	6	14	133	9.5	4	4	0	24	0
2002—Indianapolis NFL		3	0	2	17	8.5	0	0	0	0	1
—Carolina NFL		11	1	8	45	5.6	1	1	0	6	0
2003—Carolina NFL		16	11	8	80	10.0	1	1	0	6	0
Pro totals (4 years)		61	20	50	482	9.6	8	8	0	48	2

W

WILCOX, DANIEL — TE

PERSONAL: Born March 23, 1977, in Atlanta, Ga. ... 6-1/229.
HIGH SCHOOL: Decatur (Ga.).
JUNIOR COLLEGE: Georgia Military College.
COLLEGE: Appalachian State.
TRANSACTIONS/CAREER NOTES: Signed as non-drafted free agent by New York Jets (April 26, 2001). ... Released by Jets (August 2, 2001). ... Re-signed by Jets (August 20, 2001). ... Released by Jets (September 2, 2001). ... Re-signed by Jets to practice squad (September 3, 2001). ... Activated (September 19, 2001); did not play. ... Released by Jets (October 10, 2001). ... Re-signed by Jets to practice squad (October 11, 2001). ... Activated (November 15, 2001). ... Released by Jets (August 28, 2002). ... Re-signed by Jets to practice squad (September 2, 2002). ... Signed off Jets practice squad by Tampa Bay Buccaneers (December 18, 2002). ... Released by Buccaneers (August 24, 2003). ... Re-signed by Buccaneers (September 5, 2003). ... Released by Buccaneers (September 16, 2003).
CHAMPIONSHIP GAME EXPERIENCE: Member of Buccaneers for NFC championship game (2002 season); inactive. ... Member of Super Bowl championship team (2002 season); inactive.

			RECEIVING				TOTALS			
Year Team	G	GS	No.	Yds.	Avg.	TD	TD	2pt.	Pts.	Fum.
2001—New York Jets NFL	1	0	0	0	0.0	0	0	0	0	0
2003—Tampa Bay NFL	2	0	0	0	0.0	0	0	0	0	0
Pro totals (2 years)	3	0	0	0	0.0	0	0	0	0	0

WILEY, CHUCK — DE — VIKINGS

PERSONAL: Born March 6, 1975, in Baton Rouge, La. ... 6-5/275. ... Full name: Samuel Charles Wiley Jr.
HIGH SCHOOL: Southern University Lab (Baton Rouge, La.).
COLLEGE: Louisiana State.
TRANSACTIONS/CAREER NOTES: Selected by Carolina Panthers in third round (62nd pick overall) of 1998 NFL draft. ... Signed by Panthers (June 10, 1998). ... On injured reserve with heel injury (August 30, 1998-entire season). ... Claimed on waivers Atlanta Falcons (August 28, 2000). ... Granted unconditional free agency (March 1, 2002). ... Signed by Minnesota Vikings (May 2, 2002).

			TOTALS			INTERCEPTIONS			
Year Team	G	GS	Tk.	Ast.	Sks.	No.	Yds.	Avg.	TD
1998—Carolina NFL	Did not play.								
1999—Carolina NFL	16	16	32	4	0.0	0	0	0.0	0
2000—Atlanta NFL	16	0	25	14	4.0	0	0	0.0	0
2001—Atlanta NFL	16	1	12	5	1.0	1	1	1.0	0
2002—Minnesota NFL	16	0	7	3	0.0	0	0	0.0	0
2003—Minnesota NFL	7	4	5	0	1.0	0	0	0.0	0
Pro totals (5 years)	71	21	81	26	6.0	1	1	1.0	0

WILEY, MARCELLUS — DE — COWBOYS

PERSONAL: Born November 30, 1974, in Compton, Calif. ... 6-4/275. ... Full name: Marcellus Vernon Wiley.
HIGH SCHOOL: Santa Monica (Calif.).
COLLEGE: Columbia.
TRANSACTIONS/CAREER NOTES: Selected by Buffalo Bills in second round (52nd pick overall) of 1997 NFL draft. ... Signed by Bills (June 20, 1997). ... Granted unconditional free agency (March 2, 2001). ... Signed by San Diego Chargers (March 6, 2001). ... Released by Chargers (March 2, 2004). ... Signed by Cowboys (March 11, 2004).
HONORS: Played in Pro Bowl (2001 season).

			TOTALS			INTERCEPTIONS			
Year Team	G	GS	Tk.	Ast.	Sks.	No.	Yds.	Avg.	TD
1997—Buffalo NFL	16	0	12	4	0.0	0	0	0.0	0
1998—Buffalo NFL	16	3	17	7	3.5	0	0	0.0	0
1999—Buffalo NFL	16	1	18	8	5.0	1	52	52.0	0
2000—Buffalo NFL	16	15	40	25	10.5	0	0	0.0	0
2001—San Diego NFL	14	14	38	10	13.0	0	0	0.0	0
2002—San Diego NFL	14	14	31	5	6.0	1	40	40.0	0
2003—San Diego NFL	16	16	38	13	3.0	0	0	0.0	0
Pro totals (7 years)	108	63	194	72	41.0	2	92	46.0	0

WILHELM, MATT — LB — CHARGERS

PERSONAL: Born February 2, 1981, in Oberlin, Ohio. ... 6-4/245.
HIGH SCHOOL: Elryia Catholic (Lorain, Ohio).
COLLEGE: Ohio State.
TRANSACTIONS/CAREER NOTES: Selected by San Diego Chargers in fourth round (112th pick overall) of 2003 NFL draft. ... Signed by Chargers (July 19, 2003).

			TOTALS			INTERCEPTIONS			
Year Team	G	GS	Tk.	Ast.	Sks.	No.	Yds.	Avg.	TD
2003—San Diego NFL	2	0	0	0	0.0	0	0	0.0	0

W

WILKERSON, JIMMY — DE — CHIEFS

PERSONAL: Born January 4, 1981, in Omaha, Texas. ... 6-2/271.
HIGH SCHOOL: Paul H. Pewitt (Omaha, Texas).
COLLEGE: Oklahoma.

TRANSACTIONS/CAREER NOTES: Selected after junior season by Kansas City Chiefs in sixth round (189th pick overall) of 2003 NFL draft. ... Signed by Kansas City Chiefs (July 14, 2003).

Year Team	G	GS	TOTALS Tk.	Ast.	Sks.
2003—Kansas City NFL	12	0	6	3	0.0

WILKINS, JEFF — K — RAMS

PERSONAL: Born April 19, 1972, in Youngstown, Ohio. ... 6-2/205. ... Full name: Jeff Allen Wilkins.
HIGH SCHOOL: Austintown Fitch (Youngstown, Ohio).
COLLEGE: Youngstown State.
TRANSACTIONS/CAREER NOTES: Signed as non-drafted free agent by Dallas Cowboys (April 28, 1994). ... Released by Cowboys (July 18, 1994). ... Signed by Philadelphia Eagles (November 14, 1994). ... Released by Eagles (August 14, 1995). ... Signed by San Francisco 49ers (November 8, 1995). ... Granted unconditional free agency (February 14, 1997). ... Signed by St. Louis Rams (March 6, 1997). ... Granted unconditional free agency (March 2, 2001). ... Re-signed by Rams (March 2, 2001).
CHAMPIONSHIP GAME EXPERIENCE: Played in NFC championship game (1999 and 2001 seasons). ... Member of Super Bowl championship team (1999 season). ... Played in Super Bowl 36 (2001 season).
HONORS: Played in Pro Bowl (2003 season).
RECORDS: Holds NFL single-season record for most PATs without a miss—64 (1999). ... Shares NFL single-season record for highest field-goal percentage—100.0 (2000). ... Shares NFL single-season record for most field goals made—39 (2003). ... Shares NFL record for most field goals made, one quarter (4), vs. Baltimore (November 9, 2003, fourth quarter).
POST SEASON RECORDS: Shares NFL postseason single-game records for most field goals made—5; and most field goals attempted—6 (January 10, 2004, vs. Carolina).

Year Team	G	FIELD GOALS 1-29	30-39	40-49	50+	Tot.	Pct.	Lg.	TOTALS XPM	XPA	Pts.
1994—Philadelphia NFL	6	0-0	0-0	0-0	0-0	0-0	0.0	0	0	0	0
1995—San Francisco NFL	7	6-6	5-5	1-2	0-0	12-13	92.3	40	27	29	63
1996—San Francisco NFL	16	16-16	7-8	7-10	0-0	30-34	88.2	49	40	40	130
1997—St. Louis NFL	16	8-9	8-12	7-14	2-2	25-∞37	67.6	52	32	32	107
1998—St. Louis NFL	16	4-5	8-8	5-7	3-6	20-26	76.9	‡57	25	26	§85
1999—St. Louis NFL	16	6-6	6-7	7-11	1-4	20-28	71.4	51	*64	*64	‡124
2000—St. Louis NFL	11	7-7	6-6	3-3	1-1	17-17	*100.0	51	38	38	89
2001—St. Louis NFL	16	11-11	5-5	6-12	1-1	23-29	79.3	54	*58	*58	127
2002—St. Louis NFL	16	5-5	8-10	6-9	0-1	19-25	76.0	47	37	37	94
2003—St. Louis NFL	16	16-16	11-13	8-9	4-4	*39-*42	92.9	53	46	46	*163
Pro totals (10 years)	136	79-81	64-74	50-77	12-19	205-251	81.7	57	367	370	982

WILKINS, MARCUS — LB — PACKERS

PERSONAL: Born January 2, 1980, in Austin, Texas. ... 6-2/235. ... Full name: Marcus Wesley Wilkins.
HIGH SCHOOL: Westwood (Austin, Texas).
COLLEGE: Texas.
TRANSACTIONS/CAREER NOTES: Signed as non-drafted free agent by Green Bay Packers (April 25, 2002). ... On injured reserve with calf injury (January 11, 2004-remainder of 2003 season). ... Granted free agency (March 3, 2004). ... Re-signed by Packers (March 11, 2004).

Year Team	G	GS	TOTALS Tk.	Ast.	Sks.	INTERCEPTIONS No.	Yds.	Avg.	TD
2002—Green Bay NFL	5	0	1	1	0.0	0	0	0.0	0
2003—Green Bay NFL	7	0	0	0	0.0	0	0	0.0	0
Pro totals (2 years)	12	0	1	1	0.0	0	0	0.0	0

WILKINS, TERRENCE — WR — DOLPHINS

PERSONAL: Born July 29, 1975, in Washington, DC. ... 5-10/180. ... Full name: Terrence Olondo Wilkins.
HIGH SCHOOL: Bishop Denis J O'Connell (Arlington, Va.).
COLLEGE: Virginia.
TRANSACTIONS/CAREER NOTES: Signed as non-drafted free agent by Indianapolis Colts (April 22, 1999). ... Granted free agency (March 1, 2002). ... Re-signed by Colts (April 15, 2002). ... Traded by Colts to St. Louis Rams for undisclosed draft pick (April 15, 2002). ... Released by Rams (July 22, 2003). ... Signed by Carolina Panthers (July 28, 2003). ... Waived by Panthers (August 30, 2003). ... Signed by Indianapolis Colts (November 10, 2003). ... Granted unconditional free agency (March 3, 2004). ... Signed by Miami Dolphins (March 16, 2004).
CHAMPIONSHIP GAME EXPERIENCE: Member of Colts for AFC championship game (2003 season); inactive.
SINGLE GAME HIGHS (regular season): Receptions—9 (September 25, 2000, vs. Jacksonville); yards—148 (September 25, 2000, vs. Jacksonville); and touchdown receptions—1 (December 3, 2000, vs. New York Jets).
STATISTICAL PLATEAUS: 100-yard receiving games: 1999 (1), 2000 (2). Total: 3.

Year Team	G	GS	RUSHING Att.	Yds.	Avg.	TD	RECEIVING No.	Yds.	Avg.	TD	PUNT RETURNS No.	Yds.	Avg.	TD	KICKOFF RETURNS No.	Yds.	Avg.	TD	TOTALS TD	2pt.	Pts.
1999—Ind. NFL	16	11	1	2	2.0	0	42	565	13.5	4	41	388	9.5	1	51	1134	22.2	▲1	7	0	42
2000—Ind. NFL	14	7	3	8	2.7	0	43	569	13.2	3	29	240	8.3	0	15	279	18.6	0	3	0	18
2001—Ind. NFL	11	4	0	0	0.0	0	34	332	9.8	0	21	219	10.4	1	44	1007	22.9	0	1	0	6
2002—StL. NFL	13	0	6	56	9.3	0	5	31	6.2	0	25	242	9.7	0	47	1074	22.9	0	0	0	0
2003—Ind. NFL	3	0	0	0	0.0	0	0	0	0.0	0	7	25	3.6	0	14	325	23.2	0	0	0	0
Pro totals (5 years)	57	22	10	66	6.6	0	124	1497	12.1	7	123	1114	9.1	2	171	3819	22.3	1	11	0	66

W

WILKINSON, DAN — DT — LIONS

PERSONAL: Born March 13, 1973, in Dayton, Ohio. ... 6-4/353.
HIGH SCHOOL: Paul L. Dunbar (Dayton, Ohio).
COLLEGE: Ohio State.

TRANSACTIONS/CAREER NOTES: Selected after sophomore season by Cincinnati Bengals in first round (first pick overall) of 1994 NFL draft. ... Signed by Bengals (May 5, 1994). ... Designated by Bengals as franchise player (February 11, 1998). ... Tendered offer sheet by Washington Redskins (February 25, 1998). ... Bengals declined to match offer (February 26, 1998); Bengals received first-(LB Brian Simmons) and third-round (G Mike Goff) picks as compensation. ... On injured reserve with calf injury (December 5, 2002-remainder of season). ... Released by Redskins (July 29, 2003). ... Signed by Detroit Lions (August 17, 2003).

HONORS: Named defensive lineman on THE SPORTING NEWS college All-America first team (1993).

			TOTALS			INTERCEPTIONS			
Year Team	**G**	**GS**	**Tk.**	**Ast.**	**Sks.**	**No.**	**Yds.**	**Avg.**	**TD**
1994—Cincinnati NFL	16	14	37	7	5.5	0	0	0.0	0
1995—Cincinnati NFL	14	14	30	10	8.0	0	0	0.0	0
1996—Cincinnati NFL	16	16	37	7	6.5	1	7	7.0	0
1997—Cincinnati NFL	15	15	24	10	5.0	0	0	0.0	0
1998—Washington NFL	16	16	38	7	7.5	1	4	4.0	0
1999—Washington NFL	16	16	23	9	8.0	1	88	88.0	1
2000—Washington NFL	16	16	15	5	3.5	0	0	0.0	0
2001—Washington NFL	16	16	19	6	4.0	2	0	0.0	0
2002—Washington NFL	12	11	12	4	0.0	0	0	0.0	0
2003—Detroit NFL	16	16	18	7	2.0	0	0	0.0	0
Pro totals (10 years)	153	150	253	72	50.0	5	99	19.8	1

WILLIAMS, AENEAS — S — RAMS

PERSONAL: Born January 29, 1968, in New Orleans, La. ... 5-11/200. ... Full name: Aeneas Demetrius Williams. ... Name pronounced: uh-NEE-us.

HIGH SCHOOL: Fortier (New Orleans).

COLLEGE: Southern University.

TRANSACTIONS/CAREER NOTES: Selected by Phoenix Cardinals in third round (59th pick overall) of 1991 NFL draft. ... Signed by Cardinals (July 26, 1991). ... Granted free agency (February 17, 1994). ... Cardinals franchise renamed Arizona Cardinals for 1994 season. ... Re-signed by Cardinals (June 1, 1994). ... Granted unconditional free agency (February 16, 1996). ... Re-signed by Cardinals (February 27, 1996). ... Designated by Cardinals as franchise player (February 22, 2001). ... Re-signed by Cardinals (April 21, 2001). ... Traded by Cardinals to St. Louis Rams for second- (DB Michael Stone) and fourth-round (DT Marcus Bell) picks in 2001 draft (April 21, 2001). ... On injured reserve with broken ankle (October 21, 2002-remainder of season). ... Released by Rams (February 27, 2003). ... Re-signed by Rams (March 1, 2003).

CHAMPIONSHIP GAME EXPERIENCE: Played in NFC championship game (2001 season). ... Played in Super Bowl 36 (2001 season).

HONORS: Named cornerback on THE SPORTING NEWS NFL All-Pro team (1995, 1997 and 2001). ... Played in Pro Bowl (1994-1999, 2001 and 2003 seasons).

RECORDS: Shares NFL record for longest fumble recovery return for touchdown—104 yards (November 5, 2000, vs. Washington).

POST SEASON RECORDS: Shares NFL single-game postseason record for most interceptions returned for touchdown—2 (January 20, 2002, vs. Green Bay). ... Holds NFL postseason record for most consecutive games with an interception—4 (1998-2001).

			TOTALS			INTERCEPTIONS			
Year Team	**G**	**GS**	**Tk.**	**Ast.**	**Sks.**	**No.**	**Yds.**	**Avg.**	**TD**
1991—Phoenix NFL	16	15	38	10	0.0	∞6	60	10.0	0
1992—Phoenix NFL	16	16	40	8	0.0	3	25	8.3	0
1993—Phoenix NFL	16	16	37	5	0.0	2	87	43.5	1
1994—Arizona NFL	16	16	40	1	0.0	†9	89	9.9	0
1995—Arizona NFL	16	16	52	10	0.0	6	86	14.3	†2
1996—Arizona NFL	16	16	65	12	1.0	6	89	14.8	1
1997—Arizona NFL	16	16	49	14	0.0	6	95	15.8	∞2
1998—Arizona NFL	16	16	57	13	1.0	1	15	15.0	0
1999—Arizona NFL	16	16	49	7	0.0	2	5	2.5	0
2000—Arizona NFL	16	16	48	14	0.0	5	102	20.4	0
2001—St. Louis NFL	16	16	56	17	0.0	4	69	17.3	†2
2002—St. Louis NFL	6	6	23	6	0.0	1	3	3.0	0
2003—St. Louis NFL	16	16	60	15	1.0	4	82	20.5	1
Pro totals (13 years)	198	197	614	132	3.0	55	807	14.7	9

WILLIAMS, ANDREW — DE — 49ERS

PERSONAL: Born April 18, 1979, in Tampa, Fla. ... 6-2/263. ... Full name: Andrew B. Williams.

HIGH SCHOOL: Hillsborough (Tampa, Fla.).

JUNIOR COLLEGE: Hinds Community College (Miss.).

COLLEGE: Miami (Fla.).

TRANSACTIONS/CAREER NOTES: Selected by San Francisco 49ers in third round (89th pick overall) of 2003 NFL draft. ... Signed by 49ers (July 24, 2003).

			TOTALS		
Year Team	**G**	**GS**	**Tk.**	**Ast.**	**Sks.**
2003—San Francisco NFL	2	0	1	0	0.0

WILLIAMS, BOBBIE — G — BENGALS

PERSONAL: Born September 25, 1976, in Jefferson, Texas. ... 6-3/320.

HIGH SCHOOL: Jefferson (Texas).

COLLEGE: Arkansas.

TRANSACTIONS/CAREER NOTES: Selected by Philadelphia Eagles in second round (61st pick overall) of 2000 NFL draft. ... Signed by Eagles (July 17, 2000). ... Inactive for 16 games (2000). ... Granted unconditional free agency (March 3, 2004). ... Signed by Cincinnati Bengals (March 26, 2004).

PLAYING EXPERIENCE: Philadelphia NFL, 2000-2003. ... Games/Games started: 2001 (1/1), 2002 (16/0), 2003 (16/11), Total: 33/12.

CHAMPIONSHIP GAME EXPERIENCE: Member of Eagles for NFC championship game (2001 season); inactive. ... Played in NFC championship game (2002 and 2003 seasons).

WILLIAMS, BOO TE SAINTS

PERSONAL: Born June 22, 1979, in Tallahassee, Fla. ... 6-4/270. ... Full name: Eddie Lee Williams.
HIGH SCHOOL: Lincoln (Tallahassee, Fla.).
JUNIOR COLLEGE: Coffeyville (Kan.) Community College.
COLLEGE: Arkansas.
TRANSACTIONS/CAREER NOTES: Signed as non-drafted free agent by New Orleans Saints (April 26, 2000). ... Released by Saints (September 2, 2001). ... Re-signed by Saints to practice squad (September 3, 2001). ... Activated (October 27, 2001).
SINGLE GAME HIGHS (regular season): Receptions—9 (November 23, 2003, vs. Philadelphia); yards—110 (November 23, 2003, vs. Philadelphia); and touchdown receptions—2 (November 18, 2001, vs. Indianapolis).
STATISTICAL PLATEAUS: 100-yard receiving games: 2003 (1). Total: 1.

			RECEIVING				TOTALS			
Year Team	G	GS	No.	Yds.	Avg.	TD	TD	2pt.	Pts.	Fum.
2001—New Orleans NFL	11	4	20	202	10.1	3	3	0	18	0
2002—New Orleans NFL	16	3	13	143	11.0	2	2	1	14	0
2003—New Orleans NFL	16	6	41	436	10.6	5	5	0	30	0
Pro totals (3 years)	43	13	74	781	10.6	10	10	1	62	0

WILLIAMS, BRIAN CB VIKINGS

PERSONAL: Born July 2, 1979, in High Point, N.C. ... 5-11/198.
HIGH SCHOOL: Southwest Guilford (N.C.).
COLLEGE: North Carolina State.
TRANSACTIONS/CAREER NOTES: Selected by Minnesota Vikings in fourth round (105th pick overall) of 2002 NFL draft. ... Signed by Vikings (July 24, 2002).

			TOTALS			INTERCEPTIONS			
Year Team	G	GS	Tk.	Ast.	Sks.	No.	Yds.	Avg.	TD
2002—Minnesota NFL	16	7	32	5	0.0	1	2	2.0	0
2003—Minnesota NFL	16	16	54	16	3.0	5	†205	41.0	1
Pro totals (2 years)	32	23	86	21	3.0	6	207	34.5	1

WILLIAMS, BROCK CB BEARS

PERSONAL: Born August 11, 1979, in Hammond, La. ... 5-10/195.
HIGH SCHOOL: Hammond (La.).
COLLEGE: Notre Dame.
TRANSACTIONS/CAREER NOTES: Selected by New England Patriots in third round (86th pick overall) of 2001 NFL draft. ... Signed by Patriots (September 10, 2001). ... On injured reserve with knee injury (September 10, 2001-remainder of season). ... Released by Patriots (September 1, 2002). ... Re-signed by Patriots to practice squad (September 3, 2002). ... Released by Patriots (October 18, 2002). ... Signed by Oakland Raiders to practice squad (October 23, 2002). ... Waived by Raiders (August 26, 2003). ... Signed by Chicago Bears (August 27, 2003).

			TOTALS			INTERCEPTIONS			
Year Team	G	GS	Tk.	Ast.	Sks.	No.	Yds.	Avg.	TD
2003—Chicago NFL	10	0	2	0	0.0	0	0	0.0	0

WILLIAMS, CHAD S RAVENS

PERSONAL: Born January 22, 1979, in Birmingham, Ala. ... 5-9/207.
HIGH SCHOOL: Wenonah (Birmingham, Ala.).
COLLEGE: Southern Mississippi.
TRANSACTIONS/CAREER NOTES: Selected by Baltimore Ravens in sixth round (209th pick overall) of 2002 NFL draft. ... Signed by Ravens (July 25, 2002).

			TOTALS			INTERCEPTIONS			
Year Team	G	GS	Tk.	Ast.	Sks.	No.	Yds.	Avg.	TD
2002—Baltimore NFL	16	0	29	3	0.0	3	98	32.7	1
2003—Baltimore NFL	16	1	20	4	1.0	1	52	52.0	1
Pro totals (2 years)	32	1	49	7	1.0	4	150	37.5	2

WILLIAMS, GRANT T RAMS

PERSONAL: Born May 10, 1974, in Hattiesburg, Miss. ... 6-7/320.
HIGH SCHOOL: Clinton (Miss.).
JUNIOR COLLEGE: Hinds Community College (Miss.).
COLLEGE: Louisiana Tech.
TRANSACTIONS/CAREER NOTES: Signed as non-drafted free agent by Seattle Seahawks (April 22, 1996). ... Granted unconditional free agency (February 11, 2000). ... Signed by New England Patriots (March 17, 2000). ... Granted unconditional free agency (March 1, 2002). ... Re-signed by Patriots (April 19, 2002). ... Traded by Patriots to St. Louis Rams for seventh-round pick (traded to Tennessee) in 2003 draft (August 19, 2002). ... On injured reserve with ankle injury (October 15, 2002-remainder of season). ... Granted unconditional free agency (February 28, 2003). ... Re-signed by Rams (April 16, 2003).

PLAYING EXPERIENCE: Seattle NFL, 1996-1999; New England NFL, 2000-2001; St. Louis NFL, 2002-2003. ... Games/Games started: 1996 (8/0), 1997 (16/8), 1998 (16/0), 1999 (16/15), 2000 (15/8), 2001 (14/4), 2002 (5/3), 2003 (16/0). Total: 106/38.
CHAMPIONSHIP GAME EXPERIENCE: Played in AFC championship game (2001 season). ... Member of Super Bowl championship team (2001 season).

WILLIAMS, JAMAL — DT — CHARGERS

PERSONAL: Born April 28, 1976, in Washington, D.C. ... 6-3/305.
HIGH SCHOOL: Archbishop Carroll (Washington, D.C.).
COLLEGE: Oklahoma State.
TRANSACTIONS/CAREER NOTES: Selected by San Diego Chargers in second round of 1998 supplemental draft (July 9, 1998). ... Signed by Chargers (August 7, 1998). ... Granted free agency (March 2, 2001). ... Re-signed by Chargers (May 11, 2001). ... On injured reserve with knee injury (October 3, 2001-remainder of season). ... On injured reserve with ankle injury (December 2, 2002-remainder of season).

			TOTALS			INTERCEPTIONS			
Year Team	**G**	**GS**	**Tk.**	**Ast.**	**Sks.**	**No.**	**Yds.**	**Avg.**	**TD**
1998—San Diego NFL	9	0	5	1	0.0	1	14	14.0	1
1999—San Diego NFL	16	2	22	4	1.0	0	0	0.0	0
2000—San Diego NFL	16	16	46	7	1.0	0	0	0.0	0
2001—San Diego NFL	3	3	2	0	0.0	0	0	0.0	0
2002—San Diego NFL	12	10	20	4	2.5	0	0	0.0	0
2003—San Diego NFL	15	15	24	9	1.0	0	0	0.0	0
Pro totals (6 years)	71	46	119	25	5.5	1	14	14.0	1

WILLIAMS, JAMES — WR

PERSONAL: Born March 6, 1978, in Vicksburg, Miss. ... 5-10/186. ... Full name: James L. Williams.
HIGH SCHOOL: Warren Central (Vicksburg, Miss.).
JUNIOR COLLEGE: Hinds Community College (Miss.).
COLLEGE: Marshall.
TRANSACTIONS/CAREER NOTES: Selected by Seattle Seahawks in sixth round (175th pick overall) of 2000 NFL draft. ... Signed by Seahawks (June 22, 2000). ... Granted free agency (February 28, 2003). ... Re-signed by Seahawks (April 2, 2003). ... Released by Seahawks (August 25, 2003). ... Signed by Detroit Lions (December 2, 2003). ... Released by Lions (May 7, 2004).
SINGLE GAME HIGHS (regular season): Receptions—4 (December 30, 2001, vs. San Diego); yards—101 (December 30, 2001, vs. San Diego); and touchdown receptions—1 (December 30, 2001, vs. San Diego).
STATISTICAL PLATEAUS: 100-yard receiving games: 2001 (1). Total: 1.

			RECEIVING				KICKOFF RETURNS				TOTALS			
Year Team	**G**	**GS**	**No.**	**Yds.**	**Avg.**	**TD**	**No.**	**Yds.**	**Avg.**	**TD**	**TD**	**2pt.**	**Pts.**	**Fum.**
2000—Seattle NFL	10	0	8	99	12.4	0	3	76	25.3	0	0	0	2	0
2001—Seattle NFL	6	2	12	212	17.7	1	9	175	19.4	0	1	0	6	1
2002—Seattle NFL	13	2	9	99	11.0	0	21	354	16.9	0	0	0	0	0
2003—Detroit NFL	1	0	0	0	0.0	0	0	0	0.0	0	0	0	0	0
Pro totals (4 years)	30	4	29	410	14.1	1	33	605	18.3	0	1	0	8	1

WILLIAMS, JAY — DE — DOLPHINS

PERSONAL: Born October 13, 1971, in Washington, DC. ... 6-3/275. ... Full name: Jay Omar Williams.
HIGH SCHOOL: St. John's (Washington, D.C.).
COLLEGE: Wake Forest.
TRANSACTIONS/CAREER NOTES: Signed as non-drafted free agent by Miami Dolphins (April 28, 1994). ... Released by Dolphins (August 28, 1994). ... Signed by Los Angeles Rams to practice squad (September 27, 1994). ... Activated (December 7, 1994); did not play. ... Rams franchise moved from Los Angeles to St. Louis (April 12, 1995). ... On physically unable to perform list with forearm injury (July 31-November 18, 1996). ... Released by Rams (November 20, 1996). ... Re-signed by Rams (December 11, 1996). ... Granted free agency (February 12, 1999). ... Re-signed by Rams (May 4, 1999). ... Granted unconditional free agency (February 11, 2000). ... Signed by Carolina Panthers (February 16, 2000). ... Traded by Panthers to Miami Dolphins for DE Al Wallace and fourth-round pick (DB Colin Branch) in 2003 draft (July 19, 2002).
CHAMPIONSHIP GAME EXPERIENCE: Played in NFC championship game (1999 season). ... Member of Super Bowl championship team (1999 season).

			TOTALS			INTERCEPTIONS			
Year Team	**G**	**GS**	**Tk.**	**Ast.**	**Sks.**	**No.**	**Yds.**	**Avg.**	**TD**
1994—Los Angeles Rams NFL			Did not play.						
1995—St. Louis NFL	7	0	0	0	0.0	0	0	0.0	0
1996—St. Louis NFL	2	0	0	0	0.0	0	0	0.0	0
1997—St. Louis NFL	16	2	4	3	1.0	0	0	0.0	0
1998—St. Louis NFL	16	1	10	4	1.0	0	0	0.0	0
1999—St. Louis NFL	16	0	13	1	4.0	0	0	0.0	0
2000—Carolina NFL	16	14	21	6	6.0	0	0	0.0	0
2001—Carolina NFL	16	13	27	12	1.0	1	0	0.0	0
2002—Miami NFL	16	0	17	5	6.0	0	0	0.0	0
2003—Miami NFL	16	0	8	4	2.5	0	0	0.0	0
Pro totals (9 years)	121	30	100	35	21.5	1	0	0.0	0

WILLIAMS, JIMMY — CB — 49ERS

PERSONAL: Born March 10, 1979, in Baton Rouge, La. ... 5-11/190.
HIGH SCHOOL: Episcopal (Baton Rouge, La.).
COLLEGE: Vanderbilt.

TRANSACTIONS/CAREER NOTES: Selected by Buffalo Bills in sixth round (196th pick overall) of 2001 NFL draft. ... Signed by Bills (June 13, 2001). ... Released by Bills (September 2, 2001). ... Signed by San Francisco 49ers to practice squad (September 5, 2001). ... Activated (October 16, 2001). ... On injured reserve with knee injury (December 10, 2002-remainder of season). ... Granted free agency (March 3, 2004). ... Re-signed by 49ers (March 30, 2004).

			TOTALS			INTERCEPTIONS				PUNT RETURNS				KICKOFF RETURNS				TOTALS			
Year Team	G	GS	Tk.	Ast.	Sks.	No.	Yds.	Avg.	TD	No.	Yds.	Avg.	TD	No.	Yds.	Avg.	TD	TD	2pt.	Pts.	Fum.
2001—S.F. NFL	10	0	0	0	0.0	0	0	0.0	0	0	0	0.0	0	0	0	0.0	0	0	0	0	0
2002—S.F. NFL	13	0	0	0	0.0	0	0	0.0	0	20	336	*16.8	1	35	765	21.9	0	1	0	6	2
2003—S.F. NFL	15	0	9	1	0.0	1	6	6.0	0	35	240	6.9	0	11	207	18.8	0	0	0	0	3
Pro totals (3 years)	38	0	9	1	0.0	1	6	6.0	0	55	576	10.5	1	46	972	21.1	0	1	0	6	5

WILLIAMS, JOSH — DT — COLTS

PERSONAL: Born August 9, 1976, in Denver, Colo. ... 6-3/290. ... Full name: Josh Sinclair Williams.
HIGH SCHOOL: Cypress Creek (Houston).
COLLEGE: Michigan.
TRANSACTIONS/CAREER NOTES: Selected by Indianapolis Colts in fourth round (122nd pick overall) of 2000 NFL draft. ... Signed by Colts (June 27, 2000). ... Granted free agency (February 28, 2003). ... Re-signed by Colts (April 15, 2003).
CHAMPIONSHIP GAME EXPERIENCE: Played in AFC championship game (2003 season).

			TOTALS		
Year Team	G	GS	Tk.	Ast.	Sks.
2000—Indianapolis NFL	14	7	26	16	3.0
2001—Indianapolis NFL	16	16	30	19	3.0
2002—Indianapolis NFL	7	3	10	4	1.0
2003—Indianapolis NFL	16	4	13	4	1.0
Pro totals (4 years)	53	30	79	43	8.0

WILLIAMS, KARL — WR/PR — CARDINALS

PERSONAL: Born April 10, 1971, in Albion, Mich. ... 5-10/177.
HIGH SCHOOL: Garland (Texas).
COLLEGE: Texas A&M-Kingsville.
TRANSACTIONS/CAREER NOTES: Signed as non-drafted free agent by Tampa Bay Buccaneers (April 23, 1996). ... Granted unconditional free agency (March 1, 2002). ... Re-signed by Buccaneers (April 17, 2002). ... Released by Buccaneers (March 2, 2004). ... Signed by Arizona Cardinals (March 18, 2004).
CHAMPIONSHIP GAME EXPERIENCE: Played in NFC championship game (1999 and 2002 seasons). ... Member of Super Bowl championship team (2002 season).
SINGLE GAME HIGHS (regular season): Receptions—6 (September 13, 1998, vs. Green Bay); yards—87 (December 7, 1997, vs. Green Bay); and touchdown receptions—2 (November 2, 1997, vs. Indianapolis).

			RECEIVING				PUNT RETURNS				KICKOFF RETURNS				TOTALS			
Year Team	G	GS	No.	Yds.	Avg.	TD	No.	Yds.	Avg.	TD	No.	Yds.	Avg.	TD	TD	2pt.	Pts.	Fum.
1996—Tampa Bay NFL	16	0	22	246	11.2	0	13	274	21.1	1	14	383	27.4	0	1	0	6	2
1997—Tampa Bay NFL	16	7	33	486	14.7	4	46	‡597	13.0	∞1	15	277	18.5	0	5	0	30	5
1998—Tampa Bay NFL	13	6	21	252	12.0	1	10	83	8.3	0	0	0	0.0	0	1	0	6	0
1999—Tampa Bay NFL	13	4	21	176	8.4	0	20	153	7.7	0	1	15	15.0	0	0	0	0	2
2000—Tampa Bay NFL	13	0	2	35	17.5	0	31	286	9.2	1	19	453	23.8	0	1	0	6	2
2001—Tampa Bay NFL	15	3	24	314	13.1	1	35	366	10.5	†1	2	35	17.5	0	2	0	12	3
2002—Tampa Bay NFL	16	2	7	77	11.0	1	43	410	9.5	1	3	49	16.3	0	2	0	12	0
2003—Tampa Bay NFL	13	0	7	114	16.3	0	15	110	7.3	0	1	15	15.0	0	0	1	2	0
Pro totals (8 years)	115	22	137	1700	12.4	7	213	2279	10.7	5	55	1227	22.3	0	12	1	74	14

WILLIAMS, KEVIN — DE — VIKINGS

PERSONAL: Born August 16, 1980, in Arkadelphia, Ark. ... 6-5/311.
HIGH SCHOOL: Fordyce (Ark.).
COLLEGE: Oklahoma State.
TRANSACTIONS/CAREER NOTES: Selected by Minnesota Vikings in first round (ninth pick overall) of 2003 NFL draft. ... Signed by Vikings (July 25, 2003).

			TOTALS			INTERCEPTIONS			
Year Team	G	GS	Tk.	Ast.	Sks.	No.	Yds.	Avg.	TD
2003—Minnesota NFL	16	16	37	15	10.5	1	3	3.0	0

W

WILLIAMS, MAURICE — T — JAGUARS

PERSONAL: Born January 26, 1979, in Detroit, Mich. ... 6-5/310. ... Full name: Maurice Carlos Williams.
HIGH SCHOOL: Pershing (Detroit).
COLLEGE: Michigan.
TRANSACTIONS/CAREER NOTES: Selected by Jacksonville Jaguars in second round (43rd pick overall) of 2001 NFL draft. ... Signed by Jaguars (July 25, 2001). ... On injured reserve with leg injury (October 14, 2002-remainder of season).
PLAYING EXPERIENCE: Jacksonville NFL, 2001-2003. ... Games/Games started: 2001 (16/16), 2002 (5/5), 2003 (16/16). Total: 37/37.

WILLIAMS, MELVIN — DE — SAINTS

PERSONAL: Born February 2, 1979, in St. Louis, Mo. ... 6-2/269.
HIGH SCHOOL: Mehlville (St. Louis, Mo.).
COLLEGE: Kansas State.

TRANSACTIONS/CAREER NOTES: Selected by New Orleans Saints in fifth round (155th pick overall) of 2003 NFL draft. ... Signed by Saints (June 2, 2003).

Year Team	G	GS	TOTALS Tk.	Ast.	Sks.
2003—New Orleans NFL	14	2	6	6	0.0

WILLIAMS, MIKE T BILLS

PERSONAL: Born January 11, 1980, in Dallas, Texas. ... 6-6/370. ... Full name: Michael D. Williams.
HIGH SCHOOL: The Colony (Texas).
COLLEGE: Texas.
TRANSACTIONS/CAREER NOTES: Selected by Buffalo Bills in first round (fourth pick overall) of 2002 NFL draft. ... Signed by Bills (July 28, 2002).
PLAYING EXPERIENCE: Buffalo NFL, 2002-2003. ... Games/Games started: 2002 (14/14), 2003 (13/13). Total: 27/27.
HONORS: Named offensive tackle on THE SPORTING NEWS college All-America second team (2001).

WILLIAMS, MOE RB VIKINGS

PERSONAL: Born July 26, 1974, in Columbus, Ga. ... 6-1/205. ... Full name: Maurice Jabari Williams.
HIGH SCHOOL: Spencer (Columbus, Ga.).
COLLEGE: Kentucky.
TRANSACTIONS/CAREER NOTES: Selected after junior season by Minnesota Vikings in third round (75th pick overall) of 1996 NFL draft. ... Signed by Vikings (July 22, 1996). ... On injured reserve with foot injury (December 8, 1998-remainder of season). ... Granted free agency (February 12, 1999). ... Re-signed by Vikings (April 30, 1999). ... Granted unconditional free agency (February 11, 2000). ... Re-signed by Vikings (March 20, 2000). ... Released by Vikings (September 2, 2001). ... Signed by Baltimore Ravens (September 4, 2001). ... Granted unconditional free agency (March 1, 2002). ... Re-signed by Vikings (May 21, 2002). ... Granted unconditional free agency (February 28, 2003). ... Re-signed by Vikings (March 13, 2003).
CHAMPIONSHIP GAME EXPERIENCE: Played in NFC championship game (2000 season).
SINGLE GAME HIGHS (regular season): Attempts—24 (December 2, 2001, vs. Indianapolis); yards—111 (December 2, 2001, vs. Indianapolis); and rushing touchdowns—2 (October 5, 2003, vs. Atlanta).
STATISTICAL PLATEAUS: 100-yard rushing games: 2001 (1), 2002 (1), 2003 (1). Total: 3. 100-yard receiving games: 2003 (1). Total: 1.

			RUSHING				RECEIVING				KICKOFF RETURNS				TOTALS			
Year Team	G	GS	Att.	Yds.	Avg.	TD	No.	Yds.	Avg.	TD	No.	Yds.	Avg.	TD	TD	2pt.	Pts.	Fum.
1996—Minnesota NFL	9	0	0	0	0.0	0	0	0	0.0	0	0	0	0.0	0	0	0	0	0
1997—Minnesota NFL	14	0	22	59	2.7	1	4	14	3.5	0	16	388	24.3	0	1	0	6	0
1998—Minnesota NFL	12	1	0	0	0.0	0	1	64	64.0	0	2	19	9.5	0	0	0	0	1
1999—Minnesota NFL	14	0	24	69	2.9	1	1	12	12.0	0	10	240	24.0	1	2	0	12	0
2000—Minnesota NFL	16	0	23	67	2.9	0	4	31	7.8	0	10	214	21.4	0	0	1	2	0
2001—Baltimore NFL	15	2	65	291	4.5	0	23	210	9.1	0	0	0	0.0	0	0	0	0	1
2002—Minnesota NFL	16	0	84	414	4.9	11	27	251	9.3	0	24	516	21.5	0	11	0	66	1
2003—Minnesota NFL	16	7	174	745	4.3	5	65	644	9.9	3	0	0	0.0	0	8	0	48	2
Pro totals (8 years)	112	10	392	1645	4.2	18	125	1226	9.8	3	62	1377	22.2	1	22	1	134	5

WILLIAMS, PAT DT BILLS

PERSONAL: Born October 24, 1972, in Monroe, La. ... 6-3/315. ... Full name: Patrick Williams.
HIGH SCHOOL: Wossman (Monroe, La.).
JUNIOR COLLEGE: Navarro College (Texas).
COLLEGE: Texas A&M.
TRANSACTIONS/CAREER NOTES: Signed as non-drafted free agent by Buffalo Bills (April 25, 1997). ... Granted free agency (February 11, 2000). ... Re-signed by Bills (March 23, 2000).

Year Team	G	GS	TOTALS Tk.	Ast.	Sks.
1997—Buffalo NFL	1	0	0	0	0.0
1998—Buffalo NFL	13	0	11	1	3.5
1999—Buffalo NFL	16	0	25	7	2.5
2000—Buffalo NFL	16	4	37	18	2.5
2001—Buffalo NFL	13	13	41	18	1.5
2002—Buffalo NFL	16	16	53	31	0.5
2003—Buffalo NFL	16	16	54	28	0.0
Pro totals (7 years)	91	49	221	103	10.5

W

WILLIAMS, RANDAL WR COWBOYS

PERSONAL: Born May 21, 1978, in Bronx, N.Y. ... 6-3/220. ... Full name: Randal Ellison Williams.
HIGH SCHOOL: Deerfield Academy (Maine).
COLLEGE: New Hampshire.
TRANSACTIONS/CAREER NOTES: Signed as non-drafted free agent by Jacksonville Jaguars (April 27, 2001). ... Claimed on waivers by Dallas Cowboys (October 29, 2001). ... Granted free agency (March 3, 2004). ... Re-signed by Cowboys (April 19, 2004).

			RECEIVING				KICKOFF RETURNS				TOTALS			
Year Team	G	GS	No.	Yds.	Avg.	TD	No.	Yds.	Avg.	TD	TD	2pt.	Pts.	Fum.
2001—Dallas NFL	7	0	0	0	0.0	0	0	0	0.0	0	0	0	0	0
2002—Dallas NFL	11	0	0	0	0.0	0	0	0	0.0	0	0	0	0	0
2003—Dallas NFL	15	0	0	0	0.0	0	2	60	30.0	1	1	0	6	0
Pro totals (3 years)	33	0	0	0	0.0	0	2	60	30.0	1	1	0	6	0

WILLIAMS, RICKY — RB — DOLPHINS

PERSONAL: Born May 21, 1977, in San Diego, Calif. ... 5-10/226. ... Full name: Errick Lynne Williams.
HIGH SCHOOL: Patrick Henry (San Diego).
COLLEGE: Texas.
TRANSACTIONS/CAREER NOTES: Selected by New Orleans Saints in first round (fifth pick overall) of 1999 NFL draft. ... Signed by Saints (May 14, 1999). ... Traded by Saints with fourth-round pick (TE Randy McMichael) in 2002 draft to Miami Dolphins for first-(DE Charles Grant) and fourth-round (DB Keyuo Craver) picks in 2002 draft and first-round pick (traded to Arizona) in 2003 draft (March 8, 2002).
HONORS: Named running back on THE SPORTING NEWS college All-America first team (1997 and 1998). ... Doak Walker Award winner (1997 and 1998). ... Heisman Trophy winner (1998). ... Walter Camp Award winner (1998). ... Maxwell Award winner (1998). ... Named College Football Player of the Year by THE SPORTING NEWS (1998). ... Played in Pro Bowl (2002 season). ... Named Outstanding Player of Pro Bowl (2002). ... Named running back on the THE SPORTING NEWS NFL All-Pro team (2002).
RECORDS: Shares NFL record for most consecutive games with 200 or more yards rushing—2 (December 1-9, 2002).
SINGLE GAME HIGHS (regular season): Attempts—42 (September 21, 2003, vs. Buffalo); yards—228 (December 1, 2002, vs. Buffalo); and rushing touchdowns—3 (October 22, 2000, vs. Atlanta).
STATISTICAL PLATEAUS: 100-yard rushing games: 1999 (2), 2000 (5), 2001 (5), 2002 (10), 2003 (7). Total: 29.

			RUSHING				RECEIVING				TOTALS			
Year Team	G	GS	Att.	Yds.	Avg.	TD	No.	Yds.	Avg.	TD	TD	2pt.	Pts.	Fum.
1999—New Orleans NFL	12	12	253	884	3.5	2	28	172	6.1	0	2	0	12	6
2000—New Orleans NFL	10	10	248	1000	4.0	8	44	409	9.3	1	9	0	54	6
2001—New Orleans NFL	16	16	313	1245	4.0	6	60	511	8.5	1	7	0	42	8
2002—Miami NFL	16	16	*383	*1853	4.8	16	47	363	7.7	1	17	0	102	7
2003—Miami NFL	16	16	*392	1372	3.5	9	50	351	7.0	1	10	0	60	7
Pro totals (5 years)	70	70	1589	6354	4.0	41	229	1806	7.9	4	45	0	270	34

WILLIAMS, RICKY — RB — COLTS

PERSONAL: Born August 29, 1978, in Dallas, Texas. ... 5-7/195. ... Full name: Ricky Antwan Williams.
HIGH SCHOOL: Duncanville (Texas).
COLLEGE: Texas Tech.
TRANSACTIONS/CAREER NOTES: Signed as non-drafted free agent by New Orleans Saints (April 23, 2002). ... Traded by Saints to Indianapolis Colts for conditional pick (traded to New England) in 2003 draft (September 1, 2002). ... Granted free agency (March 3, 2003). ... Re-signed by Colts (April 15, 2003).
CHAMPIONSHIP GAME EXPERIENCE: Played in AFC championship game (2003 season).
SINGLE GAME HIGHS (regular season): Attempts—17 (October 12, 2003, vs. Carolina); yards—57 (October 12, 2003, vs. Carolina); and rushing touchdowns—2 (October 6, 2003, vs. Tampa Bay).

			RUSHING				RECEIVING				KICKOFF RETURNS				TOTALS			
Year Team	G	GS	Att.	Yds.	Avg.	TD	No.	Yds.	Avg.	TD	No.	Yds.	Avg.	TD	TD	2pt.	Pts.	Fum.
2002—Indianapolis NFL	10	0	11	35	3.2	0	1	20	20.0	1	2	35	17.5	0	1	0	6	0
2003—Indianapolis NFL	13	4	48	155	3.2	2	22	157	7.1	1	4	67	16.8	0	3	0	18	2
Pro totals (2 years)	23	4	59	190	3.2	2	23	177	7.7	2	6	102	17.0	0	4	0	24	2

WILLIAMS, ROLAND — TE — RAIDERS

PERSONAL: Born April 27, 1975, in Rochester, N.Y. ... 6-5/265. ... Full name: Roland Lamar Williams.
HIGH SCHOOL: East (Rochester, N.Y.).
COLLEGE: Syracuse.
TRANSACTIONS/CAREER NOTES: Selected by St. Louis Rams in fourth round (98th pick overall) of 1998 NFL draft. ... Signed by Rams (July 13, 1998). ... Granted free agency (March 2, 2001). ... Re-signed by Rams (April 20, 2001). ... Traded by Rams to Oakland Raiders for fourth-round pick (traded to Arizona) in 2001 draft (April 21, 2001). ... On injured reserve with knee and toe injuries (January 18, 2003-remainder of 2002 season). ... Released by Raiders (August 26, 2003). ... Signed by Tampa Bay Buccaneers (November 12, 2003). ... Waived by Buccaneers (March 2, 2004). ... Signed by Oakland Raiders (April 10, 2004).
CHAMPIONSHIP GAME EXPERIENCE: Played in NFC championship game (1999 season). ... Member of Super Bowl championship team (1999 season).
SINGLE GAME HIGHS (regular season): Receptions—7 (September 15, 2002, vs. Pittsburgh); yards—55 (September 15, 2002, vs. Pittsburgh); and touchdown receptions—2 (October 24, 1999, vs. Cleveland).

			RECEIVING				TOTALS			
Year Team	G	GS	No.	Yds.	Avg.	TD	TD	2pt.	Pts.	Fum.
1998—St. Louis NFL	13	9	15	144	9.6	1	1	0	6	0
1999—St. Louis NFL	16	15	25	226	9.0	6	6	0	36	0
2000—St. Louis NFL	16	11	11	102	9.3	3	3	1	20	0
2001—Oakland NFL	16	15	33	298	9.0	3	3	0	18	0
2002—Oakland NFL	16	12	27	213	7.9	0	0	0	0	1
2003—Tampa Bay NFL	1	0	0	0	0.0	0	0	0	0	0
Pro totals (6 years)	78	62	111	983	8.9	13	13	1	80	1

WILLIAMS, ROOSEVELT — CB — BROWNS

PERSONAL: Born September 10, 1978, in Jacksonville, Fla. ... 6-0/196.
HIGH SCHOOL: Terry Parker (Jacksonville, Fla.).
COLLEGE: Tuskegee.
TRANSACTIONS/CAREER NOTES: Selected by Chicago Bears in third round (72nd pick overall) of 2002 NFL draft. ... Signed by Bears (June 28, 2002). ... Claimed on waivers by Denver Broncos (September 1, 2003). ... Waived by Broncos (September 17, 2003). ... Signed by Cleveland Browns (September 24, 2003).

Year Team	G	GS	Tk.	Ast.	Sks.	No.	Yds.	Avg.	TD
			TOTALS			INTERCEPTIONS			
2002—Chicago NFL	13	2	9	1	0.0	0	0	0.0	0
2003—Cleveland NFL	7	3	11	3	0.0	0	0	0.0	0
Pro totals (2 years)	20	5	20	4	0.0	0	0	0.0	0

WILLIAMS, ROY — S — COWBOYS

PERSONAL: Born August 14, 1980, in Redwood City, Calif. ... 6-0/235.
HIGH SCHOOL: James Logan (Union City, Calif.).
COLLEGE: Oklahoma.
TRANSACTIONS/CAREER NOTES: Selected after junior season by Dallas Cowboys in first round (ninth pick overall) of 2002 NFL draft. ... Signed by Cowboys (July 26, 2002).
HONORS: Named strong safety on THE SPORTING NEWS college All-America first team (2001). ... Jim Thorpe Award winner (2001). ... Bronko Nagurski Award winner (2001). ... Named safety on THE SPORTING NEWS NFL All-Pro team (2003). ... Played in Pro Bowl (2003 season).

Year Team	G	GS	Tk.	Ast.	Sks.	No.	Yds.	Avg.	TD
			TOTALS			INTERCEPTIONS			
2002—Dallas NFL	16	16	81	11	2.0	5	90	18.0	2
2003—Dallas NFL	16	16	53	16	2.0	2	69	34.5	0
Pro totals (2 years)	32	32	134	27	4.0	7	159	22.7	2

WILLIAMS, SAM — DE — RAIDERS

PERSONAL: Born July 28, 1980, in Clayton, Calif. ... 6-5/265.
HIGH SCHOOL: Clayton Valley (Clayton, Calif.).
COLLEGE: Fresno State.
TRANSACTIONS/CAREER NOTES: Selected by Oakland Raiders in third round (83rd pick overall) of 2003 NFL draft. ... Signed by Raiders (July 24, 2003). ... On injured reserve with knee injury (November 19, 2003-remainder of season).

Year Team	G	GS	Tk.	Ast.	Sks.
			TOTALS		
2003—Oakland NFL	1	0	0	0	0.0

WILLIAMS, SHAUN — S — GIANTS

PERSONAL: Born October 10, 1976, in Los Angeles, Calif. ... 6-2/218. ... Full name: Shaun LeJon Williams.
HIGH SCHOOL: Crespi (Encino, Calif.).
COLLEGE: UCLA.
TRANSACTIONS/CAREER NOTES: Selected by New York Giants in first round (24th pick overall) of 1998 NFL draft. ... Signed by Giants (July 24, 1998). ... Granted unconditional free agency (March 1, 2002). ... Re-signed by Giants (March 29, 2002). ... On injured reserve with knee injury (November 19, 2003-remainder of season).
CHAMPIONSHIP GAME EXPERIENCE: Played in NFC championship game (2000 season). ... Played in Super Bowl 35 (2000 season).
HONORS: Named free safety on THE SPORTING NEWS college All-America second team (1997).

Year Team	G	GS	Tk.	Ast.	Sks.	No.	Yds.	Avg.	TD
			TOTALS			INTERCEPTIONS			
1998—New York Giants NFL	13	0	19	5	0.0	2	6	3.0	0
1999—New York Giants NFL	11	0	13	3	0.0	0	0	0.0	0
2000—New York Giants NFL	16	16	68	17	0.0	3	52	17.3	0
2001—New York Giants NFL	16	16	77	19	1.0	3	25	8.3	0
2002—New York Giants NFL	16	16	64	26	2.0	2	-2	-1.0	0
2003—New York Giants NFL	10	10	44	14	1.5	1	14	14.0	0
Pro totals (6 years)	82	58	285	84	4.5	11	95	8.6	0

WILLIAMS, TANK — S — TITANS

PERSONAL: Born June 30, 1980, in Gulfport, Miss. ... 6-3/223. ... Full name: Clevan Williams.
HIGH SCHOOL: Bay (Bay St. Louis, Miss.).
COLLEGE: Stanford.
TRANSACTIONS/CAREER NOTES: Selected by Tennesse Titans in second round (45th pick overall) of 2002 NFL draft. ... Signed by Titans (July 22, 2002).
CHAMPIONSHIP GAME EXPERIENCE: Played in AFC championship game (2002 season).

Year Team	G	GS	Tk.	Ast.	Sks.	No.	Yds.	Avg.	TD
			TOTALS			INTERCEPTIONS			
2002—Tennessee NFL	16	16	46	15	2.0	1	0	0.0	0
2003—Tennessee NFL	16	16	52	22	0.5	2	0	0.0	0
Pro totals (2 years)	32	32	98	37	2.5	3	0	0.0	0

WILLIAMS, TONY — DT — BENGALS

PERSONAL: Born July 9, 1975, in Germantown, Tenn. ... 6-2/296. ... Full name: Anthony Demetric Williams.
HIGH SCHOOL: Oakhaven (Memphis, Tenn.), then Germantown (Tenn.).
COLLEGE: Memphis.

TRANSACTIONS/CAREER NOTES: Selected by Minnesota Vikings in fifth round (151st pick overall) of 1997 NFL draft. ... Signed by Vikings (June 17, 1997). ... Granted free agency (February 11, 2000). ... Re-signed by Vikings (May 18, 2000). ... Granted unconditional free agency (March 2, 2001). ... Signed by Cincinnati Bengals (March 6, 2001).
CHAMPIONSHIP GAME EXPERIENCE: Played in NFC championship game (1998 and 2000 season).

			TOTALS		
Year Team	**G**	**GS**	**Tk.**	**Ast.**	**Sks.**
1997—Minnesota NFL	6	2	9	3	0.0
1998—Minnesota NFL	14	9	26	10	1.0
1999—Minnesota NFL	16	12	30	15	5.0
2000—Minnesota NFL	14	12	27	6	4.0
2001—Cincinnati NFL	13	13	15	23	5.0
2002—Cincinnati NFL	16	16	30	12	5.0
2003—Cincinnati NFL	16	16	28	10	2.0
Pro totals (7 years)	95	80	165	79	22.0

WILLIAMS, TYRONE CB FALCONS

PERSONAL: Born May 31, 1973, in Bradenton, Fla. ... 5-11/193. ... Full name: Upton Tyrone Williams.
HIGH SCHOOL: Manatee (Bradenton, Fla.).
COLLEGE: Nebraska.
TRANSACTIONS/CAREER NOTES: Selected by Green Bay Packers in third round (93rd pick overall) of 1996 NFL draft. ... Signed by Packers (May 15, 1996). ... Granted free agency (February 12, 1999). ... Re-signed by Packers (May 17, 1999). ... Granted unconditional free agency (February 28, 2003). ... Signed by Atlanta Falcons (March 16, 2003). ... On suspended list for conduct detrimental to team (October 1- 6, 2003).
CHAMPIONSHIP GAME EXPERIENCE: Played in NFC championship game (1996 and 1997 seasons). ... Member of Super Bowl championship team (1996 season). ... Played in Super Bowl 32 (1997 season).

			TOTALS			INTERCEPTIONS			
Year Team	**G**	**GS**	**Tk.**	**Ast.**	**Sks.**	**No.**	**Yds.**	**Avg.**	**TD**
1996—Green Bay NFL	16	0	22	3	0.0	0	0	0.0	0
1997—Green Bay NFL	16	15	49	17	0.0	1	0	0.0	0
1998—Green Bay NFL	16	16	61	8	0.0	5	40	8.0	0
1999—Green Bay NFL	16	16	53	12	0.0	4	12	3.0	0
2000—Green Bay NFL	16	16	50	8	0.0	4	105	26.2	1
2001—Green Bay NFL	16	16	77	12	0.0	4	117	29.2	1
2002—Green Bay NFL	15	15	60	9	1.0	1	0	0.0	0
2003—Atlanta NFL	6	6	18	2	0.0	0	0	0.0	0
Pro totals (8 years)	117	100	390	71	1.0	19	274	14.4	2

WILLIAMS, WILLIE CB STEELERS

PERSONAL: Born December 26, 1970, in Columbia, S.C. ... 5-9/182. ... Full name: Willie James Williams Jr.
HIGH SCHOOL: Spring Valley (Columbia, S.C.).
COLLEGE: Western Carolina.
TRANSACTIONS/CAREER NOTES: Selected by Pittsburgh Steelers in sixth round (162nd pick overall) of 1993 NFL draft. ... Signed by Steelers (July 9, 1993). ... Granted free agency (February 16, 1996). ... Re-signed by Steelers (June 12, 1996). ... Granted unconditional free agency (February 14, 1997). ... Signed by Seattle Seahawks (February 18, 1997). ... Granted unconditional free agency (March 2, 2001). ... Re-signed by Seahawks (May 3, 2001). ... Granted unconditional free agency (February 28, 2003). ... Re-signed by Seahawks (May 2, 2003). ... Granted unconditional free agency (March 3, 2004). ... Signed by Pittsburgh Steelers (May 26, 2004).
CHAMPIONSHIP GAME EXPERIENCE: Played in AFC championship game (1994 and 1995 seasons). ... Played in Super Bowl 30 (1995 season).

			TOTALS			INTERCEPTIONS			
Year Team	**G**	**GS**	**Tk.**	**Ast.**	**Sks.**	**No.**	**Yds.**	**Avg.**	**TD**
1993—Pittsburgh NFL	16	0	7	2	0.0	0	0	0.0	0
1994—Pittsburgh NFL	16	1	3	0	0.0	0	0	0.0	0
1995—Pittsburgh NFL	16	15	69	8	0.0	§7	122	17.4	▲1
1996—Pittsburgh NFL	15	14	66	10	1.0	1	1	1.0	0
1997—Seattle NFL	16	16	58	9	0.0	1	0	0.0	0
1998—Seattle NFL	14	14	53	13	0.0	2	36	18.0	1
1999—Seattle NFL	15	14	66	6	0.0	5	43	8.6	1
2000—Seattle NFL	16	15	51	9	1.0	4	74	18.5	1
2001—Seattle NFL	14	14	60	12	0.0	4	24	6.0	0
2002—Seattle NFL	15	1	21	4	1.0	1	2	2.0	0
2003—Seattle NFL	15	0	11	3	0.0	0	0	0.0	0
Pro totals (11 years)	168	104	465	76	3.0	25	302	12.1	4

WILLIG, MATT T PANTHERS

PERSONAL: Born January 21, 1969, in Santa Fe Springs, Calif. ... 6-8/315. ... Full name: Matthew Joseph Willig.
HIGH SCHOOL: St. Paul (Santa Fe Springs, Calif.).
COLLEGE: Southern California.
TRANSACTIONS/CAREER NOTES: Signed as non-drafted free agent by New York Jets (May 5, 1992). ... Released by Jets (August 24, 1992). ... Re-signed by Jets to practice squad (September 2, 1992). ... Activated (December 24, 1992). ... Active for one game (1992); did not play. ... Signed by Jets (February 14, 1995). ... Released by Jets (April 23, 1996). ... Signed by Atlanta Falcons (May 2, 1996). ... Granted unconditional free agency (February 13, 1998). ... Signed by Green Bay Packers (May 5, 1998). ... Released by Packers (February 23, 1999). ... Signed by Cleveland Browns (August 17, 1999). ... Released by Browns (September 5, 1999). ... Signed by St. Louis Rams (November 30, 1999). ... Granted unconditional free agency (February 11, 2000). ... Signed by San Francisco 49ers (June 7, 2000). ... Granted unconditional-

al free agency (March 1, 2002). ... Re-signed by 49ers (March 7, 2002). ... Granted unconditional free agency (February 28, 2003). ... Signed by Carolina Panthers (August 1, 2003). ... Granted unconditional free agency (March 3, 2004). ... Re-signed by Panthers (May 1, 2004).
PLAYING EXPERIENCE: New York Jets NFL, 1993-1995; Atlanta NFL, 1996-1997; Green Bay NFL, 1998; San Francisco NFL, 2000-2002; Carolina NFL, 2003. ... Games/Games started: 1993 (3/0), 1994 (16/3), 1995 (15/12), 1996 (12/0), 1997 (16/13), 1998 (16/0), 2000 (16/3), 2001 (15/0), 2002 (11/3), 2003 (13/0). Total: 133/34.
CHAMPIONSHIP GAME EXPERIENCE: Member of Rams for NFC championship game (1999 season); inactive. ... Member of Super Bowl championship team (1999 season); inactive. ... Played in NFC championship game (2003 season). ... Played in Super Bowl 38 (2003 season).

WILLIS, DONALD — G — CHIEFS

PERSONAL: Born July 15, 1973, in Goleta, Calif. ... 6-3/325. ... Full name: Donald Kirk Willis.
HIGH SCHOOL: Cabrillo (Lompoc, Calif.).
COLLEGE: North Carolina A&T.
TRANSACTIONS/CAREER NOTES: Signed as non-drafted free agent by Seattle Seahawks (April 27, 1995). ... Claimed on waivers by New Orleans Saints (December 1, 1995). ... Inactive for 16 games (1995). ... Released by Saints (September 8, 1997). ... Signed by Tampa Bay Buccaneers (December 30, 1997). ... Released by Buccaneers (August 30, 1998). ... Signed by Kansas City Chiefs (March 12, 1999). ... Released by Chiefs (September 6, 1999). ... Re-signed by Chiefs (March 6, 2000). ... Granted unconditional free agency (March 1, 2002). ... Re-signed by Chiefs (April 4, 2002).
PLAYING EXPERIENCE: New Orleans NFL, 1996; Kansas City NFL, 2000-2003. ... Games/Games started: 1996 (4/0), 2000 (16/2), 2001 (14/4), 2002 (13/0), 2003 (16/0). Total: 63/6.

WILSON, ADRIAN — S — CARDINALS

PERSONAL: Born October 12, 1979, in High Point, N.C. ... 6-3/222.
HIGH SCHOOL: T.W. Andrews (High Point, N.C.).
COLLEGE: North Carolina State.
TRANSACTIONS/CAREER NOTES: Selected after junior season by Arizona Cardinals in third round (64th pick overall) of 2001 NFL draft. ... Signed by Cardinals (July 24, 2001). ... Granted free agency (March 3, 2004). ... Re-signed by Cardinals (2004).

			TOTALS			INTERCEPTIONS			
Year Team	**G**	**GS**	**Tk.**	**Ast.**	**Sks.**	**No.**	**Yds.**	**Avg.**	**TD**
2001—Arizona NFL	16	0	15	7	0.5	2	97	48.5	1
2002—Arizona NFL	14	14	66	27	1.5	4	35	8.8	0
2003—Arizona NFL	16	15	70	9	0.0	0	0	0.0	0
Pro totals (3 years)	46	29	151	43	2.0	6	132	22.0	1

WILSON, AL — LB — BRONCOS

PERSONAL: Born June 21, 1977, in Jackson, Tenn. ... 6-0/240. ... Full name: Aldra Kauwa Wilson.
HIGH SCHOOL: Central Merry (Jackson, Tenn.).
COLLEGE: Tennessee.
TRANSACTIONS/CAREER NOTES: Selected by Denver Broncos in first round (31st pick overall) of NFL draft. ... Signed by Broncos (July 21, 1999).
HONORS: Named inside linebacker on THE SPORTING NEWS college All-America second team (1998). ... Played in Pro Bowl (2001 and 2003 seasons). ... Named to play in Pro Bowl (2002 season); replaced by Kendrell Bell due to injury.

			TOTALS			INTERCEPTIONS			
Year Team	**G**	**GS**	**Tk.**	**Ast.**	**Sks.**	**No.**	**Yds.**	**Avg.**	**TD**
1999—Denver NFL	16	12	58	16	1.0	0	0	0.0	0
2000—Denver NFL	15	14	47	13	5.0	3	21	7.0	0
2001—Denver NFL	16	16	72	13	3.0	0	0	0.0	0
2002—Denver NFL	16	15	100	32	5.0	0	0	0.0	0
2003—Denver NFL	16	16	70	18	1.0	0	0	0.0	0
Pro totals (5 years)	79	73	347	92	15.0	3	21	7.0	0

WILSON, CEDRICK — WR — 49ERS

PERSONAL: Born December 17, 1978, in Memphis, Tenn. ... 5-10/183.
HIGH SCHOOL: Melrose (Memphis, Tenn.).
COLLEGE: Tennessee.
TRANSACTIONS/CAREER NOTES: Selected by San Francisco 49ers in sixth round (169th pick overall) of 2001 NFL draft. ... Signed by 49ers (July 24, 2001). ... Granted free agency (March 3, 2004). ... Re-signed by 49ers (April 14, 2004).
SINGLE GAME HIGHS (regular season): Receptions—5 (December 27, 2003, vs. Seattle); yards—57 (September 14, 2003, vs. St. Louis); and touchdown receptions—1 (December 27, 2003, vs. Seattle).

			RECEIVING				PUNT RETURNS				KICKOFF RETURNS				TOTALS			
Year Team	**G**	**GS**	**No.**	**Yds.**	**Avg.**	**TD**	**No.**	**Yds.**	**Avg.**	**TD**	**No.**	**Yds.**	**Avg.**	**TD**	**TD**	**2pt.**	**Pts.**	**Fum.**
2001—San Francisco NFL	6	0	0	0	0.0	0	2	4	2.0	0	6	127	21.2	0	0	0	0	0
2002—San Francisco NFL	16	0	15	166	11.1	1	8	59	7.4	0	10	195	19.5	0	1	0	6	0
2003—San Francisco NFL	16	3	35	396	11.3	2	1	12	12.0	0	37	836	22.6	1	3	0	18	1
Pro totals (3 years)	38	3	50	562	11.2	3	11	75	6.8	0	53	1158	21.8	1	4	0	24	1

WILSON, EUGENE — CB — PATRIOTS

PERSONAL: Born August 17, 1980, in Merrillville, Ind. ... 5-10/195. ... Full name: Eugene W. Wilson II.
HIGH SCHOOL: Merrillville (Ind.).
COLLEGE: Illinois.

TRANSACTIONS/CAREER NOTES: Selected by New England Patriots in second round (36th pick overall) of 2003 NFL draft. ... Signed by Patriots (July 21, 2003).
CHAMPIONSHIP GAME EXPERIENCE: Played in AFC championship game (2003 season). ... Member of Super Bowl championship team (2003 season).

			TOTALS			INTERCEPTIONS			
Year Team	G	GS	Tk.	Ast.	Sks.	No.	Yds.	Avg.	TD
2003—New England NFL	16	15	47	14	0.0	4	18	4.5	0

WILSON, JERRY S CHARGERS

PERSONAL: Born July 17, 1973, in Alexandria, La. ... 5-10/190. ... Full name: Jerry Lee Wilson Jr.
HIGH SCHOOL: La Grange (Lake Charles, La.).
COLLEGE: Southern University.
TRANSACTIONS/CAREER NOTES: Selected by Tampa Bay Buccaneers in fourth round (105th pick overall) of 1995 NFL draft. ... Signed by Buccaneers (May 9, 1995). ... On injured reserve with knee injury (August 31, 1995-entire season). ... Released by Buccaneers (August 20, 1996). ... Signed by Miami Dolphins to practice squad (October 29, 1996). ... Activated (November 5, 1996). ... Granted unconditional free agency (March 2, 2001). ... Signed by New Orleans Saints (January 2, 2002). ... Granted unconditional free agency (March 1, 2002). ... Re-signed by Saints (May 2, 2002). ... Released by Saints (September 1, 2002). ... Re-signed by Saints (September 10, 2002). ... Released by Saints (November 12, 2002). ... Signed by San Diego Chargers (November 19, 2002). ... Granted unconditional free agency (February 28, 2003). ... Re-signed by Chargers (March 17, 2003). ... Granted unconditional free agency (March 3, 2004). ... Re-signed by Chargers (March 17, 2004).

			TOTALS			INTERCEPTIONS			
Year Team	G	GS	Tk.	Ast.	Sks.	No.	Yds.	Avg.	TD
1996—Miami NFL	2	0	0	0	0.0	0	0	0.0	0
1997—Miami NFL	16	0	9	1	2.0	0	0	0.0	0
1998—Miami NFL	16	0	13	2	0.0	1	0	0.0	0
1999—Miami NFL	16	1	14	1	3.0	1	13	13.0	0
2000—Miami NFL	16	0	30	9	0.5	1	19	19.0	0
2001—New Orleans NFL	1	0	0	0	0.0	0	0	0.0	0
2002—New Orleans NFL	7	0	4	0	0.0	0	0	0.0	0
—San Diego NFL	5	0	3	0	0.0	0	0	0.0	0
2003—San Diego NFL	16	16	63	19	1.0	1	-2	-2.0	0
Pro totals (8 years)	95	17	136	32	6.5	4	30	7.5	0

WINBORN, JAMIE LB 49ERS

PERSONAL: Born May 14, 1979, in Wetumpka, Ala. ... 5-11/242.
HIGH SCHOOL: Wetumpka (Ala.).
COLLEGE: Vanderbilt.
TRANSACTIONS/CAREER NOTES: Selected after junior season by San Francisco 49ers in second round (47th pick overall) of 2001 NFL draft. ... Signed by 49ers (July 25, 2001). ... On injured reserve with knee injury (January 2, 2003-remainder of 2002 season). ... On injured reserve with neck injury (November 15, 2003-remainder of season).

			TOTALS			INTERCEPTIONS			
Year Team	G	GS	Tk.	Ast.	Sks.	No.	Yds.	Avg.	TD
2001—San Francisco NFL	14	4	34	11	0.5	2	40	20.0	0
2002—San Francisco NFL	3	3	18	6	1.0	0	0	0.0	0
2003—San Francisco NFL	9	0	34	3	3.0	0	0	0.0	0
Pro totals (3 years)	26	7	86	20	4.5	2	40	20.0	0

WINEY, BRANDON T REDSKINS

PERSONAL: Born January 27, 1978, in Lake Charles, La. ... 6-7/315.
HIGH SCHOOL: Washington-Marion (Lake Charles, La.).
COLLEGE: Louisiana State.
TRANSACTIONS/CAREER NOTES: Selected by Miami Dolphins in sixth round (164th pick overall) of 2001 NFL draft. ... Signed by Dolphins (June 15, 2001). ... Released by Dolphins (September 2, 2001). ... Re-signed by Dolphins to practice squad (September 3, 2001). ... Signed by Denver Broncos off Dolphins practice squad (December 11, 2001). ... Released by Broncos (August 26, 2002). ... Signed by Seattle Seahawks to practice squad (September 2, 2002). ... Released by Seahawks (January 6, 2003). ... Signed by Washington Redskins (August 2, 2003).
PLAYING EXPERIENCE: Washington NFL, 2003. ... Games/Games started: 2003 (11/3). Total: 11/3.
HONORS: Named offensive tackle on THE SPORTING NEWS college All-America third team (2000).

WINFIELD, ANTOINE CB VIKINGS

PERSONAL: Born June 24, 1977, in Akron, Ohio. ... 5-9/180. ... Full name: Antoine D. Winfield.
HIGH SCHOOL: Garfield (Ohio).
COLLEGE: Ohio State.
TRANSACTIONS/CAREER NOTES: Selected by Buffalo Bills in first round (23rd pick overall) of 1999 NFL draft. ... Signed by Bills (July 30, 1999). ... On injured reserve list with shoulder injury (November 22, 2000-remainder of season). ... Granted unconditional free agency (March 3, 2004). ... Signed by Minnesota Vikings (March 5, 2004).
HONORS: Named cornerback on THE SPORTING NEWS college All-America second team (1997). ... Jim Thorpe Award winner (1998). ... Named cornerback on THE SPORTING NEWS college All-America first team (1998).

Year Team	G	GS	TOTALS Tk.	Ast.	Sks.	INTERCEPTIONS No.	Yds.	Avg.	TD
1999—Buffalo NFL	16	2	38	1	0.0	2	13	6.5	0
2000—Buffalo NFL	11	11	34	8	0.0	1	8	8.0	0
2001—Buffalo NFL	16	16	69	12	0.0	2	0	0.0	0
2002—Buffalo NFL	13	13	51	5	0.0	0	0	0.0	0
2003—Buffalo NFL	16	16	94	15	1.0	1	11	11.0	0
Pro totals (5 years)	72	58	286	41	1.0	6	32	5.3	0

WIRE, COY S BILLS

PERSONAL: Born November 7, 1978, in Camp Hill, Pa. ... 6-0/205.
COLLEGE: Stanford.
TRANSACTIONS/CAREER NOTES: Selected by Buffalo Bills in third round (97th pick overall) of 2002 NFL draft. ... Signed by Bills (July 3, 2002).

Year Team	G	GS	TOTALS Tk.	Ast.	Sks.	INTERCEPTIONS No.	Yds.	Avg.	TD
2002—Buffalo NFL	16	15	67	25	3.0	0	0	0.0	0
2003—Buffalo NFL	16	1	10	3	1.0	0	0	0.0	0
Pro totals (2 years)	32	16	77	28	4.0	0	0	0.0	0

WISTROM, GRANT DE SEAHAWKS

PERSONAL: Born July 3, 1976, in Webb City, Mo. ... 6-4/272. ... Full name: Grant Alden Wistrom.
HIGH SCHOOL: Webb City (Mo.).
COLLEGE: Nebraska.
TRANSACTIONS/CAREER NOTES: Selected by St. Louis Rams in first round (sixth pick overall) of 1998 NFL draft. ... Signed by Rams (July 18, 1998). ... Granted unconditional free agency (March 3, 2004). ... Signed by Seattle Seahawks (March 4, 2004).
CHAMPIONSHIP GAME EXPERIENCE: Played in NFC championship game (1999 and 2001 seasons). ... Member of Super Bowl championship team (1999 season). ... Played in Super Bowl 36 (2001 season).
HONORS: Named defensive end on THE SPORTING NEWS college All-America first team (1996 and 1997).

Year Team	G	GS	TOTALS Tk.	Ast.	Sks.	INTERCEPTIONS No.	Yds.	Avg.	TD
1998—St. Louis NFL	13	0	14	6	3.0	0	0	0.0	0
1999—St. Louis NFL	16	16	33	6	6.5	2	131	65.5	†2
2000—St. Louis NFL	16	16	51	12	11.0	0	0	0.0	0
2001—St. Louis NFL	15	15	47	9	9.0	2	-4	-2.0	0
2002—St. Louis NFL	15	14	45	2	4.5	1	2	2.0	0
2003—St. Louis NFL	16	16	50	11	7.5	0	0	0.0	0
Pro totals (6 years)	91	77	240	46	41.5	5	129	25.8	2

WITHERSPOON, WILL LB PANTHERS

PERSONAL: Born August 19, 1980, in San Antonio, Texas. ... 6-1/234. ... Full name: William Cordell Witherspoon.
HIGH SCHOOL: Rutherford (Panama City, Fla.).
COLLEGE: Georgia.
TRANSACTIONS/CAREER NOTES: Selected by Carolina Panthers in third round (73rd pick overall) of 2002 NFL draft. ... Signed by Panthers (June 20, 2002).
CHAMPIONSHIP GAME EXPERIENCE: Played in NFC championship game (2003 season). ... Played in Super Bowl 38 (2003 season).

Year Team	G	GS	TOTALS Tk.	Ast.	Sks.	INTERCEPTIONS No.	Yds.	Avg.	TD
2002—Carolina NFL	15	8	49	14	1.5	0	0	0.0	0
2003—Carolina NFL	16	16	73	24	1.0	1	10	10.0	0
Pro totals (2 years)	31	24	122	38	2.5	1	10	10.0	0

WITHROW, CORY C VIKINGS

PERSONAL: Born April 5, 1975, in Spokane, Wash. ... 6-2/287.
HIGH SCHOOL: Mead (Spokane, Wash.).
COLLEGE: Washington State.
TRANSACTIONS/CAREER NOTES: Signed as non-drafted free agent by Minnesota Vikings (April 23, 1998). ... Released by Vikings (August 30, 1998). ... Signed by Cincinnati Bengals to practice squad (December 18, 1998). ... Released by Bengals (April 15, 1999). ... Signed by Vikings (April 30, 1999). ... Released by Vikings (September 5, 1999). ... Re-signed by Vikings to practice squad (September 6, 1999). ... Activated (October 26, 1999); did not play. ... Released by Vikings (November 30, 1999). ... Re-signed by Vikings to practice squad (December 1, 1999). ... Granted free agency (February 28, 2003). ... Re-signed by Vikings (April 9, 2003). ... Granted unconditional free agency (March 3, 2004). ... Re-signed by Vikings (April 25, 2004).
PLAYING EXPERIENCE: Minnesota NFL, 2000-2003. ... Games/Games started: 2000 (12/0), 2001 (16/1), 2002 (16/0), 2003 (8/0). Total: 52/1.
CHAMPIONSHIP GAME EXPERIENCE: Played in NFC championship game (2000 season).

W

WITTEN, JASON TE COWBOYS

PERSONAL: Born May 6, 1982, in Elizabethton, Tenn. ... 6-5/257. ... Full name: Christopher Jason Witten.
HIGH SCHOOL: Elizabethon (Tenn.).
COLLEGE: Tennessee.

TRANSACTIONS/CAREER NOTES: Selected after junior season by Dallas Cowboys in third round (69th pick overall) of 2003 NFL draft. ... Signed by Cowboys (July 26, 2003).
SINGLE GAME HIGHS (regular season): Receptions—8 (November 27, 2003, vs. Miami); yards—58 (November 27, 2003, vs. Miami); and touchdown receptions—1 (December 21, 2003, vs. New York Giants).

			RECEIVING				TOTALS			
Year Team	G	GS	No.	Yds.	Avg.	TD	TD	2pt.	Pts.	Fum.
2003—Dallas NFL	15	7	35	347	9.9	1	1	0	6	0

WOHLABAUGH, DAVE — C — RAMS

PERSONAL: Born April 13, 1972, in Hamburg, N.Y. ... 6-3/296. ... Full name: David Vincent Wohlabaugh. ... Name pronounced: WOOL-uh-buh.
HIGH SCHOOL: Frontier (Hamburg, N.Y.).
COLLEGE: Syracuse.
TRANSACTIONS/CAREER NOTES: Selected by New England Patriots in fourth round (112th pick overall) of 1995 NFL draft. ... Signed by Patriots (June 26, 1995). ... Granted free agency (February 13, 1998). ... Re-signed by Patriots (May 28, 1998). ... Granted unconditional free agency (February 12, 1999). ... Signed by Cleveland Browns (February 16, 1999). ... Released by Browns (February 26, 2003). ... Signed by St. Louis Rams (February 28, 2003).
PLAYING EXPERIENCE: New England NFL, 1995-1998; Cleveland NFL, 1999-2002; St. Louis NFL, 2003. ... Games/Games started: 1995 (11/11), 1996 (16/16), 1997 (14/14), 1998 (16/16), 1999 (15/15), 2000 (12/12), 2001 (16/16), 2002 (12/12), 2003 (16/16). Total: 128/128.
CHAMPIONSHIP GAME EXPERIENCE: Played in AFC championship game (1996 season). ... Played in Super Bowl 31 (1996 season).

WOMACK, FLOYD — T — SEAHAWKS

PERSONAL: Born November 15, 1978, in Cleveland, Miss. ... 6-4/333. ... Full name: Floyd Seneca Womack.
HIGH SCHOOL: East Side (Cleveland, Miss.).
COLLEGE: Mississippi State.
TRANSACTIONS/CAREER NOTES: Selected by Seattle Seahawks in fourth round (128th pick overall) of 2001 NFL draft. ... Signed by Seahawks (June 22, 2001). ... Granted free agency (March 3, 2004). ... Re-signed by Seahawks (April 4, 2004).
PLAYING EXPERIENCE: Seattle NFL, 2001-2003. ... Games/Games started: 2001 (6/0), 2002 (11/10), 2003 (11/4). Total: 28/14.

WONG, JOE — G — RAIDERS

PERSONAL: Born February 24, 1976, in Waimanalo, Hawaii. ... 6-6/315. ... Full name: Joseph H.L. Wong.
HIGH SCHOOL: Kailua (Honolulu).
COLLEGE: Brigham Young.
TRANSACTIONS/CAREER NOTES: Selected by Miami Dolphins in seventh round (244th pick overall) of 1999 NFL draft. ... Signed by Dolphins (July 27, 1999). ... On injured reserve with knee injury (August 31, 1999-entire season). ... Released by Dolphins (July 7, 2000). ... Signed by Philadelphia Eagles (February 9, 2001). ... Assigned by Eagles to Amsterdam Admirals in 2001 NFL Europe enhancement allocation program (February 19, 2001). ... Released by Eagles (August 31, 2001). ... Signed by Oakland Raiders (October 9, 2002). ... Released by Raiders (November 16, 2002). ... Re-signed by Raiders to practice squad (January 15, 2003). ... Activated (February 5, 2003). ... Waived by Raiders (August 31, 2003). ... Re-signed by Raiders to practice squad (October 8, 2003). ... Released by Raiders (October 23, 2003). ... Re-signed by Raiders to practice squad (October 31, 2003). ... Released by Raiders (November 16, 2003). ... Re-signed by Raiders (December 19, 2003).
PLAYING EXPERIENCE: Miami NFL, 1999; Oakland NFL, 2003. ... Games/Games started: 2003 (2/0), Total: 2/0.

WONG, KAILEE — LB — TEXANS

PERSONAL: Born May 23, 1976, in Eugene, Ore. ... 6-2/250.
HIGH SCHOOL: North Eugene (Ore.).
COLLEGE: Stanford.
TRANSACTIONS/CAREER NOTES: Selected by Minnesota Vikings in second round (51st pick overall) of 1998 NFL draft. ... Signed by Vikings (July 25, 1998). ... On injured reserve with leg injury (December 31, 1998-remainder of season). ... Granted free agency (March 2, 2001). ... Re-signed by Vikings (April 16, 2001). ... Granted unconditional free agency (March 1, 2002). ... Signed by Houston Texans (March 7, 2002).
CHAMPIONSHIP GAME EXPERIENCE: Played in NFC championship game (2000 season).

			TOTALS			INTERCEPTIONS			
Year Team	G	GS	Tk.	Ast.	Sks.	No.	Yds.	Avg.	TD
1998—Minnesota NFL	15	0	12	2	1.5	0	0	0.0	0
1999—Minnesota NFL	13	8	34	12	0.0	0	0	0.0	0
2000—Minnesota NFL	16	16	83	28	2.0	2	28	14.0	0
2001—Minnesota NFL	16	16	83	16	3.0	1	27	27.0	1
2002—Houston NFL	16	16	34	10	5.5	0	0	0.0	0
2003—Houston NFL	16	16	49	13	3.0	0	0	0.0	0
Pro totals (6 years)	92	72	295	81	15.0	3	55	18.3	1

W

WOODARD, CEDRIC — DT — SEAHAWKS

PERSONAL: Born September 5, 1977, in Bay City, Texas. ... 6-2/310. ... Full name: Cedric Darnell Woodard.
HIGH SCHOOL: Sweeny (Texas).
COLLEGE: Texas.
TRANSACTIONS/CAREER NOTES: Selected by Baltimore Ravens in sixth round (191st pick overall) of 2000 NFL draft. ... Signed by Ravens (June 15, 2000). ... Claimed on waivers by Seattle Seahawks (September 6, 2000). ... Granted free agency (February 28, 2003). ... Re-signed by Seahawks (April 9, 2003). ... Granted unconditional free agency (March 3, 2004). ... Re-signed by Seahawks (March 9, 2004).

Year Team	G	GS	TOTALS Tk.	Ast.	Sks.
2001—Seattle NFL	16	0	3	1	0.0
2002—Seattle NFL	12	0	0	1	0.0
2003—Seattle NFL	16	13	41	16	0.0
Pro totals (3 years)	44	13	44	18	0.0

WOODEN, SHAWN S DOLPHINS

PERSONAL: Born October 23, 1973, in Philadelphia, Pa. ... 5-11/205. ... Full name: Shawn Anthony Wooden.
HIGH SCHOOL: Abington (Pa.).
COLLEGE: Notre Dame.
TRANSACTIONS/CAREER NOTES: Selected by Miami Dolphins in sixth round (189th pick overall) of 1996 NFL draft. ... Signed by Dolphins (July 10, 1996). ... On injured reserve with knee injury (September 15, 1998-remainder of season). ... Granted free agency (February 12, 1999). ... Re-signed by Dolphins (April 23, 1999). ... Granted unconditional free agency (February 11, 2000). ... Signed by Chicago Bears (March 6, 2000). ... Released by Bears (June 26, 2001). ... Signed by Dolphins (June 29, 2001). ... Released by Dolphins (March 11, 2003). ... Re-signed by Dolphins (April 24, 2003). ... Granted unconditional free agency (March 3, 2004). ... Re-signed by Dolphins (March 6, 2004).

			TOTALS			INTERCEPTIONS			
Year Team	G	GS	Tk.	Ast.	Sks.	No.	Yds.	Avg.	TD
1996—Miami NFL	16	11	54	13	0.0	2	15	7.5	0
1997—Miami NFL	16	15	56	27	0.0	2	10	5.0	0
1998—Miami NFL	2	1	10	0	0.0	0	0	0.0	0
1999—Miami NFL	15	6	36	15	0.0	0	0	0.0	0
2000—Chicago NFL	11	0	8	3	0.0	0	0	0.0	0
2001—Miami NFL	13	0	2	0	0.0	0	0	0.0	0
2002—Miami NFL	16	2	12	6	0.0	1	0	0.0	0
2003—Miami NFL	15	0	1	0	0.0	0	0	0.0	0
Pro totals (8 years)	104	35	179	64	0.0	5	25	5.0	0

WOODS, JEROME S CHIEFS

PERSONAL: Born March 17, 1973, in Memphis, Tenn. ... 6-2/210.
HIGH SCHOOL: Melrose (Memphis, Tenn.).
JUNIOR COLLEGE: Northeast Mississippi Community College.
COLLEGE: Memphis.
TRANSACTIONS/CAREER NOTES: Selected by Kansas City Chiefs in first round (28th pick overall) of 1996 NFL draft. ... Signed by Chiefs (August 12, 1996). ... Granted unconditional free agency (February 11, 2000). ... Re-signed by Chiefs (February 11, 2000). ... On injured reserve with broken leg (August 26, 2002-entire season). ... Granted unconditional free agency (March 3, 2004). ... Re-signed by Chiefs (March 3, 2004).
HONORS: Played in Pro Bowl (2003 season).

			TOTALS			INTERCEPTIONS			
Year Team	G	GS	Tk.	Ast.	Sks.	No.	Yds.	Avg.	TD
1996—Kansas City NFL	16	0	5	1	0.0	0	0	0.0	0
1997—Kansas City NFL	16	16	67	19	1.0	4	57	14.3	0
1998—Kansas City NFL	16	16	56	25	0.0	2	47	23.5	0
1999—Kansas City NFL	15	15	70	9	0.0	1	5	5.0	0
2000—Kansas City NFL	16	16	74	8	2.0	2	0	0.0	0
2001—Kansas City NFL	16	16	74	13	1.0	3	48	16.0	0
2002—Kansas City NFL	Did not play.								
2003—Kansas City NFL	16	16	61	18	0.0	3	125	41.7	†2
Pro totals (7 years)	111	95	407	93	4.0	15	282	18.8	2

WOODS, LEVAR LB CARDINALS

PERSONAL: Born March 15, 1978, in Cleveland, Ohio. ... 6-3/244.
HIGH SCHOOL: West Lyon (Inwood, Iowa).
COLLEGE: Iowa.
TRANSACTIONS/CAREER NOTES: Signed as non-drafted free agent by Arizona Cardinals (April 23, 2001). ... Granted free agency (February 27, 2003). ... Re-signed by Cardinals (March 16, 2003).

			TOTALS			INTERCEPTIONS			
Year Team	G	GS	Tk.	Ast.	Sks.	No.	Yds.	Avg.	TD
2001—Arizona NFL	15	0	8	0	0.0	0	0	0.0	0
2002—Arizona NFL	15	2	22	7	0.5	0	0	0.0	0
2003—Arizona NFL	16	3	17	4	1.0	0	0	0.0	0
Pro totals (3 years)	46	5	47	11	1.5	0	0	0.0	0

W

WOODSON, CHARLES CB RAIDERS

PERSONAL: Born October 7, 1976, in Fremont, Ohio. ... 6-1/200.
HIGH SCHOOL: Ross (Fremont, Ohio).
COLLEGE: Michigan.
TRANSACTIONS/CAREER NOTES: Selected after junior season by Oakland Raiders in first round (fourth pick overall) of 1998 NFL draft. ... Signed by Raiders (July 20, 1998). ... Designated by Raiders as franchise player (February 24, 2004).

CHAMPIONSHIP GAME EXPERIENCE: Played in AFC championship game (2000 and 2002 seasons). ... Played in Super Bowl 37 (2002 season).
HONORS: Named cornerback on THE SPORTING NEWS college All-America second team (1996). ... Heisman Trophy winner (1997). ... Jim Thorpe Award winner (1997). ... Maxwell Award winner (1997). ... Bronko Nagurski Award winner (1997). ... Named College Football Player of the Year by The Sporting News (1997). ... Named cornerback on THE SPORTING NEWS college All-America first team (1997). ... Played in Pro Bowl (1998-2000 seasons). ... Named cornerback on THE SPORTING NEWS NFL All-Pro team (2001). ... Named to played in Pro Bowl (2001 season); replaced by Ty Law due to injury.

			TOTALS			INTERCEPTIONS				PUNT RETURNS				TOTALS			
Year Team	G	GS	Tk.	Ast.	Sks.	No.	Yds.	Avg.	TD	No.	Yds.	Avg.	TD	TD	2pt.	Pts.	Fum.
1998—Oakland NFL	16	16	61	3	0.0	5	118	23.6	1	0	0	0.0	0	1	0	6	0
1999—Oakland NFL	16	16	52	9	0.0	1	15	15.0	1	0	0	0.0	0	1	0	6	0
2000—Oakland NFL	16	16	66	13	0.0	4	36	9.0	0	0	0	0.0	0	0	0	0	0
2001—Oakland NFL	16	15	40	13	2.0	1	64	64.0	0	4	47	11.8	0	0	0	0	0
2002—Oakland NFL	8	7	35	2	0.0	1	3	3.0	0	4	6	1.5	0	0	0	0	0
2003—Oakland NFL	15	15	56	14	1.0	3	67	22.3	0	0	0	0.0	0	0	0	0	0
Pro totals (6 years)	87	85	310	54	3.0	15	303	20.2	2	8	53	6.6	0	2	0	12	0

WOODSON, DARREN S COWBOYS

PERSONAL: Born April 25, 1969, in Phoenix, Ariz. ... 6-1/219. ... Full name: Darren Ray Woodson.
HIGH SCHOOL: Maryvale (Phoenix).
COLLEGE: Arizona State.
TRANSACTIONS/CAREER NOTES: Selected by Dallas Cowboys in second round (37th pick overall) of 1992 NFL draft. ... Signed by Cowboys (April 26, 1992). ... On injured reserve with broken forearm (December 14, 2000-remainder of season). ... Granted unconditional free agency (March 1, 2002). ... Re-signed by Cowboys (March 1, 2002). ... On injured reserve with abdominal injury (November 27, 2002-remainder of season).
CHAMPIONSHIP GAME EXPERIENCE: Played in NFC championship game (1992-1995 seasons). ... Member of Super Bowl championship team (1992, 1993 and 1995 seasons).
HONORS: Named strong safety on THE SPORTING NEWS NFL All-Pro team (1994-1996 and 1998). ... Played in Pro Bowl (1994-1996 and 1998 seasons). ... Named to play in Pro Bowl (1997 season); replaced by John Lynch due to injury.

			TOTALS			INTERCEPTIONS			
Year Team	G	GS	Tk.	Ast.	Sks.	No.	Yds.	Avg.	TD
1992—Dallas NFL	16	2	28	5	1.0	0	0	0.0	0
1993—Dallas NFL	16	15	89	66	0.0	0	0	0.0	0
1994—Dallas NFL	16	16	58	19	0.0	5	140	28.0	1
1995—Dallas NFL	16	16	84	11	0.0	2	46	23.0	1
1996—Dallas NFL	16	16	62	16	3.0	5	43	8.6	0
1997—Dallas NFL	14	14	53	20	2.0	1	14	14.0	0
1998—Dallas NFL	16	15	66	12	3.0	1	1	1.0	0
1999—Dallas NFL	15	15	59	10	1.0	2	5	2.5	0
2000—Dallas NFL	11	11	62	10	0.0	2	12	6.0	0
2001—Dallas NFL	16	16	70	11	0.0	3	11	3.7	0
2002—Dallas NFL	10	10	41	9	0.0	1	1	1.0	0
2003—Dallas NFL	16	16	59	20	1.0	1	-2	-2.0	0
Pro totals (12 years)	178	162	731	209	11.0	23	271	11.8	2

WOODSON, ROD S RAIDERS

PERSONAL: Born March 10, 1965, in Fort Wayne, Ind. ... 5-11/205. ... Full name: Roderick Kevin Woodson.
HIGH SCHOOL: R. Nelson Snider (Fort Wayne, Ind.).
COLLEGE: Purdue.
TRANSACTIONS/CAREER NOTES: Selected by Pittsburgh Steelers in first round (10th pick overall) of 1987 NFL draft. ... On reserve/unsigned list (August 31-October 27, 1987). ... Signed by Steelers (October 28, 1987). ... Granted roster exemption (October 28-November 7, 1987). ... Granted free agency (February 1, 1991). ... Re-signed by Steelers (August 22, 1991). ... Granted unconditional free agency (February 14, 1997). ... Signed by San Francisco 49ers (July 17, 1997). ... Released by 49ers (February 9, 1998). ... Signed by Baltimore Ravens (February 20, 1998). ... Granted unconditional free agency (March 2, 2001). ... Re-signed by Ravens (May 7, 2001). ... Released by Ravens (February 27, 2002). ... Signed by Oakland Raiders (April 30, 2002). ... On injured reserve with knee injury (November 28, 2003-remainder of season).
CHAMPIONSHIP GAME EXPERIENCE: Played in AFC championship game (1994, 2000 and 2002 seasons). ... Member of Steelers for AFC championship game (1995 season); inactive. ... Played in Super Bowl 30 (1995 season). ... Played in NFC championship game (1997 season). ... Member of Super Bowl championship team (2000 season). ... Played in Super Bowl 37 (2002 season).
HONORS: Named defensive back on THE SPORTING NEWS college All-America second team (1985). ... Named kick returner on THE SPORTING NEWS college All-America first team (1986). ... Named kick returner on THE SPORTING NEWS NFL All-Pro team (1989). ... Played in Pro Bowl (1989-1994, 1996, 1999-2002 seasons). ... Named cornerback on THE SPORTING NEWS NFL All-Pro team (1990 and 1992-1994).
RECORDS: Holds NFL career records for most yards on interceptions—1,483; and most touchdowns by interception return—12.
MISCELLANEOUS: Active NFL leader for career interceptions (71). ... Shares Baltimore Ravens all-time record for most interceptions (20).

			TOTALS			INTERCEPTIONS				PUNT RETURNS				KICKOFF RETURNS				TOTALS			
Year Team	G	GS	Tk.	Ast.	Sks.	No.	Yds.	Avg.	TD	No.	Yds.	Avg.	TD	No.	Yds.	Avg.	TD	TD	2pt.	Pts.	Fum.
1987—Pit. NFL	8	0	15	5	0.0	1	45	45.0	1	16	135	8.4	0	13	290	22.3	0	1	0	6	3
1988—Pit. NFL	16	16	78	10	0.5	4	98	24.5	0	33	281	8.5	0	37	850	23.0	†1	1	0	6	3
1989—Pit. NFL	15	14	67	13	0.0	3	39	13.0	0	29	207	7.1	0	§36	§982	*27.3	†1	1	0	6	3
1990—Pit. NFL	16	16	54	12	0.0	5	67	13.4	0	§38	§398	10.5	†1	35	764	21.8	0	1	0	6	3
1991—Pit. NFL	15	15	60	11	1.0	3	72	24.0	0	28	320	§11.4	0	*44	§880	20.0	0	0	0	0	3
1992—Pit. NFL	16	16	85	15	6.0	4	90	22.5	0	32	364	§11.4	1	25	469	18.8	0	1	0	6	2
1993—Pit. NFL	16	16	79	16	2.0	8	§138	17.3	▲1	42	338	8.0	0	15	294	19.6	0	1	0	6	2
1994—Pit. NFL	15	15	67	16	3.0	4	109	27.2	2	39	319	8.2	0	15	365	24.3	0	2	0	12	2
1995—Pit. NFL	1	1	0	1	0.0	0	0	0.0	0	0	0	0.0	0	0	0	0.0	0	0	0	0	0

Year	Team	G	GS	TOTALS Tk.	Ast.	Sks.	INTERCEPTIONS No.	Yds.	Avg.	TD	PUNT RETURNS No.	Yds.	Avg.	TD	KICKOFF RETURNS No.	Yds.	Avg.	TD	TOTALS TD	2pt.	Pts.	Fum.
1996—Pit. NFL		16	16	57	10	1.0	6	121	20.2	1	0	0	0.0	0	0	0	0.0	0	2	0	12	1
1997—S.F. NFL		14	14	43	5	0.0	3	81	27.0	0	1	0	0.0	0	0	0	0.0	0	0	0	0	0
1998—Bal. NFL		16	16	76	12	0.0	6	108	18.0	▲2	0	0	0.0	0	0	0	0.0	0	2	0	12	0
1999—Bal. NFL		16	16	54	12	0.0	†7	195	27.9	†2	2	0	0.0	0	0	0	0.0	0	2	0	12	1
2000—Bal. NFL		16	16	67	10	0.0	4	20	5.0	0	0	0	0.0	0	0	0	0.0	0	0	0	0	0
2001—Bal. NFL		16	16	56	20	0.0	3	57	19.0	1	0	0	0.0	0	0	0	0.0	0	1	0	6	0
2002—Oak. NFL		16	16	70	12	0.0	†8	§225	28.1	▲2	0	0	0.0	0	0	0	0.0	0	2	0	12	0
2003—Oak. NFL		10	10	41	10	0.0	2	18	9.0	0	0	0	0.0	0	0	0	0.0	0	0	0	0	0
Pro totals (17 years)		238	229	969	190	13.5	71	1483	20.9	12	260	2362	9.1	2	220	4894	22.2	2	17	0	102	23

WOODY, DAMIEN — C — LIONS

PERSONAL: Born November 3, 1977, in Beaverdam, Va. ... 6-3/320. ... Full name: Damien Michael Woody.
HIGH SCHOOL: Patrick Henry (Beaverdam, Va.).
COLLEGE: Boston College.
TRANSACTIONS/CAREER NOTES: Selected after junior season by New England Patriots in first round (17th pick overall) of 1999 NFL draft. ... Signed by Patriots (July 30, 1999). ... On injured reserve with knee injury (January 9, 2003-remainder of 2002 season). ... On injured reserve with leg injury (January 17, 2004-remainder of 2003 season playoffs). ... Granted unconditional free agency (March 3, 2004). ... Signed by Detroit Lions (March 5, 2004).
PLAYING EXPERIENCE: New England NFL, 1999-2003. ... Games/Games started: 1999 (16/16), 2000 (16/16), 2001 (16/15), 2002 (16/15), 2003 (14/14). Total: 78/76.
CHAMPIONSHIP GAME EXPERIENCE: Played in AFC championship game (2001 season). ... Member of Super Bowl championship team (2001 season).
HONORS: Played in Pro Bowl (2002 season).

WOOLFOLK, ANDRE — CB — TITANS

PERSONAL: Born January 26, 1980, in Denver, Colo. ... 6-1/197.
HIGH SCHOOL: Thomas Jefferson (Denver).
COLLEGE: Oklahoma.
TRANSACTIONS/CAREER NOTES: Selected by Tennessee Titans in first round (28th pick overall) of 2003 NFL draft. ... Signed by Titans (July 24, 2003). ... On injured reserve with ankle injury (December 23, 2003-remainder of season).

Year	Team	G	GS	TOTALS Tk.	Ast.	Sks.	INTERCEPTIONS No.	Yds.	Avg.	TD
2003—Tennessee NFL		6	1	14	4	0.0	1	4	4.0	0

WORD, MARK — DE — BROWNS

PERSONAL: Born November 23, 1975, in Miami, Fla. ... 6-5/305. ... Full name: Mark Bernard Word.
HIGH SCHOOL: Southridge (Miami).
JUNIOR COLLEGE: Hinds Community College (Miss.).
COLLEGE: Jacksonville State.
TRANSACTIONS/CAREER NOTES: Signed as non-drafted free agent by Kansas City Chiefs (April 20, 1999). ... Released by Chiefs (August 27, 2000). ... Signed by Hamilton Tiger-Cats of CFL (September 3, 2000). ... Signed by St. Louis Rams (January 12, 2001). ... Assigned by Rams to Rhein Fire in 2001 NFL Europe enhancement allocation program (February 19, 2001). ... Released by Rams (July 2, 2001). ... Signed by Cleveland Browns (July 20, 2001). ... Released by Browns (August 22, 2001). ... Signed by Hamilton Tiger-Cats of CFL (August 22, 2001). ... Re-signed by Browns (August 31, 2001). ... On injured reserve with shoulder injury (September 1, 2001-entire season).

Year	Team	G	GS	TOTALS Tk.	Ast.	Sks.
1999—Kansas City NFL		6	0	0	0	0.0
2002—Cleveland NFL		16	2	18	3	8.0
2003—Cleveland NFL		16	2	11	4	4.0
Pro totals (3 years)		38	4	29	7	12.0

WORRELL, CAMERON — S — BEARS

PERSONAL: Born December 14, 1979, in Merced County, Calif. ... 5-11/199.
HIGH SCHOOL: Chowchilla (Calif.).
JUNIOR COLLEGE: Fresno City College (Calif.).
COLLEGE: Fresno State.
TRANSACTIONS/CAREER NOTES: Signed as non-drafted free agent by Chicago Bears (May 4, 2003).

Year	Team	G	GS	TOTALS Tk.	Ast.	Sks.	INTERCEPTIONS No.	Yds.	Avg.	TD
2003—Chicago NFL		14	0	1	0	0.0	0	0	0.0	0

WRIGHSTER, GEORGE — TE — JAGUARS

PERSONAL: Born April 1, 1981, in Memphis, Tenn. ... 6-3/260. ... Full name: George Fredrick Wrighster III.
HIGH SCHOOL: Sylmar (Calif.).
COLLEGE: Oregon.

TRANSACTIONS/CAREER NOTES: Selected after junior season by Jacksonville Jaguars in fourth round (104th pick overall) of 2003 NFL draft. ... Signed by Jaguars (July 18, 2003).

SINGLE GAME HIGHS (regular season): Receptions—3 (October 26, 2003, vs. Tennessee); yards—30 (December 21, 2003, vs. New Orleans); and touchdown receptions—1 (October 26, 2003, vs. Tennessee).

			RECEIVING				TOTALS			
Year Team	**G**	**GS**	**No.**	**Yds.**	**Avg.**	**TD**	**TD**	**2pt.**	**Pts.**	**Fum.**
2003—Jacksonville NFL	15	2	13	150	11.5	2	2	0	12	0

WRIGHT, ANTHONY QB RAVENS

PERSONAL: Born February 14, 1976, in Vanceboro, N.C. ... 6-1/211.

HIGH SCHOOL: West Craven (N.C.).

COLLEGE: South Carolina.

TRANSACTIONS/CAREER NOTES: Signed as non-drafted free agent by Pittsburgh Steelers (April 18, 1999). ... Active for one game (1999); did not play. ... Released by Steelers (August 27, 2000). ... Signed by Dallas Cowboys to practice squad (August 30, 2000). ... Activated (November 21, 2000). ... On injured reserve with knee injury (November 2, 2001-remainder of season). ... Released by Cowboys (September 1, 2002). ... Signed by Baltimore Ravens to practice squad (September 3, 2002). ... Activated (October 15, 2002). ... Granted free agency (February 28, 2003). ... Re-signed by Ravens (April 7, 2003). ... Granted unconditional free agency (March 3, 2004). ... Re-signed by Ravens (March 12, 2004).

SINGLE GAME HIGHS (regular season): Attempts—37 (November 23, 2003, vs. Seattle); completions—20 (November 23, 2003, vs. Washington); yards—319 (November 23, 2003, vs. Seattle); and touchdown passes—4 (November 23, 2003, vs. Seattle).

STATISTICAL PLATEAUS: 300-yard passing games: 2003 (1). Total: 1.

MISCELLANEOUS: Regular-season record as starting NFL quarterback: 6-6 (.500). ... Post-season record as starting NFL quarterback: 0-1 (.000).

			PASSING									RUSHING				TOTALS		
Year Team	**G**	**GS**	**Att.**	**Cmp.**	**Pct.**	**Yds.**	**TD**	**Int.**	**Avg.**	**Skd.**	**Rat.**	**Att.**	**Yds.**	**Avg.**	**TD**	**TD**	**2pt.**	**Pts.**
1999—Pittsburgh NFL	Did not play.																	
2000—Dallas NFL	4	2	53	22	41.5	237	0	3	4.47	12	31.7	12	36	3.0	0	0	0	0
2001—Dallas NFL	4	3	98	48	49.0	529	5	5	5.40	5	61.1	17	57	3.4	0	0	0	0
2003—Baltimore NFL	7	7	178	94	52.8	1199	9	8	6.74	19	72.3	28	73	2.6	0	0	0	0
Pro totals (3 years)	15	12	329	164	49.8	1965	14	16	5.97	36	62.4	57	166	2.9	0	0	0	0

WRIGHT, KENNY CB TEXANS

PERSONAL: Born September 14, 1977, in Ruston, La. ... 6-1/205. ... Full name: Kenneth D. Wright.

HIGH SCHOOL: Ruston (La.).

COLLEGE: Northwestern State.

TRANSACTIONS/CAREER NOTES: Selected after junior season by Minnesota Vikings in fourth round (120th pick overall) of 1999 NFL draft. ... Signed by Vikings (July 21, 1999). ... Granted free agency (March 1, 2002). ... Re-signed by Vikings (April 16, 2002). ... Claimed on waivers by Houston Texans (August 1, 2002). ... Re-signed by Texans (April 2, 2003). ... On injured reserve with knee injury (December 22, 2003-remainder of season).

CHAMPIONSHIP GAME EXPERIENCE: Member of Vikings for NFC championship game (2000 season); inactive.

			TOTALS			INTERCEPTIONS			
Year Team	**G**	**GS**	**Tk.**	**Ast.**	**Sks.**	**No.**	**Yds.**	**Avg.**	**TD**
1999—Minnesota NFL	16	12	64	10	0.0	1	11	11.0	0
2000—Minnesota NFL	16	7	34	6	0.0	0	0	0.0	0
2001—Minnesota NFL	15	8	34	5	0.0	0	0	0.0	0
2002—Houston NFL	16	0	24	5	1.0	0	0	0.0	0
2003—Houston NFL	15	5	39	7	1.0	3	-2	-0.7	0
Pro totals (5 years)	78	32	195	33	2.0	4	9	2.3	0

WRIGHT, KENYATTA LB JETS

PERSONAL: Born February 19, 1978, in Vian, Okla. ... 6-0/240.

HIGH SCHOOL: Vian (Okla.).

COLLEGE: Oklahoma State.

TRANSACTIONS/CAREER NOTES: Signed as non-drafted free agent by Buffalo Bills (April 23, 2000). ... Granted free agency (March 1, 2002). ... Signed by New York Jets (April 17, 2003). ... Granted free agency (March 3, 2004). ... Re-signed by Jets (March 25, 2004).

			TOTALS			INTERCEPTIONS			
Year Team	**G**	**GS**	**Tk.**	**Ast.**	**Sks.**	**No.**	**Yds.**	**Avg.**	**TD**
2000—Buffalo NFL	16	0	13	3	0.0	0	0	0.0	0
2001—Buffalo NFL	11	1	26	8	1.5	0	0	0.0	0
2002—	Did not play.								
2003—New York Jets NFL	16	0	2	1	0.0	0	0	0.0	0
Pro totals (3 years)	43	1	41	12	1.5	0	0	0.0	0

WUNSCH, JERRY T/G SEAHAWKS

PERSONAL: Born January 21, 1974, in Eau Claire, Wis. ... 6-6/339. ... Full name: Gerald Wunsch. ... Name pronounced: WUNCH.

HIGH SCHOOL: West (Wausau, Wis.).

COLLEGE: Wisconsin.

TRANSACTIONS/CAREER NOTES: Selected by Tampa Bay Buccaneers in second round (37th pick overall) of 1997 NFL draft. ... Signed by Buccaneers (July 18, 1997). ... Granted unconditional free agency (March 2, 2001). ... Re-signed by Buccaneers (April 10, 2001). ... Released by Buccaneers (August 25, 2002). ... Signed by Seattle Seahawks (August 27, 2002). ... Granted unconditional free agency (February 28, 2003). ... Re-signed by Seahawks (March 18, 2003). ... On injured reserve with ankle injury (December 26, 2003-remainder of season).

PLAYING EXPERIENCE: Tampa Bay NFL, 1997-2001; Seattle NFL, 2002-2003. ... Games/Games started: 1997 (16/0), 1998 (16/1), 1999 (16/13), 2000 (16/16), 2001 (16/16), 2002 (15/5), 2003 (12/0). Total: 107/51.

CHAMPIONSHIP GAME EXPERIENCE: Played in NFC championship game (1999 season).

WYCHECK, FRANK TE

PERSONAL: Born October 14, 1971, in Philadelphia, Pa. ... 6-3/253. ... Name pronounced: WHY-check.

HIGH SCHOOL: Archbishop Ryan (Philadelphia).

COLLEGE: Maryland.

TRANSACTIONS/CAREER NOTES: Selected after junior season by Washington Redskins in sixth round (160th pick overall) of 1993 NFL draft. ... Signed by Redskins (July 15, 1993). ... On suspended list for anabolic steroid use (November 29, 1994-remainder of season). ... Released by Redskins (August 17, 1995). ... Signed by Houston Oilers (August 18, 1995). ... Granted free agency (February 16, 1996). ... Re-signed by Oilers (June 28, 1996). ... Oilers franchise moved to Tennessee for 1997 season. ... Oilers franchise renamed Tennessee Titans for 1999 season (December 26, 1998). ... Announced retirement (January 23, 2004).

CHAMPIONSHIP GAME EXPERIENCE: Played in AFC championship game (1999 and 2002 seasons). ... Played in Super Bowl 34 (1999 season).

HONORS: Played in Pro Bowl (1998-2000 seasons).

SINGLE GAME HIGHS (regular season): Receptions—10 (December 5, 1999, vs. Baltimore); yards—100 (October 21, 2001, vs. Detroit); and touchdown receptions—2 (November 23, 2003, vs. Atlanta).

STATISTICAL PLATEAUS: 100-yard receiving games: 2001 (1). Total: 1.

			RECEIVING				KICKOFF RETURNS				TOTALS			
Year Team	**G**	**GS**	**No.**	**Yds.**	**Avg.**	**TD**	**No.**	**Yds.**	**Avg.**	**TD**	**TD**	**2pt.**	**Pts.**	**Fum.**
1993—Washington NFL	9	7	16	113	7.1	0	0	0	0.0	0	0	0	0	1
1994—Washington NFL	9	1	7	55	7.9	1	4	84	21.0	0	1	0	6	0
1995—Houston NFL	16	10	40	471	11.8	1	0	0	0.0	0	2	0	12	0
1996—Houston NFL	16	16	53	511	9.6	6	2	5	2.5	0	6	0	36	2
1997—Tennessee NFL	16	16	63	748	11.9	4	1	3	3.0	0	4	1	26	0
1998—Tennessee NFL	16	16	70	768	11.0	2	1	10	10.0	0	2	0	12	2
1999—Tennessee NFL	16	16	69	641	9.3	2	0	0	0.0	0	2	0	12	0
2000—Tennessee NFL	16	16	70	636	9.1	4	0	0	0.0	0	4	0	24	2
2001—Tennessee NFL	16	16	60	672	11.2	4	0	0	0.0	0	4	0	24	0
2002—Tennessee NFL	15	15	40	346	8.7	2	0	0	0.0	0	2	0	12	1
2003—Tennessee NFL	10	6	17	165	9.7	2	0	0	0.0	0	2	0	12	0
Pro totals (11 years)	155	135	505	5126	10.2	28	8	102	12.8	0	29	1	176	8

WYMS, ELLIS DE BUCCANEERS

PERSONAL: Born April 12, 1979, in Indianola, Miss. ... 6-3/279. ... Full name: Ellis Rashad Wyms.

HIGH SCHOOL: Gentry (Indianola, Miss.).

COLLEGE: Mississippi State.

TRANSACTIONS/CAREER NOTES: Selected by Tampa Bay Buccaneers in sixth round (183rd pick overall) of 2001 NFL draft. ... Signed by Buccaneers (July 16, 2001). ... On injured reserve with knee injury (December 16, 2003-remainder of season).

CHAMPIONSHIP GAME EXPERIENCE: Played in NFC championship game (2002 season). ... Member of Super Bowl championship team (2002 season).

			TOTALS		
Year Team	**G**	**GS**	**Tk.**	**Ast.**	**Sks.**
2001—Tampa Bay NFL	4	0	3	0	0.0
2002—Tampa Bay NFL	14	0	27	8	5.5
2003—Tampa Bay NFL	13	0	20	4	2.0
Pro totals (3 years)	31	0	50	12	7.5

WYNN, RENALDO DE REDSKINS

PERSONAL: Born September 3, 1974, in Chicago, Ill. ... 6-3/292. ... Full name: Renaldo Levalle Wynn.

HIGH SCHOOL: De La Salle Institute (Chicago).

COLLEGE: Notre Dame.

TRANSACTIONS/CAREER NOTES: Selected by Jacksonville Jaguars in first round (21st pick overall) of 1997 NFL draft. ... Signed by Jaguars (July 21, 1997). ... On injured reserve with groin injury (December 25, 1998-remainder of season). ... Granted unconditional free agency (March 1, 2002). ... Signed by Washington Redskins (March 28, 2002).

CHAMPIONSHIP GAME EXPERIENCE: Played in AFC championship game (1999 season).

			TOTALS		
Year Team	**G**	**GS**	**Tk.**	**Ast.**	**Sks.**
1997—Jacksonville NFL	16	8	23	5	2.5
1998—Jacksonville NFL	15	15	23	11	1.0
1999—Jacksonville NFL	12	10	10	7	1.5
2000—Jacksonville NFL	14	14	31	5	3.5
2001—Jacksonville NFL	16	16	29	11	5.0
2002—Washington NFL	16	16	30	11	2.5
2003—Washington NFL	16	16	22	7	2.0
Pro totals (7 years)	105	95	168	57	18.0

WYRICK, JIMMY CB

PERSONAL: Born December 31, 1976, in DeSoto, Texas. ... 5-9/176.
HIGH SCHOOL: DeSoto (Texas).
COLLEGE: Minnesota.
TRANSACTIONS/CAREER NOTES: Signed as non-drafted free agent by Detroit Lions (April 28, 2000). ... On injured reserve with ankle injury (October 16, 2000-remainder of season). ... Granted free agency (February 28, 2003). ... Re-signed by Lions (February 28, 2003). ... Released by Lions (November 15, 2003). ... Signed by Miami Dolphins (December 1, 2003). ... Granted unconditional free agency (March 3, 2004).

			TOTALS			INTERCEPTIONS			
Year Team	G	GS	Tk.	Ast.	Sks.	No.	Yds.	Avg.	TD
2000—Detroit NFL	6	0	1	3	0.0	0	0	0.0	0
2001—Detroit NFL	16	0	13	2	0.0	0	0	0.0	0
2002—Detroit NFL	15	0	8	0	0.0	0	0	0.0	0
2003—Detroit NFL	7	1	7	0	0.0	0	0	0.0	0
—Miami NFL	4	0	0	0	0.0	0	0	0.0	0
Pro totals (4 years)	48	1	29	5	0.0	0	0	0.0	0

YATES, BILLY G DOLPHINS

PERSONAL: Born April 15, 1980, in Fort Worth, Texas. ... 6-2/305. ... Full name: Billy L. Yates.
HIGH SCHOOL: Corsicana (Texas).
COLLEGE: Texas A&M.
TRANSACTIONS/CAREER NOTES: Signed as non-drafted free agent by Miami Dolphins (April 28, 2003).
PLAYING EXPERIENCE: Miami NFL, 2003. ... Games/Games started: 2003 (3/0). Total: 3/0.

YODER, TODD TE JAGUARS

PERSONAL: Born March 18, 1978, in New Palestine, Ind. ... 6-4/250.
HIGH SCHOOL: New Palestine (Ind.).
COLLEGE: Vanderbilt.
TRANSACTIONS/CAREER NOTES: Signed as non-drafted free agent by Tampa Bay Buccaneers (April 17, 2000). ... Granted free agency (February 28, 2003). ... Re-signed by Buccaneers (April 4, 2003). ... Granted unconditional free agency (March 3, 2004). ... Signed by Jacksonville Jaguars (March 5, 2004).
CHAMPIONSHIP GAME EXPERIENCE: Played in NFC championship game (2002 season). ... Member of Super Bowl championship team (2002 season).
SINGLE GAME HIGHS (regular season): Receptions—4 (October 12, 2003, vs. Washington); yards—28 (October 12, 2003, vs. Washington); and touchdown receptions—2 (October 12, 2003, vs. Washington).

			RECEIVING				TOTALS			
Year Team	G	GS	No.	Yds.	Avg.	TD	TD	2pt.	Pts.	Fum.
2000—Tampa Bay NFL	9	0	1	1	1.0	0	0	0	0	1
2001—Tampa Bay NFL	16	1	4	48	12.0	0	1	0	6	0
2002—Tampa Bay NFL	16	0	2	26	13.0	0	0	0	0	0
2003—Tampa Bay NFL	16	1	7	68	9.7	2	2	0	12	0
Pro totals (4 years)	57	2	14	143	10.2	2	3	0	18	1

YOUNG, BRIAN DT SAINTS

PERSONAL: Born July 8, 1977, in Lawton, Okla. ... 6-2/290. ... Full name: James Brian Young.
HIGH SCHOOL: Andress (El Paso, Texas).
COLLEGE: Texas-El Paso.
TRANSACTIONS/CAREER NOTES: Selected by St. Louis Rams in fifth round (139th pick overall) of 2000 NFL draft. ... Signed by Rams (July 7, 2000). ... Granted free agency (February 28, 2003). ... Re-signed by Rams (April 25, 2003). ... Granted unconditional free agency (March 3, 2004). ... Signed by New Orleans Saints (March 7, 2004).
CHAMPIONSHIP GAME EXPERIENCE: Played in NFC championship game (2001 season). ... Played in Super Bowl 36 (2001 season).

			TOTALS			INTERCEPTIONS			
Year Team	G	GS	Tk.	Ast.	Sks.	No.	Yds.	Avg.	TD
2000—St. Louis NFL	11	0	4	2	0.0	0	0	0.0	0
2001—St. Louis NFL	16	16	33	7	6.5	1	25	25.0	0
2002—St. Louis NFL	16	3	25	9	2.0	0	0	0.0	0
2003—St. Louis NFL	16	12	27	9	2.0	0	0	0.0	0
Pro totals (4 years)	59	31	89	27	10.5	1	25	25.0	0

YOUNG, BRYANT DT 49ERS

PERSONAL: Born January 27, 1972, in Chicago Heights, Ill. ... 6-3/291. ... Full name: Bryant Colby Young.
HIGH SCHOOL: Bloom (Chicago Heights, Ill.).
COLLEGE: Notre Dame.
TRANSACTIONS/CAREER NOTES: Selected by San Francisco 49ers in first round (seventh pick overall) of 1994 NFL draft. ... Signed by 49ers (July 26, 1994). ... On injured reserve with broken leg (December 2, 1998-remainder of season). ... On physically unable to perform list with leg injury (July 30-August 10, 1999).
CHAMPIONSHIP GAME EXPERIENCE: Played in NFC championship game (1994 and 1997 seasons). ... Member of Super Bowl championship team (1994 season).
HONORS: Named defensive tackle on THE SPORTING NEWS NFL All-Pro team (1996 and 1998). ... Played in Pro Bowl (1996, 1999, 2001 and 2002 seasons).

Year	Team	G	GS	TOTALS Tk.	Ast.	Sks.
1994	San Francisco NFL	16	16	45	4	6.0
1995	San Francisco NFL	12	12	25	3	6.0
1996	San Francisco NFL	16	16	61	15	11.5
1997	San Francisco NFL	12	12	39	6	4.0
1998	San Francisco NFL	12	12	43	11	9.5
1999	San Francisco NFL	16	16	36	5	11.0
2000	San Francisco NFL	15	15	33	12	9.5
2001	San Francisco NFL	16	16	33	6	3.5
2002	San Francisco NFL	16	16	28	8	2.0
2003	San Francisco NFL	16	16	29	6	3.5
Pro totals (10 years)		147	147	372	76	66.5

YOUNG, CHRIS — S — BRONCOS

PERSONAL: Born January 23, 1980, in Senoia, Ga. ... 6-0/210. ... Full name: Christopher Lamont Young.
HIGH SCHOOL: East Cowetta (Ga.).
COLLEGE: Georgia Tech.
TRANSACTIONS/CAREER NOTES: Selected by Denver Broncos in seventh round (228th pick overall) of 2002 NFL draft. ... Signed by Broncos (June 11, 2002). ... Released by Broncos (September 1, 2002). ... Re-signed by Broncos to practice squad (September 3, 2002). ... Activated (December 31, 2002). ... Assigned by Broncos to Frankfurt Galaxy in 2003 NFL Europe enhancement allocation program (February 4, 2003).

Year	Team	G	GS	TOTALS Tk.	Ast.	Sks.	INTERCEPTIONS No.	Yds.	Avg.	TD
2003	Denver NFL	11	0	0	1	0.0	0	0	0.0	0

YOUNG, DAVID — S — BROWNS

PERSONAL: Born May 17, 1979, in Columbia, S.C. ... 6-1/209. ... Full name: David F. Young.
HIGH SCHOOL: Keenan (Columbia, S.C.).
COLLEGE: Georgia Southern.
TRANSACTIONS/CAREER NOTES: Selected by Jacksonville Jaguars in sixth round (179th pick overall) of 2003 NFL draft. ... Waived by Jaguars (September 8, 2003). ... Signed by Cleveland Browns to practice squad (September 12, 2003). ... Signed by New York Jets off Browns practice squad (October 15, 2003). ... Waived by Jets (December 17, 2003). ... Signed by Browns to practice squad (December 22, 2003).

Year	Team	G	GS	TOTALS Tk.	Ast.	Sks.	INTERCEPTIONS No.	Yds.	Avg.	TD
2003	New York Jets NFL	5	0	0	0	0.0	0	0	0.0	0

YOUNG, MICHAEL — LB — CARDINALS

PERSONAL: Born June 1, 1978, in St. Louis, Mo. ... 6-2/245. ... Full name: Michael Young.
HIGH SCHOOL: Hazelwood East (Hazelwood, Mo.).
COLLEGE: Illinois.
TRANSACTIONS/CAREER NOTES: Signed as non-drafted free agent by Arizona Cardinals (April 23, 2001). ... Released by Cardinals (August 27, 2001). ... Re-signed by Cardinals to practice squad (September 3, 2001). ... Released by Cardinals (September 12, 2003). ... Re-signed by Cardinals (November 18, 2003). ... Granted free agency (March 4, 2004). ... Re-signed by Cardinals (April 8, 2004).

Year	Team	G	GS	TOTALS Tk.	Ast.	Sks.	INTERCEPTIONS No.	Yds.	Avg.	TD
2002	Arizona NFL	16	2	13	4	0.0	0	0	0.0	0
2003	Arizona NFL	6	0	0	0	0.0	0	0	0.0	0
Pro totals (2 years)		22	2	13	4	0.0	0	0	0.0	0

YOUNG, RYAN — T

PERSONAL: Born June 28, 1976, in St. Louis, Mo. ... 6-5/320.
HIGH SCHOOL: Parkway Central (Chesterfield, Mo.).
COLLEGE: Kansas State.
TRANSACTIONS/CAREER NOTES: Selected by New York Jets in seventh round (223rd pick overall) of 1999 NFL draft. ... Signed by Jets (June 25, 1999). ... Selected by Houston Texans from Jets in NFL expansion draft (February 18, 2002). ... Granted unconditional free agency (February 28, 2003). ... Signed by Dallas Cowboys (March 5, 2003). ... Released by Cowboys (March 2, 2004).
PLAYING EXPERIENCE: New York Jets NFL, 1999-2001; Houston NFL, 2002; Dallas NFL, 2003. ... Games/Games started: 1999 (15/7), 2000 (16/16), 2001 (16/16), 2002 (10/8), 2003 (11/8). Total: 68/55.

Year	Team	G	GS	RECEIVING No.	Yds.	Avg.	TD	TOTALS TD	2pt.	Pts.	Fum.
2003	Carolina NFL	7	0	0	0	0.0	0	0	0	0	0

YOUNG, WALTER — WR — PANTHERS

PERSONAL: Born December 7, 1979, in Chicago Heights, Ill. ... 6-5/214. ... Full name: Walter Young Jr.
HIGH SCHOOL: Rich East (Park Forest, Ill.).
COLLEGE: Illinois.
TRANSACTIONS/CAREER NOTES: Selected by Carolina Panthers in seventh round (226th pick overall) of 2003 NFL draft. ... Signed by Panthers (May 22, 2003). ... On injured reserve with wrist injury (December 20, 2003-remainder of season).

Year	Team	G	GS	RECEIVING No.	Yds.	Avg.	TD	TOTALS TD	2pt.	Pts.	Fum.
2003	Carolina NFL	7	0	0	0	0.0	0	0	0	0	0

Z

ZASTUDIL, DAVE — P — RAVENS

PERSONAL: Born October 26, 1978, in Bay Village, Ohio. ... 6-3/210.
HIGH SCHOOL: Bay Village (Ohio).
COLLEGE: Ohio.
TRANSACTIONS/CAREER NOTES: Selected by Baltimore Ravens in fourth round (112th pick overall) of 2002 NFL draft. ... Signed by Ravens (July 26, 2002).
HONORS: Named punter on THE SPORTING NEWS college All-America third team (2001).

		PUNTING					
Year Team	G	No.	Yds.	Avg.	Net avg.	In. 20	Blk.
2002—Baltimore NFL	16	81	3368	41.6	33.7	31	2
2003—Baltimore NFL	16	89	3649	41.0	35.2	21	0
Pro totals (2 years)	32	170	7017	41.3	34.5	52	2

ZELENKA, JOE — TE/LS — JAGUARS

PERSONAL: Born March 9, 1976, in Cleveland, Ohio. ... 6-3/261. ... Full name: Joseph John Zelenka.
HIGH SCHOOL: Benedictine (Cleveland).
COLLEGE: Wake Forest.
TRANSACTIONS/CAREER NOTES: Signed as non-drafted free agent by San Francisco 49ers (April 23, 1999). ... Traded by 49ers to Washington Redskins for seventh-round pick (TE Eric Johnson) in 2001 draft (April 17, 2000). ... Released by Redskins (March 9, 2001). ... Signed by Jacksonville Jaguars (August 13, 2001). ... Granted unconditional free agency (February 28, 2003). ... Re-signed by Jaguars (February 28, 2003). ... Granted unconditional free agency (March 3, 2004). ... Re-signed by Jaguars (March 3, 2004).
PLAYING EXPERIENCE: San Francisco NFL, 1999; Washington NFL, 2000; Jacksonville NFL, 2001-2003. ... Games/Games started: 1999 (13/0), 2000 (16/0), 2001 (16/0), 2002 (16/0), 2003 (16/0). Total: 77/0.

ZELLNER, PEPPI — DE

PERSONAL: Born March 14, 1975, in Forsyth, Ga. ... 6-5/262. ... Full name: Hunndens Guiseppi Zellner.
HIGH SCHOOL: Mary Persons (Forsythe, Ga.).
JUNIOR COLLEGE: Georgia Military College.
COLLEGE: Fort Valley (Ga.) State.
TRANSACTIONS/CAREER NOTES: Selected by Dallas Cowboys in fourth round (132nd pick overall) of 1999 NFL draft. ... Signed by Cowboys (July 27, 1999). ... On injured reserve with knee injury (December 12, 2000-remainder of season). ... On physically unable to perform list with knee injury (July 22-August 14, 2001). ... Granted unconditional free agency (February 28, 2003). ... Signed by Washington Redskins (May 13, 2003). ... Granted unconditional free agency (March 3, 2004).

			TOTALS		
Year Team	G	GS	Tk.	Ast.	Sks.
1999—Dallas NFL	13	0	9	0	1.0
2000—Dallas NFL	12	0	7	3	2.0
2001—Dallas NFL	16	15	36	10	3.0
2002—Dallas NFL	16	2	22	7	0.0
2003—Washington NFL	16	0	12	2	1.0
Pro totals (5 years)	73	17	86	22	7.0

ZEREOUE, AMOS — RB — RAIDERS

PERSONAL: Born October 8, 1976, in Hempstead, N.Y. ... 5-8/212. ... Name pronounced: zer-O-way.
HIGH SCHOOL: W.C. Mepham (Hempstead, N.Y.).
COLLEGE: West Virginia.
TRANSACTIONS/CAREER NOTES: Selected after junior season by Pittsburgh Steelers in third round (95th pick overall) of 1999 NFL draft. ... Signed by Steelers (July 30, 1999). ... Granted free agency (March 1, 2002). ... Re-signed by Steelers (June 13, 2002). ... Released by Steelers (March 11, 2004). ... Signed by Oakland Raiders (April 29, 2004).
CHAMPIONSHIP GAME EXPERIENCE: Played in AFC championship game (2001 season).
HONORS: Named running back on THE SPORTING NEWS college All-America third team (1997).
SINGLE GAME HIGHS (regular season): Attempts—37 (November 10, 2002, vs. Atlanta); yards—123 (November 10, 2002, vs. Atlanta); and rushing touchdowns—2 (December 29, 2002, vs. Baltimore).
STATISTICAL PLATEAUS: 100-yard rushing games: 2002 (3). Total: 3.

			RUSHING				RECEIVING				KICKOFF RETURNS				TOTALS			
Year Team	G	GS	Att.	Yds.	Avg.	TD	No.	Yds.	Avg.	TD	No.	Yds.	Avg.	TD	TD	2pt.	Pts.	Fum.
1999—Pittsburgh NFL	8	0	18	48	2.7	0	2	17	8.5	0	7	169	24.1	0	0	0	0	0
2000—Pittsburgh NFL	12	0	6	14	2.3	0	0	0	0.0	0	0	0	0.0	0	0	0	0	0
2001—Pittsburgh NFL	14	0	85	441	5.2	1	13	154	11.8	1	0	0	0.0	0	2	0	12	3
2002—Pittsburgh NFL	16	5	193	762	3.9	4	42	341	8.1	0	0	0	0.0	0	4	0	24	2
2003—Pittsburgh NFL	16	6	132	433	3.3	2	40	310	7.8	0	0	0	0.0	0	2	0	12	0
Pro totals (5 years)	66	11	434	1698	3.9	7	97	822	8.5	1	7	169	24.1	0	8	0	48	5

ZGONINA, JEFF — DT — DOLPHINS

PERSONAL: Born May 24, 1970, in Chicago, Ill. ... 6-2/285. ... Full name: Jeffrey Marc Zgonina. ... Name pronounced: ska-KNEE-na.
HIGH SCHOOL: Mount Carmel (Chicago).
COLLEGE: Purdue.

TRANSACTIONS/CAREER NOTES: Selected by Pittsburgh Steelers in seventh round (185th pick overall) of 1993 NFL draft. ... Signed by Steelers (July 16, 1993). ... Claimed on waivers by Carolina Panthers (August 28, 1995). ... Granted free agency (February 16, 1996). ... Re-signed by Panthers (April 11, 1996). ... Released by Panthers (August 19, 1996). ... Signed by Atlanta Falcons (October 8, 1996). ... Granted unconditional free agency (February 14, 1997). ... Signed by St. Louis Rams (March 17, 1997). ... Released by Rams (August 30, 1998). ... Signed by Oakland Raiders (October 13, 1998). ... Released by Raiders (October 18, 1998). ... Signed by Indianapolis Colts (November 25, 1998). ... Granted unconditional free agency (February 12, 1999). ... Signed by Rams (April 5, 1999). ... Released by Rams (April 1, 2002). ... Re-signed by Rams (April 2, 2002). ... Granted unconditional free agency (February 28, 2003). ... Signed by Miami Dolphins (March 31, 2003).

CHAMPIONSHIP GAME EXPERIENCE: Played in AFC championship game (1994 season). ... Played in NFC championship game (1999 and 2001 seasons). ... Member of Super Bowl championship team (1999 season). ... Played in Super Bowl 36 (2001 season).

			TOTALS			INTERCEPTIONS			
Year Team	**G**	**GS**	**Tk.**	**Ast.**	**Sks.**	**No.**	**Yds.**	**Avg.**	**TD**
1993—Pittsburgh NFL	5	0	11	5	0.0	0	0	0.0	0
1994—Pittsburgh NFL	16	0	6	5	0.0	0	0	0.0	0
1995—Carolina NFL	2	0	2	0	0.0	0	0	0.0	0
1996—Atlanta NFL	8	0	7	5	1.0	0	0	0.0	0
1997—St. Louis NFL	15	0	19	2	2.0	0	0	0.0	0
1998—Indianapolis NFL	2	0	0	0	0.0	0	0	0.0	0
1999—St. Louis NFL	16	0	26	5	4.5	0	0	0.0	0
2000—St. Louis NFL	16	11	30	7	2.0	0	0	0.0	0
2001—St. Louis NFL	13	13	32	6	0.0	0	0	0.0	0
2002—St. Louis NFL	16	16	29	9	4.0	0	0	0.0	0
2003—Miami NFL	16	3	22	17	3.0	1	0	0.0	0
Pro totals (11 years)	125	43	184	61	16.5	1	0	0.0	0

ZUKAUSKAS, PAUL — T — BROWNS

PERSONAL: Born July 12, 1979, in Weymouth, Mass. ... 6-5/320. ... Full name: Paul Malcolm Zukauskas.

HIGH SCHOOL: Boston College (Ma.).

COLLEGE: Boston College.

TRANSACTIONS/CAREER NOTES: Selected by Cleveland Browns in seventh round (203rd pick overall) of 2001 NFL draft. ... Signed by Browns (July 20, 2001). ... Released by Browns (September 1, 2001). ... Re-signed by Browns to practice squad (September 3, 2001). ... Activated (November 21, 2001). ... Granted free agency (March 3, 2004). ... Re-signed by Browns (April 8, 2004).

PLAYING EXPERIENCE: Cleveland NFL, 2001-2003. ... Games/Games started: 2001 (1/0), 2002 (16/3), 2003 (12/10). Total: 29/13.

HONORS: Named guard on THE SPORTING NEWS college All-America second team (2000).

2004 DRAFT PICKS

ABNEY, DEREK — WR — RAVENS

PERSONAL: Born December 19, 1980, in Mosinee, Wisc. ... 5-9/179. ... Full name: Derek Allen Abney.
HIGH SCHOOL: D.C. Everest (Schofield, Wisc.).
COLLEGE: Kentucky.
TRANSACTIONS/CAREER NOTES: Selected by Baltimore Ravens in seventh round (244th pick overall) of 2004 NFL draft.

		RECEIVING				PUNT RETURNS				KICKOFF RETURNS				TOTALS	
Year Team	G	No.	Yds.	Avg.	TD	No.	Yds.	Avg.	TD	No.	Yds.	Avg.	TD	TD	Pts.
2000—Kentucky	11	40	413	10.3	3	1	1	1.0	0	0	0	0.0	0	3	18
2001—Kentucky	11	66	741	11.2	6	22	212	9.6	1	33	739	22.4	0	7	42
2002—Kentucky	12	40	569	14.2	4	36	544	15.1	4	30	804	26.8	2	10	60
2003—Kentucky	12	51	616	12.1	5	29	285	9.8	1	32	772	24.1	0	6	38
College totals (4 years)	46	197	2339	11.9	18	88	1042	11.8	6	95	2315	24.4	2	26	158

ADIBI, NATHANIEL — DE — STEELERS

PERSONAL: Born January 25, 1981, in Hampton, Va. ... 6-3/254. ... Full name: Nathaniel Barnell Adibi.
HIGH SCHOOL: Phoebus (Hampton, Va.).
COLLEGE: Virginia Tech.
TRANSACTIONS/CAREER NOTES: Selected by Pittsburgh Steelers in fifth round (145th pick overall) of 2004 NFL draft.
HONORS: Named defensive lineman on THE SPORTING NEWS Freshman All-America first team (2000).

Year Team	G	SACKS
2000—Virginia Tech	11	5.0
2001—Virginia Tech	11	1.0
2002—Virginia Tech	14	9.0
2003—Virginia Tech	12	5.5
College totals (4 years)	48	20.5

ALLEN, JARED — DE — CHIEFS

PERSONAL: Born April 3, 1982, in Los Gatos, Calif. ... 6-6/265.
HIGH SCHOOL: Los Gatos (Calif.).
COLLEGE: Idaho State.
TRANSACTIONS/CAREER NOTES: Selected by Kansas City Chiefs in fourth round (126th pick overall) of 2004 NFL draft.

			INTERCEPTIONS			
Year Team	G	Sks.	No.	Yds.	Avg.	TD
2000—Idaho State	8	4.0	1	0	0.0	0
2001—Idaho State	10	6.5	1	38	38.0	1
2002—Idaho State	11	10.5	1	0	0.0	0
2003—Idaho State	12	17.0	0	0	0.0	0
College totals (4 years)	41	38.0	3	38	12.7	1

ALLEN, WILL — DB — BUCCANEERS

PERSONAL: Born June 17, 1982, in Dayton, Ohio. ... 6-2/190.
HIGH SCHOOL: Wayne (Dayton, Ohio).
COLLEGE: Ohio State.
TRANSACTIONS/CAREER NOTES: Selected by Tampa Bay Buccaneers in fourth round (111th pick overall) of 2004 NFL draft.

			INTERCEPTIONS			
Year Team	G	Sks.	No.	Yds.	Avg.	TD
2000—Ohio State	11	0.0	0	0	0.0	0
2001—Ohio State	11	1.0	1	32	32.0	0
2002—Ohio State	13	1.0	2	0	0.0	0
2003—Ohio State	13	0.0	2	107	53.5	1
College totals (4 years)	48	2.0	5	139	27.8	1

AMANO, EUGENE — G — TITANS

PERSONAL: Born August 1, 1982, in San Pedro, Calif. ... 6-3/295.
HIGH SCHOOL: Rancho Bernardo (San Diego, Calif.). **COLLEGE:** Southeast Missouri.
TRANSACTIONS/CAREER NOTES: Selected by Tennessee Titans in seventh round (239th pick overall) of 2004 NFL draft.
PLAYING EXPERIENCE: Southeast Missouri State, 2000-2003. ... Games played: 2000 (11), 2001 (11), 2002 (12), 2003 (12). Total: 46.

ANDERSON, CHARLIE — DE/LB — TEXANS

PERSONAL: Born December 8, 1981, in Jackson, Miss. ... 6-4/240. ... Full name: Charlie Alexander Anderson.
HIGH SCHOOL: Provine (Jackson, Miss.).
COLLEGE: Mississippi.
TRANSACTIONS/CAREER NOTES: Selected by Houston Texans in sixth round (200th pick overall) of 2004 NFL draft.

Year Team	G	SACKS
2000—Mississippi	11	1.0
2001—Mississippi	11	2.5
2002—Mississippi	13	3.5
2003—Mississippi	13	5.5
College totals (4 years)	48	12.5

ANDERSON, COURTNEY — TE — RAIDERS

PERSONAL: Born November 19, 1980, in Greenville, Texas. ... 6-7/267.
HIGH SCHOOL: Richmond (Calif.).
COLLEGE: Contra Costa, then San Jose State.
TRANSACTIONS/CAREER NOTES: Selected by Oakland Raiders in seventh round (245th pick overall) of 2004 NFL draft.

		RECEIVING			
Year Team	**G**	**No.**	**Yds.**	**Avg.**	**TD**
2002—San Jose State	13	13	155	11.9	2
2003—San Jose State	10	23	322	14.0	5
College totals (2 years)	23	36	477	13.3	7

ANDERSON, TIM — DT — BILLS

PERSONAL: Born November 22, 1980, in Clyde, Ohio. ... 6-4/289.
HIGH SCHOOL: Clyde (Ohio).
COLLEGE: Ohio State.
TRANSACTIONS/CAREER NOTES: Selected by Buffalo Bills in third round (74th pick overall) of 2004 NFL draft.

			INTERCEPTIONS			
Year Team	**G**	**Sks.**	**No.**	**Yds.**	**Avg.**	**TD**
2000—Ohio State	7	2.0	0	0	0.0	0
2001—Ohio State	11	3.0	1	4	4.0	0
2002—Ohio State	12	2.5	0	0	0.0	0
2003—Ohio State	13	3.5	0	0	0.0	0
College totals (4 years)	43	11.0	1	4	4.0	0

ANDREWS, SHAWN — T — EAGLES

PERSONAL: Born December 25, 1982, in Camden, Ark. ... 6-5/370. ... Brother of Stacy Andrews, offensive tackle, Cincinnati Bengals.
HIGH SCHOOL: Fairview (Camden, Ark.).
COLLEGE: Arkansas.
TRANSACTIONS/CAREER NOTES: Selected after junior season by Philadelphia Eagles in first round (16th pick overall) of 2004 NFL draft.
PLAYING EXPERIENCE: Arkansas, 2001-2003. ... Games played: 2001 (11), 2002 (13), 2003 (12). Total: 36.
HONORS: Named offensive tackle on THE SPORTING NEWS Freshman All-America first team (2001). ... Named offensive tackle on THE SPORTING NEWS college All-America first team (2002 and 2003).

ANDREWS, STACY — T — BENGALS

PERSONAL: Born June 2, 1981, in Camden, Ark. ... 6-5/330. ... Full name: Stacy Dewayne Andrews. ... Brother of Shawn Andrews, offensive tackle, Philadelphia Eagles.
HIGH SCHOOL: Fairview (Camden, Ark.).
COLLEGE: Mississippi.
TRANSACTIONS/CAREER NOTES: Selected by Cincinnati Bengals in fourth round (123rd pick overall) of 2004 NFL draft.
PLAYING EXPERIENCE: Mississippi, 2003. ... Games played: 2003 (5). Total: 5.

ASKEW, MATTHIAS — DT — BENGALS

PERSONAL: Born July 1, 1982, in Fort Lauderdale, Fla. ... 6-5/308.
HIGH SCHOOL: Dillard (Fort Lauderdale, Fla.).
COLLEGE: Michigan State.
TRANSACTIONS/CAREER NOTES: Selected after junior season by Cincinnati Bengals in fourth round (114th pick overall) of 2004 NFL draft.

			INTERCEPTIONS			
Year Team	**G**	**Sks.**	**No.**	**Yds.**	**Avg.**	**TD**
2001—Michigan State	10	0.0	0	0	0.0	0
2002—Michigan State	12	1.0	1	2	2.0	0
2003—Michigan State	13	6.0	0	0	0.0	0
College totals (3 years)	35	7.0	1	2	2.0	0

BABIN, JASON — LB/DE — TEXANS

PERSONAL: Born May 24, 1980, in Kalamazoo, Mich. ... 6-4/265.
HIGH SCHOOL: Paw Paw (Mich.).
COLLEGE: Western Michigan.
TRANSACTIONS/CAREER NOTES: Selected by Houston Texans in first round (27th pick overall) of 2004 NFL draft.
HONORS: Named defensive end on THE SPORTING NEWS college All-America second team (2003).

Year Team	**G**	**SACKS**
2000—Western Michigan	12	1.0
2001—Western Michigan	11	7.0
2002—Western Michigan	12	16.0
2003—Western Michigan	12	15.0
College totals (4 years)	47	39.0

BALL, DAVE — DE — CHARGERS

PERSONAL: Born January 4, 1981, in Fairfield, Calif. ... 6-6/275. ... Full name: David Stewart Ball.
HIGH SCHOOL: Dixon (Dixon, Calif.).
COLLEGE: UCLA.
TRANSACTIONS/CAREER NOTES: Selected by San Diego Chargers in fifth round (133rd pick overall) of 2004 NFL draft.
HONORS: Named defensive end on THE SPORTING NEWS college All-America first team (2003).

Year Team	G	SACKS
2000—UCLA	11	2.0
2001—UCLA	11	1.0
2002—UCLA	13	11.0
2003—UCLA	13	16.5
College totals (4 years)	48	30.5

BELL, JACOB — G — TITANS

PERSONAL: Born March 2, 1981, in Euclid, Ohio. ... 6-5/300.
HIGH SCHOOL: St. Ignatius (Euclid, Ohio).
COLLEGE: Miami of Ohio.
TRANSACTIONS/CAREER NOTES: Selected by Tennessee Titans in fifth round (138th pick overall) of 2004 NFL draft.
PLAYING EXPERIENCE: Miami of Ohio, 2000-2003. ... Games played: 2000 (11), 2001 (2), 2002 (12), 2003 (14). Total: 39.

BELL, TATUM — RB — BRONCOS

PERSONAL: Born March 2, 1981, in Dallas, Texas. ... 5-11/190.
HIGH SCHOOL: DeSoto (Texas).
COLLEGE: Oklahoma State.
TRANSACTIONS/CAREER NOTES: Selected by Denver Broncos in second round (41st pick overall) of 2004 NFL draft.

		RUSHING				RECEIVING				TOTALS	
Year Team	G	Att.	Yds.	Avg.	TD	No.	Yds.	Avg.	TD	TD	Pts.
2000—Oklahoma State	9	49	251	5.1	1	5	42	8.4	0	1	6
2001—Oklahoma State	10	197	776	3.9	6	18	97	5.4	0	6	36
2002—Oklahoma State	11	175	1096	6.3	11	4	59	14.8	2	13	78
2003—Oklahoma State	12	213	1286	6.0	16	9	60	6.7	0	16	96
College totals (4 years)	42	634	3409	5.4	34	36	258	7.2	2	36	216

BERRIAN, BERNARD — WR — BEARS

PERSONAL: Born December 27, 1980, in Winton, Calif. ... 6-1/190.
HIGH SCHOOL: Atwater (Winton, Calif.).
COLLEGE: Fresno State.
TRANSACTIONS/CAREER NOTES: Selected by Chicago Bears in third round (78th pick overall) of 2004 NFL draft.
HONORS: Named kick returner on THE SPORTING NEWS college All-America fourth team (2001).

		RUSHING				RECEIVING				PUNT RETURNS				KICKOFF RETURNS				TOTALS	
Year Team	G	Att.	Yds.	Avg.	TD	No.	Yds.	Avg.	TD	No.	Yds.	Avg.	TD	No.	Yds.	Avg.	TD	TD	Pts.
1999—Fresno State	9	0	0	0.0	0	6	58	9.7	1	0	0	0.0	0	0	0	0.0	0	1	6
2000—Fresno State	9	1	2	2.0	0	36	543	15.1	4	15	158	10.5	1	8	128	16.0	0	5	32
2001—Fresno State	13	6	101	16.8	0	76	1270	16.7	13	39	552	14.2	1	27	668	24.7	1	15	92
2002—Fresno State	1	0	0	0.0	0	2	54	27.0	1	1	1	1.0	0	0	0	0.0	0	1	6
2003—Fresno State	14	13	171	13.2	2	63	668	10.6	4	42	429	10.2	1	26	631	24.3	0	7	44
College totals (5 years)	46	20	274	13.7	2	183	2593	14.2	23	97	1140	11.8	3	61	1427	23.4	1	29	180

BINGHAM, RYON — DT — CHARGERS

PERSONAL: Born June 6, 1981, in Sandy, Utah. ... 6-3/303.
HIGH SCHOOL: Alta (Sandy, Utah).
COLLEGE: Nebraska.
TRANSACTIONS/CAREER NOTES: Selected by San Diego Chargers in seventh round (204th pick overall) of 2004 NFL draft.

Year Team	G	SACKS
2001—Nebraska	12	0.5
2002—Nebraska	14	1.0
2003—Nebraska	11	2.0
College totals (3 years)	37	3.5

BOCKWOLDT, COLBY — LB — SAINTS

PERSONAL: Born April 14, 1981, in Ogden, Utah. ... 6-1/225.
HIGH SCHOOL: Northridge (Sunset, Utah).
COLLEGE: Brigham Young.
TRANSACTIONS/CAREER NOTES: Selected by New Orleans Saints in seventh round (240th pick overall) of 2004 NFL draft.

Year Team	G	Sks.	INTERCEPTIONS No.	Yds.	Avg.	TD
2000—Brigham Young	7	0.0	0	0	0.0	0
2001—Brigham Young	13	1.0	0	0	0.0	0
2002—Brigham Young	12	3.0	0	0	0.0	0
2003—Brigham Young	12	4.5	2	8	4.0	0
College totals (4 years)	44	8.5	2	8	4.0	0

BOULWARE, MICHAEL — SS/LB — SEAHAWKS

PERSONAL: Born September 17, 1981, in Columbia, S.C. ... 6-3/220. ... Brother of Peter Boulware, linebacker, Baltimore Ravens.
HIGH SCHOOL: Spring Valley (Columbia, S.C.).
COLLEGE: Florida State.
TRANSACTIONS/CAREER NOTES: Selected by Seattle Seahawks in second round (53rd pick overall) of 2004 NFL draft.

Year Team	G	Sks.	INTERCEPTIONS No.	Yds.	Avg.	TD
2000—Florida State	9	0.0	0	0	0.0	0
2001—Florida State	11	0.0	3	52	17.3	1
2002—Florida State	14	1.0	2	1	0.5	0
2003—Florida State	13	2.5	0	0	0.0	0
College totals (4 years)	47	3.5	5	53	10.6	1

BRAMLET, CASEY — QB — BENGALS

PERSONAL: Born in Wheatland, Wyo. ... 6-4/209. ... Full name: Corey Bramlet.
HIGH SCHOOL: Wheatland (Wyo.).
COLLEGE: Wyoming.
TRANSACTIONS/CAREER NOTES: Selected by Cincinnati Bengals in seventh round (218th pick overall) of 2004 NFL draft.

		PASSING								RUSHING				TOTALS	
Year Team	**G**	**Att.**	**Cmp.**	**Pct.**	**Yds.**	**TD**	**Int.**	**Avg.**	**Rat.**	**Att.**	**Yds.**	**Avg.**	**TD**	**TD**	**Pts.**
2000—Wyoming	5	57	24	42.1	288	1	1	5.05	86.8	8	-22	-2.7	0	0	0
2001—Wyoming	11	432	225	52.1	3069	9	20	7.10	109.4	89	-21	-0.2	6	6	38
2002—Wyoming	12	464	277	59.7	3290	24	18	7.09	128.6	101	35	0.3	5	5	34
2003—Wyoming	12	425	241	56.7	3037	22	9	7.15	129.6	98	-101	-1.0	3	3	18
College totals (4 years)	40	1378	767	55.7	9684	56	48	7.03	121.1	296	-109	-0.4	14	14	90

BROOKS, GREG — CB — BENGALS

PERSONAL: Born December 16, 1980, in New Orleans, La. ... 5-11/175.
HIGH SCHOOL: Shaw (New Orleans, La.).
COLLEGE: Southern Mississippi.
TRANSACTIONS/CAREER NOTES: Selected by Cincinnati Bengals in sixth round (183rd pick overall) of 2004 NFL draft.

Year Team	G	Sks.	INTERCEPTIONS No.	Yds.	Avg.	TD
2000—Southern Mississippi	11	0.0	0	0	0.0	0
2001—Southern Mississippi	11	1.0	3	0	0.0	0
2002—Southern Mississippi	13	0.0	3	0	0.0	0
2003—Southern Mississippi	11	1.0	3	24	8.0	0
College totals (4 years)	46	2.0	9	24	2.7	0

BUA, TONY — LB — DOLPHINS

PERSONAL: Born February 11, 1980, in River Ridge, La. ... 5-11/218. ... Full name: Anthony Bua.
HIGH SCHOOL: John Curtis (River Ridge, La.).
COLLEGE: Arkansas.
TRANSACTIONS/CAREER NOTES: Selected by Miami Dolphins in fifth round (160th pick overall) of 2004 NFL draft.

Year Team	G	Sks.	INTERCEPTIONS No.	Yds.	Avg.	TD
2000—Arkansas	10	0.0	0	0	0.0	0
2001—Arkansas	10	1.0	2	17	8.5	0
2002—Arkansas	13	4.0	2	13	6.5	0
2003—Arkansas	13	1.0	2	0	0.0	0
College totals (4 years)	46	6.0	6	30	5.0	0

BUBIN, SEAN — T — JAGUARS

PERSONAL: Born January 26, 1981, in Rantoul, Ill. ... 6-7/300. ... Full name: Sean Christopher Bubin.
HIGH SCHOOL: Rantoul (Rantoul, Ill.).
COLLEGE: Illinois.
TRANSACTIONS/CAREER NOTES: Selected by Jacksonville Jaguars in fifth round (159th pick overall) of 2004 NFL draft.
PLAYING EXPERIENCE: Illinois, 2001-2003. ... Games played: 2001 (11), 2002 (12), 2003 (12). Total: 35.

BUTLER, KELLY — T — LIONS

PERSONAL: Born July 24, 1982, in Grand Rapids, Mich. ... 6-8/299. ... Full name: Kelly Don Butler.
HIGH SCHOOL: Union (Grand Rapids, Mich.).
COLLEGE: Purdue.
TRANSACTIONS/CAREER NOTES: Selected after junior season by Detroit Lions in sixth round (172nd pick overall) of 2004 NFL draft.
PLAYING EXPERIENCE: Purdue, 2001-2003. ... Games played: 2001 (11), 2002 (13), 2003 (13). Total: 37.

CAREY, VERNON — G — DOLPHINS

PERSONAL: Born July 13, 1981, in Miami, Fla. ... 6-5/363. ... Full name: Vernon A. Carey.
HIGH SCHOOL: Northwestern (Miami, Fla.).
COLLEGE: Miami (Fla.).
TRANSACTIONS/CAREER NOTES: Selected by Miami Dolphins in first round (19th pick overall) of 2004 NFL draft.
PLAYING EXPERIENCE: Miami (Fla.), 2000-2003. ... Games played: 2000 (8), 2001 (11), 2002 (12), 2003 (11). Total: 42.

CARROLL, AHMAD — CB — PACKERS

PERSONAL: Born August 4, 1983, in Atlanta, Ga. ... 5-11/190.
HIGH SCHOOL: Douglass (Atlanta, Ga.).
COLLEGE: Arkansas.
TRANSACTIONS/CAREER NOTES: Selected after junior season by Green Bay Packers in first round (25th pick overall) of 2004 NFL draft.
HONORS: Named cornerback on THE SPORTING NEWS Freshman All-America third team (2001).

			INTERCEPTIONS			
Year Team	**G**	**Sks.**	**No.**	**Yds.**	**Avg.**	**TD**
2001—Arkansas	10	0.0	1	43	43.0	0
2002—Arkansas	13	1.0	0	0	0.0	0
2003—Arkansas	13	0.0	3	0	0.0	0
College totals (3 years)	36	1.0	4	43	10.8	0

CARTER, DREW — WR — PANTHERS

PERSONAL: Born September 5, 1981, in Solon, Ohio. ... 6-4/200.
HIGH SCHOOL: Solon (Solon, Ohio).
COLLEGE: Ohio State.
TRANSACTIONS/CAREER NOTES: Selected by Carolina Panthers in fifth round (163rd pick overall) of 2004 NFL draft.

		RECEIVING			
Year Team	**G**	**No.**	**Yds.**	**Avg.**	**TD**
2000—Ohio State	11	6	75	12.5	0
2002—Ohio State	14	10	147	14.7	0
2003—Ohio State	8	25	410	16.4	1
College totals (3 years)	33	41	632	15.4	1

CAVKA, MARKO — T — JETS

PERSONAL: Born April 7, 1981, in Cypress, Calif. ... 6-7/294.
COLLEGE: Sacramento State.
TRANSACTIONS/CAREER NOTES: Selected by New York Jets in sixth round (178th pick overall) of 2004 NFL draft.
PLAYING EXPERIENCE: Sacramento State, 2000-2003. ... Games played: 2000 (7), 2001 (11), 2002 (12), 2003 (11). Total: 41.

CAYLOR, DREW — C — STEELERS

PERSONAL: Born January 27, 1981, in Kensington, Md. ... 6-6/270.
HIGH SCHOOL: Bethesda Chevy Chase (Kensington, Md.).
COLLEGE: Stanford.
TRANSACTIONS/CAREER NOTES: Selected by Pittsburgh Steelers in sixth round (197th pick overall) of 2004 NFL draft. ... Signed by Steelers (May 17, 2004).
PLAYING EXPERIENCE: Stanford, 2001-2003. ... Games played: 2001 (10), 2002 (11), 2003 (11). Total: 32.

CHAMBERS, KIRK — T — BROWNS

PERSONAL: Born March 19, 1979, in Provo, Utah. ... 6-7/307.
HIGH SCHOOL: Provo (Utah).
COLLEGE: Stanford.
TRANSACTIONS/CAREER NOTES: Selected by Cleveland Browns in sixth round (176th pick overall) of 2004 NFL draft.
PLAYING EXPERIENCE: Stanford, 2000-2003. ... Games played: 2000 (11), 2001 (11), 2002 (11), 2003 (11). Total: 44.

CHILLAR, BRANDON — LB — RAMS

PERSONAL: Born October 21, 1982, in Los Angeles, Calif. ... 6-3/230. ... Full name: Brandon Oneil Chillar.
HIGH SCHOOL: Carlsbad (Calif.).
COLLEGE: UCLA.

TRANSACTIONS/CAREER NOTES: Selected by St. Louis Rams in fourth round (130th pick overall) of 2004 NFL draft.

			INTERCEPTIONS			
Year Team	G	Sks.	No.	Yds.	Avg.	TD
2000—UCLA	11	0.0	0	0	0.0	0
2001—UCLA	11	4.5	1	20	20.0	0
2002—UCLA	13	5.0	1	0	0.0	0
2003—UCLA	13	2.0	1	0	0.0	0
College totals (4 years)	48	11.5	3	20	6.7	0

CLARKE, ADRIEN — G — EAGLES

PERSONAL: Born March 26, 1981, in Shaker Heights, Ohio. ... 6-5/330.
HIGH SCHOOL: Shaker Heights (Shaker Heights, Ohio).
COLLEGE: Ohio State.
TRANSACTIONS/CAREER NOTES: Selected by Philadelphia Eagles in seventh round (227th pick overall) of 2004 NFL draft.
PLAYING EXPERIENCE: Ohio State, 2001-2003. ... Games played: 2001 (11), 2002 (13), 2003 (12). Total: 36.
HONORS: Named offensive lineman on THE SPORTING NEWS Freshman All-America first team (2000).

CLAUSS, JARED — DT — TITANS

PERSONAL: Born April 7, 1981, in West Des Moines, Iowa. ... 6-5/280.
HIGH SCHOOL: Valley (West Des Moines, Iowa).
COLLEGE: Iowa.
TRANSACTIONS/CAREER NOTES: Selected by Tennessee Titans in seventh round (230th pick overall) of 2004 NFL draft.

Year Team	G	SACKS
2000—Iowa	12	1.0
2001—Iowa	11	1.0
2002—Iowa	13	6.0
2003—Iowa	11	2.0
College totals (4 years)	47	10.0

CLAYTON, MICHAEL — WR — BUCCANEERS

PERSONAL: Born October 13, 1982, in Baton Rouge, La. ... 6-4/197. ... Full name: Michael Rashard Clayton.
HIGH SCHOOL: Christian Life Academy (Baton Rouge, La.).
COLLEGE: Louisiana State.
TRANSACTIONS/CAREER NOTES: Selected after junior season by Tampa Bay Buccaneers in first round (15th pick overall) of 2004 NFL draft.

		RECEIVING			
Year Team	G	No.	Yds.	Avg.	TD
2001—Louisiana State	12	47	754	16.0	6
2002—Louisiana State	13	57	749	13.1	5
2003—Louisiana State	14	78	1079	13.8	10
College totals (3 years)	39	182	2582	14.2	21

COBBS, CEDRIC — RB — PATRIOTS

PERSONAL: Born January 9, 1981, in Little Rock, Ark. ... 6-1/225.
HIGH SCHOOL: Fair (Little Rock, Ark.).
COLLEGE: Arkansas.
TRANSACTIONS/CAREER NOTES: Selected by New England Patriots in fourth round (128th pick overall) of 2004 NFL draft.

		RUSHING				RECEIVING				KICKOFF RETURNS				TOTALS	
Year Team	G	Att.	Yds.	Avg.	TD	No.	Yds.	Avg.	TD	No.	Yds.	Avg.	TD	TD	Pts.
1999—Arkansas	11	116	668	5.8	3	11	60	5.5	1	12	328	27.3	1	5	30
2000—Arkansas	3	70	291	4.2	4	2	26	13.0	0	0	0	0.0	0	4	24
2001—Arkansas	9	102	340	3.3	7	2	-2	-1.0	0	3	56	18.7	0	7	42
2002—Arkansas	11	74	399	5.4	2	3	20	6.7	0	6	117	19.5	0	2	12
2003—Arkansas	12	227	1320	5.8	10	8	34	4.3	0	0	0	0.0	0	10	60
College totals (5 years)	46	589	3018	5.1	26	26	138	5.3	1	21	501	23.9	1	28	168

COLBERT, KEARY — WR — PANTHERS

PERSONAL: Born May 21, 1982, in Oxnard, Calif. ... 6-2/210.
HIGH SCHOOL: Hueneme (Oxnard, Calif.).
COLLEGE: Southern California.
TRANSACTIONS/CAREER NOTES: Selected by Carolina Panthers in second round (62nd pick overall) of 2004 NFL draft.

		RECEIVING			
Year Team	G	No.	Yds.	Avg.	TD
2000—Southern California	12	33	480	14.5	3
2001—Southern California	11	32	404	12.6	2
2002—Southern California	13	71	1029	14.5	5
2003—Southern California	13	69	1013	14.7	9
College totals (4 years)	49	205	2926	14.3	19

COLCLOUGH, RICARDO — CB — STEELERS

PERSONAL: Born April 18, 1982, in Sumter, S.C. ... 5-10/186. ... Full name: Ricardo Sanchez Colclough.
HIGH SCHOOL: Sumter (S.C.).
COLLEGE: Tusculum.
TRANSACTIONS/CAREER NOTES: Selected by Pittsburgh Steelers in second round (38th pick overall) of 2004 NFL draft.

			INTERCEPTIONS				PUNT RETURNS				KICKOFF RETURNS				TOTALS	
Year Team	**G**	**Sks.**	**No.**	**Yds.**	**Avg.**	**TD**	**No.**	**Yds.**	**Avg.**	**TD**	**No.**	**Yds.**	**Avg.**	**TD**	**TD**	**Pts.**
2002—Tusculum	9	0.0	4	27	6.8	0	5	75	15.0	1	4	27	6.8	0	0	0
2003—Tusculum	11	0.0	11	111	10.1	1	19	270	14.2	1	19	552	29.1	2	2	12
College totals (2 years)	20	0.0	15	138	9.2	1	24	345	14.4	2	23	579	25.2	2	2	12

COLEMAN, ERIK — DB — JETS

PERSONAL: Born May 6, 1982, in Sacramento, Calif. ... 5-10/200. ... Full name: Erik James Coleman.
HIGH SCHOOL: Lewis and Clark (Spokane, Wash.).
COLLEGE: Washington State.
TRANSACTIONS/CAREER NOTES: Selected by New York Jets in fifth round (143rd pick overall) of 2004 NFL draft. ... Signed by Jets (May 26, 2004).

			INTERCEPTIONS				PUNT RETURNS				KICKOFF RETURNS				TOTALS	
Year Team	**G**	**Sks.**	**No.**	**Yds.**	**Avg.**	**TD**	**No.**	**Yds.**	**Avg.**	**TD**	**No.**	**Yds.**	**Avg.**	**TD**	**TD**	**Pts.**
2000—Washington State	8	0.0	0	0	0.0	0	1	17	17.0	0	8	203	25.4	0	0	0
2001—Washington State	10	0.0	3	47	15.7	1	7	48	6.9	0	7	151	21.6	0	1	6
2002—Washington State	13	0.0	2	25	12.5	1	0	9	0.0	0	8	154	19.3	0	3	18
2003—Washington State	13	1.0	7	22	3.1	0	1	10	10.0	0	0	0	0.0	0	0	0
College totals (4 years)	44	1.0	12	94	7.8	2	9	84	9.3	0	23	508	22.1	0	4	24

COOLEY, CHRIS — TE — REDSKINS

PERSONAL: Born July 11, 1982, in Powell, Wyo. ... 6-4/252.
HIGH SCHOOL: Logan (Utah).
COLLEGE: Utah State.
TRANSACTIONS/CAREER NOTES: Selected by Washington Redskins in third round (81st pick overall) of 2004 NFL draft.

		RECEIVING			
Year Team	**G**	**No.**	**Yds.**	**Avg.**	**TD**
2000—Utah State	8	0	0	0.0	0
2001—Utah State	11	3	21	7.0	1
2002—Utah State	11	31	502	16.2	4
2003—Utah State	10	62	732	11.8	6
College totals (4 years)	40	96	1255	13.1	11

COOPER, MARQUIS — LB — BUCCANEERS

PERSONAL: Born March 11, 1982, in Mesa, Ariz. ... 6-4/215.
HIGH SCHOOL: Highland (Gilbert, Ariz.).
COLLEGE: Washington.
TRANSACTIONS/CAREER NOTES: Selected by Tampa Bay Buccaneers in third round (79th pick overall) of 2004 NFL draft.

			INTERCEPTIONS			
Year Team	**G**	**Sks.**	**No.**	**Yds.**	**Avg.**	**TD**
2000—Washington	11	0.0	0	0	0.0	0
2001—Washington	11	0.0	0	0	0.0	0
2002—Washington	13	3.0	1	0	0.0	0
2003—Washington	12	4.0	2	58	29.0	1
College totals (4 years)	47	7.0	3	58	19.3	1

CORDOVA, JORGE — LB — JAGUARS

PERSONAL: Born September 25, 1981, in Murrieta, Calif. ... 6-2/250.
HIGH SCHOOL: Murrieta (Calif.).
COLLEGE: Nevada.
TRANSACTIONS/CAREER NOTES: Selected by Jacksonville Jaguars in third round (86th pick overall) of 2004 NFL draft.

Year Team	**G**	**SACKS**
2000—Nevada	11	5.0
2001—Nevada	8	4.0
2002—Nevada	11	8.5
2003—Nevada	12	11.5
College totals (4 years)	42	29.0

COTCHERY, JERRICHO — WR — JETS

PERSONAL: Born June 16, 1982, in Birmingham, Ala. ... 6-1/200.
HIGH SCHOOL: Phillips (Birmingham, Ala.).
COLLEGE: North Carolina State.

TRANSACTIONS/CAREER NOTES: Selected by New York Jets in fourth round (108th pick overall) of 2004 NFL draft.

Year Team	G	RUSHING Att.	Yds.	Avg.	TD	RECEIVING No.	Yds.	Avg.	TD	PUNT RETURNS No.	Yds.	Avg.	TD	TOTALS TD	Pts.
2000—North Carolina State	11	1	5	5.0	0	6	75	12.5	0	0	0	0.0	0	0	0
2001—North Carolina State	11	6	57	9.5	1	41	483	11.8	4	10	100	10.0	0	5	30
2002—North Carolina State	14	4	8	2.0	0	67	1192	17.8	7	20	109	5.5	0	8	48
2003—North Carolina State	13	7	32	4.6	0	86	1369	15.9	10	0	0	0.0	0	10	62
College totals (4 years)	49	18	102	5.7	1	200	3119	15.6	21	30	209	7.0	0	23	140

CRAMER, CASEY — TE — BUCCANEERS

PERSONAL: Born January 5, 1982, in Middleton, Wisc. ... 6-2/235 ... Full name: Casey R. Cramer.
COLLEGE: Dartmouth.
TRANSACTIONS/CAREER NOTES: Selected by Tampa Bay Buccaneers in seventh round (228th pick overall) of 2004 NFL draft.

Year Team	G	RUSHING Att.	Yds.	Avg.	TD	RECEIVING No.	Yds.	Avg.	TD	TOTALS TD	Pts.
2000—Dartmouth	10	2	5	2.5	0	18	240	13.3	2	2	12
2001—Dartmouth	9	13	40	3.1	0	37	525	14.2	6	6	36
2002—Dartmouth	10	0	0	0.0	0	72	1017	14.1	7	7	42
2003—Dartmouth	10	1	-2	-2.0	0	58	695	12.0	6	6	38
College totals (4 years)	39	16	43	2.7	0	185	2477	13.4	21	21	128

CRAYTON, PATRICK — WR — COWBOYS

PERSONAL: Born April 7, 1979, in De Soto, Texas. ... 6-1/205.
COLLEGE: Northwestern Oklahoma State.
TRANSACTIONS/CAREER NOTES: Selected by Dallas Cowboys in seventh round (216th pick overall) of 2004 NFL draft.

Year Team	G	RUSHING Att.	Yds.	Avg.	TD	RECEIVING No.	Yds.	Avg.	TD	PUNT RETURNS No.	Yds.	Avg.	TD	KICKOFF RETURNS No.	Yds.	Avg.	TD	TOTALS TD	Pts.
2000—Northwestern (Okla.)	13	4	34	8.5	1	18	320	17.8	3	16	325	20.3	2	7	141	20.1	0	0	0
2001—Northwestern (Okla.)	10	20	174	8.7	3	27	543	20.1	3	19	508	26.7	3	6	134	22.3	0	0	4
2002—Northwestern (Okla.)	8	12	117	9.8	0	20	324	16.2	7	21	384	18.3	3	8	172	21.5	0	0	2
2003—Northwestern (Okla.)	13	173	1426	8.2	13	15	331	22.1	4	16	279	17.4	2	18	476	26.4	2	0	0
College totals (4 years)	44	209	1751	8.4	17	80	1518	19.0	17	72	1496	20.8	10	39	923	23.7	2	0	6

DANSBY, KARLOS — LB — CARDINALS

PERSONAL: Born November 3, 1981, in Birmingham, Ala. ... 6-5/235.
HIGH SCHOOL: Woodlawn (Birmingham, Ala.).
COLLEGE: Auburn.
TRANSACTIONS/CAREER NOTES: Selected by Arizona Cardinals in second round (33rd pick overall) of 2004 NFL draft.

Year Team	G	Sks.	INTERCEPTIONS No.	Yds.	Avg.	TD
2001—Auburn	12	0.5	5	41	8.2	0
2002—Auburn	12	4.0	3	66	22.0	0
2003—Auburn	13	5.5	0	0	0.0	0
College totals (3 years)	37	10.0	8	107	13.4	0

DARILEK, TREY — G — EAGLES

PERSONAL: Born April 23, 1981, in San Antonio, Texas. ... 6-6/290.
HIGH SCHOOL: Robert E. Lee (San Antonio, Texas).
COLLEGE: Texas-El Paso.
TRANSACTIONS/CAREER NOTES: Selected by Philadelphia Eagles in fourth round (131st pick overall) of 2004 NFL draft.
PLAYING EXPERIENCE: Texas-El Paso, 2000-2003. ... Games played: 2000 (12), 2001 (11), 2002 (7), 2003 (13). Total: 43.

DARLING, DEVARD — WR — RAVENS

PERSONAL: Born April 16, 1982, in the Bahamas. ... 6-1/213.
HIGH SCHOOL: Austin (Houston, Texas).
COLLEGE: Florida State, then Washington State.
TRANSACTIONS/CAREER NOTES: Selected after junior season by Baltimore Ravens in third round (82nd pick overall) of 2004 NFL draft.

Year Team	G	RECEIVING No.	Yds.	Avg.	TD	KICKOFF RETURNS No.	Yds.	Avg.	TD	TOTALS TD	Pts.
2000—Florida State	4	2	36	18.0	1	0	0	0.0	0	1	6
2002—Washington State	13	54	800	14.8	11	7	128	18.3	0	12	72
2003—Washington State	13	50	830	16.6	7	0	0	0.0	0	7	42
College totals (3 years)	30	106	1666	15.7	19	7	128	18.3	0	20	120

DAVID, JASON — CB — COLTS

PERSONAL: Born June 12, 1982, in Convina, Calif. ... 5-8/165. ... Full name: Jason Aeron Walter David.
HIGH SCHOOL: Charter Oak (Convina, Calif.).
COLLEGE: Washington State.

TRANSACTIONS/CAREER NOTES: Selected by Indianapolis Colts in fourth round (125th pick overall) of 2004 NFL draft.

		INTERCEPTIONS				PUNT RETURNS				KICKOFF RETURNS				TOTALS	
Year Team	**G**	**No.**	**Yds.**	**Avg.**	**TD**	**No.**	**Yds.**	**Avg.**	**TD**	**No.**	**Yds.**	**Avg.**	**TD**	**TD**	**Pts.**
2000—Washington State	9	0	0	0.0	0	0	0	0.0	0	0	0	0.0	0	0	0
2001—Washington State	11	3	73	24.3	1	0	0	0.0	0	11	208	18.9	0	0	0
2002—Washington State	10	7	101	14.4	0	0	0	0.0	0	0	0	0.0	0	0	0
2003—Washington State	13	6	144	24.0	2	4	35	8.8	0	0	0	0.0	0	3	18
College totals (4 years)	43	16	318	19.9	3	4	35	8.8	0	11	208	18.9	0	3	18

DAVIS, ROD — LB — VIKINGS

PERSONAL: Born April 21, 1981, in Gulfport, Miss. ... 6-3/246.
HIGH SCHOOL: Gulfport (Miss.).
COLLEGE: Southern Mississippi.
TRANSACTIONS/CAREER NOTES: Selected by Minnesota Vikings in fifth round (155th pick overall) of 2004 NFL draft.
HONORS: Named linebacker on THE SPORTING NEWS Freshman All-America second team (2000). ... Named linebacker on THE SPORTING NEWS college All-America fourth team (2001) and second team (2003).

			INTERCEPTIONS			
Year Team	**G**	**Sks.**	**No.**	**Yds.**	**Avg.**	**TD**
2000—Southern Mississippi	11	1.0	2	33	16.5	0
2001—Southern Mississippi	11	3.0	2	20	10.0	0
2002—Southern Mississippi	13	10.5	2	29	14.5	0
2003—Southern Mississippi	12	4.0	0	0	0.0	0
College totals (4 years)	47	18.5	6	82	13.7	0

DOCKETT, DARNELL — DT — CARDINALS

PERSONAL: Born May 27, 1981, in Burtonsville, Md. ... 6-4/280.
HIGH SCHOOL: Paint Branch (Burtonsville, Md.).
COLLEGE: Florida State.
TRANSACTIONS/CAREER NOTES: Selected by Arizona Cardinals in third round (64th pick overall) of 2004 NFL draft.
HONORS: Named defensive lineman on THE SPORTING NEWS Freshman All-America first team (2000). ... Named defensive tackle on THE SPORTING NEWS college All-America second team (2003).

Year Team	**G**	**SACKS**
1999—Florida State	3	0.0
2000—Florida State	12	7.0
2001—Florida State	11	0.0
2002—Florida State	13	2.0
2003—Florida State	13	1.5
College totals (5 years)	52	10.5

DORSEY, NAT — T — VIKINGS

PERSONAL: Born September 9, 1983, in New Orleans, La. ... 6-6/324. ... Full name: Nathaniel Willie Dorsey III.
HIGH SCHOOL: St. Augustine (New Orleans, La.).
COLLEGE: Georgia Tech.
TRANSACTIONS/CAREER NOTES: Selected after junior season by Minnesota Vikings in fourth round (115th pick overall) of 2004 NFL draft.
PLAYING EXPERIENCE: Georgia Tech, 2001-2003. ... Games played: 2001 (12), 2002 (11), 2003 (13). Total: 36.
HONORS: Named offensive tackle on THE SPORTING NEWS Freshman All-America first team (2001).

DUFF, VONTEZ — CB — TEXANS

PERSONAL: Born March 8, 1982, in Kentucky. ... 6-1/194. ... Full name: Vontez Douglas Duff.
HIGH SCHOOL: Copperas Cove (Copperas Cove, Texas).
COLLEGE: Notre Dame.
TRANSACTIONS/CAREER NOTES: Selected by Houston Texans in sixth round (170th pick overall) of 2004 NFL draft.

			INTERCEPTIONS				PUNT RETURNS				KICKOFF RETURNS				TOTALS	
Year Team	**G**	**Sks.**	**No.**	**Yds.**	**Avg.**	**TD**	**No.**	**Yds.**	**Avg.**	**TD**	**No.**	**Yds.**	**Avg.**	**TD**	**TD**	**Pts.**
2000—Notre Dame	11	0.0	1	4	4.0	0	0	0	0.0	0	0	0	0.0	0	0	0
2001—Notre Dame	11	0.0	3	37	12.3	0	9	80	8.9	0	12	358	29.8	1	1	6
2002—Notre Dame	13	0.0	1	33	33.0	1	40	385	9.6	1	19	526	27.7	1	3	18
2003—Notre Dame	12	0.0	2	55	27.5	0	24	260	10.8	0	16	346	21.6	0	0	0
College totals (4 years)	47	0.0	7	129	18.4	1	73	725	9.9	1	47	1230	26.2	2	4	24

DUGAN, JEFF — TE — VIKINGS

PERSONAL: Born April 8, 1981, in Allison Park, Pa. ... 6-4/261. ... Full name: Jeffery Steven Dugan.
HIGH SCHOOL: Central Catholic (Allison Park, Pa.).
COLLEGE: Maryland.
TRANSACTIONS/CAREER NOTES: Selected by Minnesota Vikings in seventh round (220th pick overall) of 2004 NFL draft.

		RECEIVING			
Year Team	**G**	**No.**	**Yds.**	**Avg.**	**TD**
2000—Maryland	11	25	319	12.8	1
2001—Maryland	11	7	64	9.1	1

Year Team	G	RECEIVING No.	Yds.	Avg.	TD
2002—Maryland	14	9	91	10.1	1
2003—Maryland	13	14	175	12.5	0
College totals (4 years)	49	55	649	11.8	3

EARL, GLENN — DB — TEXANS

PERSONAL: Born June 10, 1981, in Southfield, Mich. ... 6-1/205.
HIGH SCHOOL: Naperville North (Lisle, Ill.).
COLLEGE: Notre Dame.
TRANSACTIONS/CAREER NOTES: Selected by Houston Texans in fourth round (122nd pick overall) of 2004 NFL draft.

Year Team	G	Sks.	INTERCEPTIONS No.	Yds.	Avg.	TD
2000—Notre Dame	11	0.0	1	0	0.0	0
2001—Notre Dame	8	2.0	0	0	0.0	0
2002—Notre Dame	13	1.0	2	9	4.5	0
2003—Notre Dame	7	1.0	1	0	0.0	0
College totals (4 years)	39	4.0	4	9	2.3	0

ECHEMANDU, ADIMCHINOBE — RB — BROWNS

PERSONAL: Born November 21, 1980, in Lagos, Nigeria. ... 5-10/225.
HIGH SCHOOL: Hawthorne (Calif.).
COLLEGE: California.
TRANSACTIONS/CAREER NOTES: Selected by Cleveland Browns in seventh round (208th pick overall) of 2004 NFL draft.

		RUSHING				RECEIVING				KICKOFF RETURNS				TOTALS	
Year Team	G	Att.	Yds.	Avg.	TD	No.	Yds.	Avg.	TD	No.	Yds.	Avg.	TD	TD	Pts.
1999—California	9	10	24	2.4	0	4	44	11.0	1	0	0	0.0	0	1	6
2000—California	11	58	215	3.7	3	7	35	5.0	1	22	516	23.5	0	4	24
2003—California	13	238	1195	5.0	13	22	185	8.4	0	0	0	0.0	0	13	80
College totals (3 years)	33	306	1434	4.7	16	33	264	8.0	2	22	516	23.5	0	18	110

EDWARDS, DWAN — DT — RAVENS

PERSONAL: Born May 16, 1981, in Billings, Mont. ... 6-2/305. ... Full name: Dwan Sedaine Edwards. ... Name pronounced: Duh-wan.
HIGH SCHOOL: Columbus (Columbus, Montana).
COLLEGE: Oregon State.
TRANSACTIONS/CAREER NOTES: Selected by Baltimore Ravens in second round (51st pick overall) of 2004 NFL draft.

Year Team	G	SACKS
2000—Oregon State	11	5.0
2001—Oregon State	10	2.0
2002—Oregon State	13	3.5
2003—Oregon State	13	3.0
College totals (4 years)	47	13.5

EILAND, DEANDRE' — DB — VIKINGS

PERSONAL: Born June 4, 1982, in Tupelo, Miss. ... 5-11/200.
HIGH SCHOOL: Tupelo (Miss.).
COLLEGE: South Carolina.
TRANSACTIONS/CAREER NOTES: Selected by Minnesota Vikings in sixth round (184th pick overall) of 2004 NFL draft.
HONORS: Named defensive back on THE SPORTING NEWS Freshman All-America second team (2000).

Year Team	G	Sks.	INTERCEPTIONS No.	Yds.	Avg.	TD
2000—South Carolina	10	0.0	4	12	3.0	0
2001—South Carolina	10	0.0	2	31	15.5	0
2002—South Carolina	12	0.0	1	69	69.0	1
2003—South Carolina	12	0.0	2	19	9.5	0
College totals (4 years)	44	0.0	9	131	14.6	1

EUHUS, TIM — TE — BILLS

PERSONAL: Born October 2, 1980, in Eugene, Ore. ... 6-5/247.
HIGH SCHOOL: Churchill (Eugune, Ore.).
COLLEGE: Oregon State.
TRANSACTIONS/CAREER NOTES: Selected by Buffalo Bills in fourth round (109th pick overall) of 2004 NFL draft. ... Signed by Bills (May 18, 2004).

Year Team	G	RECEIVING No.	Yds.	Avg.	TD
2000—Oregon State	11	0	0	0.0	0
2001—Oregon State	11	27	316	11.7	1
2002—Oregon State	13	22	385	17.5	1
2003—Oregon State	13	49	645	13.2	7
College totals (4 years)	48	98	1346	13.7	9

EVANS, LEE — WR — BILLS

PERSONAL: Born March 11, 1981, in Bedford, Ohio. ... 5-11/202.
HIGH SCHOOL: Bedford (Ohio).
COLLEGE: Wisconsin.
TRANSACTIONS/CAREER NOTES: Selected by Buffalo Bills in first round (13th pick overall) of 2004 NFL draft.
HONORS: Named wide receiver on THE SPORTING NEWS college All-America second team (2001).

		RECEIVING			
Year Team	**G**	**No.**	**Yds.**	**Avg.**	**TD**
1999—Wisconsin	8	3	76	25.3	1
2000—Wisconsin	12	30	548	18.3	3
2001—Wisconsin	12	75	1545	20.6	9
2003—Wisconsin	13	64	1213	19.0	13
College totals (4 years)	45	172	3382	19.7	26

FERRERA, CHRISTIAN — DT — 49ERS

PERSONAL: Born February 21, 1981, in Livingston, N.J. ... 6-4/295. ... Full name: Christian Scott Ferrera.
HIGH SCHOOL: West Essex Regional (North Caldwell, N.J.).
COLLEGE: Syracuse.
TRANSACTIONS/CAREER NOTES: Selected by San Francisco 49ers in seventh round (226th pick overall) of 2004 NFL draft.

Year Team	**G**	**SACKS**
2000—Syracuse	11	0.0
2001—Syracuse	12	4.5
2002—Syracuse	10	0.0
2003—Syracuse	12	3.0
College totals (4 years)	45	7.5

FITZGERALD, LARRY — WR — CARDINALS

PERSONAL: Born August 31, 1983, in Minneapolis, Minn. ... 6-3/225. ... Full name: Larry Darnell Fitzgerald.
HIGH SCHOOL: Academy of Holy Angels (Minn.), then Valley Forge Military Academy (Pa.).
COLLEGE: Pittsburgh.
TRANSACTIONS/CAREER NOTES: Selected after sophomore season by Arizona Cardinals in first round (third pick overall) of 2004 NFL draft.
HONORS: Fred Biletnikoff Award winner (2003). ... Walter Camp Award winner (2003). ... Named wide receiver on THE SPORTING NEWS Freshman All-America first team (2002). ... Named wide receiver on THE SPORTING NEWS college All-America first team (2003).

		RECEIVING			
Year Team	**G**	**No.**	**Yds.**	**Avg.**	**TD**
2002—Pittsburgh	13	69	1005	14.6	12
2003—Pittsburgh	13	92	1672	18.2	22
College totals (2 years)	26	161	2677	16.6	34

FLEMING, TROY — RB — TITANS

PERSONAL: Born October 1, 1980, in Franklin, Tenn. ... 6-2/230. ... Full name: Troy Majors Fleming.
HIGH SCHOOL: Battle Ground Academy (Franklin, Tenn.).
COLLEGE: Tennessee.
TRANSACTIONS/CAREER NOTES: Selected by Tennessee Titans in sixth round (191st pick overall) of 2004 NFL draft.

		RUSHING				RECEIVING				TOTALS	
Year Team	**G**	**Att.**	**Yds.**	**Avg.**	**TD**	**No.**	**Yds.**	**Avg.**	**TD**	**TD**	**Pts.**
2000—Tennessee	11	9	35	3.9	0	6	71	11.8	0	0	0
2001—Tennessee	10	24	102	4.3	0	10	39	3.9	3	3	18
2002—Tennessee	13	34	162	4.8	1	21	120	5.7	0	1	6
2003—Tennessee	13	17	43	2.5	0	36	262	7.3	2	2	12
College totals (4 years)	47	84	342	4.1	1	73	492	6.7	5	6	36

FOX, KEYARON — LB — CHIEFS

PERSONAL: Born January 24, 1982, in Atlanta, Ga. ... 6-3/220. ... Full name: Keyaron James Fox. ... Name pronounced: key-AIR-un.
HIGH SCHOOL: Westlake (Atlanta, Ga.).
COLLEGE: Georgia Tech.
TRANSACTIONS/CAREER NOTES: Selected by Kansas City Chiefs in third round (93rd pick overall) of 2004 NFL draft.

			INTERCEPTIONS			
Year Team	**G**	**Sks.**	**No.**	**Yds.**	**Avg.**	**TD**
2000—Georgia Tech	8	0.0	0	0	0.0	0
2001—Georgia Tech	12	2.0	0	0	0.0	0
2002—Georgia Tech	12	3.0	1	35	35.0	0
2003—Georgia Tech	13	4.0	0	0	0.0	0
College totals (4 years)	45	9.0	1	35	35.0	0

FRANCIS, CARLOS — WR — RAIDERS

PERSONAL: Born January 3, 1981, in Fort Worth, Texas. ... 5-10/197. ... Full name: Carlos Miguel Francis.
HIGH SCHOOL: Southwest (Fort Worth, Texas).
COLLEGE: Texas Tech.

TRANSACTIONS/CAREER NOTES: Selected by Oakland Raiders in fourth round (98th pick overall) of 2004 NFL draft.

Year Team	G	RUSHING Att.	Yds.	Avg.	TD	RECEIVING No.	Yds.	Avg.	TD	TOTALS TD	Pts.
2000—Texas Tech	12	0	0	0.0	0	41	519	12.7	2	2	12
2001—Texas Tech	11	4	28	7.0	0	50	703	14.1	3	3	18
2002—Texas Tech	13	3	19	6.3	1	50	632	12.6	7	8	48
2003—Texas Tech	13	8	42	5.3	0	75	1177	15.7	9	9	54
College totals (4 years)	49	15	89	5.9	1	216	3031	14.0	21	22	132

FURIO, DOMINIC C EAGLES

PERSONAL: Born June 4, 1981, in San Pedro, Calif. ... 6-3/295. ... Full name: Dominic Joseph Furio.
HIGH SCHOOL: San Pedro (Calif.).
COLLEGE: Nevada-Las Vegas.
TRANSACTIONS/CAREER NOTES: Selected by Philadelphia Eagles in seventh round (243rd pick overall) of 2004 NFL draft.
PLAYING EXPERIENCE: UNLV, 2001-2003. ... Games played: 2001 (10), 2002 (12), 2003 (12). Total: 34.

GAINES, MICHAEL TE PANTHERS

PERSONAL: Born March 30, 1980, in Tallahassee, Fla. ... 6-3/280.
HIGH SCHOOL: Florida (Tallahassee, Fla.).
COLLEGE: Central Florida.
TRANSACTIONS/CAREER NOTES: Selected by Carolina Panthers in seventh round (232nd pick overall) of 2004 NFL draft.

Year Team	G	RECEIVING No.	Yds.	Avg.	TD
2001—Central Florida	11	11	115	10.5	1
2002—Central Florida	12	11	191	17.4	2
College totals (2 years)	23	22	306	13.9	3

GALLERY, ROBERT T RAIDERS

PERSONAL: Born July 26, 1980, in Masonville, Iowa. ... 6-7/307.
HIGH SCHOOL: East Buchanan (Masonville, Iowa).
COLLEGE: Iowa.
TRANSACTIONS/CAREER NOTES: Selected by Oakland Raiders in first round (second pick overall) of 2004 NFL draft.
PLAYING EXPERIENCE: Iowa, 2000-2003. ... Games played: 2000 (12), 2001 (11), 2002 (13), 2003 (13). Total: 49.
HONORS: Outland Award winner (2003). ... Named offensive tackle on THE SPORTING NEWS All-America first team (2003).

GAMBLE, CHRIS CB PANTHERS

PERSONAL: Born March 11, 1983, in Sunrise, Fla. ... 6-2/194.
HIGH SCHOOL: Dillard (Sunrise, Fla.).
COLLEGE: Ohio State.
TRANSACTIONS/CAREER NOTES: Selected after junior season by Carolina Panthers in first round (28th pick overall) of 2004 NFL draft.
HONORS: Named cornerback on THE SPORTING NEWS college All-America second team (2002 and 2003).

Year Team	G	Sks.	INTERCEPTIONS No.	Yds.	Avg.	TD	PUNT RETURNS No.	Yds.	Avg.	TD	KICKOFF RETURNS No.	Yds.	Avg.	TD	TOTALS TD	Pts.
2001—Ohio State	10	0.0	0	0	0.0	0	5	82	16.4	0	1	16	16.0	0	0	0
2002—Ohio State	14	0.0	4	40	10.0	1	35	293	8.4	0	11	253	23.0	0	2	12
2003—Ohio State	13	0.0	3	0	0.0	0	20	92	4.6	0	6	115	19.2	0	0	0
College totals (3 years)	37	0.0	7	40	5.7	1	60	467	7.8	0	18	384	21.3	0	2	12

GARDNER, GILBERT LB COLTS

PERSONAL: Born May 9, 1982, in Angleton, Texas. ... 6-2/234. ... Full name: Gilbert Ravelle Gardner II.
HIGH SCHOOL: Angleton (Texas).
COLLEGE: Purdue.
TRANSACTIONS/CAREER NOTES: Selected by Indianapolis Colts in third round (69th pick overall) of 2004 NFL draft.

Year Team	G	Sks.	INTERCEPTIONS No.	Yds.	Avg.	TD
2000—Purdue	11	1.0	0	0	0.0	0
2001—Purdue	8	1.0	1	51	51.0	0
2002—Purdue	13	0.0	0	0	0.0	0
2003—Purdue	13	1.5	2	0	0.0	0
College totals (4 years)	45	3.5	3	51	17.0	0

GARDNER, RICH CB TITANS

PERSONAL: Born February 1, 1981, in Chicago, Ill. ... 5-11/185. ... Full name: Richard James Gardner.
HIGH SCHOOL: Hales Franciscan (Chicago, Ill.).
COLLEGE: Penn State.
TRANSACTIONS/CAREER NOTES: Selected by Tennessee Titans in third round (92nd pick overall) of 2004 NFL draft.

Year	Team	G	Sks.	INTERCEPTIONS No.	Yds.	Avg.	TD
2000—Penn State		10	0.0	0	0	0.0	0
2001—Penn State		11	0.0	0	0	0.0	0
2002—Penn State		13	0.0	2	86	43.0	2
2003—Penn State		12	0.0	1	22	22.0	0
College totals (4 years)		46	0.0	3	108	36.0	2

GEATHERS, ROBERT — DE — BENGALS

PERSONAL: Born August 11, 1983, in Georgetown, S.C. ... 6-3/270. ... Full name: Robert L. Geathers.
HIGH SCHOOL: Carvers Bay (Georgetown, S.C.).
COLLEGE: Georgia.
TRANSACTIONS/CAREER NOTES: Selected by Cincinnati Bengals in fourth round (117th pick overall) of 2004 NFL draft.

Year	Team	G	Sks.	INTERCEPTIONS No.	Yds.	Avg.	TD
2001—Georgia		11	0.0	1	9	9.0	0
2002—Georgia		14	2.0	0	0	0.0	0
2003—Georgia		14	3.0	1	0	0.0	0
College totals (3 years)		39	5.0	2	9	4.5	0

GORDON, AMON — DT — BROWNS

PERSONAL: Born October 13, 1981, in San Diego, Calif. ... 6-3/275.
HIGH SCHOOL: Mira Mesa (San Diego, Calif.).
COLLEGE: Stanford.
TRANSACTIONS/CAREER NOTES: Selected after junior season by Cleveland Browns in fifth round (161st pick overall) of 2004 NFL draft.

Year	Team	G	SACKS
2001—Stanford		11	1.0
2002—Stanford		11	4.0
2003—Stanford		11	2.0
College totals (3 years)		33	7.0

GREEN, RODERICK — LB — RAVENS

PERSONAL: Born April 26, 1982, in Brenham, Texas. ... 6-2/243.
HIGH SCHOOL: Brenham (Texas).
JUNIOR COLLEGE: Blinn (Texas).
COLLEGE: Central Missouri State.
TRANSACTIONS/CAREER NOTES: Selected by Baltimore Ravens in fifth round (153rd pick overall) of 2004 NFL draft.

Year	Team	G	Sks.	INTERCEPTIONS No.	Yds.	Avg.	TD
2002—Central Missouri State		12	6.0	0	0	0.0	0
2003—Central Missouri State		11	7.0	0	0	0.0	0
College totals (2 years)		23	13.0	0	0	0.0	0

GROVE, JAKE — C — RAIDERS

PERSONAL: Born January 22, 1980, in Johnson City, Tenn. ... 6-3/286. ... Full name: Charles Jacob Grove.
HIGH SCHOOL: Jefferson Forest (Forest, Va.).
COLLEGE: Virginia Tech.
TRANSACTIONS/CAREER NOTES: Selected by Oakland Raiders in second round (45th pick overall) of 2004 NFL draft.
PLAYING EXPERIENCE: Virginia Tech, 2000-2003. ... Games played: 2000 (12), 2001 (11), 2002 (14), 2003 (13). Total: 50.
HONORS: Named center on THE SPORTING NEWS college All-America first team (2003).

HACKETT, D.J. — WR — SEAHAWKS

PERSONAL: Born July 31, 1981, in Fontana, Calif. ... 6-2/199. ... Full name: DeAndre James Hackett.
HIGH SCHOOL: San Dimas (Calif.).
COLLEGE: Cal State Northridge, then Colorado.
TRANSACTIONS/CAREER NOTES: Selected by Seattle Seahawks in fifth round (157th pick overall) of 2004 NFL draft.

Year	Team	G	RECEIVING No.	Yds.	Avg.	TD
2000—Cal State Northridge		10	47	728	15.5	7
2001—Cal State Northridge		10	53	778	14.7	10
2002—Colorado		13	18	211	11.7	4
2003—Colorado		12	78	1013	13.0	7
College totals (4 years)		45	196	2730	13.9	28

HADNOT, REX — G/C — DOLPHINS

PERSONAL: Born January 28, 1982, in Lufkin, Texas. ... 6-2/310. ... Full name: Rex Hadnot Jr.
HIGH SCHOOL: Lufkin (Lufkin, Texas).
COLLEGE: Houston.
TRANSACTIONS/CAREER NOTES: Selected by Miami Dolphins in sixth round (174th pick overall) of 2004 NFL draft.
PLAYING EXPERIENCE: Houston, 2000-2003. ... Games played: 2000 (11), 2001 (11), 2002 (12), 2003 (13). Total: 47.

HALL, ANDY — QB — EAGLES

PERSONAL: Born November 26, 1980, in Cheraw, S.C. ... 6-2/210. ... Full name: Andrew Steven Hall.
HIGH SCHOOL: Cheraw (S.C.).
COLLEGE: Georgia Tech, then Delaware.
TRANSACTIONS/CAREER NOTES: Selected by Philadelphia Eagles in sixth round (185th pick overall) of 2004 NFL draft.

		PASSING								RUSHING				TOTALS	
Year Team	**G**	**Att.**	**Cmp.**	**Pct.**	**Yds.**	**TD**	**Int.**	**Avg.**	**Rat.**	**Att.**	**Yds.**	**Avg.**	**TD**	**TD**	**Pts.**
2000—Georgia Tech	6	16	4	25.0	37	0	0	2.31	44.4	15	37	2.5	1	1	6
2001—Georgia Tech	3	27	15	55.6	262	1	2	9.70	134.5	9	46	5.1	0	0	0
2002—Delaware	11	306	159	52.0	1832	9	5	5.99	108.7	153	863	5.6	7	7	42
2003—Delaware	16	378	234	61.9	2764	25	7	7.31	141.4	163	710	4.4	8	8	50
College totals (4 years)	36	727	412	56.7	4895	35	14	6.73	125.3	340	1656	4.9	16	16	98

HALL, DEANGELO — CB — FALCONS

PERSONAL: Born November 19, 1983, in Chesapeake, Va. ... 5-11/200. ... Full name: DeAngelo Eugene Hall.
HIGH SCHOOL: Deep Creek (Chesapeake, Va.).
COLLEGE: Virginia Tech.
TRANSACTIONS/CAREER NOTES: Selected after junior season by Atlanta Falcons in first round (eighth pick overall) of 2004 NFL draft.
HONORS: Named cornerback on THE SPORTING NEWS Freshman All-America fourth team (2001). ... Named cornerback on THE SPORTING NEWS college All-America second team (2003).

			INTERCEPTIONS			PUNT RETURNS				TOTALS		
Year Team	**G**	**Sks.**	**No.**	**Yds.**	**Avg.**	**TD**	**No.**	**Yds.**	**Avg.**	**TD**	**TD**	**Pts.**
2001—Virginia Tech	11	0.0	3	37	12.3	0	1	0	0.0	0	0	0
2002—Virginia Tech	12	0.0	4	124	31.0	1	22	352	16.0	2	3	18
2003—Virginia Tech	13	0.0	1	0	0.0	0	33	487	14.8	3	6	36
College totals (3 years)	36	0.0	8	161	20.1	1	56	839	15.0	5	9	54

HAMILTON, DERRICK — WR — 49ERS

PERSONAL: Born November 30, 1981, in Dillon, S.C. ... 6-4/200. ... Full name: Derrick T. Hamilton.
HIGH SCHOOL: Dillon (Dillon, S.C.).
COLLEGE: Clemson.
TRANSACTIONS/CAREER NOTES: Selected after junior season by San Francisco 49ers in third round (77th pick overall) of 2004 NFL draft.
HONORS: Named wide receiver on THE SPORTING NEWS Freshman All-America second team (2001).

		RUSHING				RECEIVING				PUNT RETURNS				KICKOFF RETURNS				TOTALS	
Year Team	**G**	**Att.**	**Yds.**	**Avg.**	**TD**	**No.**	**Yds.**	**Avg.**	**TD**	**No.**	**Yds.**	**Avg.**	**TD**	**No.**	**Yds.**	**Avg.**	**TD**	**TD**	**Pts.**
2001—Clemson	11	4	21	5.3	0	49	590	12.0	3	2	11	5.5	0	15	476	31.7	1	4	24
2002—Clemson	13	21	208	9.9	2	52	602	11.6	2	35	377	10.8	0	32	696	21.8	0	4	24
2003—Clemson	13	17	111	6.5	0	62	1026	16.5	10	29	218	7.5	0	11	380	34.5	1	11	66
College totals (3 years)	37	42	340	8.1	2	163	2218	13.6	15	66	606	9.2	0	58	1552	26.8	2	19	114

HARDWICK, NICK — C — CHARGERS

PERSONAL: Born September 12, 1981, in Indianapolis, Ind. ... 6-4/282. ... Full name: Nicholas Adam Hardwick.
HIGH SCHOOL: Lawrence North (Indianapolis, Ind.).
COLLEGE: Purdue.
TRANSACTIONS/CAREER NOTES: Selected by San Diego Chargers in third round (66th pick overall) of 2004 NFL draft.
PLAYING EXPERIENCE: Purdue, 2002-2003. ... Games played: 2002 (10), 2003 (13). Total: 23.

HARGROVE, TONY — DE — RAMS

PERSONAL: Born July 20, 1983, in Punta Gorde, Fla. ... 6-4/255. ... Full name: Anthony La'Ron Hargrove.
HIGH SCHOOL: Port Charlotte (Punta Gorde, Fla.).
COLLEGE: Georgia Tech.
TRANSACTIONS/CAREER NOTES: Selected after junior season by St. Louis Rams in third round (91st pick overall) of 2004 NFL draft.

Year Team	**G**	**SACKS**
2001—Georgia Tech	11	2.0
2002—Georgia Tech	13	4.0
College totals (2 years)	24	6.0

HARRIOTT, CLAUDE — DE — BEARS

PERSONAL: Born April 8, 1981, in Belle Glade, Fla. ... 6-4/255. ... Full name: Claude Desmond Harriott.
HIGH SCHOOL: Glades Central Community (Belle Glade, Fla.).
COLLEGE: Pittsburgh.
TRANSACTIONS/CAREER NOTES: Selected by Chicago Bears in fifth round (147th pick overall) of 2004 NFL draft.

Year Team	**G**	**SACKS**
2000—Pittsburgh	11	1.0
2001—Pittsburgh	10	1.0
2002—Pittsburgh	13	9.5
2003—Pittsburgh	13	2.0
College totals (4 years)	47	13.5

HARRIS, JOSH — QB — RAVENS

PERSONAL: Born September 9, 1982, in Westerville, Ohio. ... 6-3/238.
HIGH SCHOOL: North (Westerville, Ohio).
COLLEGE: Bowling Green State.
TRANSACTIONS/CAREER NOTES: Selected by Baltimore Ravens in sixth round (187th pick overall) of 2004 NFL draft.

		PASSING								RUSHING				TOTALS	
Year Team	G	Att.	Cmp.	Pct.	Yds.	TD	Int.	Avg.	Rat.	Att.	Yds.	Avg.	TD	TD	Pts.
2000—Bowling Green	6	48	23	47.9	243	0	2	5.06	82.1	69	292	4.2	2	2	12
2001—Bowling Green	10	133	81	60.9	1022	9	3	7.68	143.3	126	614	4.9	8	9	54
2002—Bowling Green	12	353	198	56.1	2425	18	11	6.87	124.4	186	737	4.0	20	22	134
2003—Bowling Green	14	494	325	65.8	3813	27	12	7.72	143.8	215	830	3.9	13	14	84
College totals (4 years)	42	1028	627	61.0	7503	54	28	7.30	134.2	596	2473	4.1	43	47	284

HARRIS, TOMMIE — DT — BEARS

PERSONAL: Born October 29, 1983, in Killeen, Texas. ... 6-3/289.
HIGH SCHOOL: Ellison (Killeen, Texas).
COLLEGE: Oklahoma.
TRANSACTIONS/CAREER NOTES: Selected after junior season by Chicago Bears in first round (14th pick overall) of 2004 NFL draft.
HONORS: Lombardi Award winner (2003). ... Named defensive tackle on THE SPORTING NEWS Freshman All-America first team (2001). ... Named defensive tackle on THE SPORTING NEWS college All-America second team (2002) and first team (2003).

Year Team	G	SACKS
2001—Oklahoma	12	2.0
2002—Oklahoma	12	2.0
2003—Oklahoma	14	5.0
College totals (3 years)	38	9.0

HARTSOCK, BEN — TE — COLTS

PERSONAL: Born July 5, 1980, in Chillicothe, Ohio. ... 6-4/264.
HIGH SCHOOL: Uniote (Chillicothe, Ohio).
COLLEGE: Ohio State.
TRANSACTIONS/CAREER NOTES: Selected by Indianapolis Colts in third round (68th pick overall) of 2004 NFL draft.

		RECEIVING			
Year Team	G	No.	Yds.	Avg.	TD
2000—Ohio State	11	1	11	11.0	0
2001—Ohio State	11	6	77	12.8	1
2002—Ohio State	14	17	137	8.1	2
2003—Ohio State	13	33	290	8.8	2
College totals (4 years)	49	57	515	9.0	5

HENDERSON, DEVERY — WR — SAINTS

PERSONAL: Born March 26, 1982, in Lafayette, La. ... 5-11/190. ... Full name: Devery Vaughn Henderson.
HIGH SCHOOL: Opelousas (La.).
COLLEGE: Louisiana State.
TRANSACTIONS/CAREER NOTES: Selected by New Orleans Saints in second round (50th pick overall) of 2004 NFL draft.

		RECEIVING			
Year Team	G	No.	Yds.	Avg.	TD
2000—Louisiana State	10	4	25	6.3	0
2001—Louisiana State	10	1	2	2.0	0
2002—Louisiana State	11	23	447	19.4	8
2003—Louisiana State	14	53	861	16.2	11
College totals (4 years)	45	81	1335	16.5	19

HILL, MARQUISE — DE — PATRIOTS

PERSONAL: Born August 7, 1982, in New Orleans, La. ... 6-6/297.
HIGH SCHOOL: De La Salle (New Orleans, La.).
COLLEGE: Louisiana State.
TRANSACTIONS/CAREER NOTES: Selected by New England Patriots in second round (63rd pick overall) of 2004 NFL draft.

Year Team	G	SACKS
2001—Louisiana State	12	1.0
2002—Louisiana State	13	3.0
2003—Louisiana State	13	6.0
College totals (3 years)	38	10.0

HILTON, ISAAC — DE — GIANTS

PERSONAL: Born February 26, 1981, in Long Beach, Calif. ... 6-3/251.
HIGH SCHOOL: St. Andrews Parish (Charleston, S.C.).
COLLEGE: Hampton.

TRANSACTIONS/CAREER NOTES: Selected by New York Giants in seventh round (253rd pick overall) of 2004 NFL draft.

Year Team	G	SACKS
2000—Hampton	6	1.0
2001—Hampton	10	5.0
2002—Hampton	12	13.0
2003—Hampton	11	5.0
College totals (4 years)	39	24.0

HUTCHINS, VON — CB — COLTS

PERSONAL: Born February 14, 1981, in Natchez, Miss. ... 5-11/184. ... Full name: Tahaya De'Von Hutchins.
HIGH SCHOOL: Cathedral (Natchez, Miss.).
COLLEGE: Mississippi.
TRANSACTIONS/CAREER NOTES: Selected by Indianapolis Colts in sixth round (173rd pick overall) of 2004 NFL draft.

			INTERCEPTIONS			
Year Team	G	Sks.	No.	Yds.	Avg.	TD
2000—Mississippi	10	0.0	0	0	0.0	0
2001—Mississippi	11	0.0	1	18	18.0	0
2002—Mississippi	12	0.0	6	28	4.7	0
2003—Mississippi	13	1.5	4	5	1.3	0
College totals (4 years)	46	1.5	11	51	4.6	0

JACKSON, STEVEN — RB — RAMS

PERSONAL: Born July 22, 1983, in Las Vegas, Nev. ... 6-3/229. ... Full name: Steven Rashad Jackson.
HIGH SCHOOL: Eldorado (Las Vegas, Nev.).
COLLEGE: Oregon State.
TRANSACTIONS/CAREER NOTES: Selected after junior season by St. Louis Rams in first round (24th pick overall) of 2004 NFL draft.

		RUSHING				RECEIVING				TOTALS	
Year Team	G	Att.	Yds.	Avg.	TD	No.	Yds.	Avg.	TD	TD	Pts.
2001—Oregon State	10	74	390	5.3	5	5	45	9.0	1	7	42
2002—Oregon State	13	319	1690	5.3	15	17	165	9.7	2	17	102
2003—Oregon State	13	350	1545	4.4	19	44	470	10.7	3	22	132
College totals (3 years)	36	743	3625	4.9	39	66	680	10.3	6	46	276

JENKINS, MICHAEL — WR — FALCONS

PERSONAL: Born June 18, 1982, in Tampa, Fla. ... 6-5/215.
HIGH SCHOOL: Leto (Tampa, Fla.).
COLLEGE: Ohio State.
TRANSACTIONS/CAREER NOTES: Selected by Atlanta Falcons in first round (29th pick overall) of 2004 NFL draft.

		RECEIVING				PUNT RETURNS				TOTALS	
Year Team	G	No.	Yds.	Avg.	TD	No.	Yds.	Avg.	TD	TD	Pts.
2000—Ohio State	11	0	0	0.0	0	0	0	0.0	0	0	0
2001—Ohio State	11	41	836	20.4	3	0	0	0.0	0	3	18
2002—Ohio State	14	61	1076	17.6	6	1	11	11.0	0	6	36
2003—Ohio State	13	55	834	15.2	7	20	178	8.9	1	8	48
College totals (4 years)	49	157	2746	17.5	16	21	189	9.0	1	17	102

JENSEN, ERIK — TE — RAMS

PERSONAL: Born October 11, 1980, in Appleton, Wisc. ... 6-3/259.
HIGH SCHOOL: East (Appleton, Wisc.).
COLLEGE: Iowa.
TRANSACTIONS/CAREER NOTES: Selected by St. Louis Rams in seventh round (237th pick overall) of 2004 NFL draft.

		RECEIVING			
Year Team	G	No.	Yds.	Avg.	TD
2000—Iowa	9	2	37	18.5	1
2001—Iowa	10	3	22	7.3	1
2002—Iowa	8	2	33	16.5	0
2003—Iowa	12	16	182	11.4	1
College totals (4 years)	39	23	274	11.9	3

JOE, LEON — LB — BEARS

PERSONAL: Born October 26, 1981, in Clinton, Md. ... 6-1/223.
HIGH SCHOOL: Friendly (Clinton, Md.).
COLLEGE: Maryland.
TRANSACTIONS/CAREER NOTES: Selected by Chicago Bears in fourth round (112th pick overall) of 2004 NFL draft.

			INTERCEPTIONS			
Year Team	G	Sks.	No.	Yds.	Avg.	TD
2000—Maryland	11	0.0	0	0	0.0	0
2001—Maryland	11	1.0	1	8	8.0	0
2002—Maryland	13	1.0	0	0	0.0	0
2003—Maryland	13	1.0	1	23	23.0	0
College totals (4 years)	48	3.0	2	31	15.5	0

JOHNSON, LANDON — LB — BENGALS

PERSONAL: Born March 13, 1981, in Lubbock, Texas. ... 6-2/211. ... Full name: Landon Tremone Johnson.
HIGH SCHOOL: Coronado (Lubbock, Texas).
COLLEGE: Purdue.
TRANSACTIONS/CAREER NOTES: Selected by Cincinnati Bengals in third round (96th pick overall) of 2004 NFL draft.

			INTERCEPTIONS			
Year Team	**G**	**Sks.**	**No.**	**Yds.**	**Avg.**	**TD**
2000—Purdue	10	2.0	0	0	0.0	0
2001—Purdue	11	4.0	2	2	1.0	0
2002—Purdue	11	1.0	0	0	0.0	0
2003—Purdue	13	1.5	2	26	13.0	0
College totals (4 years)	45	8.5	4	28	7.0	0

JOHNSON, SHAWN — DE — RAIDERS

PERSONAL: Born March 24, 1980, in Fairport, N.Y. ... 6-4/273.
HIGH SCHOOL: Fairport (N.Y).
COLLEGE: Duke, then Delaware.
TRANSACTIONS/CAREER NOTES: Selected by Oakland Raiders in sixth round (166th pick overall) of 2004 NFL draft.

Year Team	**G**	**SACKS**
2000—Duke	11	1.0
2001—Duke	11	2.0
2002—Duke	12	12.0
2003—Delaware	16	13.5
College totals (4 years)	50	28.5

JOHNSON, TERRY — DT — BEARS

PERSONAL: Born December 7, 1981, in Temple, Ariz. ... 6-4/285.
HIGH SCHOOL: McClintock (Temple, Ariz.).
COLLEGE: Washington.
TRANSACTIONS/CAREER NOTES: Selected by Chicago Bears in second round (47th pick overall) of 2004 NFL draft.

			INTERCEPTIONS			
Year Team	**G**	**Sks.**	**No.**	**Yds.**	**Avg.**	**TD**
2001—Washington	10	0.0	0	0	0.0	0
2002—Washington	13	5.0	1	0	0.0	1
2003—Washington	12	10.0	0	0	0.0	0
College totals (3 years)	35	15.0	1	0	0.0	1

JOHNSON, TREVOR — DE — JETS

PERSONAL: Born February 26, 1981, in Gordon, Neb. ... 6-4/255.
HIGH SCHOOL: Northeast (Lincoln, Neb.).
COLLEGE: Nebraska.
TRANSACTIONS/CAREER NOTES: Selected by New York Jets in seventh round (234th pick overall) of 2004 NFL draft.

Year Team	**G**	**SACKS**
2000—Nebraska	10	0.0
2001—Nebraska	12	0.0
2002—Nebraska	14	3.0
2003—Nebraska	13	4.0
College totals (4 years)	49	7.0

JONES, ADRIAN — T — JETS

PERSONAL: Born June 10, 1981, in Dallas, Texas. ... 6-5/265.
HIGH SCHOOL: Carter (Dallas, Texas).
COLLEGE: Kansas.
TRANSACTIONS/CAREER NOTES: Selected by New York Jets in fourth round (132nd pick overall) of 2004 NFL draft.
PLAYING EXPERIENCE: Kansas, 2000-2003. ... Games played: 2000 (7), 2001 (10), 2002 (12), 2003 (13). Total: 42.

JONES, DONNIE — P — SEAHAWKS

PERSONAL: Born July 5, 1980, in Baton Rouge, La. ... 6-2/222. ... Full name: Donald Scott Jones Jr.
HIGH SCHOOL: Catholic (Baton Rouge, La.).
COLLEGE: Louisiana State.
TRANSACTIONS/CAREER NOTES: Selected by Seattle Seahawks in seventh round (224th pick overall) of 2004 NFL draft.

		PUNTING				
Year Team	**G**	**No.**	**Yds.**	**Avg.**	**In. 20**	**Blk.**
2000—Louisiana State	11	57	2174	38.1	17	0
2001—Louisiana State	12	47	2052	43.7	13	1
2002—Louisiana State	13	64	2813	44.0	17	4
2003—Louisiana State	14	65	2757	42.4	22	1
College totals (4 years)	50	233	9796	42.0	69	6

JONES, GREG — RB — JAGUARS

PERSONAL: Born May 4, 1981, in Beaufort, S.C. ... 6-1/248.
HIGH SCHOOL: Battery Creek.
COLLEGE: Florida State.
TRANSACTIONS/CAREER NOTES: Selected by Jacksonville Jaguars in second round (55th pick overall) of 2004 NFL draft.

		RUSHING				RECEIVING				TOTALS	
Year Team	**G**	**Att.**	**Yds.**	**Avg.**	**TD**	**No.**	**Yds.**	**Avg.**	**TD**	**TD**	**Pts.**
2000—Florida State	10	41	266	6.5	2	2	16	8.0	0	2	12
2001—Florida State	11	134	713	5.3	6	3	11	3.7	0	6	36
2002—Florida State	10	161	938	5.8	8	10	74	7.4	0	8	48
2003—Florida State	13	144	618	4.3	7	9	52	5.8	0	7	42
College totals (4 years)	44	480	2535	5.3	23	24	153	6.4	0	23	138

JONES, JULIUS — RB — COWBOYS

PERSONAL: Born August 14, 1981, in Big Stone Gap, Va. ... 5-10/210. ... Full name: Julius Andre Maurice Jones. ... Brother of Thomas Jones, running back, Chicago Bears.
HIGH SCHOOL: Powell Valley (Big Stone Gap, Va.).
COLLEGE: Notre Dame.
TRANSACTIONS/CAREER NOTES: Selected by Dallas Cowboys in second round (43rd pick overall) of 2004 NFL draft.

		RUSHING				RECEIVING				PUNT RETURNS				KICKOFF RETURNS				TOTALS	
Year Team	**G**	**Att.**	**Yds.**	**Avg.**	**TD**	**No.**	**Yds.**	**Avg.**	**TD**	**No.**	**Yds.**	**Avg.**	**TD**	**No.**	**Yds.**	**Avg.**	**TD**	**TD**	**Pts.**
1999—Notre Dame	12	75	375	5.0	3	3	90	30.0	0	15	195	13.0	1	26	603	23.2	0	4	24
2000—Notre Dame	10	162	657	4.1	7	6	50	8.3	0	4	35	8.8	0	15	427	28.5	1	8	48
2001—Notre Dame	11	168	718	4.3	6	9	57	6.3	1	18	192	10.7	0	18	405	22.5	0	7	42
2003—Notre Dame	12	229	1268	5.5	10	10	53	5.3	0	1	4	4.0	0	13	243	18.7	0	10	60
College totals (4 years)	45	634	3018	4.8	26	28	250	8.9	1	38	426	11.2	1	72	1678	23.3	1	29	174

JONES, KEVIN — RB — LIONS

PERSONAL: Born August 21, 1982, in Chester, Pa. ... 5-11/211. ... Full name: Kevin S. Jones.
HIGH SCHOOL: Cardinal O'Hara (Chester, Pa.).
COLLEGE: Virginia Tech.
TRANSACTIONS/CAREER NOTES: Selected after junior season by Detroit Lions in first round (30th pick overall) of 2004 NFL draft.
HONORS: Named running back on THE SPORTING NEWS Freshman All-America second team (2001). ... Named running back on THE SPORTING NEWS college All-America first team (2003).

		RUSHING				RECEIVING				TOTALS	
Year Team	**G**	**Att.**	**Yds.**	**Avg.**	**TD**	**No.**	**Yds.**	**Avg.**	**TD**	**TD**	**Pts.**
2001—Virginia Tech	12	175	957	5.5	5	6	47	7.8	0	5	30
2002—Virginia Tech	13	160	871	5.4	9	4	21	5.3	0	9	54
2003—Virginia Tech	13	281	1647	5.9	21	14	161	11.5	0	21	126
College totals (3 years)	38	616	3475	5.6	35	24	229	9.5	0	35	210

JONES, MARK — WR — BUCCANEERS

PERSONAL: Born November 3, 1980... 5-9/185. ... Full name: Mark Christopher Jones.
HIGH SCHOOL: Strath Haven (Wallingford, Pa.).
COLLEGE: Tennessee.
TRANSACTIONS/CAREER NOTES: Selected by Tampa Bay Buccaneers in seventh round (206th pick overall) of 2004 NFL draft.

		RECEIVING				PUNT RETURNS				TOTALS	
Year Team	**G**	**No.**	**Yds.**	**Avg.**	**TD**	**No.**	**Yds.**	**Avg.**	**TD**	**TD**	**Pts.**
2000—Tennessee	10	0	0	0.0	0	0	0	0.0	0	0	0
2001—Tennessee	12	0	0	0.0	0	0	0	0.0	0	0	0
2002—Tennessee	13	0	0	0.0	0	26	240	9.2	0	1	6
2003—Tennessee	13	36	556	15.4	5	20	303	15.2	1	6	36
College totals (4 years)	48	36	556	15.4	5	46	543	11.8	1	7	42

JONES, NATE — DB — COWBOYS

PERSONAL: Born June 15, 1982, in Scotch Plains, N.J. ... 5-10/180. ... Full name: Nathan Jones.
HIGH SCHOOL: Scotch Plains-Fanwood (N.J.).
COLLEGE: Rutgers.
TRANSACTIONS/CAREER NOTES: Selected by Dallas Cowboys in seventh round (205th pick overall) of 2004 NFL draft.

			INTERCEPTIONS				KICKOFF RETURNS				TOTALS	
Year Team	**G**	**Sks.**	**No.**	**Yds.**	**Avg.**	**TD**	**No.**	**Yds.**	**Avg.**	**TD**	**TD**	**Pts.**
2000—Rutgers	10	0.0	0	0	0.0	0	0	0	0.0	0	0	0
2001—Rutgers	11	0.0	1	70	70.0	1	37	677	18.3	0	1	6
2002—Rutgers	12	0.0	2	30	15.0	0	26	736	28.3	2	2	12
2003—Rutgers	12	0.0	2	0	0.0	0	19	489	25.7	1	1	6
College totals (4 years)	45	0.0	5	100	20.0	1	82	1902	23.2	3	4	24

JONES, SEAN — DB — BROWNS

PERSONAL: Born December 28, 1983, in Atlanta, Ga. ... 6-2/212.
HIGH SCHOOL: Westlake (Atlanta, Ga.).
COLLEGE: Georgia.
TRANSACTIONS/CAREER NOTES: Selected after junior season by Cleveland Browns in second round (59th pick overall) of 2004 NFL draft.

			INTERCEPTIONS				PUNT RETURNS				TOTALS		
Year Team	**G**	**Sks.**	**No.**	**Yds.**	**Avg.**	**TD**	**No.**	**Yds.**	**Avg.**	**TD**	**TD**	**TD**	**Pts.**
2001—Georgia	11	0.0	0	0	0.0	0	0	0	0.0		0	0	0
2002—Georgia	14	0.0	2	58	29.0	0	10	160	16.0		0	0	0
2003—Georgia	12	1.0	5	42	8.4	0	0	0	0.0		0	1	6
College totals (3 years)	37	1.0	7	100	14.3	0	10	160	16.0		0	1	6

JOSEPH, CARLOS — T — CHARGERS

PERSONAL: Born July 14, 1980, in Miami, Fla. ... 6-6/334. ... Brother of William Joseph, defensive tackle, New York Giants.
HIGH SCHOOL: Edison (Miami, Fla.).
COLLEGE: Miami (Fla.).
TRANSACTIONS/CAREER NOTES: Selected by San Diego Chargers in seventh round (254th pick overall) of 2004 NFL draft.
PLAYING EXPERIENCE: Miami (Fla.), 2001-2003. ... Games played: 2001 (8), 2002 (13), 2003 (11). Total: 32.

KAEDING, NATE — K — CHARGERS

PERSONAL: Born March 26, 1982, in Coralville, Iowa. ... 6-0/187.
HIGH SCHOOL: Iowa City West (Coralville, Iowa).
COLLEGE: Iowa.
TRANSACTIONS/CAREER NOTES: Selected by San Diego Chargers in third round (65th pick overall) of 2004 NFL draft.
HONORS: Named kicker on THE SPORTING NEWS Freshman All-America third team (2000). ... Named kicker on THE SPORTING NEWS college All-America first team (2002).

		KICKING						
Year Team	**G**	**50+**	**Tot.**	**Pct.**	**Lg.**	**XPM**	**XPA**	**Pts.**
2000—Iowa	12	0-0	14-22	63.6	49	20	20	62
2001—Iowa	11	0-1	8-11	72.7	47	48	49	72
2002—Iowa	13	3-3	21-24	87.5	55	57	58	120
2003—Iowa	13	2-2	20-21	95.2	55	40	40	100
College totals (4 years)	49	5-6	63-78	80.8	55	165	167	354

KARNEY, MIKE — FB — SAINTS

PERSONAL: Born July 6, 1981, in Kent, Wash. ... 5-11/254.
HIGH SCHOOL: Kentwood (Kent, Wash.).
COLLEGE: Arizona State.
TRANSACTIONS/CAREER NOTES: Selected by New Orleans Saints in fifth round (156th pick overall) of 2004 NFL draft.

		RUSHING				RECEIVING				TOTALS	
Year Team	**G**	**Att.**	**Yds.**	**Avg.**	**TD**	**No.**	**Yds.**	**Avg.**	**TD**	**TD**	**Pts.**
2000—Arizona State	11	14	42	3.0	0	4	42	10.5	0	0	0
2001—Arizona State	11	6	18	3.0	0	6	39	6.5	1	1	6
2002—Arizona State	14	8	20	2.5	0	13	121	9.3	0	0	2
2003—Arizona State	10	4	-2	-0.5	0	14	106	7.6	0	0	0
College totals (4 years)	46	32	78	2.4	0	37	308	8.3	1	1	8

KIMBALL, DAVID — K — COLTS

PERSONAL: Born January 13, 1982, in Fredericksburg, Va. ... 6-1/209. ... Full name: David Wayne Kimball.
HIGH SCHOOL: State College Area (Penn.).
COLLEGE: Penn State.
TRANSACTIONS/CAREER NOTES: Selected by Indianapolis Colts in seventh round (229th pick overall) of 2004 NFL draft.

		KICKING						
Year Team	**G**	**50+**	**Tot.**	**Pct.**	**Lg.**	**XPM**	**XPA**	**Pts.**
2000—Penn State	12	0-1	0-3	0.0	0	2	2	2
2001—Penn State	11	0-0	0-0	0.0	0	1	2	1
2002—Penn State	13	0-0	0-0	0.0	0	3	4	3
2003—Penn State	12	0-1	2-5	40.0	48	4	4	10
College totals (4 years)	48	0-2	2-8	25.0	48	10	12	16

KOUTOUVIDES, NIKO — LB — SEAHAWKS

PERSONAL: Born March 25, 1981, in Plainville, Conn. ... 6-3/226. ... Full name: Niko Stelios Koutouvides.
HIGH SCHOOL: Milford Academy (Conn.).
COLLEGE: Purdue.
TRANSACTIONS/CAREER NOTES: Selected by Seattle Seahawks in fourth round (116th pick overall) of 2004 NFL draft.

Year Team	G	Sks.	INTERCEPTIONS No.	Yds.	Avg.	TD
2000—Purdue	11	0.0	0	0	0.0	0
2001—Purdue	11	0.0	0	0	0.0	0
2002—Purdue	13	4.0	3	21	7.0	0
2003—Purdue	13	0.0	2	24	12.0	0
College totals (4 years)	48	4.0	5	45	9.0	0

KRANCHICK, MATT — TE — STEELERS

PERSONAL: Born December 13, 1979, in Carlisle, Pa. ... 6-8/253. ... Full name: Matthew Alan Kranchick.
HIGH SCHOOL: Trinity (Carlisle, Pa.).
COLLEGE: Penn State.
TRANSACTIONS/CAREER NOTES: Selected by Pittsburgh Steelers in sixth round (194th pick overall) of 2004 NFL draft. ... Signed by Steelers (May 17, 2004).

Year Team	G	RECEIVING No.	Yds.	Avg.	TD
2000—Penn State	1	0	0	0.0	0
2001—Penn State	1	0	0	0.0	0
2002—Penn State	7	2	15	7.5	0
2003—Penn State	12	22	337	15.3	1
College totals (4 years)	21	24	352	14.7	1

KRAUSE, RYAN — TE — CHARGERS

PERSONAL: Born June 16, 1981, in Omaha, Neb. ... 6-2/244.
COLLEGE: Nebraska-Omaha.
TRANSACTIONS/CAREER NOTES: Selected by San Diego Chargers in sixth round (169th pick overall) of 2004 NFL draft.

Year Team	G	RECEIVING No.	Yds.	Avg.	TD
2000—Nebraska-Omaha	10	8	139	17.4	0
2001—Nebraska-Omaha	10	22	468	21.3	3
2002—Nebraska-Omaha	11	54	893	16.5	8
2003—Nebraska-Omaha	11	67	1066	15.9	11
College totals (4 years)	42	151	2566	17.0	22

KRENZEL, CRAIG — QB — BEARS

PERSONAL: Born July 1, 1981, in Sterling Heights, Mich. ... 6-4/225.
HIGH SCHOOL: Henry Ford II (Sterling Heights, Mich.).
COLLEGE: Ohio State.
TRANSACTIONS/CAREER NOTES: Selected by Chicago Bears in fifth round (148th pick overall) of 2004 NFL draft.

Year Team	G	PASSING Att.	Cmp.	Pct.	Yds.	TD	Int.	Avg.	Rat.	RUSHING Att.	Yds.	Avg.	TD	TOTALS TD	Pts.
2000—Ohio State	6	6	3	50.0	41	0	0	6.83	107.4	5	-11	-2.2	0	0	0
2001—Ohio State	2	41	22	53.7	282	1	3	6.88	104.8	8	-12	-1.5	0	0	0
2002—Ohio State	14	249	148	59.4	2110	12	7	8.47	140.9	125	368	2.9	3	3	18
2003—Ohio State	11	278	153	55.0	2040	15	10	7.34	127.3	109	255	2.3	3	3	18
College totals (4 years)	33	574	326	56.8	4473	28	20	7.79	131.4	247	600	2.4	6	6	36

LABOY, TRAVIS — DE — TITANS

PERSONAL: Born August 10, 1981, in San Rafael, Calif. ... 6-4/249.
HIGH SCHOOL: Marin Catholic (San Rafael, Calif.).
COLLEGE: Utah State, then Hawaii.
TRANSACTIONS/CAREER NOTES: Selected by Tennessee Titans in second round (42nd pick overall) of 2004 NFL draft.

Year Team	G	Sks.	INTERCEPTIONS No.	Yds.	Avg.	TD
2001—Hawaii	9	4.0	0	0	0.0	0
2002—Hawaii	12	7.0	0	0	0.0	0
2003—Hawaii	13	13.0	2	17	8.5	0
College totals (3 years)	34	24.0	2	17	8.5	0

LACY, BO — T/G — STEELERS

PERSONAL: Born November 22, 1980, in Newport, Ark. ... 6-4/303. ... Full name: Gay Lacy.
HIGH SCHOOL: Newport (Ark.).
COLLEGE: Arkansas.
TRANSACTIONS/CAREER NOTES: Selected by Pittsburgh Steelers in sixth round (177th pick overall) of 2004 NFL draft.
PLAYING EXPERIENCE: Arkansas, 2000-2003. ... Games played: 2000 (8), 2001 (8), 2002 (14), 2003 (13). Total: 43.

LAVALAIS, CHAD — DT — FALCONS

PERSONAL: Born April 15, 1979, in Marksville, La. ... 6-1/293. ... Full name: Chad Douglas Lavalais.
HIGH SCHOOL: Marksville (La.).
COLLEGE: Louisiana State.
TRANSACTIONS/CAREER NOTES: Selected by Atlanta Falcons in fifth round (142nd pick overall) of 2004 NFL draft.

			INTERCEPTIONS			
Year Team	**G**	**Sks.**	**No.**	**Yds.**	**Avg.**	**TD**
2000—Louisiana State	11	1.0	0	0	0.0	0
2001—Louisiana State	11	2.0	0	0	0.0	0
2002—Louisiana State	13	2.0	0	0	0.0	0
2003—Louisiana State	14	7.0	1	-5	-5.0	0
College totals (4 years)	49	12.0	1	-5	-5.0	0

LAWRIE, NATE — TE — BUCCANEERS

PERSONAL: Born October 17, 1981... 6-7/265. ... Full name: Nathan Earl Lawrie.
HIGH SCHOOL: Roncalli (Indianapolis, Ind.).
COLLEGE: Yale.
TRANSACTIONS/CAREER NOTES: Selected by Tampa Bay Buccaneers in sixth round (181st pick overall) of 2004 NFL draft.

		RECEIVING			
Year Team	**G**	**No.**	**Yds.**	**Avg.**	**TD**
2000—Yale	2	0	0	0.0	0
2001—Yale	9	3	46	15.3	0
2002—Yale	10	41	505	12.3	4
2003—Yale	10	72	810	11.3	3
College totals (4 years)	31	116	1361	11.7	7

LECKEY, NICK — G — CARDINALS

PERSONAL: Born March 12, 1982, in Grapevine, Texas. ... 6-4/285.
HIGH SCHOOL: Grapevine (Texas).
COLLEGE: Kansas State.
TRANSACTIONS/CAREER NOTES: Selected by Arizona Cardinals in sixth round (167th pick overall) of 2004 NFL draft.
PLAYING EXPERIENCE: Kansas State, 2001-2003. ... Games played: 2001 (11), 2002 (13), 2003 (15). Total: 39.

LEE, ANDY — P — 49ERS

PERSONAL: Born August 11, 1982, in Westminster, S.C. ... 6-2/205. ... Full name: Andy Paul Lee.
HIGH SCHOOL: West-Oak (Westminster, S.C.).
COLLEGE: Pittsburgh.
TRANSACTIONS/CAREER NOTES: Selected by San Francisco 49ers in sixth round (188th pick overall) of 2004 NFL draft.

		PUNTING				
Year Team	**G**	**No.**	**Yds.**	**Avg.**	**In. 20**	**Blk.**
2000—Pittsburgh	7	30	1177	39.2	8	0
2001—Pittsburgh	11	64	2630	41.1	13	2
2002—Pittsburgh	13	73	3147	43.1	17	2
2003—Pittsburgh	13	77	3399	44.1	23	0
College totals (4 years)	44	244	10353	42.4	61	4

LEHMAN, TEDDY — LB — LIONS

PERSONAL: Born November 18, 1981, in Fort Gibson, Okla. ... 6-2/243.
HIGH SCHOOL: Fort Gibson (Fort Gibson, Okla.).
COLLEGE: Oklahoma.
TRANSACTIONS/CAREER NOTES: Selected by Detroit Lions in second round (37th pick overall) of 2004 NFL draft.
HONORS: Chuck Bednarik Award winner (2003). ... Dick Butkus Award winner (2003). ... Named linebacker on THE SPORTING NEWS college All-America first team (2002 and 2003).

			INTERCEPTIONS			
Year Team	**G**	**Sks.**	**No.**	**Yds.**	**Avg.**	**TD**
2000—Oklahoma	11	0.0	0	0	0.0	0
2001—Oklahoma	12	2.0	1	2	2.0	1
2002—Oklahoma	14	2.0	2	51	25.5	0
2003—Oklahoma	14	2.0	1	0	0.0	0
College totals (4 years)	51	6.0	4	53	13.3	1

LEISLE, RODNEY — DT — SAINTS

PERSONAL: Born February 5, 1981, in Fresno, Calif. ... 6-3/294. ... Full name: Rodney Allen Leisle.
HIGH SCHOOL: Ridgeview (Bakersfield, Calif.).
COLLEGE: UCLA.
TRANSACTIONS/CAREER NOTES: Selected by New Orleans Saints in fifth round (139th pick overall) of 2004 NFL draft.
HONORS: Named defensive lineman on THE SPORTING NEWS Freshman All-America third team (2000).

Year Team	G	Sks.	INTERCEPTIONS No.	Yds.	Avg.	TD
2000—UCLA	12	1.0	1	3	3.0	0
2001—UCLA	11	2.0	0	0	0.0	0
2002—UCLA	9	0.0	0	0	0.0	0
2003—UCLA	12	3.0	3	55	18.3	1
College totals (4 years)	44	6.0	4	58	14.5	1

LESUEUR, JEREMY — CB — BRONCOS

PERSONAL: Born October 5, 1980, in Holly Springs, Miss. ... 6-1/200.
HIGH SCHOOL: Holly Springs (Miss.).
COLLEGE: Michigan.
TRANSACTIONS/CAREER NOTES: Selected by Denver Broncos in third round (85th pick overall) of 2004 NFL draft.

			INTERCEPTIONS				KICKOFF RETURNS				TOTALS	
Year Team	G	Sks.	No.	Yds.	Avg.	TD	No.	Yds.	Avg.	TD	TD	Pts.
1999—Michigan	1	0.0	0	0	0.0	0	0	0	0.0	0	0	0
2000—Michigan	12	1.0	0	0	0.0	0	0	0	0.0	0	0	0
2001—Michigan	12	0.0	1	0	0.0	0	0	0	0.0	0	0	0
2002—Michigan	13	0.0	1	0	0.0	0	26	583	22.4	0	0	0
2003—Michigan	12	1.0	2	87	43.5	1	9	189	21.0	0	2	12
College totals (5 years)	50	2.0	4	87	21.8	1	35	772	22.1	0	2	12

LEWIS, ALEX — LB — LIONS

PERSONAL: Born June 11, 1981, in Delran, N.J. ... 6-1/237.
HIGH SCHOOL: Delran (Delran, N.J.).
JUNIOR COLLEGE: SUNY-Morrisville(N.Y.).
COLLEGE: Wisconsin.
TRANSACTIONS/CAREER NOTES: Selected by Detroit Lions in fifth round (140th pick overall) of 2004 NFL draft.

			INTERCEPTIONS			
Year Team	G	Sks.	No.	Yds.	Avg.	TD
2002—Wisconsin	14	1.0	0	0	0.0	0
2003—Wisconsin	13	9.0	0	0	0.0	0
College totals (2 years)	27	10.0	0	0	0.0	0

LEWIS, KEITH — DB — 49ERS

PERSONAL: Born October 20, 1981, in Sacramento, Calif. ... 6-0/202. ... Full name: Keith D'Andre Lewis.
HIGH SCHOOL: Valley (Sacramento, Calif.).
COLLEGE: Oregon.
TRANSACTIONS/CAREER NOTES: Selected by San Francisco 49ers in sixth round (198th pick overall) of 2004 NFL draft.

			INTERCEPTIONS			
Year Team	G	Sks.	No.	Yds.	Avg.	TD
2000—Oregon	11	1.0	1	0	0.0	0
2001—Oregon	10	1.0	2	32	16.0	0
2002—Oregon	13	0.0	5	16	3.2	0
2003—Oregon	13	0.0	3	31	10.3	1
College totals (4 years)	47	2.0	11	79	7.2	1

LOCKLEAR, SEAN — G — SEAHAWKS

PERSONAL: Born May 29, 1981, in Lumberton, N.C. ... 6-5/296.
HIGH SCHOOL: Lumberton (Lumberton, N.C.).
COLLEGE: North Carolina State.
TRANSACTIONS/CAREER NOTES: Selected by Seattle Seahawks in third round (84th pick overall) of 2004 NFL draft.
PLAYING EXPERIENCE: North Carolina State, 2000-2003. ... Games played: 2000 (11), 2001 (11), 2002 (14), 2003 (13). Total: 49.

LORD, JAMMAL — DB — TEXANS

PERSONAL: Born January 10, 1981, in Brooklyn, N.Y. ... 6-2/220.
HIGH SCHOOL: Bayonne (N.J.).
COLLEGE: Nebraska.
TRANSACTIONS/CAREER NOTES: Selected by Houston Texans in sixth round (175th pick overall) of 2004 NFL draft.

		PASSING								RUSHING				TOTALS	
Year Team	G	Att.	Cmp.	Pct.	Yds.	TD	Int.	Avg.	Rat.	Att.	Yds.	Avg.	TD	TD	Pts.
2000—Nebraska	6	16	9	56.3	116	0	1	7.25	104.7	28	130	4.6	4	4	24
2001—Nebraska	6	8	5	62.5	65	0	1	8.13	105.8	22	83	3.8	2	2	12
2002—Nebraska	14	204	95	46.6	1362	12	12	6.68	110.3	251	1412	5.6	8	8	48
2003—Nebraska	13	176	85	48.3	1305	6	8	7.41	112.7	215	948	4.4	10	10	60
College totals (4 years)	39	404	194	48.0	2848	18	22	7.05	111.0	516	2573	5.0	24	24	144

LOSMAN, J.P. — QB — BILLS

PERSONAL: Born March 12, 1981, in Venice, Calif. ... 6-3/220. ... Full name: Jonathan Paul Losman.
HIGH SCHOOL: Venice (Calif.).
COLLEGE: Tulane.
TRANSACTIONS/CAREER NOTES: Selected by Buffalo Bills in first round (22nd pick overall) of 2004 NFL draft.

		PASSING								RUSHING				TOTALS	
Year Team	**G**	**Att.**	**Cmp.**	**Pct.**	**Yds.**	**TD**	**Int.**	**Avg.**	**Rat.**	**Att.**	**Yds.**	**Avg.**	**TD**	**TD**	**Pts.**
2000—Tulane	10	114	58	50.9	722	4	2	6.33	112.1	59	133	2.3	1	1	6
2001—Tulane	3	49	31	63.3	487	4	1	9.94	169.6	13	9	0.7	1	1	6
2002—Tulane	13	401	230	57.4	2468	19	10	6.15	119.7	88	19	0.2	6	6	38
2003—Tulane	12	422	251	59.5	3077	33	14	7.29	139.9	77	80	1.0	2	2	12
College totals (4 years)	38	986	570	57.8	6754	60	27	6.85	130.0	237	241	1.0	10	10	62

LUKE, TRIANDOS — WR — BRONCOS

PERSONAL: Born in Phenix City, Ala. ... 5-10/190.
HIGH SCHOOL: Central (Phenix City, Ala.).
COLLEGE: Alabama.
TRANSACTIONS/CAREER NOTES: Selected by Denver Broncos in sixth round (171st pick overall) of 2004 NFL draft.

		RECEIVING				KICKOFF RETURNS				TOTALS	
Year Team	**G**	**No.**	**Yds.**	**Avg.**	**TD**	**No.**	**Yds.**	**Avg.**	**TD**	**TD**	**Pts.**
2000—Alabama	7	2	6	3.0	0	0	0	0.0	0	0	0
2001—Alabama	11	15	152	10.1	3	3	60	20.0	0	3	18
2002—Alabama	13	41	482	11.8	2	10	196	19.6	0	2	14
2003—Alabama	13	32	432	13.5	4	0	0	0.0	0	4	24
College totals (4 years)	44	90	1072	11.9	9	13	256	19.7	0	9	56

MADDOX, ANTHONY — DT — JAGUARS

PERSONAL: Born November 22, 1978, in Funston, Ga. ... 6-1/308.
HIGH SCHOOL: Monroe (Albany, Ga.).
JUNIOR COLLEGE: Jones County (Ellisville, Miss.).
COLLEGE: Delta State.
TRANSACTIONS/CAREER NOTES: Selected by Jacksonville Jaguars in fourth round (118th pick overall) of 2004 NFL draft.

Year Team	**G**	**SACKS**
2002—Delta State	11	5.5
2003—Delta State	11	5.5
College totals (2 years)	22	11.0

MANN, MAURICE — WR — BENGALS

PERSONAL: Born September 14, 1982, in Seaside, Calif. ... 6-2/185.
HIGH SCHOOL: Monterey (Seaside, Calif.).
JUNIOR COLLEGE: Monterey (Calif.) Peninsula.
COLLEGE: Nevada.
TRANSACTIONS/CAREER NOTES: Selected by Cincinnati Bengals in fifth round (149th pick overall) of 2004 NFL draft.

		RECEIVING				KICKOFF RETURNS				TOTALS	
Year Team	**G**	**No.**	**Yds.**	**Avg.**	**TD**	**No.**	**Yds.**	**Avg.**	**TD**	**TD**	**Pts.**
2002—Nevada	12	18	233	12.9	3	0	0	0.0	0	3	18
2003—Nevada	8	35	594	17.0	2	15	311	20.7	0	2	12
College totals (2 years)	20	53	827	15.6	5	15	311	20.7	0	5	30

MANNING, ELI — QB — GIANTS

PERSONAL: Born January 3, 1981, in New Orleans, La. ... 6-5/218. ... Full name: Elisha Nelson Manning. ... Son of Archie Manning, quarterback with New Orleans Saints (1971-82), Houston Oilers (1982-83) and Minnesota Vikings (1983-84). ... Brother of Peyton Manning, quarterback, Indianapolis Colts.
HIGH SCHOOL: Isadore Newman (New Orleans, La.).
COLLEGE: Mississippi.
TRANSACTIONS/CAREER NOTES: Selected by San Diego Chargers in first round (first pick overall) of 2004 NFL draft. ... Traded by Chargers to New York Giants for QB Philip Rivers, a third-round pick (K Nate Kaeding) in 2004 draft and 2005 first- and fifth-round draft choices (April 24, 2004).
HONORS: Maxwell Award winner (2003). ... Johnny Unitas Award winner (2003). ... Named quarterback on THE SPORTING NEWS college All-America second team (2003).

		PASSING								RUSHING				TOTALS	
Year Team	**G**	**Att.**	**Cmp.**	**Pct.**	**Yds.**	**TD**	**Int.**	**Avg.**	**Rat.**	**Att.**	**Yds.**	**Avg.**	**TD**	**TD**	**Pts.**
2000—Mississippi	6	33	16	48.5	170	0	1	5.15	85.7	7	4	0.6	0	0	0
2001—Mississippi	11	408	259	63.5	2948	31	9	7.23	144.8	34	9	0.3	0	0	0
2002—Mississippi	13	481	279	58.0	3401	21	15	7.07	125.6	39	-120	-3.1	2	2	12
2003—Mississippi	13	441	275	62.4	3600	29	10	8.16	148.1	48	-28	-0.6	3	3	18
College totals (4 years)	43	1363	829	60.8	10119	81	35	7.42	137.7	128	-135	-1.1	5	5	30

MARSHALL, ALFONSO — CB — BEARS

PERSONAL: Born January 17, 1981... 6-1/186. ... Full name: Alfonso Lanard Marshall.
HIGH SCHOOL: Clewiston (Fla.).
COLLEGE: Miami (Fla.).

TRANSACTIONS/CAREER NOTES: Selected by Chicago Bears in seventh round (215th pick overall) of 2004 NFL draft.

Year Team	G	Sks.	INTERCEPTIONS No.	Yds.	Avg.	TD
2000—Miami (Fla.)	9	0.0	0	0	0.0	0
2001—Miami (Fla.)	10	0.0	0	0	0.0	0
2002—Miami (Fla.)	13	0.0	0	0	0.0	0
2003—Miami (Fla.)	13	0.0	2	5	2.5	0
College totals (4 years)	45	0.0	2	5	2.5	0

MAUCK, MATT — QB — BRONCOS

PERSONAL: Born February 12, 1979, in Evansville, Ind. ... 6-1/213. ... Full name: Matthew Ryan Mauck.
HIGH SCHOOL: Jasper (Ind.).
COLLEGE: Louisiana State.
TRANSACTIONS/CAREER NOTES: Selected after junior season by Denver Broncos in seventh round (225th pick overall) of 2004 NFL draft.

		PASSING								RUSHING				TOTALS	
Year Team	G	Att.	Cmp.	Pct.	Yds.	TD	Int.	Avg.	Rat.	Att.	Yds.	Avg.	TD	TD	Pts.
2001—Louisiana State	3	41	18	43.9	224	0	2	5.46	80.0	20	73	3.7	2	2	12
2002—Louisiana State	6	130	63	48.5	782	9	2	6.02	118.8	50	175	3.5	2	2	12
2003—Louisiana State	14	358	229	64.0	2825	28	14	7.89	148.2	79	97	1.2	1	1	8
College totals (3 years)	23	529	310	58.6	3831	37	18	7.24	135.7	149	345	2.3	5	5	32

MCCLOVER, DARRELL — LB — JETS

PERSONAL: Born August 25, 1981... 6-2/219. ... Full name: Darrell A. McClover.
HIGH SCHOOL: Coconut Creek (Fla.).
COLLEGE: Miami (Fla.).
TRANSACTIONS/CAREER NOTES: Selected by New York Jets in seventh round (213th pick overall) of 2004 NFL draft.

Year Team	G	Sks.	INTERCEPTIONS No.	Yds.	Avg.	TD
2000—Miami (Fla.)	9	0.0	0	0	0.0	0
2001—Miami (Fla.)	9	0.0	0	0	0.0	0
2002—Miami (Fla.)	11	2.0	0	0	0.0	0
2003—Miami (Fla.)	13	2.0	0	0	0.0	0
College totals (4 years)	42	4.0	0	0	0.0	0

MCCOWN, LUKE — QB — BROWNS

PERSONAL: Born July 12, 1981, in Jacksonville, Texas. ... 6-3/208. ... Brother of Josh McCown, quarterback, Arizona Cardinals.
HIGH SCHOOL: Jacksonville (Texas).
COLLEGE: Louisiana Tech.
TRANSACTIONS/CAREER NOTES: Selected by Cleveland Browns in fourth round (106th pick overall) of 2004 NFL draft.

		PASSING								RUSHING				TOTALS	
Year Team	G	Att.	Cmp.	Pct.	Yds.	TD	Int.	Avg.	Rat.	Att.	Yds.	Avg.	TD	TD	Pts.
2000—Louisiana Tech	8	369	244	66.1	2544	21	15	6.89	134.7	55	-29	-0.5	3	3	18
2001—Louisiana Tech	11	469	277	59.1	3337	28	14	7.12	132.6	87	144	1.7	4	4	24
2002—Louisiana Tech	12	505	296	58.6	3539	19	19	7.01	122.4	61	30	0.5	2	2	12
2003—Louisiana Tech	12	432	246	56.9	3246	19	14	7.51	128.1	71	-80	-1.1	1	1	6
College totals (4 years)	43	1775	1063	59.9	12666	87	62	7.14	129.0	274	65	0.2	10	10	60

MCCRAY, BOBBY — DE — JAGUARS

PERSONAL: Born November 1, 1981, in Miami, Fla. ... 6-6/245.
HIGH SCHOOL: Homestead (Miami, Fla.).
COLLEGE: Florida.
TRANSACTIONS/CAREER NOTES: Selected by Jacksonville Jaguars in seventh round (249th pick overall) of 2004 NFL draft.

Year Team	G	SACKS
2000—Florida	3	0.0
2001—Florida	8	2.5
2002—Florida	13	2.3
2003—Florida	12	9.5
College totals (4 years)	36	14.3

MCFARLAND, DYLAN — T — BILLS

PERSONAL: Born July 11, 1980, in Kalispell, Mont. ... 6-6/245.
HIGH SCHOOL: Flathead (Kalispell, Mont.).
COLLEGE: Montana.
TRANSACTIONS/CAREER NOTES: Selected by Buffalo Bills in seventh round (207th pick overall) of 2004 NFL draft. ... Signed by Bills (May 25, 2004).
PLAYING EXPERIENCE: Montana, 2000-2003. ... Games played: 2000 (6), 2001 (12), 2002 (14), 2003 (13). Total: 45.

2004 DRAFT PICKS

MCHUGH, SEAN — FB — TITANS

PERSONAL: Born September 4, 1983, in Drexel Hill, Pa. ... 6-3/284.
HIGH SCHOOL: Monsignor Bonner (Drexel Hill, Pa.).
COLLEGE: Penn State.
TRANSACTIONS/CAREER NOTES: Selected by Tennessee Titans in seventh round (241st pick overall) of 2004 NFL draft.

		RUSHING				RECEIVING				TOTALS	
Year Team	G	Att.	Yds.	Avg.	TD	No.	Yds.	Avg.	TD	TD	Pts.
2000—Penn State	12	0	0	0.0	0	2	12	6.0	0	0	0
2001—Penn State	4	8	20	2.5	0	7	47	6.7	0	0	0
2002—Penn State	13	20	46	2.3	3	8	53	6.6	0	3	18
2003—Penn State	12	54	256	4.7	3	27	185	6.9	1	4	24
College totals (4 years)	41	82	322	3.9	6	44	297	6.8	1	7	42

MCINTYRE, JERIS — WR — CHIEFS

PERSONAL: Born July 4, 1981, in Tampa, Fla. ... 5-11/207.
HIGH SCHOOL: Catholic (Tampa, Fla.).
COLLEGE: Auburn.
TRANSACTIONS/CAREER NOTES: Selected by Kansas City Chiefs in sixth round (195th pick overall) of 2004 NFL draft.

		RECEIVING			
Year Team	G	No.	Yds.	Avg.	TD
2000—Auburn	12	6	36	6.0	0
2001—Auburn	11	12	187	15.6	0
2002—Auburn	13	10	129	12.9	1
2003—Auburn	13	41	621	15.1	3
College totals (4 years)	49	69	973	14.1	4

MILLER, CALEB — LB — BENGALS

PERSONAL: Born September 3, 1980, in Sulpher Springs, Texas. ... 6-3/225.
HIGH SCHOOL: Sulpher Springs (Sulpher Springs, Texas).
COLLEGE: Arkansas.
TRANSACTIONS/CAREER NOTES: Selected by Cincinnati Bengals in third round (80th pick overall) of 2004 NFL draft.

			INTERCEPTIONS			
Year Team	G	Sks.	No.	Yds.	Avg.	TD
2000—Arkansas	11	1.0	0	0	0.0	0
2001—Arkansas	11	1.5	4	62	15.5	0
2002—Arkansas	14	4.0	0	0	0.0	0
2003—Arkansas	13	1.0	0	0	0.0	0
College totals (4 years)	49	7.5	4	62	15.5	0

MIREE, BRANDON — RB — BRONCOS

PERSONAL: Born April 14, 1981, in Cincinnati, Ohio. ... 5-11/237. ... Full name: Brandon C. Miree.
HIGH SCHOOL: Winton Woods (Cincinnati, Ohio).
COLLEGE: Alabama, then Pittsburgh.
TRANSACTIONS/CAREER NOTES: Selected by Denver Broncos in seventh round (247th pick overall) of 2004 NFL draft.

		RUSHING				RECEIVING				TOTALS	
Year Team	G	Att.	Yds.	Avg.	TD	No.	Yds.	Avg.	TD	TD	Pts.
2000—Alabama	11	94	426	4.5	6	1	11	11.0	0	6	36
2001—Alabama	2	3	2	0.7	0	0	0	0.0	0	0	0
2002—Pittsburgh	13	214	943	4.4	4	11	123	11.2	0	4	24
2003—Pittsburgh	6	115	573	5.0	6	16	130	8.1	1	7	42
College totals (4 years)	32	426	1944	4.6	16	28	264	9.4	1	17	102

MOLINARO, JIM — T — REDSKINS

PERSONAL: Born April 27, 1981, in Hatfield, Pa. ... 6-6/301. ... Full name: James Anthony Molinaro Jr.
HIGH SCHOOL: Catholic (Bethlehem, Pa.).
COLLEGE: Notre Dame.
TRANSACTIONS/CAREER NOTES: Selected by Washington Redskins in sixth round (180th pick overall) of 2004 NFL draft.
PLAYING EXPERIENCE: Notre Dame, 2000-2003. ... Games played: 2000 (1), 2001 (6), 2002 (13), 2003 (12). Total: 32.

MOORE, CLARENCE — WR — RAVENS

PERSONAL: Born September 24, 1982, in Bellflower, Calif. ... 6-5/211. ... Full name: Clarence Kelly Moore.
COLLEGE: Northern Arizona.
TRANSACTIONS/CAREER NOTES: Selected by Baltimore Ravens in sixth round (199th pick overall) of 2004 NFL draft.

Year Team	G	RECEIVING No.	Yds.	Avg.	TD
2000—Northern Arizona	10	15	289	19.3	4
2001—Northern Arizona	12	51	797	15.6	5
2002—Northern Arizona	11	61	925	15.2	9
2003—Northern Arizona	13	63	1184	18.8	12
College totals (4 years)	46	190	3195	16.8	30

MOORE, MEWELDE — RB — VIKINGS

PERSONAL: Born July 24, 1982, in Hammond, La. ... 6-1/210. ... Full name: Mewelde Jaem Cadere Moore.
HIGH SCHOOL: Belaire (Baton Rouge, La.).
COLLEGE: Tulane.
TRANSACTIONS/CAREER NOTES: Selected by Minnesota Vikings in fourth round (119th pick overall) of 2004 NFL draft. ... Signed by Vikings (May 18, 2004).
HONORS: Named running back on THE SPORTING NEWS Freshman All-America second team (2000).

		RUSHING				RECEIVING				TOTALS	
Year Team	G	Att.	Yds.	Avg.	TD	No.	Yds.	Avg.	TD	TD	Pts.
2000—Tulane	10	174	890	5.1	2	33	350	10.6	1	3	20
2001—Tulane	12	262	1421	5.4	8	65	756	11.6	7	15	90
2002—Tulane	13	288	1138	4.0	6	52	545	10.5	3	9	56
2003—Tulane	9	185	915	4.9	5	39	408	10.5	4	9	54
College totals (4 years)	44	909	4364	4.8	21	189	2059	10.9	15	36	220

MORANT, JOHNNIE — WR — RAIDERS

PERSONAL: Born December 7, 1981, in Newark, N.J. ... 6-4/229. ... Full name: Johnnie E. Morant.
HIGH SCHOOL: Parsippany (N.J.).
COLLEGE: Syracuse.
TRANSACTIONS/CAREER NOTES: Selected by Oakland Raiders in fifth round (134th pick overall) of 2004 NFL draft.

		RECEIVING				KICKOFF RETURNS				TOTALS	
Year Team	G	No.	Yds.	Avg.	TD	No.	Yds.	Avg.	TD	TD	Pts.
2000—Syracuse	3	0	0	0.0	0	0	0	0.0	0	0	0
2001—Syracuse	11	18	409	22.7	2	0	0	0.0	0	2	12
2002—Syracuse	9	24	327	13.6	0	4	121	30.3	0	1	6
2003—Syracuse	12	46	799	17.4	5	18	403	22.4	0	5	30
College totals (4 years)	35	88	1535	17.4	7	22	524	23.8	0	8	48

MORTON, CHRISTIAN — CB — PATRIOTS

PERSONAL: Born April 28, 1981, in St. Louis, Mo. ... 6-1/180.
HIGH SCHOOL: Riverview Gardens (St. Louis, Mo.).
COLLEGE: Illinois.
TRANSACTIONS/CAREER NOTES: Selected by New England Patriots in seventh round (233rd pick overall) of 2004 NFL draft.

			INTERCEPTIONS				KICKOFF RETURNS				TOTALS	
Year Team	G	Sks.	No.	Yds.	Avg.	TD	No.	Yds.	Avg.	TD	TD	Pts.
2000—Illinois	10	0.0	0	0	0.0	0	27	539	20.0	0	1	6
2001—Illinois	11	0.0	4	104	26.0	2	7	115	16.4	0	2	12
2002—Illinois	12	0.0	1	0	0.0	0	1	17	17.0	0	0	0
2003—Illinois	11	1.0	0	0	0.0	0	0	0	0.0	0	0	0
College totals (4 years)	44	1.0	5	104	20.8	2	35	671	19.2	0	3	18

NAVARRE, JOHN — QB — CARDINALS

PERSONAL: Born September 9, 1980, in Cudahy, Wis. ... 6-6/236.
HIGH SCHOOL: Cudahy (Wis.).
COLLEGE: Michigan.
TRANSACTIONS/CAREER NOTES: Selected by Arizona Cardinals in seventh round (202nd pick overall) of 2004 NFL draft.

		PASSING								RUSHING				TOTALS	
Year Team	G	Att.	Cmp.	Pct.	Yds.	TD	Int.	Avg.	Rat.	Att.	Yds.	Avg.	TD	TD	Pts.
2000—Michigan	12	77	40	51.9	583	8	1	7.57	147.2	11	-34	-3.1	0	0	0
2001—Michigan	12	346	186	53.8	2195	17	12	6.34	116.3	45	-100	-2.2	0	0	0
2002—Michigan	13	448	248	55.4	2905	21	7	6.48	122.2	40	-16	-0.4	2	2	12
2003—Michigan	13	456	270	59.2	3331	24	10	7.30	133.6	48	-91	-1.9	0	1	6
College totals (4 years)	50	1327	744	56.1	9014	70	30	6.79	126.0	144	-241	-1.7	2	3	18

ODOM, ANTWAN — DE — TITANS

PERSONAL: Born September 24, 1981, in Bayou LaBatre, Ala. ... 6-5/279.
HIGH SCHOOL: Alma (Bryant, Ala.).
COLLEGE: Alabama.

TRANSACTIONS/CAREER NOTES: Selected after junior season by Tennessee Titans in second round (57th pick overall) of 2004 NFL draft.

Year Team	G	SACKS
2000—Alabama	11	3.0
2001—Alabama	2	0.0
2002—Alabama	13	10.0
2003—Alabama	13	8.0
College totals (4 years)	39	21.0

OLIVEA, SHANE — T — CHARGERS

PERSONAL: Born October 7, 1981, in Cedarhurst, N.Y. ... 6-5/320.
HIGH SCHOOL: Lawrence (Cedarhurst, N.Y.).
COLLEGE: Ohio State.
TRANSACTIONS/CAREER NOTES: Selected by San Diego Chargers in seventh round (209th pick overall) of 2004 NFL draft.
PLAYING EXPERIENCE: Ohio State, 2000-2003. ... Games played: 2000 (5), 2001 (11), 2002 (11), 2003 (12). Total: 39.

OLSHANSKY, IGOR — DT — CHARGERS

PERSONAL: Born May 3, 1982, in Dnepropetrovsk, Ukraine. ... 6-5/309.
HIGH SCHOOL: St. Ignatius (San Francisco, Calif.).
COLLEGE: Oregon.
TRANSACTIONS/CAREER NOTES: Selected after junior season by San Diego Chargers in second round (35th pick overall) of 2004 NFL draft.

			INTERCEPTIONS			
Year Team	**G**	**Sks.**	**No.**	**Yds.**	**Avg.**	**TD**
2001—Oregon	11	1.0	0	0	0.0	0
2002—Oregon	13	4.0	1	37	37.0	0
2003—Oregon	13	6.5	0	0	0.0	0
College totals (3 years)	37	11.5	1	37	37.0	0

ORR, RAHEEM — DE — TEXANS

PERSONAL: Born November 8, 1980, in Elizabeth, N.J. ... 6-4/260.
HIGH SCHOOL: Elizabeth (N.J.).
COLLEGE: Rutgers.
TRANSACTIONS/CAREER NOTES: Selected by Houston Texans in seventh round (210th pick overall) of 2004 NFL draft.

Year Team	G	SACKS
2001—Rutgers	7	0.0
2002—Rutgers	12	4.5
2003—Rutgers	12	8.5
College totals (3 years)	31	13.0

PAPE, TONY — T — DOLPHINS

PERSONAL: Born September 29, 1981, in Clarendon Hills, Ill. ... 6-6/299.
HIGH SCHOOL: Hindsdale South (Clarenton Hills, Ill.).
COLLEGE: Michigan.
TRANSACTIONS/CAREER NOTES: Selected by Miami Dolphins in seventh round (221st pick overall) of 2004 NFL draft.
PLAYING EXPERIENCE: Michigan, 2000-2003. ... Games played: 2000 (7), 2001 (12), 2002 (13), 2003 (13). Total: 45.

PARKER, SAMIE — WR — CHIEFS

PERSONAL: Born March 25, 1981, in Long Beach, Calif. ... 5-11/177. ... Full name: Samie Jabar Parker.
HIGH SCHOOL: Long Beach Poly (Long Beach, Calif.).
COLLEGE: Oregon.
TRANSACTIONS/CAREER NOTES: Selected by Kansas City Chiefs in fourth round (105th pick overall) of 2004 NFL draft.

		RECEIVING			
Year Team	**G**	**No.**	**Yds.**	**Avg.**	**TD**
2000—Oregon	11	11	201	18.3	0
2001—Oregon	11	32	586	18.3	3
2002—Oregon	13	49	724	14.8	8
2003—Oregon	13	77	1088	14.1	7
College totals (4 years)	48	169	2599	15.4	18

PERRY, BRUCE — RB — EAGLES

PERSONAL: Born March 22, 1981, in Philadelphia, Pa. ... 5-9/196.
HIGH SCHOOL: George Washington (Philadelphia, Pa.).
COLLEGE: Maryland.
TRANSACTIONS/CAREER NOTES: Selected by Philadelphia Eagles in seventh round (242nd pick overall) of 2004 NFL draft.

		RUSHING				RECEIVING				TOTALS	
Year Team	G	Att.	Yds.	Avg.	TD	No.	Yds.	Avg.	TD	TD	Pts.
1999—Maryland	7	30	195	6.5	0	1	9	9.0	0	0	0
2001—Maryland	11	219	1242	5.7	10	40	359	9.0	2	12	72
2002—Maryland	6	72	341	4.7	1	6	68	11.3	0	1	6
2003—Maryland	10	147	713	4.9	6	8	42	5.3	0	6	38
College totals (4 years)	34	468	2491	5.3	17	55	478	8.7	2	19	116

PERRY, CHRIS — RB — BENGALS

PERSONAL: Born December 27, 1981, in Advance, N.C. ... 6-1/235.
HIGH SCHOOL: Fork Union Military (Va.).
COLLEGE: Michigan.
TRANSACTIONS/CAREER NOTES: Selected by Cincinnati Bengals in first round (26th pick overall) of 2004 NFL draft.
HONORS: Doak Walker Award winner (2003). ... Named running back on THE SPORTING NEWS college All-America first team (2003).

		RUSHING				RECEIVING				TOTALS	
Year Team	G	Att.	Yds.	Avg.	TD	No.	Yds.	Avg.	TD	TD	Pts.
2000—Michigan	10	77	417	5.4	5	0	0	0.0	0	5	30
2001—Michigan	11	112	456	4.1	2	6	46	7.7	0	2	12
2002—Michigan	13	267	1110	4.2	14	14	156	11.1	0	14	84
2003—Michigan	13	338	1674	5.0	18	44	367	8.3	2	20	120
College totals (4 years)	47	794	3657	4.6	39	64	569	8.9	2	41	246

PETERMAN, STEPHEN — G — COWBOYS

PERSONAL: Born January 11, 1982, in Gulfport, Miss. ... 6-4/300. ... Full name: Stephen Frederick Peterman.
HIGH SCHOOL: St. Stanislaus (Waveland, Miss.).
COLLEGE: Louisiana State.
TRANSACTIONS/CAREER NOTES: Selected by Dallas Cowboys in third round (83rd pick overall) of 2004 NFL draft.
PLAYING EXPERIENCE: Louisiana State, 2000-2003. ... Games played: 2000 (9), 2001 (11), 2002 (13), 2003 (14). Total: 47.
HONORS: Named guard on THE SPORTING NEWS college All-America first team (2003).

PHILLIPS, SHAUN — DE — CHARGERS

PERSONAL: Born May 13, 1981, in Willingboro, N.J. ... 6-3/260. ... Full name: Shaun Jamal Phillips.
HIGH SCHOOL: Willingboro (N.J.).
COLLEGE: Purdue.
TRANSACTIONS/CAREER NOTES: Selected by San Diego Chargers in fourth round (98th pick overall) of 2004 NFL draft.

			INTERCEPTIONS			
Year Team	G	Sks.	No.	Yds.	Avg.	TD
2000—Purdue	11	7.0	0	0	0.0	0
2001—Purdue	11	6.0	0	0	0.0	0
2002—Purdue	12	6.0	0	0	0.0	0
2003—Purdue	13	14.5	1	0	0.0	0
College totals (4 years)	47	33.5	1	0	0.0	0

PICKETT, CODY — QB — 49ERS

PERSONAL: Born June 30, 1980, in Caldwell, Idaho. ... 6-4/220.
HIGH SCHOOL: Caldwell (Caldwell, Idaho).
COLLEGE: Washington.
TRANSACTIONS/CAREER NOTES: Selected by San Francisco 49ers in seventh round (217th pick overall) of 2004 NFL draft.

		PASSING								RUSHING				TOTALS	
Year Team	G	Att.	Cmp.	Pct.	Yds.	TD	Int.	Avg.	Rat.	Att.	Yds.	Avg.	TD	TD	Pts.
1999—Washington	1	4	0	0.0	0	0	1	0.00	-50.0	0	0	0.0	0	0	0
2000—Washington	2	2	1	50.0	12	0	0	6.00	100.4	0	0	0.0	0	0	0
2001—Washington	10	301	169	56.1	2403	10	14	7.98	124.9	83	60	0.7	5	5	30
2002—Washington	13	612	365	59.6	4458	28	14	7.28	131.4	86	-185	-2.2	3	3	18
2003—Washington	12	454	257	56.6	3043	15	13	6.70	118.1	80	-61	-0.8	3	3	18
College totals (5 years)	38	1373	792	57.7	9916	53	42	7.22	125.0	249	-186	-0.7	11	11	66

POOLE, WILL — CB — DOLPHINS

PERSONAL: Born July 24, 1981, in St. Albans, N.Y. ... 5-10/190.
HIGH SCHOOL: Christ the King (St. Albans, N.Y.).
JUNIOR COLLEGE: Ventura (Calif.).
COLLEGE: Boston College, then Southern California.
TRANSACTIONS/CAREER NOTES: Selected by Miami Dolphins in fourth round (102nd pick overall) of 2004 NFL draft.

			INTERCEPTIONS			
Year Team	G	Sks.	No.	Yds.	Avg.	TD
2000—Boston College	11	1.0	1	0	0.0	0
2003—Southern California	13	3.0	7	70	10.0	1
College totals (2 years)	24	4.0	8	70	8.8	1

POPE, DERRICK — LB — DOLPHINS

PERSONAL: Born May 4, 1982, in Huntsville, Ala. ... 6-1/223.
HIGH SCHOOL: Butler (Huntsville, Ala.).
COLLEGE: Alabama.
TRANSACTIONS/CAREER NOTES: Selected by Miami Dolphins in seventh round (222nd pick overall) of 2004 NFL draft.

			INTERCEPTIONS			
Year Team	G	Sks.	No.	Yds.	Avg.	TD
2002—Alabama	13	1.0	1	61	61.0	0
2003—Alabama	12	5.0	1	0	0.0	0
College totals (2 years)	25	6.0	2	61	30.5	0

POPE, KENDYLL — LB — COLTS

PERSONAL: Born May 9, 1981, in Ft. White, Fla. ... 6-2/220.
HIGH SCHOOL: Columbia (Ft. White, Fla.).
COLLEGE: Florida State.
TRANSACTIONS/CAREER NOTES: Selected by Indianapolis Colts in fourth round (107th pick overall) of 2004 NFL draft.
HONORS: Named linebacker on THE SPORTING NEWS Freshman All-America first team (2000).

			INTERCEPTIONS			
Year Team	G	Sks.	No.	Yds.	Avg.	TD
2000—Florida State	12	0.0	1	4	4.0	0
2001—Florida State	11	2.0	2	6	3.0	0
2002—Florida State	14	0.0	2	17	8.5	1
2003—Florida State	10	3.0	0	0	0.0	0
College totals (4 years)	47	5.0	5	27	5.4	1

PRUITT, ETRIC — DB — FALCONS

PERSONAL: Born August 16, 1980, in Theodore, Ala. ... 6-0/197.
HIGH SCHOOL: Theodore (Ala.).
COLLEGE: Southern Mississippi.
TRANSACTIONS/CAREER NOTES: Selected by Atlanta Falcons in sixth round (186th pick overall) of 2004 NFL draft.

			INTERCEPTIONS				PUNT RETURNS				TOTALS	
Year Team	G	Sks.	No.	Yds.	Avg.	TD	No.	Yds.	Avg.	TD	TD	Pts.
2000—Southern Mississippi	10	0.0	0	0	0.0	0	0	0	0.0	0	0	0
2001—Southern Mississippi	11	0.5	2	16	8.0	0	1	21	21.0	0	0	0
2002—Southern Mississippi	13	1.5	6	96	16.0	1	2	22	11.0	0	1	6
2003—Southern Mississippi	13	0.0	3	32	10.7	0	0	0	0.0	0	0	0
College totals (4 years)	47	2.0	11	144	13.1	1	3	43	14.3	0	1	6

RATLIFF, KEIWAN — CB — BENGALS

PERSONAL: Born April 19, 1981, in Columbus, Ohio. ... 5-10/178.
HIGH SCHOOL: Whitehall-Yearling (Columbus, Ohio).
COLLEGE: Florida.
TRANSACTIONS/CAREER NOTES: Selected by Cincinnati Bengals in second round (49th pick overall) of 2004 NFL draft.
HONORS: Named cornerback on THE SPORTING NEWS college All-America first team (2003).

			INTERCEPTIONS			
Year Team	G	Sks.	No.	Yds.	Avg.	TD
2000—Florida	12	0.0	0	0	0.0	0
2001—Florida	11	0.0	2	16	8.0	0
2002—Florida	13	2.0	1	62	62.0	1
2003—Florida	13	0.0	9	182	20.2	2
College totals (4 years)	49	2.0	12	260	21.7	3

REED, J.R. CB EAGLES

PERSONAL: Born February 11, 1982, in Tampa, Fla. ... 5-11/190. ... Full name: Herbert Lee Reed Jr.
HIGH SCHOOL: Hillsborough (Tampa, Fla.).
COLLEGE: South Florida.
TRANSACTIONS/CAREER NOTES: Selected by Philadelphia Eagles in fourth round (129th pick overall) of 2004 NFL draft.

			INTERCEPTIONS				KICKOFF RETURNS				TOTALS	
Year Team	G	Sks.	No.	Yds.	Avg.	TD	No.	Yds.	Avg.	TD	TD	Pts.
2000—South Florida	11	0.0	0	0	0.0	0	0	0	0.0	0	0	0
2001—South Florida	11	0.0	5	48	9.6	0	0	0	0.0	0	1	6
2002—South Florida	11	1.0	6	34	5.7	1	0	0	0.0	0	1	6
2003—South Florida	11	0.0	7	45	6.4	0	18	570	31.7	1	2	12
College totals (4 years)	44	1.0	18	127	7.1	1	18	570	31.7	1	4	24

REEVES, JACQUES CB COWBOYS

PERSONAL: Born October 8, 1982... 6-1/183. ... Full name: Jacques D. Reeves.
HIGH SCHOOL: Lancaster (Texas).
COLLEGE: Purdue.
TRANSACTIONS/CAREER NOTES: Selected by Dallas Cowboys in seventh round (223rd pick overall) of 2004 NFL draft.

			INTERCEPTIONS			
Year Team	G	Sks.	No.	Yds.	Avg.	TD
2000—Purdue	10	0.0	0	0	0.0	0
2001—Purdue	11	0.0	2	8	4.0	0
2002—Purdue	13	0.0	3	15	5.0	0
2003—Purdue	12	1.0	2	0	0.0	0
College totals (4 years)	46	1.0	7	23	3.3	0

REID, DEXTER DB PATRIOTS

PERSONAL: Born March 18, 1981, in Norfolk, Va. ... 5-11/200.
HIGH SCHOOL: Granby (Norfolk, Va.).
COLLEGE: North Carolina.
TRANSACTIONS/CAREER NOTES: Selected by New England Patriots in fourth round (113th pick overall) of 2004 NFL draft.
HONORS: Named defensive back on THE SPORTING NEWS Freshman All-America third team (2000).

			INTERCEPTIONS			
Year Team	G	Sks.	No.	Yds.	Avg.	TD
2000—North Carolina	11	1.0	1	2	2.0	0
2001—North Carolina	12	2.0	2	66	33.0	1
2002—North Carolina	12	1.0	0	0	0.0	0
2003—North Carolina	12	0.0	0	0	0.0	0
College totals (4 years)	47	4.0	3	68	22.7	1

REYNOLDS, ROBERT LB TITANS

PERSONAL: Born May 20, 1981, in Bowling Green, Ky. ... 6-3/242.
HIGH SCHOOL: Bowling Green (Ky.).
COLLEGE: Ohio State.
TRANSACTIONS/CAREER NOTES: Selected by Tennessee Titans in fifth round (165th pick overall) of 2004 NFL draft.

			INTERCEPTIONS			
Year Team	G	Sks.	No.	Yds.	Avg.	TD
2000—Ohio State	11	1.0	0	0	0.0	0
2001—Ohio State	11	1.0	1	0	0.0	0
2002—Ohio State	14	1.0	0	0	0.0	0
2003—Ohio State	12	2.0	1	19	19.0	0
College totals (4 years)	48	5.0	2	19	9.5	0

RIMPF, BRIAN T RAVENS

PERSONAL: Born February 11, 1981, in Raleigh, N.C. ... 6-6/318.
HIGH SCHOOL: Leesville Road (Raleigh, N.C.).
COLLEGE: East Carolina.
TRANSACTIONS/CAREER NOTES: Selected by Baltimore Ravens in seventh round (246th pick overall) of 2004 NFL draft.
PLAYING EXPERIENCE: East Carolina, 2000-2003. ... Games played: 2000 (10), 2001 (11), 2002 (12), 2003 (12). Total: 45.

RIVERS, PHILIP — QB — CHARGERS

PERSONAL: Born December 8, 1981, in Athens, Ga. ... 6-5/236.
HIGH SCHOOL: Athens (Ga.).
COLLEGE: North Carolina State.
TRANSACTIONS/CAREER NOTES: Selected by New York Giants in first round (fourth pick overall) of 2004 NFL draft. ... Traded by Giants with a third-round pick (K Nate Kaeding) in 2004 draft and 2005 first- and third-round draft choices to San Diego Chargers for QB Eli Manning (April 24, 2004).
HONORS: Named running back on THE SPORTING NEWS Freshman All-America first team (2000).

		PASSING								RUSHING				TOTALS	
Year Team	G	Att.	Cmp.	Pct.	Yds.	TD	Int.	Avg.	Rat.	Att.	Yds.	Avg.	TD	TD	Pts.
2000—North Carolina State	11	441	237	53.7	3054	25	10	6.93	126.1	73	-85	-1.2	2	3	18
2001—North Carolina State	11	368	240	65.2	2586	16	7	7.03	134.8	44	-26	-0.6	2	2	12
2002—North Carolina State	14	418	262	62.7	3353	20	10	8.02	141.1	57	100	1.8	10	10	60
2003—North Carolina State	13	483	348	72.0	4491	34	7	9.30	170.5	78	109	1.4	3	3	18
College totals (4 years)	49	1710	1087	63.6	13484	95	34	7.89	144.2	252	98	0.4	17	18	108

ROBINSON, DUNTA — CB — TEXANS

PERSONAL: Born April 11, 1982, in Athens, Ga. ... 6-0/180.
HIGH SCHOOL: Clarke Central (Athens, Ga.).
COLLEGE: South Carolina.
TRANSACTIONS/CAREER NOTES: Selected by Houston Texans in first round (10th pick overall) of 2004 NFL draft.

			INTERCEPTIONS			
Year Team	G	Sks.	No.	Yds.	Avg.	TD
2000—South Carolina	8	0.0	0	0	0.0	0
2001—South Carolina	10	0.0	0	0	0.0	0
2002—South Carolina	12	0.0	4	63	15.8	0
2003—South Carolina	12	0.0	1	29	29.0	1
College totals (4 years)	42	0.0	5	92	18.4	1

ROETHLISBERGER, BEN — QB — STEELERS

PERSONAL: Born March 2, 1982, in Findlay, Ohio. ... 6-5/240.
HIGH SCHOOL: Findlay (Ohio).
COLLEGE: Miami of Ohio.
TRANSACTIONS/CAREER NOTES: Selected after junior season by Pittsburgh Steelers in first round (11th pick overall) of 2004 NFL draft.
HONORS: Named quarterback on THE SPORTING NEWS Freshman All-America third team (2001).

		PASSING								RUSHING				TOTALS	
Year Team	G	Att.	Cmp.	Pct.	Yds.	TD	Int.	Avg.	Rat.	Att.	Yds.	Avg.	TD	TD	Pts.
2001—Miami of Ohio	12	381	241	63.3	3105	25	13	8.15	146.5	120	189	1.6	3	3	18
2002—Miami of Ohio	12	428	271	63.3	3238	22	11	7.57	138.7	82	-54	-0.7	1	1	6
2003—Miami of Ohio	14	495	342	69.1	4486	37	10	9.06	165.8	67	111	1.7	3	3	18
College totals (3 years)	38	1304	854	65.5	10829	84	34	8.30	151.3	269	246	0.9	7	7	42

ROGERS, JACOB — T — COWBOYS

PERSONAL: Born August 17, 1981, in Oxnard, Calif. ... 6-6/305.
HIGH SCHOOL: Oxnard (Calif.).
COLLEGE: Southern California.
TRANSACTIONS/CAREER NOTES: Selected by Dallas Cowboys in second round (52nd pick overall) of 2004 NFL draft.
PLAYING EXPERIENCE: Southern California, 2000-2003. ... Games played: 2000 (12), 2001 (11), 2002 (12), 2003 (13). Total: 48.
HONORS: Named offensive tackle on THE SPORTING NEWS college All-America second team (2003).

RYAN, SEAN — TE — COWBOYS

PERSONAL: Born March 27, 1980, in Buffalo, N.Y. ... 6-5/264.
HIGH SCHOOL: St. Joseph (Buffalo, N.Y.).
COLLEGE: Boston College.
TRANSACTIONS/CAREER NOTES: Selected by Dallas Cowboys in fifth round (144th pick overall) of 2004 NFL draft.

		RECEIVING			
Year Team	G	No.	Yds.	Avg.	TD
2000—Boston College	11	0	0	0.0	0
2001—Boston College	11	17	223	13.1	3
2002—Boston College	13	23	280	12.2	3
2003—Boston College	13	35	447	12.8	6
College totals (4 years)	48	75	950	12.7	12

SAM, P.K. WR PATRIOTS

PERSONAL: Born December 26, 1983, in Buford, Ga. ... 6-3/195.
HIGH SCHOOL: Buford (Ga.).
COLLEGE: Florida State.
TRANSACTIONS/CAREER NOTES: Selected after junior season by New England Patriots in fifth round (164th pick overall) of 2004 NFL draft.

		RECEIVING				PUNT RETURNS				KICKOFF RETURNS				TOTALS	
Year Team	G	No.	Yds.	Avg.	TD	No.	Yds.	Avg.	TD	No.	Yds.	Avg.	TD	TD	Pts.
2001—Florida State	9	11	158	14.4	2	4	11	2.8	0	4	74	18.5	0	2	12
2002—Florida State	11	15	173	11.5	0	2	19	9.5	0	0	0	0.0	0	0	0
2003—Florida State	13	50	735	14.7	5	0	0	0.0	0	0	0	0.0	0	5	30
College totals (3 years)	33	76	1066	14.0	7	6	30	5.0	0	4	74	18.5	0	7	42

SAMPSON, KEVIN T CHIEFS

PERSONAL: Born June 19, 1981, in Westwood, N.J. ... 6-4/308. ... Full name: Kevin M. Sampson.
HIGH SCHOOL: Westwood (N.J.).
COLLEGE: Syracuse.
TRANSACTIONS/CAREER NOTES: Selected by Kansas City Chiefs in seventh round (231st pick overall) of 2004 NFL draft.
PLAYING EXPERIENCE: Syracuse, 2000-2003. ... Games played: 2000 (6), 2001 (12), 2002 (12), 2003 (12). Total: 42.

SANDER, B.J. P PACKERS

PERSONAL: Born July 29, 1980, in Cincinnati, Ohio. ... 6-3/212.
HIGH SCHOOL: Roger Bacon (Cincinnati, Ohio).
COLLEGE: Ohio State.
TRANSACTIONS/CAREER NOTES: Selected by Green Bay Packers in third round (87th pick overall) of 2004 NFL draft.
HONORS: Ray Guy Award winner (2003). ... Named punter on THE SPORTING NEWS Freshman All-America first team (2000).

		PUNTING				
Year Team	G	No.	Yds.	Avg.	In. 20	Blk.
1999—Ohio State	2	2	49	24.5	0	0
2000—Ohio State	11	33	1402	42.5	7	2
2001—Ohio State	2	4	119	29.8	0	0
2003—Ohio State	13	82	3553	43.3	39	0
College totals (4 years)	28	121	5123	42.3	46	2

SANDERS, BOB DB COLTS

PERSONAL: Born February 24, 1981, in Erie, Pa. ... 5-8/200.
HIGH SCHOOL: Cathedral Prep (Erie, Pa.).
COLLEGE: Iowa.
TRANSACTIONS/CAREER NOTES: Selected by Indianapolis Colts in second round (44th pick overall) of 2004 NFL draft.

			INTERCEPTIONS			
Year Team	G	Sks.	No.	Yds.	Avg.	TD
2000—Iowa	12	1.0	0	0	0.0	0
2001—Iowa	10	1.0	4	24	6.0	0
2002—Iowa	12	1.0	2	15	7.5	0
2003—Iowa	10	1.0	1	0	0.0	0
College totals (4 years)	44	4.0	7	39	5.6	0

SCHAUB, MATT QB FALCONS

PERSONAL: Born September 25, 1981, in Pittsburgh, Pa. ... 6-5/235. ... Full name: Matthew Rutledge Schaub. ... Name pronounced: Shob.
HIGH SCHOOL: West Chester East (West Chester, Pa.).
COLLEGE: Virginia.
TRANSACTIONS/CAREER NOTES: Selected by Atlanta Falcons in third round (90th pick overall) of 2004 NFL draft.

		PASSING								RUSHING				TOTALS	
Year Team	G	Att.	Cmp.	Pct.	Yds.	TD	Int.	Avg.	Rat.	Att.	Yds.	Avg.	TD	TD	Pts.
2000—Virginia	4	8	7	87.5	50	0	1	6.25	115.0	3	-1	-0.3	0	0	0
2001—Virginia	12	240	140	58.3	1524	10	8	6.35	118.8	33	-13	-0.4	2	2	12
2002—Virginia	14	418	288	68.9	2976	28	7	7.12	147.5	70	95	1.4	2	2	14
2003—Virginia	11	403	281	69.7	2952	18	10	7.33	141.0	26	-23	-0.9	1	1	8
College totals (4 years)	41	1069	716	67.0	7502	56	26	7.02	138.4	132	58	0.4	5	5	34

SCHOBEL, BO — DE — TITANS

PERSONAL: Born March 24, 1981, in Columbus, Texas. ... 6-5/268. ... Full name: Robert Edward Schobel.
HIGH SCHOOL: Columbus (Columbus, Texas).
COLLEGE: Texas Christian.
TRANSACTIONS/CAREER NOTES: Selected by Tennessee Titans in fourth round (103rd pick overall) of 2004 NFL draft.

Year Team	G	SACKS
2000—Texas Christian	11	4.0
2001—Texas Christian	1	0.0
2002—Texas Christian	12	7.5
2003—Texas Christian	13	17.0
College totals (4 years)	37	28.5

SCHWEIGERT, STUART — DB — RAIDERS

PERSONAL: Born June 21, 1981, in Saginaw, Mich. ... 6-3/208. ... Full name: Stuart Eric Schweigert.
HIGH SCHOOL: Heritage (Saginaw, Mich.).
COLLEGE: Purdue.
TRANSACTIONS/CAREER NOTES: Selected by Oakland Raiders in third round (67th pick overall) of 2004 NFL draft.
HONORS: Named defensive back on THE SPORTING NEWS Freshman All-America first team (2000). ... Named safety on THE SPORTING NEWS college All-America fourth team (2001) and second team (2003).

			INTERCEPTIONS			
Year Team	G	Sks.	No.	Yds.	Avg.	TD
2000—Purdue	11	0.0	5	2	0.4	0
2001—Purdue	11	0.0	6	110	18.3	0
2002—Purdue	12	0.0	2	2	1.0	0
2003—Purdue	13	2.5	4	62	15.5	0
College totals (4 years)	47	2.5	17	176	10.4	0

SCOBEE, JOSH — K — JAGUARS

PERSONAL: Born June 23, 1982, in Longview, Texas. ... 6-1/191.
HIGH SCHOOL: Longview (Texas).
COLLEGE: Louisiana Tech.
TRANSACTIONS/CAREER NOTES: Selected by Jacksonville Jaguars in fifth round (137th pick overall) of 2004 NFL draft.

		KICKING						
Year Team	G	50+	Tot.	Pct.	Lg.	XPM	XPA	Pts.
2000—Louisiana Tech	12	1-4	10-17	58.8	51	39	41	69
2001—Louisiana Tech	11	0-1	18-22	81.8	48	44	45	98
2002—Louisiana Tech	12	1-2	16-21	76.2	51	30	35	78
2003—Louisiana Tech	12	4-7	21-31	67.7	53	31	31	94
College totals (4 years)	47	6-14	65-91	71.4	53	144	152	339

SCOTT, DARRION — DE — VIKINGS

PERSONAL: Born October 25, 1980, in Charleston, W. Va. ... 6-3/280.
HIGH SCHOOL: Capital (Charleston, W. Va.).
COLLEGE: Ohio State.
TRANSACTIONS/CAREER NOTES: Selected by Minnesota Vikings in third round (88th pick overall) of 2004 NFL draft.

Year Team	G	SACKS
2000—Ohio State	11	0.0
2001—Ohio State	11	2.0
2002—Ohio State	13	8.5
2003—Ohio State	11	4.0
College totals (4 years)	46	14.5

SCOTT, GUSS — DB — PATRIOTS

PERSONAL: Born May 21, 1982, in Jacksonville, Fla. ... 5-11/195.
HIGH SCHOOL: Trinity Christian (Jacksonville, Fla.).
COLLEGE: Florida.
TRANSACTIONS/CAREER NOTES: Selected by New England Patriots in third round (95th pick overall) of 2004 NFL draft.

			INTERCEPTIONS			
Year Team	G	Sks.	No.	Yds.	Avg.	TD
2000—Florida	12	2.0	0	0	0.0	0
2001—Florida	11	3.5	0	0	0.0	0
2002—Florida	13	1.0	2	62	31.0	1
2003—Florida	13	1.0	2	47	23.5	1
College totals (4 years)	49	7.5	4	109	27.3	2

SCOTT, JAKE — T — COLTS

PERSONAL: Born April 16, 1981, in Lewiston, Idaho. ... 6-5/283.
HIGH SCHOOL: Lewiston (Idaho).
COLLEGE: Idaho.
TRANSACTIONS/CAREER NOTES: Selected by Indianapolis Colts in fifth round (141st pick overall) of 2004 NFL draft.
PLAYING EXPERIENCE: Idaho, 2000-2003. ... Games played: 2000 (11), 2001 (11), 2002 (12), 2003 (12). Total: 46.

SEIGLER, RICHARD — LB — 49ERS

PERSONAL: Born October 19, 1980, in Las Vegas, Nev. ... 6-3/239. ... Full name: Richard Joseph Seigler.
HIGH SCHOOL: Chaparral (Las Vegas, Nev.).
COLLEGE: Oregon State.
TRANSACTIONS/CAREER NOTES: Selected by San Francisco 49ers in fourth round (127th pick overall) of 2004 NFL draft.
HONORS: Named linebacker on THE SPORTING NEWS Freshman All-America first team (2000).

			INTERCEPTIONS			
Year Team	G	Sks.	No.	Yds.	Avg.	TD
2000—Oregon State	11	2.0	3	15	5.0	0
2001—Oregon State	11	2.0	0	0	0.0	0
2002—Oregon State	13	0.5	3	102	34.0	1
2003—Oregon State	13	2.5	3	32	10.7	0
College totals (4 years)	48	7.0	9	149	16.6	1

SEWELL, JOSH — C — BRONCOS

PERSONAL: Born July 26, 1981, in Lincoln, Neb. ... 6-2/300.
HIGH SCHOOL: Southeast (Lincoln, Neb.).
COLLEGE: Indiana State, then Nebraska.
TRANSACTIONS/CAREER NOTES: Selected by Denver Broncos in sixth round (190th pick overall) of 2004 NFL draft.
PLAYING EXPERIENCE: Indiana State, 2000; Nebraska, 2002-2003. ... Games played: 2000 (10), 2002 (5), 2003 (13). Total: 28.

SHIVERS, JASON — DB — RAMS

PERSONAL: Born November 4, 1982, in Phoenix, Ariz. ... 6-1/193.
HIGH SCHOOL: South Mountain (Phoenix, Ariz.).
COLLEGE: Arizona State.
TRANSACTIONS/CAREER NOTES: Selected after junior season by St. Louis Rams in fifth round (134th pick overall) of 2004 NFL draft.
HONORS: Named free safety on THE SPORTING NEWS Freshman All-America first team (2001).

			INTERCEPTIONS			
Year Team	G	Sks.	No.	Yds.	Avg.	TD
2001—Arizona State	11	1.0	0	0	0.0	0
2002—Arizona State	14	0.0	3	0	0.0	0
2003—Arizona State	11	1.0	3	85	28.3	0
College totals (3 years)	36	2.0	6	85	14.2	0

SHOATE, JEFF — DB — BRONCOS

PERSONAL: Born March 23, 1981, in San Diego, Calif. ... 5-11/175.
HIGH SCHOOL: Serra (San Diego, Calif.).
COLLEGE: Montana, then San Diego State.
TRANSACTIONS/CAREER NOTES: Selected by Denver Broncos in fifth round (152nd pick overall) of 2004 NFL draft.

			INTERCEPTIONS			
Year Team	G	Sks.	No.	Yds.	Avg.	TD
1999—Montana	11	0.0	1	11	11.0	0
2001—San Diego State	11	0.0	3	18	6.0	0
2002—San Diego State	13	0.0	2	0	0.0	0
2003—San Diego State	12	0.0	1	8	8.0	0
College totals (4 years)	47	0.0	7	37	5.3	0

SIAVII, JUNIOR — DT — CHIEFS

PERSONAL: Born November 14, 1978, in Tafuna, American Samoa. ... 6-4/323. ... Full name: Saousoalii Poe Siavii Jr.
JUNIOR COLLEGE: Dixie College (Utah), Butte College (Calif.).
COLLEGE: Oregon.

TRANSACTIONS/CAREER NOTES: Selected by Kansas City Chiefs in second round (36th pick overall) of 2004 NFL draft.

Year Team	G	SACKS
2002—Oregon	12	0.5
2003—Oregon	13	2.0
College totals (2 years)	25	2.5

SMILEY, JUSTIN — G — 49ERS

PERSONAL: Born November 11, 1981, in Ellabell, Ga. ... 6-4/296.
HIGH SCHOOL: Southeast Bulloch (Ellabell, Ga.).
COLLEGE: Alabama.
TRANSACTIONS/CAREER NOTES: Selected after junior season by San Francisco 49ers in second round (46th pick overall) of 2004 NFL draft.
PLAYING EXPERIENCE: Alabama, 2001-2003. ... Games played: 2001 (11), 2002 (13), 2003 (11). Total: 35.
HONORS: Named guard on THE SPORTING NEWS Freshman All-America third team (2001).

SMITH, ANTONIO — DE — CARDINALS

PERSONAL: Born October 21, 1981, in Oklahoma City, Okla. ... 6-3/274.
COLLEGE: Oklahoma State.
TRANSACTIONS/CAREER NOTES: Selected by Arizona Cardinals in fifth round (135th pick overall) of 2004 NFL draft.

Year Team	G	SACKS
2002—Oklahoma State	13	3.5
2003—Oklahoma State	11	5.0
College totals (2 years)	24	8.5

SMITH, DARYL — LB — JAGUARS

PERSONAL: Born April 14, 1982, in Albany, Ga. ... 6-2/235.
HIGH SCHOOL: Dougherty County (Albany, Ga.).
COLLEGE: Georgia Tech.
TRANSACTIONS/CAREER NOTES: Selected by Jacksonville Jaguars in second round (39th pick overall) of 2004 NFL draft.
HONORS: Named linebacker on THE SPORTING NEWS Freshman All-America first team (2000).

			INTERCEPTIONS			
Year Team	G	Sks.	No.	Yds.	Avg.	TD
2000—Georgia Tech	11	4.0	2	75	37.5	1
2001—Georgia Tech	9	3.0	0	0	0.0	0
2002—Georgia Tech	13	5.0	1	14	14.0	0
2003—Georgia Tech	13	3.5	0	0	0.0	0
College totals (4 years)	46	15.5	3	89	29.7	1

SMITH, FREDDIE — WR — BILLS

PERSONAL: Born November 28, 1981, in Argyle, Ga. ... 5-10/194. ... Full name: Jonathan Dewayne Smith.
HIGH SCHOOL: Cinch County (Homerville, Ala.).
COLLEGE: Georgia Tech.
TRANSACTIONS/CAREER NOTES: Selected by Buffalo Bills in seventh round (214th pick overall) of 2004 NFL draft.

		RECEIVING				PUNT RETURNS				TOTALS	
Year Team	G	No.	Yds.	Avg.	TD	No.	Yds.	Avg.	TD	TD	Pts.
2000—Georgia Tech	9	7	80	11.4	0	0	0	0.0	0	0	2
2001—Georgia Tech	12	53	590	11.1	4	2	35	17.5	0	5	30
2002—Georgia Tech	12	36	430	11.9	3	6	78	13.0	0	3	20
2003—Georgia Tech	13	78	1138	14.6	5	31	364	11.7	2	7	42
College totals (4 years)	46	174	2238	12.9	12	39	477	12.2	2	15	94

SMITH, KEITH — CB — LIONS

PERSONAL: Born March 20, 1980, in Leesville, La. ... 5-11/192.
HIGH SCHOOL: Leesville (La.).
COLLEGE: McNeese State.
TRANSACTIONS/CAREER NOTES: Selected by Detroit Lions in third round (73rd pick overall) of 2004 NFL draft.

			INTERCEPTIONS			
Year Team	G	Sks.	No.	Yds.	Avg.	TD
2000—McNeese State	11	0.0	0	0	0.0	0
2001—McNeese State	10	0.0	1	0	0.0	0
2002—McNeese State	15	1.0	1	22	22.0	0
2003—McNeese State	12	0.0	4	8	2.0	0
College totals (4 years)	48	1.0	6	30	5.0	0

SMITH, WILL DE SAINTS

PERSONAL: Born July 4, 1981, in Utica, N.Y. ... 6-4/265.
HIGH SCHOOL: Proctor (Utica, N.Y.).
COLLEGE: Ohio State.
TRANSACTIONS/CAREER NOTES: Selected by New Orleans Saints in first round (18th pick overall) of 2004 NFL draft.
HONORS: Named defensive end on THE SPORTING NEWS college All-America second team (2003).

			INTERCEPTIONS			
Year Team	**G**	**Sks.**	**No.**	**Yds.**	**Avg.**	**TD**
2000—Ohio State	11	3.0	0	0	0.0	0
2001—Ohio State	11	4.0	0	0	0.0	0
2002—Ohio State	14	5.5	1	0	0.0	0
2003—Ohio State	13	10.5	0	0	0.0	0
College totals (4 years)	49	23.0	1	0	0.0	0

SMOKER, JEFF QB RAMS

PERSONAL: Born June 13, 1981, in Manheim, Pa. ... 6-3/223.
HIGH SCHOOL: Manheim Central (Pa.).
COLLEGE: Michigan State.
TRANSACTIONS/CAREER NOTES: Selected by St. Louis Rams in sixth round (201st pick overall) of 2004 NFL draft.

		PASSING								RUSHING				TOTALS	
Year Team	**G**	**Att.**	**Cmp.**	**Pct.**	**Yds.**	**TD**	**Int.**	**Avg.**	**Rat.**	**Att.**	**Yds.**	**Avg.**	**TD**	**TD**	**Pts.**
2000—Michigan State	9	197	103	52.3	1365	6	7	6.93	113.4	74	-11	-0.1	2	2	14
2001—Michigan State	11	230	144	62.6	2227	18	7	9.68	163.7	72	-75	-1.0	2	2	12
2002—Michigan State	7	203	114	56.2	1593	13	10	7.85	133.4	38	-39	-1.0	0	0	0
2003—Michigan State	13	488	302	61.9	3395	21	14	6.96	128.8	63	-116	-1.8	3	3	18
College totals (4 years)	40	1118	663	59.3	8580	58	38	7.67	134.1	247	-241	-1.0	7	7	44

SNEE, CHRIS G GIANTS

PERSONAL: Born January 8, 1982, in Montrose, Pa. ... 6-3/331. ... Full name: Christopher Snee.
HIGH SCHOOL: Montrose (Pa.).
COLLEGE: Boston College.
TRANSACTIONS/CAREER NOTES: Selected by New York Giants in second round (34th pick overall) of 2004 NFL draft.
PLAYING EXPERIENCE: Boston College, 2001-2003. ... Games played: 2001 (9), 2002 (13), 2003 (12). Total: 34.

SOMMERSELL, ANDRE LB RAIDERS

PERSONAL: Born June 26, 1980, in Guyana. ... 6-3/200. ... Full name: Andre Lawrence Sommersell.
HIGH SCHOOL: Fountain Valley (Calif.).
COLLEGE: Colorado State.
TRANSACTIONS/CAREER NOTES: Selected by Oakland Raiders in seventh round (255th pick overall) of 2004 NFL draft.

			INTERCEPTIONS			
Year Team	**G**	**Sks.**	**No.**	**Yds.**	**Avg.**	**TD**
2000—Colorado State	9	0.0	0	0	0.0	0
2001—Colorado State	11	2.0	0	0	0.0	0
2002—Colorado State	10	0.0	0	0	0.0	0
2003—Colorado State	13	2.0	0	0	0.0	0
College totals (4 years)	43	4.0	0	0	0.0	0

SOPOAGA, ISAAC DT 49ERS

PERSONAL: Born September 4, 1981, in Pago Pago, American Samoa. ... 6-3/315.
HIGH SCHOOL: Samoana (Pago Pago, American Samoa).
JUNIOR COLLEGE: College of the Canyons (Santa Clarita, Calif.).
COLLEGE: Hawaii.
TRANSACTIONS/CAREER NOTES: Selected by San Francisco 49ers in fourth round (104th pick overall) of 2004 NFL draft.

Year Team	**G**	**SACKS**
2002—Hawaii	14	0.0
2003—Hawaii	11	4.0
College totals (2 years)	25	4.0

SORGI, JIM — QB — COLTS

PERSONAL: Born December 3, 1980, in Fraser, Mich. ... 6-3/194.
HIGH SCHOOL: Fraser (Mich.).
COLLEGE: Wisconsin.
TRANSACTIONS/CAREER NOTES: Selected by Indianapolis Colts in sixth round (193rd pick overall) of 2004 NFL draft.

		PASSING								RUSHING				TOTALS	
Year Team	G	Att.	Cmp.	Pct.	Yds.	TD	Int.	Avg.	Rat.	Att.	Yds.	Avg.	TD	TD	Pts.
2000—Wisconsin	5	67	45	67.2	592	6	1	8.84	168.0	17	8	0.5	0	0	0
2001—Wisconsin	11	132	64	48.5	1096	9	8	8.30	128.6	30	-34	-1.1	2	2	12
2002—Wisconsin	11	70	38	54.3	536	1	2	7.66	117.6	23	-3	-0.1	0	0	0
2003—Wisconsin	12	248	140	56.5	2251	17	9	9.08	148.1	67	-10	-0.1	2	2	12
College totals (4 years)	39	517	287	55.5	4475	33	20	8.66	141.5	137	-39	-0.3	4	4	24

SPENCER, CODY — LB — RAIDERS

PERSONAL: Born June 1, 1981, in Port Lavaca, Texas. ... 6-3/235.
HIGH SCHOOL: Grapevine (Texas).
COLLEGE: North Texas.
TRANSACTIONS/CAREER NOTES: Selected by Oakland Raiders in sixth round (182nd pick overall) of 2004 NFL draft.

			INTERCEPTIONS			
Year Team	G	Sks.	No.	Yds.	Avg.	TD
2000—North Texas	8	0.0	0	0	0.0	0
2001—North Texas	11	0.0	1	7	7.0	0
2002—North Texas	10	5.0	3	61	20.3	0
2003—North Texas	13	2.0	3	37	12.3	0
College totals (4 years)	42	7.0	7	105	15.0	0

SPENCER, SHAWNTAE — CB — 49ERS

PERSONAL: Born February 22, 1982, in Ranken, Pa. ... 6-1/181.
HIGH SCHOOL: Woodland Hills (Pa.).
COLLEGE: Pittsburgh.
TRANSACTIONS/CAREER NOTES: Selected by San Francisco 49ers in second round (58th pick overall) of 2004 NFL draft.

			INTERCEPTIONS			
Year Team	G	Sks.	No.	Yds.	Avg.	TD
2000—Pittsburgh	11	0.0	2	0	0.0	0
2001—Pittsburgh	11	0.0	1	68	68.0	1
2002—Pittsburgh	13	0.0	3	49	16.3	0
2003—Pittsburgh	13	0.0	2	0	0.0	0
College totals (4 years)	48	0.0	8	117	14.6	1

STARKS, MAX — T — STEELERS

PERSONAL: Born January 10, 1982, in Orlando, Fla. ... 6-7/349. ... Son of Ross Browner, defensive end with Cincinnati Bengals (1978-86) and Green Bay Packers (1987).
HIGH SCHOOL: Lake Highland Prep (Orlando, Fla.).
COLLEGE: Florida.
TRANSACTIONS/CAREER NOTES: Selected by Pittsburgh Steelers in third round (75th pick overall) of 2004 NFL draft.
PLAYING EXPERIENCE: Florida, 2000-2003. ... Games played: 2000 (7), 2001 (11), 2002 (13), 2003 (12). Total: 43.

STARKS, RANDY — DT — TITANS

PERSONAL: Born December 14, 1983, in Waldorf, Md. ... 6-4/302.
HIGH SCHOOL: Westlake (Waldorf, Md.).
COLLEGE: Maryland.
TRANSACTIONS/CAREER NOTES: Selected after junior season by Tennessee Titans in third round (71st pick overall) of 2004 NFL draft.
HONORS: Named defensive tackle on THE SPORTING NEWS Freshman All-America fourth team (2001). ... Named defensive tackle on THE SPORTING NEWS college All-America second team (2003).

Year Team	G	SACKS
2001—Maryland	11	3.5
2002—Maryland	14	6.5
2003—Maryland	13	7.5
College totals (3 years)	38	17.5

STEPANOVICH, ALEX — C — CARDINALS

PERSONAL: Born September 25, 1981, in Berea, Ohio. ... 6-4/300.
HIGH SCHOOL: Berea (Berea, Ohio).
COLLEGE: Ohio State.
TRANSACTIONS/CAREER NOTES: Selected by Arizona Cardinals in fourth round (100th pick overall) of 2004 NFL draft.
PLAYING EXPERIENCE: Ohio State, 2000-2003. ... Games played: 2000 (7), 2001 (10), 2002 (13), 2003 (9). Total: 39.

STRAIT, DERRICK — CB — JETS

PERSONAL: Born August 27, 1980, in Austin, Texas. ... 5-11/195.
HIGH SCHOOL: Lanier (Austin, Texas).
COLLEGE: Oklahoma.
TRANSACTIONS/CAREER NOTES: Selected by New York Jets in third round (76th pick overall) of 2004 NFL draft.
HONORS: Bronko Nagurski Award winner (2003). ... Jim Thorpe Award winner (2003). ... Named defensive back on THE SPORTING NEWS Freshman All-America second team (2000). ... Named cornerback on THE SPORTING NEWS college All-America first team (2003).

			INTERCEPTIONS			
Year Team	**G**	**Sks.**	**No.**	**Yds.**	**Avg.**	**TD**
2000—Oklahoma	12	2.0	2	32	16.0	1
2001—Oklahoma	12	0.0	3	63	21.0	1
2002—Oklahoma	14	0.0	6	175	29.2	1
2003—Oklahoma	14	0.0	3	127	42.3	0
College totals (4 years)	52	2.0	14	397	28.4	3

STROJNY, DREW — T — GIANTS

PERSONAL: Born June 30, 1981, in Wrentham, Mass. ... 6-8/300. ... Full name: Andrew Strojny.
HIGH SCHOOL: Xaverian Brothers (Mass.).
COLLEGE: Duke.
TRANSACTIONS/CAREER NOTES: Selected by New York Giants in seventh round (203rd pick overall) of 2004 NFL draft.
PLAYING EXPERIENCE: Duke, 2000-2003. ... Games played: 2000 (11), 2001 (11), 2002 (12), 2003 (12). Total: 46.

SYMONS, B.J. — QB — TEXANS

PERSONAL: Born November 19, 1980, in Houston, Texas. ... 6-2/215.
HIGH SCHOOL: Cypress Creek (Houston, Texas).
COLLEGE: Texas Tech.
TRANSACTIONS/CAREER NOTES: Selected by Houston Texans in seventh round (248th pick overall) of 2004 NFL draft.

		PASSING								RUSHING				TOTALS	
Year Team	**G**	**Att.**	**Cmp.**	**Pct.**	**Yds.**	**TD**	**Int.**	**Avg.**	**Rat.**	**Att.**	**Yds.**	**Avg.**	**TD**	**TD**	**Pts.**
2000—Texas Tech	5	25	8	32.0	56	0	0	2.24	50.8	3	12	4.0	0	0	0
2001—Texas Tech	4	35	23	65.7	160	2	2	4.57	111.5	6	22	3.7	1	1	6
2002—Texas Tech	9	43	28	65.1	329	5	1	7.65	163.1	12	31	2.6	0	0	0
2003—Texas Tech	13	719	470	65.4	5833	52	22	8.11	151.3	79	143	1.8	5	5	30
College totals (4 years)	31	822	529	64.4	6378	59	25	7.76	147.1	100	208	2.1	6	6	36

TAPEH, THOMAS — FB — EAGLES

PERSONAL: Born March 28, 1980, in Monrovia, Liberia. ... 6-1/233.
HIGH SCHOOL: Johnson (St. Paul, Minn.).
COLLEGE: Minnesota.
TRANSACTIONS/CAREER NOTES: Selected by Philadelphia Eagles in fifth round (162nd pick overall) of 2004 NFL draft.

		RUSHING				RECEIVING				TOTALS	
Year Team	**G**	**Att.**	**Yds.**	**Avg.**	**TD**	**No.**	**Yds.**	**Avg.**	**TD**	**TD**	**Pts.**
2000—Minnesota	7	81	344	4.2	2	3	36	12.0	1	3	18
2001—Minnesota	10	29	138	4.8	3	1	4	4.0	0	3	18
2002—Minnesota	13	181	906	5.0	8	7	93	13.3	2	10	60
2003—Minnesota	13	119	570	4.8	11	8	86	10.8	0	11	66
College totals (4 years)	43	410	1958	4.8	24	19	219	11.5	3	27	162

TAYLOR, ERIC — DE — STEELERS

PERSONAL: Born December 14, 1981, in Winchester, Tenn. ... 6-3/265.
HIGH SCHOOL: Franklin City (Winchester, Tenn.).
COLLEGE: Memphis.

TRANSACTIONS/CAREER NOTES: Selected by Pittsburgh Steelers in seventh round (212th pick overall) of 2004 NFL draft.

Year Team	G	Sks.	INTERCEPTIONS No.	Yds.	Avg.	TD
2000—Memphis	6	0.0	0	0	0.0	0
2001—Memphis	11	1.0	0	0	0.0	0
2002—Memphis	11	1.0	0	0	0.0	0
2003—Memphis	13	4.0	1	52	52.0	1
College totals (4 years)	41	6.0	1	52	52.0	1

TAYLOR, JAMAAR WR GIANTS

PERSONAL: Born February 25, 1981, in Giessen, West Germany. ... 6-1/194. ... Full name: Henry Jamaar Taylor.
HIGH SCHOOL: Mission (Texas).
COLLEGE: Texas A&M.
TRANSACTIONS/CAREER NOTES: Selected by New York Giants in sixth round (168th pick overall) of 2004 NFL draft.

		RECEIVING				KICKOFF RETURNS				TOTALS	
Year Team	G	No.	Yds.	Avg.	TD	No.	Yds.	Avg.	TD	TD	Pts.
2001—Texas A&M	10	39	489	12.5	3	0	0	0.0	0	3	18
2002—Texas A&M	10	44	760	17.3	3	2	27	13.5	0	3	18
2003—Texas A&M	6	25	456	18.2	4	4	70	17.5	0	4	24
College totals (3 years)	26	108	1705	15.8	10	6	97	16.2	0	10	60

TAYLOR, SEAN DB REDSKINS

PERSONAL: Born April 1, 1983, in Miami, Fla. ... 6-3/220. ... Full name: Sean Michael Taylor.
HIGH SCHOOL: Gulliver Prep (Miami, Fla.).
COLLEGE: Miami (Fla.).
TRANSACTIONS/CAREER NOTES: Selected after junior season by Washington Redskins in first round (fifth pick overall) of 2004 NFL draft.
HONORS: Named safety on THE SPORTING NEWS college All-America first team (2003).

			INTERCEPTIONS				PUNT RETURNS				TOTALS	
Year Team	G	Sks.	No.	Yds.	Avg.	TD	No.	Yds.	Avg.	TD	TD	Pts.
2001—Miami (Fla.)	9	0.0	0	0	0.0	0	0	0	0.0	0	0	0
2002—Miami (Fla.)	13	0.0	4	122	30.5	0	3	101	33.7	1	2	12
2003—Miami (Fla.)	12	1.0	10	184	18.4	3	5	53	10.6	0	3	18
College totals (3 years)	34	1.0	14	306	21.9	3	8	154	19.3	1	5	30

TERRILL, CRAIG DT SEAHAWKS

PERSONAL: Born June 26, 1980, in Lebanon, Ind. ... 6-3/284. ... Full name: Craig Adam Terrill.
HIGH SCHOOL: Lebanon (Ind.).
COLLEGE: Purdue.
TRANSACTIONS/CAREER NOTES: Selected by Seattle Seahawks in sixth round (189th pick overall) of 2004 NFL draft.

Year Team	G	SACKS
2000—Purdue	11	6.0
2001—Purdue	11	2.0
2002—Purdue	12	4.0
2003—Purdue	13	8.5
College totals (4 years)	47	20.5

TERRY, JEB G BUCCANEERS

PERSONAL: Born April 10, 1981, in Dallas, Texas. ... 6-6/308.
HIGH SCHOOL: Culver Military Academy (Bloomington, Ind.).
COLLEGE: North Carolina.
TRANSACTIONS/CAREER NOTES: Selected by Tampa Bay Buccaneers in fifth round (146th pick overall) of 2004 NFL draft.
PLAYING EXPERIENCE: North Carolina, 1999-2003. ... Games played: 1999 (5), 2001 (12), 2002 (12), 2003 (12). Total: 41.

THOMAS, DONTARRIOUS LB VIKINGS

PERSONAL: Born September 2, 1980, in Perry, Ala. ... 6-2/241. ... Full name: Dontarrious Donta Thomas.
HIGH SCHOOL: Perry (Ala.).
COLLEGE: Auburn.
TRANSACTIONS/CAREER NOTES: Selected by Minnesota Vikings in second round (48th pick overall) of 2004 NFL draft.

Year Team	G	Sks.	INTERCEPTIONS No.	Yds.	Avg.	TD
2000—Auburn	12	1.0	0	0	0.0	0

Year Team	G	Sks.	INTERCEPTIONS No.	Yds.	Avg.	TD
2001—Auburn	12	1.5	1	33	33.0	0
2002—Auburn	12	3.0	0	0	0.0	0
2003—Auburn	13	0.0	1	0	0.0	0
College totals (4 years)	49	5.5	2	33	16.5	0

THOMAS, JOEY CB PACKERS

PERSONAL: Born August 29, 1980, in Burien, Wash. ... 6-0/195. ... Full name: Joseph Thomas.
HIGH SCHOOL: John F. Kennedy (Burien, Wash.).
COLLEGE: Montana State.
TRANSACTIONS/CAREER NOTES: Selected by Green Bay Packers in third round (70th pick overall) of 2004 NFL draft.

Year Team	G	Sks.	INTERCEPTIONS No.	Yds.	Avg.	TD
2000—Montana State	11	0.0	2	0	0.0	0
2001—Montana State	11	0.0	5	17	3.4	1
2002—Montana State	7	1.0	0	0	0.0	0
2003—Montana State	12	1.0	4	28	7.0	0
College totals (4 years)	41	2.0	11	45	4.1	1

THOMAS, SLOAN WR TEXANS

PERSONAL: Born December 22, 1981, in Clarksville, Tenn. ... 6-2/200. ... Full name: Sloan Edward Thomas.
HIGH SCHOOL: Klein (Houston, Texas).
COLLEGE: Texas.
TRANSACTIONS/CAREER NOTES: Selected by Houston Texans in seventh round (211th pick overall) of 2004 NFL draft.

		RECEIVING				KICKOFF RETURNS				TOTALS	
Year Team	G	No.	Yds.	Avg.	TD	No.	Yds.	Avg.	TD	TD	Pts.
2000—Texas	8	9	208	23.1	3	0	0	0.0	0	3	18
2001—Texas	12	29	435	15.0	5	0	0	0.0	0	5	30
2002—Texas	13	30	383	12.8	2	0	0	0.0	0	2	12
2003—Texas	13	20	336	16.8	2	6	108	18.0	0	2	12
College totals (4 years)	46	88	1362	15.5	12	6	108	18.0	0	12	72

THOMPSON, CHRIS CB JAGUARS

PERSONAL: Born May 19, 1982, in New Orleans, La. ... 6-0/191. ... Full name: Christopher J. Thompson.
HIGH SCHOOL: Holy Cross (New Orleans, La.).
COLLEGE: Nicholls State.
TRANSACTIONS/CAREER NOTES: Selected by Jacksonville Jaguars in fifth round (150th pick overall) of 2004 NFL draft.

Year Team	G	Sks.	INTERCEPTIONS No.	Yds.	Avg.	TD
2000—Nicholls State	3	0.0	0	0	0.0	0
2001—Nicholls State	11	0.0	5	17	3.4	0
2002—Nicholls State	11	1.0	5	77	15.4	1
2003—Nicholls State	11	0.0	1	0	0.0	0
College totals (4 years)	36	1.0	11	94	8.5	1

THORNTON, BRUCE CB COWBOYS

PERSONAL: Born January 31, 1980, in LaGrange, Ga. ... 5-11/195.
HIGH SCHOOL: LaGrange (LaGrange, Ga.).
COLLEGE: Georgia.
TRANSACTIONS/CAREER NOTES: Selected by Dallas Cowboys in fourth round (121st pick overall) of 2004 NFL draft.

Year Team	G	Sks.	INTERCEPTIONS No.	Yds.	Avg.	TD
2000—Georgia	11	0.0	0	0	0.0	0
2001—Georgia	11	0.0	0	0	0.0	0
2002—Georgia	14	0.0	2	71	35.5	1
2003—Georgia	14	0.0	2	4	2.0	0
College totals (4 years)	50	0.0	4	75	18.8	1

TORBOR, REGGIE LB GIANTS

PERSONAL: Born January 25, 1981, in Baton Rouge, La. ... 6-3/242.
HIGH SCHOOL: Lee (Baton Rouge, La.).
COLLEGE: Auburn.

TRANSACTIONS/CAREER NOTES: Selected by New York Giants in fourth round (97th pick overall) of 2004 NFL draft.

			INTERCEPTIONS			
Year Team	G	Sks.	No.	Yds.	Avg.	TD
2000—Auburn	12	3.0	0	0	0.0	0
2001—Auburn	12	2.5	0	0	0.0	0
2002—Auburn	10	3.5	0	0	0.0	0
2003—Auburn	13	9.5	0	0	0.0	0
College totals (4 years)	47	18.5	0	0	0.0	0

TROUPE, BEN — TE — TITANS

PERSONAL: Born September 1, 1982, in Augusta, Ga. ... 6-4/262.
HIGH SCHOOL: Butler (Augusta, Ga.).
COLLEGE: Florida.
TRANSACTIONS/CAREER NOTES: Selected by Tennessee Titans in second round (40th pick overall) of 2004 NFL draft.
HONORS: Named tight end on THE SPORTING NEWS college All-America second team (2003).

		RECEIVING			
Year Team	G	No.	Yds.	Avg.	TD
2000—Florida	4	1	22	22.0	0
2001—Florida	11	9	98	10.9	1
2002—Florida	11	15	200	13.3	1
2003—Florida	13	39	638	16.4	5
College totals (4 years)	39	64	958	15.0	7

TUBBS, MARCUS — DT — SEAHAWKS

PERSONAL: Born May 16, 1981, in Dallas, Texas. ... 6-4/310. ... Full name: Marcus Dwayne Tubbs.
HIGH SCHOOL: DeSoto (DeSoto, Texas).
COLLEGE: Texas.
TRANSACTIONS/CAREER NOTES: Selected by Seattle Seahawks in first round (23rd pick overall) of 2004 NFL draft.

Year Team	G	SACKS
2000—Texas	11	5.5
2001—Texas	12	2.0
2002—Texas	10	2.5
2003—Texas	13	5.5
College totals (4 years)	46	15.5

TUFTS, SEAN — LB — PANTHERS

PERSONAL: Born March 26, 1982, in Englewood, Colo. ... 6-4/245.
HIGH SCHOOL: Cherry Creek (Englewood, Colo.).
COLLEGE: Colorado.
TRANSACTIONS/CAREER NOTES: Selected by Carolina Panthers in sixth round (196th pick overall) of 2004 NFL draft. ... Signed by Panthers (May 21, 2004).

			INTERCEPTIONS			
Year Team	G	Sks.	No.	Yds.	Avg.	TD
2000—Colorado	6	0.5	0	0	0.0	0
2001—Colorado	12	0.0	0	0	0.0	0
2002—Colorado	7	0.0	0	0	0.0	0
2003—Colorado	12	0.0	0	0	0.0	0
College totals (4 years)	37	0.5	0	0	0.0	0

TURNER, LARRY — C — RAMS

PERSONAL: Born March 8, 1982, in New Carlisle, Ohio. ... 6-2/280. ... Full name: Lawrence Turner.
HIGH SCHOOL: Wayne (Huber Heights, Ohio).
COLLEGE: Eastern Kentucky.
TRANSACTIONS/CAREER NOTES: Selected by St. Louis Rams in seventh round (238th pick overall) of 2004 NFL draft.
PLAYING EXPERIENCE: Eastern Kentucky, 2001-2003. ... Games played: 2001 (9), 2002 (12), 2003 (12). Total: 33.

TURNER, MICHAEL — RB — CHARGERS

PERSONAL: Born February 13, 1982, in Chicago, Ill. ... 5-10/223.
HIGH SCHOOL: North Chicago (Chicago, Ill.).
COLLEGE: Northern Illinois.

TRANSACTIONS/CAREER NOTES: Selected by San Diego Chargers in fifth round (154th pick overall) of 2004 NFL draft.
HONORS: Named running back on THE SPORTING NEWS college All-America second team (2003).

		RUSHING				RECEIVING				KICKOFF RETURNS				TOTALS	
Year Team	G	Att.	Yds.	Avg.	TD	No.	Yds.	Avg.	TD	No.	Yds.	Avg.	TD	TD	Pts.
2000—Northern Illinois	11	200	983	4.9	7	4	45	11.3	0	0	0	0.0	0	7	42
2001—Northern Illinois	10	92	395	4.3	3	10	76	7.6	0	9	319	35.4	1	4	24
2002—Northern Illinois	12	338	1915	5.7	19	10	100	10.0	0	10	269	26.9	1	20	120
2003—Northern Illinois	12	310	1648	5.3	14	19	230	12.1	3	3	58	19.3	0	17	102
College totals (4 years)	45	940	4941	5.3	43	43	451	10.5	3	22	646	29.4	2	48	288

UDEZE, KENECHI — DE — VIKINGS

PERSONAL: Born March 5, 1983, in Los Angeles, Calif. ... 6-4/285.
HIGH SCHOOL: Verbum Dei (Los Angeles, Calif.).
COLLEGE: Southern California.
TRANSACTIONS/CAREER NOTES: Selected after junior season by Minnesota Vikings in first round (20th pick overall) of 2004 NFL draft.
HONORS: Named defensive end on THE SPORTING NEWS Freshman All-America second team (2001). ... Named defensive end on THE SPORTING NEWS college All-America first team (2003).

			INTERCEPTIONS			
Year Team	G	Sks.	No.	Yds.	Avg.	TD
2001—Southern California	12	4.0	0	0	0.0	0
2002—Southern California	13	7.5	1	0	0.0	0
2003—Southern California	13	16.5	0	0	0.0	0
College totals (3 years)	38	28.0	1	0	0.0	0

VAN PELT, BRADLEE — QB — BRONCOS

PERSONAL: Born July 3, 1980, in Owosso, Mich. ... 6-2/231.
HIGH SCHOOL: San Marcos (Santa Barbara, Calif.).
COLLEGE: Colorado State.
TRANSACTIONS/CAREER NOTES: Selected by Denver Broncos in seventh round (250th pick overall) of 2004 NFL draft.

		PASSING								RUSHING				TOTALS	
Year Team	G	Att.	Cmp.	Pct.	Yds.	TD	Int.	Avg.	Rat.	Att.	Yds.	Avg.	TD	TD	Pts.
2001—Colorado State	11	194	94	48.5	1247	8	10	6.43	105.7	100	546	5.5	4	5	34
2002—Colorado State	14	287	150	52.3	2072	10	7	7.22	119.5	148	835	5.6	11	11	66
2003—Colorado State	13	297	180	60.6	2845	19	13	9.58	153.4	170	909	5.3	10	10	60
College totals (3 years)	38	778	424	54.5	6164	37	30	7.92	129.0	418	2290	5.5	25	26	160

VASHER, NATHAN — CB — BEARS

PERSONAL: Born November 17, 1981, in Wichita Falls, Texas. ... 5-11/180. ... Full name: Nathanael DeWayne Vasher.
HIGH SCHOOL: Texas (Texarkana, Texas).
COLLEGE: Texas.
TRANSACTIONS/CAREER NOTES: Selected by Chicago Bears in fourth round (110th pick overall) of 2004 NFL draft. ... Signed by Bears (May 24, 2004).
HONORS: Named kick returner on THE SPORTING NEWS college All-America third team (2001).

			INTERCEPTIONS				PUNT RETURNS				TOTALS	
Year Team	G	Sks.	No.	Yds.	Avg.	TD	No.	Yds.	Avg.	TD	TD	Pts.
2000—Texas	11	1.0	0	0	0.0	0	3	26	8.7	0	0	0
2001—Texas	12	0.0	7	17	2.4	0	37	554	15.0	1	1	6
2002—Texas	11	1.0	4	3	0.8	0	26	370	14.2	1	1	6
2003—Texas	13	0.0	6	12	2.0	0	28	364	13.0	0	0	0
College totals (4 years)	47	2.0	17	32	1.9	0	94	1314	14.0	2	2	12

VILMA, JONATHAN — LB — JETS

PERSONAL: Born April 16, 1982, in Coral Gables, Fla. ... 6-2/220. ... Full name: Jonathan Polynice Vilma.
HIGH SCHOOL: Coral Gables (Fla.).
COLLEGE: Miami (Fla.).
TRANSACTIONS/CAREER NOTES: Selected by New York Jets in first round (12th pick overall) of 2004 NFL draft.

			INTERCEPTIONS			
Year Team	G	Sks.	No.	Yds.	Avg.	TD
2000—Miami (Fla.)	11	0.0	0	0	0.0	0
2001—Miami (Fla.)	10	1.0	1	16	16.0	0
2002—Miami (Fla.)	13	2.0	0	0	0.0	0
2003—Miami (Fla.)	13	1.0	0	0	0.0	0
College totals (4 years)	47	4.0	1	16	16.0	0

WADDELL, MICHAEL CB TITANS

PERSONAL: Born January 9, 1981, in Ellerbe, N.C. ... 5-11/183.
HIGH SCHOOL: Richmond County (Ellerbe, N.C.).
COLLEGE: North Carolina.
TRANSACTIONS/CAREER NOTES: Selected by Tennessee Titans in fourth round (124th pick overall) of 2004 NFL draft.

		INTERCEPTIONS				PUNT RETURNS				KICKOFF RETURNS				TOTALS	
Year Team	**G**	**No.**	**Yds.**	**Avg.**	**TD**	**No.**	**Yds.**	**Avg.**	**TD**	**No.**	**Yds.**	**Avg.**	**TD**	**TD**	**Pts.**
2000—North Carolina	11	1	16	16.0	0	0	0	0.0	0	1	24	24.0	0	0	0
2001—North Carolina	12	0	0	0.0	0	4	98	24.5	1	3	81	27.0	0	1	6
2002—North Carolina	10	2	33	16.5	0	17	72	4.2	0	0	0	0.0	0	0	0
2003—North Carolina	11	0	0	0.0	0	11	159	14.5	0	15	475	31.7	1	1	6
College totals (4 years)	44	3	49	16.3	0	32	329	10.3	1	19	580	30.5	1	2	12

WARD, DERRICK RB JETS

PERSONAL: Born August 30, 1980, in Los Angeles, Calif. ... 5-11/233.
COLLEGE: Fresno State, then Ottawa (Kan.).
TRANSACTIONS/CAREER NOTES: Selected by New York Jets in seventh round (235th pick overall) of 2004 NFL draft.

		RUSHING				RECEIVING				TOTALS	
Year Team	**G**	**Att.**	**Yds.**	**Avg.**	**TD**	**No.**	**Yds.**	**Avg.**	**TD**	**TD**	**Pts.**
1999—Fresno State	12	147	875	6.0	7	0	0	0.0	0	6	36
2000—Fresno State	7	45	189	4.2	4	3	49	16.3	0	4	24
College totals (2 years)	19	192	1064	5.5	11	3	49	16.3	0	10	60

WARE, MATT CB EAGLES

PERSONAL: Born December 2, 1982, in Santa Monica, Calif. ... 6-3/213. ... Full name: Matthew Jesse Ware.
HIGH SCHOOL: Loyola (Malibu, Calif.).
COLLEGE: UCLA.
TRANSACTIONS/CAREER NOTES: Selected after junior season by Philadelphia Eagles in third round (89th pick overall) of 2004 NFL draft.
HONORS: Named cornerback on THE SPORTING NEWS Freshman All-America first team (2001).
MISCELLANEOUS: Selected by Seattle Mariners organization in 21st round of free-agent baseball draft (June 6, 2001); did not sign.

			INTERCEPTIONS			
Year Team	**G**	**Sks.**	**No.**	**Yds.**	**Avg.**	**TD**
2001—UCLA	11	0.0	5	56	11.2	0
2002—UCLA	13	1.0	1	0	0.0	0
2003—UCLA	10	0.0	2	12	6.0	0
College totals (3 years)	34	1.0	8	68	8.5	0

WASHINGTON, DONNELL DT PACKERS

PERSONAL: Born February 6, 1981, in Beaufort, S.C. ... 6-6/320. ... Full name: Donnell M. Washington.
HIGH SCHOOL: Battery Creek (Beaufort, S.C.).
COLLEGE: Clemson.
TRANSACTIONS/CAREER NOTES: Selected after junior season by Green Bay Packers in third round (72nd pick overall) of 2004 NFL draft.
HONORS: Named defensive tackle on THE SPORTING NEWS Freshman All-America second team (2001).

Year Team	**G**	**SACKS**
2001—Clemson	11	3.0
2002—Clemson	13	1.0
2003—Clemson	13	4.0
College totals (3 years)	37	8.0

WASHINGTON, RASHAD DB JETS

PERSONAL: Born March 15, 1980, in Wichita, Kan. ... 6-3/210.
HIGH SCHOOL: Wichita Southeast (Wichita, Kan.).
COLLEGE: Kansas State.
TRANSACTIONS/CAREER NOTES: Selected by New York Jets in seventh round (236th pick overall) of 2004 NFL draft.

			INTERCEPTIONS			
Year Team	**G**	**Sks.**	**No.**	**Yds.**	**Avg.**	**TD**
2000—Kansas State	11	0.0	0	0	0.0	0
2001—Kansas State	10	0.0	0	0	0.0	0
2002—Kansas State	13	0.0	1	40	40.0	1
2003—Kansas State	15	3.0	2	67	33.5	1
College totals (4 years)	49	3.0	3	107	35.7	2

WATSON, BEN — TE — PATRIOTS

PERSONAL: Born December 18, 1980, in Rock Hill, S.C. ... 6-3/255. ... Full name: Benjamin Watson.
HIGH SCHOOL: Northwestern (Rock Hill, S.C.).
COLLEGE: Duke, then Georgia.
TRANSACTIONS/CAREER NOTES: Selected by New England Patriots in first round (32nd pick overall) of 2004 NFL draft.

		RECEIVING			
Year Team	G	No.	Yds.	Avg.	TD
1999—Duke	11	8	93	11.6	1
2001—Georgia	11	11	187	17.0	1
2002—Georgia	14	31	341	11.0	3
2003—Georgia	12	23	324	14.1	2
College totals (4 years)	48	73	945	12.9	7

WATSON, COURTNEY — LB — SAINTS

PERSONAL: Born September 18, 1980, in Sarasota, Fla. ... 6-1/234.
HIGH SCHOOL: Riverview (Sarasota, Fla.).
COLLEGE: Notre Dame.
TRANSACTIONS/CAREER NOTES: Selected by New Orleans Saints in second round (60th pick overall) of 2004 NFL draft.

			INTERCEPTIONS			
Year Team	G	Sks.	No.	Yds.	Avg.	TD
2000—Notre Dame	11	0.0	0	0	0.0	0
2001—Notre Dame	11	2.0	1	31	31.0	1
2002—Notre Dame	10	3.0	4	123	30.8	1
2003—Notre Dame	11	3.5	2	48	24.0	0
College totals (4 years)	43	8.5	7	202	28.9	2

WATTS, DARIUS — WR — BRONCOS

PERSONAL: Born December 19, 1981, in Atlanta, Ga. ... 6-2/181. ... Full name: Darius Orlando Watts.
HIGH SCHOOL: Banneker (College Park, Ga.).
COLLEGE: Marshall.
TRANSACTIONS/CAREER NOTES: Selected by Denver Broncos in second round (54th pick overall) of 2004 NFL draft.
HONORS: Named wide receiver on THE SPORTING NEWS college All-America fourth team (2001).

		RUSHING				RECEIVING				KICKOFF RETURNS				TOTALS	
Year Team	G	Att.	Yds.	Avg.	TD	No.	Yds.	Avg.	TD	No.	Yds.	Avg.	TD	TD	Pts.
2000—Marshall	11	7	52	7.4	0	36	616	17.1	6	10	203	20.3	0	6	36
2001—Marshall	12	2	8	4.0	0	91	1417	15.6	18	2	31	15.5	0	18	112
2002—Marshall	12	1	28	28.0	0	71	1030	14.5	12	3	20	6.7	0	12	72
2003—Marshall	12	11	100	9.1	0	74	968	13.1	11	0	0	0.0	0	11	66
College totals (4 years)	47	21	188	9.0	0	272	4031	14.8	47	15	254	16.9	0	47	286

WELLS, SCOTT — C — PACKERS

PERSONAL: Born January 7, 1981, in Spring Hill, Tenn. ... 6-2/300. ... Full name: Scott Darvin Wells.
HIGH SCHOOL: Brentwood Academy (Spring Hill, Tenn.).
COLLEGE: Tennessee.
TRANSACTIONS/CAREER NOTES: Selected by Green Bay Packers in seventh round (251st pick overall) of 2004 NFL draft.
PLAYING EXPERIENCE: Tennessee, 2000-2003. ... Games played: 2000 (11), 2001 (13), 2002 (13), 2003 (13). Total: 50.
HONORS: Named offensive lineman on THE SPORTING NEWS Freshman All-America third team (2000).

WHARTON, TRAVELLE — T — PANTHERS

PERSONAL: Born May 19, 1981, in Fountain Inn, S.C. ... 6-4/300.
HIGH SCHOOL: Hillcrest (Fountain Inn, S.C.).
COLLEGE: South Carolina.
TRANSACTIONS/CAREER NOTES: Selected by Carolina Panthers in third round (94th pick overall) of 2004 NFL draft.
PLAYING EXPERIENCE: South Carolina, 2000-2003. ... Games played: 2000 (11), 2001 (11), 2002 (11), 2003 (12). Total: 45.
HONORS: Named offensive lineman on THE SPORTING NEWS Freshman All-America second team (2000).

WILFORD, ERNEST — WR — JAGUARS

PERSONAL: Born January 14, 1979, in Richmond, Va. ... 6-4/216. ... Full name: Ernest Lee Wilford Jr.
HIGH SCHOOL: Armstrong/Franklin Military (Richmond, Va.), then Fork Union Military Academy (Va.).
COLLEGE: Virginia Tech.

TRANSACTIONS/CAREER NOTES: Selected by Jacksonville Jaguars in fourth round (120th pick overall) of 2004 NFL draft.

Year Team	G	RECEIVING No.	Yds.	Avg.	TD
2000—Virginia Tech	11	12	141	11.8	0
2001—Virginia Tech	11	8	100	12.5	1
2002—Virginia Tech	14	51	925	18.1	7
2003—Virginia Tech	13	55	886	16.1	3
College totals (4 years)	49	126	2052	16.3	11

WILFORK, VINCE — DT — PATRIOTS

PERSONAL: Born November 4, 1981, in Boynton Beach, Fla. ... 6-2/350. ... Full name: Vince Lamar Wilfork.
HIGH SCHOOL: Santaluces (Boynton Beach, Fla.).
COLLEGE: Miami (Fla.).
TRANSACTIONS/CAREER NOTES: Selected after junior season by New England Patriots in first round (21st pick overall) of 2004 NFL draft.

Year Team	G	SACKS
2001—Miami (Fla.)	11	1.0
2002—Miami (Fla.)	12	7.0
2003—Miami (Fla.)	13	6.0
College totals (3 years)	36	14.0

WILLIAMS, COREY — DT — PACKERS

PERSONAL: Born August 17, 1980, in Harmony Grove, Ark. ... 6-4/292.
HIGH SCHOOL: Harmony Grove (Ark.).
COLLEGE: Arkansas State.
TRANSACTIONS/CAREER NOTES: Selected by Green Bay Packers in sixth round (179th pick overall) of 2004 NFL draft.

Year Team	G	SACKS
2000—Arkansas State	11	2.5
2001—Arkansas State	11	2.0
2002—Arkansas State	11	9.0
2003—Arkansas State	10	1.0
College totals (4 years)	43	14.5

WILLIAMS, DEMORRIO — LB — FALCONS

PERSONAL: Born July 6, 1980, in Beckville, Texas. ... 6-1/210.
HIGH SCHOOL: Beckville (Texas).
JUNIOR COLLEGE: Kilgore (Texas).
COLLEGE: Nebraska.
TRANSACTIONS/CAREER NOTES: Selected by Atlanta Falcons in fourth round (101st pick overall) of 2004 NFL draft.

Year Team	G	Sks.	INTERCEPTIONS No.	Yds.	Avg.	TD
2002—Nebraska	14	1.0	1	34	34.0	0
2003—Nebraska	13	11.0	1	2	2.0	0
College totals (2 years)	27	12.0	2	36	18.0	0

WILLIAMS, D.J. — LB — BRONCOS

PERSONAL: Born July 20, 1982, in Pittsburg, Calif. ... 6-2/247. ... Full name: Genos Derwin Williams.
HIGH SCHOOL: Concord De La Salle (Pittsburg, Calif.).
COLLEGE: Miami (Fla.).
TRANSACTIONS/CAREER NOTES: Selected by Denver Broncos in first round (17th pick overall) of 2004 NFL draft.
HONORS: Named linebacker on THE SPORTING NEWS college All-America second team (2003).

Year Team	G	Sks.	INTERCEPTIONS No.	Yds.	Avg.	TD
2000—Miami (Fla.)	10	0.0	0	0	0.0	0
2001—Miami (Fla.)	11	1.0	0	0	0.0	0
2002—Miami (Fla.)	13	4.0	0	0	0.0	0
2003—Miami (Fla.)	13	6.0	0	0	0.0	0
College totals (4 years)	47	11.0	0	0	0.0	0

WILLIAMS, LENNY — CB — BUCCANEERS

PERSONAL: Born December 16, 1981, in Lake Charles, La. ... 6-0/190.
COLLEGE: Southern.
TRANSACTIONS/CAREER NOTES: Selected by Tampa Bay Buccaneers in seventh round (252nd pick overall) of 2004 NFL draft.

Year Team	G	Sks.	INTERCEPTIONS No.	Yds.	Avg.	TD
2000—Southern	11	0.0	2	0	0.0	0
2001—Southern	11	0.0	4	73	18.3	1
2002—Southern	12	0.0	6	0	0.0	0
2003—Southern	13	1.0	3	120	40.0	1
College totals (4 years)	47	1.0	15	193	12.9	2

WILLIAMS, MADIEU — DB — BENGALS

PERSONAL: Born October 18, 1981, in Sierra Leone, West Africa. ... 6-1/193.
HIGH SCHOOL: DuVal (Lanham, Md.).
COLLEGE: Towson State, then Maryland.
TRANSACTIONS/CAREER NOTES: Selected by Cincinnati Bengals in second round (56th pick overall) of 2004 NFL draft.

Year Team	G	Sks.	INTERCEPTIONS No.	Yds.	Avg.	TD
1999—Towson State	11	0.0	1	14	14.0	0
2000—Towson State	11	0.0	0	0	0.0	0
2002—Maryland	14	1.0	4	0	0.0	0
2003—Maryland	13	0.0	3	10	3.3	0
College totals (4 years)	49	1.0	8	24	3.0	0

WILLIAMS, REGGIE — WR — JAGUARS

PERSONAL: Born May 17, 1983, in Laadstuhl, Germany. ... 6-4/225.
HIGH SCHOOL: Lakes (Lakewood, Wash.).
COLLEGE: Washington.
TRANSACTIONS/CAREER NOTES: Selected after junior season by Jacksonville Jaguars in first round (ninth pick overall) of 2004 NFL draft.
HONORS: Named wide receiver on THE SPORTING NEWS Freshman All-America first team (2001).

Year Team	G	RECEIVING No.	Yds.	Avg.	TD
2001—Washington	11	55	973	17.7	3
2002—Washington	13	94	1454	15.5	11
2003—Washington	12	89	1109	12.5	8
College totals (3 years)	36	238	3536	14.9	22

WILLIAMS, ROY — WR — LIONS

PERSONAL: Born December 20, 1981, in Odessa, Texas. ... 6-4/210. ... Full name: Roy Eugene Williams.
HIGH SCHOOL: Permian (Odessa, Texas).
COLLEGE: Texas.
TRANSACTIONS/CAREER NOTES: Selected by Detroit Lions in first round (seventh pick overall) of 2004 NFL draft.
HONORS: Named wide receiver on THE SPORTING NEWS Freshman All-America second team (2000).

		RUSHING				RECEIVING				TOTALS	
Year Team	G	Att.	Yds.	Avg.	TD	No.	Yds.	Avg.	TD	TD	Pts.
2000—Texas	11	2	75	37.5	2	40	809	20.2	8	10	62
2001—Texas	12	5	47	9.4	0	67	836	12.5	7	7	42
2002—Texas	12	5	85	17.0	1	64	1142	17.8	12	13	78
2003—Texas	13	4	36	9.0	0	70	1079	15.4	9	9	56
College totals (4 years)	48	16	243	15.2	3	241	3866	16.0	36	39	238

WILSON, GIBRIL — DB — GIANTS

PERSONAL: Born November 12, 1981, in San Jose, Calif. ... 6-1/190.
HIGH SCHOOL: Northwest Whitfield (San Jose, Calif.).
JUNIOR COLLEGE: City College of San Francisco (Calif.).
COLLEGE: Tennessee.
TRANSACTIONS/CAREER NOTES: Selected by New York Giants in fifth round (136th pick overall) of 2004 NFL draft.

Year Team	G	Sks.	INTERCEPTIONS No.	Yds.	Avg.	TD
2002—Tennessee	13	2.5	0	0	0.0	0
2003—Tennessee	13	3.0	3	1	0.3	0
College totals (2 years)	26	5.5	3	1	0.3	0

WILSON, KRIS — TE — CHIEFS

PERSONAL: Born August 22, 1981, in Lancaster, Pa. ... 6-3/250. ... Full name: Kristopher Wilson.
HIGH SCHOOL: J.P. McCaskey (Lancaster, Pa.).
COLLEGE: Pittsburgh.

TRANSACTIONS/CAREER NOTES: Selected by Kansas City Chiefs in second round (61st pick overall) of 2004 NFL draft.

Year Team	G	RECEIVING No.	Yds.	Avg.	TD
2000—Pittsburgh	11	7	127	18.1	2
2001—Pittsburgh	11	19	272	14.3	2
2002—Pittsburgh	13	18	389	21.6	2
2003—Pittsburgh	13	44	643	14.6	9
College totals (4 years)	48	88	1431	16.3	15

WILSON, MARK — T — REDSKINS

PERSONAL: Born November 11, 1980, in McArthur, Calif. ... 6-6/295.
HIGH SCHOOL: Fall River (McArthur, Calif.).
COLLEGE: California.
TRANSACTIONS/CAREER NOTES: Selected by Washington Redskins in fifth round (151st pick overall) of 2004 NFL draft.
PLAYING EXPERIENCE: California, 2000-2003. ... Games played: 2000 (11), 2001 (11), 2002 (12), 2003 (14). Total: 48.
HONORS: Named offensive lineman on THE SPORTING NEWS Freshman All-America third team (2000).

WILSON, QUINCY — RB — FALCONS

PERSONAL: Born April 26, 1981, in Weirton, W.Va. ... 5-9/210. ... Son of Otis Wilson, linebacker, Chicago Bears (1980-87) and Los Angeles Raiders (1989).
HIGH SCHOOL: Weir (Weirton, W. Va.).
COLLEGE: West Virginia.
TRANSACTIONS/CAREER NOTES: Selected by Atlanta Falcons in seventh round (219th pick overall) of 2004 NFL draft.

		RUSHING				RECEIVING				TOTALS	
Year Team	G	Att.	Yds.	Avg.	TD	No.	Yds.	Avg.	TD	TD	Pts.
1999—West Virginia	10	26	147	5.7	1	1	8	8.0	0	1	6
2001—West Virginia	11	25	181	7.2	1	1	8	8.0	0	1	6
2002—West Virginia	13	140	901	6.4	6	8	36	4.5	0	6	36
2003—West Virginia	12	282	1380	4.9	12	15	95	6.3	1	13	78
College totals (4 years)	46	473	2609	5.5	20	25	147	5.9	1	21	126

WINSLOW, KELLEN — TE — BROWNS

PERSONAL: Born July 21, 1983, in San Diego, Calif. ... 6-5/233. ... Full name: Kellen Boswell Winslow II. ... Son of Kellen Winslow Sr., Hall of Fame tight end, San Diego Chargers (1979-87).
HIGH SCHOOL: Scripps Ranch (San Diego, Calif.).
COLLEGE: Miami (Fla.).
TRANSACTIONS/CAREER NOTES: Selected after junior season by Cleveland Browns in first round (sixth pick overall) of 2004 NFL draft.
HONORS: John Mackey Award winner (2003). ... Named tight end on THE SPORTING NEWS college All-America second team (2002) and first team (2003).

Year Team	G	RECEIVING No.	Yds.	Avg.	TD
2001—Miami (Fla.)	11	2	34	17.0	0
2002—Miami (Fla.)	13	57	726	12.7	8
2003—Miami (Fla.)	13	60	605	10.1	1
College totals (3 years)	37	119	1365	11.5	9

WOODS, RASHAUN — WR — 49ERS

PERSONAL: Born October 17, 1980, in Oklahoma City, Okla. ... 6-2/185. ... Full name: Rashaun Dorrell Woods.
HIGH SCHOOL: Millwood (Oklahoma City, Okla.).
COLLEGE: Oklahoma State.
TRANSACTIONS/CAREER NOTES: Selected by San Francisco 49ers in first round (31st pick overall) of 2004 NFL draft.
HONORS: Named wide receiver on THE SPORTING NEWS college All-America first team (2002).

Year Team	G	RECEIVING No.	Yds.	Avg.	TD
2000—Oklahoma State	11	29	329	11.3	0
2001—Oklahoma State	11	80	1023	12.8	10
2002—Oklahoma State	13	107	1695	15.8	17
2003—Oklahoma State	13	77	1367	17.8	15
College totals (4 years)	48	293	4414	15.1	42

WYNN, DEXTER — CB — EAGLES

PERSONAL: Born February 25, 1981, in Sumpter, S.C. ... 5-9/165.
HIGH SCHOOL: Rampart (Colorado Springs, Colo.).
COLLEGE: Colorado State.

TRANSACTIONS/CAREER NOTES: Selected by Philadelphia Eagles in sixth round (192nd pick overall) of 2004 NFL draft.

			INTERCEPTIONS				PUNT RETURNS				KICKOFF RETURNS				TOTALS	
Year Team	**G**	**Sks.**	**No.**	**Yds.**	**Avg.**	**TD**	**No.**	**Yds.**	**Avg.**	**TD**	**No.**	**Yds.**	**Avg.**	**TD**	**TD**	**Pts.**
2000—Colorado State	10	0.0	0	0	0.0	0	7	159	22.7	0	10	350	35.0	1	1	6
2001—Colorado State	10	2.0	1	0	0.0	0	14	214	15.3	0	12	313	26.1	1	1	6
2002—Colorado State	14	1.0	2	56	28.0	0	35	568	16.2	1	22	490	22.3	0	1	6
2003—Colorado State	13	2.0	1	6	6.0	0	35	445	12.7	0	27	782	29.0	0	0	0
College totals (4 years)	47	5.0	4	62	15.5	0	91	1386	15.2	1	71	1935	27.3	2	3	18

HEAD COACHES

BELICHICK, BILL — PATRIOTS

PERSONAL: Born April 16, 1952, in Nashville. ... Full name: William Stephen Belichick. ... Son of Steve Belichick, fullback with Detroit Lions (1941); head coach at Hiram (Ohio) College (1946-49); assistant coach, Vanderbilt (1949-53); assistant coach, North Carolina (1953-56); assistant coach, Navy (1956-83); and administrative assistant, Navy (1983-89).
HIGH SCHOOL: Annapolis (Md.) and Phillips Academy (Andover, Mass.).
COLLEGE: Wesleyan University.

COACHING RECORD

BACKROUND: Assistant special teams coach, Baltimore Colts NFL (1975). ... Assistant special teams coach, Detroit Lions NFL (1976-77). ... Assistant special teams coach/assistant to defensive coordinator, Denver Broncos NFL (1978). ... Special teams coach, New York Giants NFL (1979-80). ... Special teams/linebackers coach, Giants (1981-82). ... Linebackers coach, Giants (1983-84). ... Defensive coordinator/linebackers coach, Giants (1985-88). ... Defensive coordinator/secondary coach, Giants (1989-90). ... Assistant head coach/secondary coach, New England Patriots NFL (1996). ... Assistant head coach/secondary coach, New York Jets NFL (1997-99).
HONORS: Named NFL Coach of the Year by THE SPORTING NEWS (2003).

	REGULAR SEASON					POST-SEASON	
	W	L	T	Pct.	Finish	W	L
1991—Cleveland NFL	6	10	0	.375	3rd/AFC Central Division	0	0
1992—Cleveland NFL	7	9	0	.438	3rd/AFC Central Division	0	0
1993—Cleveland NFL	7	9	0	.438	3rd/AFC Central Division	0	0
1994—Cleveland NFL	11	5	0	.688	2nd/AFC Central Division	1	1
1995—Cleveland NFL	5	11	0	.313	4th/AFC Central Division	0	0
2000—New England NFL	5	11	0	.313	5th/AFC Eastern Division	0	0
2001—New England NFL	11	5	0	.688	1st/AFC Eastern Division	3	0
2002—New England NFL	9	7	0	.563	2nd/AFC East Division	0	0
2003—New England NFL	14	2	0	.875	1st/AFC East Division	3	0
Pro totals (9 years)	75	69	0	.521	**Pro totals (3 years)**	7	1

NOTES:
1994—Defeated New England, 20-13, in first-round playoff game; lost to Pittsburgh, 29-9, in conference playoff game.
2001—Defeated Oakland, 16-13 (OT), in conference playoff game; defeated Pittsburgh, 24-17, in AFC championship game; defeated St. Louis, 20-17, in Super Bowl 36.
2003—Defeated Tennessee, 17-14, in first-round playoff game; defeated Indianapolis, 24-14, in AFC championship game; defeated Carolina, 32-29, in Super Bowl 38.

BILLICK, BRIAN — RAVENS

PERSONAL: Born February 28, 1954, in Fairborn, Ohio. ... Full name: Brian Harold Billick. ... Played tight end.
HIGH SCHOOL: Redlands (Calif.).
COLLEGE: Air Force, then Brigham Young.
TRANSACTIONS/CAREER NOTES: Selected by San Francisco 49ers in 11th round of 1977 NFL draft. ... Signed by 49ers for 1977 season. ... Released by 49ers (August 30, 1977). ... Signed by Dallas Cowboys (May 1978). ... Released by Cowboys before 1978 season.

COACHING RECORD

BACKROUND: Assistant coach, University of Redlands (1977). ... Graduate assistant, Brigham Young (1978). ... Assistant public relations director, San Francisco 49ers NFL (1979-80). ... Assistant coach and recruiting coordinator, San Diego State (1981-85). ... Offensive coordinator, Utah State (1986-88). ... Assistant coach, Stanford (1989-91). ... Tight ends coach, Minnesota Vikings (1992). ... Offensive coordinator, Minnesota Vikings (1993-98).

	REGULAR SEASON					POST-SEASON	
	W	L	T	Pct.	Finish	W	L
1999—Baltimore NFL	8	8	0	.500	3rd/AFC Central Division	0	0
2000—Baltimore NFL	12	4	0	.750	2nd/AFC Central Division	4	0
2001—Baltimore NFL	10	6	0	.625	2nd/AFC Central Division	1	1
2002—Baltimore NFL	7	9	0	.438	3rd/AFC North Division	0	0
2003—Baltimore NFL	10	6	0	.625	1st/AFC North Division	0	1
Pro totals (5 years)	47	33	0	.588	**Pro totals (3 years)**	5	2

NOTES:
2000—Defeated Denver, 21-3, in first-round playoff game; defeated Tennessee, 24-10, in conference playoff game; defeated Oakland, 16-3, in AFC championship game; defeated New York Giants, 34-7, in Super Bowl 35.
2001—Defeated Miami, 20-3, in first-round playoff game; lost to Pittsburgh, 27-10, in conference playoff game.
2003—Lost to Tennessee, 20-17, in first-round playoff game.

CAPERS, DOM — TEXANS

PERSONAL: Born August 7, 1950, in Cambridge, Ohio. ... Full name: Dominic Capers.
HIGH SCHOOL: Meadowbrook (Byesville, Ohio).
COLLEGE: Mount Union (Ohio), then Kent State.

COACHING RECORD

BACKROUND: Graduate assistant, Kent State (1972-74). ... Graduate assistant, Washington (1975). ... Defensive backs coach, Hawaii (1976) ... Defensive backs coach, San Jose State (1977). ... Defensive backs coach, California (1978-79). ... Defensive backs coach, Tennessee (1980-81). ... Defensive backs coach, Ohio State (1982-83). ... Defensive backs coach, Philadelphia Stars USFL (1984). ... Defensive backs coach, Baltimore Stars USFL (1985). ... Defensive backs coach, New Orleans Saints NFL (1986-91). ... Defensive coordinator, Pittsburgh Steelers NFL (1992-94). ... Defensive coordinator, Jacksonville Jaguars NFL (1999 and 2000).
HONORS: Named NFL Coach of the Year by THE SPORTING NEWS (1996).

					REGULAR SEASON	POST-SEASON	
	W	L	T	Pct.	Finish	W	L
1995—Carolina NFL	7	9	0	.438	4th/NFC Western Division	0	0
1996—Carolina NFL	12	4	0	.750	1st/NFC Western Division	1	1
1997—Carolina NFL	7	9	0	.438	2nd/NFC Western Division	0	0
1998—Carolina NFL	4	12	0	.250	4th/NFC Western Division	0	0
2002—Houston NFL	4	12	0	.250	4th/AFC South Division	0	0
2003—Houston NFL	5	11	0	.313	4th/AFC South Division	0	0
Pro totals (6 years)	39	57	0	.406	**Pro totals (1 year)**	1	1

NOTES:

1996—Defeated Dallas, 26-17, in conference playoff game; lost to Green Bay, 30-13, in NFC championship game.

COUGHLIN, TOM — GIANTS

PERSONAL: Born August 31, 1946, in Waterloo, N.Y. ... Full name: Thomas Richard Coughlin.
HIGH SCHOOL: Waterloo (N.Y.) Central.
COLLEGE: Syracuse.

COACHING RECORD

BACKROUND: Graduate assistant, Syracuse (1969). ... Quarterbacks/offensive backfield coach, Syracuse (1974-76). ... Offensive coordinator, Syracuse (1977-80). ... Quarterbacks coach, Boston College (1980-83). ... Receivers coach, Philadelphia Eagles NFL (1984-85). ... Receivers coach, Green Bay Packers NFL (1986-87). ... Receivers coach, New York Giants NFL (1988-90).

					REGULAR SEASON	POST-SEASON	
	W	L	T	Pct.	Finish	W	L
1970—Rochester Tech	4	3	0	.571	Eastern College Athletic Conference	0	0
1971—Rochester Tech	5	2	1	.714	Eastern College Athletic Conference	0	0
1972—Rochester Tech	4	5	0	.444	Eastern College Athletic Conference	0	0
1973—Rochester Tech	3	5	1	.375	Eastern College Athletic Conference	0	0
1991—Boston College	4	7	0	.364	7th/Big East Conference	0	0
1992—Boston College	8	2	1	.800	3rd/Big East Conference	0	1
1993—Boston College	9	3	0	.750	3rd/Big East Conference	1	0
1995—Jacksonville NFL	4	12	0	.250	5th/AFC Central Division	0	0
1996—Jacksonville NFL	9	7	0	.563	2nd/AFC Central Division	2	1
1997—Jacksonville NFL	11	5	0	.688	2nd/AFC Central Division	0	1
1998—Jacksonville NFL	11	5	0	.688	1st/AFC Central Division	1	1
1999—Jacksonville NFL	14	2	0	.875	1st/AFC Central Division	1	1
2000—Jacksonville NFL	7	9	0	.438	4th/AFC Central Division	0	0
2001—Jacksonville NFL	6	10	0	.375	5th/AFC Central Division	0	0
2002—Jacksonville NFL	6	10	0	.375	3rd/AFC South Division	0	0
College totals (7 years)	37	27	3	.578	**College totals (2 years)**	1	1
Pro totals (8 years)	68	60	0	.531	**Pro totals (4 years)**	4	4

NOTES:

1992—Lost to Tennessee, 38-23, in Hall of Fame Bowl.
1993—Defeated Virginia, 31-13, in Carquest Bowl.
1996—Defeated Buffalo, 30-27, in first-round playoff game; defeated Denver, 30-27, in conference playoff game; lost to New England, 20-6, in AFC championship game.
1997—Lost to Denver, 42-17, in first-round playoff game.
1998—Defeated New England, 25-10, in first-round playoff game; lost to New York Jets, 34-24, in conference playoff game.
1999—Defeated Miami, 62-7, in conference playoff game; lost to Tennessee, 33-14, in AFC championship game.

COWHER, BILL — STEELERS

PERSONAL: Born May 8, 1957, in Pittsburgh. ... Full name: William Laird Cowher. ... Played linebacker.
HIGH SCHOOL: Carlynton (Carnegie, Pa.).
COLLEGE: North Carolina State.
TRANSACTIONS/CAREER NOTES: Signed as non-drafted free agent by Philadelphia Eagles (May 8, 1979). ... Released by Eagles (August 14, 1979). ... Signed by Cleveland Browns (February 27, 1980). ... On injured reserve with knee injury (August 20, 1981-entire season). ... Traded by Browns to Eagles for ninth-round pick (WR Don Jones) in 1984 draft (August 21, 1983). ... On injured reserve with knee injury (September 25, 1984-remainder of season).
PLAYING EXPERIENCE: Cleveland NFL, 1980-82; Philadelphia, 1983-84. ... Games: 1980 (16), 1982 (9), 1983 (16), 1984 (4). Total: 45.

COACHING RECORD

BACKROUND: Special teams coach, Cleveland Browns NFL (1985-86). ... Defensive backs coach, Browns (1987-88). ... Defensive coordinator, Kansas City Chiefs NFL (1989-91).
HONORS: Named NFL Coach of the Year by THE SPORTING NEWS (1992).

					REGULAR SEASON	POST-SEASON	
	W	L	T	Pct.	Finish	W	L
1992—Pittsburgh NFL	11	5	0	.688	1st/AFC Central Division	0	1
1993—Pittsburgh NFL	9	7	0	.563	2nd/AFC Central Division	0	1
1994—Pittsburgh NFL	12	4	0	.750	1st/AFC Central Division	1	1
1995—Pittsburgh NFL	11	5	0	.688	1st/AFC Central Division	2	1
1996—Pittsburgh NFL	10	6	0	.625	1st/AFC Central Division	1	1
1997—Pittsburgh NFL	11	5	0	.688	1st/AFC Central Division	1	1
1998—Pittsburgh NFL	7	9	0	.438	3rd/AFC Central Division	0	0

	REGULAR SEASON					POST-SEASON	
	W	L	T	Pct.	Finish	W	L
1999—Pittsburgh NFL	6	10	0	.375	4th/AFC Central Division	0	0
2000—Pittsburgh NFL	9	7	0	.563	3rd/AFC Central Division	0	0
2001—Pittsburgh NFL	13	3	0	.813	1st/AFC Central Division	1	1
2002—Pittsburgh NFL	10	5	1	.667	1st/AFC North Division	1	1
2003—Pittsburgh NFL	6	10	0	.375	3rd/AFC North Division	0	0
Pro totals (12 years)	115	76	1	.602	**Pro totals (8 years)**	7	8

NOTES:

1992—Lost to Buffalo, 24-3, in conference playoff game.
1993—Lost to Kansas City, 27-24 (OT), in first-round playoff game.
1994—Defeated Cleveland, 29-9, in conference playoff game; lost to San Diego, 17-13, in AFC championship game.
1995—Defeated Buffalo, 40-21, in conference playoff game; defeated Indianapolis, 20-16, in AFC championship game; lost to Dallas, 27-17, in Super Bowl 30.
1996—Defeated Indianapolis, 42-14, in first-round playoff game; lost to New England, 28-3, in conference playoff game.
1997—Defeated New England, 7-6, in conference playoff game; lost to Denver, 24-21, in AFC championship game.
2001—Defeated Baltimore, 27-10, in conference playoff game; lost to New England, 24-17, in AFC championship game.
2002—Defeated Cleveland, 36-33, in first-round playoff game; lost to Tennessee, 34-31 (OT), in conference playoff game.

DAVIS, BUTCH — BROWNS

PERSONAL: Born November 17, 1951, in Tahlequah, Okla. ... Full name: Paul Hilton Davis.
HIGH SCHOOL: Bixby (Okla.).
COLLEGE: Arkansas.

COACHING RECORD

BACKROUND: Assistant coach, Fayetteville (Ark.) High School (1973). ... Assistant coach, Pawhuska (Okla.) High School (1974-75). ... Assistant coach, Sand Springs (Okla.) High School (1976-77). ... Head coach, Rogers High School, Tulsa, Okla. (1978). ... Assistant coach, Oklahoma State (1979-83). ... Assistant coach, University of Miami (1984-88). ... Assistant coach, Dallas Cowboys NFL (1989-92). ... Defensive coordinator, Cowboys (1993-94).

	REGULAR SEASON					POST-SEASON	
	W	L	T	Pct.	Finish	W	L
1995—Miami (Fla.)	8	3	0	.727	T1st/Big East Conference	0	0
1996—Miami (Fla.)	9	3	0	.750	T1st/Big East Conference	1	0
1997—Miami (Fla.)	5	6	0	.455	T5th/Big East Conference	0	0
1998—Miami (Fla.)	9	3	0	.750	T2nd/Big East Conference	1	0
1999—Miami (Fla.)	9	4	0	.692	2nd/Big East Conference	1	0
2000—Miami (Fla.)	11	1	0	.917	1st/Big East Conference	1	0
2001—Cleveland NFL	7	9	0	.438	3rd/AFC Central Division	0	0
2002—Cleveland NFL	9	7	0	.563	2nd/AFC North Division	0	1
2003—Cleveland NFL	5	11	0	.313	4th/AFC North Division	0	0
College totals (6 years)	51	20	0	.718	**College totals (4 years)**	4	0
Pro totals (3 years)	21	27	0	.438	**Pro totals (1 year)**	0	1

NOTES:

1996—Defeated Virginia, 31-21, in Carquest Bowl.
1998—Defeated North Carolina State, 46-23, in Micron PC Bowl.
1999—Defeated Georgia Tech, 28-13, in Gator Bowl.
2000—Defeated Florida, 37-20, in Sugar Bowl.
2002—Lost to Pittsburgh, 36-33, in first-round playoff game.

DEL RIO, JACK — JAGUARS

PERSONAL: Born April 4, 1963, in Castro Valley, Calif. ... Full name: Jack Del Rio, Jr.
HIGH SCHOOL: Hayward (Calif.).
COLLEGE: Southern California.
TRANSACTIONS/CAREER NOTES: Selected by Los Angeles Express in 1985 USFL territorial draft. ... Selected by New Orleans Saints in third round (68th pick overall) of 1985 NFL draft. ... Signed by Saints (July 31, 1985). ... Traded by Saints to Kansas City Chiefs for fifth-round pick (TE Greg Scales) in 1988 draft (August 17, 1987). ... On injured reserve with knee injury (December 13, 1988-remainder of season). ... Claimed on waivers by Dallas Cowboys (August 31, 1989). ... Granted free agency (February 1, 1991). ... Re-signed by Cowboys (July 25, 1991). ... Granted unconditional free agency (February 1, 1992). ... Signed by Minnesota Vikings (March 3, 1992). ... Released by Vikings (February 13, 1996). ... Signed by Miami Dolphins (June 2, 1996). ... Released by Dolphins (August 5, 1996).
HONORS: Played in Pro Bowl (1994 season).
MISCELLANEOUS: Selected by Toronto Blue Jays organization in 22nd round of free-agent baseball draft (June 8, 1981); did not sign.

			TOTALS			INTERCEPTIONS			
Year Team	G	GS	Tk.	Ast.	Sks.	No.	Yds.	Avg.	TD
1985—New Orleans NFL	16	9	51	17	0.0	2	13	6.5	0
1986—New Orleans NFL	16	1	14	6	0.0	0	0	0.0	0
1987—Kansas City NFL	10	7	32	12	3.0	0	0	0.0	0
1988—Kansas City NFL	15	10	45	32	1.0	1	0	0.0	0
1989—Dallas NFL	14	12	40	18	0.0	0	0	0.0	0
1990—Dallas NFL	16	16	48	56	1.5	0	0	0.0	0
1991—Dallas NFL	16	16	77	53	0.0	0	0	0.0	0
1992—Minnesota NFL	16	16	113	40	2.0	2	92	46.0	1
1993—Minnesota NFL	16	16	108	61	0.5	4	3	0.8	0

Year	Team	G	GS	TOTALS Tk.	Ast.	Sks.	INTERCEPTIONS No.	Yds.	Avg.	TD
1994—Minnesota NFL		16	16	56	43	2.0	3	5	1.7	0
1995—Minnesota NFL		9	9	32	21	3.0	1	15	15.0	0
Pro totals (11 years)		160	128	646	359	13.0	13	128	9.8	1

COACHING RECORD

BACKROUND: Linebackers coach/assistant strength coach, New Orleans Saints NFL (1997-98). ... Linebackers coach, Baltimore Ravens NFL (1999-2001). ... Defensive coordinator, Carolina Panthers NFL (2002).

	REGULAR SEASON W	L	T	Pct.	Finish	POST-SEASON W	L
2003—Jacksonville NFL	5	11	0	.313	3rd/AFC South Division	0	0

DUNGY, TONY — COLTS

PERSONAL: Born October 6, 1955, in Jackson, Mich. ... Full name: Anthony Kevin Dungy. ... Name pronounced: DUN-gee. ... Played defensive back and quarterback.

HIGH SCHOOL: Parkside (Jackson, Mich.).

COLLEGE: Minnesota.

TRANSACTIONS/CAREER NOTES: Signed as non-drafted free agent by Pittsburgh Steelers (May 1977). ... Traded by Steelers to San Francisco 49ers for 10th-round pick in 1980 draft (August 21, 1979). ... Traded by 49ers with RB Mike Hogan to New York Giants for WR Jimmy Robinson and CB Ray Rhodes (March 27, 1980).

CHAMPIONSHIP GAME EXPERIENCE: Played in AFC championship game (1978 season). ... Played in Super Bowl 13 (1978 season).

Year	Team	G	INTERCEPTIONS No.	Yds.	Avg.	TD
1977—Pittsburgh NFL		14	3	37	12.3	0
1978—Pittsburgh NFL		16	6	95	15.8	0
1979—San Francisco NFL		15	0	0	0.0	0
Pro totals (3 years)		45	9	132	14.7	0

COACHING RECORD

BACKROUND: Defensive backs coach, University of Minnesota (1980). ... Defensive assistant, Pittsburgh Steelers NFL (1981). ... Defensive backs coach, Steelers (1982-83). ... Defensive coordinator, Steelers (1984-88). ... Defensive backs coach, Kansas City Chiefs NFL (1989-91). ... Defensive coordinator, Minnesota Vikings NFL (1992-95).

	REGULAR SEASON W	L	T	Pct.	Finish	POST-SEASON W	L
1996—Tampa Bay NFL	6	10	0	.375	4th/NFC Central Division	0	0
1997—Tampa Bay NFL	10	6	0	.625	2nd/NFC Central Division	1	1
1998—Tampa Bay NFL	8	8	0	.500	3rd/NFC Central Division	0	0
1999—Tampa Bay NFL	11	5	0	.688	1st/NFC Central Division	1	1
2000—Tampa Bay NFL	10	6	0	.625	2nd/NFC Central Division	0	1
2001—Tampa Bay NFL	9	7	0	.563	3rd/NFC Central Division	0	1
2002—Indianapolis NFL	10	6	0	.625	2nd/AFC South Division	0	1
2003—Indianapolis NFL	12	4	0	.750	1st/AFC South Division	2	1
Pro totals (8 years)	76	52	0	.594	**Pro totals (6 years)**	4	6

NOTES:

1997—Defeated Detroit, 20-10, in first-round playoff game; lost to Green Bay, 21-7, in conference playoff game.
1999—Defeated Washington, 14-13, in conference playoff game; lost to St. Louis, 11-6, in NFC championship game.
2000—Lost to Philadelphia, 21-3, in first-round playoff game.
2001—Lost to Philadelphia, 31-9, in first-round playoff game.
2002—Lost to New York Jets, 41-0, in first-round playoff game.
2003—Defeated Denver, 41-10, in first-round playoff game; defeated Kansas City, 38-31, in conference playoff game; lost to New England, 24-14, in AFC championship game.

EDWARDS, HERMAN — JETS

PERSONAL: Born April 27, 1954, in Fort Monmouth, N.J. ... Full name: Herman Lee Edwards. ... Played cornerback.

HIGH SCHOOL: Monterey (Calif.).

JUNIOR COLLEGE: Monterey (Calif.) Peninsula College.

COLLEGE: California, then San Diego State.

TRANSACTIONS/CAREER NOTES: Signed as non-drafted free agent by Philadelphia Eagles (May 1977). ... Released by Eagles (September 8, 1986). ... Signed by Los Angeles Rams (September 15, 1986). ... Released by Rams (October 20, 1986). ... Signed by Atlanta Falcons (November 3, 1986). ... Announced retirement (November 11, 1986).

CHAMPIONSHIP GAME EXPERIENCE: Played in NFC championship game (1980 season). ... Played in Super Bowl 15 (1980 season).

Year	Team	G	INTERCEPTIONS No.	Yds.	Avg.	TD
1977—Philadelphia NFL		14	6	9	1.5	0
1978—Philadelphia NFL		16	7	59	8.4	0
1979—Philadelphia NFL		16	3	6	2.0	0
1980—Philadelphia NFL		16	3	12	4.0	0
1981—Philadelphia NFL		16	3	1	0.3	0
1982—Philadelphia NFL		9	5	3	0.6	0

Year Team	G	INTERCEPTIONS No.	Yds.	Avg.	TD
1983—Philadelphia NFL	16	1	0	0.0	0
1984—Philadelphia NFL	16	2	0	0.0	0
1985—Philadelphia NFL	16	3	8	2.7	1
1986—Los Angeles Rams NFL	4	0	0	0.0	0
—Atlanta NFL	3	0	0	0.0	0
Pro totals (10 years)	142	33	98	3.0	1

COACHING RECORD

BACKROUND: Defensive backs coach, San Jose State (1987-89). ... Scout, Kansas City Chiefs NFL (1990, 1991 and 1995). ... Defensive backs coach, Chiefs (1992-94). ... Assistant head coach/defensive backs coach, Tampa Bay Buccaneers NFL (1996-2000).

	REGULAR SEASON W	L	T	Pct.	Finish	POST-SEASON W	L
2001—New York Jets NFL	10	6	0	.625	3rd/AFC Eastern Division	0	1
2002—New York Jets NFL	9	7	0	.563	1st/AFC East Division	1	1
2003—New York Jets NFL	6	10	0	.375	4th/AFC East Division	0	0
Pro totals (3 years)	25	23	0	.521	**Pro totals (2 years)**	1	2

NOTES:

2001—Lost to Oakland, 38-24, in first-round playoff game.
2002—Defeated Indianapolis, 41-0, in first-round playoff game; lost to Oakland, 30-10, in conference playoff game.

ERICKSON, DENNIS — 49ERS

PERSONAL: Born March 24, 1947, in Everett, Wash.
HIGH SCHOOL: Everett (Wash.).
COLLEGE: Montana State.

COACHING RECORD

BACKROUND: Graduate assistant, Montana State (1969). ... Graduate assistant, Washington State (spring 1970). ... Head coach, Billings (Mont.) Central High (1970; record: 7-2). ... Offensive backs coach, Montana State (1971-73). ... Offensive coordinator, Idaho (1974-75). ... Offensive coordinator, Fresno State (1976-78). ... Offensive coordinator, San Jose State (1979-81)
HONORS: Named College Football Coach of the Year by The Sporting News (1992 and 2000).

	REGULAR SEASON W	L	T	Pct.	Finish	POST-SEASON W	L
1982—Idaho	8	3	0	.727	T2nd/Big Sky Conference	1	1
1983—Idaho	8	3	0	.727	T3rd/Big Sky Conference	0	0
1984—Idaho	6	5	0	.545	T3rd/Big Sky Conference	0	0
1985—Idaho	9	2	0	.818	1st/Big Sky Conference	0	1
1986—Wyoming	6	6	0	.500	T4th/Western Athletic Conference	0	0
1987—Washington State	3	7	1	.300	9th/Pacific-10 Conference	0	0
1988—Washington State	8	3	0	.727	T3rd/Pacific-10 Conference	1	0
1989—Miami (Fla.)	10	1	0	.909	Independent	1	0
1990—Miami (Fla.)	9	2	0	.818	Independent	1	0
1991—Miami (Fla.)	11	0	0	1.000	Independent	1	0
1992—Miami (Fla.)	11	0	0	1.000	1st/Big East Conference	0	1
1993—Miami (Fla.)	9	2	0	.818	2nd/Big East Conference	0	1
1994—Miami (Fla.)	10	1	0	.909	1st/Big East Conference	0	1
1995—Seattle NFL	8	8	0	.500	3rd/AFC Western Division	0	0
1996—Seattle NFL	7	9	0	.438	5th/AFC Western Division	0	0
1997—Seattle NFL	8	8	0	.500	3rd/AFC Western Division	0	0
1998—Seattle NFL	8	8	0	.500	3rd/AFC Western Division	0	0
1999—Oregon State	7	5	0	.583	5th/Pacific 10 Conference	0	1
2000—Oregon State	11	1	0	.917	1st/Pacific 10 Conference	1	0
2001—Oregon State	5	6	0	.455	7th/Pacific 10 Conference	0	0
2002—Oregon State	8	4	0	.667	4th/Pacific 10 Conference	0	1
2003—San Francisco NFL	7	9	0	.438	3rd/NFC West Division	0	0
College totals (17 years)	139	51	1	.732	**College totals (12 years)**	6	7
Pro totals (5 years)	38	42	0	.475			

NOTES:

1982—Defeated Montana, 21-7, in first round of NCAA Division I-AA playoffs; lost to Eastern Kentucky, 38-30, in second round of NCAA Division I-AA playoffs.
1985—Lost to Eastern Washington, 42-38, in first round of NCAA Division I-AA playoffs.
1988—Defeated Houston, 24-22, in Aloha Bowl.
1989—Defeated Alabama, 33-25, in Sugar Bowl.
1990—Defeated Texas, 46-3, in Cotton Bowl.
1991—Defeated Nebraska, 22-0, in Orange Bowl.
1992—Lost to Alabama, 34-13, in Sugar Bowl.
1993—Lost to Arizona, 29-0, in Fiesta Bowl.
1994—Lost to Nebraska, 24-17, in Orange Bowl.
1999—Lost to Hawaii, 23-17, in O'ahu Bowl.
2000—Defeated Notre Dame, 41-9, in Fiesta Bowl.
2002—Lost to Pittsburgh, 38-13, in Insight.com Bowl.

FISHER, JEFF — TITANS

PERSONAL: Born February 25, 1958, in Culver City, Calif. ... Full name: Jeffrey Michael Fisher. ... Played safety.
HIGH SCHOOL: Taft (Woodland Hills, Calif.).
COLLEGE: Southern California.
TRANSACTIONS/CAREER NOTES: Selected by Chicago Bears in seventh round (177th pick overall) of 1981 NFL draft. ... On injured reserve with broken leg (October 24, 1983-remainder of season). ... On injured reserve with ankle injury entire 1985 season.
CHAMPIONSHIP GAME EXPERIENCE: Played in NFC championship game (1984 season).

		INTERCEPTIONS				PUNT RETURNS				KICKOFF RETURNS				TOTALS			
Year Team	G	No.	Yds.	Avg.	TD	No.	Yds.	Avg.	TD	No.	Yds.	Avg.	TD	TD	2pt.	Pts.	Fum.
1981—Chicago NFL	16	2	3	1.5	0	43	509	11.8	1	7	102	14.6	0	1	0	6	3
1982—Chicago NFL	9	3	19	6.3	0	7	53	7.6	0	7	102	14.6	0	0	0	0	2
1983—Chicago NFL	8	0	0	0.0	0	13	71	5.5	0	0	0	0.0	0	0	0	0	0
1984—Chicago NFL	16	0	0	0.0	0	57	492	8.6	0	0	0	0.0	0	0	0	0	4
1985—Chicago NFL	Did not play.																
Pro totals (4 years)	49	5	22	4.4	0	120	1125	9.4	1	14	204	14.6	0	1	0	6	9

COACHING RECORD

BACKROUND: Defensive backs coach, Philadelphia Eagles NFL (1986-88). ... Defensive coordinator, Eagles (1989-90). ... Defensive coordinator, Los Angeles Rams NFL (1991). ... Defensive backs coach, San Francisco 49ers NFL (1992-93). ... Defensive coordinator, Houston Oilers NFL (February 9-November 14, 1994). ... Oilers franchise moved to Tennessee for 1997 season.

	REGULAR SEASON					POST-SEASON	
	W	L	T	Pct.	Finish	W	L
1994—Houston NFL	1	5	0	.167	4th/AFC Central Division	0	0
1995—Houston NFL	7	9	0	.438	3rd/AFC Central Division	0	0
1996—Houston NFL	8	8	0	.500	4th/AFC Central Division	0	0
1997—Tennessee NFL	8	8	0	.500	3rd/AFC Central Division	0	0
1998—Tennessee NFL	8	8	0	.500	2nd/AFC Central Division	0	0
1999—Tennessee NFL	13	3	0	.813	2nd/AFC Central Division	3	1
2000—Tennessee NFL	13	3	0	.813	1st/AFC Central Division	0	1
2001—Tennessee NFL	7	9	0	.438	4th/AFC Central Division	0	0
2002—Tennessee NFL	11	5	0	.688	1st/AFC South Division	1	1
2003—Tennessee NFL	12	4	0	.750	2nd/AFC South Division	1	1
Pro totals (10 years)	88	62	0	.587	**Pro totals (4 years)**	5	4

NOTES:

1994—Replaced Jack Pardee as head coach (November 14) with 1-9 record and club in fourth place.
1999—Defeated Buffalo, 22-16, in first-round playoff game; defeated Indianapolis, 19-16, in conference playoff game; defeated Jacksonville, 33-14, in AFC championship game; lost to St. Louis, 23-16, in Super Bowl 34.
2000—Lost to Baltimore, 24-10, in conference playoff game.
2002—Defeated Pittsburgh, 34-31 (OT), in conference playoff game; lost to Oakland, 41-24, in AFC championship game.
2003—Defeated Baltimore, 20-17, in first-round playoff game; lost to New England, 17-14, in AFC conference playoff game.

FOX, JOHN — PANTHERS

PERSONAL: Born February 8, 1955, in Virginia Beach, Va.
HIGH SCHOOL: Castle Park (Chula Vista, Calif.).
JUNIOR COLLEGE: Southwestern Junior College (Calif.).
COLLEGE: San Diego State.

COACHING RECORD

BACKROUND: Graduate assistant, San Diego State (1978). ... Assistant coach, U.S. International University, Calif. (1979). ... Secondary coach, Boise State (1980). ... Secondary coach, Long Beach State (1981). ... Secondary coach, University of Utah (1982). ... Secondary coach, University of Kansas (1983). ... Secondary coach, Iowa State (1984). ... Secondary coach, Los Angeles Express USFL (1985). ... Defensive coordinator/secondary coach, University of Pittsburgh (1986-88). ... Secondary coach, Pittsburgh Steelers NFL (1989-91). ... Secondary coach, San Diego Chargers NFL (1992-93). ... Defensive coordinator, Los Angeles Raiders NFL (1994). ... Defensive coordinator, Oakland Raiders NFL (1995). ... Consultant, St. Louis Rams NFL (1996). ... Defensive coordinator, New York Giants NFL (1997-2001).

	REGULAR SEASON					POST-SEASON	
	W	L	T	Pct.	Finish	W	L
2002—Carolina NFL	7	9	0	.438	4th/NFC South Division	0	0
2003—Carolina NFL	11	5	0	.688	1st/NFC South Division	3	1
Pro totals (2 years)	18	14	0	.563	**Pro totals (1 year)**	3	1

NOTES:

2003—Defeated Dallas, 29-10, in first-round playoff game; defeated St. Louis, 29-23 (2OT), in conference playoff game; defeated Philadelphia, 14-3, in NFC championship game; lost to New England, 32-29, in Super Bowl 38.

GIBBS, JOE — REDSKINS

PERSONAL: Born November 25, 1940, in Mocksville, N.C. ... Full name: Joe Jackson Gibbs.
HIGH SCHOOL: Spring (Santa Fe, Calif.).
JUNIOR COLLEGE: Cerritos (Calif.).
COLLEGE: San Diego State.

COACHING RECORD

BACKROUND: Graduate assistant, San Diego State (1964-65). ... Assistant coach, San Diego State (1966). ... Assistant coach, Florida State (1967-68). ... Assistant coach, Southern California (1969-70). ... Assistant coach, Arkansas (1971-72). ... Assistant coach, St. Louis Cardinals NFL (1973-77). ... Assistant coach, Tampa Bay Buccaneers NFL (1978). ... Assistant coach, San Diego Chargers NFL (1979-80).

HONORS: Named NFL Coach of the Year by THE SPORTING NEWS (1982, 1983 and 1991).

	REGULAR SEASON					POST-SEASON	
	W	L	T	Pct.	Finish	W	L
1981—Washington NFL	8	8	0	.500	4th/NFC Eastern Division	0	0
1982—Washington NFL	8	1	0	.889	1st/NFC	4	0
1983—Washington NFL	14	2	0	.875	1st/NFC Eastern Division	2	1
1984—Washington NFL	11	5	0	.688	1st/NFC Eastern Division	0	1
1985—Washington NFL	10	6	0	.625	3rd/NFC Eastern Division	0	0
1986—Washington NFL	12	4	0	.750	2nd/NFC Eastern Division	2	1
1987—Washington NFL	11	4	0	.733	1st/NFC Eastern Division	3	0
1988—Washington NFL	7	9	0	.438	3rd/NFC Eastern Division	0	0
1989—Washington NFL	10	6	0	.625	3rd/NFC Eastern Division	0	0
1990—Washington NFL	10	6	0	.625	3rd/NFC Eastern Division	1	1
1991—Washington NFL	14	2	0	.875	1st/NFC Eastern Division	3	0
1992—Washington NFL	9	7	0	.563	3rd/NFC Eastern Division	1	1
Pro totals (12 years)	124	60	0	.674	**Pro totals (8 years)**	16	5

NOTES:

1982—Defeated Detroit, 31-7, in first-round playoff game; defeated Minnesota, 21-7, in conference playoff game; defeated Dallas, 31-17, in NFC championship game; defeated Miami, 27-17, in Super Bowl 17.

1983—Defeated Los Angeles Rams, 51-7, in conference playoff game; defeated San Francisco, 24-21, in NFC championship game; lost to Los Angeles Raiders, 38-9, in Super Bowl 18.

1984—Lost to Chicago, 23-19, in conference playoff game.

1986—Defeated Los Angeles Rams, 19-7, in first-round playoff game; defeated Chicago, 27-13, in conference playoff game; lost to New York Giants, 17-0, in NFC championship game.

1987—Defeated Chicago, 21-17, in conference playoff game; defeated Minnesota, 17-10, in NFC championship game; defeated Denver, 42-10, in Super Bowl 22.

1990—Defeated Philadelphia, 20-6, in first-round playoff game; lost to San Francisco, 28-10, in conference playoff game.

1991—Defeated Atlanta, 24-7, in conference playoff game; defeated Detroit, 41-10, in NFC championship game; defeated Buffalo, 37-24, in Super Bowl 26.

1992—Defeated Minnesota, 24-7, in first-round playoff game; lost to San Francisco, 20-13, in conference playoff game.

GREEN, DENNIS — CARDINALS

PERSONAL: Born February 17, 1949, in Harrisburg, Pa.

HIGH SCHOOL: John Harris (Harrisburg, Pa.).

COLLEGE: Iowa.

COACHING RECORD

BACKROUND: Graduate assistant, University of Iowa (1972). ... Running backs/receivers coach, Dayton (1973). ... Running backs/receivers coach, Iowa (1974-76). ... Running backs coach, Stanford (1977-78). ... Special teams coach, San Francisco 49ers NFL (1979). ... Offensive coordinator, Stanford (1980). ... Receivers coach, 49ers (1986-88).

	REGULAR SEASON					POST-SEASON	
	W	L	T	Pct.	Finish	W	L
1981—Northwestern	0	11	0	.000	10th/Big Ten Conference	0	0
1982—Northwestern	3	8	0	.273	T8th/Big Ten Conference	0	0
1983—Northwestern	2	9	0	.182	T8th/Big Ten Conference	0	0
1984—Northwestern	2	9	0	.182	9th/Big Ten Conference	0	0
1985—Northwestern	3	8	0	.273	T9th/Big Ten Conference	0	0
1989—Stanford	3	8	0	.273	T7th/Pacific-10 Conference	0	0
1990—Stanford	5	6	0	.455	T6th/Pacific-10 Conference	0	0
1991—Stanford	8	3	0	.727	T2nd/Pacific-10 Conference	0	1
1992—Minnesota NFL	11	5	0	.688	1st/NFC Central Division	0	1
1993—Minnesota NFL	9	7	0	.563	2nd/NFC Central Division	0	1
1994—Minnesota NFL	10	6	0	.625	1st/NFC Central Division	0	1
1995—Minnesota NFL	8	8	0	.500	4th/NFC Central Division	0	0
1996—Minnesota NFL	9	7	0	.563	2nd/NFC Central Division	0	1
1997—Minnesota NFL	9	7	0	.563	4th/NFC Central Division	1	1
1998—Minnesota NFL	15	1	0	.938	1st/NFC Central Division	1	1
1999—Minnesota NFL	10	6	0	.625	2nd/NFC Central Division	1	1
2000—Minnesota NFL	11	5	0	.688	1st/NFC Central Division	1	1
2001—Minnesota NFL	5	10	0	.333		—	—
College totals (8 years)	26	62	0	.295	**College totals (1 year)**	0	1
Pro totals (10 years)	97	62	0	.610	**Pro totals (8 years)**	4	8

NOTES:

1991—Lost to Georgia Tech, 18-17, in Aloha Bowl.

1992—Lost to Washington, 24-7, in first-round playoff game.

1993—Lost to New York Giants, 17-10, in first-round playoff game.

1994—Lost to Chicago, 35-18, in first-round playoff game.

1996—Lost to Dallas, 40-15, in first-round playoff game.

1997—Defeated New York Giants, 23-22, in first-round playoff game; lost to San Francisco, 38-22, in conference playoff game.

1998—Defeated Arizona, 41-21, in conference playoff game; lost to Atlanta, 30-27, in NFC championship game.

1999—Defeated Dallas, 27-10, in first-round playoff game; lost to St. Louis, 49-37, in conference playoff game.

2000—Defeated New Orleans, 34-16, in conference playoff game; lost to New York Giants, 41-0, in NFC championship game.

2001—Replaced as head coach by Mike Tice (January 4, 2002) and club in fourth place.

GRUDEN, JON — BUCCANEERS

PERSONAL: Born August 17, 1963, in Sandusky, Ohio. ... Son of Jim Gruden, scout, San Francisco 49ers; and brother of Jay Gruden, quarterback with Tampa Bay Storm of Arena League (1991-96) and current head coach, Orlando Predators of Arena League.
HIGH SCHOOL: Clay (South Bend, Ind.).
COLLEGE: Dayton, then Tennessee.

COACHING RECORD

BACKROUND: Graduate assistant, Tennessee (1986-87). ... Passing game coordinator, Southeast Missouri State (1988). ... Wide receivers coach, Pacific (1989). ... Assistant coach, San Francisco 49ers NFL (1990) ... Wide receivers coach, University of Pittsburgh (1991). ... Offensive/quality control coach, Green Bay Packers NFL (1992). ... Wide receivers coach, Packers (1993-94). ... Offensive coordinator, Philadelphia Eagles NFL (1995-97).

	REGULAR SEASON					POST-SEASON	
	W	L	T	Pct.	Finish	W	L
1998—Oakland NFL	8	8	0	.500	2nd/AFC Western Division	0	0
1999—Oakland NFL	8	8	0	.500	4th/AFC Western Division	0	0
2000—Oakland NFL	12	4	0	.750	1st/AFC Western Division	1	1
2001—Oakland NFL	10	6	0	.625	1st/AFC Western Division	1	1
2002—Tampa Bay NFL	12	4	0	.750	1st/NFC South Division	3	0
2003—Tampa Bay NFL	7	9	0	.438	3rd/NFC South Division	0	0
Pro totals (6 years)	57	39	0	.594	**Pro totals (3 years)**	5	2

NOTES:
2000—Defeated Miami, 27-0, in conference playoff game; lost to Baltimore, 16-3, in AFC championship game.
2001—Defeated New York Jets, 38-24, in first-round playoff game; lost to New England, 16-13 (OT), in conference playoff game.
2002—Defeated San Francisco, 31-6, in conference playoff game; defeated Philadelphia, 27-10, in NFC championship game; defeated Oakland, 48-21, in Super Bowl 37.

HASLETT, JIM — SAINTS

PERSONAL: Born December 9, 1957, in Pittsburgh. ... Full name: James Donald Haslett. ... Played linebacker.
HIGH SCHOOL: Avalon (Pittsburgh).
COLLEGE: Indiana University, Pa.
TRANSACTIONS/CAREER NOTES: Selected by Buffalo Bills in second round (51st pick overall) of 1979 NFL draft. ... On injured reserve with back injury (September 13-November 17, 1983). ... On injured reserve with broken leg (September 1, 1986-entire season). ... Released by Bills (September 7, 1987). ... Signed by New York Jets as replacement player (September 30, 1987). ... On injured reserve with back injury (October 20, 1987-remainder of season).
HONORS: Played in Pro Bowl (1980 and 1981 seasons).

		INTERCEPTIONS			
Year Team	G	No.	Yds.	Avg.	TD
1979—Buffalo NFL	16	2	15	7.5	0
1980—Buffalo NFL	16	2	30	15.0	0
1981—Buffalo NFL	16	0	0	0.0	0
1982—Buffalo NFL	6	0	0	0.0	0
1983—Buffalo NFL	5	0	0	0.0	0
1984—Buffalo NFL	15	0	0	0.0	0
1985—Buffalo NFL	16	1	40	40.0	0
1986—Buffalo NFL	Did not play.				
1987—New York Jets NFL	3	1	9	9.0	0
Pro totals (8 years)	93	6	94	15.7	0

COACHING RECORD

BACKROUND: Linebackers coach, University of Buffalo (1988). ... Defensive coordinator, University of Buffalo (1989-90). ... Defensive coordinator, Sacramento Surge W.L. (1991-92). ... Linebackers coach, Los Angeles Raiders NFL (1993-94). ... Linebackers coach, New Orleans Saints NFL (1995). ... Defensive coordinator, Saints (1996). ... Defensive coordinator, Pittsburgh Steelers NFL (1997-99).

	REGULAR SEASON					POST-SEASON	
	W	L	T	Pct.	Finish	W	L
2000—New Orleans NFL	10	6	0	.625	1st/NFC Western Division	1	1
2001—New Orleans NFL	7	9	0	.438	3rd/NFC Western Division	0	0
2002—New Orleans NFL	9	7	0	.563	3rd/NFC South Division	0	0
2003—New Orleans NFL	8	8	0	.500	2nd/NFC South Division	0	0
Pro totals (4 years)	34	30	0	.531	**Pro totals (1 year)**	1	1

NOTES:
2000—Defeated St. Louis, 31-28, in first-round playoff game; lost to Minnesota, 34-16, in conference playoff game.

HOLMGREN, MIKE — SEAHAWKS

PERSONAL: Born June 15, 1948, in San Francisco. ... Full name: Michael George Holmgren. ... Played quarterback.
HIGH SCHOOL: Lincoln (San Francisco).
COLLEGE: Southern California.
TRANSACTIONS/CAREER NOTES: Selected by St. Louis Cardinals in eighth round of 1970 NFL draft. ... Released by Cardinals (1970).

COACHING RECORD

BACKROUND: Coach, Lincoln High, San Francisco (1971). ... Assistant coach, Sacred Heart Cathedral Prep School, San Francisco (1972-73). ... Assistant coach, Oak Grove High School, San Jose, Calif. (1975-80). ... Offensive coordinator/quarterbacks coach, San Francisco State (1981). ... Quarterbacks coach, Brigham Young (1982-85). ... Quarterbacks coach, San Francisco 49ers NFL (1986-88). ... Offensive coordinator, 49ers (1989-91).

	REGULAR SEASON					POST-SEASON	
	W	L	T	Pct.	Finish	W	L
1992—Green Bay NFL	9	7	0	.563	2nd/NFC Central Division	0	0
1993—Green Bay NFL	9	7	0	.563	3rd/NFC Central Division	1	1
1994—Green Bay NFL	9	7	0	.563	2nd/NFC Central Division	1	1
1995—Green Bay NFL	11	5	0	.688	1st/NFC Central Division	2	1
1996—Green Bay NFL	13	3	0	.813	1st/NFC Central Division	3	0
1997—Green Bay NFL	13	3	0	.813	1st/NFC Central Division	2	1
1998—Green Bay NFL	11	5	0	.688	2nd/NFC Central Division	0	1
1999—Seattle NFL	9	7	0	.563	1st/AFC Western Division	0	1
2000—Seattle NFL	6	10	0	.375	4th/AFC Western Division	0	0
2001—Seattle NFL	9	7	0	.563	2nd/AFC Western Division	0	0
2002—Seattle NFL	7	9	0	.438	3rd/NFC West Division	0	0
2003—Seattle NFL	10	6	0	.625	2nd/NFC West Division	0	1
Pro totals (12 years)	116	76	0	.604	**Pro totals (8 years)**	9	7

NOTES:

1993—Defeated Detroit, 28-24, in first-round playoff game; lost to Dallas 27-17, in conference playoff game.
1994—Defeated Detroit, 16-12, in first-round playoff game; lost to Dallas, 35-9, in conference playoff game.
1995—Defeated Atlanta, 37-20, in first-round playoff game; defeated San Francisco, 27-17, in conference playoff game; lost to Dallas, 38-27, in NFC championship game.
1996—Defeated San Francisco, 35-14, in conference playoff game; defeated Carolina, 30-13, in NFC championship game; defeated New England, 35-21, in Super Bowl 31.
1997—Defeated Tampa Bay, 21-7, in conference playoff game; defeated San Francisco, 23-10, in NFC championship game; lost to Denver, 31-24, in Super Bowl 32.
1998—Lost to San Francisco, 30-27, in first-round playoff game.
1999—Lost to Miami, 20-17, in first-round playoff game.
2003—Lost to Green Bay, 33-27 (OT), in first-round playoff game.

LEWIS, MARVIN — BENGALS

PERSONAL: Born September 23, 1958, in McDonald, Pa.
HIGH SCHOOL: Fort Cherry (McDonald, Pa.).
COLLEGE: Idaho State.

COACHING RECORD

BACKROUND: Linebackers coach, Idaho State (1981-84). ... Linebackers coach, Long Beach State (1985-86). ... Linebackers coach, University of New Mexico (1987-89). ... Outside linebackers coach, University of Pittsburgh (1990-91). ... Linebackers coach, Pittsburgh Steelers NFL (1992-95). ... Defensive coordinator, Baltimore Ravens NFL (1996-2001). ... Defensive coordinator/assistant head coach, Washington Redskins NFL (2002).

	REGULAR SEASON					POST-SEASON	
	W	L	T	Pct.	Finish	W	L
2003—Cincinnati NFL	8	8	0	.500	2nd/AFC North Division	0	0

MARIUCCI, STEVE — LIONS

PERSONAL: Born November 4, 1955, in Iron Mountain, Mich. ... Full name: Steven Mariucci. ... Played quarterback.
HIGH SCHOOL: Iron Mountain (Mich.).
COLLEGE: Northern Michigan.
TRANSACTIONS/CAREER NOTES: Signed with Hamilton Tiger-Cats of CFL for 1978 season.

COACHING RECORD

BACKROUND: Quarterbacks/running backs coach, Northern Michigan (1978-79). ... Quarterbacks/special teams coordinator, Cal State Fullerton (1980-82). ... Assistant head coach, Louisville (1983-84). ... Receivers coach, Orlando Renegades USFL (1985). ... Quality control coach, Los Angeles Rams NFL (fall 1985). ... Wide receivers/special teams coach, University of California (1987-89). ... Offensive coordinator/quarterbacks coach, University of California (1990-91). ... Quarterbacks coach, Green Bay Packers NFL (1992-95).

	REGULAR SEASON					POST-SEASON	
	W	L	T	Pct.	Finish	W	L
1996—California	6	6	0	.500	T5th/Pacific-10 Conference	0	1
1997—San Francisco NFL	13	3	0	.813	1st/NFC Western Division	1	1
1998—San Francisco NFL	12	4	0	.750	2nd/NFC Western Division	1	1
1999—San Francisco NFL	4	12	0	.250	4th/NFC Western Division	0	0
2000—San Francisco NFL	6	10	0	.375	4th/NFC Western Division	0	0
2001—San Francisco NFL	12	4	0	.750	2nd/NFC Western Division	0	1
2002—San Francisco NFL	10	6	0	.625	1st/NFC West Division	1	1
2003—Detroit NFL	5	11	0	.313	4th/NFC North Division	0	0
College totals (1 year)	6	6	0	.500	**College totals (1 year)**	0	1
Pro totals (7 years)	62	50	0	.554	**Pro totals (4 years)**	3	4

NOTES:

1996—Lost to Navy, 42-38, in Aloha Bowl.
1997—Defeated Minnesota, 38-22, in conference playoff game; lost to Green Bay, 23-10, in NFC championship game.
1998—Defeated Green Bay, 30-27, in first-round playoff game; lost to Atlanta, 20-18, in conference playoff game.
2001—Lost to Green Bay, 25-15, in first-round playoff game.
2002—Defeated New York Giants, 39-38, in first-round playoff game; lost to Tampa Bay, 31-6, in conference playoff game.

MARTZ, MIKE — RAMS

PERSONAL: Born May 13, 1951, in Sioux Falls, S.D.
HIGH SCHOOL: Madison (San Diego).
JUNIOR COLLEGE: San Diego Mesa Community College.
COLLEGE: UC Santa Barbara, then Fresno State.

COACHING RECORD

BACKROUND: Assistant coach, Bullard High School, Fresno, Calif. (1973). ... Assistant coach, San Diego Mesa Community College (1974, 1976 and 1977). ... Assistant coach, San Jose State (1975). ... Assistant coach, Santa Ana College (1978). ... Assistant coach, Fresno State (1979). ... Assistant coach, Pacific University (1980-81). ... Running backs coach, University of Minnesota (1982). ... Quarterbacks/receivers coach, Arizona State (1983, 1986 and 1987). ... Offensive coordinator, Arizona State (1984 and 1988-91). ... Offensive assistant, Los Angeles Rams NFL (1992-93). ... Quarterbacks coach, Rams (1994). ... Wide receivers coach, St. Louis Rams NFL (1995-96). ... Quarterbacks coach, Washington Redskins NFL (1997-98). ... Offensive coordinator, Rams (1999).

	REGULAR SEASON					POST-SEASON	
	W	L	T	Pct.	Finish	W	L
2000—St. Louis NFL	10	6	0	.625	2nd/NFC Western Division	0	1
2001—St. Louis NFL	14	2	0	.875	1st/NFC Western Division	2	1
2002—St. Louis NFL	7	9	0	.438	2nd/NFC West Division	0	0
2003—St. Louis NFL	12	4	0	.750	1st/NFC West Division	0	1
Pro totals (4 years)	43	21	0	.672	**Pro totals (3 years)**	2	3

NOTES:

2000—Lost to New Orleans, 31-28, in first-round playoff game.
2001—Defeated Green Bay, 45-17, in conference playoff game; defeated Philadelphia, 29-24, in NFC championship game; lost to New England, 20-17, in Super Bowl 36.
2003—Lost to Carolina, 29-23 (2OT), in conference playoff game.

MORA, JIM — FALCONS

PERSONAL: Born November 19, 1961, in Los Angeles. ... Full name: Jim Mora Jr. ... Son of Jim Mora, coach, New Orleans Saints (1986-96) and Indianapolis Colts (1998-2001).
HIGH SCHOOL: Interlake (Bellevue, Wash.).
COLLEGE: Washington.

COACHING RECORD

BACKROUND: Assistant coach, University of Washington (1984). ... Assistant secondary coach, San Diego Chargers NFL (1986-88). ... Secondary coach, Chargers (1989-91). ... Secondary coach, New Orleans Saints NFL (1992-96). ... Defensive backs coach, San Francisco 49ers NFL (1997-98). ... Defensive coordinator, 49ers (1999-2003).

MULARKEY, MIKE — BILLS

PERSONAL: Born November 19, 1961, in Fort Lauderdale, Fla. ... Full name: Michael Rene Mularkey. ... Played tight end.
HIGH SCHOOL: Northeast (Fort Lauderdale).
COLLEGE: Florida.
TRANSACTIONS/CAREER NOTES: Selected by Tampa Bay Bandits in 1983 USFL territorial draft. ... Selected by San Francisco 49ers in ninth round (229th pick overall) of 1983 NFL draft. ... Signed by 49ers (June 1, 1983). ... Released by 49ers (August 29, 1983). ... Claimed on waivers by Minnesota Vikings (August 30, 1983). ... On injured reserve with ankle injury (September 30, 1983-remainder of season). ... On injured reserve with knee injury (September 8-October 31, 1987). ... Crossed picket line during players strike (October 7, 1987). ... Returned to picket line (October 12, 1987). ... Granted unconditional free agency (February 1, 1989). ... Signed by Pittsburgh Steelers (March 31, 1989). ... Granted unconditional free agency (February 1-April 1, 1991). ... Re-signed by Steelers for 1991 season. ... On injured reserve with back injury (December 6, 1991-remainder of season). ... Granted unconditional free agency (February 1-April 1, 1992). ... Re-signed by Steelers for 1992 season. ... Released by Steelers (June 29, 1992).

			RECEIVING			
Year Team	G	GS	No.	Yds.	Avg.	TD
1983—Minnesota NFL	3	...	0	0	0.0	0
1984—Minnesota NFL	16	...	14	134	9.6	2
1985—Minnesota NFL	15	...	13	196	15.1	1
1986—Minnesota NFL	16	...	11	89	8.1	2
1987—Minnesota NFL	9	...	1	6	6.0	0
1988—Minnesota NFL	16	...	3	39	13.0	0
1989—Pittsburgh NFL	14	...	22	326	14.8	1
1990—Pittsburgh NFL	16	...	32	365	11.4	3
1991—Pittsburgh NFL	9	...	6	67	11.2	0
Pro totals (9 years)	114	...	102	1222	12.0	9

COACHING RECORD

BACKROUND: Offensive line coach, Concordia (Minn.) College (1993). ... Quality control coach, Tampa Bay Buccaneers NFL (1994). ... Tight ends coach, Buccaneers (1995). ... Tight ends coach, Pittsburgh Steelers NFL (1996-2000). ... Offensive coordinator, Steelers (2001-03).

PARCELLS, BILL — COWBOYS

PERSONAL: Born August 22, 1941, in Englewood, N.J. ... Full name: Duane Charles Parcells.
HIGH SCHOOL: River Dell (Oradell, N.J.).
COLLEGE: Colgate, then Wichita State.

COACHING RECORD

BACKROUND: Defensive assistant coach, Hastings (Neb.) College (1964). ... Defensive line coach, Wichita State (1965). ... Linebackers coach, Army (1966-69). ... Linebackers coach, Florida State (1970-72). ... Defensive coordinator, Vanderbilt (1973-74). ... Defensive coordinator, Texas Tech (1975-77). ... Assistant coach, New York Giants NFL (1979). ... Linebackers coach, New England NFL (1980). ... Defensive coordinator/linebackers coach, New York Giants NFL (1981-82). ... NFL Analyst, NBC Sports (1991-92).

HONORS: Named NFL Coach of the Year (1986).

	REGULAR SEASON					POST-SEASON	
	W	L	T	Pct.	Finish	W	L
1978—Air Force	3	8	0	.273	Independent	0	0
1983—New York Giants NFL	3	12	1	.200	5th/NFC Eastern Division	0	0
1984—New York Giants NFL	9	7	0	.563	2nd/NFC Eastern Division	1	1
1985—New York Giants NFL	10	6	0	.625	2nd/NFC Eastern Division	1	1
1986—New York Giants NFL	14	2	0	.875	1st/NFC Eastern Division	3	0
1987—New York Giants NFL	6	9	0	.400	5th/NFC Eastern Division	0	0
1988—New York Giants NFL	10	6	0	.625	2nd/NFC Eastern Division	0	0
1989—New York Giants NFL	12	4	0	.750	1st/NFC Eastern Division	0	1
1990—New York Giants NFL	13	3	0	.813	1st/NFC Eastern Division	3	0
1993—New England NFL	5	11	0	.313	4th/AFC Eastern Division	0	0
1994—New England NFL	10	6	0	.625	2nd/AFC Eastern Division	0	1
1995—New England NFL	6	10	0	.375	4th/AFC Eastern Division	0	0
1996—New England NFL	11	5	0	.688	1st/AFC Eastern Division	2	1
1997—New York Jets NFL	9	7	0	.563	3rd/AFC Eastern Division	0	0
1998—New York Jets NFL	12	4	0	.750	1st/AFC Eastern Division	1	1
1999—New York Jets NFL	8	8	0	.500	4th/AFC Eastern Division	0	0
2003—Dallas NFL	10	6	0	.625	2nd/NFC East Division	0	1
College totals (1 year)	3	8	0	.273			
Pro totals (16 years)	148	106	1	.583	**Pro totals (9 years)**	11	7

NOTES:

1984—Defeated Los Angeles Rams, 16-13, in wild-card playoff game; lost to San Francisco, 21-10, in conference playoff game.
1985—Defeated San Francisco, 17-3, in wild-card playoff game; lost to Chicago, 21-0, in conference playoff game.
1986—Defeated San Francisco, 49-3, in conference playoff game; defeated Washington, 17-0, in NFC championship game; defeated Denver, 39-20, in Super Bowl 21.
1989—Lost to Los Angeles Rams, 19-13 (OT), in conference playoff game.
1990—Defeated Chicago, 31-3, in conference playoff game; defeated San Francisco, 15-13, in NFC championship game; defeated Buffalo, 20-19, in Super Bowl 25.
1994—Lost to Cleveland, 20-13, in first-round playoff game.
1996—Defeated Pittsburgh, 28-3, in conference playoff game; defeated Jacksonville, 20-6, in AFC championship game; lost to Green Bay, 35-21, in Super Bowl 31.
1998—Defeated Jacksonville, 34-24, in conference playoff game; lost to Denver, 23-10, in AFC championship game.
2003—Lost to Carolina, 29-10, in first-round playoff game.

REID, ANDY — EAGLES

PERSONAL: Born March 19, 1958, in Los Angeles. ... Full name: Andrew Walter Reid.

HIGH SCHOOL: John Marshall (Los Angeles).

JUNIOR COLLEGE: Glendale (Calif.).

COLLEGE: Brigham Young.

COACHING RECORD

BACKROUND: Graduate assistant, Brigham Young University (1982). ... Offensive coordinator, San Francisco State (1983-85). ... Offensive line coach, Northern Arizona University (1986). ... Offensive line coach, University of Texas-El Paso (1987-88). ... Offensive line coach, University of Missouri (1989-91). ... Tight ends coach, Green Bay Packers NFL (1992-96). ... Quarterbacks coach, Packers (1997-98).

HONORS: Named NFL Coach of the Year by THE SPORTING NEWS (2000 and 2002).

	REGULAR SEASON					POST-SEASON	
	W	L	T	Pct.	Finish	W	L
1999—Philadelphia NFL	5	11	0	.313	5th/NFC Eastern Division	0	0
2000—Philadelphia NFL	11	5	0	.688	2nd/NFC Eastern Division	1	1
2001—Philadelphia NFL	11	5	0	.688	1st/NFC Eastern Division	2	1
2002—Philadelphia NFL	12	4	0	.750	1st/NFC East Division	1	1
2003—Philadelphia NFL	12	4	0	.750	1st/NFC East Division	1	1
Pro totals (5 years)	51	29	0	.638	**Pro totals (4 years)**	5	4

NOTES:

2000—Defeated Tampa Bay, 21-3, in first-round playoff game; lost to New York Giants, 20-10, in conference playoff game.
2001—Defeated Tampa Bay, 31-9, in first-round playoff game; defeated Chicago, 33-19, in conference playoff game; lost to St. Louis, 29-24, in NFC championship game.
2002—Defeated Atlanta, 20-6, in conference playoff game; lost to Tampa Bay, 27-10, in NFC championship game.
2003—Defeated Green Bay, 20-17 (OT), in conference playoff game; lost to Carolina, 14-3, in NFC championship game.

SCHOTTENHEIMER, MARTY — CHARGERS

PERSONAL: Born September 23, 1943, in Canonsburg, Pa. ... Full name: Martin Edward Schottenheimer. ... Played linebacker. ... Brother of Kurt Schottenheimer, defensive backs coach, Green Bay Packers; father of Brian Schottenheimer, quarterbacks coach, San Diego Chargers.

HIGH SCHOOL: Fort Cherry (McDonald, Pa.).

COLLEGE: Pittsburgh.

TRANSACTIONS/CAREER NOTES: Selected by Buffalo Bills in seventh round of 1965 AFL draft. ... Released by Bills (1969). ... Signed by Boston Patriots (1969). ... Patriots franchise renamed New England Patriots for 1971 season. ... Traded by New England Patriots to Pittsburgh Steelers for OT Mike Haggerty and a draft choice (July 10, 1971). ... Released by Steelers (1971).

CHAMPIONSHIP GAME EXPERIENCE: Member of AFL championship team (1965 season). ... Played in AFL championship game (1966 season).
HONORS: Played in AFL All-Star Game (1965 season).

Year Team	G	INTERCEPTIONS No.	Yds.	Avg.	TD
1965—Buffalo AFL	14	0	0	0.0	0
1966—Buffalo AFL	14	1	20	20.0	0
1967—Buffalo AFL	14	3	88	29.3	1
1968—Buffalo AFL	14	1	22	22.0	0
1969—Boston AFL	11	1	3	3.0	0
1970—Boston NFL	12	0	0	0.0	0
AFL totals (5 years)	67	6	133	22.2	1
NFL totals (1 year)	12	0	0	0.0	0
Pro totals (6 years)	79	6	133	22.2	1

COACHING RECORD

BACKROUND: Linebackers coach, Portland Storm WFL (1974). ... Linebackers coach, New York Giants NFL (1975-76). ... Defensive coordinator, Giants (1977). ... Linebackers coach, Detroit Lions NFL (1978-79). ... Defensive coordinator, Cleveland Browns NFL (1980-October 22, 1984).

	REGULAR SEASON W	L	T	Pct.	Finish	POST-SEASON W	L
1984—Cleveland NFL	4	4	0	.500	3rd/AFC Central Division	0	0
1985—Cleveland NFL	8	8	0	.500	1st/AFC Central Division	0	1
1986—Cleveland NFL	12	4	0	.750	1st/AFC Central Division	1	1
1987—Cleveland NFL	10	5	0	.667	1st/AFC Central Division	1	1
1988—Cleveland NFL	10	6	0	.625	2nd/AFC Central Division	0	1
1989—Kansas City NFL	8	7	1	.533	2nd/AFC Western Division	0	0
1990—Kansas City NFL	11	5	0	.688	2nd/AFC Western Division	0	1
1991—Kansas City NFL	10	6	0	.625	2nd/AFC Western Division	1	1
1992—Kansas City NFL	10	6	0	.625	2nd/AFC Western Division	0	1
1993—Kansas City NFL	11	5	0	.688	1st/AFC Western Division	2	1
1994—Kansas City NFL	9	7	0	.563	2nd/AFC Western Division	0	1
1995—Kansas City NFL	13	3	0	.813	1st/AFC Western Division	0	1
1996—Kansas City NFL	9	7	0	.563	2nd/AFC Western Division	0	0
1997—Kansas City NFL	13	3	0	.813	1st/AFC Western Division	0	1
1998—Kansas City NFL	7	9	0	.438	4th/AFC Western Division	0	0
2001—Washington NFL	8	8	0	.500	2nd/NFC Eastern Division	0	0
2002—San Diego NFL	8	8	0	.500	3rd/AFC West Division	0	0
2003—San Diego NFL	4	12	0	.250	4th/AFC West Division	0	0
Pro totals (18 years)	165	113	1	.594	**Pro totals (11 years)**	5	11

NOTES:

1984—Replaced Sam Rutigliano as head coach (October 22) with 1-7 record and club in third place.
1985—Lost to Miami, 24-21, in conference playoff game.
1986—Defeated New York Jets, 23-20 (2 OT), in conference playoff game; lost to Denver, 23-20 (OT), in AFC championship game.
1987—Defeated Indianapolis, 38-21, in conference playoff game; lost to Denver, 38-33, in AFC championship game.
1988—Lost to Houston, 24-23, in wild-card playoff game.
1990—Lost to Miami, 17-16, in first-round playoff game.
1991—Defeated Los Angeles Raiders, 10-6, in first-round playoff game; lost to Buffalo, 37-14, in conference playoff game.
1992—Lost to San Diego, 17-0, in first-round playoff game.
1993—Defeated Pittsburgh, 27-24 (OT), in first-round playoff game; defeated Houston, 28-20, in conference playoff game; lost to Buffalo, 30-13, in AFC championship game.
1994—Lost to Miami, 27-17, in first-round playoff game.
1995—Lost to Indianapolis, 10-7, in conference playoff game.
1997—Lost to Denver, 14-10, in conference playoff game.

SHANAHAN, MIKE — BRONCOS

PERSONAL: Born August 24, 1952, in Oak Park, Ill. ... Full name: Michael Edward Shanahan.
HIGH SCHOOL: East Leyden (Franklin Park, Ill.).
COLLEGE: Eastern Illinois.

COACHING RECORD

BACKROUND: Graduate assistant, Eastern Illinois (1973-74). ... Running backs/wide receivers coach, Oklahoma (1975-76). ... Backfield coach, Northern Arizona (1977). ... Offensive coordinator, Eastern Illinois (1978). ... Offensive coordinator, University of Minnesota (1979). ... Offensive coordinator, University of Florida (1980-83). ... Receivers coach, Denver Broncos NFL (1984). ... Offensive coordinator, Broncos (1985-1987 and 1991). ... Quarterbacks coach, Broncos (1989-90). ... Offensive coordinator, San Francisco 49ers NFL (1992-94).

	REGULAR SEASON W	L	T	Pct.	Finish	POST-SEASON W	L
1988—Los Angeles Raiders NFL	7	9	0	.438	3rd/AFC Western Division	0	0
1989—Los Angeles Raiders NFL	1	3	0	.250	3rd/AFC Western Division	0	0
1995—Denver NFL	8	8	0	.500	4th/AFC Western Division	0	0
1996—Denver NFL	13	3	0	.813	1st/AFC Western Division	0	1
1997—Denver NFL	12	4	0	.750	2nd/AFC Western Division	4	0
1998—Denver NFL	14	2	0	.875	1st/AFC Western Division	3	0
1999—Denver NFL	6	10	0	.375	5th/AFC Western Division	0	0
2000—Denver NFL	11	5	0	.688	2nd/AFC Western Division	0	1

					REGULAR SEASON	POST-SEASON	
2001—Denver NFL	8	8	0	.500	3rd/AFC Western Division	0	0
2002—Denver NFL	9	7	0	.563	2nd/AFC West Division	0	0
2003—Denver NFL	10	6	0	.625	2nd/AFC West Division	0	1
Pro totals (11 years)	99	65	0	.604	**Pro totals (5 years)**	7	3

NOTES:

1989—Replaced as Raiders coach by Art Shell (October 3) with club tied for fourth place.
1996—Lost to Jacksonville, 30-27, in conference playoff game.
1997—Defeated Jacksonville, 42-17, in first-round playoff game; defeated Kansas City, 14-10, in conference playoff game; defeated Pittsburgh, 24-21, in AFC championship game; defeated Green Bay, 31-24, in Super Bowl 32.
1998—Defeated Miami, 38-3, in conference playoff game; defeated New York Jets, 23-10, in AFC championship game; defeated Atlanta, 34-19, in Super Bowl 33.
2000—Lost to Baltimore, 21-3, in first-round playoff game.
2003—Lost to Indianapolis, 41-10, in first-round playoff game.

SHERMAN, MIKE — PACKERS

PERSONAL: Born December 19, 1954, in Norwood, Mass. ... Full name: Michael Francis Sherman.
COLLEGE: Central Connecticut State.

COACHING RECORD

BACKROUND: Head coach, Stamford High School, Stamford, Conn. (1978). ... Head coach, Worcester (Mass.) Academy (1979-80). ... Graduate assistant, University of Pittsburgh (1981-82). ... Offensive line coach, Tulane (1983-84). ... Offensive line coach, Holy Cross (1985-87). ... Offensive coordinator, Holy Cross (1988). ... Offensive line coach, Texas A&M (1989-93). ... Offensive line coach, UCLA (1994). ... Offensive line coach, Texas A&M (1995-96). ... Tight ends coach, Green Bay Packers NFL (1997-98). ... Offensive coordinator/tight ends coach, Seattle Seahawks NFL (1999).

	REGULAR SEASON					POST-SEASON	
	W	**L**	**T**	**Pct.**	**Finish**	**W**	**L**
2000—Green Bay NFL	9	7	0	.563	3rd/NFC Central Division	0	0
2001—Green Bay NFL	12	4	0	.750	2nd/NFC Central Division	1	1
2002—Green Bay NFL	12	4	0	.750	1st/NFC North Division	0	1
2003—Green Bay NFL	10	6	0	.625	1st/NFC North Division	1	1
Pro totals (4 years)	43	21	0	.672	**Pro totals (3 years)**	2	3

NOTES:

2001—Defeated San Francisco, 25-15, in first-round playoff game; lost to St. Louis, 45-17, in conference playoff game.
2002—Lost to Atlanta, 27-7, in first-round playoff game.
2003—Defeated Seattle, 33-27 (OT), in first-round playoff game; lost to Philadelphia, 20-17 (OT), in conference playoff game.

SMITH, LOVIE — BEARS

PERSONAL: Born May 8, 1958, in Big Sandy, Texas.
HIGH SCHOOL: Big Sandy (Texas).
COLLEGE: Tulsa.

COACHING RECORD

BACKROUND: Assistant coach, Big Sandy (Tex.) High School (1980). ... Assistant coach, Cascia Hall (Okla.) Prep (1981). ... Linebackers coach, Tulsa (1983-86). ... Linebackers coach, Wisconsin (1987). ... Linebackers coach, Arizona State (1988-91). ... Outside linebackers coach, Kentucky (1992). ... Defensive backs coach, Tennessee (1993-94). ... Defensive backs coach, Ohio State (1995). ... Linebackers coach, Tampa Bay Buccaneers NFL (1996-2000). ... Defensive coordinator, St. Louis Rams NFL (2001-02). ... Assistant head coach/defensive coordinator, Rams (2003).

TICE, MIKE — VIKINGS

PERSONAL: Born February 2, 1959, in Bayshore, N.Y. ... Full name: Michael Peter Tice. ... Brother of John Tice, tight end, New Orleans Saints (1983-1992).
HIGH SCHOOL: Central Islip (N.Y.).
COLLEGE: Maryland.
TRANSACTIONS/CAREER NOTES: Signed as non-drafted free agent by Seattle Seahawks (April 30, 1981). ... On injured reserve with fractured ankle (October 15-December 7, 1985). ... Granted unconditional free agency (February 1, 1989). ... Signed by Washington Redskins (February 20, 1989). ... Released by Redskins (September 4, 1990). ... Signed by Seahawks (November 28, 1990). ... Granted unconditional free agency (February 1-April 1, 1991). ... Re-signed by Seahawks (July 19, 1991). ... Granted unconditional free agency (February 1, 1992). ... Signed by Minnesota Vikings (March 18, 1992). ... On injured reserve with back injury (September 25-October 21, 1992). ... Granted unconditional free agency (March 1, 1993). ... Re-signed by Vikings (May 4, 1993). ... Released by Vikings (August 30, 1993). ... Re-signed by Vikings (August 31, 1993). ... Granted unconditional free agency (February 17, 1994). ... Re-signed by Vikings (December 7, 1995). ... Granted unconditional free agency (February 16, 1996).
CHAMPIONSHIP GAME EXPERIENCE: Played in AFC championship game (1983 season).

			RECEIVING				KICKOFF RETURNS				TOTALS			
Year Team	**G**	**GS**	**No.**	**Yds.**	**Avg.**	**TD**	**No.**	**Yds.**	**Avg.**	**TD**	**TD**	**2pt.**	**Pts.**	**Fum.**
1981—Seattle NFL	16	3	5	47	9.4	0	0	0	0.0	0	0	0	0	0
1982—Seattle NFL	9	9	9	46	5.1	0	0	0	0.0	0	0	0	0	0
1983—Seattle NFL	15	1	0	0	0.0	0	2	28	14.0	0	0	0	0	0
1984—Seattle NFL	16	8	8	90	11.3	3	0	0	0.0	0	3	0	18	0
1985—Seattle NFL	9	2	2	13	6.5	0	1	17	17.0	0	0	0	0	0

Year Team	G	GS	RECEIVING No.	Yds.	Avg.	TD	KICKOFF RETURNS No.	Yds.	Avg.	TD	TOTALS TD	2pt.	Pts.	Fum.
1986—Seattle NFL	16	15	15	150	10.0	0	1	17	17.0	0	0	0	0	0
1987—Seattle NFL	12	12	14	106	7.6	2	0	0	0.0	0	2	0	12	0
1988—Seattle NFL	16	16	29	244	8.4	0	1	17	17.0	0	0	0	0	1
1989—Washington NFL	16	5	1	2	2.0	0	0	0	0.0	0	0	0	0	0
1990—Seattle NFL	5	2	0	0	0.0	0	0	0	0.0	0	0	0	0	0
1991—Seattle NFL	16	15	10	70	7.0	4	3	46	15.3	0	4	0	24	0
1992—Minnesota NFL	12	9	5	65	13.0	1	0	0	0.0	0	1	0	6	0
1993—Minnesota NFL	16	12	6	39	6.5	1	0	0	0.0	0	1	0	6	1
1995—Minnesota NFL	3	1	3	22	7.3	0	0	0	0.0	0	0	0	0	0
Pro totals (14 years)	177	110	107	894	8.4	11	8	125	15.6	0	11	0	66	2

COACHING RECORD

BACKROUND: Tight ends coach, Minnesota Vikings NFL (1996). ... Offensive line coach, Vikings (1997-2000). ... Assistant head coach/offensive line coach, Vikings (2001).

	REGULAR SEASON W	L	T	Pct.	Finish	POST-SEASON W	L
2001—Minnesota NFL	0	1	0	.000	4th/NFC Central Division	0	0
2002—Minnesota NFL	6	10	0	.375	2nd/NFC North Division	0	0
2003—Minnesota NFL	9	7	0	.563	2nd/NFC North Division	0	0
Pro totals (3 years)	15	18	0	.455			

NOTES:

2001—Replaced Dennis Green as head coach (January 4) with 5-10 record and club in fourth place.

TURNER, NORV — RAIDERS

PERSONAL: Born May 17, 1952, in LeJeune, N.C. ... Full name: Norval Eugene Turner. ... Brother of Ron Turner, head coach, University of Illinois.

HIGH SCHOOL: Alhambra (Calif.).

COLLEGE: Oregon.

COACHING RECORD

BACKROUND: Graduate assistant, Oregon (1975). ... Receivers coach, Southern California (1976-79). ... Defensive backs coach, USC (1980). ... Quarterbacks coach, USC (1981-83). ... Offensive coordinator, USC (1984). ... Receivers coach, Los Angeles Rams NFL (1985-90). ... Offensive coordinator, Dallas Cowboys NFL (1991-93).

	REGULAR SEASON W	L	T	Pct.	Finish	POST-SEASON W	L
1994—Washington NFL	3	13	0	.188	5th/NFC Eastern Division	0	0
1995—Washington NFL	6	10	0	.375	3rd/NFC Eastern Division	0	0
1996—Washington NFL	9	7	0	.563	3rd/NFC Eastern Division	0	0
1997—Washington NFL	8	7	1	.533	2nd/NFC Eastern Division	0	0
1998—Washington NFL	6	10	0	.375	4th/NFC Eastern Division	0	0
1999—Washington NFL	10	6	0	.625	1st/NFC Eastern Division	1	1
2000—Washington NFL	7	6	0	.538		—	—
Pro totals (7 years)	49	59	1	.454	**Pro totals (1 year)**	1	1

NOTES:

1999—Defeated Detroit, 27-13, in first-round playoff game; lost to Tampa Bay, 14-13, in conference playoff game.

VERMEIL, DICK — CHIEFS

PERSONAL: Born October 30, 1936, in Calistoga, Calif. ... Full name: Richard Albert Vermeil. ... Brother of Al Vermeil, conditioning coach with San Francisco 49ers (1979-82) and brother-in-law of Louie Giammona, running back with Philadelphia Eagles (1978-82).

HIGH SCHOOL: Calistoga (Calif.).

JUNIOR COLLEGE: Napa College.

COLLEGE: San Jose State (master's degree in physical education, 1959).

COACHING RECORD

BACKROUND: Assistant coach, Del Mar High School, San Jose, Calif. (1959). ... Head coach, Hillsdale High School, San Mateo, Calif. (1960-62; record: 17-9-1). ... Assistant coach, College of San Mateo (1963). ... Assistant coach, Stanford (1965-68). ... Assistant coach, Los Angeles Rams NFL (1969 and 1971-73). ... Offensive coordinator, UCLA (1970).

HONORS: Named NFL Coach of the Year by THE SPORTING NEWS (1979 and 1999).

	REGULAR SEASON W	L	T	Pct.	Finish	POST-SEASON W	L
1964—Napa College	8	1	0	.889	2nd/Golden Valley Conference	0	0
1974—UCLA	6	3	2	.667	T3rd/Pacific-8 Conference	0	0
1975—UCLA	8	2	1	.800	T1st/Pacific-8 Conference	1	0
1976—Philadelphia NFL	4	10	0	.286	4th/NFC Eastern Division	0	0
1977—Philadelphia NFL	5	9	0	.357	4th/NFC Eastern Division	0	0
1978—Philadelphia NFL	9	7	0	.563	2nd/NFC Eastern Division	0	1
1979—Philadelphia NFL	11	5	0	.688	2nd/NFC Eastern Division	1	1
1980—Philadelphia NFL	12	4	0	.750	1st/NFC Eastern Division	2	1

	REGULAR SEASON					POST-SEASON	
	W	L	T	Pct.	Finish	W	L
1981—Philadelphia NFL	10	6	0	.625	2nd/NFC Eastern Division	0	1
1982—Philadelphia NFL	3	6	0	.333	5th/NFC Eastern Division	0	0
1997—St. Louis NFL	5	11	0	.313	5th/NFC Western Division	0	0
1998—St. Louis NFL	4	12	0	.250	5th/NFC Western Division	0	0
1999—St. Louis NFL	13	3	0	.813	1st/NFC Western Division	3	0
2001—Kansas City NFL	6	10	0	.375	4th/AFC Western Division	0	0
2002—Kansas City NFL	8	8	0	.500	4th/AFC West Division	0	0
2003—Kansas City NFL	13	3	0	.813	1st/AFC West Division	0	1
College totals (2 years)	14	5	3	.737	**College totals (1 year)**	1	0
Pro totals (13 years)	103	94	0	.523	**Pro totals (6 years)**	6	5

NOTES:

1975—Defeated Ohio State, 23-10, in Rose Bowl.
1978—Lost to Atlanta, 14-13, in conference playoff game.
1979—Defeated Chicago, 27-17, in first-round playoff game; lost to Tampa Bay, 24-17, in conference playoff game.
1980—Defeated Minnesota, 31-16, in conference playoff game; defeated Dallas, 20-7, in NFC championship game; lost to Oakland, 27-10, in Super Bowl 15.
1981—Lost to New York Giants, 27-21, in conference playoff game.
1982—Only nine of 16 games were played due to the cancellation of games because of a players strike.
1999—Defeated Minnesota, 49-37, in conference playoff game; defeated Tampa Bay, 11-6, in NFC championship game; defeated Tennessee, 23-16, in Super Bowl 34.
2003—Lost to Indianapolis, 38-31, in conference playoff game.

WANNSTEDT, DAVE — DOLPHINS

PERSONAL: Born May 21, 1952, in Pittsburgh. ... Full name: David Raymond Wannstedt.
HIGH SCHOOL: Baldwin (Pittsburgh).
COLLEGE: Pittsburgh.
TRANSACTIONS/CAREER NOTES: Selected by Green Bay Packers in 15th round (376th pick overall) of 1974 NFL draft. ... On injured reserve with neck injury for entire 1974 season.

COACHING RECORD

BACKROUND: Graduate assistant, University of Pittsburgh (1975). ... Assistant coach, University of Pittsburgh (1976-78). ... Defensive line coach, Oklahoma State (1979-80). ... Defensive coordinator, Oklahoma State (1981-82). ... Defensive line coach, Southern California (1983-85). ... Defensive coordinator, Miami, Fla. (1986-88). ... Defensive coordinator, Dallas Cowboys NFL (1989-92). ... Assistant head coach, Miami Dolphins NFL (1999).

	REGULAR SEASON					POST-SEASON	
	W	L	T	Pct.	Finish	W	L
1993—Chicago NFL	7	9	0	.438	4th/NFC Central Division	0	0
1994—Chicago NFL	9	7	0	.563	4th/NFC Central Division	1	1
1995—Chicago NFL	9	7	0	.563	3rd/NFC Central Division	0	0
1996—Chicago NFL	7	9	0	.438	3rd/NFC Central Division	0	0
1997—Chicago NFL	4	12	0	.250	5th/NFC Central Division	0	0
1998—Chicago NFL	4	12	0	.250	5th/NFC Central Division	0	0
2000—Miami NFL	11	5	0	.688	1st/AFC Eastern Division	1	1
2001—Miami NFL	11	5	0	.688	2nd/AFC Eastern Division	0	1
2002—Miami NFL	9	7	0	.563	3rd/AFC East Division	0	0
2003—Miami NFL	10	6	0	.625	2nd/AFC East Division	0	0
Pro totals (10 years)	81	79	0	.506	**Pro totals (3 years)**	2	3

NOTES:

1994—Defeated Minnesota, 35-18, in first-round playoff game; lost to San Francisco, 44-15, in conference playoff game.
2000—Defeated Indianapolis, 23-17 (OT), in first-round playoff game; lost to Oakland, 27-0, in conference playoff game.
2001—Lost to Baltimore, 20-3, in first-round playoff game.